ISBN 978-0-282-51855-4
PIBN 10854642

J.J. Little & Ives Co. N.Y.
Printers and Bookbinders

TO

THE THOUSANDS OF PRACTICAL HOUSEKEEPERS,

READERS OF SUCCESS MAGAZINE,

AND OTHERS,

WHOSE DISCOVERIES ARE EMBODIED

IN THIS VOLUME

ONE CENT A WORD

We will pay for new household discoveries, including all practical recipes and processes, not contained in this volume, one cent a word for all we can use in future editions of Household Discoveries. Corrections of errors or misstatements, utilized by us, will be paid for at the same rate. If you have saved money or have been otherwise benefited by using one of our recipes, write us all about it.

SUCCESS COMPANY'S BRANCH OFFICES.

NOTICE

Household Discoveries is not offered for sale through the book stores, and can only be obtained of our regular authorized solicitors or from the publishers direct. Anyone desiring a copy may address the publishers at address below and full information will be given by mail, or one of our representatives will be asked to call. We are always in want of canvassing agents. The price of Household Discoveries, because of its genuine worth (so apparent), sells the book readily and it always gives satisfaction. We will pay a good salary to the right person. The work is both pleasant and profitable.

SUCCESS COMPANY'S BRANCH OFFICES,
Petersburg, New York.

PREFACE

The main object of this book is economy. If rightly used, it will save a great deal of money in every household. It will also save time and labor, which are the equivalent of money.

The publishers have long felt that there is a great need for a new book of this sort upon the market. To be sure, there are a number of standard dictionaries and encyclopedias of applied science. But these cost from five to ten dollars and upward. And they contain a great deal of information about commercial processes not suitable to household use. There are also a number of popular books of recipes published. But most of these are old books. Others are made up scrapbook fashion by the republication of old material without proper editorial supervision.

In the course of the preparation of this volume, our attention was necessarily called to the fact that a number of so-called "new" books republish, word for word, recipes and processes that have been formerly published in six or eight other books, some of which appeared before the Civil War. Recent science has introduced many new substances and processes then unknown. All these have been availed of in the present volume.

Moreover, the old-fashioned popular book of recipes leaves something to be desired in its manner as well as its matter. The enormous sale and reputation of a number of old books that contain some recipes of great practical value, but accompanied by comment which no sane person can possibly read without a sense of humor or a feeling of disgust, is the strongest possible evidence of the value of this kind of information. We believe that what has made these old books popular is their practical part and not their silly part. We believe that the public will approve a volume that sets forth what to do, how to do, and the reasons why, in simple, direct, and dignified language, and saves space for additional recipes and other information by omitting "horseplay" and all unnecessary remarks and commentaries.

This is a modern book. All who have owned or used one

PackingID: PGFB-058790

Packing List

PGFB-05879
OrderDate 10/21/2020

your Order

From:

Ship Code: Media Mail
Freight Collect
ShippingAcctNum

	Quantity Packed	Box#
ia of Practical Recipes and Processes (Classic	1	1
	1	**1**

on of claim including number of items damaged, condition of carton, etc.

Country of Origin: United States

Thank you fc

PONumber: 112-6009928-4121817
Ship To:
Christine Barkman
PO BOX 344

CLAYSBURG, PA - 16625-0344 US
+1 415-851-9136 ext. 1129

Quantity Ordered	Product	Title
1	9780282518554	Household Discoveries: An Encyclopaec Reprint)
1	**Total Quantity enclose**	

Claim Policy:

Please report damage claims within 3 business days of receipt of shipment.
Please call 630-221-1850 with tracking number, contact name, telephone and descrip

of the old-time books of recipes know that hardly a week passes that they do not find occasion to refer to it. They will, we believe, appreciate the importance of having the latest and best information along these lines obtainable. Others, who have no good collection of this sort, will appreciate without argument the value of purchasing a new book rather than an old one.

Thus we feel that there is a universal necessity for HOUSEHOLD DISCOVERIES, and we have therefore put the price so low as to bring it within the reach of every family, in the confident expectation of distributing at least a million copies throughout the continent of North America.

THE PUBLISHERS.

INTRODUCTION

THERE are a number of other books of recipes, but the present volume is unique in three ways: what it contains, what it omits, and the way it is arranged.

WHAT THE BOOK CONTAINS

As to the *first* of these three features, the title HOUSEHOLD DISCOVERIES is suggestive. We all have our own ways of doing things. We learn to do by doing. But we are all the time trying new ways, to save time, to save money, and to do things better. Every now and then, through a happy combination of circumstances, we make a "Discovery." We hit upon a better way than we have known before. Nothing pleases us more than to tell our friends about it. They in turn like to tell us ways they have discovered to do this or that. Women thus exchange household recipes. Men swap ideas on carpentering, painting, tinkering, and odd jobs generally. The value of these homely ideas thus passing throughout the country, from lip to lip, from friend to friend, and from neighbor to neighbor, is enormous. Some persons are able to store up large numbers of such practical ideas in memory. Others keep notebooks or scrapbooks in which to record them. But the stock of most persons is limited to a few score or a few hundreds, whereas others, equally good, are in existence to the number of many thousands.

The present volume is made up of practical ideas of this character. More than twenty-five thousand persons contributed from one to half a dozen of their own tried "Discoveries." All were practical housekeepers. Their ideas were the direct product of their experience. They were proud of them and they had reason to be. The writer appreciated to the full the value of this material and obtained permission to edit it and prepare it for the press.

Valuable as are the "Discoveries" of practical housekeepers in themselves, they have, in their suggestiveness, an added value. They show what kind of information housekeepers need and want. But they also reveal the fact that many women of great practical experience lack scientific knowledge. It has therefore been necessary to supplement this wealth of ideas derived from experience. And this has been done in two ways: ***First,*** the discoveries contributed by housekeepers have been carefully checked against the best scientific authorities, errors have been corrected, impractical ideas discarded. *Second,* the whole has been augmented by the addition of the most approved practical and scientific formulæ. As a result, it turned out to be necessary to rewrite the entire volume.

"Discoveries" are usually *how to do* this or that. But many persons also want to know why. And all can work better if they understand the nature and properties of the various substances. These are of several sorts. In removing stains and spots, for instance, what to do depends upon the kind of fabric, whether animal or vegetable fiber; its condition, whether white or colored, bleached or unbleached; the nature of the staining substance; and the nature of the cleanser to be employed. Hence, the nature and the properties of the particular kinds of substances in common household use are carefully stated. Distinctions are made, and closely adhered to, between the treatment of different classes of substances, as animal versus vegetable fibers and the like. Poisons, explosives, and other dangerous substances are recommended only with the proper cautions, and all possible safeguards have been thrown about the use, by ordinary persons, of the various recipes recommended.

WHAT THE BOOK OMITS

The *second* feature that makes this book unique is what it omits. The writer has closely examined about fifty thousand recipes contributed by housekeepers, and more than fifty published books of recipes (embracing all that have appeared in the English language in the past fifty or sixty years) or a total (including duplicates) of nearly one hundred thousand recipes. This book contains the cream of them all. It is like apple butter boiled down from cider. It is sound wheat winnowed free from chaff. It was not necessary to leave out any good recipes that were adapted to household use. They are all here. Nothing had to be left out but waste words, duplicates (the same thing said in another way), gush, and braggadocio.

A favorite way of padding books of recipes has been to occupy more space boasting about the wonders the recipes will do than it takes to give the recipe and the directions. Nearly half of one of the most celebrated books of recipes is thus taken up with "Remarks" that are of no possible use to anybody. If the mass of trivialities contained in some of the most widely known books of recipes now in use could be struck out and the contents "boiled down" or "churned" or "winnowed" in a thorough manner, it would surprise everyone to find how little space the recipes themselves take up.

And a boiled-down book is much more valuable. The recipes are still the same and they are a great deal more convenient. By thus avoiding unnecessary words, all the best recipes for household purposes extant have been combined into one volume. They are given on their merits in a plain, direct, and simple way. And full information is given in regard to the nature and properties of the various substances. Thus anyone can select the best recipe for a given use, and he will discover its virtues for himself without paying extra to read about them beforehand. "The proof of the pudding is in the eating thereof."

THE WAY IN WHICH THE CONTENTS ARE ARRANGED

The *third* feature in which this book is unique is the way it is arranged. The contents are pictorial. Each chapter is a picture, or rather a series of moving pictures, from daily life. If a moving-picture machine could follow a good housekeeper around from morning until night, seven days in the week and fifty-two weeks in the year, and then throw the series of pictures thus taken upon a screen, the result would be similar to the contents of this volume. The book goes right with the housekeeper when furnishing and decorating all parts of the house, and makes a series of pictures that suggest what to do. It gives helpful pictures of the best method of heating, lighting, water supply, and refrigeration. It goes right through the day's work and makes pictures of the different processes, of the kindling and care of fires, dishwashing, cleaning lamps, chamber work, and preparations for the night.

It goes through the week's work and makes a picture of getting ready for wash day by removing spots and stains from the linen and by dry cleaning all sorts of fabrics; of the different kinds of soap and how to make them; of wash day, ironing day, mending, sweeping and cleaning days, and all of their different processes.

It goes through the year's work also, the spring and fall house cleaning; the fight against moths, cockroaches, ants, fleas, mosquitoes, flies, rats and mice, and other household pests; and even takes up packing to travel or to move away.

And on wash day, for example, just when the picture is complete—including the piles of soiled garments, the utensils of the laundry, and the various soaps and other cleansing mixtures—all of the recipes are given that can be found in any published book of good repute and many "Discoveries" that have never been published elsewhere. Thus, a young bride—or an experienced housekeeper, too, for that matter—can take up the book the night before wash day and read over exactly the information she will need to put in practice on the morrow. Or the book can be kept at hand in the laundry closet and picked up with wet hands if need be. The cover (in one style of binding) is made of oilcloth and it will not be damaged in the least. What the housekeeper wants to know about any kind of housework can be found at the very time she wants it, and all in one place. Contrast with this books that are arranged in *a b c* order like an encyclopedia, and you will see why HOUSEHOLD DISCOVERIES is, in arrangement, the most practical and convenient book of recipes ever published.

Take, for instance, the family workroom. It is a picture of what is needed to make a man handy about the house. Everything is described in such a simple way that anyone can fix up such a workroom and always have at hand paste, mucilage, glue, and cement for all kinds of uses; paints and varnishes; soldering tool and solder and other forms of simple metal work; oils and lubricators; and all sorts of similar contrivances. Every recipe and process is described in the simplest language. And this part of the book alone is worth, to the man of the house, many times the cost of the entire volume. It will save the family the price of the book several times over every year that it is in the house.

Upward of one hundred thousand recipes include a great many different ways of doing the same things. And by omitting all waste words and boiling down everything to the last degree it has been possible to include more of these ways than any one person would be likely to want. It has seemed best, however, to include them all. Circumstances differ. And many men are of many minds. From the variety of the recipes given, it is believed that any housekeeper or practical man can, in most cases, make up a recipe for a given purpose from what is at hand in the house or at any rate what can easily be had in the neighborhood. And thus the book is adapted to all parts of the country, and to the use of every individual and family in the land.

THE AUTHOR.

CONTENTS

CHAPTER VI

PREVENTABLE DISEASES OF CHILDREN

CHAPTER VII

THE CARE OF BABIES

CHAPTER VIII

OUTDOOR PROBLEMS OF THE HOUSEHOLDER

CHAPTER IX

THE DAY'S ROUTINE

CHAPTER X

REMOVAL OF SPOTS AND STAINS

CHAPTER XI

WASH DAY

CHAPTER XII

IRONING DAY

CHAPTER XIII

SWEEPING DAY

CHAPTER XIV

HOUSE CLEANING

CHAPTER XV

HOUSEHOLD AND GARDEN PESTS

CHAPTER XVI

ADHESIVES, PAINTS, AND VARNISHES

CHAPTER XVII

LEATHER, INK, AND MISCELLANEOUS

CHAPTER XVIII

THE TOILET AND BATH

CHAPTER XIX

TOILET PREPARATIONS

CHAPTER XX

HAIRDRESSING BOTH FOR MEN AND WOMEN

CHAPTER XXI

THE TEETH

CHAPTER XXII

FOOD VALUES AND ADULTERATIONS

CHAPTER XXIII

PRESERVING AND CANNING FRUIT AND VEGETABLES

CHAPTER XXIV

VINEGAR, PICKLES, AND PICKLING

CHAPTER XXV

PRESERVATION OF MEAT AND VEGETABLES

CHAPTER XXVI

CANDIES AND CANDY MAKING

CHAPTER XXVII

WEIGHTS AND MEASURES

CHAPTER XXVIII

BEVERAGES

CHAPTER XXIX

BREAD

CHAPTER XXX

BAKING-POWDER BREADS

CHAPTER XXXI

STALE BREAD

CHAPTER XXXII

SANDWICHES

CHAPTER XXXIII

CEREALS AND FLOUR PASTE

CHAPTER XXXIV

CEREAL LEFT-OVERS

CHAPTER XXXV

EGGS

CHAPTER XXXVI

SOUPS

CHAPTER XXXVII

FISH

CHAPTER XXXVIII

FISH LEFT-OVERS

CHAPTER XXXIX

SHELLFISH

CHAPTER XL

MEATS

CHAPTER XLI

LEFT-OVERS OF BEEF

CHAPTER XLII

LAMB AND MUTTON

CHAPTER XLIII

LAMB LEFT-OVERS

CHAPTER XLIV

VEAL

CHAPTER XLV

VEAL LEFT-OVERS

CHAPTER XLVI

PORK

CHAPTER XLVII

PORK AND HAM LEFT-OVERS

CHAPTER XLVIII

POULTRY

CHAPTER XLIX

LEFT-OVER CHICKEN AND TURKEY

CHAPTER L

MEAT OR FISH SAUCES

CHAPTER LI

VEGETABLES

CHAPTER LII

LEFT-OVER VEGETABLES

CHAPTER LIII

POTATOES

CHAPTER LIV

LEFT-OVER POTATOES

CHAPTER LV

SALADS

CHAPTER LVI

PUDDINGS MADE FROM STALE BREAD AND CAKE

CHAPTER LVII

PUDDING SAUCES

CHAPTER LVIII

FROZEN DESSERTS

CHAPTER LIX

PUFF PASTE

CHAPTER LX

COOKIES, CAKES, AND DOUGHNUTS

CHAPTER LXI

CAKE

CHAPTER LXII

CAKE FILLINGS AND ICINGS

CHAPTER LXIII

FIRELESS COOKERY

CHAPTER LXIV

FAVORITE DISHES IN FAMOUS HOMES

CHAPTER LXV

SOME KITCHEN KINKS

APPENDIX CHAPTER I

ECONOMICAL USE OF MEAT IN THE HOME

APPENDIX CHAPTER II

CHEESE AND ITS ECONOMICAL USES IN THE DIET

APPENDIX CHAPTER III

PREPARATION OF VEGETABLES FOR THE TABLE

CHAPTER I

HOUSE FURNISHING AND DECORATING

HOUSE FURNISHING — FURNITURE — WALL COVERINGS — FLOOR COVERINGS — CURTAINS, SHADES AND DRAPERIES — MISCELLANEOUS OBJECTS — LIVING ROOMS — SLEEPING ROOMS — DINING ROOM — KITCHEN, STOREROOM, AND PANTRY — SMALL ECONOMIES

HOUSE FURNISHING

The subject of house furnishing is more important than is often realized. It has a moral and social as well as an economic side. The relation is very close between the character, or at least the reputation, of men and their surroundings. Everyone is free to change his surroundings. Hence the furniture and the decorations of a house, and the condition of the house and grounds, are properly considered an index to the character of its occupants.

Furniture, decorations, and other surroundings that are disorderly or in bad taste tend to keep refined and thoughtful people away from such homes. They have an even worse effect on the character of the inmates. Those who live in such circumstances become used to them, and no longer notice their badness. But the worst effect is upon the impressionable minds of growing children. Young children naturally take their own homes as models. What they see in childhood tends to fix their standards for life. Hence, neat, tasteful, and orderly homes, but not necessarily expensive in their appointments, have a very important educational influence.

The problem of furnishing and decorating comes up in two ways: originally, as in the formation of a new home, in the furnishing of additional rooms, or in moving into a new and larger dwelling; or, secondarily, in refurnishing from time to time, and purchasing additions to the family stock, usually in connection with the semiannual housecleaning.

All of these occasions give rise to many problems that require good judgment. But these can usually be referred to a few simple rules that are not difficult to understand or to apply. Styles and fashions in these matters change more slowly than some other fashions, as in dress; but they do change, and while it is proper and desirable that the fur-

"Simplicity, Harmony, and Durability."

nishings in the home should be to some extent original and express the individuality of its owners, it is natural and convenient for everyone to conform in a general way to the tendencies of the times in which he lives. Hence it is important to know in what direction the current of thought is moving, so as to keep in advance or abreast of it, rather than to lag behind.

Simplicity, harmony, and durability

are the keynotes of the modern tendency. The general intention seems to be to avoid everything that is superfluous, everything that has a tendency to catch and hold dust or dirt, or to add to the discomforts and dangers of dust and dirt by quickly wearing out. Hence carpets are being largely replaced by hard-wood floors and rugs; wooden bedsteads, by beds of iron or brass; stuffed and upholstered furniture, by articles of plain wood or wood and leather. Wall papers are often discarded for walls tinted or calcimined with washable materials. "Bric-a-brac," flounces, valances, and all other superfluous articles are much less fashionable than formerly.

Good and Bad Taste.—The same trend can be seen in decoration. Wall papers in solid colors, and hard-wood floors or solid-colored floor coverings, with rugs of Oriental patterns, are preferred to the large figured carpets, rugs, and wall papers with their so-called "cheerful" or bright and contrasted colors. Stuffed plush, and other upholstered articles of furniture

"Much Less Purchased than Formerly."

in bright colors, or large figured designs, are being much less purchased than formerly.

All this is a result of the Arts-and-Crafts movement originating in England with William Morris, inventor of the Morris chair. A number of popular magazines are devoted to these and kindred subjects, which occupy a good deal of space in general periodicals of all classes.

Formerly there was little opportunity for persons in small towns and remote rural districts either to become familiar with the right standards or to obtain the more approved styles of furniture. But the general prosperity of recent years has resulted in many country homes being tastefully and elegantly furnished. The possibility of buying desirable styles on the mail-order plan has forced local dealers to keep better and more up-to-date stocks of all household articles. Moreover, the great demand for simplicity of design has reduced the cost. There is now a good selection of household furniture in the less expensive grades upon the same models as the most costly and tasteful articles.

FURNITURE

Furniture should be chosen for simplicity and durability. The most simple designs are usually the most artistic, and the most durable articles are likely to be the most sanitary. Quiet and subdued colors and dull finishes are the most restful and generally satisfactory, although the high polish of such furniture as mahogany is preferred by many people. To produce a soothing and restful effect all the colors in a given room should be in harmony. The artistic quality that makes an article of furniture an object of beauty as well as of use should be sought in the lines of the design itself, rather than in additions by way of decoration. Cheap furniture stamped with scrolls and other designs in imitation of carving or the torturing of the natural lines of a piece of furniture into various fanciful knobs, curves, and scrolls, sometimes facetiously called "gingerbread," have little to recommend them. The modern Craftsman and Mission styles of furniture indicate a change in the right direction. Not all of these designs are of equal value;

but for the most part they are simple, durable, and derive their beauty from their appropriateness and the natural lines on which they are constructed. Dainty white and gold spider-legged

"*Modern Craftsman and Mission Styles.*"

furniture has no place except in drawing-rooms of wealth and extreme conventionality.

Antique Furniture.—The craze for second-hand or antique furniture is, on the whole, rather absurd. Very few persons indeed are able to distinguish a real antique from an imitation. Dealers in these goods may not only willfully deceive, but are often deceived themselves by persons who have so-called antiques, manufactured in America, shipped abroad and reshipped to this country. The wood is not infrequently given the appearance of age by being buried in the ground, eaten with acids, or riddled with fine shot in imitation of worm holes.

Even the cloth or leather in which the goods are upholstered may be given the effect of wear by mechanical means, and the whole may be placed on the market by fraud in such a way as to suggest that the articles are heirlooms.

Modern furniture, made on the same models, can be obtained at much lower prices, and is much more satisfactory than these supposed antiques. But, as a rule, antique pieces are not desirable unless a room can be furnished with them and can have all its appointments in harmony with the antique style.

Furnishing.—William Morris says: "Have nothing in your home that you do not know to be useful or believe to be beautiful." It is a good rule in furnishing a new home to buy first only what is absolutely necessary, and not to buy an article that is not immediately required because it is beautiful or cheap, or for any other reason. After living for a while with only the few articles that are absolutely necessary, it will be easier to see just what is required that will harmonize with the articles already purchased and their surroundings and help to make a satisfactory whole.

Moreover, the longer one lives without unnecessary furnishings the more he is likely to appreciate the wisdom of simplicity. Every new article purchased is a new care, and a few objects of good quality in a room give a much more elegant effect than a large number of less desirable pieces. Hence there is no reason why any family, whether in the city or the country, cannot furnish their home in a thoroughly modern way that will always be in good taste and will be in good style for many years to come.

Refurnishing.—It would, of course, very rarely happen that a family could afford or would wish to discard serviceable articles because they are not in good style or good taste according to present fashion. But as such articles wear out and have to be replaced, or as additions are made from time to time, it is quite possible to refurnish in such a way that in comparatively few years the entire contents of the home will be modernized. Hence the importance of some knowledge of the subjects of harmony and color, simplicity, design, and durability in material and in modes.

Color Schemes.—The most pleasing effects in decoration are obtained by treating each room or group of connected rooms in such a way as to get a harmonious general effect or color scheme. And the color scheme must, of course, be chosen with reference to the purpose for which the room is intended, its shape and size, and the amount of sunlight it receives. Rooms can be so treated as to seem higher or broader than they are, the amount of light can be increased or subdued, and each room can be given a distinct tone and individuality appropriate to the uses to which it is put. This way of decorating does not necessarily cost any more than any other. It merely requires some knowledge and skill that can easily be acquired.

The basis of the color scheme is, of course, in the background provided by the wall and floor coverings and the woodwork. But all the furnishings should be selected so as to form, with the background, a harmonious whole. Hence the subject naturally divides itself into the separate topics of woodwork, wall coverings, floor coverings, and furniture. And the last topic can be best taken up in connection with each of the different rooms, as the living room, dining room, bedrooms, etc.

Color and Light.—Some colors reflect a large part of the light that falls upon them; others absorb it. The various shades of green are the greatest thieves of light. A dark-green wall will absorb about 85 per cent of the light; a dark brown perhaps 70 per cent; a light green, 50 per cent; an orange or yellow, 25 or 30 per cent; light blue, 35 per cent; and soft, delicate tints about 10 per cent. But of course these figures are only approximate. Pure white absorbs about 15 per cent of the light thrown upon it. Hence suitable color schemes for rooms facing south that need toning down are greens or the dull shades of blue, écru, or tan.

For rooms facing west the lighter shades of green, with rose, terra cotta, or white, are appropriate. White enamel furniture with brass trimmings is suitable for such apartments.

North and east rooms require warm tones of yellow, with which yellow oak furniture harmonizes, or warm shades of red, which harmonizes with Mission oak.

Most men would agree to Eugene Field's remark that "almost any color suited him, so long as it was red." Hence red is a suitable color for the furnishing of a man's room or den.

For the dining room, provided it is a bright, sunny room, a suitable color is blue or grayish blue, harmonizing with the tones of delft china. Or, if the dining room is less well lighted, a rich warm tone of yellow gives a sunny atmosphere to the room. But avoid yellow of a greenish or lemon cast.

For the hall, a suitable color is green. And for the living room, green or a warm shade of russet brown, to harmonize with the green of the hall.

Bedrooms should be preferably in light and delicate colors.

WALL COVERINGS

The materials commonly used for wall coverings are chiefly of three sorts, paper, cloth, and paint, or washes applied direct to the walls. The last method is much more generally used than formerly. Wall papers are cheaper but less durable than cloth. Suitable tints and stains in water colors and calcimine are cheaper than either, and also more durable.

Wall Papers.—Perhaps the commonest wall coverings are the wall papers of various grades, from the ordinary wood-pulp paper costing but a few cents a roll, to the highest grades of cartridge, ingrain, or duplex papers, imitations of leather, and other specialties.

Wall papers are very cheap, and anyone can readily learn how to hang them. Hence there is no reason why rooms should not be repapered as often as is necessary to keep them fresh and clean.

Wall papers are especially suitable to walls that are rough or uneven, and to walls of houses that are not sufficiently well built. By suitable treatment paper can be hung on almost any wall, and it assists in keeping the rooms tight and warm.

Colors and Patterns.—The plain cartridge, ingrain, or duplex papers in solid colors are the most approved and among the most satisfactory wall papers, especially for living rooms in general use. The absence of any pattern or design brings out in full relief the pictures upon the walls and other ornaments, and helps to give a quiet air of luxury to the apartment. But these are somewhat more expensive than ordinary wall papers, and require a smoother wall surface and better care in hanging. The edges must be trimmed on both sides and "butted," or brought together side by side, tight enough not to show the wall between them, instead of being overlapped, as with ordinary papers. Otherwise the thickness of the paper would make a ridge which, on account of the solid color, would be plainly visible. This requires some skill, but with a little practice can be done by anyone. The edge should be trimmed with a sharp knife by means of a straightedge rather than with shears.

Next to the ingrain papers, the two-toned or double-toned papers, having a subdued pattern in another shade or tint of the same color as the groundwork, are preferred for the living room.

Good taste demands the selection of a paper having a comparatively small and simple design, and without large figures or striking and glaring contrasts of color. Large-figured papers deprive pictures and other ornaments of all artistic effect and make the wall, which should be merely a background, stand out obtrusively.

How to Choose Wall Paper.—The effect of wall papers cannot be well judged from small samples. Hence when possible choose from the stock itself and have two or three widths unrolled side by side to get the general effect. Remember that vertical stripes make a room seem higher than it is, that large figures and dark colors make it seem smaller, and that a simple design in natural outlines, as a landscape or flowers and foliage, has perspective and tends to give an effect of greater width. Hence it may be suitable for halls or narrow apartments.

Figured papers in dainty patterns, as poppies, roses, or other natural blossoms, are more suitable for bedrooms than for living rooms. They can be selected to suit almost any kind of color scheme. Solid colors seem to make the walls retire; hence they give the effect of broadening and enlarging the apartment. This is especially true of the lighter shades. Mother Goose and other figured papers in suitable designs may be had for children's rooms and nurseries, imitation leather for dining rooms and halls, and waterproof oilcloth papers for bathrooms, kitchens, etc.

Ceilings.—Various desirable effects may be produced in wall coverings by the treatment of the ceiling. Low rooms may be given an effect of greater height by the use of a two-toned paper in narrow, vertical stripes, carried clear to the ceiling without a border, and by fastening the picture molding as close to the ceiling as it will go. On the other hand, rooms that are too narrow in proportion to other dimensions may be given a better effect by lowering the picture molding one to two feet or more and papering up to the molding, but not above, the upper part of the wall being whitewashed or calcimined in the same materials as the ceiling.

"Vertical Stripes Carried Clear to the Ceiling."

Ceilings that have rough or crooked

places which cannot be repaired may be hung with a paper of the same quality as the walls, but usually of a lighter tint. The border may be put on around the edge of the ceiling instead of around the top of the wall, thus giving the room the effect of greater height.

Or ceilings may be whitewashed or calcimined, or tinted with water colors, with or without stenciled borders or frescoes.

Dadoes.—The effect of any room may be improved by a chair rail around the walls three feet from the floor. Suitable material can be procured from dealers in picture moldings. This will, of course, be painted the same color as the woodwork.

On the wall below hang cotton or linen cloth previously painted with boiled linseed oil and well dried, or cheap ingrain paper, and when dry paint this wall covering the same color as the woodwork.

Or this dado may be developed with picture molding, the corners being mitered the same as picture frames. With the aid of a homemade miter-box anyone who is handy with tools can do this work.

Test for Wall Paper.—To test green wall paper for the presence of arsenic in dangerous quantities dip a sample in aqua ammonia. If arsenic is present, the paper will turn from green to blue.

Or light a piece of the paper with a match, and when burning briskly blow it out. The presence of arsenic may be detected by an odor similar to that of garlic.

Wall Coverings — Cloth.—Various grades of prepared cloth wall coverings are obtainable, as silk, linen, and burlap. These are more expensive than paper, and are objected to by some on the ground that they catch dust and are unsanitary, unless regularly swept and dusted every day. But these materials when of good quality are very durable, and furnish perhaps the most artistic of all backgrounds for pictures and other decorations. Burlap is more suitable for outer halls or rooms furnished with heavy oak or Mission furniture. Silks and linens harmonize with mahogany and with the lighter and more graceful furniture of parlors and drawing-rooms.

To Color Walls. — The Arts-and-Crafts movement is introducing the custom of tinting walls in waterproof

"Stencil Added Above."

colors without the use of cloth or paper hangings, either in solid colors or with the addition of designs by means of stencils. The wall is usually tinted in a solid color, and the stencil added above the picture molding by way of border.

"Protected by Means of a Dado."

Or the walls may be painted for half or two thirds of their height and sanded and tinted above, a light molding of simple design being used to divide the two surfaces. The molding should be painted the same color as the woodwork.

Or a chair rail and painted dado may be used, and the walls tinted above.

Stairways. — Paper for stairways may be the same as the hall paper. It often becomes soiled along the bottom, and may be protected by means of a dado about three feet high carried around the hall and up the stairway, and surmounted by a light wooden molding painted to correspond to the adjacent woodwork.

FLOOR COVERINGS

The principal kinds of floor coverings in common use are rugs of various kinds, both Oriental and domestic; carpets, and oilcloths, including linoleum. Of carpets, the most important in the order of their value and desirability are Chenille Axminster, Wilton Axminster, Moquette, Velvet, Brussels, Tapestry Brussels, Ingrain or Kidderminster, two or three ply, Venetian, and old-fashioned rag carpet.

Chenille Axminster is an imported carpet, consisting of worsted chenille woven in strips upon a jute backing. It comes three fourths of a yard wide in rolls, and may also be obtained in whole rugs or carpets specially designed for any kind of room. These are imported, principally from Scotland.

Domestic Axminster and **Moquette** are much alike. They have a thick, high, tufted pile, which is very durable. The Axminster is usually of better material and construction than the Moquette. The groundwork of these carpets is jute or cotton. The pile consists of tufts of soft woolen yarn fastened upon the groundwork so as to make the design. As each color in the design of these carpets is furnished from a separate roll, acting independently, any number of colors may be employed. Hence the most elaborate patterns and shadings of color may be had in these carpets.

Wilton and **Brussels** are made upon a groundwork of linen with a face of worsted in raised loops. In Brussels carpet these loops remain uncut, whereas in Wilton they are cut and the pile is sheared smooth. These loops are formed of woolen threads of continuous colors which, to form the design, are thrust through the warp threads at intervals by means of wires. As each color comes to the surface independently of the others, the designs are exceptionally clear and perfect, but the number of threads that can be employed conveniently is limited; hence there are fewer colors and much less shading in these carpets than in Axminster or Moquette.

Velvet and **Tapestry Brussels** are constructed on the same principle as Wilton and Brussels, except that the worsted threads which form the surface are not of continuous colors, but have the colors forming the design printed upon them before the fabric is woven; hence, without any additional expense, any number of colors may be employed. For this reason the designs of Velvet and Tapestry Brussels are much more elaborate in color and shading than the Wilton or Brussels carpets. Tapestry carpets are more commonly used than any other kind except Ingrains, and hence they give rise in this country to the most important branch of carpet manufacture.

Ingrain or **Kidderminster** carpet is the only kind of which both warp and woof is of wool. Hence it may be turned and worn on either side, although it shows a right and a wrong side in point of color. Its name of "Kidderminster" is derived from the city in which it was formerly manufactured on a large scale. The names "Ingrain" and "three-ply" arise from the fact that there are two grades, one of which consists of two layers interwoven or "ingrained" to cause the colors of the design to change or mingle, whereas the other has three layers similarly put together.

Venetian is made on a coarse ground of hemp filling with a woolen warp. It usually comes in stripes and is largely manufactured for stair coverings.

Oilcloth consists of a foundation of burlap covered with a number of coatings of coarse paint. The pattern is printed on the surface with wooden blocks, one for each color. Oilcloth may be obtained in any width from three feet to twenty-four feet, but is ordinarily sold in narrow widths and medium weights.

In purchasing oilcloth first look at the back and choose a grade of cloth the background of which is closely woven. Next see that the coating of paint is of good weight or thickness, and choose a cloth having a smooth surface rather than one which is coarse or has a raised pattern. These portions are the first to wear.

Oilcloth improves with age as the paint hardens; hence select, if possible, a piece which has been a long time in stock.

Linoleum is a coined word for a floorcloth consisting of a mixture of oxidized linseed oil and pulverized cork. This is laid upon a foundation of coarse burlap and made to adhere by pressure. Linoleum was invented by an Englishman, William Walton, and was formerly sold at rather high prices on account of a monopoly in the use of the patents in the United States. The patents have now expired and linoleum is being sold in competition with oilcloths for floor coverings. It presents a better appearance, is much more durable, and hence is cheaper in the long run. Oilcloths and linoleums, if of good quality and properly laid, are perhaps the best of all floor coverings for kitchen, pantry, laundry, or any other room where wet or greasy substances are likely to be spilled or where there is a great deal of wear. A good grade of linoleum in a solid color also makes a desirable background for Oriental or other rugs as a substitute for a hard-wood floor.

To Lay Oilcloth. — The floors of many rooms, especially in houses that have been standing for many years, become very rough. The cracks widen, and some boards wear or settle more than others, making the surface uneven. This condition presents two difficulties: the cracks admit draughts from beneath, and the sharp and uneven edges wear the floor coverings. Linoleums and oilcloths being stiff and brittle are especially liable to wear and break along these cracks; hence, before laying these floor coverings, put down a number of thicknesses of newspapers. These will also prevent the floor covering, when heated by the sun or by the heat of a stove, from sticking to the floor.

Or use carpet felt or carpet linings obtainable from dealers for this purpose.

Or cover the floor evenly with sawdust by working it into the cracks as much as possible.

Or spread over the floor a rather thick coating of fine dry sand.

Any of these methods makes a solid filling that increases the life of the oilcloth many years.

To Varnish Oilcloths.—Oilcloth and linoleum may be much improved in appearance, and also indefinitely preserved by an occasional coat of varnish. To apply a fresh coat once in three months is not too often. This freshens the colors, prevents the oilcloth from cracking, and, by lessening friction, makes it much easier to clean. If linoleum is used as a background for rugs in bedrooms or living rooms it may be painted, in imitation of various colors of wood, with any of the modern varnish paints which contain stains, and dry with a smooth, glossy surface. When so treated a good linoleum makes an imitation of a hardwood floor, which can hardly be excelled either for beauty or durability. It is especially useful in those cases where a large rug is used for the center of the room with an open border about it. It is, of course, much better in such cases to cover the entire room with linoleum, and to lay the rug upon this.

To Renew Linoleum.—Old pieces of linoleum may often be made as good as new by first washing them with a strong solution of sal soda, ammonia, and soapsuds to remove the original color. Then apply a coat of any good light-colored paint, and lay over this any desired color of varnish paint in imitation of the woodwork. Instructions as to what paint to use may be had from the dealers. Always allow paint and varnish to become thoroughly dry and hard before walking upon it.

Use of Floor Coverings.—Floor coverings doubtless originated in the use by our primitive ancestors of the skins of animals as rugs, and the earliest floor coverings used by civilized nations were in the form of rugs. This usage still continues in the Orient.

The later custom of manufacturing carpets and other floor coverings in long, narrow strips, to be joined together, grew out of the desire to cheapen the process of manufacture by adapting the size of the fabrics to the uses of the loom. The custom of covering the entire floor of a room with carpet or other floor covering doubtless arose, in great degree, from the desire to cover cracks, knots, and other unsightly defects in cheap and badly made floors, to prevent soft-wood floors from wearing, and also to lessen draughts from the cracks between floor boards.

The present tendency among well-to-do people is back to the original idea of scattering rugs upon a smooth, polished surface. The ideal floor is undoubtedly of hard wood, properly laid and highly polished. This is the most sanitary, durable, and beautiful of all floors. It is the easiest to clean, and furnishes an ideal foundation as a basis for any interior decoration. The growing wealth of farmers as a class throughout the great central West and elsewhere, by reason of improved machinery and modern scientific methods of agriculture, has resulted in the building and furnishing of many homes having floors of this sort in the smallest towns and rural districts throughout the United States. Moreover, modern means of transportation, as trolley systems, interurban electric railways, automobiles, and the upbuilding of local telephone systems, have promoted the building in rural neighborhoods of a vast number of summer homes. There is hardly a community in the United States where modern houses constructed with polished hard-wood floors and furnished with Oriental or domestic rugs as floor coverings is not to be seen.

Another great educator has been the periodicals devoted to home making and especially catering to the class of suburban residents above mentioned. These models have set the fashion for bare floors and rugs, and there is no doubt but that as time goes on this custom will become increasingly popular.

Hard-wood floors may be laid under certain conditions over old floors, and be all the better for having another flooring beneath them, but they are somewhat expensive. Hence numerous ingenious methods have been used to secure the same result by imitation.

To Imitate Hard-wood Floors.—Obtain a suitable hard-wood filler, and

"Apply a Good Stain."

press it into the cracks in the floor according to directions. Take care to smooth the filler exactly level after the cracks have been filled. When this substance hardens, the floor will be smooth and even, and all danger from draughts will be permanently done away. Next apply a good stain of any desired color to match the woodwork, or apply a suitable paint mixed with varnish that will dry, leaving a hard, smooth, glossy surface.

Soluble Glass for Floors.—Instead of the old-fashioned method of using wax for polished floors, etc., soluble glass is now employed to great advantage. For this purpose the floor is first well cleaned, and then the cracks are well filled up with a cement of water glass and powdered chalk or gypsum. Afterwards a water glass of 60° to 65°, of the thickness of sirup, is applied by means of a stiff brush. Any desired color may be imparted to the floor in a second coat of the water glass, and additional coats given until the requisite polish is obtained. A still higher finish may be given by pumicing off the last layer, and then putting on a coating of oil.

Or denim of good quality in solid colors may be laid upon the floor as a background for the rugs. But when this material is used the rugs must be large enough and numerous enough to cover most of the surface and receive the greater part of the wear.

Or use heavy building paper pasted smoothly to the floors, and apply to this two or more coats of varnish paint. This material wears well and presents a good appearance.

Or heavy unbleached cotton or denim may be treated by tacking it against a building or laying it on a floor which is not in use, and applying with a paint brush one or two coats of linseed oil. After this is dry, apply a coat of varnish or "lac" paint, let dry and apply a second coat. Afterwards apply a coat of varnish. Let the cloth dry thoroughly before using. This is a good and cheap substitute for oilcloth and linoleum for kitchen floors and all other purposes.

Or matting may be used, especially in bedrooms, sewing room, sitting room, and even in the parlor if the rugs are of the right size and number and of sufficiently good quality.

Or the floor may be covered, especially in the sitting room, where there is more or less tracking in of mud and dirt, and in bedrooms, with a good quality of linoleum, which may be stained and painted in imitation of a hard-wood floor, or to correspond with the woodwork.

The great advantage offered by the bare wood or a smooth surface such as linoleum is that it can be readily kept clean and free from dust, dirt, and all sorts of vermin. Rugs may be taken up and beaten out of doors and thoroughly aired on the line, and every particle of dust and dirt can be readily removed by wiping over the floor with a damp cloth drawn bag-fashion over the head of a broom. Good rugs, both Oriental and domestic, are no more expensive than the same grades of carpet, and their use is to be decidedly recommended for artistic and sanitary reasons as well as from a labor-saving standpoint.

Denim.—Denim is perhaps the most generally popular floor covering as a background for rugs when cost is taken into account. But it is not, of

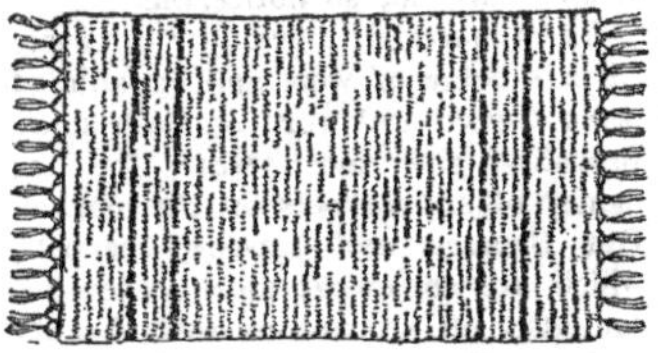

"Filling . . . Transformed into Rugs."

course, as durable as carpet, and does not come in fast colors. When partly worn, however, denim may be woven into rugs or converted into carpet rags.

Filling.—An all-wool ingrain "filling" in greens and other solid colors is another popular floor covering much used as a background for rugs. This is very durable, but like denim tends to fade in comparatively few years, and must then be redyed or transformed into rugs.

To Choose Carpets.—The effect of design in carpets is much the same as in wall paper. Large patterns tend to make a room seem small, and borders about the carpet have the same effect. The present tendency favors carpets in solid colors or having small and delicate patterns. Large patterns and all sorts of glaring contrasts of color should be avoided. Both very dark and very light carpets are difficult to keep clean, and carpets containing blue, green, or other delicate colors, when exposed to sunlight, tend to fade.

As to color, carpets should, of course, harmonize with the general color scheme of the room. But as they cannot be changed as frequently as the wall coverings, they should, as a rule, be in neutral colors that will harmonize with almost any other scheme that may be adopted.

A point in favor of carpets having small patterns is that the two webs of which the carpet consists are much more closely interwoven if the design is small than if the pattern is a large one. Hence the carpet having a small design is likely to be more durable. Moreover, where there are no large patterns to attract the eye the results of wear are not so noticeable.

As to material, ingrain or three-ply carpets being of wool and capable of being turned and worn on both sides, probably give most wear for the money of any carpets on the market. But Brussels and tapestry carpets, which are somewhat more expensive, are also, on account of their beauty and excellent wearing qualities, in very general use.

Rag Carpet.—This is the cheapest carpet of all and can readily be made on a hand loom at home. It makes a thick and serviceable covering for the floors of kitchen or living rooms in winter. To make rag carpet, use a warp of strong cotton thread, and weave in any kind of rags twisted into small rolls.

To Color Rag-carpet Warp.—First use a strong cotton yarn reeled into skeins of five knots. About one skein to the yard of carpet will be required, with about three knots additional for binding at the end of each breadth.

For tan color first soak the warp thoroughly with lime water; next boil it in a brass or copper kettle in a strong solution of extract of hemlock bark in water. This is used by tanners for making leather, and may be obtained through a tanner or dealer in dye stuff.

For black color soak the warp in strong copperas water instead of lime water, and use iron or tin vessels instead of brass or copper. Afterwards boil in the hemlock solution.

For slate color use weaker solutions of copperas and hemlock.

For brown use a weak solution of copperas and a strong solution of hemlock. Thus, by a little experimenting, the shades of color may be varied at will.

Carpet Rags.—The contents of the rag bag should be first picked over, and rags intended to be used as carpet rags should be washed and ironed and afterwards ripped apart. Seams and worn spots should be rejected. They should then be sorted according to the colors of materials, and if not needed at once, stored away for future use in paper bags. Woolen rags should be protected against moths by pasting the tops of the bags together.

Rags of fast and satisfactory colors need not be dyed. But better effects may often be obtained by dyeing all rags to suitable colors.

To cut carpet rags, trim around the outside of the rag, clipping off square corners, and continue cutting round and round until the rag is all cut up. By this means small pieces may be utilized, the rags will be of satisfactory length, and will require less sewing. Cotton rags and rags of fine dress goods make a smoother and better-looking carpet than rags of heavy woolen colors. Hence the latter had better be kept separate and made into rugs or kitchen carpets.

The quantity of rags required for a carpet may be estimated by weight. For each yard one and one half to two pounds of rags, depending upon the material, will be required. In sewing, it is better to mix the different shades of the same color so that the stripes will be of an even and uniform shade. Thus the breadths will present the same appearance. But if the pepper-and-salt pattern is desired all the colors may be mixed together. For this kind of carpet short pieces may be utilized. Rag carpets also come by the piece and may be bought in shops by the yard, the same as others. But when made at home or woven to order they can be ordered to fit the room, the breadths being made exactly to measure and bound up at the ends. Allowance in ordering should be made for shrinkage, as the breadths tend to become a little shorter and wider with wear.

To Cut Carpets.—Before cutting a new carpet, unroll a little more than twice the length of the room, double this in the middle so that the edges will come side by side, and work it back and forth so as to match the pattern at a length a little longer than that of the room. The required number of strips can thus be cut in such a way that the pattern will be matched exactly without waste.

Try both ways on the floor before cutting, as it may be more economical to cut the lengths for the short way of the floor. Any pieces wasted in matching the pattern may be used to make rugs or foot stools, or to fill in recesses.

To Sew Carpets.—Sew with the through-and-tbrough stitch, very close together.

Straw Matting.—When purchasing straw matting it is advisable to buy the best grade of fine white or unfigured matting for all rooms alike; thus as it wears out it can be readily matched or replaced by putting good matting from two rooms together in one.

Matting Rugs.—Cut suitable lengths of matting and hem with twine string for use as summer rugs. Two or more breadths may be attached together if desired to make wide rugs. Use plain, or apply paint, or stain of any desired color. A large square rug can be made in this way to occupy the center of the floor, a border being made by painting or staining the floor, or covering with green denim or drugget.

Rag Rugs.—Very durable and useful rugs may be made of all sorts of old rags in the same fashion as a rag carpet, or by braiding, or they may be knitted or drawn through burlap or canvas as in embroidery. Small pieces may be utilized by commencing at one side and cutting the width of a carpet rug almost to the end, then turning a corner and cutting along the side, and so going around the outside until the piece is cut up. After clipping off the square corners the rag will be found to be of convenient length. Carpet rags should be wound into balls of uniform size. They catch less dust, and do not become tangled. When ready to tack them, have a sewing bee, or run them up on the sewing machine. This will enable you to do them very quickly.

Old stocking legs make especially pretty rugs.

To Make Drawn Rugs.—First prepare a frame by nailing together four pieces of lathe or other light pine stuff, and stretch on this a piece of strong burlap or coarse canvas. Prepare the rags by cutting them in a uniform width of one half inch or less, and wind each color in a separate ball. Draw the rags through the burlap by means of a hook, that can be extemporized from a piece of wire. Insert the hook from above between the warp and woof of the burlap, and draw the rag up from below so as to form loops projecting at uniform heights above the burlap. This is the principle upon which Axminster carpet is made. A design may be traced on the burlap by means of chalk or charcoal, and the outlines drawn with two or three rows of rags in different colors. A little experience will indicate how closely together to draw the loops, which should project a half inch or less above the burlap. If desired, the loops may afterwards be clipped, as is done with the Wilton carpets, by means of a sharp pair of scissors.

CURTAINS, SHADES, AND DRAPERIES

The use of curtains originated before the invention of glass, when windows were either open or imperfectly protected against draughts. They originally hung straight down across the sash.

At present the object of window shades and curtains is primarily to regulate the amount of light in the room, and to screen the interior, when desired, from observation from without. It is a prime rule of good taste in decoration that it must not be allowed to interfere with the purpose for which a thing is intended. Hence curtains and draperies that cannot be drawn aside to admit the light, or let fall to exclude it, are objectionable. Curtains for French windows should be arranged with cords and pulleys so as to be brought out of the way when the windows are opened, or adjusted on rods long enough so that they can be drawn to one side.

Window Curtains. — Some city houses have three or four sets of

"Simpler Methods . . . Are Gaining Favor."

curtains, but the simpler methods of country houses are gaining in favor. One set is sufficient, and more than two are undesirable. A thin semi-transparent curtain of lace, net, or muslin, in white or écru, may be used next the glass. This may either be crossed at the top and hang straight down or be draped at the middle sash with a band. This is a question of taste and depends upon the proportions of the room and the window. When an inner curtain of heavy material is used the lace or net curtain should usually be draped to soften the outlines. Lace or net curtains are usually, but not always, used downstairs, and less expensive curtains of muslin are used for bedrooms and other upstairs windows.

Materials for Window Curtains.— Lace curtains may be purchased ready made. Or curtains may be made of bobbinet or similar material and edged with ruffles or suitable lace. Or Cluny lace may be used by way of insertion. Plain scrim, with no other decoration than hemstitched hems, makes handsome curtains. They launder easily and well. If they bleach with time they can be restored to their original color by being dipped in dilute coffee. The best materials for bedrooms are dotted Swiss or other muslins. Other serviceable materials are India linen, Aberdeen linen, Persian cotton, cretonnes, and linen taffetas. The reps of various fabrics—cotton, wool, and silk—all hang well and are soft and graceful.

Any suitable material may be scalloped along the edge by means of a tumbler. Mark around this with chalk or pencil. Buttonhole the scallops and work in them polka dots or other simple design.

Muslin Curtains. — For bedroom curtains it pays to buy various cotton materials like dimity and muslin by the piece, and to make them all the same style. It is wise to keep to the same pattern, as dots or small rings, and to buy new pieces the same as the old, or as nearly so as they can be matched. Then new curtains can be used with the old. As the curtains begin to wear they can be put together as pairs, or changed from room to room as long as any two are left.

Or when curtains from the living rooms wear on the edges, trim them off, hem them neatly, and turn the edged border toward the sash. They will make good curtains for bedrooms or other inconspicuous windows that will last for years.

Dyeing Curtains.—All cotton materials can be readily dyed by dipping them in dye stuff after they have been washed and rinsed in the laundry. Thus the curtains can be made to conform to any desired color shade.

Cheese cloth when dyed in suitable colors makes pretty and inexpensive curtains. Hemmed bands or borders of striped silkoline or other suitable material add a decorative effect. Dark green trimmed with a stripe in Oriental design and coloring makes a very pretty curtain.

Or take cheese cloth or unbleached sheeting which may be any old material as old sheets, from which pieces of suitable size can be cut for curtains, and dye them in any suitable shade. White cotton dipped in a deep brown dye and afterwards in a deep green gives a beautiful gray-green color.

"Decorative Border in Oil Paints."

Or unbleached cotton sheeting can be stenciled or hand painted with a decorative border in oil paints thinned slightly with turpentine, and thus given a very artistic effect. Cut the curtain wide enough so that the inner edge of each pair may be turned over eight inches. Fold this strip top and bottom into squares. Mark the squares by means of a stencil and paint any design to form the border.

To Hang Lace Curtains.—To hang lace curtains without assistance, first adjust the pole; throw the top of the curtain loosely over the pole; then, by means of a common pin or tack, fasten each scallop to the skirting board just above the carpet or along the floor. The curtain may then be drawn up rather firmly over the pole so that when the pins are removed the curtain will have been stretched just enough to lift it off the floor. This, without jumping down to look, insures the curtain hanging evenly.

To Mend Lace Curtains.—To mend delicate lace and net curtains when they first show a tear, take very fine thread and a hook and fill up the space with a single crochet stitch. When laundered the mend will defy detection.

Or when lace curtains are much worn, take one or two of the worst for patches, and after the others are laundered cut a patch to match the design of the torn part, dip it in thick starch, lay it carefully over the rent, and iron it down. The starch will cause it to adhere until the curtains are laundered again. Strips of net or illusion may also be used in the same way.

Sash Curtains.—Use partly worn muslin or silk curtains for sash curtains. The tops and bottoms of old curtains that have not had the direct rays of the sun will usually be found best for sash curtains. The middle part can be discarded. Make a wide hem top and bottom through which to run the rod. A wide hem is not so likely to tear, and the curtains can be used either end up. Slip a round-headed hat pin into the hollow of the rod to run them in the hems, and they will pass easily through. Rods may be fixed inside the sash so as to be elevated with the window and not to lean against the screen. Cords tacked across the window will prevent the sash curtain from beating against the screen.

Or instead of rods use quarter-inch iron wire painted over with gold paint or otherwise gilded or silvered. This makes the wire look better and prevents it from rusting. This wire is suitable for shams, mantels, and closet curtains, and many similar purposes in house decoration. It answers the same purpose as brass rods, and is much cheaper. It can be purchased at any hardware store, cut to any desired length.

Flour Sacks. — Large flour sacks may be utilized for sash curtains by carefully washing out the print and finishing with a suitable design in fancy work.

Curtains for Broad Windows.—Divide a broad, low window, or two windows together, by running two shelves across, one at the top of each sash. Paint or stain these to match the woodwork. Fit sash curtains to both shelves by means of rods or quarter-inch iron or copper iron, and hang

"Divide a Broad Low Window."

from brass rings. Let the hangings match the woodwork or conform to the color scheme of the room. The upper shelves may be treated as a plate rail, and the lower shelf may hold pots of ferns or other green plants.

Window Shades.—A double set of window shades—an inner dark shade to harmonize with the color scheme of the room, and an outer white shade—are desirable, but both are not necessary. It saves carpets and other things from fading to exclude the sunshine when a room is not in use, and also assists in keeping sunny rooms cool in summer. Hence, a dark or tan shade is to be preferred, unless the house is fitted with blinds. In that case only the white shade is necessary.

To Renew Window Shades.—Trim off the soiled or worn part at the bottom, make a new hem, and put back the stick. To do this lay on an ironing board, curled side down, the part of the shade that has been curled up over the roller and press it with a hot iron. This makes it easy to turn a hem, which may be stitched on the sewing machine. Let the stitch out as far as it will go so that the fabric will not pucker.

Or, if the shade is too short to trim, change the ends by opening the hem at the bottom, taking the shades from the roller and tacking the bottom of the shade to the roller. Make a new hem and put back the stick.

To Hang Window Shades.—To adjust the spring on new window shades, roll them tight, fasten them into the sockets, and draw them down full length. Take them out of their sockets, roll them up again by hand, and again draw them down until the spring is as strong as desired.

To Prevent Blowing Window Shades. — To prevent the window shades from being drawn out at the top of the window or blowing back and forth when the upper sash is lowered for ventilation, attach the cord from the bottom of the shade to the back of a chair, and move it a sufficient distance from the window to give a free circulation of air underneath it.

Substitute for Window Shades.—To economize on window shades, the upper rooms of a house may be fitted with shades of white cotton, having the selvage on one side and a very fine hem on the other. By the addition of a little glue size or gum arabic to the starch, they can be made very stiff. They look from outside almost equal to ordinary shades of Holland linen. They can, of course, readily be laundered when soiled.

Draperies. — Portières and other draperies must be selected with due regard to the size and shape of the room, as well as to the color scheme. Heavy, thick draperies make a small room look close and stuffy. But light, airy hangings are equally out of place in a large room. To improve the effect of a room that is too narrow and high between joints, or a room having too high and narrow doors and windows, lower the window shades twelve or fifteen inches from the top and fill in the

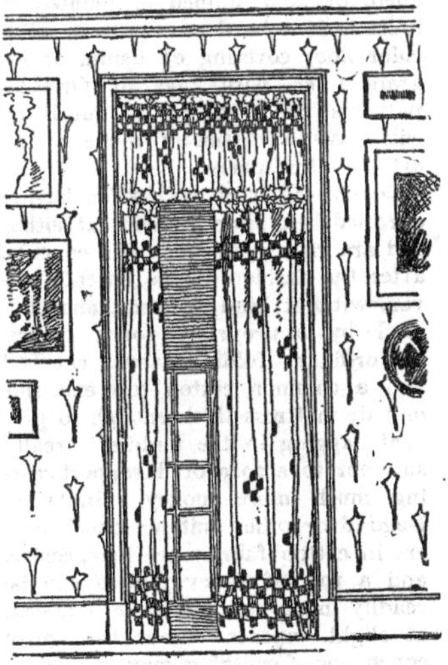

"Lower the Rod."

space with a grill, a rope network, a shirring of silk, or similar decoration. If the doors open outward, or if a door is taken down and hung with draperies, lower the rod twelve or fifteen inches and fill in above with shirred silk or silkoline to harmonize with the portières or draperies.

Or run a shelf or plate rack across the top of the door on a level with the top of the window shades; by these means the room is made to seem lower and larger in proportion to its height.

Or lower the curtain from the pole by means of cords to match the drapery. Lace over the pole and through the hooks on the pins.

Portiéres.—In addition to the various grades of draperies on the market, burlap and other suitable fabrics may be made up for this purpose at much less expense.

Or brown leather scraps may be purchased from bookbinders at a few cents a pound, cut in strips about half an inch wide, and tied in lots after the manner of carpet rags. These make very cheap and effective draperies for libraries and living rooms.

Choose preferably materials that will not catch and hold dust more than is necessary, and avoid flounces, fringes, and tassels coarse enough to allow dust to accumulate in them. It is a good plan in summer to take down heavy draperies, shake and clean them, and pack them away until fall in a moth-proof box or chest. They will last longer, and the house will be much cleaner, more airy, and comfortable without them.

Or, if desired, replace the winter draperies with cheap draperies of dark green or other color of burlap. Lower the pole a foot or more from the casing to let the air pass through, and let them swing clear of the floor.

Curtain Rings.—Rub the curtain poles occasionally with a rag dipped in kerosene oil to make the rings slip easily.

To Clean Draperies.—Draperies and tapestries hung upon the walls may be cleaned by pouring gasoline into a shallow pan, and brushing them with this by means of a soft brush or whisk broom.

LIVING ROOMS

The old custom of setting apart a "best room" or parlor to be used only on special occasions, as for weddings, funerals, or the entertainment of company, is happily passing away. Only very wealthy people now have drawing rooms reserved for state occasions. The present tendency is to call all the lower rooms of the house "living rooms," and to have all the members of the family use them freely. A room set apart from ordinary use, and hence shut up much of the time from sun and air, is not good for the physical or moral health of the household. Hygiene demands that sun and air should be admitted freely to all parts of the house. The furnishings themselves, if good care is given them, will be improved rather than injured by ordinary wear, and guests will receive a far pleasanter impression from the easy and graceful atmosphere imparted to a room by daily use, than from the stiff and formal restraints imposed by the old-fashioned parlor. A hostess who takes her friends into a sitting room and tells them frankly that she prefers to "live in her own parlor" will have more friends than critics. The arrangement is plainly for the good of the family, and all who visit such a home will enjoy being taken into the wholesome family life.

When possible, it is pleasant and convenient to have two living rooms thrown together by folding or sliding doors, with a grill and portières or other suitable draperies across the opening. The effect of many country homes could be greatly improved by cutting an arch or square opening about the width and height of two ordinary doors placed side by side or slightly wider, so as to throw two living rooms into one. Suitable folding or sliding doors, while desirable, are not necessary, as the opening can be closed by means of heavy hangings sliding on a rod.

"Front Room."—Large houses and ample means will, of course, suggest other living rooms, as the library, music room, a special sewing room, and the like. But these are neither necessary nor possible in ordinary households, and the "front room" may be made not only more habitable but also more attractive to callers and guests by the presence of a piano or other musical instrument, and by low bookcases built along the walls, three or four shelves high, to hold the family collection of books, and stained or painted to match the woodwork. The top of these bookcases may be finished by a shelf about breast high, or slightly lower, on which plaster-of-Paris casts, vases, or flowers and other appropriate objects may be displayed. A "front room" having the walls hung with suitable cloth or paper in solid colors, or two-toned shades of brown or green, with shades of green or tan, and hangings to match the wall coverings; a hard-wood floor waxed and oiled, or floor stained or painted in imitation of hard wood, or a solid-color floor covering of denim or ingrain filler, with rugs of Oriental patterns and appropriate furniture, will have a distinctly modern and artistic atmosphere.

Couch.—Couches and sofas having a raised headpiece or arms at either end are giving place to plain couches, after the fashion of the Oriental divan, without head or arms, and covered by appropriate couch covers. An ordinary folding canvas cot bed and a common cotton top excelsior or hair mattress thick enough to prevent sagging in the middle is really superior to a sofa or davenport costing much more money. Imitation Bagdad or other suitable couch covers in cotton fabrics are inexpensive, and a row of fancy pillows can be readily made of washable material at slight expense. Thus the entire couch and furnishing may be had at the cost of but a few dollars.

On the other hand, by purchasing an iron or steel couch with wire-spring top and hair mattress, and adding a real Bagdad or other Oriental couch cover and pillows to correspond, a couch may be had that will be in keeping with the most luxurions surroundings.

Center Table.—Have a low center table, with a reading lamp or a hanging lamp suspended over it, drawn out from the wall, and covered with books and periodicals, so that all the members of the family can gather about it. Cover this with a suitable cloth to harmonize with the color scheme of the room. The opportunity thus suggested of drawing up a number of chairs invites just the sort of informal social life that is so much needed in every community, and that cements the family bond as well as strengthens the ties of neighborliness.

"Have a Low Center Table."

Tea Table.—Have, if possible, in one corner of the room a small, low table with an alcohol lamp and suitable tea things for making a cup of tea without going for it to the kitchen. This simple expression of hospitality gives a note of good cheer that is much needed in modern social life. There need be no formality suggested by a cup of tea offered to a caller even in the most quiet neighborhoods, and having all of the needful articles at hand helps to give the serving of tea an air of grace and naturalness.

Chairs.—Select chairs as other furniture for simplicity and durability, and avoid complicated affairs such as the patent rockers, carved or stamped furniture, and all elaborate designs and decorations. The lines of the Morris chair suggest ease and comfort, and they are to be strongly recommended. Chairs of willow and wicker work are graceful, comfortable, and satisfactory. Of course, mahogany and

"The Lines of the Morris Chair."

other hard woods will be selected by those who can afford them. As to design, the Colonial models and the Craftsman and Mission styles of furniture are among the most satisfactory.

Taboret.—The low stand or taboret holding a graceful fern or other potted plant in a suitable jardinière adds an agreeable touch of grace and color to the living room.

Music. — The modern invention of the mechanical piano player has unlocked many a dusty piano and opened the whole world of music to thousands of homes. Heretofore the cost of a musical education has restricted the natural love of music in most families to but a few simple hymns and tunes that almost anyone could play. Hence the piano need no longer be regarded as necessarily confined to homes where some member of the family has a pronounced musical talent. Certainly nothing signifies more, with the possible exception of a collection of good books, than a musical instrument in the family living room.

Care of Piano.—To keep the piano or organ in good condition, arrange to have the atmosphere of the room dry, but not too dry, and at a moderate and even temperature. If the atmosphere is damp, there is a tendency for the wires to rust and the keys to stick. A dry heat without any moisture in the air will tend to check the varnish and also to injure the adjustment of a musical instrument. Hence, if rooms are heated by hot air, hang a small galvanized iron pail containing water from the under side of the register, so that the heated draught in coming up will bring a small amount of moisture with it.

Or, if gas or coal stoves are used for heating, place a suitable vessel of water on the top of the stove. The slight resulting moisture will be beneficial to all the furniture, although the piano will perhaps suffer most from the lack of it. The slight humidity is also good for the health of the family.

Do not stand the piano close against an outer wall, which may be damp or chilled from frost in winter, and if possible keep it out of a direct draught. If an upright piano, tack a dust cover of denim or other suitable material across the back to exclude dust, leaving flaps wide enough to be thrown over the piano when sweeping. These can hang down behind the piano when not in use. Take care that no small articles laid on the keys find their way inside of the instrument. Have a music cabinet, so as to keep the top of the instrument free from books and sheet music. Keep the piano closed when not in use, and have it tuned three or four times a year, or oftener, if necessary. If it is not kept up to pitch it will not stay in tune when required. An hour or two of practice on a piano each day will keep it in the best condition. But, if possible, every key on the keyboard should be struck at least once daily.

Care of Sheet Music.—Have a music cabinet, homemade if necessary, with shelves large enough for a piece of sheet music, and close enough together to admit of keeping the pieces classified. Bind two or more pieces of music of the same general kind together as desired by means of brass brads sold by stationers. The use of these is very simple. Lay the sheets one upon the other in the order desired, cut a slot top, bottom, and middle a half inch from the back edge with a penknife, insert the brad and turn down the edges.

Or, to bind music together, take a piece of strong manila or other tough paper two inches or more in width, and as long as the music is high. Fold this lengthwise in the middle and paste one side to one piece of music, the other to another. Run over this with a hot flatiron to insure its drying quickly and evenly without wrinkles. If the sheets tear apart, insert a similar strip between the torn sheets, and when all have been reënforced in this way take a similar strip of tough paper or muslin wide enough to go round the back of the whole collection and lap over an inch or more on either side. Slush the back well with paste or glue, lay on this strip, rub down tightly, and let dry under a weight. A manila folder or cover the same size as the music itself may be "drawn on" in a similar way to correspond to the cover of a bound book.

Pictures—Good and Bad Taste.—A good illustration of what to avoid is found in the family photographs enlarged by the carbon or imitation pastel process, and surrounded by massive frames at the recommendation of enterprising manufacturers, whose profits are in proportion to the size of the frame and the elaborateness of the molding. Only the eloquence of the venders could give such pictures even a temporary popularity, but they are seen everywhere. Family photographs should be, as a rule, confined to sleeping apartments rather than displayed in living rooms, and much better re-

"Much Less Seen than Formerly."

productions can be had in smaller sizes than upon a large scale. Carbon and other reproductions have little decorative value, and even when enlarged should be framed as simply and unobtrusively as possible. This work can usually be done at a lower rate and of a better quality by a local photographer. The difference in expense will usually furnish the living room with a good photographic reproduction of one of the masterpieces of the world, that will be equally interesting to strangers and instructive to the inmates of the home. Happily, public taste is rapidly improving in these matters. Heavy and elaborate moldings with intricate designs made of putty and covered with gilt paint, or oak molding stamped in imitation of hand carving, and the like monstrosities are much less seen than formerly. The object of picture molding is, of course, twofold—to protect and to define the picture; hence the frame itself should be unobtrusive and should in no way attract the eye to itself. If the wall coverings are in solid colors or quiet two-toned effects, and the picture frames are simple and appropriate, the picture itself stands out in all of its natural beauty. Thus the object is attained for which the picture was hung. A few pictures of reasonable size and real merit, simply but appropriately framed, give a much more artistic effect than does a wall crowded with a large number of subjects among which those that are inferior must necessarily suffer by contrast.

Pictures to Choose.—Select for living rooms landscapes, reproductions of still life, ideal heads and faces, and reproductions of masterpieces portraying scenes or subjects that might properly be the subject of conversation in the social circle.

For the music room, photographs of eminent composers and other musicians, or reproductions of paintings suggested by the use of the room, are appropriate.

For the library, photographs of literary and other public men, and reproductions of public buildings of all ages and in all parts of the world, are in order.

Reserve for the privacy of sleeping apartments photographs of friends or relatives of the family, children, and all other pictures that, however interesting they may be to the owner, can

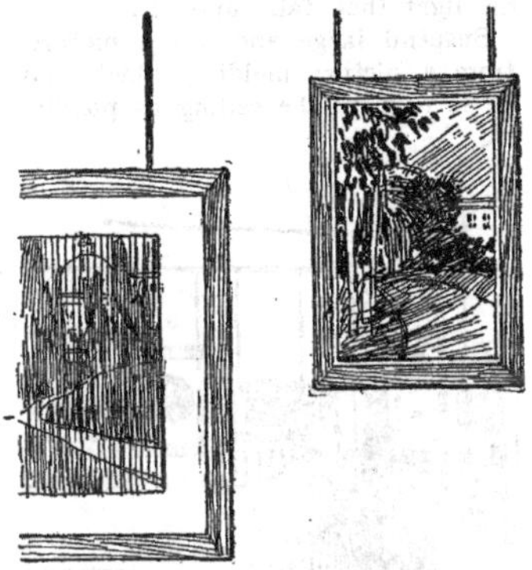

"The Frame Should Be Unobtrusive."

be of no general concern to those who are not members of the family.

To Hang Pictures.—Do not make the common mistake of hanging pictures above the line of sight, so as to make it necessary to strain the eyes in looking up at them. Pictures should not, as a rule, hang more than five and one half feet from the floor—about on a level with the eyes of a person of average height when standing. But, of course, the different pictures, for the sake of variety, are hung slightly above or below this line, according to their size and other circumstances, and not at a uniform level. Remember that in looking at a picture the eye falls, not at the exact center, but at a point about intermediate between the center and the top of the picture, or at about one third of its depth from the top. Hence, if a picture is hung so that the line of sight of a person of average height when standing falls on this point, it is displayed to the best advantage.

Do not hang a picture in direct light, as exactly opposite a sunny window. When possible, a picture should be located with reference to windows and other openings so that it will be lighted as the artist intended; that is, the shadows in the picture should appear to be cast by the light that falls upon it.

Suspend large and heavy pictures from a picture molding which may be as near to the ceiling as possible

On a Level with the Eyes."

to give a low room the effect of greater height, or lower it from the ceiling to give a high room a broader effect. Use as little picture wire as may be. Two wires and hooks, one near either end of a large picture, rather than a single hook with wire running from it diagonally in either direction, are to be preferred. Suspend small pictures preferably from small hooks or tacks driven into the wall behind the picture itself, and by means of rings or screw eyes in the back of the frame, all of which will be concealed from sight when the picture is hung. That is, have as little picture wire visible as possible. Ordinary woven picture wire is now inexpensive and can be used again and again. It not only looks better but is safer than cord. Ordinary "silver" wire is suitable for most purposes. It can be touched up with a little bronze paint to hang gilt frames, or when it becomes tarnished. Picture hooks of brass may be painted white or otherwise, to conform to the color of the picture molding and thus be less conspicuous.

In order to get the most effective arrangement, when in doubt where to hang pictures, do the experimental grouping on the floor. Thus the pictures may be shifted about until the most tasteful way is found. This saves many trips up and down the stepladder. When taking down pictures from the molding, make a dot with a pencil point on the wall back of the molding, where it will not show, exactly where the hook was hung, or leave the hook in place so that the picture when cleaned may be returned to its place without the necessity of measuring again. But if the wall coverings are of material that shows the effect of fading, as do most solid colors, especially greens and browns in ingrain papers, burlap, and the like, change the position of the pictures occasionally. Otherwise the wall covering behind the picture will not fade, and when for any reason a change becomes necessary the outlines will be unsightly.

Mats for Pictures.—Use common ingrain or moiré wall papers of various colors in place of mats or picture mounts. It is cheaper and equally effective. Mount the pictures on the mats as photographs are mounted.

Magazine Covers.—The cover designs and full-page illustrations of several of the leading monthly and other periodicals are reproductions of the best works of prominent artists and illustrators. These are freely used in many homes to decorate the walls of libraries, dens, and sometimes living rooms, either framed or bound in passepartout binding or merely neatly trimmed with a straightedge, and attached to the wall by means of brass-headed tacks or thumb tacks. A series of cover designs of one or more periodicals makes a very interesting and attractive frieze for the den or library.

SLEEPING ROOMS

The objects and nature of sleep should be understood as a basis for the intelligent furnishing and care of the bed and bedroom. Perhaps no other subject in connection with the household is more important or less understood. Where more than one person occupies a sleeping room each individual should have a separate bed, even if the requirements of space or other conditions make it necessary for two or more beds to stand side by side. It is especially important that children, after a very early age, should have separate cradles or cribs provided for them and be taught to occupy them. The reason for this custom is that individuals vary greatly in the amount of heat required to keep the body in a normal condition during sleep. Children require less covering than grown persons, and aged persons require much more covering than those in middle life. Separate beds admit of each individual adjusting the covering to his own requirements. Again, while the bodily sensations are dormant during sleep, they are not absent, or else a person could not be awakened. The body is still sensitive to outer impressions. Hence the motions of another sleeper or the changes in temperature produced by the addition or removal of coverings to accommodate a bedfellow may awaken a sleeper who by his restless motions will keep his companion awake, and no sound sleep may be enjoyed by either person. Fortunately, the invention of cast-iron and other cheap metallic bedsteads that may be obtained in half and three-quarter sizes makes it possible for many families to afford separate beds, a luxury which would formerly have been denied them.

The introduction of iron and brass bedsteads in many homes on sanitary and hygienic grounds, and the consequent discarding of old-fashioned wooden bedsteads that are heavy, difficult to clean, and that by collecting dust and furnishing harboring places for vermin are constantly contributing to the labor of the housekeeper, gives an opportunity to introduce this

"The Introduction of Iron and Brass Beds."

cleanly, healthful, and agreeable custom. Moreover, single or half beds can be readily moved from one room to another and from place to place, and are easier to care for.

Ventilation of Bedrooms.—The effect of entire lack of ventilation is illustrated by the celebrated case of the "Black Hole of Calcutta." About 150 Europeans taken at the capture of Fort Williams in Calcutta in 1756 were confined in a dungeon about twenty feet square, having two small windows. The following morning only twenty-three remained alive. In a similar case, on the steamer *Londonderry,* 150 passengers were confined in a small cabin for a number of hours. Of these, seventy died from constantly rebreathing the air contaminated in the lungs and by various exhalations of the human body. In breathing (and also in the combustion of fuel, as wood or coal, or of oil or gas for illumination), a part of the oxygen of the air which is necessary for human life is converted into carbonic-acid gas. The atmosphere consists of about 78 per cent of nitrogen, 20.96 per cent of oxygen, 1 per cent of argon, and .04 per cent of carbonic-acid gas mixed together. Each breath converts about one fourth of the available oxygen in the air into carbonic-acid gas; hence in an air-tight space death from suffocation would very quickly ensue.

Ordinary dwellings are, of course, by no means air-tight, and are partially ventilated through the narrow openings about window frames, by the occasional opening of doors, and through various cracks and crevices. But these sources are not sufficient to supply the volume of pure air required for human breathing. Rooms occupied by a number of persons are almost invariably so close that a great deal of air is necessarily breathed again and again. The results upon bodily health are in their nature the same as those which produce death by suffocation. Only the exhaustion is more gradual and extends over a longer period of time.

The effects of insufficient ventilation are perhaps less during our waking hours than during sleep. Most persons move about a good deal during the day and are in and out of doors. Moreover, the lungs are active, and if the air is impure, they may make up the deficiency by more frequent respiration. When a person is conscious, the discomfort of close air, resulting in headaches and a sense of incipient suffocation, affords warning that it is time to change the air in the room or take a walk outside. But a sleeper is usually unconscious of any warning sensations. The respiration is slower, and there is nothing to check the evil effects of breathing again and again the air that has been robbed of its oxygen. The result is the impairment of all the vital processes that normally make up during sleep for the daily wastes of the body. Hence sleeping in poorly ventilated rooms leads immediately to headaches, a sense of having rested badly, with exhaustion and fatigue, and eventually to such wasting diseases as consumption, catarrh, and other affections of the head, throat, and lungs.

The Fresh-air Cure.—It is now well known that consumption, the most wasting and fatal of all human diseases, can be cured in many cases by simply breathing pure air out of doors, both day and night. Modern sanitariums have sleeping porches of canvas or tents in which patients sleep out of doors, even in cold climates in winter, the body being protected by suitable covering. The contrast between slow suffocation from lack of ventilation and the cure of consumption by breathing pure air both day and night should impress upon everyone the absolute necessity of thorough ventilation, especially in sleeping apartments.

When to Ventilate.—It is a sure indication that, when the air in a room seems close and has a musty odor to a person coming in from outdoors, it is so impure as to be injurious to health. If, after stepping into the open air in the morning and taking a few deep breaths, one returns to a sleeping room and finds the air insufferably close, the room has not been sufficiently ventilated during the night, and evil consequences are sure to follow.

Or place a shallow glass dish containing lime water in a room to determine the presence of carbonic-acid gas. If there is much of this substance present the water will quickly become cloudy.

Or, to test for marsh gas, sewer gas, and the like containing sulphureted hydrogen, expose to the air moist carbonate of lead, which will turn black if this substance is present.

Night Air.—There is a superstition prevalent in many parts of the country that night air is injurious. There may be some ground for this belief where the Anopheles mosquito is abroad in malarial districts, or the vicinity of swamps wherever a mist may arise at night and spread contamination. But in most localities this notion is entirely groundless and misleading. If we do not breathe night air at night, pray what shall we breathe? Either it is necessary to breathe over and over the air that has been in the sleeping room all day, or else to admit fresh air from outdoors, and whatever the danger in breathing night air, it is certainly less immediate than quick or slow suffocation from lack of ventilation.

To Ventilate Bedrooms.—The problem of ventilation is twofold: first, to let in the pure air; second, to let out that which is impure. There should be windows on two sides of the bedroom, and also, if possible, a fireplace for ventilation. The bed should be located so that the air will circulate freely around and beneath it without a draught. If possible, the door when open should screen the bed, or a screen should be interposed when necessary between the bed and the open door or window.

The simplest means of ventilation is to lower the upper sash of a window for several inches and raise the lower sash either of the same window or of one on the opposite side of the room. If there is an open fireplace in the room, it will remove the impure air by creating a draught and causing suction.

Or lower the upper sashes of two windows opposite one another.

Or open the bedroom door and admit the fresh air to an adjacent room or hall by means of two or more windows in such a way that a draught passing near the bedroom door will create suction and draw the impure air out of it. The direction of these air currents may be determined by holding a lighted match or candle in them.

Just before retiring open all the windows and change the air in the room.

To Prevent Draughts.—To prevent a direct current of air crossing the bed on raising a window sash, take a piece of any firm, tightly woven cloth, as duck or light canvas or strong flannel goods, the width of the window and about eighteen inches deep. Make a heading at top and bottom to admit sash-curtain rods. Adjust one rod at the bottom of the window frame and the other about twelve or fourteen inches higher up. Thus when the sash is lifted as high as the upper rod the entering current of air will cause the cloth to belly out into the room, and the current will be turned on both sides and driven along the wall. A current of air, like a current of water,

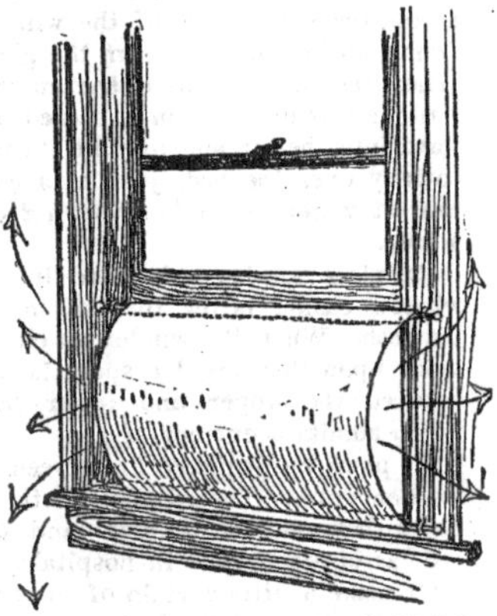

"The Air Will Follow Along the Wall."

has a tendency to stick to any surface over which it flows; hence the air will follow along the wall, and even to some extent around the corners of the room, as can be seen by testing with the flame of a candle.

Or either end of this cloth screen may be closed by means of a pin or buttonhole and button, and the entire current turned in the opposite dircetion. Ordinary sash-curtain rods or even rollers such as are used for curtain shades or sticks used for the lower part of curtain shades may be adjusted permanently for this purpose in sleeping rooms.

Or the patent spring sash-curtain rods, that have a spring inside and rubber tips at the end to keep them adjusted, may be utilized to make one or more removable screens. These can be adjusted according to conditions from time to time on any windows in any part of the house.

Or stretch a piece of cheese cloth over the opening and tack it fast.

Or tack cheese cloth on a small removable frame that will fit into the opening.

Or put a sheet of finely perforated metal in place of one of the upper panes of glass in one of the windows.

Or tack a strip of thin wood or stiff cardboard eight to twelve inches wide across the lower part of the window frame, an inch or two from the glass. When the sash is raised the current striking this obstruction is turned upward into the air and may be thrown entirely over the bed, just as a current of water might be thrown from a hose.

Or place a piece of board in the window casing below the bottom of the sash. When the window is closed down upon this board a space is left between the upper and lower sash which admits a current of air.

Or place an ordinary fire screen or wooden frame covered with cloth or paper between the window and the bed, as is often done in hospitals.

Or make a little curtain of sheeting to fit the head of the bed and tie at the four corners by means of tape.

Any of these devices may be used to ventilate other than sleeping apartments.

Sleeping Porch.—In the vicinity of the great sanitariums where sleeping out of doors has been proved to be a cure for consumption and other diseases, many persons have formed the habit of sleeping thus. Any porch somewhat excluded from view and in a sheltered location can be utilized. The porch should be screened and provided with storm curtains of tent canvas that can be drawn and buttoned like the curtains of a carriage. If the porch is used during the day a bunk or folding bed may be hinged to the wall on one side, with legs that will let down on the other. When folded up this may be concealed by a waterproof curtain. Or one of the so-called hammock beds may be suspended by hooks from the ceiling.

"The Porch Should be Screened."

If suitable blankets are provided it is possible to sleep out of doors the year round in most parts of the United States, with the exception of a very few nights, and probably no practice would be more invigorating, healthful, or pleasurable, especially in the summer months.

Bedrooms.—Furnishings and decorations of bedrooms should conform to the object for which the room is intended. Simplicity should be the keynote. Wall coverings in geometrical designs or large-figured patterns of any sort and all bric-a-brac and useless flounces and decorations should be avoided. The fewer objects not actually necessary in the room the better. Finish the woodwork in natural colors, oiled or stained, and preferably with oil paint or varnish. Tint the walls or hang them with a solid colored or double-toned paper, or a simple stripe. Hang at the windows light muslin or cheese-cloth curtains, either white or dyed to conform to the general color scheme. If the floors are smooth, oil and wax them, or stain or paint them with any of the lac paints or varnishes. Floors not smooth may be covered with either linoleum or matting as preferred. Avoid, as a rule, the use of carpets in bedrooms. A plain stained or painted wood floor with rugs is much easier to keep clean and is more sanitary.

Beds.—Iron or brass beds fitted with woven wire or other suitable wire springs are to be preferred. The iron beds in white enamel harmonize well with birch and other light-colored woods and enameled furniture; and brass beds with mahogany, walnut, and other hard woods in darker colors. The furniture should be of simple design, without carving or unnecessary decoration. The mattress should be of hair or cotton felt, of good quality, and made in two parts, for convenience in turning and airing. The bed clothing should be light and warm, consisting of linen or cotton sheets, blankets, and a white spread.

Beds and Bedding.—The ideal bed for health and comfort is of metal, either white enameled iron or brass, with a box spiral shelf spring or woven wire spring having enough spiral springs through the middle so that it will not sag. Iron and brass beds are now so cheap that they are being rapidly substituted for wooden bedsteads in all parts of the country. In choosing enamel beds see that the brass fittings are of good quality and well put on. The brass parts are the first to show wear, especially if they are loosely adjusted; and if they come off, the loss will spoil the appearance of the bed.

Enameled beds may be renovated by going over them with white or black enamel paint; to make them look like brass use gilt enamel. Any of these can be washed with soap and water. Thus a metal bed can be easily kept in perfect sanitary condition, free from dust, dirt, or vermin. Happily, the old-fashioned slat and cord bedsteads are rapidly becoming things of the past.

Mattresses.—The bed should not be softer than is necessary for comfort, and the surface should be smooth and nearly level. Feather beds are advisable for healthy adults only in extremely cold weather or cold climates, and in unheated rooms. They may be used for children or the aged in ordinary temperatures, but they should rather be packed tightly in thin ticks than loosely in large masses. Mattresses with suitable springs and bed coverings are to be preferred in most cases. The best material for mattresses is curled hair, although the much-advertised modern mattresses of felted cotton are also good and cheaper. Mattresses of excelsior and husks with cotton tops and ticks filled with clean hay or straw, or even beach-tree and other leaves are still used in many

"The Much Advertised Modern Mattress."

parts of the country. Any of these are hygienic and comfortable, and are to be preferred for adults in good health to feather beds.

The best material for pillows is curled hair, but if feathers are used the pillows should be tightly packed so that they will not allow the head to sink into them. The use of thick pillows is inadvisable. The pillow should be of just about the right thickness to support the head in its natural position when lying on the side, or to allow it to incline slightly backward.

Bed Springs.—The upholstered or box springs are the best. Make a cover of heavy unbleached drilling slightly larger than the springs, or cover them with a worn sheet or faded quilt. Fasten brass rings in the corners of the cover and attach them to brass-headed tacks or nails driven into the under side of the spring. This prevents the cover from slipping, but makes it removable for dusting. Or with a darning needle and cord tack the cover neatly and firmly in place. This prevents the springs from staining the mattress with rust.

Bed Covers.—As the muscles are entirely quiescent during sleep the body generates much less heat than in waking hours. Hence the bedclothes should furnish greater warmth than the ordinary clothing. On the other hand, the bed should not be warm enough to interfere with normal evaporation or overheat the body so as to cause undue perspiration.

Light bed covers of a suitable nonconducting material, as wool or eiderdown, are much better than heavy or numerous covers of cotton, as homemade quilts and comforters. Wool blankets are perhaps the best of all bed covers, and nothing else except a suitable coverlet for the purpose of decoration should be used if blankets can be afforded. Linen sheets are preferable to cotton for the reason that they are more absorbent. Hence they take up more readily the perspiration of the body. For the same reason they are much cooler in summer. They are more durable and it will be found a wise economy in the long run to purchase sheeting of unbleached linen rather than of cotton material.

Bedspreads.—Net, with lace insertion and edges, over an inexpensive lining of any color to match the other furnishings, makes an attractive bedspread.

Or dimity or dotted muslin may be used.

Or an old pair of lace curtains may be utilized by sewing the scalloped edges together to form the middle of the spread, and lining with any suitable colored fabric.

Valances.—The use of a valance is much less customary than formerly, as it is now thought more sanitary to allow the sunlight to penetrate to all parts of the room and the air to circulate freely. But if a valance is used, it should not be fastened to the frame of the bed, but so adjusted as to be easily removable for the laundry. Hence, to make a valance, cut a sheet to the size of the top of the mattress; make the valance in four sections, one for each side and for the top and bottom of the bed, and just long enough, allowing for the hem, to reach from the bottom of the mattress to the floor. Baste these sections to the edge of the sheet like a ruffle. Do not join the top and bottom to the sides, but leave the corners open. Try this on to see that it fits exactly before stitching. When completed, spread the sheet over the springs, and put the mattress on over it, so that the valance will hang down on all sides like a ruffle. Thus the valance always stays in place, but can easily be removed for washing, and the old sheet to which it is attached serves to protect the mattress from the springs. Delicate swiss or other light washable fabrics are more suitable for this purpose than cretonne or other heavy figured material.

Use of Feather Beds.—Formerly feather beds were much-valued luxuries, and the possession of a store of them was a matter of family pride. Happily, however, they are rapidly being replaced by mattresses, which, on account of improved methods of manufacture and the use of new material, are much better and cheaper than they were formerly. Feather beds are open to many objections. They are difficult to keep clean and they conform too closely to the shape of the body; hence they heat the body and do not admit of proper ventilation. Their use is always debilitating, and can only be justified by extreme cold weather, or for infants or very aged persons.

Feathers for Beds and Pillows.—The best feathers for this purpose are live geese feathers or other feathers plucked from the live birds; but chicken, goose, or duck feathers may be preserved and used for beds or pillows by putting all the soft feathers together in a barrel as they are picked from the birds after scalding. Leave the barrel open to the sun and rain, simply covering it with an old screen to prevent the feathers from blowing about.

Or purchase the feathers in quantity from the nearest poulterer and purify them yourself. Thus you can obtain plenty of feathers for pillows and feather beds at very little expense.

Feather Pillows.—Feathers are open to the same objections when used in pillows as in feather beds. By conforming to the shape of the head they prevent ventilation and tend to overheat the scalp. This weakens it and may lead to premature baldness or other affliction. Curled hair should be substituted for feathers whenever possible.

To Fill Feather Pillows.—To transfer feathers from an old feather bed to pillow ticks, or from one pillow tick to another, open a small part of the seam in the tick containing the feathers, draw over it the opening in the tick to be filled, and tack it to the full tick with basting thread, using large stitches. Feathers can then be shaken from one tick to the other without the white fluff getting about. Remove the basting threads and pin the openings together until you have time to stitch them firmly. This can be done in such a way as not to lose a single feather.

To Make Pillow Cases.—Pillow slips and bolster cases usually give out first at the corners from being hung on the line with clothespins and from the impact of irons against the sewed ends. Hence, by leaving both ends of the case open, you can distribute the wear over it all and double its life. Such cases are also much easier to iron. Both ends may be trimmed with lace or insertion, and two or three buttons and buttonholes may be left at each end to button the pillow in. Pillows thus trimmed will not need pillow shams.

To Protect Ticks.—To protect mattresses and pillow cases from becoming soiled make covers for them of unbleached cotton cloth or any suitable washable material, cut the cloth to measurements of the mattress and pillows, and finish one side or end with buttons and buttonholes, so that the cover can be easily slipped off and cleaned when necessary. Or the mattress protector may be tied on with tape. Bed linen often falls short of covering the mattress completely while in use, hence the extra slip is needed, especially to protect from the dust the under side of the mattress. These slips can be removed and laundered twice a year or oftener when housecleaning; the pillow covers may be removed oftener if desired. Ticking treated in this way will be fresh and clean at the end of a dozen years' hard usage, when otherwise it would be so worn and soiled as to be unfit for use. A dozen or two yards of cheap material will make cases for all the ticks in an ordinary household.

Or old sheets, pillow cases, or wornout garments may be utilized for this purpose. Cloth flour sacks make excellent pillow covers. Of course, the usual bed linen will be needed in addition to these.

Mattress Top.—A soft top for a husk or excelsior mattress may be made of old cotton or woolen blankets that have outworn their original use. Place between the blankets several thicknesses of cotton batting and tie the same as for comforters.

Sheets.—Linen is, of course, the best material for sheeting, for comfort, appearance, and durability, but cotton sheeting is more commonly used, because it is less expensive. Buy unbleached linen or cotton for sheets and pillow slips, as it is not only less expensive, but much more durable and can be easily bleached when being laundered.

To Make Sheets.—When making sheets, tear off one length, pin the first end of this length to the sheet and measure off the next. Then sew up as you have pinned. Thus the threads run the same way and the sheets will never pucker in the middle when washed.

Look over sheets before they go to the laundry and mend any tears at once. Sheets usually wear first and split in the middle. When this happens tear them down the middle, sew together the outer selvage edges to make the middle of new sheets, and hem the torn sides. This should be done as soon as the sheets begin to wear thin, without waiting for them to tear. It will double the life of the sheet.

Bathroom.—When possible, cover the floor of the bathroom with tile, cement, or other washable material, but linoleum is a good substitute for these. Or use cork carpet, which is warm to the feet and is washable and desirable, although it spots easily.

Hang the walls with waterproof paper. Or tint the walls with a natural cement that has no glue and does not require a glue size.

THE DINING ROOM

Besides the regular dining-room furniture, tables, chairs, sideboard, and serving table, the addition of a plate rail or rack for plates, pitchers, and other decorative china objects, and of a china cabinet with glass doors for displaying the best china, help to give a room character and beauty. The effect of these articles will be very much heightened if the wall coverings are in solid or double-toned colors, and, as in other living rooms, hard-wood floors or floor coverings in solid colors, with a large rug or drugget coming within a few feet of the wall all around, make perhaps the most effective treatment. The color scheme of the dining room should preferably be in cheerful tones, as blues, yellows, or reds, according to the amount of light the room receives.

China Closet.—The china cabinet is a useful and beautiful article of furniture, but in the absence of such a cabinet any ordinary closet opening into a dining room may be utilized as a china closet by removing the door and replacing it with a decorative door with diamond panes of glass, and lining the interior with denim to correspond in color with the furnishings of the room.

Or the door may be removed and replaced by a suitable drapery hanging from a rod, and drawn aside when the dining room is in use. Screw hooks on the inside of the shelves of the china cabinet or closet from which to hang cups to display them, save space, and prevent breakage. Tack a narrow strip of board two or three inches from the back of each shelf, as a rim to hold up the plates. Or put in a row of brass tacks standing an eighth of an inch above the shelf for this purpose.

Table Pad.—A pad of table felt sold for the purpose should be laid over the dining-room table, both to protect the polish and to save the linen tablecloth. But an old blanket or thick cotton flannel may be used for this purpose, or clean carpet lining can be utilized by covering it with white muslin smoothly pasted on. This will last for months and can be readily replaced.

To Store Table Leaves.—Fasten under the lower shelf of the pantry the frame in which the extra boards of the extension dining table come, and slide the boards in. Thus they take up no extra space and are always at hand.

China.—Select a stock pattern when buying china, and preferably a standard design of some sort, as the well-known willow or onion design, or some other that can be readily replaced as pieces are broken. When possible it is, of course, a good plan to have two sets of china, one for best, to be displayed in the china cabinet and only used upon special occasions, and another for ordinary wear, which may be less delicate and expensive.

THE KITCHEN, STOREROOM, AND PANTRY

The kitchen, as the workshop of the house, is the room in which many housekeepers spend most of their waking hours. Hence it should be perhaps the lightest, airiest, and most cheerful room in the house. It is safe to say that much more attention might well be given to the matter of kitchen conveniences than they usually receive. There are very few housekeepers indeed who could not, by intelligent forethought in planning and arranging the contents of the kitchen, pantry and storeroom, save themselves daily miles of useless traveling to and fro.

Color for Kitchen.—Try to make the kitchen a room in harmonizing tints by painting or tinting the walls in light greens and the floor in dark green. Or a clear, light yellow is a good color for the kitchen walls, with the floor in brown. Or, if the room has a southern or western exposure, gray walls, with the floor in drab or slate color, will give a cooler effect.

Kitchen Walls. — Kitchen walls should be covered with washable materials; hence ordinary wall paper

"The Cracks May be Filled."

and calcimine are less suitable in the kitchen than in other parts of the house. If the walls are new and smooth, tint them in waterproof cement or paint them with water colors and coat with soluble glass. Both these processes are inexpensive.

Or washable paper is excellent. It can be washed and kept perfectly clean, and does not absorb grease or moisture.

Or paint the walls with common oil paint of good quality and finish with a coat of enamel paint or soluble glass, so that they can be mopped the same as the floor. For this purpose fit a large sponge into a mop handle. But paint is not as easy to wash down as washable paper or oilcloth, hence, where the walls are in good condition, the latter is preferable.

Kitchen Floor. — A tight, smooth floor of unpainted wood, hard enough not to splinter and to admit of being scrubbed, is perhaps the best floor for a kitchen. But if the floor is of soft wood, or is uneven and has unsightly cracks in it, the cracks may be filled and the floor painted with oil paints, and varnish or "lac" paints containing varnish may be used.

Or the floor may be covered with linoleum, which is perhaps, all things considered, the most satisfactory floor covering. Before laying the linoleum on a rough floor, cover the floor with a layer of sand, or sawdust, or old newspapers, to prevent its being worn by the cracks, and give the linoleum a coat of paint and varnish three or four times a year. When thus treated it is practically indestructible.

Or oilcloth may be substituted for linoleum and cared for in the same fashion. This is inexpensive, and with proper care will last a long time.

Kitchen Sinks.—The sink may be of iron or other metal, with or without enamel, or of stone, or even of wood lined with lead, tin, or zinc. But it should stand on four legs, and all the waste pipe should be exposed to sun and air. Take away all woodwork from about the sink, and paint the pipes and under part the same color as the walls and woodwork.

If the air is admitted freely to all parts, no moisture can accumulate to cause the decay of organic matter which produces diphtheria, typhoid and other fevers. Physicians say that when these diseases occur in any household, the first thing they look at is the sink and the arrangements for drainage about the kitchen door. Each day rinse the dishpan with boiling water in which dissolve a tablespoonful or more of washing soda or aqua ammonia, and pour it down the spout boiling hot. Once a week flush the pipes by filling the sink with boiling water, in which dissolve a teacupful of chloride of lime. Use a quantity of water great enough so that it will run through the pipes with force. This is the best disinfectant, is cheap, and just as good as any patent preparation.

Have the drainage carried to a sufficient distance from the house into a covered cesspool, whence it will leach off into the soil, and see that it does not leach into the well. Never throw dishwater from the kitchen door. Have a receptacle for all garbage, and feed it regularly to the chickens, or, if no fowls are kept, see that it is burned, buried, or at least removed to a distance from the house. Scald the garbage receptacle with a solution of chloride of lime—half a teacupful to a quart of water—twice a week.

Kitchen Table.—A bench or table, homemade if necessary, at the left of

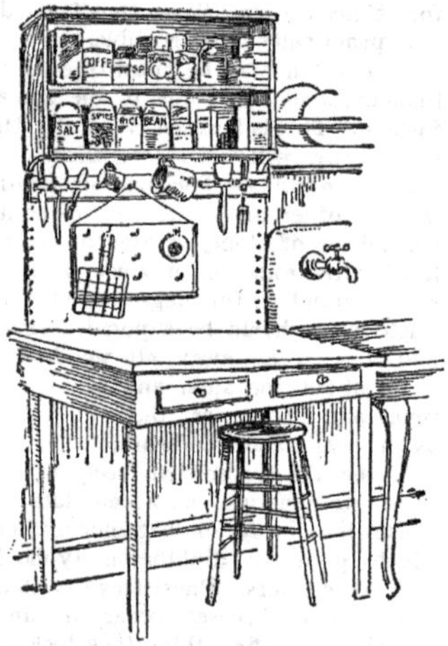

"Homemade if Necessary"

the kitchen sink and as large as the room will admit, is indispensable to saving steps in the kitchen. Have this overlap the edge of the sink and cover with zinc, which will not rust. Turn up the zinc over a molding around the sides of the table, except at the end over the sink, so that water will drain back from it into the latter. Carry the zinc, if possible, eighteen inches or two feet up the kitchen wall behind the table and the sink. This is lasting, easily kept clean, and is not injured by hot pans or kettles. If scrubbed clean it can be used as a molding board. Particles of dough which adhere to it can easily be scraped off with a knife. Zinc that has done duty under a stove may be used for a kitchen table. Cut a V out of the corners, lap over the edges, and nail closely with long, sharp steel tacks.

Or cover the kitchen table with oilcloth. This will last a long time if the table is padded with sheet wadding or several thicknesses of newspaper covered with an old sheet. Draw the padding smooth and tack it under the edge of the table.

Kitchen Rack for Utensils.—Cover the wall back of the kitchen table and sink with zinc or oilcloth about two feet in height, tacking a strip of inch-thick pine or other soft wood about three inches wide along the top. Along the middle of this fasten a narrow strip of leather or a strip of doubled oilcloth, with tacks at intervals of one and a half or two inches, making loops through which cooking spoons, knives, forks, can openers, etc., may be thrust. Thus these articles are always in sight and ready for use. Above put up a number of six- or eight-inch shelves to any desired height to hold breakfast foods, coffee, salt, pepper and other spices, glass jars or tin cans containing nuts, rice, beans, sugar, and various dry groceries. On the upper shelves can be stored soap, canned goods, and the like. Insert hooks on the under side of the lower shelf to hold measuring cups, tin pails, or anything that can be hung up out of the way. Cover the shelves with oilcloth so that they can be kept clean. Hang from the cleat against the wall a board of any desired size; say 16 by 24, which may be of weathered oak or any hard-wood stuff cleated to prevent warping. In this screw small brass hooks on which to hang the strainer, baking spoon, egg whip, roasting fork, meat cleaver, bread toaster, etc. These shelves and the rack save thousands of steps to the pantry and take the place of a costly kitchen cabinet.

Blotters in the Kitchen.—Obtain a supply of ordinary desk blotters and have a place for them on the rack above the kitchen table. If fruit juice or grease spatters or spills on clothing or table linen apply the edge or corner of a clean blotter, and most of the liquid will be taken up.

Or, if grease is spilled on the floor, a blotter will take it up quickly while warm and save the labor of removing a grease spot that has soaked into the boards.

Tin Rack.—Hang near the range a plate rack, which may be homemade, or fasten a cleat against the wall for tin lids, kettle covers, pie tins, and the like. Thus these are always dry and convenient.

Pantry Shelves.—Paint the pantry shelves white, or cover them with a coat of white enamel. Wash the shelves with cold water as soon as the enamel dries, and it will harden quickly. Such shelves will not require oilcloth or paper, can be easily wiped off with a damp cloth, and always show when perfectly clean.

Or cover the shelves with white oilcloth. Cut the oilcloth to exactly fit the shelf, turn down over the edge, and paste on. While somewhat expensive, this lasts for years, cleans easily, and always looks well.

Or use ordinary building paper, which is better than newspaper and by the roll is very cheap. It can be wiped off with a damp cloth almost as easily as paint.

Or use washable paper, the same as kitchen walls are hung with, pasting it to the shelves.

Or, if newspapers are used, fold a whole newspaper the longest way of the full sheets and place the fold in the front of the shelf. Then when cleaning the pantry it is only necessary to slip a paper cutter in the fold of the outer sheet, cut it clear across, and take off the soiled upper part.

Tack a narrow strip of wood (any left-over pieces of picture molding will do) along the back of the pantry shelves, about three inches from the wall. To save space, stand platters and large plates with their edges resting against this.

Run a one-inch strip of wood against the wall, held away from it by wooden brackets; in this put kettle lids and covers of all sizes.

Screw suitable hooks on the under side of the shelves for dishes having handles, as pitchers, cups, and the like.

Dampness in Closets.—Place a bowl of quicklime in a damp pantry, cupboard, or closet. This not only removes dampness, but kills all odors.

Range Shelves.—Have near the range a shelf to hold the many things needed in cooking, as pepper, salt, and other seasonings, flavorings, and the like, to save steps to the pantry or to the shelves over the kitchen table. Have another shelf covered with zinc on which to put down hot kettles and articles taken fresh from the baking oven.

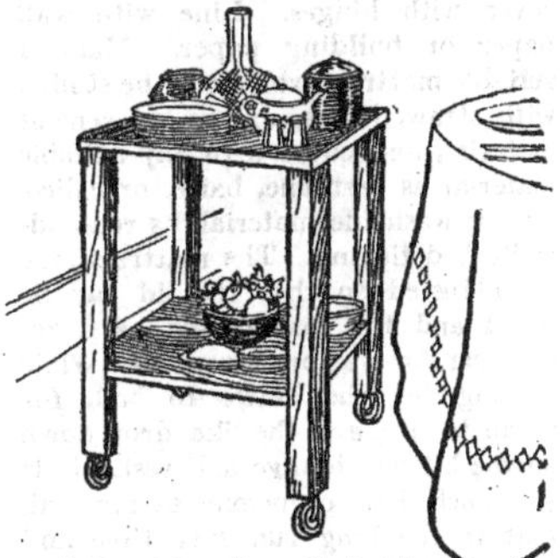

"Mounted on Large Casters."

Rolling Table.—Have made at home or by a carpenter a small, strong table about 2 feet or $2\frac{1}{2}$ by 3 feet, mounted on large casters or small wheels, which can be bought at small expense at a hardware store. Have a shelf part way down in addition to the top. When clearing or setting the dining-room table load this serving table and draw it to and from the kitchen. Thus one trip will do for all.

Kitchen Slate.—Try making a programme each morning of the things to be done through the day. Or jot down from time to time those that must be done at the first opportunity. You will be surprised to find how quickly these things will be disposed of. When cooking or preparing company dinner, make a list of the articles to be prepared, and glance at it occasionally.

Homemade Receipt Book.—Have at hand a blank book in which to paste or copy valuable recipes. Cover this with white oilcloth neatly pasted on. Have a special part of this book or a separate book for menus. This will help to solve the problem of what to have for dinner.

Kitchen Lounge.—Remove the old sofa to the kitchen, and put in its place a modern couch with an artistic couch cover.

Or make a homemade lounge out of a long packing box or tack together two of the right height. Put on a cover with hinges. Line with wall paper or building paper. Make a suitable mattress which may be stuffed with straw, husks, or any convenient material, and cover with any suitable material as cretonne, baize, or calico. Or use washable material, as red-and-white bed ticking. The mattress may be adjusted so that the lid can be lifted and the inside used as a receptacle for various purposes. While waiting for the kettle to boil, for bread to rise, and the like, drop down on the kitchen lounge and rest. It is just such little economies of strength that in the long run save time and preserve health.

SMALL ECONOMIES

The reason many things are wasted in every household is that the family has not formed the habit of making uses for them. The following ways to use string, paper bags, wrapping paper and newspapers, lard pails, and various cans and bottles that come into the house every day from the grocers and other merchants, will be found not only useful small economies but also valuable household conveniences.

Uses of Common Twine.—Save all bits of string or twine, and teach the children to sort them and knot the different sizes together. Roll the common white twine up into a ball, drop it inside a box, with the end protruding through a hole in the lid. Or use the accumulated twine to knit or crochet dishcloths eight to twelve inches square. Bath slippers can also be made of it.

Wind coarse twine on a roller or fishline reel and hang it up on the back of the pantry door.

Paper Bags.—These are not only convenient to wrap up articles, but are especially useful to polish stoves and lamp chimneys, to wipe up milk, grease, or what not, as they can be quickly disposed of by burning when soiled.

Tissue Paper.—This is useful for polishing glass, wrapping up laces, ribbons, and other delicate articles.

Oiled Papers.—Oiled papers that come over butter and lard may be used for papering cake tins. The waxed papers that come on the inside of cracker or biscuit boxes are useful to wrap up cheese and other articles which will deteriorate if exposed to the air, also for wrapping lunches, for school and factory lunch pails, and picnics.

Wrapping Paper.—This may be used to slice bread and cake upon, roll crackers, pare apples or potatoes, and dress chickens on, after which it may be rolled up and dropped into the garbage pail.

Or it may be spread over the garbage pail and all garbage placed on it to save trouble in cleaning.

Flour Bags.—Large paper flour bags are useful for bleaching gloves and other small articles with the fumes of sulphur, and dry cleaning with magnesia, corn meal, and similar substances. The cloth sacks may be used for dish towels and dishcloths.

When emptying flour sacks, a small amount of flour will adhere to the sack. Turn the sack inside out, lay it over the molding board, and knead the bread upon it. This will cleanse it effectually.

Newspapers. — Spread clean newspapers under the carpet, especially if the floor is rough. They make a smooth surface, prevent wear, and also check draughts through the floor cracks. Also use them for polishing windows, mirrors, lamp chimneys, stove tops, and nickel.

Spread a newspaper before the stove when taking up ashes. Light newspaper in the open grate when taking up ashes, or shaking down a grate fire. The resulting draught will carry the dust up the chimney.

Cover plants on frosty nights with newspapers, or if indoors, put them between the plants and the windows. Fold a newspaper across the chest and attach with safety pins under the cloak or coat when exposed for a long time in cold winds, as in sleighriding.

Also use newspapers for wrapping furs, velvets, and other articles when storing them to protect them from moths.

Tin Cans. — Lard, kerosene, and other oils are sold in various parts of the country in five-gallon cans. These can be obtained from the grocer for a small sum and make excellent boilers to wash out small articles too dainty for the regular wash. They can also be used with a small washboard as tubs.

Or they may be used as flour bins, bread or cake boxes, and the like.

Or, by removing the top and making holes at each side and attaching short pieces of copper wire with a broom handle between, convenient pails may be made out of them. These pails may be made of any desired depth by cutting off the can with a cold chisel and hammer and turning back the sharp edges.

Such cans are also convenient to salt down pickles, steam fruit, etc.

Lard Pails.—These may be used for storing sugar, coffee, cereals, and rice. Or for potting plants, especially as hanging baskets. They are also useful both in five- and ten-pound sizes for steaming brown bread and Indian puddings. A five-pound lard pail placed inside a ten-pound pail, and slightly raised from the bottom of the latter by small stones or otherwise, forms a good substitute for a double boiler.

Or an earthen jar or common saucepan may be used for the outer receptacle, and rice, cracked wheat, oatmeal, prunes, etc., may be cooked without danger of burning.

They are also useful for storing and carrying milk, butter, and eggs.

Baking-powder and Cocoa Cans.—One of these cans, with a few nail holes in each end, is a good soap shaker. This will utilize all the scraps of soap.

Or soak off the wrappers, paint these cans with any color of enameled paint, and label them with gilt or any other colored letters. Use these for all sorts of spices, which may be bought in bulk much cheaper than in cans. These cans are air-tight and will preserve the strength of the contents.

Or use for this purpose empty vaseline and cold-cream jars with screw tops. These being of glass, their contents can be seen at a glance, and no labeling is required.

Cereal Boxes.—The stiff pasteboard boxes in which breakfast foods are sold may be labeled and set in a row on the pantry shelf. When paper bags of dry groceries come from the grocer's, they may be dumped in the proper box, thus saving the time and trouble of opening first one sack and then another to find the right article. Use these for rice, beans, tapioca, corn meal, oatmeal, starch, salt, hominy, buckwheat, sugar, etc.

Labels. — Everything should be labeled for the convenience of every member of the family. Beat up the white of an egg and dilute with a pint of warm water. On ironing day apply this both to the label and to the glass or tin, and afterwards run a hot iron over the surface to set it. Tack pasteboard tags on wooden boxes, and on bags containing pieces of cloth of all descriptions tie cloth labels.

Kitchen Cabinet.—A good kitchen cabinet, with metal bins for flour, meal, and other substances that mice are fond of, is an investment which will save time and strength for the

"A Good Kitchen Cabinet."

housekeeper and will be a money saver in the long run. These bins should be removable, so that they can be regularly washed, scalded, and dried.

To Order Groceries.—A child's school slate hung on a nail in the wall of a kitchen, with a slate pencil attached by a strong cord, will be found a great convenience in ordering groceries. When any supplies run low, make a note on the slate of what is wanted. The whole family will soon get into the habit of making these memoranda, and many steps in running errands will be saved. Also make an alphabetical list of groceries in a little indexed alphabetical memorandum book and hang this up on the same nail. When the grocer calls run over this list to refresh your mind.

If the various dry groceries, as tapioca, rice, raisins, etc., are kept in glass jars, it will be easy to see what is wanted, and they will be protected from mice and insects. Fruit jars of various sizes are useful for this purpose.

Or use a pad and pencil to keep memoranda of articles wanted. The paper can then be detached when going to market and forms a convenient memorandum.

Storeroom.—A cellar having a cement floor and water-tight walls, if kept clean and sanitary, makes an ideal storeroom, but many houses do not have one. A small storeroom can be made in a corner of the cellar at much less cost than is commonly supposed, by putting up walls of concrete made of sand or gravel and cement. Rough boards may be knocked together with very little trouble to make a mold. The cellar walls, if they are tight and dry, will make two sides; or they can be faced with cement by building a board-retaining wall an inch or two from the surface of the cellar wall and pouring the cement back of it. The whole, including the floor, can thus be made solid concrete at a trifling cost. When furnished with a suitable door, this storeroom will be damp proof and free from dust, germs, and all other unsanitary pests. There should be a cellar window protected on the outside by wire netting, and having on the inside a removable screen of cheese cloth to keep out the dust.

Slat shelves painted with white paint and a coat of enamel may be built up in this storeroom in the same manner as book stacks in a library, i. e., back to back, with just enough room between them for a person to walk. On these shelves preserves, pickles, canned goods, butter, eggs, and other groceries can be stored the year round in perfect safety.

In a cellar thus equipped can be stored canned goods and other groceries bought at wholesale when prices are low, thus saving in many cases 25 per cent of the cost of such articles.

Door Mat.—A great deal of mud is tracked in at the kitchen door. Make door mats of several thicknesses of old carpets, turning in the raw edges and sewing them together with carpet tacks. Attach stout loops to the corners and fasten these over strong nails on the porch floor. These keep the mat in shape and place, and allow it to be readily removed and cleaned.

Verandas.—One of the most notable changes that have come over American

"Living Out of Doors."

life in recent years is the increase in the custom of living out of doors. The old-fashioned porch, formerly a mere rain shed over the doorstep, or small outer vestibule, is being generally replaced by a wide structure ex-

CHAPTER II

HEATING, LIGHTING, AND REFRIGERATION

KINDS OF FUEL—HEATING SYSTEMS—CHIMNEYS AND FLUES—FIRE EXTINGUISHERS AND FIRE ESCAPES—FIREPROOFING AND WATERPROOFING—ARTIFICIAL ILLUMINATION—COAL GAS, GASOLINE GAS, AND ACETYLENE—KEROSENE OIL—ICE AND REFRIGERATION

KINDS OF FUEL

The principal kinds of fuel used in this country are anthracite or hard, and bituminous or soft, coal, coke, gas, petroleum or kerosene, and wood, either hard or soft. Peat or turf fuel is quite common in European countries, and some attempts have been made to introduce it in the United States in the form of "briquettes" and "eggettes," but thus far without much success. The cost of the various kinds of fuel naturally varies according to local conditions, but where all kinds are equally plentiful, wood is the most expensive. About eighteen cords of the best hard wood is required to heat the home of an average family for a year. At six dollars a cord this would cost nine dollars a month. Anthracite or hard coal is the next most expensive fuel; its first cost is higher and it is not an economical fuel to use, the estimated cost of heating an average home with hard coal being about seven dollars a month. The cheapest forms of fuel in common use are bituminous or soft coal and coke. Where plenty of coke is available it may be regarded as perhaps the cheapest fuel, its cost being estimated on an average of about five dollars a month in temperate latitudes. Bituminous coal is, ton for ton, cheaper than coke, but as somewhat more is required for fuel, the cost may be regarded as practically the same. Gas is, perhaps, the ideal fuel. It is clean, convenient, and when the price is not unduly advanced by monopolistic control, it is cheaper than any other fuel. Under present conditions it is usually somewhat more expensive, although the extra cost is, perhaps, more than made up by increased convenience and efficiency.

Coal as Fuel.—Coal in its natural state consists of solid carbon combined with various proportions of hydrocarbons (or compounds of carbon with hydrogen, which may be driven off in the form of illuminating gas) and various impurities. Thus coal is really made up of two kinds of fuel: coke—which is practically all carbon—and ordinary illuminating gas. It is much more convenient and satisfactory to use coal in these two separate forms than in its natural state. Very little bituminous or soft coal is used for domestic purposes in most parts of the United States, notwithstanding its cheapness, because of the dirt, dust, coal gas, and cinders consequent upon its use. Anthracite or hard coal is somewhat less troublesome, but its use is wasteful because little more than the hydrocarbons driven off as gas is really consumed, the remainder being left in the form of cinders, which are usually thrown away.

Sizes of Coal.—The large sizes of coal are the most wasteful, as the volatile gases are rarely all driven off and the heart of the large chunks is not usually consumed. The result is a residue of cinders and clinkers that choke up the grate and create a great deal of labor and discomfort. By the use of suitable grates and some care and attention, the smallest sizes of coal (which are also ton for ton much cheaper) may be utilized.

Coal — Small Sizes to Use. — The smallest size of coal in ordinary use is known as "pea coal." This requires a special grate, but after a fire has been kindled in an ordinary grate, and a good bed of coals has been made, pea coal may be used if care is taken not to shake down all the ashes at once. There is a still smaller size known as "buckwheat coal," which is even cheaper than pea coal. This may be used in place of cinders to bank down the fires at night, the advantage being that when coke or larger coal is added to the fire next morning, the buckwheat coal will be entirely consumed, whereas a bank of cinders tends to deaden the fire during the day.

Coke as Fuel.—Coke is produced in large quantities as a by-product of illuminating gas, and in the vicinity of gas plants in cities it is usually sold at low prices. Coke is cleaner than coal (whether hard or soft), easier to kindle, burns more freely, and leaves a much smaller residue of ash, with practically no cinders or clinkers. The principal objection to its use is, that unless care is taken it may produce too hot a fire. But this difficulty may be overcome by banking the fire after it is well kindled with buckwheat or pea coal.

Gas as Fuel.—The advantages of gas as fuel are manifold, and its use, especially for cooking purposes, is being rapidly extended. It is clean, convenient, and efficient, and will be the most economical fuel when proper arrangements are made for selling it to the public at a reasonable profit. It is probable that good gas can be manufactured and sold to the public in most localities in the neighborhood of fifty cents a thousand, and that under stress of competition new and approved appliances might be produced that would decrease still further the cost of manufacture. Even at prices ranging from $1 to $1.50 and upward per thousand, the use of gas, if proper care is observed, must be regarded as economical.

HEATING SYSTEMS

The principal systems of heating dwelling houses are the use of steam, hot water or hot air, generated by furnaces (located usually in a basement or cellar), and the use of closed coal, oil, or gas stoves, or of open grates, which may be placed in stoves or in fireplaces. Each of these systems has its advantages and disadvantages, but, disregarding the first cost, it is probable that, from the double standpoint of efficiency and economy, they may all be rated about as follows: First, steam; second, hot water; third, hot air; fourth, the open grate; fifth, the closed coal stove; sixth, closed oil stove; seventh, closed gas stove.

Furnaces. — Furnaces vary greatly in the amount of coal that they con-

"Most Notable is the Underfeed System."

sume to produce a given temperature. At best only a small percentage of the actual heat value of the fuel is realized, and the future will doubtless witness great improvement in this direction. At present a number of new devices are on the market, of which one of the most notable is the underfeed system. This furnace is so constructed that the fuel is deposited in a chamber below the fire box, where it is gradually warmed before being forced from below by means of a lever into the fire box. Thus the heat is saved which is wasted in other types of furnaces by raising the temperature of cold fuel thrown directly upon the blaze, and less fuel is consumed to produce a given increase of temperature. There is also less unnecessary combustion. The difference may be illustrated by the burning of two candles, one right side up and the other upside down. The former con-

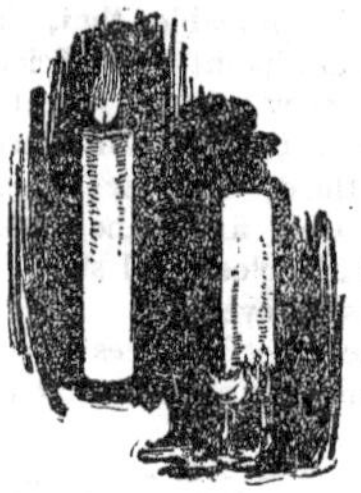

"*An Inevitable Waste.*"

sumes no more fuel than is necessary; the latter produces an inevitable waste.

Another device consists in a perforated plate of metal, placed across the fire box so that the flame is broken up into a large number of small jets of burning gas. The plate also becomes exceedingly hot and thus assists the combustion of the gases.

Other important devices are means to prevent heat from being wasted by radiation in the cellar or basement or by escaping up the chimney. The indirect-draught furnace contains a device which causes the heated products of combustion to circulate in such a way, before going up the chimney, as to heat every part of the furnace. The saving in the use of these devices would far exceed the difference in the first cost, even if they were much

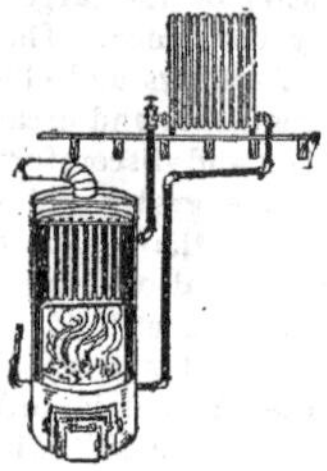

"*Hot-water Radiation.*"

more expensive than other types of heating apparatus, which is not necessarily the case. Hence, their universal use is to be recommended.

Steam and Hot-water Heating Systems.—The first cost of installing a steam or hot-water system is considerable, and both require a good deal of care to produce satisfactory results. They also demand some provision for ventilation, which is an additional expense. Both steam heat and hot water are difficult to adjust to sudden changes of temperature. In mild weather, steam heat is not economical, because the furnace must be kept hot enough to boil water in order to produce any steam at all, and hot-water heat is inconvenient, since, if the weather becomes suddenly mild when the pipes are filled with hot water, the house will be too warm. On the other hand, if the water is allowed to cool and the temperature again changes, considerable time is required in either system to reheat the boiler.

Thermostat.—The most satisfactory results with the steam and hot-water systems are obtained by the installation of the thermostat, an instrument which can be adjusted at any given temperature, so that if the heat falls below this standard the furnace draught will be automatically opened; if it rises above, the furnace draught will be closed. Thus a uniform temperature can be maintained with the least possible attention.

The Ideal System. — Probably the ideal system of heating is the so-called vacuum steam system, by which a partial vacuum is formed in the steam

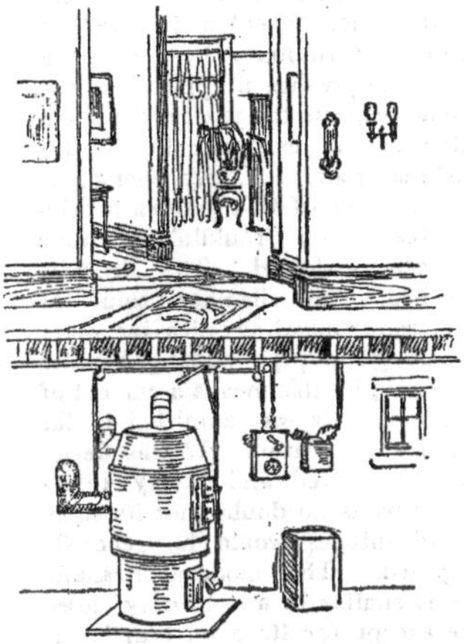

"If the Heat Falls . . . the Draught Opens."

pipes. Thus, steam may be produced in the pipes at a temperature below 212°. An attachment, known as the automatic vacuum valve, which produces a similar effect, can be supplied to ordinary steam radiators. Probably, then, an underfeed, indirect-draught furnace with a system of ventilation and a suitable thermostat, while somewhat expensive to install, would give the most perfect and satisfactory results.

Hot-air Systems.—The advantages of the hot-air system of heating, after the first cost of installation, are that it does not require a supplementary system of ventilation, can be easily cared for, and readily adjusted to changes in temperature. The disadvantages oftenest complained of are the dust and gases that sometimes rise from the register, the difficulty caused by high winds blowing into the cold-air boxes, and dryness of the atmosphere caused by delivering the heated air at too high a temperature. But these disadvantages may be overcome by proper construction and installation.

To Prevent Dust.—Dust may find its way either from above or from below into the stream of warm air that rises from the register. To prevent its rise from below, the outer opening of the cold-air box may be screened with cheese cloth or other thin fabric, and over the seams of the cold-air box and flues may be placed a metal protector with tightly soldered joints. Thus the gases and any foul air that may be in the cellar will be excluded from the draught, and the supply of air coming in from out of doors will be fresh and pure as well as warm. To prevent dust from entering the flue from above, the registers should be closed while sweeping and should be removed each day after sweeping and dusted out of the window; one or more thicknesses of cheese cloth or netting should be stretched under the register and across the flue so as to screen the current of air as it rises. Registers set in the wall naturally receive less dust from sweeping than floor registers do. They also give the warm air a somewhat better circulation.

How to Regulate Hot Air.—Hot air is a misnomer. Overheated air is detrimental to health and also injurious to woodwork and furniture. The term "warm air" is preferred by most authorities, and the best results are secured by having a relatively large furnace that, by delivering a large quantity of air at a moderate temperature, will heat the house comfortably in the coldest weather. The air should not be delivered at a temperature greater than 120°, and under no circumstance should the fires be allowed to rage until the fire box is red hot.

To Overcome Dryness. — The dryness of the atmosphere caused by the warm-air furnace may be overcome by keeping a supply of water in the receptacle usually furnished for that purpose inside the jacket of the furnace; or by hanging a small tin pail of galvanized iron from a hook below one or more of the registers in the room, so that the current of air therefrom will receive a small amount of moisture.

Hot Air — To Prevent Waste. — A great saving can be effected by casing the jacket of the furnace and the hot-air pipes with several thicknesses of asbestos paper to prevent direct radiation in the basement. Heat which would otherwise be wasted may also be utilized by the addition of a hot-water attachment. This combination of the hot-air and hot-water systems affords, perhaps, the greatest

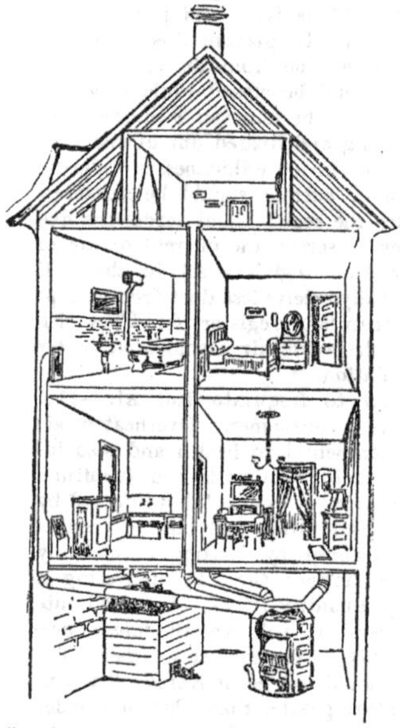

"The Same Flue Will Serve Two Registers."

possible economy in fuel. The hot-water piping may be used in distributing the heat to any parts of the house not equipped with the hot-air system. When possible, the hot-air flues should be so adjusted that the same flue will serve two or more registers. Thus, by closing the register in the lower rooms, the heat can be diverted through the same flue to the upper part of the house, with the least possible number of pipes and waste of heat.

The Franklin Stove. — The celebrated device invented in 1782 by Benjamin Franklin, and called by him the "Pennsylvania fireplace," is still in some respects the most satisfactory contrivance in existence for heating individual rooms. Oddly enough, in modern stoves of this pattern a principal feature of Franklin's invention has been neglected. The Franklin stove had an air chamber behind the grate, communicating with the outer air through a pipe passing beneath the hearth; by this means a current of pure, warm air was admitted to the room for ventilation. If this device could be revived and widely advertised, there is no doubt that its superior advantages would be generally recognized. The modern Franklin stove is similar to an ordinary closed stove except for its open hearth. It combines the cheerful open grate of a fireplace with economy of the heat lost in a fireplace by passing up the chimney. The Franklin stove can be connected by means of stovepipe with an ordinary flue.

Closed Stoves.—Closed stoves burning coal, oil, or gas as fuel are, of course, in very general use for heating individual apartments. Of these, the coal stove has the very decided advantage that the products of combustion pass through the stovepipes into the chimney, whereas both gas and oil stoves vitiate the air with carbonic-acid gas and other injurious substances. For this reason, gas logs and gas grates should not be used except immediately under a chimney flue, nor should small gas stoves or oil stoves be used in living rooms or bedchambers without abundant ventilation.

Open Grates. — The old-fashioned open fireplace is the most cheerful and sanitary means of heating, and would be by all means to be preferred were it not that so much of the heat escapes up the chimney. It has been estimated that only 5 per cent of it is thrown into the room. A recent invention known as the ventilating grate overcomes this difficulty. This is an open furnace, to which fresh outdoor air is introduced by pipes which pass below the hearth and are heated by circulating around the grate, and flues through which the products of combustion escape. The pure air thus warmed is admitted into the rooms through registers. By a suitable arrangement of the flues, the warm air from the ventilating grate can be distributed through the walls to adjacent or upper rooms, and thus two or more of these grates can heat a house of six or eight rooms at less cost than a furnace.

Open fireplaces may also be profitably utilized for supplementary heat in connection with different systems, as they afford the most perfect system of ventilation obtainable.

Economy of Stove Heat.—The heat from an ordinary stove or a Franklin stove may be economized and utilized in upper rooms by adjusting a modern drum radiator to the stovepipe. A number of small tubes within the drum absorb the heat and radiate it into the apartment. The open flames of lamps and gas jets also give a good deal of heat which can be utilized by equipping them with small detachable radiators that operate on the same principle.

Gasoline Stoves.—Those who have generator gasoline stoves often complain that the gasoline smokes and ruins wall paper. To avoid this generate the fire with wood alcohol. Keep the alcohol in a glass bottle holding about a quart. Or a machine-oil can holding about a pint will be found convenient. If the latter is used, a piece of cork should be inserted in the end of the spout to keep the gasoline from evaporating. Or use a piece of Irish potato for this purpose.

Pour a little alcohol in the generator cup, and light it the same as gasoline.

Gas Stoves.—These are of two sorts, adapted for heating and cooking respectively. Gas stoves for heating may be obtained in a variety of sizes, from small cylinders to large-sized stoves of the radiator pattern. These are cleanly, cheap, and efficient, and have nothing about them to get out of order. Gas stoves for cooking may be had in all sizes, from the one-burner stove of the hot-plate type, costing about $1, to the gas kitchen range, ranging in price up to $50. The average type is a two-oven range that will broil, roast, or bake, and can be fitted with laundry conveniences. The standard size has two 16- or 18-inch ovens, and is provided on top with one double and three single burners. These are equal to every requirement of a complete kitchen range, and

"Demonstrate Superiority in Summer."

unlike the latter have no fire brick to burn out, or other parts likely to become warped, cracked, or injured. A gas range has every possibility of service of a coal range except heating, but of course demonstrates its greatest superiority in the summer months, when cooking can be done with a minimum of heat and fuel consumption.

The temperature of a gas oven can always be accurately gauged, and it is possible to have a slow fire and a hot fire at the same time, on different parts of the gas range, which is impossible with a coal range. Further, a gas range is always clean, requires no blacking, kindling, or carrying of coal, removal of ashes, and similar nuisances.

Gas Water Heaters.—A gas water-heating appliance attached to an ordinary kitchen boiler will consume about thirty feet of gas in an hour for a thirty-gallon boiler, or forty to forty-five feet for a sixty- to eighty-gallon boiler. A smaller quantity of hot water for ordinary household purposes can be heated in ten or fifteen minutes at a cost of less than one cent. A similar appliance may be put into the bathroom, which would heat water sufficient for a bath at a cost of from two to three cents. This is an ideal summer arrangement. But care must be taken that accidents do not occur with these, by persons locking the bathroom door and being overcome by the gas.

CHIMNEYS AND FLUES

Chimneys have a twofold object—to remove the smoke and gases produced by combustion, and to produce a draught to increase the rate of combustion. They were first introduced in Europe about the twelfth century. The first chimney in Rome was built in 1368. Chimneys did not come into general use in Europe until the seventeenth century. Formerly—and to this day in many parts of the world—fires were built on stone or earthen hearths in the center of the room, the products of combustion being allowed to escape through a hole in the middle of the roof.

The draught produced by a chimney depends upon its height and proportions. The higher the chimney, the better the draught. The flue should be about one fifth or one sixth the area of the grate.

Chimneys are the best of ventilators, hence there should be one or more extending from the bottom of the cellar and opening by means of suitable fines and fireplaces into every living room in the house.

To Prevent Dampness in Chimneys.—Let the chimney start from the bottom of the cellar, or, if built at the side of the house, from the foundation wall, and rest on a flat stone laid in water cement. This will prevent the bricks from absorbing moisture. A chimney resting on a foundation in the upper part of the house may accumulate water during a rain storm, which will saturate the bricks and communicate dampness to adjacent walls.

Chimneys—To Prevent Soot.—Mix salt freely with the mortar in which the bricks on the inside of a chimney are laid. This will cause them to attract moisture in damp weather, which will loosen the soot and cause it to fall. It will also prevent the chimney from becoming infested with chimney swallows.

To Ventilate Chimneys.—An open fireplace communicating with the chimney is an ideal ventilator; or a chimney may be built double, having two columns side by side or one within the other, one being reserved for ventilation and communicating with each room through an opening in the ceiling.

Or a double chimney may have one column within the other, the air space between the two being connected with the rooms by ventilators.

Chimneys — To Prevent Smoke.—Build a long, narrow flue 4 or 5 inches deep and 15 to 18 inches wide, thus having an opening of 60 to 90 square inches. Let the flue open into an air chamber in the chimney of twice its size, i. e., an area of 120 to 180 square inches or 11 to 16 inches square, but this may be reduced toward the top of the chimney if desired. Carry the chimney as high above the roof as good taste will permit, and let the flue approach the chimney at an angle, or, if possible, by a number of turns. Usually the more crooked the flue the better the draught. A straight funnel does not usually draw well.

To Cure a Smoky Chimney.—First note the cause. Either too much air is admitted below, or the draught is insufficient, or the wind blows down into the chimney from above. Hence, according to circumstances, contract the draught by narrowing the entrance to the grate or fireplace, or increase the height or crookedness of the flue and shaft, or place on the top of the chimney a wind shield or turn cap, which will revolve with the wind in such a way as to prevent the gusts from blowing down the chimney.

The draught is caused by the fact that hot air rises and tends to create a vacuum, which by suction draws cold air after it. Hence, anything that chills the column of air in the chimney tends to check the draught. Therefore avoid admitting, across the top of the fire in a grate or fireplace, enough cold air to cool the flue. The fire should be located in such relation to the flue that the rising current of hot air will have the right of way and tend to fill the flue, to the exclusion of the cold air of the room; thus the latter will be sucked up through the fire itself, assisting the combustion and strengthening the draught.

To Kindle Fires without Smoke.—To start a draught without smoke, on kindling a fire in an open grate when the air in the chimney is cold and the first flame is feeble, use a sufficient quantity of very combustible substances, as kindlings, to create flames. These will heat the air in the chimney before cold or solid fuel is added, which burns less perfectly.

Or reduce the opening to the grate or fireplace by means of a blower or light screen lined with asbestos and placed across the opening so as to admit air only in the required quantity and beneath the grate.

To Prevent Smoke.—A hot fire will consume its own smoke. Hence, to prevent the formation of smoke, heat a hot bed of coals and add fresh fuel in such limited quantity as not to lower the heat of the fire below the smoke-consuming point. Push the coals back and put on fresh fuel so that the smoke will pass over the bed of live coals, where it will be consumed.

Or adjust a wire screen having forty or more wires to the inch, to prevent the escape of smoke.

To Clean Chimneys.—Prepare a bed of hot coals in the stove, throw open the draughts and dampers, and throw on the coals some pieces of old zinc, as the zinc from an old washboard. This will clean out all soot from the chimney.

Or the chimney may be swept if the shaft is straight by attaching a heavy stone or other weight to the butt of a small pine or hemlock sapling and fastening a rope to its upper part. The weight will carry the sapling down the chimney, and when it is dragged back the extending branches will sweep clean the soot. Care must be taken to use a rope sufficiently strong and a sapling not too large, so as to prevent the rope from parting or the brush from lodging in the shaft.

To Stop Leaks in Chimneys.—Make a cement of coal tar and sand, and apply as may be convenient within or without.

To Put Out Fires in Chimneys.—Throw sulphur on the fire so that the fumes will ascend the flue. Take precautions not to breathe the fumes of burning sulphur.

Or ascend to the roof and throw salt down the chimney. Or shut off the draught from below if possible by covering the opening to the fireplace with wet blankets or otherwise. Or, if the fire is not too strong, put a tight cover over the top of the chimney.

FIRE EXTINGUISHERS AND FIRE ESCAPES

To Extinguish Fires.—The objects to be attained in putting out fire are principally two: to cut off its source of supply in the oxygen of the air, and to lower the temperature of the burning substances below the point of combustion. Drenching the burning parts with water accomplishes both objects. It prevents the access of air and chills the burning parts.

A heavy woolen cloth thrown over or wrapped about burning objects smothers the fire by shutting off the air, and if wet, also assists by lowering the temperature.

Chemical fire extinguishers produce noninflammable gas, as carbon dioxide, which flows over the burning parts the same as water, temporarily shutting off the supply of air; hence the following suggestions for extinguishing fires:

Close the doors and windows to prevent draughts. Seize the burning objects if small and movable, as lamps, curtains, and the like, and throw them out of the window, or wrap them in rugs or woolen table covers or bed covers.

Or, if solid, heavy objects are on fire, seize a woolen blanket or other heavy woolen article, and if possible beat out the flames. If a small quantity of water is at hand, dip the woolen cloth into it and beat the fire with that. A single pail of water will go further if soaked up in a blanket than if dashed directly on the flames.

Or, if plenty of water is at hand, dip a mop in it and beat the flames, or dash it on the fire in small quantities from a dipper, directing it intelligently to cover as much space as possible.

To Put Out Burning Garments.—If a person's clothing takes fire, he should be rolled up in a woolen rug, overcoat, table cover, or blanket to smother the fire.

Or, if alone, he should roll himself up in one of these articles as quickly as possible; roll over and over on the floor or bed; or tear up the carpet and roll up in that.

To Extinguish Fire with Chemicals.—To make a chemical fire extinguisher, prepare a mixture of substances that will produce carbonic-acid gas in the presence of water, and arrange so that a stream of mingled gas and water will be thrown upon the flames by the expansive power of the gas. This is the celebrated patent of William A. Graham of Lexington, Va., that was contested during nearly fifty years in the United States courts. It is the principle of most chemical fire extinguishers now upon the market.

The substances most commonly mixed to produce carbonic-acid gas are common soda and sulphuric acid, or oil of vitriol. Numerous practical devices have been patented for storing these two, or other substances, in a suitable receptacle side by side, but

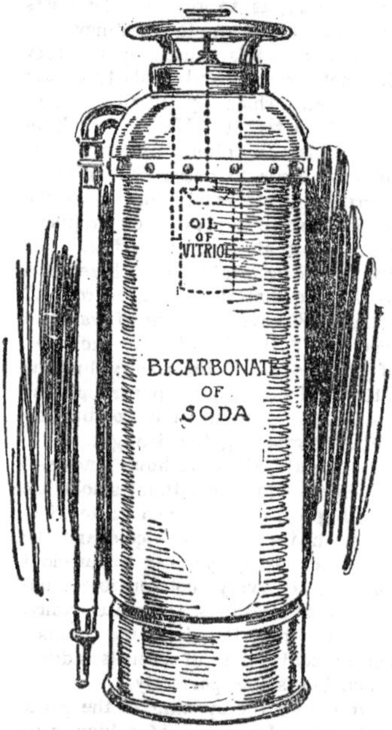

"The Celebrated Patent of Graham."

so arranged that they will not mingle until wanted. Then, by turning the receptacle upside down, or turning a stopcock, the acid is precipitated into a solution of bicarbonate of soda in water and the water is thereby charged with carbonic-acid gas, which, by its expansive power, ejects the stream of mingled gas and water through a flexible rubber tube and a nozzle.

One device consists of a tank or jar containing a strong solution of bicarbonate of soda or common baking soda in water in which is immersed a tightly stoppered bottle containing oil of vitriol. The stopper of the bottle may be pulled out by means of a wire running through the cover of the tank, thus allowing the acid to mingle with the soda solution and produce carbonic-acid gas. To imitate this device, take an old milk can or a five-gallon oil can and have a tinsmith fit it with a screw top and a stopcock fitted with a flexible rubber tube and a nozzle. Plain rubber tubing or flexible gas pipe is suitable for this purpose. The longer, the better. Fasten to the removable screw top by means of wire a glass bottle containing sulphuric acid and having a glass stopper. Fasten another wire about the neck of this stopper, let it protrude through the cover, and end in a ring by means of which the stopper may be withdrawn. But care must be taken to use wires strong enough so that, should the stopper stick, the bottle may be broken off if need be without removing the screw top of the can. When required, carry the extinguisher to the vicinity of the fire, pull out the stopper, and shake the can to mix the oil and soda solution. Turn the stopcock and direct the resulting stream of water charged with carbonic-acid gas upon the flame.

Or an ordinary pair of pliers or nippers used to handle wire may be set in the screw top of the can to hold the neck of the bottle of acid between their teeth. Then by closing the handle of the nippers the neck of the vial may be broken, allowing the acid to drop into the soda solution. This should be a little below the mouth of the can, so that the pliers themselves will not be immersed. They may be protected from rust by coating with rust-proof varnish.

Or get a cylinder or pipe of tin, zinc, or other suitable material, and by means of a perforated partition near one end divide into two compartments, one much larger than the other. Fit the opposite end with a stopcock, a flexible tube, and a nozzle. The larger compartment contains the solution of bicarbonate of soda in water; the smaller contains sulphuric acid in the form of a dry powder or crystals too coarse to pass through the perforations in the partition. This cylinder when not in use must, of course, be kept upright so that the soda solution will not come in contact with the acid; when required for use it must be inverted, the soda solution will then fall through the perforations upon the dry acid, and the mixture will produce carbonic-acid gas.

Or the partition may be operated by means of a plunger which will knock it out of the way so that the dry soda will fall into the soda solution. Any tinsmith or person of mechanical ingenuity can construct at a very nominal cost either of these devices and charge it with the same materials as are used in the most expensive fire extinguisher upon the market. But take care to use a strong receptacle or to open the stopcock so as to give the mixture a vent by means of a suitable tube and nozzle as soon as the acid and the soda solution are brought into combination. This will prevent an explosion. Take care also to combine the materials in the right proportion.

The proportions in which sulphuric acid and bicarbonate of soda unite to form carbonic-acid gas are 5 parts of sulphuric acid and 6 parts of bicarbonate of soda (which is ordinary baking soda), by weight. Commercial bicarbonate of soda requires 13 times its weight of water to fully dissolve it. Hence a sufficiently large receptacle would require 6 pounds of baking soda dissolved in 78 pounds of water and 5 pounds of sulphuric acid so arranged as to be poured into the soda solution when required.

To fill a smaller tank in the same proportions, place the tank on the scales and note its weight. Now fill about two thirds or more with water. Note the total weight and subtract the weight of the tank. Divide this amount expressed in pounds by 13, and the result will be the number of pounds of soda required. The weight of acid required will be five sixths the weight of the soda. Dissolve the soda in the water and place the sulphuric acid in a glass bottle so arranged that when required for use the bottle may be turned over by a crank or otherwise and the acid spilled into the charge of soda water. Carbonic-acid gas will be generated at once under strong enough pressure to force the whole contents with considerable power through a nozzle directed against the fire.

Or dissolve copperas or ferrous sulphate, 5 parts; ammonium sulphate, 20 parts, in water, 125 parts.

Or dissolve in 75 parts water, calcium chloride, 20 parts; salt, 5 parts.

The two last may be kept conveniently at hand for use with a hand pump.

Hand Fire Extinguisher.—Another device consists of a mixture of suitable substances combined in a glass vessel, which must be thrown upon the fire with sufficient force to break the glass. To make hand grenades or fire extinguishers of this sort take pint or quart fruit jars or any large bottles and charge them with a mixture of equal parts of sugar of lead, alum, and common salt, dissolved in water. Keep these tightly corked in various parts of the house. To extinguish a fire throw one or more of these bottles into or just above the burning parts, so that the liquid will fall upon the wood or flames.

Or charge these bottles with a mixture made of 2 pounds of common salt, 1 pound of muriate of ammonia, and 3 quarts of water. Dissolve, bottle, cork, and keep at hand in various parts of the house for emergency. Throw the bottles into the fire with force enough to break them.

Or dissolve pearlash, soda, wood ashes, or common salt in the water which is being dashed upon the flames from pails or pitchers, or in which are soaked cloths to beat out the flames.

Fire Extinguisher Hand Grenades.—Fill round bottles of thin blue glass with a mixture of equal parts of common borax and sal ammoniac or calcium chloride. Add just enough water to dissolve these substances, thus making strong saturated solutions.

Fire Drills.—Boys should be encouraged to prepare, under proper supervision, one or more of these fire extinguishers, and practice with them in putting out fires made out of doors for this purpose. A few experiments will insure that the directions have been understood, and will give valuable practice as a sort of fire drill in advance of the emergency, as there is always danger of fire, whether from lightning or other cause, in isolated farmhouses and other buildings, not within reach, as in cities, of a fire department. A conflagration may not only destroy the results of the labor of a lifetime, but also lead to loss of life from the flames or from consequent exposure in severe weather. Hence the importance of such preparation can hardly be overestimated, especially when it can be done at very little expense. Moreover, such experiments have an important educational influence.

To Extinguish Kerosene Fire.—Do not throw water on the flames of burning kerosene, gasoline, benzine, naphtha, or other petroleum products. The water will spread the flames and not put them out. Instead use milk, which forms an emulsion with the oil and extinguishes it.

Fire Escapes.—You may remember Mark Twain's story of the "poor white" in Arkansas whose roof leaked so badly that the bed in which he slept was wet by every storm. When asked why he did not mend the roof, he replied that he could not do so when it rained without getting wet, and when the weather was fair it was not necessary.

That is the attitude of many persons in regard to fire escapes. Suitable provision for escape from attics, chambers, and other upper rooms is rarely thought of, except in the actual moment of danger, when stairways may be choked with smoke and flames. Many persons have escaped from upper windows of cottages and other low dwellings by knotting sheets and other bed covers together to form a strong rope, fastening one end to the bedpost, and sliding down this to the ground. This plan should be talked over in the family circle so as to be

"Suitable Provisions for Escape."

clearly understood by children and others in case of emergency.

Or, if the rooms are too high from the ground to admit of this mode of escape, fasten a strong iron hook to the window casing, and have at hand a knotted rope long enough to reach to the ground.

Or, if this is not to be had, the bed may be thrown out of the window to assist in breaking the shock, and the person may make a rope of the bed covers and slide down as far as possible before dropping on the bed. A skylight should be cut in the roof of every dwelling and a permanent ladder fixed to give access to this, and also from thence to the edge of the roof and to the ground. This will admit of escape if the staircase should take fire and fall.

To Escape from Fires. — As the heated air, smoke, and noxious gases produced by combustion tend to rise, the purest air is next the floor. Hence, in escaping from fires, creep or crawl with the face near the floor. If time admits, a handkerchief or other thin cloth dipped in water and held over the nostrils will to some extent prevent drawing smoke into the lungs. Bystanders may assist in the escape of persons who are obliged to jump by holding a horse blanket or other large, strong cloth or canvas to receive them. The larger the cloth, the more persons holding it, and the higher it is held from the ground, the better.

FIREPROOFING AND WATER-PROOFING

To Prevent Fires.—The following substances are recommended for fireproofing cloth and other materials: Alum, borax, vitriol, copperas, sulphate of ammonia, soluble glass, tungstate of soda, and phosphate of ammonia; also various combinations and preparations of these.

To Fireproof Cloth. — Mix equal quantities of alum, borax, and vitriol, or copperas; dissolve with boiling water or a thin size made by melting an ounce of glue or gum arabic in a gallon of water. Use no more water than is necessary to dissolve perfectly. Dilute the mixture to liquid form and soak the fabric in this. This preparation is for articles to be used about stoves and flames, as holders, fire screens, and the like.

To Fireproof Garments.—Mix tungstate of soda with boiled starch, or dissolve alum in water, or both. The tungstate of soda does not interfere with the ironing and is the best substance to fireproof children's garments, lace curtains, and other light fabrics which are in danger of taking fire.

To Fireproof Fabrics.—Dissolve 12 ounces of borax and 9 ounces of sulphate of magnesia in 5 pounds of boiling water. In this immerse the fabric when cool.

Or dip the fabric in soluble glass,

diluted with boiling water to 25° B. Hang to drip dry without wringing. While still damp, immerse in a solution of 1 pound of sulphate of alumina and 1 pound of sulphate of copper in 10 pounds of water. Dry without wringing in the open air.

To Fireproof Canvas.—To fireproof canvas awnings or other coarse materials, make a hot solution of 3 parts of alum and 1 part of copperas. Immerse the articles three times, letting them drip dry between each immersion. Finally let dry and by means of a brush apply a solution of copperas mixed with pipe clay to the consistency of paint. This is a celebrated German recipe.

To Fireproof Wood.—To fireproof wood impregnate it with alum, borax, or copperas, or a mixture of these.

Or mix 2½ pounds sulphate of zinc, 1 pound of potash, 2 pounds of alum, and 1 pound of manganic oxide with lukewarm water in an iron kettle. Stir and add slowly 1 pound of sulphuric acid, 60 per cent pure. Dissolve the same proportions by weight for larger quantities. To apply, build up the pieces of wood corncob fashion, and wrap them at their points of juncture with sufficient wire to keep them at least an inch apart. This method admits of immersing the greatest quantity of wood in the smallest bulk of liquid. Place the wood thus prepared in an old iron sink or tank and pour the liquid over it. Allow it to soak three or four hours, afterwards to drip dry, and season under shade in the open air.

To Waterproof Cloth. — Substances recommended for waterproofing cloth are alum, acetate of lead (sugar of lead), linseed oil, and solutions of India rubber, isinglass, and wax in turpentine and other solvents, or mixtures of the above in varying proportions. India rubber and other close waterproof fabrics are impervious to air as well as moisture; hence they are hot, close, and uncomfortable, besides being unhealthful. Ordinary fabrics, as wool, linen, or cotton, duck, canvas, and the like, may be made waterproof by immersing in any of the above mixtures without affecting their porous qualities.

The following methods are recommended: Dissolve in a wash boiler 1 ounce of yellow soap in 4 gallons of water and bring it to a boil. Allow the liquid to cool and when cold immerse the fabric for twenty-four hours. Remove without wringing, and let it drip till partially dry. While still moist immerse it in a solution of ½ pound of alum and ½ pound of sugar of lead in 3 gallons of water. Dissolve these substances separately each in 1½ gallons of water, stir vigorously, and mix the two solutions. Soak the fabric in this for three or four hours, and hang it up to drip dry. When nearly dry it may be dipped again if desired.

Or, for delicate fabrics, allow the mixture to settle, pour off the clear liquid from the sediment, and immerse in this. Fabrics thus treated are partially fireproof as well as waterproof.

Or dissolve one pound of alum in a gallon of boiling water. Allow the liquid to cool and soak the fabric in it, but this is not equal to the mixture of alum and sugar of lead.

Or put 5 pounds of sulphate of alumina in 1½ gallons of water; in a separate receptacle dissolve 2 pounds of oleic acid and 1½ quarts of alcohol. Stir vigorously until dissolved. Now add the sulphate of alumina in a thin stream, mix and allow it to settle for twenty-four hours. Pour off the clear liquid, which may be discarded. Dry the residue with heat, and pulverize. Make a solution of this substance at the rate of 1 pound to 10 gallons of water to waterproof any silk, linen, or woolen fabric. Immerse the cloth or garment until it is thoroughly saturated, and afterwards allow it to drip dry.

Or mix 4 ounces of isinglass, 4 ounces of alum, and 2 ounces of yellow soap, and dissolve in hot water to form an emulsion about the consistency of milk. Apply with a stiff brush to the wrong side of the fabric, rubbing thoroughly. Remove the ex-

a b c d e f

a. Incandescent gas or gasoline gas at $1 per 1,000 ft. costs $\frac{1}{8}$c. per hour. Equals breath of 3 persons; b. Acetylene gas costs $\frac{3}{8}$c. per hour. Equals 2 or 3 persons; c. Kerosene lamp costs $\frac{3}{8}$c. Equals 7 or 8 persons; d. Open flame gas costs $\frac{3}{4}$c. Equals 6 persons; e. Electric bulb costs $1\frac{1}{4}$c. Consumes no oxygen; f. Candles cost $6\frac{1}{4}$c. Each candle equals 12 persons.

cess by sponging with water, or with a brush dipped in water, and rub smooth with a dry brush.

Or dissolve pure India rubber and turpentine to a thin solution, and apply with a brush. Afterwards apply a coating of sugar of lead dissolved in water.

To Waterproof and Color Black.—Raise to a boil 4 quarts of linseed oil and stir in 1 ounce of burnt umber, 1 ounce of acetate of lead, and 15 ounces of lampblack. Dry and apply a second coat of the same solution, leaving out the sugar of lead. Allow this to dry and rub it down with a stiff bristle brush. Apply a third coat if desired.

Or raise to a boil 4 quarts of linseed oil. Add 3 ounces of burnt umber, 2 ounces of sugar of lead, $1\frac{1}{2}$ ounces of sulphate of zinc, 2 ounces of Prussian blue, and $1\frac{1}{2}$ ounces of verdigris. Stir these into the oil and add 10 ounces of lampblack, stirring vigorously. Apply with a brush as in painting. Two or three coats of either of these mixtures should give a hard, durable waterproof surface of a black color and having a high gloss.

To Waterproof Canvas Tents or Awnings.—Mix 8 pounds of white lead with one fourth by bulk spirits of turpentine. Stir in 1 ounce of sugar of lead and 1 ounce of white vitriol. Dilute with boiled linseed oil to the consistency of paint.

First boil the fabric in suds and rinse clean. Or scrub with soap and water and a stiff brush, afterwards applying water with a brush to remove all traces of soap. Apply the waterproofing with a painter's brush and stretch tightly while drying.

ARTIFICIAL ILLUMINATION

Use of Systems of Illumination.—Artificial light is the third most important of the necessities of civilization, taking rank after the items of clothing and shelter. A comparative statement of the annual value of illumination in the United States shows the following results: Acetylene (estimated), about $11,000,000; illuminating gas, $60,000,000; kerosene, $133,000,000; electricity, $150,000,000; or total of $360,000,000, being about $4 for every man, woman, and child in the United States. Probably 10 per cent of the light thus generated is wasted through misuse and ignorance, which would amount to forty cents per capita for the entire population of the country, or a total of $36,000,000. Including all items pertaining to the lighting industry, it is probable that the grand total of expenditure would reach annually $500,000,000.

Cost of Lighting Systems.—An average period for the burning of artificial light per twenty-four hours is perhaps from 6 to 10 P.M., or about four hours. A careful comparison of the cost of different systems of lighting shows that each twenty-four candle power of light produced from gas at $1 a thousand with a Welsbach burner, or from gasoline gas with a Welsbach burner, would be $\frac{2}{3}$ cent for four hours, or about $2.46 a year; the same candle power produced from acetylene would be $1\frac{6}{10}$ for four hours, or $5.85 a year; from kerosene, $2\frac{2}{5}$ cents a day, or $8.76 a year. From gas at $1 per thousand without a Welsbach burner, 3 cents a day, or $10.95 a year; from incandescent electric lamps, 5 cents a day, or $18.25 a year. But of course allowance must be made for varying prices and other local conditions.

Effect of Artificial Light on Health.—It is not commonly known that most ordinary lights vitiate the atmosphere of living rooms to a greater extent than does the breathing of several persons. The incandescent electric light has a great advantage in this respect, as it is inclosed in a vacuum, and so consumes no oxygen and gives off very little heat. The next least injurious form of lighting is the Welsbach burner with any illuminating gas, which consumes about the same amount of air as three persons. The ordinary gas jet without the Welsbach burner vitiates the air about as rapidly as the breathing of five persons; the common oil lamp, about the same as that of eight persons; and the ordinary tallow candle is equal to the breath of twelve persons in the amount of atmospheric oxygen it consumes.

COAL GAS, GASOLINE GAS, AND ACETYLENE

Gas. — Gas for illuminating purposes was invented by William Murdoch in 1792 at Redrutch, Cornwall, England. It was first used in the United States in 1806 by David Melville, of Newport, R. I. It was introduced in Boston in 1822, and in New York the year following. Gas is now used for heating and cooking as well as for illuminating purposes by upward of half the population of the United States. As its convenience and economy become better known, the number of towns and villages to introduce gas will no doubt steadily increase.

Coal gas is made by distilling bituminous coal with heat in a retort, condensing and separating it from the water, vapor of tar, and other solid substances, and purifying the resulting product to remove the compounds of sulphur and carbonic-acid gas. A by-product of this process is coke, about one-third of which is required for heating the retorts; the rest is sold. Other by-products are ammonia water and coal tar.

Illuminating gas consists of nearly equal parts of hydrogen (which burns with a blue flame, giving heat but no light), marsh gas, and other hydrocarbons (which burn with a luminous flame, but deposit soot if not fully consumed), and small quantities of carbonic oxide, and nitrogen, which are impurities and diminish the illuminating power of the gas.

Gas, after being purified, is usually stored in a cylindrical tank with a conical top made of iron plates floating in a cistern of water. This is so arranged as to exert a uniform pressure on the gas equal to that of a column of water 6 inches high. The pressure serves to distribute the gas in the mains. These are usually made of cast iron from 24 inches down to 3 inches in diameter and laid about 3 feet under ground. The mains are connected with the buildings of consumers by service pipes, which should be below the frost line. Otherwise they may be closed by hoarfrost caused by the freezing of the watery vapor contained in the gas. The gas is measured by means of a house meter before being distributed.

Gas Meters.—The gas meter is not constructed like a clock, as the dial seems to suggest; hence, contrary to common belief, a gas meter in good order cannot run either too fast or too slow. The meter is an engine in which the gas is the motive power. Unless the gas actually passes through the meter, the latter does not move. The dials mechanically and actually record the number of revolutions in cubic feet. The popular notions that gas meters are often inaccurate, and that an increased pressure or the practice of turning on the gas with full force when first lighted may make the meter spin faster and record against the consumer, are erroneous. Of course the meter records all gas which passes, including that which is wasted as well as that which is used. Hence gas jets should be regulated so as to prevent "blowing" or the passing of unconsumed gas. This regulation neutralizes the effect of any increase in the pressure in the gas mains. Contrary to common belief, most injuries to a meter work against the company. Any apertures caused by use in the interior of the meter may allow the gas to get through without being recorded. Not infrequently the valves of a meter become fixed so as to let gas through without being registered. Hence meters are tested at intervals by inspectors, who pass a certain number of cubic feet through them and note whether or not the dials make proper record.

Amount of Gas Consumed.—Learn to read the gas meter and thus note what amount of gas is being consumed. The ordinary flat-flame burner should consume 5 or 6 feet of gas an hour. If badly adjusted or of faulty construction, it may consume 10 to 15 cubic feet an hour. A Welsbach burner uses only about 3 feet an hour. A medium-sized two-oven range with all burners lighted consumes about 60 feet an hour. A gas cylinder stove about 24 feet an hour. At least once a month make a test by reading the gas meter in the morning, noting carefully the time each burner is lighted, and again reading the gas meter at night. If the quantity consumed is greatly in excess of the above figures it indicates that the burners are poorly adjusted. In that case notify the gas company, whose duty it is to regulate the burners, and to keep them in order. Gas is the most economical of fuels if used with intelligence and care.

To Burn Gas.—There are a right way and a wrong way to burn gas. In other words the illumination obtained from the gas burned depends

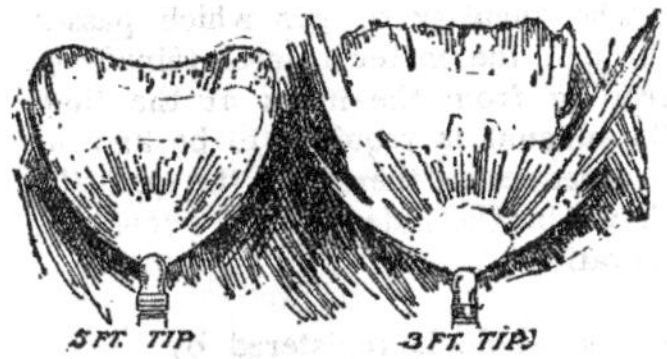

"A Right Way and a Wrong Way."

upon perfect combustion at the burner tip. And this combustion cannot take place unless the tip itself is in good condition.

The picture on the left shows a 5-foot tip; the shape of the flame is full and regular, giving the fullest illuminating power of the gas consumed. On the other hand, the picture on the right shows a 3-foot tip burning 5 feet of gas per hour and giving poor light; the flame is irregular and the combustion imperfect, due to the use of a burner tip not designed to burn over 3 cubic feet.

It is obvious, then, that it is highly important to see that the burners and tips are intelligently selected and that they are kept in good condition, if gas is to be used economically, and the full illuminating power of the gas consumed obtained.

To Read the Gas Meter.—The figures on the index at the right hand denote even hundreds. When the hand completes the entire circle it denotes

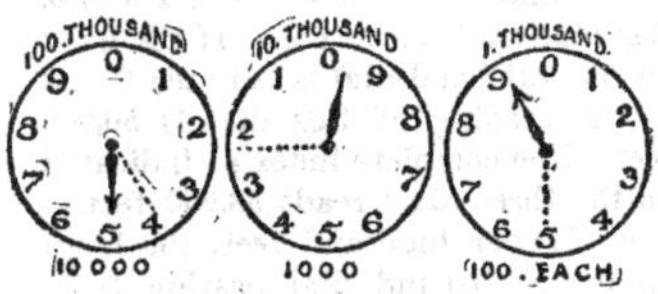

"The Figures on the Index."

ten hundred, and is registered by the hand in the center circle pointing to 1; each figure in the center circle denotes a thousand, this entire circle being ten thousand, which is registered at 1 on the index of the left-hand circle by the hand, each figure there denoting ten thousand.

The quantity of gas which passes through the meter is ascertained by reading from the index at the time the amount is required to be known, and deducting therefrom the quantity shown by the index at a previous observation.

If the whole is registered by the hands on the three circles above, it indicates..........	49,900
Amount at previous observation, as shown by the dotted lines	42,500
Amount which passed through since last taken off........	7,400

The register at all times shows the quantity that has passed through since the meter was first set. Deducting from this the amount that has been paid for (without any regard to the time when), the remainder shows what is unpaid.

Or, in different words, the dial on the right hand (marked 1,000) indicates 100 feet from one figure to the next. The middle dial (marked 10,-000) indicates 1,000 feet from one figure to the next. The dial on the left (marked 100,000) indicates 10,000 feet from one figure to the next.

If the hand on the right-hand dial is between the figures 2 and 4, the lesser of the two numbers is read, the index reading 200 feet. If the hand on the middle dial is between 1 and 0, this dial reads 3,000 feet. If the hand on the left-hand dial is between 0 and 6, the reading of this dial is 50,000 feet. The complete index as indicated on the three dials reads 53,200 feet.

At $1 per thousand feet, the hand on the right-hand dial passing from the zero point 0 to the figure 1, would indicate that ten cents' worth of gas has been registered on the meter. This hand would have to make one entire revolution of this dial and reach the zero point again to register $1 worth of gas, and the hand on the middle dial will have moved just one point, or from the zero point 0 to the figure 1, indicating the 1,000 feet of gas which has been registered in hundreds on the right-hand dial.

The small (2-foot) dial which is on the face of the consumer's meter is not read except for testing purposes, and registers only two feet of gas for each revolution of the hand.

Shades and Chimneys.—The use of shades and chimneys causes a very considerable loss of light on account of the conversion of the light from flame into heat. The loss from a clear glass is 10 per cent or 11 per cent, from ground glass about 30 per cent, opal glass over 50 per cent, orange-colored glass about 35 per cent, purple, ruby, or green, over 80 per cent, or transparent porcelain over 95 per cent. Hence care should be used that the kind of shade or chimney employed does not interpose to cut off the direct rays of light upon the objects to be illuminated. The Argand chimneys are of two kinds: the straight and the bulb varieties. Of these the straight variety is to be preferred.

Gas Burners.—Gas burners are of three kinds: the common bat-wing burner with a slit, the fish-tail with two oblique holes facing each other, and the Argand, a circular burner with a ring of small holes, a glass chimney, and an interior supply of air. In addition to these are the Welsbach burner having a fiber cap, and the Bunsen burner, used for heating in chemical laboratories.

Burners are constructed in varying sizes to burn 1, 2, 3, 4, or 5 cubic feet of gas per hour, according to the size of the flame when turned on full. Under equal conditions the larger burners are more economical than the smaller. That is, a burner which consumes 4 feet of gas gives twice as much light as two burners that consume each 2 feet. Hence there is great economy in the use of a few large burners over many small ones.

Pressure of Gas.—Gas is frequently supplied at a much higher pressure than is necessary to give the best results. Hence if the jet is turned on full some of the gas will escape, causing the well-known "blowing" noise.

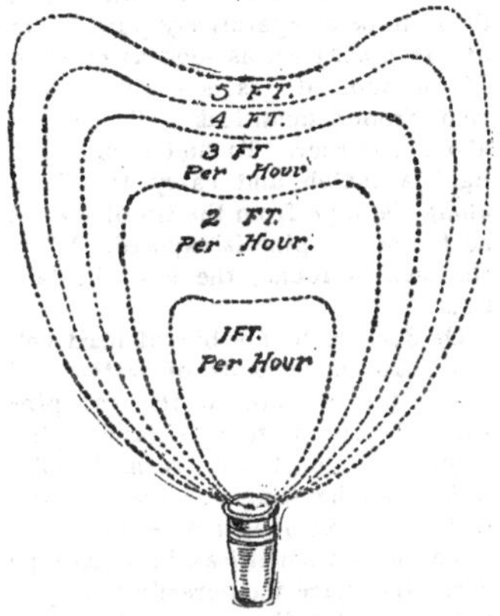

"Burners in Varying Sizes."

To prevent this, always on lighting the jet turn the stopcock backward as much as possible without perceptibly decreasing the light. This practice alone, if adhered to, will make a very important difference in the consumption of gas.

Or the gas may be partially turned off at the meter, or a check can be introduced into the burner. One of the best checks is to screw a burner

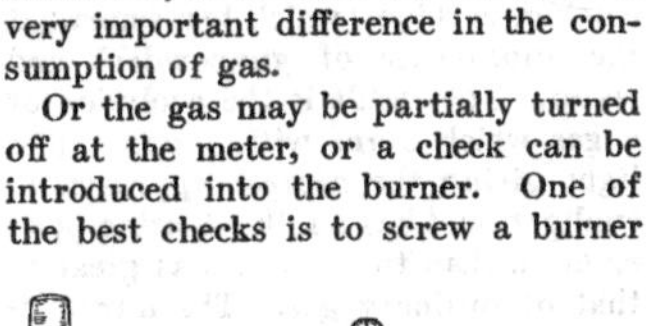

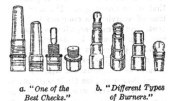

a. *"One of the Best Checks."* b. *"Different Types of Burners."*

intended to consume 5 or 6 feet of gas an hour over a 3- or 4-foot burner. A low pressure with a burner which secures a supply of air just enough to prevent smoking gives a maximum amount of light.

A Welsbach burner having a cap or mantle constructed on the well-known principle of the miner's safety lamp consumes from 3 to 3½ feet of gas an hour and gives about 60 candle power, as against the 16 candle power of the ordinary electric light bulb. In a well-regulated Welsbach burner there should be no smoke. The blackening of the mantle is caused by the improper adjustment of the air shutter and consequent clogging of the wire gauze or air holes in the burner which produces an improper mixture of gas and air.

To prevent the heat of the Welsbach light from discoloring the ceiling, put a mica dome over it. This is made to fit into or clamp to the top of the lamp chimney. Or suspend a glass smoke bell from the ceiling. If Welsbach lights, after being used for a month or two, become dim, probably the wire gauze of the burner is rusted or dirty. It should be removed and cleaned before a new mantle is adjusted.

To Change a Mantle on a Welsbach Lamp.—To change a cap mantle take it up gently and put it down on a steady base, say, on the mantelpiece, handling it by the base or cap. To change a loop mantle, disengage the supporting rod by setting back the set screw. Lift the mantle off carefully by raising the supporting wire. Slip a stiff wire or knitting needle through the loop in the top of the mantle at right angles with it. Hang the mantle in a pitcher having the ends of the knitting needle rest on each side. Be careful not to jar or knock the mantle in raising or replacing it. The best of these mantles are exceedingly delicate and will fall to pieces at a touch.

Gas Troubles.—If the gas goes out, send for the gas fitter or notify the office of the company. But as this may occur at night when help cannot be obtained it is well to know how to meet the emergency. The cause may be a deficiency of water or an excess of water, freezing of the meter, freezing of the service pipes, or the condensation of water in the house pipes. Close the cocks of all the burners except one. When approaching the meter with a candle or open-flame lamp, keep the light at a distance to prevent an explosion. Turn off the gas at the main cock between the street surface pipe and the meter. Unscrew the plug of the waste-water system to let out any excess of water.

If the meter is frozen, cover it with a flannel cloth and pour boiling water over it. Afterwards wrap it in dry flannel or protect it by felt, straw, tan bark, sawdust, or sand. If the surface pipe is frozen outside the house, it will be necessary to uncover it and apply heat.

If water has condensed in the pipes it will cause the gas to jump up and down for some days before it finally puts the gas out. Hence, when it jumps or flickers, the gas company should be notified.

Or, on emergency, remove a burner and blow violently into the pipe. This will sometimes force the water below the hollow. If the trouble persists, the location of the meter should be changed to a lower one, and the pipes inclined so that all condensed water will trickle back to the meter.

Gas Arc Lamps.—These lamps are intended to give a maximum light with a minimum consumption of gas. They are composed of four burners of the incandescent burner or Welsbach type, and give a wonderfully high illuminating power, especially adapted for use in rooms of large area like stores, assembly halls, and churches having lofty ceilings. They are made for both outside and interior lighting, and are especially valuable for commercial purposes.

Gas Leaks.—If a strong odor of gas is detected, probably a stopcock has been left open and the gas thus escapes at full force. Do not go near such an open gas jet with a light, as gas mingled with air is a highly explosive mixture. To enter a room filled with gas, first open adjacent doors and windows to create a draught, throw the doors wide open, rush across the room, and throw the windows wide open, meantime holding the breath. The air is purest next the floor; hence if in danger of being overcome lie face down on the floor, where the air is likely to be comparatively pure. Turn off the open cock as soon as possible. If the odor of gas is slight, it may come from a small leak in the pipe or about a burner. To find such a leak light a match and carry the flame along the pipe from the tip of the jet as far as the pipe is exposed. When the leak is found, the gas will take fire.

Or dissolve half a bar of hard yellow soap in 1½ pints of water, and apply the mixture to the gas pipe with a brush. If there is gas escaping through holes it will form bubbles which can be seen and the leak detected without danger of explosion.

To mend a small leak in a gas pipe cover the place temporarily with yellow soap; stop it permanently with a cement made of white lead and boiled linseed oil.

Acetylene Gas.—The use of acetylene gas for lighting purposes marks an era in artificial illumination. Acetylene is produced by the contact of calcium carbide (which has somewhat the appearance of gunpowder) and water. The result is the evolution of a gas which burns with a pure white light giving the nearest approach to sunlight, and has an illuminating power more than twelve times as great as that of ordinary gas. The introduction of acetylene is comparatively recent, and some prejudice against it has been aroused by defects in the style of generators first placed upon the market. The experimental period is now well-nigh passed, and the National Board of Fire Underwriters has approved a large number of generators. If a proper apparatus is selected, acetylene may be regarded to be as safe as any other illuminant. The various generators on the markets are of two types: one, in which the gas is produced by placing the calcium carbide in a suitable receptacle and allowing water to gradually fall upon it; the other, in which a receptacle is filled with a relatively large quantity of water and the calcium carbide is allowed to drop into the water in small

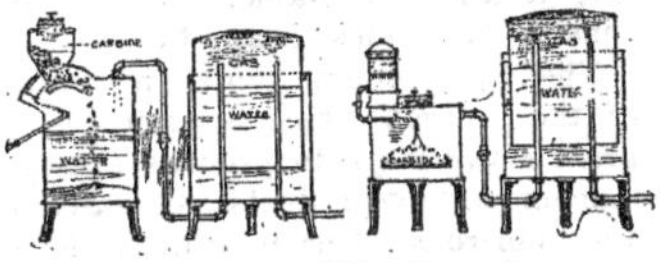

"*Generators of Two Types.*"

quantities. The latter type of generator is the safer and is consequently to be preferred. The brilliancy of acetylene flame is so great that a small one the size of a copper cent is sufficient to light an ordinary living room. Hence the air is vitiated much less than by most other forms of illumination. Recent experiments at Cornell University show that the light furnished by acetylene has, to a considerable degree, the power that sunlight has in promoting the growth of vegetation. It is much less trying to the eyes than electricity or ordinary gas,

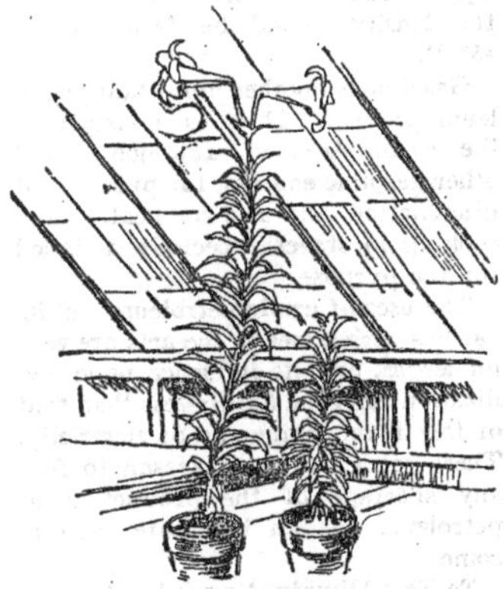

"*The Power of Sunlight in Promoting Growth.*"*

* Both lilies had the same treatment except that the larger was exposed at night to the light of acetylene gas.

and is likely to become increasingly popular.

Gasoline Gas.—Perhaps the cheapest method of illumination in localities that are not supplied with illuminating gas or that are furnished with the gas at high prices, is the use of gasoline gas. A tank of gasoline is located outside of the dwelling house and buried six or eight feet under ground. To produce the gas it is only necessary to pass a current of air across the surface of the gasoline. A very simple contrivance for this purpose is a blower, which may be operated by windmill, water power, or by means of weights and pulleys installed in the cellar. Of course the necessary piping must be provided to carry the gasoline gas to various parts of the dwelling as required, and also an automatic air mixer. When the gasoline tank is outside the premises and underground, there is no possibility of explosion. The entire apparatus is very simple, and while the first cost has to be taken into account, the cost of operation is very low, probably not more than one half that of an equal number of kerosene lamps.

Welsbach Burner. — The incandescent principle of light, as applied in the well-known Welsbach burner, consists in heating a gauze mantle, impregnated with certain rare earths, to a white heat by means of a mixture of gas and air. The result is a flame five or six times as strong in proportion to the gas consumed as that produced by an ordinary open gas burner. The air in the room is also vitiated much less, and less heat is given off. The Welsbach burner may be used with any form of gas, but is especially useful in connection with gasoline gas, as it admits of a proper mixture of air with the gas, and does away with the necessity of providing an automatic air mixer.

KEROSENE OIL

Kerosene Lamps.—The use of kerosene in rural districts and small villages is practically universal. Formerly, the oil of the sperm whale was the principal source of illumination in those localities, and before the discovery of petroleum the problem of lighting for country districts was a very serious one. Petroleum had been known for many years before the first well was driven in northwestern Pennsylvania, in 1837, but from that time to this the use of kerosene and other petroleum products has increased rapidly.

To Choose Oil Lamps.—Practically all the standard makes of kerosene lamps are now safe and reliable, but the best results are those made on the principle of the German student lamp, having a reservoir of oil placed at a distance from the wick. If the wick protrudes directly from the reservoir of oil below it, the light decreases as the oil is consumed.

Petroleum and Its Products.—Petroleum is a liquid containing bitumen, which occurs in a natural state in various parts of the world. It is also called rock oil and mineral oil. It ranges from a light straw color to black, depending upon the locality in which it is found. It sometimes occurs in springs, but is more often obtained by drilling wells.

Petroleum is now conveyed to markets and refineries through pipe lines, and the various oils derived from it are handled in tank cars, in steamships, and in barrels. Among the products of petroleum are gasoline, naphtha, benzine, kerosene, lubricating oils, paraffine, vaseline, and other substances too numerous to mention.

These are obtained by distilling petroleum in an iron still having a condenser of wrought-iron pipes immersed in water. When heat is applied to the still the lightest or most volatile constituents are first driven off in the form of a gas. The next heaviest constituents condense at ordinary temperatures as crude naphtha. These are afterwards distilled into gasoline and A B C naphthas. They have a specific gravity of 65° to 58° B.

When the stream of oil has a gravity of 59° B. it is turned from the naphtha tank to the kerosene tank until it reaches a gravity of about 38° B., or until the color becomes yellow. The stream is then turned into the paraffine tank until it ceases to flow at a gravity of about 25° B. The residuum contained in the still consists of a thick, heavy tar.

This is, of course, only an outline of the process, which is varied in a great many ways to produce a large number of by-products, as vaseline and numerous others used in medicine and in the arts. The following is a fair average composition of petroleum: Gasoline, 1½ per cent; naphthas, 14 per cent; kerosene, 55 per cent; lubricating oil, 17½ per cent; paraffine, 2 per cent; waste, 10 per cent.

Or, by another process, the same oil could be made to produce: Naphthas, 20 per cent; kerosene, 66 per cent; waste, 14 per cent.

Kerosene, or common illuminating oil, is the most important product of petroleum. Its appearance and principal properties are well known. Its density should be from 43° to 45° B.

Gasoline is another important petroleum product. It is used largely in the carburetors of automobile and other gasoline engines, for purposes of illumination, and also for heating and cooking in stoves especially designed for the purpose.

The uses of crude petroleum and its various derivatives in the arts are very numerous, and its influence upon civilization has been hardly less than that of the steam engine and of electricity. There seems to be no reason to fear any shortage of the production of petroleum for an indefinite time to come.

To Test Illuminating Oil.—At ordinary temperatures kerosene oil should extinguish a match as readily as water. It should not give off any inflammable gas below 110° F., nor take fire below 125° F. Kerosene is usually freed from naphtha by spraying. If kerosene contains even a very small quantity of naphtha it is highly inflammable and explosive; therefore it is required by law to be tested before it is sold.

There are two kinds of tests: the "flash test," which determines the lowest temperature at which oil gives off an inflammable vapor, and the "burning test," which determines the lowest temperature at which the oil takes fire. This test is made commercially by means of an apparatus having a cup to hold the oil, in which the bulb of a thermometer is immersed, and which is surrounded by a vessel of water heated by an alcohol lamp. The temperature is slowly increased at the rate of about 2 per cent a minute. The oil is stirred at intervals, a flame applied, and the point noted at which an inflammable vapor is given off, and also at which the oil takes fire.

A rough test for ordinary purposes may be made by filling a cup with water, inserting an ordinary thermometer, and bringing the temperature to 110° over a slow fire. Pour a tablespoonful of oil on the water, and apply a lighted match. If the oil takes fire it is unsafe and is liable to explode. Dealers who sell oil that will not stand this test at 110° are liable to prosecution by law. They should be compelled to take back the oil and refund the price paid for it.

To Purify Kerosene.—The adulteration of oil by means of a heavier oil than standard kerosene causes a dimness of the flame and charring of the wick. The best kerosene oil is clear and nearly colorless, like water. To purify kerosene oil, add to 100 pounds of oil 1 pound of chloride of lime, mixed with 12 pounds of water to the consistency of cream. This must be done in a lead-lined vat, as iron or copper will be corroded by the process. Thoroughly mix these materials, let stand over night, and add 1 or 2 pounds of sulphuric acid diluted with 20 to 50 parts of water and boil with gentle heat, stirring constantly until a sample tested on a glass plate is perfectly clear. Let the mixture settle, when the oil will rise to the top and can be drawn off, leaving the impurities in the form of sediment mixed with the acidulated water.

The following four paragraphs are adapted from Macbeth's "*Index*."

The Care of Lamps.—Lamps smell and give poor light: first, because they are not kept clean; or secondly, the wick is poor or clogged by having been used too long; or thirdly, the chimney is wrong.

Trim, clean, and fill daily, and wipe the whole lamp.

Trim by rubbing the char off the wick; this leaves it even. Don't cut it; you can't cut it even.

Keep the holes in the floor of the burner clear for draught.

Don't fill quite full; the oil expands with heat and runs over.

Boil the burner a few minutes once a month in sal soda or lye water.

Empty the fount occasionally for sediment.

Don't open the lamp when hot; there is explosive vapor in it.

Light it with the wick turned low and turn up gradually, or you will get it too high and make smoke.

Move with care a lamp that has been burning long enough to get hot; or, better still, don't move it.

Use the American Fletcher or Hyatt wick; and renew it every month or two, no matter how fresh it looks; it gets clogged and doesn't feed freely.

Use oil of not less than 110° flash for safety; the higher the flash the safer the oil.

Lamp Chimneys.—The object of lamp chimneys is to supply the flame with exactly the amount of air it needs for perfect combustion, no more and no less, with an even draught on both sides of the flame; they must, of course, be clear and transparent. This calls for fit in the full meaning of the word and for clear glass that will stay clear. Thus there is something to know about chimneys beyond the mere size of the bottom. The ordinary notion of fit is a chimney that will stay on the lamp and not fall off. That is part of the fit. The rest is such a shape as to make the right draught for that particular lamp. It includes the seat, bulb, shaft, proportion, sizes in all parts, and length. Good chimneys that fit well give more light than common ones. This is due to perfection of shape and proportion and the right balance of draughts.

To Select Chimneys.—Use the chimney recommended by the maker of the lamp, or write to a manufacturer of lamp chimneys for his catalogue and order according to directions.

If compelled to buy from stock, try one chimney after another, turning up the wick in each case till you get the most light it will give. When you have the right one, you can turn the wick higher and get more light than you can from others, in some cases perhaps twice as much. It pays to select chimneys with care for two reasons: one is, the right chimney gives more light; the other is, it lasts longer. Chimneys are usually made in three grades, of which it always pays to buy the best. Comparing bad chimneys with good ones, the breakage is ten to one, the light is half, and the price is half.

The Breaking of Chimneys.—Chimneys break from misuse. A wrong number may break or melt; if the burner is foul, the glass may break; a gust of cold air on a hot chimney may break it; a gas chimney may break or melt from a hole in the mantle; the hole lets a jet of flame directly against the chimney, the explosion of lighting breaks the mantle, and the broken mantle breaks the chimney.

Whenever the chimney is touched by the flame it melts or breaks. Its shape prevents touching, unless through some misuse. In central-draught lamps the flame is between two draughts—the central and the outer one. When the burner is foul, this outer draught is partly stopped, and the flame gets pushed too near or against the chimney, and breaks or melts it.

Chimneys cannot be made to resist misuse or accidents.

To Prevent Explosions of Lamps.—One common cause of explosions is the upsetting of a lamp; hence select a lamp which has a broad, solid base rather than one that appears top heavy.

Never fill a lamp while it is burning. To avoid this, buy lamps that have no opening but the one made for the wick. While it is a convenience to have a lamp with a special opening for filling, it is not safe, as children and others will sometimes undertake to fill it while burning, which may lead to an explosion. Also, when lamps have a special opening for filling, the wick is likely to be neglected until it becomes charred and the burner gets clogged up and dirty. In this condition the lamp is very apt to explode, because the charred portion of a wick takes fire, the oil that runs over burns, and heat is generated so low down in the burner that any volatile gases thrown off by the oil may become ignited. The best oil commences to evaporate at about 110° and ignites at 125°, and this vapor, like that which rises from gasoline, benzine, or naphtha, is highly inflammable and explosive. Hence do not let a lamp stand with little oil in it, or light one which has stood partly empty for a long time.

The best lamps have an extinguisher to put out the flame, but if this is lacking, do not blow out the lamp without first turning down the wick, especially if the lamp has been burned for some time and the burner and adjacent parts are hot. The fact that you may have done this safely many times does not prove that under certain conditions a volatile gas from the oil may not meet the flame and cause explosion.

Always turn the lamp low when carrying it about, as movement from place to place in sudden draughts may bring the flame in contact with the gases that form when oil is burning, and that are more or less disturbed by the jar of walking.

Chemistry of Lamps. — The chemistry of burning kerosene is very simple. The oil is composed of two inflammable substances, a gas (hydrogen), which burns with a blue flame and a very intense heat, and a solid (carbon), which consists of very minute particles in chemical combination with the hydrogen. When the lamp is lit the flame is raised to a temperature that admits of chemical union with the oxygen of the air. The hydrogen first burns, and produces sufficient heat to allow the oxygen to ignite with the carbon. When for any reason there is an excess of oil as when a lamp is turned too high, or when the heat of the flame is reduced as when the lamp is turned too low, the heat of the burning hydrogen is not sufficient to ignite all of the solid carbon, some of which escapes in the form of a finely divided black solid, and we say that the lamp smokes. This solid carbon is what we call soot, or lampblack. Commercial lampblack is thus obtained.

When we breathe the air, a very similar process takes place in our lungs, the oxygen of the air uniting with the waste substances in the blood and purifying them by a kind of combustion. Hence every flame in a room robs the air of a certain amount of oxygen that is essential to human life.

This process, both in the lamp and in the lungs, produces a compound of oxygen and carbon called carbon dioxygen, or carbonic-acid gas. Human beings would immediately suffocate in a room quite filled with carbonic-acid gas, as it contains no free oxygen in the form available for human use. When unburned particles of carbon are thrown off in the form of smoke or soot, the finest of them are suspended in the air and find their way into the lungs. Nothing offers so much resistance to chemical and vital forces as pure carbon; hence these particles are difficult to dislodge and exceedingly harmful.

Meantime the lamp in burning generates a certain amount of heat. This extends from the burner to the adjacent parts of the lamp, and in many cases makes the receptacle containing the oil quite hot. The temperature of the oil is thus raised, and at a certain point it gives off a volatile inflammable gas similar to gasoline, benzine, or naphtha, which, if the lamp should leak, may come in contact with the open flame and cause an explosion.

Or, under certain circumstances, it may be exploded by a sharp jar.

If these facts and principles are understood and proper cautions are observed, there need be no danger in the use of kerosene. The fact that kerosene is used in practically every household and that explosions are very rare proves this, but it does not prove that proper precautions must not be observed. Modern lamps are so constructed as to reduce to a minimum the dangers due to ignorance and carelessness, but the fact that explosions do take place occasionally shows that care and intelligence are still necessary.

Cautions to Observe.—Buy the best lamps and the best oil. Trim the wicks and fill the lamps daily. Adjust the wick neither too high nor too low.

After turning up the wick to the right height, set the screw by a slight turn backward, which will prevent the wick from crawling up as it expands with the increase of heat. Try this, and the sense of touch will tell you what is necessary. Do not leave lamps or carry them when turned too high or too low. Adjust the flame midway and set back the screw.

Night Lamps.—Do not use ordinary lamps as night lamps by turning them low. Instead obtain a small night lamp that will admit of burning a tiny flame turned on full. Or turn up the ordinary lamp until the flame is clear and bright and then shade it from the eyes. The flame of an ordinary lamp turned low throws off a large amount of unconsumed carbon and volatile gases, which impregnate the atmosphere and are taken into the lungs with many evil consequences, that are usually attributed to other sources.

Student Lamps. — These are provided with an oil tank at some little distance from the burner and at a lower level. Great care must be observed to keep a student lamp exactly level. If the oil tank is raised above the level of the burner, the latter will be overflowed with dangerous results. When filling the lamp, care must be taken not to leave air bubbles in the oil, otherwise the pipe conveying the oil to the burner will be clogged and the light will be made dim.

Lamps on Fire.—When a lamp overflows or for any reason gets on fire, seize it and throw it out of the window. A moment's delay may result in an explosion that will scatter burning kerosene all about and lead to a conflagration. Or seize as quickly as possible a heavy woolen rug, table cover, or couch cover, and wrap it tightly around the lamp. This prevents the oxygen of the air from reaching the flame, and it is quickly smothered. If a person's clothing takes fire from kerosene flames, do not throw water upon him or allow him to run about. Wrap him quickly in a large rug or other woolen cloth, which will extinguish the flames. If, by the explosion of a lamp or otherwise, burning oil is scattered about a room, do not throw water upon it, as it will only spread it. Throw on milk or any dry, heavy substance, as flour, corn meal, sand, or earth.

Kerosene for Lighting Fires.—Kerosene should not be used for lighting fires, but it is so convenient and efficient that persons will always be found who prefer to take their chances of an explosion. The only caution that must be observed is not to pour oil into the stove from a can, else it will become ignited and the flame following the stream will find its way into the can and explode the oil. Even if the fire is supposed to be out, there may be coals or sparks in the ashes sufficient to ignite the fine stream of kerosene. If oil is to be used it should be poured into an old cup, saucer, or other open vessel and dashed at once on the kindling wood. The worst possible result to follow if oil is thus ignited will be a puff of flame, that will do no harm if it does not catch light garments or other inflammable substances.

Some persons soak corncobs in kerosene and use these as fire lighters. When this is done the vessel in which they are kept should be provided with a tight cover and kept in a cool place.

Foot Warmer.—When driving or sleighriding in winter, fill a sirup can having a screw top with hot water. This will keep warm for a long time. It may be used in place of a hot-water bottle.

Or make a square box of pine, 6 or 8 inches deep and large enough to just fit about the base of an ordinary lantern. Leave this open at the top, and have the bottom broad enough so that the box will not readily tip over. Bore a few holes near the bottom of the box to admit the air, and when driving in winter set a lantern in the box and let it stand on the carriage or sleigh bottom under the robes at the driver's feet. If these suggestions are observed the lantern will burn with a clear, steady flame, without smoking, will not tip over or soil robes or garments, and will keep the driver comfortable in freezing weather.

To Improve Kerosene Oil.—Put a teaspoonful of common salt in an ordinary hand lamp, and a tablespoonful in a large lamp with a B burner. This gives a more brilliant light, and tends to prevent smoking, and hence to keep the wicks and chimneys clean.

Chinese Lanterns.—When using these lanterns for holiday occasions, put a few handfuls of sand in the bottom of the paper lantern about the candle. This keeps them from swaying, and also tends to prevent them from taking fire.

Vest-pocket Light.—Put a piece of phosphorus in a 1- or 2-ounce glass vial and fill with olive oil. Cork tightly. When the oil is heated by the warmth of the body or otherwise, the phosphorus will emit light enough to read the time on the dial of a watch in the darkest night. Should the vial become broken do not touch the phosphorus with the fingers, as it will eat the flesh and produce an ulcer.

Take it up between two sticks or otherwise and drop it into water. To give good results it must be kept from the air.

Bonfires.—To make brilliant bonfires and signal fires, mix 8 pounds of saltpeter, 4 pounds of flower of sulphur, 1 pound of antimony, and ½ pound of camphor. Powder these ingredients, mix and tamp them into an iron socket. When ignited, they will burn for some time with great brilliancy.

ICE AND REFRIGERATION

Nature of Ice.—Ice is one of a number of substances that occupy a greater volume in the solid than in the liquid state. At the moment of freezing it expands with great force about one-eleventh in bulk, as is testified by the bursting of frozen water pipes.

An interesting experiment consists in passing a wire through a solid block of ice without cutting it in two. The ice should be supported at both ends, leaving the middle free, and the wire over it with weights attached to either end. The pressure on the wire raises the temperature of the ice to the melting point and allows the wire to sink; but the wire absorbs some of the heat, and causes the water to freeze upon its upper surface; hence the seam is closed, and after the passage of the wire the block of ice remains intact. Its course, however, can be traced by the air bubbles which it leaves behind.

Under ordinary conditions water freezes at 32° F., and does not melt until the temperature is raised above that point; but under pressure, as above noted, ice will be converted into water at a lower temperature, having been melted under high pressure at 18° C. If water is perfectly still it may be lowered to 22° F. before freezing, but the slightest jar will cause it to freeze when the temperature rises to 32° F.

Uses of Ice.—In addition to its natural service in transforming lakes and rivers during winter in northern climates into solid roadways, ice is in great demand as an antiseptic or preserving agent. Formerly it was supposed that meats and carcasses of animals intended for food must be frozen to be preserved. The discovery of the practicability of preserving meats and vegetables by means of ice, but without freezing them, is comparatively recent. Now, in addition to the household refrigerator, refrigerating cars convey beef, fruit, and vegetables across continents, and refrigerating steamships take tropical fruits and other products from southern to northern climes and return with dairy products, northern fruits, and other perishable articles that could not otherwise be obtained in tropical countries. In many cities cold-storage houses also preserve, with a very slight percentage of loss, dairy products, meats, fruits, and vegetables for periods varying from months to years. Cold-storage vaults protect furs and valuable garments from the ravages of moths and other insects. Ice is also now regarded as absolutely necessary in the summer months to preserve the bodies of the dead until the time of burial.

To Harvest Commercial Ice.—Ice has been an important article of commerce since the time of Nero, and in cold countries family ice houses are very common. Sometimes these storage places are merely pits or caves under ground, or partly under ground, but an ice house wholly above ground is to be preferred.

Ice from salt or brackish water is nearly pure, as freezing expels the mineral ingredients, but it is sufficiently contaminated on the surface to be unfit for many purposes. Hence the best ice crop is usually gathered from fresh-water ponds, or lakes, or in rivers above tide water. A great deal of ice is also manufactured artificially. Commercial ice houses are usually built of wood, having hollow walls that may be double, triple, or quadruple, the spaces between being filled with sawdust, spent tan bark, or some other poor conductor of heat.

In harvesting ice the usual practice is to scrape the snow from the surface of the ice by means of a scraper drawn by horses, to plane off the soft porous top of the ice if necessary by means of a horse planer, and to mark the ice into blocks by running a series of grooves about 5 feet apart and 3 inches deep so as to make blocks 5 feet square. Ice is usually cut when it is about 2 feet thick. After the ice has been marked one row of blocks is usually cut through by means of a handsaw, and pushed under out of the way or pulled up on the ice. The succeeding blocks are pried off with a crowbar, towed to the landing place, and loaded into wagons or run up an inclined plane to the storehouse and packed away. The blocks are stood on end in a solid mass. A space is left between the ice and the walls of the ice house in which are gutters and drainways to receive and carry off the drainage from the melted ice.

Ice—Domestic Harvest.—To gather ice for home use, cut it as soon as it is thick enough, and before the surface has been covered with snow or has had a chance to freeze and thaw a number of times. If a light snow

"To Gather Ice for Home Use"

falls before the ice is gathered it is advisable to clear off a sufficient space before a thaw sets in. A horse plow for marking the ice is desirable, and one can usually be borrowed if necessary, but a crosscut saw may be used. After one row of blocks has been sawed out it is only necessary to saw across the ends of the blocks. They may be separated lengthwise by marking with an ax and splitting off with an ice pick or chisel. It is not desirable to cut cakes larger than 2 by 3 feet if the work is to be done by hand. Provide a runway or ice ladder about 26 inches wide and 12 feet long to reach from the sled into the water. Drive two upright planks or timbers into the ice, and attach a crossbar at the top of the sled on which to support one end of the runway, the other reaching down in the water. Two men with ice hooks can pull a cake 3 feet long, 2 feet wide, and 18 inches or more in depth up this runway and load it upon the sled without undue exertion.

To Preserve Ice.—The two requisites to preserve ice are the exclusion of heat and outer air, and the drainage of the water produced by melting without at the same time allowing the cold air surrounding the ice to escape. A piece of ice of 50 pounds weight exposed at a temperature of 80°, but placed on cross slats so as to be perfectly drained, will not melt under twenty-four hours. But if exposed at the same temperature in a tight vessel that will retain the water produced by melting, it will dissolve in six or seven hours. Hence ice houses, refrigerators, or ice boxes should have double sides, bottom and top, with a space between the casings filled with nonconducting materials to keep out the external heat, all doors and other apertures should be sealed as nearly air-tight as possible, and the contents should be arranged to provide perfect drainage. All water must be removed at once, and the drainage pipe must be fitted with a trap so that cold air cannot escape nor outer air be admitted. If these principles are observed, any ingenious person can build an ice house or refrigerator, or design one to be built by a local carpenter that will answer all practical purposes.

To Make an Ice House.—The size of an ice house must, of course, be determined by the number of persons that are to make use of it. The interior should be so proportioned as to admit of packing cakes of any preferred size, as 2 by 3 feet, in a solid mass, but with an air space between the outside of the cakes and the wall of the ice house to admit of drainage. Hence an ice house 14 by 20 feet inside dimensions will admit of a layer of twenty-four cakes with a space of 1 foot clear all around.

Such an ice house carried up eight or ten layers would last two or three ordinary families for a year. It costs but little more to build a good-sized ice house, and often two or three neighbors can club together to advantage, both to reduce the cost of building the house, and also the labor of filling it.

Or, if more ice is harvested than one family requires, it can frequently be sold to neighbors at a profit sufficient to admit of paying for the first cost and for the labor of harvesting the ice each year.

To Build Ice Houses, make a frame of two or three joists, supported on posts raised a foot or more from the ground, and have a shed roof sloping to the north. Board up the outside and make another frame inside 10 or 12 inches from the outer boarding, and fill in the space between with shavings, sawdust, or spent tan bark packed as solidly as possible. Lay a solid plank floor and give it a pitch toward one corner with an outlet for drainage. Build double doors, reaching from the outer to the inner wall and packed solidly with nonconducting material. Or have a separate door in each wall, but the former is the better method.

To Fill an Ice House.—First cover the floor with sawdust, tan bark, or other suitable material at least 2 feet in thickness. Lay on this successive layers of ice in a solid mass, but leave a space of 12 inches all around. Cover the ice and fill the pitch of the building to a thickness of several feet with nonconducting material, but leave an air space between the top of this material and the roof. As the ice is removed from day to day for use, carefully replace the covering.

Homemade Tackle.

To Protect an Ice House.—Build a cheap trellis of slats or rough poles 8 or 10 inches from the walls all around, and also extending over the roof, and train the common woodbine or English ivy, or even clematis, morning glory, or other similar trailing vine to run over it. This can readily be done in most localities and forms a cheap and effective shade, that is a perfect defense against the direct rays of the sun. The trellis will prevent the plants from causing the boards of the ice house to decay, and by leaving a space between for circulation of air, will greatly assist in lowering the temperature. A mantle of vines also covers the bare ugliness of the cheap boarding of an ice house and tends to make it an object of beauty.

Or a skeleton ice house may be built by driving posts in the ground to make a frame and boarding them up to any desired height. Sawdust may be laid directly on the ground, but to prevent washouts and provide drainage it is better to throw in a few large stones, level them roughly, and lay a loose board floor a foot or more from the ground. Cover this with a layer of coarse hay or straw to prevent the sawdust from falling through, and on this put a foot or more of sawdust. Lay the ice in the middle in a solid mass, but leave a space of 2 feet all around between the ice and the boards and pack this space and cover the ice with nonconducting material, and lay a roof of loose boards over all, with an air space between. Such an ice house can be thrown up and boarded in a day while the ice is being drawn, and the planks can be taken down and stored away, if desired, as rapidly as the ice is removed in summer.

Or ice may be stored in a pen made of rails built up corncob fashion as the ice is put in. A floor of rails should be laid a foot or so from the ground and covered with straw, on which sawdust should be packed a foot or more deep. Lay the ice in a solid mass, pack with sawdust all around, cover the top with 2 feet of sawdust, and thatch with coarse straw. Over this lay a shed roof of boards tacked down with a few nails.

If morning glories or other quick-growing vines can be trained to run over the rails, it will greatly assist in preserving the ice in summer.

Or a load of sawdust may be thrown on the ground, a pile of ice built up on this, and a rough board frame merely tacked together at the corners about 2 feet distant all around from the pile. This space must, of course, be filled with sawdust, the top covered over to an equal depth, and rough boards or canvas thrown over all.

To Make an Ice Chest.—A practical ice chest may be made by building a tight box of matched boards with double sides 6 inches apart, having an inner chamber 3 feet long, 2 feet deep, and 2 feet wide. This will hold a block of 100 pounds or more of ice, and leave room all around for milk, butter, fresh meat, and other articles. This ice box must be furnished with a double lid packed with charcoal or sawdust and fitting tightly so as to exclude the outer air. It will preserve ice practically as well as an expensive refrigerator. The inner compartment must be furnished with a small pipe to carry off the water from the melting ice.

Or a cheap ice box may be made by simply setting one dry-goods box inside of another. There must be a space of 6 inches all around between the two. Pack this space closely with powdered charcoal or sawdust, and make a double lid, packed in the same manner, to fit the larger box. Provide a drainage pipe to remove the melting ice.

Or place a small cask or half barrel inside of a large cask and fill the space all around with charcoal. A tube from the bottom of the lower cask will carry off the melted ice. Furnish the inner cask with a removable lid and the outer cask with double cover packed with charcoal. Also provide a charcoal bag a foot thick or more to lay over the top of the inner cask. By filling the inner cask two thirds full of powdered ice, or with snow in winter, ices may be frozen in it, or by putting in a cake of ice it may be used as an ordinary refrigerator.

Ice Bags.—To preserve small quantities of ice, make two bags of heavy woolen goods, one of which should be 2 or 3 inches wider on all sides than the other. Place the smaller bag inside of the larger and stuff the space between with canvas. A block of ice placed in a bag of this description will be preserved as long as in an ordinary ice box. A small bit of rubber tubing should be inserted at one corner to provide drainage.

A Cooling Box.—In tropical regions where ice is scarce, or unobtainable, it is customary to construct a water-tight box, say 28 inches square and 10 inches deep, which should be filled with water. A shelf 30 by 30 inches is suspended from this by four posts, 2 by 2 inches and 36 inches long. Common burlap sacks are tacked closely about the sides. Pieces of woolen stuff, such as old woolen underwear, are placed around the edge of the box, with one end in the water and the other hanging outside and resting on the burlap. The whole is suspended in a shady place where the air can circulate freely around and through it, and where the sun will not shine on it. The air passing through the burlap causes evaporation of the water, and the burlap is kept dripping wet by the woolen stuff drawing water from the box as evaporation takes place. This is the principle by which the box is cooled. When the box is first filled the burlap should be thoroughly wet. Afterwards, if filled regularly, it will keep saturated.

The box is filled with water. On one side the burlap is allowed to hang free over the suspended shelf. This curtain is the door of the cooler. Butter placed on the shelf will keep perfectly solid. Even where ice is plentiful this is a convenient way to cool hot dishes that you do not wish to put in the refrigerator.

Care of the Refrigerator.—Put a saucer of unslacked lime in the refrigerator to keep it sweet. Place in the ice chest two or three lumps of charcoal as large as an egg, changing them two or three times a month. They will absorb all odors of cooked food and the like. Keep everything in the refrigerator covered. Have a number of glass fruit jars with screw tops in which to place liquids, and a glass jar for drinking water. This will save cracking off ice.

Few housekeepers take the necessary pains to keep the ice box scrupulously clean. It should be wiped out daily, and when the ice is exhausted, before a new piece is put in, a strong solution of caustic potash or sal soda should be poured through the waste pipes to cleanse and disinfect them.

To Break Ice.—Use an awl or a darning needle and tap it gently with a hammer. Make a row of holes across the ice, which will crack straight through beneath.

To Preserve Ice.—To preserve ice it must be isolated and surrounded with nonconducting material. There must be no access of the outer air to the ice except on top. Cold air is heavier than warm, hence the air which has been cooled by the melting of the ice settles upon its surface and cannot be displaced by the warmer air from above unless the cold air is allowed to escape or is displaced by a current, which must be avoided. The larger and colder a block of ice is, and the less it is exposed to warmth before being placed in the refrigerator, the longer it will keep.

Ice varies in temperature all the way from below zero to 30° F. before melting. Hence the fact that a piece of ice is not all melted by exposure to warm air is no criterion that it is not losing heat and rapidly approaching the melting point. If a piece of ice must be exposed to warm air for a time before being placed in the refrigerator it should be wrapped up in a heavy cloth or newspapers. If these are left on after the ice has been put in the refrigerator, so much the better. The larger the block of ice, the slower it melts. Hence it is economy to purchase ice in as large quantities as the refrigerator will hold.

CHAPTER III

HOME SANITATION AND HYGIENE

LOCATION OF BUILDINGS—DANGER FROM ARTIFICIAL HEATING SYSTEMS—WATER SUPPLY—DISPOSAL OF HOUSEHOLD WASTES —ELIMINATION OF FLIES

Not many years ago disease was most often deemed the act of Providence as a chastening or visitation for moral evil. Many diseases are now known to be merely human ignorance and uncleanliness out on public exhibition. The sins for which humanity suffers in the common communicable (and many other) diseases are violations of the laws of sanitation and hygiene, or simply the one great law of absolute sanitary cleanliness. The duty of supervising conditions affecting the public health is taken over by the community itself in the larger centers of population, but in many small towns and in the open country the chief responsibility for sanitary conditions in and about the home devolves upon each individual householder. Every symptom of preventable disease, especially diseases of the respiratory system (bronchitis, pneumonia); all fevers (typhoid fever, malaria, etc.); and all other communicable diseases (diphtheria, scarlet fever and the like) should suggest the question: "Is the cause of this illness any unsanitary condition within my control which can and should be remedied?"

Not infrequently landlords and parents shirk responsibility for illness due to unsanitary conditions upon the ground that the cost of the proper remedy would be prohibitive. Such conditions as dampness in cellars, or the pollution of air, soil or water supply by seepage from barnyard manure piles, privy vaults and open drains, are often thought to be determined for all future time by the location of dwellings and outbuildings and are believed to be incurable without greater expense than the owner can afford. Men are too apt to say under such circumstances, "What can't be cured must be endured," and to think that the members of their families must take their chance of sickness along with the other risks of life. Such a mode of reasoning is most reprehensible. As sanitary knowledge increases it will undoubtedly be corrected by law.

The most important asset not only of the individual and family but also of the community is not mere property, but rather the physical vigor of its members. The cost of bringing an average child to maturity has been estimated at from two to five thousand dollars. The value to the family of each of its adult members may be taken as their normal earning capacity for the average period of expectation of life. On this basis courts usually grant damages on death claims at the rate of from five thousand dollars upward. And the average of such awards appears to be steadily on the increase. Hence on the economic side alone, it is false economy to risk the loss of one or more lives worth five thousand dollars each and upwards, in order to avoid making improvements costing a small fraction of that sum.

Moreover, with the progress of sanitary science, additional stress is being laid upon the moral aspect of sanitation. Persons who should expose in open vessels solutions of strychnine, arsenic or other virulent poisons would be held guilty of criminal negligence if accidental death by poisoning should result. Yet some of the gases, liquids and micro-organisms with which the air, soil and water supply in and about dwellings may become contaminated, are now known to be as fatal under some common circumstances as the most deadly poisons. The only possible excuse for permitting the existence of these nuisances is ignorance. And with the present rapid spread of scientific information that excuse will not much longer avail. Another generation will doubtless see laws passed holding property owners and heads of families responsible for illness resulting from preventable causes. Consider not alone the economic loss and moral wrong involved. Think of the pain and suffering of illness, the labor and anxiety of nursing, the expense of medicines and medical attendance and the cost of funerals! Above all must we regard the desolation and heart-break caused by the loss of those near and dear to us! When all these are cast into the scale, the expense of proper sanitation, however great, is clearly seen to be necessary and even negligible.

At first thought it might seem that information regarding the proper location and construction of the home and its appurtenances would be of value only to those who are about to build a new dwelling. And of course the founding of a new home affords the best opportunity to put the principles of hygiene and sanitation into effect. Yet perhaps a majority of the entire population occupy rented dwellings and are free to remove from them at will. In all such cases a knowledge of the demands of proper sanitation is directly applicable to the question whether or not to renew the leasehold of one's present dwelling. In the event of removal it applies equally to the selection of another home. Moreover, the conditions surrounding buildings improperly located may often be remedied by permanent improvements. Or such buildings may be removed bodily to new foundations at an expense trifling in comparison to the original cost of the structures. If, however, necessary improvements to insure sanitation cannot be made, it is far better to sell property even at a sacrifice and remove from it, before sickness or death have brought about their inevitable loss. A knowledge of the laws of sanitation is also of vital importance in the selection of temporary homes, such as summer hotels, boarding places and summer camps. Indeed, so fundamental is this subject to human health and happiness that it should be regarded as an essential part of the fund of knowledge which is or should be common to every normal person.

The conditions essential to proper sanitation are simply an abundance of sunshine, pure air and pure water, with necessary shade in summer, or, negatively, freedom from pollution of the air, soil or water supply with noxious micro-organisms (germs) or other poisons. Within the dwelling, artificial heat and light must be provided by means which give off into the air a minimum of the noxious products of combustion. And these must be promptly removed by a proper system of ventilation. To accomplish these results attention must be given to both the location and construction of the home and its necessary outbuildings, and to the installation of suitable systems of heating, lighting and ventilation, water supply, drainage and sewage disposal. These will be the topics under consideration in the present chapter.

LOCATION OF BUILDINGS

If a house stands on low damp ground, or if there is swampy or wet land in the immediate vicinity, sickness will follow as sure as night follows day. It is far better not to build at all than to occupy such a location unless the site and all adjacent pools or swamp are first improved by efficient drainage. Moisture in and about the foundations of a home adds to the humidity of the atmosphere. This makes the occupants more susceptible to both heat and cold. Swamps or pools of standing water afford breeding grounds for mosquitoes. Thus in many localities they condemn in advance members of the family and their guests to attacks of debilitating malaria. If, however, a house stands in a damp spot which cannot be drained, it should at least be lifted well above the surface of the soil on damp-proof posts or other foundations. Or the cellar, if there is one, should be made thoroughly damp-proof. These steps with proper artificial heat will aid in protecting the family from the ill effects of excessive humidity.

Relative Position of House and Other Things.—The danger from lack of proper drainage is greatly increased if the moisture in the soil is polluted by seepage from any sort of nuisance. No such conditions should be tolerated. Even the choice of a proper site for the house where the soil is porous and there is good natural drainage will not protect the health of the family if the stable or other outbuildings are so located that there is a gradual seepage of polluted water through the ground into and around the foundations of the house. Nor should there be an open sink drain contaminating the earth adjacent to the foundations. Not infrequently buildings of prosperous farmers are so placed that the land slopes from the barn, stable or pigpen toward the dwelling. In addition to constant seepage through the soil, a flood of filthy surface water during heavy rains flows toward and around the house and cellar. The inevitable result is illness which is most often attributed to other causes. It must also be borne in mind that the underground strata of the soil do not always coincide with the surface condition. Thus there may be a gentle elevation between the farm buildings and the house which would appear to protect the latter from soil pollution. Yet below the ground there may be a shelf of hardpan covered with a layer of loose sand and gravel dipping direct from under the barn or stable toward the foundations of the house. All such conditions must be carefully observed and studied. The object is to so locate the buildings that the drainage from the outbuildings occupied by animals cannot carry pollution toward the house.

Air Drainage.—Next only in importance to a well drained soil is the question of air drainage. C. G. Hill says: "A hollow, however porous and well drained the soil, will prove a cold and frosty spot in winter, a hot and sultry one in summer. A site too closely shut in by timber will lose what it may gain in shade by the absence of free circulation of air. Every breeze will be cut off during the sultry days of summer and in winter the absence of sunlight will be a drawback. All things considered a gentle hillside slope offers the greatest advantages. If the highest land is to the north or west little more is to be desired. . . . The prevailing breezes must also be considered and the outbuildings or any fixtures or places which may become sources of offensive odors should be located well to the leeward of the house."

Shade and Shelter. — While the house should stand in direct sunshine and be exposed to thorough ventilation from prevailing winds, the shelter of a strip of timber or a windbreak to the north and west is very desirable, especially in cold climates. This helps to keep the house comfortably warm in cold weather with economy of fuel. It also adds to the comfort of live stock and of those who are obliged to care for them. Every owner of a home should take pride in improving the lawn and grounds and planting suitable shade trees. Yet the choice of a site for a new home, other things being equal, may well be determined by the presence of one or more fine old trees already capable of yielding the shade which is so grateful and necessary in summer.

Arrangement of Rooms.—When possible, the living rooms and work rooms of the house should be on the east side so as to receive a good share of sunshine. This side is also advantageous for sleeping rooms so that the morning sun may stream into these rooms and upon the beds before they are made up. Nor should they be made up too early. Moreover, this side of the house does not receive the intense rays of the afternoon sun in summer, nor is it exposed to the prevailing winter winds. Artificial heat also tends from the west toward the east side of a building. The latter has therefore the advantage of being cooler in summer and more sheltered and warmer in winter. Vestibules, halls, stairs and the least used rooms may sometimes be so placed as to afford protection to other apartments. All these considerations are of course equally as important in choosing a house for rental as in building a home for one's own occupancy.

Cellar or Basement.—The vital importance of a clean dry cellar is due to the danger of the contamination of the air from soil pollution. The artificial heat in a house, especially in winter, rises and creates suction from the soil beneath and around the cellar. Thus the building as a whole acts as a flue. It draws up and transports to the rooms above whatever noxious air or gases the earth may contain. Moisture in the atmosphere of the cellar is thus quickly communicated to all parts of the house. These facts have been abundautly proved by experiment.

A new cellar should be so drained as to keep the water level below the cellar floor. Or if this precaution has been neglected, such a drain may be put in after the house has been built, provided a proper outlet can be secured.

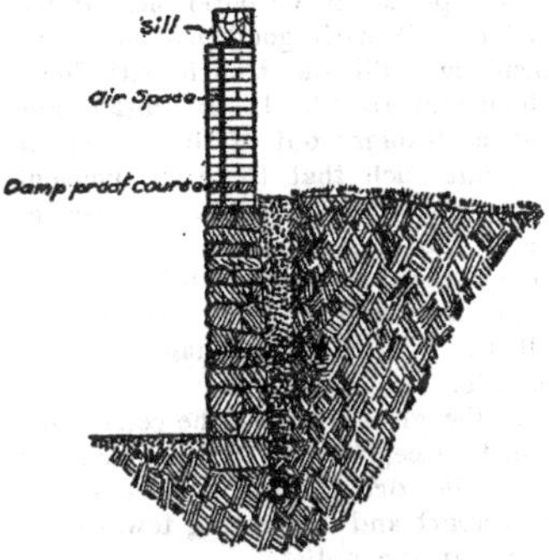

Method of draining cellar walls. Courtesy State Board of Health of Maine.

The cellar wall laid up dry and then chinked and "pointed" on the inside should be avoided, especially in damp localities. The open crevices admit the water freely from the outside. The plaster or cement on the inside then becomes wet and eventually falls off. Cellar walls should preferably be built of concrete or stone laid solidly in cement-mortar and brought to a good smooth face both inside and outside, particularly the latter. This will exclude all vermin as well as moisture. Such a wall, especially if backed with gravel, coarse sand or fine rubble, as shown in the illustration, turns the water and allows it to drain off rapidly through the tile surrounding the foundation.

To drain a cellar after a house has been built, dig a trench outside the foundation wall to a depth at least 12 inches below the cellar bottom and lay 2-inch unglazed tile all around the foundation wall outside of and close to it. Give the tile a slope of 10 or 12 inches on an even grade from the corner of the house diagonally opposite, around both sides and down to the outlet. If the drain must then enter a sewer, insert a trap well outside the cellar wall with a deep water seal which will not go dry at any season. If the ground is very damp, point up the outer side of the cellar wall with good hydraulic cement and fill the trench with loose stone and gravel. If the outlet pipe can be brought out of the ground at a point such that there is sufficient fall, this will provide perfect drainage. Take care not to disturb the foundations. If the earth is not very firm, dig the trench in sections and fill it as fast as the drainage pipe can be laid.

If the ground under the cellar bottom is exceptionally wet, underlay it with tile drains not more than 12 feet apart and converging toward the point of the outlet.

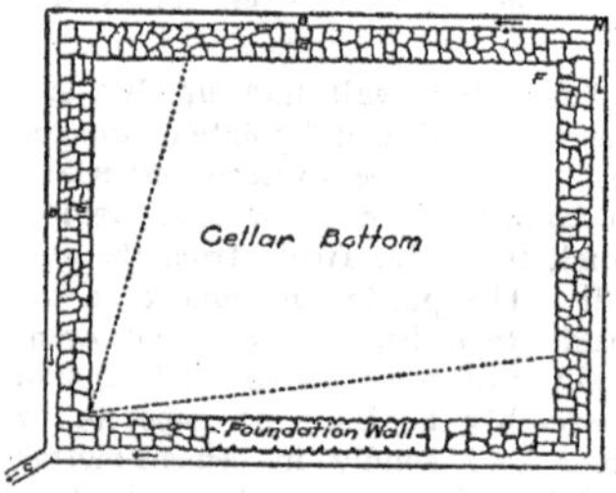

Method of draining cellar bottom. Courtesy State Board of Health of Maine.

Damp-proof Courses.—Some kinds of building materials used for foundation and the underpinning of houses are porous. These readily absorb water from the soil and transmit dampness to the structure and the rooms above. Brick is the worst offender, but concrete and some kinds of building stone are almost equally as bad. Hence insert a damp-proof course laid completely across the foundation wall and extending all around the building. This may consist of a half-inch layer of asphalt or of slate embedded in cement. It must necessarily be above grade so that the ground may not come in contact with the work above it.

In many old brick houses, or wooden houses with brick underpinnings, the ground comes in contact with the brickwork. This is a standing and very cordial invitation to serious forms of illness to visit the occupants. Hence remove, sectionally, a course of brick all the way around the house above the ground line and below the sills or floor timbers, and insert a damp-proof course.

DANGERS FROM ARTIFICIAL HEAT

The various kinds of fuel and systems of heating have been considered elsewhere from the standpoint of their efficiency. We are concerned here only with their sanitary and hygienic effect. The most common danger to health is perhaps from over-heating. E. C. Jordan says: "Cold, pure air is a wonderful tonic. It improves the appetite, increases the red corpuscles of the blood and tones up the system generally. Many American children and adults emerge from their hibernation in the spring anemic and weak. This is largely due to the faults in our methods of heating. We customarily overheat our houses and offices. Seventy degrees or more of artificial heat is enervating. We should accustom ourselves to being comfortable at a temperature at least a few degrees below 70.

"A second serious danger is from the products of combustion. Burning coal, wood, oil or gas generate certain very harmful gases. The utmost care should be taken to exclude these from the air we breathe. Yet leakage of gas from stoves or furnaces not properly constructed or managed is very common. The use of oil and gas heaters is perilously imprudent. They should never be used unless the products of combustion are carried from the room by means of a pipe connecting with the chimney flue.

"A third fault and danger is want of ventilation. In unventilated living rooms the air is rendered unsuitable for breathing by these four things: (1) An insufficient percentage of oxygen; (2) the poisonous products of respiration; (3) the deleterious products of combustion from lights or leakage from heaters; (4) disease-producing bacteria. One principal reason why grip, pneumonia, diphtheria, smallpox, and some other diseases are more prevalent in winter than in summer, is that in winter the doors and windows are closed and the bacterial causes of these diseases are concentrated.

"It is a serious yet common mistake to put in a heating apparatus which cannot easily do the work required of it in cold weather. Such a heating plant is then sure to be crowded and overheated, its period of usefulness is shortened, the greatest practicable amount of heat is not obtained from the fuel, and deleterious products escape into the rooms.

"Another prolific source of ill health for those who breathe artificial air is the unintelligent use of dampers. Everybody who uses coal knows that, if the damper is turned too soon, we get into our rooms an ill-smelling sulphurous gas. That gas is also dangerously poisonous. But unfortunately most people are unaware that after the damper is turned so that the draft is too slight, another gas, without odor to reveal its presence, continues to leak out. This is carbonic oxide.

"Of the two carbon gases found in vitiated air, both will cause death by suffocation if the percentage in the air is large enough. If he is rescued in time and carried into the open air, the victim of carbonic acid gas will quickly recover, and apparently without permanent injury. But in cases of partial asphyxiation from carbonic oxide gas, resuscitation and ultimate recovery are very doubtful. The red corpuscles of the blood seem to suffer destruction, or a great diminution of their oxygen-carrying capacity. Recovery, when it occurs, is usually very slow and incomplete. The person chronically poisoned by habitually breathing this gas in small quantities is having his blood corpuscles slowly destroyed. He comes out in the spring pale and weak, and with his general health impaired. Many persons, with no suspicion of the cause of their illness, feel the need of the recuperation which they can gain in the summer season to enable them to endure the next winter's chronic foul-air poisoning. Any perceptible odor of gas from the furnace or other heating apparatus is always an indication of serious danger to health and should have immediate attention."

WATER SUPPLY

Water should be brought into the house and also to the barn whenever possible, and pipes should then be laid to remove the waste water from house and barn and to so dispose of it as to avoid breeding grounds for the bacteria that cause filth diseases. There are important reasons why water should be brought to the barn, but if it is not possible to bring it to both places, the house should have the preference. L. H. Bailey says: "The first thing I would now do for the farm home is to put in sanitary water works for the care and comfort of the person. Nothing would so soon lift the home ideals."

Every dwelling should have good kitchen sinks, water closets and a bathroom. Drinking water should be brought in by pipes. Such a water supply means additional comfort, better health, protection against fire, saving of labor and a supply of water for lawn and garden. Various methods are in use, as gravity from high springs or creeks, or power from windmills, hydraulic rams, small gas or hot air engines, or from tanks which may be filled by pneumatic pumps operated either by power or by hand. The location of the storage tank and the best means of forcing water into it depend upon local conditions. The source of supply, the amount of water required, the need of power for other purposes, th available fuel and the cost of labor all have a bearing on the matter, in addition to the first cost of installation.

A small hydraulic ram can be installed for $50 or less, pipe not included. This will be practicable if there is a fall of 18 inches or more from the source of supply. The illustration shows the method of setting a hydraulic ram.

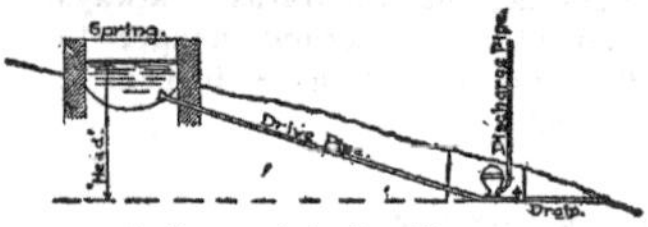

Setting of hydraulic ram.
(E. T. Wilson.)

The height of the source of supply above the ram—i. e., the head—determines the distance and elevation to which the water can be forced. The head may be increased by damming a stream so as to create a reservoir or, if a drain can be secured to keep the outlet free from water, by sinking the ram in a pit. A ram keeps going all the time and requires very little attention. The expense of maintenance is small. Hence a small ram with a very low head makes a cheap and adequate source of water supply. The water can be forced into an elevated tank or pneumatic tank as desired. The overflow can be utilized by a water motor for pumping cistern water, shelling corn or any of the other numerous ways for saving hand labor. The water which is pumped need not be the same as the power water. By means of a compound ram, impure water can be used to pump the pure water without danger of mixing. The size of the ram required will depend upon the head, the amount of water required and the height and distance to which it must be delivered. After the pipes are laid, keep them uncovered until they are given a test. This will discover any leaks.

Windmills.—A properly constructed windmill is a good and simple way of securing a supply of water and can be equipped at small cost with a device which will also furnish power for grinding feed, shelling corn, sawing wood, washing, churning, and many other purposes with no expense for fuel. The first cost of a windmill varies greatly according to the conditions. But this is perhaps the most economical means of obtaining power. The wind is free and the cost of repairs is very small. The tank should hold a week's supply or about 2,000 gallons for the house, and twice as much for the house and barn, say a tank 10 feet across and 6 feet deep. A windmill to supply such a tank should be at least a 12-footer.

Gas or Hot Air Engines.—These devices are now manufactured expressly for pumping water to elevated or pneumatic tanks to furnish supplies for houses and barns. Such engines may be had to burn any kind of fuel—natural gas, gasoline, kerosene, coal or wood. They are not difficult to operate and may be used for other purposes when not needed for pumping. The pipes should be laid as straight as possible and free from elbows and sharp bends. The cost ranges from $60 upwards for 2 or 3 h.p. The cost of fuel is very small. A half hour's pumping a day will furnish a supply of water for an average family.

Distribution of Water.—Whatever the source of supply or method of pumping employed, the water must be collected in some sort of storage tank for distribution throughout the house. This may be an elevated outdoor tank, a tank in the attic, or a pneumatic tank in the cellar. An elevated outdoor tank must be protected from freezing in cold weather by enclosing the exposed pipes in two or more wooden cases with air spaces between. The outer case may be of matched boards and painted. Equip a storage tank in the attic with a suitable float to shut off the supply pipe when the water reaches a certain height and admit the water again when the water level of the tank is lowered. Also to protect against freezing, the possibility of leakage or other costly accident equip the attic tank with an overflow pipe to carry off surplus water, if the float valve fails to shut it off when the

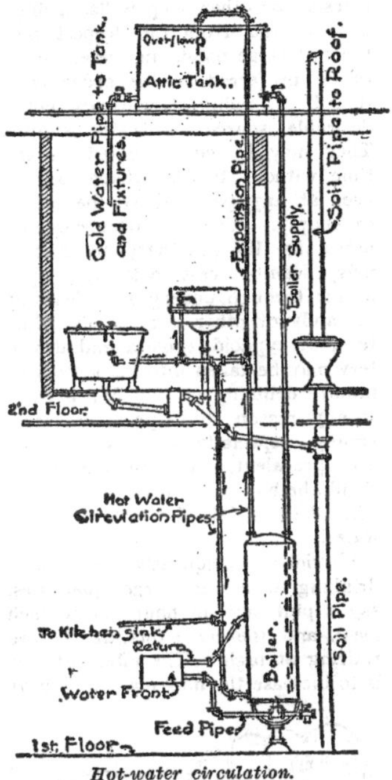

Hot-water circulation.
(E. T. Wilson.)

tank is full. Take care to avoid stoppage of this pipe in winter by freezing. As a rule indoor elevated tanks are not advisable in cold climates unless the whole house can be kept warm by an adequate heating system. An outdoor tank properly protected against the weather is safer.

Pneumatic Tank.—To avoid these difficulties use the modern pneumatic tank built of steel plates. Locate this in the cellar, or protect it by a small building outdoors, or even bury it in the ground. Water is distributed from these tanks by means of air which is pumped into them with the water. This may be done by hand by means of an ordinary force pump, or by any of the above means of using power. The return of the air and water is prevented by means of a check valve in the pipe. The air in the upper part of the tank is compressed by the water which is forced in from below. The pressure is increased by pumping more water into the tank. It decreases as the water is drawn off. A 10-pound pressure will raise the water 22 feet, or a 15-pound pressure 33 feet. A 40-pound pressure will deliver water to points 85 feet above the tank. A little pumping each day will maintain an average pressure of 50 pounds. A tank 30 inches in diameter and 10 feet long will supply the needs of an ordinary family of five. It can be filled in from 10 to 20 minutes a day with a good hand force pump. But if more than 100 gallons a day are required, it would be better to employ some kind of mechanical power. If an engine is used, a large tank is more economical. Twenty minutes pumping once or twice a day should furnish the supply.

The first cost of a small tank for an ordinary family of five will be from $100 upward. The expense for repairs and maintenance is slight. A large neighborhood plant with a pneumatic tank and suitable engine or other source of power capable of supplying water to several houses could be installed at greatly reduced cost to each householder. This would give a much higher pressure in case of fire.

The pipes should be run as nearly as possible in straight lines and free from sharp bends or elbows. The farther they are carried horizontally the larger they should be. This decreases the loss of pressure by friction. If a windmill is used, it should be supplied with an automatic regulator which will throw it out of gear when the pressure reaches a given amount and start it again when the pressure is relieved. The advantages of this system are complete security against freezing in winter, coolness of the water in summer and incidental fire protection. The tank is wholly closed to dust and light and has the advantage of resting upon the ground.

Hand Force Pump.—If water cannot be supplied by gravity or power

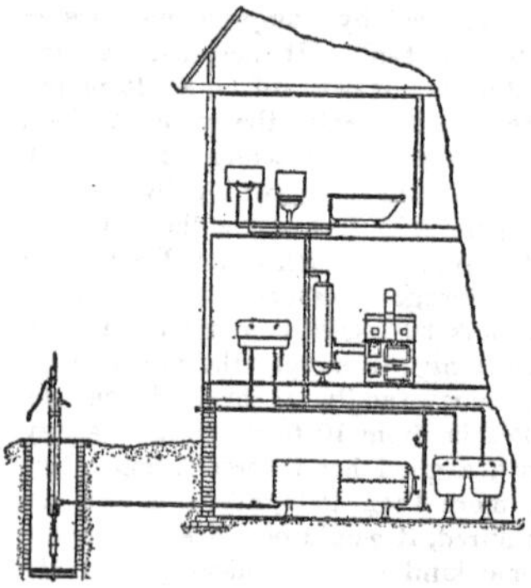

Water distribution by pneumatic tank system. Courtesy State Board of Health of Maine.

it should certainly be brought from the cistern or well to the kitchen sink and also to the bathroom, if any, by means of a small hand force pump. The steps saved and health gained make a convenient water supply a necessity rather than a luxury. A small force pump may be located at one end of the kitchen sink with a suction pipe reaching to the cistern. If an attic tank is used, this may be connected with the rainfall leader and supplied with an automatic cut-off which will send the water to the eistern when the attic tank is full. The kitchen force pump can also be connected with the tank and used to fill it in dry seasons.

Sources of Water Supply.—For domestic purposes water should preferably be what is known as soft rather than hard, and must be clear, pure and palatable. The essentials are freedom from disease germs, turbidity, color, odor or taste. The source of supply of drinking water should be absolutely pure. It is a good plan to have drinking water, especially from wells and cisterns, tested at least twice a year. Water from artesian or other deep wells, springs, cisterns and from the deepest portions of large ponds and reservoirs is to be preferred in the order mentioned. Running streams are not a desirable source of water supply. They may be contaminated at any time without the knowledge of the user at any point above the source of supply. Water is often contaminated by its proximity to stables, privy vaults, cess-pools and open drains through underground leaching in sandy or other porous soil. Bacteria of typhoid, cholera and dysentery may be taken into the system by impure drinking water. When there is any reason to suspect the water supply, especially if these diseases are prevalent, all drinking water should be boiled. A little lemon juice will take away the flat taste of boiled water.

Physicians frequently recommend drinking water in large quantities, say a pint half an hour before each meal, and the same quantity before retiring at night. The effect of this is to increase the muscular activity of

Pollution of water supply from open privy vault and manure pile.

certain internal organs by distention, and to dissolve certain poisonous secretions—as, for instance, uric acid which causes rheumatism. The same course is also recommended in cases of threatened diabetes or kidney disease. It is probable that few persons drink as much water as is advisable from a hygienic standpoint.

But, of course, the more water taken into the system the more important it is that the source of supply be pure. Approximately four-fifths of the human body consists of liquids, of which over 60 per cent is water. This fact suggests the importance of supplying drinking water of the best quality.

SOURCES OF WATER SUPPLY

Wells.—An artesian or other deep well driven through hardpan and drawing water from a deep underground stream by means of a tight pipe is perhaps the purest and best source of permanent water supply. The first cost is considerable, but such a well may be regarded as much the most desirable of all permanent improvements. Open shallow wells dug just deep enough to strike running water, usually not more than 20 or 30 feet, are the ordinary source of supply in most localities. Such wells may become contaminated in two ways: by surface water washing into them, or by underground seepage from some source of pollution. It was formerly taken for granted by most persons that the soil acted as a natural filter and freed the water passing through it from all its impurities. Recent experiments have shown that this is far from being the case. The capacity of the soil to purify water by filtration varies greatly. It depends upon the nature of the soil, the lay and dip of the various strata and the kind and extent of the contamination. Under favorable conditions organic matter and most visible impurities will be filtered out of polluted water before it reaches the well. The water may then be clear and cold, taste all right and be free from odor, but it may, nevertheless, contain chemical poisons in solution. It may also contain the germs of typhoid and other filth diseases in great quantities. For these are entirely colorless and so small as to be wholly invisible without the aid of the microscope.

Another common mistake is to assume that underground percolation follows the same lines as surface drainage. This, too, is by no means the case. If the top of a well is on higher ground than the open vault or drain, cess-pool or other source of pollution, it will be protected from surface washing. But if the bottom is lower than any of these nuisances there may be a dip of the hardpan underground from them toward the bottom of the well. This, if covered with a layer of porous soil or loose gravel, may be almost as good a conduit for polluted water as an open drain or sewer. The continued pollution of the soil causes these underground strata to become charged with various impurities in ever increasing volume. With the lapse of time these creep steadily into closer proximity to the well. Eventually attention is attracted to the danger by the presence of a marked taste or odor. But meantime various degrees of ill health may be observed in the family. Or even an epidemic of sickness may break out from this cause. Yet these diseases may have been attributed to some other source.

As a general rule it may be taken for granted that a shallow well anywhere within convenient distance of a barnyard or an open vault or drain is dangerous to health. This danger is constantly increasing with the passing years, although meanwhile the family may be lulled into a false sense of security. Among the remedies which suggest themselves are piping water from high springs or other suitable sources beyond contamination, the use of cistern water, or if the shallow well seems a necessity, a change in the location of the barnyard and the elimination of open vaults and drains by means elsewhere recommended.

Dug wells should be lined all the way up either with stone laid in water cement and smoothly faced on the inside with a trowel, or preferably with large tiles or tile piping. This compels the water to come in from the bottom. It thus increases the depth of the soil which serves as a filter. The lining of a well, whether of stone or tile, should be

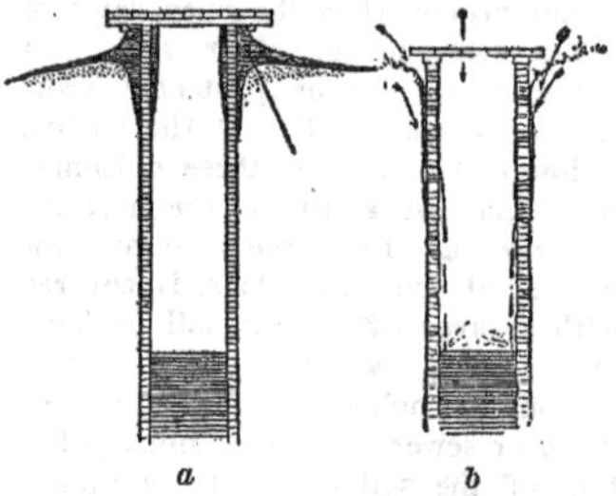

(*a*) *Proper method of walling up and protecting private wells from surface drainage;* (*b*) *unprotected private well.* (*Ritchie's Primer of Sanitation. Copyright, 1909, by World Book Company, Yonkers, New York.*)

brought 18 inches or 2 feet above the surface of the soil and banked up with a mound of earth. This will prevent contamination from surface leaching. Take care that the upper 4 or 5 feet is made absolutely watertight. Then lay a heavy tight-fitting stone over the mouth to keep out small animals, angleworms, dead leaves and other organic matter. When cleaning old wells not thus protected, the skeletons of these animals are frequently found.

Never lay a sewer pipe or waste drain near a well. Never dig a new well in their vicinity. Such pipes and drains are seldom watertight. Or if a sewer pipe must be run near a well, use cast-iron pipe and seal all joints watertight. Never locate a cess-pool, open vault or drain or throw slop water on the ground anywhere on the same piece of ground as a well. Otherwise in the course of time the well water is almost certain to become contaminated. The only means of insuring the purity of the water supply is to take adequate steps to keep the soil in the vicinity free from pollution.

Springs.—Spring water is usually pure and good for drinking purposes, but often contains minerals in solution. It is then known as hard water. But springs may become contaminated in the same manner as wells if located near possible sources of pollution. Hence a spring intended to be a source of water supply should be carefully tested. If the water supply is to be piped from a spring as a permanent source of supply, first find out two things: Is the spring high enough above the house? Is the quantity of water sufficient? You can measure the overflow of the spring by pailfuls. The house alone for a family of ten will need about 600 gallons in twenty-four hours. To get this, the spring should flow fast enough to fill a 10-quart pail in five minutes. If the spring is high above the house and near at hand, ¾-inch pipe may be sufficient. But if the spring is not high, or if the pipe is long, inch pipe is safer and better.

The spring should be dug out, walled up, and covered with wood, brick, stone or concrete—to be preferred in the order mentioned. The pipe may be either iron, lead, wood or sewer pipe. Sewer pipe costs about six cents a running foot, and ¾-inch wrought-iron pipe about the same.

If the pressure is high—especially at the lower end, it is better to use iron. Wood or lead pipe is nowadays rarely used.

Cisterns.—Rain water when properly collected at a distance from large towns is pure and soft. In towns and cities it is often contaminated by smoke and fumes in the atmosphere. Cistern water in such localities should therefore be filtered and boiled before drinking. The rainfall collected in cisterns is a valuable source of water supply in localities where it is difficult or costly to drive a well and also in regions where the water is hard. In some localities this is the only source of water supply available. Rain water is soft and hence especially adapted to laundry purposes.

Cisterns must be carefully screened with wire netting to exclude insects, toads and other vermin and should be so arranged as not to admit surface water. They should be kept scrupulously clean. The first rainfall should be excluded to allow the accumulated dirt to wash off the roof and out to the gutters. For this purpose place a cut-off on the rain water pipe to divert the flow from the cistern. Various automatic devices of this sort are on the market. Locate a cistern close to the house for convenience, or construct it in a corner of the basement or cellar.

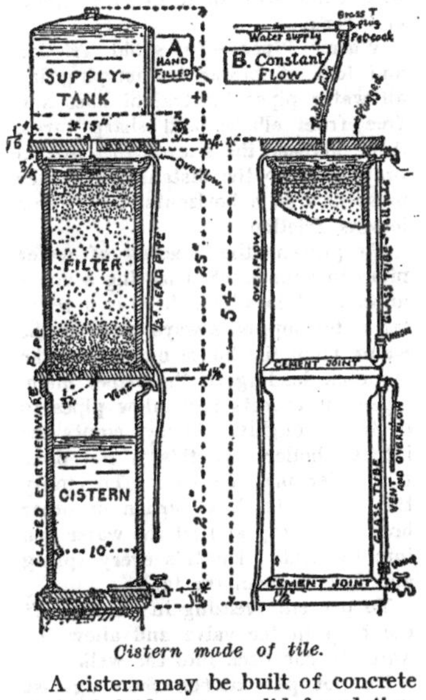

Cistern made of tile.

A cistern may be built of concrete or brick laid upon a solid foundation, and may be either round or rectangular. A round or egg-shaped cistern is preferable to one with square corners. It is more difficult to build but is stronger and easy to keep clean, especially for drinking purposes. A cheap and convenient small cistern and filter may be built of tile. Two styles of this kind of cistern are shown in the illustration. A little ingenuity used in the construction of a cistern and filter will be amply com-proper sizes and wash them clean and free from loam and other impurities. Carry the wall between the inlet chamber (A) and the filter (B) to the top or above the level of the overflow pipe. Plaster it on both sides with cement to prevent the water from seeping through and fouling the brick. But leave in the bottom of this partition a number of openings the size of a half brick to admit the water from the inlet chamber (A) into the bottom of the filter. Thence it passes upward through the filtering material and overflows into the storage tank (C), its fall being broken by the ledge of projecting bricks at F.

Build the floor of the inlet chamber (A) and the filter (B) so as to slope to the outer side of A. Much of the coarse dirt and sediment will then settle at this point and may be readily removed. This relieves the filter and facilitates cleansing. Occasionally on a very rainy day, pump or bale out the inlet chamber and shift the inlet pipe from the inlet chamber (A) over to the top of the

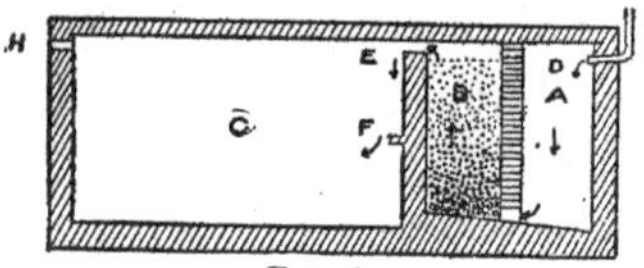

FIG. A.

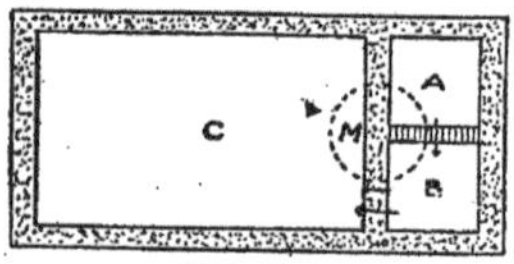

FIG. B.

Plan of brick cistern. Courtesy State Board of Health of Maine.

filter (B). This will reverse the filtering process and flush out the filter chamber. (D) is the inlet pipe which brings the water from the roof and (H) is the overflow from the cistern.

The linear arrangement of the three compartments in Fig. A is to show a cross section of the filter chamber, but in actual construction the ground plan of the filter should be as shown in Fig. B. This cistern may be built of brick laid in Portland cement mortar, or of concrete. It should preferably be arched over or covered with reinforced concrete leaving a good-sized manhole to serve as a common entrance to all three compartments. Or, it may be provided with a perfectly tight plank cover to keep out small animals, insects and the like.

Equip both inlet and overflow pipe with a fine strainer to exclude insects and vermin.

Water Pipes.—To avoid friction and loss of power in pumping lay all water pipes in straight lines and free from elbows and sharp turns. Also increase the size of the pipe in proportion to the distance the water must flow in a horizontal line. This lessens friction.

To prevent the freezing of water pipes in winter, when leaving a house unoccupied in which there is a regular water supply, always turn off the water from the house by turning the stopcock leading to the street main. Open all faucets and allow pipes to drain thoroughly. Always empty the kitchen boiler. If this is not done the boiler may collapse. To empty the boiler attach a garden or other hose to the top and let the water run into the sink. Do this every spring and fall to clean the tank.

To prevent freezing in pumps, lift the trap in the valve and allow the water to run back into the well.

Do not put kitchen sinks against the outer wall of a house. If this has been done and the sink cannot be changed, purchase circular tubes of asbestos and fit over the pipes, or line the wall with asbestos. But on cold nights it is safer to turn the water off.

Frozen Water Pipes.—While the pipes are frozen take care not to build a fire in furnace or range. Direct heat from the pipes will generate steam and severe explosions may follow. At the very least pipes will burst and the plumbers' bills for repairs will be heavy. Pipes that are slightly stuck may be thawed by wrapping around them flannel or other cloth and pouring on hot water. Plumbers use gasoline or kerosene gas in lamps which blow around the frozen pipe. They move the lamp back and forth so as not to apply too much heat at any one spot.

To Soften Water.—Boiling hard water from twenty to thirty minutes is the best way to soften it for drinking purposes. This also has the effect of killing all germs of disease it may contain. Carbonic-acid gas passes off with the steam, and carbonate of lime is left as a sediment. A clean oyster shell put in the tea kettle will attract this and other sediments that are deposited from boiling water and will thus prevent an unpleasant crust from gathering on the inside of the tea kettle.

Or baking soda (bicarbonate of soda) in small quantities will soften hard water by removing the excess of lime.

Or, for the laundry, hard water may be softened by the addition of a little borax.

Or quicklime is also recommended. Dissolve ½ ounce in 10 quarts of water, and pour this solution into a barrel of hard water. The whole will be softened.

To Make Boiled Water More Palatable.—The flat taste of boiled water is objectionable to many. This may be obviated by pouring the water rapidly from one pitcher to another, holding the two pitchers some distance apart. This process aerates the water, renders it sparkling, and restores its natural flavor. A few drops of lemon juice contribute to this effect.

To Keep Water Cool Without Ice.—In summer or in warm climates drinking water may be kept in unglazed earthenware pitchers. Place the pitcher on a board lying across a tub or pail containing water. Wrap several folds of cheese cloth around the outside of the pitcher and let the ends hang down into the water. Place this contrivance in a draught. The evaporation of the moisture from the cheese cloth tends to cool the contents of the pitcher.

To Test Water.—Fill a number of tumblers half full of the suspected water, and employ the following tests:

To test for lime, use a small quantity of oxalic acid. The lime will be revealed in a white precipitate.

To test for carbonate of iron, use a tincture of galls. This will yield a black precipitate.

To test for vegetable and animal matter, use a small quantity of sulphuric acid. The water will become black.

To test for copper, dip a penknife in the water. The copper will be deposited in a yellow coating.

To Purify Water.—When water in wells or other receptacles smells bad, suspend in it lumps of charcoal in a basket or net, so that they can be removed and replaced at intervals.

To Clarify Water.—Water in springs, wells and streams often becomes muddy after heavy rains, and the water of some streams always holds a large amount of liquid mud and other impurities in solution. In such cases it becomes important to clarify the water. This not only makes it more palatable and attractive. It is imperative when filters are used. Otherwise the filter soon clogs up and becomes useless.

Alum is the universal agent for precipitating impurities in suspension or even in solution. It is very commonly employed along the Missouri and Mississippi Rivers and other muddy streams.

To quickly clarify a pitcher of drinking water, tie a lump of alum to a string and swing it about in the water. The sediment will settle.

Or, for larger quantities, use 1 teaspoonful of pulverized alum to 4 gallons of drinking water. Stir the water before putting in the alum. After the water has settled draw it off in such a way as not to disturb the sediment. A tablespoonful of alum will settle the contents of a hogshead of water. The alum itself, if too much is not used, will settle and be carried off in the sediment.

Or lime is recommended, used in the form of certain salts of lime, either chloride, nitrate, or bicarbonate of lime, or caustic lime. Use 1 part of any of these salts of lime to 1,000 parts of water.

Or sulphate of alumina is recommended for clarifying water containing vegetable or animal matter. The formula is as follows: Bisulphate of alumina (neutral solution), 1 ounce; water, 435 gallons.

Or dissolve 2 ounces of saltpeter in 1 quart of warm water and throw the solution into the cistern or well.

Or, to purify putrid water: Water, 1 pound; sulphuric acid, 8 drops. Mix and filter through charcoal.

Or water, 8 gallons; powdered alum, 1 ounce. Dissolve with agitation, then allow it to rest for twenty-four hours, decant into another vessel, and add a solution of carbonate of soda until it ceases to produce a precipitate.

Or instead of alum add 7 or 8 grains of red sulphate of iron, then proceed as before.

Or add a little aqueous chlorine to the foul water.

Or arrange a suitable pipe at the end of a pair of bellows (double bellows are best), and force the air through the water for a time, then allow it to settle for use.

Water Filters. — The ordinary household appliances for filtering water are rarely preventives of disease. Such filters are not ordinarily cleansed often enough. Hence they become receptacles for disease germs instead of means of prevention.

The better practice is to boil drinking water from twenty minutes to half an hour when there is danger of contamination. The following are a number of devices that may be recommended to make muddy or otherwise contaminated water clear for appearance sake. It must be borne in mind, however, that these processes and all other filters merely strain the water in a mechanical way. They do not remove or destroy the germs of contagious diseases. These cannot be destroyed without boiling the water, as just recommended.

Homemade Water Filters.—Rainwater collected in barrels from a roof or otherwise is a necessity in some localities, and is often more wholesome for drinking purposes than hard water. The following is a cheap and easy way to make a filter just as good as a patent filter costing ten times as much:

Take a new vinegar barrel or an oak tub that has never been used, either a full cask or half size.

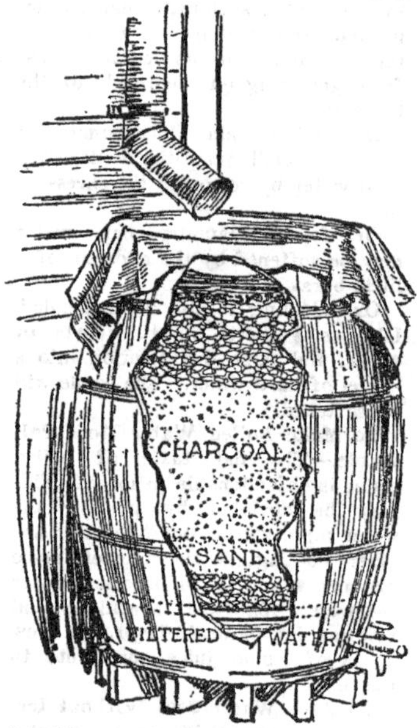

"A Cheap and Easy Way to Make a Filter."

Stand it on end raised on brick or stone from the ground. Insert a faucet near the bottom. Make a tight false bottom three or four inches from the bottom of the cask.

Perforate this with small gimlet holes, and cover it with a piece of clean white canvas. Place on this false bottom a layer of clean pebbles three or four inches in thickness; next, a layer of clean washed sand and gravel; then coarsely granulated charcoal about the size of small peas. Charcoal made from hard maple is the best. After putting in a half bushel or so, pound it down firmly. Then put in more until the tub is filled within one foot of the top. Add a three-inch layer of pebbles, and throw over the top a piece of canvas as a strainer. This canvas strainer can be removed and washed occasionally and the cask can be dumped out, pebbles cleansed, and charcoal renewed every spring and fall, or once a year may be sufficient.

This filter may be set in the cellar and used only for drinking water. Or it may be used in time of drouth for filtering stagnant water, which would otherwise be unpalatable, for the use of stock. This also makes a good cider filter for the purpose of making vinegar. The cider should first be passed through cheese cloth to remove all coarser particles.

Or a small cheap filter may be made from a flower pot. A fine sponge may be inserted in the hole and the pot filled about as directed for the above filter. It may be placed in the top of a jar, which will receive the filtered water.

Or a valuable substitute for charcoal in the above filters is sponge iron obtained by burning finely divided iron ore with charcoal. This can be obtained in the locality of iron mines or smelting furnaces. This is much more powerful than charcoal, and is said to completely purify contaminated water.

DISPOSAL OF WASTES

The sanitary disposal of household wastes presents three distinct problems: The removal (1) of solid excreta; (2) of slops; and (3) of garbage. If an adequate water supply is available from an elevated or pneumatic storage tank, the first two problems can be jointly solved by a house drainage system equipped with water closets, bath tubs and sinks. Such a system can be installed with somewhat less trouble and expense when the house is first built. Yet it can be put into any house at modcrate cost. From a sanitary standpoint it is perhaps the most desirable of all permanent improvements. All pipes and drains should be exposed to full view. Hence there need be no interference with walls or partitions. The only carpentry necessary will be openings through the floors. These with the necessary repairs to ceilings and the like will not add greatly to the expense.

House Drains and Soil Pipes.—The main feature of a house drainage system is a 4-inch cast iron pipe calked with lead at all joints so as to be completely water-tight. Start this soil pipe at least 5 feet outside the house and support it from being crushed where it passes through the foundation wall by means of a suitable arch. Just inside the cellar, insert a running trap to exclude sewer gas and supply this trap with an inspection hole closed with a tight cover but easily accessible. Just beyond this trap insert a fresh air inlet pipe of the same size and material as the soil pipe. Extend this outward through the foundation wall, by means of a suitable arch, and bring it above the surface of the ground, but not near any doors or windows. Now carry the soil pipe upward by as straight a course as possible to a point 4 or 5 feet above the roof. Cover it only with a wire screen to exclude twigs, leaves and the like. The warmth of the house will cause a current of air to be drawn through the soil pipe from the fresh air inlet. This will help to destroy and carry away the organic matter that clings to its inner surface. In cold climates increase the diameter of the soil pipe to about 6 inches from a point just beneath the roof to the top. This prevents the upper end from being closed with hoarfrost. If the soil pipe opens into a sewer, or if there is provision for drainage below the level of the cellar bottom, it may be carried along the cellar wall or rest upon the cellar floor exposed to view in an open

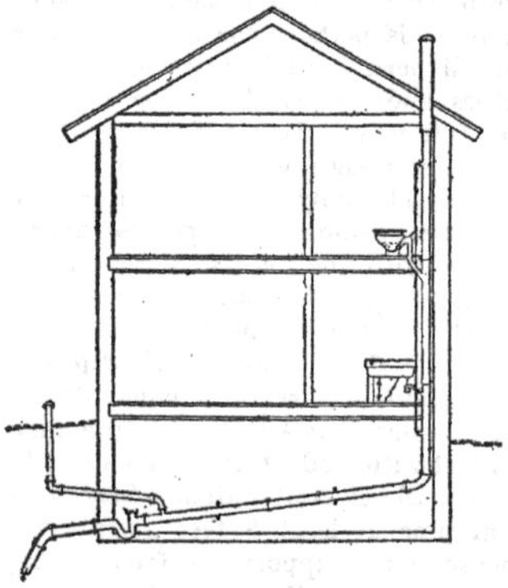

Plan of soil pipe for house sewage disposal system. Courtesy State Board of Health of Maine.

trench. Or, if there are no plumbing fixtures in the cellar and the outlet of the drainage system is at a higher point, the soil pipe may be carried under the cellar floor and fastened to the rafters by wire or other supports at suitable intervals.

Arrangement of Fixtures. — The bath room, sinks, and other fixtures should be located as nearly as possible over one another and in close proximity to the soil pipe. The cost of plumbing will be much less and the system will work better. Both the bath room fixtures and kitchen or pantry sink should be adjacent to an outer wall and near windows to insure abundant light and ventilation. But the soil pipe must be sufficiently far from the outer wall to avoid danger of freezing. When practicable it should be placed on the east, south or southeast side of the house. The soil pipe and all other plumbing fixtures should be entirely open. They will not be objectionable in appearance if painted to correspond with the woodwork in the different rooms. It is a fixed rule of modern sanitation to admit sunlight freely to every part.

Sinks.—The sink should be of slate, enameled iron or porcelain. It should not be boarded up. An open sink is not only more sanitary but more convenient for use. There is an open space beneath it for the toes when standing and for the knees when sitting. Thus great relief may be had while doing certain work by using a stool of proper height. Equip the sink spout with a brass strainer screwed in place and provide a trap to exclude sewer gas.

Water Closets. — The choice of water closets should be confined to those which have the bowl and trap in one piece, are simple in construction, self cleansing and provided with a safe water seal. None should be considered except the short hopper, the washout, the washdown, the syphonic and the syphonic jet styles. The last of these is the best, and they are to be preferred in reverse order. The washout closet has too shallow a pool of water to receive the soil. Nor do the trap below and portion above the trap receive a sufficient scouring from the flush. The washdown closet is an improvement over the former. It has a deeper basin and water seal, a smaller surface uncovered by water and a more efficient scouring action.

The syphonic closet differs from the washdown style chiefly in having a more contracted outlet. The filling

a b c d

Types of sanitary water-closets; (a) washout, (b) washdown, (c) syphonic, (d) syphonic jet.

of this outlet when the closet is flushed forms a syphon. The resulting pressure of air upon the surface of water in the basin drives the water into the soil pipe with much force. When the syphon is broken enough water remains in the trap to preserve the seal. In the syphonic jet closet there is an additional jet of water which helps drive the water in the bowl more rapidly into the outlet. The last mentioned styles are also more nearly noiseless than others and should be preferred. The flush tanks should be well built, ample in size and connected with the closet by means of pipes large enough to insure thorough and efficient flushing.

Sewer Connections.—The connection between the end of the soil pipe and the public sewer or other point of disposal should be made with a good vitrified sewer pipe of the same dimension as the soil pipe, or an inch larger in diameter, laid as shown in the illustration. Or, if a sewer pipe must be carried near a well, use cast iron pipe and take care that the joints are absolutely water-tight. In any case the joints of the sewer pipe should be carefully cemented so that there may be no leakage into the ground near the house. Otherwise sewer gas will find its way through the soil into the cellar and thence to all parts of the house. It is also important to exclude the ground water from the sewage in certain systems of local sewage disposal, since it increases the bulk of the waste to be disposed of.

Sewage Disposal.—Since the danger to health of soil pollution from cess-pools has been clearly recognized, sanitary engineers have given a great deal of attention to the problem of sewage disposal for farmhouses, summer cottages and other isolated dwellings. Various plans have been devised whereby liquid household wastes may be disposed of either on or beneath the surface of ordinary soil, or upon artificially prepared filtration beds. All of these methods are in practical operation and either may be chosen according to local conditions. The working principle is the same in all cases. The upper layer of the earth's surface teems with millions of bacteria which have the power to convert organic matter into earth again. The effect of these changes is to improve the soil both from the agricultural and hygienic standpoint. It becomes more porous, the oxygen of the air penetrates it more freely, and its capacity for holding moisture is improved. These bacteria are active only in the presence of the oxygen of the air. They cannot work if the air is permanently excluded, as when the soil is saturated with water. Hence it is necessary to dispose of sewage near the surface of the ground by what is known as the "intermittent" system. That is, the household wastes must be collected in some suitable receptacle and emptied upon the soil only at intervals sufficiently far apart to permit the liquids to leach away and allow the soil to become dry enough so that the bacteria can perform their function. These facts emphasize the danger from leaking sewer pipes, deep vaults, or cess-pools, located so far below the surface of the ground that the air is excluded. Here the bacteria which purify the soil are unable to live and work.

Septic Tanks.—If the liquid household wastes consist only of kitchen slops they may be discharged directly upon the soil, provided they are first collected in a suitable tank so arranged as to release them at regular intervals. But if solid excreta are present it is better to provide what is known as a septic tank. Here the sewage is liquefied and to some extent purified before being discharged. The work of purifying organic matter is done in two distinct stages by two different kinds of organisms. One of these is called anaerobic bacteria. They work in the dark and do not require the presence of oxygen. They break down the particles of insoluble organic matter or sludge in the sewage and convert them into a form such that the second set of bacteria may complete the process of purification. The latter are called aerobic bacteria. These must have an abundance of oxygen supplied by the air. A septic tank interposed between the house and the patch of ground which is to do the work of filtration greatly assists the process, especially for a system of sub-surface irrigation, by eliminating the grease and dissolving the solid matter which tends to clog the pipes.

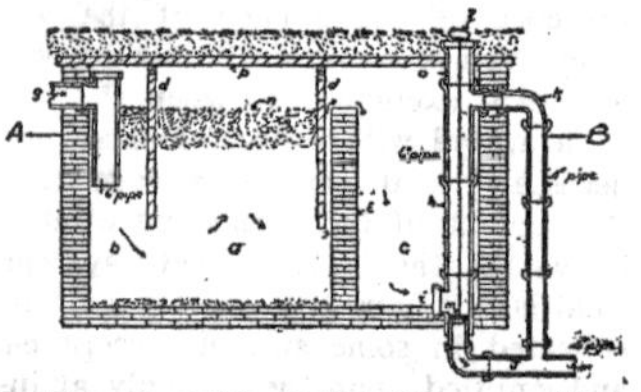

Section of septic tank. Courtesy State Board of Health of Maine.

A septic tank consists of two chambers. One receives the sewage and retains it while the anaerobic bacteria are doing their work. The second receives the overflow from the first chamber (when the process of liquefaction has been completed) and thence discharges it at suitable intervals upon the filtration beds. This may be accomplished either by hand —by means of a gate valve as shown in the illustration—or better by means of a syphonic device of which there are several styles upon the market.

To build a septic tank such as that shown in the illustration, first determine the size which would be required. The volume of sewage is practically equal to the water consumption. The solids, exclusive of garbage and kitchen refuse, which should, of course, be otherwise disposed of, will amount to not over 1 pound to 120 gallons of water. An average family will consume from 60 to 100 gallons a day for each person. Hence a flush tank for a family of six, to empty every twenty-four hours, must contain at least 360 gallons of liquid matter, or have a capacity of 48 cubic feet. In the style of tank here illustrated, this applies only to the second chamber. The first chamber must be sufficiently large to retain the total sewage for a number of days—say a week—which would require a capacity of 336 cubic feet. Thus, a tank having the first chamber 6 feet wide, 6 feet deep and 10 feet in length, and the second chamber of equal width and depth but only 3 feet in length, would accommodate the sewage of a family of 6 persons and would require to be emptied only every forty-eight hours.

To make such a tank build the walls and partition between the two tanks of concrete or brick set in Portland cement mortar. Carefully cement the inside to prevent leakage. Admit the sewage into the first chamber through the 6-inch vitrified inlet pipe (g). Extend this at least 2 feet below the water level fixed by the top of the partition between the two chambers. Extend the two baffle boards (dd) to about two-thirds the depth of the tank. The first is designed to break the force of the inrush of water through the inlet pipe. The second keeps the scum on the surface of the first chamber from flowing over the partition.

As soon as the sewage is brought into the first chamber the anaerobic bacteria attack the sludge at the bottom of the tank. At the same time a scum begins to form on the surface of the sewage. This soon mats into a tough mass a foot or more in thickness. It excludes the light and air and provides the conditions required by the anaerobic bacteria for their work. Under these conditions so much of the sludge at the bottom of the tank will be liquefied and will escape between the second baffle board and the partition into the second chamber that the removal of the sludge by other means will be required only at long intervals of time.

The stand pipe (h) of 6-inch vitrified tile with its tee and connecting bend of 4-inch pipe at (k) serves as an overflow, and at (i) and the discharge pipe (j) there is an arrangement which permits the discharge of the whole contents of the second chamber, when intermittent irrigation is desired, by drawing the plug (m) above the opening (i). This can be done by pulling upward the handle (l). The top of the stand pipe at (l) serves as an exit for the gases formed in the second chamber and also as an inlet for air into the sub-soil or irrigation pipes. A series of holes should be bored in the upper part of the two baffle boards above the water level. These afford an inter-communication of gases between the separate chambers of the tank. Also provide an opening into the stand pipe at (o) to serve as a means of escape for the accumulated gas, otherwise an explosion might occur. The whole tank is covered tightly with the plank (p). All the materials required for this tank may be had in any locality. The construction is simple and the expense is chiefly for labor. A better plan, however, is to provide an automatic syphon of which there are several styles on the market, so that the sewage may be discharged at required intervals without constant attention.

Syphon Tanks.—The principle of the automatic syphon is well known. It consists simply of a section of pipe so curved that one leg is longer than the other. The long leg is erected vertically to a proper height in the second chamber of the tank and covered at the top by a suitable bell. It is connected by means of the short leg with the outlet pipe. When the liquid sewage enters the second chamber it rises under the bell, flows into the long leg of the syphon and seals the trap at the bottom of the bend. As the depth of sewage increases, it compresses the air in the long leg of the syphon until, at the proper level, the pressure becomes great enough to force the water in the bottom of the trap out through the short leg and the outlet pipe and thereby creates sufficient suction to empty the second chamber. Once the level of the fluid descends below the mouth of the bell, air is admitted, the syphon is broken and no further discharge can occur until the tank is again refilled.

Flush Tank. — The two-chamber septic tank above described may be deemed necessary for proper sub-surface irrigation, and is desirable in all cases. But for surface irrigation a simple flush tank having a single chamber and operated by hand by means of a check valve, or by an automatic syphon, may be sufficient. The accompanying illustration shows a simple form of flush tank designed

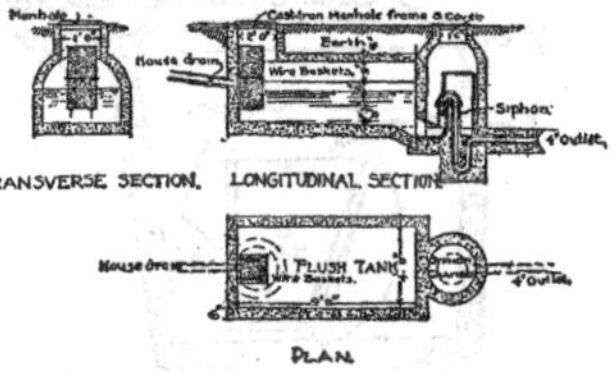

Simple flush tank. (*E. T. Wilson.*)

to be constructed of concrete. The sewage from the house-drain is first screened by means of a wire basket so arranged as to be removable through a convenient manhole with a cast iron or other solid cover —a second basket being substituted while the first is emptied and cleaned. The small residue caught by the basket should be promptly spaded into the ground.

The object of this flush tank is merely to collect the household wastes for a period of from 12 to 24 hours to admit of their intermittent discharge at fixed intervals. Hence the tank, if equipped with an automatic syphon as shown in the illustration, need be only large enough to hold the household wastes for the desired period between the automatic discharges. A capacity of 48 cubic feet is sufficient for a family of 6 using 60 gallons of water a day for each person. The depth of the tank may be determined by the syphon, the other two dimensions to give the required cubic capacity being a matter of convenience. The necessary concrete "forms" for this flush tank or the septic tank previously illustrated can be built by any carpenter or person handy with tools from the accompanying drawings. The concrete for the walls can be mixed and laid by any householder who will follow the instructions elsewhere given. The average cost for material in most localities for this flush tank will be about $25. For the septic tank previously shown about $150.

Tilting Tank.—In houses where a sewerage system is not available and

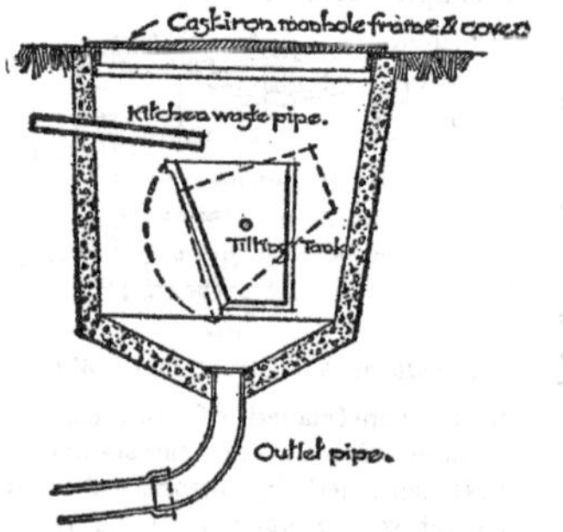

Tilting tank. (E. T. Wilson.)

the liquid waste consists only of kitchen slops, these may be accumulated by means of a tilting tank as shown in the illustration. Install this in a suitable concrete trough with a convenient manhole and equip it with an outlet pipe of 4-inch vitrified tile. Furnish the sinks and laundry tubs emptying into this tank with brass strainers to prevent the entrance of anything which might clog the kitchen waste pipe or outlet pipe. The tilting tank collects the irregular flow and discharges only when full. This provides for the necessary intermittent discharge.

Or provide a concrete or other suitable tank of sufficient capacity to hold the sink drainage and domestic slops for 24 hours or more and equip it with a check valve to be operated by hand. Furnish a tell-tale to show when this tank is sufficiently full to require attention.

Or provide a simple wire pan into which the slops may be poured from pails. All these devices require an outlet of vitrified drain pipe with tight joints long enough to carry waste water without leakage to a point where it may be finally disposed of.

Or to make a cheap temporary drain for waste water from the kitchen sink use 4-inch vitrified tile costing about 7 cents a foot. Run a drain about 25 feet in the opposite direction from the well, and convey the waste to a tub or barrel. Thence run it off to the garden by a small pipe or carry it away in pails. If a barrel can be provided with two wheels, and a tongue like a cart, it can be easily drawn away from time to time and emptied. The expense of such a drain is nominal: 25 feet of vitrified tile, $1.75; sink, $1.25; pipe and trap, $1. Total, $4.

Irrigation Beds. — Whether the liquid household wastes are collected in a septic tank, a simple flush tank, tilting tank or otherwise, provision must be made for their final reception and purification by contact with

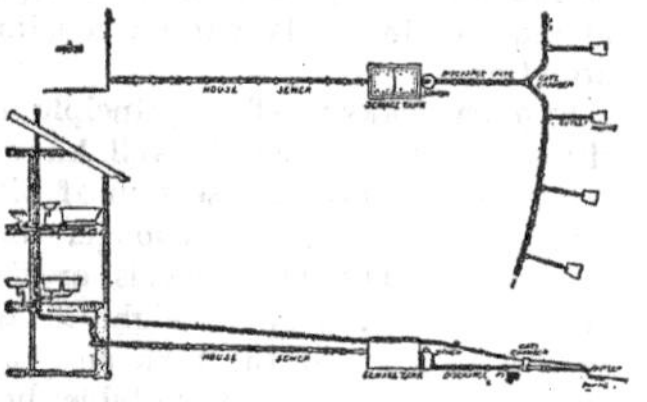

Details of a typical surface irrigation plant in plan and section. Courtesy State Board of Health of North Carolina.

the ordinary surface soil, or by specially prepared filtration beds.

Surface Irrigation.—The final disposal of household sewage—preferably after it has passed through a septic tank to remove grease and dissolve solid substances—may be on the surface of the ground. But in such case it must be carried not less than 300 feet—and the farther the better—from buildings, and with due care not to contaminate any source of water supply. Select for this purpose preferably a sloping tract of grass land, where the soil is a porous sandy or gravelly loam. If the soil is of clay, a much larger tract will be required. If wet, it must be under-drained. Carry the drain pipe along the side of the ridge and let it discharge at intervals upon the surface. Or receive the sewage into a transverse drain pipe across the head of the irrigation field and provide a series of outlets closed by suitable check valves or gates to admit of irrigating different portions of the field at intervals. Mark off the field into plats by means of low dykes and broad shallow ditches, or by means of furrows made with a plow.

Or, if the land is flat, with proper grading the sewage may be disposed broadly over the surface. The amount of solids in household sewage is so small that, if discharged intermittently at rather frequent intervals and in such a way as to give the different portions of the field enough rest to prevent them from becoming saturated, this system will prove by far the best and cheapest for isolated dwellings. If a suitable piece of land is available it can be operated without the slightest offense.

Filtration Beds.—This plan consists in receiving the sewage upon a specially prepared bed of sand. It may be preferred where the amount of land available is small, or the soil is of clay and poorly drained. Make

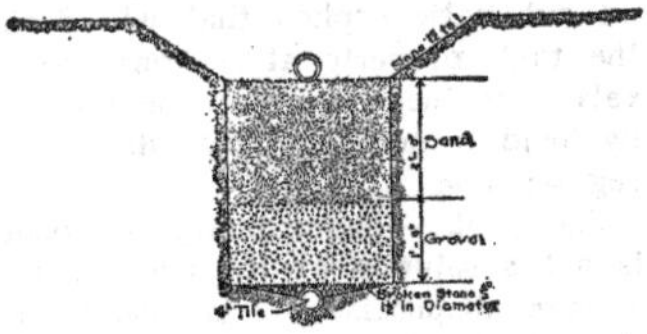

Section of filter bed. (E. T. Wilson.)

an excavation from 3 to 5 feet deep and under-drain with 3-inch red unglazed land drainage tiles. A filter bed from 15 to 20 feet square having an area of from 225 to 400 square feet should be sufficiently large for a family of five persons. Discharge the sewage intermittently from a septic or flush tank and distribute evenly over the surface by means of wooden troughs, 4-inch red drain tile, or a 6-inch galvanized roof gutter pierced with small holes at frequent intervals. The efficiency of the filtration bed increases with the lapse of time, especially if the surface is raked over to the depth of an inch or more each week. The capacity of the septic or flush tank may be reduced at least one-half if a filter bed is used instead of sub-surface irrigation.

Sub-Surface Irrigation.—The advantage of this system, when properly installed, is that household sewage may be disposed of without offense beneath the lawn or garden and within a very limited distance of the house. The first cost is greater than that of surface irrigation or a filtration bed, but such a system may be regarded as the best and most sanitary method of sewage disposal. A well-made septic or flush tank if properly covered is free from odor. It may be located as near the house as may be desired, provided the tank and outlet pipe are made watertight up to the point of sewage disposal. This admits of convenient access, especially if no automatic syphon is provided and the sewage must be discharged by means of a check valve by hand.

To provide for a system of subsurface irrigation it is first necessary to under-drain the land provided it is hard or clayey and not naturally dry. Lay the drain tiles for this purpose 3 or 4 feet below the surface and carry off the ground water by means of a suitable outfall. But this will not be necessary if the soil is a porous, sandy, or gravelly loam. Now open a system of trenches from 8 to 12 inches deep, distinct from the trenches for under-drainage, if any, and in these lay red unglazed land drainage tiles to receive the sewage. Select tile 3 inches in diameter and 1 foot in length. Lay them end to end with the joints open for a space of ⅛ to ¼ of an inch between the tiles and with a very slight grade of about 2 inches to 100 feet. If the grade is much greater the lower end of the system will be flooded.

After laying the tile, fill in the trench so as to cover them 2 or 3 inches deep with small pebbles, gravel or very coarse sand. This will assist in distributing the sewage through the soil. Lay down the tract to grass or cultivate it as a kitchen garden, taking care to work the ground when necessary with a spade or fork and not deep enough to disturb the tiles. The total capacity of these tiles should equal that of the discharge tank from which the sewage comes. Hence the total length of irrigation tiles needed for the family consuming 360 gallons of water a day would be not to exceed 1,000 feet. And probably in porous well drained soil, 25 per cent less or 800 feet would be sufficient. To ascertain the number of tiles required divide the total number of gallons reckoned as 60 for each member of the family, by the capacity of each tile. This may be estimated roughly as one-third of a gallon.

The system of tile may be laid out in any form best suited to the size, shape and contour of the available land, provided that the lines should be laid at least from 3 to 5 feet apart. The plot of ground occupied may be as broad as it is long. A header or central pipe may be used to throw the sewage into long branches. Or laterals may be thrown off from the main drain at intervals of 4 or 5 feet at any angle or to any desired distance. Or preferably the drains may be so laid as to constitute two or more distinct systems. Thus the sewage may be diverted from one to another so as to allow the land intervals of rest. The accompanying illustrations show a number of the various schemes that may be devised. The importance of the intermittent discharge of sewage is greatest in subsurface irrigation. A septic tank must be provided large enough to hold at least a 24 hours' supply with an automatic syphon that will flush the tank properly at 24-hour intervals. Or the tank must be flushed by hand if necessary each day at a regular time.

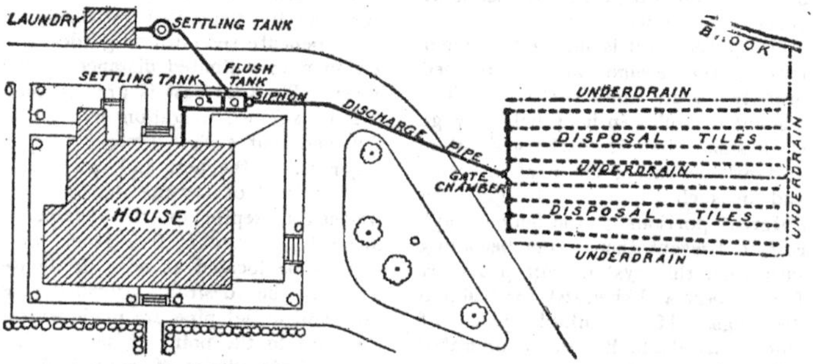

Rectangular tanks close to house. Separate settling tank for laundry building. Underdrains in disposal area to drain out underlying ground water and water from purified sewage in naturally wet or dense soil. Courtesy State Board of Health of North Carolina.

Cess-pools.—The ordinary cess-pool is not a solution of the problem of sewage disposal. It is merely a method of getting the sewage out of sight. It is now regarded as absolutely unsanitary and highly objectionable. The necessary depth of a cess-pool is such as to contaminate the soil beyond the reach of the purifying bacteria which require the presence of oxygen. The ground surrounding the cess-pool becomes contaminated for a constantly increasing radius and eventually the resulting poisonous liquids and gases find their way to strata of the soil through which they reach and pollute the air of cellars or sources of water supply. If, however, a cess-pool is deemed necessary, it may be converted into a rude form of septic tank by turning down the inlet pipe to a point below the water level and providing an outlet pipe similarly turned down so that the inward and outward flow of sewage will not disturb the processes which are going on in the surface scum and in the sludge at the bottom. Such a cess-pool should preferably be made water-tight by lining it with concrete or stone set in Portland cement mortar. The effluent from the outlet must then be carried to a considerable distance from the house and disposed of by surface irrigation, or by means of a small filtration bed as above suggested.

Where water sewage is not available, proper sanitation demands a strictly separate method of disposal of the three kinds of waste matters, namely, solid excreta, slops and garbage. The garbage should be fed to pigs or chicken, burned or buried in a trench at a suitable distance from dwellings and sources of water supply. Kitchen drainage and domestic slops should invariably be disposed of by one of the methods above recommended. They should never be thrown on the surface of the ground near the house or well, allowed to accumulate in an open drain or pool, or deposited in an open privy vault. The cost of a simple system of disposal of these liquid wastes is slight and the danger to health requires that this, at least, be done at any sacrifice.

The Sanitary Privy.—A recent investigation of the subject of soil pollution from open vaults of the ordinary type has been made by Charles Wardell Stiles in connection with his study of the spread of the hookworm disease, especially in the southern states. The following suggestions are condensed and adapted from his report to the Surgeon-General. This plan if generally adopted throughout the United States would eliminate a nuisance which is practically universal and which is perhaps the greatest menace to health now existing in the vicinity of most rural dwellings.

HOW TO BUILD A PRIVY

The following are the essential features: There is a closed portion (box) under the seat for the reception (in a receptacle) and safeguarding of the excreta; a room for the occupant; and, proper ventilation.

The average style of privy found in the South. It is known as a surface privy, open in back. Notice how the soil pollution is being spread, and how flies can carry the filth to the house and thus infect the food.

The receptacle consists practically of a box, with a top represented by the seat, with a floor which is a continuation of the floor of the room, with a front extending from the seat to the floor, with a hinged back which should close tightly, and with two sides continuous with the sides of the room and provided with wire screened ventilators, the upper margin of which is just under the level of the seat. The seat should have one or more holes according to the size of the privy desired, and each hole should have a hinged lid which lifts up toward the back of the room; there should be a piece of wood nailed across the back, on the inside of the room, so as to prevent the lids from being lifted sufficiently to fall backward and so as to make them fall forward of their own accord as soon as the person rises. In this box there should be one or more water-tight tubs, half barrels, pails, or galvanized cans, corresponding to the number of holes in the seat. This receptacle should be high enough to reach nearly to the seat, or, better still, so as to fit snugly against the seat, in order

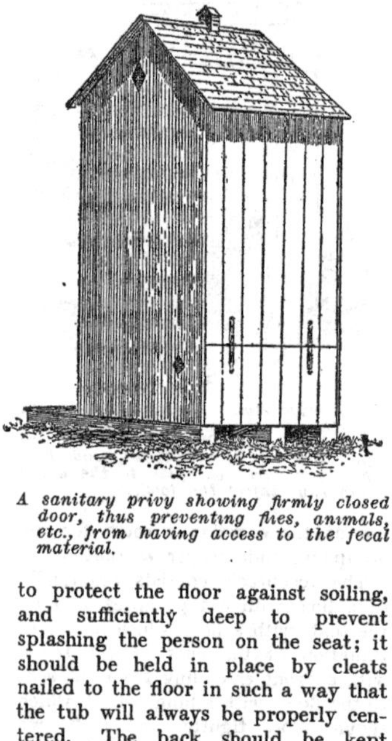

A sanitary privy showing firmly closed door, thus preventing flies, animals, etc., from having access to the fecal material.

to protect the floor against soiling, and sufficiently deep to prevent splashing the person on the seat; it should be held in place by cleats nailed to the floor in such a way that the tub will always be properly centered. The back should be kept closed, as shown in the illustration.

The room should be water-tight and should be provided in front with a good, tightly fitting door. The darker this room can be made the fewer flies will enter. The roof may have a single slant, or a double slant, but while the double slant is somewhat more sightly, the single slant is less expensive in first cost. The room should be provided with two or three wire-screened ventilators, as near the roof as possible.

The ventilators are very important additions to the privy, as they permit a free circulation of air and thus not only reduce the odor but make the outhouse cooler. These ventilators should be copper wire screened in order to keep out flies and other insects. There should be at least 4 (better 5) ventilators, arranged as follows: One each side of the box; one each side the room near the roof; and a fifth ventilator, over the door, in front, is advisable.

Latticework, Flowers and Vines.—At best, the privy is not an attractive addition to the yard. It is possible, however, to reduce its unattractiveness by surrounding it with a latticework on which are trained vines or flowers. This plan, which adds but little to the expense, renders the building much less unsightly and much more private.

Disinfectant.—It is only in comparatively recent years that the privy has been thought worthy of scientific study, and not unnaturally there is some difference of opinion at present as to the best plan to follow in regard to disinfectants.

Top Soil.—Some persons prefer to keep a box or a barrel of top soil, sand, or ashes in the room and to recommend that each time the privy is used the excreta be covered with a shovelful of the dirt. While this has the advantage of simplicity, it has the disadvantage of favoring carelessness, as people so commonly (in fact, as a rule) fail to cover the excreta; further, in order to have the best results, it is necessary to cover the discharges very completely; finally, at best, our knowledge as to how long certain germs and spores will live under these conditions is very unsatisfactory.

Lime. — Some persons prefer to have a box of lime in the room and to cover the excreta with this material. Against this system there is the objection that the lime is not used with sufficient frequency or liberality to keep insects away, as is shown by the fact that flies carry the lime to the house and deposit it on the food.

Water and Oil.—A very cheap and simple method is to pour into the tub about 2 or 3 inches of water; this plan gives the excreta a chance to ferment and liquefy so that the disease germs may be more easily destroyed. If this plan is followed a cup of oil (kerosene will answer) should be poured on the water in order to repel insects.

Cresol.—Some persons favor the use of a 5 per cent crude carbolic acid in the tub, but probably the compound solution of cresol (U. S. P.) will be found equally or more satisfactory if used in a strength of 1 part of this solution to 19 parts of water.

If a disinfectant is used the family should be warned to keep the reserve supply in a place that is not accessible to the children, otherwise accidents may result.

Cleaning the Receptacle.—The frequency of cleaning the receptacle depends upon (*a*) the size of the tub, (*b*) the number of persons using the privy, and (*c*) the weather. In general, it is best to clean it about once a week in winter and twice a week in summer.

An excellent plan is to have a double set of pails or tubs for each privy. Suppose the outhouse is to be cleaned every Saturday: Then pail No. 1 is taken out (say January 1), covered, and set aside until the following Saturday; pail No. 2 is placed in the box for use; on January 8 pail No. 1 is emptied and put back in the box for use while pail No. 2 is taken out, covered, and set aside for a week (namely, until January 15); and so on throughout the year. The object of this plan is to give an extra long time for the germs to be killed by fermentation or by the action of the disinfectant before the pail is emptied.

Each time that the receptacle is emptied, it is best to sprinkle into it a layer of top soil about a quarter to half an inch deep before putting it back into the box.

Disposal of the Excreta.—For the present, until certain very thorough investigations are made in regard to the length of time that the eggs of parasites and the spores of certain other germs may live, it is undoubtedly best to burn or boil all excreta; where this is not feasible, it is best to bury all human discharges at least 300 feet away and down hill from any water supply (as the well, spring, etc.).

Many farmers insist upon using the fresh night soil as fertilizer. In warm climates this is attended with considerable danger, and if it is so utilized, it should never be used upon any field upon which vegetables are grown which are eaten uncooked; further, it should be promptly plowed under.

In our present lack of knowledge as to the length of time that various germs (as spores of the ameba which produce dysentery, various eggs, etc.) *may live, the use of fresh, unboiled night soil as a fertilizer is false economy which may result in loss of human life. This is especially true in warm climates.*

Directions for Building a Sanitary Privy.—In order to put the construction of a sanitary privy for the home within the carpentering abilities of boys, a practical carpenter has been requested to construct models to conform to the general ideas expressed in this article, and to furnish estimates of the amount of lumber, hardware, and wire screening required. Drawings of these models have been made during the process of construction and in completed condition. The carpenter was requested to hold constantly in mind two points, namely, economy and simplicity of construction. It is believed that any 14-year-old schoolboy of average intelligence and mechanical ingenuity can, by following these plans, build a sanitary privy for his home at an expense for building materials, exclusive of receptacle, of $5 to $10, according to locality. It is further believed that the plans submitted cover the essential points to be considered. They can be elaborated to suit the individual taste of persons who prefer a more elegant and more expensive structure. For instance, the roof can have a double

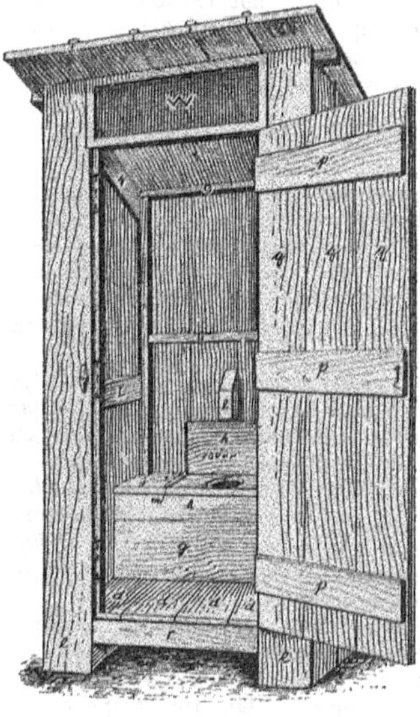

The sanitary privy. Front view.

instead of a single slant, and can be shingled; the sides, front, and back can be clapboarded or they can be shingled. Instead of one seat, there may be two, three, four, or five seats, etc., according to necessity.

A Single-Seated Privy for the Home.—Nearly all privies for the home have seats for two persons, but a single privy can be made more economically.

Framework.—The lumber required for the framework of the outhouse shown is as follows:

A. Two pieces of lumber (scantling) 4 feet long and 6 inches square at ends.

B. One piece of lumber (scantling) 3 feet 10 inches long; 4 inches square at ends.

C. Two pieces of lumber (scantling) 3 feet 4 inches long; 4 inches square at ends.

D. Two pieces of lumber (scantling) 7 feet 9 inches long; 2 by 4 inches at ends.

E. Two pieces of lumber (scantling) 6 feet 7 inches long; 2 by 4 inches at ends.

F. Two pieces of lumber (scantling) 6 feet 3 inches long; 2 by 4 inches at ends.

G. Two pieces of lumber (scantling) 5 feet long; 2 by 4 inches at ends.

H. One piece of lumber (scantling) 3 feet 10 inches long; 2 by 4 inches at ends.

I. Two pieces of lumber (scantling) 3 feet 4 inches long; 2 by 4 inches at ends.

J. Two pieces of lumber (scantling) 3 inches long; 2 by 4 inches at ends.

K. Two pieces of lumber (scantling) 4 feet 7 inches long; 6 inches wide by 1 inch thick. The ends of K should be trimmed after being nailed in place.

L. Two pieces of lumber (scantling) 4 feet long, 6 inches wide, and 1 inch thick.

First lay down the sills marked A and join them with the joist marked B; then nail in position the two joists marked C, with their ends 3 inches from the outer edge of A; raise the corner posts (D and F), spiking them at bottom to A and C, and joining them with L, L_2, G, and K; raise door posts E, fastening them at J, and then spike I, in position; H is fastened to K.

Sides.—Each side requires four boards (a) 12 inches wide by 1 inch thick and 8 feet 6 inches long; these are nailed to K, L, and A. The corner boards must be notched at G, allowing them to pass to bottom of roof; next draw a slant from front to back at G-G, on the outside of the boards, and saw the four side boards to correspond with this slant.

Back. — The back requires two boards (b) 12 inches wide by 1 inch thick and 6 feet 11 inches long, and two boards (c) 12 inches wide by 1 inch thick and 6 feet 5 inches long. The two longest boards (b) are nailed next to the sides; the shorter

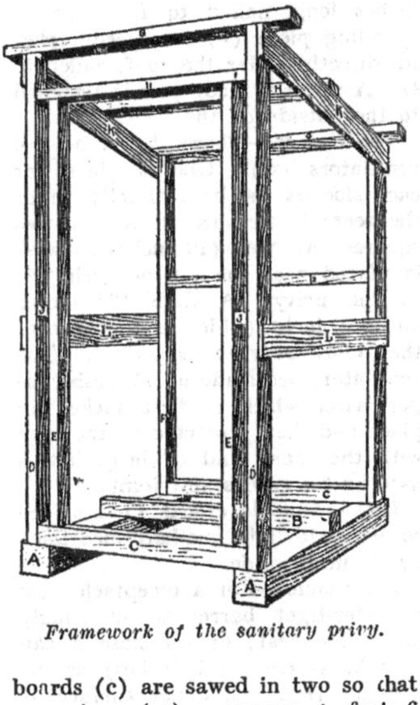

Framework of the sanitary privy.

boards (c) are sawed in two so that one piece (c^1) measures 4 feet 6 inches, the other (c^2) 1 foot 11 inches; the longer portion (c^1) is nailed in position above the seat; the shorter portion (c^2) is later utilized in making the back door.

Floor. — The floor requires four boards (d) which (when cut to fit) measure 1 inch thick, 12 inches wide, and 3 feet 10 inches long.

Front.—The front boards may next be nailed on. The front requires (aside from the door) two boards (e) which (when cut to fit) measure 1 inch thick, 9 inches wide, and 8 feet 5 inches long; these are nailed next to the sides.

Roof.—The roof may now be finished. This requires five boards (f) measuring (when cut to fit) 1 inch thick, 12 inches wide, and 6 feet long. They are so placed that they extend 8 inches beyond the front. The joints (cracks) are to be broken (covered) by laths one-half inch thick, 3 inches broad, and 6 feet long.

Box.—The front of the box requires two boards, 1 inch thick and 3 feet 10 inches long. One of these (g) may measure 12 inches wide, the other (h) 5 inches wide. These are nailed in place, so that the back of the boards is 18 inches from the inside of the backboards. The seat of the box requires two boards, 1 inch thick, 3 feet 10 inches long; one of these (i) may measure 12 inches wide, the other (j) 7 inches wide. One must be jogged (cut out) to fit around the back corner posts (F). An oblong hole, 10 inches long and 7½ inches wide, is cut in the seat. The edge should be smoothly rounded or beveled. An extra (removable) seat for children may be made by cutting a board 1 inch thick, 15 inches wide, and 20 inches long; in this seat a hole is cut, measuring 7 inches long by 6 inches wide; the front margin of this hole should be about 3 inches from the front edge of the board; to prevent warping, a cross cleat is nailed on top near or at each end of the board.

A cover (k) to the seat should measure 1 inch thick by 15 inches wide by 20 inches long; it is cleated on top near the ends, to prevent warping; it is hinged in back to a strip 1 inch thick, 3 inches wide, and 20 inches long, which is fastened to the seat. Cleats (m) may also be nailed on the seat at the sides of the cover. On the inside of the backboard, 12 inches above the seat, there should be nailed a block (l), 2 inches thick, 6 inches long, extending forward 3½ inches; this is intended to prevent the cover from falling backward and to make it to fall down over the hole when the occupant rises.

On the floor of the box (underneath the seat) two or three cleats (n) are nailed in such a position that they will always center the tub; the position of these cleats depends upon the size of the tub.

Back Door.—In making the back of the privy the two center boards (c) were sawed at the height of the bottom of the seat. The small portions (c^2) sawed off (23 inches long) are cleated (o) together so as to form a back door which is hinged above; a bolt or a button is arranged to keep the door closed.

The sanitary privy. Rear and side view.

Front Door.—The front door is made by cleating (p) together three boards (q) 1 inch thick, 10 inches wide, and (when finished) 6 feet 7 inches long; it is best to use three cross cleats (p) (1 inch thick, 6 inches wide, 30 inches long), which are placed on the inside. The door is hung with two hinges (6-inch "strap" hinges will do), which are placed on the right as one faces the privy, so that the door opens from the left. The door should close with a coil spring (cost about 10 cents) or with a rope and weight, and may fasten on the inside with a catch or a cord. Under the door a cross-piece (r) 1 inch thick, 4 inches wide, 30 inches long (when finished) may be nailed to the joist. Stops (s) may be placed inside the door as illustrated in the cut. These should be 1 inch thick, 3 inches wide, and 6 feet 6 inches long, and should be jogged (cut out) (t) to fit the cross cleats (p) on the door. Close over the top of the door place a strip (v) 1 inch thick, 2 inches wide, 30 inches long, nailed to I. A corresponding piece (v) is placed higher up directly under the roof, nailed to G. A strap or door pull is fastened to the outside of the door.

Ventilators.—There should be five ventilators (w). One is placed at each side of the box, directly under the seat; it measures 6 to 8 inches square. Another (12 inches square) is placed near the top on each side of the privy. A fifth (30 inches long, 8½ inches wide) is placed over the door, between G and I_1. The ventilators are made of 15-mesh copper wire, which is first tacked in place and then protected at the edge with the same kind of lath that is used on the cracks and joints.

Lath.—Outside cracks (joints) are covered with lath one-half inch thick by 3 inches wide.

Receptacle.—For a receptacle, saw a water-tight barrel to fit snugly under the seat; or purchase a can or tub, as deep (17 inches) as the distance from the under surface of the seat to the floor. If it is not possible to obtain a tub, barrel, or can of the desired size, the receptacle used should be elevated from the floor by blocks or boards so that it fits snugly under the seat. A galvanized can measuring 16 inches deep and 16 inches in diameter can be purchased for about $1, or even less. An empty candy bucket can be purchased for about 10 cents.

Order for Material.—The carpenter has made out the following order for lumber (pine, No. 1 grade) and hardware to be used in building a privy such as here illustrated:

1 piece scantling, 6 by 6 inches by 8 feet long, 24 square feet.

1 piece scantling, 4 by 4 inches by 12 feet long, 16 square feet.

5 pieces scantling, 2 by 4 inches by 16 feet long, 54 square feet.

3 pieces board, 1 by 6 inches by 16 feet long, 24 square feet.

2 pieces board, 1 by 9 inches by 9 feet long, 14 square feet.

3 pieces board, 1 by 10 inches by 7 feet long, 18 square feet.

15 pieces board, 1 by 12 inches by 12 feet long, 180 square feet.

12 pieces board, $\frac{1}{2}$ by 3 inches by 16 feet long, 48 square feet.

2 pounds of 20-penny spikes.

6 pounds of 10-penny nails.

2 pounds of 6-penny nails.

7 feet screen, 15-mesh, copper, 12 inches wide.

4 hinges, 6-inch "strap," for front and back doors.

2 hinges, 6-inch "T," or 3-inch "butts," for cover.

1 coil spring for front door.

According to the carpenter's estimate, these materials will cost from $5 to $10, according to locality.

There is some variation in the size of lumber, as the pieces are not absolutely uniform. The sizes given in the lumber order represent the standard sizes which should be ordered, but the purchaser need not expect to find that the pieces delivered correspond with mathematical exactness to the sizes called for. On this account the pieces must be measured and cut to measure as they are put together.

Elimination of Flies.—A link between the subject of home sanitation and hygiene and that of the prevention of disease has been forged by the discovery that the deadly germs of enteric diseases,—such as typhoid fever, cholera, cholera infantum and tropical dysentery—are frequently communicated to man by the common house fly. Other diseases which are less commonly transmitted by flies are tuberculosis, anthrax, bubonic plague (black death), trachoma, septicemia, erysipelas, leprosy, yaws, and, perhaps, smallpox. The problem of eliminating the house fly belongs to the subject of sanitation because flies commonly become infected with noxious bacteria from feeding upon infected garbage or

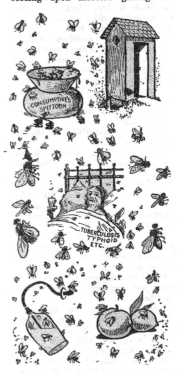

The agency of flies in communicating disease. Courtesy of the State Board of Health of Florida.

other domestic refuse or the excreta of persons suffering from typhoid or other communicable disease, or those of healthy carriers. The elimination of these nuisances by the various methods of disposal above recommended is half the battle in the prevention of disease. Flies infest and feed upon decaying organic matter of all sorts, such as accumulations of swill in the vicinity of pig pens, garbage and animal excreta. If these substances are exposed in the vicinity of dwellings they will become infested with flies in such enormous numbers that it will be practically impossible to keep them out of the house, or to avoid their coming into contact with human food.

The following catechism, which is being distributed in great numbers by boards of health in many cities throughout the world, is a digest of scientific opinion on this subject.

Where is the fly born? In manure and filth.

Where does the fly live? In every kind of filth.

Is anything too filthy for the fly to eat? No.

Where does he go when he leaves the vault and the manure pile and the spittoon? Into the kitchen and dining room.

What does he do there? He walks on the bread, fruit and vegetables; he sticks in the butter; he swims in the milk.

Does the fly visit the patient sick with consumption, typhoid fever and cholera infantum? He does and may call on you next.

Is the fly dangerous? He is man's worst pest, and more dangerous than wild beasts.

What diseases does the fly carry? He carries typhoid fever, tuberculosis and summer complaint. How? On his wings and hairy feet. What is his correct name? Typhoid fly.

Did he ever kill anyone? He killed more American soldiers in the Spanish-American war than the bullets of the Spaniards.

Where are the greatest number of cases of typhoid fever, consumption, and summer complaint? Where there are the most flies.

Where are the most flies? Where there is the most filth.

Why should we kill the fly? Because he may kill us.

How shall we kill the fly? Destroy all the filth about the house and yard; pour lime into the vault and on the manure; kill the fly with a wire screen paddle or sticky paper or kerosene oil.

Kill the fly in any way, but kill the fly.

Extirpation of Flies.—A very great deal of attention has been drawn to this subject by recent scientific investigations and many practicable suggestions have been made since the publication of the first edition of this volume. The control of the house fly is now regarded as one of the most important of all sanitary problems. A nation-wide campaign to this end has been set on foot. It has been shown by actual experience during the last few years that the method of excluding flies from horse manure as elsewhere recommended, will greatly lessen the number observed in the locality. Several cities have adopted ordinances providing

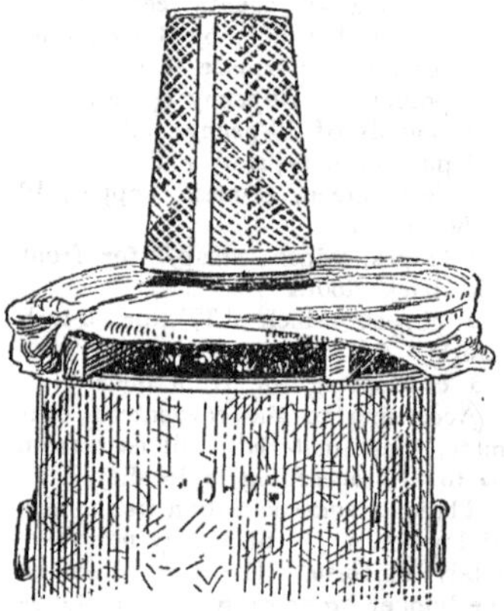

Simple and very successful fly trap for a garbage can. Cloth curtain turned up to show cleats. It catches the flies outside the house. Flies enter the garbage can through the crack between the cover and the can, and also around the edge of the trap placed over a two or three inch hole in the can. After feeding they fly toward the light and come out this hole in the cover into the trap. (C. F. Hodge.)

that the floors of stables shall be solid and free from cracks, and that horse manure shall be collected in tight cans or barrels, covered so as to exclude flies, and removed daily beyond the city limits. Some such means of depriving flies of their natural breeding places is the most essential step in the warfare against these pests. Any householder may greatly abate this nuisance by proper sanitary precautions on his own premises. And such means will be found very effective in localities where dwellings are fairly distant from one another. But since flies may come from considerable distances and bring with them infection from sources beyond one's control, it will still be found necessary to adopt preventive measures. In addition to those elsewhere recommended several ingenious methods of trapping flies in large numbers have recently been devised and may here be recommended.

Trapping Flies. — Prof. C. F. Hodge offers a number of practical suggestions derived from experience in catching flies in large quantities to feed bob-white and partridge chicks. His method is, in substance, to provide a number of large traps and either to bait them artificially with garbage and meat scraps in considerable quantities or set them at the flies' natural feeding grounds. The working principle of these traps is that a fly seeks its food entirely by smell and will crawl to it through any dark crack. Thence, after feeding, it will fly or crawl toward the light. Hence, if a suitable trap is placed over the garbage can or swill barrel, or in a room or shed in homes, hotels, restaurants or markets, in which waste matter is collected, the great bulk of the flies which are drawn to these feeding grounds from the entire locality can be captured and disposed of.

Small traps of wire net can be bought for about 10 cents apiece in most localities. Or they can be readily made at home of two pieces of ordinary wire netting. The outer may be of any shape and size desired. The inner is merely an inverted cone with an opening just large enough to permit the flies to crawl in. One or more of these traps may be attached to the lid of the garbage pail, swill barrel, or hog trough over a hole through which the flies may find their way into the trap after feeding. Lift the lid or cover of the receptacle a little way to admit the flies and hang something over the edge so as to keep out the light. Or a strip of burlap from an old potato sack may be thrown over the lid to keep the sun out.

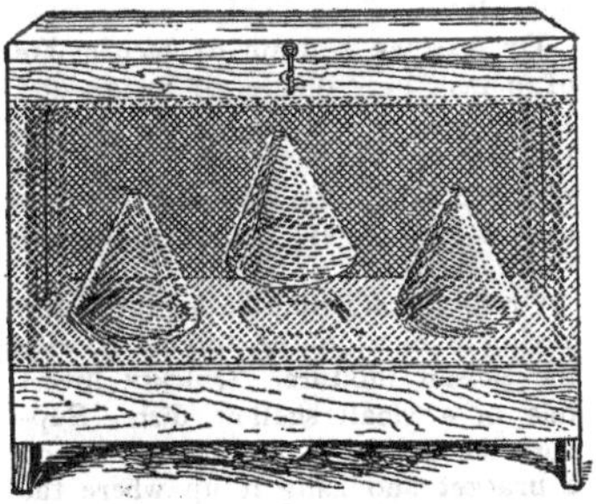

Box fly trap designed by C. F. Hodge.

Or if there is no accumulation of garbage, swill or other natural feeding ground for flies in the locality, construct one or more large traps in the form of a screened box, as shown in the illustration. Artificially bait these by placing, in old tomato cans or other receptacles, meat scraps and similar refuse beneath the platform on which the traps are located. Bring the side boards below this platform nearly to the ground so that the space beneath, where the bait is placed, may be dark. The cones in the illustration may be readily made from pieces of ordinary wire netting. One small boy in Worcester, Mass., has a record of capturing about three bushels of flies in a trap of this kind during a single summer.

If the small woven wire traps are

used, the files may be killed by immersing them in boiling water. Or hold the traps over the flames of burning newspaper. Or if the large screen boxes are employed, equip them with one or more small vessels containing liquid fly poison. A good fly killer consists of a teaspoonful of 40 per cent solution of formaldehyde and one-half teaspoonful of sugar dissolved in a cup of water. This may be exposed inside the fly trap in a shallow vessel, as an earthenware plate or pie tin, and also in saucers or other suitable receptacles, in any part of the house. While deadly to flies it is nonpoisonous, in small quantities, to children or domestic animals.

Or dissolve 1 dram of bichromate of potash in 2 ounces of water, add a little sugar and expose in shallow receptacles. These poisons are quickly effective in fly traps because the flies cannot get to any other source of water supply.

Or fill a half pint or a pint bottle having a nick in the top of it with the poison mixture. Quickly invert this in a small shallow dish. Support the bottle in that position upon a bracket and hang it up where the flies abound. A nick of the right depth in the mouth of the bottle will keep in the dish a shallow pool of poison all the time.

Or to make an efficient, cheap and safe fly poison, for use in the household, markets, store windows, etc., mix 1 cupful milk, 1 cupful water, 1 teaspoonful 40 per cent solution of formaldehyde, 1 tablespoonful sugar.

Pour enough of this solution over a small slice of bread placed on a saucer to thoroughly saturate it and leave surplus liquid in the saucer. Place these saucers on window sills and other places where flies swarm, but out of reach of children and animals.

Another ingenious method suggested by Prof. Hodge is to attach a small wire trap to the wire screen with which windows and doors are protected against insects in summer. Two small guide boards tacked on the screen lead the flies to a small opening near the top and thence through a hole in the screen into the trap. A similar trap may be attached to the inside of the same or another window and thus flies may be

Device for poisoning flies.

caught both "coming and going." This method is equally well adapted to the house and to the barn and stable.

A little ingenuity and reasonable pains in providing and caring for a sufficient number of traps of this character will, according to Prof. Hodge, reduce the number of flies in most localities to a point such that the few that do finally get into the house may be readily killed with the ordinary fly swatter. The importance of the campaign against flies from the standpoint of sanitation and the prevention of disease can hardly be overestimated.

CHAPTER IV

INFECTION AND DISINFECTION

CONTACT INFECTION—DISINFECTION—STANDARD SOLUTIONS—FUMIGATION OR GASEOUS DISINFECTION—FORMALDEHYDE AND SULPHUR FUMIGATION—ADDITIONAL DISINFECTION

CONTACT INFECTION

Before the germ theory of disease became fully established, a distinction was made between what were called "infectious" as opposed to "contagious" diseases. These words are now used interchangeably. It was formerly supposed that "infectious" diseases could be "caught" by merely breathing the air in the vicinity of the patient. A superstition to this effect still lingers in some localities. Many persons, otherwise well informed, attempt to hold their breath while passing pest houses or dwellings where patients with virulent communicable diseases are quarantined. This notion that the germs of disease are usually communicated through the air has been completely exploded. On the other hand it was formerly supposed that "contagious" in the sense opposed to "infectious" diseases, could be communicated only by actual contact of the diseased part with the body of another person. Some diseases were thought to be both contagious and infectious. Many cases of the transmission of disease were observed, however, which could not be explained upon either of these theories. Hence there was formerly a good deal of doubt, even among medical men, as to the exact way in which certain diseases were communicated.

This confusion of thought is now to a large extent cleared away. The contact infection theory may be said to be fully established. According to this theory the living bacteria, or germs, which cause contagious diseases are most commonly transmitted from a diseased to a well person within a comparatively short space of time, and through the medium of some solid object or liquid, rather than through the air. Two kinds, or types, of infection are loosely distinguished — direct and secondary. Direct infection is, in general, that which gives rise to new cases in families or on premises that have been previously free from disease. Indirect, or secondary, infection is that whereby a disease is communicated from a patient to his nurse or other attendant, or to other members of the same household. Direct infection is thought to occur chiefly through the contamination of the sources of water or milk supply, or by chance contact with persons in the early stages of a communicable disease, or those suffering from mild cases, or from healthy "carriers." Especial attention has also been directed of late to the part played by insects, especially the house fly, as carriers of disease. The bedbug, the body louse, the various species of fleas, mosquito and ticks have also been found to communicate the germs of disease from certain animals to man and from one person to another.

Direct infection may, and often does, occur from unavoidable accident. But secondary infection is invariably the result of ignorance or carelessness. The most usual vehicles of secondary infection are thought to be the bed covers or clothing of the patient; his handkerchief; his discharges; remnants of food and drink left by him on the tray, or the dishes or other utensils by means of which he is served; and the person or clothing of the nurse or other bedside visitors. The cardinal principle of preventive medicine is that secondary infection must and shall not occur.

According to the contact infection theory all the germs of disease by which healthy persons are infected had quite recent origin in the body of some diseased person. They left the patient through some of his discharges, as his sputum or excreta, possibly through perspiration, or in the case of smallpox, chickenpox, or scarlet fever, through the scabs or scaling of the outer surface of the body. Thence they were transmitted to the neighborhood of the infected person, through some fairly direct route, by the agency of solid bodies or liquids, and under conditions reasonably favorable to germ life. They then found their entrance into his body through some of its main orifices, usually by being breathed in or swallowed. When these essential principles are well understood and sufficiently considered, they will usually enable the responsible head of a family to trace a case of infection to its source. Steps may then be taken to avoid further infection and prevent the spread of the disease.

The open vault, sink drain, or accumulation of garbage or other filth, so located as to contaminate the soil or the sources of the water supply, and the flies or other insects which feed in and about them, may be compared to an unloaded gun. Their deadly possibilities are latent until they become infested (loaded) with the living germs of typhoid or other communicable diseases. Such germs are not the product of putrefaction. They do not develop spontaneously in fecal or decayed matter such as night-soil, garbage, and kitchen slops. Nor do disease germs multiply in such locations. Indeed, the bacteria which cause human diseases will ordinarily die out within a comparatively short time when deliberately added to such substances for the purpose of scientific investigation. When a case of typhoid or other contagious disease occurs, through the pollution of the soil or water supply, or through the medium of flies, by contagion from an open vault or drain or similar nuisance, the real source is often overlooked and disregarded, because these nuisances have existed before the patient was taken sick and no one had previously been made ill by them. The explanation of science is that only at rare intervals and as a consequence of direct infection from some diseased person, do these nuisances become active sources of contagion and deadly menaces to the public health. The danger is that this may happen unknown to the responsible head of the family. The result may be an epidemic in which many lives are needlessly sacrificed.

A good illustration may be found in a case reported by a milk inspector of a western city. An outbreak of typhoid was traced to the milk supply from a certain farm dairy. On investigation it was found that two of the dairyman's children were convalescing from that disease. The family water supply used for drinking purposes and also for cleansing milk pails and other receptacles was a dug well in the farmer's yard. It was located not far from an outhouse of the open vault type. The milk inspector suggested that the well water might be contaminated from this source. The dairyman responded that this could not be the case because the water was clear, cold and tasteless. A few days later this farmer called up the milk inspector on the telephone and inquired if the germs of typhoid fever would make water pink. The inspector responded, No! but that if the well water was pink, it might be due to a quantity of red dye which he had poured into the vault of the outhouse. Later, the dairyman himself succumbed to typhoid fever. The milk supply from this dairy having been shut off, further spread of the disease among its patrons was prevented.

A practical suggestion may be drawn from this incident for cases where it is suspected that the source of drinking water may be contaminated from open vaults, drains or similar sources. A bushel or more of coarse salt may be deposited in the vault or drain and care taken to observe whether or not the water, especially after the next heavy rain, tastes in the least salty.

But, as the amount of salt that might be transmitted in solution through the soil may not be enough to be detected when diluted by the contents of a deep well, it is safer and better in all such cases to have a bacteriological test of the water made at the State laboratory. The commissioner of health in most States will forward on request a suitable bottle properly packed for mailing, with full directions how to select and forward the necessary sample. In some States such tests will be made free. But in any case the cost will hardly exceed that of a doctor's visit. The result may be the saving of one or many lives.

The bacteria which cause germ diseases are parasites, that is, they do not normally occur in nature outside the bodies of men or other animals. These they regard as their natural home. Hence they can thrive and multiply only under very similar conditions of warmth, moisture, absence of direct sunlight and presence of a supply of food suitable to their necessities. They are so exceedingly small as to be totally invisible to the naked eye, and are without color, taste or odor. Hence the presence in an ordinary well of bacteria sufficient to kill all the inhabitants of a great city could not be detected without the use of a microscope except through their fatal consequences.

It was formerly supposed that the introduction into the human body of one or more germs of any contagious ailment was certain to result in the contraction of a typical case of the disease. The use of the microscope has proved that this is by no means the case. The germs of pneumonia, diphtheria, tuberculosis and others are often found in the throat and lungs of perfectly healthy persons. The germs of various diseases may be swallowed without injurious results. The likelihood of contagion depends in part upon the number of the bacteria that may gain lodgment in the system, in part upon their vitality, and in part upon the state of health of the afflicted person. Most germs tend to breed and multiply in colonies. They do not live long outside of the human body, or other living host, except under favorable conditions, and the body when in perfect health has considerable power to resist their invasion.

The vitality of different species, or of the same species under different conditions, varies considerably. The germ which causes consumption, the tubercle bacillus, is among the most resistant. The germs expectorated by the consumptive may be found in a state of full vitality, in the dry sputum of the patient, floating in the air as dust. With this exception, however, it is believed that exposure to dry heat and especially to direct sunlight kills most disease germs or greatly weakens them. The effect of cold is merely to suspend their activities. Freezing for an indefinite time does not injure most germs. But all are destroyed by exposure to heat at or near the temperature of boiling water, or by contact with various substances known as germicides or disinfectants.

The most virulent bacteria will die of themselves within a comparatively short time after they are thrown off from the body of a diseased person, unless by chance they find congenial lodgment in warm, dark places such as open vaults or drains or in another human body.

The germs of diphtheria, typhoid and some other diseases will multiply quite rapidly in fresh milk, although they are commonly destroyed by the lactic acid which forms in milk in the process of souring. They will, however, live for some time in cheese and butter. Hence contamination of the milk supply is one of the most frequent sources of infection. Bacteria do not appear to multiply in ordinary drinking water. On the contrary, it is believed that the germs of typhoid will die out of wells and cisterns in about a week or ten days if there is no further contamination in that interval. The contamination of water supplies is, however, among the most frequent causes of fatal epidemics of typhoid and some other diseases. The pollution is usually continuous and often increases in amount and virulence until attention is drawn to it by an outbreak of disease.

The discharges of patients suffering from typhoid and similar diseases contain myriads of the living bacteria. When these find their way by seepage, or surface drainage from open vaults to streams, springs, wells and cisterns, or through the outflows of sewage being in too close proximity to the intake of water supplies, the number of germs swallowed is almost sure to bring on the disease in its most virulent form.

Other common sources of infection are vegetables, contaminated by polluted soil, pet cats and other animals, and, in short, anything which may serve as a vehicle to transport the living germs in a fairly direct route from one human body to another.

While a person in perfect health may come in contact with the germs of disease with impunity, especially if they are few in number, and if their vitality has been impaired by exposure to drying heat or otherwise, yet every precaution that science can suggest should be taken to avoid such contagion. Persons in the best of health may become susceptible to the attacks of bacteria by the lowering of tone due to over-fatigue, to a sudden cold, or similar causes. Or the disease may be taken in such mild form that its true character may not be recognized. Such an attack may cause the patient little inconvenience, but may result, in the absence of proper precautions, in the spread of the disease to others in its most virulent form. Indeed, such cases, and those called healthy "carriers" are known to be among the most common agencies in the spread of epidemics.

Healthy "carriers" of disease, in medical parlance, are patients who have recovered and become immune to the bacteria of a germ disease, but who are still breeding such germs in large numbers in their bodies. Ordinarily, the germs of disease disappear at or near the time of the patient's recovery, but in exceptional cases persons have been known to be "carriers" for many months or even years. Such persons are especially dangerous, because the liability of infection from them is not usually suspected. Yet, in the absence of absolute cleanliness and proper precautionary measures, they may be the means of infecting others, or contaminating sources of water supply. A typical case is that known to medical men as "Typhoid Mary." This woman is known to have infected about twenty-four persons in six different families where she was employed as a cook. Another recorded instance is that of a dairyman, a carrier of typhoid, who caused no fewer than three epidemics in a western city through the contamination of the water supply which was used by him for cleansing milk cans and other receptacles.

Prevention of Contact Infection.—There are two distinct lines of action which must be adopted to insure against infection. The first consists in preventing all possibility of the contamination of the soil, pollution of water supply, or transmission of the germs of disease by flies and other insects. This may be done by abolishing all open vaults and drains and by the sanitary disposition of all slops, garbage, dead animals and other household or farm refuse. Statistics show that such steps, if properly taken, will reduce the likelihood of infection about one-half. Thus, in the city of Springfield, Ill., the death rate from typhoid continued to increase even after the introduction of an efficient water supply and sanitary sewerage. An investigation by the Board of Health disclosed that only about one-third of the property owners were availing themselves of these improvements. Two-thirds of the families were still dependent upon cess-pools and open vaults. When these were abolished by city ordinance, the death rate from typhoid was reduced about one-half. A similar result was observed in the city of Providence after all cess-pools and open vaults were abolished by municipal ordinance.

The other line of defense consists in the observance of absolute sanitary cleanliness and the proper use of disinfectants, especially in times of epidemic or when there are cases of contagious illness in the family or neighborhood. It has been proved beyond question that, if proper precautions are taken to avoid infection from milk or water supplies, insects and similar causes, and if sanitary precautions are observed, a patient with any contagious disease may be nursed in his own home without infecting other members of the family. In certain high-class French hospitals, patients suffering from all sorts of contagious diseases, such as diphtheria, smallpox, typhoid fever, scarlet fever and others, are treated in the same open wards and waited upon by the same physicians, nurses and attendants. The only separation of one patient from another is by means of low screens or partitions made of cotton cloth. Even these are sometimes omitted and the space allotted to each patient is defined merely by a line of tape or by marks chalked or painted upon the floor. The object of these is simply to call the nurse's attention to the necessity of observing sanitary precautions before crossing the territory of one patient into that of another.

No object which has touched the person of a patient or been contaminated by any of his discharges is permitted to touch the person of any other patient. The nurse and the attending physicians wash their hands in a disinfectant solution each time they touch or handle the patient or anything which has come into contact with him, before approaching the bedside of another sufferer. Under this plan, which is known as the French cubicle system, instances in which a patient suffering from one contagious disease has become infected with another are extremely rare, while all are being treated in the same room and are breathing the same air.

DISINFECTION

The purpose of disinfection is to kill the germs of contagious diseases after they leave the body of the patient and before they find another victim. This may be done by means of heat by boiling, baking or burning the infected material, or by means of various chemical poisons known as disinfectants or germicides. These are usually applied in liquid or gaseous form. Germs can be killed by heat or disinfectants only under the following conditions: The heat must be sufficiently intense or the disinfectant sufficiently strong; the germs must be thoroughly exposed to the heat or disinfectant; and for a sufficient length of time.

Disinfection by heat may be by fire, boiling water or live steam. No special apparatus is needed if fire or boiling water is used. The infected articles are simply burned or boiled. Articles to be disinfected by boiling should be weighted, if necessary, and kept under the water while actually boiling for not less than half an hour. The addition of common washing soda to the water, at the rate of one moderate tablespoonful to each gallon of water, increases its efficiency.

Steam disinfection, on a small scale, may be accomplished by means of an ordinary wash boiler containing a wooden rack resting upon bricks, or otherwise suspended above the level of the boiling water. Pack the articles to be disinfected closely upon this rack, put the cover on tight and boil briskly at least an hour. Be sure to use enough water so that the boiler will not go dry. Many kinds of clothing and other objects which would be injured by boiling can be safely disinfected in this manner.

All stains should be removed before disinfection by steam or boiling water, as heat tends to fix them.

Disinfection in General.—Most of the so-called disinfection practiced in families is inefficient and useless. The burning of coffee, tar, or other substances in the sick room or elsewhere in the presence of the patient or others, operates at most only as a deodorizer. Such fumes do not destroy the germs of disease. Open vessels containing chloride of lime, carbolic acid or other disagreeable-smelling substances have no value for disinfecting purposes, unless the infected material is actually immersed in them. If bad odors exist, remove the source and admit an abundance of fresh air. Never use disinfectants not vouched for by reliable authorities. Disinfectants, germ killers, and the like, sold like patent medicines are most often expensive and worthless. They should never be relied upon. The following solutions are for use during illness and for general family use as directed.

Allow nothing to go from the sick room in case of communicable diseases without having been disinfected with one of these solutions. It should be an unceasing duty of the nurse or other attendants to see that disinfection as here indicated is carried out to the minutest particular.

STANDARD DISINFECTANT SOLUTIONS

Substances recommended as reliable disinfectants for general external use in contagious diseases are (1) chloride of lime; (2) quick lime; milk of lime; (3) bichloride of mercury (corrosive sublimate), either with or without the addition of muriate of ammonia, or permanganate of potash; (4) carbolic acid, and (5) solution of formaldehyde (formalin). Such substances as Lysol, Kreolin, Tri-Kresol and other much advertised patented preparations are no better than the above and are too expensive for general external use in sufficient quantities. The following standard disinfectant solutions are those endorsed and recommended by public health authorities throughout the United States. They are the cheapest, best known and most reliable disinfectants. No others need be employed for general external use. Most of these solutions are highly poisonous. None are suitable for washing out the mouth, gargling the throat, or other internal use.

No. 1. Standard Solution of Chloride of Lime (chlorinated lime).—This is one of the most effective and highly recommended disinfectants. It is used in the form of an aqueous solution, i. e., dissolved in water, in strength varying from 3 per cent (weak) to 10 per cent (strong) solution. For a 10 per cent solution add 1 pound of good chloride of lime to 1 gallon of water and mix thoroughly. For a 5 per cent solution use ½ pound to the gallon of water, and for a 3 per cent solution use 1 pound to 3 gallons or 5⅓ ounces to the gallon. Authorities variously recommend from 5½ to 6½ ounces chloride of lime to the gallon of water, or a solution of slightly more than 3 per cent, as a standard solution for free general use.

Chloride of lime is not fully soluble in water. A clear solution may be obtained by filtration or decantation, but the insoluble sediment does no harm and this is an unnecessary refinement. The solution should stand at least ten minutes before using.

The chloride of lime must be of the best quality. It should contain at least 25 per cent of available chlorine. Poor chloride of lime is useless. Prepare only as needed and keep, preferably, in a stone jug with a tight-fitting stopper. Do not depend upon this solution unless freshly prepared from chloride of lime of good quality. This substance ought to be obtained anywhere for about 10 cents a pound retail or about 3½ cents wholesale, making the cost of a 3 per cent solution only about 1 to 3 cents a gallon. Hence, in addition to being among the most effective disinfectants and germicides available for general use, it is also one of the cheapest.

Directions for Use.—Use one quart of the half-strength (5 per cent) solution for each discharge from a patient suffering from any contagious or infectious disease. Mix well and leave in the vessel for an hour or more before throwing into privy vault or water closet. The same for vomited matter. For a very copious discharge, especially in cholera, use a larger quantity; and for solid or semi-solid matter, use the full strength (10 per cent) solution. Receive discharges from the mouth or throat in a cup half full of the half-strength (5 per cent) solution, and those from the nostrils upon soft cotton or linen rags. Burn these immediately.

As the fecal discharges of the sick are the chief vehicles of communication in many contagious diseases, their disinfection should be thoroughly performed. Especially should care be taken as to their disposal, so that no portion of them can gain access, either directly or indirectly, by surface drainage, percolation, filtration, or otherwise, to any water-supply.

Use a quart or more of the solution full-strength (10 per cent) each day in an offensive vault, and such quantities as may be necessary in other places. Use it in a sprinkler in stables, and elsewhere. In the sick room place it in vessels, cuspidors, etc. Immerse sheets and other clothing used by the patient in a pail or tub of this solution, diluted one gallon of the full-strength (10 per cent) solution to ten of water, for two hours, or until ready for the wash room or laundry. This solution is non-poisonous and does not injure white clothing. It should be used, however, only for white, cotton or linen fabrics. It bleaches colored goods and injures wool, silk and other animal fibers. Body and bed linen thus treated should afterwards be thoroughly cleansed by boiling for a half hour in soap and water and by two or more rinsings.

It may also be used in one-third strength (3 per cent) solution for washing the hands or parts of the body which may have been exposed to infection from excreta, etc.

For a free and general use in privy-vaults, sewers, sink drains, refuse heaps, stables, and wherever else the odor of the disinfectant is not objectionable, this is perhaps the cheapest and most effective disinfectant and germicide available for general use. It should be used so freely as to wet everything required to be disinfected. Its odor does not disinfect. It only covers up other odors.

Chloride of lime in dry form may also be applied in large quantities to vaults and cess-pools. Dilute it for this purpose with 9 parts of plaster of Paris or the same proportion of clean dry sand to admit of more conveulent application.

No. 2. Standard Solution Milk of Lime (quick lime).—Slake a quart of freshly-burnt lime (in small pieces) with ⅗ of a quart of water—or to be exact, 60 parts of water (by weight) with 100 of lime. A dry product of slaked lime (hydrate of lime) results.

Make from this, milk of lime, immediately before it is to be used, by mixing 1 part of this dry hydrate of lime with 8 parts (by weight) of water. The dry hydrate may be preserved for some time if enclosed in a covered fruit jar or other air-tight container.

Or, prepare milk of lime by slaking freshly burnt quick lime in about four times its volume of water, i. e., about 1 pound of fresh unslaked lime to 1 gallon of water. Milk of lime must be used within a day or two after preparation or its value as a disinfectant is lost. It should be kept in some air-tight container, preferably an earthenware jug and closely stoppered.

Air-slaked lime has no value as a disinfectant and should not be used for this purpose.

Quick lime is one of the cheapest of disinfectants, and may take the place of chloride of lime if desired. Use freely in a quantity equal in amount to the material to be disinfected. Use also to whitewash exposed surfaces, to disinfect excreta in the sick room, or on the surface of the ground, in sinks, vaults, drains, stagnant pools and the like.

No. 3. Standard Solution of Bichloride of Mercury (corrosive sublimate).—The most convenient way to prepare this solution is by the use of bichloride of mercury tablets which can be obtained at any drug store. The directions for using these tablets are given on the package. But if large quantities of bichloride solutions are to be used, it will be found cheaper to have a strong solution prepared by a druggist and then add at home, under his direction, sufficient water to reduce it to the required strength. Two tablets dissolved in 1 pint of water, or sixteen tablets (2 drams) corrosive sublimate to the gallon, makes a solution of 1 to 500. This may be improved by adding 2 ounces of common salt to the gallon of water.

Or, dissolve corrosive sublimate and muriate of ammonia in water in the proportion of 2 drams, 120 grains or ¼ ounce of each to the gallon.

Or, dissolve corrosive sublimate and permanganate of potash, 2 drams each to 1 gallon of water.

Or, dissolve corrosive sublimate, permanganate of potash and muriate of ammonia in pure soft water in the proportion of 2 drams each to the gallon.

All the above substances may be obtained at any first-class drug store. The simple solution of bichloride in water first mentioned is a good disinfectant and may be preferred whenever it is necessary to practice economy. But, if the additional cost of such substances as muriate of ammonia (sal ammoniac) and permanganate of potash can be afforded, the solution will be more efficient and will keep better. If permanganate of potash is not used, it is a good plan to add a little blue vitriol or common bluing to color the solution. This lessens the danger of its being swallowed by accident.

Cautions.—All the above solutions or others containing bichloride of mercury (corrosive sublimate) will corrode metals and even tarnish gold. In so doing their disinfecting power is lost. Hence, these solutions must be mixed in a wooden tub, barrel or pail, or an earthen crock. They must be kept in a glass or earthenware receptacle—as a glass fruit jar or earthenware jug—tightly stoppered to prevent evaporation, and labeled "Poison". They should never be poured into metal drains without thorough and repeated flushing. Otherwise they will injure plumbing. Nor should they be permitted to come into contact with the metal fixtures of the bath room. The better plan is to bury them, after using, at least one foot deep in the ground. Rings must be removed from the hands before they are immersed in the bichloride solutions.

Use any of the above solutions full strength (1 : 500) to disinfect excreta in the same manner and quantity as the Chloride of Lime Solution

No. 1. They are equally as effective but slower in action. Hence it is necessary to let the mixture, disinfectant and infected matter, stand at least four hours. It is best to empty the mixture into a wooden pail and leave it for twenty-four hours. It may then be thrown into a vault or buried. The chief advantage of these solutions over No. 1 is that they possess no odor. Hence they may be preferred for use in vessels, cuspidors and the like, if Solution No. 1 is objectionable on account of its smell. They are not as good disinfectants for vaults, sink drains, sewers and the like as the chloride of lime solution, nor are they trustworthy as a disinfectant of fresh sputum.

Also use any of these solutions one-half strength, that is, diluted with an equal quantity of water (1 : 1,000), for the disinfection of soiled underclothing, bed linen and other fabrics. Mix the solution well by stirring and immerse the articles for two hours. Then wring them out and boil at least half an hour. Bichloride solutions tend to fix stains. Hence remove stains by appropriate process before disinfection.

Also use one-half strength (1 : 1,000) of any of these solutions for washing all hard surfaces not metallic, as walls, floors, furniture and the like, and for moistening cloths with which to wipe off dust from the woodwork and furniture. For washing metallic surfaces use disinfectant No. 5, 2 per cent solution of formaldehyde.

Also use this solution one-half strength (1 : 1,000) for washing the hands and general body surfaces of the attendants and convalescents—the latter, however, only by direction of the physician.

Bichloride of mercury, either in solid form or in mixtures is a violent corrosive poison. One ounce of any of the above solutions, full strength, contains nearly a grain of corrosive sublimate and will quickly cause death by poison if swallowed. Hence all these solutions must be labeled "Poison" and kept out of reach of children. Their use should always be under the direction of some intelligent person.

Antidote.—If by accident one of these solutions is swallowed, send for a physician at once. Do not wait, however, until he arrives. Give the proper antidote quickly. Give freely white of egg mixed with water, or if this is not at hand, give wheat flour mixed with water, or give milk. Try to provoke vomiting so as to empty the stomach. For this purpose give mustard and water, or salt and water, or tickle the back of the throat.

No. 4. Standard Solution of Carbolic Acid.—Carbolic acid is one of the most generally useful disinfectants in the sick room, but is rather expensive when properly used and its odor is objectionable to some persons. Carbolic acid may be used dissolved in water in a strength from a 2 per cent (weak) to a 5 per cent (strong) solution. For a 5 per cent solution add 1 pint or pound of either the crude or purified liquid carbolic acid to 2½ gallons of hot water, or about 6 ounces to the gallon. Stir frequently until no red or colorless droplets remain in the bottom of the mixture. The keeping power and efficiency of this solution may be increased by the addition of 12 to 14 ounces of common salt to each gallon, when used for the disinfection of excreta or other uses where the salt is not objectionable. Use this 5 per cent solution in the same way and for the same purposes as Standard Solution No. 1 of Chloride of Lime.

Use one-half strength, i. e., diluted in an equal quantity of water (2½ per cent solution) for the tub in which body or bed linen is immersed. Also for washing woodwork, floors and other hard surfaces and for the hands and person. Immerse fabrics four hours, then rinse and boil for half an hour.

Antidote.—Carbolic acid, like bichloride of mercury, is a violent corrosive poison. Hence take great care to see that it is properly labeled and kept out of reach of children. In case of poisoning send for a physician at once, but do not wait until he arrives. Diluted alcohol is the best antidote. Give this in the form of whisky, brandy or cologne water, if pure alcohol is not at hand. Do not use wood alcohol, which is itself poisonous. Epsom salts or glauber salts, in doses of one tablespoonful, rank next to alcohol as antidotes. All cases, however, require the immediate attendance of a physician. Olive oil, castor oil and glycerine are also antidotes for carbolic acid. Try to provoke vomiting so as to empty the stomach. For this purpose give mustard and water, salt and water or tickle the back of the throat.

Pure carbolic acid will burn the skin. Should an accident of this kind happen, immediately apply ordinary alcohol, whisky, brandy or cologne water.

No. 5. Standard Solution of Formaldehyde (formalin).—Dissolve 12 ounces 40 per cent solution of formaldehyde (formalin) in 1 gallon pure soft water. This mixture contains $6\frac{2}{3}$ per cent of formaldehyde. It should be kept in tightly corked bottles to prevent loss of strength by evaporation of the gas. This solution, while somewhat more expensive, is preferable for the disinfection of clothing and other fabrics, since it does not bleach or injure them. Use full strength for cuspidors, vessels and sputum cups in the sick room. Dilute one-half for the tub in which fabrics are immersed and for washing floors, woodwork and the like. It is especially recommended for washing furniture, woodwork and metallic surfaces and for washing the hands and person of both nurse and patient.

Formaldehyde is a gas. It is sold in a solution containing 40 per cent of formaldehyde either under the simple designation, "Forty per cent solution of formaldehyde," or under the proprietary designations, "Formalin" and "Formal"; always ask for "formaldehyde" else you may pay extra for the same thing. For disinfecting, it may be used either in solution or in gaseous form. In household disinfection it is generally used as a gas. Formaldehyde tends to fix stains. Hence they should be removed by appropriate processes before disinfection. Formaldehyde in gaseous form does not injure even the most delicate fabrics. It has a slightly corrosive action on polished steel, but does not affect other metals.

Antidote.—If by chance formaldehyde solution is swallowed, give at once one to two tablespoonfuls of solution of acetate of ammonia (spirit of mindererus), or 1 teaspoonful of aromatic spirits of ammonia, diluted with water; or 10 to 20 drops of ordinary ammonia, well diluted with cold water. Send for a physician at once. The doses stated are for adults. The dose for children must be in proportion to their age. But none of the antidotes mentioned are poisonous, and they can be given in any approximately correct quantity without fear.

FUMIGATION OR GASEOUS DISINFECTION

Preparations.—The sick room in all cases and preferably every room in the house, especially in case of smallpox, diphtheria, typhoid and other virulent diseases, should be thoroughly disinfected by fumigation. This may be accomplished by formaldehyde gas or by the fumes of burning sulphur. During convalescence following cases of scarlet fever, smallpox or measles, the body of the patient should be daily rubbed with vaseline to prevent scales and dry particles of dead skin from being carried by air currents. When sufficiently recovered, the patient should have a warm bath every day until the skin has ceased to peel. When the patient leaves the sick room he should be given a disinfectant bath in Standard Solution No. 3 or No. 5 (bichloride 1:1,000 or formaldehyde 2 per cent). This should be followed by a cleansing bath including a shampoo or thorough washing of the hair and scalp. The patient should then be dressed in clean garments and should not again enter the infected room until it has been disinfected and cleansed. The nurse or attendant should exercise the same precautions against spreading the infection. After the room has been vacated by the patient and nurse it is ready for final disinfection. This should be done preferably by a duly qualified officer of the Board of Health, but may be done successfully by any one if the following directions are carefully observed.

Fumigation by Formaldehyde.—First send to the drug store for the necessary materials. To ascertain the quantity required measure the room and find the length, breadth and height in feet. Multiply the figures together, disregarding fractions. This gives the cubical contents of the room in feet. Divide by 1,000 (point off three places) to find the number of thousand cubic feet in the room. For example, a room 10 feet square and 10 feet high contains 1,000 cubic feet. Use 6¾ ounces crystals of potassium permanganate for each 1,000 cubic feet of room space, or 10 ounces when the temperature is below 60 degrees F. Over these pour 16 ounces of 40 per cent aqueous solution of formaldehyde (formalin) for each 1,000 cubic feet of room space, or 24 ounces when the temperature is below 60 degrees F.

Thoroughly seal the room from within so as to prevent the escape of the gas until disinfection has been accomplished. Carefully close all windows and doors except one door for exit. Leave the windows unlocked so that they may be opened from without. Securely paste wet strips of paper over all registers, transoms, keyholes and cracks above, beneath and at the sides of windows and doors, over stove holes and all openings in walls, ceilings and floor. Use several thicknesses of paper if the openings are large. Gummed paper put up in rolls is made for this purpose. Or adhesive surgeon's plaster may be used. But common newspaper cut into narrow strips will do. It should be thoroughly wet with the Standard Solution No. 3 or No. 5 (bichloride 1:500 or formaldehyde 5 per cent), in order to disinfect the surfaces upon which it is used. Soft soap may be used for pasting paper strips so that they may later be easily washed off. Or use paperhanger's paste, which may be prepared, and afterwards removed, by methods described elsewhere in this volume. After the strips are in place go over them on the outside with the brush dipped in the paste so as to wet them thoroughly.

Stop up the fire place with a sheet of tin or zinc and paste strips of paper around the edges. Or securely paste large sheets of heavy wrapping paper over the opening so that they cannot be displaced by the draft. There must be no opening through which gas can escape.

Now spread out on chairs, or clothes-racks, all articles that cannot be boiled. Clothing, bed covers and the like should be hung on a line stretched across the room. Open the mattresses and set them on edge. Stretch the window shades and curtains to their full length. Open the doors of closets or clothes-presses. Lift the lids of trunks or chests and remove and spread out their contents. Open one of the long seams of pillows so that the fumes can reach the feathers. Do not pile articles together. Open books and spread out the leaves. In short, arrange the room and its contents so as to secure free access of gas to all parts and to every object. If the room has been properly cleansed and ventilated during the course of the disease and especially if it was stripped of carpets and unnecessary furniture when first set apart as a sick room, the difficulties of disinfection will be greatly reduced.

Humidity.—When all is in readiness make the air of the room damp. This is absolutely necessary for disinfection either by sulphur or formaldehyde. Dampness may be produced by boiling a quantity of water in a wash boiler on a gas or gasoline stove, by pouring boiling water from a tea kettle into a tub, or by pouring cold water onto hot bricks or stones, or dropping hot bricks or stones into vessels containing cold, or preferably hot water. Under no circumstances is efficient disinfection possible without in some way making the air of the room quite damp. The temperature should be from 60 to 70 degrees F. or over, the higher the better, but there must not be any fire or exposed flame in the room.

Formaldehyde Generators. — Formaldehyde is a gas which may be generated in large quantities by the addition of formaldehyde solution (formalin) to crystals of potassium permanganate in the right proportions. A number of patented generators and processes for disinfection with formaldehyde have been placed upon the market. Many of these are inefficient and the use of any of them is an unnecessary expense. A homemade device equal to the best patent generator ever devised may be arranged by means of a common wood or fiber wash tub, two or more ordinary red bricks and a tin or galvanized iron pail, such as a common milk or water pail, having the seams rolled, not soldered. Place the tub in the middle of the room with the pail inside resting upon two or more bricks standing edgewise. Now fill the tub with water nearly but not quite up to the level of the top of the bricks and the generator is ready for use. If the bricks can be previously heated in a very hot oven and the water poured in at, or near the boiling point, so as to give off a quantity of steam, so much the better.

Before the pail is put in place spread the potassium permanganate crystals evenly over the bottom. Meantime have in readiness wet strips of paper and paste, or adhesive plaster, with which to seal up the cracks of the door immediately on leaving the room. When everything is in readiness and the pail containing the permanganate crystals is in place, pour over them the formaldehyde solution. Leave the room and seal up the door on the outside as quickly as possible. The formaldehyde is promptly liberated in great quantities. Hence the necessity that all preparations be made in advance and that the operator leave the room at once on the combination of the two chemicals. Leave the room closed for at least four hours.

Quantities and Proportions.—Care must be taken not to put too much formaldehyde into a single container. The reaction is violent and there is great effervescence and bubbling. If the rooms are large, as in the case of school rooms, public halls and the like, more than one container should be used.

The following quantities may be used safely in the containers recommended:

10 or 12-quart milk-pail.
Formaldehyde, 16 ounces,
Permanganate, $6\frac{3}{4}$ ounces.

14-quart milk-pail.
Formaldehyde, 24 ounces.
Permanganate, 10 ounces.

A receptacle of ample capacity, not less than mentioned above, should always be used, as otherwise, the effervescence resulting from the reaction between the two substances may carry the mixture, or some of it, over the sides of the receptacle and stain the carpet or floor. As permanganate of potassium is liable to stain anything with which it comes into contact, use great care in handling it.

Remember that the permanganate must always be put in before the formaldehyde solution.

Conservation of Heat. — If the bricks and water which are placed in the tub are cold, it is a good plan to set the tin pail snugly into a wooden or pulp bucket. Or wrap it tightly with several layers of asbestos paper. This is done to retain within the generator the heat, which is very important to the proper generation of the gas. If the bricks and water are hot this will not be necessary.

Selection of Materials.—The chemicals required for formaldehyde disinfection are not expensive and the best quality should be obtained from a reliable dealer. Secure the highest grade 40 per cent aqueous solution of formaldehyde on the market. An inferior gradé may fail to do its work and thus bring about unfortunate results by giving a false sense of security. The fine needle-shaped crystals of potassium permanganate are better than the rhomboid. See that you get this substance in crystals. Do not accept the dust which often contains impurities. Never use formaldehyde candles. They are not reliable. Do not rely upon advertised apparatus, disinfectants, and processes. Nothing can be better or cheaper than the plan above set forth.

Formaldehyde Solution.—The fairly rapid liberation of gas may be secured by sprinkling 40 per cent formaldehyde solution over sheets hung in the room requiring disinfection and containing the articles to be disinfected. One pint of formaldehyde should be used for every 1,000 cubic feet of air space in the apartment, if there is not too much opportunity for the escape of the gas through cracks, windows, doors, etc. If the gas can find easy escape, proportionately more of the solution must be used. Since by either the permanganate method or by the sheet method, formaldehyde gas is rapidly liberated, it is essential that all preparations be made in advance for the operator to leave the room promptly. The door should be closed and sealed and the room left closed for not less than six hours, after which the door and windows may be opened and the room aired.

The odor of formaldehyde, if it persists so as to be objectionable, can be removed, or at least moderated, by hanging up towels or sheets in the room and sprinkling them with ammonia water.

Cautions. — Formaldehyde is intensely irritating to the eyes, nose and mouth. It kills the upper layers of the skin if applied in too strong solutions. The inhalation in ordinary quantities of such formaldehyde as is given off while sprinkling sheets in a room about to be disinfected, is uncomfortable, but not dangerous. The discomfort may be lessened by tying a moist towel over the mouth and nose while engaged in such work. Injury to the hands can be avoided by greasing them well before they come into contact with the formaldehyde solution, or by wearing rubber gloves.

Sulphur Fumigation.—Sulphur will be found a thoroughly reliable gaseous disinfectant of considerable penetrating power if it is intelligently employed. To obtain satisfactory results the following essentials of successful disinfection, established by repeated experiments, must be observed: (a) the infected room, or rooms, must be thoroughly closed, every crack and crevice sealed; (b) sufficient sulphur must be used; (c) there must be ample moisture in the room; (d) the time of exposure must be sufficient. Ten hours is the minimum.

If sulphur is preferred for disinfection, use four pounds of powdered sulphur to every thousand cubic feet in the room. Seal and otherwise prepare the room in all respects as for disinfection with formaldehyde. Place a common wood or fiber tub on a table—not on the floor. In this place an iron pot or earthenware crock supported by two or more bricks placed edgewise. Pour in water to the level of the top of the bricks. The disinfecting apparatus will then be in working order. Now fill the room with steam. Fumigation with sulphur is not efficient unless the air is very moist. Pile the sulphur in the form of a low cone with a depression on top about as large as the bowl of a tablespoon. Fill this with alcohol, turpentine or coal oil, and set it on fire. Immediately leave the room and close and seal the door. The sulphur in burning throws off sulphurous acid gas which, in the presence of steam, kills all infection. Keep the room closed for ten hours at least and preferably for twenty-four hours after starting the fumes. Then open the windows from the outside for ventilation and thoroughly air the room before using.

Sulphur candles can be used instead of crude sulphur but take care to use sufficient candles. The average candle on the market contains one pound of sulphur. Four of these will be required in the disinfection of a small room 10x10x10. Do not use a smaller number, no matter what directions may accompany the candle. The water-jacketed candle is to be preferred. Partly fill the tin around candles with water and place them in a pan on a table, not on the floor. Let one-half pint of water be vaporized with each candle.

Cautions.—There is one serious objection to the use of sulphur, which must be fully understood. The fumes have a destructive action on fabrics of wool, silk, cotton and linen as tapestries and draperies and tend to injure brass, copper, steel and gilt work. Colored fabrics are frequently changed in appearance and the strength impaired. Hence such articles should be separately disinfected, as hereafter described, and removed from the room before it is disinfected by sulphur.

Sulphur fumigation has the advantage over formaldehyde that it kills insects and thus prevents their conveying the disease. An ideal plan of fumigation is to use first one method and then the other.

Additional Disinfection.—After the sick room has been fumigated with formaldehyde or sulphur, thoroughly wash the floor and woodwork and all out of the way places, window ledges, picture moulding, etc., and thoroughly wet all dust and dirt in cracks with the half-strength Standard Solution No. 3, Bichloride of Mercury (1:1,000). Follow this up with hot soap suds, afterwards rinse with cloths wet in the disinfectant. Do not attempt to mix soap suds with the disinfectant solution. Scrape off and burn the wall paper. Whitewash the ceiling and walls before re-papering and open the room to sunlight and air for several days. Apply a fresh coat of paint to the woodwork.

Cotton Fabrics.—Disinfect all cotton and linen fabrics by immersing them in Solution No. 3 (1:1,000); No. 4 (5 per cent) or No. 5 (10 per cent), for four hours, after which boil them for at least half an hour, then launder as usual. Immerse soiled clothing in a disinfectant solution before it is dried. Before transporting dry clothing or other infected material from the sick room to any other part of the house, wrap the articles in a sheet wet in No. 3 (1:1,000), or No. 4 (5 per cent), or in the absence of these wet in water.

Woolen Fabrics.—Disinfect woolen goods with formaldehyde fumigation in an empty trunk, wooden box or wash boiler, or in tight closets or other air-tight enclosed spaces. All unwashable clothing, bed clothing, mattresses and similar objects may be disinfected in this manner. Place one layer at a time in any air-tight enclosure having a close fitting door, lid or other cover. Sprinkle each successive layer with a 40 per cent solution of formalin, full strength, by means of a sprayer or small sprinkling pot, at the rate of about two tablespoonfuls of the solution to each garment. Protect silks or other delicate fabrics which might be spotted by direct contact with the drops of moisture by means of cotton sheets or towels placed between each layer. Spray the formalin on this protective covering. Now close the receptacle, seal all cracks and crevices by means of wet strips of paper and leave it unopened in a warm room for at least twelve hours. Afterwards expose the articles for a day or more to direct sunshine. If the smell of formaldehyde persists, sprinkle a little aqua ammonia on the articles to remove it.

Or, disinfect by soaking in corrosive sublimate or formaldehyde solutions No. 3 (1:1,000), and No. 5 (6⅔ per cent), in a wooden or fiber wash tub. Afterwards boil for half an hour and launder as usual.

Money, jewelry, letters, valuable papers and similar articles may be disinfected by spraying with a 40 per cent solution of formalin, full strength, by means of a hand atomizer. Place them in a small wooden or pasteboard box with a tight-fitting cover, seal and keep in a warm room for twelve hours. Burn all books, magazines, newspapers and other articles the value of which is not great enough to warrant disinfection.

Bedding.—Throw straw beds out of the window, empty out and burn the straw, and disinfect the tick as for cotton clothing. Disinfect feather beds, pillows, quilts, comforters and blankets in a steam disinfector when practical, or if not soiled, with formaldehyde in large quantities. If mattresses have been soiled by the patient's discharges and steaming disinfection is not practical, burn them.

Rugs and Carpets.—These should be removed from the sick room before the patient is installed, but if they remain and become infected, disinfect with steam or by soaking in corrosive sublimate or formaldehyde solutions. If their value is slight burn them.

Lounges, Couches and Other Upholstered Furniture.—Leave in place when the room is fumigated. Strip off and disinfect the covering as for cotton and linen clothing. Burn the filling and replace with new.

The hands of nurses and others who have attended to the wants of the sick should be disinfected with thorough and prolonged washing and scrubbing with hot soap and water, and then immersed for several minutes in a carbolic, bichloride or formaldehyde solution.

Sputum.—Receive on pieces of paper or rag or in paper sputum cups and burn. Or receive in cuspidors containing carbolic or formaldehyde solutions.

Disinfection of the Dead.—Bodies of persons dying of smallpox, scarlet fever, diphtheria, membranous croup or measles, should be wrapped in several thicknesses of cloth wrung out of full strength corrosive sublimate, carbolic or formaldehyde solution and should not thereafter be exposed to view. The funeral should be private and no persons except the undertaker and his assistant, the clergyman and the immediate family of the deceased should attend. Carriages used by persons attending the funeral ceremony should be fumigated. No person should enter the sick room until it has been thoroughly disinfected.

Rules for the Sick Room.—Sunlight kills disease germs and should be admitted freely to the sick room unless the patient is suffering from some condition which renders darkness necessary.

Proper ventilation diminishes the number of disease germs in the sick room by carrying some such germs into the open air. The number of germs likely to pass from an ordinarily well-kept sick room into the open air by means of ventilation is so small that such germs cannot be regarded as dangerous to people on the outside. Moreover, such organisms speedily die because they are not adapted to live in the open air. The ventilation of a sick room should not, however, be such as to permit air to pass from the sick room into the rest of the house.

Have all utensils and materials necessary for disinfection placed where they can be used with the least possible trouble. Failure to disinfect is often due to the fact that proper facilities for disinfecting are not conveniently at hand.

See that every bottle and box containing a disinfectant is properly labeled and see that all such bottles and boxes are kept apart from bottles and boxes containing medicines for internal use. Accidental poisoning may be thus avoided.

CHAPTER V

PREVENTION OF COMMUNICABLE DISEASE

TYPHOID FEVER—THE SICK ROOM—TUBERCULOSIS OR CONSUMPTION—SMALLPOX—VACCINATION—CHICKENPOX—MALARIA—YELLOW FEVER—HOOKWORM DISEASE—FOREIGN DISEASES—CONTAGIOUS DISEASES OF ANIMALS

Since the rise of the germ theory there has been a complete revolution in the attitude of well-informed persons toward the subject of disease. A large number of the most common and heretofore fatal enemies of mankind are now well known to be absolutely preventable.

The appearance of the first case of any communicable malady may be due to unavoidable accident; the spread of the disease must be attributed to ignorance or to criminal carelessness. In cities, persons ill with contagious diseases are either isolated in hospitals set apart for that purpose, or quarantined in their own homes by law. The necessary sanitary regulations are enforced by trained inspectors under the authority of the Board of Health. The absence of such officials in most rural neighborhoods shifts this responsibility to the head of the family. Unless parents in such localities take the pains to inform themselves so that they can intelligently co-operate with the attending physician, unnecessary deaths from preventable diseases will continue to occur.

No attempt will be made here to discuss the treatment of contagious or other diseases. In all suspected cases a physician should be promptly summoned. Our purpose here is simply to make clear the causes of preventable disease and to describe the ordinary sources and channels of infection. When these are fully understood and proper preventive measures taken, the likelihood of infection will be reduced to a minimum. Or, if by some unhappy accident a member of a family becomes infected, such knowledge will enable those in charge of the patient to prevent the spread of the disease. A careful study has been made of all the recent publications of Boards of Health of city, state and nation throughout the United States. The most essential knowledge which they impart is here condensed for ready reference. Many of these bulletins, however, contain detailed information on each of the principal contagious diseases which would extend far beyond the limits of the present chapter. Hence, on the appearance of any contagious disease, in any family or neighborhood, address a postal card to the Secretary of the Board of Health at the nearest metropolitan city. Address another to the Secretary of the State Board of Health at the State Capital. Also a third to the Surgeon-General of the United States, Washington, D. C. Name the disease and request copies of all available circular matter relating to it. Three cents thus spent on postal cards will bring back, without charge, full detailed practical information and instruction of great value. Also ask to have copies of these bulletins mailed to the heads of other families where contagious diseases have broken out, or where, through ignorance or neglect, conditions are so unsanitary as to threaten the public health.

No ordinary person would knowingly give poison to the members of his own family or those of his neighbor. Yet, through ignorance, many well meaning persons are permitting the existence of conditions within their control which result directly in the poisoning of others through the germs of contagious diseases.

Contagious Diseases. — The most usual communicable diseases among adults are consumption (tuberculosis), typhoid fever (typhus fever), smallpox, and, in some localities, yellow fever, malaria and hookworm disease.

Several other communicable diseases are most common among children, as diphtheria (membranous croup, diphtheritic sore throat), scarlet fever (scarlatina, scarlet rash), measles (German measles), chickenpox, mumps, and whooping cough. Another class is most prevalent among small infants, as infantile paralysis (anterior poliomyelitis), cerebrospinal meningitis, summer complaint, congenital blindness (ophthalmia neonatorum). The preventable diseases of children are discussed in the succeeding chapter.

There is a small class of virulent contagious diseases the infection from which may usually be traced to immigration from foreign parts. These include Asiatic cholera, bubonic plague and leprosy. Another communicable disease to which especial attention has been directed in recent years is hookworm disease. In addition, pediculosis, trachoma, ringworm, scabies and impetigo contagiosa, are held to be so contagious as to be dangerous to the public health.

Most of the above diseases are known to be preventable. It is confidently believed that all can be controlled and their communication from one person to another prevented, if certain well understood precautions are observed.

TYPHOID FEVER

Typhoid Fever (Enteric Fever, Abdominal Typhus) is an infectious disease caused by a specific germ known as the typhoid bacillus. This is a low form of vegetable life belonging to the group of bacteria. It was discovered by Eberth in 1880. Each germ is a minute vegetable cell shaped like a cylinder with round ends. Each is equipped with a number of long, leg-like processes called flagella which give it the power of swimming rapidly in liquids. These bacteria can be seen only by the aid of the most powerful microscope. They are so small that half a million would scarcely cover the head of a pin. Yet, each is descended from another germ of the same kind, has its own individual life and can be produced in no other way. These germs, under favorable conditions, multiply very rapidly. Each splits into two, each two into four, each four into eight and so on. A single colony of a few score germs may, within forty-eight hours, develop into a billion.

We do not "catch" typhoid, we swallow it. The germs invariably enter the system through the mouth. Thence they pass into the stomach. Here they may be destroyed by the acids present in the gastric juice, a fact which may explain why some persons who are known to have swallowed the germs do not develop typhoid fever. But if not destroyed in the stomach, they pass on into the intestine. The conditions present in the lower third of the small intestine seem especially to favor their growth. Here they multiply rapidly and become very active. It takes anywhere from seven days to three weeks to bring on the symptoms of the disease after the germs are swallowed. This is called the incubation period. The average is from ten to twelve days. The germ attacks primarily the glands of the intestines, causing small abscesses by which the intestinal walls are often perforated through and through. It also attacks other organs during the course of the disease and may attack any part of the body.

Typhoid fever exists at all seasons of the year, but is most prevalent in autumn. The greatest number of deaths occur in September and October.

Symptoms.—Typhoid fever is a very insidious disease since there may be no symptoms whatever during the period of incubation, that is, on an average, for ten to twelve days after infection has taken place. It is often difficult to determine the day on which the disease begins to make itself manifest. Cases are usually dated from the day on which the patient gives up work and takes to his bed. The disease may then have been in existence for a considerable time. In cases known as "walking" typhoid, the patient is never prostrated. The patient and his family may be unaware of the nature of the disease. Yet germs are being given off which may infect others with typhoid in its most malignant form. For these reasons it is advisable to summon a physician promptly in all suspected cases and to treat every case of fever as typhoid until the physician has completed his diagnosis.

Every case of so-called "typhomalarial fever" and every case of doubtful origin continuing more than seven days, should be reported to the local health officer, and due precautions taken.

Painless diarrhœa, or simple "looseness of the bowels," occurring in one who has never had typhoid fever should excite suspicion if the disease is known to exist in the neighborhood. The mild, "walking" cases are by no means uncommon. Hence it is advisable that *all* diarrhœal discharges should be disinfected especially during the existence of typhoid fever in a community.

As a rule the disease comes on slowly. The first symptoms are headache, with a general sense of fatigue and loss of appetite. The headache may be severe and confined to the top of the head, or may consist of more or less general soreness. Abdominal pain occurs in about one-third of all cases. A low fever is almost always present from the outset. But this may be so slight that the patient is unaware of it. Women or children in the first stages of the disease often keep up about the house, or they may be compelled to lie down a part of the day. Men frequently give up work for a day or two and after a little rest go to work again. When such symptoms are observed as tiring easily, digestive disturbauces, headache, drowsiness, and abdominal pain that cannot be attributed to any special condition, a physician should be promptly consulted.

If the onset of the disease is more sudden, there may be nausea and vomiting, accompanied by a chill and high fever. A slight cough and occasional nosebleed may be present. Whenever there is doubt as to the diagnosis, the attending physician should have a blood test made. The Widal test is made free for health officers and physicians in the public laboratories of most states.

Prognosis.—During the first week of the disease, the symptoms gradually grow worse, fever develops and the patient suffers chilly sensations. The temperature gradually rises to a height of 102 to 105 degrees F. In severe forms of the disease, diarrhœa commences during the first week and is then continuous.

During the second week the above symptoms become more severe. Nervousness and delirium develop. Minute reddish spots resembling flea bites are frequently observed over the chest, abdomen and thighs. These spots disappear after a few days. Then a fresh crop appears in other situations. The bronchial tubes frequently become inflamed. Sometimes pneumonia develops. Bleeding from the bowels is an occasional symptom in the second week of this disease and is highly characteristic.

During the third week, in normal cases, the symptoms gradually abate. The fever lessens. The diarrhœa improves. The nervous symptoms and delirium diminish. The patient, though much emaciated, gradually returns to a normal condition. Or the symptoms may increase in severity, the patient become profoundly prostrated, the delirium deepen and death occur. The hemorrhage from the bowels in some instances may be so severe that death is produced even in comparatively early stages of the infection. This is quite as frequent in the mild cases known as walking typhoid as in others; hence the patient should receive equally careful attention.

The mortality varies from five to twenty per cent, depending upon the character of the disease and the nature of the nursing and treatment. A physician should be summoned and his directions implicitly followed. Nothing in this disease is of more importance than careful nursing. It is absolutely necessary that the patient receive only liquid diet until the physician permits other food. Solid food given prematurely will cause death.

Modes of Infection.—There is a common opinion among the laity that typhoid fever is contracted from foul drains and other things which contaminate the atmosphere; this is probably never the case, although such conditions may be injurious to health.

The germs, or typhoid bacilli, can enter the body in no other way than through the mouth. Direct infection is thought to occur most often through contaminated milk or drinking water, but secondary infection—that is, where one member of a family "catches" the disease from another—is believed to occur chiefly by transmitting the germs to the mouth with the fingers. This may come about by handling the patient or something which has come in contact with him, or by means of food or other articles which have been handled by the nurse or others with unwashed hands after coming into contact with the patient. A little reflection will show how easily the virus may get upon cooking utensils, drinking cups, bed linen, door knobs and similar articles, or may be carried from place to place by pets or insects, particularly flies.

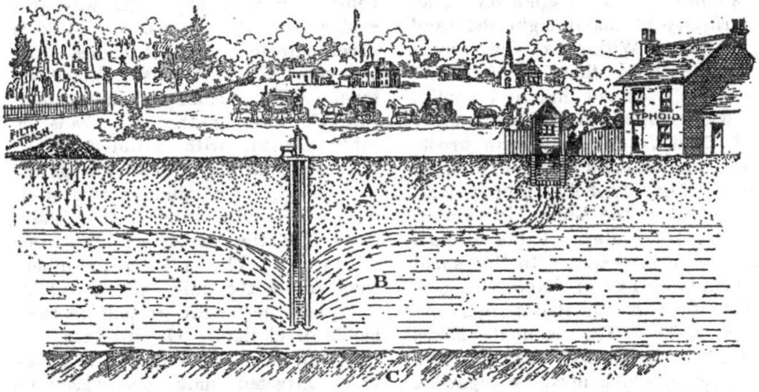

Privy vaults and wells which connect underground lead to funeral processions.

The germs leave the patient's body in the discharges of the bowels and bladder, in some cases in the sputum and possibly in perspiration. Especially must it be borne in mind that the urine of a typhoid fever patient is even more dangerous than the stools.

The germs may be found in very large numbers in these discharges, upon the bed linen, in the water with which the patient is bathed and upon the utensils used in nursing and feeding him. They are probably never carried on dust through the air. If every typhoid germ was destroyed as soon as it left the human body the disease would be speedily eradicated. But this, unfortunately, is by no means the case.

Infection from Water Supply.—Investigation has shown that most epidemics of the disease are caused by the excreta of the patient having been thrown upon the ground or into an open vault or drain, whence by seepage or surface drainage they were carried into a spring, well, or other source of water supply. A well-known instance is an epidemic in an eastern city of about eight thousand population. Within a few weeks there were more than one thousand cases and over one hundred deaths. The water supply of this community is obtained from a mountain brook. It was contaminated by the discharges from a single typhoid fever patient thrown upon the snow, in winter, near the headwaters of the stream. The consequent expense to this small community in loss of wages and care of the sick was estimated as in excess of $100,000. The annual losses throughout the United States from this disease, which must be regarded as almost entirely preventable, are estimated at many hundred thousand dollars. Investigation shows that milk is usually contaminated indirectly through an infected water supply. Hence due precautions to secure the purity of the water supply is of prime importance in the prevention of this disease.

Well water is frequently a cause of the disease. Too often we find a privy, or rather a hole in the ground containing fecal and urinary discharges, in close proximity to a well, and often upon higher ground. Unless the soil possesses the best of filtering properties, and this is frequently not the case, the well will certainly become contaminated. Infected discharges thrown on the ground may be washed into the well by the first rain storm.

Water which has a bad taste or odor, or which comes from a source that renders it likely to be impure, is dangerous, but unfortunately the reverse is not true. Dangerously contaminated water may be, and often is clear and colorless and may have no bad taste or odor.

Infected Milk Supply.—Milk is a very common and dangerous source of infection, because it is what medical men call an excellent "culture medium," that is, germs grow and multiply very rapidly in fresh milk. Nor do they cause the milk to become sour or in any other way give evidence of their presence. Milk is never infected when it comes from the cow. It is always infected by man. This usually takes place through washing the milk cans or other utensils with polluted water. Watered milk may contain the germs of typhoid, for a milkman who adulterates milk with water is not usually careful of the quality of his source of supply. The milkers or others who handle the milk may infect it, if typhoid germs are present on their hands or clothing. Or, infected flies may fall into the milk. The germs from infected milk may also be found in butter and cheese. Hence no milk or other dairy products should be sold from a dairy, farm, or house where there is a case of typhoid fever.

Infection from Ice.—The germs of typhoid fever are not destroyed by freezing. Hence ice taken from sewage-polluted rivers or lakes, or ice manufactured from such waters, is unsafe to use.

Infection from Vegetables.—Vegetables often become infected with the germs of typhoid by irrigation with polluted water, by contamination from night-soil used by farmers or market gardeners as a fertilizer, by flies and other insects. Creel, in a careful review of the results of recent scientific investigation, asserts that the typhoid bacillus may retain its vitality in privy vaults, or in night-soil used as a fertilizer for a period of several weeks, or even months, and that plants cultivated in contaminated soil may take up the germs on their leaves and stems in the process of growth. He found living typhoid bacilli on the tips of leaves that to the naked eye appeared

Where the flies come from. *Where the flies go.*

free from any particles of soil. He also proved by careful observation that rainfall will not free vegetables wholly from infected material. This source of pollution is especially dangerons in the case of such vegetables as lettuce, radishes and celery, which are eaten raw. The remedy is to thoroughly wash or scrub them free from earth and bacteria by means of a stiff brush. All vegetables should be cleaned in this manner, but the danger of infection is less from cooked vegetables, as most germs of disease are destroyed by boiling.

All fruits, such as grapes, apples, pears, berries and the like, including lemons and oranges, should be carefully washed in at least three waters or for five minutes in running water, especially in times of epidemic disease. Dried figs and dates are very commonly eaten without being cooked or washed, yet they have been exposed for an unknown space of time to all kinds of contagion from dust, flies and dirty hands. Shelled nuts purchased in the market should be washed and scalded before they are used, as they are commonly exposed to similar infection.

The Typhoid Fly.—This term has been applied to the common house fly by L. O. Howard to draw attention to the danger of infection from this insect. Flies cannot become the carriers of disease germs unless they have access to some source of infection. Hence the danger is much lessened by the elimination of all nuisances in the neighborhood of our dwellings. However, since flies may travel from considerable distances, the only assurance of safety against infection from them is to exclude them by screening or destroy them by means of traps and poisons.

Flies having access to privy vaults or sources of typhoid infection elsewhere, and then, through unscreened doors and windows, to living rooms, alighting upon food already prepared for the table or to be used without subsequent heating, are a serious danger. Some of these articles, liquid, semi-solid, or with moist surfaces, thus slightly infected, serve as congenial culture media for the rapid multiplication of the infection. A few typhoid germs brought on the hairy feet of flies may increase many fold if deposited in milk or on the surface of boiled potato.

While typhoid is not ordinarily an air-borne disease, care should be taken to avoid the typhoid patient's breath and not to come unnecessarily in his immediate vicinity especially if he has pneumonia, or an explosive cough. The sputum bearing infection may be sprayed into the air during coughing, but the range of possible danger is slight—hardly more than four or five feet.

The disease is also occasionally spread by the dust of dried urine or other excreta, which is carried through the air, thereby contaminating food or water. Some authorities

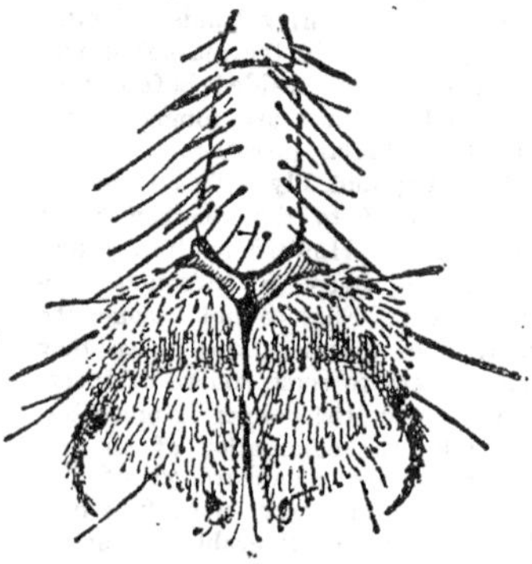

The hairy foot of a fly (magnified).

still hold that the disease may be communicated by inhaling these particles by mouth or nostrils. The diarrhœal discharge, when dry, may preserve the poison as effectually as the crusts of smallpox, the scales of scarlet fever, and the dried membrane of diphtheria preserve the specific poisons of those diseases.

Among miscellaneous sources of infection may be mentioned bread, pastry, confectionery, fruits, vegetables, meats, etc., handled by infected hands in bakeries, stores, markets and slaughterhouses, or the same articles and milk infected by flies recently arrived from sources of filth.

The general filth conditions in the homes of extremely untidy families favor the spread of typhoid infection, and in such homes or in any homes where there is neglect of the greatest possible cleanliness of the sick person, his bedding, clothing and everything else in the management of him, the danger from secondary infection is serious.

THE SICK ROOM

Care of a Typhoid Patient.—As typhoid fever is one of the most common of communicable diseases, full instructions will be given here for the management of the sick room in such a way as to preclude the possibility of other members of the family becoming infected. All of these instructions apply equally to other contagious diseases with the addition of especial precautions in certain other ailments which will be mentioned.

Isolation.—The first and most essential precaution in the case of typhoid or other communicable disease is that the patient should be completely isolated. Unless this is done, other members of the family are almost sure to contract the malady. The safest course is to send the patient to a hospital. When this is not possible, select a large airy room as the sick room. This should be located on the sunny side of the house, and should have a fire place if the weather be cold. It should be as far from living and sleeping rooms of other persons as possible. It is of the utmost consequence that the room have windows and doors by means of which it can be at all times thoroughly ventilated. At all seasons of the year a room on the lowest floor of the house is more satisfactory, since it is warmer in the winter and cooler in the summer. The room should not be uncomfortably cold, though it is much better to have the temperature too low than to have it stuffy. In most diseases ventilation is of supreme importance, and should be secured at any cost. There are no better disinfectants than pure air and sunlight. A temperature of about 70° F., if compatible with thorough ventilation, is generally considered most desirable. The sick room should have its windows always open day and night, and there should be an open fire if possible, otherwise recovery will be greatly delayed, for bad air of itself makes well persons sick. Keep the patient out of drafts.

Preparing the Sick Room.—Before installing the patient, take up the carpet and remove all rugs, ornaments, curtains, portières, bureau scarfs and hangings of every description. Empty bureau drawers, remove the contents of closets and clothes-presses, in short, take everything out of the room that is not necessary, and especially all sorts of fabrics which may serve as catch-alls for the germs of the disease. The room should contain no more furniture than is necessary. Metal bedsteads, plain wooden chairs and tables, are best. Remove all scarfs from tables and cushions, doilies and the like from chairs. Seal up door cracks and keyholes communicating with other rooms by pasting over them strips of wrapping paper. Suspend over the doorway a sheet reaching from the top to the floor, moistened with full strength carbolic or bichloride solutions No. 3 and No. 4. Tack this across the top and one side, leaving the other side free to be pushed aside to gain entrance. Only such toys, books and the like should be given the patient as can be destroyed after recovery or death.

The floor, woodwork and furniture should be frequently wiped with cloths moistened with half strength Standard Disinfectant Solution No. 3, 4 or 5. Throw away the broom and duster. Use only damp cloths moistened with half strength Solution No. 3, 4 or 5, for cleaning floor and furniture. These should be at once thrown into the disinfectant solution or burned. It is well to wash the floor each day with one of the same solutions.

Cleanliness.—Keep the premises clean. All decaying animal and vegetable matter and every kind of filth in and around the house should be removed, and disinfectants freely used. Surface drains and gutters, areas, outhouses, privies, shelters for domestic animals, fowls, etc., should receive close and constant attention. Use Standard Disinfectant No. 1 or No. 2, freely and regularly, in every such place.

Odors.—Never allow bad smells to exist. If free ventilation, sunshine and cleanliness do not keep out bad smells, sprinkle diluted formaldehyde, one part formaldehyde to 50 parts of water, upon the floor, or spray it into the air with an atomizer.

Bed and Bedding.—Place the patient's bed in the middle of the room, or at least away from the wall. Do not suffer the bed covers to come in contact with the walls or floor so as to contaminate them. The bed should be narrow. A mattress is much to be preferred to a feather bed. The cover should consist of a sheet long enough to fold back at the head over the other coverings for some distance. Blankets should be used for warmth in preference to quilts. Keep the bed scrupulously clean, and remove the linen and coverings promptly when soiled. The nurse should see to it that bread crumbs do not remain in the bed.

The best way to make up the bed for the typhoid patient is the following: (1) Over the mattress (no feather bed) spread smoothly and tuck in the sheet. Under the sheet have preferably a once-folded sheet or blanket. (2) Next spread a rubber sheet crosswise the bed, the two ends tucked smoothly under the edges of the mattress. (3) A folded sheet (draw-sheet) also crosswise over the rubber sheet. (4) A second rubber sheet. (5) Over that a second draw-sheet.

To Remove Soiled Bed Clothes.—Move the patient to one side of the bed as near the edge as possible, and loosen the sheet beneath him at the head and foot and on the opposite side. Then roll it up toward the patient and push it well up under him, leaving the side of the bed opposite to that upon which he is lying bare. Upon this place the new sheet. Tuck this under the edges of the mattress, and pull the patient back over on it. Now remove the soiled sheet and pull the edges of the fresh one over the portions of the bed still uncovered, and secure in the usual way.

Cleanliness greatly aids recovery, hence the utmost cleanliness of the patient and his surroundings should be the rule. If there is diarrhœa, the mattress should be protected by an impervious rubber sheet placed under the linen sheet, or by newspaper pads. Oilcloth cracks and wrinkles too badly to be suitable. Provide two or more rubber sheets so that they can be changed and cleaned as often as required. Sponge the rubber sheets with standard carbolic acid solution No. 4 (5 per cent) and dry and air them in the sun for several hours daily. If the condition of the patient makes it difficult to avoid the soiling of his bed, provide smaller squares of rubber sheeting and folded sheets to be placed above the ordinary sheets. Remove all soiled sheets and clothing promptly before drying occurs. (See Disinfection.) Take care to cleanse and disinfect the patient locally with a solution of corrosive sublimate 1:2,000—half a dram to the gallon of water, or one tablet to the quart.

Bathing.—All patients, if the attending physician approves, should have a daily bath, special attention being given to the hair, teeth, mouth and nails. In many cases it is necessary to wash the patient's mouth frequently with some antiseptic wash. But this should only be done on the express instructions of the doctor.

Disinfection.—A pail or tub should be kept in the room, containing a standard disinfectant solution such as No. 3, 4 or 5 for the purpose of disinfecting every article of clothing before it is carried through the house. One of these solutions should be kept standing in the tub and renewed at frequent intervals. All blankets, sheets, towels, napkins, bandages and clothing, used either by the patient or the attendant should be at once immersed in this tub and remain at least three hours. After this they should be boiled for at least one-half hour. The body linen of the patient should be changed daily or oftener if soiled. When removed it should be immersed immediately in this tub. Rags, closet paper or other material used about the person of the patient should be immediately burned.

The discharges from the throat, mouth and nose are especially dangerons and must be cared for at once. It is well to prepare a number of squares of old soft cloth—old sheets or pillow cases are good—to receive these discharges. These cloths should be burned as soon as soiled. If there is no fire in the sick room, it is convenient to have a small tub containing any strong standard disinfecting solution, to receive these cloths until they can be carried from the room and burned.

The nurse or **attendant** should wear washable clothing and over all a washable gown, preferably with a hood attachment for the protection of the hair. The gown and hood should be removed and the exposed surface disinfected when leaving the sick room, even though temporarily. A good rule is to consider that everything which has been brought into the sick room has become infected and should be carefully disinfected before it is carried out.

The hands of the attendant should be immediately washed and disinfected after any contact with the patient or his clothing. A good supply of towels and tin or porcelain basins for this purpose should be kept on hand. Probably the best disinfectant for this purpose is standard solution of corrosive sublimate No. 3, consisting of one gram to one quart of water. No one should ever leave the sick room without first thoroughly washing the hands in a disinfectant solution, or with carbolic or other antiseptic soap, with especial care to clean and scrub the finger nails. It is best to then soak the hands for two or three minutes in half strength disinfectant solution No. 3 or 4, and then wash them off in fresh water.

A large bottle of such a solution should be kept in the sick room for this purpose. Otherwise the nurse may handle something outside the room leaving the germs thereon to be picked up by some one else. It is probable that 90 per cent of all cases of secondary infection are brought about in this manner. The nurse should carefully avoid soiling door knobs or anything else which may be touched by others. While typhoid fever is both contagious and infectious there is no danger of contracting the disease if we prevent the germs from getting into our mouths. This can be easily done. The only occasion for a second case occurring in a household must come either from ignorance or carelessness. With proper disinfection of the hands and general cleanliness the nurse or attendant may take her meals at the household table. At all events she should not eat in the sick room.

Food and Drink. — The tray, dishes, and other utensils used in the sick room should be set apart for the exclusive use of the patient. Never wash them in the same pan as other dishes for the family. Use a separate dish cloth and wiping towel. First immerse these articles for an hour in a half strength standard disinfectant solution No. 3, 4 or 5 and then boil for half an hour and keep apart from all other household utensils. It is best to use paper napkins, which should be burned. If cloth napkins are used they should be immersed in the same disinfectant solution as the bed and body linen. All solid food brought into the sick room and not consumed by the patient should be placed in paper bags to be removed by the attendant and burned. Liquid foods should be poured into a disinfectant. Neither the nurse nor any other person should be permitted to eat any portion of the food remaining. Nothing should be eaten by a well person while in the sick room nor should anything which has been in the room be eaten. Nurses and attendants should always wash their hands in a disinfectant solution before eating or putting anything into their mouths. It is absolutely necessary that this rule be scrupulously observed.

If milk is delivered to the house in bottles, never let these be taken into the room of the typhoid case. If you do, these bottles may be the means of carrying the disease to someone else. Keep special bottles of your own for the patient's milk. Empty the milk into one of these as soon as received. Then scald out the dairy bottle and keep it as far as possible from the sick room until it is given back to the driver.

Quarantine.—All unnecessary visitors should be excluded from the sick room. If a nurse can be provided, all members of the family should be kept away. Otherwise, one or two persons should be detailed as attendants and all others should be excluded. Certainly there is no need that all the relatives, neighbors and friends should visit the patient. This can do no good but in the majority of instances will do harm, and they take a chance of getting the disease. The quieter the patient is kept, both during illness and convalescence, the better for him. Children, especially, should be carefully excluded. They have little or no sense of cleanliness and are constantly putting their fingers and other things into their mouths. It has been shown that children contract communicable diseases much more readily than grown persons. If visitors are permitted to see the patient they should touch nothing in the room, or if they do, should wash their hands in a disinfectant solution upon leaving. All visitors, including members of the family, should be cautioned not to shake hands with or kiss the patient. No one should sit for any length of time in the sick room unless compelled to do so.

Removal of Excretions.—The discharges from the bowels and kidneys should be received into a bedpan or vessel containing at least a quart of full-strength disinfectants No. 1 or No. 2. Enough of the same should be added to cover them and be thoroughly mixed by stirring. Solid masses should be broken up with a stick which can be burned, or a glass rod which can be disinfected. See that all lumps are thoroughly broken up. Disinfectants cannot kill germs unless they come in contact with them. They should stand in the vessel for not less than an hour. Where there are sewers they may then be emptied into the water closet, taking care not to soil the seats or covers. In the country it is best to deposit the contents of the vessels in a trench. This must be remote, and, if possible, down hill from the well or nearest watercourse. The trench should be about four feet deep and two wide. Each deposit should at once be well covered with quicklime and earth well beaten down. When half filled in this manner the trench should be covered in with earth. But care must be taken that none of the excretions from persons afflicted with typhoid are ever emptied until thoroughly disinfected. Under no circumstances should these be poured out in the neighborhood of springs or wells. It should also be remembered that the water in which typhoid fever patients are bathed necessarily becomes infected. This should also be thoroughly disinfected before being emptied out. Vomited matter and the sputum from the patient also contains the germs of typhoid and should receive the same care and thorough disinfection. These precautions should be continued for some time after the patient has recovered. About three per cent of all cases are carriers of the disease for many months or even years. It is well to request the attending physician to ascertain by means of blood tests whether or not the germs of typhoid have left the system.

A great responsibility rests upon the household in the management of a case of typhoid fever. To pour out the discharges from a patient in the back yard or expose them in open vaults or drains may be, and often is, equivalent to the murder of innocent neighbors by poisoning. Yet this is being done, in many thousands of instances, as the result of ignorance of the fatal nature of the invisible germs of the disease.

Vermin.—Steps should be taken, if necessary, to destroy all such vermin as fleas, bedbugs, lice and especially rats and mice, by means described elsewhere in this volume. The sick room should be carefully screened against flies and mosquitoes. Insects worry sick people and hinder recovery. Above everything else flies should not be permitted to enter the room, or, if they get in, should be killed before they get out. Screens are cheaper than additional cases of typhoid in the family. If flies are numerous in the vicinity a number of vessels containing fly poison should be exposed in the room. If sticky fly paper is used, it must be burned at frequent intervals. Fly traps may be used if care is taken to destroy the insects with boiling water and to burn their bodies or deposit them in a disinfectant. Or single flies may be killed by means of the ordinary fly swatter and then dropped into a disinfectant solution.

After recovery and during convalescence the patient is to be considered dangerous so long as the intestinal discharges continue to be more copious, liquid and frequent than natural; and these should be disinfected until the attending physician advises that it is no longer necessary.

In the event of death the body must be wrapped in a sheet thoroughly soaked in full-strength Standard Disinfectant No. 3 or 4, and placed in an air-tight coffin. This must remain in the sick room until removed for burial. Public funerals and wakes over such bodies are forbidden.

Quarantine. — It is entirely unnecessary to quarantine a case of typhoid fever, or the premises in which it exists, provided proper care is given to all the details of the sick room, as recommended. The use of placards has been largely discontinued in this disease. If the disinfection is practiced as strictly as it should be, there is no danger of the disease being communicated to others from a given case; but constant cleanliness and disinfection are absolutely necessary to secure such result.

Anti-Typhoid Vaccination. — Typhoid fever in normal cases is a self-limiting disease. That is, unless the patient dies, the body develops within itself the power of resisting the virus. The patient then recovers and regains his health even though the germs are still developed in large numbers in the intestines. In recent years many attempts have been made by scientific men to perfect a serum for anti-typhoid vaccination and a number of different typhoid vaccines are now upon the market. The use of typhoid vaccine was first publicly advocated in 1896 by Pfeiffer and Kolle in Germany and by A. Wright in England. In 1904 elaborate experiments were made and since that time the results obtained have been very encouraging. The degree of immunization obtained has not yet been equal to that secured by vaccination against smallpox, but statistics indicate that the likelihood of infection is greatly reduced by this means and that the death rate may be reduced at least one-half. It has been shown that, if proper precautions are observed, anti-typhoid vaccination in healthy persons is harmless and that the personal discomfort caused by its application is ordinarily very slight. The duration of immunity is not yet determined, but it is thought to be at least two and a half years and probably longer. It is the most effective method of protection yet devised against the chronic bacillus carrier. Every member of the American army from the Secretary of War down is now required to be vaccinated against typhoid. And this is believed to be the principal cause of the immunity of the troops in recent army maneuvers.

Anti-typhoid vaccination should always be done by a competent physician. The infection often gives rise to slight fever and some painful local and general symptoms. These disappear in from 24 to 48 hours. It may also result in temporarily weakening the power to resist infection. Hence preventive vaccination should be undertaken before the usual time that epidemics appear. Persons vaccinated should take the strictest precautions to avoid the chance of typhoid infection by carefully boiling all water that is drunk and cleansing the food that is eaten and by rigorous personal hygiene and cleanliness. These precautions need only be taken during a period of two or three weeks at most. No one should be vaccinated who has been exposed to typhoid fever or during the beginning of an attack. In such cases vaccination may aggravate the disease. It should be practiced only upon perfectly healthy subjects, free from all organic or other defects and from local or general ailments no matter what their nature, especially tuberculosis. The vaccination of debilitated or delicate persons should be avoided. Anti-typhoid vaccination is especially recommended for physicians, internes, medical students, male and female nurses in hospitals; persons, members of families in which bacillus carriers have been found; and the population of localities where the disease is frequent, especially young persons of both sexes who have recently come to such localities from more salubrious regions.

MALARIA

This is a germ disease produced by a parasite belonging to the very lowest order of animal life. It attacks and destroys the red cells of the blood. It also produces a toxin or poison that causes the characteristic symptoms of the disease.

Symptoms. — The most common and well-recognized symptoms occur in the cases known as malarial or intermittent fever, fever and ague, or chills and fever. Chilly sensations occur at intervals for several days together with a feeling of fullness in the head and general bodily depression. Then come chills followed by a high fever, with subsequent profuse perspiration. After a few hours the patient returns to a normal condition and feels about as usual until the next attack occurs. The paroxysms of chills and fever occur at various intervals depending upon the particular parasite which produces them. A common form is that which produces a chill every other day. Or there may be a continuous slow fever, or attacks of fever at irregular intervals. In severe cases the brain becomes affected and the malady often terminates in chronic Bright's disease.

Treatment. — Home doctoring is often thought sufficient for malaria, quinine usually being considered a specific. But the constitutional effects of this disease are so serious that a physician should be consulted and his recommendations implicitly followed.

Prevention.—The germ or parasite which causes malaria can be communicated to man only by the bite of the Anopheles mosquito. This species as shown in the illustration has a body which is placed parallel to and almost on the same plane with the front portions of the insect. Hence, when at rest on walls or other objects, the back portion sticks out almost or quite at right angles with the surface upon which it is resting. Observe that the back portion of the common mosquito forms an angle with the front part of its body. Hence both ends of the mosquito point toward the object upon which it rests. There are other differences that clearly differentiate the malarial from the common mosquito, but the one given serves to distinguish between them. The malarial mosquito is preëminently a house gnat. It is scarcely ever seen in the woods or open, but may be found oftentimes in great numbers in all malarial localities, lying quietly during the day in dark corners of rooms or stables. This mosquito practically never bites in the day, but will do so in a darkened room, if a person will remain perfectly quiet. Their favorite time for feeding is in the early part of the night and about daybreak. This accounts for the fact, long observed, that malarial fever is almost invariably contracted at night.

The malarial mosquito bites and then goes back to some dark corner

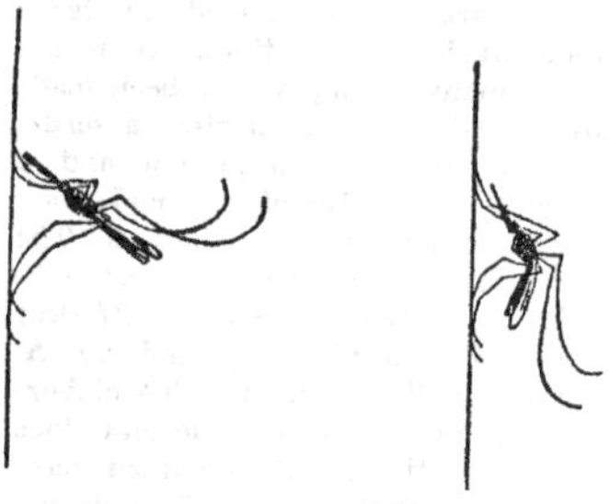

a *Anopheles* (*Malarial Mosquito*) *b* *Culex* (*Common Mosquito*)
Courtesy State Board of Health of Georgia.

where it remains quiescent for forty-eight hours. Then it again comes out to feed. Contrary to the general opinion mosquitoes bite many times. They frequently remain alive for months. The malarial mosquito, particularly, oftentimes lives in cellars and attics throughout the entire winter. If one of these mosquitoes bites a person with malaria, the parasites are sucked in along with the blood. They pass into the stomach of the gnat and make their way ultimately into the body substance. Here the parasites undergo a series of multiplications. A single bacterium sometimes produces as many as ten thousand young malarial parasites. After these have developed fully, which requires eight days in warm weather, they make their way into the venom gland of the mosquito. Here they remain until it bites. They are then injected into the body of the individual attacked along with the poison.

After getting into the human blood, each parasite attacks a red blood cell, bores into it, and grows at the expense of the cell until it reaches maturity. It then divides up into from seven to twenty-five young parasites which are liberated and each in turn attacks a new cell. This process goes on until a sufficient number of parasites are produced in the individual to cause the symptoms of malaria. The new subject of the disease thereafter becomes a source of danger to others in the vicinity through the intervention of still other malarial mosquitoes.

Hence the proper way to avoid malaria is to screen houses so that mosquitoes cannot enter them. Persons in malarial districts should not sit on open porches at night. They should also be very careful to sleep under properly constructed nets. If these measures are taken there is absolutely no danger of any one ever contracting the disease. These precautions are not necessary in the daytime.

Those who have the disease are a constant source of danger to people living in the vicinity. Hence they should be doubly careful to avoid being bitten by mosquitoes at night. They should vigorously treat the disease until the parasites are no longer present in their bodies. They then cease to be a menace to others.

Many children have malaria without showing symptoms. If allowed to sleep without being properly covered with a net, they are very apt to infect a large number of malarial mosquitoes. The blood of children in malarial localities should be examined from time to time. If the parasites be found they should be given the proper remedies until a cure is effected.

Almost all negroes in malarial localities harbor the parasites, though very few of them show symptoms of their presence. It is, therefore, very important that they be treated properly. Their white neighbors should see to it, for their own safety, that negroes do not sleep in houses unprotected by nets.

If the precautions herein detailed were properly carried out everywhere for even a few months, malaria would practically cease to exist. Nor could it recur in any locality until individuals suffering from the disease imported it from other places.

Yellow Fever.—Yellow fever like malaria can be communicated to man only by the bites of mosquitoes, in this case the Stegomyia Calopus variety. From the standpoint of preventive medicine the procedure indicated for the two diseases is entirely similar.

TUBERCULOSIS OR CONSUMPTION

A nation-wide campaign has been set on foot for the extermination of consumption — often called "The Great White Plague" — the ravages of which justify the characterization of this disease as "the captain of the men of death." Several voluntary associations are engaged in this campaign and a number of the great insurance companies are giving their active co-operation. The following is a summary of the latest scientific information upon this subject prepared under the supervision of the Metropolitan Life Insurance Company of New York:

Its Nature.—This disease, known also as "phthisis," is caused by a living germ, called the "bacillus tuberculosis," which multiplies with great rapidity. The germ is called "bacillus" because it resembles a little rod, this being the meaning of the word "bacillus." A picture of these germs, much magnified, is shown on another page.

Outside of the human body, the germ may live in warm, moist, dark places for a long time. By direct sunlight the germ is killed in a few hours, in a few days by ordinary daylight, and immediately by boiling water. If the germ finds its way into the lungs it rapidly increases in number. A strong, healthy person will resist the germs, but in an individual who is weak, they rapidly multiply until the lungs are consumed and the person dies.

The germ generally obtains access to the body through the mouth, and most frequently lodges in the air passages of the lungs. It may, however, get into the glands of the neck, attack the throat, the bowels, the kidneys, the brain, or any other organ of the body as well as the bones of the joints. Fortunately, strong, healthy people possess the power of resisting these germs, otherwise it is likely that the disease would kill off whole communities. Nearly everybody at some period of his life breathes in the living germs of the disease, but owing to the power of resistance of a healthy body they are not able to multiply. If they do not immediately die they produce little lumps called "tubercles," from which comes the name "tuberculosis." If these form in the lungs, they continue to grow, soften, break open, and are eventually expelled by coughing or otherwise. For this reason, the sputum, or "spit," of an individual who has consumption is filled with the germs of tuberculosis.

How the germs of consumption are carried from the sick to the well.

Consumption's allies—avoid them and you are safeguarding against the disease.

In early stages of the disease the germ is found in small numbers in the sputum, in larger numbers as the disease progresses, and in countless millions in the later stages. Unless this sputum is destroyed by burning or by disinfectants, it may become the most common method of carrying tuberculosis to other individuals.

Not Hereditary.—It is generally believed now that consumption is not inherited. It is true that the children of consumptives are frequently of low vitality and generally of poor physique. This does not mean, however, that they are bound to become consumptives. They will get consumption only if the germ enters their body. Being weak, however, and being unable to resist the action of the bacillus, they are more susceptible than individuals who are physically well and strong. There is no reason whatever why such children, if properly cared for, should not grow to healthy and well-developed men and women who will never be consumptive.

It is possible to have the disease for some time and not know it or suspect it. An examination of the patient's chest by a competent physician and a microscopical examination of the sputum may discover it, but if both of these tests fail, it does not definitely mean that tuberculosis is not present.

Repeated examinations should be made from time to time if the earlier symptoms of tuberculosis are present. Among these (if they are present, the individual should consult a physician at once) are the following: Slight cough, lasting a month or longer; loss of weight; slight fever, each afternoon; bleeding from the lungs; tired feeling. We repeat, if these symptoms are present, do not delay, but consult a physician at once.

From what has been said above, it will be seen that as consumption is a germ disease, it is a communicable disease and as such a preventable disease. If it is treated properly in its early stages it is a curable disease.

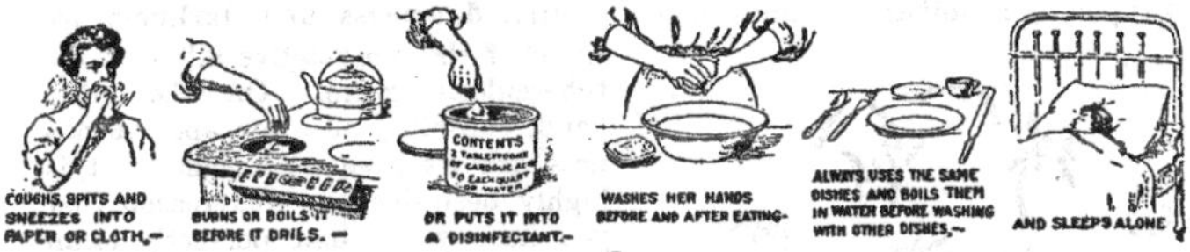

A careful consumptive—not dangerous to live with.

In case of consumption look to these for cure.

The Extent of the Disease.—Tuberculosis is the great disease of middle life. It causes about one-third of all the deaths that occur between the ages of twenty and fifty years. More deaths result from consumption than from any other disease. It is estimated that two hundred thousand people die each year in the United States from tuberculosis. Between the ages of fifteen and forty-five years, one-third of all deaths are from tuberculosis. Between the ages of twenty and thirty-five, one-half of all deaths are from tuberculosis. During the four years of the Civil War, the total loss of life was two hundred and five thousand and seventy. In the same time, the tubercle bacillus destroyed in the United States alone over seven hundred thousand people.

When we hear of yellow fever, we make every possible effort to stamp out the disease at once. The same is true of smallpox and other so-called contagious diseases, and yet it is estimated that the total number of deaths from yellow fever in the

United States during one hundred years was only one hundred thousand. The annual economic loss from consumption in the United States is $330,000,000.

The Spread of the Disease.—The great medium for the spread of the disease is the consumptive's spit. When the consumptive coughs or sneezes, he fills the air before him with particles of moisture, almost too small to be seen, which are filled with germs. When he spits upon the floor, or the walk, millions of germs are deposited, and are ready to find their way upon the clothes or hands and

Bacteria of consumption.

thus into the mouths and into the lungs, stomach and intestines of children who play upon the floor, or walk. The careless consumptive's handkerchief, the pocket in which he carries it, the bedding, especially the pillow cover, and the towel used by him, are laden with germs.

When a member of the family has consumption and the spit is not carefully collected and destroyed, the house is apt to become infected and other members of the family take the disease.

When a consumptive removes or dies, and other persons move into the house, some of them are very apt to take the disease unless the house is thoroughly cleaned and disinfected, particularly the floors and walls.

Impure air and deficient sunlight favor the development of the bacillus. For this reason a consumptive is more frequently met with in the crowded parts of cities, where houses are built closely together, air cannot circulate freely, and sunlight does not enter. Overcrowded, poorly ventilated houses, offices and workshops, all tend to spread the disease. Consumption is much less common where people live in separate houses.

Dirt, dampness and darkness are three of the most active allies of the tuberculosis germ. On the other hand, sunshine, pure air and cleanliness are its greatest enemies. It is highly desirable for this reason that you keep your home perfectly clean and constantly remove from it dust and dirt. Every room should have a thorough spring and fall house cleaning each year. Rooms which have been occupied by consumptives frequently become infected with the germs. Such rooms should never be used without having been previously disinfected. Remember that the most active agent for spreading tuberculosis is the spit of the consumptive. If this is thoroughly burned or destroyed at once, there is little danger of infection.

If the body is weakened by overwork, or by dissipation or by excesses of any kind, the individual is more apt to contract tuberculosis than if he keeps himself strong and well. In fact, healthy persons, living a proper life, when infected frequently get over the disease so quickly and so readily that they do not even know that they have had it.

People addicted to the use of alcohol in any form are more likely to have tuberculosis than others.

The Cure of the Disease.—Consumption is no longer the hopeless disease of the past—it is curable. The earlier it is detected in an individual case, the surer the cure. Therefore, help your friend, your neighbor, your relative, to recognize and treat his disease at the start.

If you should be unfortunate enough to be afflicted with tuberculosis or consumption, first of all get the advice of a reliable physician, and follow his instructions conscientiously and religiously. There is no antitoxin for treating tuberculosis such as is used for diphtheria. The only cure we know for tuberculosis is to increase the bodily strength, so that the body will resist and gradually destroy the germ. This is a slow process. Its principal means are plenty of fresh air all the time, plenty of good food, rest, freedom from worry and out-of-door life. Medicines are of comparatively little use in the cure of consumption. Patent medicines do not cure consumption. Most of them are alcoholic drinks in disguise, which are dangerous to the consumptive.

Sanatoria.—For the best treatment of tuberculosis, so as to afford the patient outdoor treatment as much as possible, special hospitals, called sanatoria, have been erected in all parts of the United States and Europe. It is highly desirable, in order to cure the consumptive as rapidly as possible, that he be treated in such a sanatorium. There are, however, as yet not sufficient of these to accommodate everybody, and for this and for other reasons it is frequently necessary for the patient to be treated at home. If the latter method be resorted to, it should be done under the advice of a physician.

Home Treatment.—The physician will tell you how to carry on this home treatment in the best manner. A person who has pulmonary tuberculosis, or consumption, is not dangerons to have in the house if he is careful and clean, and if he follows the usual rules laid down to prevent infection of other members of the family. The patient's window should be open day and night and he should occupy the room alone. Preferably there should be no carpet or rug on the floor. The sheets and the body linen should be frequently washed and well boiled. The room should be dusted with a damp cloth or a damp broom. The food which he eats should be used by him exclusively and should be well boiled.

The Prevention of the Disease.—To prevent consumption, two things are required: (1) the removal of the source of contagion; (2) the removal of the predisposing cause. These can be accomplished, (1) by collecting and destroying the germs in the consumptive's spit, and (2) by keeping the body in good general health, so that it will be able to resist the germs.

The consumptive, if he carefully destroys all his spit, is harmless. He should preferably use paper napkins, which can be burned immediately. They should not be carried loose in the pocket after using. When coughing or sneezing, he should hold one of these before his mouth. If the handkerchief is ever used for this purpose it should be immediately disinfected, by being placed either in boiling water or in a 3 per cent solution of carbolic acid.

He should spit into a pasteboard sputum cup, which at the end of each day can be burned, or into a vessel which can be easily and completely cleaned daily. The ordinary spittoon is most difficult to clean, and should never be used by a consumptive. When the consumptive is at work, riding on the street car, or traveling, he should use a pocket sputum cup or flask which can be kept tightly closed until he can empty it at night.

The Careful Consumptive is Not Dangerous.—Tuberculosis is not contagious by the breath (except when the consumptive coughs or sneezes), or in the same way as smallpox, or diphtheria, or scarlet fever, but through the sputum.

Even though every effort is made to collect and destroy the germ it is probable that every one of us, on account of the prevalence of the disease and the large number of consumptives who are careless or do not understand the importance of destroying their spit, will receive at some time or other the germs in our lungs. It is most important, therefore, that the lungs be in proper condition and that the general health be good.

Thorough ventilation of bedrooms is one of the most important means to this end. Too often the bedroom is small, dark and unventilated, the windows sometimes being nailed shut. To nail one's bedroom window shut is to drive a nail in one's coffin. We spend more hours each day in our bedrooms than in any other room in the house, yet they are usually the smallest, worst lighted, and least ventilated.

Sleeping out of doors is urged upon the consumptive, and it is probable that most of us would be in far better condition to resist tuberculosis if we slept out of doors a good portion of the year.

Excessive hours of hard work, whether on the farm or in the factory, lower the vitality. Insufficient food or indigestible food also injures the health. The steady drinking of alcoholic liquors, whether or not we become drunk, injures the body.

SMALLPOX AND CHICKENPOX

Smallpox is an acute, contagious, infectious disease characterized by the well-known eruption of small boils or pustules all over the body. Varioloid and variola are terms sometimes applied to mild cases of smallpox under the mistaken impression that they are a different and less virulent disease. This is not the case. The mildest cases communicate the disease in its most malignant form. Smallpox is sometimes called by false names, such as Cuban itch, Porto Rico itch, Porto Rico scratches, or elephant itch, to conceal its existence in the community. There are, in fact, no such diseases and this practice is most reprehensible. Smallpox has all the characteristics of a germ disease, but the germ which causes it has not yet been identified. It may occur at any season of the year, but is most prevalent in winter.

History.—No other disease, not excepting the bubonic plague or "Black Death," has contributed an equally interesting chapter to the history of mankind. It is known to have prevailed in the far east many centuries before the Christian era. Europe was first visited with smallpox in the sixth century. Later it was widely disseminated by the crusades. It depopulated an entire colony in Greenland in the thirteenth century, contributed largely to the conquest of Mexico by Cortez in the sixteenth century, and destroyed far larger numbers of the American Indians than did the firearms and fire water of the white man. By the eighteenth century smallpox was distributed throughout Great Britain and the continent of Europe. Over 90 per cent of the population is said to have been affected and about one-tenth of the entire mortality was caused by this disease. More than one-half of all the living are said to have been scarred and disfigured by it. Historians aver that women whose faces were not pockmarked were the exception. Not a little of the great reputation of famous beauties of this period is said to have been due to chance immunity from this disease. Smallpox before the days of vaccination spared neither high nor low. It spread its terrors alike in the homes of rich and poor, and even penetrated into the palaces of princes. More than a score of deaths in royal families were thus caused. A half dozen reigning monarchs were attacked but recovered. More than once it threatened the total extinction of representative European dynasties. George Washington, during his early manhood, was "strongly attacked by the smallpox" while on a visit to the West Indies.

Smallpox is now a rare malady and

is rapidly vanishing. This great change has been wrought in a single century by the discovery of vaccination on May 14, 1796, by Edward Jenner. On that day Jenner performed the first vaccination on a human being. Eight weeks later he fearlessly exposed his patient in smallpox hospitals and brought him into contact with smallpox patients without causing him to contract the disease. Vaccination has been called the greatest discovery ever made for the preservation of the human species. Millions of lives have been saved by it, and a thorough and continuous practice of vaccination will undoubtedly blot out smallpox from the face of the earth.

Jenner's discovery was based on a widespread belief that persons who had become infected with a similar disease of cattle, known as cowpox, were thereafter immune from smallpox infection. A remark made in his presence to this effect by a milkmaid was the "awakening impulse which after years of study and experiment culminated in the discovery which has conferred the greatest benefits upon the human race."

The practice of vaccination up to a comparatively recent date was not always surrounded by proper sanitary safeguards. The vaccine was sometimes impure and sufficient care was not always taken to prevent infection of the sore with the germs of tetanus (lockjaw) and other diseases. The progress of modern science has now overcome all these dangers. Vaccination at the hands of a competent physician is not only an entirely safe and almost painless operation: it is an absolute preventive of smallpox and the only possible safeguard against its ravages. Vaccination against smallpox is compulsory upon all inhabitants by law in Germany and Japan. In both countries it has been practically stamped out. The vaccination of school children is compulsory by regulation of the school board or board of health in many American cities, but is not enjoined upon the general public by state or national legislation. Hence sporadic outbreaks are constantly occurring. The disease invariably attacks persons who have never been vaccinated and may also attack those who were vaccinated in childhood, but have not been revaccinated after an interval of ten or more years. In such cases, however, the disease assumes a milder form.

Opposition to compulsory vaccination when not due to mere ignorance or prejudice is based upon one of the following grounds: i. e., (1) that vaccination does not protect, (2) that it may transmit other diseases or is otherwise harmful or dangerous, or (3) that compulsory vaccination is an invasion of the rights of an individual. The experience of Japan and Germany, and especially the immunity of the German army as the result of vaccination during the Franco-Prussian war, 1870-1 (when the opposing French army was ravaged by smallpox), and the universal testimony of expert sanitarians, proves that the first of these objections is totally unfounded.

The chance that vaccination may transmit other diseases, or otherwise prove injurious to the patient has now been entirely overcome. Arm to arm vaccination was formerly the custom, i. e., the scab from a successful vaccination was used as a vaccine for others. Occasionally such diseases as tuberculosis and syphilis were transmitted in this way. But this method is a practice of the past. The only vaccine now employed is prepared from healthy young calves under Government supervision. It is true that there is the possibility of blood poisoning or lockjaw if the sore become infected. But this will not occur if the vaccination is properly performed and protected by a suitable dressing. The danger from this source is much less than that from pricks and scratches from thorns or minute splinters, or the claws of domestic pets. In a word, the possible danger from vaccination is grossly exaggerated. Pure vaccine is harmless and it is doubtful whether a single death has been caused by vaccination conducted in a proper manner.

The notion that compulsory vaccination is an invasion of the rights of an individual might be sustained if a person could suffer from the disease without requiring the care of other members of society, and subjecting them to the dangers of infection. The loathesomeness of smallpox, the helplessness of the sufferer and the necessity of providing pesthouses for the treatment of patients of this disease bring the subject of vaccination well within the police power of state and nation. Every effort should be made to arouse public sentiment in favor of a state and national compulsory vaccination law.

A Vaccination Creed. — Seven years ago the Department of Health of Chicago made the following declaration of their faith in vaccination:

"First.—That true vaccination—repeated until it no longer 'takes'—always prevents smallpox. Nothing else does.

"Second.—That true vaccination—that is, vaccination properly done on a clean arm with pure lymph and kept perfectly clean and unbroken afterwards—never did and never will make a serious sore.

"Third.—That such a vaccination leaves a characteristic scar, unlike that from any other cause, which is recognizable during life, and is the only conclusive evidence of a successful vaccination.

"Fourth.—That no untoward results ever follow such vaccination; on the other hand thousands of lives are annually sacrificed through the neglect to vaccinate—a neglect begotten of lack of knowledge."

How to Vaccinate.—Vaccination should, as a rule, be performed only by a competent physician, but may be safely performed by anyone if the following instructions are carefully observed: Secure the pure vaccine from a first-class drug store, or if there is no drug store in the vicinity, write or telegraph the state board of health at the capital city of your state, and ask them to forward through the mails enough vaccine for the required number of persons. If buying from a drug store ask for glycerinized lymph. It is both safer and more reliable than the vaccine from dried points. A good plan is to make the inoculation on the inside of the arm above the elbow where the scar will be out of sight. But if preferred, the wound may be made on the leg or, indeed, on any part of the body. The part should be thoroughly washed with soap and hot water. Then rinse with a 50 per cent solution of alcohol. But this must be allowed to fully evaporate. Otherwise it may kill the vaccine. The operator's hands should be thoroughly scrubbed with hot water and soap, preferably carbolic or green soap, with especial attention to the finger nails. If the virus comes on bone points, it is best not to use a knife at all. Scrape the parts with the point over a spot about as large as the little finger nail, until the upper layers of the skin have been rubbed away and serum appears and mingles with the virus which thus gains entrance into the system. If a knife is used for scarifying the parts thoroughly disinfect it in standard solution No. 4, carbolic acid (5 per cent) and afterwards rinse free of the antiseptic solution in boiling water. In either case dry the parts thoroughly before the operation is attempted. If the knife is used, scarify very lightly and stop as soon as the serum appears *and before the red blood commences to flow.* If the wound is deep enough to draw blood there is much more danger of infection and, moreover, the flow of blood tends to wash the virus away.

When the serum begins to run, rub in the vaccine with the knife or vaccine point. If the virus is dry, first dip the point in tepid water which has been freshly boiled. After the virus has been thoroughly rubbed in, leave the scar uncovered until it is dry. Now cover the wound with antiseptic gauze or sterilized gauze, or cotton, and bandage with great care so that the bandage will not get out of place and the wound become infected. The best plan, after covering the wound with gauze, is to cover the gauze and adjacent parts with strips of adhesive surgeon's plaster. The dressing should be changed every day or two until the scab falls off. Sanitary precautions must be taken at every dressing to avoid infecting the wound.

If the vaccination "takes" a small red spot appears at the site of inoculation on the third day. The temperature rises slightly on the third or fourth day, and may continue a little above normal until the eighth or ninth day. On the eleventh or twelfth day the soreness begins to subside and a brownish scab forms over the wound. This becomes dry and hard and falls off on the twenty-first to the twenty-fifth day. It leaves a circular pitted scar. The sore must be kept clean and free from irritation and disturbance. It must not be rubbed or scratched. If, after six or seven days there is an undue degree of inflammation, a physician should be consulted. Practically every case of ill effects from vaccination is due to scratching or picking at the sore, or otherwise handling or dressing it with dirty hands or fingers.

A successful vaccination usually confers immunity from smallpox for life. In other cases the power of resistance seems to decrease with time. Hence adults vaccinated in childhood should be revaccinated if exposed to smallpox or if an epidemic of the disease breaks out in a community. The second vaccination will "take" only on those who need it.

When to Vaccinate.—Every child should be vaccinated during the first year and again at the age of puberty, i. e., twelve or fourteen years of age. If a case of smallpox occurs in the family or neighborhood, or even if it is known to exist in the community, every member of the family should be promptly revaccinated. Inoculation within three days after exposure has been found to give immunity, and if performed as late as the fifth day the attack will be averted or much modified. This is especially the case when revaccination is performed In one recorded case a mother and three small children were vaccinated after the father was taken down with the smallpox. The wife nursed her husband during the disease and took care of her children, but no other member of the family became infected.

Symptoms.—The period of incubation varies from 7 to 20 days, the average being 12 days. Inoculation shortens the time to 7 or 8 days. During this period the symptoms are very slight. The invasion of the disease is sudden. It begins with a chill which may be followed by others. There is severe aching in the small of the back, sometimes in the limbs, intense headache, vomiting and fever. The pulse is rapid and strong. Convulsions often occur in children. An initial rash in the form of a diffused redness somewhat similar to the rash of scarlet fever occurs in a few cases on the second day. The distinctive eruption appears on the third day on the forehead, around the mouth, and on the wrists. Now the temperature, which has been continuously high, begins to fall. Within twenty-four hours the eruption spreads all over the body, and at this stage the disease strongly resembles measles. On the fourth and fifth days the eruption is papular and a characteristic "shotty" sensation is obtained by passing the fingers over the skin.

In the milder cases commonly called varioloid or variola, the fever falls at once after the appearance of the eruption on the third or fourth day, and the patient feels comfortable. The eruption is slight, scattered, and often limited to the face and hands.

There is danger that this disease may be mistaken for measles, scarlet fever, chickenpox or some other infection. The characteristic symptoms are the severity of the attack together with chills, backache, headache and vomiting. The presence of these symptoms associated with a high fever from $102\frac{2}{10}$ to $105\frac{8}{10}$ F. continuing for three or four days and falling on the appearance of an eruption should excite suspicion of smallpox, especially when the disease is prevalent.

The symptoms of measles have been described elsewhere. The cruption occurs about the fourth or fifth day without the fall of temperature which is characteristic of smallpox. In scarlet fever the eruption appears on the second day and gradually fades after two or three days.

Chickenpox (Varicella).—This is a mild disease of children of importance chiefly because the mild cases of smallpox may be mistaken for this disease. Chickenpox is ordinarily confined to children under six years of age. The initial symptoms are much milder than smallpox, although there may be fever, vomiting and pains in the back and legs. The eruption appears during the first twenty-four hours on the back, chest, or face in the form of red pimples which in a few hours become filled with a clear or turbid fluid. In three or four days the eruption dries up into scabs which soon fall off. There is little or no scarring.

Prognosis of Smallpox.—From the sixth to the eighth day after the onset of the disease the vesicles change to pustules with a slight depression in the center surrounded by a red border or halo. The temperature rises again, what is known as the secondary fever sets in, and the general symptoms return. Pustules are especially thick on the face which is much swollen and disfigured. On the twelfth or thirteenth day, about four or five days from their first appearance, the pustules begin to dry up. A few days later the scabs begin to fall off first from the face and later from other parts of the body. The temperature falls to normal and convalescence begins.

Or, in severe cases such as the confluent form or hemorrhagic smallpox, the symptoms become more severe and death occurs, usually at the state of maturation, about the tenth or eleventh day. When recovery takes place, the process of desquamation, or peeling off of the scales, is usually completed in three or four weeks, but may extend to six or eight weeks.

Modes of Infection.—The virus of smallpox has an extraordinary vitality. Infected clothing and other articles may transmit the disease after an interval of months or even years. Contagion may be direct from contact with the patient, or may be carried from the sick room on the person or clothing of the nurse or physician or by means of bedding and other articles. All who enter the sick room should wear a washable hooded gown. This should be disinfected on leaving the room as elsewhere recommended. After leaving the room the hands, face and hair should be washed in a disinfectant solution. The contagion exists in all the secretions and excretions of the body, and the exhalations from the lungs and perspiration. The pus from the pustules is the most fertile source of contagion and the dust from dried pus scales is the usual medium of its dissemination. The disease is most contagious while the eruption is in active progress, but begins to be contagious before the eruption appears and so continues until the process of scaling is complete.

Quarantine.—As soon as the case is known to be smallpox, convey the patient if practicable to a hospital or pesthouse, or isolate in a sick room prepared in all respects as for typhoid fever. Placard the premises. Vaccinate every member of the family. Allow no one to leave the house until the vaccination "takes" or it appears that the person is immune by reason of previous vaccination. The bread-winners may then leave the premises, after proper disinfection under the advice of a physician or public health officer, but must board and room elsewhere during the progress of the disease. Do not allow the nurse and other members of the family to leave the premises or mingle with other persons. All members of the family who have been successfully vaccinated and revaccinated at the outbreak of the disease will be immune. They are in no danger from the disease themselves, but should not come in contact with other persons as they may communicate the disease on their person or clothing. Household pets, flies and insects should be rigidly excluded from the premises. No visitors should be admitted under any pretext. Every sanitary precaution described under typhoid fever should be observed with redoubled vigilance on account of the virulence of the germs. All excreta should be thoroughly disinfected and afterwards buried. After the recovery or death of the patient, not only the sick room but every room in the dwelling should be thoroughly fumigated with formaldehyde or sulphur or preferably with both.

Quarantine should be observed until the process of desquamation is complete. The length of time will depend entirely on the individual case. A safe rule is to await the disappearance of the peculiar red specks at the bottom of the pits or scars. As long as these spots are visible the desquamation is going on.

HOOKWORM DISEASE

This disease has existed from time immemorial, but especial attention has been directed to it in the United States in recent years. Investigations by Dr. Chas. Wardell Stiles of the United States Public Health and Marine Hospital Service and those made under the supervision of the Rockefeller Institution, have proved that this disease is widely prevalent, especially in the southern states, and is of enormous economic importance. It is caused by soil pollution. The eggs and larvæ of the hookworm are passed in large numbers in the discharges of infected persons. Thence they may be communicated to others by contaminated food or water or directly from the soil through the skin. This mode of infection is perhaps the most common in rural districts where all children and many adult members of the population go barefoot in summer and are thus more or less constantly in contact with infected soil. In the rural sections of the southern states all the factors necessary for the propagation of this disease are found. The conditions most favorable to its development are warmth, moisture, an open porous soil and infected people who pollute the soil. North of the Ohio and Potomac Rivers the climate is too cold and in the arid west too dry to favor the disease.

The adult hookworm is about one-third or two-thirds of an inch in

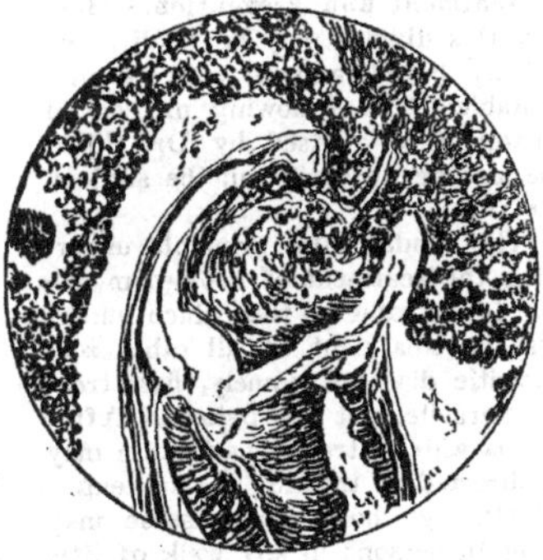

This shows the head of a hookworm as the parasite is feeding, attached to the wall of the bowels. (P. H. & M. H. Service.)

length and about the thickness of a small hairpin, or a No. 30 thread. Its head bends back on its neck like a hook, hence the name. The mouth is equipped with lances which pierce the flesh and make openings through which the blood can escape. These carry a poisonous secretion from a gland in the worm's head which keeps the blood from clotting. In severe cases, the worms occur in enormous numbers and take large quantities of blood from the system. Much more is lost from constant oozing of the wounds. The secretion injected by the worm is poisonous and causes a chronic inflammation which impairs digestion. The wound also affords entrance for disease-producing bacteria to the system. There is also a general lowering of the body tone which exposes the victim to all sorts of diseased conditions.

The symptoms in general are those of malnutrition and may be mild, medium or severe. In general the patient becomes very much weakened, the body looks bloodless and development is stunted. The proverbial laziness of the Georgia "cracker" and other so-called "poor whites" in southern states is now believed to be the result of hookworm infection.

Treatment and Prevention.—Happily this disease may be readily and quickly cured and is entirely preventable. The following method of treatment is advised by Dr. Stiles, the leading authority on the subject. He says:

"The fundamental principle underlying the treatment of hookworm disease is the same as that which underlies the treatment of all other zooparasitic diseases, namely, first treat the parasite, not the patient. After the parasite is treated, attention may be directed to treating the patient.

"Although hookworm disease may occur in persons in any walk of life, it is particularly among the poorer classes that it is found, and the average hookworm patient (children excepted, to a certain extent) can not afford to lose several days' wages to undergo treatment. It is therefore frequently expedient to conduct the treatment Saturday evenings and Sunday mornings. It will often be found difficult to arouse the interest of a community in regard to the presence of hookworm disease and the need of treatment. This can frequently be done, however, if it is borne in mind that the resulting anemia is, in common with other anemias, a frequent cause of amenorrhea.

Warning.—"Notwithstanding that primarily we are to treat the parasite, not the patient, it should be remembered that if too great a quantity of thymol is absorbed by the patient, alarming symptoms and even death may occur. Accordingly, the patient and the patient's family should be carefully warned not to permit the patient under any circumstances to have on the Sunday during which the treatment is given any food or drink containing alcohol, fats, or oil. Patent medicines should be mentioned in particular, because of the alcohol many of them contain, and even milk and butter should be forbidden. I know of one case of serious thymol poisoning which followed promptly after the patient took a copious drink of milk the day thymol was taken.

Preliminary Treatment.—"On Saturday evening give a dose of Epsom salts. The reason is this: The hookworms are surrounded by more or less mucus and partially digested food. Unless this is removed, the thymol may not reach the parasites, but may reach the patient, and this is contrary to what is desired, as thymol is intended for the parasite, not the patient.

Thymol Treatment on Sunday.—"Position of patient: Instruct the patient to lie on his right side immediately before taking the drug and to remain in that position for at least half an hour. The reason for this is that many of these patients have enlarged stomachs, and if they lie on their right side, the drug has the benefit of gravity in passing rapidly from the stomach to the intestine; but if any other position is assumed, the drug may remain in the dilated cardiac portion of the stomach for some hours and result in considerable complaint on the part of the patient and delay of the drug reaching the worms.

"Time of dosage: The time of giving and size of dose should be arranged on one of two plans, depending on existing conditions.

"The plan usually followed is: At 6 a. m., one-half of the total dose of thymol; at 8 a. m., one-half of the total dose of thymol; at 10 a. m., Epsom salts (never castor oil).

"If the case is an especially severe one, or if the patient has, upon the first Sunday's treatment, complained of burning or other effects of thymol, the following plan is adopted: At 6 a. m., one-third of the total dose of thymol; at 7 a. m., one-third of the total dose of thymol; at 8 a. m., one-third of the total dose of thymol (if unpleasant symptoms, as a sensation of severe burning in the stomach, have appeared this third dose should be omitted); at 10 a. m., Epsom salts (never castor oil).

"Food: No food is allowed until after the 10 o'clock dose of Epsom salts, but the patient is permitted to take a glass or so of water after the thymol, if he desires.

"Thymol: Finely powdered thymol in capsules, preferably in five-grain capsules, should be used.

"General rule as to age: In the table of dosage given in the next paragraph, the maximum dose per day to be adopted as a routine is given for various age groups. In determining the dose, however, the rule should be followed of taking the apparent rather than the real age and of not hesitating to cut down the dose even lower in case of unusually severe cardiac symptoms or other unfavorable conditions. Thus for a boy sixteen years old, who appears to be only twelve years old, or in whom the anemia is especially marked, resulting in severe cardiac symptoms, the quantity of thymol should be reduced to the twelve or even the eight-year dose. Some authors give the impression that it is useless to give thymol for this disease unless the full dose is administered. This view is not in harmony with my experience.

"Size of dose: The following doses represent the maximum amount to be used during one day's treatment for the age groups in question. It is practically the same table that the Porto Rican Commission has been using:

	Grains.
Under 5 years old..............	7½
From 5 to 9 years old.........	15
From 10 to 14 years old......	30
From 15 to 19 years old.....	45
From 20 to 59 years old........	60
Above 60 years old.......	30 to 45

Total dose, to be divided as previously indicated.

Repetition of Treatment.—"The foregoing treatment is repeated once a week, preliminary treatment Saturday evening and thymol on Sunday morning, until the patient is discharged.

Duration of Treatment.—"To recognize whether the parasites are all expelled, and therefore to determine when to end the thymol treatment, either of two plans may be adopted, namely:

"Microscopic examination: On Saturday morning make ten microscopic preparations of a fresh stool. If eggs are still present repeat the treatment; if eggs are not found, discontinue the thymol. It takes about forty to sixty minutes to make this examination of ten slides thoroughly.

"Cheese-cloth method: A much easier way of recognizing the completion of the treatment, and for practical results nearly as satisfactory as the miscroscopic examination, is the following: Instruct the patient to wash all of his stools Sunday, Monday and Tuesday, through a cheese cloth and to keep the cheese cloth moist and bring it to the office on Tuesday. While the fecal material will wash through, the worms will be retained in the cloth. Continne treatment as long as worms are found in the cheese cloth.

Other Treatment. — "If desired, iron may be administered on the days on which the thymol is not taken. It is a good plan, however, not to give iron during the first week, for it is quite important to convince the patient that the thymol treatment is the one which is really accomplishing the lasting good. If the drug is taken Sunday, the patient is likely to begin to feel some benefit by Wednesday or Thursday; his family is likely to notice it on Thursday or Friday. If iron is given during the first week, the conclusion may possibly be drawn by the patient that it is really the iron which is causing the improvement, and he may discontinue the thymol. Of the two, the thymol is, of course, the far more important, for it reaches the parasite, while the iron reaches only the patient."

The prevention of hookworm disease lies in proper sanitation to prevent soil pollution, and especially in the construction of sanitary privies. State laws to this end, if properly enforced by an adequate system of local supervision, would undoubtedly put an end to the disease within comparatively few years. Those interested in this subject should address a letter or postal card to the Surgeon-General of the United States, Washington, D. C., requesting detailed information.

FOREIGN DISEASES

A small class of communicable diseases sometimes occur in the United States as the result of infection from foreign parts. Notable among these are Asiatic cholera, bubonic plague and leprosy.

Asiatic Cholera.—This disease is native to India. Thence it has spread in epidemic form from time to time throughout the civilized world. It is caused by a specific micro-organism sometimes called the "comma" bacillus on account of its shape. The presence of this is often the only test by which this disease can be distinguished from gastro-enteritis, ptomaine poisoning and other similar diseases. Asiatic cholera closely resembles typhoid fever as regards modes of infection, and should be treated in an entirely similar manner. Like typhoid it may be spread by healthy carriers and communicated by the mild or "walking" cases of the disease. There is an anti-cholera vaccine similar to the anti-typhoid vaccine, by means of which the death rate has been greatly lowered. This disease is entirely preventable if the precautions recommended under typhoid fever are observed. Needless to say a physician should always be summoned even in the mildest cases.

The period of incubation is from one to five days, although it may be greatly prolonged. The symptoms are similar to ptomaine poisoning: vomiting, diarrhœa, sub-normal temperature, loss of pulse, suppression of urine and collapse. They are common to the action of various poisons and can only be distinguished by a competent physician.

Bubonic Plague (Black Death).—This historic disease which destroyed upwards of 50 per cent of the population of England in the fourteenth century has, from time to time, ravaged nearly every part of the civilized world. It is caused by a vegetable micro-organism, the Bacillus pestis. Rats and other small rodents are very susceptible to this disease and it is communicated by them to man through the medium of fleas. There are three types of plague: (a) bubonic, characterized by glandular swelling. This is the form transmitted from rats to man by means of fleas; (b) pneumonic, which is very much like pneumonia and which may be transmitted by contact infection in the same manner as typhoid fever; (c) septicemic, in which the patient is literally saturated with plague bacilli. This is transmitted by contact infection. The mortality ranges from 15 per cent up to as high as 50 per cent or 75 per cent. Death in the septicemic type is a matter of hours; in the pneumonic type, of days; and in the bubonic type, of one or two weeks. In rats the disease may become chronic. It is most prevalent among rats when they are shut up in their holes in winter, but is most often communicated to human beings during summer. Then the rats are abroad and the fleas which have bitten the infected rodents are widely scattered through the community. The disease, however, may be communicated at any season of the year. The only remedy is the destruction of rats by means elsewhere recommended.

Leprosy.—Leprosy is a communicable disease of the skin occurring very rarely in the United States, fewer than three hundred cases having been reported. The chief interest in this malady is due to its supposed frequency in Biblical times. An almost insane fear of leprosy has been caused by a general knowledge of what is said about it in the Bible, but its virulence, at least in modern times, is believed to be greatly exaggerated. There are said to be fifty or more lepers engaged in various occupations in the city of London. These are not regarded as dangerous to the public health.

CONTAGIOUS DISEASES OF ANIMALS

There is a small group of contagions diseases of animals which are occasionally contributed to man. These include, notably, anthrax, glanders and rabies. Anthrax and glanders may be communicated by contact infection, but rabies occurs only from the bite of dogs or other infected animals. A veterinary physician should be promptly sent for in all cases of anthrax, glanders or farcy and his recommendations faithfully observed. Carcasses of animals dead of these diseases should be immediately buried in a grave not less than six feet deep. Eight or ten inches of unslaked lime should be placed in the bottom of the grave and a similar amount spread over the carcass before the earth is filled in. The site for burial should be distant from any stream or other source of water supply and a strong fence should be erected to enclose it. Stables and all objects with which the dead animal has come in contact should be thoroughly disinfected. The germs of these diseases and their spores often retain their vitality for many years. Hence too much care cannot be given to the process of disinfection.

Rabies (Hydrophobia).—This is a specific communicable disease which affects chiefly the canine race, although all warm-blooded animals, including man, are susceptible to it. There is a widely prevalent belief that if persons or animals are bitten by a dog they are liable to become rabid if the dog should contract the disease at any future time. It will be a great comfort to many persons who have been bitten by animals to know that there is no foundation for this impression. Rabies is transmitted only by animals that are actually diseased at the time the bite is inflicted. Every animal or person bitten does not necessarily develop the disease. This depends on the location and size of the wound, the flow of blood produced and other conditions. The nearer the bite is located to the central nervous system and the deeper it is, the greater danger of a fatal result. Rabies is believed to be caused by a specific germ but this has not yet been identified.

Symptoms.—There are two types of rabies: (1) the furious, violent or irritable; (2) the dumb or paralytic. Cases of furious rabies in a dog usually develop between three weeks and three months after the animal has been infected. A marked change in the disposition of the animal should arouse suspicion. An affectionate dog may become morose and depressed. A snappy, treacherous dog may become mild or affectionate. Then comes an irresistible tendency to roam. A dog will fight or bite at any restraint which interferes with its freedom. He may roam about for several days, aimlessly, in a nervous and irritable condition. He tends to eat or chew indigestible objects such as rags, leather, straw, feathers, sticks and the like. He becomes unable to swallow and his saliva becomes frothy from constant champing of the jaws. But foaming at the mouth is not a reliable symptom, nor is fear of water, since rabid dogs sometimes swim streams. When tired of roving a dog tends to return home and hide in some secluded place.

Paralysis of the throat sets in early. This changes the normal bark of the affected dog to a long, resonant, peculiarly drawn-out cry, like the yelp of a coyote. Later the paralysis extends to the muscles of the jaw. This causes the lower jaw to drop and the tongue to hang out, collect dirt and appear dry and black in color. The pupil of the eye dilates, the paralysis extends to the hind legs and the dumb form of the disease results. Death follows in from four to eight days after development of the first symptoms.

The dumb or paralytic form of rabies in the dog is much more infrequent. The dog is depressed and seeks quiet spots in which to hide. The first symptom observable is often paralysis of the lower jaw, suggesting that the animal may have a bone in its throat. Paralysis quickly progresses and death results in from one to three days.

Rabies in Cattle.—The symptoms are similar to those of the dog. There is loss of appetite, stoppage of the secretion of milk, great restlessness, anxiety, manifestation of fear and change in the disposition of the animal. Then comes excitation or madness, loud bellowing, violent butting, with an insane desire to attack other animals and sometimes the desire to bite. The paralysis progresses rapidly with loss of flesh and finally the animal lies in a comatose condition and dies, usually in from four to six days. The temperature remains normal or even sub-normal.

Rabies in Cats.—The animal hides in a dark corner and dies unobserved in the course of a day or two, or becomes violent and suddenly attacks animals or persons, especially children. The cat loses its voice or mews hoarsely. It becomes emaciated and succumbs within a few days.

Other animals as horses, sheep, goats, hogs, chickens and wild animals exhibit much the same symptoms.

Rabies appear to be spreading, but can be readily controlled by proper local regulations for licensing and muzzling dogs, since the disease is almost always spread to other animals by dogs. As many as sixteen persons have been bitten by a single small dog, which also wounded a great many other animals.

Treatment for Rabies. — Any wound made by a dog or other animal showing symptoms of rabies should be promptly cauterized. Go to a doctor or drug store, if there is one at hand. Otherwise cauterize the wound with nitric acid, carbolic acid or if necessary red-hot iron. Or tincture of iodine may be used, if nothing better is at hand. The best agent is nitric acid. Carry this on a swab or glass rod to every recess and part of the wound. Carbolic acid and other acids are less efficient; nitrate of silver is useless. A red-hot iron is not as effective as a suitable acid, is very painful and makes a wound more severe than is necessary. Great care must be observed when using strong acids or red-hot iron about the face. Children or very nervous subjects should preferably be put under an anæsthetic before the cautery is used.

Capture the suspected animal alive, if possible, by means of a lasso or net, or by turning a box or barrel over it. Or snare it by means of a loop of stout cord on the end of a pole. Put the animal into a stout box or pen but take care not to injure or mistreat it, or deprive it of food and water. If it remains alive and well for ten days there is no danger of rabies. But if it dies or the symptoms become unmistakable, send the head to the nearest laboratory for examination.

In killing an animal suspected of rabies avoid shooting through the head or beating on the head. This may interfere with a proper examination. Shoot the animal through the back or behind the shoulders. Cut off the head close to the shoulders, wrap it in a cloth wrung out of a standard solution of bichloride of mercury (1:500), place it in a new tin pail with a tight-fitting cover and pack the pail in a larger bucket or box surrounded by ice. Ship by express to the laboratory and notify the director by telegram of the shipment.

Should the investigation show the existence of rabies, the only method of treatment which offers any protection is immunization by the Pasteur vaccine. This requires about three weeks and usually demands attendance at a hospital or sanitarium, but may be given by any competent physician. The Pasteur treatment, if given in time, is almost always successful. The proportion of failures is less than 1 per cent, whereas from 10 per cent to 15 per cent of untreated persons who have been bitten by rabid animals develop the disease.

CHAPTER VI

PREVENTABLE DISEASES OF CHILDREN

SAVE THE BABIES—HEALTH AND DISEASE—DISEASES OF THE EYES—DIGESTIVE DISTURBANCES—SOOTHING SIRUP—SYMPTOMS OF COMMUNICABLE DISEASES—INFANTILE PARALYSIS—CEREBRO-SPINAL MENINGITIS—DIPHTHERIA—SCARLET FEVER—MEASLES—CHICKENPOX—WHOOPING COUGH—MUMPS—PARASITIC DISEASES

SAVE THE BABIES

A normal, well born baby is hard to kill. Nature intends that every such baby shall be well and strong, and grow to maturity. Yet the census shows that of the two and one-half million babies born every year in the United States, one-half die before they reach their twenty-third year. One-fourth never reach their fifth birthday; one-eighth, or nearly one-third of a million, die within the first year of life. One-third of all deaths occur under the fifth year of age; one-fifth, during the first year of life. The chance of living a week is less for a new born child than for a man of ninety. The chance of living a year is less than for a man of four score.

Since the rise of the germ theory of disease, wonderful discoveries have been made by the high power microscope as to the effects of germ life upon human health. It has now been proved that a large part of the mortality among infants is due to preventable causes. Much of this death rate is due to dirt. By this is not necessarily meant uncleanliness in the ordinary sense of dirt which can be seen, but a lack of sanitary precautions in the scientific sense, resulting in dirt invisible to the naked eye but which under the microscope is seen to contain millions of injurious bacteria. The best proof of the vitality of infants is that so many do live and grow up in spite of the unsanitary conditions with which they are surrounded, and the poisonous milk and other substances they are compelled to swallow.

Now that science has shown that so many deaths among infants are preventable, a nation-wide campaign to save the babies has been set on foot. A special effort has been made to discover the sanitary and other rules that must be followed by mothers to keep their babies well, and cause them to thrive and grow strong. The following is a collection of these rules as laid down by the public health authorities throughout

Save the babies.

the United States. It contains the latest and most authentic scientific information obtainable.

What Kills Babies?—Out of every hundred deaths under two years of age, thirty-five are the result of improper food and feeding. About ninety-five per cent of these are avoidable. Twenty-six are due to accidents and defects at birth. About one-half are avoidable. Eighteen are caused by impure air diseases (pneumonia and bronchitis); seventy-five per cent avoidable. Two are caused by tuberculosis and six by acute contagious diseases. All of these are avoidable. The remainder are due to miscellaneous causes, many of which could be and ought to be avoided.

The two principal factors which multiply the deaths of infants are the denial of its birthright—its mother's breasts—and the heat of summer. In other words, the bottle feeding of infants in warm weather is what causes the death rate to run extremely high. Ten times as many bottle-fed babies succumb to diarrhœal diseases as breast-fed babies. When the mother from necessity or convenience takes away the natural food of the child—her own breasts—she takes from it nine-tenths of its chance of life. Hot weather in itself has little to do with the death rate of infants from diarrhœa, as breast-fed children do not show much, if any, increase of death rate during the summer months. The two factors that bring about the high death rate, namely, bottle feeding and the hot season, combine to produce a single condition, namely, milk containing a dangerous quantity of injurious bacteria or germs. When the child takes nourishment from its mother's breast it gets a practically sterile or germ-free food. When it is fed modified cow's milk or other artificial food from a bottle, especially in hot weather, it may be, and often is, swallowing a quick or slow poison. This, however, is wholly preventable if proper sanitary precautions to insure strict scientific cleanliness are observed.

HEALTH AND DISEASE

Fontanelles.—In the middle line from before backwards on the top of a baby's head in the early weeks of his life, are two openings or soft places not yet covered with bony formation. The one in front is called the "anterior fontanelle." This closes in five or six weeks. But the larger one, just back of the forehead, is usually not closed until the child is a year and a half old or a little older. If widely open as the time for closure approaches, or if the closure is much delayed, it may indicate rickets or other serious diseased condition. In such cases the advice of the family physician should be had.

Respiration. — Trustworthy information about respiration, pulse and temperature are a great help in judging when to send for the doctor. The normal standards are given below. But remember that the action of a baby's lungs and heart is quickly accelerated by exercise or by excitement. And respiration, pulse and temperature are often much affected by causes which are comparatively trivial. Both the pulse-rate and respiration are more regular and slower in sleep than while awake. There is a progressive decrease in the rapidity of the pulse and respiration from infancy to adult life.

Approximately, the number of respirations per minute at different ages are:

At birth,	35 or more
" 1 year,	27
" 2 years,	25
" 6 "	22
" 12 "	20
In adult life,	15 to 17

In serious illness, as, for instance, in pneumonia, young children may breathe as rapidly as 60 to 80 times in the minute.

Pulse.—The rate of the pulse in health at different ages is:

In the first month,	120 to 140
At 1 year,	110 to 120
" 2 years,	100 to 110
" 6 "	90 to 95
" 12 "	80 to 88
In adult life,	72 or lower.

These are the rates while at rest. During infancy a rise of twenty, thirty or more beats per minute is not uncommon as the result of slight effort or disturbance. In the serious acute diseases, as in scarlet fever or pneumonia, the pulse may run to 160, 180, or higher.

Temperature.—A training in motherhood should include the use of the clinical thermometer so that correct observations on the temperature and its variations may reveal indications of the approach of serious conditions. Buy a good clinical thermometer at your drug store. Or ask your physician to get one for you and explain to you how to use it.

The normal temperature of the human body is about 98½° F. In early infancy, it is slightly higher than from later childhood on. The temperature of 100° indicates the presence of fever; 102° to 103° constitutes moderate fever; 104° to 105° shows a high fever; above 105° means a very high and very dangerous fever.

DISEASES OF THE EYES

Ophthalmia Neonatorum (Infantile Blindness).—About 15 per cent of all cases of total blindness are caused by inflammation of the eyes in new-born babies. This disease is always due to an infection entering the eyes of the baby at the time of, or shortly after birth. It may be almost always prevented by proper care and by early and correct treatment. If precautions are not taken, and the disease develops and runs its course unchecked, the sight is totally destroyed, often within a fortnight.

For All Mothers.—All women during pregnancy should thoroughly perform daily external cleansing with soap and water and a clean wash cloth. Should the pregnant woman have any irritating discharges, or even profuse white discharge, she should be instructed to immediately consult her physician or the nearest dispensary.

For All Children. — Immediately after the delivery of the head, and before the delivery of the body, the eyelids should be carefully cleaned by means of absorbent cotton or a soft linen cloth, dipped into warm water that has been boiled or boric acid (saturated) solution. A separate cloth should be used for each eye, and the lids washed, from the nose outward, free from all mucus, blood or discharges. All wipes should be burned after using. No opening of the lids should be attempted. At this time also the lips and nose should be wiped free of mucus in like manner, and the little finger, wrapped with a piece of moist linen, should be passed into the child's mouth and any accumulated mucus removed by an outward sweep of the finger. As soon after birth as possible, the eyelids should be again wiped clean of mucus, and two drops of a one per cent solution of nitrate of silver should be dropped into each eye. One application only of the silver solution should be made. Ordinarily no further attention should be given the eyes for several hours.

The silver nitrate solution is best kept in a dark-colored bottle with a ground glass stopper. The neck of the bottle should measure about half an inch in diameter. The glass rod used is six inches long, very smooth and round at each end. The silver solution will keep for many months, but it is best to renew it about once in six weeks.

Each time that the child is bathed, the eyes should be first wiped clean, as above described, with the boric acid solution. The hands of the person charged with the care of the child must be washed with soap and dried with a clean towel before the eyes of the child are touched. Everything that is brought near the eyes must be, in every instance, absolutely clean.

The cotton that is used on the eyes of the child must, in every instance, be immediately burned after using. The water, towels, old linen and the cotton that have been used on the mother must, under no circumstances, be applied to the child. The air of the bedroom must be kept as pure as possible, and the linen should never be dried in the sick room.

Inflammation of the Eyes.—Should the lids become red and swollen, or gummed along their borders, or should a mattery discharge be mixed with the tears as the child sleeps or cries, call an oculist or a physician immediately, or take the child to the nearest dispensary. Each hour of delay adds to the danger. While waiting, bathe the child's eyes every half hour with pledgets of cotton dipped in a warm solution of boric acid. Open the lids wide and allow the warm solution to flood the eyes and wash out any matter which may have gathered there.

All of those in the home should be warned of the danger of catching the disease by getting the matter into their own eyes. Do not fondle the child. Take care that nothing which has been used about its eyes or face shall be used for any other purpose. Do not listen to those who say it will amount to nothing, or to those who say to bathe the eyes of the child with the mother's milk. Such advice is bad. The milk is a means of spreading the germs of this disease. The slightest delay may result in blindness.

Trachoma.—This is an infectious disease of the eyelids which often results in total blindness. It occurs chiefly among children who are brought up under unsanitary conditions. Contributory causes are lack of cleanliness and lack of proper nourishment. It may be communicated from one person to another by the use of a common towel, by interchanging or lending handkerchiefs, or by the contact of infected hands among children at play. This disease is most prevalent among school children and in institutions, work-shops, army camps and other places where large numbers of persons are herded together and toilet or other facilities are used in common.

Any symptoms of redness, or inflammation of the eyes, or granulation of the eyelids should be brought to the attention of a physician, especially if accompanied by pain, sensitiveness to light, swelling or discharge. About 15 per cent of all cases of preventable blindness are due to this disease. Diligent effort should be made to prevent it from spreading. When a case occurs, all possibility of the infection of other persons should be eliminated. The patient should have separate towels, wash basins and the like set apart for individual use. Children with this disease should be excluded from the public schools until the acute stage is over. Under proper treatment, if taken in its early stages, blindness can ordinarily be prevented.

INTESTINAL DISEASES

Summer Complaint (Cholera Infantum).—This fatal disease which kills thousands of infants every year attends continued high temperature. Excessive heat if long endured profoundly affects the nerves and fretfulness (nervousness) always precedes attacks of cholera infantum. The digestion is depressed by nervousness. Then if the child happens to over-eat, or to be fed unwholesome food, it quickly develops this dreaded disease. The micro-organisms (germs) which cause this and other intestinal diseases of infancy are most numerous and active in hot weather. Thus they are always at hand to attack infants when their powers of resistance have become lessened by a long continued heated term.

Cholera Morbus (summer diarrhœa and dysentery) also occurs

principally during the summer and autumn. This is caused by improper food and sudden chilling of the body after exposure to great heat. Certain substances will produce it in certain persons, as, for instance, veal or shell fish. And all dishes cooked with milk such as rice pudding, cream puffs and even ice cream, are dangerons when they have been kept too long. Take care that the baby does not get any remnants of stale food. Under-ripe and over-ripe fruit—especially if taken with large draughts of ice water—will cause this disease. But sound ripe fruit is a natural food in hot weather for children over two years of age, and wholesome. Avoid chills during sleep. In temperate and changeable climates have a light blanket always at hand to draw over an infant, if the weather suddenly becomes cold during the night. Persistent summer diarrhœa is sometimes caused by malaria or impure water. Any conditions liable to contaminate air and water should be carefully sought out and remedied. Water of doubtful purity can and should be rendered safe by boiling. Mosquitoes and flies should be exterminated. As dysentery is often epidemic, it is wise to consider every case as a possible source of danger to others and to disinfect all diarrhœal discharges with the greatest care.

Symptoms of Intestinal Diseases.—Vomiting of soured and partly digested food (not simple regurgitation or "raising" of milk from overfeeding in young infants) is often the first sign of approaching illness. Vomiting may indicate one of the serious diseases of childhood or, more commonly in hot weather, "summer complaint" or simple diarrhœa. Diarrhœa does not come from teething but from too much food, too frequent feeding, too little water, too little sleep and too much handling. The most frequent cause is overfeeding. This often causes prolonged sickness and finally death. Vomiting due to this cause may be the first sign of trouble. The bowels may not become loose until several days later. A certain symptom of danger is loose, green passages from the bowels, or passages containing mucus or curds. A healthy bottle-fed infant should have at least one and not more than two or three movements of the bowels each day. These should be yellow or "gingerbread color" and not too hard to be passed easily. If they become greenish, frothy, or otherwise unnatural, and more frequent than two or three a day, consult your doctor. In summer it is dangerous to wait. Any diarrhœa or simple looseness of the bowels indicates the presence of some irritation in the intestinal tract.

These diseases are often mild at the beginning. There may be no fever and the child may show no signs of illness other than diarrhœa or vomiting. Such a baby—often in a few hours—may become dangerously, if not fatally, ill. The simplest cases of diarrhœa and vomiting during the summer must not be ignored. Neglect of the first symptoms of indigestion may lead to infection and inflammation and be followed by the death of the child. If taken in hand promptly, this condition will almost always yield to simple remedies and serious trouble may be averted. If the movements remain green in color and increase in number to five or six or more in twenty-four hours, the baby is beginning to have bowel trouble or summer diarrhœa.

Causes and Remedies.—When the baby vomits or has diarrhœa the first thing to do is to find and remove the cause. The trouble is probably due to improper feeding or over-feeding. The child may be given too much food, the milk may be too strong for its age, or it may be dirty and unsanitary. A child gets diarrhœa more often in summer than in winter because the heat makes him weak and spoils his food, and because you fail to realize that he needs less food in hot weather. Stop all food at once. Every drop of milk that goes into the baby's mouth after this warning simply adds to the poison that is already there. You will cause serious or fatal illness by feeding your baby after the bowels become loose and the movements green in color. Give nothing but pure boiled water or barley water. Send for the doctor and do not begin feeding the baby again without the doctor's orders. Meantime stop the milk at once. Give only cool boiled water or barley water until the child can be seen by a physician.

Do not give any medicine, except perhaps a teaspoonful of lime water every hour, to modify the acidity of the stomach. If the baby should have a convulsion before the doctor comes, put it in a warm bath and pour cool water on its head. But this must not be done if the convulsion occurs immediately after a meal. Do not give any "cordials" or "teas" or diarrhœa mixtures to stop vomiting or check the bowels. Nothing but harm can be done by such means.

If you cannot get a doctor promptly, give the baby two teaspoonfuls of castor oil to remove the irritating matter from the bowels. Also wash out the bowels with an enema of tepid water containing two level teaspoonfuls of salt to the quart. This should be given from a fountain syringe. Do not hold the bag more than eighteen inches or two feet above the baby, so that the water will run slowly. Babies under fifteen months almost invariably pass part of the water back by the side of the tube while it is flowing in.

When vomiting occurs give the baby as much water as it will take. This will help to wash the remaining undigested food out of the stomach. After this for eight or ten hours give only one or two teaspoonfuls of boiled water every ten or fifteen minutes, if wanted. A larger amount will be vomited. Give no food for at least six hours after the vomiting has stopped, then give barley water or rice water in gradually increasing quantities, or give broth or white of egg. Later, when the child is entirely well, it may be gradually worked back to its regular food. A weak mustard plaster on the pit of the stomach, left until there is a rosy color, then promptly removed, will assist in counteracting vomiting.

OTHER DISEASES OF INFANCY

Fever.—If the child becomes weak in hot weather, is fretful and especially if it has fever and the skin is hot and dry, take off all its clothes except the diaper and put on a night dress. Sponge it all over with cool water at frequent intervals and do not wipe it quite dry. Let the water evaporate and thus carry off some of the fever. Give it all the cool water it will drink. No matter how high the fever a baby with bowel trouble always does better out of doors in pleasant weather than in a hot, stuffy room. A child with fever will not take cold if you keep it out of strong, cold drafts.

Great care must be exercised in treating for fever. There are two principal kinds. In outer or surface fever, the hands and feet are warm and the skin hot. Place cold applications to the head, hot water bottle to the feet and bathe in cold water. In case of inward fever the hands and feet are cold and the skin cool and pale and mottled. Place cold applications at the head, a hot water bottle to the feet and bathe in hot mustard water to bring the blood to the surface. A sense of touch is unreliable as to fever. Every mother should have a clinical thermometer and ask her physician to instruct her in its use.

Eruptions.—If the baby has any eruption or breaking out of the skin, consult the doctor promptly. Every rash is not prickly heat. It may be some serious disease like scarlet fever, smallpox or chickenpox and may require the promptest possible treatment.

Teething. — A few words as to baby's teething. The first teeth—

the two lower front ones—are usually cut when the baby is from six to seven months old. Some babies cut their teeth with little trouble; others are restless, uneasy and wakeful. The latter is especially the case if the baby is constipated.

The teeth are usually cut in pairs: First the two lower (in the center), next the two upper, then the outside two above, then two below, next to those first cut. These teeth usually are all present by the twelfth month. The cutting, however, does not always follow the above order, and all children do not cut their first teeth by the sixth or seventh month.

Symptoms of difficult teething are fever, restlessness, sleeplessness and, locally, swollen or tender gums. There is often loss of appetite and thirst caused by fever. These symptoms are present only in severe cases. When a child's teeth begin to come, it should be given less food and more water. It will often take more food than it can digest because it is thirsty and the food is liquid. The result is diarrhœal trouble due to intestinal irritation from over-feeding. This is often mistakenly supposed to be due to teething, whereas if babies are properly fed and hygienic rules observed, very few will have any bowel trouble during the first or second year regardless of whether teeth are coming or not.

For the sleeplessness and irritability which so often accompany teething, much can be done by the mother. Drugs should not be given, except under the direction of a physician. A hot foot bath will often have a soothing effect by relieving the congestion in the head and mouth. Mustard can often be added to the foot bath with benefit. A little castor oil will be beneficial, for a good movement of the bowels will relieve congestion in the gums. The mother's finger dipped in sirup of lettuce can be gently carried over the tender and inflamed gum, and now and then by a little firmer pressure may allow the point of the tooth to free its way through. The baby may be allowed to bite on a small chicken or ham bone, or if over nine months, on a piece of rare roast beef.

Beware of soothing sirups which merely "dope" the baby, and often cause great harm.

Constipation.—If a bottle-fed baby is constipated, wash out the bowels with an enema of tepid water containing salt in the proportion of a level teaspoonful to the pint. Give one or two teaspoonfuls of castor oil. If this does not afford relief within four hours consult your physician. At this time you will be able to prevent a serious summer complaint with which the baby is threatened.

When the food does not agree with the baby it will fail to gain weight or will be constipated, have colic, "rolling of gases in the stomach" (flatulence), loose stools and diarrhœa. Consult your doctor without delay. Remember the stitch in time. The fact that an infant under one year of age does not gain in weight may show that it needs a different kind of liquid food, but does not indicate that it requires any sort of solid food and under no circumstances should solid food be given to babies under twelve or thirteen months of age. In hot weather reduce the amount of food and give more water. Pour out about one-fourth of the milk, replace with water and make the feedings farther apart, giving water between. These simple rules are intended to help you take care of the baby when it is well and to prevent its becoming sick. But the first thing to do when the baby is sick is to send for your physician. The home remedies above given will help you to check the trouble and keep it under control until the doctor comes and prescribes the proper course of treatment.

DON'T DRUG YOUR BABY

Soothing Sirups.—There is no such thing as a harmless soothing sirup, teething powder or "baby's friend", as such drugs are ironically called by unprincipled manufacturers. This is a fact which all right-thinking mothers should take to heart and seek to impress upon others who are responsible for the care of infants. Hundreds of thousands of children have been poisoned to death in infancy by such compounds. Other children have survived their use with weakened constitutions, or have become the victims of drug habits in later life from the effects of these mixtures. The chief active agents in most of these compounds are opium, morphine, heroin, codein, chloroform and chloral hydrate—all active poisons and especially deadly to children.

Since the passage of the Pure Food Law, the manufacturers of preparations containing habit-forming drugs, or drugs dangerous to life, have been compelled to print on the label a list of these substances. Hence mothers should read carefully the labels of any cough mixtures, soothing sirups or other preparations recommended for children and discard them if they are found to contain any of these ingredients. You may safely regard with grave suspicion the manufacturer, dealer or physician who tells you that these substances are not likely to occur, in the widely advertised preparations, in quantities dangerous to your baby's health or life.

Mrs. Winslow's Soothing Sirup is a well known preparation with which thousands of helpless infants have been drugged into insensibility by ignorant or indifferent mothers and nurses for more than a generation. It contains opium in the form of morphine sulphate. There is little doubt but that this nostrum has caused the death of many children and has done incalculable injury to others. Collier's Weekly—to which much credit is due for its exposure of the nostrums which are such a menace to the lives and health of the American people—tells the following story: "A prominent New York lawyer was asked by his office scrubwoman to buy a ticket to some association ball. He replied: 'How can you go to these affairs, Nora, when you have two young children at home?' 'Sure, they're all right,' she returned blithely. 'Just wan tayspoonful of Winslow's and they lay like the dead till marnin'.' "

The great demand for soothing sirup by mothers who wish their babies to "stay put" has produced a rival to the late Mrs. Winslow under the touching name of "Kopp's Baby's Friend." This also contains opium. Collier's states that it is made of sweetened water and morphine sulphate. It is well styled "the king of baby soothers," since it is said to contain in each teaspoonful enough morphine to kill an infant. Morphine should be given to a child under ten years of age only in very rare instances and never except under the direction of a physician. Read carefully the following list of such preparations and what they contain. This was compiled by the Bureau of Chemistry of the United States Department of Agriculture:

Mrs. Winslow's Soothing Sirup, *morphine sulphate.*

Children's Comfort, *morphine sulphate.*

Dr. Fahrney's Pepsin Anodyne Compound, *morphine sulphate.*

Dr. Fahrney's Teething Sirup, *morphine and chloroform.*

Dr. Fowler's Strawberry and Peppermint Mixture, *morphine.*

Dr. Grove's Anodyne for Infants, *morphine sulphate.*

Hooper's Anodyne, the Infants' Friend, *morphine hydrochloride.*

Jadway's Elixir for Infants, *codein.**

Dr. James' Soothing Sirup Cordial, *heroin.**

Kopp's Baby's Friend, *morphine sulphate.*

Dr. Miller's Anodyne for Babies, *morphine sulphate and chloral hydrate.*

*Heroin and Codein are derivatives of opium, the same as morphine, and their action is similar.

Dr. Moffett's Teethina, Teething Powders, *powdered opium.*

Victor Infant Relief, *chloroform and cannabis indica.*

To allay the fears of mothers, manufacturers and dealers often print on the label of such preparations statements of the following character: "Contains nothing injurious to the youngest babe"; or "Mothers need not fear giving this medicine, as no bad effects will come from its continued use." All such statements associated with the presence of opium or any of its derivatives—morphine, codein, heroin — chloroform, cannabis indica (hasheesh) or chloral hydrate, are deliberate falsehoods made with the calculated intention to deceive. There is always danger that an undue proportion of these drugs may be present in a given bottle or that an over-dose may be given and the baby put to sleep never to awake again. Numerous such cases are on record. In other instances when the remedy is freely used, the child does not succumb but develops a craving for the drug comparable to a drug habit in adults. As soon as one dose

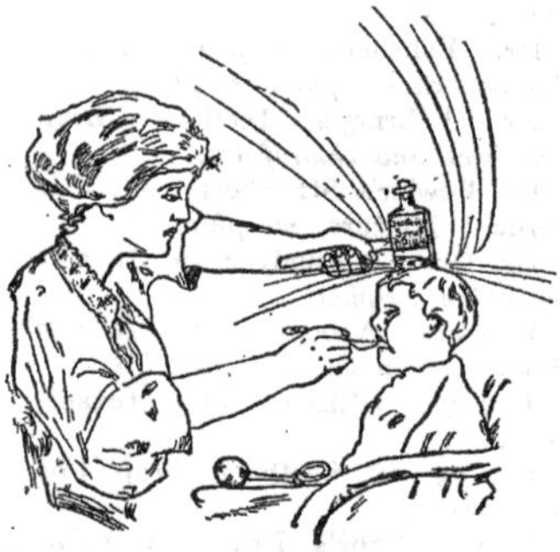

Soothing sirups are poisons to babies. They contain opium. Opium kills babies. Don't dope your baby.

of the drug passes away, the child becomes irritable and fretful with the result that another dose is administered. When the craving is thus met the child is quieted and the mother or nurse feels justified in "recommending" the remedy to her neighbors. Sometimes such children look plump and healthy when, as a matter of fact, their flesh is soft and flabby and they are poorly prepared to withstand the attack of disease.

Don't Dope Colicky Babies.—Soothing sirup is most often recommended and used in case of colic. Paregoric, whisky, brandy or soothing sirup are improper remedies for that disease. Colic is often a symptom of some condition which needs attention. Drugging the baby into insensibility, or making it drunk, will not remove the cause of illness. Colic is often due to constipation, in which case an enema of warm water—with the addition of salt at the rate of a level teaspoonful to the pint—is required followed by one or two teaspoonfuls of castor oil or other gentle laxative medicine.

Or, colic may come from cold hands and feet. Keep a flannel belly band on a "colicky" baby both summer and winter, but don't dope or drug the baby. When it is sick enough to need soothing sirup, it is sick enough to need a doctor. Proper feeding will usually overcome the trouble. In correcting errors in feeding a physician is your best advisor.

SYMPTOMS OF COMMUNICABLE DISEASES

Mothers, school teachers and other persons in immediate charge of small children should be constantly upon the look-out for symptoms of communicable diseases and other common conditions requiring medical attention. In general, any marked departure from the normal is a danger signal. The most common symptoms of acute contagious diseases are as follows: very red or pale face; red or discharging eyes, ears or nose; unusual dullness or sleepiness; evidences of sore throat; coughing, vomiting or diarrhœal discharges.

Eruptions of any sort demand especially prompt attention. Chronic diseases may be suggested by emaciation; defective vision of one or both eyes; deafness; mouth constantly open; marked odors from the ear, nose, mouth or person; peculiar postures when sitting or walking; frequent requests to go out or to the toilet; pain or swelling, or constant scratching of any part of the body.

The following summary will be found convenient for ready reference:

Symptoms of Fever. — Headache, dullness or sleepiness and indisposition for play or study; languid expression of the eyes; sometimes flushed cheek and other times pallor; heat of skin and increased frequency of pulse, all indicate fever. Take the child's temperature promptly with a clinical thermometer. A normal temperature is between 98° and 99°.

Eruptions.—The rash of scarlet fever is of a bright color. It usually appears on the neck and chest spreading thence to the face. A very characteristic symptom is a pale ring about the mouth. There is usually sore throat.

The eruption of measles is a rose or purple red. It occurs in blotches about the size of a pea. It appears first on the face and is associated with running of the nose and eyes.

The eruption of chickenpox appears first as small red pimples which quickly become small red blisters.

Colds and Sore Throat.—Symptoms of a cold in the head with running eyes, sneezing and discharges from the nose and sore throat may mean nothing more than coryza or tonsilitis. But very often they indicate diphtheria, scarlet fever or measles. A thin watery nasal discharge which irritates the nostrils and upper lip indicates diphtheria. Weak and running eyes indicate measles.

Coughs.—A cough may mean a simple cold or slight bronchitis. But a spasmodic cough which occurs in paroxysms and is uncontrollable indicates whooping cough. A croupy cough—harsh and ringing—indicates diphtheria. A painful cough indicates diseases of the lungs, especially pleurisy or pneumonia. A long-continned, hacking cough indicates tuberculosis.

Vomiting.—This may mean only some digestive disturbance. But it may indicate the onset of diphtheria, smallpox or scarlet fever.

Quarantine.—All children or other persons exposed to infection from the following diseases should be kept under observation and excluded from schools and other public places during the following period of incubation dated from the latest exposure to such infection: Infantile paralysis (anterior poliomyelitis), 14 days; diphtheria, 8 days; scarlet fever, 8 days; measles, chickenpox, whooping cough and mumps each 14 days. Patients convalescing from any of the above diseases should be isolated for the following periods reckoned from the date of onset or final diagnosis of the disease, namely: Infantile paralysis (anterior poliomyelitis), 28 days; chickenpox, 15 days and thereafter until all scabs have fallen off; diphtheria, 15 days and thereafter until two successive negative cultures have been obtained from the site of the disease secured at least twenty-four hours apart; measles, 21 days and thereafter until all catarrhal symptoms have ceased; mumps, 21 days and thereafter until all glandular swelling has disappeared; scarlet fever, 42 days and thereafter until desquamation (peeling) is complete and all discharges from mucous membranes have stopped; whooping cough, 35 days and thereafter until all spasmodic cough and whooping have ceased.

Children afflicted with ringworms, scabies or impetigo contagiosa should be kept from school and contact with other persons until the disease is cured, or until a reliable physician can certify that they are not liable to spread infection.

Diphtheria. — This disease often runs a very mild course. A child may hardly feel sick enough to take to its bed. Such cases may, and often do, give other children the form that kills. Hence every case of fever with sore throat in children should be looked on with suspicion. Look out especially for nasal diphtheria marked by a thin watery discharge from the nose which irritates the nostrils and may cause bleeding from the nose and sores about the nostrils and upper lip. Any hoarseness or thickness of the voice should suggest an examination of the throat. If the tonsils, the palate and surrounding mucous membrane are inflamed and swollen, and particularly if there are white patches in any part of the throat, have a culture taken and tested for diphtheria.

Scarlet Fever.—A sudden attack of vomiting, redness of the throat, headache and fever suggests scarlet fever. The rash appears on the first, or more often the second day and extends from the back of the neck to the chest and thence all over the body. It is usually uniformly scattered but may be patchy. The color is a characteristic deep red which may become more livid, approaching purple. A very characteristic sign is a pale ring about the mouth. The eruption lasts from three to five days and fades. Peeling follows in the shape of scales and persists for several weeks.

Measles.—The early symptoms are those of a feverish cold. Observe especially that the eyes are red and sensitive to the light. There is a discharge from the nose, sneezing and a dry hacking cough. Look for Koplik's sign, i. e., minute, pearly white blisters on the inside membrane of the mouth near the molar teeth. This is a sure sign. But observe that these may be few in number and not surrounded by any inflammation. Hence be sure to examine the patient carefully in a good light. The rash comes out the third or fourth day, first on the forehead and face and then over the front and down the sides. As the red spots increase in number they form distinct crescent-shaped figures composed of papules just raised above the skin. In severe cases the color may deepen to purple. The rash lasts four or five days, then fades and is followed by peeling. The disease is highly contagious from the beginning of the symptoms.

Whooping Cough. — A persistent paroxysmal cough frequently accompanied by vomiting is indicative of whooping cough, whether or not there is any distinct whoop. But as a rule, whooping cough comes in distinct spasms. During these the face is puffed and reddened, the eyes congested and watery, and the characteristic whooping sound is made. A paroxysm is often followed by vomiting.

Mumps. — Any swelling of the glands behind the angle of the jaw should suggest mumps. The swelling extends just in front, just behind and below the ear and is extremely painful. A very frequent symptom is swelling inside the mouth and opposite the second molar tooth.

Smallpox.—The first symptoms are severe headache, backache, rapid rise of temperature and vomiting. The eruption appears about the third day. Then the fever subsides and the patient sometimes feels perfectly well. In mild cases a child may be able to play or return to school. The symptoms in mild cases are very similar to chickenpox. But observe that smallpox cannot occur if a child has been successfully vaccinated. If not, it is best to be on the safe side and promptly call a physician.

Chickenpox.—The symptoms are those of a cold in the head with a slight fever. The characteristic rash breaks out the first or second day in the form of small blisters. A few of these may be seen about the roots of the hair, but they occur mostly on the body. These soon break and produce a drying scab.

Scabies (Itch).—Small pimples are noticed on the back of the hands and especially the spaces between the fingers or on the arms or whole body. These are caused by an animal parasite which burrows in the skin. They are seldom seen on the face or scalp. Itching and an irresistible desire to scratch are the principal symptoms. These become more intense when the patient stands near a hot fire or about the time of going to bed at night.

Pediculosis (Lice).—Intense itching and scratching of the hair and scalp are indications of vermin. Constant scratching may cause in-

Protect your baby from the preventable perils surrounding it.

flammation of the scalp and skin of the neck. Look for the eggs (nits) which are always stuck on to the hair and not readily brushed off.

Ringworm.—All eruptions of the skin in the form of circles or rings should be examined by a physician for ringworm. This is a vegetable parasitic skin disease which is communicable.

Impetigo.—This is a contagious disease which is often spread by towels, toys and other things handled by children. It is characterized by large or small pustules (boils) or festers upon the skin. These usually appear on the face, neck or hands and occasionally upon the scalp.

INFANTILE PARALYSIS (ACUTE POLIOMYELITIS)

This is a communicable disease which has become epidemic in recent years and seems to be spreading rapidly throughout the United States. It is due to a germ which attacks the spinal cord and to a less extent the brain. It injures and destroys the tissues, and causes temporary or permanent paralysis of the muscles.

It attacks chiefly young children during the first year of teething, but may also be communicated to older children, and adults are not exempt. Hence the name infantile paralysis is somewhat misleading. The nature and source of this disease were formerly obscure, but recently Flexner has proved it to have all the characteristics of a germ disease and early in 1913 he announced that the specific germ by which it is caused has been isolated.

If the germs of this disease become as widespread as those of measles or scarlet fever, the result will be appalling. Not only is the death rate high, but the after effects, in about three-fourths of all cases, are more or less severe permanent paralysis of the arms or legs, or other parts of the body. About 20,000 cases have been reported in the last few years in the United States, with 5,000 deaths and upwards of 15,000 children crippled. The death rate varies in different localities from 5 per cent to 20 per cent. The disease is most prevalent in July, August and September. In respect to its permanent after effects it is one of the saddest of all diseases.

Modes of Infection.—The germs gain entrance into the system through the mucous surfaces of the nose and throat. Infection may be direct by inhaling germs from the breath laden with infection from the mucous surfaces of the patient's nose and throat; or indirect, from the clothing of the nurse, physician, or other bedside visitor, or from objects contaminated in the sick room. There is danger also from the healthy carriers of the disease. Epidemics are probably due to mild cases and to "carriers" attending day or Sunday schools, fairs, or other public gatherings.

Symptoms.—The period of incubation is from one to fourteen days. The average is from five to ten days. This is one of the most difficult of all diseases to recognize, unless the physician is put on guard by the presence of other cases in the locality. It is especially difficult to recognize in the case of children. The onset of the disease is usually sudden. The fever rises from 101° to 103° in the first twenty-four hours. There is usually malaise, profuse sweating, vomiting and general severe pains in the arms and back, sometimes referred to the joints. Convulsions frequently occur in children. Tenderness, generally in the lower extremities, less frequently in the spine and trunk, but sometimes in the upper limbs and neck, is a frequent and highly important symptom.

Paralysis of one or both legs generally occurs within from twelve hours to three or four days, but the paralysis may extend to any part of the body. The fever lasts from five to nine days, accompanied by delirium, but rarely rises above 104° even in fatal cases. Diarrhœa often sets in on the second day.

This disease often occurs in a milder form without paralysis, and these cases may give the form that kills. A physician should be promptly summoned in suspicious cases, especially if this disease has been reported in the locality. The patient should be isolated until a positive diagnosis can be made.

Prevention.—The work of Flexner gives strong hope of the discovery of an antitoxin for poliomyelitis, but at present there is no certain means of cure. Hence the only safety lies in preventive measures. Children should be kept absolutely away from homes in which this disease has appeared and from association with members of the afflicted families, even though they are apparently well. The patient should be isolated and the sick room should be prepared in all respects as for typhoid, and every sanitary precaution suggested for that disease should be observed. As the infection is present chiefly in the discharges from the nose and throat, special care should be taken to receive them on soft cloths which should be promptly burned. The nurse and physician should take the precaution to suspend a cloth moistened in a disinfectant solution over their mouth and nostrils when approaching the patient closely enough to take his infected breath.

The use of a 10 per cent solution of peroxide of hydrogen as a gargle or spray for the throat is advised both for the patient and also for the nurse, physician and members of the family, or others who may have been exposed to the infection. Contact with this substance kills all germs of this disease.

Special care should be taken to disinfect all excreta from the patient. The germs have great vitality, and being extremely small, it is probable they may be scattered through the air on particles of dust. Hence special care should be observed to wash floors, rather than sweep them, and to dust only with cloths wet with a disinfectant. After the death or recovery of the patient, the room should be disinfected with about double the ordinary quantity of sulphur or formaldehyde, and on account of the extreme vitality of the germ, the entire exposed floor and all surfaces, woodwork and furnishings should also be washed with full strength standard solution, No. 3, bichloride of mercury.

Quarantine. — Most boards of health now require all cases to be reported, the premises to be placarded, and strict quarantine maintained. No one except the nurse and physician should be admitted to the sick room during the sickness, or for some months after recovery. There is danger that the patient may continue to carry the germs of the disease. Several epidemics have been stamped out by strict quarantine. The period of infection is not precisely known, but is supposed to be chiefly while the fever lasts—usually about three weeks. The quarantine of the other members of the family than the patient need not extend beyond this period. The bread winners should board and room elsewhere, especially during the quarantine period and for three weeks after their last exposure. They should avoid all public gatherings and mingle as little as possible with other persons. Or, preferably, the patient should be removed to a hospital at the outset of the disease.

CEREBROSPINAL MENINGITIS

This malady, also called spotted fever, or simply meningitis, was formerly one of the most terrible and fatal of all diseases, the mortality in some local epidemics running up to as high as 100 per cent. It is an inflammation of the membrane cover-

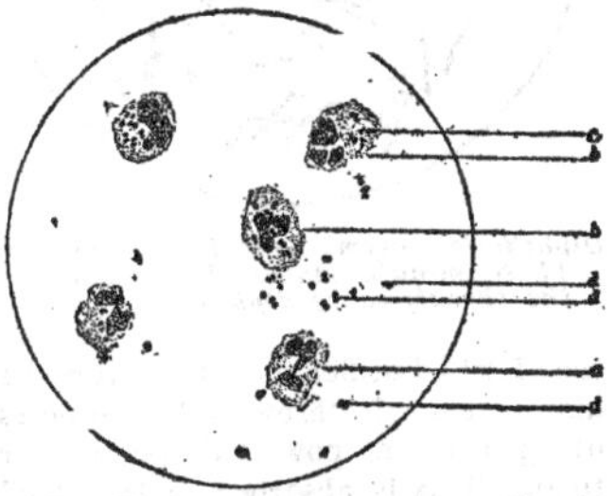

Germs of cerebrospinal meningitis: a, pus-cell; b, pus-cell containing germs of meningitis shown at c; d, the same germ lying outside of pus-cells.

ing the brain and spinal cord and is caused by a specific germ.

Flexner has discovered a serum which cures this disease and leads to the hope that a similar antitoxin may be discovered for the control of infantile paralysis. The germ of this disease has been identified, and is always present in the brain and spinal cord of the patient, and in the spinal fluid. It may also occur in the nasal passages of the patient and of healthy carriers who have been infected from him. It attacks most frequently children between one and ten years of age. It is most prevalent in the late winter and spring months, especially in March, April and May. It is always present in certain neighborhoods and may occur at any season of the year.

Modes of Infection. — The germ of meningitis occurs in the discharges from the mouth, nose and ears of the patient, and the infection may be spread by direct contact with the patient or healthy carriers, or by objects infected by them. The germ is not thought to live long outside the human body. Hence the spread of the disease is easily controlled by the isolation of the patient and by proper sanitary precautions.

Symptoms.—The first symptoms of infection are those of an ordinary cold. But when the brain is attacked, the onset of the disease becomes very sudden. There is usually a chill with intense headache, vomiting, restlessness, and a great dread of noises and bright light. In many cases the reddish spots appear beneath the skin, which suggests the name, spotted fever. These spots are usually quite tender on pressure. The muscles of the neck become very stiff and contract, drawing the head backward. This is a characteristic symptom. The chill is followed by irregular temperatures, sometimes very high. After a few hours or days, unless the antitoxin serum is injected, the patient becomes unconscious and shortly dies. Or, in mild cases, the symptoms quickly subside and recovery is rapid.

Prevention.—The symptoms of an ordinary cold in the head should be regarded with suspicion during an epidemic of meningitis. A physician should be summoned in all suspicious cases, and the patient isolated in the sick room as for typhoid fever, until a positive diagnosis can be made. This may be done by withdrawing a sample of the spinal fluid from the spinal column by means of a hypodermic needle. This is a simple procedure when performed by a competent physician, and quite free from danger. If the germs of meningitis are present, both local and state health authorities should be promptly notified and the Flexner serum should be obtained and injected into the spinal column by an experienced physician. Prompt action is imperative, as death will occur in most cases within a few days unless this remedy is administered.

The sick must be kept away from the well. All discharges, especially from the nose and throat, must be thoroughly disinfected. The nurse or attendant in the sick room, the physician and all the members of the family who may have been infected before the nature of the disease was recognized, should thoroughly disinfeet the nasal passages and throat by a spray or gargle of one part peroxide of hydrogen to three parts of water, or with equal parts of water and liquor antisepticus U. S. P. This should be followed by a spray of menthol, gum camphor and liquid alboline. As an immunizing dose, about 10 c. c. of Flexner serum may be injected for three or four days, twenty-four hours apart, in cases of known exposure.

The use of urotropin in doses of from 5 to 10 grains dissolved in water an hour after meal time, three times a day—under the advice of a physician—as a preventive, is also recommended. Observe that if this drug is taken too soon after eating, digestive disturbances may result.

These measures with the ordinary sanitary precautions in the sick room, including disinfection of all excreta, have been found to thoroughly control this disease. Fresh air and sunshine quickly destroy the germs.

Quarantine. — Placard the premises and keep the members of the family to themselves until cultures taken from their nasal passages are found to be free from germs of the disease. After recovery or death, disinfect the house thoroughly with formaldehyde or sulphur. The effect of sanitary precautions is shown from the fact that nurses and attendants very rarely contract this disease.

DIPHTHERIA

Diphtheria is a germ disease caused by the growth of the diphtheria bacillus, usually in the throat, nose or bronchial tubes. This bacillus was discovered by Klebs (1803) and shown to be the cause of diphtheria by Loeffler (1884), hence it is called

Diphtheria germs greatly magnified. These minute plants, by growing in the throat, cause diphtheria.

the Klebs-Loeffler bacillus after its discoverers. It throws off in process of growth a powerful poison, or toxin. This is absorbed in the blood and tissues and produces the symptoms of the disease. Adults are not as susceptible to this poison as are children over one year old, nor are all persons equally susceptible. Hence all cases are not equally severe. The germs are often found in the throat or nasal passages of persons who are perfectly well or who may exhibit only the mildest symptoms. But if there is any redness or soreness in the throat and the diphtheria bacillus is present, the disease should be regarded as diphtheria and treated accordingly. These bacilli frequently live and grow for months and even years in the throats and noses of persons who have recovered from diphtheria even after they have become quite well and strong. Recovery from the disease does not necessarily mean freedom from the germs that caused it.

Symptoms. — The symptoms of diphtheria vary from a mild redness of the throat to the formation, in severe cases, of a thick, grayish-white membrane which may cover the whole throat and cause death by choking. It is extremely important to recognize this disease at the outset, since there is an antitoxin which cures diphtheria if administered promptly. It is the delay in securing treatment that kills. A case treated on the first day very rarely terminates in death. Every case of simple sore throat in children should be suspected as possibly diphtheritic. Call the doctor early. Give antitoxin as soon as a diagnosis of diphtheria is made.

The patient first complains of sore throat. This gradually grows worse and in a few hours fever is observed. But sometimes the throat is not complained of until the fever has appeared. Or nausea and vomiting may be the first symptoms. After the fever appears the child usually becomes sleepy. This condition is brought about by the absorption of the poisonous product of the germs. In severe cases this drowsiness may pass into a stupor from which the child is hard to rouse. The germs do not usually circulate in the blood but grow in masses in the throat. First a small whitish speck will appear on one or both tonsils. The extent of this growth varies with the severity of the disease from small patches to the entire surface of the throat. Any grayish deposit on the tonsils or other part of the throat, if attended with the slightest fever, should arouse suspicion and a physician should be promptly consulted.

The first symptom of membranous croup or diphtheria of the larynx may be a harsh cough or difficulty in breathing. Croupy conditions, not promptly relieved by ordinary remedies, should always be suspected as possibly diphtheritic, especially if there is diphtheria in the community. Diphtheria of the lining membrane of the nose is frequently mistaken for ordinary cold. The discharges, however, are different, being frequently tinged with blood and causing lip sores. Such conditions when diphtheria is prevalent should be regarded as suspicious.

Diphtheria occurs chiefly in children between the ages of two and fifteen years. Girls are attacked in larger numbers than boys. But adults are not infrequently infected. The disease is most prevalent in late fall. It prevails more in winter than in summer. It develops in from two to seven days, oftenest two days after exposure.

If a child or adult has sore throat with the formation of a thick gray-white membrane in any part of the mouth, throat or nose, the disease is diphtheria. The sick room should be made ready, as recommended under typhoid fever, and the patient promptly isolated. If there is no membrane formation, but the patient appears to be stupid, drowsy or much prostrated, the case may be diphtheria and should be isolated until a positive diagnosis can be obtained. A "culture" should be taken from the throat of all persons who have come into contact with the patient before he was isolated. If the germs of diphtheria are present they should be protected by an immunizing dose of 1,000 units of diphtheria antitoxin.

Prevention and Disinfection. — Isolate the patient in a sick room prepared as recommended for typhoid fever and observe all the precautions therein suggested to prevent secondary infection. The germs are most numerous in the discharges from the nose and throat. Hence take especial care to receive the sputum on soft rags which should be promptly burned, or in a sputum cup containing disinfectants No. 4, carbolic acid (5 per cent), or No. 5, formalin (5 per cent). The nurse and attending physician should wear a gown of washable material, preferably with a hood, to avoid carrying the infection in their hair and clothing. After the recovery or death of the patient, the sick room should be thoroughly disinfected by formaldehyde or sulphur fumigation.

Quarantine.—Quarantine the entire household as recommended under scarlet fever. Keep children from day and Sunday school. Keep the members of the family indoors and arrange for the bread-winners to board and room elsewhere. Quarantine must be continued until the diphtheria bacilli disappear from the throat of the patient. This will ordinarily require about four weeks after recovery. "Cultures" should then be taken by the physician and quarantine should not be lifted until the bacilli are found to be absent from two successive "cultures." Remember that the mild cases and well persons who are carrying the germs of the disease are the most dangerous sources of infection. The only sure precaution is the bacteriological test made by a competent physician and the isolation of all infected persons until the bacillus disappears.

SCARLET FEVER

Scarlet fever has all the characteristics of a germ disease, though the specific germ which causes it has not yet been identified. Hence there is no antitoxin against scarlet fever and no efficient method for its control. Scarlatina, scarlet rash, canker rash, fever rash and Duke's disease are merely other names for scarlet fever. They are often applied to the mild cases under the mistaken belief that these are a different and less dangerous malady, but this is not the case. The mild cases will give the form that kills. Scarlet fever is highly contagious, but, like other germ diseases, is wholly preventable. It is, or should be, among the most dreaded of all the acute diseases of childhood. It attacks chiefly children between the ages of one and 10 years, although about 5 per cent of all cases occur in adult life. The death rate is about one out of every fifteen or twenty cases.

Occasionally parents expose a child to a mild case from the mistaken notion that all children must have the disease and that it is best to have it light. Parents frequently permit children suffering from mild cases or convalescing to play about the house or even run about the neighborhood at will. Such contacts of infected with healthy children are of great assistance in spreading the disease. Persons who knowingly permit them often cause cases of death, and with the increase of sanitary knowledge the law will undoubtedly recognize such crimes and visit them with appropriate penalties. After childhood the liability to take the disease is very much lessened. Many persons who escape the disease in childhood have been immune to it although many times exposed in later life. Two-thirds of all deaths occur in children under five. When the disease does not kill it frequently leaves its victim crippled for life. The commonest after-effects are inflammation of the kidneys, heart, ears, glands and joints. Deafness sometimes results. Hence, although one attack usually renders a patient immune, the utmost care should be taken to protect all children from exposure.

Symptoms.—The period of incubation after exposure varies from one to fourteen days. Hence, a child exposed to scarlet fever should be carefully watched during the following two weeks. Upon the first symptoms of shivering, lassitude, headache, frequent pulse, hot, dry skin, flushed face, furred tongue with much thirst and loss of appetite, the sick room should be prepared as for typhoid fever and the patient isolated until a positive diagnosis can be made by a physician.

Vomiting is usually among the first positive symptoms. Other symptoms are sore throat, intense fever with headache or backache, and the characteristic scarlet rash. This usually appears in from twelve to twenty-four hours, first upon the lower part of the neck and adjacent parts of the chest and afterwards gradually spreading over the entire body. This disease, like typhoid or diphtheria, appears in varying degrees of severity. It may cause death within twenty-four hours or may be so mild that the patient does not feel sick enough to stay in bed. There are many true cases of this malady with a very low fever and without vomiting or other acute symptoms, or even without the characteristic rash. A child with a sore throat is under suspicion of scarlet fever or diphtheria and should be kept away from school and from other children until a positive diagnosis can be made.

Running Ear.—During the third or fourth week of the disease, it is possible that the ears may become diseased and lead to what is known as a "running ear." The child by this time has had no fever for a number of days. He suddenly becomes more or less feverish and restless, and complains at the same time of pain in the ear. This is a danger signal and calls for immediate action by the doctor. If this condition goes untreated, it may result in a running ear which sometimes lasts for years. With proper treatment, however, most of these cases are soon cured.

Acute Nephritis, or inflammation of the kidneys, develops, at times, in the third to the fifth week of the disease. The child, who has seemed to be almost well, suddenly develops a fever. He complains of headache, usually vomits and may have convulsions. The amount of urine passed is small. The patient may complain of trouble with the eyes, and of not being able to see distinctly. Should any of these symptoms develop, the doctor should be called immediately.

Modes of Infection.—This disease is spread through carelessness. Every case comes directly, or indirectly, from some previous case, either by direct infection from inhaling the breath of a scarlet fever patient, or by secondary contact infection. Most cases of direct infection are due to neglect of mild cases and carelessness of those recovering from the disease. If every case could be thoroughly isolated — quarantined — the disease would disappear from the face of the earth. The only safe course to pursue is to isolate the patient and to quarantine and disinfect the sick room in all respects as for typhoid fever.

The nurse and attending physician should wear a hooded gown of washable material to avoid carrying infection from the sick room upon the hair or clothing. On leaving the sick room this gown may be disinfected by sprinkling it with one or two tablespoonfuls of 40 per cent solution of formaldehyde and packing it in a small valise or other tightly closed receptacle. Both the nurse and physician should avoid direct infection from the patient's breath. No one else should be permitted to enter the sick room.

The chief danger from contact infection is from scales from the skin, the spittle from the throat and mouth and the nose and ear discharges. But all the discharges of the patient should be disinfected as for typhoid fever. By confining the patient absolutely to the sick room until the danger of infection is passed and by proper and efficient disinfection, as elsewhere recommended, the spread of the disease can be absolutely prevented.

The germs of scarlet fever are very long-lived. They may communicate the infection after many months and at long distances by means of clothing, playthings, books, magazines, bedding, towels or any articles of household furniture or other objects on which the contagion from the patient may have lodged. Hence nothing should be removed from the sick room without having first been thoroughly disinfected.

Quarantine.—Most cities require strict quarantine in cases of scarlet fever. Keep the children from both day and Sunday school. Take care that the nurse and all members of the family remain indoors. Arrange for the bread-winners to room and board elsewhere during the course of the disease. Have milk and groceries left at the door and disinfect all articles even including letters and postal cards. This may be done by baking them in a suitable receptacle at a temperature of about 250 degrees.

Or, place the articles in an air-tight receptacle with a closely-fitting cover, sprinkle them freely with a 40 per cent solution of formaldehyde, cover tightly and leave the receptacle in a warm room for at least four hours. No milk or groceries should be sold in, or accepted from, premises quarantined for scarlet fever. Milk from infected dairies is a frequent source of contagion.

Desquamation or "Peeling" is a highly characteristic phase of scarlet fever. After the rash begins to fade the fever disappears and the patient usually feels good and is anxious to get out and play. The skin affected by the rash now begins to scale or peel from all parts of the body, sometimes in large or small flakes, but often in the form of a dry mealy powder. This is charged with the virus of the disease in its most infectious form. The process of peeling occupies a variable time from ten days to six weeks and this is the most contagious period of the disease. The infectious dry skin is easily spread about the room and may be carried elsewhere upon the clothing of members of the family, or other objects. Or it may remain attached to articles of furniture, or as dust in out-of-the-way places, to infect others with whom it may come in contact. To prevent all this, the patient must be confined to the sick room and bathed daily, under the advice of the attending physician, with soap and warm water. Bathing with disinfectants is not advisable. But the water used for the bath must afterwards be thoroughly disinfected.

After the bath the patient should be anointed with sweet or olive oil containing a little oil of Eucalyptus, or 3 per cent of carbolic acid, or with 2 per cent carbolized vaseline, or a boracic acid ointment at the discretion of the attending physician. This will not only allay the itching from the rash, but will confine the dry scales to the body and bed linen and facilitate the work of disinfection. This should be continued until the skin is entirely smooth. The soles of the feet and palms of the hand are usually the last to peel.

Duration of Quarantine.—The length of time during which a scarlet fever patient is dangerous to others differs widely. Isolation must be enforced until all peeling or scaling off of the skin is completed, and until there is no further discharge from the ears, nose, throat, suppurating glands or inflammation of the kidneys. The time required for scaling varies from four to eight weeks. The soles of the feet and palms of the hands are the last to peel. Mild cases with very little scaling and without ear, nose, throat, kidney and glandular complications, should be isolated not less than four weeks, and severe cases not less than six weeks. This period must be prolonged if the ears, nose, throat, glands or kidneys continue to be diseased. The advice of a reliable physician should be followed in all cases.

Disinfection.—After death or recovery disinfect the sick room and its contents thoroughly as elsewhere described.

MEASLES

Measles is the most contagious eruptive disease of childhood. It is probably a germ disease, but the germ by which it is caused has not yet been identified. German measles—more properly Rotheln or Rubella—is not a form of measles nor is it a mild type of scarlet fever. It is a distinct disease. Black measles—the malignant type of the disease—is very fatal. The black color is due to hemorrhages in the skin. Measles may occur at any time during the year, but is most prevalent in the fall and winter months.

Symptoms.—The period of incubation is from ten to fourteen days after exposure. The symptoms for the first two or three days are very much like those of an ordinary cold in the head. The eyes become red and watery and are sensitive to light. The nose is stopped up or there is a discharge from the nose, with sneezing. The throat is sore and there is a dry, hard, high-pitched cough. The tonsils may be swollen or red, headache, fever, loss of appetite, drowsiness and irritability are usually observed.

Occasionally the disease comes on suddenly with vomiting and high fever, but usually the fever is not very high. It may disappear on the second or third day with improvement of all the other symptoms. Then the temperature again rises and continues very high until the fourth day when the eruption appears. The disease is contagious from the outset of the earliest symptoms. Hence any one suffering from these symptoms should be isolated and kept under observation for three or four days, especially if measles is prevalent. Children should be kept from both day and Sunday school.

The characteristic skin eruption appears on the fourth day on the face and neck and thence over the whole body as dull red blotches a little raised, and later running together. It gives the skin a peculiar mottled appearance. Before this occurs one cannot be positive that the case is one of measles. But generally there is an eruption of some light red spots on the inside of the cheeks two or three days before the external eruption. If care is taken to be on the lookout for this symptom the nature of the disease may be determined early. The eruption lasts usually four or five days and disappears as the other symptoms improve. It is followed by a fine bran-like desquamation or peeling, which is usually complete in about a week.

Prognosis.—Measles is quite commonly regarded as a slight and trivial disorder. Hence parents not infrequently expose young children to this malady from the mistaken notion that they are certain to contract it some time and the sooner it is over the better. It is true that the disease is more severe in adult life. But on the other hand it is a very fatal disease among young children. It causes about three times as many deaths as smallpox and nearly as many as scarlet fever. Measles and whooping cough together cause nearly as many deaths as diphtheria. The mortality from measles is much higher than is generally supposed. Ninety-five per cent of all deaths occur in children under five years of age, and far more deaths occur under than over two years of age. The death rate from measles in times of epidemic ranges from 4 per cent to 6 per cent and not infrequently exceeds that from scarlet fever.

The danger from measles is chiefly due to complication with other diseases, such as whooping cough and bronchial pneumonia, or to after-effects, such as consumption, paralysis, meningitis, diseases of the skin and nervous disorders. Inflammation of the ear is a not infrequent complication of measles. This often leads to deafness or worse. Latent tuberculosis in a child often becomes active after an attack of measles. If a child "seems to have caught cold" after measles consult a doctor at once. Hence exposure to infection should be avoided and every case should receive skilled medical attention.

Modes of Infection.—Measles is contagious from the beginning of the symptoms—usually three or four days before the eruption occurs. It is during this first stage of the disease, when the symptoms can hardly be distinguished from those of an ordinary cold in the head, that direct infection is most often communicated. The disease is usually conveyed to others by direct exposure but may be conveyed by the discharges of the nose and throat and possibly from the fragments of skin thrown off from the surface of the body during peeling. Infection may be carried by the clothing of the patient, or those who come in contact with him, and by other objects. But the germs are not nearly so long-lived as those of diphtheria and scarlet fever. Hence the danger from secondary infection is much less. Mild cases may give the disease in its most malignant form and are equally as contagious.

Quarantine. — When measles is prevalent and especially if there is likelihood that exposure has occurred, children should be kept under close observation for ten days to two weeks and promptly isolated on the appearance of the first symptoms. If red spots are not observed on the inside of the cheeks within two days, or if the eruption does not break out within four or five days after the first feverish symptoms, the case may be regarded as a simple cold in the head. But if there is any evidence of eruption, however mild, isolate the child in the sick room prepared as for typhoid fever and promptly summon a physician.

Practically everyone is susceptible to measles. One attack usually protects a person against others, but this rule is by no means invariable. The course of the disease is usually more severe in adult life, hence in the management of the sick room observe all the usual sanitary precautions.

Quarantine.—Isolate all suspicious cases, especially during periods of epidemic. Placard the premises. Keep all visitors out of the sick room. Protect, especially, children under five years of age and adults who have never had the disease. The disease is communicable until the peeling is complete, which will be, as a rule, within three weeks from the onset of the malady.

The quarantine must be continued until the patient's temperature has been normal for forty-eight hours. Persons exposed to measles and who have never had the disease should be quarantined for two weeks from time of exposure. Adults who have had the disease may go about their ordinary business, providing they keep entirely away from the sick room. But no person from a home quarantined for measles should attend school, church, theater, or other public gathering. Everything coming from the patient's room should be disinfected. After recovery or death the sick room should be thoroughly disinfected with formaldehyde or sulphur as elsewhere recommended.

WHOOPING COUGH

This is a highly contagious disease characterized by severe inflammation of the bronchial tubes and accompanied by a peculiar cough ending in the familiar "whoop." It has all the characteristics of a germ disease but the germ which causes it has not yet been identified. Persons of all ages are liable to the attacks of this malady but practically all deaths occur under the age of five years. One-half of these occur under one year of age. The average age of death is one and a half years.

Whooping cough, when severe, is a debilitating disease at any time of life. It lasts for several weeks and is not infrequently complicated with pneumonia. It often leads to chronic invalidism from exhaustion, with heart and lung changes which may be permanent. The disease may occur at any time of the year but the greatest mortality is in July and August. Children should never be knowingly exposed to whooping cough and great care should be taken to protect children under five years of age from infection. After this period the likelihood of infection is much lessened and the danger of death from this disease is practically over. Many persons escape this malady altogether.

Symptoms.—The period of incubation is from four to fourteen days after exposure. The symptoms for the first few days are those of an ordinary cold or simple catarrh but with less fever than measles. The cough is more severe than the other symptoms seem to warrant and grows harsher from day to day. After a week or ten days the characteristic whoop develops. This continues with varying degrees of severity for a month or six weeks. Then the paroxysms cease, often leaving a simple catarrhal cough which may last indefinitely.

Modes of Infection.—Infection is ordinarily by direct and fairly intimate contact between the infected and healthy person. The virus of the disease is not as long lived as that of diphtheria or scarlet fever and hence not so likely to be conveyed from the sick room on the hands and clothing of the nurse or by means of other objects. The disease is probably not spread through the air except within the range of the fine spray thrown from the mouth of the patient while coughing.

Quarantine.—Isolate the patient in a sick room prepared as recommended for typhoid fever, especially if there is an infant in the family under two years of age. Keep on the safe side by observing all the sanitary precautions recommended for the sick room in other communicable diseases and disinfect the sick room after the death or recovery of the patient.

MUMPS

Mumps is a glandular swelling in the angle between the jaw and the ear. It is a highly contagious but wholly unnecessary and preventable disease. It chiefly affects children, but may attack older persons who have not become immune from having had the disease in childhood. It usually develops in from two to three weeks after exposure.

Symptoms.—The early symptoms are fever with pain below the ear on one or both sides. A slight swelling below one ear may be first noticed. Within two days there is great enlargement of the neck and side of the cheek. The other side usually becomes affected within a day or two. The swelling persists from seven to ten days then gradually subsides. A second or even a third attack may occur and troublesome complications are quite common. It is always advisable to consult a physician.

Quarantine.—Isolate the patient in the sick room and exclude other children and adults who have not had the disease. Keep children from school for a period of three weeks following their last exposure.

PARASITIC DISEASES

Pediculosis (Lice).—There are three varieties of these parasites which infest human beings, the head louse, body louse and crab louse. A single family of children so infested may communicate them to many others through the contacts of outer clothing hung up in school dressing rooms, or in play, or otherwise. In most states such children may be excluded from schools until these parasites have been exterminated. The following methods of treatment for killing parasites and nits are recommended:

Add two teaspoonfuls of chloronaphtholeum disinfectant to a pint of warm water. Wet the hair with this mixture. Put a towel around the head and let it dry on. When the hair is dry comb with a fine comb. Repeat this two or three times until the head is clear of vermin. The nits may be removed by combing the hair after it has been moistened with vinegar.

Or obtain half a pint of crude petroleum at a drug store and wet the hair thoroughly with this. Keep it wet for three hours. Then wash the whole head with warm water and soap. Repeat this process on three successive days. The nits may then be removed by combing the hair very carefully with a fine-tooth comb wet with vinegar. Repeat the combing for several days until no more nits can be found. To make the treatment easier and more thorough, the hair may be cut short, if there is no objection.

All the children in a family are likely to be affected, and should also be treated as above.

Brushes and combs should be cleansed by putting them in boiling water for a few minutes.

Or head lice may promptly be destroyed with common kerosene. Pour a little into a small dish. Moisten a small rag with it. After squeezing the rag somewhat, moisten the hair with the kerosened rag. Do this in the afternoon, after the children return from school, or in the evening. Before morning the oil will have evaporated so that little or no odor will remain. Or remove both oil and odor with soap and water. Or to disguise the odor of kerosene, pour a small quantity into a vial, and add an equal amount, or less, of oil of sassafras. Shake until there is a complete mixture.

Or, dip a small, clean hairbrush into kerosene oil or oil of sassafras poured into a shallow dish. Then brush and moisten the hair with it.

Make these applications by daylight and be very careful not to let the children go near fire or lights. For the night, cover the head with a cap, which can be improvised by knotting the corners of a handkerchief, or wrap a cloth around it. Repeat this treatment several times to ensure complete destruction of the lice and nits. Applied as recommended, kerosene is not in any way injurious to the scalp or hair.

Body Lice (Pediculus Vestimentorum).—This parasite belongs to the same family as head lice but is somewhat larger. It is found comnouly on the body, where it goes only for the purpose of feeding. In the adult form it can be differentiated from the head louse by dark transverse bands across the back. The parasite lives and reproduction occurs chiefly in the various folds and seams of the clothing, and especially where the skin is most conveniently reached. Hence the various lesions are to be found most often around the neck, across the shoulders, the upper part of the back, around the waist and the outside of the thighs.

Treatment should be directed to the infested clothing where the parasite and nits are to be found. In order to destroy these, all garments should be thoroughly baked, boiled or lightly sprinkled and gone over with a very hot iron.

However, it has been observed that some of the ova or nits are attached to the fine hairs (lanugo) of the body surface. Hence a general tub bath disinfected with corrosive sublimate is advisable. Eight tablets of bichloride of mercury to a tub of water makes a strong enough solution. After the bath, flush the tub thoroughly to avoid injury to the plumbing and fixtures.

Or clothing, beds and bedding, and the like may be rid of these insects and parasites of all other kinds, by fumigation with sulphur.

Crab Lice (Phthirius Inguinalis).—These are a smaller species of the same family as head or body lice but are quite distinct on account of their shape. They are nearly as wide as long. Their strong legs, spread out laterally, give them the appearance of crabs. They are of whitish color, somewhat shaded on the shoulders, and the legs have a slightly red tinge. Each is about one-tenth of an inch in length. They are to be found on the various hairy regions of the body other than the scalp. They do not thrive among the fine hairs of the head, though they have often been observed in the eyebrows.

Treatment. — Repeated washings with vinegar or diluted acetic acid will free the hairs of ova. This should be followed by a careful daily shampoo of all the regions involved. After the shampoo, apply freely a solution of corrosive sublimate containing one tablet to a pint of water. If not desirable to use the mercury wash, apply a lotion consisting of tincture of larkspur, ½ ounce; commercial ether, 8 ounces. Or use a stronger solution, consisting of equal parts of the two ingredients. Afterwards cover the parts with a closely applied dressing.

Cautions. — Corrosive sublimate (bichloride of mercury) is a powerful poison. Ether is highly inflammable.

The Itch Mite.—This is a minute bug which gives rise to the condition commonly known as "Itch," "Seven-Year Itch," "Army Itch," "Jackson Itch" and many other synonymous names. The female burrows into the superficial skin forming a tortuous or, at times, a straight, dotted, slightly elevated line. This varies in length from one-eighth to one-half inch. The burrow is dark gray or blackish in color, thread-like, and may be slightly more elevated at one end.

This mite is transmitted from one individual to another by occupancy, either of the same bed, or of one on which the sheets have not been changed. It may also be transmitted by the use of a common towel and by shaking hands. It is commonly found in the moist surfaces of the body, such as between the fingers, on the hands or folds of the wrist, in the folds under the shoulder, the lower portion of the abdomen and about the neck. Its entire existence is spent on its human host. It is believed not to have any power to transmit disease, but may be inimical to the health of the individual from secondary infection of the burrows or of the excoriations produced by scratching. There may be also varying degrees of papular or pustular lesions over the infected regions.

These mites usually thrive best in unsanitary conditions. To destroy them, thoroughly boil or bake all bed linen and clothing used by the infected individual. If woolens are in use, bake them or sprinkle lightly and thoroughly iron them with a very hot iron. Take a hot bath, and rub down with a coarse washcloth or brush. This opens up the burrows and exposes the eggs for destruction. After the bath, rub in an ointment made up as follows: Sublimed sulphur, 1 dram (1 teaspoonful); balsam of Peru, 1 dram (1 teaspoonful); vaseline, 1 ounce (2 tablespoonfuls). Repeat morning and evening from two to four days. In particularly serious cases, repeat this entire treatment at the end of one week.

Or use either of the following preparations:

(1) Mix equal parts of balsam of Peru and lard. Rub these together thoroughly in a shallow plate with a steel table knife to form an ointment. Or use vaseline in place of lard, or still better, lanolin.

(2) Or mix flowers of sulphur, 1 tablespoonful; balsam of Peru, two tablespoonfuls; lard or vaseline, 8 tablespoonfuls. Make into an ointment.

Take a hot bath and give the whole body a thorough scrubbing with soap and hot water. Dry the body well. Now with the palm of the hand, rub one of these ointments thoroughly into every part of the body from the neck downward, or, at least, anoint all parts of the body which are affected. Sometimes the only parts affected at first are the hands and the arms to the elbows. To make sure work, particularly in bad cases, make two or three applications within twenty-four or thirty-six hours. Take another hot bath twelve hours or so after the last application. Thorough scrubbing and cleanliness go a long way toward effecting a cure.

To avoid reinfection put on clean clothes, particularly underclothing, and change sheets and blankets, particularly after the last soap and water bath. Deposit all infected clothing and bed linen in a standard disinfectant solution of carbolic acid (5 per cent), or formaldehyde (3 per cent), or boil in soap and water at least one hour.

Balsam of Peru is sometimes painted on pure, or mixed with an equal amount of glycerine. To make this mixture fill a bottle half full, heat by putting the bottle in moderately hot water and shake vigorously.

Contagious Impetigo.—This cruption first appears on the exposed surfaces of the body, particularly on the face, hands or wrists. It takes the form of a simple-looking pimple or pustule. This enlarges in size and the patch becomes covered by a brownish or yellowish crust. Other patches then appear caused by conveyance of the infection by the fingers or otherwise. Medical advice should be promptly taken. Contagions impetigo sometimes spreads rapidly in schools, but it can be readily cured by medical treatment.

CHAPTER VII

THE CARE OF BABIES

BEFORE THE BABY COMES—THE NEW BORN CHILD—SAVE THE BABIES — GENERAL RULES — BREAST FEEDING — ARTIFICIAL FEEDING—MILK MODIFICATION—MATERIALS FOR MILK MODIFICATION — BOTTLE FEEDING — ARTIFICIAL FOODS — OTHER FOODS FOR INFANTS—DRUGS—CARE OF MILK IN THE HOME

BEFORE THE BABY COMES

A poorly fed or sickly mother cannot give birth to a vigorous, healthy infant and successfully nurse it. Such a mother rarely carries her baby for the full nine months. A woman who has had repeated miscarriages or whose previous labors have come on before time should, early in pregnancy, consult her physician in order that the underlying cause may be cured or alleviated. During pregnancy and especially in the latter months, the expectant mother must have abundant rest and spare herself as much as possible. An extra amount of sleep is required and daytime rest for an hour or two is desirable. Select and consult your physician early in pregnancy. Keep yourself in good health. Hard household labor or factory work during the latter months tend to bring about miscarriages or the birth of puny and undersized children.

Exercise.—Exercise in the open air in the form of walks should be taken throughout the entire course of pregnancy. Violent exercise in any form should be prohibited. Unnecessary stair climbing must be avoided in the latter months. The sewing machine must not be used towards the end. Should labor be threatened before the proper time, go to bed at once and remain perfectly quiet until the danger is well passed.

Care of the Breasts.—Small, flattened or depressed nipples should be drawn out with the forefinger and thumb and held for five minutes night and morning during the two months before the baby is born. The nipples should also be carefully anointed each night with white vaseline. This will soften and remove the milky substance which is secreted at this time, and which may otherwise form hard crusts, and ulcerate the soft tissues beneath. Wash the nipples every day with castile soap and water and put boracic acid solution on them, a heaping tablespoonful to the pint of water. Or better, use warm water, two-thirds, and alcohol, one-third. Proper attention to the care of the nipples will make nursing a pleasure and satisfaction, instead of a pain and discomfort.

After the baby comes, always wash the nipples carefully both before and after nursing, in pure, cold water containing a teaspoonful of baking soda to each pint of water. This will prevent them from becoming tender.

Food for the Baby.—No food is as good for a baby as its mother's milk. This is why so many more bottle babies are sick and die than breast babies. One or two feedings a day from the breast are a great deal better than none at all. Hence keep the body well nourished before the birth of the baby in order to secure a good supply of milk. Exercise, freedom from excessive worry and massage of the breast and nipples before the child is born will, in nearly every instance, insure the child being nursed. Every mother should expect and plan to nurse her child.

Diet.—The diet should be carefully regulated, but abundant. A full, wholesome and liberal diet is essential. What to eat, however, will depend largely on individual tastes and habits, as food which agrees with one will not agree with another. Highly seasoned or very rich food should be avoided as well as fatty foods and coarse vegetables.

The following dietary is recommended during pregnancy and nursing:

Soup—Any kind.

Fish—Fresh fish, of any kind, boiled or broiled. Raw oysters and raw clams.

Meats—Chicken, beef, ham or bacon, veal, lamb, tender lean mutton. Red meat in moderation but only once a day.

Cereals—Hominy, oatmeal, farina, cream of wheat, rice mush, shredded wheat biscuits, etc.

Breads—Stale bread, corn bread, Graham bread, rye bread, brown bread, toast, crackers.

Vegetables—Potatoes, onions, spinach, cauliflower, asparagus, green corn, green peas, beans, lettuce or other salads, with oil.

Desserts—Plain puddings, custard, junket, ripe raw fruits, stewed fruits, ice cream. No pastry.

Drinks—Tea and coffee very sparingly, never more than one cup a day. No alcoholic beverages, beer, or liquors. At least two quarts of water a day. Milk, buttermilk, cocoa, malted milk.

At least one satisfactory movement of the bowels should take place daily; if there is any difficulty about this, consult the doctor. But observe that strong medicines must not be used to open the bowels. Costiveness can be avoided by sufficient exercise and suitable food as brown bread, stewed vegetables, fruit and abundance of water.

Work.—The expectant mother may do her usual work, but should not work hard enough to get very tired. Work in stores and mills is not good. It should be stopped as soon as possible, at least four weeks before the expected birth of the child. She should go out of doors every day, but must not run for cars, or jump, or over-exert herself in any way.

Once in four weeks, at the times when the woman would have been unwell, if she were not to have a baby, she should be even more careful than usual about over-exertion, because at these times there is more danger of miscarriage.

Clothing.—All clothing should be loose. As soon as she begins to show her condition, the mother should leave off her corsets, and have nothing about the waist that is at all tight. A loose corset waist should be worn. To this attach side garters instead of wearing circular ones about the legs.

Baths.—It is important to keep the skin in a healthy condition, and this is best done by frequent bathing. Sea-bathing is not good, however, because it is too violent.

When the Baby Comes.—Send for the doctor when the labor pains begin. He prefers being called too early than too late. A sudden gush of water signifies that the membranes have ruptured and the mother should go to bed at once.

The bed should be prepared as follows: Place a rubber sheet or several thicknesses of newspapers next to the mattress and over this a clean sheet. Next place three thicknesses of newspapers over the middle and edge of the side of the bed and cover with a folded sheet and then cover with a clean sheet. This top layer of papers and sheets can be easily removed after the labor and the mother will lie on a clean, dry sheet.

Everything should be in readiness for the reception and care of the baby. Have at hand a warmed flannel blanket in which to place the baby after birth, and hot water bottles with which to surround it if the room is cold. Expose the baby as little as possible during the bath. The clothes and diapers should be warmed. Everything that comes in contact with the baby. should be scrupulously clean.

The mother should insist that a drop of silver solution be placed in the baby's eyes. This will prevent blindness. If the baby weighs less than four pounds it can best be taken care of in incubators which are to be found in any well-equipped hospital. Your physician is required to make a prompt report of the birth to the registrar or local board of health. This is a matter of great importance. Don't let him forget it. The mother should remain in bed for at least two weeks after confinement. The womb does not return to its normal state for five or six weeks and no hard work or active exercise should be taken during this period.

THE NEW BORN CHILD

If a new born infant is to live its first requirement is air, its second warmth. It is extremely sensitive to cold and may be seriously or fatally injured by slight exposure to cool air. Wrap up the child quickly and carefully and do not expose it, except momentarily, to a temperature below blood heat. Do not handle the baby during the first few days more than is required to insure local cleanliness.

The death rate among infants is at its highest point the first week. The second week it drops enormously. Many babies die thus early because the care which they receive within the first few hours or days is not intelligent. The first bath coming too early kills many. A full bath should not be given before the child is ten or twelve days old. The first cleansing of the skin can be done much better with olive oil or even lard. Apply this to only a small portion of the body at a time, then wipe it off with pieces of old, soft cotton or linen.

Next to air and warmth among the life needs of the new born child is sleep. After it has had its initial cry, see that the breathing is well established and the child is made comfortable. Then let the infant sleep undisturbed during the first two or three days, eighteen or twenty hours out of the twenty-four.

Immediately after birth of a child two drops of a 1 per cent fresh solution of nitrate of silver should be placed in each eye by the nurse or attending physician. This preparation costs about two cents and will prevent blindness. The eyes should be carefully shielded from the light until they gradually become accustomed to it. The need of food is not immediate. Nature does not usually provide a supply of food for the first two or three days and sometimes not for the first five or six days. Hence it is safe to infer that a preliminary fast is the best and safest for the baby. Observation shows that feeding within this time is most often injurious.

When a baby is well it will sleep twelve hours or more in every twenty-four, without being rocked. It will nurse every three or four hours during the daytime, and after the sixth month will be satisfied without nursing in the night. It will gain about six ounces in weight every week. It will have a movement of the bowels every day, soft and yellow in color, without the aid of medicine or other help. It will be happy and contented. It will cut its first tooth at about the sixth month; sit up without aid at the seventh or eighth month; creep at the ninth or tenth month; walk at from the twelfth to the fourteenth month, and talk at about the fifteenth month of age.

To keep a baby well you must satisfy its needs in respect of the following essentials, namely: food, clothing, fresh air, bathing (with sanitary cleanliness of both the baby's body and clothing), sleep at night and naps in the daytime with all the rest and quiet possible. The following simple rules sum up a world of practical wisdom on this subject:

Give the baby pure outdoor air both night and day. Give it no food but mother's milk or milk or food from a clean bottle as directed by the physician. Let the baby alone when not feeding or bathing it. Whenever it cries or is fretful, don't offer it food, but give it water. Be sure that it gets sleep and at least two naps during the day. Don't wake the baby to feed it. Don't put too much clothing on it. Bathe it in a tub every day.

Why Babies Cry.—Because they are tired of lying on one side and are unable to turn over. Turn a baby once in a while. Because their diapers are wet or soiled and therefore uncomfortable. Because their hands or feet are cold. Because they are thirsty. Babies must have water (boiled and cooled, but not iced) to drink. Because they are too warm (sweating) and possibly irritated by "prickly heat." Because they are sleepy and wish to lie down and be let alone. Because the air of the room is foul and smelly. Babies require lots of fresh air. Because their clothes are too tight, or perhaps a pin is sticking into them. Because crying is the only way they have to tell you something is wrong with them.

Of course babies cry when in pain from colic or other cause, but you should find out if it is not some of the above stated causes before deciding that it is pain which is causing the crying. *Above all else, get the notion out of your head that every time the baby cries it is hungry.* If you are sure that none of the things spoken of above are the cause of the crying, then the most probable cause is intestinal indigestion and the quickest way to relieve it is by an enema of salt solution (a level teaspoonful of salt in a pint of warm water).

Children often cry when put down to sleep. If they are let alone they will soon stop crying and go to sleep. Don't get nervous about it. Don't fear that the crying child will rupture itself. Crying is one way in which children learn to develop their lungs. If children were let alone and allowed to have their cry out, instead of being tossed and petted and hushed, they would be far better for it.

Many babies suffer because they are used to amuse older people and are tossed about and excited when they should be resting or sleeping. Try to have people leave the baby alone. Think how tired and irritable you get yourself on a hot day and shield the baby as much as possible from excitement and "attention."

Kissing.—There are many serious objections to babies being kissed by other children and by older people. Tuberculosis, diphtheria, and other dangerous diseases may be communicated in this way.

GENERAL RULES

Clothing.—The clothing of infants should be simple, warm, light in weight and not too tight fitting. For the first four or five months provide an abdominal band of thin, soft wool or flannel about six inches wide and twenty inches long. This will prevent serious effects from sudden changes of temperature. It should be only wide enough to cover the belly and should be wound two or three times around the body, according to the season of the year. This bellyband, or pinning blanket, should be wound smooth and free from creases or folds, and fastened with safety pins, or preferably with a few stitches of soft darning cotton. It must not be pinned so tightly as to interfere with the movements of the child's bowels or it will tend to cause diarrhœa. Nor should it be wide enough to impede the free movement of the legs, else it will prevent proper exercise and make the child fretful. All the baby's clothing should at all times be loose enough to allow it to breathe and move its limbs easily and to admit of the free circulation of blood. Never use clothing with tight waistbands. Skirts should be supported from the shoulders by straps. Never, for appearance sake, put starched, stiff or uncomfortable clothing on a baby.

Infants are very susceptible to changes of temperature. The clothing should be modified with each change in the weather. Either overheating or sudden chill tends to produce stomach or intestinal complaints. Healthy infants are, however, warm blooded and need less covering than adults, especially in hot weather. Cool outdoor air will not harm them even in winter or in cold climates, if they are well wrapped up, protected from changes of temperature and kept out of drafts.

More babies are made sick by being wrapped up too warmly, especially in summer or in hot climates, than by taking cold. Babies feel the heat more than grown folks. Keep them cool in summer. They will not take cold. All through the hot season dress the child very lightly and keep it cool. Unless the baby is very delicate, limit its clothing in hot weather to a shirt, petticoat, cotton dress, narrow bellyband of thin wool, and the diaper. During the height of summer one thin piece, as a loose muslin slip or gauze shirt, is enough both day and night, in addition to a narrow bellyband of light wool and a diaper. On very hot days take off all the clothing but the diaper, unless the baby is under four months old, or is delicate or colicky, in which case the bellyband should be worn.

A baby with fever should never be wrapped up. It will not take cold. Remove nearly all the clothing and give a sponge bath every two or three hours. If the baby breaks out with nettle rash or "prickly heat" add to the basin of water a teaspoonful of baking soda or a tablespoonful of vinegar. After bathing with this mixture leave a slight moisture on the skin. Remove all clothing except the diaper and lay the baby in a cool place, but not in a draft. Keep the feet warm, the head cool. It is a mistake to suppose that babies must be kept wrapped up in flannel at all seasons of the year.

The Diapers.—Use great care in the selection of the baby's diapers at all times, and especially during the summer months when it is so easy to overheat and irritate the bladder and the bowels. Make the diapers of the softest cotton cloth. Change them promptly when wet or soiled and keep them in a bucket or other receptacle containing water in which baking soda has been dissolved in the proportion of about one teaspoonful to the pint. Cover tightly to prevent odors and to exclude flies. A big lard pail or tin cracker box is suitable. Remember that summer diarrhœa and cholera infantum are infectious diseases and contagion may be carried to other children or grown persons by flies. Wash soiled diapers as soon as possible with pure refined soap or, preferably, in hot soda water. Rinse, air and dry thoroughly before using again. Never dry and use a diaper a second time before washing it. Boil all diapers at least once a week. Diapers freshly washed should never be put on a child suffering from diarrhœa. If there are no more at hand which have been washed several days previous, go through the house and gather all the clean soft pieces of old linen and muslin you can find. Cut these into proper shape for temporary use. If the supply is still insufficient, borrow from someone else. In summer, diarrhœa diapers must never be used until they have been exposed several days to sunlight and fresh air to kill the germs which they contain.

After every movement of the bowels change the diaper promptly. Babies often get sick from being left with soiled diapers on. Wash the baby well and pay especial attention to the creases in the flesh. The baby may become sore and chafed because it is not well washed, or because baby powder is put on when it is still dirty, or because the diapers are not washed out but only dried and used again. If the baby is chafed apply to the irritated surfaces a little zinc oxide ointment, sweet oil or olive oil instead of powder.

Clothing worn during the day which is to be worn again should be hung up to air, preferably out of doors, weather permitting. Garments worn at night should be hung up to air during the day. Both the baby and its clothing should be kept at all times clean, sweet and free from odor.

Bathing.—Give the baby a tub bath every morning, preferably at a certain regular hour. A clean baby is happier and healthier than a dirty baby. A daily bath helps the baby to stand heat and, in hot weather, it may be well to bathe the baby twice or three times a day. Never bathe within an hour after feeding. A good plan is to give the baby its bath, then its bottle and then a nap. The first full bath should not be given for a week or ten days after birth. The water should not be below blood heat, which is between 98° and 99°. Or, better, make the water one or two degrees warmer than your own or the baby's temperature. If the infant is vigorous, the temperature may gradually be reduced to 95° at six months, to 90° at one year of age, and to 80° at the age of two and a half years.

Every mother should have a clinical thermometer. This can be obtained at any drug store. If you have one, use it when preparing the baby's bath. If not, test the water by putting your face in it. Never test it by the arm or hand. Until the infant is able to sit up unsupported, it should have only a sponge bath, but do not use a sponge. They cannot be kept clean. Use instead pieces of soft old toweling, or cheese cloth which can be balled up in the hand. As soon as the baby can sit up, obtain a small bath tub or use a wash tub. If the water is neither too cold nor too warm, the child will always enjoy its bath. The reason that some children do not like

Bathing the baby.

the bath is because they have been put into water that is too hot or too cold. Remember that an infant does not react quickly from a cold bath and is depressed or injured by water that seems only slightly cool to an adult. Children's skin is very sensitive and the baby must not be permitted to take cold. It should be bathed in a room warmed to a temperature of at least 75° and carefully guarded against drafts.

A cold bath indoors or outdoor fresh water or surf bathing, should not be permitted under three years. A child of two years may be allowed to run about on the sand with its bare feet and occasionally step in the water, but much harm has been done by immersing young babies in cold water. It is a good plan to sponge the neck and feet of a baby over twelve months old with cold water at night and follow with brisk rubbing. This in many cases will prevent its taking cold.

Take good care of the baby's skin. If it is irritated the baby will be uncomfortable, and will tend to become fretful and unhealthy. Buy only the purest kind of soap for the baby's bath and use it sparingly. The green castile Zanti soap is the best and can be procured through your druggist. If this is not available, white castile soap is the next choice. Do not use soap if the skin is irritated or raw. Place a cheese cloth bag containing a teacupful of bran in the baby's bath and squeeze it until the water becomes slightly milky.

On very warm days, sponge the baby two to four times with lukewarm water in which dissolve a little salt in the proportion of a teaspoon to each pint, or use a like amount of alcohol (not wood alcohol) instead of salt. For nettle rash or "prickly heat" bathe the affected skin with water containing a teaspoonful of baking soda or a tablespoonful of vinegar, but remember that roughened or inflamed skin may be the sign of infectious disease. If it does not yield to this treatment consult your physician.

If the baby has fever, sponge it in cool vinegar water every two or three hours and place cool wet cloths on its head. Sponge the baby whenever the diapers are changed. Take especial care to cleanse the creases of the body, particularly after movements of the bowels. Dry the skin thoroughly after sponging and if talcum powder is used, buy only the unscented.

Don't let the baby crawl on a dirty floor where it may pick up the germs of tuberculosis or other disease and transmit them to its mouth. Keep the floor clean and wash the baby's hands after crawling.

Care of the Mouth. — Wash out the mouth at least twice a day with a soft clean cloth wet in water containing a teaspoonful of borax or baking soda to the pint, but never put your fingers in the baby's mouth without first washing them. Don't let the baby put dogs or cats close to its mouth.

Fresh Air.—Fresh air is as important to the baby's health as fresh food. Children, like growing plants, thrive best in the open air. Keep the baby in the largest, coolest, best ventilated room you have. Screen the windows and doors against flies

Keep the baby cool.

and destroy those that get in. Also protect the baby from flies, mosquitoes and other insects by screens and mosquito netting. Insects often carry the germs of malaria, typhoid and other contagious diseases. Keep the room clean and free from garbage, soiled clothes and rubbish. Even in winter and in cold climates, the airing of the baby's room may be begun when he is not more than a month old. Thereafter the windows may be kept open for a gradually lengthened period of time from a few minutes to an hour or several hours at a time depending on the weather. Protect the baby when thus exposed to the fresh air by putting on his bonnet and coat the same as for an airing out of doors. If thus habituated to fresh air the baby is much less liable to colds than if reared in foul or stagnant air.

In summer keep as little fire as possible. In very hot weather keep the doors and windows wide open night and day. Always keep one or more windows open in the baby's sleeping room winter and summer, night and day, and whether the baby is sick or well, as soon as it has been properly accustomed to fresh air. Some ignorant persons have a superstition that night air is injurious to health. Night air is the only kind of air there is at night and fresh outdoor air is far more wholesome than that which has been shut up in the house and breathed over and over again. In summer sleep out of doors with the baby if you can.

Keep the baby out of the kitchen or other overheated rooms, especially

Keep the baby outdoors in summer.

if you are cooking or washing. Take it out of doors in the early morning when the air is free from dust, and if the weather is good keep it out of doors, if you can, all day. Avoid the sun on hot days. Keep on the shady side of the street, under the trees, or in some shady place. Walk and move around slowly. Have a basket for the baby to sleep in, which you can hang up outdoors in some shady place away from dust and sudden winds. But when you place the baby in the shade be very careful to alter its position as the sun moves around. Be careful not to let the sun shine on the baby's eyes. Its sight may be injured if it is left staring up into the hot sun. During the fly season see that the baby is covered with a suitable net. Keep it away from crowds and crowded places. Babies are very susceptible to the germs of contagious diseases.

A trip to the country for city babies, or any change to a higher altitude or cooler climate, may save the baby's life if summer complaint or diarrhœa should set in during the heat of midsummer. Choose preferably some place near a large body of water. An ideal spot is a heavy wooded region on the banks of a lake or bay. Too much sunshine is harmful—natural shade is necessary to health and comfort. Even a few hours in the park every day or two may save the life of a baby living in a crowded city. When traveling with a sick baby, carry sufficient food —cow's milk, condensed milk or other manufactured foods — to last the baby during the trip. Also carry a supply of pure or boiled water for the baby to drink and for use in mixing its food. There is a traveling basket on the market lined with metal and felt, or mineral wool, which contains chambers for ice and milk bottles. In this, milk can be kept the same as in a refrigerator. This basket will also carry an alcohol stove and supply of alcohol, ex-

Traveling basket for baby's food.

tra nipples, brushes and other accessories to the nursing bottle.

Sleep and Rest.—Under no circumstances should a baby sleep with its mother, nurse or any other person. Very young babies have often been smothered by their mothers overlying them in sleep. There is also a temptation to frequent nursing at night which is harmful to both the baby and mother. If there is no crib, a bed for the baby may be made up on a couple of chairs at the mother's bedside. The baby will be much more comfortable in such a bed and will neither disturb others nor be disturbed. The backs of the chairs will keep the baby from falling. A Morris chair makes a good substitute for an infant's crib and can be utilized during the daytime. Lay the back down flat with something under it for a support and use the cushions as a mattress.

The Baby's Bed.—The best kind of a bed for a baby is a mattress made of excelsior covered with cheese cloth. A good quality of excelsior may be obtained at any furniture store or factory for a few cents, and cheese cloth may be found in any dry goods store at three or four cents a yard. Such a bed is always cool, clean and comfortable. It helps the child to keep strong and well and free from colds and coughs. Should it become soiled, the excelsior can be removed, the cover washed and another cover stuffed with excelsior substituted. This bed is highly recommended for sick children, especially in summer months. If an ordinary mattress is used it should be firm and hard.

Never put a baby to sleep on a feather pillow or lay it on a rubber cloth or oil cloth upon a bed. Such beds overheat the baby's back and head, so that when taken up it is wet with sweat, and very apt to take cold. Never use feather pillows. Provide a crib for the baby and let it sleep alone at night. Keep the bed and bed clothes scrupulously clean. Change them promptly if they become soiled. Cover the bed or crib with mosquito netting. Flies not only make the baby restless, but may communicate the germs of malaria, typhoid, or other contagious diseases.

Sleep and Naps.—Let the baby sleep all it will. Authorities differ as to whether or not a well child should be awakened from its nap to be fed at its regular feeding time. The prevailing opinion seems to be that the child should be allowed to awaken naturally, but that, if put down for its naps at regular hours and not handled or disturbed, it will sleep about the same length of time each day and can thus be trained in regular habits of sleep which will not interfere with the regularity of its feedings or turn night into day. Babies under three years of age should have regular two-hour naps morning and afternoon. Up to six months old they should have eighteen hours' sleep and thereafter at least twelve hours' sleep at night, besides the daily naps. Older children should have at least one nap during the day. The want of sufficient sleep is a very serious hindrance to the child's growth and development. Get the baby into the habit of going to sleep without being held or rocked. This is much better for the baby and saves time for the mother or other members of the family. Lay the baby down in a suitable place and let it alone. Children often cry when put down to sleep. If they are let alone and not handled or talked to they stop crying and go to sleep. Don't fear that the baby will rupture itself by crying. Don't keep a child at the breast or bottle while putting it to sleep.

Handling.—When the baby is awake don't get it into the habit of being held by its mother or other children. Most babies suffer because they are used to amuse older people and are forced to laugh or are tossed about and excited when they need to rest or be quiet. Constant holding and passing from one arm to the other tend to make the baby fretful, cross and sick. No man or woman would like to be held, tossed or tumbled around for several hours daily by a much larger person. This is just what frequently happens to the child. He likes to play by himself. Therefore, let him alone with some one to watch him, and don't handle him.

Quieting the Baby.—Never give a child soothing sirup to make him sleep. Such preparations contain some form of opium or other poisonous, habit-forming drugs. Don't let it suck a nipple, "comforter" or "pacifier." All artificial devices for quieting babies are harmful. Pacifiers often cause thrush or other infections of the mouth. Their use causes a constant flow of saliva which interferes with digestion. They sometimes cause deformities of the mouth and teeth, and may lead to the habit of sucking the fingers. They are wholly unnecessary and their use should be discontinued.

Standing and Walking.—The free use of the muscles is essential to health even in early infancy. Do not swathe the baby's limbs so closely as to prevent their movements. Even in the early months it is a good plan, under proper conditions of warmth, to take off babies' outer wraps and let them kick. It is good for them. Do not encourage the baby to stand or try to teach it to walk. It will walk when it gets ready. The bones of an infant are plastic and if its weight is thrown upon them too soon there will be danger of bow-legs or other deformities. It is a mistake to encourage a child to stand or walk too early. Few babies can walk at twelve months and none should be allowed to do so.

BREAST FEEDING

If you love your baby nurse it. Its chance for life will be nearly ten times greater than the chance of the bottle-fed baby. Nursing will also lay the foundations of a good constitution with which to resist the attacks of summer complaint, consumption, convulsions and rickets (bow-legs), and the contagious diseases of infancy. Children never fully recover from the effects of a lack of proper nourishment during the first few months of life. The chief advantage of breast feeding over bottle feeding is that breast milk is the cleanest milk obtainable. Taken directly from the maternal breast to the stomach of the infant the natural food of infancy is not exposed to anything that might contaminate or pollute it. Careful observation shows that it is not the hot weather itself that causes the high mortality among infants in summer, for breast-fed babies do not die excessively in hot weather. The difference is due to the freedom of breast milk from the micro-organisms, or germs in dirty cow's milk, which cause intestinal disease. Even the difference in the composition of breast milk and bot-

The baby's birthright.

tle milk seems to play a very minor rôle in the high summer death rate, because in the winter there is very little difference in the death rate as between breast-fed and bottle-fed babies.

There is no perfect substitute for mother's milk. The milk of the cow, goat, and other animals, condensed milk, and the artificial manufactured foods so widely advertised, are unnatural and unsatisfactory makeshifts. Even the milk of the wet nurse will not agree with the infant as well as that of its mother. All of these substitutes have been often analyzed and the difference between them and the natural food of infancy is clearly understood. The milk of the she ass and the mare most closely resemble that of women through their percentage of casein. Cow's milk comes next. Goat's milk holds only the fourth place. It has no advantage over cow's milk. Condensed milk contains too much sugar, and not enough fat. None of the manufactured foods most commonly used contain sufficient fat; some contain too much starch, others too much sugar. At times some of these substitutes may be used to advantage, but none of them can take the place of mother's milk, nor be safely used alone.

Almost every mother can nurse her baby if she will. Even though there is but little milk at first, don't become discouraged; be patient and try, try again. There are very few mothers whose breasts will not give sufficient milk if they will encourage the baby to suck. This keeps the milk flowing and increases the flow. Even though you feel weak, you can nurse the baby without danger to yourself. Only a few serious diseases forbid nursing. If you are in doubt, consult your doctor. His advice is better than that of your neighbors or relatives.

Even though the breast milk is scanty, you should cherish it as you value your baby's life and health. A single swallow of such food is better than nothing. In such a case do not alternate the breast with the bottle feeding. This will tend to let the breasts dry up. Nurse regularly to the extent of the supply, and if required, immediately make up the shortage at each feeding from the bottle.

Care of the Nursing Mother.—A nursing mother must keep herself well in order to keep her baby well. Breast-fed babies often vomit or have diarrhœa because the mother is sick or tired out, or because the milk is poor. Causes which weaken the mother and injure her milk are improper food, irregular meals, exhaustion from over-work or lack of sleep, and too frequent or prolonged nursing. Mothers must not overwork, worry, or get over-heated. They should sleep as much as possible, and preferably outdoors, or in rooms with windows wide open. The above causes may render the milk less nutritious or even dangerous. They act especially in hot weather. If you feel that you cannot nurse your baby or think that you ought not to do so, consult your doctor before using any kind of artificial food. There are cases in which it is better to remove the baby from the breast, but the dangers are such that the mother should not assume this responsibility but should be guided by the doctor's advice.

Nursing mothers should therefore keep themselves well and their milk in good condition, by eating at regular hours three plain, well-cooked meals a day, consisting of milk, meat, vegetables and cereals. They should drink freely between meals of pure cold water. The notion that large quantities of tea, coffee and beer improve the quality of the mother's milk is mistaken. Beer and tea are always harmful and large quantities are positively dangerous. Mothers should keep their bowels regular. Constipation in a nursing mother often causes colic in her child. If the mother is ill or run down, or the baby has diarrhœa and vomiting, she should consult a doctor at once, and before giving the baby other foods or bottle feeding.

Diet of the Nursing Mother.—Both the quantity and the quality of the mother's milk may be improved by improving her health and by modification of her diet.

The first rule of a good diet for the nursing mother is that it must agree with her and keep her in a good state of health. Hence a diet adopted to increase the quantity or quality of the milk must not be adhered to unless it proves wholesome to the mother. Some foods, as tomatoes, strawberries and lettuce, which may be eaten by some nursing mothers without affecting their babies, cannot be eaten by others. For most mothers these fresh foods are of great value and may be eaten freely. The mother must be in good health to produce good milk.

The quantity of the milk may be increased by the use of liquid foods. Drink plenty of pure water and good rich milk. A quart or more of milk a day may often be taken to advantage. The diet may be varied by the use of tea, coffee (taken sparingly), cocoa and soup, in addition to milk. Take care not to brew tea and coffee long enough to extract from them the tannin, caffein and other harmful substances they contain. Never boil tea or put the teapot over the fire. Simply put in the tea and pour boiling water over it. Pour as soon as it is strong enough, which will be in about three minutes. Do not allow coffee to boil. Use preferably a coffee percolator and remove from the fire as soon as it begins to boil. Drink freely of pure water, but avoid all sour, salt or highly spiced foods and alcoholic drinks of all kinds. Also avoid saline purgatives (salts)—they are highly injurious.

Quality of Mother's Milk.—If the breast milk is plentiful and of good quality, yet fails to nourish the infant, a change of the mother's diet and habits will be found to give excellent results. The richness of the milk may be increased by eating plenty of meat, eggs, animal broths, and other animal foods; or decreased by omitting or decreasing these foods and by eating freely of fruits and cereals. If the infant does not increase in weight, the use of fats and oils by the mother will soon cause improvement.

Roth's Rules for Influencing Breast Milk.—To increase the total quantity, increase proportionately the liquids in the mother's diet and encourage her to believe that she will be enabled to nurse her infant; or to decrease the quantity, decrease the liquids proportionately.

To increase the total solids, shorten the nursing intervals and decrease the exercise and the proportion of liquids in the mother's diet. To decrease the total solids, prolong the nursing intervals and increase the exercise and the proportion of liquid diet. To increase the fats, increase the proportion of meat in the diet and of the fats which are in a readily digestible form. To decrease the fats, decrease the proportion of meat and fat in the diet. To increase the proteids, decrease the exercise; or to decrease the proteids, increase the exercise up to the limit of fatigue for the individual.

When to Nurse.—The mother's milk does not always come immediately after the birth of the child. Sometimes it is unusually late in coming. In these cases, the rule should be to wait and be sure before resorting to bottle feeding. Take the advice of the family doctor. This is too serious a matter to be settled offhand and without the best advice. Sometimes a good flow of milk is not established until the fourth, fifth or sixth day. Some young mothers make the serious mistake of giving other food to their babies during this time. It may be taken for granted that nature's method cannot be improved upon. The baby will not starve. If it is given anything except the mother's milk, it may be seriously injured. Put the child to the breast every six hours the first day, and every four hours the second day after birth, or oftener if it fails to nurse or obtain nourishment. But do not awaken it to nurse. Undisturbed rest is what it needs. In the interval between nursings give it a clean linen rag moistened with pure, boiled water to suck. After the milk comes, usually from the third day on, the frequency of nursing during the first year is shown in the following table from Holt:

Period.	Nursings in 24 hours.	Interval by day.	Night nursings (10 P. M. to 6 A.M.)
1st and 2d day..	4	6 hrs.	1
3 days to 6 wks...	10	2 "	2
6 wks. to 3 mos...	8	$2\frac{1}{2}$ "	2
3 to 5 months....	7	3 "	1
5 to 12 months...	6	3 "	0

After the third day and for the next six weeks, nurse the baby every two hours during the day time, and not more than twice at night, or a total of not more than ten nursings in the twenty-four hours. The healthy child will take one or more naps each day. It should not be awakened for feeding, but aside from this should be fed regularly every two hours.

The interval between nursings may be increased from the sixth week to the third month to two and one-half hours with one nursing at night, or a total of eight nursings in twenty-four hours. The interval may be further increased to three hours during the day time with one nursing at night from the third to the fifth month. From the fifth to the twelfth month the times of feeding remain the same, but the night feeding should be discontinued. If the child wakes up in the night, give it a drink of cooled boiled water, or thin barley water without milk. It needs nothing more. After a short time, if it is well, it will sleep through the night.

It is easy to get the baby into good habits, and hard to get it out of bad habits. By adopting regular habits of nursing, the mother is given more freedom and more rest and is in better condition to take good care of her child. Form the habit of nursing your baby by the clock. It will soon learn to expect its nursing at the proper time, and not at any other time. It is a good plan to write on a slip of paper a memorandum of the hours for nursing with the date on which the hours are to be changed to longer intervals, and also which breast is to be used at each nursing. It is much better to use but one breast at each feeding alternating, than to let the baby nurse at both breasts at each feeding. Such a memorandum during the first six weeks would read:

Right, 5 A. M.; Left, 7 A. M.; Right, 9 A. M.; Left, 11 A. M.; Right, 1 P. M.; Left, 3 P. M.; Right, 5 P. M.; Left, 7 P. M.; Right, 9 P. M.; Change to $2\frac{1}{2}$ hours between nursings on (date).

Do not nurse except at the regular intervals. It is a great, but very common mistake to put the baby to the breast every time it cries. It is more likely to be thirsty or suffering from over-feeding than to be hungry. Give it a drink of water, but do not nurse it until the regular time. If you nurse oftener, your milk will become unfit. Babies when nursed too often or whenever they cry get indigestion and then cry harder from pain. If a baby is not sick or uncomfortable from heat or from the pricking of a pin, it will get no harm from crying. Indeed, every baby should cry during the day. It helps to develop its lungs. Crying, especially during the first few days of life is perfectly natural, and often beneficial. It does not necessarily indicate illness or hunger at any time, and food or medicine should not be given merely because the child cries.

The nursing should not last more than twenty minutes. Never let the baby go to sleep with the nipple in its mouth. Never nurse the baby when you are very tired or very much wrought up with grief, anger, or other very strong emotion. Your milk under such conditions will often be unfit for food. It may give the baby convulsions. In such cases it is often better to draw off the milk and give the infant some other food until you regain self control. Do not take drugs while nursing your baby, except by the direction of your physician. Opium, senna, rhubarb, and some other drugs may affect the milk so as to poison the child.

Care of Nursing Bottles.—If the baby must be fed from a bottle absolute sanitary cleanliness is the price of safety. A baby cannot get clean milk out of a dirty bottle or through a dirty nipple. Sore mouth, colic and summer complaint often come from improper care of bottles and nipples. It is true that some babies have lived in filthy surroundings and survived dirty food, but it is equally true that others have been killed by them. The only safe course is to take no chances. It is better to be safe than to be sorry.

Clean the nursing bottle immediately after each feeding. First rinse with clear cold water. Hot water changes the casein of milk into an insoluble glue which is very hard to wash off. Stale milk curds sticking to the inside of the bottle become poisonous after a few hours and may contaminate fresh food. After rinsing, put the bottle to soak in soda or borax water or soap suds. Finally, scrub the inside with a clean wire or other bottle brush; rinse with hot water and boil for twenty minutes. Turn the bottle upside down in a clean dish without wiping, and place in a clean place to dry and cool. Or, preferably fill the bottle with clean boiled

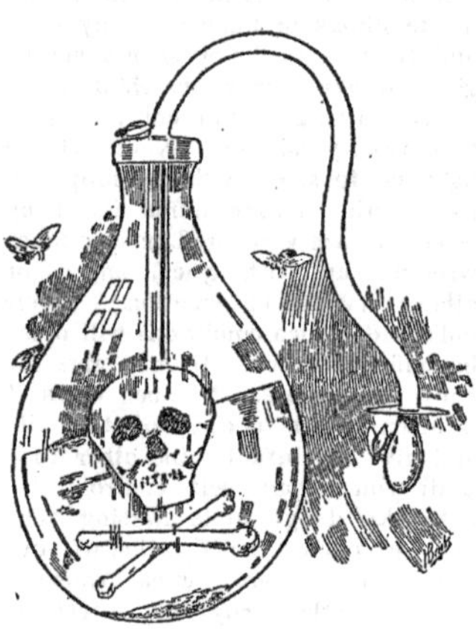

There's death in the dirty bottle.

water and a little piece of cooking soda the size of a pea and let the water stand in the bottle until the next feeding. Never let the bottle stand with milk in it. Never try to save what is left from one feeding until the next.

Nursing Bottles. — Never use square or paneled bottles. Sour milk and dirt cannot be removed from the corners. This filth remaining will afterwards contaminate the fresh food. Also avoid nursing bottles with tubes of either glass or rubber. They may be handy for you, but they are death to your baby. Indigestion and bowel complaint are the

a *b*

(a) Avoid corners or a tube; (b) use a bottle like this.

result. Their use cannot be too strongly condemned. They cannot be properly cleaned and milk taken through them, especially in hot weather, soon becomes filthy and absolutely poisonous to the infant. Square bottles and nursing tubes are baby killers and their sale has been forbidden in many states by law. Select bottles with round corners and with the kind of nipple that fits over the neck and can be turned and washed both inside and out. Nipples of black rubber are better than those of white or red.

No person ailing or sick with a contagious disease, or who is known or suspected of having been exposed to such diseases, should be allowed to touch or come near the baby's milk or other food, or any of the utensils in which it is prepared or served. A small cluster of bacteria from a contaminated finger may develop to a colony of several billions in a bottle of warm milk within a short time.

Care of Rubber Nipples.—Use the kind of nipple which is slipped over the neck of the bottle. Have at least two nipples, or preferably buy a half dozen at a time and keep some on hand to replace those that are lost or injured. After each feeding, turn the nipple inside out, rinse with cold water, and scrub with a brush kept for that purpose. Wash thoroughly with hot water inside and out, and drop into a cup containing about a teaspoonful of soda or borax to the pint of water, until needed for use. Boil the nipple at least once daily for twenty minutes while the milk bottles are being boiled. Rinse the nip-

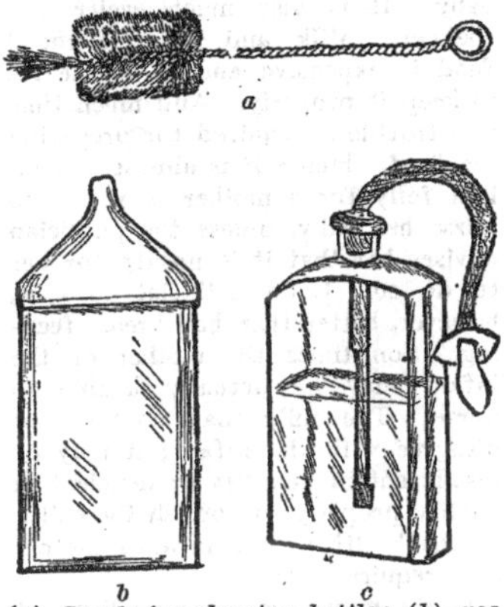

(a) Brush for cleaning bottle; (b) use a bottle and nipple like this; (c) don't use a "baby killer" like this.

ple in boiling water before using it. Don't put it into your mouth to find out whether the milk is warm enough, nor let the nurse do so. To test its temperature, let a few drops of milk fall on your wrist.

Weaning.—Ask your doctor how long you ought to nurse your baby. It will depend partly upon your state of health, and partly upon the season of the year. Some mothers ought to wean their infants at six months, others may nurse them a full year. The average is about nine or ten months. Nursing the child too long is an unnecessary drain upon the mother. There is also great danger of injury to the child. Don't wean your baby as long as he is gaining in weight, and never do so except by the advice of your physician. His advice is better than that of your neighbors. If the baby remains well but stops gaining weight, don't conclude that your milk does not agree with it. Consult your physician about the use of some artificial food to help you out. Wean gradually by giving one breast meal less each week and teach the baby to drink from a cup or bottle. This is better for the baby. Sudden weaning is apt to cause serious illness.

With the advice and consent of your physician, you may begin during the fifth or sixth month to teach the baby to take food and water from a bottle. Thus the baby will be fed for some time with both breast milk and artificial food, and there will be time for his stomach to adjust itself to the change. This plan will materially decrease both the difficulties and dangers of weaning. It also helps you to extend the period of nursing. Every drop of breast milk the baby gets adds to his health and strength as no other food ever can.

In changing from breast milk to cow's milk, the milk used first should be very much diluted and modified unless the baby has been given a bottle in addition to the mother's milk. In weaning a six months old baby give the milk usually given to an infant one month old. If the baby is ten months old, give the milk usually given to a three months old baby.

Wet Nurses.—A true foster mother in good health and spirits and equally as devoted to the welfare of the child as though it were her own, would be the ideal substitute for an infant deprived of its mother's milk. In practice, there are so many objections to the employment of the wet nurse that this plan is by no means as popular as in years past. The cost for board and wages is considerable and the difficulty of finding a suitable person is very great. The mother who yields her natural function to another must remember that if the nurse is not perfectly healthy she may infect the child with disease; if careless and ignorant, she may cause the death of the child through neglect; and if her own baby should chance to suffer through her employment, she may grieve or become so nervously excited as to make her milk unwholesome. She may also leave at any moment without warning. Hence, a wet nurse should never be hired unless she is known to be reliable and of good moral character and is pronounced by a competent physician to be free from disease. Inquiries should be made as to the circumstances surrounding her own child. Reasonable assurance should be had that she is likely to be free from anxiety or worry.

The same care should be devoted to the nurse's habits of life and diet as the nursing mother should exercise in her own behalf. As a rule it is necessary that the nurse should have the sort of food and the amount of exercise to which she has previously been accustomed, rather than that she be fed upon rich foods and suffered to lead a life of idleness.

ARTIFICIAL FEEDING

All doctors of experience agree that the problem of the artificial feeding of infants is one of the most serious which they are called upon to face. Some babies have to be put on the bottle at birth or during the first few weeks or months of life. All must be weaned sooner or later. Hence, this is a problem which must be worked out for every single child. There are certain facts and principles which every mother should know, because they are of equal importance in all cases. But every mother should clearly understand that no set of rules can be laid down which will be adapted in all respects to any child. Each baby needs a combination suited to his digestion. The mixture upon which some other baby is thriving may be too strong or too weak for your baby. The only way to learn what food will agree with your baby is by experience. The facts and principles herein stated are condensed from the official publications of boards of health throughout the United States. They may be relied upon as the consensus of the best medical opinion. But if your baby does not thrive upon artificial food prepared as here suggested, you should consult your family physician and be guided by his advice.

It is much better for her own health as well as that of the child for the mother to nurse her own baby. It is also much easier and cheaper. Milk and other artificial food is expensive and so is the ice to keep it properly. And much time and trouble is required for preparing the food. Hence it is almost a criminal folly for a mother to refuse to nurse her baby, unless the physician advises her that it is unsafe for her to do so. Good artificial food is, however, better than bad breast feeding. Sometimes the mother or the infant may be actually unable to nurse. The milk may continue to disagree with the infant; it may be insufficient in quantity or deficient in quality properly to nourish the child; or the health of the infant's mother may require weaning.

If the milk is good in quality, but insufficient in quantity, it is far better to continue the breast feeding and to give the baby some artificial food in addition, to help the mother out. Mother's milk is not only the most easily digested and the most nutritious of all baby foods. It contains a ferment such that a very small quantity helps to digest a larger quantity of cow's milk. It also contains certain antitoxin substances which afford a large degree of protection against diarrhœal diseases, the ordinary infectious diseases, and some others. Hence, even if the supply of breast milk is not sufficient for the total nourishment of the child, this partial supply is of such great value that it should be kept up as long as possible.

Even when the mother's milk has nearly disappeared it may sometimes be brought back. If the inclination of the child has not been spoiled by feeding from a cup or spoon it will, by regular application to the breast, help to stimulate the secretion of milk. The flow can also be encouraged by proper attention to the diet. But if the mother is suffering from disease which impairs the healthfulness of the milk, breast feeding must be wholly discontinued and artificial food adopted.

When Not to Nurse.—When the mother is consumptive or suffers from any other chronic disease or is very delicate, nursing may be too severe a drain upon her and may be unwholesome for the child. Nursing a consumptive mother is not only dangerous to the child; it may hasten the progress of the mother's disease and make fatal its termination. Breast feeding is also out of the question when serious complications follow the child's birth, such as severe hemorrhage, childbed fever, blood poisoning, kidney disease, or when the mother suffers from epilepsy or St. Vitus Dance, or other chronic nervous affliction.

Contrary to common opinion the nursing mother may become pregnant, in which case her baby should be promptly weaned. The milk is then deficient in quality and to continue nursing may work irreparable injury to both mother and child. The importance of this fact cannot be over-estimated, as some mothers from a mistaken opinion to the contrary nurse their children for several months after they should be weaned and suffer the most unfortunate consequences.

The menstruation of the mother does not affect the milk as much as usually believed. It may cause slight indigestion, but is not sufficient reason to stop nursing. Extreme sensitiveness of the breasts to the point of intense pain in nursing is not a good reason for discontinuing. Persistence for a few days will allow nature time to effect a cure.

MILK MODIFICATION

Cow's milk undiluted and unmodified is entirely unfit for infants under one year old, but when properly diluted and mixed it is the best substitute for mother's milk. Cow's milk must be diluted on account of its richness in curds. The cheesy matter it contains forms large curds in the child's stomach which are harder to digest than the smaller curds in mother's milk. Hence it is necessary to dilute the cow's milk, both to lessen the amount of cheesy matter and to break up the curds into small particles so that the child can digest the milk more easily. When diluted, however, it contains too little fats and sugar. Hence after dilution, it is necessary to add cream and sugar to the milk. This process imitates the milk of the mother as nearly as can be done. It is commonly known as milk modification. Milk so treated is called modified milk. This is now accepted by all authorities as the best food for the infant deprived of breast milk. Cow's milk can be diluted either by water, by decoctions of cereals such as barley or oatmeal, or, toward the end of the first year, by beef or mutton broth. Both oatmeal and beef broth have a tendency to loosen the bowels. Changes have to be made from time to time to suit the infant's digestion. Your physician will advise you as to how this can be done.

Good cow's milk contains about four per cent of butter fat and may be called 4% milk. After standing

(a) Upper third 10% milk; (b) upper half 7%; (c) whole milk 4%. Courtesy State Board of Health of Illinois.

until the cream rises to the top, the upper third of a bottle of good milk contains ten per cent of butter fat. This is called 10% milk, or cream. The upper half contains seven per cent of butter fat and is known as 7% milk. Always buy whole milk, i. e., 4% milk, never skimmed milk.

Materials Required for Milk Mixing.—It is good economy to equip yourself at the outset with a full set of proper utensils for mixing the baby's milk. The best are none too good. The whole cost will hardly equal the doctor's fees which may result from a single illness due to improper feeding. You will require an eight-ounce glass graduate, a glass funnel, a cream dipper, a dozen nursing bottles, a half dozen black rubber nipples, and three bottle brushes for washing out the bottles. If you buy milk in bottles and measure it in a glass graduate you will not need to use pitchers, cups, or other measures. But whatever utensils you do use for mixing the baby's food should be kept by themselves, washed separately, boiled and drained without wiping, and not put into the dish water or wiped with a dish towel in the ordinary way.

The Materna Measure.—This is a sixteen-ounce measure with six panel sides. It affords a simple means of milk mixing in the home. On each side is marked the exact amount of sugar, lime water, water, milk and cream to be used in feeding. The six panels are labeled to measure the food suitable to as many ages of infancy. If your druggist does not carry this measure in stock ask him to order one for you. It will help you to avoid making mistakes.

All utensils used in preparing baby food should be of glass, china, porcelain or granite-ironware. These will not rust nor present crevices for the accumulation of dirt. Never use vessels or utensils which are cracked or have rough edges or surfaces. Select nursing bottles with round bottoms and free from angles. The best bottles are marked with a scale of ounces so that the exact amount given may be measured at each feeding. It is advisable to purchase a dozen bottles because it is much more convenient to mix in the morning the food for the entire day. Put enough for each feeding in a sepa-

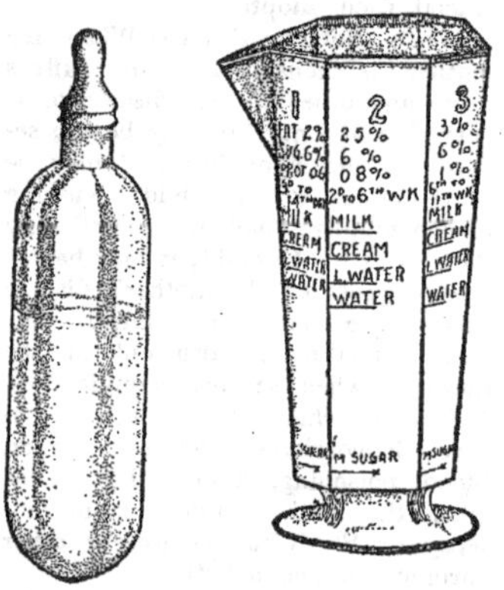

a b

(a) Best style of nursing bottle; (b) materna measure.

rate bottle and then place the bottles on ice. Ten feedings will be required for small infants and it is well to have extra bottles on hand in case of breakage. Fewer bottles may be used, but no mother should attempt to get along with less than two. It is better to have plenty of bottles so that the same bottles will not have to be used too frequently.

MATERIALS FOR MILK MODIFICATION

Water.—The purity of water with which infants' food is diluted is equally as important as the purity of the milk. The benefits of clean milk are entirely lost if it is diluted with dirty water. Pure spring water, which can be purchased in bottles in many localities, is to be preferred for diluting infants' food, but if it is necessary to use water from cisterns, wells, or streams of doubtful purity, boil the water for half an hour and store it in clean glass bottles stoppered with cotton wool or antiseptic gauze. Do not allow it to stand over six hours.

Lime Water.—Lime water is used to overcome the acidity of cow's milk and to lessen the consistency of the curd. There are some infants with whom it does not agree, and if used too freely it may cause constipation. Vichy water is a good substitute for lime water and should be used if the latter does not agree. Either can be obtained from a druggist. But in buying material of any kind for infant feeding, patronize only druggists in whom you can have confidence. Some unscrupulous druggists sell ordinary unfiltered tap water for lime water.

Sugar.—Sugar is not added to cow's milk to sweeten it and make it more palatable, but to make it conform as nearly as possible to mother's milk. Milk sugar is best if you can get a pure article from a reliable druggist. But milk sugar often contains impurities. Hence, unless you are very sure of the reliability of your dealer, use cane sugar; this is rarely adulterated or impure. Loaf sugar is the purest form of sugar and among the purest of all foods. Use only half the quantity of cane sugar that you would of milk sugar.

Barley Water.—This is often used in diluting milk for infant feeding to make the curds of milk more easily digestible. Barley flour * is preferable to pearl barley. To make barley water use two tablespoonfuls of barley flour or meal, and a small pinch of salt, to a quart of cold water. First stir the barley flour with a little of the water into a thin paste. Then add the remainder of the water, stir and boil fifteen to twenty minutes. If pearl barley is used it must be thoroughly cooked. Place two tablespoonfuls in one quart of water and boil from two to three hours. Add more water from time to time so that the quantity in the end will be one quart. Strain through a clean piece of cheese cloth sterilized by baking in a hot oven. Barley water should not be kept from day to day, but should be made fresh every morning.

A prominent physician of northern Illinois, who has been practicing for thirty-two years, says: "My food for babies is invariably one heaping tablespoonful of pearl (store) barley, ground in a coffee-mill, and boiled in one quart of water, down to a pint. Strain, add the same quantity of milk, and let the baby have it. Hundreds of mothers have used this preparation on my direction, and the result has been healthy, growing, fat babies. I think that Professor Jacobi recommended this many years ago. At any rate I always use it, and with constant success."

Oatmeal Water.—This is used in the same way as barley water, especially if a laxative effect is desired. To make it, stir two tablespoonfuls of oatmeal with a pinch of salt in a quart of boiling water. Cover and let simmer for two or three hours. Replace the water as it evaporates so that there will be a quart when done. Strain the same as for barley water and make fresh every day.

Or, for oatmeal or rice water, put three tablespoonfuls of oatmeal (H-O) or rice into a quart of water. Soak three hours or overnight. Then boil steadily for two hours keeping the quantity up to a quart with more water as needed. Add a pinch of salt and strain as for barley water. Keep in an ice box or other cool place and make fresh daily.

BOTTLE FEEDING

The best plan is to prepare each morning enough food to last for twenty-four hours and place the required quantity for each nursing in a separate nursing bottle. Plug the

---

* Robinson's patent barley or the prepared barley of the Health Food Company are standard preparations of barley flour and can be obtained at almost any drug store.

bottles with baked absorbent cotton, cotton wool or antiseptic gauze.

Or, if you do not have enough nursing bottles, prepare enough food for twenty-four hours and place it in a clean, freshly boiled fruit jar with a glass clamp top. Do not use the screw-top jars. They are not so easy to keep clean. Do not use the rubber ring, it is hard to keep clean and is not necessary.

Get together all the necessary utensils, and put them in a saucepan, preferably of agate ware. Cover them with cold or luke-warm water, and bring them slowly to a boil. Clear off a table top to work on and cover it with a freshly laundered towel or other clean cloth. See that everything that comes in contact with the milk is absolutely clean. Wash your hands with soap and water and scrub them with a stiff brush with especial attention to the finger nails. Put the water to be used in mixing the food on the fire in a covered saucepan. Bring it to a boil and keep it, until ready for use, in the same vessel in which it was boiled. Now mix the food exactly as the doctor directs, or in accordance with the formula you have adopted. Always mix it exactly the same way. As soon as the food has been placed in nursing bottles or fruit jar, and stoppered properly, put these on ice or in the coolest place you can find. Work quickly and do not let the milk or prepared food stand in a warm room any longer than is necessary.

Or, if the milk is not perfectly fresh, or has not been freshly pasteurized, it may be pasteurized after it has been prepared and placed in the nursing bottles. This is perhaps the safest course, as it avoids all possibility of contamination from the time the food is prepared until it is fed. After the nursing bottles are filled stand them up on a plate in the bottom of a saucepan filled with luke-warm water up to within two or three inches of the tops of the bottles. Bring the water slowly to a boil. Then remove the saucepan from the fire and let the bottles stand in the hot water for fifteen or twenty minutes. Now cool the water surrounding the bottles by pouring in cold water. But take care not to cool the bottles so quickly as to crack them. As soon as they are cold enough to handle, plug with cotton stoppers and put them on the ice.

Or, if you have no ice, springhouse or other means of keeping milk cool, especially in summer weather, it is better to sterilize the milk absolutely by leaving the saucepan on the fire and keeping the water just at the boiling point for 20 minutes. Then chill thoroughly with cold water. Plug with cotton and keep as cool as you can. Such milk is not as wholesome as pasteurized or fresh milk would be if kept on ice, but it contains no living germs and is therefore safer than unsterilized milk which cannot be kept cool at 40 degrees F. or under.

Feeding the Baby.—Keep the food on ice until ready for use and heat it when the baby needs it. Never let the bottle stand in a warm room with milk in it. Be sure not to heat a bottle when you go to bed and keep it in bed until nursing time, because you do not want to go to the ice box for it. This is certain to make the baby sick. Do not attempt to keep milk at a luke-warm temperature at night or any other time in a thermos bottle or by any other arrangement. Such a device simply acts as an incubator for germs which, at this temperature, quickly grow to enormous numbers and render the milk dangerous.

Place the nursing bottle in hot water when needed and warm the food to about body heat. Do not give the baby cold milk. Do not give the baby hot milk. Make the temperature just right. Wash your hands in soap and water before adjusting the nipple. Never put the nipple in your own mouth to find out whether the milk is warm enough. Try it on your wrist. Taste a little from a spoon. If the milk is not sweet do not give it to the baby. Shake the bottle before using it.

Don't feed a baby under six months of age from a cup or spoon. Sucking is the natural way by which a baby takes its food. It needs the sucking action of the lips, mouth and tongue to mix its food with the fluids of the mouth, and for the proper development of the mouth and teeth.

How and When to Feed.—In feeding your baby from the bottle follow as nearly as you can the same rule as feeding from the breast. Write down on a slip of paper the hours for feeding and feed by the clock at regular intervals. Break away from

TABLE OF TIMES AND AMOUNTS FOR INFANT FEEDING FOR THE FIRST YEAR

AGE	Hours between feeding	Number of feedings between 10 P. M. and 7 A. M.	Number of feedings in 24 hours	Ounces to each feeding	Ounces in 24 hours
3rd to 7th day	2	2	10	1–1½	10–15
2nd to 3rd week	2	2	10	1½–3	15–30
4th to 5th week	2	1	10	2½–3½	25–35
6th week to 3rd month	2½	1	8	3–5	25–40
3rd to 5th month	3	1	7	4–6	28–42
5th to 9th month	3	0	6	5–7½	30–45
9th to 12th month	4	0	5	7–9	35–45

FEEDING ACCORDING TO BABY'S WEIGHT, THE BEST WAY, OR BY AGE

Child's Weight in Pounds for Age in Mos.	Total Amts. for 24 hours			At each feeding			How Often	In 24 Hours	From 6 A. M. to 6 P. M.	From 6 P. M. to 6 A. M.
	Milk	Water	Teaspoonfuls Sugar	Milk	Water	Teaspoonfuls Sugar				
6, 7 and 8 up to 2 Mos.	8 oz.	16 oz.	5	1 oz.	2 oz.	½	1 bottle every 2 hours	8 bottles	6 bottles	2 bottles
9 and 10, 2–3 Mos.	12 oz.	20 oz.	5	1½ oz.	2½ oz.	½	1 bottle every 2 hours	8 bottles	6 bottles	2 bottles
11, 12, 13 and 14 3–6 Mos.	18 oz.	18 oz.	6	2½ oz.	2½ oz.	¾	1 bottle every 2½ hours	7 bottles	5 bottles	2 bottles
15 and 16, 6–8 Mos.	24 oz.	18 oz.	7	3½ oz.	2½ oz.	1	1 bottle every 2½ hours	7 bottles	5 bottles	2 bottles
17 and 18, 8–10 Mos.	30 oz.	12 oz.	6	5 oz.	2 oz.	1	1 bottle every 3 hours	6 bottles	5 bottles	1 bottle
19 and 20, 10–12 Mos.	48 oz.			8 oz.	0	1½	1 bottle every 3 hours	6 bottles	5 bottles	1 bottle

Two tablespoonfuls make one ounce.

night feedings as soon as possible. Hold the baby in the same position as for nursing at the breast and take care to tip the bottle so that the neck is always full. The baby should not take its food in less than ten minutes. If it sucks too rapidly, withdraw the bottle occasionally for a minute or two, or use a nipple with a smaller hole. But do not prolong the feeding over fifteen or twenty minutes. Never let the child suck the empty bottle. Do not let it go to sleep with the nipple in its mouth. If you start right and get the baby into the habit of nursing at regular intervals, it will not cry for food at other times. If the baby cries, look at the clock, if not feeding time the trouble is something else. Infants and children are frequently fretful from thirst.

How Much to Feed.—Measure the food and give regular amounts at each feeding. Never coax the baby to take more food than it wants. Too much food and too frequent feeding does greater harm than too little. It over-taxes the digestion and leads to stomach and intestinal disturbances. Regurgitation, or the "raising" of the milk after feeding indicates over-feeding. Cut down the amount and avoid digestive troubles and diarrhœa. If the baby does not take the whole feeding throw it away. Do not attempt to save it for the next time.

During days of extreme heat give not more than half the usual food at each feeding, but give the baby all the cold boiled water—not ice water—that it craves. At all seasons take care to give the baby water at frequent intervals in sufficient quantities to quench its thirst.

Feeding Problems.—If a bottle-fed baby does not thrive the difficulty may be that the food is too rich, or not rich enough; that the amount fed is too much, or too little; or that the food spoils before it is fed from not being kept clean and cold. The food must be kept clean and cold to be wholesome at any age. But the quality of the food, the amount to be given at each feeding, and the frequency of the feedings must be modified and adapted to the needs of the growing child. It is usual to give rules for feeding according to the age of the child, but regard must also be had to its weight in pounds. There is a relation between the weight of the baby and size of the stomach. Large babies require more food than small babies. Most authorities agree that a child should not be fed oftener than once in two hours, nor more than ten times in each twenty-four hours during the first few weeks of life, and that the intervals between feedings should be lengthened and the number of feedings decreased progressively up to the end of the first year. The exact time to make these changes must be determined in each case by the state of the baby's health, but the tables on the opposite page may be taken as a fair general average and will be found helpful and suggestive.

It is best to begin with a weak food, as the first milk mixture in the accompanying table, for babies from birth to three or four months of age. The food should be increased gradually both in strength and quality. Do not increase the quantity more than half an ounce at a time. Never increase both the quantity and the richness of the food at the same time. Never feed oftener than suggested by this table. The child's stomach needs some rest. Too rich food or too much food at the beginning makes later feeding difficult. Over-feeding at any time will upset the baby's digestion and may lead to serious illness.

Weight and Height.—The age of a child alone is not a trustworthy guide as to the amount or strength of the food which it should have. The weight is a much more correct index. Weigh the baby every week. Measure its length (or height) and keep a record for future reference. Compare this record with the following standard table of the growth and development of a normal infant.

This will show you at once whether or not your baby is enjoying a normal development. The average weight of a child at birth is 7 or 7½ pounds. During the first week there is a loss of a few ounces. Thereafter the normal gain is about six ounces a week for the first three months, and after that about four ounces a week to the end of the first year.

All weights during the first year should be taken without any clothing. Loss of weight is a danger signal which must not be ignored. If your baby does not gain weight every week consult your doctor and be guided by his advice. In doubtful cases the weighing should be daily or every other day. Use suitable baby scales and record the weight for continuous reference. The weighing of children often brings surprises. Loss of weight indicates that the milk is insufficient in quantity or in nutritive value, or there are faults of digestion and assimilation. Weighing of a breast-fed baby just before and then just after nursing will show the quantity of breast milk obtained.

The growth of the child in length (or height) is another important aid in proper feeding and care of infauts. A normal increase of weight does not prove a normal development. An unsuitable food, such as condensed milk, may increase the weight rapidly enough, or even fatten the baby too much, yet the development may be faulty and the degree of resistance against disease low. Hence both weight and height should be taken into consideration.

LENGTH AND WEIGHT OF A NORMAL BABY

Age	Length	Weight
At birth	19.5 in.	7 lbs.
1 Mo.	20.5 in.	7¾ lbs.
2 Mo.	21. in.	9½ lbs.
3 Mo.	22. in.	11 lbs.
4 Mo.	23. in.	12½ lbs.
5 Mo.	23.5 in.	14 lbs.
6 Mo.	24. in.	15 lbs.
7 Mo.	24.5 in.	16 lbs.
8 Mo.	25. in.	17 lbs.
9 Mo.	25.5 in.	18 lbs.
10 Mo.	26. in.	19 lbs.
11 Mo.	26.5 in.	20 lbs.
12 Mo.	27. in.	21 lbs.

The character of the stools is a most important guide in infant feeding. Foul smelling, frothy or greenish passages indicate illness and may be the forerunner of fatal sickness. When the stools are unnatural in character or more frequent than four a day, a physician should be promptly called.

Milk Mixtures. — The following method of preparing the milk mixtures given in the accompanying tables is recommended by the Illinois State Board of Health as the most convenient and satisfactory for those using bottled milk.

Set apart a separate quart of milk for the baby and do not shake it or

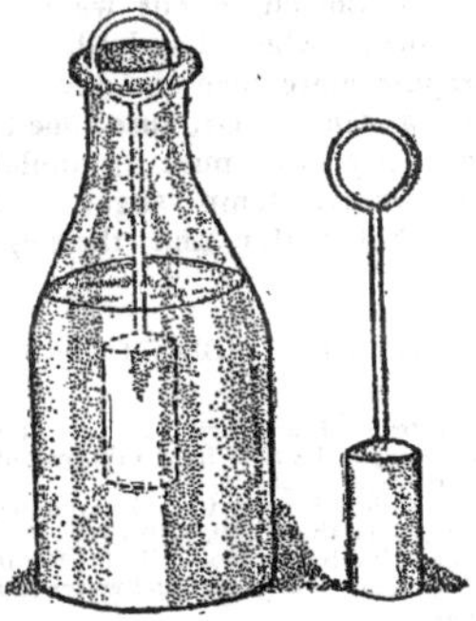

The Chapin cream dipper. Courtesy State Board of Health of Illinois.

pour any milk out of it until after the baby's food has been prepared. Then what is left may be used by others. The top part of the milk, the upper third, or upper half, as required, may be taken off with a spoon by tilting the bottle gently without shaking, and dipping from it with care not to lose sight of the cream line. But it is much better to order through your druggist what is known as the Chapin cream dipper. This inexpensive little device is shown in the illustration. It holds just one ounce and is convenient both for dipping and measuring. If a spoon is used, remember that eight teaspoons are equivalent to one ounce, or four dessertspoons, or two tablespoons.

The 10% milk required by the table for milk mixtures from birth to three or four months of age, may be secured from the upper third of a bottle of good 4% milk, or by mixing two parts of good whole milk with one part of cream. The 7% milk required by the table from the third or fourth month to the end of the ninth or tenth month may be secured from the upper half of a bottle of whole milk, or by mixing three parts of whole milk with one part of cream. A pinch of salt may be added to the food if desired.

The milk sugar required should always be dissolved in hot water. It sours quickly when dissolved, so do not prepare more than one day's supply at a time. Or, use one-half the quantity of pure granulated or, preferably, lump sugar. Dissolve in hot water and thoroughly mix.

The quantity given in the first table is twenty ounces. This is the amount that will be used by an average baby during the first four weeks of life if fed every two hours at the rate of about two ounces each feeding. It is easy to estimate the quantities required for larger amounts. For a twenty-five ounce mixture add one-fourth more of each ingredient. For a thirty ounce mixture, add one-half more of each ingredient. If the baby is fed artificially from birth, begin with mixture No. 1 in the first table. Substitute the succeeding mixtures gradually until the third or fourth month. Observe carefully how the baby thrives and especially any change in weight. After the fourth month the above mixtures are not strong enough and those given in the second table should be substituted.

When weaning older infants use the mixture suited to its age from one of the accompanying tables.

TABLE FOR MILK MODIFICATION PREPARED BY STATE BOARD OF HEALTH OF ILLINOIS

Milk Mixtures.—(From Birth to Three or Four Months of Age.)

1. Milk-sugar, 1 oz. (3 level tablespoonfuls.)
   Lime water, 1 oz.
   Enough hot * water to make 20 ounces. After the milk-sugar is dissolved add two ounces of upper third milk (10% fat).

This is a suitable modified milk for the infant immediately after birth.

2. Milk sugar, lime water and water same as for No. 1, with the addition of 3 ounces of upper third milk.
3. Milk sugar, lime water and water as in No. 1, with the addition of 4 ounces of upper third milk.
4. Milk sugar, lime water and water as in No. 1, with the addition of 5 ounces of upper third milk.
5. Milk sugar, lime water and water as in No. 1, with the addition of 6 ounces of upper third milk.
6. Milk sugar, lime water and water as in No. 1, with the addition of 7 ounces of upper third milk.

(From the Third or Fourth Month to the end of the Ninth or Tenth Month.)

1. Milk sugar, 1 oz. (3 level tablespoonfuls.)
   Lime water, 1 oz.
   Enough hot * water to make 20 ounces. After the milk sugar is dissolved add 3 ounces of upper half milk.
2. Milk sugar, lime water and water as in No. 1, with the addition of 4 ounces of upper half milk.
3. Milk sugar, lime water and water as in No. 1, with the addition of 5 ounces of upper half milk.
4. Milk sugar, lime water and water as in No. 1, with the addition of 6 ounces of upper half milk.
5. Milk sugar, lime water and water as in No. 1, with the addition of 7 ounces of upper half milk.
6. Milk sugar, lime water and water as in No. 1, with the addition of 8 ounces of upper half milk.
7. Milk sugar, lime water and water as in No. 1, with the addition of 9 ounces of upper half milk.
8. Milk sugar, lime water and water as in No. 1, with the addition of 10 ounces of upper half milk.
9. Milk sugar, ¾ oz.
   Lime water, 1 oz.
   Enough water to make 20 ounces. To this add 12 ounces of upper half milk.

Of the above formulas, it is seldom necessary for the healthy infant to use a mixture of less strength than No. 5. Nos. 1, 2, 3 and 4 are of value, however, during temporary disturbances of digestion when it is desired to relieve the digestive organs of as much work as possible.

The infant which can take Mixture No. 9 of the above formulas without difficulty is usually able to begin on No. 5 of the following formulas, in which whole milk (4%) is used.

---

* Not boiled.

Milk Mixtures.—(For the latter part of the First Year.)

1. Milk sugar, 1 oz.
   Lime water, 1 oz.
   Enough hot * water to make 20 ounces. After the milk sugar is dissolved add 5 ounces of whole milk.
2. Milk sugar, lime water and water as in No. 1, with the addition of 6 ounces of whole milk.
3. Milk sugar, lime water and water as in No. 1, with the addition of 8 ounces of whole milk.
4. Milk sugar, lime water and water as in No. 1, with the addition of 10 ounces of whole milk.
5. Milk sugar, ½ oz.
   Lime water, 1 oz.
   Enough water to make 20 ounces. To this add 12 ounces of whole milk.
6. Milk sugar, lime water and water as in No. 5, with the addition of 14 ounces of whole milk.
7. Milk sugar, lime water and water as in No. 5, with the addition of 16 ounces of whole milk.

* Not boiled.

Other Mixtures.—For mothers who cannot get milk in bottles and who have difficulty in using the mixtures given in the above tables, the following are recommended by the Illinois State Board of Health. They are easily prepared and prove satisfactory for most healthy infants.

For a new-born baby, or one a month or two old, take one ounce of fresh milk; three ounces of water; one ounce of fresh cream, and two level teaspoonfuls of milk sugar. This makes about five ounces. For twenty ounces use four times as much of each ingredient. This closely resembles mother's milk.

For older babies, take two ounces of fresh milk; two ounces of water; one ounce of fresh cream; two level teaspoonfuls of milk sugar and a teaspoonful of lime water. Larger quantities may be made by increasing the amounts of each ingredient in proper proportion. More milk and less water will be used as the infant increases in age.

If cream disagrees with the infant its use should be stopped temporarily. The following is a good substitute for mother's milk suitable for an infant of three months or less: Pure milk, cupful; water, two cupfuls; sugar of milk, one heaping tablespoonful; lime water, one tablespoonful.

The following table contains the milk mixtures recommended by the Providence (R. I.) Health Department:

For Babies Under One Month.—Milk, 5 ounces; lime water, 1 ounce; boiled water, 15 ounces; milk sugar, 1¼ tablespoons.

Dissolve the sugar in the boiling water and then add the milk and lime water. Keep in a cool place. Give the baby 2 ounces every 2 hours during the day and once at night. In all 10 feedings. Add a little more milk to the whole mixture every few days and give the baby a little more in each bottle.

One Month to Three Months.—Milk, 12 ounces; lime water, 1¼ ounces; boiled water, 24 ounces; milk sugar, 1½ tablespoons.

Dissolve the sugar in the boiling water and then add the milk and lime water. Keep in a cool place. Give the baby 3½ ounces every 2 hours during the day and once at night. Ten feedings. Add a little more milk to the whole mixture every few days and give the baby a little more in each bottle.

Three Months to Six Months.—Milk, 1 pint; lime water, 2 ounces; boiled water, 1½ pints; milk sugar, 2 tablespoons.

Dissolve the sugar in the boiled water and then add the milk and lime water. Keep in a cool place. Give the baby 5 ounces every 2½ hours during the day and once at night. Eight feedings. Add a little more milk to the whole mixture every few days and give the baby a little more in each bottle.

Six Months to Ten Months.—Milk, 1½ pints; lime water, 2 ounces; boiled water, 1½ pints; milk sugar, 2 tablespoons.

Dissolve the sugar in the boiled water and then add the milk and lime water. Keep in a cool place. Give the baby 6 or 7 ounces or about 1 cupful every 3 hours during the day.

Seven feedings. Every few days put 1 tablespoon less water and 1 tablespoon more milk into this mixture.

Use of Barley Water and Oatmeal Water.—Some authorities recommend the use of barley water from birth in place of the plain water used for the dilution of infants' food in the above mixtures, and in the same proportions. But others who have made a special study of feeding infants, think that the use of barley water or oatmeal water is not advisable until after six months of age. The use of barley water has been found, in practice, to enable some young infants to digest the curds of milk who would otherwise have been unable to do so. But as a rule it is probable that these cereal waters are not required until after the sixth or seventh month. They should not be fed to very young infants except under the direction of a physician.

The late Prof. A. Jacoby of New York, an author of international reputation, stated that if he were restricted to the use of any one food in addition to cow's milk, it would be barley meal or oatmeal water, and that he preferred barley water to oatmeal water for a steady diet because the latter tends to relax the bowels. Hence after the sixth or sevcuth month use barley water to dilute the baby's food in place of plain water unless you find from experience that it does not agree with your child. When the infant is constipated, substitute oatmeal water for the barley water. As the barley water is added the amount of sugar should be reduced.

ARTIFICIAL FOODS

Condensed Milk for Infants.—Condensed milk is the artificial food most commonly used, especially among the poor, but is not easily digestible especially by very young and frail infants. Its effects are not satisfactory. It contains too much sugar and not enough fat. Babies fed on condensed milk alone are often fat but seldom strong. A fat baby is not always a healthy baby. Practically every baby raised on condensed milk alone shows signs of rickets or other disease. It may serve a good purpose when traveling or at other times of emergency when pure, fresh milk cannot be secured. Between dirty, impure and stale cow's milk and condensed milk, choose the latter. When traveling or when the milk supply fails, condensed milk may be used to tide the infant over a period of danger, but do not use it any longer than is really necessary. It should never be used without the addition of fats—fresh cream if possible. Or, if good cream cannot be had, give cod liver oil at the rate of five to twenty drops at each feeding. If you use condensed milk get the best that can be had. Borden's Eagle Brand is known to be well prepared and reliable.

Manufactured Foods.—Do not be misled by the statements of any manufacturer of condensed milk or other artificial food that his product is a perfect substitute for mother's milk. All such statements are false. There is no perfect substitute for mother's milk, nor is there any artificial food that is equally as good as pure fresh cow's milk properly modified. The most commonly used foods upon the market may be classed as milk foods, malted foods and farinaceous foods. Horlick's, Borden's (malted) milk, and Mellin's are examples of the second class, and Eskay's of the third. None of these foods contain sufficient fat. Some of them have an excess of starch which makes them unsuitable for an infant until the latter part of the first year. Some contain too much sugar. None of these foods should be used alone. Some authorities claim that they are harmful and that certain diseases have followed their prolonged use. Others consider them of considerable value. Many advocate combining their use with the breast milk to help the mother out during the latter part of the nursing period, especially after the fifth or sixth month.

Notwithstanding the difference of opinion regarding the value of these foods, they are recommended by competent physicians and are used to seeming advantage by many infants, although they do not agree with others. They should be used under the advice of a physician, if at all, and mixed with diluted cow's milk for the purpose of breaking up the tough curds and rendering the milk more digestible. Barley water and oatmeal water are used for the same purpose, but do not contain all the food elements to be found in the best types of prepared foods.

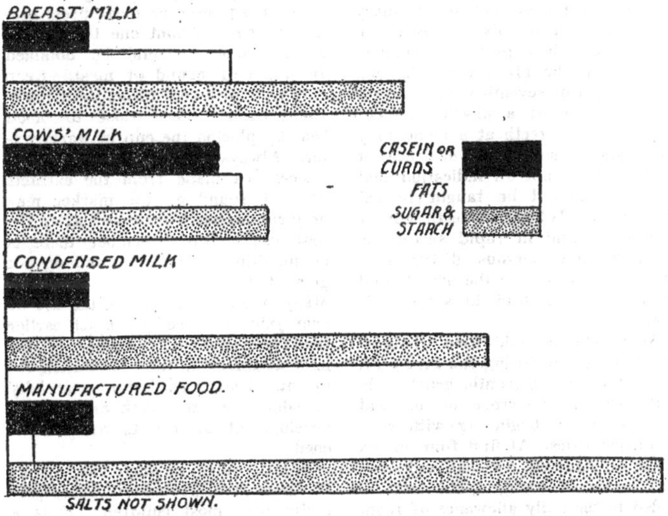

The manufactured food is shown as mixed with water alone. Mixed with milk, as usually directed, the comparison would show it much more like breast milk. Courtesy State Board of Health of Illinois.

The manufacturers of Horlick's Malted Milk assert that it does not require the addition of cow's milk; that it is composed of pure, rich cow's milk reduced to dryness and combined with an extract of malted wheat and barley. This food may perhaps be used alone, temporarily; but for continued use, milk should be added.

Mellin's Food is said to be a dry extract from wheat and malt, and free from cane sugar and starch.

Eskay's Food, according to the manufacturers, contains the more easily digested cereals combined with egg albumen.

An analysis of Horlick's Malted Milk shows that it contains less fat than mother's milk and more sugar, and that it is free from starch. Mellin's Food alone has practically no fats or starch and much more sugar than mother's milk. It should be used with milk.

Eskay's Food, when properly mixed with milk, resembles breast milk very closely, except that there is some starch present. It is stated, however, that this starch is thoroughly broken up and easily digested, and that the egg albumen contained is more easily digested than similar amounts of the albumen or curds of milk.

The chart on the preceding page shows a comparison of breast milk, cow's milk, condensed milk and a widely advertised manufactured food.

OTHER FOODS FOR INFANTS

Keep your baby largely on milk until well into the second year. This is the chief secret of successful infant feeding. There is far less necessity for a mixed diet of ordinary foods than is generally supposed. No other food than properly modified milk should be given until the end of the sixth or seventh month, except on the order of a physician. The appearance of teeth at a moderately early age is simply an evidence of health. It is not an indication that the baby should be taught to eat solid food. When the teeth appear very early and in rapid succession, nutritive and nervous disturbances are apt to occur and the use of solid food may then lead to serious illness.

As a rule no solid food whatever should be given during the first year. After the seventh month, gruel made with barley, arrowroot or oatmeal may be given, beginning with very small quantities. At first four ounces of thick strained oatmeal and one-half ounce of orange juice may be added to the daily allowance of food. The quantity of gruel may be gradually increased as the child grows older. The addition of a pinch of salt will make the food more palatable.

After the ninth month pure whole milk may be allowed in some cases and the child may have a crust of bread, or a small piece of zwieback.

After the tenth month beef, mutton or chicken broth thoroughly strained may be substituted for or added to a child's regular food.

Soups and broths for infants should be very carefully prepared so as to be free from any excess of fat or bits of meat. They should be very sparingly seasoned. Fresh beef juice may be given in the latter part of the first year and in some cases even earlier in quantities of not over two teaspoonfuls a day.

To prepare beef juice cut a half pound of fresh lean beef into small pieces and put them into a clean dry pan. Place the pan over a slow fire and turn the pieces of meat with a fork until the outside is gray. Broil very lightly. Express the juice with a lemon squeezer or meat press into a clean cup. About one to one and a half ounces should be obtained from a half pound of meat. Keep on ice, or in a cool place, until ready for feeding. Then raise to blood heat by placing the cup in warm water. Always use the same day.

Beef tea made from the extracts of beef found on the market may be given in small quantities after the first year. But remember there is no nutrition in beef tea and do not give it in place of regular food. Many practitioners advise the use of beef juice and beef tea much earlier than here stated, especially if the milk disagrees or fails to nourish the infant. They regard it as especially valuable when the teeth are slow in development or rickets are threatened.

Orange juice in such cases is of the greatest value and will agree perfectly with most children. It is a safe precaution, especially if pasteurized or cooked milk, or condensed milk or manufactured infants' food is given, to feed half an ounce of orange juice each day to all children over six months of age.

Meat Broth Plain and Thickened.—Chop into small pieces one pound of lean beef, chicken or neck of mutton including some of the bone. Add a quart of water and let stand for two hours, then add salt and boil slowly for two hours down to one pint. While boiling add two tablespoonfuls of crushed barley, rice or oatmeal. Strain through muslin, cool and skim off the grease.

Egg Water.—This may sometimes be used to advantage in case of intestinal disturbances, such that the baby cannot digest milk. To prepare, stir the white of a fresh egg into one pint of boiled water. Add a pinch of salt, shake thoroughly and strain. Keep in the ice box or other cool place and use the same day.

Whey.—Warm one pint of milk to blood heat and add one teaspoonful of essence of pepsin or one junket tablet. Let stand until it jellies, then break up the curds with a fork and strain through muslin. Whey is sometimes used to advantage when the baby cannot digest cow's milk.

Solid Foods.—The cutting of the eighth incisor or front teeth, which occurs usually during the twelfth month, may be taken as nature's indication that the child requires other food than milk. At this time if the infant is well and strong, a little stale bread, at least one day old, may be given with fresh milk in place of one of the regular feedings. This may soon be supplemented by a small quantity of well cooked hominy, oatmeal or cornmeal mush. But keep in mind constantly the fact that milk is the most important article of the diet, and that these foods are merely supplementary. Do not feed the baby any of the ready-cooked or pre-digested breakfast foods. Buy the natural cereals and cook them at home. Cereals should be cooked at least three hours in a double boiler, or preferably over night in a fireless cooker. They should be strained through cheese cloth or muslin.

If the above foods are taken without difficulty and no bad results are observed, give stale bread liberally buttered. This satisfies the infant's desire for solid food and also affords an easily digested and nourishing form of fat.

At fifteen months, a soft boiled egg may be given as the noon feeding. About the middle of the second year, or when sixteen teeth have developed, other and more solid foods may be given. But throughout the entire period of infancy, food other than milk should be selected and prepared with the greatest care and given in moderation. During the second year children are almost invariably overfed.

Diet of Older Children.—Between one and a half and two and a half years of age a child may have bread and butter, orange, potatoes and certain other vegetables, certain fruits and certain meats. The bread should be at least one day old and may include toast, zwieback, graham, oatmeal and gluten crackers. Porridge may be oatmeal, rice (cooked three hours), hominy (cooked six hours), farina (cooked one hour), cornmeal (cooked two hours), barley meal or wheaten grits. All should be thoroughly cooked for the time stated, or over night in a fireless cooker. Strain through cheese cloth or muslin and serve with certified or pasteurized milk. The meat may be rare roast beef, fresh cooked mutton or chicken. All should be finely minced. The vegetables may be well cooked spinach or potato. The latter should be fed in small quantities, freshly baked and lightly broken up and salted. Potato is a starchy food and hard for an infant to digest. It is much more wholesome baked than boiled. The fruit may be ripe apples (better baked), grapes, freed from the stones and skins, stewed prunes and orange pulp, freed from the fibrous portion. Fruit should be given in great moderation, if at all, in summer. Other suitable foods are baked custards or junket.

A piece of rare roast beef to suck, bread with dish gravy (not the heavy thickened and highly seasoned gravy) and soft boiled or poached eggs may form additions to the dietary which may be extended gradually to meet developments as the baby grows into childhood. But either for an infant or a child, overfeeding is far more injurious than underfeeding.

Improper Foods.—Hundreds of infants have been killed by the mistakes of parents in giving them other and improper foods. Never feed the baby at the table from the food prepared for other members of the family. The table foods may be poisonous to the infant. Never give a child under two years of age ham, bacon, or pork in any other form; cabbage, pickles or other succulent vegetables; coffee, tea, beer, wine, cider or any other alcoholic liquor of any kind; bananas, berries or other fruit except orange juice or pulp, prune juice and stewed or baked apple. Do not give pie or pastry, nuts, cake, candy, ice cream, or any other kind of sweets. Above all never dope your baby with drugs, nostrums, or patent foods of any kind, relying upon the statements of unprincipled manufacturers, druggists or other venders, or those who have "tried and can recommend them." Such advice is often as ignorant as it is well intended. The kind of medicine or food preparation which may agree with your neighbor's baby may totally disagree with yours. Don't experiment with your baby. If you think it needs medicine or a change of food consult a competent physician to find out what is the matter. Then be guided implicitly by his advice.

Home Pasteurization of Milk.—Pasteur, the French chemist (whose name has become a household word from his discovery of a treatment which prevents hydrophobia), was once employed by the French Government to study the causes of fermentation in wines and beer. He found that these changes were brought about by the action of microorganisms (germs). He further discovered that these germs could be destroyed at the comparatively low temperature of 140° F. by maintaining this degree of heat for twenty minutes. Hence this process is called "pasteurization."

The germs which cause fermentation or souring of milk or other food products can be destroyed more quickly at or near 212°, the temperature of boiling water. This process is called "sterilization." But this destroys much of the flavor and nutritive value of milk as food. The advantage of pasteurization, when properly conducted, is that neither the flavor nor the food value of the milk is affected.

To pasteurize milk in bottles, place a saucer in the bottom of a small tin pail and stand the bottle of milk on this with the cap on. Now fill the pail up to within three or four inches of the top of the bottle with hot water—but not so hot as to break the bottle—and then stand the pail and its contents on the stove. The instant the water begins to boil (not simmer) remove it from the pail and cool it as rapidly as possible.

Home pasteurization of milk. Courtesy State Board of Health of Wisconsin.

Milk properly pasteurized is not injurious to infants, although it is not considered quite so good as clean, pure unpasteurized milk. Most doctors think it is entirely wholesome. Others suspect that its prolonged use may tend to cause scurvy or rickets. If such results are feared, orange juice, or its equivalent, may be given as a preventive. The dangers from pasteurized milk, if any, are slight in comparison with those from unpasteurized milk of doubtful origin, especially in summer where milk has to be transported any considerable distance before delivery. Pasteurization, if the milk is afterwards kept clean until used, will certainly eliminate all danger of diarrhœal or other intestinal trouble. But observe that this process merely kills the living bacteria then present in the milk. It does not eliminate dirt, nor any chemical poisons cast off by germs which the milk may contain. Nor does it prevent the milk from afterwards becoming contaminated with other bacteria. Pasteurization, in other words, is not a panacea for making dirty milk wholesome. Nor is it a substitute for painstaking cleanliness in the home. It is a makeshift at best, but nevertheless should be adopted whenever the milk delivered at your door is known or suspected to be warm, stale or dirty. As a rule unless you can afford to buy certified milk, it is better to pasteurize the milk and be on the safe side. But it is a good plan, before doing so, to consult your physician.

Sterilization of Milk.—Pasteurization is always to be preferred over sterilization, provided milk can afterwards be kept clean and cold. Sterilization makes milk harder to digest and decreases its food value. The prolonged use of such milk leads to stomach and intestinal diseases, rickets, loss of weight, failure of bones to grow properly, and other harmful conditions. But between dirty milk and cooked milk, sterilization is the lesser evil. Those who cannot obtain ice, and especially those who are obliged to live in unsanitary conditions such that the milk is sure to become contaminated, would better sterilize rather than pasteurize the milk, especially in summer. In winter the milk can be kept cool by means of a window box. This will afford the baby some relief from the evil effects of sterilization.

To scald or sterilize milk which comes in bottles place the bottle on a saucer in the bottom of a tin pail as for pasteurization. Leave the cap on. Fill up the pail to within three or four inches of the top and bring to a boil. The instant the water begins to boil (not simmer) remove the boiler from the stove. Take care that the milk does not boil. If it should boil, throw it away. Boiled or over-heated milk, if fed to a baby for any considerable length of time, will produce a most distressing type of scurvy. Remove the boiler from the stove and let the bottle of milk stand in the water for about twenty minutes. Then cool as quickly as possible.

Or, if milk is bought in bulk, pour it into a sterilized glass fruit jar as recommended for pasteurization and proceed as for bottled milk.

Observe that sterilized milk is more susceptible to contamination from germs than raw milk. Hence take care that everything that comes in contact with scalded milk is scrupulously clean. Remember that the ice box cannot be cleaned too often.

When to Pasteurize or Sterilize.—Certified milk or good fresh milk which has been kept clean and cold needs no preservative. Do not "scald," sterilize or pasteurize such milk. But if milk is dirty, or sours quickly, or if there is other evidence that it has not been kept clean or cold, the sooner it is pasteurized or sterilized after it comes into the house, the better. If the milk is to be kept in the original bottle or in a glass fruit jar or similar receptacle during the day, and the baby's bottle is to be filled from this as required, the best plan is to pasteurize or sterilize the milk as soon as it is received and before it is put into the ice box. But if milk is to be modified, and especially if there are enough bottles so that a separate bottle can be prepared for each feeding, the better plan is to pasteurize or sterilize the modified milk or prepared food after it has been mixed and placed in the baby's bottles or other receptacles in which it is to be kept for the day.

Adulteration of Milk.—There are still some dairymen and dealers who think it is cheaper to kill the bacteria in dirty, warm, stale milk by means of germicides than to adopt means to keep the milk clean, cool and sweet. Such adulteration is forbidden by law in many states, and all offenders should be vigorously prosecuted. Keep a sharp lookout for adulterated milk and occasionally test the milk you receive for boric acid, borax, formaldehyde or bicarbonate of soda by methods elsewhere recommended. Or request your physician, or the health officials of your community, if any, to test it for you. Never use such preservatives yourself, nor buy milk from a dealer who uses them. You can never tell how much he has used, nor how much may have been used by others before the milk came to him. Preservatives are never harmless and if present in large quantities may be very injurious or even poisonous.

CARE OF MILK IN THE HOME

If the milk producer and the milk dealer have done their duty there is daily left at the consumer's door a bottle of clean, cold, unadulterated milk. By improper treatment in the home the milk may become unfit for food, especially for babies. This bad treatment consists in placing it in unclean vessels; in exposing it unnecessarily to the air; in failing to keep it cool up to the time of using it; and in exposing it to flies.

Milk absorbs impurities—collects bacteria—whenever it is exposed to the air or placed in unclean vessels. If there is a sediment in the bottom of the container, after the milk has stood an hour or two, it indicates filthy habits on the part of the producer. The remedy is, change milkmen. This sediment is almost invariably fecal matter (manure) that has fallen into the milk pail from filthy cows. Most farmers who allow this matter to get into the milk are careful to strain it out, but they cannot strain out the unmistakable flavor which it imparts to milk. Remember that clean, pure milk is nearly free from taste or odor. If milk tastes or smells of the stable it is probably dirty.

To test milk for dirt place a good-sized button in the bottom of an ordinary tin funnel and upon this a piece of dampened absorbent cotton about the size of a twenty-five cent piece and about one-sixteenth of an inch in thickness. Carefully pour the entire contents of the milk bottle into this funnel and let it filter. The cotton will catch every particle of sediment or dirt which the milk may contain. Remove the cotton and place it upon a piece of white paper near the stove to dry. If much dirt is shown, ask your milkman to take a look at it. Or, if you live in a city mail it, with a complaint, to the Board of Health.

The danger to health from dirty methods of keeping and milking cows, dirty milkers and dirty milk vessels increases with every moment milk is allowed to stand in a temperature over 40° or 45° F. Injurious spores and bacteria remain dormant or increase very slowly at lower temperatures, but as the temperature rises up to 60° or 70° F., or thereabouts, they develop and multiply with astonishing rapidity. A bottle of dirty milk standing in the sun for an hour or two in the early morning may breed millions of injurious bacteria and become totally unfit for human food.

The feeding of cow's milk to infants, to be at all safe, entails the following tedious and never-ending operations: Securing fresh milk every day; home pasteurization; sterilization of all milk containers including boiling of feeding bottles, nipples, etc., for each and every feeding; refrigeration—storage in scrupulously clean ice boxes — and milk modification, all to be carefully performed and varied according to age or condition of the child.

Even if the milk is clean, fresh and cool when it is delivered at your door, or if you then kill the germs which it may contain by home pasteurization, it may afterwards become unfit for food, especially for babies, by improper treatment. This may occur if you place it in unclean vessels, expose it unnecessarily to the air, or fail to keep it cool up to the time of using it. Hence the following suggestions.

Buy bottled milk, at least for your baby, if you can. Keep milk in the original bottle till needed for immediate consumption. Carefully wipe or rinse the bottle, especially the mouth, before pouring any milk from it, so that dust or dirt which may have gathered thereon or on the cap will not get into the milk. Do not pour back into the bottle milk which has been exposed to the air by being placed in other vessels. Keep the bottle covered with a paper cap as long as milk is in it and when not actually pouring from it. If the paper cap has been punctured, cover the bottle with an inverted tumbler.

The sanitary containers that are used but once and then destroyed are preferable to those of glass, but the consumer seems to object to them because, not being transparent, no cream line can be seen. When their value from a health standpoint is understood the sanitary containers will be universally adopted as they already have been in some cities.

Dipping milk from large cans and pouring it into customers' receptacles on the street, expose it to contamination from the air and otherwise. Drawing milk from the faucet of a retailer's can is objectionable for another reason. The milk is not thoroughly mixed. Hence some consumers receive less than their due proportion of cream. But if you must buy dipped milk, do not set out over night an uncovered vessel to receive it. Cats, dogs or tramps may contaminate the milk by drinking from it. At best it will collect thousands of bacteria from street dust before morning. Have the milk received by some member of the family if possible, or set out a bowl covered with a plate, or better still, provide yourself with several glass preserving jars kept for this special purpose. Use jars with the clamp glass top. Avoid the screw tops. Omit the rubber band. They are difficult to keep clean. Do not use a pitcher. It cannot be tightly covered on account of the projecting spout.

Take the milk into the house as soon as possible after delivery, particularly in hot weather. Sometimes milk delivered as early as 4 a. m. remains outdoors until 9 or 10 o'clock. This is wrong. If you cannot receive the milk as soon as delivered provide a small wooden box or other shelter to protect it from the sun and insist that the milkman use it.

The best way of serving milk on the table, from a sanitary standpoint, is in the bottle or fruit jar in which it is received. At all events, pour out only what is needed for immediate use and keep the rest in the original receptacle. Never pour the milk into a bowl or pitcher for storage, nor pour back into the bottle or jar milk which has been exposed to the air. In fact, do not mix milk —the mixture always descends to the quality of its worst part. Milk deteriorates by exposure to the air of the nursery, kitchen, pantry or refrigerator in two ways: by contamination from germs and by absorption of odors. Cover milk when not actually pouring from it by turning over the jar or bottle a small bowl or tumbler, or use a cork or cap of sterilized gauze or cotton wool, both of which are germ-proof. Never expose uncovered milk in a refrigerator containing any kind of food, especially strong-smelling foods like fish, cabbage or onions.

Milk cannot be properly kept without ice. If you have a refrigerator put the milk into it promptly. Unless it comes into actual contact with the ice, it will keep best in the bottom of the ice box. The cold air descends. If you can get ice but have no refrigerator, you can make a cheap ice box that can be operated for less than three cents a day in which to preserve a baby's milk, as follows:

A Cheap Ice Box.—Secure an ordinary wooden box, 13 by 18 inches, with a depth of 11½ inches, from your grocer. In the bottom of the box place a substantial layer of sawdust. On this set a tin pail or can, 8 inches in diameter and high enough to hold a quart bottle of milk. Care should be taken that the pail rests on sawdust—not on the wood bottom of the box. Around the pail place a cylinder of tin a little larger than the pail, then pack sawdust about the cylinder—not between pail and cylinder—up to top of the cylinder. On the cover of the box nail about fifty layers of newspaper. Set the

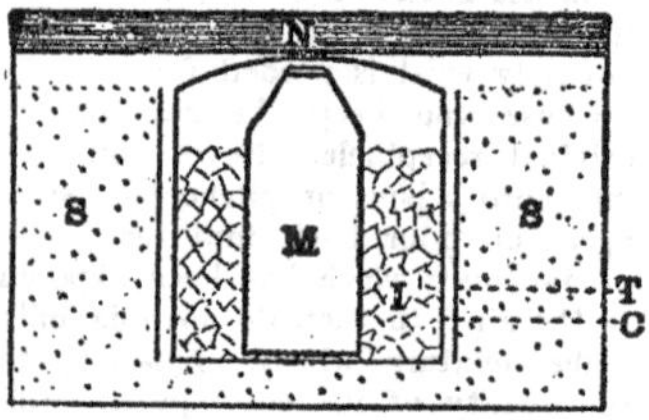

Vertical section of homemade milk refrigerator; S, sawdust; T, cylinder of tin or galvanized iron; C, can or pail, in which is placed the milk bottle M, surrounded by broken ice, I; N, newspapers nailed to lid of case. Courtesy Health Department of Chicago.

milk bottle in the pail and pack broken ice about the bottle. A refrigerator of this description will hold two quart bottles of milk, or four eight-ounce feeding bottles. It can be operated for about two cents per day. To prevent rusting, a little soda may be placed in the can each day. The little expense involved is nothing as compared with the cost of sickness and death.

Or, get a box about 18 inches square from your grocer, take the boards off the top and cleat them together to form a lid. Tack to the

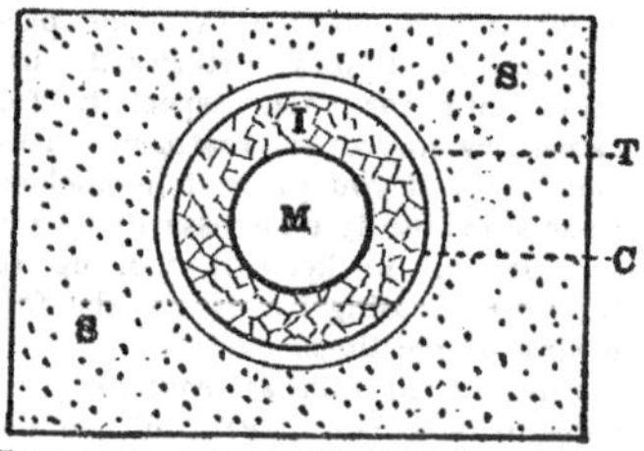

Horizontal section of homemade milk refrigerator; M, milk bottle; I, broken ice; C, can or pail for holding ice; T, tin or galvanized iron cylinder to prevent sawdust, S, from falling into space when can is removed for purpose of emptying water. Courtesy Health Department of Chicago.

under side of this lid a number of thicknesses of old newspapers up to an inch or more in depth, trimming around the edges so that they will set down in the box, and, preferably, protecting them by an inner cover of thin boards or a number of cleats. Now put three inches of sawdust in the bottom. Place two pails in this sawdust one inside of the other and fill the space between the inner and outer with sawdust. Fill the space between the outer pail and box with sawdust. Place the nursing bottle filled with milk in the inner pail and cover it with a tin cover. Now fill the outer pail over and around the inner pail with cracked ice. Put on the lid and keep the ice box in a cool shady place.

Or, to make a still cheaper ice box, get a large soap box from your grocer and another box about half as large. Line the smaller box with tin or zinc. This will hold your ice and milk bottles. Now, put a layer at least three inches deep of sawdust in the bottom of the larger box, set the smaller box on this and fill in around the sides with sawdust. Line the cover with newspapers fastened on by means of tacks or cleats and keep the box tightly closed.

Or, if you cannot get ice, milk may be kept fairly cool as follows: Procure an ordinary butter or lard tub or a half barrel cask. Put on the bottom a layer of sawdust three inches or more thick and place on this a large earthenware jar. Surround this with sawdust. Cork the milk bottles to protect the contents from dust, stand them up in the jar and surround them up to the necks of the bottles with the coldest water you can get. Put on the lid of the jar and fit over the jar a cushion stuffed with sawdust or fine hay that will just fill the top of the tub. Keep this in the coolest place that can be found. Change the water at least once in twenty-four hours. The temperature of the milk will remain nearly stationary and about one degree warmer than the water.

A Window Box.—Most families discontinue taking ice for the refrigerator during half the year or more. During such times, if milk is allowed to stand in the pantry it quickly becomes warm and unfit for infants' food. Yet the outdoor temperature would keep the milk sweet for some time. A window box may be constructed with sides made of old blinds, slats, or boards perforated with auger holes for ventilation, and provided with a solid bottom and tight slanting roof. Attach this outside the pantry window where it can be reached by simply raising the sash. Line with wire netting to keep out insects, especially flies. Such a box costs next to nothing, and serves to keep not only the baby's milk, but butter, meat and other provisions when the refrigerator is not in use.

Or stand a deep dish or pail of water by an open window away from the sun. Put a narrow board or wire screen across the top and on this stand the milk bottles or jars. Wrap the bottles in a wet cloth and let the end of the cloth extend to the bottom of the water. The cloth will be kept wet by capillary attraction and the water, by evaporation, will cool the milk.

By some such method you must keep the milk and cream cool until used if you desire to safeguard your baby's health.

Care of the Ice Box.—Keep the refrigerator sweet and clean. Personally inspect it at least once a week. See that the outlet for melted ice is kept open and the space under the ice rack is clean. Scald the place where food is kept every week with a strong sal soda solution. A single drop of spoiled milk or small particle of other neglected food will contaminate a refrigerator in a few days.

Care of Milk Bottles.—As soon as a milk bottle is empty, rinse it in clear lukewarm or cold water until it looks clean and set it bottom side up to drain. Do not use it for any other purpose than holding milk. Never return filthy bottles. Rinse, wash and scald all utensils with which milk comes in contact every time they are used. Do not wash them in dish water or wipe with an ordinary dish towel. This will only serve to smear them with an invisible coating of grease. Boil them in clean water containing a little borax or washing soda and set them away unwiped. If a case of typhoid, scarlet fever or diphtheria breaks out in a family do not return any milk bottles to the milkman except with the knowledge of the attending physician and under conditions prescribed by him. Never accept milk from any family, dairyman or dealer when you know, or suspect, that there are contagious diseases in his family, or that they have recently been exposed to such contagion. The above suggestions apply to cream as well as to milk.

CHAPTER VIII

OUTDOOR PROBLEMS OF THE HOUSEHOLDER

THE LAWN AND HOME GROUNDS—FLOWER, FRUIT AND VEGETABLE GARDENS—TREES AND SHRUBBERY—TREE PROPAGATION BY CUTTINGS, GRAFTS AND BUDS—PRUNING ORCHARD AND SHADE TREES—THE FRIENDS AND ENEMIES OF ORCHARD AND GARDEN —CLEARING NEW LAND—CONCRETE CONSTRUCTION—PRESERVATION OF TIMBER AND SHINGLES—GOOD ROADS—LIGHTNING CONDUCTORS

The natural and wholesome tendency toward a normal life in open spaces, where fresh air and sunlight abound, has been much encouraged in recent years by the development of such means of rapid transit as the automobile and the interurban street car. A great number of city dwellers have returned to the land and many more are planning to take this beneficial step. Persons already thus pleasantly situated in life manifest greater contentment, coupled with a pardonable pride in their country or suburban homes. A determination is observable on the part of many owners of such homes to make the most of their advantages of location by all sorts of permanent improvements.

Therefore, apart from the indoor problems of house furnishing, cleanliness, cookery, sanitation and other affairs which make up the routine of daily life and work, there is a great and growing interest everywhere in what may be called the outdoor problems of the householder. These embrace such subjects as the laying down and subsequent care of lawns, the proper selection, location, planting and care of shade trees and shrubbery, and their defense against all sorts of insects and other pests; the construction and maintenance of out-buildings and their appurtenauces such as fences, gates and the like; and the development and care of fruit and vegetable gardens. All of these are matters with which every householder may have to do, whether he occupies a rented dwelling or owns his own home. They are of especial interest to the large class of persons who have recently bought home-sites with the intention of building, or are planning so to do. The object of this chapter is to furnish practical information, which has been carefully compiled from the best and most recent authorities, on these various subjects.

THE LAWN AND HOME GROUNDS

Nothing can add so much to the outward attractiveness of a home as a well laid and well kept lawn. The cost is not great, under ordinary conditions, nor the work difficult. Yet many persons who have a suitable open space adjacent to their dwellings have been prevented from making a lawn by a wrong impression as to the expense or by lack of necessary information.

The existing condition and nature of the soil is the first and most important consideration. A fairly deep surface soil of good mechanical quality and rich in humus, with good under-drainage, is essential. If the land already produces a good grass or other crop every year, the soil conditions are probably favorable. No great difficulty or expense will be encountered in making a good lawn unless the surface soil has been removed or covered with sub-soil in the process of grading. Neither lawn grass nor other ordinary plants will thrive in sub-soil, until it has been mixed with humus and mellowed by the mechanical action of frosts and other natural agencies. And this requires time. Hence unless you can afford the expense of resurfacing your lawn with a layer of good garden or other fertile soil, you must take care, in grading, not to lose the valuable surface soil either by removing or covering it.

Grading.—First settle the grade or contour you desire the surface to have. As a general rule avoid terraces, or other banks or sharp curves on any part of your grounds. They are ordinarily more expensive to grade and much more difficult to maintain. They are liable to injury from frost and to erosion or "washing" by rains. They are also diffi-

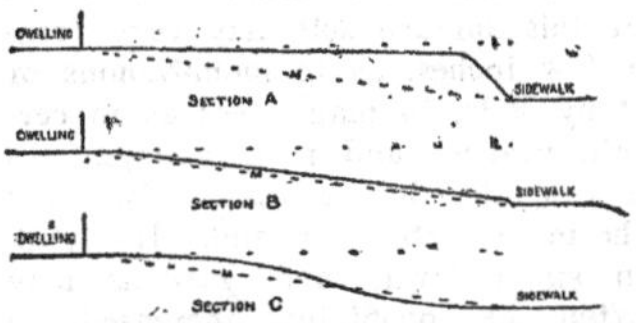

Cross sections of bad and good grading of small front yards. L indicates the level of the house foundation, and M a straight line from the top of the house foundation to the sidewalk level. Section A: Bad, with the rare exception of where a strictly formal treatment is admissible. Section B: Bad. Section C: Good. This ogee curve may be short or long to accommodate the difference in height between the dwelling and sidewalk, and the distance between them. (L. C. Corbett.)

cult to trim and keep in order. Most grounds will admit of the long sweeping curve shown in the accompanying illustration. This is greatly to be preferred to the more costly and less attractive terrace bank. If the ground is level, it is most unwise to build artificial banks or terraces to be covered with turf, or otherwise to incur needless expense to produce the effect of slopes or curves. A perfectly flat lawn, if well kept, may be very beautiful.

The less grading done, the better. The best landscape engineers seek to conform to the natural contours of the soil. Modify these only when necessary, either to produce a more pleasing symmetry, or to bring them into pleasant relations with the adjacent street, walks and drives, and the home with its accompanying buildings.

Most often all that is necessary in grading is to take soil from a high point upon the grounds with which to fill up a nearby hollow. This course is always preferable because the work can be done with a scraper much cheaper than by shoveling the soil into carts. But take care in all such cases to first scrape from the ground the surface soil. This extends to a depth of four to six inches and may easily be distinguished by its color and texture. Bank this at one side to be returned to its original position after the grading of the sub-soil has been done. Otherwise the top of the hill will be cut down to a hard sub-soil and the surface soil in the hollow will be covered with sub-soil. Such spots can be seeded with great difficulty, if at all. Moreover, the grass which springs up on them will almost certainly dry up at the first drouth thus giving the lawn a spotty appearance. After all the sub-soil that is needed to fill the hollows has been taken from the high ground, break up the sub-soil which remains on the crest of the knoll, to the depth of four to six inches with a plow. This will make it correspond more nearly in mechanical condition to the sub-soil which was removed. Then level carefully with a harrow or rake and replace the surface soil in its original position.

Preparation of the Soil.—Lawn grass, like other plant crops, thrives best upon a porous, well drained soil, rich in humus, and abundantly supplied with moisture. A deep and fairly heavy soil, as a clay or sand loam with a clay sub-soil, is perhaps an ideal condition. It is necessary, however, as a rule, to accept the existing conditions as a basis, and then take such measures to modify them in the direction of this ideal as circumstances will admit. It is always well to treat the entire home lot—including not only the lawn but also the flower garden, and the vegetable garden, if any—as a single unit. The characteristics of the soil and its requirements as to drainage and fertilization will most often be the same. This is not the place to discuss the question of soils and soil fertilization from the standpoint of raising farm crops, i. e., of general agriculture. A few words, however,

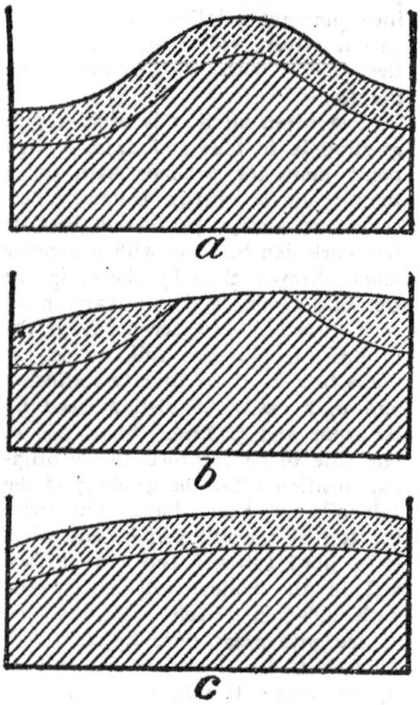

Proper and improper soil grading. (a) Soil to be graded; (b) improper grading, showing exposure of subsoil; (c) proper grading. (L. C. Corbett.)

are necessary as to the different kinds of soil and methods of treatment since the two subjects are intimately related.

Two general classes of soil are first to be distinguished, i. e., heavy or clay soils and light or sandy soil. Each class may be of various degrees of fineness due to the mixture of different kinds of material. Heavy soils may be classified as clay, clay loams, silt loams, or loam soils. They are formed by the admixture of clay with silt or fine earth in varying proportions. Light or sandy soils may be coarse or fine sandy soils or sandy loams. The basis of this case is sand which is mixed with fine earth and loam in various proportions.

The distinction between surface soil and sub-soil has been mentioned. At some distance below the surface of the ground in most localities, a change will be observed in both the color and texture of the soil. The surface soil is usually darker and more porous. This is due to the effects of vegetable and animal life and to other influences. The depth of this surface soil may vary from a few inches, as in mountainous or stony soils, to many feet as in certain prairies and river valleys. As a rule the deeper the surface soil the more fertile the land. Its depth in small lawns and gardens may often be profitably increased in either or both of two ways: (1) a layer of suitable soil from some other locality may be added; or (2) the surface soil may be deepened by the use of an ordinary plow or spade, or by sub-soiling. The kind of soil to add upon the surface will depend upon the nature of that already in position. This may be readily understood from a brief statement of the chief characteristics of the different kinds of soils.

A light or sandy soil is usually "leachy." The soil water tends to drain off too rapidly and to carry with it soluble plant food. Such soils, therefore, tend to become deficient both in plant food and moisture. And this tendency is much enhanced if the sub-soil is a porous sand or gravel. In such cases, measures are required to solidify the soil and increase its proportion of humus. This may be done by adding a layer of two or three inches of clay, by the liberal application of stable manure, or by liming.

Heavy soils, upon the other hand, are sometimes not sufficiently open to admit as much oxygen as the plant roots and the soil bacteria require. Moreover, such soils do not drain freely and evenly enough. The surface of the ground tends to become baked and hard. Yet there may be too much water beneath and about the roots of the plants. Such conditions are best overcome by good under-drainage with tile, by careful cultivation, by the adding of an inch or two of sand and fine loam, by liberal top dressing with strawy stable manure, or by green manuring. The use of lime is especially beneficial.

Drainage.—A prime consideration to the growth of lawn grasses, shade trees, shrubbery, garden plants, and, indeed, all sorts of crops, is an abundance of moisture coupled with good drainage in the soil. The movement of soil water above hard-pan is principally up and down. There is very little lateral movement except that caused by the dip of hard-pan, usually at some distance below the surface. The free water in the soil tends to settle to a uniform level over a larger or smaller area depending upon the nature of the sub-soil. This level is known as the "water table." When rains fall, that portion of the rain water which is not carried off by surface drainage sinks into the soil and settles to the level of the water table which is thereby raised. In times of drouth, the water which evaporates from the surface is replaced from this reservoir of free water beneath by the process called capillarity. The principle is that by which oil is fed to the flame through the wick of a lamp. The water table is thereby lowered. A sandy soil may resist drouth poorly for two reasons: the water table may be too low or it may not have enough of this property of capillarity, its particles being too far apart. A clay soil may be too wet either because the water table is too high so that the plants have "wet feet", that is, their roots are surrounded with standing water, or it may be deficient in capillarity for an opposite reason, its particles being too close together. A well drained soil is one in which the water table lies normally several inches below the roots of the growing plants but which has strong capillarity properties. Its particles must be neither too far apart nor too close together, as a good wick is one which is neither too loosely nor too tightly woven.

Reasoning from the above principles it is apparent that a sandy soil or fine, light, clay loam may not require under-drainage unless it lies upon a clay or other impervious sub-soil or receives excessive moisture from springs or underground streams. On the other hand most heavy soils are improved by under-drainage, especially if the land is low and springy or marshy, or if it contains pools of standing water at any period of the year.

The first step is evidently to find out what the soil conditions are. They may often be observed from cuts, such as the excavation of cellars, wells, roadways, planting of shade trees and other purposes, or in the course of grading operation. But unless such cuts are well distributed over the grounds, it is a good plan to make a few openings here and there. Especially make observations at the highest and lowest points to learn the nature and relations of the surface soil, sub-soil and hard-pan and the dip of the various strata. This may be done with some labor by means of spades or the implements used to dig post holes. But a much more convenient tool is the soil auger. By means of this the soil can be tested on any part of the grounds with very little effort or interference with existing conditions.

Soil auger for collecting soil samples and useful in exploring sub-soil conditions in lawns. Such an instrument entirely prevents the disfigurement which would be unavoidable if a larger hole had to be dug in a lawn. (L. C. Corbett.)

Tile Drains.—Unless investigation shows that both surface and sub-soil are so porous as to admit of abundant drainage, it may be assumed that an appropriate system of tile drainage will be a substantial benefit to both lawn and garden. To accomplish the best results treat the entire plot as a single unit. Lay the tile lines at a distance of from five to twenty feet apart according to the amount of water to be removed and the texture of the soil. Lay them at a depth of between three and four feet according to climate. This places them well below the frost line and out of the way of injury from plowing or other operations such as installing a sewage disposal system, digging fence posts, tree planting and the like. All tile should have a gradual inclination toward a common outlet. This may be the street sewer, if any, or in the absence of a sewerage system, any low point of ground, the farther from the house, the better. Take care to see that the outfall does not become a stagnant pool, else it will afford a breeding place for mosquitoes.

Use the four-inch red agricultural tile laid with open joints according to the directions of the manufacturer. First prepare a plan to show the exact location of every line of tile and mark the end of each in some suitable manner as by an iron rod or stone set in the ground. Thus it can readily be found and uncovered if the drains should become stopped up.

The effect of an adequate system of tile drainage is to remove all surplus surface water from the soil and to lower the water table to a uniform point below the roots of the growing plants. If the sub-soil is reasonably compact and if the surface soil contains a fair proportion of clay or loam and is well supplied with humus, the result will be an ideal condition for growing plants.

Take care both in opening and filling ditches made for tile, to throw the surface soil to one side and the sub-soil to the other. Refill the ditch so that the two kinds of soil will be in their former relation. Otherwise the grass will not grow equally as well over the lines of the ditches and they may be clearly observable in the finished lawn.

To clear tile drain pipes which have become obstructed by roots of trees or otherwise use a stiff wire brush on the end of a wire cable. Open the end of the obstructed drain most remote from the outlet, attach the brush to the cable and thrust it along the tile until the obstruction has been reached. If the obstruction resists the brush, its exact location can be measured by the length of the cable under ground. An opening can then be made at a point such that the obstructed tile can be removed and cleaned.

After the tile are laid and the grading operations finished, give the entire lawn and garden the same treatment as a field intended for an especially valuable farm crop. Plow or spade the land to a depth depending upon that of the surface soil and the nature of the sub-soil. If the surface soil is thin and the sub-soil is of a markedly different character,—if, for example, a thin layer of loam lies over a hard gravel or clay—do not plow deeply enough to mix the raw sub-soil with the surface soil. Rather, turn over the surface soil and add a layer of suitable soil from some other locality. Or use the sub-soil plow to deepen the soil. This loosens and breaks up the sub-soil without turning or lifting it. Both before and after plowing, take great care to pick up and remove all pieces of board, broken brick, slate, tile, or other building material and also all roots, branches and trunks of trees, loose stone, roots of grasses and weeds, and other rubbish of every description. Not infrequently odds and ends of this sort are deliberately carted in to fill up the lawn. Or they may be carelessly left lying scattered about and merely covered to a depth of a few inches with surface soil. Such obstructions cut off the grass roots from their supply of water and their presence is revealed at the first drouth by a spot of dead grass in the lawn.

Fertilization.—The lawn is to be permanently seeded to a single crop. And the gardens are to be subjected to an annual cropping of plants and flowers. Hence it would seem that they could hardly be made too rich. The best authorities recommend that well composted and rotted stable manure be applied to the surface at the rate of from forty to sixty two-horse wagon loads to the acre, and turned in with the plow. But take care that this is free from detrimental weed seeds. If the soil is raw, from admixture with sub-soil from cellars or grading operations, or if it is light, thin or poor in plant food and humus, it may be very much improved by sowing it for a year or more with some crop suitable for green manuring. Cow-peas and soy-beans are recommended for latitudes south of Washington, D. C., and red clover, vetches and Canadian peas for northern districts. Let these reach their maximum growth and then plow under. This will improve the structure of the soil and make it more retentive of moisture and soluble plant food.

Then apply about 1,000 pounds of lime to the acre and later,—at the time of preparing the seed bed,—apply from 500 to 1,000 pounds of fine ground bone, together with 300 to 500 pounds of a high grade fertilizer containing about 3 per cent nitrogen, 6 to 8 per cent phosphoric acid and about 8 per cent potash, upon each acre. This is, in substance, the recommendation of the United States Department of Agriculture.

Or if the soil is so raw that it will not grow a good forage crop suitable for green manuring, manure even more heavily and grow such crops as corn or potatoes for a year or two in order to improve its tilth by the process of cultivation.

Selection of Lawn Grass Seeds.—Among the qualities most sought for in lawn grasses are a close turf, soft, rather than wiry, of pleasing color and with capacity to resist drouth and other climatic conditions under repeated clipping. Under ideal conditions a better lawn can be made with one kind of lawn grass than with a mixture. Kentucky blue grass is the prime favorite. It thrives best on a comparatively retentive, strong and well drained soil where there is an abundance of moisture. It is adapted to most parts of the United States. Where conditions are not ideally adapted to blue grass—as, for example, on lighter soils—a better lawn may be secured by the admixture of other grasses as Rhode Island red top. The preferred mixture in most localities is two parts by weight of Kentucky blue grass, to one of red top. This mixture is a leader with the principal seedsmen. White clover seed is often added, as a nurse crop, to protect the young grasses the first year. It springs up quickly and makes a good lawn, but is soon crowded out under close cutting in the presence of a good stand of the best lawn grasses. On very light land Rhode Island bent may be substituted for Kentucky blue grass in the above mixture. These are the standard lawn grasses but others as Canadian blue grass, the fescue grasses, wood meadow grass and sweet vernal grass are useful for special purposes.

Shady Nook Mixtures. — Rhode Island bent, creeping bent and Canadian blue grass do well in the shade and so do red fescue and sheep fescue, especially if used in mixtures under heavy seeding. The best plan is to try a mixture of a number of these grasses and seed heavily. Only the grass or grasses which prove best adapted to the location will survive.

Kentucky blue grass stands shade well and mixed with wood meadow grass makes perhaps the best of all shade mixtures, but as the latter is very high in price, its use in recent years has been very limited.

In seeding a lawn it is sound economy to procure the best select or recleaned seeds and to seed heavily. Pure blue grass weighs about 23 pounds to the bushel, whereas, an ordinary market grade averages only about 12 pounds. Pure red top should weigh 24 pounds to the bushel, although it ranges as low as 10 pounds. A fair grade should weigh not less than 16 to 20 pounds to the bushel. A standard mixture of blue grass with the bent grasses and the fescues should be sown at the rate of 3 to 5 bushels of seed an acre. Blue grass alone should be sown at a rate of from 50 to 70 pounds to the acre. White clover may be added in either case at the rate of one peck to the acre.

For latitudes north of Washington, D. C., under ideal conditions of soil and seed bed, sow a mixture of 50 pounds blue grass, 25 pounds red top and 6 quarts of white clover to the acre on fairly heavy soils. But increase the proportion of red top on light soils to equal parts by weight with the blue grass, or 37½ pounds of each with 6 quarts of white clover, to the acre.

Planting the Lawn.—Lawn grass seed may be sowed either in the spring or fall depending upon the climate, nature of the soil and other conditions. If the soil is not protected by snow in winter, so that the seed bed is liable to washing from rains and upheaval from alternate frosts and thaws, it will be found better to prepare a fresh seed bed for spring planting. The chief objection to this plan is the liability to delay from unfavorable soil conditions in spring, especially in clay land or other wet or heavy soils. This difficulty may be overcome by good under-drainage, and by fall plowing or other previous cultivation, to bring the land into a good state of tilth. If the ground is broken in the fall the first crop of weeds will come up early in the spring and may be turned under when preparing the seed bed. Keep down weeds which spring up later by frequent clipping with the lawn mower. They will soon be killed out by the growing stand of grass, particularly if white clover is added as a nurse crop.

Plant the lawn as early in the spring as the soil is dry enough to work properly and there is enough heat to germinate the seed and bring along the crop. If the planting is too late, the tender young plants will be injured by the heat and drouth of summer. In the northern half of the United States, fall planting may be done from the latter part of August to October according to location. In the South the best time for fall planting comes later and that for spring planting earlier, according to climatic conditions.

Maintenance of the Lawn.—Close clipping will eradicate most weeds except those having broad, flat heads such as plantain, dandelion and dock. These must be cut out by the use of a knife or trowel. A short-handled asparagus knife is suitable for this purpose. But if dandelions or dock come up in great numbers, it is often cheaper to plow and remake the lawn.

Fertilization.—The basis of a good lawn is to bring the seed bed into a proper state of tilth by the liberal application of well rotted barnyard manure, bone phosphate, lime or green manuring, as above suggested. A winter mulch of well rotted stable manure will lessen the danger from alternate frosts and thaws and enrich the soil. Apply a light covering in the late fall and rake off the coarse residue when the grass starts in the spring. Or if the grass clippings are allowed to remain on the lawns they serve much the same purpose.

As a rule fertilizers should be applied to lawns in the fall. A good plan for a small lawn is a three year rotation of a complete commercial fertilizer the first year, followed by ground bone the next two years and so continued. But any of the standard fertilizing materials may be employed. These have the advantage over stable manure that they contain no weed seeds.

Nitrate of soda scattered over the lawn at the rate of 100 pounds per acre in the spring will stimulate its growth and give it a richer color. This should be done after the grass begins to grow and just before a rain or sprinkling. Or the nitrate may be dissolved in water and sprinkled upon the lawn. Later applications at the rate of 50 pounds to the acre will help to keep the lawn green during the heated summer. An application of well slaked lime scattered broadcast, at the rate of 500 to 1,000 pounds to the acre, will be found beneficial on some soils. On those especially which are sour, as shown by the presence of sorrel or those which have a tendency to bake and crack as clays, or heavy clay loams, the use of lime is indicated. Lime tends to favor such desirable grasses as blue grass and white clover.

THE VEGETABLE GARDEN

"God Almighty," says Bacon, "first planted a garden eastward in Eden and walked there in the cool of the day." And there can be no purer nor more wholesome pleasure than that which the gardener enjoys when observing the growth of plants and flowers. Not only is gardening a source of the liveliest and most unfailing delight. If properly conducted, it is an educational process of the greatest value. A good flower garden exerts a powerful influence upon the æsthetic side of the home life. The home vegetable garden also contributes to the health and physical well being of the family and is, moreover, an important measure of economy.

The custom of setting apart a portion of the home grounds for flower and vegetable gardens, while nearly universal in New England and many other of the older and more thickly settled portions of the United States, is much less widely practiced over the whole national area than it ought to be. Garden vegetables grown as farm crops are commonly used as articles of summer diet everywhere. But this custom can by no means vie with a well kept kitchen garden, either in the variety or quality of the wholesome eatables which it affords. An area of land cultivated as a kitchen garden will easily supply the family table with one hundred dollars' worth of vegetables every year. The advantage to the housewife of a bountiful supply of good vegetables, close at hand, is apparent.

Many of the best varieties of garden vegetables lose much of their proper flavor within a few hours after gathering. Hence these are rarely, if ever, seen in the market. Their places are commonly taken by inferior sorts which have better keeping qualities. Moreover, fresh vegetables in the home garden are clean and not liable to infection from handling and exposure.

Location of the Garden.—On small grounds the garden site may be confined of necessity to one location. But if choice is afforded, select preferably a spot having a gentle slope and southern exposure. A prime consideration is to secure the best possible crops of early vegetables as a wholesome change from the monotony of winter diet. A windbreak either of trees, buildings or hedges, or even a high board fence or stone wall, will be an aid to this end by breaking the force of the cold spring winds. Some persons prefer, where space admits, to change the location of the garden every five or six years. But by proper rotation of crops and suitable cultivation, it has been found possible to continue growing garden crops with equal, or even increasingly good results, upon the same piece of ground for many years.

The subject of drainage and the original preparation of the soil have already been considered. The proper treatment in after years depends upon the nature of the soil. A clay or other heavy soil should be plowed in the fall so that it may be mellowed by the frosts. A lighter soil may be plowed in the spring as soon as the ground is dry enough to be worked. The rule is to grasp a handful of soil firmly in the hand and observe whether or not it crumbles when released. If so, the soil may be worked with safety. The finer the soil, the better the crops will be. Hence, some gardeners go over the soil in the spring with the disc harrow before plowing so that, when turned over, the bottom soil will be fine. They also use the disc harrow after plowing so as to mellow the soil through and through.

Fertilization.—Only well rotted stable manure or high grade commercial fertilizer should be used. The latter may be applied in the fall on heavy soil and plowed under. Or on light soil it may be applied either in the fall or spring and turned under at the spring plowing. Fertilizer may be applied either broadcast or in the hill; or better, part one way and part the other. A handful of fertilizer sprinkled in the hill over a space about as large as a dinner plate and worked into the soil with a hoe will help to give any vegetable, and especially early crops, a flying start. But never dump a handful of fertilizer in the bottom of the hill without mixing it thoroughly with soil. Otherwise some of the roots will not come in contact with it at all, and those which do will be burned. Hence for the time being it will be somewhat worse than wasted.

Garden Seeds and Plants.—The selection of seeds and plants for the garden, the depth at which they should be planted, and many other particulars about the different garden crops vary so greatly by reason of climatic and other conditions that they cannot be properly discussed in this place. Send for the catalogs of the principal seedsmen in your section and follow carefully the directions which they give. For further information apply by letter to the State Experiment Station of the Department of Agriculture in your own State or to the Secretary of Agriculture at Washington.

Tables for Planting.—The tables on the following pages for planting flowers and vegetables are taken from "The Garden Annual" of the Chicago Sunday Tribune. The times of planting are calculated for the latitude of New York. Allow ten days for each one hundred miles north or south of that latitude. The date for indoor planting applies to seeds started in the house, in a hot bed, or in a cold frame, but observe that cold snaps and other weather conditions may affect these dates. The table for planting vegetables is planned especially for those having small gardens in which most or all of the work must be done by hand.

Hot Beds.—To start early plants in the northern half of the United States build a hot bed. This is simply a box sunk in the ground and heated from below by means of a bed of stable manure or otherwise. It contains a layer of soil for the seed bed and is protected by a cover of window sash filled with glass. Hot beds may be either temporary or permanent.

To Build a Temporary Hot Bed.—Select a sheltered, well drained location and shake out a pile of manure in a broad flat heap 8 or 9 feet

NAME	WHEN TO PLANT		SEED NEEDED FOR 100 FT.	PLANTING DEPTH (INCHES)	DISTANCE APART (INCHES)	COMMENT
	INDOORS	OUTDOORS				
Asparagus	....	April.	1 oz.	1	3 to 5	Give asparagus rich, well-drained soil.
Asparagus plants	....	April-May.	50–80	8	12	Plant one-year-old roots and grow two years before cutting. Mulch with manure in the fall.
Beans (bush)	....	May-August.	1 pt.	2	3 to 6 ft.	Make successive plantings.
Beans (pole)	....	May.	½ pt.	2	3 to 4 ft.	Plant several kinds to determine which succeeds best in your soil.
Beets	....	April-August.	2 oz.	1	18	Plant an abundance to allow for beet greens. Use Early Egyptian.
Cabbage (early)	March.	May.	¼ oz.	½	18	For very early cabbages sow seed in the hot bed and transplant to cold frame in March.
Cabbage (late)	....	May.	¼ oz.	½	24	Be sure to try the Savoy. It is unrivalled.
Carrot	....	April-July.	1 oz.	½	3 to 8	Grow French Forcing and plant for a succession. Danvers Half-long is good for winter.
Cauliflower	March.	May.	¼ oz.	½	20	Likes a cool, rich, moist soil.
Celery	March.	May-June.	¼ oz.		4 to 8	Grow Paris Golden for an early crop and Boston Market later.
Corn	April.	May-June.	¼ pt.	1½	30 to 35	Golden Bantam planted every two weeks will give a long succession.
Cucumber	March.	April-July.	½ oz.	1	Hills 4 ft.	Get early "cukes" by starting seeds in the house or in a cold frame.
Egg Plant	March.	April-May.	⅓ oz.	½	16 to 24	Needs a long season.
Endive	....	April-September.	1 oz.	½	6 to 12	Grow like lettuce, and tie up the leaves to blanch them two or three weeks before wanted.
Kale	....	May.	1 oz.	½	24	Kale is best after the frost has touched it.
Lettuce	Feb.-March.	April-Aug. 10.	½ oz.	¼	6	Must be grown rapidly to be good.
Muskmelon	April.	May-June.	¼ oz. for 15 hills.	1	Hills 6 ft.	Grow an early kind like Netted Gem, in the North. Put manure in the hill.

NAME	WHEN TO PLANT		SEED NEEDED FOR 100 FT.	PLANTING DEPTH (inches)	DISTANCE APART (inches)	COMMENT
	INDOORS	OUTDOORS				
Melon (Watermelon)	....	May-June.	½ oz. for 15 hills	1	Hills 8 ft.	Ask your seedsman to recommend a variety. Use manure in the hill.
Onions	Feb.	April.	1 oz.	½	3	Plant Danvers Yellow Globe and keep the ground well cultivated.
Parsley	....	April.	½ oz.	¼	6	Soak the seed over night in lukewarm water.
Parsnip	....	April.	½ oz.	½	6	Use the Student in the home garden.
Peas	....	March-June.	1 qt.	2½	Thick	Make the ground very fine and plant for a succession.
Peppers	March.	May-June. (Set out plants.)	⅓ oz.	½	2 ft.	Must be started under cover.
Potato (Irish)	....	May-June.	1 pk. for 100 hills.	Early 2 Late 5	12 or more.	Irish Cobbler is a good early sort and Green Mountain a reliable late variety.
Pumpkin	....	May-July.	½ oz. for 15 hills.	1½	Hills 6 ft.	Pumpkins may be planted in the corn or beside the compost heap.
Radish	Feb.-March.	April-September.	1 oz.	½	2	Plant every ten days for a long season.
Rhubarb Roots	....	Spring or Fall.	30	3	3 ft.	Rhubarb craves heavy feeding with manure every fall.
Salsify (Oyster Plant)	....	April.	1	1	5	May be left in the ground like parsnips until spring.
Spinach	....	Mar.-May and Oct.	1	1	3	Sowed in the fall and covered with a light litter spinach will give an early spring crop.
Squash	....	May-June.	⅓ oz. for 25 hills.	1½	Hills 5 ft.	Grow on the edge of the garden and let the vines run on the grass to save garden space.
Tomato	March.	May-June.	¼ oz. for 250 plants.	½	36	Feed the plants during the season instead of making the ground very rich.
Turnip	....	April-July.	½	½	4	Grow Extra Early White Milan and White Egg.

NAME	WHEN TO PLANT		DISTANCE APART (INCHES)	FLOWERING PERIODS	COLOR	COMMENT
	INDOORS	OUTDOORS				
Achillea (Sneezewort)	....	June-Oct.	12	July-Oct.	White.	A perennial, two feet high. The Pearl is a good variety.
Ageratum	March.	May.	6	June-Oct.	Blue, white.	Annual, grown from seeds or cuttings. Fine for borders. Blues are most popular.
Alysum (Annual)	....	May-June.	4	June-Oct.	White.	Excellent annual for borders.
Alysum (Perennial)	....	June-Sept.	6	July-Oct.	Yellow.	Used for edgings and rock work.
Aquilegia (Columbine)	....	June 15-Sept.	8	June-Sept.	White, yellow, blue, pink.	Hardy perennial. Blooms the second year.
Asters (China)	March-April.	May-June.	9	July-Oct.	White, pink, yellow, red, purple, lavender.	Bedding annual. Use wood ashes when setting plants.
Balsam	....	May.	9	July-Sept.	Red, white, pink, yellow.	Annual, to grow in clumps in the sun.
Calendula (Pot marigold)	....	May-June.	6	June-Oct.	Yellow, orange.	Easily grown annuals, that self-sow. Fill vacant spots with them.
Calliopsis	....	May.	6	July-Oct.	Yellow, brown.	Showy annuals, good for cutting. Easy to grow, but they like the sun.
Campanula (Canterbury Bells)	....	June-Aug.	12	June-Aug.	Blue, pink, white.	Perennial, blooming the second year.
Celosia (Cockscomb)	April.	May.	6	June-Oct.	White, red, pink, yellow.	Annual. Combs may be dried for winter bouquets.
Candytuft	....	May 15-June 15.	4	June-Oct.	Pink, white, red, purple.	Annuals, for beds, borders or to cut. Make successive sowings.
Centaurea (Corn flower)	....	April.	6	June-Oct.	Blue, white, pink.	Annual, to grow in masses. Self-sown. Keep flowers picked.
Chrysanthemum (Annual)	April.	May.	6	July-Oct.	White, yellow, red.	Annuals, for massing at a distance.
Cobea	April.	....	8	July-Oct.	Purple.	Climbing vine. Plant seeds edgewise.
Cosmos (Early)	April.	May.	12	July-Sept.	White. red, pink.	Tender annuals. Pinch back to make bushy plants.
Cosmos (Late)	March-May.	May.	12	Sept.-Oct.	White, pink, orange.	Tie to stakes if exposed to winds.
Dahlia	March-April.	....	36	Aug.-Oct.	White, yellow, pink, red.	Late-started plants give largest flowers.
Delphinium (Larkspur)	....	June-Aug.	12	July-Oct.	Blue, yellow, white.	Fine tall perennials. Bloom the second year. Blues are best.
Dianthus (Pinks)	March-May.	May.	6	July-Oct.	White, red, striped.	Perennial, blooming the first year.
Digitalis (Foxglove)	....	July-Aug.	9	July-Aug.	Pink, white, blue.	Fine in hardy border. Bloom the second year.
Eschscholtzia (California poppy)	....	May.	4	July-Aug.	Yellow, orange.	Do not transplant. Foliage is pretty.
Gaillardia	April.	May.	6	July-Sept.	Yellow, red.	Showy annual, for beds.
Gourds	March-April.	May.	4	Sept.-Oct.	Fruit-bearing.	Excellent to hide unsightly objects.
Four O'Clocks	April.	May.	8	July-Sept.	White, pink.	Annuals, for borders or beds.
Gypsophilia	April.	May.	10	July-Sept.	White.	Fine to use in bouquets. Grow Elegant.

NAME	WHEN TO PLANT		DISTANCE APART (INCHES)	FLOWERING PERIODS	COLOR	COMMENT
	INDOORS	OUTDOORS				
Helianthus (Sunflower)	....	May.	12	July-Oct.	Yellow.	Make a good [illegible]en. Try the new [illegible]ds.
Hollyhock	March-April.	June 15–July.	15	Aug.-Sept.	White, red, yellow, pink.	[illegible]al. Spray with [illegible]x.
Kochia (Summer Cypress)	....	[illegible].	12		No flowers.	[illegible] turns [illegible]ed in the fall.
Larkspur (Annual)	March-April.	May-June.	6	June-Sept.	Red, white, blue, pink.	Grow in [illegible]. The [illegible] are good for cutting.
Lobelia	April.	May.	4	June-Sept.	Blue, white.	Lobelia Erinus is very [illegible] for low [illegible]. It is [illegible]. Use manure [illegible] for Lobelias.
Marigold	April.	May.	6	July-Oct.	Brown, red, yellow.	[illegible]
Mignonette	March-April.	May.	6	July-Oct.	....	[illegible] ive sowings. Like [illegible]
Myosotis (Forget-me-not)	March-April.	[illegible].	6	June-Aug.	Blue, pink, white.	Perennial, [illegible] the first [illegible]
Nasturtium	April.	May.	6	June-Oct.	Various colors.	[illegible]
Nicotiana (Tobacco plant)	April.	May.	9	July-Oct.	White, pink.	[illegible]
Pansy	March-May.	[illegible]-Oct.	4	April-Oct.	Many colors.	[illegible]
Petunia	Feb.-April.	May.	6	June-Oct.	Red, pink, white.	[illegible] -flowering an-[illegible]. Don't [illegible]
Phlox (Annual)	March-April.	May.	8	July-Oct.	Red, white, yellow, pink.	[illegible]
Poppy (Annual)	....	[illegible].	4	June-Sept.	Red, white, pink, yellow.	Very [illegible]. Do not [illegible]. Make [illegible] sowings.
Poppy (Perennial)	....	June-Sept.	9	June-Aug.	Red, white, pink, yellow.	Fine to give bright [illegible].
Portulaca	....	May-July.	4	July-Oct.	Red, pink, yellow, white.	Unexcelled for [illegible] and many [illegible].
Pyrethrum	....	June-Sept.	12	July-Aug.	Red, white, pink.	Grow in [illegible]. Good to [illegible].
Ricinus (Castor Oil Plant)	April.	May.	36	No bloom.	No flowers.	Very [illegible]. Best started in the [illegible]
Salpiglossis	April.	May.	6	July-Oct.	White, brown, red.	Good [illegible] and easy to grow.
Salvia	Feb.-March.	May.	18	Aug.-Oct.	Scarlet.	[illegible] a green [illegible]
Scabiosa (Mourning Bride)	April.	May.	9	July-Sept.	White, yellow, pink.	Long-flowering [illegible].
Stocks	Feb.-April.	May.	12	July-Oct.	Pink, white, scarlet, yellow.	Good for [illegible] and to [illegible].
Sweet Pea	....	[illegible].	3	July-Sept.	Many colors.	[illegible] in the [illegible]
Verbena	Feb.-April.	May.	6	June-Oct.	White, red, blue, pink.	[illegible] in the [illegible].
Zinnia	March-April.	May.	6	June-Oct.	Red, yellow, white, pink.	Good [illegible], and [illegible] easy to grow.

wide. Pack by tramping to a solid mass 18 or 24 inches deep. The length will depend upon the number of sash to be employed. Select for this purpose horse manure containing sufficient litter to spring lightly when trodden. Now adjust the frames facing to the south. These are merely an open box without top or bottom. Build them of any sound inch lumber, 6 feet wide, and long enough to accommodate any required number of sash. Standard garden sash 3 by 6 feet in size can be purchased of seedsmen or dealers in garden supplies. Or suitable frames to hold the glass can be made at home or by a local carpenter. Including the item of labor, however, this method is likely to be more expensive. Make the front from 4 to 6 inches lower than the back so as to incline the glass enough to afford good drainage. Now spread 3 to 5 inches of good garden loam, or special prepared soil, evenly over the manure within the frame, put the sash on and let the bed heat. At first the temperature will be high: Do not plant seed until it falls to 80°. This will be in about three days.

Or, to make a permanent hot bed, dig a pit about 30 inches deep and 6 feet wide to any desired length and line the walls with brick or 2-inch plank. Fill this with manure. Or, if convenient, install a suitable heating system. Care must be taken to adjust this so that the temperature within the hot bed will not exceed 80° F.

Provide board shutters, straw matting, burlap or old carpet to cover the frames during cold nights. Also have at hand a supply of straw, or loose stable manure, to throw over them during cold snaps.

Place the hot bed near the house or barn, convenient to some walk which is used several times a day, and keep it under close and constant observation. When the sun shines on the glass, ventilate the hot bed by raising the sash a little on the side opposite the wind. Take care to keep the plants from a draft of cold air. Toward evening close the sash and let the bed warm up for the night. Water only on bright days and in the early morning. Watering in the evening or on cloudy days may chill the bed and expose it to frosts. After watering, ventilate to let surplus moisture escape, else the plants may be lost by damping-off fungus or mildew.

Cold Frames.—These are made precisely the same as hot beds except that they rest on the bare earth and are not heated. Place a cold frame near the hot bed in northern climates and transplant to it plants that have been started in the hot bed, to harden them before transplanting to the garden. But in the South, the cold frame may take the place of the hot bed in starting early plants. Ventilate and water cold frames the same as hot beds.

Earth for Seed Beds.—To prepare earth for seeds or small plants, for filling pots, window boxes, hot beds, cold frames or for certain purposes in the open garden, mix one part by bulk of well rotted manure, two parts of good garden loam and one part of sharp fine sand. Choose for this purpose manure which has been thoroughly rotted but not exposed to leaching from the weather. Mix all together in a heap, stir well with the shovel, sift and place in boxes or in the bed prepared for the seed. If convenient, bake the soil for an hour in a hot oven. This will kill all weed seed and spores of fungous disease.

Seeding. — Sow all garden seeds which are to be transplanted in straight rows 2 inches or more apart according to kind and convenience. Water just often enough to keep the soil in such condition that a handful will crumble freely after being pressed in the hand.

Thin the plants as soon as they can be handled and before they begin to "draw" or grow tall and spindling. Remove the centers of the thick bunches so as leave uniform spaces but preserve as far as possible the best plants.

Hardening Off and Transplanting.—Do not transplant seedlings grown in the house, hot bed or cold frame to the open garden without first accustoming them to effects of sun and wind. To "harden off" plants, increase gradually the ventilation and reduce the amount of watering. But do not let the ground become so dry that the plant will wilt. After a few days leave the plants uncovered throughout the day and on mild nights. They can then be transplanted without loss. Transplant preferably twice; first from the hot bed to the cold frame or especially prepared seed bed in the open garden and, afterwards, thence to the permanent location. This strengthens and improves most plants by increasing the size and vigor of the root system.

Others as melons, cucumbers and beans, do not transplant readily from the seed bed to the open ground. Start each hill of these in a pint or quart berry box, or on the bottom of a piece of sod 2 or 3 inches thick and 5 or 6 inches square placed root side up in the hot bed or cold frame. Then bury the box or sod in its proper place in the garden a little below the surface of the earth. Cut out the bottom of the berry box with a sharp knife before planting. By these means the roots of the growing plants are not disturbed.

Choose for transplanting a cool, cloudy day or work in the evening and preferably when the soil is moist but not wet. Soak the earth in the seed bed a few hours before transplanting. Separate the plants from one another by cutting the soil into cubes by means of a knife or trowel. Remove preferably enough earth from the seed bed to protect the roots. Or, should the earth fall from the roots, "puddle" the plant by dipping the roots in a thin slime consisting of clay, cow manure and water, mixed in a pail or tub. Pick up the plants in small bunches and "puddle" until the roots are coated with moist earth. This protects them from air and affords direct contact of the roots with the soil.

Have the seed bed smooth, fine and level. Mark the location of the rows by a cord fastened to stakes at either end and drawn taut. But do not open the holes or separate the plants until ready to insert them so that the soil will be moist and fresh. Should the earth be dry, pour a little water in the hole and cover with dry soil to prevent baking. Set the plants upright a little deeper than they stood in the seed bed. Press the earth about them with the fingers so that no open spaces are left. The time of planting must depend upon climatic and other local conditions. If in doubt, ask some experienced local gardener.

To protect small plants from heat in hot climates drive stakes into the ground slanting toward the north and lean boards against them so as to shade the rows. Or use light frames on lath or wooden slats and cover them with cotton cloth. To protect crops planted in winter from cold and give an early start in the spring, set the stakes slanting to the south and lean boards against them on the north side. Or cover with a mulch of manure, straw or leaves. But take care that this is not so thick as to keep the air from the plants and also see that it is free from injurious weeds.

Cultivation of Gardens. — Horse cultivation is to be preferred when possible. It is cheaper and likely to be more thorough. In this case make the rows as long as possible and plant potatoes, or other crops not easily injured by tramping, in the space required for turning at the ends. The objects of cultivation are to keep down the weeds and conserve soil moisture by providing a surface mulch. Stirring the top soil to a depth of 2 or 3 inches after every rain accomplishes both. Frequent shallow cultivation is the rule with all good gardeners, the more frequent, the better. A light mulch of fine manure, lawn clippings, or the like for ten or twelve inches around young plants will help to preserve the moisture. This is essential for strawberries to keep the fruit from contact with the ground. But do not make this mulch so heavy as to exclude the air. Do not cultivate too soon after a rain. Test the soil by squeezing it in the hand.

It is sound economy to provide a full set of garden tools. A complete outfit of hand tools should include spade and spading fork, steel rake, common hoe, narrow hoe, dibbles and trowels for transplanting, weeders, watering can and wheelbarrow. A wheel hoe is also a great convenience, especially if a horse cultivator is not available.

Combined Fruit and Vegetable Garden.—It is quite surprising how much can be accomplished upon a very small area by wise selection and proper modes of culture. Often two kinds of crops can be grown upon the same space as by growing small fruits, like the currant or raspberry, between the rows of apple or other fruit trees. Or strawberries may be grown between rows of grapevines. Or grapevines may be used to screen out-buildings or porches. Or a grape arbor may be utilized as a summer house. Some flowering plants as pansies or violets—and some garden vegetables—as radishes—may also be grown between grapevines, or fruit trees. Asparagus grows well in such a location. There are many plans for combining fruit and vegetable garden which may readily be adapted to local conditions. The following suggestions are made by the Department of Agriculture:

An area of 60 by 80 feet set apart as a fruit garden will accommodate 442 fruit-bearing plants of the kinds designated, while an area of 40 by 80 feet will be sufficient for quite a variety of vegetable plants. On these areas, if carefully planned, the following fruit and vegetable plants may be grown:

Thirty-two grapevines, dispersed at intervals of 10 feet around the entire garden; three rows, each containing 6 trees dwarf pears, 18 specimens in all (rows Nos. 2, 10, 14); one row, 6 specimens, peaches (row No. 4); one row, 6 specimens, cherries (row No. 8); one row, 6 specimens, dwarf apples (row No. 6); one row, 6 specimens, plums (row No. 12); one row, 20 specimens, blackberries (row No. 1); two rows, 40 specimens, blackcaps (rows Nos. 3 and 5); two rows, 40 specimens, red raspberries (rows Nos. 7 and 9); three rows, 300 specimens, strawberries (rows Nos. 11, 13 and 15).

Vegetable Plants That Can Be Grown on an Area of 40 by 80 Feet.—One row, ½ row rhubarb, ½ row asparagus (occupying four feet); one row, salsify (1½ feet); one row, parsnips (1½ feet); two rows, beets (3 feet); one row, eggplant—plants set 18 inches apart—2 dozen (3 feet); two rows, tomatoes, plants set 2 feet apart—2 dozen (6 feet); one row, summer squash, 12 hills, 3 feet apart (3 feet); two rows, cucumbers, 24 hills, 3 feet apart (1 foot); two rows, early cabbage, 4 dozen plants, set 18 inches apart (4 feet); two rows, late cabbage, 4 dozen plants, set 18 inches apart (4 feet); one row, early celery, 6 dozen plants, set 6 inches apart (2 feet); eight rows, peas, plant in double rows, 4 inches apart, follow by 6 rows late celery, 36 dozen plants (16 feet); two rows, lima beans, 4 dozen hills, 18 inches apart (4 feet); six rows, bunch beans, in succession sow seeds in drills, placing seeds about 6 inches apart in the row; follow by late cabbage, turnips, or spinach (12 feet); two rows, radishes, 4 sowings, planted in double rows 6 inches apart (3 feet); two rows, lettuce, two sorts, adapted for early and late use (3 feet); one row, parsley and peppergrass (1½ feet). The space occupied by the last three plants may be given over to winter squashes by planting these before other crops are off the ground.

This general plan will serve as a

guide to planting in any portion of the United States, but the sorts chosen must be suited to each particular section of the country.

As will be seen, this garden is planned to utilize the space to the best possible advantage. In order to secure large returns, the soil must be kept cultivated and well enriched. Walks, if any are to be maintained as permanent features, should only exist where necessary for ease and comfort in getting about. A permanent walk should divide the fruit garden from the vegetable garden. This is best made of gravel or some other loose material, which will preserve a dry passageway without preventing rain from penetrating the soil beneath it. The fruit trees which stand beside it will need the moisture which it gathers. On account of the small area occupied and the close planting necessary to secure the results desired, the culture of such a garden must of necessity be by hand. If the grapevines are trained on the high renewal system, they will serve both as a screen for the rest of the garden and as a source of fruit supply. A good wire fence should, however, be constructed on the line between adjoining properties, and the grape border planted not farther than 2 feet from the boundary fence.

TREES AND SHRUBBERY

A good, well-kept lawn affords a natural background against which to display shade trees and shrubbery. These may be purely ornamental objects. Or such useful trees and shrubs as fruit trees and currant or barberry bushes may be chosen with both ornament and utility in view. Both these thoughts should be kept in mind in the selection of trees and shrubs and in making the decision where to plant them. As above suggested, to secure best results, treat all of the available space about the home site as a single tract. The work of grading, breaking, manuring and otherwise preparing the soil can be done both cheaper and better all at one time. And the treatment requisite for the lawn and garden will prepare the soil for the reception of trees and shrubs.

First make a plan of the home site, to scale, with pencil and paper. On this mark the location of all buildings and other cultural objects and landmarks. This will greatly assist in securing pleasing effects in laying out even the smallest and simplest of home grounds. Mark the dimensions and outlines of the portion to be reserved for lawn and greensward.

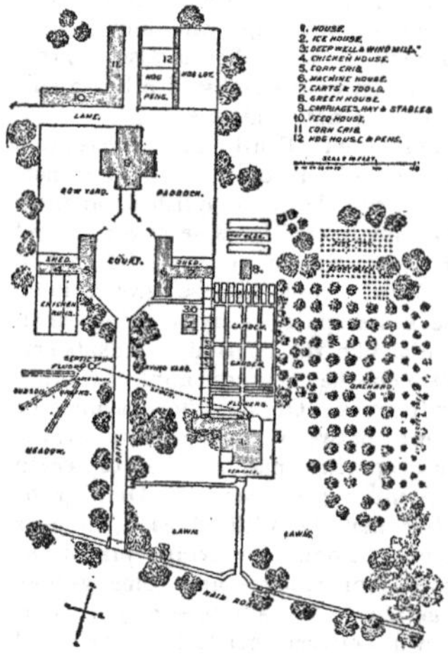

General plan for farmhouse grounds.

Set apart spaces for vegetable and flower gardens. Now sketch in the necessary pathways, walks and drives. Finally consider how to secure against this background the most desirable effects by the planting of trees and shrubbery. The size of the home grounds and their location and surroundings—including climatic and other conditions—vary so widely that the problem of beautifying them is necessarily an individual one. However, experience has suggested certain general principles which are of universal value. These may be briefly stated.

General Design.—Observe the main lines of travel and, unless there should be some good reason for changing, make these the basis for permanent paths and walks. Custom is very persistent and usual lines of travel will not only prove as a rule to be the most convenient, but will be difficult to change. They may result, if changed unwisely, in unsightly foot

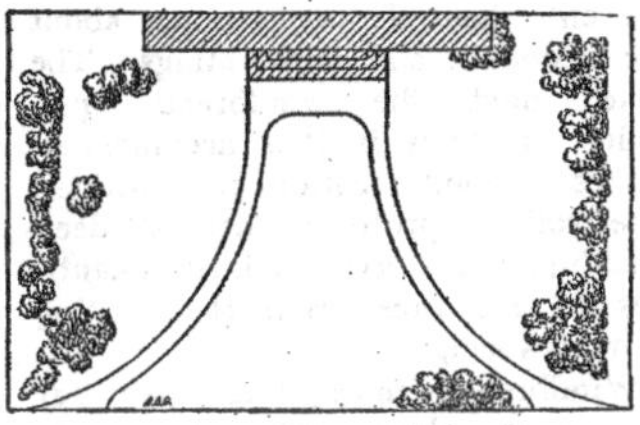

Group planting.

paths across the lawn. Short walks and drives of less than 100 feet should preferably be straight. If longer they may be gently curved to provide bays in which trees and shrubs may be planted. Observe carefully the outlook from all the doors and windows to determine which parts of the landscape should be retained in view and what objects should be cut off from sight by trees and shrubs.

The best practice is to confine trees and shrubs to the borders of the grounds or the lines of walks or drives. Leave the lawn lying in unbroken stretches. But such borders need not be continuous around the grounds. They should be broken here and there to preserve attractive views of the exterior landscape. Often a continuous belt of trees is desirable across the rear or at the sides of the lot to afford protection. But since the rear views may be as attractive as those toward the front, these belts may also be broken at intervals. Great care must be taken, however, not to leave openings which will cause snow to drift in the vicinity of the house and outbuildings.

Formal arrangements of trees in straight rows are sometimes desirable to screen public highways, or as borders. But more pleasing effects can usually be produced by spacing the trees irregularly. The width of a belt of trees may properly be varied. Let them project in some places into the interior open space and retreat, in others, almost to the limit of the grounds.

The best effects may be secured from a variety of kinds of trees. Group each kind by itself. Vistas of the more distant landscape opening between groups of trees irregularly spaced are among the most pleasing views imaginable. A few elms, a group of oaks, or a clump of graceful birches scattered about the grounds gives character to the planting from a near view and, when seen at a distance, makes a pleasingly diversified sky-line.

Shrubbery is properly placed when planted in clumps against belts of trees, in bays or corners, or when employed to screen a rough foundation wall, to soften the outlines of

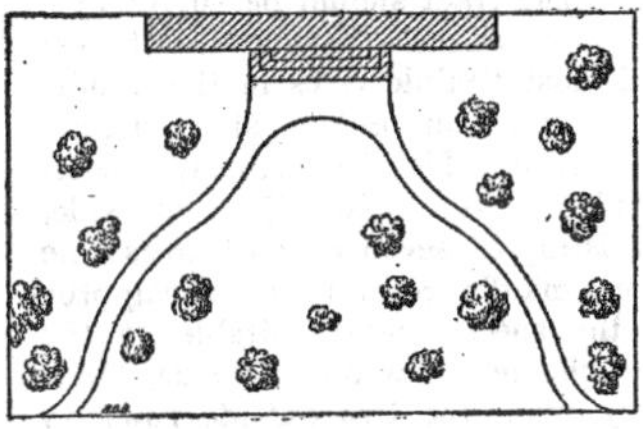

Scattered plantations.

unsightly objects or to hide them wholly from view.

Walks may properly follow the contour of the ground.

Windbreaks. — Many homes are naturally sheltered by adjacent hills or timber. But countless thousands of dwellings, school-houses, barns and other occupied buildings stand on hills, or treeless plains, such that some suitable protection is required. Such a windbreak, recommended by the Department of Agriculture for the northern half of the United States, consists of thirteen rows of trees parallel to one another and 6 feet 10 inches apart. The first two rows on the north and west edges of the belt are Russian wild olive; the third and fourth, arborvitæ; fifth and sixth, box elder; seventh and eighth, white elm; ninth and tenth, white willow; and the remaining three rows, common cottonwood. Such a windbreak when the trees are matured will appear like the side and top of a building having a sloping roof.

For the southern part of the United States, to afford protection from south and west winds, the following is advised: The first two rows on the south and west edges of the belt to be Russian mulberry or Osage orange; the third and fourth, Chinese arborvitæ; the fifth and sixth, black locust; seventh and eighth, green ash; ninth and tenth, white elm; the remaining three rows, honey locust or common cottonwood.

For portions of the Pacific slope where damaging winds may come from either southwest or northeast, the whole tract should be surrounded by a windbreak having the tallest and most flexible trees in the middle and those on either side sloping downward. The Department recommends a windbreak $2\frac{1}{2}$ rods wide, consisting of seven rows of trees; the three middle rows to be eucalyptus of the species most suitable to the site; the next row on each side, Monterey pine; the two outside rows on both edges, Monterey cypress. Or any number of rows of these varieties of trees may be planted in the same relative proportions.

Such windbreaks not only protect the land for a distance approximately ten times their height. They also provide timber for the repair of buildings and many similar purposes. An objection to windbreaks is that trees adjacent to lawns and gardens may injure them by their shade and may also rob the soil of plant food and moisture. Such loss is more than offset — in localities where windbreaks are most needed—by the conservation of moisture which would otherwise be removed by prevailing winds, and by the favorable modification both of summer's heat and winter's cold.

Leave an opening in the windbreak, in Northern latitudes, from 75 to 100 feet in width to the north and west of buildings and orchards. This will act as a snow trap. It will catch the drifts during winter storms and prevent them from forming about the residence and outbuildings. The space next the windbreak upon which the snow is thus accumulated makes a good location for gardens. The soil is protected against deep freezing, yet stores up large quantities of moisture from the melting snow in spring.

Windbreaks more than pay for themselves, when needed, by economizing the feed required by domestic animals and also the fuel necessary to warm dwellings in winter. They protect fruit trees against frosts, and lawns and gardens against the effeets of drouth. They may, therefore, be regarded as among the most desirable permanent improvements.

Orchards.—When space admits, a small orchard of apple, pear and other desirable fruit trees, according to climate, will add greatly to the resources of any householder and enhance the value of any piece of property. The selection of varieties must depend upon the amount of space available, and climatic and other conditions. But as a rule, the greater variety of kinds of fruits obtainable from the home orchard, the better. A separate plot of ground set apart as an orchard presents some advantages over the plan of scattering fruit trees over the lawn and grounds for shade and ornament. More care can be taken to select for a separate orchard a site having the right kind of soil, with suitable exposure and protection from prevailing winds and frosts. Fruit trees are also easier to cultivate when growing together in an orchard and, especially, to protect against the attacks of insects by spraying. But if space does not admit of a separate orchard, fruit trees, if properly located, pruned and cared for, make very desirable shade trees. Indeed, they are regarded by many as among the most decorative objects which can be used to beautify the lawn and grounds.

Ornamental Trees and Shrubs.—Choose, preferably, for shade and ornamental purposes, the kinds of trees and shrubs which may be observed growing wild and the species which seem to flourish best in the locality. Many persons neglect the beautification of their grounds by tree planting either from motives of false economy or from lack of necessary information. The cost of planting a number of trees required by the ordinary home grounds is very small. The process is simple. And if ordinary care is taken there will be little danger that the trees may not thrive. It is quite surprising how quickly a few seedlings will spring up and how much they will add both to the beauty and comfort of the home surroundings.

The cost, if any, of nursery stock will be the principal item of expense. Even this expense can be saved, in many localities, by transplanting growing seedlings from neighboring forests. These can be had in most cases for the asking and at very slight cost for removal. Or grow the young trees themselves from seed in a little nursery in a corner of the kitchen garden. This is one of the most interesting experiments which can be made by any family and has great educative value for children.

The Home Nursery.—The seeds of most trees can be purchased from seedsmen the same as garden seed. Or they may be collected from trees growing in the vicinity. Most tree seeds mature in the fall. Gather them as soon as ripened. A few, such as silver maple and elm, ripen in the spring. Collect these when ripe and plant immediately. Such tree seeds as those of the honey locust, acorns, and the various nuts, may be gathered from the ground. But the small, thin-coated seeds, like those of maple, box elder, ashes, and elms should preferably be picked from the tree by hand. Collect these after the first seeds have fallen from the tree; since the sterile or infertile seeds are the first to fall. Dry the seeds for a few weeks to remove surplus moisture and prevent molding. Spread acorns and other nuts on a dirt floor and smaller seeds on boards in a dry place. If there are signs of mold spread out thinner. If the kernels shrink, they are drying too rapidly; cover with clean sand or chaff. For permanent storage, place acorn and other nuts in a close covered wooden box mixed with dry chaff or straw. Sink this in the ground in some well drained place to within a few inches of the top. Heap over it a mound of earth to protect it from rains and frost.

When planting time comes, cut open a number of seeds and examine the kernels. If these are plump and firm the seeds are good; if withered,

Seed-testing device. (*Dick J. Crosby.*)

the seeds are not fit to plant. A good plan is to make a germination test by sprouting a few seeds between pieces of clean wet blotting paper or in shallow boxes of sand. To test small seeds count a certain number—as one hundred or more—and spread them on a piece of moist blotting paper. Lay this on a plate and cover with another layer of blotting paper. Place over all another plate or a pane of glass. Set in a warm sunny room at a temperature of 68° to 86° F. Keep the blotting paper constantly moist but not wet. Keep a record of the kind and number of the seeds and the date. Look at them every day for two weeks or more, depending upon the kind of seed, until all that will are sprouted. Count the number which fail to germinate and figure the percentage of good seed. In general the percentages which should germinate in the different kinds of trees are as follows: ash, 35 to 50; basswood, 35 to 50; beach, 70 to 80; box elder, 40 to 60; catalpa, 40 to 75; cherry, 78 to 80; Kentucky coffee tree, 70 to 75; cottonwood, 75 to 95; elm, 50 to 75; hackberry, 70 to 80; hickory, 50 to 75; locust, 50 to 75; maple, 25 to 60; mulberry, 75 to 95; oak, 75 to 95; Osage orange, 60 to 95; poplar, 5 to 10; walnut, 75 to 80.

If the percentage shown by testing falls much below this standard the seeds are poor. Either reject them or sow more thickly than usual. To test large seeds such as nuts, cherry and other pits, use shallow boxes of moist sand under similar conditions.

Prepare soil for the nursery as for the lawn or garden. But the seed bed should not be too much exposed to the sun. It should preferably be sheltered to the east or north by a group of trees or buildings. A heavy dressing of well rotted stable manure plowed under in fall, followed by spring plowing will bring about an ideal condition. A nursery only one square rod in size, with eleven rows 18 inches apart, will produce about fifty seedlings to each row or 550 trees in all. And each row may be devoted to a single species of tree if desired. It will thus be seen that a very small space will grow all the trees that will be required for the grounds of an ordinary dwelling.

The best time to plant tree seeds is as early in the spring as the ground can be worked. Exceptions to this rule, already noted, are the seeds of the silver maple and white elm. These mature in the late spring and should be planted at once. Other exceptions are those of the basswood and yellow poplar. These ripen in autumn and must be planted in the fall. As a rule tree seeds may be planted at the same time the earliest vegetable seeds are planted in the garden. Fresh nuts, acorns of good quality, or cherry and peach pits may be planted 2 or 3 inches apart in rows. Seeds of which the average germination is from 45 to 75 per cent should be spaced from 1½ inch to 1½ inches apart. Those whose germinating powers are very low—as the basswood and yellow poplar—should be sown thickly, three or four seeds deep in the row; the others, in proportion to their power of germination. Cover tree seeds very lightly; the rule is, about twice their average diameter.

Care of Seed Beds.—Cultivate seedlings the same as garden crops. Keep down the weeds with a hoe. Stir the surface of the soil to a depth of 1 or 2 inches every few days especially after rains. In time of drouth this forms a surface mulch and conserves soil moisture. If the rains do not keep the soil moist, the seedlings must be watered or irrigated. The best plan is to dig a trench between the rows and fill this with water at night or early morning, so that it will not be drunk up by the sun. The soil must be moistened to a depth of 6 inches. Merely sprinkling water on the soil does little or no good. To carry the seedlings through the winter, hill them up 4 to 6 inches and cover with a mulch of straw, leaves or moss from 6 inches to 1 foot in depth. Hold this in place by branches or poles.

Transplanting Trees. — Seedlings of broad leaf trees—i. e., other than evergreen—should be, at the end of the first year, transplanted from the seed bed to some other part of the garden where they will have more room in which to grow. They should not be placed in permanent position in the lawn or road-side until they are two to five years old and have been transplanted once or more.

As a rule small trees can be handled more safely and conveniently than large ones. But with care forest trees 8 or 10 feet high, or even larger, may be transplanted. These are somewhat less liable to injury after planting. If nursery stock is to be used, the less distance the stock has to travel and the shorter time it is on the road, the better. Take care to insure shipment by the most direct and fastest route. Receive the stock and plant it promptly or "heel it in" on arrival. The likelihood to injury is in direct proportion to the amount of exposure to drying winds or sun. But if seedlings from the home nursery or adjacent forests are available, and if proper precautions are observed, there need be no such danger.

To take up seedlings one year old, drive a spade as deep into the soil as possible 5 or 6 inches to the side

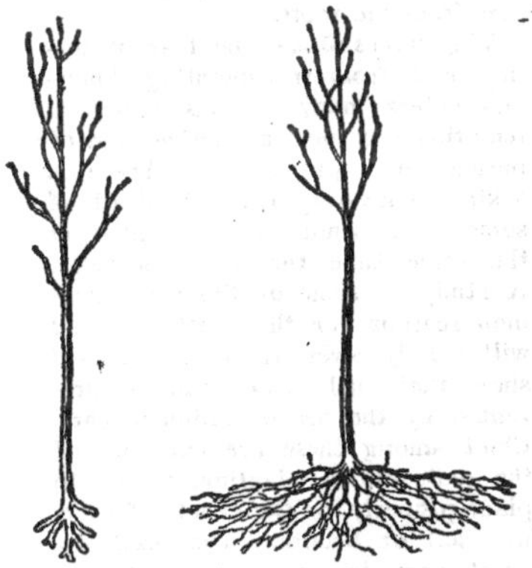

a b

(a) The relation of root to top in a nursery tree lifted for shipment; (b) how the roots are cut at digging time. (*L. C. Corbett.*)

of the tree and pry upward until the earth about the roots is thoroughly loosened, then grasp them by the stem close to the ground and gently raise them from the soil.

To take up large trees cut off the lateral roots proportionately further from the trunk, and dig more deeply into the ground so as to pry up a considerable ball of earth surrounding the root system. The object is not only to take up the main laterals and as much of the tap root as possible, but also to prevent stripping from these larger roots their net-like tracery of fine rootlets. The best results in transplanting very large trees are obtained in winter. A large ball of frozen earth surrounding the roots can then be taken up with the tree. It can thus be moved to its new location without disturbing the most delicate rootlets. The less injury these sustain, the better the tree will flourish when transplanted.

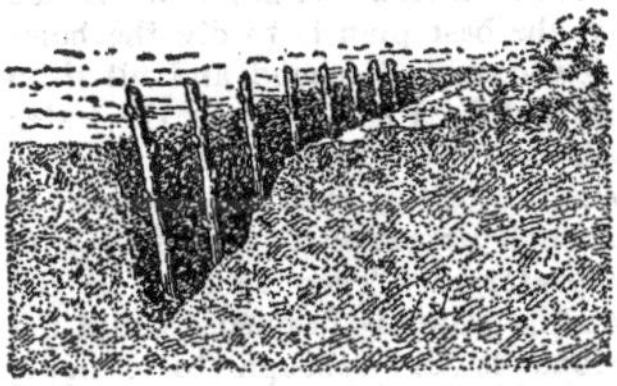

Cuttings set in trench. (*L. C. Corbett.*)

To protect nursery stock or other seedlings from injury after being taken up, if there should be any delay in planting them, "heel them in" or plant them in temporary trenches. Dig for this purpose a trench deep enough to bury the roots and about half the tops. Extend this east and west and have its south bank slope at an angle of about 30° with the surface of the ground. Place in this a layer of trees with their tops leaning south and cover the roots and trunk with fresh, fine earth taken from the north side of the trench. Add another layer of trees in the trench thus formed and so continue until all the stock is heeled in. The trees may be safely left in this condition until ready for planting.

To Plant a Tree.—The best time to plant trees in Northern and temperate climates is as early in the spring as the ground can be worked. But in warm regions trees planted in fall secure some root growth which gives them an early start in spring. Avoid sunny and windy weather. Select, rather, a cool, wet or cloudy day. Deciduous trees may be planted as soon as the ground stops freezing; evergreens, even up to the time the young growth begins to start.

Carry the trees to the site in a barrel half filled with a thin mixture of earth and water. Lift them out only as needed. The slightest exposure of the delicate roots to sun or air will dry and injure them. To secure good results the soil should be well drained. If there is standing water in the soil, postpone planting. The earth surrounding the trees should be moist, but not wet. If too dry, the best plan is to dig the holes a few days beforehand and fill them with water. Refill them as the water soaks away and persist until the surrounding soil is well moistened. A thorough irrigation of dry soil is to be preferred. Then as soon as the standing water is drained off and the ground is dry enough to crumble freely, the trees may be planted.

Dig holes for trees big enough so that the roots may be spread out flat in about their normal condition. Dig deep enough so that the trunk or stem will be 2 or 3 inches lower in the soil than its former position. Make the holes for seedlings one year old at least two feet in diameter and 1 foot deep in good soil; but make them 4 feet across in poor soil. Make holes for older trees larger in proportion. Have the sides perpendicular and the bottom flat. Loosen the soil in the bottom of the hole to the full depth of the spade. Spread 2 or 3 inches of fine top soil, free from sod or other decomposible organic matter over the bottom of the hole. If fertile garden earth can be procured for this purpose, so much the better. At all events the root system of a young tree must not be immediately surrounded by raw subsoil. On top of this layer of earth place the roots of the tree and spread them as evenly as possible over the bottom of the hole. Extend the roots in their natural position. Now carefully pack about them fine loam soil free from stone and rubbish. Work the soil about each root separately and pack it solidly with the foot. Now fill the hole and compact the earth about the roots to hold them firmly in place by treading. But do not tamp the soil with a bar or otherwise. This tends to prevent the circulation of air in the soil which is necessary to supply oxygen.

Make the last two or three inches of soil very fine and let it lie perfectly loose. This forms a mulch to conserve the soil moisture. Hill up the soil a few inches above the level of the ground.

The above practice makes it unnecessary to use water at the time of planting when it might be injurious. The presence of free water, especially in clay soils, tends to cause the earth to puddle or cake. And this tends to shut off the supply of oxygen from the roots.

Why Trees Die.—The fear of losing trees from transplanting doubtless deters many persons from attempting this most attractive kind of permanent improvements. There is a kind of mystery about the death of some trees, while others planted at the same time thrive prosperously. A study of some of the more common reasons for the death of trees will usually reveal the cause. It will show that such losses can be prevented by the use of ordinary care. Chief among these are exposure of the roots before planting, failure to plant properly, or the effects of overwet soil or drouth. The need for great care to avoid injury to the rootlets and exposure to sun and dry air has been emphasized. Failure to pack the soil tightly about the roots is a common error. This not only leaves the tree unstable, it partially prevents the rootlets from absorbing nutriment. This they cannot do unless they come into very close contact with the soil. Turf, manure or rubbish of any kind should not be brought into contact with roots. Only fine loamy soil should be used. Compact this firmly against the roots by the foot and weight of the body. Another error is false economy of time and labor in digging too small or too shallow holes. Standing water in or about the roots of the trees not only prevents the air from reaching them. It causes the soil to become puddled in the process of planting. When dry it then bakes into a hard lump which excludes the air. Drying out of soil from drouth is always injurious to newly transplanted trees. This may be largely overcome by proper cultivation. Small trees are frequently injured by stock and other accidents. If standing in exposed locations they should be protected by suitable fencing. If, however, the rules above stated are carefully followed there need be little or no loss from transplanting trees under ordinary conditions.

Care of Trees.—Even well planted and thrifty young trees sometimes die for lack of proper care. They must be protected against injury from stock and other accident by suitable fencing; and against drouth by irrigation, or other steps to increase the supply of moisture when necessary, and by frequent cultivation to conserve moisture in the soil. Artificial watering is not usually desirable. But surface water from an adjacent hill can sometimes be conducted to the home grounds by a trench made by turning a few furrows with the plow along the contour lines of the slope. In the Northwest, trees planted as windbreaks a few rods from the northwest side of the home grounds will cause drifts of snow to form just under the edge of the windbreak. They thus protect the orchard and ornamental trees and shrubbery from breakage and conserve a supply of moisture along the edge of the grounds.

Deep cultivation with the plow or spade in orchards or beneath shade trees is not desirable. It injures the root system. If the seed bed has been properly prepared, the only cultivation necessary is to stir the ground to a depth of 2 or 3 inches with a cultivator or hoe to keep down weeds and grass and conserve soil moisture by maintaining a surface mulch of fine, loose, dry earth.

TREE PROPAGATION BY CUTTINGS, GRAFTS AND BUDS

A tree may reproduce itself either by seeds or buds. Hence a valuable tree or shrub once established may be made to supply as many other specimens as may be desired. Or cuttings, scions, or buds may be exchanged with neighbors, or obtained from them for the asking or at slight expense. Many trees can be propagated by cuttings and nearly all can be grafted and budded.

Grafting. — The following is, in substance, the method of grafting recommended by the Department of Agriculture:

A scion is a portion cut from a plant to be inserted upon another (or the same) plant, with the intention that it shall grow. The wood for scions should be taken while in a dormant or resting condition. The time usually considered best is after the leaves have fallen, but before severe freezing begins. Tie the scions in bunches and bury in moist sand where they will not freeze and yet will be kept cold enough to prevent growth. Good results in cleft grafting often follow cutting scions in the

(1) Grafting tool; (2) cleft grafting: a, scion; b, scions inserted in cleft; (3) cross section of stock and scion, (L. C. Corbett.)

spring just before or at the time of grafting. But spring cutting of scions for whip grafting is not desirable. Not enough time is given for a proper union to take place.

The stock is the plant or part of a plant upon which or into which the bud or scion is inserted. For best results in grafting it is essential that the stock be in such condition that active growth can be quickly brought about.

Grafting.—The cleft style of graft is particularly adapted to large trees when for any reason it becomes necessary to change the variety. Branches too large to be worked by other methods can be cleft grafted.

To Make a Cleft Graft.—Select a branch 1 or 1½ inches in diameter and sever it with a saw. Take care not to loosen the bark from any

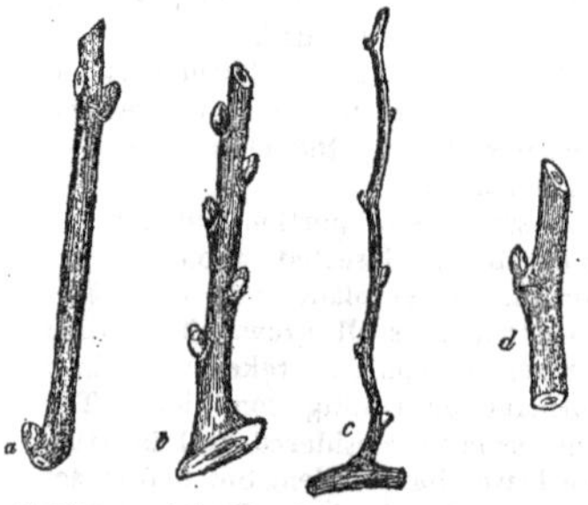

Cuttings: (a) Simple cutting; (b) heel cutting; (c) mallet cutting; (d) single-eye cutting. (L. C. Corbett.)

portion of the stub. Split the exposed end with a broad, thin chisel or grafting tool. Then with a wedge, or the wedge-shaped prong at the end of the grafting tool, spread the cleft so that the scion may be inserted as shown in the illustrations.

The scion should consist of a portion of the previous season's growth and should be long enough to have two or three buds. The lower end of the scion, which is to be inserted into the cleft, should be cut into the shape of a wedge, having the outer edge thicker than the other. In general, it is a good plan to cut the scion so that the lowest bud will come just at the top of this wedge. Thus it will be near the top of the stock. The advantage of cutting the wedge thicker on one side is shown in the illustration. This shows how the pressure of the stock is brought upon the outer growing parts of both scion and stock. Were the scion thicker on the inner side, the conditions would be reversed and its death would follow.

The importance of having an intimate connection between the growing tissues of both scion and stock can not be too strongly emphasized. Upon this alone the success of grafting depends. To make this contact of the growing portions doubly certain, the scion is often set at a slight angle with the stock into which it is inserted. This causes the growing portions of the two to cross.

After the scions have been set, the operation of cleft grafting is completed by covering all cut surfaces with a layer of grafting wax.

Whip Grafting.—The style known as whip grafting is the one almost universally used in root grafting. It has the advantage of being well adapted to small plants only 1 or 2 years of age. It can be done in-

Whip grafting: (a) The stock; (b) the scion; (c) stock and scion united. (L. C. Corbett.)

doors during the comparative leisure of winter.

To Make a Whip Graft.—Cut the stock off diagonally with one long smooth cut with a sharp knife.

Leave about three-fourths of an inch of cut surface, as illustrated. Place the knife about one-third of the distance from the end of the cut surface at right angles to the cut, and split the stock in the direction of its long axis. Cut the lower end of the scion in like manner. When the two are forced together, as shown in the illustration, the cut surfaces will fit neatly, and, if the scion and stock are of the same size, one will nearly cover the other. A difference in diameter of the two parts to be united may be disregarded unless it be too great. After the scion and stock have been locked together they should be wrapped with five or six turns of waxed cotton to hold the parts firmly.

While top grafting may be done in this way, it is in root grafting that the whip graft finds its distinctive field. When the roots are cut into lengths of from 2 to 5 or 6 inches to be used as stocks, the operation is known as piece-root grafting. Sometimes the entire root is used.

The roots are dug and the scions are cut in the autumn and stored. The work of grafting may be done during the winter months. When the operation has been completed, the grafts are packed away in moss, sawdust or sand, in a cool cellar, to remain until spring. It is important that the place of storage be cool, else the grafts may start into growth and be ruined, or heating and rotting may occur. If the temperature is kept low—not above 40° F.—there will be no growth except callousing and the knitting together of stock and scion.

In ordinary propagation by means of whip grafts, the scion is cut with about three buds, the stock being nearly as long as the scion. The grafted plant is so set as to bring the union of stock and scion below the surface of the ground.

When whip grafting is employed above the ground, the wound must be protected, as in cleft grafting, either with a mass of grafting wax or a bandage of waxed muslin.

Grafting Wax.—A good grafting wax may be made of the following ingredients: Resin, 4 parts; beeswax, 2 parts; tallow or linseed oil, 1 part by weight. If a harder wax is needed, 5 parts of resin and 2½ of beeswax may be used with 1 part of tallow.

Break the resin and beeswax up fine and melt together with the tallow. When thoroughly melted pour the liquid into a vessel of cold water. When hard enough to handle take it out, pull and work it until it becomes tough and has the color of very light-colored manila paper. To apply wax by hand grease the hands well with tallow. Or apply the wax with a hot brush. But take care to avoid injury.

Spread the wax carefully over all cut or exposed surfaces and press closely, so that upon cooling it will form a sleek coating impenetrable to air or moisture.

To prepare waxed string put a ball of No. 18 knitting cotton into a kettle of melted grafting wax. In five minutes it will be thoroughly saturated. It will remain in condition for use indefinitely.

Budding.—This is one of the most economical forms of artificial reproduction, and each year witnesses its more general use. Some nurserymen go so far as to use it as a substitute for all modes of grafting save whip grafting in the propagation of the dwarf pear. Budding is economical in the amount of wood used from which to take buds. A single bud does the work of the three or more upon the scion used in grafting. But while economical of wood, it is expensive in the use of stocks. A seedling is required for each tree, while, with the piece-root system of grafting, two, three, or more stocks can be made from a single seedling.

The operation of budding is simple, and can be done with great speed by expert budders. The expense of the operation is, therefore, not more than that of whip grafting, although the work has usually to be done in

July, August, or early September. The usual plan is for a man to set the buds and a boy to follow closely and do the tying.

The bud should be taken from wood of the present season's growth. Since the work of budding is done during the season of active growth, the bud sticks are prepared so that the petiole or stem of each leaf is left attached to serve as a handle to aid in pushing the bud home when inserting it beneath the bark of the stock. This is what is usually called a shield bud. It is cut so that a small portion of the woody tissue of the branch is removed with the bud. A bud stick and the operation of cutting the bud are illustrated.

(a) Cutting the bud; (b) a bud stick. (L. C. Corbett.)

The Stock.—The stock for budding should be at least as thick as an ordinary lead pencil. With the apple and pear, a second season's growth will be necessary to develop this size. With the peach a single season will suffice. Hence peach stocks can be budded the same season the pits are planted. Consequently the peach is left until as late in the season as is practicable in order to obtain stocks of suitable size. The height at which buds are inserted varies with the operator. In general, the nearer the ground the better.

To Bud a Plant.—Make a cut for the reception of the bud in the shape of a letter T, as shown in the illustration. Usually the cross-cut is not quite at right angles with the body of the tree, and the stem to the T starts at the cross-cut and extends toward the root for an inch or more. Loosen the flaps of bark caused by the intersection of the two cuts with the ivory heel of the budding knife,

Budding: (a) Inserting the bud; (b) tying; (c) cutting off the top. (L. C. Corbett.)

grasp the bud by the leaf stem as a handle, insert it under the flaps and push it firmly in place until its cut surface is entirely in contact with the peeled body of the stock. Tie a ligature tightly about it, above and below the bud, to hold it in place until a union shall be formed. Bands of raffia or wrapping cotton, about 10 or 12 inches long, make the most convenient tying material. As soon as the buds have united with the stock cut the ligature to prevent girdling the stock. This done, the operation is complete until the following spring. Then all the trees in which the buds have "taken" should have the top cut off just above the bud. The various processes are illustrated.

Cuttings.—Some trees, as the willow, cottonwood and poplars, are difficult to grow from seed but may be propagated readily from cuttings. These should be made some time in February or March, just before the spring growth begins. Select a smooth branch or sprout of the previous season's growth and from one-fourth to three-fourths of an inch in diameter. Cut off a section about 10 inches long squarely at both ends with a sharp hatchet. Let the upper cut be just above a bud. Arrange the cuttings with the tops together, tie them in bundles and bury them in moist sand or earth until they are ready for planting. They will not be injured by frost.

Prepare the soil the same as for a seed bed, as soon as it can be worked in the spring. Set the cuttings so that but one bud remains above the surface. They may be merely thrust into the soil—if it is sufficiently mellow—or planted with the aid of the plow or spade. To secure better contact with the soil set cuttings at a slight angle. The growth will be erect. Pack the soil lightly with the foot or tamping block. Give the same after cultivation as for seedlings.

PRUNING ORCHARD AND SHADE TREES

Pruning Orchards.—The objects of pruning fruit trees are many. Among them are protection against breakage from wind and loading with snow, during storms; checking the growth of the tree to increase its fruitfulness, or, under other conditions, accelerating growth; rejuvenating old trees; limiting the fruit production, to avoid exhausting the trees; and controlling such diseased conditions as pear blight, plum and peach rot and others.

Forming the Head.—For most deciduous, ornamental and orchard trees, the object is to form symmetrical open crowns such that all the space will be occupied and as large a quantity of foliage as possible exposed to sun and air. Avoid forming a thick bushy head such that the branches will shade one another. Commence to form the head of a young tree at planting time by selecting three to five branches according to the kind of tree to form the main framework for aftergrowth. Cut these back to a point about 8 inches from the main stem and just above an outside bud, i. e., a bud facing toward the outside of the tree. Cut back the main stem to a point just above the topmost of these branches and remove all other branches and buds.

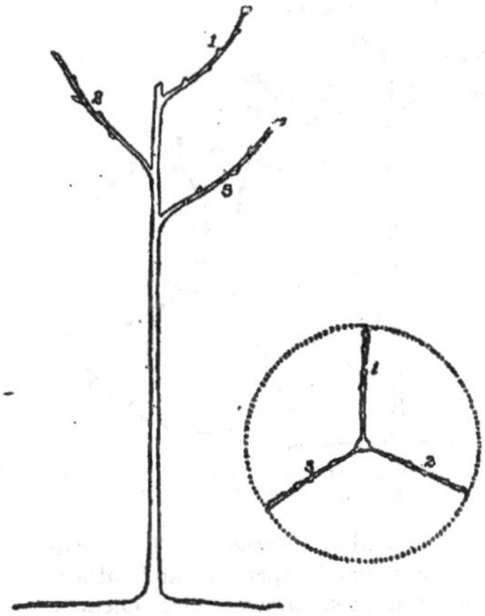

Plan of tree at planting time.
(L. C. Corbett.)

Choose branches disposed at equal distances about the main stem or axis of the plant and springing thence at intervals of several inches one above the other. The branches when viewed from above should radiate from the stem like spokes from the hub of a wheel and at about equal angles from one another. Thus all the space will be occupied and a symmetrical development will result. Two or more branches which spring from the trunk side-by-side or opposite to one another, at the same level, must never be allowed to develop. This makes a weak joint which tends to split under pressure when loaded with fruit, or snow, or when twisted by storms. Some trees such as the elm and silver maple have a tendency to form branches by twos in this manner. This must be corrected by careful pruning.

The best orchardists now form the heads of apple, pear and all small fruit trees very low, not over 18 or 20 inches from the ground. Such low lying trees are not only better protected against injury from weather

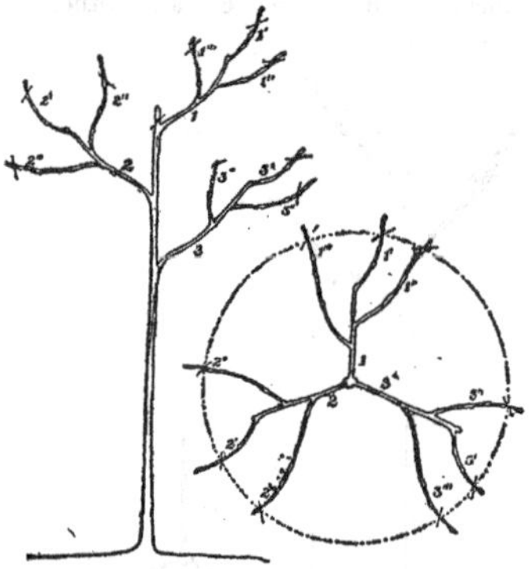

Plan of top after one year's growth in the orchard. (L. C. Corbett.)

conditions at all seasons. They can also be pruned, sprayed and otherwise cultivated much more cheaply and easily. And a large part of the annual fruit crop can be picked from the ground.

After Pruning.—At the close of the first season treat each of the principal branches as if it were a new tree. Select three of its branches for future growth. Cut these back to 8 inches in length from the main branch and remove all other branches. Repeat the operation at the end of the third year. But observe that the number of branches suffered to remain should now be reduced to two. Take equal care throughout not to allow branches to spring side-by-side or opposite from one another upon any part of the branch system.

Observe that some trees have an erect and others a lateral system of branch development. The former may be improved by pruning the branches just above an outside bud so that the new growth will tend to shoot in an outward direction and vice versa. A careful study of the accompanying illustrations will fix clearly in mind the principal types of tree development sought by expert men.

Pruning Large Branches. — Remove large branches with a clean sharp cut by means of a saw. Cut off as nearly flush with the trunk of the tree as possible. Avoid leaving any stub, breaking any part of the branch, or stripping the bark so as to leave a rough, uneven surface. Such wounds accumulate dirt and moisture, and invite the entrance of the fungous diseases which cause decay and the attentions of squirrels and woodpeckers. All stubs tend to decay back to the heart wood of the trunk. They thus become the most fruitful cause of hollow trees and branches. A wound flush with the main stem is quickly covered with new growth. It is thus not only protected from injury but actually hidden from view.

To remove large branches without injury make two cuts, one about 18 inches or 2 feet from the trunk of the tree to get rid of the weight of the limb, the other flush with the stump. The stub remaining after the

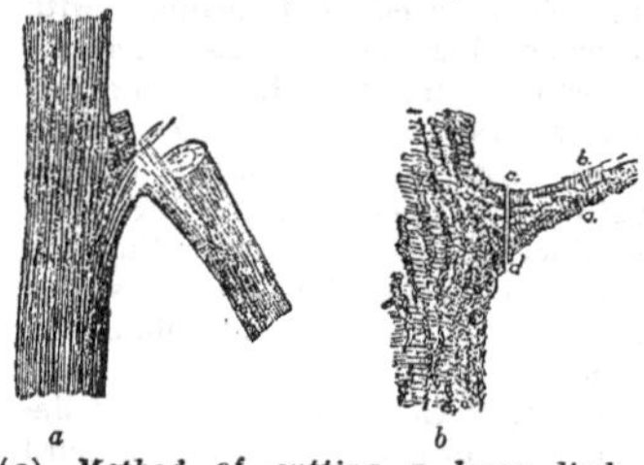

(a) Method of cutting a large limb which should be avoided; (b) proper method of cutting off a large limb. (L. C. Corbett.)

first cut can be supported until completely severed, with one hand, while the saw is being used with the other. Always begin to cut from the bottom of the branch and continue as long as the saw can be moved freely. Cut especially through the bark around the lower half of the limb. Then finish the cut from above. Take care to meet the lower cut accurately. There will then be little danger of the limb breaking or of stripping the bark.

Paint the wounds made by removing large branches with good white lead paint, yellow ochre, coal tar or grafting wax. The only object to be attained is to keep out moisture and insects until the wound has time to heal naturally. Antiseptics and patented preparations are wholly unnecessary.

Hollow Trunks.—To fill hollows caused by the decay of old stumps in valuable orchard or shade trees, first clean out the hole and remove all diseased wood from the interior with a sharp gouge or chisel. Cut away until sound wood is exposed. Now, preferably, spray the inside with a solution of copper sulphate at the rate of one pound to five or six gallons of water. This kills the organisms which cause decay. Choose for this purpose a dry day, preferably with hot sun and wind. Before the surface of the cavity can become in any way infected, fill it with a thin mortar made by mixing one part Portland cement with three parts clean sharp sand.

Remember that Portland cement will set in twenty minutes. Hence have everything in readiness to pour it soon after it has been mixed. After the mortar has set stiff, but not too hard, point up the exposed surface with a mixture of one part sand and one part cement. Take care to exclude the entrance of moisture to the cavity.

Pinching and Disbudding. — "Pinching" or "stopping" are technical terms which mean simply removing the extreme points of growing shoots, in summer, with a pinch between the finger and thumb. This retards the shoot from growing longer and encourages other buds and shoots to grow upon its sides. It also promotes the growth of other less thrifty shoots.

"Disbudding" means rubbing off superfluous buds to prevent waste caused by the growth of shoots that are not desired. It diverts the sap to the remaining shoots and thus tends to produce branches, flowers and fruit of superior quality. If practiced with care, pinching and disbudding take the place of all after pruning, since if no shoots are allowed to develop where not wanted, there will be no useless branches to be pruned away. But the inexperienced gardener should experiment on a small scale for a year or two and carefully observe the effects of these methods before adopting them extensively. If too much foliage is removed by them, they may irreparably injure the tree.

When to Prune.—The old rule used to be "prune when your knife is sharp." This is not bad general practice. But recent study has suggested some important modifications. Small branches of most trees may be removed at any convenient time during winter or the early spring months. But large branches should be pruned, preferably, during the season of most rapid growth. This may or may not be when the tree is in flower. It must be determined for each species by special observation. But defer pruning peach trees and other species liable to suffer from winter killing until the amount of injury from this cause can be determined. This will be just previous to the beginning of growth. Then remove all dead or injured branches. But take care to make allowance for the amount of winter killing. Do not prune so severely as to prevent the development of a full crop. For most fruit trees pruning can be done in February or March as well as at any other season. But pruning grapevines, which produces a heavy flow of sap, should preferably be done in the late fall or early winter months. Still if there is danger of winter killing, it may be best to delay pruning the vines as late as possible.

Pruning Implements.—The hawk-bill knife, pruning shears, lopping shears, hedge shears, double-edged curved-blade pruning saw and a special device for cutting small limbs on tall trees, are the most conveni-

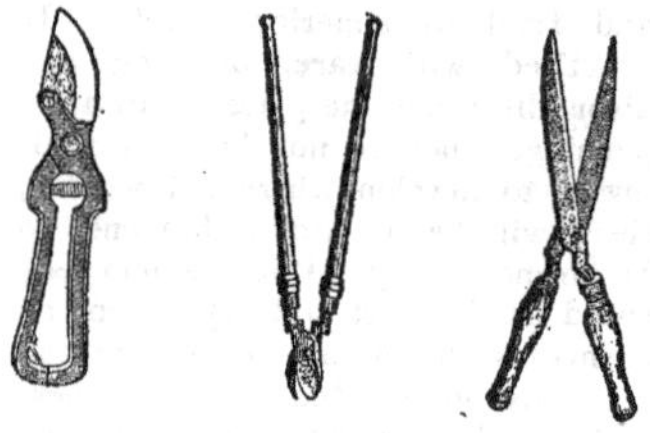

a b c
(a) Pruning shears; (b) lopping shears; (c) hedge shears. (L. C. Corbett.)

ent tools for pruning. These are shown in the accompanying illustrations. The advantage of the special saw illustrated is that the operator can use it to cut off branches within arm's reach overhead. The upper edge of the blade is convenient to make the first cut on the under side of the limb. The curve of the lower edge and inward slant of the teeth

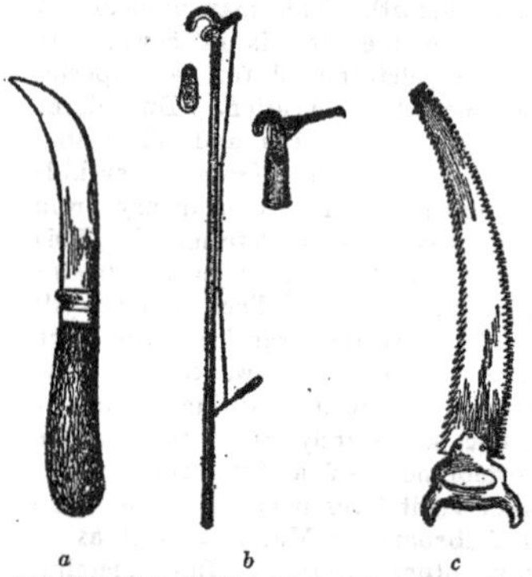

a b c
(a) The hawkbill knife; (b) device for cutting small limbs on tall trees; (c) double-edged curved-blade pruning saw. (L. C. Corbett.)

cause it to cut deeply on the back or downward stroke.

Pruning Pear Trees.—Form the heads of four or five main branches distributed about the stem at equal spaces and different heights. Cut back to ten or twelve inches at the end of the first year. From each, start two or three new shoots and cut these back to twelve inches at the second year. So continue until the tree comes into full bearing. The annual growth will then not exceed 6 or 8 inches.

Pear Blight.—The only effectual way to control pear blight is by pruning. The spores of this disease gain entrance to the tree through its flowers. These are borne upon spurs. If spurs are permitted to grow upon the trunk of the tree or any of its principal branches, and if they become diseased, the entire trunk or

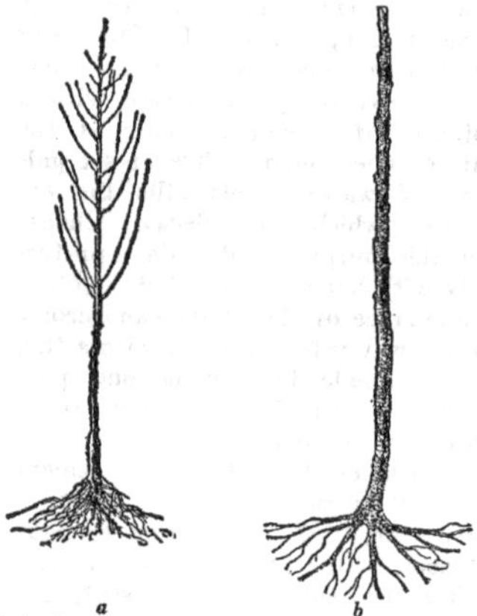

a b
(a) Peach tree from the nursery; (b) peach tree pruned for orchard planting. (L. C. Corbett.)

branch is infected and must be destroyed. Hence to control pear blight, all fruit spurs must be disbudded or rubbed from the main stems and branches. The flowers must be suffered to grow only upon the external branches of the tree. These must then be closely observed. The moment they are found to be infected they must be cut away and burnt. Thus the tree can be rid of blight without serious or permanent injury.

Pruning Peach Trees.—Buy yearling stock and reduce the young plant to a single whip or stem. Form the head at the end of the first year, from the shoots which develop along the body of the tree, by rubbing off the buds which are not desired. Start three or four branches 18 or

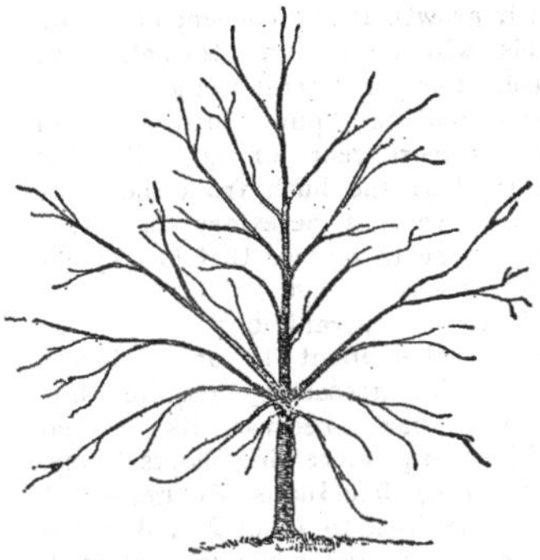

Sour cherry; good form.
(L. C. Corbett.)

20 inches from the ground. Cut them off to about 12 inches in length at the end of the first season's growth. Allow each to divide into three or four branches the next season and at the season's end cut these back to 12 inches in length and so continue. Defer pruning until all danger of freezing is past. Then gauge the amount of wood, if any, which has been winter killed. Prune so as to leave only outside buds and thus cause the tree to form a broad, round head.

Pruning Plum and Cherry Trees.—Prune the plum and cherry tree upon the same general principles as the preceding. But take special care to prevent limbs forming at the same level or with a close angle between them. Such branches are almost sure to split off when loaded with fruit. Rub off all shoots which spring from the roots or trunk of the tree and confine the flowering and fruit production to the other branches. The desired form for these two trees is shown in the illustrations.

Pruning the Grapevine. — There are various methods of pruning grapevines of which that known as the modified Kniffen system is here recommended. Plant the roots in rows and provide a trellis of two wires, one 6 feet above the ground, the other 18 or 20 inches lower. Support the wires on any kind of post. But for a permanent vineyard use, preferably, posts of concrete or creosoted wood. Carry two main trunks from each root, one to the lower and the other to the upper wire. Preserve two shoots of new cane to extend along the wires from each trunk. Cut these back to six or eight buds and tie them to the two wires of the trellis. Preserve also two spurs at the head of each main trunk to furnish fruiting canes for the following season. The style of pruning, construction of the trellis and method of renewing the wood, are shown in the illustration. By this system the fruit branches are lifted so far above the ground that the annual growth falls from the supporting wires in a natural way. This does away with the labor and expense of tying. The fruit is also

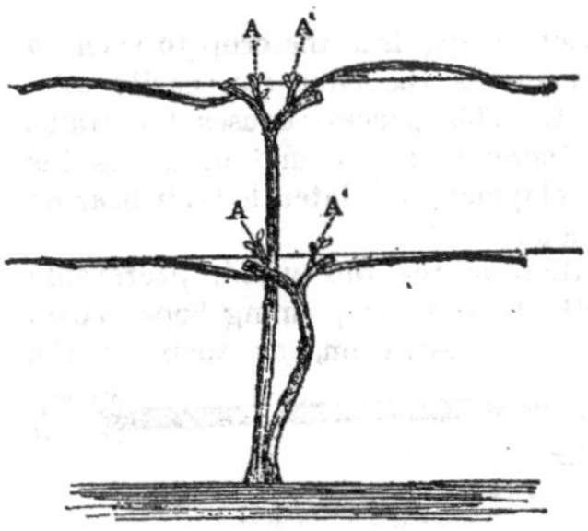

Vine trained by modified Kniffen system; two stem. (L. C. Corbett.)

further from the ground, and, hence, less liable to injury from mildew and rot.

Pruning the Raspberry and Blackberry.—Set the plants in rows six or eight feet apart and three feet apart in the row. No trellises are necessary. Let the young shoots spring up a little over 2 feet high. Then break off 3 or 4 inches from the top with the fingers, leaving the shoot 20 or 22 inches in height. No knife or shears will be needed. About blooming time, pinch back and shorten the lateral branches which have developed from the central

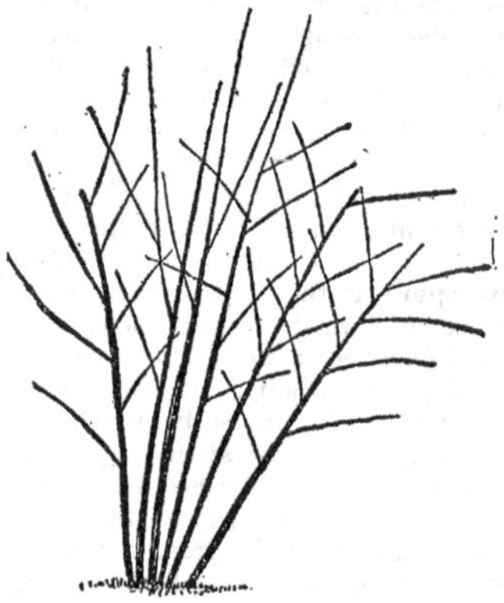

Typical raspberry after pruning. *(L. C. Corbett.)*

shoot, to regulate the crop to such an amount as the cane can easily support. This process causes the stalks to increase in size and promotes the development of lateral fruit-bearing shoots.

Remove the old wood, preferably with the type of pruning hook shown in the illustration, as soon as the

Pruning hook for brambles. *(L. C. Corbett.)*

crop has been harvested. It is then easy to tell the new from the old wood. By cutting out the latter the energy of the root is preserved for next year's crop.

Observe the same general plan in pruning blackberries except that the annual shoots should be allowed to grow somewhat higher before being broken.

Pruning the Currant and Gooseberry.—Train both these plants in bush form. Let new wood spring up annually from the roots to replace any canes which may be destroyed by borers, or otherwise become diseased. Break off the new shoots to stop their growth at any convenient height. This will induce the formation of fruit spurs on lateral branches. Observe that the spurs form on wood two or more years of age. But the renewal of the bush from the roots year-by-year is necessary to insure fresh cane to replace that lost by injury, disease or age.

Prune a currant bush to six or eight stalks about 18 or 20 inches high. The gooseberry requires less heading back because its normal habit is to produce side shoots freely.

Pruning Deciduous Hedges.—Cut back the plant to about 2 or 3 inches from the ground when transplanted. Again cut back to 6 or 8 inches in height at the end of the first season. Prune all lateral growth to within 1 inch of the main stem. The second season pinch back the strong upright shoots to divert the sap into the weaker shoots and to promote an even growth in height and desirable breadth of base. During the following winter prune into shape as a pointed pyramid with sides 8 or 10 inches from the center.

Pruning Evergreens.—Evergreens, such as arborvitæ, naturally assume a pyramidical form. Pinch back the more vigorous shoots to encourage lateral growth and trim annually just before growth commences in the spring. A hedge 5 feet high should be about 3 feet wide at the surface of the ground. Hence, prune with this object in view.

Pruning Street Trees. — Keep street trees under nursery culture until they reach the height of 8 to 10 feet. Then remove all side shoots to a height of at least 6 feet. Do not cut off the main stem. On the contrary if it is divided into two or more shoots which rival one another, select the most vigorous to remain and remove the others. The object is to cultivate a well defined central stem with symmetrically set branches subordinate to it. Hence, pinch back the more vigorous side branches to divert the sap to the weaker limbs and promote uniform development.

Remove the lower branches from time to time as they interfere with traffic. But cut off first the ends which droop over the street. Postpone the removal of such branches close up to the trunk until it becomes absolutely necessary.

To prune large trees remove every second or third branch. But never "head down" the tree, i. e., cut off part of the main stem or of each branch. Seek rather to remove one-third or more of the branches, flush with the trunk, so skillfully that the tree will retain its natural appearance.

Pruning Forest Trees.—Set the trees quite closely together and encourage a single upright stem as with street trees. The tops will be drawn toward the light and the side branches in the shade will die off. Thus natural pruning will be effected. As the trees become overcrowded, thin by removing inferior specimens. Later remove branches two or more inches in diameter from especially valuable trees by cutting off flush with the trunk. Cover the wound with paint, tar, or the like.

Pruning Flowering Shrubs. — Avoid cutting back the summer growths of flowering shrubs. The flower buds grow on the new wood and the effect of its removal is to lessen the number of blossoms the following year. Instead, pinch back the more vigorous shoots during summer to promote symmetrical growth and remove only the oldest branches or a few of the young shoots if they are too dense. Cut these off close to the root.

FRIENDS AND ENEMIES OF THE ORCHARD AND GARDEN

Our Common Birds.—Common observation of the feeding habits of some well known birds has led to widespread prejudice against birds in general as enemies of the orchard and garden. The robin, cat bird, cedar bird, and others are often accused as thieves of fruit. The king bird is thought to rob the apiary. The woodpecker is said to injure orchard and forest trees by girdling them or excavating hollows in their trunks and branches. The crow, blackbird, and others, rob the grain fields both at planting time and harvest. The blue jay destroys the nests and eggs of other birds. And many similar charges are brought against different species of the feathered tribe. The existing prejudice against birds is the more unfortunate, since recent scientific studies indicate that, almost without exception, our common birds are among the best friends of the orchardist and gardener. Any harm they may do to fruit crops or otherwise is more than compensated, in the opinion of scientists, by the enormous numbers of injurious insects, grubs and larvæ that they annually destroy.

Scientific analyses have been made of the stomach contents of most common kinds of birds throughout the United States. These prove beyond question that the great bulk of the diet of most species consists of noxious weed seeds and injurious insects or other grubs and larvæ. With the exception of a very few species, the proportion of fruit, grain or other farm or garden crops found in the stomachs of birds has been very small. Hence, it seems certain that bird life in the vicinity of our farms and gardens should be encouraged by every means within our power.

It is true that some birds which are beneficial under ordinary circumstances or during the greater part of the year, may do considerable injury during periods of scarcity of food, or under special circumstances, as during the sowing of grain, the ripening of early fruits, or when grain is in the stook or ear. A special remedy for each such injury should be sought according to the circumstances, rather than the destruction of the birds themselves.

To enumerate the kinds of birds whose feeding habits are beneficial to the gardener and orchardist would require a review of practically every existing species. On the contrary, a few words will suffice to draw attention to the few species which are actually injurious and to indicate how their ravages may be prevented. In general, among the most useful birds are the quail, or bobwhite; all the woodpeckers including the flicker, but excepting the true sapsucker, which is injurious; the night hawk; all of the fly catchers, including the king bird, Arkansas king bird and Phœbe; the blue jay, but not the Pacific Coast jays which are injurious; the crow, the bobolink (in Northern latitudes), which is, however, injurious to the Southern rice crops under the name of reed bird; all of the blackbirds; the orioles, larks, sparrows, finches; all of the grosbeaks, which are highly beneficial; all of the swallows; the robin, cedar bird, cat bird, and brown thresher; the house wren and titmice, including the chickadees which are highly beneficial; and the humming bird.

Among larger birds, the prairie chicken, California quail, ruffed grouse, upland plover, killdeer, horned grebe, Franklin gull, and various species of terns are all beneficial. Cooper's hawk—the well-known chicken hawk—is injurious; but the rough legged hawk, the sparrow hawk, the long-eared owl and the screech owl are all beneficial. Their food consists chiefly of meadow mice and other small rodents injurious to crops or mischievous in and about farm buildings.

Sapsuckers. — Only three of the twenty-three species of woodpeckers in the United States are properly classed as sapsuckers. Unlike the true woodpeckers who feed on wood borers and other enemies of trees, the sapsuckers live chiefly upon ants. But they also feed upon the inner bark of trees and drink a great deal of their sap. Sometimes they completely girdle and thus destroy a tree with holes which go clear through the bark and even into the wood. These are usually made in rings around the trunk or limbs. They often fall in a vertical series and they may be either vertically or horizontally connected. These holes disfigure ornamental trees by causing pitch to exude and sometimes induce serious permanent injury. The evidence of their work depreciates the value of forest trees as lumber to the extent of many thousand dollars a year. The two species which do most injury are the red-breasted sapsucker and the yellow-bellied sapsucker. The first lives west of the Rocky Mountains and is the only woodpecker of that region having the whole head and throat red. The second has a transcontinental range and is the only woodpecker having the front of the head, i. e., from bill to crown, red in combination with a black patch on the breast. The majority of woodpeckers seen are not sapsuckers but are among the birds most beneficial to both orchard and forest. Hence great care should be taken to distinguish them. To destroy sapsuckers, mix thoroughly ⅛ ounce powdered strychnine (alkaloid) with one pint of honey or thick sugar. Apply to the injured tree just above the rows of fresh punctures. Or put small pinches of the powdered strychnine directly into the freshest sap pits.

The King Bird.—This bird is often accused of feeding upon honey bees but the examination of their stomachs prove that extremely small numbers of worker bees are eaten and that any loss from this source is far more than offset by the destruction of great numbers of injurious insects. More than 90 per cent of the diet of the king bird is shown to belong to the latter class.

Blue Jay.—The common blue jay of the Eastern States is often accused of eating the eggs and young of small birds and of stealing corn. While both accusations are doubtless true to a limited extent, investigation has proved that, roughly speaking, half of the blue jay's diet consists of nuts and acorns, about one-fifth of injurious insects and the remainder of a great miscellany of foods. Only a small fraction consists of corn, most of which is gleaned from the fields after harvest. The blue jay may occasionally rob the fields of corn at planting time but this may be prevented by coating the corn with tar. Such other sins as he may commit do not appear to justify his extirpation. The well known California jay of the Pacific Coast, however, is a notorious fruit stealer and robber of hens' nests. He is so prolific in that region that efforts to reduce his numbers are not without justification.

The Crow.—The crow pulls up sprouting corn, destroys chickens, robs the nests of small birds and sometimes eats beneficial toads and small snakes. But in his diet the crow makes amends by eating large numbers of grasshoppers, bugs and caterpillars and many cut worms. The crow rarely, if ever, eats hard, dry corn or otherwise robs the harvest field; but he sometimes does great injury at planting time and occasionally attacks corn before it is ripe and while still in milk. The best way to prevent crows from pulling up corn is by coating it with tar before planting.

Experience has also shown that crows and many other birds may be kept from the corn throughout the season by "stringing" the field. Use for this purpose common twine supported by a row of light poles. Saplings 10 or 12 feet long, 2 inches in diameter at the base, make suitable poles for this purpose. Thrust these into the ground in holes made by a crowbar around the edge of the garden or other field. Set them at considerable distance apart and suspend the twine high enough from the ground to be out of the way during horse cultivation. If these and other ordinary precautions are taken to protect corn and young poultry against the depredation of crows, it is believed that the season's balance will be found overwhelmingly in their favor.

The crow blackbird sometimes steals grain and fruits and robs the nests of other birds. But about one-third of his food consists of injurious insects. The amount of damage done is small except when large flocks settle upon the grain crops at harvest time. For this there seems to be no adequate remedy, except shooting which is ordinarily too expensive.

Swallows.—The various kinds of swallows are especially useful birds. Their diet consists almost wholly of injurious or annoying insects. Their presence may be encouraged in case of eave swallows, by providing a quantity of mud to be used by them as mortar. Cut small holes in the gables of barns for barn swallows and furnish suitable boxes for the white-bellied swallows and martins. Place these preferably upon a tall pole or other high location.

Cedar Bird, Cat Bird and Robins.—These birds are most often accused of stealing cherries, strawberries or other small fruit. The first is sometimes called the "cherry bird" on account of this well known propensity. Close observation indicates that the damage done by these and other small birds is confined chiefly to very early fruit crops, since these mature in advance of the wild fruits which form their ordinary summer diet. Most of this damage can be prevented by planting near the garden or orchard a few such trees as the Russian mulberry, the fruit of which they ordinarily prefer. During the remainder of the year these birds are highly beneficial. Hence their presence should be encouraged.

The house wren is a particularly useful bird. To invite his company place suitable nesting boxes, or even gourds or tin cans or empty jars about the house and orchard for his reception. An opening about 1 inch in diameter will admit the wren and yet afford him protection by excluding the English sparrow. One pair of wrens annually rears from twelve to sixteen young. Hence each family consumes an enormous number of injurious insects.

The blue bird is another species not only harmless but highly beneficial. It does not eat fruit but destroys large numbers of injurious insects. Every householder can afford to provide suitable nesting boxes for his occupancy.

English Sparrows. — The English sparrow among birds, like the rat among animals, is cunning, destructive and filthy. It was introduced into America about sixty years ago. It is now widely distributed throughout the United States and Southern Canada. Its ability to live everywhere, upon all sorts of food and to fight its own way, together with its extraordinary fecundity, make it a dangerous rival of such native birds as blue birds, purple martins and the different kinds of swallows. It drives these away by destroying their eggs and usurping their nesting places. It also drives off other attractive species as the robin, wren, red-eyed vireo, cat bird and mocking bird. It injures and destroys all sorts of fruit, garden and farm crops, and also the buds and flowers of cultivated trees, shrubs and vines. It defiles buildings and ornamental trees and shrubs with its excrement and bulky nests. It has no song, but is noisy and vituperative. Nowhere is it included among the birds protected by law.

To protect blue birds, martins and wrens from English sparrows, construct bird houses having a hinged top, bottom or side to admit of removing the nests and eggs of the sparrow as soon as the latter have been laid. A convenient method is to make a hinged bottom which will fall when unhooked. This allows the contents to drop to the ground. Take care to construct a tight nest box and cleat the hinged side so as to prevent warping. In common with other birds, the sparrow does not like drafty nesting places and will not occupy a box the inside of which is exposed to drafts.

To destroy sparrows or clear them from any neighborhood, drive them from their roosts at night by turning upon them a stream of water from a garden hose, or balls of fire from small Roman candles. Or destroy their nests at intervals of ten to twelve days throughout the breeding season. These can be readily torn down by means of a long pole having an iron hook at the tip. But take care to have this work done by competent persons. Otherwise the nests of useful native birds may be destroyed.

Or capture the sparrows by providing one-room bird houses and driving them thence into a net held over the opening by means of a long pole. This may be done by tapping on the side of the box after they have gone to roost at night.

Or scatter grain over a long narrow area and shoot the sparrows at this feeding place. If they infest poultry yards, place the bait on a horizontal board so that they can be safely shot over the heads of the poultry.

Or trap the birds alive, for which purpose a number of ingenious plans are recommended. One simple device is the use of an ordinary square wire sieve such as are commonly used for screening ashes.

Or, preferably, construct large boxes not less than 4 feet square open upon one side and covered with wire on the other. Place a small sliding door near one corner. Adjust the trap supported by a stick 18 inches long with a chip between the top and the stick and carry it around a neighboring corner or to any convenient point of observation. Or an old door or similar device may be employed as a dead fall. It is a good plan to keep the trap set and baited for a few days until the sparrows have become accustomed to it. Meantime to avoid its being sprung prematurely, hold it firmly by a stake driven into the ground. This trap is very effective but has the disadvantage of requiring attendance.

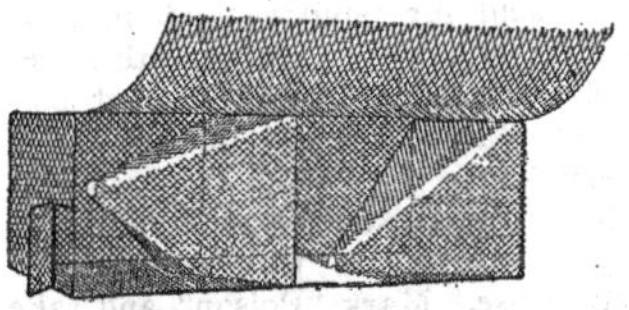

Funnel trap. (Side raised to show interior.) (Ned Dearborn.)

Or a more convenient device is the funnel trap shown in the illustration. This is easy to construct and the cost of material is very slight. It weighs little and when painted green or gray is inconspicuous.

The following directions are given by the Department of Agriculture: "The essential parts of this trap are: (1) A half funnel leading into (2) an antechamber, which ends in (3) a complete funnel leading into (4) a final chamber. It is made of woven-wire poultry netting of ¾-inch mesh and is reinforced around the open end and along the sides at the bottom by No. 8 or No. 10 wire. This is used also around the aperture for the door and around the door itself. The angles between the first funnel and the walls of the antechamber are floored with netting. The final chamber is floored with the same material. The accompanying drawings will enable anybody handy with tools to construct one of these traps in a few hours. These plans are for a trap 3 feet long, a foot and a half wide, and a foot high. At ordinary retail prices the cost of material will be about 70 cents.

"Paper patterns for the two funnels can be made by first drawing the concentric circles, as shown in the illustrations, and then laying off the straight lines, beginning with the longest. The wavy outlines indicate that the pattern is to be cut half an inch outside of the straight lines.

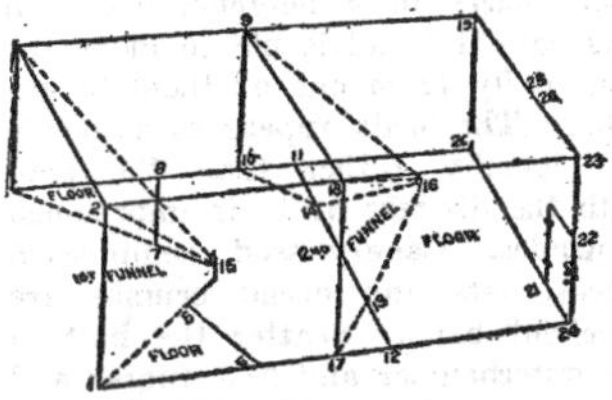

Outline of funnel trap. (Ned Dearborn.)

This allows extra wire for fastening the cones to the top and sides of the trap. The illustrations also show how all parts of a trap having the above dimensions may be cut from a piece of netting 4 feet wide and 6 feet long. The full lines in this figure indicate where the netting is to be cut and the broken lines where it

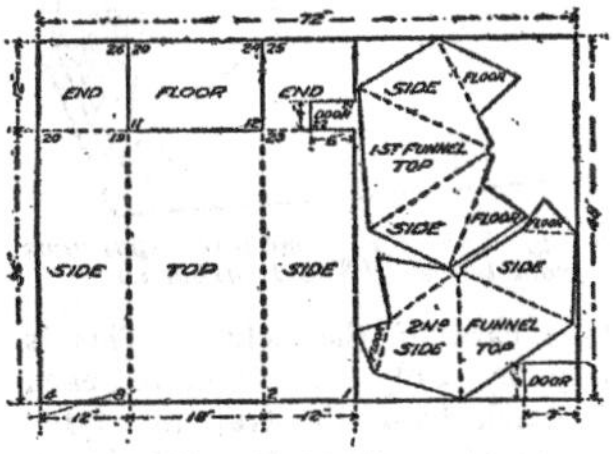

Diagram for cutting out the parts of a funnel trap 36 x 18 x 12 inches. (Ned Dearborn.)

is to be bent. The numbers at the angles in the pattern correspond with those in the illustration which shows in outline the relation of the different parts as they appear when assembled.

"A trap of the above dimensions is as small as can be used satisfactorily. Where sparrows are very numerous a larger size is recommended.

A trap 4 feet long, 2 feet wide, and 15 inches high may be made from a piece of netting 4 by 10 feet. This is a very good size for parks and large private grounds.

"In setting a funnel trap select a place where sparrows are accustomed to assemble. Often there are several such places in a neighborhood. In this case it is advisable to move the trap daily from one of them to another. The birds appear to associate the locality rather than the trap with the distress of their imprisoned comrades. Canary seed, hemp seed, wheat, oats and bread crumbs are excellent baits. Scatter the bait in the antechamber and first funnel and also, sparingly, outside about the entrance. A live sparrow kept in the trap as a decoy will facilitate a catch. In case native birds enter a trap they may be released without harm. Trapping may begin at any time after young sparrows are able

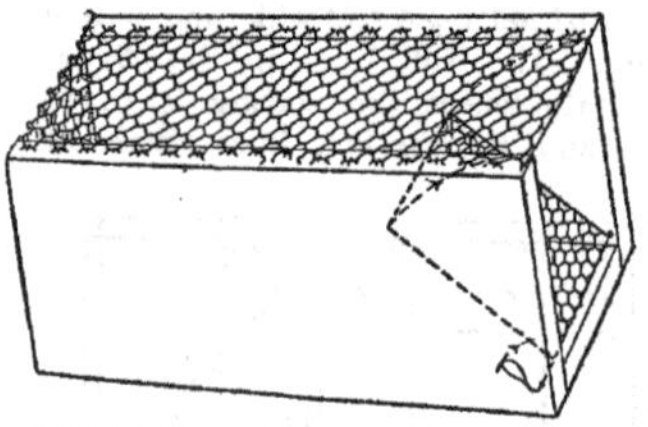

Receiving box for removing sparrows from traps. (Ned Dearborn.)

to take care of themselves. This is usually by July 1. Remove each day's catch from the trap at nightfall, and if a decoy is used, house it comfortably and otherwise care for it when off duty.

"In removing sparrows from either a funnel or a sieve trap the receiving box illustrated will be found useful. It should be about 6 inches square and 18 inches long, inside measurements. The door, hinged at the bottom and turning inward, is controlled by the part of its wire frame extending through the side of the box to form a handle. The box as it appears in the figure is ready to be placed before the open door of a trap from which birds are to be driven."

To poison sparrows, where this is not prohibited by law, put ⅛ ounce of pulverized strychnia in three-fourths of a gill of hot water. Add 1½ teaspoonfuls of starch or wheat flour moistened with a few drops of cold water and heat. Stir constantly until the mixture thickens. Now place a quart of whole wheat, such as is sold for poultry food, in a 2-quart glass fruit jar or other receptacle and pour on it the hot poisoned starch. Shake or stir until every kernel is coated. Spread out thin on a flat surface and use when dry. Or put into jars to keep for future use. Mark "Poison" and take care to cleanse all dishes employed for this purpose by careful washing.

Or spread thin slices of bread with the strychnia-starch mixture.

Choose preferably the early morning after a snow storm when other food is covered. Clear the ground of snow and scatter the poisoned bait over a considerable surface. Remove and destroy promptly all dead and dying birds, as some are sickened but do not die. Change the feeding grounds at intervals. To avoid danger to poultry, use preferably enclosed back yards, roofs or unused poultry runs. Or to keep out doves or poultry, make small pens of coarse wire netting and raise the sides 1½ inches above the ground. The best plan is to use various kinds of traps until the sparrows are thinned out and become wary. Then poison the survivors.

English Sparrows as Food.—These birds have been utilized for food in the old world for centuries. Their flesh is palatable and wholesome, especially when broiled or baked in the form of pies. Any recipe for pigeon or chicken pies, or for broiling small birds may be adapted for cooking sparrows. The birds may be trapped and kept alive, sheltered from storms and cold winds, in large outdoor cages, until wanted. But remember that they eat daily more than half their own weight. Feed table scraps or any food suitable for chickens, and provide a supply of clear water.

To kill them mercifully, place the thumb nail at the base of the skull and dislocate the neck by hard and quick pressure. Cut off the legs, the wings at the outer joint and the neck close to the body. Strip off the skin beginning at the neck. Now make a cut through the body wall extending from the neck along the backbone till the ribs are severed, then around between the legs to the tail, and remove the viscera. If sparrows are to be broiled, save only the breasts. This method of cooking so shrivels and parches the lesser parts as to render them worthless. In this case tear off a strip of skin from wing to wing across the back; grasp the wings, in front of the body, in one hand and the neck in the other, and by a quick pull separate the breast from the ribs. Turn the breast out of the skin that covers it, and sever the wings at the second joint. The whole operation requires but a fraction of a minute and can be done by the fingers alone.

Sparrows may be cooked by any of the methods employed for reed-birds or quail. When boned, broiled, buttered, and served on toast they are particularly good and compare favorably with the best kinds of small game.

Toads.—Many strange prejudices and traditions attach to toads such as the unfounded notion that they cause warts on the hands, poison infants by their breath, bring good fortune to the house in whose new-made cellar they take up their abode, or cause bloody milk in cows if killed by accident or design.

Toads feed chiefly on insects, a large percentage of which are injurious to gardeners and orchardists. Analysis of the contents of their stomachs prove that they are among the most useful friends to orchard and garden. They are very sensitive to heat and hence secrete themselves in rubbish during the day. This fact suggests means by which they may be encouraged to frequent gardens and vineyards. Place a number of large flat stones or pieces of 2-inch plank about the edge of the garden supported a couple of inches from the ground by means of half brick or small stones. Throw a sack or square of old carpet or matting over these to exclude the light. Leave an entrance only on the north side.

Or dig shallow holes in the earth and partially cover them with boards or flat stone.

Encourage children to feed toads with captured flies and other insects. This may be readily done when they come to the entrance of their lairs about twilight. This will impress upon children the value of the services of the toad and the importance of their protection. Many English and some other gardeners purchase young toads and colonize them to rid greenhouses and gardens of insects and snails. A shallow pool having a small but constant water supply will encourage their breeding on the premises.

Field Mice and Moles.—There are a large number of species of field mice and moles, ground squirrels and other small rodents throughout the United States which do great injury to lawns, orchards, gardens and farm crops by burrowing through the soil and eating the roots of plants, bark of trees and the like. Orchard and shade trees are often completely girdled by field mice in winter and destroyed. In some localities the number of mice increases at times to enormous proportions as during the celebrated plague of mice in the Humboldt Valley, Nevada, in 1907. All field crops and trees were largely destroyed. The damage so done amounted to many hundred thousands of dollars. Experiments during this and other plagues indicate that the most effective mode of destroying mice is by poisoning. Yellow phosphorus and carbon bisulphide are sometimes employed. But the former is dangerous to handle and may cause disastrous fires. The latter is highly explosive. Wheat and grain poisoned by these substances are also eaten readily by many useful birds. The most effective method employed was the use of alfalfa hay, or crushed wheat, poisoned with strychnia sulphate. The advantage of the former when available is that it is without danger to birds.

Choose for this purpose alfalfa hay which is fresh and green, rather than bleached. Chop into 2-inch lengths in an ordinary feed cutter and mix in a large metal receptacle such as a galvanized iron pail or tub. Use one ounce of strychnia sulphate to 30 pounds of chopped alfalfa hay, moistened in five or six gallons of water, or as much as the hay will absorb. Place the chopped hay in the receptacle and moisten with about half of the water. Dissolve the poison in the rest of the water by heating in a closed vessel. Now sprinkle over the dampened hay, mix until the moisture is all taken up, and sack for use. Use within two or three days as it spoils quickly. Distribute by hand. Place a small pinch equal to a teaspoonful near the entrance of each burrow or scatter along the surface trails. Place the poison a little to one side of the entrance to prevent its being covered by the earth thrown out. Or in winter drop into the entrance of the burrows. The amount of poison likely to be taken up by stock is small. No such accidents have been reported. But for safety, stock may be kept out of the fields a few days after the poison has been distributed.

Or in summer use green alfalfa at the rate of 45 pounds of hay to one ounce of strychnia sulphate moistened in 1½ gallons of water. Dissolve the strychnia in ½ gallon of water by heating in a closed vessel. Add one gallon of cold water, sprinkle slowly over the alfalfa and mix until the moisture is all taken up. Distribute in the same manner, placing the bait in the holes or along runways.

Or use crushed wheat at the rate of 60 pounds to the ounce of strychnia sulphate, dissolved in 2 gallons of water. Heat and stir the sulphate in the water in a closed vessel until completely dissolved. Sprinkle over the wheat and mix well. Add two teaspoonfuls of powdered borax to prevent fermentation. Place preferably near the burrows and along runways. But remember that poisoned grain will be taken up freely by birds. Hence the use of alfalfa is preferable.

To protect trees from mice and moles use thin wooden wrappers called "tree protectors." Or apply liberally to the exposed roots and trunks the lime and sulphur wash used for spraying. Do this with a brush at the beginning of winter.

Great numbers of field mice are destroyed by owls, hawks and other natural enemies, especially skunks and weasels. The two latter animals are especially worthy of protection.

Woodchucks.—These animals hole up in August and hibernate until the following March. The young—usually five in a litter—are born during the latter part of April and are able to eat green vegetables by early June. They are very injurious to clover and hay and also to early truck and garden crops. In many localities they also act as hosts of the wood tick which is the source of spotted fever. Hence for many reasons they merit complete extermination. To poison woodchucks, use a mixture of about 2 gallons of dandelion heads, clover tops or alfalfa hay. Coat either of these with one pint of flour paste containing 3 ounces of arsenic. This spoils quickly. Hence mix in the afternoon and place after dark at the entrance of the woodchucks' burrow. It will then be at hand when they come out in the morning.

Or employ steel traps which may be set in the mouths of the burrows or about the entrance, preferably concealed with paper or dry grass. Use a rather large size "jump" trap, preferably No. 1½.

Insect Pests.—To control insects and diseases that infest garden crops gather all refuse from crops, pile at some convenient place and burn promptly. Many injurious insects find protection for the winter under loose material remaining in the garden. Moreover, the dead vines of plants are likely to be covered with spores of various diseases. Such refuse has little or no value as a fertilizer. The gain from prompt burning will more than offset any loss of humus to the soil.

CLEARING NEW LAND

Such conditions as remodeling old farm houses and surrounding them with attractive lawns and gardens, or the purchase of homesites on land which is more or less timbered, often require clearing away trees, stumps and under-brush. The quickest and simplest way to remove large stumps is by the use of dynamite. The cost will vary from ten to twenty cents for each stump. Dynamite is a mixture of nitroglycerine with a granular absorbent in varying proportions. It comes in cylindrical sticks of different sizes. Pure nitroglycerine is one of the most powerful and dangerous of all explosives. While dynamite is somewhat less liable to cause accident from careless handling it is always better to employ an experienced person to handle it.

To blow up a stump with dynamite dig down beside the stump far enough to admit of boring a hole into it with an auger so that the charge will explode as nearly as possible in the middle of the stump at the bottom. Select a low grade dynamite containing about 30 per cent nitroglycerine. This explodes more slowly and tends rather to upheave than to shatter. Insert a suitable charge in the auger hole with cap and fuse attached. Cover with earth to the level of the ground and tamp gently. Light the fuse and retreat to a safe distance. Should the stump be located near buildings or greenhouses, the danger of breaking window glass may be lessened by covering it with earth in cloth bags or throwing over it a number of logs chained together surmounted by pieces of heavy canvas or an old horse blanket. Or a dynamite cartridge may be exploded against the side of a stump, without boring, in a hollow dug in the earth. The resulting fragments may then be readily dug up with the mattock.

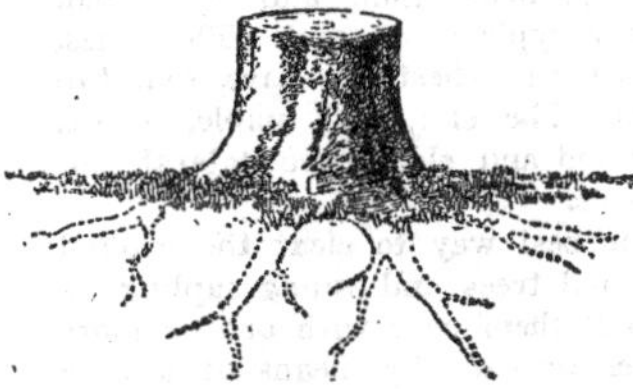

Showing dynamite cartridge in position. (Franklin Williams, Jr.)

To Pull Stumps.—There are numerous stump-pulling machines on the market and sometimes one can be hired to advantage to remove the few large stumps. But such machines as a rule are expensive to operate as compared with other methods. There are three principal types of root development: the tap root, semi-tap root and root with lateral branches. The first goes straight down into the ground without branching. The second forms branches just below the

Uprooting sapling with horse and chain. (Franklin Williams, Jr.)

surface which go somewhat deeply into the ground at various angles. The third forms branches which extend parallel with the surface in all directions, but do not penetrate deeply. The best method of removing a stump depends, therefore, upon the character of its root system. The hickory, black gum and white oak have a typical tap root. The pines, papaw and chestnuts have semi-tap roots. The elm, soft maple, locust, dogwood and elder have lateral root systems.

The best way to clear the ground of small trees and young saplings is to pull them over with one or more horses or oxen by means of a long log chain fastened as high above the ground as the stiffness of the trunk will admit. The object is to secure as good leverage as possible. A steady horse or team, or preferably a pair of oxen, is required. While the tree is bent forward with a steady pull, separate the roots on the opposite side with a sharp axe. This method can be used successfully to remove quite dogwood and elder have lateral root systems.

Or to pull out the stumps of large trees having lateral or semi-tap root systems, with a team of horses or pair of oxen, first remove the sod and loosen the earth about the principal roots. Then attach a log chain to one of the largest branch roots at some distance from the stump, carry the chain across the top of the stump and pull in a direction opposite to that in which the root extends. The object is to secure a leverage over the top of the stump. This leverage can be increased by means of two pieces of timber about six feet high bolted together in the form of the letter A or ordinary harrow. To the top of this is attached a chain or wire rope four or five feet long terminating in a hook. The A leans against one side of the stump and the hook is attached to a large root on the other side. The power is then applied slowly and steadily to the top of the A and, as this is raised up, the stump is tilted over.

Or to secure greater leverage when necessary, use two triple blocks and 200 or 300 feet of one-inch rope. Anchor one block to a solid stump and the other to the stump it is desired to pull.

Or bore a hole in the center of a large stump in the fall with a 1-inch auger. Pour into it a half pound of vitriol and drive in a tight wooden plug. In the spring, the whole stump and roots will be found so thoroughly rotted that they can easily be dug or plowed up.

Or bore a hole 18 inches deep in the center of the stump in the fall. Put in an ounce of saltpeter, fill up the hole with water and drive in a tight wooden plug. In the spring, pour in a half gill of kerosene and set it on fire. The whole stump will be burned out. But take care not to use this method in dry, mucky or peaty soil or in forests surrounded by dry leaves, else it may cause a disastrous forest fire.

Or to pull out brush and stumps, attach a log chain around the trunk or stem close to the ground and carry the chain up and over a grooved wheel, such as the wheel of an old corn planter and start the team. The wheel gives a good leverage and, by turning, lessens friction. The same device may be used to pull up fence posts.

To Remove Underbrush.—Use the mattock. Give this tool a sharp edge with a file and keep it in good working condition.

Pasturing. — Another means of clearing tracts of new land is by pasturing with any kind of stock. The angora goat is the best land clearer. And goats or sheep are always to be preferred. But horses and cattle, or even hogs, will assist in clearing land if confined to small tracts so as to be forced to obtain a considerable part of their food by browsing. All sprouts and green bushes which stock fail to subdue should be cut down with the axe or mattock in the late summer.

If time is not an object, trees of considerable size may be removed by natural forces. To use this method dig a trench around the base of the tree and cut all the lateral roots, leaving only the tap root, and await the action of wind and rain. The water which accumulates in the trenches softens the soil and causes it to be upheaved by frosts. The wind pressing against the top of the tree will then sway the trunk, in course of time, with sufficient force to throw it and thus pry the tap root completely out of the ground.

A few trees, notably the sassafras, persimmon and locust are very persistent. The entire root system should be removed from the ground.

After all trees, saplings and underbrush have been removed and the stumps pulled, new ground may be completely subdued by fall plowing one way and cross plowing the following spring. Carry an axe attached to the handle-bars of the plow and sever every root which the plow cannot break through. New land should preferably be cultivated for a year or two before being laid down as a permanent lawn or other greensward. Good crops for new land perhaps are corn, tomatoes or potatoes.

Or the land may be sown to clover or other crops suitable for green manuring.

CONCRETE CONSTRUCTION

The growing scarcity of timber in many localities and its constantly increasing cost, have led to a widespread revival of interest in concrete construction. This material was anciently used very much more than in modern times, notably among the Romans. Many of the most famous buildings and public works in ancient Rome were thus built. The materials for making concrete—Portland cement, sand, gravel and water—are so cheap and readily available in most localities, and the process is so simple, that this material promises to come into well-nigh universal application. It is suitable for walks and drives; fence posts and garden benches; cellar walls and floors; foundation walls and floors for all sorts of outbuildings; partition walls for cisterns and store rooms in cellars; privy vaults and bins for the accumulation of stable manure to prevent access of flies; watering troughs, and countless other uses too numerous to mention.

The two chief problems in the use of concrete are mixing the materials and the construction of the necessary forms or retaining walls.

To mix concrete properly requires a suitable mixing board and a few ordinary utensils. The construction of forms calls merely for a small quantity of cheap lumber, the most common carpenters' tools and very ordinary skill in carpentry. Excellent results can be secured by any householder by the application of good common sense with ordinary care and sagacity. Concrete is far superior to lumber, brick or other building stone on account of its durability, economy and safety from fire loss. It is also the best possible material for rat-proof construction.

Concrete is simply a manufactured stone formed by mixing cement, sand and crushed stone or gravel (i. e., pebbles) together with water. Cement is, therefore, only one part

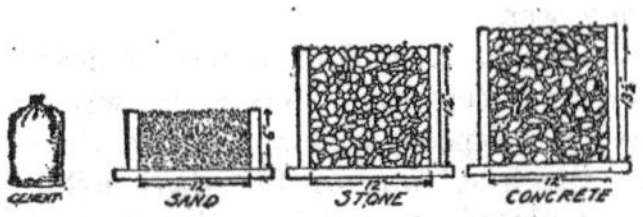

Required quantities of cement, sand, and stone or gravel for a 1:2:4 concrete mixture and the resulting quantity of concrete. (Office of Public Roads.)

of a concrete mixture. The great bulk of concrete is gravel and sand. The object to be obtained in mixing is to fill all the spaces or voids between the stone or gravel with sand, and the spaces between the particles of sand with cement. And such is an ideal mixture. In other words, only sufficient cement is required, in theory, to cover the surface of the particles of sand, gravel and stone with a thin coating of wet cement sufficient to stick or glue them firmly together. To secure such an ideal mixture it is necessary to observe the proper proportions of the different ingredients. These proportions have been determined by experience and if the following rules are followed, good results will be assured.

Cement.—Buy, preferably, Portland cement in cloth sacks, rather than in paper bags or wooden barrels. Keep dry until ready for use by storing on boards raised from the floor by means of wooden blocks and covered with canvas or roofing paper. Keep indoors in a dry place. Otherwise cement will absorb moisture from the atmosphere and become lumpy or often a solid mass. Such cement is worthless and must be thrown away. But lumps caused by pressure may be easily broken up and such cement is perfectly good. Dry cement mixed with water forms a soft sticky paste. This begins to "set" or harden in about half an hour. Any disturbance of concrete after it begins to set weakens it, or if the set is well under way, destroys it. Hence, Portland cement concrete must be mixed in small quantities, as needed, and placed in position within twenty or thirty minutes after first being wet.

Cautions.—Avoid extremes of heat. Portland cement concrete is weakened by exposure to a hot sun during the first four or five days after being placed in position. Or it may be injured by freezing while being mixed and before being placed in positiou, or even after having been placed, if subjected to a heavy load. Hence, avoid mixing in freezing weather, i. e., if the temperature is below 32° F. Do not cover when green with fresh manure to protect it from freezing as this will soil the surface and weaken the concrete.

Sand and Gravel.—The term sand, as used by concrete mixers, includes all grains and small pebbles that pass through a wire screen with ¼-inch mesh and are retained upon a screen having 40 meshes to the linear inch. Gravel in general is pebbles and stone retained upon a ¼-inch screen. It is quite commonly supposed that any kind of sand or gravel will make a good concrete mixture but this is far from being the case. Sand from pits or gravel banks varies greatly in character. Hence to secure the best results, care must be exercised in selecting materials. Coarse, hard sand, free from clay or dirt, produces the best and strongest concrete and requires much less cement than if fine, soft or dirty.

To procure good sand and gravel, screen the material at the bank twice. First use a ¼-inch screen to keep out the gravel. Set the screen upright at an angle of 45°. Then screen a second time, on a 40-mesh screen, the sand which has thus been freed from gravel. Reject all the fine sand and earth which will pass through the 40-mesh screen. The result will be material, both sand and gravel, of known character. By mixing these in exact proportions, not only will the finished work be more reliable, but enough cement can be saved to more than pay for the labor of screening.

Or fine loam and clay can be removed from the sand by washing. To test the material, fill a pint preserving jar with an average sample to the depth of 4 inches. Fill the jar with clear water to within 1 inch of the top, fasten on the lid and shake vigorously. Now set the jar upright and let the contents settle. The sand will fall to the bottom, next the clay, next the loam, and the water will come to the top. If there is a layer of more than ½ inch of clay or loam the sand must be rejected or washed.

To Wash Sand or Gravel.—Build a loose board platform 10 or 15 feet long. Have one end 12 inches higher than the other. Nail 2 by 6-inch plank across the lower end and along both sides to hold the sand. Spread out the sand on this platform in a layer 3 or 4 inches thick and wash with a ¾-inch garden hose. Begin at the upper end and let the water run through the sand and over the 2 by 6 edge at the bottom.

Reinforced Concrete. — For reinforced concrete and most ordinary purposes, reject stones over 1 inch in diameter. But for heavy foundation or abutment work, include larger stones and pebbles up to 2 inches or more in diameter. For best results use a mixture of sizes of gravel from ¼ to 1 inch or more in diameter. In ordering crushed stone specify the size of the stone and screenings wanted. The crusher dust should be washed out.

Measurements of Materials. — First figure the number of cubic feet of concrete that will be required for the job. Next determine the proportions of material, i. e., the kind of concrete you will employ. Finally figure the amount of each kind of material that will be necessary. The two most usual formulæ are 1:2:4 and 1:2½:5. The proportions are always measured by volume. A 1:2:4 mixture means 1 part cement, twice as much sand and 4 times as much stone or gravel. The whole mixture thus consists of 7 parts. A 1:2½:5 mixture means 1 part cement, 2½ times as much sand and 5 times as much stone or gravel. The whole consists of 8½ parts. In other words $\frac{1}{7}$ of a 1:2:4 mixture is cement and somewhat less than ⅛ of a 1:2½:5 mixture. The 1:2:4 mixture is, therefore, stronger and is to be preferred for foundations and other work carrying heavy loads.

The accompanying table, prepared by the national Office of Public Roads, gives the size of measuring boxes required for a two-bag batch of concrete. These boxes are made with straight sides of any kind of rough boards. They have no top or bottom. A bag of Portland cement is practically one cubic foot. A barrel contains four cubic feet or bags. The sand, stone or gravel are measured loosely in the box, not packed. For a four-bag batch of concrete double the quantities given in this table.

QUANTITIES OF MATERIALS AND THE RESULTING AMOUNT OF CONCRETE FOR A TWO-BAG BATCH

Kinds of concrete mixture	Proportions by parts			Materials			Concrete (cubic feet)	Sizes of measuring boxes (inside measurements)		Water for medium wet mixture (gallons)
	Cement	Sand	Stone or gravel	Cement (bags)	Sand (cubic feet)	Stone or gravel (cubic feet)		Sand	Stone or gravel	
1 : 2 : 4.......	1	2	4	2	3¾	7½	8½	2 feet by 2 feet by 11½ inches.	2 feet by 4 feet by 11½ inches.	10
1 : 2½ : 5.....	1	2½	5	2	4¾	9½	10	2 feet by 2 feet 6 inches by 11½ inches.	2 feet 6 inches by 4 feet by 11½ inches.	12½

To determine the total quantities of material required, multiply the total number of cubic feet of concrete needed for the job by the number given under the proper column as shown by the table on the next page, given by the Office of Public Roads. This will give the amount of cement, sand and stone or gravel needed.

Example: Let us suppose that the work consists of a concrete silo requiring in all 935 cubic feet of concrete, of which 750 cubic feet are to be 1:2:4 concrete, and 185 cubic feet are to be 1:2½:5 concrete. Enough sand and cement are also needed to paint the silo inside and outside, amounting in all to 400 square yards of surface, with a 1:1 mixture of sand and cement. One cubic foot of 1:1 mortar paints about 15 square yards of surface and requires 0.1856 barrel of cement and 0.0263 cubic yard of sand. The problem thus works out as follows:

QUANTITIES OF MATERIALS IN ONE CUBIC FOOT OF CONCRETE

Mixture of Concrete	Cement (by barrels)	Sand (by cubic yards)	Stone or gravel (by cubic yards)
1 : 2 : 4	0.058	0 0163	0.0326
1 : 2½ : 5	.048	.0176	.0352

CEMENT:	Barrels
For the 750 cubic feet of 1 : 2 : 4 concrete (750x0.058)	43.5
For the 185 cubic feet of 1 : 2½ : 5 concrete (185x0.048)	8.9
For painting (400–15x0.1856)	4.9
Total amount of cement	57.3
SAND:	Cubic yards
For 750 cubic feet of 1 : 2 : 4 concrete (750x0.0163)	12.23
For 185 cubic feet of 1 : 2½ : 5 concrete (185x0.0176)	3.26
For painting (400–15x0.0263)	.70
Total amount of sand	16.19
STONE OR GRAVEL:	Cubic yards
For 750 cubic feet of 1 : 2 : 4 concrete (750x0.0326)	24.5
For 185 cubic feet of 1 : 2½ : 5 concrete (185x0.0352)	6.5
Total amount of stone or gravel	31.0

Thus the necessary quantities of materials are about 57½ barrels of Portland cement, about 16¼ cubic yards of sand, and 31 cubic yards of stone or gravel. It is always wise to order two or three extra barrels of cement if the dealer is at considerable distance, as this avoids any possible trouble that a shortage might cause.

Equipment for Mixing.—This consists of a concrete mixing board, board "runs" for wheelbarrows, measuring boxes for sand, stone and gravel, a No. 3 square point shovel for each workman; at least two wheelbarrows, preferably having sheet iron bed; garden rake, water barrel, two 2-gallon water buckets; 4 by 4-inch tamper, 2 feet 6 inches in length with handles nailed to it; garden spade; and 2 screens, one a ¼-inch mesh, the other 40 meshes to the inch. These may be made by nailing a section of screen 2½ by 5 feet in size to a frame made of boards 2 by 4 feet.

To make a concrete board for two men to mix a 2-bag batch, order 9 pieces ⅞ by 12 inches by 10 feet boards, preferably tongue and groove roofers, planed and free from knots. Also 5 pieces 2 inch by 4 inch by 9 feet rough boards for cleats; 2 pieces 2 inch by 2 inch by 10 feet rough, for edge boards at the sides; and 2 pieces 2 inch by 2 inch by 9 feet rough, for edge boards at the two ends. The object of the edge boards is to prevent the loss of concrete grout by running over the edges.

For the same reason plug or close all knot holes by a strip nailed across them on the under side. The board must be tight to prevent waste of concrete grout, smooth to permit of easy shoveling—which should always be in the direction that the cracks run—firm and level. A board for a 4-bag batch of concrete should be 12 feet by 10 feet in size and will require a correspondingly larger amount of lumber. Have the boards run the shorter or 10-foot way.

Place the concrete board as handy to the job as may be and store the piles of sand, stone and pebbles close by. Support the board on blocks so that it will be level and cannot sag under the weight of the concrete. Build wheelbarrow "runs" of good smooth plank 2 to 3 inches in thickness and from 12 to 30 inches wide, depending upon the distance above the ground.

The following are specifications for measuring boxes for sand, stone or gravel.

For a 2-bag batch with the 1:2:4 mixture:

4 pieces 1 inch by 11½ inches by 2 feet, rough (for ends of the sand and stone boxes).

2 pieces 1 inch by 11½ inches by 4 feet, rough (for the sides of the sand box).

2 pieces 1 inch by 11½ inches by 6 feet, rough (for the sides of the stone box).

(It should be noted that the 2 pieces 4 feet long and the 2 pieces 6 feet long have an extra foot in length at each end for the purpose of serving as a handle.)

For a 2-bag batch with the 1:2½:5 mixture:

2 pieces 1 inch by 11½ inches by 2 feet (for the ends of the sand box).

2 pieces 1 inch by 11½ inches by 2½ feet (for the ends of the stone box).

2 pieces 1 inch by 11½ inches by 4½ feet (for the sides of the sand box).

2 pieces 1 inch by 11½ inches by 6 feet (for sides of the stone box).

(As in the preceding case, the 2 pieces 4½ feet long and the 2 pieces 6 feet long have an extra foot in length at each end to serve as handles.)

Mixing Concrete.—First place the mixing board and wheelbarrow runs in position and wheel two loads of sand upon the board. Place the sand measuring box about 2 feet from one of the 10-foot sides of the board. Fill the box, lift it off and spread the sand over the board with a rake in a layer 3 or 4 inches thick. Now spread 2 bags of cement as evenly as possible over the sand. Station two men facing one another at opposite ends of the board and let them start mixing the sand and cement in such a way that each man may turn over the half on his side of a line dividing the board in two. Let each man start at his feet and shovel away from himself taking a full shovel load and, in turning the shovel, not merely dumping off the sand and cement but shaking the materials from the end and sides of the shovel so that they will be mixed as they fall. Then let the men turn and work back from the board a second time in the same manner. Thus the material will be thoroughly mixed while being shoveled from one side of the board to the other.

After the sand and cement have thus been well mixed, spread them out carefully and add the gravel or stone. Place the proper measuring boxes on one side of the board and fill from the gravel pile. Now shovel the gravel on top of the sand and cement and spread out evenly. Or place the gravel measuring box on top of the level sand and cement mixture and with great care spread the gravel on top without extra shoveling. But this requires more experience.

Now dash about three-fourths of the required amount of water over the top of the pile as evenly as possible from a bucket. Take care not to get too much water near the edges lest it flow off and wash away some of the cement. Now start two men in the same way as with the sand and cement and shovel over the mixture. But let the men dump the whole shovel load instead of shaking it from the shovel and drag it back towards them with the square shovel point. This causes the wet gravel to pick up the sand and cement and insures a thorough mixture. Add water, as required, to the dry spots, until the total amount needed has been used. Now turn the mass back again as was done with the sand and cement. Experienced men will mix the concrete sufficiently in three such turnings but if it shows streaky or dry spots, turn it a fourth time and finally shovel in a compact pile. It is now ready for placing, which must be done promptly.

Only two men are required for mixing, but a third man can assist by supplying water and serving other materials and by raking dry or unmixed spots. Four men will be required for the 4-bag batch. This requires a board 10 feet by 12 feet. Start in the middle of the board and let each pair of men mix as for a 2-bag batch. But have them shovel the whole into a big mass each time the concrete is turned upon the center of the board.

Placing Concrete.—Place the concrete at once when mixed, since it will set within 20 or 30 minutes. Employ any means of conveying the concrete to the job that is most convenient. Deposit it in layers about 6 inches thick by means of a shovel or by pouring.

Three kinds of concrete mixtures are used. Each requires slightly different treatment. (1) A very wet mixture, which will run off a shovel when handled, is used for reinforced work, thin walls and the like. No ramming is necessary. (2) An ordinary or medium weight mixture of jelly-like consistency is in most general use for foundation floors and most other purposes. This should be rammed with a tamper enough to remove all air bubbles and fill voids. (3) A dry mixture about like damp earth is used for foundations when quick work is desirable. Spread this in layers 4 to 6 inches thick and tamp until the water flushes to the surface. The chief difference is that the dryer mixture sets more quickly.

Finishing Concrete.—To give the exposed surface of a concrete wall a smooth finish, run a spade or flattened shovel between the concrete and face of the form and work it up and down. This pushes the stone and gravel back slightly and causes cement grout to flow against the face of the form and harden in a smooth even surface. The same effect can be produced on thin side or partition walls by the use of a board 1 by 4 inches sharpened on one side like a chisel. The flat side should be placed against the form.

To protect new concrete from the sun while hardening, sprinkle it with water both morning and evening for the first five or six days. Or hang pieces of old canvas, sheeting, or burlap an inch or so from the face of the concrete and keep them wet. Or leave the forms in position for a week or ten days. The object of this precaution is to prevent the outside from drying more rapidly than the center.

Concrete Forms.—These are merely boxes or retaining walls of boards which serve to hold concrete in place until it is hardened. They thus fix its shape and give it a surface finish. Almost any kind of material which will hold the concrete will serve as a form. Sometimes foundations for buildings can be poured in shallow trenches dug for the purpose in the soil. The earth up to the ground line will serve as a form. Molds of wet sand are used for ornamental work. And metal molds may be had for certain purposes. But most forms are made of wood because it is both cheaper and easier to handle. Use preferably green lumber for forms, either rough or planed as desired. If the forms are to be used many times, as in casting fence posts, or if a handsome smooth surface is desired, matched boards with planed surfaces are to be preferred. But for ordinary work when the forms are to be used but once rough green lumber will answer every purpose. In such cases, use as few pieces of lumber and nails as possible. The forms may then be easily taken apart and the lumber used for other purposes. If nails are used do not drive them all the way in. Screws are preferable, since they can be more easily removed.

Build the forms strong enough to hold the concrete without bulging. Otherwise there will be leakage through the cracks. This will cause hollows on the surface and weaken the concrete. As a rule time and money will be well spent in making the forms rigid and true, and giving them an even surface. The oftener they are to be used the more nearly perfect they should be. Fill cracks and knot holes with stiff clay and tack strips over them on the outside.

Cleaning Tools and Forms.—Clean the concrete board at the beginning of each half day's work. Give the forms a dressing of linseed or cylinder oil or soft soap to prevent the concrete from sticking. Never use kerosene. Go over them before they are erected to protect them from dust and dirt. Remove all objects which fall inside the forms while being erected, else they will be cast in the concrete and may weaken it. On taking down the forms, clean them and scrape off the concrete which adheres to them with a sharp short handled hoe. Follow with a wire brush. But take care not to spoil the surface. Repaint with oil or soft soap any spots which appear dry.

Concrete Fence Posts.—Concrete is the best possible substance for ornamental gate and fence posts since they may be cast in any desirable shape or size. The same material may also be used for walks, retaining walls and similar purposes. Thus a uniform and harmonious decorative scheme can be carried out. Concrete posts usually cost less than first class wooden posts, according to locality, but are far more durable since their strength increases with age. They never need repairs as they are injured neither by fire nor weather. Barring unusual accident, concrete posts, once properly seasoned, will last forever.

Molds for line fence posts may be of steel or wood and either single or built in sets or "gangs." There are many patented steel molds on the market which have some advantages. If the posts are simple in form, these are light and easy to handle and give a post of neat finish and of any desired shape. But wooden molds made of ordinary white pine are in very common use. Two-inch plank dressed on both sides are to be preferred. But lighter lumber may be used if well braced. Molds for square posts are the simplest and easiest to make. They are merely long boxes and are often built in sets or gangs, side-by-side, with continuous bottom and end pieces. Any person having the tools can construct such molds without difficulty. They are usually laid flat. Thus when the concrete is poured into them, the two ends and three sides of the post are shaped by the mold. The fourth or top side is then smoothed with the trowel. Thus no lid or cover for the fourth side of the mold is required. To avoid sharp ragged corners, strips of canvas may be tacked along the two lower corners of the mold so that the corners of the finished post will be slightly rounded. The two upper corners can be similarly shaped by the use of a trowel or special tool called an "edger." Or clay may be plastered in the corners of the mold, or wooden strips may be tacked to the side boards and shaped properly with a gouge to answer the same purpose. The end pieces may be hinged to admit of the ready removal of the finished posts. Other forms are preferred by many such as posts tapering either on two or all four sides. A suitable size for this purpose are molds 4½ inches deep, 6 inches wide at the butt, 4½ inches square at the top and 7 feet long. Or molds 5 inches by 6 inches wide at the butt, 3 inches deep by 4 inches wide at the top and 7 feet long. Triangular posts are also a favorite style. These are easily constructed in sets or gangs. The corners should be slightly rounded.

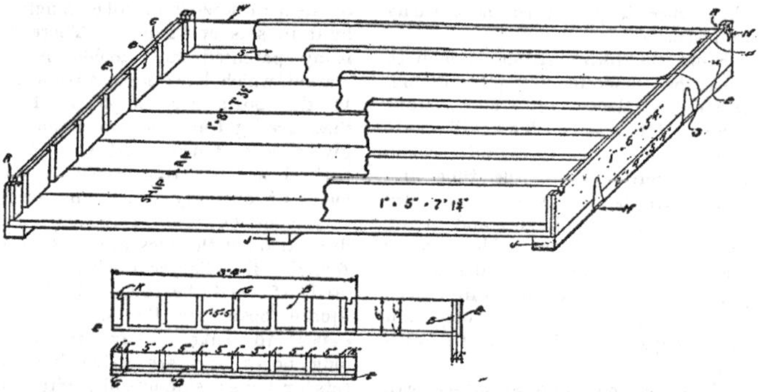
Gang mold for posts without taper. (*Office of Public Roads.*)

Oiling Molds.—Apply soft soap or crude oil, not kerosene, rather sparingly. Pour a quart of oil into a pail of water, stir, and apply the mixture with a mop or stiff broom to scrub out the molds after they have been used five or ten times. Or apply more often if necessary to prevent sticking.

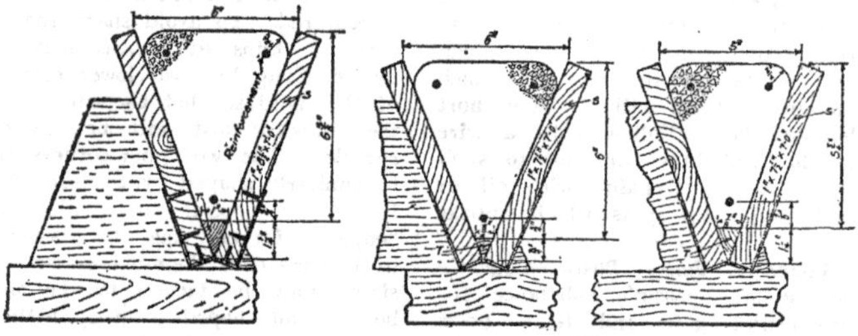
Molds for triangular posts. (*Office of Public Roads.*)

Reinforcement. — Concrete posts are somewhat brittle and may be greatly improved by reinforcing them with steel in the form of rods or wire properly buried in the concrete. Rods $\frac{3}{16}$ or $\frac{1}{4}$ inch in diameter are most used in posts. The kind especially made for this purpose is preferable to the ordinary stock kept by blacksmiths and hardware merchants. Ordinary ungalvanized fencing wire either single No. 8 or 2 No. 13 wires twisted is a suitable reinforcement for ordinary line posts. But this must be obtained straight from dealers, in the necessary lengths, and not in coils. The reinforcement should be placed within $\frac{3}{4}$ to 1 inch of the outside of the post. Care must be taken that it is not so located as to be exposed when the corners are rounded off.

"Fool-Proof Spacer."—To keep the

reinforcement in place use the little device known as the "fool-proof spacer." This consists of a No. 10 wire cut to such a length that, when twisted once around each of the two reinforcing wires or rods, the ends will nearly touch the sides of the molds. The distance from the twists to the end of the short wire or spacer is equal to the distance from the reinforcement to the side of the mold. On triangular molds such a spacer can be used only on the two rods or wires near the top of the mold. A shorter and similar device with only

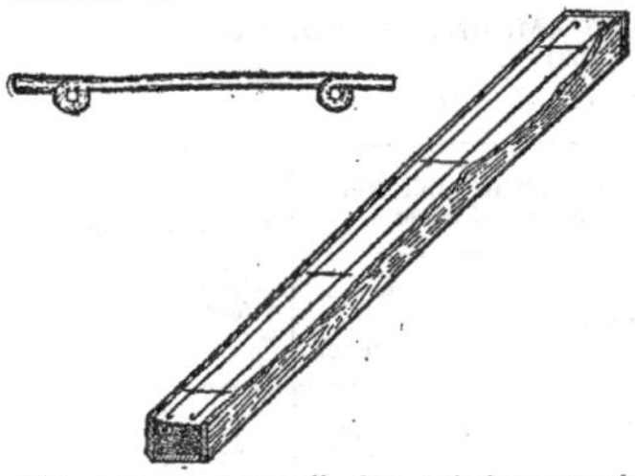

"Fool-proof spacer" for reinforcement. (Office of Public Roads.)

one twist may be used on the lower reinforcement. Place at least three spacers on each piece of reinforcement; one at the middle and the other two not far from the ends of the post. Metal slightly rusted may be used. Galvanizing is not necessary. There will be no rusting once the metal is encased in concrete.

It is a good plan to have the reinforcing wire 2 inches longer than the posts and turned back an inch on each end in the form of a hook. For posts subject to rubbing and crowding as in barn-yards, short extra reinforcing pieces 2 feet long are sometimes placed in the lower end to prevent the posts from snapping at the surface of the ground.

Mixing a Six-post Batch of Concrete.—The table on the next page, prepared by the Office of Public Roads, gives the approximate quantities of material for six posts 7 feet long and of the sizes named. To make larger numbers of posts increase the quantities in like proportion.

Molding Posts.—Oil or soap the molds and pour the concrete in them as soon as it has been mixed. If it stands thirty minutes after mixing throw it away. It is worthless. Fill the molds evenly to the depth of ¾ or 1 inch as desired and lay in the reinforcement properly spaced by means of at least 3 "fool-proof" wire spacers. Now pour in concrete until the molds are filled within ¾ to 1 inch of the top. Add the remaining reinforcement and fill the mold. Now place a crow bar or pinch bar under each outer corner of the molds, by turns, and move it up and down quickly. This vibration shakes out the air bubbles and makes the concrete more compact. Now level the exposed corners, if desired, with the edger. Finish the surface with the trowel as soon as the surface water has been absorbed but before the concrete has become hard. Use green lumber and soak the materials with water so the concrete will not cause them to swell and crack the posts. Do not work in hot sun or wind. In freezing weather work under cover.

Curing Posts.—Leave green posts in the mold two or three days to harden. The molds proper may then be removed from square posts and used on another bottom board but the posts must lay on their own bottom board, in the shade, undisturbed, for at least a week or ten days. Triangular posts may be slid gently from the molds to a smooth floor covered evenly with a cushion of sand but remember that the strain of lifting or the slightest jar may cause invisible cracks. These will greatly weaken the posts. During the first two days keep green posts wet and covered with wet canvas, burlap or any similar material. Wet sand may be used after the concrete has become hard. But manure will stain green posts and otherwise injure them. Continue sprinkling up to the tenth day. Then pile on end, leaning slightly together. But remember that a drop of 6 inches may break a green post. Or the jar of hauling them to the field over rough roads may injure them. Concrete posts gain strength rapidly up to a year or more. They should never be used until they have seasoned three months. The longer they can be made in advance, before using, the better.

Use of Concrete Posts.—Set 7 ft. concrete posts about 2½ feet deep and compact the soil about them by tamping. Attach the wire by means of short pieces of wire, one size smaller than the fence wire, in either of two ways: (1) carry the wire fastener around the post and then twist it first upon itself and then around the fence wire; (2) or twist one end around the fence wire, carry it around the post and twist on the other side to the same wire. This is known as the "Western Union Twist." Draw the fastener tight to keep the fence wire from sagging and from being slipped up or down by stock thrusting their heads through them. If necessary roughen the posts at the fastening point with a cold chisel. The kinks in woven wire fence take up the expansion and contraction from heat and cold. Hence do not hesitate to make a tight fastening. There are other methods of fastening wire, such as setting staples in the green cement, casting holes in the post or imbedding wooden strips in them. But all others than the above are unsatisfactory.

Special Posts.—Corner posts, gate posts, hitching posts and the like may be made of any desired design from special molds which can easily be constructed by anyone having ordinary skill in carpentry. Holes may be made for bolt hinges and fasteners by inserting a piece of gas pipe in the concrete. But wrought iron clamp straps going completely around the posts are to be preferred. These can be obtained to order from any blacksmith. Concrete makes excellent arbor posts and posts for vineyards, and trellises for all sorts of vines and clinging plants. Woven wire may be strung from post to post to support the vines and fastened in the manner above suggested.

Warning.—Do not buy molds or

QUANTITIES OF MATERIAL AND RESULTING AMOUNT OF CONCRETE FOR A SIX-POST BATCH

TRIANGULAR POSTS—LENGTH, 7 FEET

Size of post	Proportions of materials by parts, measured in volume			Materials in cubic feet, measured loose			Concrete tamped, cubic feet	Water for mixing, gallons
	Cement	Sand	Gravel or rock	Cement	Sand	Stone or gravel		
Heavy	1	2	4	1.4	2.8	5.6	6.2	11
	1	....	4	1.5	....	6.0	6.2	11
Medium	1	2	4	1.3	2.6	5.2	5.5	10
	1	....	4	1.4	....	5.6	5.5	10
Light	1	2	4	1.1	2.2	4.4	4.8	9
	1	....	4	1.2	....	4.8	4.8	9

RECTANGULAR POSTS—LENGTH, 7 FEET

Size of post	Cement	Sand	Gravel or rock	Cement	Sand	Stone or gravel	Concrete tamped, cubic feet	Water for mixing, gallons
Straight, 5 by 5	1	2	4	1.7	3.4	6.8	7.3	13
	1	....	4	1.8	....	7.2	7.3	13
Taper on two sides, 4½ by 6, 4½ by 4½	1	2	4	1.6	3.2	6.4	6.9	12
	1	....	4	1.7	....	6.8	6.9	12
Full taper, 5 by 6, 4 by 3	1	2	4	1.5	3.0	6.0	6.7	12
	1	....	4	1.6	....	6.4	6.7	12

means for mixing or molding concrete in blocks, posts or otherwise, or patent rights for the sale of such materials or processes, from traveling agents concerning whom you know nothing. Pay no attention whatever to assertions of such persons that you have been infringing their patent rights or that you may do so in future. Refer all such claimants to your attorney. You will never hear anything more about them. The methods above recommended are not

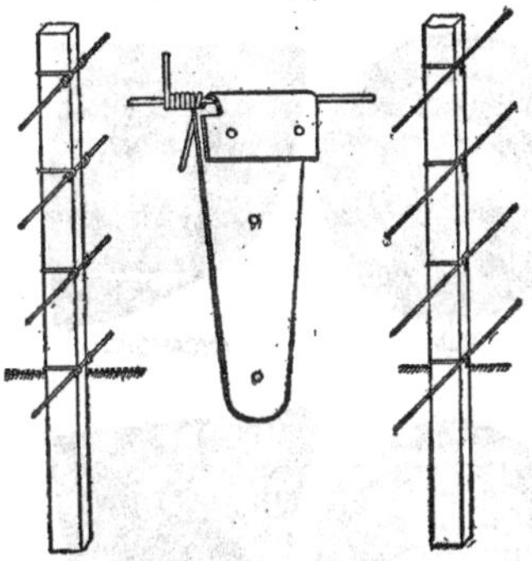

Methods of attaching fence wire to concrete posts. (Office of Public Roads.)

patented and are equally as useful for all ordinary purposes as any patented process or processes whatever.

PRESERVATION OF WOOD FENCE POSTS AND OTHER TIMBERS

When concrete is not available some method of preserving fence posts and other timbers from decay will add greatly to their life and will be found a valuable economy. Decay consists in the destruction of wood tissue by low forms of plant life called fungi. These require air, warmth and moisture. Wood decays most rapidly when in contact with the surface of the ground because the conditions of heat and moisture are there most favorable to fungous growth. Hence the objects of treatment for preservation of timber are to exclude air and moisture, to keep the fungi from coming in contact with the wood or to destroy them by antiseptics. Among the most common methods are peeling and seasoning, charring, painting, whitewashing, or the application of various coal-tar products, either by painting or dipping. The method to be employed will depend in part upon climatic conditions, and in part upon the use to which the timber is to be put. A more thorough and extensive method of preservation is justified for warm, moist climates than would be required for cool and dry localities. Those timbers, or portions of timbers, which come in contact with the soil—as the sills of buildings or the lower part of fence posts—require most thorough treatment.

All fence posts and similar timbers should be peeled and seasoned before used. Bark retards the evaporation of moisture and encourages the work of insects and fungi. Sometimes green posts are set surrounded by stone upon the theory that they will season in the ground. But experience does not indicate that the expense of this method is justified by the results. Moisture will reach timbers set among stone about as readily as if in actual contact with the soil. The most desirable preservatives are petroleum-tar creosote, by-products of the manufacture of water gas; coal-tar creosote, by-products of the manufacture of coal gas, and of coke; and various products of these. Both have antiseptic properties. But creosote, and some other products, made from coal-tar, are more efficient than petroleum products. Therefore, they are to be preferred although they are somewhat more expensive.

Charring.—To obtain good results by charring, first season the wood, then hold over an open fire. Take care not to let it check or split from the heat and do not char deep enough to weaken the post. It does not pay, as a rule, to char the entire post, but only the lower end up to about a foot above the ground and also the top of the post where water may accumulate.

Painting.—To treat posts with the brush, first peel and season them thoroughly. Then apply whitewash, any good paint or any of the coal-tar or petroleum-tar products. This method is not effective unless the posts have been thoroughly seasoned. Otherwise the surface coating will be cracked as the wood shrinks and moisture will enter. However, no such coatings are really durable. The various antiseptic coal-tar products are best suited to this purpose. Two or more coats should be applied hot. A fifty gallon barrel of creosote will give 300 posts 3 coats for the butts and 2 for the tops.

Dipping.—A somewhat better result may be secured by dipping the timbers so that the preservative can soak into the cracks and checks. This plan takes less labor than painting but consumes more of the preservative, since the tank or barrel must be kept full to the proper depth. Either petroleum-tar or coal-tar creosote may be applied by this method. The plan of dipping the butts of posts in cement is not recommended.

Still better results can be obtained by soaking the timbers in the preservative for ten hours at ordinary temperatures. Coal-tar and crude petroleum are not as suitable for this purpose as creosote. This is liquid at ordinary temperatures, soaks into the timber readily and has strong antiseptic properties. Coal-tar creosote must be warmed slightly to liquefy it. All timber thus treated must be thoroughly seasoned and dried to get as much water as possible out of the cells and thus allow the oil to come in and take its place. The kinds of woods most suitable to this treatment are beech, cottonwood, the gums, pin and red oak, the pines, sycamore and tulip tree.

Impregnation with Creosote.—Undoubtedly the best method is the impregnation of timbers with creosote by the so-called "open tank process." This consists in heating the wood so as to expand its cells and drive out of them a portion of the

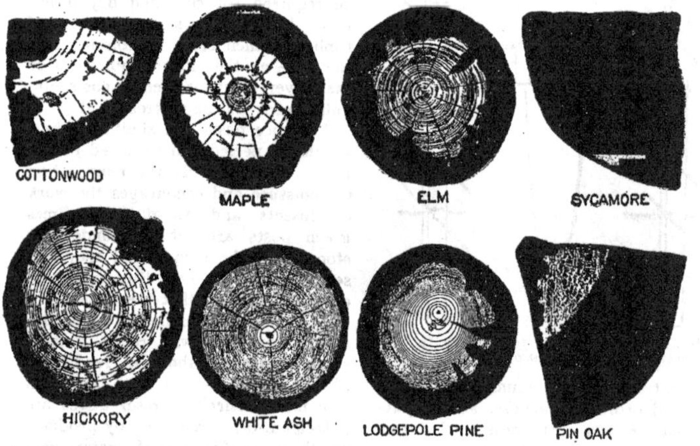

Sections of posts of various woods treated with creosote by the open-tank process. All the posts are drawn to the same scale, and are approximately 5 inches across. The black areas show the creosote penetration, which corresponds generally to the sapwood. (C. P. Willis.)

air and water they contain and then emersing the timber in a preservative bath to cool. As the air and water remaining in the cells contract during the cooling process, a partial vacuum is formed. The cool preservative is then forced into this by atmospheric pressure. The illustrations show sections of different kinds of woods treated by this process.

Materials and Equipment. — To thoroughly impregnate posts and other farm timbers with creosote requires one or more barrels or tanks with some suitable provision for heating their contents. Two common creosote barrels may be used. Set these about 7 or 8 feet apart and connect them by a 3 or 4-inch iron pipe fitted with lock (jamb) nuts. Build a fire under the middle of the pipe. Shield the sides of the barrel from direct heat by an apron or screen, preferably of some kind of metal as an old piece of sheet iron, tin or zinc. This outfit is inexpensive and, while the barrels are neither large nor deep enough for the best results and will usually leak after a few days, they answer well enough for a small number of posts or other timbers or shingles. A single barrel may be heated by means of a U made of 1½-inch pipe. Set the barrels in shallow boxes or on a platform provided with a gutter to carry off the oil to a neighboring tub, if the barrels suddenly spring a leak.

But if many posts are to be treated, and especially if one desires to preserve timber for sale or do this class of work for others on a commercial basis, the best plan is to purchase a light (14 gauge) cylindrical galvanized iron tank. Such a tank 3 feet in diameter by 4 feet high, fitted with a U of 3-inch pipe, will cost about twelve or fifteen dollars. With good care it will last indefinitely. Or a similar tank can be set in brick or masonry in such a way as to be heated from beneath like a set kettle. In addition, a rectangular tank for the cold bath about 8 feet long, 8 feet wide and 3 feet deep will be necessary if the entire post is to be immersed. Provision must be made to heat this, when necessary, to a temperature of about 100° or 120° F. to liquefy the creosote and cause it to penetrate freely. A thermometer reading to 250° F. is necessary.

Preparation of Posts.—Select preferably round posts not exceeding 5 inches average diameter, of soft and porous wood as gum, pine, maple and the like. These are cheaper than hard wood, easier to treat, yet when properly treated are equally as durable. Do not attempt to treat hard woods which are naturally durable in contact with the ground such as cedar, locust, white oak and black walnut. Do not treat split posts having highly colored heart wood such as oak and yellow pine. The creosote will not penetrate hard wood and such posts will readily decay. In fact the advantage of this process is to make cheap posts of small size and soft wood, durable. Bevel the top of the post, preferably with an axe, so as to leave a smooth slanting surface to shed rain. Peel carefully. Remove even the papery inner bark, especially from pine and basswood. Season at least five weeks. Treat only when bone dry and not less than three or four days after exposure to heavy rains. To test posts when seasoning, weigh an average sample at intervals of five days. If the loss of moisture in that period is less than one pound per post of 5-inch average diameter, it may be safely used.

Treatment.—This differs according to the kind of wood and the method employed. Soft wood absorbs more than hard wood. But, as a rule, limit the absorption to 0.4 gallon per post, if only the butt is treated, or 0.6 gallon, if the top is also impregnated. The best method is that which gives the deepest penetration in the shortest time.

To treat posts with creosote fill the tank with oil to such a point that the butts will be submerged 6 inches higher than they will stand in the ground when set. Raise the temperature to 220° F. before putting in the post, and keep it there throughout the bath. If only one tank is used, the cold bath is brought about by removing the fire and leaving the

Barrel Outfit. (*C. P. Willis.*)

posts in the tank to cool until sufficient oil has been absorbed. More oil must be added from time to time to keep them submerged to the proper depth.

If two tanks are used, liquefy the oil in the cold bath by warming to a temperature of from 100° to 120° F. Transfer the posts from the hot to the cold bath as quickly as possible. Immerse to the same point as the post stood in the hot liquid. Add more oil from time to time to keep the posts immersed at that level. Or, if desired, only the butts may be heated but the whole post may be submerged in the cold bath. Thus the butts will receive a heavy, and the tops a light treatment. The cost varies with the kind of wood, cost of materials and method of treatment employed. It may be estimated at from twelve to fifteen cents per post exclusive of fuel and labor. If posts are properly creosoted they will last twenty years. Roughly speaking, this process will result in a net saving equal to the original value of the post.

The best results may be secured by treating the various woods about as follows, assuming that all posts are round, peeled, seasoned and average about 5 inches in diameter. Use the single tank treatment as follows for the following woods, viz., white ash, immerse in hot oil 5 hours, cooling oil 12 hours; cottonwood, hot oil 1 hour, cooling oil 12 hours; butternut, white elm and bitternut hickory, hot oil 6 hours, cooling oil 12 hours. Use the double tank treatment as follows: basswood, sweet (bay) magnolia and sycamore, hot oil 1 hour, cold oil ½ hour; for beech, sweet (red) gum, pin oak and red oak, hot oil 1 hour, cold oil ¾ hour; for black gum, cotton (tupelo) gum, hot oil 1 hour, cold oil 1 hour; for loblolly and lodgepole pine, hot oil 1½ hours, cold oil 1 hour; for slippery elm, hot oil 1½ hours, cold oil 1½ hours; for tulip tree, hot oil 2 hours, cold oil ½ hour; for river birch, pitch pine and short leaf pine, hot oil 3 hours, cold oil 1 hour; for sugar maple and scrub pine, hot oil 2 hours, cold oil 2 hours; for white willow, hot oil 4 hours, cold oil 1 hour; for red maple, hot oil 3 hours, cold oil 2 hours; for white poplar, hot oil 6 hours, cold oil 12

Light iron tank heated by the pipe method of direct heating. (*C. P. Willis.*)

hours. White willow requires an especially thorough seasoning.

Preserving Shingles.—Shingles are sometimes preserved from warping and decay by painting or applying other preservatives with a brush. But this process is not to be recommended. To dip the shingles separately in paint or coal-tar derivatives is a better method. But far more satisfactory results can be had by impregnating shingles with creosote by the above plan. Cheap pine shingles, clear and free from knots, can by this process be made superior to the best cedar shingles. And the life of the best shingles can be much prolonged. An apparatus similar to that used for posts may be employed or any kind of tank used in which one or more bundles of shingles can be immersed. But choose a deep tank rather than a shallow one to prevent loss of oil from volatilization. The exact treatment required for a given lot of shingles can be determined only by experiment. Weigh a sample bundle before and after treatment and time the treatment so that the shingles will absorb from twelve to thirteen pounds of oil per bundle or six gallons per 1,000 shingles. The cost should range from $1.25 to $1.50 per thousand. Have the hot bath relatively longer than the cold. Objections to this process are that creosote has a strong odor, contaminates cistern water and gets on shingle nails so that the workmen cannot hold them in their mouths. All these difficulties may be obviated by treating the shingles a few weeks in advance. Or a shingle nailing machine may be employed. The water may be diverted from the cistern for three or four days or a week; no taint will then be observed. The odor also passes away after a few days.

To color creosote shingles red or reddish brown, mix eight to twelve ounces of the required pigment ground in oil with an equal bulk of linseed oil and add to each gallon of the preservative. To color green, it is necessary to dip or paint the shingles. The green pigment is too expensive to mix with the creosote.

Other Timbers. — In addition to posts and shingles, the life of other timbers which come in contact with the soil or are exposed to moisture may be greatly increased by the above method. Among these may be mentioned foundations, sills, beams, wooden walks and planking, the lower portion of board fences, and all lumber used near the ground in sheds or barns. The treatment to be given is similar to that for posts.

Creosoted Wood Pavement.—Creosoted wood blocks are in many respects the most satisfactory material for walks and drives. They are far superior to planking. While somewhat more expensive than brick or concrete, they cost less than a good grade of asphalt and under ordinary conditions about the home are practically indestructible. The cost in quantities is from $2.50 to $3.00 per superficial square yard laid. Wood blocks may be sawed from any well-seasoned lumber of the kinds above mentioned and treated with creosote by the open tank process. But the commercial product treated by the vacuum pressure method is to be preferred.

To lay wood block pavement first prepare a foundation of concrete four to six inches in thickness depending upon the amount of wear to which it will be subjected. Bring the surface to a true level, cover

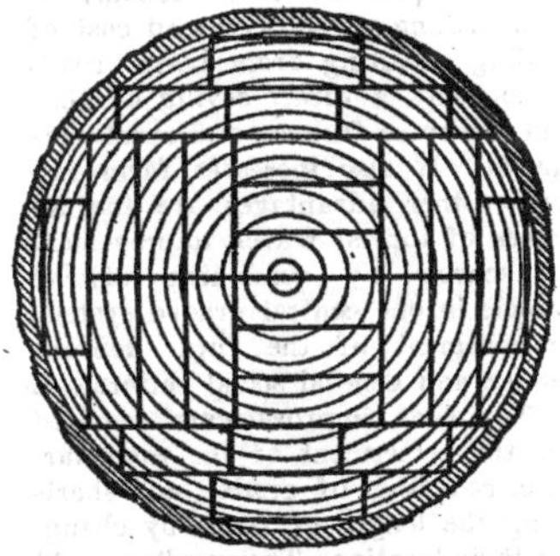

Method of cutting planks from logs. (*C. L. Hill.*)

with a thin layer of Portland cement mortar, mixed slightly, damp and lay the blocks in the damp cement with pains to keep the surface true and even. Or let the cement harden and cover with a layer of tar in which set the blocks. Or lay over them a cushion of sand. But do not use sand on hillsides or other steep grades where it may be washed out and derange the pavement. The blocks must be sawed to uniform height. The illustration shows the method of cutting the planks from logs.

Cover the pavement when laid with a layer of fine sand to fill the interstices. Or cover with coal-tar pitch heated to about 300° F. to insure perfect fluidity and scatter over this a top dressing of screened sharp sand or finely crushed stone about one-half inch in thickness. Should the pitch become soft in hot weather cover with a light dressing of sand.

GOOD ROADS

A nation-wide movement is on foot for improved roads throughout the United States. This has been brought about in part by the rapid extension of the use of the automobile among farmers and other rural residents. But it is also due to a better understanding both of the economic value of good roads and the principles of true economy in road making. The decreased cost of hauling resulting from better roads is not only a direct saving of time and money to farmers and rural merchants. It also increases farm values. Other advantages are the increase of tourist travel, improvement of schools by combining district schools in one central graded system, improvement of the rural delivery service and general social betterment.

The chief improvements required are the betterment of the road surface, reduction of grades, and shortening the length of roads by changing their location. The results sought are increased speed in hauling and ability to carry increased loads, or both. The average load which a horse can draw on a muddy earth road varies from nothing up to 800 pounds; on a smooth dry earth road, from 1,000 to 2,000 pounds; on a gravel road in bad condition, from 1,000 to 1,500 pounds or, if in good condition, about 3,300; on a macadam road, from 2,000 to 5,000 pounds; and on a brick road, from 5,000 to 8,000 pounds. The effect of a good macadam road is therefore to increase the capacity of every horse from three to five times. The actual monetary loss in the United States from bad roads if computed in dollars and cents would stagger the imagination. Several states have adopted the policy of building high grade macadam roads under state supervision in localities where counties or other local civil divisions agree to share the cost. All such movements should have the co-operation of every good citizen. But since the cost of first class macadam roads is prohibitive in many localities from lack of available material and many other reasons, a knowledge of cheaper methods of road making is of universal importance.

Earth Roads.—A considerable majority of all the public roads in the United States are of earth. These vary in character according to the soil of each locality. Some communities are favored by nature with a convenient supply of gravel, or of stone suitable for road making when treated by the stone crusher. But elsewhere are large tracts of country in which no such materials are to be had. Reliance must usually be placed upon means of treating the native soils over which the road passes. These vary from pure sand, through all sorts of admixture of sand, loam, marl and clay, to solid beds of clay. Pure sand or pure clay present among the most difficult of all conditions.

Sand Clay and Burnt Clay Roads.—While pure sand or pure clay are extreme types of bad roads, a proper combination of the two materials makes a type of road surface almost equal to macadam. Natural sand and clay roads are sometimes found. But more often there is a deficiency of either sand or clay. One or the other must then be supplied to produce a satisfactory surface. Clays vary in binding power between two extreme types. One kind is very "plastic" or sticky when wet. This is called "ball clay" because a lump of it placed in water will keep its shape. The opposite type is less sticky but will readily crumble when wet. Ball clay is somewhat more difficult to handle but makes a better road because it has more binding power. Some clays contain more or less sand, loam, or other constituents. Hence the method of road making varies somewhat according to the available materials. It is a good plan to experiment with clays from different beds and choose those which give the best results, even if they must be hauled greater distances.

The ideal combination of sand and clay is in proportion such that the voids or spaces between the grains of sand are just filled with the finer clay particles. Any excess of clay defeats the object of the mixture by enabling the particles of sand to slip loosely over one another.

To test the soil and ascertain the exact proportion of clay required, fill one of two glass tumblers level full of an average sample of sand from the roadbed and the other level full of water. Now gently pour enough of the water over the sand to fill the voids between the particles of sand up to the brim of the glass. Measure the quantity of water remaining. The proportion taken up by the sand to the quantity remaining will show the proportion of clay which will make an ideal combination. In practice, the mixture of sand and clay should be about four or five inches in depth. Thus by measurements of the road surface to be covered, the quantity of material required can be readily estimated. But somewhat larger proportions of sand or clay will usually have to be added from time to time to take the place of that lost by washing and to mix with clay brought up from below in the process of road making, or by traffic.

To Make a Sand Clay Road Over a Sandy Sub-soil. — First provide proper drainage. Then crown the roadbed slightly beginning nearest the source of clay. Now dump the

Cross section of road, showing clay cover on "deep" sand sub-soil. (Wm. L. Spoon.)

first load of clay at the point nearest the clay bed and spread it out evenly before driving over it. Finally crown the clay to a depth of six or eight inches in the middle of a twelve-foot road and taper to a thin edge at each side. Cover to the required depth with a layer of clean sand. If the clay tends to crumble when wet it may not require any further treatment, except to add more sand from time to time to keep the surface smooth and prevent the formation of mud. But if it is of a plastic and lumpy character it will be necessary to plow or harrow it by turns to break up the lumps and thoroughly mix the clay and sand together. Choose for this purpose a time when the road has been thoroughly wet by heavy rains and turn the surface to a depth of about four or five inches with the plow. Follow with a cutaway or disc harrow. This is a hard job since the clay forms a thick, pasty mud. But if properly done, it produces a surface which will stand traffic almost as well as first class macadam and at about one-sixth the cost.

The best clays for road making are usually red or mottled red and white. If such can be found it will pay to haul them considerable distances.

To Construct a Sand Clay Road Upon a Clay Sub-soil.—Take special care to provide proper drainage. Crown the clay at the rate of at least one-half inch per foot. Now turn over the surface to a depth of at least four inches with the plow and thoroughly pulverize with the harrow. Choose for this purpose a time when the road is comparatively dry. Apply clean sharp sand to a depth of six to eight inches in the middle of the road and slope at the rate of one-half inch per foot, toward each side. Mix with the plow and harrow. Finish the road by puddling with the harrow after a rain. Apply more sand to the surface from time to time, to keep it smooth and prevent its becoming sticky.

To maintain a sand clay road, shape the surface with the scraper while wet and soft, but defer rolling until it has been thoroughly puddled by means of the harrow or by traffic. A sand clay road is not finished until a proper combination of the sand and clay has been effected under the influence of care and traffic, however long this may require. Hence, the cost of maintenance during the early stages may be properly included in the cost of construction. But when a proper combination is effected, the surface will be found practically as hard and durable as macadam. The total cost will be much less, usually at the rate of about $600.00 a mile.

Burnt Clay Roads.—Where sand is not available, clay roads may be improved by burning or "clinkering" the clay to destroy its plasticity or sticky quality. Instructions for this process will be furnished by the Office of Public Roads connected with the Department of Agriculture at Washington, D. C., on request.

The Split Log Drag.—The best and cheapest means of maintaining all kinds of earth roads is the use of the split log drag. The average annual cost of maintenance of earth roads by other methods is from forty to fifty dollars a mile. Whereas earth roads can be kept in first class condition under ordinary circumstances with the split log drag at from two to five dollars a mile. The cost of such a drag is nominal. There is no reason why any householder, who owns a team and has private roads to maintain upon his own lands, should not have a drag of his own. Incidentally, he can work the public road in front of his own premises, both with an eye to his own convenience and as an object lesson to others.

To Make a Split Log Drag.—Select preferably a dry red cedar log ten or twelve inches in diameter and seven or eight feet long. Split it carefully down the middle. Red elm or walnut when thoroughly dry are suitable, and either box elder, soft maple or weeping willow are preferable to oak, hickory or ash. Select the heavier and better slab for the front. Bore three holes with a two-inch auger; one, four inches from the end that is to be in the middle of the road, another twenty-two inches from the opposite end, and the third half way between the two. These are to receive the cross stakes. Now bore three corresponding holes in the back slab; the first, twenty inches from the end which is to be at the middle of the road, the second six inches from the opposite end, and the third in the middle as before. Take care to hold the auger plumb so that the stakes will fit properly.

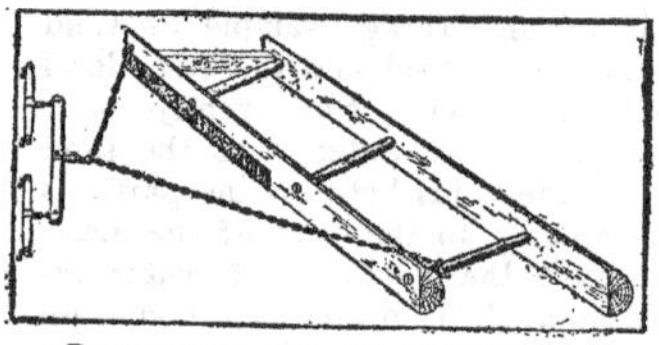

Perspective view of split-log drag. (D. Ward King.)

Select for the stakes straight grained timber, which will fit snugly in the two-inch holes. Cut these to such a length that the slabs will be kept thirty inches apart. Taper them gradually toward the end so that there will be no shoulder at the point where they enter the slab. Now bring the holes opposite one another, insert the stakes and fasten them solely by means of wedges. Insert a two-by-four brace diagonally to the stakes at the ditch end, as shown in the illustration. Drop this on the front slab so that the lower edge will be within one inch of the ground. Rest the other end between the slab and the end stake.

Shoe the ditch end of the front slab with a strip of ¼ inch iron or steel about 3½ feet long and 4 inches wide. Bolt this to the front slab with flat head bolts, countersunk. Locate this shoe half an inch below the lower edge of the slab at the ditch end and flush with the edge of the slab at the middle of the road. Insert a wedge between the lower edge of this shoe and the slab so as to give it a set like the bit of a plane. Lay a platform of 1 inch boards, held together by three cleats, on the stakes between the slabs. Separate the boards an inch or more apart to let the earth fall through them. Let the cleats clear the stakes and extend them an inch on either side of the finished platform.

Bore another 2 inch auger hole 4 inches from the ditch end of the front slab to receive one end of a trace chain and hold it by a pin passed through a link. Pass the other end of the trace chain over the front slab and wrap it around the rear stake. This allows the earth to drift past the face of the drag.

Plank may be used instead of split logs if preferred by strengthening them along their middle line by a 2 inch by 6 inch strip of timber.

To maintain an earth road in good condition use the drag when the soil is moist but not sticky, and will move freely along the faces of the slabs. Drive the team with one horse on either side of the right hand wheel pit or rut for the full length of the portion to be dragged. Return upon the other half of the roadway. This moves the earth toward the center, gives it a proper crown and fills the ruts. The fresh earth will be packed by traffic.

There are many fine points about the use of the split log drag which can best be learned by experience. In general, fasten the snatch link or clevis nearer the ditch end, so that the drag will follow the team at an angle of 45°. To deepen the cut lengthen the hitch and vice versa. As a rule, 1½ trace chains will be sufficient. Ride the drag standing and observe how to deepen or lessen the cut, pass over obstructions and the like, by shifting your position.

Ditch Cleaner.—To make a ditch cleaner select a 2 inch guide plank 12 feet long and 12 inches wide and attach to it a mold board of 2 inch plank 12 inches by 8 feet. Brace these with a 3 foot cross piece.

Shoe the mold board with a ¼ inch iron plate 4 inches wide by 3 feet long fastened by ⅜ inch bolts, countersunk. Hollow the cross boards 3 inches on each side of the middle beginning not less than 4 inches from each end, so as not to shorten its bearing against the guide plank or mold board, or decrease the nailing space. This will keep the earth from heaping up against it. Hitch one end of the trace chain to a bolt about mid-way the intersection of the mold board and guide plank, carry the other over the top of the mold board and fasten to a hook or staple. Add a weight of about 200 pounds over the front end. Use two or more horses according to conditions. Endeavor to maintain a smooth, even surface at the bottom of the ditch over which water can flow smoothly. Hence, pass lightly over soft spots, but cut hard places down to an equal level. To do this ride the ditcher standing and shift your weight forward to depress the point or back to raise it. This type of ditcher should precede the split log drag. It will assist in preserving an even slope from the crown of the road to the bottom of the ditch. It thus facilitates drainage and prevents accidents from ditches with too abrupt slopes.

LIGHTNING CONDUCTORS

The words "lightning rod agent" have become a by-word from the fact that while the need of protection against loss from fire, or death of persons or stock from lightning strokes, is universally felt, yet the subject, in the minds of most persons, is surrounded with mystery. It has been easy for designing men to play upon this combination of ignorance and fear. Not only have many supposed contracts for lightning rods

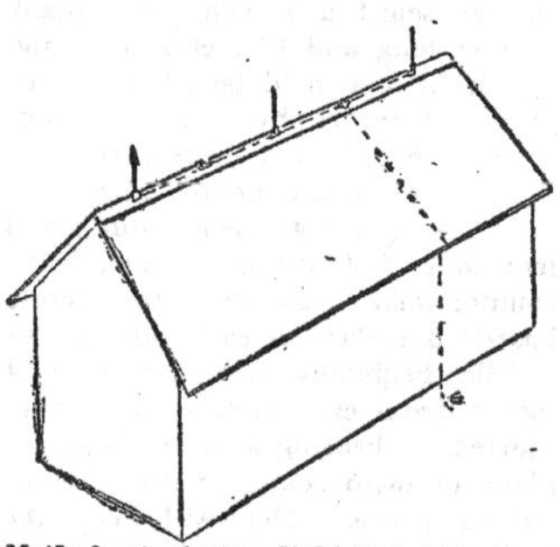

Method of placing lightning rods on a building having no cupola or chimney. Length of building, about 25 feet. (Alfred J. Henry.)

turned out to be cleverly devised promissory notes. Most often the equipment provided, if any, has proved inefficient, although the price paid was ruinously high. Hence there is a general prejudice against lightning rods and a widespread belief that, if not precisely worthless, they will not justify the expense of installation. Owing to recent experiments and discoveries any householder who is handy with tools can now equip his premises with efficient lightning conductors at very low cost. The materials can be purchased from any of the large electrical supply houses in the principal cities or from the big mail order concerns.

To wire a building with lightning conductors requires only a sufficient length of No. 3 or No. 4 double-galvanized iron telegraph wire, a pound, more or less, of galvanized iron staples, and a few connecting tees, known as "Tee conductors of ¼ inch rod." There are three grades of galvanized iron wire known as Extra Best Best (E. B. B.), Best Best (B. B.) and steel. The "extra best best" is to be preferred to either of the cheaper grades of iron wire or to copper. It is a wise economy to pay the difference for the "extra best best" double-galvanized. Observe that there are three standards of wire gauges: Brown and Sharp (B. & S.), Roebling, and the Birmingham wire gauge of England. Observe also that the size of the wire increases as the numbers diminish, i. e., No. 4 wire is smaller than No. 3. Use for small buildings such as hen houses, sheds and small barns or dwellings, No. 4 wire, B. & S. gauge. Or for large barns and resideuces, No. 3 of the same gauge or their equivalent in other gauges. If a building is large enough to require two vertical wires down each side of the building and wire along the ridge of the roof, it is advisable to use No. 3 wire.

To protect from lightning a building having a wooden roof, simply run a wire along the ridge pole and connect with this, by means of tees, one or more side wires. Extend these down the slope of the roof and sides of the building and sink their lower ends in the ground. Fasten the wires to the building by galvanized iron staples about 1 inch long. It is not necessary to insulate them in any way.

Or tack a row of small wooden blocks 1½ inches thick, 2½ inches wide and 4 inches long down the slope of the roof and side of the building at intervals of 10 feet or less, insert in each a stout screweye and pass the wire through these.

The length of wire required will depend upon the size of the building and the number of side wires employed. The rule is to space the side wires about 25 or 30 feet apart. Thus a barn 50 or 60 feet long should have at least two vertical conductors on each of its opposite sides. The simplest way to measure the length of wire required is to toss a ball of stout cotton twine over the ridge pole. Hold one end and let it unravel as it goes. Fasten the end of the cord you hold to the sill, go around to the other side of the building, and draw it taut directly opposite. But take care not to stretch it more than is necessary. Cut it off, pull it down and measure it with a tape, yardstick or any similar device. It is well to order a few yards extra to cover any possible stretching of the cord. Allow also for the ridge pole wire and the necessary terminals.

Terminals.—At every chimney, cupola or other obstruction of the roof, erect a "terminal" or vertical rod of wire about 20 inches long. Also erect terminals at each end of the ridge pole by making a right angle bend in the wire which runs along the ridge at intervals of 20 inches from the respective ends. Also erect similar terminals at each junction of a side wire with the ridge wire and elsewhere, so that there will be a terminal about every 18 or 20 feet along the ridge of the roof. Fasten each of these to the ridge wire by a tee connector.

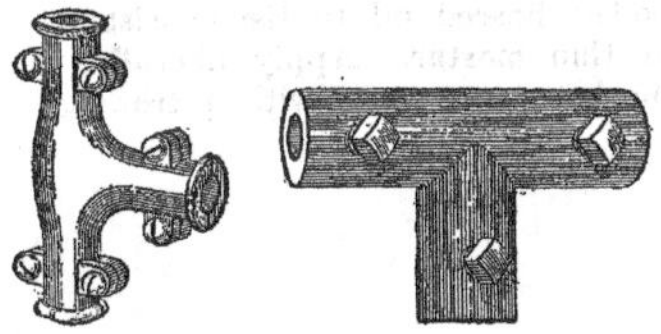

Two types of tee connections. (Alfred J. Henry.)

To put up the wires first slip the necessary tees on to the horizontal ridge wire and erect them at the points of junction with the downward direct wires and at other points where required. Fasten the horizontal wire with staples. Now insert the side wires and terminals in the tee conductors. Slip the side wires through the screweyes or fasten them by means of staples, and ground them as hereafter directed. The terminals are short and will offer little or no resistance to the wind. Do not leave the ends of the terminals blunt. File them to a cone shape.

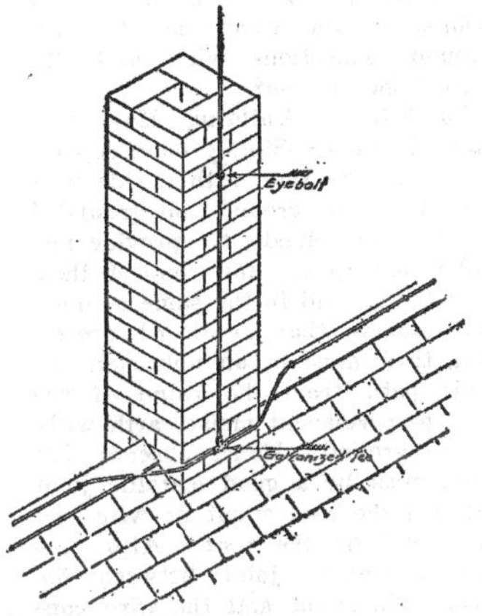

Showing method of running horizontal conductor around a chimney or cupola. (Alfred J. Henry.)

And as this removes the galvanizing, coat the tips heavily with aluminum paint to prevent rusting.

Earth Connections.—The ends of the side wires must be sunk in the ground deep enough to reach permanently moist earth at the shortest possible distance. Coil the end of the wire in a spiral about 1 foot in diameter and bury this in moist earth at whatever depth it may be found.

Or drive a 1¼ inch galvanized iron pipe into the ground at the foot of the main conductors deep enough to encounter permanently moist soil. Thrust the wire into this and fill the interstices with powdered charcoal. But before inserting the wire, provide a cap for the top of the pipe, with a hole through it big enough to admit the wire and also to allow water to drip down the wire into the inside of the pipe. Pass the wire through the cap, insert the charcoal and finally screw the cap firmly in position.

It is a good plan to bring the rain spouts down from the eaves to a point near these earth connections to keep the ground moist. Or if there are no down rain spouts bore holes, or insert a short spout over these points, in the eaves so that the ground connections will catch the drip from the roof.

To Wire a Building Having a Metallic Roof.—Simply connect each corner of the roof with a side wire running to the ground and grounded as above described. Or provide metallie rain spouts and connect them with the ground in the same manner. But observe that to afford protection, there must be an unbroken metallic path from the ridge of the roof to permanent moist earth within the ground. Hence observe that there must be a good metallic joint between the rain spout or wire and the metal of the roof. Also provide a similar joint between the metal rain spout and the wire connection to the ground. To make such a joint hammer the end of the wire into a flat tape and both bolt and solder it to the roof and also to the rain spout. Since this process destroys the galvanizing, keep the joint well coated with aluminum paint.

In putting up lightning conductors avoid bending the wire at sharp angles when passing chimneys and cupolas and also in passing around the eaves. A gooseneck bend is always to be preferred to a sharp one. Or preferably bore a hole through the overhang of the roof so as to let the wire pass the eaves close to the wall of the building.

Cautions.—Keep the lightning conductors as far as possible from gas pipes in the building, if any, but preferably connect them with water pipes, provided the latter are in good connection with the ground. See that the joints are mechanically perfect. Examine them frequently, especially after thunder storms, to make sure that they are not broken. Give the whole system two coats of aluminum paint when installed and repaint every two or three years.

To Mend Leaky Roofs.—A correspondent furnishes the following recipe for mending leaks in old tin or other metal roofs, or about chimneys, eaves or gutter spouts where the flashing has given out. He states that this formula alone has earned for him more than $200:

Mix equal parts, by bulk, of fine sifted coal ashes and whiting with boiled linseed oil to the consistency of thin mortar. Apply liberally to the holes and leaks with a trowel.

CHAPTER IX

THE DAY'S ROUTINE

CLEANING AND POLISHING STOVES — DISHWASHING — CARE OF KITCHEN WARES—CARE OF GLASSWARE AND CUT GLASS—STEEL KNIVES AND FORKS—CARE OF SILVERWARE—CARE OF SINKS AND DISPOSAL OF GARBAGE—CHAMBER WORK—CARE OF LAMPS

CLEANING AND POLISHING STOVES

Care of Kitchen Range.—Remove cinders and ashes each morning, brush out the inside of fire box and flnes, and brush off the outside with wings or a hair brush; wash off the stove, if greasy, with soda and water and a piece of flannel. Blacken and polish.

Clean steel fittings from rust with sweet oil or kerosene and polish with emery. Clean brass fittings with emery or bath brick by means of flannel, and polish with chamois. Clean the hearth with hot water and soda by means of a flannel cloth.

Care of Stoves.—The cook stove or range may be kept in good order by a daily brushing or rubbing and by a thorough blacking and polishing once a week.

Cook Stove — To Keep Clean. — Sprinkle a little salt over anything burning on the stove to remove the dirt. Have at hand small sheets of sandpaper to remove whatever adheres.

To Keep the Hands Clean.—Before polishing the stove rub lard under the finger nails.

Dilute the polish in a saucer with water or vinegar, and apply with a common dishwashing mop. Draw over the hand a small paper bag, and polish with a flannel or other cloth.

Or use a polishing mitten, but the liquid blacking will work through the polishing mitten and soil the hands, whereas the paper bags can be changed as fast as they become soiled.

If the hands become soiled with blacking, first rub them thoroughly with lard, then wash with soap and water.

Stove Blacking. — Dissolve ½ ounce of alum in 1 gill of soft water. Add 6½ pounds of plumbago mixed with 12 ounces of lampblack. Stir vigorously. Stir in 1½ gills of molasses, next ½ bar of white soap dissolved in 3 pints of water, and lastly 1 ounce of glycerin. This is a commercial article which has a great reputation.

Or beat up the whites of 3 eggs and mix in ½ pound of black lead. Dilute with sour beer or ale to the consistency of cream, and boil gently for 15 or 20 minutes.

Or mix 8 ounces of copperas, 4 ounces of bone black, and 4 ounces of black lead with water to the consistency of cream.

Or melt 1 pound of hard yellow soap with a little boiling water, and while hot stir in 1 pound of powdered soft coal. Cool, and preserve in tight fruit jars or wide-mouthed bottles for use.

Or mix 4 ounces of black lead with 2 tablespoonfuls of vinegar, 1 teaspoonful of sugar, and a piece of yellow soap the size of a butternut,

Melt the soap with gentle heat and reduce while hot to the consistency of cream with coffee strained through a cheesecloth. Stir in ½ teaspoonful of alum.

Or use vinegar instead of water for mixing any of the above. The work of polishing will not be so hard, and the polish will last longer.

Or mix with oil of turpentine. This prevents and removes rust.

Or add a little sugar or alum to any of the above; or a little benzine or naphtha to help cut the grease. If these are added the stove must be polished cold.

To Apply Polish.—Apply stove polish in liquid form by softening with a little vinegar or turpentine, and spread on with a dishwashing mop or wide painter's brush.

Or rub a piece of flannel with wet yellow soap. Dip it into dry powdered blacking and apply. This saves friction and makes the labor of polishing much easier.

Or, if a stove is much covered with grease, mix powdered blacking with gasoline and rub it on rapidly with flannel. Clean the stove thoroughly as you go, as the gasoline evaporates quickly. Of course the stove must be entirely cold.

To Polish Stoves.—Polishing cloths may be purchased, or a substitute may be made from any old glove or mitten by sewing to the palm several thicknesses of outing flannel, velveteen, or a piece of sheepskin with the wool on.

Or polish the stove with newspapers.

Or take a large paper bag, insert the hand part way, and crumple up the remainder to polish with.

Or use the paper that electric-light globes are cleaned with. This can be bought of any electrical plant, and will give a fine polish as well as economize blacking.

To Clean Nickel.—Clean the nickel or other metal trimmings on stoves with whiting. Mix to a thin paste with aqua ammonia or water, or both. Cover the parts with this and allow it to dry. Afterwards rub it off and polish with dry flannel or polishing cloth.

Or apply baking soda diluted to a thin paste with aqua ammonia.

Care of New Stoves.—A new stove should be heated gradually, and the oven door should be left open for half a day or more before it is used. If a new stove is allowed to become too hot there is danger that it may be cracked or warped. If an oven is overheated the first time it will not retain the heat well afterwards. Ironware of all kinds should first be tempered by gradual heat.

Stove Holders. — Few homemade gifts will be more appreciated than a generous supply of kitchen holders. A half dozen is not too many to have at hand in the kitchen at all times, and two or three times as many should be provided, as there will always be some in the wash. They can be made of odd pieces that would otherwise go to waste. Stove holders containing a thin sheet of asbestos between two pieces of canvas or other cloth are perhaps the best nonconductors. Thin asbestos cloth comes by the yard at a small price, and a single thickness, protected by two pieces of cloth, makes a holder that is quite fireproof.

A large pair of loose mittens of canvas or outing flannel lined with asbestos will be found very useful to take hot dishes out of the oven, and for other use about the stove. Fasten to these a stout cord or piece of tape about 2 feet long, and when much cooking is to be done slip one of them under the apron band or belt. Thus both will be suspended so that they will always be at hand.

Old stocking legs, especially of wool, which is a nonconductor, make good holders. Fold the legs inwardly three times to form a square, stitch across it, and also stitch it diagonally in a crisscross pattern, an inch or two apart, on the sewing machine, to prevent wrinkling in the wash. Two old stockings prepared in this way and stitched together at the sides and ends so as to admit of a removable square of asbestos between make the best kitchen holders. Or they may be covered with strong washable material, as denim or duck. Attach loops of strong tape at one or more corners, or sew on brass curtain rings and hang them on a nail or hook near the stove.

Or cover the holders with pieces of ticking or cretonne or worn-out overalls. Two holders fastened together by a piece of tape about 18 inches long and hung by the apron belt are a great kitchen convenience.

Uses for Asbestos.—Asbestos is a fireproof substance which is found in the earth in a natural state. It has a short fiber, but whether it is of animal or mineral origin is not known. The commercial article can be purchased in the form of cloth or boards of varying degrees of thickness, or mixed with cement in strong, smooth plates. Asbestos is the best protection possible against heat, and has numberless uses in the household. A piece of hard, smooth asbestos board under the range, cook stove, parlor stove, gas stove, or small oil stove, is superior to iron or zinc because it is durable, easier to keep clean, and presents a better appearance. The woodwork near stoves may be protected by the same material, also the collars above stovepipes where they pass through the ceiling and side walls.

Candle lamp shades may be protected by a collar or lining of asbestos; dinner mats, either square or oval, made of two thicknesses of linen, with an opening at one end to admit a square of asbestos, will prevent the hot tea or coffee pot or dishes containing hot food from injuring the tablecloth or the polished surface of the table. Holders of washable material containing a removable square of asbestos are light, fireproof, and convenient, and asbestos mats lined with wire have many uses about the stove. They may be placed in a hot oven to prevent cakes and pies from burning on the bottom, and also on the top of the stove to prevent the contents of kettles and saucepans from burning. A small asbestos mat, wire lined, with a hole cut through the asbestos in the center, but not through the wire, will be found useful for warming milk and other things in cups and small saucepans with rounded bottoms. The heat is applied to the bottom instead of the sides, and the vessel will not tip over.

To Clean Grates.—When stirring the coal or wood in an open grate fire, spread a newspaper in front of the grate, or clear across the hearth if it is a small one, and work while the paper burns. The flames will cause a rushing draught that will carry the dust up the chimney.

Or, to prevent the dust flying, if the fire is out, sprinkle a handful of wet tea leaves over the ashes.

To Clean a Hearth.—Cover grease spots on the hearth with hot ashes or live coals, or sprinkle fuller's earth on the spots. Cover with live coals and brush away after the grease has been absorbed.

To Black a Hearth.—Shave ½ bar of yellow soap into 1 pint of boiling water and stir in ¼ pound of black lead. Boil 10 or 15 minutes, stirring vigorously. Dilute with water if necessary, and apply with a brush.

Or beat up black lead with white of eggs. Lay on with a brush and polish.

Care of Matches.—Keep a stock of matches on a high and dry shelf in a covered earthen jar or tin box with a tight lid where they will be out of the way of children and safe from rats and mice. These animals are fond of phosphorus, and will gnaw match heads if they can, and often set them on fire. Have a covered match safe in each room where they are in frequent use. A match safe fastened to a piece of sandpaper will be found a great convenience. To hold burnt matches, a wineglass suspended with a bit of ribbon and hung on the gas jet or near the stove will be found useful.

To Clean a Gas Range.—Do not black a gas range, but wash the greasy parts in a strong solution of potash lye or sal soda, afterwards thoroughly clean and dry. Do not put blacking or anything else on the burners, as it is likely to clog them and interfere with the flame.

Care of a Gas Range.—Keep the gas stove clean both inside and out. It is not hot enough to burn off or absorb vegetable or animal matter. Hence it should never be blacked, as the blacking is likely to rub off on the clothing. As soon as it is dry and while still warm rub every portion, inside and out, thoroughly with an oily cloth. Use kerosene for this purpose, or a very little lard or suet, but olive oil is probably the most desirable. Do not wash the stove or apply an oily cloth while it is cold or while the burners are in use. To do so will cause rust, cakes of fat, or disagreeable odors when the stove is next lighted.

If the stove is to be detached and stored away, it should be thoroughly cleaned and given a coat of some rust-proof varnish.

Care of Burners. — Never black the top of a perforated or any other burner. Clean it with a damp cloth, and while warm wipe it off with an oily cloth to make the red burned appearance less pronounced. If the burners are removable boil them from time to time in borax water. But some burners cannot be removed unless taken apart. When this is done take care to get the burners back in their right places. Especially the giant or large burner must be attached to its right key or gas outlet, otherwise it will not get the proper flow of gas.

The burners should always be warm when washed, and after being dried should be replaced on their keys, lighted at once, and burned a few seconds or until the flame is clear. If particles that have been released in the pipe leading to the burner lodge in the pipe, tap the pipe leading from the key to the burner. This dislodges the particles and allows the gas to carry them on and out through the burner. When sweeping cover the range well, or else particles of dust may lodge on or in the burners, and be carried into the air mixture, whence they produce flames full of red specks.

Care of Air Mixers.—Just back of the keys in every gas range is a round device with from 3 to 5 slots or openings. This regulates the air supply. These may be called the lungs of the gas stove, since through them the burners take in the air necessary to insure perfect combustion. Hence these parts must be kept free and clear of any accumulation of dirt, or the flame will have a white luminous tip, which will smut pans and lessen the amount of heat. Too much care cannot be taken to keep these air spaces clear and free. They must be frequently wiped out.

Care of the Oven.—Great care must be taken to keep the racks of the oven clean, especially if they are of sheet iron or heavy wire, since they may be utilized in many ways. Remove them occasionally and scrub them with potash lye or strong solution of sal soda by means of a stiff fiber brush. Rinse with boiling water and dry thoroughly before returning to the oven. Never broil anything on the top of the stove, as the unconsumed food and grease will drop down and clog up the burners, and can only be removed by boiling in strong lye.

To clean oven doors lined with aluminum, mix whiting and potash or sal soda with water and scrub by means of a stiff brush. After baking or roasting, wipe out the oven while still warm. Use an old newspaper for this purpose. This will save much future trouble in scrubbing.

To wash the drip trays, take them out while warm, fill them with boiling water in which a little caustic potash or sal soda is dissolved, and scrub with a coarse fiber brush.

To kill the odors of cooking, put a few pieces of charcoal tied with a piece of white cheese cloth in cabbage, onions, or similar dishes. This will be a great help in reducing the odor.

To Light Gas Stoves.—In lighting the top burners do not be in a hurry. Locate the burner you wish to use, and with your eye follow the pipe from the burner down to the keys in front of the range, so as to be sure you turn the proper key. When you turn on the gas count five; meanwhile strike a match. After the fifth count apply the match to the back of the burner, bringing it forward over the burner. This method of lighting is almost sure to prevent the snapping sound sometimes heard.

If spurts of flame are not seen at all the holes in a burner, a slight breath directed across the flames will cause all the jets to light.

To prevent snapping and burning of gas in the air mixers, loosen the front of the air mixer just behind the key, and reduce the opening until the burner can be lighted. There should never be a white tip on the flame.

Waste of Gas.—Turn down the burner as soon as the food begins to cook. When water bubbles the burner should be turned down. It is a common mistake to suppose that when the water in a dish or vessel reaches the boiling point it will continue to get hotter if the gas is left turned on full. In fact, water turns to steam at the boiling point, 212° F., and does not get any hotter, but merely evaporates more quickly; and there is not only waste of gas but additional trouble in replacing the water lost by evaporation, as well as the liability of food burning or cooking into a sticky mass on the bottom of the saucepan. When food begins to cook, the valve or cock can be turned off two thirds. Do not turn on the gas and go hunting for a match in another room. Do not light the burners, and then stop to prepare vegetables or hunt up saucepans. Light the burner just as you reach the range, saucepan in hand, ready to begin cooking, and turn off the gas as soon as the saucepan is removed.

Obtain a set of two semicircular or three triangular saucepans that can be placed on a single burner at the same time. They economize space and gas, as two or three vegetables can be cooked at the same time over the same burner.

Ironing with Gas.—Get a strip of metal large enough to hold four or five flatirons, and heat the irons on this. A single gas burner will heat the metal from end to end, and thus do the work of three or four. The same strip of metal can be used for making griddlecakes. Turn over the irons a metal pan so as to save the top heat, and turn the gas down low. With care, four or five flats can be kept hot at a cost of about ten cents for an ordinary ironing. Do not put flatirons directly over a gas flame, as the watery vapor from the flame will rust and consequently roughen them.

Or get a flatiron heated with gas, which can be connected with rubber gas tubing. Several of these irons are on the market, and with proper adjustment will give satisfactory results.

Broiling with Gas.—To broil with gas, light the burner about ten minutes before the meat is put into the broiling compartment. Take off the excess of fat, wipe the meat with a damp cloth, slice the gristle to keep the edge from curling, and lay the meat on the gridiron as close to the fire as possible. Always leave the broiling-oven door open to prevent the meat from taking fire.

Put a little water in the drip pan to catch and cool the melted fat.

DISHWASHING

There is no single operation of housekeeping in which system will save so much time as in dishwashing. System is only force of habit and soon becomes second nature. The following suggestions are condensed from the practical experience of a large number of intelligent housewives.

(1) Wash the cooking utensils as soon as the food is emptied out of them and before it is placed on the table. Or, if this is not convenient, fill them with hot water and leave

them to soak. (2) After the meal is finished, and before clearing the table, prepare a place in the kitchen to receive the soiled dishes. (3) Scrape off all bits of food into one dish, using preferably a good plate scraper of sheet rubber. This will remove all food and grease, and will not injure the most delicate china. If greasy dishes are not scraped, the dishwater will become too foul, and it will be difficult to wash or wipe the dishes clean. Greasy dishwater also makes the sink difficult to clean, and tends to stop up the spout. If a little lye is scattered over very greasy dishes, it will cleanse them readily by partially transforming the grease into soap. Be careful not to use lye strong enough to injure the skin. (4) Sort the dishes and stack them up in an orderly way, with the smallest articles on top; place the glass, small china articles, silver, and other delicate pieces together; next, cups and saucers, sauce dishes and the like, and finally plates, platters, and larger objects. (5) Load these lots on a large tray in the above order, carry them to the kitchen, and keep them separate until they are washed, wiped, and put away. This method saves frequent steps to the kitchen as well as confusion in sorting them there. Lay a newspaper or piece of wrapping paper over a large pan, scrape all the garbage into that, and if possible burn it in the range. Or use a small garbage burner. Or obtain a good, odorless garbage can that can be thoroughly disinfected and cleaned. Keep at hand a grease kettle in which to preserve scraps of grease. Sprinkle a little lye on the most greasy cooking utensils, as skillets, iron kettles, and platters, and rinse them into the grease pot. The lye will keep the grease sweet and assist in the process of soap making. Save the tea leaves to be used for sweeping. (6) Next prepare a suds with soap or any washing compound. Borax is good. Wash first in hot suds the silver, glass, and delicate china, using a swab with a long wooden handle. Wipe the silver as soon as it is washed. Put the glass and china in a wire basket, and pour hot water over them. (7) Place the second lot of dishes—cups and saucers, vegetable and side dishes—in the dishwater, and allow them to soak while the first lot are being wiped. (8) Add hot water if necessary, wash the second lot of dishes, set them in the drainer, and place the third lot in the suds, or make new suds for it if necessary. (9) Next make fresh suds for milk pans, if any, and other tinware. Finally, wash the ironware—roaster, gridiron, pots, and kettles. Use for this purpose a little lye and scrape with a stiff fiber brush.

Conveniences for Dishwashing.—The process of dishwashing will be much simplified if a large bench or table can be arranged to stand beside the sink, with the china cabinet or pantry for the ordinary tableware placed just above it. In many modern kitchens (especially in city apartment houses) an arrangement which is ideal allows the dishwasher to wash, dry, and put away most of the dishes without leaving the sink. The time and steps lost in walking from the sink to the table, even if but a few feet distant, and thence to pantry or closet, is a waste of energy that can never be justified. If, for any reason, a permanent bench or table cannot be placed near the sink, get a movable folding table like a sewing table, or a shelf arranged to let down against the wall. A small shelf or cupboard above the sink to contain soap, borax, washing powder, and various utensils will be found convenient.

The sink should be placed high enough so that the dishes may be washed without stooping. The top of the adjacent table should be slightly above and overlapping the sink, and with just enough slope to let the water drain back into it. Or a small cleat may be tacked on the edges of the table, front and back, projecting about a quarter of an inch, and the whole covered with oilcloth. This will let the drainage water flow back into the sink, and the top of the table can be easily kept both dry and clean.

Provide a strong stool, high enough to allow sitting down at the sink to pare vegetables and for other purposes.

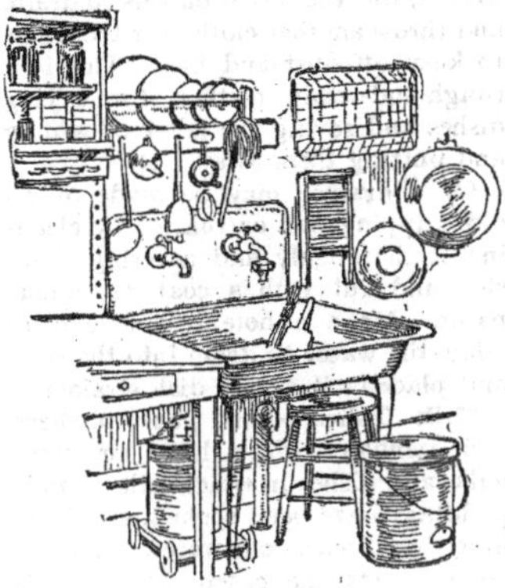

"Air is Admitted to Every Part."

Convenient utensils are: a swab made by fastening strips of linen or cotton to the end of a wooden handle; a small brush, like a nail brush, and a larger scrubbing brush for cleaning vegetables; a soap shaker, which may be homemade; a pot scraper, which may be an ordinary clam shell; and a wire dish drainer, either bought or homemade, which may be hung on a neighboring wall. A closet under the sink is not advisable. It is better to have the plumbing exposed and paint the under portion of the sink white, or cover it with white enamel. This may be done by any member of the family. The wall behind the sink should be protected by zinc, and if the table is covered with zinc instead of oilcloth, so much the better.

Or a curtain of any soft, cheap material may be hung against the wall so that the lower edge will just reach the table top. This should be of washable material so that it can be changed weekly. A line of strong cord or picture wire should be strung near at hand to hold the dishcloths and towels. The garbage can may be placed under the sink or to the right. A three-cornered wire drainer, fastened in the corner of the sink, will be found convenient to receive vegetable parings, and also to strain the dishwater. A small shovel of cast iron, similar in shape to a fire shovel, will be a great convenience to lift scraps from the sink to the garbage can.

Have one or more wood fiber brushes to clean dishes, kettles, and pans. The fibers are stiffer than bristles, and hence do more effective work. A whisk or two will clean an empty potato or gravy kettle as soon as the vessel is emptied. A convenient size for brush is 2 by 2½ inches.

Washboard.—Hang beside the sink a small washboard. Use this to rub out dishcloths, and to keep towels sweet and clean.

Hinged Table.—A hinged table or bench that can be let down, and lifted up against the wall when not in use, is often convenient in a small kitchen, or where an ordinary table would be in the way. Have this bench or table just high enough to let down over one's lap when sitting in a chair. A great deal of work can thus be done sitting.

Or use an ordinary collapsible sewing table for this purpose.

Dishwashing Machines.—Many unsuccessful attempts were made in the past to invent dishwashing machines. Some of these took more time to clean than was required to wash the dishes themselves. Good ones can now be purchased, however, that will wash the dishes not only quicker, but better, than by the old-fashioned way. These machines are simple in construction, are easily cleaned, and, if given proper attention, will last many years. They are constructed with a galvanized iron cylinder, which is to be half filled with water containing any good washing compound and brought to a boil. The dishes are put in a cylindrical basket or tray, the plates and platters placed on edge and held by brackets. Saucers, cups, and side dishes are placed beside them, the basket is lowered into the cylinder, revolved two or three times by means of a crank, reversed, and the dishes are cleansed. The tray is then taken out, and if the dishes are scalded with boiling water, very little wiping will be required. When we reflect that in many families of average size upward of three hours a day are devoted to washing dishes, or that approximately one fifth of the waking moments of thousands of intelligent women are occupied in this manner, we cannot but earnestly urge the average family to make whatever sacrifices may be necessary to provide the housewife with this and all other improved labor-saving devices. This, we think, will also be found a key to the solution of the much-vexed problem of domestic help.

Dish Draining.—If the table be covered with oilcloth or zinc, the edges raised, and the whole slightly tilted so as to empty into the sink, a wire basket may be the only dish strainer required. A homemade article may be prepared from an ordinary soap box by lining the bottom with zinc. A cleat may be tacked on the bottom at one end to tilt the box, and by boring auger holes a slit may be made at the opposite end to allow the water to escape. Place this dish drainer on the table in such a way that the open end will project over the sink. Through holes bored at intervals in the sides of the box thrust old broomsticks or other rods to hold plates and saucers upright to dry. Cover the box with oilcloth or stain it to match the kitchen woodwork.

Or an old dish pan may be used by perforating the bottom with holes by means of a hammer and round wire nails. Place the draining basket, pan, or box to the left of the dish pan to avoid unnecessary handling. If the handles are front and back, as you face the dish pan you will have fewer pieces of nicked china. If lye is used, and the dishwater is fairly hot and soapy, dishes rinsed with cold water will dry in the rack bright and shiny and not require wiping.

Or, if thoroughly rinsed with hot water, they may be allowed to dry in the same way.

Or, if the table is not wanted for immediate use, lay a large dry cloth over it, put the dishes on this to drain, and throw another cloth over the whole to keep off dust and flies. This is a rough-and-ready method for drying dishes and saving the labor of wiping and putting them away.

Or a drainer may be made of an old dripping pan or roaster by cleaning it thoroughly and covering it inside and out with a coat of enamel paint. Make a hole in one end to allow the water to drain into the sink, and place in it a wire dish strainer.

Milk Dishes.—Milk pans, pitchers, and tumblers which have contained milk, and dishes in which milk or milk puddings have been cooked, should be first rinsed with cold water. Hot water converts the casein of the milk into a kind of cement or glue which is hard to remove.

Milk Cans.—These should be filled with cold water and allowed to soak. Put them away from the stove. Rinsing with cold water will assist in keeping the milk dishes sweet and prevent the milk from souring. Afterwards pour out the cold water, wash in hot soapsuds or borax water, rinse, and scald.

To Remove Odors.—Dishes which have been used to cook fish or cabbage, or anything else having a disagreeable odor, may be cleansed by first washing them and then rinsing them with powdered charcoal.

Or set the dish after washing in a warm oven for ten or fifteen minutes.

Or fill the dish with boiling water and drop into it a piece of charcoal. A lump of charcoal left in a closed bottle or jar will keep it from becoming musty. The water in which cabbage has been cooked should not be poured down the sink, or, if this must be done, the sink should be rinsed with water containing powdered charcoal or a little chloride of lime.

A new wooden vessel, as a pail, a keg, or a churn, will often communicate a woody taste to food, whether solid or liquid. To prevent this, scald the vessel with boiling water and let it stand to soak until cold. Then wash well with a strong lye of wood ashes or caustic potash containing a small quantity of slacked lime. Repeat if necessary. Scald with hot water, and rinse with cold.

Sleeve Protectors.—An old pair of stockings may be converted into useful sleeve protectors by cutting off the feet and hemming the cut edge. These may be drawn over the sleeves of a clean gown if necessary when washing dishes. They are also useful in other kinds of housework.

Dishcloths.—Unravel coarse manila rope and use the loose mass as a dishcloth. This is especially useful for cleansing cooking, tin and ironware utensils; also for scouring and scrubbing table shelves, paint, sinks, and other rough surfaces.

Or save cloth flour sacks, sugar, salt, and corn-meal bags, and use them as dishcloths, dusters, etc. They keep white and last longer than ordinary towel stuff. To wash flour sacks, turn them wrong side out and dust the flour from them; afterwards wash in cold water. Hot water will make a paste of the flour.

Or use cheese cloth for both washing and wiping dishes. This is better than crash, especially for drying silver and glassware.

Or use scrim or cotton underwear crocheted about the edge, or folded and hemmed double.

Or make dishcloths of worn dish towels.

Or use the fiber of the so-called dishrag gourd, the seeds of which may be obtained from any seedman.

Or try grass toweling. This is, of course, fibrous material, which is easily rinsed.

Best of all for many purposes is a small dish mop which permits of the use of boiling hot water and strong washing powder. With a little practice, the hands may be kept out of the water altogether.

Dishcloths—Care of.—The dishcloth must be kept clean. A greasy dishcloth affords a breeding place for the germs of diphtheria, typhoid, and other filth diseases. Wash in soapsuds and rinse in cold water, or add lemon juice and salt to the water, or a teaspoonful of kerosene.

Dish Towels.—Any of the above fabrics recommended for dishcloths may be used for dish toweling. Large flour sacks are the right size. So are old pillow slips cut in halves, or dish towels may be made from old sheets.

Or cut up old garments of outing flannel, which has great absorbent qualities, to the size of dish towels. Hem, and add tape hangers.

Or make hangers of lamp wicking.

Or use blue and white striped ticking from old pillow cases.

Dish Towels—Care of.—Two or three dish towels should be used at each meal, and these should be washed in soap and water, rinsed and hung to dry, rather than allowed to dry when soiled with more or less greasy dishwater.

Hanging Towels.—Roller towels are perhaps most convenient and satisfactory for kitchen use, but if these are not used, sew tape hangers at each end of common towels so that they can be turned about when one end is soiled and worn equally at both ends.

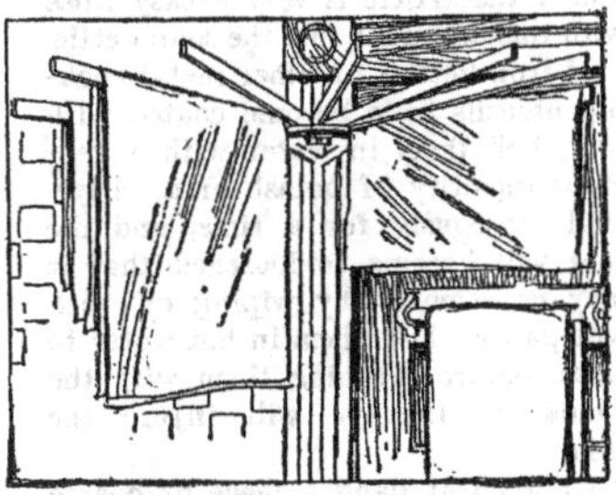

"The Best Towel Racks."

Or make hangers of small lamp wicks, one at each end, turning the ends in with the hem. Keep a stock of half a dozen or more dish towels and hanging towels, and mark them

1, 2, 3, 4, 5, 6. This makes it easy to account for them and to use them in rotation.

CARE OF KITCHEN WARES

To Keep Ironware Clean.—Rub soap thickly on the bottom of an iron kettle or saucepan which is placed directly over the fire of a coal range; this will prevent the soot burning on. Lard or other grease may also be used, but is not so good.

To Clean Cooking Utensils.—After emptying food from cooking utensils, do not take them off the range dry. Pour a little water in them, cover closely, and set them back on the range. If a steady fire is kept the steam will loosen any fragments of food so that the utensils will be very easily washed.

Or, if possible, take them to the sink and wash them immediately before placing the food on the table. They will never be easier to clean than now, and thus the most difficult part of dishwashing will be out of the way before the table dishes are brought in. Keep a can of lye dissolved in water, and if the article is very greasy rinse with this and pour into the soap kettle.

If iron kettles or other metal cooking utensils have become coated with soot, boil them in water with a generous quantity of potash or soda lye. Boil vigorously for a time, and the soot will become so loosened that it may be removed by wiping off with soft paper. Dip them in hot water to rinse, before touching them with the hands, as the lye will injure the skin.

Or keep at hand a piece of coarse sandpaper and with it rub kettles in which food is burned on. Or use a clam shell as a scraper. This is better and more convenient than a knife. Or scour with finely sifted coal ashes and a flannel rag.

A frying pan should not be scraped. Fill it with cold water containing a teaspoonful of sal soda, and let it stand until the dishes are washed for the next meal.

To Remove Rust from Ironware.—Cover the rusted article with grease, and set it in a hot oven for half an hour. Afterwards wash with soap and water, and the rust will be removed.

Copper Ware.—Copper kettles should not be used unless they are perfectly bright and clean. To polish copper ware, apply hot salt and vinegar, and scrub with a stiff nail brush. Or rub with flannel dipped in hot water and sprinkled thickly with powdered borax.

Or dip a cloth in kerosene or gasoline, sprinkle it with a mixture of bath brick or ground pumice, and polish. For large copper boilers or other utensils which are not used for the preparation of food, apply with a damp cloth or nail brush a saturated solution of oxalic acid in its own bulk of water, and scour with bath brick and pumice stone softened with olive oil. It must, of course, be borne in mind that *oxalic acid is a deadly poison.*

Enameled Ware.—Scraping ruins enameled ware. Utensils of this ware placed directly over the flame of a coal range should be protected by rubbing the bottoms thickly with soap. Any soot which burns on may then be removed by soap and water. If food burns in any enameled-ware utensils, put into them a teaspoonful of sal soda or caustic lye to a quart of water and boil for fifteen minutes. This will soften the burned food so that it can be removed without scraping. If not quite clean, scour with fine sand soap. For discolored saucepans boil a little chloride of lime in the water. Or boil in them a strong solution of baking soda.

Various Utensils.—After using the egg beater rinse it in cold water before it gets time to dry.

Before using the food chopper, run a piece of suet through it, and follow with another piece after the food has been chopped. This will keep it clean and in good condition.

Run rice or bread crumbs through the spice mill after grinding orange or lemon peel, or the coffee mill may be used for this purpose and cleaned in the same way.

Dip the colander, sieve, or grater in a pan of water to prevent drying, and afterwards clean with a stiff vegetable brush. Rinse and dry.

Fur on Kettles.—To prevent fur from gathering on the inside of a teakettle, put an oyster shell or piece of marble inside. Change this occasionally.

To remove this furry deposit from heavy iron kettles, fill with water, add a large spoonful of sal ammoniac, and bring to a boil. Empty the kettle and let it stand over the fire until very hot, when the fur will peel off. Afterwards fill with water containing sal soda, boil, and rinse.

The furry deposit may also be dissolved in a weak solution of muriatic or acetic acid, but it must be remembered that these are *deadly poisons.* Immediately fill the kettle with water, add 2 to 4 ounces of hyposulphide of soda or baking soda; and boil. Let this stand in the kettle for two or three days, and afterwards rinse with boiling water.

Teakettle.—Put an oyster shell in the teakettle to prevent its becoming incrusted with lime. Polish occasionally with a woolen rag moistened with kerosene.

Tinware.—To cleanse tinware moisten either brick dust or whiting with aqua ammonia, kerosene, or washing soda. Care must be taken not to use lye in cleaning tins, as it will injure them.

To Prevent Rust on Tinware.—After washing and wiping tinware, place it on the back of the range or other warm place until it is thoroughly dry. To protect new tinware rub lard over every part of the tin and set it in the oven until it is heated through. This makes the tin permanently rust proof.

To Prepare New Tins.—New tins are often covered with rosin or other substances which should be removed before using. Fill with boiling water and add sal soda or aqua ammonia at the rate of a tablespoonful to each quart of water. Boil and afterwards scour.

To Wash Tinware.—Fill greasy tins with water, add a tablespoonful of sal soda, and place on the back part of the range. Or use hot water containing a teaspoonful of aqua ammonia.

To Scour Tins.—Use sifted coal ashes moistened with kerosene. Or use whiting with kerosene. Or fine sand, or bath brick, followed by whiting. Or polish with brown paper moistened in vinegar. Damp flannel or dry chamois may be used for polishing tinware. Afterwards wash in soapsuds, rinse, and dry.

To Clean Coffeepots.—Rub salt on the inside of a coffeepot to remove coffee and egg. Rinse quickly and thoroughly.

To Clean Wash Boilers.—If rusty, grease with lard and wash off with sweet milk. Dry thoroughly before storing away.

To Clean Earthenware.—To clean earthenware articles, as pots or jars, yellow-ware bowls, pie plates, etc., put them in a kettle with cold water, ashes, and sal soda, bring to a boil, and after boiling let them stand twenty-four hours in the lye.

Or fill the vessels with hot lime water and let them stand twenty-four hours.

Or scour, rinse, and wash with soapsuds. Afterwards scour with charcoal powder and fill with water containing lumps of charcoal. This will remove all lingering odors.

To Repair Cracked Articles.—If earthenware or china articles begin to crack, put in them a tablespoonful of sugar and half a tumberful of water, and set over a brisk fire. Paint the inside of the vessel, especially the cracks, with the melted sugar. The sirup will enter the cracks and act as a cement. This can be used for pie plates and other earthenware utensils used in cooking.

Earthenware baking dishes in which food is burned on should not be scraped. Put in the vessel a little ashes or borax or baking soda, and fill with cold water. Set on the stove and raise slowly to a boil. Set aside to cool, and wash with hot soapsuds and a small stiff brush. Scald and wipe dry.

To remove brown stains from custard cups, pie plates, and the like, use dry whiting applied with a damp flannel, or bath brick, scouring sand, or pumice. A piece of zinc shaped like the corner of a square tin is a great convenience in cleaning the corners of baking dishes and similar utensils. Punch a hole in it and hang it on a neighboring wall.

Tea and Coffee Pots.—Metal tea and coffee pots, if allowed to stand for a time, often get a musty odor. To prevent this, put a lump of dry sugar in them before putting them away. This absorbs the dampness which produces must. To clean and brighten the inside of these articles, fill with water and add a piece of hard soap. Boil for half an hour.

Or rub on a little salt and immediately rinse thoroughly.

Kettle Lids.—When these lose their handles, substitute a small block of wood by driving a screw through a tin into the lid from beneath.

Wooden Ware.—Do not wash the bread board, wooden bread platter, or rolling-pin in hot water. Wash with warm soapsuds and rinse in clean cold water.

Copper Ware.—Copper ware was formerly quite generally used for cooking utensils, and especially for large kettles, because of its durability. This ware is now being largely replaced by aluminum ware, which is equally durable, much lighter, and free from danger.

If copper-ware utensils are used it must be borne in mind that they are acted upon by moisture and by the fatty acids contained in fats and oils, the result being a carbonate of copper, and also by acetic acid contained in vinegar, the result being acetate of copper or verdigris. Both of these are deadly poisons, hence when copper vessels are used to cook food or for other purposes they should be immediately emptied and cleaned. Wipe them dry and keep in a dry place. They should be again cleaned before they are used, by scrubbing with hot salt and vinegar, and afterwards scalding with boiling water.

Or use hot buttermilk and salt for this purpose.

To Clean Japanned Ware.—Trays and other articles of japanned ware are quite commonly used, as they are light, cheap, and convenient. They must not be washed in hot water, strong suds, or water containing free alkali in any form, as sal soda, caustic lye, and the like, or with washing powders concerning which we know little. These take off the lacquer and may cause the ware to chip and scale. Wash them with a sponge or soft cloth in suds made of hard white or other neutral soap and cold or warm water. Afterwards wipe dry and sprinkle with flour. Polish with a dry cloth or chamois skin. Do not let them stand to drain dry or to dry by evaporation, as they may be stained. Never put hot articles on them.

To remove the white marks left by heat or water stains, apply sweet oil with a flannel cloth or sponge and afterwards rub with alcohol.

CARE OF GLASSWARE AND CUT GLASS

To Wash Glassware.—Glass is a very poor conductor of heat, and more valuable glass articles are broken by hot water, perhaps, than in any other way. To prevent this various precautions may be used. Place the glass on a steel knife blade, or put a silver spoon inside. The most delicate glassware can be washed in hot water if slipped in edgewise, outside or concave side first, and quickly and completely immersed. Once make this a rule, and it soon becomes a matter of habit.

Or first immerse the glassware in lukewarm water and increase the temperature by adding hot water gradually.

Or use tepid water with soda, or clear cold water.

Chamois may be used to dry glassware, or any cloth, such as scrim, which does not have a nap.

Many persons prefer to wash glassware in hot soapsuds.

Glassware which has been used for milk should be first rinsed in cold water, as hot water causes the milk to adhere and gives the glass a cloudy appearance.

Cut Glass.—Wash cut-glass articles, one piece at a time, in warm suds made of castile or other fine white soap, and rinse in warm water containing a few drops of aqua ammonia. Save old silk handkerchiefs or other pieces of white wash silk to dry cut glass, or use a soft linen towel. Dry without draining. Polish with a soft-haired brush, such as is used by jewelers. This will penetrate every part of the pattern. A still more brilliant result can be produced by dusting the article while wet with jeweler's sawdust. This can be brushed off when dry and used repeatedly. It may be obtained of any jeweler.

To Clean Bottles.—Various substances and a number of ingenious methods are employed to clean water bottles, wine decanters, milk bottles, and medicine bottles, the inside of which cannot be reached by ordinary methods. Among these are heavy articles as tacks and shot, or lighter ones, as crushed eggshells, raw potatoes chopped fine, bits of cloth or paper to dislodge dirt and for mechanical cleansing. Also lye and various acids, as lemon juice, sour milk, and dilute hydrochloric acid.

For coarse and heavy articles, like glass milk bottles and fruit jars, use a handful of carpet tacks or common shot. Fill the jar or bottle half full of soapsuds, add the tacks or shot, and shake well. If tacks are used their sharp edges will scrape off the dirt, but will also scratch the bottle. Hence they are not suitable for wine or vinegar cruets, whether of plain or cut glass. If shot is used care must be taken that none of them are suffered to remain in the cruets, or in bottles used to contain any acid, as the action of acid upon lead produces a deadly poison.

Or use one tablespoonful of crushed eggshells in the same manner. If the bottle is greasy wash with warm water and a little soda, or run a raw potato through the meat chopper, put it in a bottle of warm water, and shake until clean. This is one of the most effective cleansers known.

Or cut into fine pieces white or brown paper or blotting paper and use with warm soapsuds. Or use a swab of cotton at the end of a long stick or wire.

To Clean with Lye.—Clean medicine bottles, vinegar cruets, fruit jars, milk bottles, and all but the most delicate glassware by putting in each a tablespoonful of wood or coal ashes. Immerse them in cold water, and gradually heat the water until it boils. Afterwards wash in soapsuds, and rinse in clear water.

Or use a tablespoonful of dissolved potash, or soda lye.

To Clean Cut Glass and Fine Glassware.—Cut glass and very fine glass water bottles, decanters, and vases may be cleaned by first placing the decanter on a steel knife blade, or dropping into it a piece of silver, and then pouring into it equal quantities of hot vinegar and salt. When the decanter has become warm put in the stopper and shake thoroughly.

Or put in two tablespoonfuls of vinegar and a tablespoonful of baking soda. This will effervesce vigorously. Hold the article over the sink, but do not put in the cork, or the vessel may burst.

Or fill with buttermilk, let stand forty-eight hours, and wash in soapsuds.

Or rinse with a weak solution of muriatic acid.

To Clean Vases.—When the inside of a glass or other delicate vase becomes discolored and stained from flower stems, put a little water into the vase and add several slices of lemon, including the rind. Let stand a day or two. Rinse with clear water.

To Sweeten Musty Bottles.—Rinse

with water containing one or two teaspoonfuls of powdered charcoal, or rinse with a dilute solution of sulphuric acid at the rate of about two ounces of acid to a pint of water.

To Wipe Glass.—Glassware should be wiped dry as soon as it is lifted from the water without waiting for it to drain. For glassware use scrim or towels which have no lint.

Or rinse the articles with cold water and allow them to dry without wiping. They will be much clearer than if wiped with a cloth.

To Polish Glassware.—Save all tissue paper to polish glassware. Or save scraps of chamois. Cut these into inch squares and string on twine with a darning needle as beads are strung. Use this to polish glassware.

STEEL KNIVES AND FORKS

Carving knives and forks, steel-blade knives used for roasts and game, and kitchen knives require special care to keep them in good order. Wrap the best knives and forks in cotton batting or strips of cotton flannel or outing flannel. Each dozen of knives and forks may be rolled up in a separate strip, or pockets may be made for them of suitable material in which they may be slipped and put away out of the reach of dampness.

To prevent rust when not in use rub the steel with sweet oil or olive oil. Dampen a cloth with the oil and wipe them lightly so as to give them a thin coating before putting away. Or put powdered quicklime in a small cheesecloth bag and dust steel knives and forks with this before they are wrapped up and put away.

Or keep in the pantry a deep box or earthen jar containing fine, dry sand and plunge the blades into this when not in use. This will prevent rust and all necessity of scouring.

To Wash.—Steel knives and forks should never be allowed to stand long before cleaning, but should be washed as soon as possible after being used. The fatty acids contained in grease, and the fruit acids contained in salad dressings, vinegar, tarts, etc., will etch and stain the metal until they are removed. Collect the steel knives and forks as soon as the dishes are cleared away and soak them in a vessel of hot water. Wash in hot suds and water and then polish.

To Scour.—Brick dust, pumice stone, rotten stone, sifted wood or coal ashes, baking soda, and bath brick are all recommended for cleaning steel knives.

Make a bag of two pieces of old carpet, one 6 inches square and the other about 2 inches longer. Place the faces together and bind the edges with cloth or tape, leaving one end open with a 2-inch flap to fold over and fasten with a button. Fill this bag one fourth full of brick dust, shake well, and polish the knives in this. They will thus be cleaned on both sides at once.

Or cut a raw potato in half and dip in brick dust or other cleanser, and with it rub the knives and forks.

Or rub with a cloth moistened with kerosene and dipped in the dry cleanser.

Or use the same as brick dust powdered charcoal, rotten stone, water, lime, or sifted wood or coal ashes.

To Remove Rust.—Moisten a rag with kerosene oil, dip it in dry brick dust and rub the knives with it.

Ivory-handled Knives.—Keep the ivory and bone handles of steel-bladed knives out of water, especially hot water. After they have been used, set them in a deep dish or pitcher so that the water will cover the blades but will not touch the handles. Do not have the water too hot, or the part which runs up into the handle will expand and crack the bone or ivory.

After washing the blades with soap and water, wipe the handles with a damp cloth.

To Fasten Knife Handles.—If a bone or an ivory handle comes off the knife, mix a little plaster of Paris with water to a thin paste, pour it into the hole in the handle, insert the blade, and when cold it will be solid.

Or fill the hole with powdered alum.

Heat the steel end quite hot and push it into the hole. When cold it will be firmly fastened.

To Bleach Ivory Knife Handles.—For whitening ivory the bleaching action of sunshine on a moist surface is recommended. Spirits of turpentine, alum, lime, potash, prepared chalk, ammonia, lemon juice, and pumice stone are also used.

Make a paste of prepared chalk with aqua ammonia and olive oil. Cover the articles with this, and when dry rub it off. Repeat if necessary. Or rub with a cloth moistened in turpentine. Or moisten a cloth in vinegar dipped in brick dust, and rub. Or dip half a lemon in salt and rub; afterwards rinse in warm water. Or make a paste of slacked lime and water, apply with a wet cloth, and rub off when dry. Or use a mixture of whiting and potash lye.

CARE OF SILVERWARE

The problems connected with the care of silverware are the daily cleaning, the daily and weekly polishing, the prevention of stains and discolorations, and the removal of these when formed. It is advisable to have a regular time for polishing silver each week, according to the convenience of the housewife. In many households this is done on Saturday with other cleaning, as a part of the general preparation for Sunday when guests are often entertained and it is desirable to have the silver looking its best.

To Pack and Store Silver.—Silverware which is not in daily use should be protected from contact with the air, which often contains traces of sulphureted hydrogen or marsh gas. This is the great enemy of silver. It occurs in illuminating gas, sewer gas, and many other compounds, and contaminates the atmosphere. Retail jewelers prevent the discoloration of silver which is exposed for sale in shop windows by coating the articles with collodion diluted with alcohol. Collodion may be obtained at any drug store or from a dealer in photographic supplies. To apply it first wash the articles, dry them, and heat them slightly over the fire. Apply the collodion with a wide, soft brush, laying it on in quick, even strokes.

Collodion is a very quick dryer, hence it is necessary to have all the silver heated and in readiness and to work quickly. Care must be taken to cover every part of the surface. One coating is sufficient. Collodion is perfectly transparent, hence does not injure the appearance of the articles, and may be removed by washing in hot water. This is perhaps the most perfect protection for silverware that has to be stored for any length of time.

Or pack the silverware in wooden starch boxes or other boxes of convenient size and cover them with dry flour. This will prevent them from tarnishing. When the flour is wiped off they will be polished and in readiness for use.

Or prepare cloth bags or pockets for silverware. Use for this purpose unbleached outing flannel, cotton flannel, or other unbleached goods. The bleaching powders and other preparations of chlorine used in whitening fabrics will discolor silverware.

Or wrap the articles in blue or other dark-colored tissue paper. White paper, like bleached fabrics, contains chemicals which discolor silver.

Or wrap the articles in green baize, which does not attract moisture. Place in each pocket or drawer in which silver is kept a lump of gum camphor. This is the best preventive against tarnish.

The best material with which to line the drawers of serving tables, trays, or boxes for silverware, or of which to make bags or pockets, is chamois skin. If the outside of the chamois skin is treated with melted white wax or beeswax applied with a soft brush and afterwards run over lightly with a hot iron, it will be nearly air-tight.

Silverware Pockets. — The most convenient method of disposing of silver for daily use is a wide, shallow drawer in a serving table or sideboard, and with or without racks and trays to receive the individual pieces of silverware. The drawer should be lined with chamois skin, velvet, or flannel, and the silverware ranged in it in orderly fashion.

Or silverware pockets may be made of outing flannel and tacked on the back of the cupboard or pantry door. Take a strip of material the width of the door and about 18 inches deep.

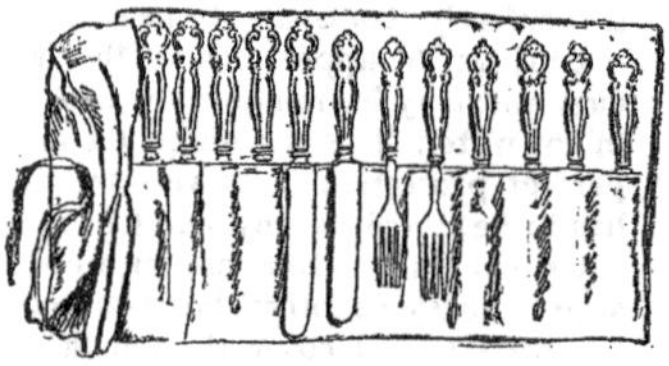

"Or Silverware Pockets May Be Made."

Fold the lower part upon the upper, leaving room for a wide hem or heading at the top. Stitch down the folded part on the sewing machine, leaving separate pockets for knives, forks, and other articles. Face the heading with a strip of canvas or other heavy material as a stay when tacking to the woodwork.

Or make a similar pocket with a lapel at the top instead of a hem. Fold or roll up in this the silver which is to be put away.

To Wash Silver.—To wash silver prepare suds with boiling water, in which dissolve about an ounce of hard white soap to a quart of water, and add a teaspoonful of soda. Into this put the silver pieces and boil them for a few minutes. Pour off the suds, pour over them clean boiling water, wipe them dry on a clean towel without draining, and polish with a piece of chamois skin.

To Polish Silver.—All plate and silverware which is in regular use and not stored in such a way as to proteet it from discoloration should be carefully polished once a week. It is best to have a regular time for this purpose. Never use sand or scouring soaps, pumice stone, or gritty washing powders for silverware, or any other polishes the nature of which you do not understand. Many of them will scratch the silver, and others will discolor it.

Articles recommended for polishing silver if not much stained are whiting—either fluid, dry, or moistened with alcohol or sweet oil—prepared chalk, cream of tartar, milk, or a solution of alum.

To apply these use chamois skin or velveteen. Or use pieces of old woolen or flannel underwear or pieces of old linen tablecloths.

Or apply with an old toothbrush or a nailbrush with soft bristles.

Or prepare and have ready polishing cloths as follows: dissolve half a cupful of scraps of castile or toilet soaps, or any hard white soap, in a cupful of water, and allow to cool. This will make a soft-soap jelly. Stir into this when cold 3 heaping tablespoonfuls of powdered whiting. In this soak suitable pieces of cloth, as old flannel underwear, pieces of tablecloths, and the like, letting them absorb as much as possible. Wring them out so they will not drip, and allow them to dry. These are convenient polishing cloths for silver, as they are always ready.

Or moisten whiting with soapy water, rub it over the silver carefully, and allow it to dry on. Then rub it off with a very soft woolen or linen cloth. Use a soft brush to remove the whiting from carvings or deep cuttings and rough surfaces of the larger silver articles.

Caution.—Care must be taken in polishing silver not to use too much force, as severe rubbing will wear solid silver and soon wear out the best of plated articles.

To Remove Stains and Discolorations.—Methods recommended for cleaning discolored silver are boiling in suds or in water containing soda, sal soda, alum, cream of tartar, borax, or lye, or rubbing with dry salt, whiting, grated potatoes, or solutions of sulphuric acid, chloride of lime, alum, or cream of tartar.

To Boil Tarnished Silver.—If the silver is much tarnished, boil for five minutes in water containing a mixture of equal parts of cream of tartar, common salt, and alum, using 1 teaspoonful of each to 1 pint of water.

Or use a strong solution of washing soda, 2 teaspoonfuls to 1 quart of water.

Or put 1 tablespoonful of borax or potash lye in 2 quarts of water, put in the silver and boil five minutes, or longer if necessary. Pour off the liquid, rinse the silver in boiling water, and polish. This method will be found a quick and easy way to cleanse a communion set or other set of numerous pieces.

To Polish Tarnished Silver.—After boiling tarnished silver, if necessary apply with a sponge or rag powdered whiting moistened with sweet oil or alcohol. Rub over the articles thoroughly with this and allow it to dry on. Afterwards rub it off with a soft cloth and polish with chamois leather.

Or use prepared chalk and alcohol. If the articles are carved or rough, use a soft bristle brush to remove the cleanser.

Or, if silver is badly tarnished, moisten whiting with ammonia, or polish with a cloth dipped in ammonia water or in a mixture of 1 teaspoonful of ammonia water and 10 teaspoonfuls of vinegar. But use the ammonia with caution, as it tends to dull the luster of the finest silver.

Or use whiting moistened with vinegar.

Or polish with flannel dipped in kerosene and afterwards in dry whiting.

Or, to remove stains that remain after boiling, take a piece of raw potato dipped in common baking soda.

Or dissolve 1 tablespoonful of alum and 1 ounce of hard white soap in 1 pint of water, and apply by rubbing.

Or the burned-out hood or mantel of a Welsbach gas burner is one of the most effective silver polishes. Drop the hood into a tin spice can or other small covered can or jar, and pulverize it with the fingers. It will fall to pieces at a touch. Moisten a cloth with water and apply the pulverized ash to the tarnished spots. One hood will clean about two dozen knives, forks, or spoons.

Or put all the silver in a shallow pan, cover with sour milk or buttermilk, and let it lie until it is bright. Afterwards wash in soapsuds and polish.

To Remove Egg Stains.—The sulphur contained in eggs speedily discolors any silver that comes in contact with it. The air is also contaminated from the sulphur in illuminating gas, other gaslights, or gas cook stoves, and from rubber. Hence silver should be kept from contact with these or any other sulphur compound. A small piece of camphor put with the silver will prevent it from staining. To remove the stains moisten a cloth in water and dip it in dry table salt. Rub with this and polish.

Or wash them in water in which potatoes have been boiled.

To Remove Medicine Stains.—Iodine and other ingredients in certain medicines may stain silver spoons. To remove such stains, rub them with a piece of cloth dipped in dilute sulphuric acid—1 part of acid to 10 parts of water. Apply the acid with a swab made by winding a bit of linen about the end of a stick, as it will injure the skin. Wash immediately afterwards with soap and water.

Silver fittings of inkstands and other silver articles often become discolored with ink. The most effective cleanser is a paste made by moistening chloride of lime with water. Rub it on the stains until they disappear. Afterwards wash with soap and water containing a little ammonia and polish.

Silver Cleansers. — For cleaning jewelry manufacturing and retail jewelers use various mixtures which are safe and reliable. If these can be obtained they are often the most satisfactory cleansers of any.

Or mix 2 ounces of jeweler's rouge with 6 ounces of prepared chalk.

Or mix 4 ounces of prepared chalk

or whiting, ¼ ounce of gum camphor, ½ ounce of alcohol, and 2 ounces of benzine. Allow this to dry on the silver before polishing.

Or mix 4 ounces of prepared chalk or whiting, 1 ounce of turpentine, 1 ounce of alcohol, and 2 drams of spirits of camphor.

To Clean Britannia Ware. — First apply sweet oil with a sponge or piece of flannel. Wash in suds and water, and polish the same as silver.

Or dissolve 4 ounces of yellow soap in 4 ounces of sweet oil, and dilute to a thick cream with alcohol. Apply with a soft sponge and polish with chamois.

To Clean China.—Cups and saucers and other articles of fine china often take on a yellow discoloration. To remove this moisten a soft cloth in water and dip into dry salt or fine coal or wood ashes, or a mixture of fuller's earth and baking soda, and rub off the stain with it. Afterwards wash with soap and water.

To Clean Candlesticks. — To clean silver candlesticks, dip them in boiling water to remove grease, and afterwards clean and polish them like other silver articles. Do not attempt to scratch off the grease or wax with a knife or melt it off with dry heat, especially if they are plated, as plated ware is often based on a composition which will run if heated.

To Clean Door Plates.—Silver door plates may be cleaned with aqua ammonia applied with a stiff brush. This is very effective for cleaning silver, but should not be used too freely upon finer silver articles, as it tends to deaden their luster.

To Clean Silver Seals.—To restore monogram and initial seals of steel or silver to usefulness after they have begun to stick to the wax, first remove as much as possible of the dried wax from the lines of the design. Then soak the seal in a moderately strong solution of oxalic acid, using a stiff brush to get at the fine lines, and remove the loosened wax which formerly adhered. When the seal is thoroughly cleaned and bright, rub well with a cloth dampened with sweet oil, to neutralize further action of the acid and prevent the wax from again sticking.

CARE OF SINKS AND DISPOSAL OF GARBAGE

Care of Sinks.—Stretch a piece of picture wire or cord over the kitchen sink. Over this hang old newspapers. Crumple one of these in the hands and use it to wipe the grease from frying pans, pots, etc., before putting them into the dishwasher. This will prevent the excess of grease from coating the sink and stopping up the sink spout. Also use newspapers to wipe off the stove, table, sink, and floor when grease and other things have been spilled on them. Throw the papers at once into the fire box of the range, where they will be consumed. Thus you will have no greasy dishwater or greasy dish cloths or towels to wash.

To Clean Sinks. — The grease in dishwater tends to coat over the sink and sink spouts and form breeding places for the germs of filth diseases, as typhoid and other fevers, diphtheria, and the like. Keep at hand on a high shelf, out of reach of children, a bottle of carbolic acid. Once a week sprinkle a few drops of this about the sink. This will not only disinfect the sink itself, but also the sink spout, drain pipes, and drain.

Or dissolve a pound of copperas in a gallon of boiling water. Pour this solution into a large glass bottle, cork, and keep out of the reach of children. Dilute half a pint with a quart of hot water and use to clean the sink daily.

Or wet the bottom of the sink and sprinkle chloride of lime over it. This will remove all stains, and when rinsed off the water will disinfect the sink spout and drain.

Or, when the sink is coated with grease or the sink spout is stopped up, put a pound or more of washing soda in a colander or strainer, and pour boiling water through it into the sink. Set the strainer into the water until the remainder of the soda is dissolved. If it does not run down after a time use force cups or partly fill the sink with water and press a rag down over the strainer. As soon as a way has been made, continue to pour hot soda and water through the pipe to flush it.

Care of Iron Sinks.—Do not use soap to wash an iron sink, but wash it in the water in which potatoes have been boiled. Use a raw or boiled potato to rub any spots that are rough or rusty; dipping the potato in bath brick will assist. Afterwards rinse clean with very hot clean water. This will keep the sink smooth and prevent rust.

To Clean a Painted Sink.—Painting a sink with white or other enamel paint prevents rusting and improves its appearance, but acids and alkalis tend to remove the paint and cause rust. Cleanse the paint with a rag moistened in kerosene and rinse with clear hot water.

Homemade Sink.—There are still many dry sinks in various parts of the country which necessitates carrying all dishwater out of doors. These relics of barbarism should not be suffered to remain in any enlightened household. A homemade sink may be made of plain boards and lined with tin or zinc at small cost. If this is set against an outer wall a foot or two of lead pipe will supply an outlet, and a wooden trough lined with lead, tin, or zinc, or merely tarred or painted, may carry away waste water to a cesspool. Make a box 4 feet long, 14 inches wide, and 5 inches deep, with open ends. Put in two partitions, leaving a 22-inch space in the center. Line this with tin or zinc, making a hole in one corner for the waste pipes. This leaves shelves at either hand for kitchen utensils, water pail, or wash pan. Have the sink at such a height that it will not be necessary to stoop when using it.

Garbage.—The problem of the disposal of garbage in small towns and villages is often a vexatious one. In cities garbage is, of course, removed by the authorities, and on farms it is usually fed to pigs and chickens. It is often remarked that the amount of food thrown away by the average American family would support a French or an Italian family of equal size and standing.

Garbage cans of galvanized iron with tightly fitting lids can be obtained at small cost, and are most satisfactory. Some of these are now fitted with a place in the cover to hold a sponge wet with an antiseptic and deodorant. Such a can prevents all bad odors and does not attract flies. A box with a hinged lid built in one corner of the porch to hold the garbage can will prevent cats and dogs from tipping it over and strewing the contents about.

Or a cheese box or other box sunk in the ground outside the door and covered with a tight lid may hold the garbage can or an ordinary garbage pail. This will keep the contents cool and prevent their being disturbed.

Or a little cayenne pepper strewed above and about the can will discourage the visits of animals. A newspaper laid inside the pail before the garbage is placed in it will keep the can in good order and make it an easy matter to clean it thoroughly. A small galvanized iron pail to stand on the kitchen or pantry table, and to be washed after each meal or at least once a day, is a convenient receptacle for the accumulation of kitchen scraps, and saves many outdoor trips to the garbage can.

CHAMBER WORK

To Air Beds.—Emanations from the body are absorbed by the sheets and through these contaminate the other bedding. Moreover, at times the air in unheated rooms contains a good deal of moisture, and this penetrates all parts of the bedding. When the weather changes, the surface of the bed will dry much more quickly than other parts; hence the object of airing a bed is to purify it and to dry it by giving the moisture a good chance to evaporate. Open the bed the first thing in the morning, remove the covers, and expose the mattress and the sheets separately to the air. If the weather is clear, open the windows if possible, but not if the outer air is damp from fog or rain. Once a week on cleaning day brush the mattress with a clean broom or stiff whisk broom, turning up the tufts and freeing it of all dust. The ideal way, from a sanitary point of view, is to leave the bed stripped all day and spread it up just before retiring. But as this is not always convenient, the next best course is to put off bed making until the last thing in the morning. A feather bed should be beaten and shaken up when it is stripped to air. In clear, dry weather it is a good plan to expose beds and bedding to outdoor air and sunshine, except the feather beds, which should be aired out of doors in a shady place. The

"A Modern Bedroom."

direct rays of the sun may cause the animal oil in the feathers if new and if not properly cleaned to become rancid. But care must be taken not to air bedding out of doors when the air is damp from fog or mist.

To Make Beds.—Spread the lower sheet with the seam down, the wide heading at the top, tucking it in all around. Spread the upper sheet with the hem up and the broad heading 6 inches above the top edge of the mattress. Tuck the lower end in firmly under the foot of the mattress. Spread the blankets with the open edges evenly together 6 inches from the head of the bed. Smooth downward. Tuck the bottom double edge firmly under the foot of the mattress.

Add quilts, if any, in the same fashion. If a white counterpane is used the bed need not be open. Or if not, turn back the upper sheet over the blankets at least 12 inches to cover them well. Do not tuck in metal beds at the sides. The spread should be long enough to hang over the mattress at the foot of the bed. A tuft or light comforter to match the furnishings of the room may be folded twice lengthwise, or square, with one edge turned over and placed across the foot of the bed. Or, if a wooden bedstead is used, the sheets and blankets may be tucked in at the sides before the spread is put on and tucked. Stand the pillows nearly erect.

In winter when the feet are so apt to be cold in unheated rooms an extra quilt or blanket spread over the lower half of the bed, and the other half folded under the mattress to prevent the clothes from pulling up, will help to keep the feet warm.

Bedroom Ware.—Clean all bedroom ware and the marble tops of washstands and tables with a rag dipped in turpentine. This not only cleanses but disinfects them.

How to Cool Bedrooms.—In summer it is often more important to keep hot air out than to let cool air in. Hence if bedrooms are aired during the early part of the day and the curtains then drawn and shutters closed until night, the bedrooms may be cooler than if they had been open to the outer air all day.

Or, when very important to cool a room quickly, wet a large cloth and suspend it over a line where, if possible, a draught will strike it. This will cool the air by evaporation approximately ten degrees according to circumstances. This plan is frequently practiced in hot climates.

To Darken Rooms. — Bedrooms should be provided with dark-green shades in addition to the white shades, or if these are not present a strip of dark-green baize or glazed calico may be pinned inside the blind or attached to the white shades when it is necessary to darken room.

CARE OF LAMPS

Lamps should be cleaned and then filled each morning and the wicks trimmed. The improved steadiness of the light will repay for the trouble. When buying a lamp, get two or three extra chimneys and burners, and a yard or two of wicking. This will save much delay and annoyance, especially when kerosene is the only light to be had, and it is not convenient to go to the store. It is very desirable, as far as possible, to have lamps and burners alike, so that the parts and supplies may be interchangeable.

Have a 5-gallon can for kerosene oil fitted with a pump. Place this on a homemade truck fitted with casters, so that it can be rolled under a shelf or into the pantry and drawn out again without lifting.

To Clean Lamps.—Collect all the lamps in the house after the chamber work has been done, and place them

"Collect All the Lamps."

on a shelf near the oil can, which may be pushed under the kitchen sink. First remove the chimneys and place them near the sink to be washed. Trim the wicks by rubbing the crust from them with the fingers or a piece of stock, as a burnt match. Do not, as a rule, use the scissors, or, if they are necessary, cut off the corners so as to round the wick up to the center instead of cutting straight across. See that the wicks are long enough to reach the bottom of the lamp. Insert a new wick when necessary. Place the lamp on the top of the oil can and fill with a pump. Or, if a 1-gallon can is used, take care that the oil does not spatter the surrounding woodwork and perhaps cause a conflagration. Wipe the lamps clean with a cloth kept for this purpose. Do not leave cloths soaked with kerosene matter together in dark corners, as they may become ignited by spontaneous combustion. Wash the lamps in soap and water; wash and put on the chimneys, and place them on a shelf ready for use.

To Clean Lamp Chimneys.—A sponge is the best thing with which to clean lamp chimneys. Select a sponge large enough to fill the biggest part of the chimney inside, thrust a stick into the center of the sponge, and fasten it with a string, wire, or tacks, dip it into soapsuds, and swab the inside of the glass. Afterwards rinse with hot water and polish.

To Polish Lamp Chimneys.—Use the small paper bags that contained groceries. Crumple and rub these together to soften them. Draw a bag on your hand like a glove, and polish with it. Hold your hand over one end of the chimney and breathe into it at the other end before polishing.

Or save tissue paper for this purpose.

Or rinse chimneys thoroughly in hot water and stand them on a hot cover of the kitchen range. They will sputter but will not break, and will dry clear and shining inside and out. If the suds are not rinsed off, however, they will leave stains.

If chimneys are smoked with soot, remove it with a dry cloth covered with salt.

Or soak them in hot water with washing soda, and wash in warm water containing aqua ammonia.

To Clean Globes.—Rough or ornamented glass globes which become smoked or grimed with dust may be placed in a vessel of cold water containing a tablespoonful of washing soda and brought to a boil. Afterwards scrub with soap and water, using a nailbrush, or with warm water containing ammonia. Rinse in warm or hot water, drain, dry and polish.

Care of Lamp Chimneys.—Lamp chimneys frequently crack when the lamp is lighted, especially if they are in a cold room. You may know if the chimney is too cold from the fact that steam will gather upon it. When this is the case keep the flame low until the chimney becomes warm enough to dispel the steam, and turn the light up by degrees.

Another cause of broken chimneys is cutting the wicks square across, which leaves a corner to flare to one side. Rub off the crust, or clip the corner so as to round up the wick toward the center.

Care of Burners.—Have at hand a complete set of extra burners. Once a month or so change the burners and boil the soiled one in a solution of sal soda or baking soda until perfectly clean and bright. Afterwards polish with sand soap, bath brick, or pumice.

When the burner becomes clogged with dirt and dust, soak it in a solution of potash or soda lye and hot water, moving it about with a stick until the dirt is moistened. Afterwards boil with baking soda until thoroughly cleaned.

Lamp Chimneys—To Prevent their Breaking.—Wrap the glass in several thicknesses of cheese cloth, cover with a strong solution of cold salt water, and bring to a boil. Boil ten or fifteen minutes, and leave the glass in the water to cool. If this is done each time the chimneys are washed they will become thoroughly toughened and practically unbreakable. If they can be put in a kettle of water on the range and boiled all day, so much the better.

Care of Lamps.—Lamps should not be allowed to stand partly empty, as the oil tends to generate a gas which may explode if ignited. They should be filled daily, but not quite full. When heated the oil expands, and if the lamp is full it will run over and drop. Fill to within half an inch or so of the top, trim, and rub dry with a soft cloth.

Metal Lamps. — Bronze lamps should be merely dusted or wiped with a flannel cloth, and care should be taken not to allow the oil to spill on them, as it has a tendency to take off the bronze. They should not be washed with soap and water.

Lacquer lamps may be washed, but not with sal soda or any strong washing powder, alcohol, or any form of naphtha, as these all may injure the lacquer.

To Mend Lamps.—The brass top of a lamp to which the burner is screwed sometimes gets broken, and may be mended either with alum or plaster of Paris. Remove the ring from the top and dig out the dry plaster of Paris with a penknife. Make a paste of fresh plaster of Paris with water, fill the threads of the brass with this, heaping on all that it will hold. Place it in position to harden. The plaster of Paris will swell and hold the top tightly.

Or fill the hollow part with powdered alum and melt it on the stove. When melted put it in place, and when cold it will be found to adhere tightly.

Lamps—To Prevent Their Smoking. — If the wick is thoroughly soaked in strong vinegar and afterwards dried it will give a clear light and prevent smoking.

Or place a small piece of rock salt close to the flame inside the burner. This not only prevents smoke but brightens the flame.

CHAPTER X

REMOVAL OF SPOTS AND STAINS

SOLVENTS FOR SPOTS AND STAINS—KINDS OF SPOTS AND STAINS—STAINS ON WHITE LINEN OR COTTON—TO REMOVE STAINS FROM VEGETABLE FIBERS—TO REMOVE STAINS FROM ANIMAL FIBERS—TO CLEAN COLORED GOODS—TO DRY-CLEAN MEN'S GARMENTS—TO DRY-CLEAN WOMEN'S GARMENTS—CLEANING AND CARE OF GLOVES—TO CLEAN FEATHERS, FURS, AND STRAW—BLEACHING VEGETABLE AND ANIMAL FIBERS

SOLVENTS FOR SPOTS AND STAINS

How to Erase Stains.—The commonest stains that have to be removed from textile fabrics are ink, grass green, iron rust, mildew, grease spots, paint, and tar. These require treatment according to the nature of the stain and the fabric. The principal chemicals that should be kept on hand in the laundry closet to remove stains are certain acids, especially oxalic, tartaric, and muriatic acid; together with ammonia and hyposulphite of soda to neutralize the effect of the acid after the stain has been removed; aqua ammonia for the same purpose; various substances that have the power of cutting or dissolving gums and resins, as alcohol, chloroform, and oil of turpentine; and certain absorbents, as chalk, French chalk, pipe clay, fuller's earth, and the like. Other useful articles—as fresh milk, sour milk, buttermilk, cream of tartar, lemon juice, salt, raw potato, etc., will usually be at hand.

Treatment of Spots and Stains.—Treatment for stains in general should be progressive, beginning with the milder remedies and reserving the more powerful ones to the last. Fresh stains are much more easily soluble than those that are allowed to remain until various chemical changes have taken place. Hence prompt treatment is always advisable. When stains are fresh, immediate application of any dry absorbent powder, as common salt, common starch, chalk, pipe clay, etc., will take up much of the staining fluid. Dipping at once into boiling water for some stains and into milk for others will assist in dissolving the stain, and various other agents may then be applied while the fabric is wet. If the stains have been suffered to dry they must usually be wet by soaking to swell the fibers of the fabric, and allow the cleansing substance to be absorbed.

The Laundry Closet.—It will be found very convenient to provide a special receptacle in the kitchen or laundry for the various articles for removing stains, and for the soaps, washing compounds, bluing, starch, and other things used in the laundry. A complete list will include hard bar soap, both white and yellow, naphtha soap, sal soda, bluing, wheat and corn starch, borax, aqua ammonia, sugar of lead, oxalic, muriatic, and tartaric acids, bleaching powder (chloride of lime), caustic potash, turpentine, benzine, and gasoline, besides various cleansing mixtures. This closet should have a strong lock or padlock, and the key should be kept beyond the reach of children. Every bottle and package of poisonous substances should be plainly labeled and should bear the word "Poison."

Utensils for Stains or Spots.—The laundry closet should also contain a number of small sponges, which can be bought for ten cents a dozen, for applying various substances to stained fabrics; likewise several sizes of small camel's-hair paint brushes, such as

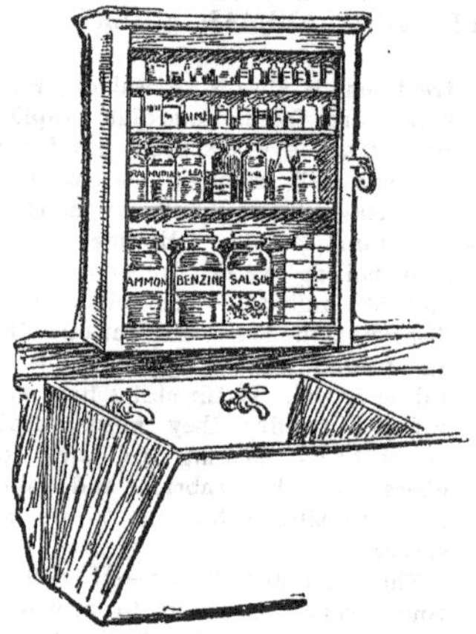

"The Laundry Closet."

are used for water colors. The stiff fibrous sponges called "loofah," which cost about ten cents apiece, are especially useful for grease stains or spots. If the goods is rough these can be used to scrape with vigorously. They can also be used with a lighter touch on delicate fabrics. They leave no lint and are easily washed and dried. When removing spots or stains, first hold the garment to the light, and if the stain is on the surface scrape off as much of it as possible with a sharp knife before wetting the fabric or applying chemicals.

Acids to Remove Stains.—The laundry cupboard should be furnished with a 4- or 6-ounce vial of oxalic and of tartaric acid and a 2-ounce vial of muriatic acid. These will be found easy to apply, and prove much more effective than many of the ordinary methods that often must be employed if they are not kept at hand.

Cautions in Use of Acids.—These acids are all poisonous and must be labeled "Poison," and locked up out of the reach of children. They must not be used on colored fabrics, and must be quickly and thoroughly rinsed out as soon as the stain has been removed. When possible, they should be followed by the use of hyposulphite of soda, ammonia, or other chemical that will neutralize the acid.

Oxalic Acid.—This is the active principle of salts of sorrel. When combined with cream of tartar it is known as salts of lemon. It may be dissolved in one part of boiling water. It is a dangerous poison, and in certain quantities will cause death in about ten minutes. It is used for cleaning leather, scouring metals, especially brass and copper, and for removing various stains. It has very much the appearance of Epsom salts, from which it must be carefully distinguished.

Use of Oxalic Acid.—Oxalic acid is especially useful in the laundry to remove iron mold, fruit stains, and ink spots produced by the old style iron-gall inks. It does not, however, remove ink stains produced by modern writing fluids or blue-black inks composed of aniline dyes. Oxalic acid may be applied to cotton, linen, woolen, silk, or any ordinary fabric if uncolored, but it bleaches colored goods. The color, can, however, in most cases be restored by aqua ammonia. When possible, it is advisable to experiment with a sample of the goods before applying oxalic acid to colored articles.

To Apply Oxalic Acid.—The acid may be applied alone, either dissolved in its own bulk of boiling water for a "saturated" solution, or in nine parts of cold water for a "dilute" solution.

Or, as salts of lemon, it may be dissolved in 1 to 10 parts of water, either hot or cold. The action of the acid is increased by heat as in boiling water.

To apply, either wet the spot in water and cover with dry oxalic acid or salts of lemon, or dip the spot into the solution, or apply the solution to the spot with a small brush, sponge, or piece of rag. If the stains are old or have penetrated through the fabric it will be necessary to rub the acid vigorously into the spot and persist patiently until successful. Oxalic acid is also recommended to bleach silk in the proportion of 4 pounds of the acid and 4 pounds of salt to 2 quarts of water for the raw silk, or 2 ounces of oxalic acid and 2 ounces of salt to 6 quarts of water for white silk that has become yellowed from washing. The latter proportions may be observed for removing vegetable or fruit stains, should it be necessary to immerse the article in the solution.

As soon as the stain disappears, rinse with clear water, and afterwards wash with soapsuds.

Uses of Citric Acid.—This is the acid principle of alum and lemon juice; it is also found in gooseberries, currants, and some other fruits. It is intensely sour, is readily soluble in water, and is used in medicine; in dyeing, to heighten certain colors, and to break up certain coloring compounds. Citric acid may be used dissolved in slightly more than its own bulk of water for a saturated solution, or in 10 or more parts for a dilute solution. It may be applied to white goods or fast-dyed cotton or woolen, by moistening the stain with a solution by means of the finger tips, a small brush, sponge, or rag. Rinse immediately in clear water. It may be used for stains from fruit, iron-gall inks, iron rust, or mildew; but for these oxalic or tartaric acids are commonly preferred. In the form of lemon juice, citric acid is a mild but useful agent, and one generally employed. With the addition of salt on colored goods it may safely be used on any ordinary fabric. To apply, saturate the spot with lemon juice, and for colored goods cover with dry salt. Expose to direct sunshine and repeat if necessary.

Or apply lemon juice and salt, and steam the fabric over a kettle.

Uses of Lactic Acid.—This is the acid which forms in milk when it turns sour and which is, therefore, contained in buttermilk. It is the presence of this acid which causes buttermilk to be employed in the process of bleaching linen. Sweet milk, sour milk, and buttermilk are all recommended for the treatment of stains in fabrics, the action being strong in proportion as the liquid sours with age. Hence, when stains are fresh they may be removed by dipping immediately in warm milk; but when they are more stubborn, they may require soaking in buttermilk for some time. The addition of common salt increases their effectiveness. This is a simple and useful means of treating ink stains from iron-gall inks, tea stains, red-wine stains, and fruit stains, especially when fresh. Sour buttermilk also erases mildew. Wet or soak the article in fresh or sour milk or buttermilk, cover with common salt—which contains chlorine, a powerful bleaching agent—and expose to sunshine in the open air.

Nature of Tartaric Acid.—This is the acid principle of cream of tartar and is found in a free state in various plants and fruits, especially the grape. It is readily soluble in either alcohol or water. If dissolved in water and allowed to stand it deteriorates, turning into acetic acid. It is the acid principle of Rochelle salts and is principally used in dyeing, in preparing effervescing beverages, and as an ingredient in baking powder. In medicine it is used as a tartar emetic.

Tartaric acid is but slightly poisonous, is much less destructive to cloth fibers than are other acids, and does not injure fast colors. It may be dissolved in less than its own bulk of water, and hence may be used in a very strong solution and readily washed out of the most delicate fabrics.

Uses of Tartaric Acid.—Tartaric acid is especially useful in grass stains, as it changes the chlorophyll and chlorophyllan into soluble substances. It is nearly as effective as oxalic acid on ink spots from iron-gall inks. It may be used on all ordinary linen, silk, cotton, woolen, or other fabrics, and if combined with salt will not cause the colors to run. The usefulness of this article in the laundry does not seem to be generally known.

To Apply Tartaric Acid.—Wet the spot with water and apply the dry acid with or without an equal quantity of salt.

Or wet the spot and cover with cream of tartar, with or without its bulk of salt. The process will be quickened if the stain is held over the steam of a teakettle or laid upon a heated dinner plate or other smooth, heated surface. The acid may be rubbed into white goods with the finger tips or the bowl of a spoon, but on colored goods it should be applied more carefully.

Or, for a saturated solution, dissolve in its own bulk or less of hot water. For a dilute solution dissolve in 10 or more parts of cold water. Apply same as oxalic acid.

Nature of Salts of Lemon.—This is a compound of equal parts in bulk of cream of tartar and salts of sorrel. It combines the effects of tartaric and oxalic acids. Its uses and methods of application are similar. It may be used on the same fabrics and requires similar caution.

Nature and Uses of Muriatic Acid.—This is a gas produced by treating common salt with sulphuric acid or oil of vitriol. It is readily soluble in water, and this solution is the commercial article. It is poisonous, has a sharp, keen smell and taste, and when inhaled causes suffocation. One part of water will absorb about 450 times its own bulk of the gas. It is a powerful corrosive, and must be provided with a glass or rubber stopper, or the cork must be smeared with vaseline, else it will eat the cork and evaporate. It corrodes metals.

To Apply Muriatic Acid.—This acid is especially useful to remove red rust stains. To apply, lay the fabric containing the spot over an earthen dish of boiling water. Allow a drop of the acid to fall on the stain from a glass stopper or medicine dropper. This will cause the stain to fade to a light yellow. Drop the cloth immediately into the water and rinse. Repeat if necessary. As soon as the stain disappears, rinse the article and dip it into ammonia water. This will neutralize any acid that was not removed by rinsing.

Muriatic acid may be used on linen or cotton fabrics, but not on silks or woolens. It can be employed on certain fast colors, but it is advisable to test a sample of the goods before applying.

To Remove Acid Stains.—The above acids and others will themselves stain certain colored goods, especially blues and blacks. To remove these stains apply aqua ammonia with a camel's-hair brush or sponge. If this is not effective apply chloroform. Either of these may be used on linen, cotton, silk, or wool.

Nature and Uses of Ammonia.—It is interesting to note that the name "ammonia" was formerly applied to common salt on account of the fact that salt was anciently found in the Libyan Desert near the Temple of Jupiter Ammon. Ammonia occurs as a colorless transparent gas with a pungent odor. It is readily soluble in water, 1 part of water absorbing about 500 volumes of the gas. A solution of ammonia in water is called aqua ammonia or "spirits of Hartshorn." Preparations sold for household purposes vary greatly in strength. Smelling salts or sal volatile is a carbonate of ammonia. Ammonia combines with acids to form soluble salts. Hence it is useful in removing fruit stains and other acids. It may be applied freely to all ordinary fabrics; to remove stains made by strong acids, red wine, iodine, nitrate of silver, and also the stains of sea water and cod-liver oil.

Uses of Alcohol.—Alcohol, as is well known, is a pure, colorless liquid with a burning taste. It burns easily, has a strong affinity for water, and dissolves many substances. Pure alcohol is called absolute or "anhydrous" alcohol, but the commercial article varies from "proof spirits," which contains about 50 per cent of alcohol by volume, to "cologne spirits," which contains from 93 to 95 per cent.

The solvent quality of alcohol makes it useful to remove stains in silk, woolen, and other delicate fabrics, provided they are soluble and do not require chemical treatment. It may be mixed with benzine or aqua ammonia or both. It is most effective when the stains are fresh.

Uses of Chloroform.—Chloroform is a colorless liquid with a sweetish taste and characteristic odor. Its anæsthetic properties are well known. It is slightly soluble in water, but readily so in alcohol and ether. It has the property of dissolving camphor, resin, wax, rubber, iodine, and other substances. Chloroform may be employed to restore certain colors that were removed by acids after the acids have been destroyed by the application of ammonia.

Uses of Turpentine.—Turpentine is a resinous oil obtained from cone-bearing trees. The commercial article is a solution of resin in a volatile oil. Turpentine has a well-known spicy odor, a bitter taste, and burns freely. Oil of turpentine, obtained by distillation, is a colorless liquid with a peculiar odor; it is insoluble in water, but dissolves readily in alcohol or ether. It also dissolves resin, gummy substances, oils, rubber, iodine, sulphur, and phosphorus. Hence its usefulness in treating stains produced by such substances. The commercial article is sold in various grades, and is used extensively in the preparation of paints and varnishes.

To Apply Turpentine.—Turpentine will remove paint, grease, or vaseline stains without injury to the most delicate fabric. Apply sufficient turpentine to soak the paint or grease spot. Use a camel's-hair brush, a common pen or feather, or, for large spots, a sponge.

Or apply by dropping from a glass bottle.

The turpentine may be mixed with alcohol, salts of lemon, or sulphuric ether.

Kinds and Uses of Absorbents.—Various absorbents are recommended to remove grease, wax, blood, ink, mildew, and other stains from fabrics. Among the most useful of these are brown paper and blotting paper. Others are chalk, French chalk (which is not chalk but ground soapstone), pipe clay, fuller's earth, magnesia, gypsum, common starch, and melted tallow.

One of the quickest and best methods to remove grease (especially when it is fresh) and spots of wax is to lay over the spot a piece of common brown paper and press with a hot iron. Care must be taken not to use an iron hot enough to change the colors of colored silks and print goods. If convenient the spot may be previously covered with French chalk.

Or any of the above powders may be applied dry. The grease or wax will be taken up more quickly if held near a stove or pressed with a hot iron.

For mildew, rub the spots with wet soap, rub in pipe clay, fuller's earth, or chalk, cover thickly with the same, and expose to sunshine.

For blood stains use cornstarch.

A mixture of 6 ounces of fuller's earth, 1 ounce of pipe clay, 1 ounce of French chalk, ¼ ounce of oil of turpentine, ½ ounce of alcohol, and 1½ ounces of melted castile soap is highly recommended.

Chlorine and Uses of Bleaching Powder.—This is the chloride of lime prepared by exposing damp slacked lime to chlorine gas. A good, fresh article contains 25 to 30 per cent of effective chlorine, which is a powerful bleaching agent. It decomposes and deteriorates with time, setting free hydrochloric acid, to which the bleaching is due. This is a pale-yellow gas that has the property of decomposing various kinds of coloring matter. Bleaching powder is one of the surest agents for removing ink stains or writing from white textile fabric or paper. Cover the spots with dry bleaching powder and moisten with a weak mineral acid, as acetic or tartaric acid. This method is not suitable for colored goods, as the bleaching powder would remove the colors. Afterwards neutralize the acid by applying aqua ammonia or hyposulphite of soda.

To Make and Use Javelle Water.—Chloride of lime or Javelle water is a colorless liquid that may be prepared from bleaching powder. It is much used for taking fruit and other stains from white textile fabrics and for bleaching wood and straw. For fruit stains dissolve ½ pound of chloride of lime in 2 quarts of boiling water. Add to this 1 pound of sal soda. Dissolve, settle, and pour off the clear liquid. This is Javelle water. Apply with a brush, rinse in clear water, and dip in ammonia water to neutralize the acid.

Or dissolve 2 ounces of chloride of lime in 1 quart of boiling water. Immerse the fabric in this for 5 minutes. Remove, add 4 quarts of cold water, and soak the article for 3 to 12 hours, depending upon the strength of the fabric. This is heroic treatment, and should only be used on coarser articles, as duck, canvas, and the like, as it tends to rot the fabric. Afterwards immerse in a solution of 4 ounces of hyposulphite of soda to 1 gallon of water to neutralize the acid. Rinse in clear water and wash in soapsuds.

Nature of Gasoline.—Gasoline is a product of the distillation of petroleum. The first liquid that passes over in the distillation of petroleum is crude naphtha. By redistillation this is separated into gasoline and the A, B, and C grades of naphtha. Gasoline is very commonly used for domestic heating and cooking in stoves especially prepared for the purpose, and also for the production of power in gasoline engines. It is highly inflammable and explosive. It gives off under ordinary temperature a volatile gas which, by contact with flame, or a hot stove, will ignite at a distance of several feet from the liquid gasoline. Great caution must, therefore, be exercised in its use.

Benzine is a substance similar to gasoline, and may be used for sponging fabrics in the same manner.

How to Use Gasoline.—Employed by the following methods gasoline will thoroughly cleanse wool, silk, velvet, and other fabrics of animal fibers, but not cotton, and will remove grease, paint, wax, and mud stains; in fact, practically all stains except acid ones, without injury to the texture or colors of the fabric. Dirt and other impurities removed will sink to the bottom and can be removed by straining through cheese cloth. Hence the same gasoline may be used again and again. The best results are obtained by using a fairly large quantity of gasoline and soaking and washing the articles in it the same as in water. The cost of cleaning with gasoline is much less than is charged by a professional cleaner, and also much less than replacing the articles. Hence it pays to purchase the best gasoline in five-gallon cans, and to provide and set aside two or three covered earthenware jars in which to use it.

Cleaning with gasoline should be done preferably out of doors, or if indoors, by daylight, and never in the vicinity of a hot stove, lamp, or other flame. Care must be taken that matches are not accidentally lighted in its vicinity.

First, shake and brush the articles to remove dust and dirt. Remove rubber dress shields or other pieces of rubber, as they will be spoiled. Tack small articles together and wash larger ones singly in an earthenware jar filled with gasoline and allow them to soak for an hour or more. If the jar can be put in a pan which is surrounded with hot water (but not on a stove or near any open flame), the gasoline will do its work quicker and better and will be less disagreeable for the hands. After soaking, work the articles about, rubbing carefully between the fingers, or rub the spots with a toothbrush or nailbrush having fairly soft bristles. Or dip the brush into a small can of gasoline set into a pan of hot water. Squeeze the gasoline out of the garments and put them into a second jar, into

"Cleaning with Gasoline Out of Doors."

which pour fresh gasoline, meantime putting other articles to soak in the first jar. A third jar may be used if necessary. After rinsing in the second or third jar squeeze the garments quite dry, stretch carefully to their proper shape, and thoroughly evaporate by airing them on a line, and afterwards pressing them with a hot iron. Hang coats or waists on a coat hanger to keep in shape while drying.

Pour the gasoline back into the can through a funnel covered with several thicknesses of cheese cloth.

Or, to remove a spot or a stain, stretch the fabric over a piece of blotting paper and pour the gasoline around it. Sponge from the center outwardly until the spot is removed. Take a dry cloth and continue rubbing in the same manner with light strokes until the article is dry.

Or sprinkle a little powdered gypsum over the spot, extending beyond the moistened part. When this is brushed off, the spot will be removed.

Or, if a benzine stain, rub French chalk into it with a piece of flannel, sprinkle a layer of the chalk over it, and let stand for twenty-four hours.

Cleansing Mixtures. — Dissolve 6 drams of gum camphor in 2 ounces of alcohol. Mix separately 2 drams of pipe clay with 4 ounces of beef's gall. Also mix separately ½ ounce each of borax, saltpeter, and honey. Shave into a saucepan large enough to hold all these ingredients 8 ounces of castile or other good hard white soap, add the mixture of gall and pipe clay, and melt with gentle heat, stirring constantly. Remove from the fire, and when cool stir in first the saltpeter, borax, and honey, then the camphor and alcohol. Lastly add ½ ounce of spirits of turpentine and ½ ounce of sulphuric ether. Pour quickly into a black glass bottle, cork tightly, and store in a dark place. This preparation contains no free alkali, will not injure any ordinary fabric, and contains solvents for practically every kind of spot or stain likely to be met with in garments. It is suitable for silks, woolens, and indeed all ordinary fabrics.

Or shave 4 ounces of castile or other hard white soap and dissolve in 2 quarts of boiling water. Remove from the fire, and when cold add ½ ounce of saltpeter, stirring until dissolved. Strain through cheese cloth, let the mixture settle, and take off the scum with a skimmer. Now add ½ pint of ammonia and bottle and cork tightly. Keep in an earthenware jug with a tight cork. This is the so-called "Magic Annihilator," which is recommended to remove grease and oil from all kinds of dress goods and other fabrics without injuring them, and for various other purposes, as scouring floors, cleaning windows, metals, etc. It must not be used on woodenware, as it will remove paint, for which purpose it is especially recommended.

Pour this liquid on both sides of the spot or article to be cleaned. Scrub with a stiff brush, sponge, or loof, and rinse with cold water. Repeat if necessary. To clean silverware and other metals mix with whiting.

Chemical Soap.—Shave 1 pound of castile soap, add ¼ pint of alcohol, ¼ pint of soft water, ½ ounce of aquafortis, ½ ounce of lampblack, ½ ounce of saltpeter, ½ ounce of potash, ½ ounce of camphor, 1 ounce of powdered cinnamon. Dissolve the soap in water, stir in the potash and saltpeter, remove from the fire, add the other ingredients, and stir until cool. Pour into molds and put away in a dry place to season. The longer it is seasoned before using the better.

Or shave 1 ounce of castile soap, cover with 1 pint of water, and boil until dissolved. Stir in 2 ounces of sal soda, ½ ounce of starch, ¼ ounce of borax. Pour into molds to cool and harden. Apply with a rag, sponge, or loof to remove grease, paint, tar, etc.

Or dissolve 1 ounce of castile soap with gentle heat in about twice its own bulk of water. Add enough hot water to make 1 pint; let cool slightly. Stir in 1 teaspoonful of saltpeter and 2 ounces of aqua ammonia.

Or mix 3 ounces of alcohol, ½ ounce of bay rum, 1 ounce of oil of wintergreen, ½ ounce of aqua ammonia, ½ ounce of chloroform, and 1 ounce of sulphuric ether. Cork tightly and let stand over night. Add 1 ounce of pulverized borax and 1 gallon of deodorized gasoline. Shake well and cork tightly.

Or mix ½ ounce of borax and ½ ounce of camphor in a quart fruit jar. Pour over them 1 pint of boiling water. Cork tightly and let stand until cool. Now add ½ pint of alcohol, shake well, and cork tightly. Use to sponge woolen dress goods, men's clothing, felt hats, and the like.

Or dissolve 1 ounce of castile soap scraped in 1 quart of boiling water. Let cool and add ½ ounce of glycerin, ½ ounce of alcohol, and ½ ounce of sulphuric ether. Bottle, cork tightly, and keep in a dark place. Use to sponge all sorts of dress goods, and especially to remove grease spots.

Or mix equal parts of turpentine, benzine, and chloroform.

Scouring Mixtures.—Mix 3 pounds of fuller's earth, ½ pound of pipe clay, 2 ounces of powdered French chalk. Mix separately 1 ounce of rectified spirits of turpentine, 1 ounce of alcohol, and 12 ounces of soap jelly. Stir the two mixtures together to a stiff paste and place in tightly covered fruit jars.

Or mix equal parts of fuller's earth and soap jelly. To apply, moisten the cloth with warm water and cover with this mixture, rubbing it well into the goods. Let stand until dry, then scour with a stiff brush and warm water.

Or mix 1 ounce of baking soda, 1 ounce of prepared chalk, 1 ounce of pumice stone, and 1 ounce of sifted wood ashes. Apply this mixture with a piece of raw white potato.

Or moisten 1 ounce of fuller's earth with lemon juice; add ½ ounce of pearlash and 1 ounce of yellow soap melted with as little water as possible. Mix the whole and knead into a stiff paste. Roll into balls the size of marbles and put them in the sun to dry. Moisten the spot with warm water and scour with one of these balls; then put in the sun to dry. Afterwards rinse with clear water.

Nature of the Fabric.—The treatment of spots and stains depends not

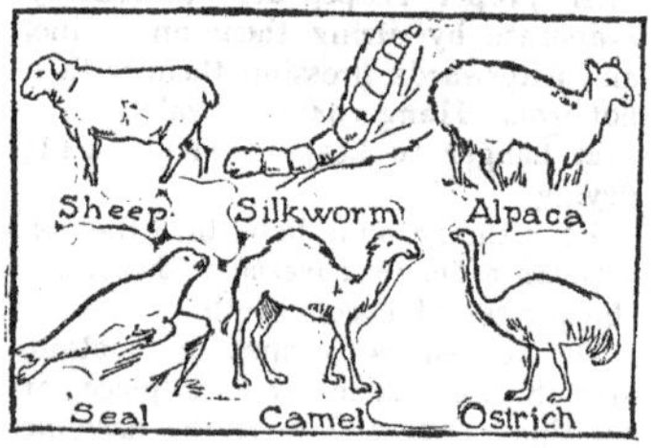

"With Animal Fibers Caution is Necessary."

only upon the kind of stain, but also upon the nature of the fabric. Fabrics are of two principal classes: vegetable fibers, which include linen and cotton goods; and animal fibers, which include wool, silk, furs, feathers, and the like. All vegetable fibers contain cellulose, a hard, woodlike substance

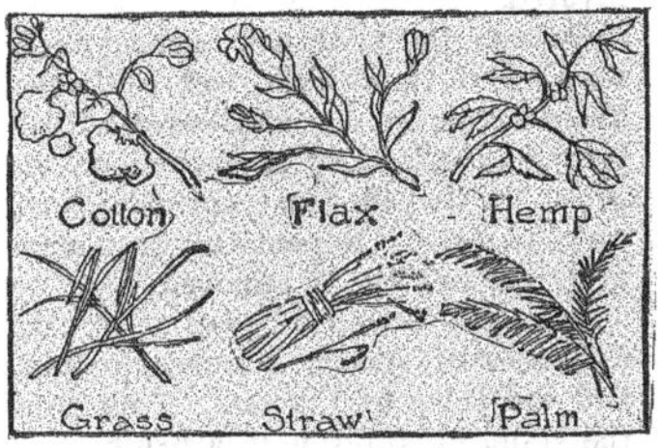

"All Vegetable Fibers Contain Cellulose."

that offers a strong resistance to the action of chemical agents, and is not easily injured by rubbing. Hence stronger acids and alkalies and more vigorous rubbing can be employed upon cottons and linens than upon wool, silk, or other animal fibers.

In the treatment of wool, caution is necessary from the fact that the fibers of wool have numerous minute hooklike projections which, by rubbing the fibers together, or by alternate expansion and contraction (as when plunged from hot water to cold water, and back again), become interlaced in such a way as to warp fabric in all directions. This is what causes the shrinking of woolen goods, so much dreaded by the laundress. Hence wool should not be rubbed or wrung out in the usual way, nor subjected to either very hot or very cold water. The water should be lukewarm or not too warm to bear the hands comfortably, and all washing and rinsing waters should be kept at a nearly uniform temperature.

A similar caution in handling silk is due to the delicacy of the fabric. Silk, if rubbed or wrung out, tends to crack or to show permanent wrinkles. It should accordingly be handled with care, and only the finer grades of soap should be employed in cleaning it.

KINDS OF SPOTS AND STAINS

The principal stains and spots the laundress has to do with are tea, coffee, and wine stains, iron rust, and ink; paint and tar, grass stains and mildew, blood stains, grease spots, and mud stains. These should all be removed from washable articles before sending them to the laundry. Hence many housekeepers set apart Tuesday for wash day, and take occasion Monday to sort the wash and carefully remove all stains, and sponge or scrub or dry-clean any articles that may require it.

Grass Stains.—White and other light-colored summer gowns, duck and flannel trousers, and children's garments frequently show grass stains in summer. The green stain is produced by chlorophyll, a coloring matter present in growing vegetation. This, when exposed to the action of the air, becomes changed into chlorophyllan, which is insoluble in water. Grass stains when fresh may be removed by sponging with alcohol, but after the chlorophyll has been converted into chlorophyllan, the action of alcohol will leave an insoluble brown stain in place of the green. Neither oxalic nor muriatic acid is effective with grass stains, but a hot solution of tartaric acid changes the green stain to light brown, that yields readily to boiling soapsuds in the laundry. If tartaric acid is not at hand, wet the stain and apply cream of tartar or salts of lemon.

Or dissolve cream of tartar in boiling water and apply hot.

Or rub grass stains with molasses and wash in clear, soft water without soap. Do not use oxalic or muriatic acid.

Tea and Coffee Stains.—These, when fresh, all yield readily to the action of boiling water, especially if the fabric be stretched tightly and the boiling water poured upon it with some force. If stains have been neglected and fixed by soap in the laundry, it may be necessary to apply dilute oxalic acid or chloride of lime, or to treat them with lemon juice and salt, salts or lemon, and other remedies, afterwards exposing the article to the air and sunshine. The stains of berries, especially of blackberries, and of plums and peaches, are very refractory. Hence, if possible, these should have immediate treatment.

Paint. — Paint and resin may be quickly dissolved by the action of turpentine, benzine, chloroform, or sulphurous ether, the treatment depending upon the nature of the fabric. Tar may be rubbed with lard and afterwards removed by washing. Oils may be dissolved by alcohol, ether, or spirits of turpentine. For colored goods, these may all be combined with ammonia and glycerin.

Mildew. — Mildew is a fungous growth of certain parasitic plants. It forms on cloth that is exposed to dampness in patches of various colors, red, black, yellow, or even green. Various substances may be used to prevent its forming. Mildew produces a stain which is very refractory. The treatment depends upon the nature of the fabric and the extent and depth of the stain, and varies from simple remedies, such as soap, lemon juice and salt, and the like, to chloride of lime and the more powerful acids. Other substances recommended are French chalk, starch, and buttermilk. These must, of course, be used with proper caution and a due regard to the liability of injury to the fabric. They should be afterwards assisted by the bleaching agencies of air and sunshine.

To Prevent Mildew.—Canvas, duck, and similar fabrics used for awnings, tents, and the like may be preserved against mildew by first soaking them in strong suds made by dissolving ½ pound of hard white or yellow soap in 2 gallons of water, and afterwards immersing the fabric, for a period of 24 hours, in a solution of 1 pound of alum dissolved in 1 gallon of water.

To Remove Mildew. — Dissolve 1 ounce of chloride of lime in 1 pint of boiling water; then add 3 pints of cold water. Soak the article in this from 3 to 12 hours. Remove, rinse thoroughly, and send to the laundry, If the chloride of lime is not thoroughly washed out the fabric may be injured.

Or rub the spot with good yellow soap, wash, and while wet rub powdered chalk into it and cover with a layer of chalk. Lay the article on the grass in the sun and sprinkle clear water over it. Repeat this treatment until the mildew is removed.

Or mix ¼ pound of soap jelly with 2 ounces of starch, 1 ounce of salt, and the juice of 1 lemon. Pour over the stain, or apply with a brush.

Iron Rust.—Stains from iron rust (or "iron mold," as they are sometimes called) yield readily to both muriatic acid and oxalic acid, but as the latter is less injurious to fabrics, a hot solution of it gives most satisfaction. Other substances recommended to remove iron rust are salts of lemon, lemon juice, salt, cream of tartar, and various admixtures of these. In all cases wet the stained fabric, apply the cleansing substance, and hold in the steam of a teakettle, or expose to direct sunshine, spreading on the grass when convenient until the stain is removed. Repeat the treatment as often as is necessary.

To make salts of lemon, mix equal parts of cream of tartar and powdered salt of sorrel. Wet the spot, and apply dry salts to the wet surface.

Or mix lemon juice with salt and cover thickly.

Or use equal parts of cream of tartar and oxalic acid, or equal parts of cream of tartar and salt.

To Remove Whitewash.—To remove whitewash stains apply strong vinegar.

Vaseline Stains.—Wash in warm soapsuds, rinse, and apply chlorinated soda.

Wax Stains.—Apply alcohol or naphtha with a camel's-hair brush, sponge, or piece of rag.

Or hold the stains within an inch

or two of a red-hot iron, and rub with a soft, clean rag.

Or lay over them a piece of brown paper, and iron with a hot iron.

Paint Stains.—Saturate the stains with gasoline and rub with a small sponge or flannel rag. Continue until the paint is absorbed, and rub with a clean cloth until dry.

Or saturate the spot for some hours with turpentine, and afterwards rub the article between the hands, when the paint will crumble and can be dusted away without injury to the fabric.

Iodine Stains.—As iodine is often applied externally to the skin, it frequently stains cotton and linen garments. To prevent this add a few drops of liquid carbolic acid to the iodine.

To remove the stains when fresh, dip the spots in aqua ammonia diluted with warm water.

Or soak the stains in a strong solution of hyposulphite of soda and water.

Or wet the fabric and cover with hyposulphite of soda until the stains are removed.

Nutgall Inks.—Formerly black ink was usually made of green vitriol dissolved in an infusion of gallnuts. Inks of this sort stain paper permanently and speedily, rapidly darken for a while, but eventually become yellow or brown with age. These old-fashioned inks were easily removed with oxalic and mineral acids, but the modern inks contain, in addition to tannate of iron (produced by the action of nutgalls upon copperas), aniline blue, indigo, and other dye stuffs that are not removable by these acids. The first inks of this sort were placed upon the market about the middle of the nineteenth century. Many of the recipes still found in print claiming to remove all sorts of ink spots were originally published more than fifty years ago. All such recipes must be regarded with suspicion. No single recipe can be given that will remove stains made by every kind of ink.

Chrome-logwood Ink. — Another modern ink known as the chrome-logwood ink is produced by the action of a solution of logwood upon potassium chromate. This is a deep purple ink, that turns darker after being exposed to the air, and has the advantage over iron-gall inks that it will not fade. Logwood is also combined with an extract of alum or chloride of aluminum. The best French copying inks are of this class. These inks may be removed by muriatic acid, which first turns the spot red. This acid must not, however, be used on stylographic inks containing eosin or nigrosine, as it will turn them into an indelible dye.

Stylographic Ink.—This is a modern ink made by dissolving in water the coal-tar product known as nigrosine. It is used for stylographic pens on account of its fluidity, as it contains no sediment. This ink is of a deep blue-black color that does not change on exposure to the air and has little luster. It does not fade, and after a lapse of years is soluble in water. Hence if paper containing it is wet the color will run. The effect upon a nigrosine ink of acids in certain recipes "guaranteed to remove any ink spot" is to mordant or set the ink, rendering it insoluble and practically indelible. Hence it is always advisable to moisten an ink spot with water, and if it blurs or smirches, thus indicating the presence of nigrosine, washing soda, caustic soda, potash lye, or any other alkali should be used, but not an acid.

Indelible Ink.—Indelible writing and marking inks are mostly finely divided carbon which, as is well known, offers great resistance to chemical agents. India and China inks are of this class. They are composed of carbon, chiefly lampblack or other soot, mixed with gum or glue. Indelible ink for marking textile fabrics is also made of nitrate of silver and other silver salts.

Various other substances are employed in ink making, but those we have given are the most common.

Treatment of Ink Stains.—If the nature of an ink is known, the proper treatment can, of course, be given; otherwise it is best to first dip the ink in water to test if nigrosine is present.

If nigrosine is not present try oxalic acid, which will remove an old style iron-gall ink or decompose a modern iron-gall ink by removing the black tannate of iron, and leaving the indigo and aniline blue dye stuffs as a stain on the fabric. If this is not effective, try muriatic acid. This will remove the stain of a logwood or copying ink. Follow this with an alkali to remove the effects of the acid.

A nitrate of silver ink stain may be removed with cyanide of potassium, which is a deadly poison.

Or apply a dilute solution of permanganate of potash with muriatic acid; follow by soaking in a solution of hyposulphite of soda, and afterwards rinse in clear water.

If all else fails, cover the spot with dry bleaching powder and moisten with dilute acetic acid. Afterwards apply ammonia, or dip in a solution of hyposulphite of soda and rinse. It must be borne in mind that strong acids and alkalies will injure the texture of animal fibers as wool and silk and bleach colored fabrics. For such articles use pyrophosphate of soda.

If a garment spotted with ink is especially valuable it would be well to try a series of experiments with the same ink on a piece of similar fabric. In the meantime cover the stain with various dry absorbents to take up the excess of ink. After these have done their work, soak the article in milk while the experiments are being made.

Or if it is small dip it immediately into pure melted tallow.

Lemon juice and salt, sour milk, and similar remedies are useful if suitable acids are not at hand, but cannot be depended on to do the work in a thorough manner.

STAINS ON WHITE LINEN OR COTTON

Ink Stains. — Substances recommended for removing ink from linen are salts of lemon, cream of tartar, citric acid, oxalic acid, lemon juice, vinegar, salt, sour milk, and chloride of lime. The treatment to be employed depends necessarily upon the nature of ink.

Ink stains should be treated as quickly as possible, before the ink has had a chance to set. While fresh, pour over them a quantity of salt, dry starch, or other absorbent, and brush it away as it absorbs the ink. Keep the spots wet, and continue applying the absorbent until the ink is removed.

Or keep the spots wet with milk, and apply dry salt until the stains come out.

Or wash the stains with sour milk and let them soak over night.

Or dip the stains alternately in strong bran water and lemon juice until they disappear.

Or use equal parts cream of tartar and powdered salts of sorrel (salts of lemon), dissolved in the smallest possible quantity of boiling water and applied hot.

Or rinse carefully in clean water and apply oxalic acid. If this produces a red tinge apply dilute aqua ammonia.

Or dip small articles, as laces, handkerchiefs, and the like, in melted tallow and after the stain has disappeared remove the tallow by boiling in hot soapsuds. This last is perhaps the simplest and best of all remedies.

To Remove Marking Ink from Linen.—Apply fresh chloride of lime mixed with water. As soon as the color fades, dip into a solution of aqua ammonia or hyposulphite of soda, and rinse well before sending to the laundry.

To Remove Indelible Ink.—Stains made by indelible ink containing nitrate of silver may be removed by applying chloride of copper. Afterwards dip the article in hyposulphite of soda.

Or apply a dilute solution of permanganate of potash and muriatic acid, and follow with hyposulphite of soda. Cyanide of potash is also used for this purpose. It is highly poisonous.

Or melt pure tallow and pour over the ink spot while hot. Remove the tallow by dipping in hot water; repeat if necessary. This is a method employed by many dyers and cleaners, and has the merit of not injuring the fabric.

To Remove Printer's Ink.—Soak the spots in turpentine for several hours. Rub them in the turpentine, as in washing. Let dry and brush thoroughly with a stiff brush.

To Remove Iron Rust.—Use lemon juice, salt, and sunshine. Or a strong solution of oxalic acid rubbed in with the fingers. Or equal parts of powdered alum and salt applied dry to the wet fabric.

Grass Stains.—Use tartaric acid or cream of tartar dissolved in boiling water. Apply hot. Or rub lard on the spot when fresh and afterwards wash as usual.

Ink Stains.—Rub promptly with a slice of lemon. Or dip in pure melted tallow. Or apply a saturated solution of oxalic acid or dilute muriatic acid or salts of lemon.

Use dilute tartaric acid for colored goods. If the colors fade, renew with dilute aqua ammonia.

Acid Stains.—Wash the article and dip in Javelle or chlorine water. For colored goods, moisten in dilute aqua ammonia.

Nitrate of Silver or Nitric-acid Stains.—Apply iodine and rub briskly with strong aqua ammonia.

Or apply a dilute solution of permanganate of potash and hydrochloric acid. Afterwards dip in a solution of hyposulphite of soda and rinse well.

Mildew.—Boil in strong borax water.

Iodine.—Soak for an hour or more in a warm solution of aqua ammonia and water. Then while still wet rub dry bicarbonate of potash into the stain until it is fully removed.

Cod-liver Oil.—Add kerosene or aqua ammonia to the suds and boil.

Red Wine.—Bleach with sulphur fumes over an inverted funnel, or dip in Javelle or chlorine water.

Tannin Stains.—These may be produced by green chestnut burs, walnut husks, or substances used for tanning leather. Dip in hot Javelle or chlorine water, remove, and rinse quickly. Or apply a strong solution of tartaric acid.

Red Stains from Colored Goods.—The dyes used for colored goods, red threads, etc., sometimes run and accidentally stain white goods. Apply fumes of sulphur through an inverted cone, or a saturated solution of oxalic acid or Javelle or chlorine water.

Mud Stains.—Dip the mud stains in kerosene before putting them in the boiler. Add kerosene to the boiling water.

Grease Spots.—Apply a hot saturated solution of alum with a sponge or brush, or dissolve in 1 quart of warm water 2 ounces of aqua ammonia, 1 teaspoonful of saltpeter, and 2 ounces of castile soap. Soak the spot in this liquid and sponge.

Or moisten the spot with butter or olive oil and rub with chloroform.

Machine Grease.—Rub sal soda or cooking soda into the spot and pour boiling water through until the spot is removed.

To Dry-clean White Goods.—Small mud stains on a clean white skirt may be concealed until ready for the laundry by pipe clay or painting over with white water-color paint.

Or if a clean white skirt or shirt waist is spattered or spotted by mud or soot, let it dry, scrape off with a penknife, and rub over the stain with white crayon or school chalk.

Rub with a clean white cloth until the spot disappears.

To Dry-clean Shirt Waists.—Put 4 quarts of corn meal into a 24-pound flour sack or a pillow slip. Put the waist into this, and rub or knead gently so that the meal will come in contact with all parts of the fabric. Leave it there for a day or two, then shake and dust thoroughly, and press with a hot iron.

To Clean Cotton Dress Skirts.—Mud stains may be removed from the bottom of a cotton dress skirt by folding several thicknesses of cloth, laying the soiled parts upon them, and scrubbing with a nailbrush, soap, and water.

TO REMOVE STAINS FROM VEGETABLE FIBERS

To Remove Stains from Linen.—All tea, coffee, milk, and other stains or spots on linen should be removed as quickly as possible. If they appear on a clean tablecloth slip beneath the spot a small dish containing hot water. Let the stain rest in the water, and rub gently with the fingers until it disappears. Smooth the cloth by putting a folded napkin underneath and applying a warm iron, and, without having been removed from the table, it will appear as fresh as when first laundered.

For strong tea stains, put a spoonful of sugar on the stain, dip into the water, and let it stand for a few minutes. Afterwards rinse with clear water.

Or, if not convenient to treat in this way, cover the stain with a quantity of powdered starch, let dry, and remove by brushing.

When dried tea, coffee, or milk stains are found in table linen, rub the stains with butter and afterwards rub in hot soapsuds before laundering.

Or apply the yolk of an egg mixed with a teaspoonful of glycerin.

Or take 10 teaspoonfuls of water, 1 teaspoonful of glycerin, and ½ teaspoonful of aqua ammonia. Dip the stain in this and allow it to dry. Repeat several times. Afterwards rub the spot between the fingers, and before sending the article to the laundry brush or scrub away the dry residue with the edge of a knife.

Mildew on Linen.—Mildew may be removed from linen as from other fabrics with powdered chalk, lemon juice, salt, and pipe clay, and afterwards exposing to sunlight. Wash the spots in soapsuds made of hard white or yellow soap. Rub in powdered chalk with a flannel cloth, cover the spot with more chalk, and lay in the sun. Repeat if necessary.

Or soak the spots in lemon juice and apply common salt. Afterwards cover with pipe clay or powdered chalk, or use equal parts powdered starch and salt.

To Remove Ink from Linen.—Treatment depends upon the nature of the ink. Stretch the linen before the steam of a teakettle and brush with a strong solution of salts of lemon.

Or use acetic or muriatic acid, not too strong. Rinse as soon as the ink disappears. Or apply salt and lemon juice. Or use the juice of a ripe tomato. Squeeze the juice upon the ink and rub with the fingers. Rinse and apply the juice again, until the stain disappears.

Linen, Marking Ink.—Apply a saturated solution of cyanide of potassium, rubbing with a glass rod. Rinse as soon as the ink disappears.

Linen, Iron Rust and Mold.—Cover the stain with salts of lemon and stretch it across the steam of a teakettle or a saucepan full of boiling water, so that the salts of lemon will be gradually dissolved by the steam and soaked into the fabric.

Or put a common dinner plate on top of a saucepan containing boiling water. Lay the linen over this, cover the stain with salts of lemon, and keep wet with hot water until the stain is removed. Afterwards rinse carefully in cold water.

Or rub the spot with butter, then add a small quantity of potash lye, and again rub the spot until the stain has disappeared. Rinse quickly in cold water.

Linen, Yellow Stains.—If linen has faded yellow or become stained from perspiration, dissolve about one tablespoonful of pipe clay in the water in which it is boiled.

Linen, Acid Stains.—Wet the article, and cover it with salts of wormwood. Rub the dry salt into the wet fabric until the stain disappears. Afterwards rinse thoroughly.

Or form a cone by twisting and pinning together a piece of paper, and under this light a number of old-fashioned brimstone matches or burn a bit of sulphur. Hold the stain so that the sulphurous-acid gas escaping through the cone will pass through it.

Linen, Iodine Stains.—Dip the spot in cold water and hold it by the fire until dry. Repeat until the stain is removed.

Linen, Fruit and Wine Stains.—While fresh put a little baking soda or washing soda on the stain, stretch it tightly over a bowl or pan, and pour boiling water upon the stain so as to dissolve the soda. No fresh fruit, wine, tea, coffee, or other common stain is likely to withstand this treatment. Let the spot sink into the water and soak until the water cools, dipping it up and down and rubbing with the fingers. When the water cools repeat, if necessary, until the stain disappears.

Or rub salts of lemon upon the stain and soak in hot water. Or dip in a weak solution of chloride of lime with water. Afterwards rinse carefully. Or rub in starch with yellow soap, then apply starch thickly moistened with water and expose to the sun. Or soak in sour buttermilk. Or apply oxalic acid.

Linen, Tea or Coffee Stains.—If tea or coffee stains are noticed at the time they are made, remove the tablecloth as soon as convenient, stretch the cloth over a pan, and pour boiling water through the stains.

Or, if they are small and the tablecloth is clean, slip a saucer or small nappy containing boiling water under the tablecloth and let the stain lie in the water. Rub gently with the fingers until it is removed. Remove the dish, put a folded napkin under the stain, and go over it with a warm iron. The cloth will then be as fresh as new without having been removed from the table. Add a little glycerin to the boiling water to remove coffee stains.

Or, if an old stain is found on a tablecloth in the laundry, first soak the spot in cold water without soap, and try to remove with boiling water and glycerin. If this is not effectual, mix the yolk of an egg with a tablespoonful of milk and a little warm water. Add a few drops of alcohol or chloroform, if convenient, and use this as soap.

Linen, Wine Stains.—Pile a little dry salt on a fresh wine stain and it will absorb the wine. Afterwards rinse in boiling water. Dip old stains in boiling milk until removed.

Linen, Blood Stains. — For fresh blood stains on white fabrics apply peroxide of hydrogen, which will immediately remove the color from the blood. This is a strong bleaching substance. Hence it must not be used on colored fabrics, and must be immediately rinsed, especially from woolen goods.

Or soak in warm water and cover with dry pepsin. This will digest the blood.

Or moisten the stain slightly with water and apply a thick layer of common starch. Afterwards rinse in cold water.

TO REMOVE STAINS FROM ANIMAL FIBERS

To Prepare Silks for Cleaning.—If silk garments are to be made over or if the silk is much soiled, rip them, remove all basting threads, and stretch out creases and wrinkles. Brush thoroughly all articles, including ribbons and small pieces, to remove dust and dirt, shake well, and stretch them to their original shape. Clear a wooden kitchen table or an ironing board, and on this stretch an old linen towel, tacking the corners down tightly. Smooth the silk out flat on the towel, and sponge first on the wrong side, afterwards on the right, applying with a small toothbrush or nailbrush or flannel cloth any of the following recipes that may be most convenient. After sponging on both sides rinse in clear cold water by dipping up and down, but without wringing or squeezing, partly dry in the shade, and press between two pieces of cloth, ironing on the wrong side with a warm, not hot, iron.

Or while wet spread the silk smoothly on a wooden polished sur-

"Clear a Wooden Kitchen Table."

face, as a varnished table top, and let it dry near the fire. It will then require no ironing.

To Remove Grease from Silk.—For removing grease spots from silk, chloroform, French chalk, essence of lemon, turpentine, white clay, magnesia, yolk of egg, and benzine are all recommended. If possible, apply any of these while the grease is still warm.

To Clean Silk and Velvet.—Substances recommended for removing grease and other spots and stains from silks, satins, and velvets are alcohol, chloroform, benzine, turpentine, juice of raw potato, magnesia, French chalk, pipe clay, yolk of egg, and various admixtures of these. Lay the stained article flat on a smooth surface and apply the cleansing fluid with a small sponge, toothbrush, or nailbrush, unless otherwise directed, until the stain is removed. Apply chloroform with a light, quick touch, using a bit of absorbent cotton or soft cotton rag. Dampen the grease, and when it disappears rub until dry with clean cloth. To use gasoline or benzine, wet the spot and also a rather large circle around it. Rub outward from the center with quick, firm strokes, and if the benzine leaves a stain hold it in the steam of a teakettle until it disappears.

Or rub grease spots with a lump of wet magnesia. This may be dusted off when dry. Or mix 4 ounces of rectified spirits of turpentine with ½ ounce of pure alcohol. Or mix 2 ounces of essence of lemon and 1 ounce of oil of turpentine. Or use turpentine alone. Or mix 2 ounces of alcohol, 1 ounce of French chalk, and 5 ounces of pipe clay. Apply as a paste to the grease spots.

Or cover grease spots thickly with French chalk, lay brown paper over them, and smooth with a hot iron. The iron will melt the grease, and the chalk and paper will absorb it.

Or if chalk is not at hand lay a piece of brown paper on the ironing board, lay the silk over this, place another piece of brown paper on top, and press with a hot iron, but not so hot as to scorch the fabric. This is a most effective method.

Or apply the yolk of an egg with or without the addition of 12 drops of chloroform or a teaspoonful of alcohol. Afterwards rinse with warm water.

To Clean Silk with Potato Juice.—Grate two fair-sized clean raw potatoes into each pint of water used and strain through cheese cloth. Let the resulting liquor stand until the potato starch it contains settles to the bottom, then pour off the clear liquid and bottle it. Lay a washboard down flat, spread over this a clean cloth, and lay the silk upon it. Apply the potato juice with a sponge until the silk is clean, and afterwards rinse it in clear cold water.

To Clean Silk with Gasoline.—Gasoline and benzine may be applied to silk with a sponge, but this should be done by daylight and never in the vicinity of an open fire or flame of any kind. These liquids are highly volatile, producing a gas which will ignite and explode if it comes in contact with an open flame. After cleansing with gasoline or benzine rinse the silk in alcohol.

Cleansing Mixtures for Silk. — Make a soap jelly by dissolving pure castile or other hard white soap or toilet soap in about four times its bulk of water. Take ¼ pound of this soap and add 4 ounces of ammonia, the white of an egg, and a wineglassful of gin or tablespoonful of brandy. Mix thoroughly and strain through cheese cloth; dilute with a small quantity of soft soap. Spread the silk smoothly on a flat surface and apply the mixture with a sponge or nailbrush to both sides, taking care not to crease or wrinkle the fabric. Rinse in cold water, adding salt and oxgall for colored articles.

Black Silk. — Various substances are recommended for cleaning black silks, including infusion of oxgall, logwood, copperas, tea, coffee, fig leaves, vinegar, and ammonia. The preparation and use of these is explained below.

Dust the article carefully, spread smooth on a flat surface, and apply, with a sponge or piece of flannel, a cold, strong infusion of black tea.

Or use equal parts of clear cold coffee and soft water. Or equal parts of coffee and aqua ammonia. Or a dilute solution of aqua ammonia in water.

Any left-over tea or coffee may be used for this purpose. Strain through cheese cloth to remove the dregs. Sponge or scrub both sides of the fabric, taking care not to crease it. Make the silk quite wet. Smooth the articles carefully and press as for other silk fabrics. Coffee removes grease and renews the silk without making it shiny.

Or make a strong solution of ivy or fig leaves by boiling 4 ounces of either with 2 quarts of water down to a pint. Strain through cheese cloth and bottle for future use. Apply with a sponge and brush or flannel cloth.

Or sponge with oxgall slightly diluted with boiling water and applied warm. Rinse in cold water from time to time and continue the oxgall until the rinsing water is clear.

Or make a strong solution of logwood by boiling 1 ounce in 2 quarts of water down to 1 pint. Wash the silk clean, immerse in the solution and simmer with gentle heat for half an hour. Remove the silk, add ½ ounce of copperas to the solution, strain through cheese cloth, and dip the silk in it.

Or save old kid gloves of all colors, and when silks require cleaning cut up a glove of the same color into small pieces and boil it in a pint of water a quarter of an hour. Let it stand twenty-four hours in a warm place, again raise it to a boil, strain through cheese cloth, and add a tablespoonful of alcohol. Sponge with this.

Or wash the articles in gasoline, dipping them up and down and rubbing lightly between the hands as in water. Care must be taken not to wrinkle or crease the fabric. This removes the dirt quickly and does not cause the colors to run.

To Remove Wax from Silk. — Scrape off the excess of wax from the surface of the fabric with a penknife. Apply French chalk made into a paste with water. Lay the silk on a piece of brown paper spread over the ironing board, put another sheet of brown paper on it, and press with a hot iron.

Or toast a piece of soft bread before the fire until quite hot, but not burned, and rub the wax spot with the hot bread until cold. Take another piece, and so continue until the wax is removed. Afterwards rub with the dry bread crumbs until perfectly clean.

Silk—To Remove Paint.—Apply a mixture of 5 parts of spirits of turpentine and 1 part of essence of lemon with a small brush, sponge, or linen rag. Or apply turpentine alone.

Silk—To Remove Tar.—Rub lard on the tar, and afterwards wash with soapsuds.

Silk, Stains of Sea Water.—Sponge with dilute aqua ammonia and water.

Silk, Acid Stains.—If the color has been taken out by acid stains, apply aqua ammonia.

To Remove Acid Stains from Violet Silk.—First apply tincture of iodine, and immediately afterwards cover the spot with hyposulphite of soda dissolved in water. Hang in the shade to dry.

To Clean Velvet.—First dust the velvet thoroughly, using for this purpose an old piece of rolled-up crape. Sponge with benzine or gasoline, same as silk. Stretch the velvet right side up over a basin of boiling water so that the steam must pass through it. While thus stretched brush with a whisk broom in the direction of the nap. The time spent depends upon the condition of the velvet, but if patiently continued the result will be entirely satisfactory. Any ingenious person can arrange a contrivance to hold the velvet in place while brushing, or an assistant may do so.

Or dampen a newspaper and set it in a hot oven until it steams. Lay this on the ironing board, cover it with a folded cotton cloth, and lay the velvet on it. While the steam is rising, brush the velvet against the pile.

Or heat a flatiron, turn it face upward, and lay a wet cotton cloth on it. Lay the velvet, nap up, over the iron, and brush while steaming.

To Revive Faded Velvet or Plush.—Brush slightly with a sponge dipped in chloroform.

To Clean Satin.—Sponge satin neckties and other small articles with a weak solution of borax, following the grain, and afterwards iron on the wrong side.

To Clean White Silk.—White silk may be washed in soapsuds the same as other delicate white fabrics, being careful not to rub or squeeze the fabric so as to cause creases or wrinkles.

Or it may be washed in gasoline, or dry-cleaned by rubbing or dusting it with magnesia and laying it away for two or three days in a paper bag covered with magnesia, afterwards brushing it with a soft, heavy brush.

Naphtha soap will remove most stains from white silk, including paint stains.

To Bleach White Silk.—When white silk articles have become yellow from the laundry or from being packed away, dip them in a solution of one tablespoonful of ammonia to a quart of warm water. Squeeze out this solution, and rinse in bluing water until fully restored. Hang in the shade to dry and while damp press between dry cloths on the wrong side.

Or dissolve 4 ounces of salt and 4 ounces of oxalic acid in 6 quarts of water. Immerse the silk in this solution until it is bleached white. This will require a half hour to an hour or more. Rinse thoroughly.

Or the silk, after having been laundered, may be bleached with the fumes of brimstone. Suspend a large-sized paper flour sack upside down, either out of doors on a still day or in an outhouse, and put in it the article to be bleached, attaching it to the sides of the bag with pins or basting thread. Put burning coke or charcoal on an iron pan, cover with flowers of sulphur, and invert a tin funnel over it so that the fumes will pass up into the bag. Afterwards sponge the article carefully and expose to air and sunshine until the odor has passed off.

To Remove Stains from Colored Silks.—To remove acid stains, apply liquid ammonia with a brush or soft rag, taking care not to rub the fabric, as the ammonia may cause the colors to fade or run. Should this happen, afterwards apply chloroform to restore the color.

Or cover the spot with cooking soda or magnesia and moisten with clear water.

TO CLEAN COLORED GOODS

Alkali Stains.—Moisten the spot with vinegar or tartaric acid, and afterwards apply chloroform to restore its color.

Grease Spots.—Cover the spot with fuller's earth, pipe clay, or French chalk. Place over this a layer of brown paper and press with a hot iron.

Fruit and Wine Stains.—Wet with a mixture of equal parts of alcohol and ammonia. Afterwards sponge gently with alcohol until the stain is removed.

Or rub the spot with soap, and apply chloride of soda with a camel's-hair brush, rinsing quickly and thoroughly.

Wax Stains.—Scrape off the surplus of wax from the surface of the fabric, dissolve with alcohol, and remove by rubbing gently with a clean flannel rag or pressing with a hot iron through brown paper.

Oil Stains.—Cover with French chalk, pipe clay, or fuller's earth, and wet with water to a thin paste. Let this dry on the fabric and remove by brushing. Repeat if necessary.

Mud Stains.—Let the mud dry thoroughly, and then remove as much as possible by brushing. When fully dry, cover with a mixture of salt and flour and keep in a dry place.

If the stains are extensive place the garment in a large paper flour sack with a quantity of salt and flour well mixed, shake vigorously, tie up the sack, and allow it to hang behind the stove for a few days. Afterwards shake out the dust and press.

Or, while the stains are wet, cover thickly with cornstarch and brush away until the stain has disappeared. When dry, make a thick paste of cornstarch with warm water, lay over the stains, and brush off when dry. Repeat if necessary.

Rust Stains.—Apply a solution of salts of lemon.

Ink Stains.—Apply 1 teaspoonful of dilute oxalic acid to 6 ounces of water. Or moisten the spots with a strong solution of citric acid. Or dip the spots in milk and cover with salt. If the colors are affected, restore them with aqua ammonia and chloroform.

Tar.—Rub lard over the tar and wash in soapsuds. Or apply oil of turpentine, rub with soap, and wash. Or soak in olive or sweet oil for twenty-four hours. Afterwards wash in soapsuds.

To Dry-clean Lace.—Stretch the lace carefully on a thick piece of wrapping paper, fastening the edges with pins. Sprinkle it quite thickly with calcined magnesia. Cover with another piece of wrapping paper, and place it under a pile of books or other heavy weight for three or four days. The magnesia can then be shaken off and the lace will appear like new. It will not only be clean, but the edges will be in perfect condition. Calcined magnesia is very cheap, and this method is well worth trying.

Or stretch the lace, if not too much soiled, on a piece of cloth, pin all the points, and work over it with the soft part of a loaf of fine bread, not too dry, and afterwards shake out the crumbs.

Or use bread crumbs, rubbing them over the lace with a soft cloth, constantly using fresh crumbs, and changing the cloth as it becomes soiled.

Or dust a mixture of flour and magnesia into the fiber of the lace, and rub it with a soft cloth. Afterwards put the lace under pressure for a few hours.

To Clean Gold and Silver Lace.—Stretch the lace and tack it down on a piece of woolen cloth, following the outline of the pattern carefully with basting thread. Brush it thoroughly free from dust. Sprinkle over it a mixture of dry crumbs or stale bread, and powdered laundry blue. Rub gently with a piece of flannel until clean.

Or use burnt alum, pulverized to a fine powder, and sifted through cheese cloth. Apply with a fine, soft brush.

Or sponge with alcohol. Afterwards polish with a piece of red velvet.

TO DRY-CLEAN MEN'S GARMENTS

To Clean Men's Clothes.—Hang the garments on a line, beat them with a carriage whip or piece of rubber hose, and brush them thoroughly with a stiff brush. To remove spots, place several thicknesses of soft cloth, like an old towel, under the spot, moisten it with water, and scour with any good cleanser, or moisten the spot thoroughly with a liquid cleanser and rub it hard. Use for this purpose a loof, a stiff, fibrous sponge, costing about ten cents. This is rough enough to scrub with vigor if the goods will stand it, or it can be used more gently on delicate goods. It leaves no lint as cloth does, but is stiffer than a sponge and can be easily washed and dried after being used. Or use one or more small scrubbing brushes of varying degrees of stiffness.

To Remove Spots.—First hold the garment up to the light to see if there is any surface dirt; if there is, scrape off with a sharp knife what can be removed (taking care not to injure the weave of the garment) before wetting the spot in water, cleansing fluid, or any sort of chemical. Next apply the cleanser and rub well, so that the dirt when dissolved may be forced through into the pad beneath. Rub with a piece of woolen

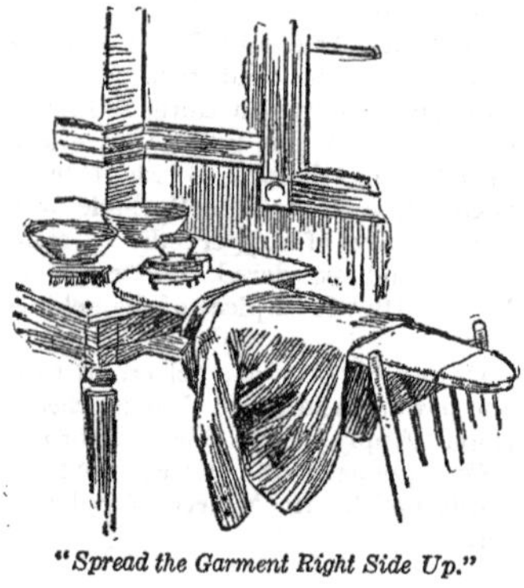

"Spread the Garment Right Side Up."

cloth folded into a tight pad. Use plenty of "elbow grease." The secret of success lies in hard rubbing.

To Press Men's Clothes.—Spread the garment right side up on an ironing board, lay over it a cotton cloth wrung out of warm water containing about 1 tablespoonful of aqua ammonia to 3 pints of water, and iron the wet cloth until both the cloth and the garment are perfectly dry. This prevents the garment from having a shiny appearance.

Black Dye for Renovating.—Put 8 ounces of logwood chips in a porcelain kettle, cover with 2 quarts of soft water, and let stand over night. Boil 30 minutes, strain through cheese cloth, and add 6 grains of prussiate of potash and 12 grains of bichromate of potash previously dissolved in as little boiling water as possible. Pour this mixture into a black glass bottle, cork tightly, and store in a dark place. This is a good black dye. To apply, first sponge or otherwise cleanse the garments, stretch them out smooth, and go over them with this dye by means of a soft brush. Let dry thoroughly before pressing.

To Clean a Mackintosh.—To clean a mackintosh, scrub both sides with soap and water, and afterwards rinse it in clear water until the soap is removed. Hang up to dry without wringing. Care must be taken not to sponge a mackintosh with alcohol, chloroform, benzine, gasoline, turpentine, or any of the chemicals which are used in sponging other fabrics, as they have the property of dissolving rubber and will injure the texture of many waterproof garments. Ammonia may be applied freely.

To Renovate Woolen Goods. — After woolen dress goods have been sponged or washed, to restore the original gloss rub the cloth with a brush dipped in a thin solution of gum arabic, cover with a dry cotton cloth, and dry under a weight. This method is useful to remove the spot caused by sponging out stains. To raise the nap on a rough woolen garment, wet it, lay it on a smooth surface, and roughen it gently with a common prickly thistle, or what is known as a teasel brush. Afterwards brush with a stiff clothes brush the way of the nap.

To Clean Men's Woolen Clothes.— Boil for half an hour 2 ounces of soap bark in 1 quart of water, and let stand all night on the dregs. Strain through cheese cloth, and use alone or combined with an equal amount of gasoline.

Or use 1 part of oxgall to 16 parts of water. Or use 1 tablespoonful of oxgall and 1 teaspoonful of cooking soda to a quart of water. Or mix 6 ounces of soap jelly or good soft soap with 4 ounces of honey, the white of 1 egg, and 1 tablespoonful of brandy or alcohol. Or mix 1 ounce of sulphuric ether, 1 ounce of aqua ammonia, and 6 ounces of water.

The most convenient way to clean men's garments is to remove the cover from an ironing board, or use some other smooth, clean, narrow board or plank, arranged to admit of laying the coat smoothly over it, or insert the board into the trousers legs. A smooth, hard, narrow board is also desirable for coat sleeves. Arrange the garment on this board and with a stiff brush apply any of the cleansers you prefer. A bristle nailbrush or horsehair brush, such as is used in the stable for smoothing the coats of horses, is a most useful implement for this purpose. Rub with, rather than against, the nap of the cloth, wetting the brush frequently.

Scrub especially spots of grease and, if much soiled by perspiration, the collar and cuffs. When the grease and dirt are thoroughly loosened, sponge with clear water until quite clean. Trousers and waistcoats may be rinsed by immersing in water and sousing up and down, but it is better not to immerse coats and jackets, as it is difficult, on account of the padded linings, to press them into shape.

To Renovate Men's Clothes.—Boil 8 ounces of logwood chips in 2 gallons of water down to 1 gallon. Strain and add 2 ounces of gum arabic, dissolved in a little hot water. Bottle for future use.

After dark, solid-colored garments, as blacks, blues, or browns, have been scrubbed and sponged, dilute this mixture to the shade of the garment, and go over it lightly with a sponge. Do not expose to direct sunshine or the heat of a stove while drying.

Or moisten a soft brush with olive oil and carefully go over the garment.

To Press Men's Clothes. — After sponging the garments, stretch them to their proper shape, lay them right side up over the ironing board, and press through linen or cotton cloth previously wrung out of clear cold water. A tablespoonful each of oxgall and salt added to every gallon of water will tend to brighten the colors. Press with a hot iron until the garment is dry.

Care must be taken that all the liquid preparations used for cleaning woolen goods be kept at the same temperature, which should be about as warm as the hands will bear comfortably.

After the garments have been pressed, brush with the nap while the steam is still rising from the cloth, and hang on suitable clothes hangers or over chairs to dry. Do not wear them for twenty-four hours or more after pressing, or until they are thoroughly dry.

TO DRY-CLEAN WOMEN'S GARMENTS

To Clean Woolen Dresses. — The most satisfactory method of cleaning waists or skirts of wool, silk, velvet, or anything except cotton goods, is to soak and wash them in gasoline. For this purpose two or three large earthen jars will be found very useful. It pays to buy the best gasoline, five gallons at a time, and use it plentifully, as the expense is much less than would be the charge of a professional cleaner, or the cost of a new garment.

First, dust the garments and rub soap on soiled or greasy spots. Nothing need be removed from them except rubber dress shields.

Next, put large pieces, one at a time, in an earthen jar and cover with gasoline. Throw a wet cloth over the jar, and press the lid down tightly. Soak for an hour or more, then rub the article well, sousing it up and down, and transfer it to a second jar containing an equal amount of fresh gasoline. Rinse in this, squeeze out the gasoline, and hang up to dry. A third jar may be used if desired.

Articles washed in this way will require to be hung out and aired for two or three days, when the odor will entirely leave them. They should not be pressed until they are thoroughly dry and all the gasoline has evaporated. The gasoline can be poured back into the cans through cheese cloth and used again, as the dirt settles to the bottom. This operation must be carried on out of doors, as much of the gasoline will evaporate. If done in the house the odor would be very unpleasant, and, besides, the vapor is explosive and might cause accident. A small bristle brush dipped in the gasoline will be found useful for removing grease spots, scrubbing collars, and the like. If a small quantity of gasoline be put in a tin can and then surrounded by a vessel of boiling water (but not on the stove), it will do the work quickly and more thoroughly.

Crape, Mourning, and Other Black Goods.—Black dress goods may be washed by observing the same caution as for other colored fabrics, whether cotton, linen, wool, or silk. To remove stains before laundering, apply a solution of 1 part of alcohol and 2 parts of water with a soft cloth, sponge, or soft bristle brush.

To remove paint, apply spirits of turpentine; for grease, apply benzine or gasoline; for mud stains, rub the spot with a piece of raw potato.

To Remove Gloss.—Sponge with a saturated solution of borax and water. Afterwards sponge with clear water.

Or boil half a handful of fig leaves in a quart of water down to a pint. Strain and apply the clear liquor.

Crape Lace. — Dissolve a square inch of sheet glue in a pint of boiling water, add a pint of skim milk, and dip the lace in this while boiling hot. When cool enough to handle, remove, stretch, and clap the lace between the hands. Pin it to a linen cloth and stretch the cloth tent fashion to dry in the shade.

White Spots.—If white spots or light-colored stains appear on black garments, apply India ink, marking ink, or common ink with a camel's-hair brush. Put a piece of blotting paper underneath the stain to absorb the surplus ink.

To Revive Faded Colors. — In 3 quarts of boiling water stir ¼ pound of green vitriol, 1 pound of logwood chips, and ½ pound of bruised galls. Boil gently for 3 hours and strain through cheese cloth.

Or mix oxgall, 4 ounces; logwood, ½ ounce; green vitriol, ½ ounce; iron filings, ½ ounce; sumac, ½ ounce, and vinegar, 1 quart.

Or make a simple solution of logwood, boiling 2 ounces of logwood in 1 gallon of water down to 1 quart.

To apply any of the above, dilute with sufficient hot water to cover the articles, and boil for half an hour. If the infusion of logwood is used alone, remove the articles, add an ounce of sulphate of iron, and boil for half an hour. Hang them up without wringing in a shady place until they cease to drip. Then rinse them in cold water, let them dry, and rub gently with a brush moistened with a little olive oil.

To Clean and Scour Woolen Goods.—Remove all dirt and dust by shaking and brushing the articles. Remove grease spots with turpentine, benzine, or gasoline. Make a strong suds of hard white or curd soap with water, and to each gallon add a tablespoonful of oxgall. Apply vigorously with a fairly stiff nailbrush. Rinse by sponging with warm water containing salt, and dry by rubbing with a piece of clean flannel.

Or, for garments which will not lose their shape, rinse in clear cold water and hang up to dry.

Sponging with stale lager beer will give some stiffness and gloss to the surface.

Or go over the surface with a brush slightly moistened with olive oil.

To Dry-clean Woolen Cloth.—Remove all spots and stains, and cover the garment with clean, damp sand, with which may be mixed a quantity of French chalk. Rub over the surface of the sand with the hands to work it into the texture of the fabric, and allow the garment to dry. Afterwards brush off the sand.

To Clean Scarlet Cloth.—Wash in bran water, and rinse in clear water containing a tablespoonful of solution of tin to each gallon.

Or add a small quantity of scarlet dye to the last rinsing water.

To Clean Light-colored Worsteds.—For delicate light-brown or buff colors apply pipe clay mixed with water to the consistency of milk. Cover the surface with this by means of a sponge or brush. Brush off when dry.

CLEANING AND CARE OF GLOVES

To Clean Gloves.—For cleaning gloves, gasoline, benzine, naphtha, and soap used with either milk or water, fuller's earth, with or without pow-

"Wash Them in Gasoline."

dered alum, cream of tartar, pipe clay, French chalk, bread crumbs, and corn meal are all recommended; for fruit and acid stains, ammonia; for ink stains, oxalic acid; and various compounds of these substances.

Gasoline.—Draw the gloves on to the hands and wash them in gasoline in the same fashion as the hands are washed in water. Wipe off surplus gasoline with a piece of flannel, and allow the gloves to partially dry on the hands. Afterwards hang on a line to dry in the sun. The soiled parts of the gloves may be rubbed with any good white hard soap during this process. But they should not afterwards be washed in soapsuds, as it shrinks and wrinkles them. For light glacé kid gloves, draw the gloves on to the hands and with a flannel cloth apply a paste composed of flour and gasoline. Rub with a clean, dry cloth until quite dry.

Turpentine.—Before the discovery of gasoline, gloves were cleaned by washing in spirits of turpentine in the same way as they are now washed in gasoline. Turpentine is to be preferred when the gloves are stained with paint or resinous substances.

Benzine.—Place the gloves in a large fruit jar full of benzine, screw on the lid and let them soak for twenty minutes or more, shaking the jar vigorously at intervals. Take them out and examine for dirt spots, which may be removed by rubbing with benzine on a flannel rag. Afterwards hang them up to dry in the open air. To remove the odor of benzine, professional cleaners dry articles cleaned in this manner in a drying room at a temperature of about 200°. But this odor will pass off after a time.

Or draw the gloves on the hands, dip a flannel rag in benzine, and allow it to become nearly dry. While slightly damp, moisten the gloves with this by rubbing the hands with it as if with a towel.

Or take part of a loaf of bread slightly moist, or dry bread crumbs, and rub lightly over the gloves until they are clean. Change the crumbs as they become soiled. Repeat if necessary.

Milk for Kid Gloves.—Draw the gloves on the hands, dip a cloth in skim milk, and wipe them on the cloth as if on a towel. Let them dry on the hands.

Or draw a glove on one hand and with the other hand dip a piece of flannel in new milk, rub on castile soap or any good hard white soap, and rub the soiled glove lightly.

Or lay the glove on a folded towel, dip a flannel cloth in milk, rub on castile soap or other white soap, and rub the glove lightly, working from the back or wrist toward the fingers.

To Dry-clean Gloves. — Delicate white kid or suède gloves may be dry-cleaned with cream of tartar, magnesia, fuller's earth, alum, pipe clay, corn meal, or various compounds of these.

A simple method is to draw the gloves on the hands and wash them thoroughly in fine corn meal.

Or place the glove in a paper bag or fruit jar, fill them with a mixture of magnesia and cream of tartar, cover them with it, shake the bag, and let it stand over night. Rub off this mixture with a flannel cloth inside and out, draw the gloves on the hands, and apply a mixture of powdered alum and fuller's earth with a small, soft brush, sponge, nailbrush, or toothbrush.

Or brush with fuller's earth without powdered alum, and dust it off.

If the gloves are not entirely clean, draw them on the hands and apply fine bran or pipe clay, or a mixture of both. None of these substances will injure the gloves, and if one is not at hand use another. Bread crumbs are also useful, especially when the gloves are much soiled. Change the crumbs as they become dirty.

To Clean Wash-leather Gloves.—Wash-leather gloves may be cleaned with soap and water. Draw them on the hands and with a shaving brush apply a lather of fine shaving or toilet soap. Wipe them on a clean towel and let them dry on the hands.

Or, if much soiled with perspiration, apply a mixture of magnesia and cream of tartar, filling and covering the gloves and letting them stand over night. Rub off with a flannel cloth, draw the gloves on the hands, and wash them in lukewarm suds made with fine white soap, rinse in warm water, and let them remain on the hands until quite dry.

To Color Wash-leather Gloves.—While the gloves are still damp they may be colored yellow by rubbing with yellow ocher, or white by rubbing with pipe clay, or any desired intermediate shade by mixing the two. Mix into a paste with stale beer or vinegar.

To Renovate Kid Gloves.—White kid gloves that are stained beyond cleaning may be dyed to a tan shade by applying two or three coats of saffron and water, drying them between the coatings. Apply to the surface with a soft brush, wetting as little as possible. Black kid or suède gloves when defaced may be improved by painting the worn spots with a mixture of black ink and olive oil. Apply it with a camel's-hair brush or feather, touch the spots lightly, and observe the effect by allowing the glove to dry before adding more color. Repeat if necessary.

Glove Cleaners.—Scrape one pound of castile or other hard white soap into a powder, place in a fruit jar, and add alcohol sufficient to make a soap jelly. Stir in a teaspoonful of ether or chloroform and keep the cover of the jar glued tight.

Or grate 1½ pounds of castile soap in 15 ounces of water and dissolve with gentle heat. Melt 3 ounces of soap in an equal bulk of water, add 2 ounces of Javelle water and 1 teaspoonful of ammonia. This will form a thick paste or jell. Apply by putting the gloves on and using a flannel cloth. Dry the gloves on the hands.

To Remove Stains. — Put a few tablespoonfuls of aqua ammonia in a large two-quart fruit jar, or other wide-mouthed bottle or can or similar receptacle, taking care not to wet the mouth or sides of the vessel. Suspend the gloves in this vessel above the ammonia, where they will be penetrated by its fumes, and cover tightly. Do not allow the gloves to touch the ammonia water. This process will not injure the most delicate colors.

To Remove Ink Stains.—First dip the stained part in melted tallow to absorb the ink. Afterwards cover with pipe clay.

Or insert a roll of brown paper inside the glove and put another piece over it; then press gently with a warm iron. Repeat if necessary.

Or, if the stain is not removed, make a solution of 1 part of oxalic acid to 10 parts of water, and gently apply it to the spot with the tip of the finger, using as little as possible. Follow with a drop of aqua ammonia.

Or wet the spot and cover with common soda to neutralize the effect of the acid.

To Clean Kid Gloves.—Shave 2 ounces of white soap and dissolve in a pint of milk with gentle heat. Add the white of 1 egg and beat up the whole with an egg beater. Add a teaspoonful of sulphuric ether, draw on the gloves, and apply the paste with a small bit of sponge until clean. It is best to keep the gloves on until they are dry. This method not only cleans but softens and revives the leather.

Or draw the gloves on the hand and go over them with a cloth dipped in skim milk. Wear them until quite dry.

Or moisten a small sponge or piece of cloth in skim milk, rub it on a cake of castile or other hard white soap, and with this sponge the gloves all over until they are clean. Wear them until dry.

Or shave fine 3 ounces of castile or other hard white soap in 2 ounces of water, and dissolve with gentle heat. Remove from the fire, and when cold stir in 2 ounces of Javelle water and 1 teaspoonful of aqua ammonia. Apply with a flannel cloth.

Or put the gloves in a large-stoppered bottle about half filled with benzine and let stand several hours, shaking frequently. Remove the gloves, sponge any spots with benzine or ether, and hang up to dry.

Or draw the gloves on to the hands and wash in benzine or turpentine. Dry on a soft muslin cloth or towel and hang up in a draught until the odor disappears.

To Polish Kid Gloves.—Apply talcum or other good toilet powder or French chalk with a piece of soft muslin.

To Clean Chamois.—To clean gloves and other articles of chamois skin, dissolve 3 tablespoonfuls of aqua ammonia in 1 quart of warm water. Soak the articles in this for an hour or more. Stir occasionally with a wooden spoon. Press out as much of the dirt as possible. Pour all into a basin of warm water, wash with the hands, rinse in clear soft water, dry in the shade, and rub between the hands until soft.

TO CLEAN FEATHERS, FURS, AND STRAW

To Clean Feathers.—Prepare suds by shaving and boiling half a bar of hard white or naphtha soap in a saucepan with sufficient water. Dilute with warm soft water. Immerse the plume in this and allow it to soak for ten or fifteen minutes, occasionally drawing it rather loosely through the hands to strip out the dirt with the suds. Rinse in water of the same temperature. If not yet clean, lay the feather on a smooth surface and with a soft toothbrush rub gently with soap and water, working outwardly from the stem. Rinse in clear warm water and afterwards, if a white feather, in bluing water. Draw through the palm of the hand to squeeze out the water, but without twisting. Pin or stitch the stem to a cloth and hang up to dry with the thick end of the stem up and the plumage hanging down. Shake occasionally while drying it, or, if time will permit, shake the feathers near the stove until dry.

Or dry out of doors in a gentle breeze. But care must be taken that the wind does not whip the feather and break the stem.

To Renovate Feathers. — Black feathers after having been washed may be restored to their original luster as follows: dissolve 1 ounce of sulphate of iron in 1 quart of hot water. Immerse the feathers in this and let them steep until the liquid is cold. Hang up in a shady place to dry. Make a solution of logwood and gallnuts by boiling ½ ounce of each in a copper vessel with 1 quart of water down to 1 pint. Remove from the fire, while hot, immerse the feathers, and allow them to remain until cool. Rinse in clear water and dry. Lay them on a smooth surface and rub from the stem outwardly with a piece of flannel slightly moistened in olive oil.

Grebe Feathers and Other Skins.—These may be washed in the same manner as ostrich plumes by first removing the lining. They must be handled with great care to prevent injury by tearing.

To Curl Feathers.—Feathers which have temporarily lost their curl from exposure to rain or fog may be improved by holding them over a fire and shaking occasionally until the matted fibers are loosened, when the curl will be restored.

When the curl has been entirely taken out by washing or soaking, it will be necessary to curl the fronds with the blunt edge of a knife or a piece of ivory. The curl will be more durable if the feather is held near the surface of a hot flatiron while curling. The feather should be bone dry. Do not take more than two or three fronds at a time, and draw them between the thumb and the blunt edge of a silver knife or ivory paper cutter. Begin at the point of the feather, and work along the stem on both sides. After a little practice feathers may be curled to look as good as new.

Swan's-down. — To clean swan's-down, first tack the strips on a piece of muslin and wash same as ostrich plumes. When partially dry, remove the muslin and rub the feather carefully between the fingers to make it pliant.

To Prepare Quills for Writing.—Cut thin, broad layers of cork wide enough to float the quills without their tipping over. Bore holes through these the right size to thrust the nibs through them so that they will be immersed when the corks float upon the water. Place the corks containing the quills in a deep kettle or other receptacle so that the cover can be put on without interfering with the quills, and so that the nibs will be immersed in water. Boil them three or four hours. Dry for twenty-four hours, remove the pith, polish with flannel, and dry in a warm oven. This method hardens the quills like bone without making them brittle, and also renders them transparent.

To Clean Fur.—The nature of fur is similar to that of wool, as both are animal fibers. Hence anything that will injure wool should not be used on fur of any description. Stains of grease or paint may be removed from fur hats or other articles by means of turpentine. Afterwards sponge with alcohol and dry.

Or other furs may be cleaned by rubbing damp corn meal through them and allowing it to dry. Afterwards remove by shaking and brushing. The coarse furs, as bear, buffalo, etc., may be scrubbed with warm suds made of pure white soap and pure water, and their appearance will be very much improved by combing with a coarse comb. To improve the luster of furs, heat corn meal in an iron skillet to a rich brown but without burning. While still hot sprinkle it over the fur and rub with a flannel cloth. Afterwards remove by shaking and brushing.

To Clean Straw Hats.—The most delicate straw goods, as Milan, Leghorn, and other straws, can be thoroughly cleaned by mixing the juice of a lemon with a tablespoonful of powdered sulphur to form a thick paste. Apply this to the hat with a nailbrush or toothbrush, first removing the band, and rub the paste thoroughly into the straw. Afterwards rinse by dashing water upon it from a glass, but without soaking. Shape the hat while still damp with a warm iron, pressing through a wet cloth until dry.

Or press into shape and dry out of doors in the sun.

Panama Hats.—Apply corn meal, slightly damp, with a fairly stiff nail-brush, changing the meal as it becomes soiled. Brush off the excess of meal while still damp, dry the hat out of doors in the sun, and afterwards brush thoroughly.

Or with a piece of flannel rub fuller's earth into the hat, cover quite thickly with it, and lay the hat away covered with a large piece of paper for four or five days. Remove the powder by brushing.

Or apply peroxide of hydrogen with a flannel cloth. Repeat if necessary.

To Size Straw Hats.—Beat up the white of an egg and apply to the hat after cleaning with a small camel's-hair brush or a sponge.

BLEACHING VEGETABLE AND ANIMAL FIBERS

Bleaching.—Bleaching is the process of treating materials in such a way as to whiten them. Bleaching is commonly applied to textile goods, as linen, cotton, wool, and silk; also to paper, pulp, straw, ivory, wax, and animal and vegetable oils. The operation of bleaching textile fabrics consists of two parts: first, removing dirt and other impurities and all foreign substances, and afterwards altering the natural coloring matter of the fabric by chemicals having specific bleaching properties. The preliminary operation of cleansing fabrics for bleaching is much the same as ordinary washing in the domestic laundry. It depends upon the action of alkaline lyes and certain acids to dissolve the resinous and fatty substances and other impurities that may either be natural or may be introduced into the fabrics in the process of manufacture.

The principal actual bleaching agents now employed are chlorine gas, usually combined with lime as chloride of lime or bleaching powder; and sulphurous acid, usually as fumes of burning sulphur. Of these the chlorine compounds are the more powerful. Like free alkali, however, they tend, after decomposing the coloring matter, to attack the fibers of the fabric itself and to injure them. Hence it is customary at the proper time to treat fabrics bleached by this agent with such substances as hyposulphite of soda to neutralize the excess of chlorine and prevent its further action.

The various vegetable fibers, as cotton, flax, and hemp, are composed of cellulose, a substance that withstands to a great degree the action both of the acids and alkalies used in preliminary cleansing and the chlorine used as a bleaching agent. Animal fibers, on the other hand, as silk, wool, feathers, and the like, contain no cellulose and are readily destroyed by these agents. Hence they are commonly bleached by the action of sulphurous-acid gas. Various other chemicals have been recommended for bleaching, but none of them are commonly employed.

Previous to the application of modern chemistry (during the latter part of the eighteenth century), bleaching was done without the use of chlorine or sulphurous acid, by soaking and washing the articles alternately in alkaline and acid liquids, exposing them on the grass to the action of air, light, and moisture, and sprinkling them with water several times a day.

The exact nature of the change which takes place in bleaching is not known, but it is supposed to be brought about by the action of ozone, or oxygen, in its active form. This is set free during the process of bleaching with chlorine, and is also known to be present in small quantities in the atmosphere. The ancient method of first soaking and washing articles in lye and acids and afterwards exposing them to the action of the elements, is still practiced in many localities, but the modern methods of bleaching by chlorides and sulphurous acid can be practiced successfully in any household.

Bleaching Linen. — The fibers of raw or unbleached linen contain a large amount of resinous and other impurities, so that the operation of bleaching reduces their original weight by about two thirds. These foreign substances protect the fiber from being injured by the alkali and acids which are used in bleaching. Hence the treatment recommended for unbleached linen is not suitable for the finer qualities of bleached fabrics, but must be modified according to the quality and condition of the goods.

The Dutch at one time had a monopoly in certain grades of fine linens, hence known as "hollands," on account of the superiority of their bleaching process. This consisted in treating the fabric by turns with alkaline and acid liquids, and exposing it on lawns or bleaching greens from March until September. Hence the origin of the word "lawn" for certain fine grades of linen. The Dutch process consisted of four different operations, frequently repeated:

(1) Steeping in alkaline lye forty-eight hours, or in pure water for several days.

(2) Boiling in alkaline lye, also called "bucking" or "bawking."

(3) Exposing on the grass for weeks at a time and sprinkling frequently with water.

(4) Souring with buttermilk.

After each operation the cloth was washed in soapsuds and rinsed with water. This method is still employed and is suitable for either raw linen or cotton. It may be shortened by the employment of dilute sulphuric acid in place of buttermilk, and also by the use, under proper conditions, of chlorine in the form of chloride of lime or bleaching powder.

Soaking in water or lye, washing, boiling in lye, and exposure on the grass, are still required, and the series of operations must be often repeated.

To Bleach Raw Linen and Cotton Cloth.—Dissolve 1 pound of chloride of lime in a small quantity of cold water by rubbing with a stick until all lumps have been dissolved. Add sufficient cold water to make 2 gallons, stirring vigorously. Preserve this liquid in an earthen jar as a bleaching fluid.

Prepare a lye by dissolving ¼ pint of caustic potash or caustic soda in 2 gallons of water.

(1) Boil the fabric in this lye for three or four hours.

(2) Wash thoroughly in soapsuds.

(3) Rinse in pure water.

(4) Steep three or four hours in 2 gallons of cold water containing 1 quart of bleaching fluid.

(5) Steep for one hour in 2 gallons of water containing 2 wineglassfuls of sulphuric acid.

(6) Wash in soapsuds.

(7) Rinse in pure water.

(8) Expose on a green lawn and sprinkle frequently with clear water.

This will illustrate the method of domestic bleaching. This series of operations must be carried on continuously, and may be repeated weekly on the regular wash day when suds are at hand in which to wash out the lye and bleaching fluid. The articles may be exposed during the week and the operations repeated on the following or subsequent wash days until the bleaching has been completed.

By reducing the strength of the lye one half the same series of operations may be carried on, a second or a third time if necessary, without "crofting," or exposure on a lawn. The latter method is, however, to be preferred. After the final operation rinse the articles in 2 gallons of water containing about 2 ounces of hyposulphite of soda and afterwards rinse in bluing water.

Various methods of bleaching ordinarily recommended and practiced in modification of these processes are of the nature of short cuts to save labor. Some of these, by employing strong bleaching agents without sufficient care, may tend to weaken the fabrics, and others are not strong enough to do the work well. The above is a standard that will serve to illustrate the principles involved.

To Bleach Brown Sheeting.—This is for an ordinary partly bleached cotton fabric. First wash with other white goods, and afterwards soak over night in strong soapsuds. Dissolve 2 pounds of chloride of lime in a wash boiler containing 2½ pails of boiling water, or about ¼ pound of chloride of lime to the gallon. Stir vigorously, and when cold pour through cheese cloth into a tub. Immerse the goods in this, stirring with a clothes stick for half an hour. Rinse thoroughly with cold water containing 1 ounce of hyposulphite of soda to the gallon. Finally rinse in bluing water and hang up to dry. Repeat if necessary. This will take mildew out of cotton or duck cloth, and restore the color of cotton goods that have been stored and yellowed.

These methods are, of course, not suitable for more delicate cotton fabrics.

Bleaching with Sal Soda.—Washing soda tends to bleach garments, but also injures them unless it is thoroughly removed by rinsing. Put no more than one teaspoonful in a boilerful of clothes.

Bleaching by Turpentine.—Dissolve 1 teaspoonful of oil of turpentine and 3 teaspoonfuls of alcohol in the last rising water.

Wool.—The process of bleaching raw wool requires five stages:

(1) It is washed on the sheep to remove sweat and dirt. Among other impurities found in sheep's wool is a substance called "suint," containing potash, which may be preserved and utilized.

(2) The wool is scoured by an ammoniacal lye consisting of stale urine dissolved in water, or by immersing in soapsuds or a weak alkaline lye at a temperature of about 130°. This removes a kind of lime soap and other impurities in it. These are the preliminary processes of cleansing, after which the wool is spun into yarn and prepared for bleaching either in the yarn or cloth.

(3) Steeping in a weak lukewarm solution of carbonate of soda and soapsuds.

(4) Washing with lukewarm soapsuds.

(5) Exposing to the fumes of sulphurous acid.

The last three operations are repeated if necessary. Afterwards the yarn or cloth is rinsed in bluing water. Operations 1 and 2 may be performed on the farm to improve the appearance of wool for the market. Operations 3, 4, and 5 may be performed in the house to bleach yarn or woolen fabrics.

Chlorine in any form, as chloride of lime or bleaching powders, must not be used for woolen articles.

To Bleach Woolen Goods with Sulphur.—An inverted barrel, cask, box, or anything that is large enough and tight enough to hold the fumes of sulphur may be employed. Place this out of doors on a still day, or in an outhouse, turned upside down and supported on three or four bricks, to admit a slight draught. Suspend the articles inside by means of hooks, or by passing cord or wire through gimlet holes and tying it about them. Afterwards fill the gimlet holes with rags or wax.

Kindle coke or charcoal, or place other live coals in an iron pan, sprinkle flowers of sulphur or pulverized brimstone on the coals, and set directly beneath. If the receptacle used is not quite tight, cover closely with a wet piece of heavy cloth or old carpet. Care must, of course, be taken not to inhale the fumes of sulphur or to permit the sulphur to blaze and scorch the goods. The articles should be first washed in soapsuds, and wrung out of weak suds without rinsing.

For Small Articles.—A paper flour sack, to which they may be attached by pins or basting threads, is light, tight, and convenient for bleaching small articles. Put the brimstone in a saucer and cover with a tin funnel, so that the fumes will be directed up into the bag. Repeat if necessary, hang the articles out of doors until the odor has passed away, and wash as usual. This method is suitable for flannels, woolen hose, yarn, and also for silk, straw, and straw goods.

To Bleach with Oxalic Acid.—Dissolve 1 ounce of oxalic acid in 1 gallon of boiling water; allow this to cool until it will bear the hands. Immerse the articles and let them steep for an hour or more, rinse thoroughly, and dry. Repeat if necessary.

To Bleach Flannel. — Dissolve 1 ounce of powdered ammonia and 1 ounce of salt in 2 quarts of water. Soak the articles in this for an hour or more.

Or dissolve 2 ounces of bisulphite of soda in 1 gallon of water acidulated slightly with hydrochloric acid.

To Bleach Silk.—Nearly one half, by weight (30 to 40 per cent), of the fibers of silk consists of various gums and coloring matter.

The operation of bleaching consists in

(1) Boiling the silks in soapsuds, with the addition of bran, to remove these impurities; (2) exposing them to sulphurous-acid gas.

Or boil in soapsuds, rinse, and expose to the sun. Or bleach with the fumes of sulphur.

To Bleach Feathers.—Make a dilute solution of bicarbonate of potassium, 1 part to 10 parts of water, slightly acidulated with nitric acid, 1 fluid ounce to the gallon. Immerse the feathers for 3 or 4 hours. Afterwards rinse in clear water, slightly acidulated with sulphuric acid, 1 fluid ounce to the gallon.

To Bleach Straw Goods. — Substances recommended for bleaching straw and straw goods, including straw hats, are sulphurous acid (i. e., fumes of burning sulphur), chlorine water (or chloride of lime), citric acid, and oxalic acid. Straw goods must be prepared for bleaching by scrubbing with lukewarm soap and water.

The safest and best method of bleaching straw is perhaps by means of the fumes of burning sulphur. This method is employed by manufacturers and milliners to bleach hats and bonnets. All bands and trimmings must first be removed.

Or apply chlorine water with a sponge, cloth, or brush. Afterwards rinse in clear water containing hyposulphite of soda.

Or make a paste of corn meal and a solution of oxalic acid in water. Spread this on the hat, allow it to dry, and remove by brushing.

Or apply a strong solution of oxalic acid and water, and rinse.

Or immerse in a weak solution of chloride of lime—2 ounces to 1 gallon of water. Rinse in water containing hyposulphite of soda.

Or make a paste of flowers of sulphur. Or pulverize brimstone with water. Cover with this, and expose to direct sunshine until dry. Repeat if necessary. Remove the sulphur by brushing. This is simple and successful.

To Bleach Straw Braid.—Dissolve 6 ounces of chloride of lime in a gallon of water.

(1) Dip the goods in this for thirty minutes.

(2) Dip in clear water acidulated with muriatic or sulphuric acid at the rate of 1 fluid ounce to the gallon.

(3) Rinse in clear water containing 1 ounce of hyposulphite of soda to the gallon.

Or dip in weak soapsuds and expose to the fumes of burning sulphur.

To Prevent White Goods from Fading.—If a suitable lawn or grassplot is available, spread white garments on the grass to dry during the warm months of the year. This is more convenient than fastening to a line and keeps the garments always bleached. Faded articles may be bleached in this way by keeping them constantly moistened with clear water.

To Bleach Unbleached Muslin. — Unbleached muslin is more durable than that which has already been bleached. Hence it pays to buy it by the piece and bleach it before making it up. Place on the stove a boilerful of strong bluing water, or use indigo instead of bluing. Unroll the cloth, put it in the boiler, and boil ten or twenty minutes. Hang it out on a clear, sunshiny day to drip; dry without wringing. When partially dry spread it on the grass to bleach.

To Whiten Lace.— First wash in strong soapsuds, rinse and immerse in fresh suds, and expose to the sun.

Or first wash and iron, stitch on cotton with basting thread, and soak for twenty minutes in olive oil. Afterwards boil for twenty minutes in suds of castile or other hard white soap and rinse in warm water.

To Bleach Faded White Goods.— All cotton and linen fabrics and garments that have been laundered tend to become yellow by the action of the alkali contained in the soap, which is imperfectly removed in rinsing. Garments that have been laid away for a time, as summer dresses, will frequently come out in the spring much yellowed or faded. Put the faded articles in a separate boiler and add ½ pound of cream of tartar. Boil until the goods are clear. Wring out of bluing water and lay on the grass to dry.

Or soak the garments over night in clear cold water, wring out, and soak for twenty-four hours in sour milk or buttermilk. If much yellowed, soak a third night in weak suds containing a little hard white soap and a tablespoonful of kerosene. Afterwards boil in suds containing a tablespoonful of kerosene. Rinse in bluing water, and hang out to drip dry.

Or boil the articles for fifteen or twenty minutes in strong soapsuds containing 1 tablespoonful of essence of turpentine and 3 tablespoonfuls of aqua ammonia, stirring occasionally. Care must be taken not to immerse the arms in suds containing turpentine. Rinse the articles, using a clothes stick, in one or two clear waters, and wash and blue in the usual way.

Washing soda should not be used for bleaching purposes, as it tends to rot the fabric.

CHAPTER XI

WASH DAY

SOAP AND SOAP MAKING—THE LAUNDRY—NATURE OF THE PROCESS—WATER FOR THE LAUNDRY—LABOR-SAVING METHODS, WASHING FLUIDS, ETC.—COLORED GOODS—LACES AND LACE CURTAINS—SILKS AND SATIN—WOOLENS, WORSTEDS, AND FLANNELS—DRYING CLOTHES

The custom of this country has established Monday as wash day. Many families, however, prefer Tuesday, in order to have an opportunity on Monday to sort over the different articles, mend tears, remove stains, and the like.

Bed clothing is usually changed on Saturday, and body clothing on Saturday or Sunday, so that all clothes may be readily collected and at hand early Monday morning.

Laundry Bags.—Each person in the family should have a laundry bag in his or her own room in which soiled garments may be kept in preparation for the weekly wash. A separate laundry bag for soiled table linen and napkins should be hung on the back of the pantry door or some other clean, dry place where mice cannot get at it. If these articles are not kept out of the way they will scent the spots of grease in table linen and gnaw their way to them.

Laundry bags may be made of heavy unbleached muslin, or worn-out pillowcases may be used, by facing them to hold a draw string.

Ordinary crash toweling, folded across and sewed at the sides, makes a convenient laundry bag.

Or ornamental bags may be made in the form of a double pocket having one opening across the middle with two bag-like receptacles.

Clothes Hamper.—In addition to these laundry bags a clothes hamper located conveniently near the laundry will be found very handy to receive soiled towels and bed linen. Covered basket hampers may be obtained at the stores.

Or a cheap clothes hamper may be made from a small barrel, by lining it inside with cambric or calico and covering the outside with cretonne or other material arranged in plaits. The lid may be covered with the same material and supplied with a covered knob in the center. The lining should be sewed together in breadths like a skirt.

Or a hamper may be made of a dry-goods box by lining and covering it in the same manner with any suitable material. By padding the top this box may be used as a seat and may be placed where a barrel would be inconvenient.

Sorting the Laundry.—Spread a white sheet on the floor and empty on this the contents of the laundry bags and hamper. Sort the small and delicate pieces of fine linen, as laces, fine waists, aprons, and petticoats, in one pile. It is a good plan to have one or two wash bags of cotton, about two feet square, in which to place these pieces to soak and boil them. Or they can be boiled separately in a kettle or small boiler.

Put the table linen, linen towels, and doilies in one pile; the bed and body linen, kitchen towels, and bath towels in another; the colored clothes, hosiery, and coarser articles in a third; and the flannels and woolens by themselves. These lots should be kept separate throughout the washing, the fine linen and table linen going into the first tub and the first boiler; bed and body linen into the second tub and second boiler; colored clothes being washed separately, but not boiled; and flannels being reserved for separate treatment. By this plan the same suds may be used in the boiler if desired, although changing the water is much to be preferred.

Laundry — To Remove Stains. — While sorting the clothes, they should be carefully looked over for stains from fruit, grass, acids, pencil marks, ink, etc., as these may be much more readily eradicated before they are touched by soap or boiling water. Pencil marks especially should be erased carefully with a rubber eraser, as the hot water will make them indelible.

SOAP AND SOAP MAKING

Properties of Soap.—Garments of linen and other fabrics become soiled principally by the oily exudations of the body, as in perspiration and the natural oil of the hair, and in the case of table linen, by animal fats, etc. The skin itself, of course, retains a considerable part of the oily substances not absorbed by the clothing. These greasy substances by their adhesive quality attract and hold particles of dirt. When soap is dissolved in water, the neutral alkali salts become in part separated into alkali which dissolves, and free fatty acid which precipitates. This explains why the transparency of clear water is disturbed by the use of soap even of the purest kind.

The detergent or cleansing properties of soap are due to the presence of free alkali, either caustic potash or soda liberated in the soapsuds. This attacks and decomposes the grease contained in soiled linen, in perspiration, and in dishwater, unites with the fatty acids, and in turn saponifies them. The process is precisely similar to that of soap-making. The union of the alkali set free in soapsuds with the grease of garments or dishwater produces a soapy substance which is readily soluble, and hence is easily removed by rinsing.

Free Alkali.—Since the cleansing properties of soap are due to the presence of free alkali, it may be asked why the alkalies themselves—as potash lye or sal soda, cannot be used without the trouble of uniting them with animal fats by soap making. It is true that lye and other strong alkalies have strong detergent properties. They attack, however, not only the grease, but also the fabrics themselves and rot or weaken them, and also irritate the skin. Hence the object of soap making is to form a compound which will release a small definite quantity of alkali at the moment that it is required.

Soap Test.—Alkali has a strong, biting taste. Hence the best test of soap is to apply the tongue to it. If it bites, the soap contains an excess of free alkali and is not suitable for the toilet or laundry. If it does not, it is good soap and will probably not injure the most delicate fabrics.

Importance of Soap.—Whether or not cleanliness is next to godliness, historians say that the degree of civilization of a nation is indicated by the quantity of soap it consumes. The kind and quality of soap and other cleansing articles used by a household is a good indication of the refinement of the family. There should be no economy in the use of soap, but since, if very freely used, it becomes quite an important item of expense, a considerable saving may be made by the use of homemade soap and other cleansing compounds.

The domestic art of soap making also has an educational value. Soap is a chemical compound and we perform a real chemical experiment every time we wash our hands or wash clothing in the laundry. Soap was made as early as the second century of the Christian era, before the modern science of chemistry was inaugurated, and good soap may be made by observing the following instructions without troubling oneself to understand the chemical principles involved. On the other hand, it is interesting, as a matter of general information, to understand the chemistry of soap making.

There is a group of substances having similar properties, which is known in chemistry as alkalies, and another group, having very different properties, which is known as acids. These two kinds of substances have a strong attraction or affinity for each other, and when brought together under suitable conditions they unite to form another class of substances, the compounds known as salts. Common salt is a good example; it consists of an alkali, sodium, and an acid, chlorine. Most of the salts are freely soluble in water.

Soaps are alkali salts of fatty acids. The alkalies commonly used in making soaps are soda and potash. All of the animal fats, and also the animal and vegetable oils, contain fatty acids. When the proper alkalies are brought into contact with animal fats or oils, under proper conditions, the alkalies attack the globules of fat or oil and unite with the fatty acids to form alkali salts of fatty acids — i. e., soap. This process is known as saponification.

To make soap it is customary to dissolve an alkali, either potash or soda, in water, forming a liquid known as lye, to dilute the lye, to then mix with it a suitable quantity of fat or oil, and to stir until saponification takes place. If the mixture is cold, the process may require several days or even months, depending upon the strength and purity of the ingredients. But if the mixture is raised to 212° F. by boiling, the process of saponification may take place in a few minutes or hours. Hence there are two processes of soap making—in the cold and by boiling.

The cold process, generally speaking, produces what is known as a soft soap. This is not true or pure soap, but contains, in addition to the actual dry alkali salts of the fatty acids—i. e., real soap—certain other ingredients, as water, glycerin (which is contained in all natural fats and is liberated in the process of soap making), more or less free alkali, and other impurities. In other words, soft soap is only partially saponified. The pure or hard soap, completing the process of saponification, is obtained by boiling soft soap until the glycerin and other impurities are absorbed by the hot lye, and by the addition of salt to remove the surplus of water. The salt, having a stronger affinity for water than the soap has, causes the water and the impurities it holds in solution to sink into the oil. The pure hard soap rises to the surface and forms a cake which may be removed. The lye, containing glycerin and other impurities, can then be discarded.

A better quality of soap may be obtained by melting the product of the first boiling a second time, and by adding more clean, strong lye and clear melted grease or oil, and stirring over the fire until complete saponification takes place.

THE LAUNDRY

Utensils for Washing.—The list of utensils for the laundry includes wash boiler, wringer, washboard, washing machine, three or four tubs, two or three pails, clothes stick, dipper, and large and small clothes baskets. Wooden tubs and pails are the most common, but those made of paper or wood pulp are to be preferred, as they are lighter and will not fall to pieces if allowed to dry.

The Boiler.—The ordinary tin boilers are commonly used, but a copper or steel boiler enameled white on the inside and painted some suitable color outside is the best. Tubs and boilers should be fitted with faucets to avoid lifting and the liability of accident in carrying hot suds from place to place. With good care a wash boiler should last a lifetime. Hence it is advisable to buy the best.

The Wringer.—The principal cost of a wringer is in the rubber rollers, and it is true economy to buy an article that has rolls made of pure rubber, and that may cost $5 or $6, rather than a cheap article having

"Utensils for the Laundry."

rollers made of a composition that will last but a short time. When the rollers begin to wear, wrap them round with straps of strong, unbleached cotton cloth. This will lengthen their usefulness many years.

Washing Machine.—We especially recommend the purchase of a good washing machine. Like the sewing machine this instrument has a very important bearing upon the welfare of the family by lessening the physical labor devolving upon the wife and mother, and thus saving much of her energy for the higher and more elevating duties of the household. We believe that any of the standard makes of washing machines are to be recommended in preference to the ordinary washboard, which is only a relic of barbarism. But we especially recommend the make which contains an inner cylinder in which the clothes are placed, and which is revolved in an outer cylinder containing water. This method tends to cleanse the clothes evenly and with the least possible wear. Other makes accomplish the result by holding the clothes stationary, agitating the water, and squeezing the goods, very much after the fashion of the old-style clothes pounder; and still others revolve the garments in the tub by means of prongs, reversing the motion from time to time. The last method is perhaps the least satisfactory. When the clothes are suddenly stopped and sent backward by the reverse motion they are subjected to a considerable strain. But even this method wears out the garments far less than does rubbing on the washboard, and we strongly recommend some washing machine to every household. If the clothes are first boiled with soap and kerosene, or other good washing fluid, they can be run through the washer in about five minutes. Colored clothes cannot, of course, be boiled, and will require a longer time to wash.

Small Utensils.—A small toy washboard is useful for washing dish towels, hand towels, handkerchiefs, hose, and light neckwear; also to take to summer resorts on vacations, as laundry bills in these places are always considerable. A small flatiron is also useful for ironing ruffles, puffings, or laces. Both these articles can be put in the trunk, and the iron can be heated over an alcohol lamp and used to press ribbons and neckwear. A 5-gallon lard can, which can be purchased for 25 cents, is a useful substitute for a boiler in washing small articles that are too dainty to put in the regular wash.

Or small articles may be inclosed in cloth bags before being put in the wash boiler.

NATURE OF THE PROCESS

Objects of Washing.—Dirt has been described as "matter which is out of place." The substances which soil garments and household linen are unobjectionable in their proper places, but become dirt when transferred to wearing apparel and linen, and require to be removed by washing. These substances are principally of three classes: fruit, acids, ink, and other things which produce stains; animal oils, grease, or fats from the oily exudations from the body in perspiration; or, in the case of table linen, from foods or from other sources; and particles of earth and other solids, either mixed with grease, or caught in the texture of the fabric. Stains require special treatment according to the nature of the substance which produces them; greasy substances, as oils or fats, require to be decomposed by the use of an alkali, in soaps or otherwise; and particles of earth and other substances, when set free from the grease in which they are usually imbedded, may be removed by the mechanical operations of rubbing and rinsing. Aside from stains, the most difficult part of washing is the decomposition, without injury to the fabrics, of greasy substances by the action of an alkali. Unless this point is clearly understood, good results in washing will come rather from good luck than from good management.

The means employed to remove dirt on fabrics are soaking, boiling, rubbing, and rinsing, with the use of an alkali either in soaps or in the various preparations known as washing powders and washing fluids.

Soaking.—The object of soaking garments is to soften the dirt and loosen it by swelling the fabric. There is no objeetion to soaking the clothes in pure soft water for a reasonable time, but soaking them over night in water with soap and washing fluids or powders is not advisable. The first effect of the alkali contained in soap is to soften the greasy substances which cause dirt to adhere to the fabric, and to render them soluble in water. But if these substances are not immediately removed by washing and rinsing, another chemical action takes place which produces compounds that, while not always visible to the eye, are very much more difficult to remove. This is especially likely to be the case if soap or other detergents are used which contain much alkali. The result is often to give the clothes a heavy or musty smell and a dingy appearance after ironing. Instead, try soaking the garments for about twenty minutes in boiling water containing borax.

Or rub soiled articles with a piece of wet soap on the morning of wash day and soak in cold water for about two hours before washing.

If clothes are soaked over night use pure soft water only, without any soap or other washing compounds. If not, put the clothes to soak in cold soft water the very first thing in the morning while the wash water is heating and breakfast is being prepared, first rubbing soiled articles, especially the greasy spots, with a piece of wet soap before putting them in the water.

Rubbing.—Rubbing is, of course, merely a mechanical operation, but it assists the action of soap and washing compounds by removing the greasy substances that have been decomposed by the alkali and by bringing what remains into contact with the alkaline suds.

Right here note a helpful labor-saving device. Instead of rubbing the clothes in the usual way, lay the washboard across the top of the tub and apply soap to them with a scrubbing brush having rather stiff bristles. Use the brush especially for the neck, wristbands, and other spots which are especially soiled or greasy. This cleanses them much more quickly than rubbing in the usual manner, besides being easier for the laundress and much less detrimental to the garment. This method is especially helpful for men's overalls, heavy blankets, and other coarse articles that are difficult to clean. Put the clothes through a wringer into the second tub and wash again, looking them over carefully for dirty spots.

Boiling.—Boiling is also a mechanical process, as the steam passing through the garments agitates them and loosens the particles of dirt contained in their texture. Boiling water and steam also increase the activity of the alkali in attacking and decomposing the grease.

Laundry—Rinsing.—Rinsing is a mechanical operation for removing the excess of soap, with the dirt, glycerin, and other impurities that have been released by the action of the washing compounds.

These processes should be firmly fixed in mind, and the nature and properties of soap and other cleansing compounds should be fully understood by all who wish to obtain satisfactory results in washing.

The principal object of rinsing clothes is to remove the excess of soap. Hence they must be thoroughly rinsed until all the suds disappear from the water. If plenty of hot water can be had it should be used for the first rinsing, as the soap contained in the garment will dissolve in hot water much more readily than in cold. It is customary, however, to lift the clothes from the boiler directly into a tub of cold rinsing water, rinse thoroughly, wring out into a second rinsing water, and continue rinsing until all trace of soap disappears. If any soap is left in the garments it will unite with the bluing and make the clothes yellow. After the final rinsing and bluing the articles must be wrung out, rolled in bundles, and sorted, starched pieces being placed in one basket and unstarched ones in another, and hung up to dry at once. It is a good idea to first spread a large, clean cloth in the bottom of the basket.

Plan for Wash Day.—The following routine is especially recommended: get up at daylight and get the washing out of the way as early as possible. It is surprising how much can be accomplished early in the morning before the regular routine of the day begins.

First Boiling.—Next fill the boiler with clear soft water, or if the water is hard, add borax to soften it. Put it on the stove and bring to a boil. Rinse out the tubs with hot water and soap to remove any dust that may have accumulated. When the clothes have been well soaked, run them through a wringer or wring them out lightly by hand, put them in tubs half filled with hot water from the boiler, and rub on the washboard, using plenty of soap. Or use the washing machine.

Second Boiling.—Run them again through the wringer and put them in a boiler with cold water over the fire. The articles may be rubbed separately with soap as they come from the wringer before being placed in the boiler, or shaved hard soap or other washing compounds may be dissolved in the water in which the clothes are boiled. If washing fluids or powders are used care must be taken to dissolve them in the water before the clothes are put in, as otherwise they may settle in the folds of the fabrics and eat holes in them with the excess of alkali they contain. Let the clothes come to a boil, pressing them down occasionally with a clothes stick. The first boiler should contain the first sorting of fine linen, and while these are coming to a boil the second sorting may be in the process of rubbing. The boiler should be emptied and refilled with cold water every time a new lot is put in. Clothes should be lifted from the boiler with a clothes stick, held up to drain slightly, and placed in a tubful of clear, cold rinsing water.

WATER FOR THE LAUNDRY

Laundry Water Supply.—All water for laundry purposes must be soft or else the clothes cannot be made clean. Hard water that contains lime and other mineral substances, or that is brackish from its vicinity to the sea, will cause the soap to curdle and float on its surface. In limestone regions and other localities where the water is hard, perhaps the best method is to collect rain water in a cistern or rain-water barrel, but hard water can be softened in various ways for laundry purposes.

To Test Water.—To find out whether or not water is fit for laundry purposes, dissolve a little good white soap in alcohol and put a few drops of this solution into a glassful of water. If the water is pure the soap solution will be dissolved and the water will continue limpid, but if it is impure the soap will form into white flakes which will tend to float on the surface.

To Soften Hard Water.—Bring the water to a boil and expose it to the air, which may be done by pouring it from some little height into a tub or other vessel, and afterwards letting it stand over night.

Or boil it with the addition of a little baking soda, and afterwards expose it to the air.

Or place a quantity of clean wood ashes in a tightly closed woolen bag and immerse the bag in a tub of water. The required amount of ashes can be ascertained by experiment.

Or use chalk, which may be put into the spring or well or used in a tub or bucket, the proper amount depending upon the extent of the impurities, and to be determined in each locality by experiment.

Or add a small quantity of borax or potash or soda lye, but care must be taken not to use too much, as otherwise the alkali they contain will injure the fabrics.

Or add 1 to 2 tablespoonfuls of quicklime to each tubful of water. Slake the lime with a little warm water, stirring it to a cream, pour it into a tubful or boilerful of water, and let stand over night or long enough to settle to the bottom. Pour off the clear water, taking care not to disturb the sediment.

Rain-water Barrel.—A cask to hold rain water should be provided with a hinged lid or other cover to prevent dust and dirt from getting in, and to keep out insects that would use it as a breeding place. It should be raised above the ground by stone or brick, and be furnished with a spigot to draw off the water for use.

To Cleanse Soapsuds. — The water supply in some localities is exceedingly limited, and periods of drought sometimes occur when it is almost impossible to obtain sufficient water for laundry purposes. Under such circumstances a tubful or boilerful of water may be made to serve for an entire washing by cleansing it when necessary. This may be done by dissolving a teaspoonful of powdered alum in half a cup of boiling water and stirring it into a tub or wash boiler of soapsuds. The soap will curdle and sink with the other impurities to the bottom, leaving the water entirely clear and free from odor. The clear water may then be poured off, taking care not to disturb the sediment, and used again.

LABOR-SAVING METHODS, WASHING FLUIDS, ETC.

Certain compounds added to the water in which the clothes are boiled are recommended as labor savers. Washing fluids and powders contain two kinds of ingredients: volatile substances, such as kerosene, turpentine, alcohol, ammonia, and camphor gum; and alkaline substances, as potash and soda lyes from wood ashes, sal soda, and various brands of commercial lye. These powerful chemicals must be used with the most intelligent caution.

First Caution. — If the hands and arms are immersed in hot water containing turpentine, alcohol, ammonia, camphor, and similar substances, these are absorbed through the pores of the skin and may seriously imperil the health. Paralysis is said to sometimes result from this cause. Hence it is best to use these compounds only in the boiler, and to take the garments out of the first rinsing water with the clothes stick, especially if hot water is used, rather than to immerse the arms therein.

When turpentine has been used in the boiling water the clothes must be very thoroughly rinsed, as if any of it remains in garments worn next the skin it may cause mischief.

Second Caution. — Substances that are strong in alkali, as potash and soda lyes and the like, are powerful cleansers, but clothes should not be allowed to lie in water that contains them for any length of time. If they are used in the boiling water the clothes must be boiled for a limited time and immediately removed and rinsed thoroughly. The alkali, as has already been explained, continues its action after decomposing greasy substances and attacks the fabrics themselves. It is injurious to the skin if not thoroughly rinsed from underwear.

Third Caution.—All washing powders should be thoroughly dissolved in the boiling water before the garments are added, so that the alkali and other ingredients may be present in equal strength in all parts of the water. If these compounds are added after the clothes have been put in they may settle in spots in the folds of the garments and eat into the fabric.

Washing Fluids. — Most washing fluids amount to neither more nor less than potash or soda lye. In other words, they are liquids containing an excess of free alkali. Their use is quite customary on the ground that they do the work quickly and well and save labor, but they are open to the objection that unless used with great caution they tend to rot the clothes and to roughen and chap the hands and arms of the laundress. They are, at best, only suitable for the coarser articles, and it is probable that their constant use weakens anything which they are employed to clean.

Caustic Soda Lye.—A common family recipe for washing fluid is caustic soda lye. Dissolve 1 pound of sal soda in 1 gallon of boiling water. Slake separately 8 ounces of fresh quicklime in 2 quarts of water. Bring the soda solution to a boil, pour in the slaked lime in a thin stream, stirring constantly, and let the mixture stand over night. Pour off the clear lye, taking care not to disturb the sediment, and preserve in glass bottles or stone jugs. When this fluid is used it is customary to soak the clothes over night in clear water, wring them out, and soap the soiled places. The boiler is then half filled with water which is brought to a boil and 1 teacupful of this fluid is stirred in thoroughly, after which the clothes are added and boiled for half an hour, when they can be cleaned with very little rubbing. The injury that the lye may do the fabric is not likely to be noticed as a result of a single washing, and the gradual weakening of the garment is likely to be attributed to ordinary wear. Hence it is often asserted that this and other washing fluids can be used without rotting ordinary fabrics. But the injury, though slight, is certain. At all events, if such fluids are used the greatest care must be taken not to let garments lie long in the suds, to rinse them very thoroughly in two or three waters and hang them out as quickly as possible. This washing fluid may be used in hot water for scrubbing floors, removing grease spots, and cleaning greasy pots, kettles, and the like. But care must be taken not to use it on tinware or aluminum or strong enough to injure the hands.

Caustic Potash Lye.—The basis of another class of washing fluids frequently recommended is potash lye, which is perhaps even more injurious than caustic soda lye, requiring the same cautions and being open to the same objections. The addition of various other ingredients, as borax, ammonia, and the like, may be regarded as beneficial, as they tend to increase the cleansing properties of the fluid, and thus lessen the amount of pure lye necessary to do the work.

Put ½ pound of concentrated lye in an earthenware jar or iron kettle and pour over it 1 gallon of cold water. Stir with a wooden stick until dissolved, and let stand until cold. Dissolve, each in a separate vessel, ½ pound of borax, ½ pound of salts of tartar, and ½ pound of lump ammonia (not aqua ammonia), using in each case as little water as possible. After the solution of lye is cold, pour into it each of the other solutions in a thin stream, stirring constantly, pour the mixture into large glass bottles or earthenware jugs, and cork tightly. Use this washing fluid in the proportion of 1 or 2 tablespoonfuls to each pailful of water. In all cases dissolve it in the wash boiler before the clothes are put in, for if the clothes are put in first and the washing fluid afterwards, it will be stronger in some places than others, and be more likely to injure the garments.

Or put 1 pound of crude potash in an earthenware jug and pour over it 1 gallon of soft water. When cold stir in ½ ounce of sal ammoniac and ½ ounce of saltpeter previously dissolved in a little soft water. Use this fluid at the rate of 1 pint to 6 or 8 gallons of water.

Or dissolve separately ½ pound of sal soda and ½ pound of potash lye, each in 2 quarts of water. Mix the two together and pour into a gallon jug. Use a teacupful to a boilerful of water.

Or put 1 can of potash lye in an earthenware jar, pour over it 2 gallons of cold water, and add 1 pound of borax and 1 pint of liquid ammonia. Pour into stone jugs and cork tightly. Use a teacupful to each boiler, and also half a bar of soap shaved fine.

Washing Fluids with Turpentine.—Turpentine as a washing fluid, with or without other ingredients, as camphor, alcohol, ammonia, and the like, is often recommended, but unless great caution is observed it is very likely to be injurious. These substances, especially turpentine and alcohol, open the pores of the skin and thus expose a person to the liability of taking cold in hanging out the clothes. Their frequent use is also debilitating. Hence these substances should not be used when washing is done by hand. They are only permissible where the clothes are pounded in the old-fashioned way, or the work is done by a washing machine. Even breathing the fumes of turpentine in the steam of the laundry may be dangerous under certain circumstances, and, on the whole, these recipes should be used only with the greatest caution. Clothes washed with turpentine should be rinsed very thoroughly to remove all traces of it before being worn, as otherwise it will be injurious to the skin.

To a boilerful of hot water add 1½ bars of hard soap shaved fine, 1 tablespoonful of spirits of turpentine, and 1 teaspoonful of aqua ammonia; bring to a boil and stir until all are dissolved before putting in the clothes.

Or, in addition to the soap, use 1 tablespoonful of spirits of turpentine and 1 tablespoonful of powdered borax.

Or to 6 or 8 gallons of water add 1 pound of hard soap shaved fine, ½ ounce of spirits of turpentine, and ½ ounce of aqua ammonia.

Or 1 tablespoonful of kerosene and 1 tablespoonful of turpentine.

Or, for a washing fluid, shave 2 pounds of hard white or yellow soap into a saucepan, pour over it 1 quart of soft water, and melt with gentle heat, stirring frequently. Stir in 1 tablespoonful of white-wine vinegar, 2 tablespoonfuls of aqua ammonia, and 6 tablespoonfuls of spirits of turpentine. Pour into large glass bottles or stone jugs and cork tightly to prevent evaporation. Use this fluid at the rate of 2 tablespoonfuls to 6 or 8 gallons of the water in which the clothes are soaked, and the same quantity in the wash boiler.

To whiten clothes take spirits of turpentine, 1 tablespoonful; powdered borax, 1 tablespoonful. Mix well and use in the water in which the clothes are boiled.

Or first soap the water in which the clothes are to be boiled, then add the following: spirits of turpentine, 1 tablespoonful; aqua ammonia, 1 tablespoonful. Housekeepers who have used this washing fluid value it highly.

Washing Fluids with Sal Soda.—Dissolve ¼ pound of sal soda and ¼ pound of borax in 1 gallon of boiling soft water. Add 2 gallons of cold soft water and 1 ounce of gum camphor dissolved in ½ pint of alcohol. Stir well and put in corked bottles or fruit jars. Add 4 teaspoonfuls of this preparation to 1 pint of soft soap or 1 bar of hard soap cut into fine shavings, and dissolve the whole in a boilerful of hot water before putting in the clothes.

Or dissolve ½ pound of washing soda and ¼ pound of borax in 4 quarts of boiling soft water. When cold add ½ teacupful of aqua ammonia and pour into corked bottles or fruit jars. Dissolve in the wash boiler in the proportion of 1 teacupful to 1 pailful of water before the clothes are put in.

Or dissolve 1 pound of sal soda and ½ pound of quicklime in 6 quarts of boiling water. When the mixture has settled, pour off and bottle the clear liquid, which is soda lye. This is a very powerful washing fluid. One cupful is added to a boilerful of hot water containing 1 pint of soft soap or 1 pound of hard soap cut in shavings will thoroughly cleanse and bleach the clothes. This fluid tends to brighten rather than to fade the colors of calico and colored flannels. The clothes must not be allowed to lie in the water. The boiling, sudsing, rinsing, and bluing must follow each other in rapid succession until the clothes are hung on the line, which should be by ten o'clock in the morning.

Dissolve in 1 gallon of cold soft water 1 pound of concentrated lye and 2 ounces each of powdered ammonia (muriate of ammonia) and salts of tartar. Preserve in glass bottles or fruit jars, tightly corked. Use a cupful of this fluid with a bar of soap and boil 15 minutes.

Or make a saponaceous lye by boiling 1 gallon of wood ashes in sufficient soft water to dissolve the ashes, then add 2 or 3 handfuls of fresh quicklime. Mix thoroughly while boiling and afterwards cool until the sediment settles. Draw off the pure water and add 1 pint of oil or melted grease strained through cheese cloth for each 20 quarts of this liquid. Ashes from hard wood are the best, but if the ashes do not contain a sufficient amount of alkali a small amount of potash or soda may be added. The result should be a milk-white liquor. Use 1 cupful to a boilerful of water with 1 pound of shaved hard soap.

Or this composition, used by the French: hard soap, 1 pound; water, 6 gallons; spirits of turpentine, ½ ounce; aqua ammonia, ½ ounce. Mix well and bottle ready for use.

Or brown soap, 2 pounds. Cut it up and put it into a clean pot, adding 1 quart of clear soft water. Set over the fire and melt thoroughly, stirring it up from the bottom occasionally. Take from the fire and stir in real white vinegar, 1 teaspoonful; aqua ammonia, 2 large teaspoonfuls; spirits of turpentine, 7 large teaspoonfuls. Stir all well together, put the mixture immediately into a stone jar, and cover without delay so that the ammonia will not evaporate. Keep it closely covered.

Washing Powders. — Commercial washing powders, such as pearline, soapine, and the like, are said by chemists to be composed of hard white soap ground to powder and mixed with pulverized sal soda in approximately equal parts. Hence they are liable to the same objections as sal soda, which is well known to contain an excess of alkali. They are, however, useful for dishwashing, scrubbing, and many other purposes. They can be made at home much more cheaply than they can be purchased.

To make washing powder, melt in a double boiler 1 ounce of good white glue in 1 gallon of hot water to make a thin glue size. Mix equal parts of granulated soda ash with granulated sal soda, pulverizing them into grains about the size of coarse sand by means of a rolling pin. Pour over this mixture the solution of glue, or use instead pure linseed oil and stir until the mass forms a stiff, thick paste. Spread out the whole on a table top or other flat surface in a warm room to dry.

Or, instead of the solution of glue, use a solution of 1 pint of linseed oil to 1 gallon of water.

Soap Jelly.—Dissolve 1 teaspoonful of any good washing powder in a cupful of hot water, or dissolve any desired quantity of shaved hard white or yellow soap in twice its own bulk of hot water, using a double boiler. Use instead of soft soap for delicate fabrics.

Kerosene for Washing.—This is a favorite labor-saving article in many households. Use for each boilerful of water 1 pound of good hard soap in shavings and 1 teaspoonful of kerosene to each pail of water, or about 2½ tablespoonfuls for a wash boiler two thirds full of water. Should it be necessary to add more water after the first or second boiling, put in ½ pound of shaved soap and 1 tablespoonful more of kerosene. This mixture will not injure fabrics and will evaporate when the clothes are laundered so as to leave no odor. When kerosene is used very little rubbing will be required.

Special Hints.—When rinsing large linen pieces, as sheets, tablecloths, and large towels, gather the middle of the piece into the hand and souse the edges in the water several times. This leaves the selvage smooth and ready for the iron.

If a little cooked starch is put into the rinsing water it will add just enough stiffness to launder properly and will give to old linen the appearance of new.

A little pipe clay dissolved in the water in which the linens are washed will assist in cleansing the more soiled articles, and also in giving them the appearance of having been bleached.

The addition of a teaspoonful of paraffin will assist in removing stains.

A small vegetable brush may be used to apply soap and water to the spots on the coarser linens, and a nail-brush is convenient to use on the delicate fabrics.

Fine cotton goods, as lawns, cambries, and muslins, should not be washed with linen, especially unbleached linen, as the latter has a tendency to discolor them.

Delicate dresses of lawn, muslin, cambric, and print goods should not be boiled or rubbed with soap. They should be washed in tepid water in which soap has been previously dissolved, rinsed quickly, and dried in the shade.

A quart of bran sewed into a tight bag and boiled in the wash boiler will assist in cleansing delicate garments.

The addition of a handful of salt helps to set the colors of light cambrics and dotted lawns.

A little beef gall will brighten yellow, purple, or green tints.

Handkerchiefs. — Handkerchiefs used by persons who have affections of the nose, throat, and lungs, as grippe, catarrh, bronchitis, and the like, should not be put in laundry bags or clothes hampers containing the family wash. The easiest and most sanitary method of handling these articles is to keep for the purpose a large tin or enameled-ware pan containing a strong solution of common salt. Drop the handkerchiefs into this, place the pan on the stove when clear from cooking, and bring to a boil. They may now be rinsed with clean water and put into the rest of the laundry, or the pan may be filled with boiling water containing a tablespoonful of any good washing powder, the handkerchiefs returned to it and boiled from twenty minutes to half an hour, then removed, rinsed, and laid aside for ironing.

To Wash Corsets.—Choose a clear, sunny day; make a strong solution of good soapsuds and a small amount of ammonia, spread the corsets on a clean board or table and scrub with a good stiff brush until thoroughly clean. Apply clear water in the same way to rinse them and hang immediately in the sun. Do not wring out. Let them drip dry, and the shape will not be changed.

Or make good warm suds, lay the corsets on a washboard and scrub thoroughly on both sides with a stiff brush. Then scald a little, rinse thoroughly, starch slightly, and dry. When ironed they look much better than when rubbed on a washboard.

Special Pieces.—In addition to the regular wash day it is often advisable to lay aside small muslins, laces, ribbons, and other delicate articles to be washed at other times when they can have special attention, rather than to put them into the weekly wash. Blankets and other heavy articles can also be washed to better advantage by themselves, and in the season when the days are long and bright.

COLORED GOODS

Care for Colored Goods.—All colored goods, especially light dress goods having delicate colors, as colored linens, muslins, lawns, or cambrics; and prints, as chintz, ginghams, and calicoes, require special care in washing. They must be handled separately from other articles, and in many respects it is better to make a special job of washing fine colored goods on another day than the regular wash day. Care must be taken in washing colored goods that the colors do not soak out or run. This may be prevented in two ways: by a special process in washing, different from the method of washing white goods, and by the addition of various substances to the washing or rinsing water to set the colors.

Cautions for Colored Goods.—The best general caution for handling colored goods is to avoid extremes of heat or cold, to avoid hard wringing, and to wash and do them up as quickly as possible. They must not be soaked or otherwise delayed in washing, boiled, scalded, or exposed to direct sunlight or the heat of a very hot iron. No form of washing soda, soft soap, or washing powders or fluids containing free alkali should be employed. Use pure white or yellow neutral soap only for this purpose. Neither must they be allowed to freeze.

To prevent the colors from running they may be set by adding certain substances to the suds or rinsing water or both.

Don'ts for Colored Goods.—Don't soak or soap colored goods over night.

Don't boil them, don't wash in hot water, don't use washing fluids, washing powders, or anything else containing the slightest particle of sal soda.

Don't put them all into the tub at once.

Don't let them lie any longer than necessary in the suds, rinsing water, or clothes basket.

Don't hang them up to dry so that the right side will be exposed to the hot sun.

Don't hang them in the sun at all if shade is available.

Don't iron them with a very hot iron.

To Wash Colored Goods.—Sort out the calicoes and other prints, colored linens, etc., and prepare suds with cold or lukewarm water and good hard white or yellow soap. Have at hand a tub of rinsing water containing alum, oxgall, or other substances to set the colors. Wash each piece separately, commencing with the lightest in color, rinse, and wring it out as quickly as possible, leaving the remaining pieces in a dry state. Wash all the colored articles as quickly as possible, turn them wrong side out, and hang them up to dry, if possible, in the shade.

To Suds Colored Goods.—Prepare suds by shaving hard white soap in soft water at the rate of about half a bar to two pailfuls of water. Bring the water to a boil, remove from the fire, and allow it to cool until it will bear the hands comfortably.

Do not rub soap on delicate colored goods. Wash the garments quickly. Put them in the water one at a time, and rub as little as possible; rather souse them up and down in the hot suds. If the suds become foul, prepare a fresh lather. Wash each garment by itself as quickly as possible.

To Wring Colored Goods.—Do not wring out delicate colored articles, but squeeze them gently as dry as possible between the hands.

To Rinse Colored Goods.—Rinse in two or three clear rinsing waters, adding various ingredients, according to the goods, to set the colors.

To Dry Colored Goods. — Select bright, clear weather to wash delicate and expensive colored garments, and when washed hang them to dry in the shade. The best goods will fade if hung in the sunshine. In freezing weather they may be dried indoors by the fire, as the colors will be irreparably injured if they are allowed to freeze.

To Wash Calicoes.—An exception to the rule against soaking colored articles is found in the custom of soaking calicoes and other print goods in a strong solution of salt before washing. Authorities variously recommend soaking the articles in strong salt water for periods of half an hour to over night. We would recommend experimenting with a sample of the goods before soaking delicate or expensive fabrics for a long period. First soak new calico garments in strong salt water. Dissolve 3 gills of salt in 1 gallon of hot water, not boiling. Put in the garments and soak until the colors are thoroughly set. The time required will vary according to the fabrics, and may be determined by experimenting with samples. We would recommend 15 minutes to a half hour as an average.

Wash same as other colored goods, using alum or oxgall in the suds and salt in the rinsing water. Use alum preferably for green.

Black calico may be washed in an infusion of potato starch. Peel two or three potatoes, scrape them, boil, and strain, washing the calico in the pure liquid.

Or wash in an infusion of wheat bran as hereinafter suggested.

Colored Goods—To Fix Their Color.—Substances recommended for fixing the colors of calicoes and other colored articles vary with the colors and the nature of the fabric. They include oxgall, salt, infusion of hay, alum, and lemon juice or vinegar; for red articles, borax, and for black goods lye and black pepper.

Of these, oxgall and salt are the most popular. The gall of an ox can be obtained from the butcher. It may be preserved by adding to it a handful of salt, and keeping it corked tightly. A bottle of this preparation should be always kept on hand in the laundry. Use 1 teacupful to 5 gallons of water.

Common salt may be used in the proportion of ½ cupful to 2 gallons of water; alum, 1 ounce to each gallon of water; borax, 1 tablespoonful to the gallon; vinegar or lemon juice, the same. Add these substances in the above proportion to both suds and rinsing water.

Or use a large tablespoonful of oxgall in the suds and a teaspoonful of vinegar in each rinsing water.

Or use alum in the suds and vinegar in the rinsing water.

Do not use both oxgall and alum.

To Fix Light, Solid Colors. — To permanently fix blue, slate, and stone colors in cotton fabrics, dissolve 1 ounce of sugar of lead in 2½ gallons of hot water. Stir with a wooden stick, and let stand until lukewarm. Immerse the garments in this solution for 1 to 2 hours, and hang up to drip dry in the shade before washing. Remember that sugar of lead is poisonous; hence, after being dried, these articles should be washed thoroughly and rinsed in plenty of clear water.

To Fix Dark, Solid Colors.—To fix black and other dark colors, dissolve 2 cupfuls of salt in 2½ gallons of water, immerse the articles until they are thoroughly saturated, and hang them up to drip dry in a shady place. Add a tablespoonful of salt to the rinsing water.

Or, to prevent black goods and hosiery from turning brown, use very strong bluing in the water. For black goods, also, add a teacupful of lye to each pailful of soapsuds in which the articles are washed. They must be washed quickly and the excess of lye thoroughly rinsed out in clear cold water to which salt has been added.

Or, for black goods, prepare an infusion of 1 tablespoonful of powdered black pepper with sufficient water to cover the articles, and steep them in it for a half hour before washing.

To Fix Pinks, Reds, and Greens.—Vinegar is especially recommended for pink, red, or green goods to brighten the color; salt for black, blue, and green colors. Hence, to fix pink or green, add ½ cupful of strong vinegar to 2½ gallons of water, immerse the articles, and let them drip dry in the shade.

To Fix Red or Scarlet.—For red or scarlet table napkins add 1 tablespoonful of borax to each gallon of soapsuds when washing.

To Fix Solid-colored Linens.—A strong infusion of common hay made by boiling the hay and straining off the clear liquor is recommended for French linens; black pepper, 1 teaspoonful for each pailful of water, for gray and brown linens.

To Wash Colored Goods with Bran.—Delicate lawn and muslin dresses, also chintz and cretonne, may be washed without soap in an infusion of wheat bran. This process cannot possibly harm the most delicate fabrics. Boil 1 quart of wheat bran in 3 quarts of water for about 15 minutes, and strain off the clear liquor into the wash water. Boil the bran again for 15 minutes in an equal quantity of water, and strain off the resulting infusion into the rinsing water.

For the wash water add to the infusion of bran about an equal quantity of clear soft water. Add also, to set the colors, a tablespoonful of oxgall or a small lump of alum. Use no soap, as the bran itself possesses sufficient cleansing properties. Wash with as little rubbing and wringing as possible.

Rinse first in the lukewarm bran water, adding salt, and afterwards in clear water containing a little gum arabic. No starch will be required. The bran after having been strained may be fed to pigs or chickens.

To Clean Colored Goods with Raw Potatoes.—Grate the potatoes to a fine pulp and mix with 1 pint of water for each pound of grated potato. Sift with a coarse sieve and let the liquid settle until the starch accumulates at the bottom. The clear liquid remaining may be bottled for future use. To apply, lay a linen towel over the washboard and spread the soiled garment upon it. Sponge with the clear liquid and afterwards rinse with clear cold water.

LACES AND LACE CURTAINS

To Wash Lace.—To wash cotton or linen lace or embroidery prepare suds of hard white soap with hot water, to which add 1 or 2 teaspoonfuls of borax. If much soiled, boil the articles in the suds before or after washing, or both. Squeeze them with the hands or draw them through the fingers in the suds until clean, rinse in clear water, add to the last water about ½ teaspoonful of granulated sugar to 1 pint of water, and iron without starching.

White Laces.—White linen and cotton laces and embroideries may be washed in soapsuds in the same manner as other delicate white goods, except that more care is required in their handling. To prepare these goods for the laundry, baste the small pieces, as doilies and smaller embroideries, Battenberg pieces, edging, and the like, on a piece of linen or cotton cloth larger than the lace. Take care to catch every point with basting thread. Several small articles can be basted on one large piece. After washing, if the cloth is stretched, the lace will dry in perfect condition without ironing. Fine lingerie, as lace waists, etc., may be basted inside a pillow case or special cotton bag prepared with a draw string for this purpose, and need not be taken out from the time it is put into the first wash water until after it is hung on the line, dried, and ready to iron. This prevents the lace from being frayed or torn by buttons catching in it, etc. Lace edging and other long pieces may be quickly basted on to a piece of cloth with the sewing machine by making the stitch long.

Or, to prepare a long piece of lace for the laundry, it may be wound around a large glass bottle. First surround the bottle with a jacket of cotton or linen cloth sewed on. Attach one end of the lace to this cloth jacket with basting thread, and roll the lace around it, overlapping carefully as in bandaging. Catch the ends and edges through the cloth jacket with basting thread.

To Soak Laces.—If lace is much soiled it may be soaked for an hour or more before washing in suds made of cold water and naphtha or curd soap. Do not use yellow soap or any form of washing compound which may contain free alkali.

To Prepare Laces for the Wash.—First remove all stains, and if much soiled by perspiration wash in soap and cold water, rubbing the soiled spots gently between the fingers. After the stains have all been removed the lace may be washed in warm suds, and, if necessary, afterwards boiled.

To Suds Laces.—Only the purest hard white curd soaps should be used for washing laces. Many persons save the scraps of fine castile and other toilet soaps, melt them with a small quantity of water in a double boiler, and make a soap jelly for use with these delicate fabrics. It is better to make soapsuds in a small kettle with soft water and fine soap in which to boil these articles than to put them in the regular boiler. If they are not much soiled do not boil them, but bring the suds to a boil and pour over the laces, letting them soak until the water is cool enough to bear the hands. Wash as other fine goods, stripping between the hands as lightly as possible and sousing up and down in the suds. Use two or more fresh suds if necessary.

To Boil Laces.—Laces that are much soiled may be, if prepared and protected in the above manner, boiled in soapsuds the same as other white goods. To boil laces rolled about a bottle, first saturate the lace with olive oil or sweet oil, prepare strong soapsuds, and stand the bottle upright. Or the bottle may merely be dropped in with other articles.

To Rinse and Dry.—Rinse laces thoroughly in clear water, pressing the water out of them with the hands and dry in the hot sun without removing from the cloth or bottle which protect them.

Point Lace and Battenberg.—Point lace may be washed as other laces if very carefully basted to a piece of fine white flannel and another piece of flannel basted over it. Care must be taken to catch all the points, using very fine basting thread. After rinsing, the flannel must be carefully stretched, and while still damp ironed, without removing the lace, until perfectly dry.

Or the professional method may be employed, which is as follows: stretch

"Stretch the Duck Out of Doors."

the lace, face down, on a piece of clean white duck and carefully tack it on, using very fine basting thread and taking pains to catch all the points. Stretch the duck tent fashion over a rod out of doors on a clear day. Make a lather of fine castile or curd soap and apply the soapsuds with a soft brush, as an old toothbrush or a nail-brush with soft bristles, or with a sponge, until it is thoroughly cleaned. Rinse by pouring over it water containing a little alum. Add a little bluing to the last rinsing water. Apply thin starch or a solution of gum arabic with a sponge, and when nearly dry lay a Turkish towel over the ironing board, put the duck on this with the lace underneath, and iron the duck. This is a perfectly safe method and gives a polish which cannot be acquired in any other way.

To Wash a White Lace Veil.—If not much soiled, first wash in cold water with castile or curd soap, squeezing between the fingers without rubbing. When stains and spots have disappeared, squeeze gently from the cold water and pour over it the hot suds. Let stand until cool enough to bear the hands, and continue squeezing with the fingers until perfectly clean, changing the suds if necessary. If much soiled, put the veil in a cotton bag and boil ten or fifteen minutes. Rinse in cold water with a little bluing, and starch with a thin solution of gum arabic, rice water, or corn starch. Stretch to its original shape and spread over a linen towel stretched tent fashion out of doors, and in the bright sun if possible. Pull the edges out to their proper shape and fasten with pins. When nearly dry iron on a Turkish towel through a piece of flannel or linen cloth.

To Wash Black Lace.—Make suds of castile or other hard white soap and boiling water, and add a tablespoonful of oxgall to set the color. Allow this to cool until it will bear the hand, then immerse the lace and cleanse by squeezing gently with the fingers. Rinse in two or more cold waters, adding salt to the first and bluing to the last. Starch with a thin solution of gum arabic or common glue made by dissolving a piece of thin glue about an inch square in a quart of boiling water. Or use thin rice water or cornstarch. Lay over black silk or cambric stretched tent fashion, stretch, and pin the edges securely. When dry arrange face down on a Turkish towel, and iron through a thin cloth, following the pattern with the point of the iron. Use a warm, not hot, iron, as much heat will turn the lace rusty.

To Sponge Black Lace.—First dust the articles thoroughly and stretch, face down, over a piece of black goods, tacking down the edges with basting thread. Sponge with dilute ammonia and water.

Or sponge with green tea.

Or use borax water in the proportion of 1 teaspoonful of borax to 1 pint of soft water.

Use, if convenient, an old black kid glove as a sponge. Press while still damp and without removing from the cloth to which it is basted. Lay the lace on a Turkish towel protected by a piece of dry black goods and iron through the protecting cloth on the wrong side, using a warm, not hot, iron.

Or a long piece of lace may be wound about a bottle and put in a warm place to dry. Avoid the direct heat of the sun or of a hot stove or iron, as these tend to give black articles a rusty appearance.

Lace Curtains—When To Launder Them.—Have a special day at house-cleaning time for lace curtains, doilies, dresser scarfs, and all articles of fancy work. These require suds made of fancy soap and more care in the laundry than ordinary articles; hence they should be handled by themselves and given special treatment. After being done up they can be laid away until house cleaning is finished, and put up as each room is cleaned.

To Air Lace Curtains.—Lace curtains may be cleaned easily and will not need washing so often if hung on the line on a clear day with a gentle breeze—not too windy—and dusted by the wind. Washing these articles is a delicate and difficult business, and they necessarily suffer more or less from the process.

To Prepare Curtains for the Laundry.—Stitch a narrow piece of tape along the hem of net or lace curtains before they go to the laundry. This keeps the curtain from pulling out of shape when ironed. Lay the curtains on an old sheet and brush them carefully with a soft brush to remove the dust. Fold them separately as a tablecloth is folded, taking care to keep the edges perfectly together until the folds are about two feet square. Baste a strip of white muslin along the edges to keep the package in order and quilt slightly with basting thread. In this shape large curtains can be put into suds and cleaned with a pounder or otherwise.

Or fold them carefully and insert in a pillowcase, running through them at intervals strong basting thread to keep them flat and prevent their bunching in the end of the case.

Or they may be carefully gathered crosswise and tied loosely in a bunch by two or three cords at intervals. Wash like other fine white goods, first, if much soiled, soaking for an hour or more in soap and cold water, next rubbing gently between the hands in warm or hot soapsuds, and afterwards boiling in one or more hot suds according to their condition. Rinse first in hot water, afterwards two or three times in cold water, adding bluing to the last. Kerosene, ammonia, or turpentine may be used in the boiling water, but no washing powders that may contain free alkali.

Or put the curtain in a large tin funnel with a wooden handle attached to it; work it through suds and rinsing water in such a way that the water will pass through the curtain and out at the bottom of the funnel, removing the dirt by suction. This process will not injure the most delicate fabrics, no matter how long it may continue.

Colored Curtains.—If there is any doubt about colors being fast, delicate-colored curtains may be cleansed with gasoline.

To Dry Curtains.—If curtains are dried out of doors, cover the line on which they are hung with one or more thicknesses of paper or throw over it a dry sheet. This will prevent the clothespin from marking the articles and keep them from being injured by the wind.

Or, if the curtains are folded and basted together with muslin, dry them before taking them out of the folds.

Or lay a blanket on the floor and spread the wet curtains on it, stretching them carefully. They will keep their place and dry without fastening.

To Stretch Curtains.—A curtain stretcher is not used in most families, and hence is something of a luxury. Sometimes two or three families in a neighborhood can combine to purchase one for their common use. As a substitute lay a sheet or clean wrapping paper on the floor, stretch the curtains over this, and fasten by means of heavy pins called bank pins, which can be obtained at the stores. Use a pin for each scallop, driving them into the floor with a tack hammer. Lay other curtains over these, hooking them on the same pins, as is done on stretchers. Several curtains may be hooked on the same set of pins. The pins may be afterwards removed and used again.

Or the curtains may be pinned to a sheet laid upon the carpet, two or three curtains by carefully matching the scallops being pinned down at the same time.

Or stretch a sheet on a quilting frame, and pin the curtains to this.

Or, while damp, hang the curtains, one at a time, on a curtain rod, and slip a heavy rod or curtain pole through the hem at the bottom. Stretch the curtains to their full width, and allow them to hang until dry. The weight of the rod at the bottom will stretch them sufficiently.

SILKS AND SATIN

To Launder Silks.—To wash silk dresses and other garments, ribbons, handkerchiefs, stockings, and the like, first rip apart made-up garments, shake, and brush thoroughly to free them from dust. Prepare soap jelly by cutting castile or other good white hard soap into shavings, pour over it about double its own bulk of water, and dissolve by gentle heat. Have ready two or three tubs or pans and fill these partly full of hot water. Thus the washing and rinsing waters will cool alike and always be of exactly the same temperature. This is the great point to observe in washing all animal fibers, as silks or woolens.

In the first receptacle dissolve enough soap jelly to make good suds, and let stand until the hands can be comfortably borne in the water. Wash each piece separately in the suds by sousing it up and down, raising it in one hand and stripping it through the fingers with the other. Continue this process until clean, but without creasing, wringing, or squeezing it. When washed clean, strip through the fingers to remove suds. If soiled spots do not come out, rub on a little soap jelly and immediately dip again into the suds. Change the suds if necessary. Rinse in clear water, following the same process as in washing, strip out the water between the fingers, or shake out the pieces without wringing, and iron at once without hanging up to dry.

Or mix 6 ounces of strained honey with 4 ounces of soft-soap jelly made of castile or other hard white soap, and add 1 pint of whisky. Rip apart made-up articles, spread the pieces flat on a smooth surface, and apply this mixture with a brush, rubbing lightly with the grain of the silk. Rinse in two or three clear waters, not too hot to bear the hands comfortably, and without wringing, creasing, or folding the silk. Add a little sugar or a tablespoonful of honey to the last rinsing water. Iron at once.

Or for delicate fabrics, as China silk, pongee, and similar dress goods, for each article, as a waist or summer gown, put 1½ pints of bran in a bag of white muslin, and pour over it sufficient boiling water to wash the garment. When the hands can be borne in it comfortably, squeeze the bag in the water to extract the solution of bran. Add 1 or 2 teaspoonfuls of powdered borax, wash, rinse in clear water, and iron at once. Use no starch, as the bran gives sufficient stiffness.

To Wash Colored Silks.—The same cautions must be observed in washing colored silks as in the case of other colored goods, with the additional caution that they must not be crushed, squeezed, or wrung when wet, or wrinkles may be formed which will not iron out. Prepare suds for silk by dissolving hard white soap in boiling water, and add oxgall or alum to set the colors. Allow the suds to cool until they will bear the hands, and immerse the silk in them. Lay the washboard across the tub, spread an old towel or piece of flannel over it, lay the silk flat on this, and apply the suds by rubbing gently with a soft cloth or a sponge, or a toothbrush or nailbrush having medium hard bristles. When the silk is clean apply cold water with the brush and afterwards souse in cold water containing salt. If the silk is of solid color, dissolve a little dye the color of the silk in the rinsing water. If the color has faded this will restore it. Silk garments rinsed in diluted dye water will come out nearly as fresh as new.

To Wash White Silk.—Prepare suds as for other delicate white goods by using hard white soap, but no soda or washing compounds containing free alkali. Cleanse the silks by applying the soapsuds with a soft cloth or brush, rinse in cold water, partially dry in the sun, and while still damp iron between two cloths on the wrong side.

To Wash Satin.—Satins may be washed in the same manner as silks, or sponge the way of the grain with a weak solution of borax.

To Wash Silk Stockings.—Prepare a lather and wash as other silk goods. For white stockings add a little bluing to the last rinsing water. For other tints add a little dye of the required color. Stretch the stockings to their proper shape, and pin or baste them between two thicknesses of a clean linen towel. Stretch this tent fashion, and the stockings will dry in their natural shape without ironing.

Or wash in bran water.

WOOLENS, WORSTEDS, AND FLANNELS

To Wash Woolen Goods and Flannels. — Washing woolen goods and flannels without shrinking them or causing them to lose their natural softness and delicate colors is one of the best tests of the skillful laundress.

Cautions for Woolen Goods.—Woolen and flannel goods must not be soaked, boiled, scalded, or wrung out by twisting. They must not be dried near a hot fire. The fibers of wool are hooked and curled, and when they are crushed together by rubbing they form knots, which thicken the fiber and shrink it in both dimensions. This is one of the principal causes of the shrinking that is so much feared. Or the expansion and contraction caused by alternate heat and cold may cause the fibers to interlace. Flannels may be shrunk, if desired, before they are made up by first placing them in cold and afterwards in hot water. But they can be washed without shrinking if proper precautions are observed.

To Suds Woolens and Flannels.—Prepare suds by dissolving 1 bar of hard white soap shaved fine in a boilerful of water and adding 2 tablespoonfuls of aqua ammonia. Do not use yellow soap which contains borax or soda in any form, or washing fluids and powders of the composition of which you know nothing. Pour the suds into a tub and allow them to become cool enough to bear the hands comfortably before putting in the flannels. Wash these articles one at a time as quickly as possible. Do not rub soap on them or rub them on the washboard. Souse them up and down in the water and rub them together with the hands until cleaned. Do not put them through the wringer or wring by twisting, but squeeze out the soapsuds with the hands, shake out carefully, stretch, and wash in a second lather prepared like the first, but not so strong. Rinse in warm water as near the temperature of the suds as possible, to which a little bluing may be added, press out the rinsing water, shake vigorously, and stretch the articles to prevent shrinking.

Pull each piece as nearly as possible into its proper shape and hang up carefully in such a way that the shape may be preserved. A clear, bright day with sunshine and a light breeze is desirable. Flannels should be taken down while still slightly damp and rolled up in a dry cloth. If the weather is not clear they may be dried indoors, but not near the stove. The object should be to avoid extreme changes of temperature, as these cause flannels to shrink and become hard.

To Wash Colored Woolens and Flannels.—Wash colored woolens and flannels same as other colored goods, adding oxgall or alum to the suds to set the colors, and salt or vinegar, or both, to the rinsing water. Omit the use of ammonia or borax. Dry delicate colored flannels in the shade.

To Wash Colored Woolen Dress Goods. — Cashmere, merino, alpaca, and llama dresses and colored worsted and flannel waists and blouses may be washed in suds prepared as for other colored woolen goods, provided the same cautions are observed. Do not soak, boil, or scald any woolen goods. Do not use any form of soda, lye, or unknown washing fluids or powders. Do not use borax or ammonia for delicate colored articles. Use pure neutral white or yellow soap shaved and dissolved in boiling water until it will bear the hands comfortably, and keep the suds and rinsing water at the same lukewarm temperature. Rub and wring as lightly as possible, rather sousing the garments up and down and squeezing out the water with the hands. Add oxgall or alum to the suds, and salt or vinegar to the rinsing water to set the colors. Dry delicate colors in the shade. Avoid direct sunlight or proximity to a hot fire. Take down before dry and iron while damp, but without sprinkling.

Soap Jelly for Woolen Goods.—To avoid preparing suds by shaving soap and boiling each time, it is convenient to prepare in advance a soap jelly, as follows: shave any amount of neutral white or yellow soap in the proportion of ½ pound of soap to 1 quart of boiling water and simmer until dissolved. When cold it will jell. Use this jelly in the proportion of 1 heaping tablespoonful to ½ gallon of warm water to prepare suds for washing all flannel or woolen goods. This saves the time required to bring the water to a boil.

To Wash Colored Flannel and Woolen Goods—Other Methods.—In addition to soapsuds, flannel and woolen goods may be washed in bran, flour starch, or rice. To use flour starch, take a teacupful of flour and rub it smooth with a little water to form a fine paste. Add boiling water slowly, stirring vigorously to make a smooth starch. Boil five or ten minutes and strain through cheese cloth into half a tubful of warm water, stirring vigorously. This will make good suds without soap.

To Wash Dress Goods with Rice.—Boil 2 pounds of rice in 12 quarts of water for 2 or 3 hours. Pour half of this into a tub, and when cool enough to bear the hands put the garments in and wash them with the soft boiled rice the same as with soap. Strain the other half through cheese cloth. Put the solid part into another tub of warm water and wash the garments once in this. Rinse in clear warm water, and a second time in warm water in which the clear rice water that was reserved for this purpose has been added. This will take the place of starch. No soap or starch need be used. The rice should be boiled a day or two in advance and kept in readiness, so that garments may be washed early in the morning and done up the same day.

Woolen Fancy Work—Crochet, etc.—Small and delicate woolen articles may be put into a cotton bag or tied up in a pillowcase and washed the same as other woolen articles. The suds and rinsing water should be plentiful. The articles need not be taken out of the bag while washing, and they may be hung up in it on the line to dry.

Woolen Table Covers.—First remove all stains and grease spots; next soak thirty minutes in strong salt water. Prepare suds, wash, rinse, and dry same as other colored woolen goods. If much soiled, apply soap and water with a scrubbing brush, laying the cloth on the washboard placed crosswise upon the tub.

To Wash Knitted Shawls.—Knitted or crocheted shawls may be folded as flat as possible and laid carefully in a pillowcase, run through at intervals with basting thread to keep flat, and treated like other flannel or woolen goods. If washed separately, observe the usual cautions for woolen goods, gently squeezing through the hands and keeping the suds and rinsing water of the same lukewarm temperature. Do not hang knitted goods up to dry, but put in the oven on a big platter, shaking and turning occasionally, or lay on a clean cloth in the bright sunshine.

Woolen Shawls.—The most delicate colored cashmere and other woolen shawls may be washed in soapsuds if proper precautions are observed. Make suds same as for other woolen goods by dissolving 1 pound of hard white soap in 2½ pailfuls of water. Add 1 tablespoonful of oxgall or 2 ounces of alum and wash the articles by sousing up and down, rubbing as little as possible. Squeeze the water out of them and rinse in two or three waters, each containing a teaspoonful of salt. Place between two dry sheets to wring out and wring lightly. Press while still damp with a warm, not hot, iron.

To Wash Blankets.—Choose a warm, sunny day with a gentle breeze. Prepare suds by dissolving in hot water ½ bar of any good white hard soap, 1 tablespoonful of borax, and 1 tablespoonful of aqua ammonia for each pair of blankets. Let the suds cool until they will bear the hands. Immerse the blankets and let them stand in the suds for an hour, keeping the temperature about as hot as the hands will bear by frequently adding hot water. Do not rub soap on the blankets nor scour nor rub them. Lay the

"Lay the Washboard Across the Tub."

washboard flat across the tub, put in one blanket at a time, raise the blanket on to the washboard and go around the edge, applying the suds with a scrubbing brush and rubbing vigorously. Meantime heat sufficient water for two more lathers. Remove from the first to a second suds prepared in the same manner, seize the blanket by the middle and souse it up and down. Squeeze and press it between the hands until clean. Rinse in three clear waters, keeping them at the same temperature as the suds, namely, as hot as the hands will bear, and run through the wringer or squeeze the water out of them rather than wring them in the usual way. Fasten by the edges to the line and frequently shake and stretch them to their proper size while drying. To have the best success in washing blankets two points must be observed, namely: to keep the water at a uniform temperature, neither boiling hot nor cold enough to chill, but as hot as the hands will bear; and not to wring or rub the blankets in such a way that the fibers will become interlaced and cause shrinking. When thoroughly dry beat the blankets while on the line with a carpet beater. This will cause the wool to become fluffy like a new blanket.

To Wash Bedspreads. — If bedspreads are changed quite frequently they will not require soaking, but if very much soiled they may be soaked by putting them in a tub and pouring over them a boilerful of hot water in which 2 tablespoonfuls of borax has been dissolved. Prepare suds by dissolving 1 bar of hard white or yellow soap in a boilerful of hot water and wash same as other white goods. Do not use any form of soda, lye, or any washing fluids or compounds. If washed on a windy day, bedspreads will need no ironing. Fold the edges together and pin them on the line with the wrong side out. This not only prevents the spread from wearing across the middle, but gives it a fresher appearance than ironing.

To Wash Comforters.—Sometimes a heavy comforter can be washed by simply tacking it smoothly on a clean shingle roof and letting the rain fall on it. It is well to previously soak it for half an hour or more in a strong solution of common salt to prevent the colors running.

Or soak the comforter for an hour or two in borax water. Prepare suds as for other colored goods, with the addition of oxgall or alum and salt. Lay the washboard across the top of the tub and apply the suds with a soft scrubbing brush, especially round the edges. Continue as in washing blankets. Those who have a supply of running water may use the garden hose for rinsing blankets, bedspreads, and comforters. Remove from the suds without wringing, hang them on a line, and drench them with water from the hose until they are rinsed thoroughly.

DRYING CLOTHES

Bag for Clothespins.—The ordinary wooden clothespins are the best. Keep clothespins for convenience in a bag made like a laundry bag of crash, linen, or other washable material, or use for this purpose a 24-pound flour sack. A wire hoop at the top of the clothespin bag is a convenience in keeping it open when clothespins are wanted.

To Preserve Clothespins.—Put the clothespin bag into a kettle of boiling water every few weeks. Remove after three to five minutes and spread the clothespins out to dry in the sun, or dry quickly near the fire. This keeps them from becoming brittle and cracking.

Dip the heads of part of the clothespins in dark paint, part in light paint, and leave the rest unpainted. Use the ones with dark heads for colored garments, those with light heads for miscellaneous pieces, as flannels, towels, and the like, and the unpainted ones for sheer white garments. This will prevent using on sheer white pieces pins that have been stained by colored garments.

To Have Clothespins Handy.—Make an apron with a large baglike pocket to contain clothespins, to wear while hanging out the clothes.

Or put clothespins into a small basket (an ordinary grape basket is convenient), and hang the basket on the clothesline by a hook made of wire, such as is used to hold the basket by apple and berry pickers. Push the basket along as you hang the clothes. It is handy, and is also out of the way.

Or hang on each clothes post a bag made of oilcloth with a lapel. Attach a sufficient number of pins to the clothesline by pieces of strong cord about a foot long. Fish line is excellent for this purpose. Make a loop of the cord over the clothesline large enough to admit of it slipping along, and fasten the pins securely at the other end. After the clothes are taken down, the clothespins will remain suspended from the line by the cords. Now shove them all along the line to the post, drop them into the bag without untying them, cover with the lapel, and leave them there for future use. But this plan necessitates leaving the clothesline out of doors.

Or set the clothes basket and clothespin bag on a child's four-wheeled cart, or even a wheelbarrow, and push them along under the line as you proceed.

To Keep the Hands Warm.—Set the clothespin bag in a kettle of boiling water. Remove and dry near the stove. The hot clothespins will help to keep the hands warm in freezing weather.

To Select and Preserve Clotheslines.—Gutta-percha clotheslines are much more satisfactory than rope. They can be left out of doors in all weathers, and wiped clean with a damp cloth. But clotheslines of rope will last longer and keep in better order if they are boiled in water for a couple of hours when first purchased, and afterwards dipped in boiling water once a month.

They must be thoroughly dried by hanging them near the fire or stretching them on the clothes posts in the sunshine. Care must be taken not to allow them to kink.

To Wash Clotheslines.—A soiled line may be cleansed and made to look like new by boiling it in strong soapsuds. For this purpose make suds of a neutral white or yellow soap, but do not use soda in any form or washing powders containing free alkali. The line is so thick that the alkali may not all be rinsed out of it and hence will be likely to rot the fiber. Wind the line into a coil around the elbow, tie it securely at both ends, and put it in the boiling suds. If it is much soiled, change the water. Pour the last suds into the tub, place the coil of line on the washboard, and apply the suds with a scrubbing brush, scrubbing downward. Dry by stretching between clothes posts in the sunshine or indoors by the fire. Take care that the line is thoroughly dry before it is put away.

To Avoid Kinks in Clotheslines.—To prevent a clothesline from becoming kinked or twisted when taken down, wind it toward you instead of from you. This tends to remove the kinkiness.

Care of Clotheslines.—Do not put out a clothesline until the clothes are ready to be hung out. When they are dry take the line down at once, coil it carefully over the elbows to avoid kinks, knot the coil at one end, and slip it into a clean cotton bag with a draw string at one end to keep it free from dust and dirt. Hang the bag in a clean, dry place.

To Hang Out Clothes.—The orderly arrangement made by sorting the clothes in the first instance should be observed in hanging them on the line. Hang the contents of the first boiler in one row, those of the second boiler in another, sheets together, towels together, napkins together, and so on. Expose plain white goods and coarser articles to the sun, but hang colored goods and delicate woolen and flannel goods in the shade. Hang up the clothes, especially colored articles, as quickly as possible after they are removed from the rinsing water. If small or delicate articles, as laces, crocheted articles, and the like, are boiled in a cotton bag or pillowcase, hang them up in this receptacle to dry. Take down woolens and flannels, including blankets, before they are quite dry. While drying, stretch them occasionally as nearly as possible to their proper shape.

To Hang Out Large Pieces.—Fold large pieces, as tablecloths, sheets, blankets, counterpanes, quilts, and the like, and pin the opposite edges to the line rather than by the middle. The articles will thus be less injured by whipping and present a better appearance. Figured counterpanes hung in this way will require no ironing, and if on account of sickness or otherwise it is necessary to save labor, sheets and even tablecloths may be used rough dry.

To Take Down Clothes. — When taking clothes from the line place the clothes basket in a child's cart or wheelbarrow. Lay a large clean cloth in the bottom, shake the wrinkles from each article, fold it carefully,

"Place the Basket in a Child's Cart."

and lay all in orderly fashion in the basket. Put the corners of the sheets, tablecloths, towels, and other similar articles exactly together, and it will be found much easier to iron them than if they were thrown into a clothes basket in a disorderly mass.

To Prevent Freezing.—The excess of soap and washing powders containing alkali which may be left in fabrics by careless rinsing will in time give white articles a dingy or yellow color. This is very much intensified by freezing. Colored articles will always be more or less faded by freezing, and all garments are injured more by one freezing than by several weeks of constant use. To prevent freezing add salt to the rinsing water. This makes the clothes less liable to freeze.

If the corners especially of towels, napkins, etc., and the edges of sheets and tablecloths be dipped in rather strong salt water they will not freeze so tightly, and there will be less danger of their tearing when whipped by the wind or when being removed from the line.

Bad Weather. — If wash day is stormy the clothes may be thoroughly wrung dry, rolled up, and laid away in covered tubs or baskets for a reasonable time while waiting for fair weather. This plan is better than to keep them soaking in a tub of water.

If the clothes are on the line and it is necessary, on account of bad weather, to take them down before they are dry, it is a good plan to put the clotheshorse in the yard, fold the pieces, and lay them over it, rather than to crowd the wet clothes into the basket. They can then be carried on the clotheshorse indoors and placed by the fire.

Or clothes may be dried indoors by special drying arrangement in the kitchen or other warm, convenient room. Place hooks or small pulleys on either side of a room opposite one another, about 3½ feet apart and at a height a few inches above the head of the tallest member of the family. Stretch the clothesline on these so that it will go back and forth across the room. Instead of allowing the clothes to hang down on the line, stretch them across horizontally, up and out of the way. Put the heaviest articles nearest the stove, and keep a good fire. Open the windows a few inches at the top for ventilation. An entire wash for a family of half a dozen persons can be thus dried without serious inconvenience in an ordinary kitchen. If there is a special room set apart for the laundry, this method will be found equally convenient.

To Dry Knit Goods. — Children's knitted underwear, woolen shirts, and other small but expensive articles which tend to shrink when drying, may be kept in shape by drying on frames. These may be purchased or can be readily made by any ingenious member of the family. They should be about an inch wider than the garment, made in two parts hinged together, and each having an arm piece with a blunt point projecting at the side. Shut the stretcher by means of the hinges, slip it into the garment while wet, insert the arm pieces, stretch it out flat, button the garment, and hang it up to dry. This not only preserves the shape and prevents shrinking, but gives the article the appearance of being new.

CHAPTER XII

IRONING DAY

BLUING AND SPRINKLING—STARCH AND STARCHING—CARE OF IRONING UTENSILS—IRONING—TO DO UP SILKS, RIBBONS, AND WOOLENS—TO DO UP LACES AND CURTAINS—TO MARK AND STORE LINEN

BLUING AND SPRINKLING

Bluing.—It is very difficult to rinse clothes quite free from all traces of soap or other washing compounds. The minute quantities of alkali left in the fabrics tend to give white articles a dingy or yellow tinge. The object of bluing is to correct this. Hence it is customary to add bluing to the last rinsing water for white articles or colored goods that have a white background. For dark colored goods it is also customary to add a liberal supply of bluing to the starch. Some laundresses do not wring from the bluing water table linens and similar articles which they desire to have a fine, clear white, but hang them up dripping in order to deepen their luster.

To Make Bluing.—In addition to the various kinds of commercial bluing upon the market, the following recipes are recommended:

Dissolve 1 ounce of the best soluble Prussian blue powder and ½ ounce of powdered oxalic acid in 1 quart of soft water.

Or dissolve 1 package of blue diamond dye for cotton in 1 quart of soft water. To prevent lumps, prepare this as you would starch. Rub the dry powder into a paste with a little water, add a little more cold water, then add the rest of the water boiling hot. Cool and bottle for use.

Sprinkling.—The object of sprinkling is to give the garments a uniform dampness, to soften wrinkles, and to prevent the iron from scorching. Hence the clothes should be sprinkled slightly and afterwards rolled up and allowed to lie until the moisture has uniformly penetrated all parts of the fabric. Delicate colored goods, flannels and other woolens, and fine linens will have a better appearance if ironed on the same day that they were washed than if allowed to become entirelv dry before ironing. Colored goods especially should not be sprinkled if it can be avoided.

Utensils for Sprinkling.—An ordinary brush broom, a child's sprinkling

"An Ordinary Brush Broom."

can, a tin baking-powder can or glass fruit jar with metal top perforated by holes made with a hammer and small nails, are all convenient utensils for sprinkling. A small fine-grain sponge and a basin of water should be at hand when ironing. If small spots of sheer goods become dry they should be dampened before ironing, or if a smudge or patch of starch appears it can be thus removed without affecting the rest of the garment.

STARCH AND STARCHING

To Make Starch.—Starch is a substance contained in various vegetables, as grains, potatoes, etc.

Starch is made from grain by steeping it in cold water until it becomes soft. It is then placed in sacks and pressed in a vat with water. The milky juice which is produced by this process is allowed to stand until it becomes clear, when the starch sinks to the bottom in the form of white powder.

Starch may be made from potatoes by grating them in water and straining and squeezing the mass through thin cloth, as cheese cloth, or a suitable sieve. The liquid is then allowed to stand until the potato starch settles at the bottom. The clear liquid from which the starch has settled has considerable cleansing properties and is especially useful to clean colored silks, woolens, and other delicate articles without injury to their color or texture. The coarse fiber of the potato removed by straining may be used in washing heavy colored woolen articles, as blankets, horse blankets, carriage robes, and the like. These articles should be soaked in water containing salt to set the colors, and afterwards scrubbed with the grated potato fibers and scrubbing brush and water.

Starch may be made from potatoes which are too small for domestic use, and a fairly good quality may also be made from frosted potatoes, although this last may have a slightly darker color. The starch from frosted potatoes may be improved by adding fresh water after the first clear liquid has been turned off, stirring, and allowing it to settle once more, and so continuing until the liquid is entirely clear.

To Prepare Starch.—The amount of starch to prepare for a given washing depends upon the articles to be starched, and must be determined in each family by experiment. The ability to do up starched linen perfectly is one of the most severe tests of the successful laundress. Hence the importance of knowing how to prepare good starch. First mix the required amount of common starch with a small quantity of cold water to the consistency of cream. Carefully rub and beat the starch with a spoon to break up all lumps and insure that the particles of starch are evenly wet through. Thin to the consistency of milk with a little more cold water. For thick cooked starch add 8 parts of boiling water to 1 of starch. For thin cooked starch add 16 parts of water to 1 of starch. Pour the water while boiling vigorously in a thin stream, and stir constantly to prevent the starch from lumping. Set the starch over the fire and continue to boil it from 3 to 5 minutes, stirring vigorously all the time. If such substances as wax, borax, oil, etc., are used, they should be mixed with the starch while cooking. Bluing should not be added until the starch is cold. Raw starch or that which has been insufficiently cooked will stick to the iron and make much trouble for the laundress. Cooked starch may be thinned by the addition of cold water.

Cornstarch. — Common cornstarch, such as is used for making puddings, is preferred by some laundresses instead of the ordinary laundry starch. It is about as cheap and in the opinion of many gives a finer gloss and more finished appearance to delicate starched articles. Try this some time when the laundry starch is out and see how you like it. A mixture of the two kinds is also much favored.

Starch with Wax.—For white cuffs, collars, and shirt bosoms melt with gentle heat white wax or a mixture of equal parts of white wax and spermaceti or a mixture of 1 part of white wax to 2 parts of spermaceti, as preferred, and stir into ordinary starch while boiling. Use a lump of wax about the size of a walnut to a quart of cooked starch, or estimate the amount of wax in the proportion of $\frac{1}{16}$ to $\frac{1}{8}$ of the bulk of *dry* starch required for the garments.

Starch with Borax.—Add 1 tablespoonful of borax to each pint of cooked starch while boiling. This makes the starch go farther by lessening the amount that adheres to each garment. It increases the gloss without giving additional stiffness and tends to prevent the irons from sticking.

Or add 1 teaspoonful of borax to 1 pint of uncooked starch for garments requiring stiffness.

Or mix 1 teaspoonful of borax and 2 tablespoonfuls of dry starch. Rub carefully in a small quantity of cold water and add enough to make $1\frac{1}{2}$ cupfuls.

Starch with Salt.—Add 1 teaspoonful of table salt to 1 pint of cooked or uncooked starch. This prevents the starch from being whipped out of the garments by the wind when drying, and also from freezing in severely cold weather.

Or add 1 teaspoonful of Epsom salts to each bowl of cooked starch while boiling. This will add stiffness and tend to prevent the articles from being scorched by hot irons.

Starch with Soap.—Make the boiling water in which starch is cooked slightly soapy with pure castile or other neutral white soap. This will assist in producing a gloss and will also prevent the irons from sticking.

Starch with Gum Arabic.—Prepare a solution of gum arabic by putting about 2 ounces of the white gum finely powdered in a glass bottle or quart fruit jar and pouring over it 1 pint of boiling water. Cork tightly and shake until the powder is dissolved. After 24 hours strain through cheese cloth and preserve the clear gum water for use. Add 1 tablespoonful to each pint of cooked starch while boiling. This is especially useful for fine dress goods, either white or colored, as lawns, muslins, calicoes, and the like, giving them much of the body and appearance of new material. Less of the gum water may be used for the finished materials, as muslins, and more may be added for cuffs, collars, and shirt cuffs to increase the stiffness and impart a gloss.

Starch with Sugar.—Add a teaspoonful of granulated sugar to each pint of starch while boiling. This assists in giving the so-called domestic finish.

Starch with Stearin.—Add a teaspoonful of stearin to each pint of starch when boiling. This substance with the addition of bluing is sold under the name of "starch luster" at a much higher price than the stearin itself costs, and is no better.

Starch with Lard.—Add half a teaspoonful of lard or butter to each quart of cooked starch when boiling. This helps to give the soft or domestic finish, and prevents the irons from sticking.

Additions to Starch.—Among the various substances added to starch for different purposes are wax, borax, salt, soap, lard, sugar, gum arabic, glue, stearin, and glycerin. Borax makes the starch more fluid, so that it goes farther, and also increases the gloss. Salt prevents the starch from freezing in garments; wax and gum arabic and stearin increase the gloss and give additional stiffness, and soap and sugar improve the gloss. These substances may also be mixed together according to various special recipes.

Special Recipes for Starch.—Melt together with gentle heat white wax, 3 ounces; spermaceti, 3 ounces; borax, $\frac{1}{2}$ pound; gum tragacanth, $1\frac{1}{2}$ ounces. Add 1 teaspoonful of the mixture to 1 pint of cooked starch while boiling.

Or, to prevent irons from sticking, rub $\frac{1}{2}$ teaspoonful of lard and 1 teaspoonful of salt into the dry starch, and proceed as with ordinary cooked starch.

Or mix 1 teaspoonful of white soap run through a grater with 1 pint of starch while boiling.

Or melt with gentle heat 1 ounce of isinglass, 1 ounce of borax, 1 teaspoonful of white glue, and 2 teaspoonfuls of white of egg. Stir into 2 quarts of cooked starch while boiling. This will give shirt bosoms a high polish.

Starch with Soda.—Add ½ teaspoonful of baking soda to 1 pint of cooked starch when boiling. This prevents the starch from whipping out of garments on the line, and also assists in giving finer finish.

To Apply Starch.—Strain the hot starch through a piece of cheese cloth and use while it is still warm. Select first the articles that require the most stiffness, as shirt bosoms, collars, and cuffs. A portion of the starch of course adheres to each, so that it becomes thinner by using. Starched clothes such as skirts, etc., should never be stiff enough to rattle. The garments to be starched should be nearly dry. Immerse them or such part of them as should be starched in the thick starch, and rub between the hands to work the starch thoroughly into their texture. Remove from the starch, squeeze out the excess, and rub once more with the hands to distribute the starch evenly through the material. If this is not done the surface will not iron smoothly. Dry the articles, sprinkle them, spread them on a clean white cloth, and roll them up in bundles so that the dampness will be evenly distributed before ironing.

To Starch Colored Clothes.—Divide the starch, set apart the required amount for colored clothes, and add bluing sufficient to make the starch quite blue. Use a liberal supply of bluing for blacks and dark colors, but not so much for light garments, especially pink. This will prevent white patches of starch from appearing on dark garments.

Or dip black or colored goods, as lawns and calicoes, in sweet or sour milk and use no starch. Milk alone will give the desired stiffness.

Or, for delicate colored goods, use a simple solution of gum arabic instead of starch.

Or rinse in dilute bran water or rice water instead of starch.

To Starch White Dress Goods.—Thin white dress goods, as white waists and summer gowns, may be starched with cold raw starch. Dry without starching. Dissolve a heaping tablespoonful of starch in sufficient water to immerse the garment, dip it into the starch until saturated, rinse in cold water, wring out, roll up in a dry cloth, and iron half an hour later.

Or dry the garments, dip a clean muslin cloth into raw starch, and lay over them long enough to dampen them. After a few minutes press them with a hot iron.

For delicate lawns and similar fabrics use a solution of gum arabic diluted to give the stiffness required.

CARE OF IRONING UTENSILS

Ironing Utensils. — Various improved implements and machines have

"An Ironing Machine for Domestic Use."

been perfected for ironing, but the old-fashioned flatiron heated on the range is still a well-nigh universal favorite. Mangles, or large heated cylinders revolving under pressure for ironing garments, have been in general use in laundries for many years, together with polishing machines and similar appliances. But until quite recently there has not been upon the market a satisfactory ironing machine suitable for domestic use. Such machines can now be obtained, and they are to be recommended for large families who can afford them.

The denatured alcohol flatiron is a cheap, practical, and serviceable, device.

The electric flatiron is an ideal utensil in homes that are supplied with electricity.

The patented flatiron which has a removable wooden handle is a great improvement over the old-fashioned solid iron which requires the use of cloth or asbestos holders.

The asbestos flatiron is an implement that is especially recommended.

To do fine ironing it is necessary to have several kinds of irons. For shirt bosoms, collars, and cuffs a ribbed or other polishing iron is necessary. Ruffles will be improved by the use of a fluting iron. The puff iron for fine tucks, puffy sleeves, and other elaborate work is especially useful. This iron is attached to a standard and the cloth is passed through it. It may be heated at the ordinary range.

Some persons are satisfied with the cold mangle, especially for table linens, linen sheets, and other linen pieces, on the theory that heat has a tendency to deteriorate the linen and also to give it a yellow tinge, but ironing by means of hot irons is still the custom.

A toy flatiron such as is sold for children is not only useful in the hands of a child for ironing dolls' clothes as a lesson in domestic economy, but is also very convenient to the laundress for tucks, fluting, and other difficult parts of dresses and similar garments. Such an iron may be packed in a trunk and taken on vacation trips. It will be found most useful in hotels, where it can be heated over the gas or by means of a small alcohol lamp, and used for doing up handkerchiefs, laces, ribbons, and other small articles, both

"*a. Device for Heating Flatirons. b. Holder. c. Emory-cloth Board. d. Wax. e. Stand.*"

as a measure of economy and also to prevent their being deteriorated by careless treatment in the laundry.

To Prevent Rust on Irons.—If irons are exposed to moisture or stored away for a time, brush or rub them when warm with a mixture of vaseline and sweet oil. Lard or vaseline alone may be used for this purpose. These substances may be removed by washing the iron in good soapsuds when ready for use.

To Keep Flatirons Clean.—In small apartments it is often convenient to store the flatirons on the back of the range. To keep them free from grease and dirt take a common pasteboard shoe box or other box of convenient shape and size, and cover with sheet asbestos glued on. Keep the irons in this, and they will be clean, dry, and always handy.

Care of Irons.—Care must be taken to prevent the roughening of irons from starch or other sticky substance adhering to them and burning on. This is especially likely to happen if raw or partly cooked starch is used. To prevent this, tack a piece of very fine sandpaper on the ironing board and rub the iron on it each time before returning to the fire.

Or use bath brick, dry salt, or powdered pumice stone spread on a smooth surface, with or without sandpaper.

Or fill a cheese-cloth bag with powdered pumice stone and rub the iron on this.

Starch may be prevented from sticking to the iron by the use of beeswax, paraffin, wax paper, or kerosene. To use beeswax, put it in a little bag of cloth or between two pieces of paper, and attach to the ironing board. Rub the iron over this. Save the paraffin on the tops of jars of jelly, melt up, and pour into a mold to cool. Put this in a cloth bag and use the same as beeswax.

Or save the wax papers that come in cracker boxes or the inside linings of laundry soap, and rub the irons on these.

Or have at hand a cloth saturated with kerosene, and rub the iron over this. These methods all tend to make the ironing easier by lessening the friction and also keep the iron clean and give polish to the fabrics.

Cautions. — Never use irons for cracking nuts or hammering nails. Never allow them to become red hot. They do not retain the heat equally throughout afterwards and will always be rough. Do not keep them on the stove when not in use without proteeting them from the heat by asbestos.

To Heat Irons. — Irons will heat more quickly and with less fuel and will keep hot longer if an iron or tin pan is turned over them while heating. A sheet-iron pan, like a bread pan, is best for this purpose, but a deep dripping pan, frying pan, or solid tin pan may be used. This will be found especially important in summer, when a hot fire is unbearable. When gas is used, if a pan is turned over the flatirons and a teakettle placed on top, hot water also may be had with the use of a single burner.

To Test the Heat of Irons.—The iron is hotter when a drop of water will run along the surface than when it is immediately evaporated. A very hot iron will form a cushion of steam which will keep the drop from the surface. Hence if a drop of water sticks and immediately evaporates, the iron is not sufficiently hot for some purposes.

Holders for Irons.—A thin sheet of asbestos between two folds of cloth makes the best holder for flatirons. A square piece of leather, cut from the top of an old boot and put between two thicknesses of cloth, is convenient and comfortable. These holders may be bound with braid.

To Hang Up an Ironing Board.—Put screw eyes on the end of the ironing board so that it can be hung from nails on the wall or the inside of pantry doors.

Covers for Ironing Boards.—Make two or three covers for the ironing board to fit tightly when drawn on, like a pillowcase. When one is soiled another may be substituted. The quickness and convenience with which these may be changed will soon pay for the labor of making them. A somewhat looser calico bag to slip over the board when not in use will keep it clean. Old sheets and discarded wrappers will furnish materials for these covers.

To Arrange the Ironing Board.—Fix two heavy screw eyes in the broad end of an ironing board and attach to these a piece of strong picture wire the same as if you intended to hang the ironing board like a picture upon

"Leaves the End Unobstructed."

the wall. Screw into the top of the baseboard, high enough from the floor to be out of the way of mops and brooms, two strong screw hooks. Now draw a stand or narrow table opposite these screw hooks in such a way that the broad end of the ironing board may rest upon it while the narrow end projects into the room. In this position the ironing board should about balance, but of course the pressure of the iron on the unsupported end would cause it to tip. Now catch the wire guys attached to the broad end of the ironing board over the two screw hooks in the baseboard. These will prevent the narrow end of the board from tipping, and leave it unobstructed, so that skirts, shirts, and other similar articles may be slipped over it conveniently.

IRONING

To Iron Shirts.—Starch the shirt bosoms, collars, and cuffs in cooked starch containing also wax or lard or other similar substance. The addition of gum arabic will increase the stiffness. First use the common iron in the usual way, making the surface smooth, but without polishing. Iron first the back and sleeves, next the collar and bosom, last the front. This dull or domestic finish, as it is called, is preferred by many persons to a high polish, but if the latter is desired use a smooth hard-wood board covered rather thickly with cloth on one side, but not on the other. First use the padded side of the board, ironing the bosom smooth, then turn the board, lay the bosom upon the hard wood, take the polishing iron, and polish by rubbing vigorously crosswise. A good polishing iron should weigh between 6 and 7 pounds and have a rounded edge at the heel. The iron is not laid down flat, but only the edge of the heel is used to give the polish. Keep the iron very hot and dampen the bosom slightly before using it by brushing with a damp cloth or sponge. If the bosom rises in wavelike blisters, dampen it slightly and go over it again. It requires a little care to use a polishing iron, but with experience any laundress can give as good a polish as can be produced in a steam laundry. A greater finish can be obtained by laying over the bosom a cloth dipped in starch just before the polishing iron is applied.

To Iron Colored Goods.—Colored goods should be ironed, when possible, before they are quite dry. They should not, as a rule, be sprinkled nor allowed to lie over night. The iron should be allowed to cool slightly, as delicate colors, especially pinks and greens, will frequently fade as soon as they are touched by a hot iron. The pink may turn to purple and the green to blue.

If, however, colored goods cannot be ironed the day they are washed, they should not be allowed to lie over night in a wet condition, but should first be thoroughly dried and then slightly dampened just before ironing by rolling them in a damp cloth and allowing them to stand for fifteen or twenty minutes.

Press colored goods on the wrong side, especially the collars and cuffs. Iron on the right side no more than is absolutely necessary to take out the wrinkles.

To Iron Black Sateen and Farmer's Satin.—Use no starch. Iron on the wrong side.

To Iron Fancy Work.—Press ribbons, lace, and embroidery on the wrong side, and iron delicate articles through a piece of linen. For colored silks and ribbons, allow the iron to cool slightly as with any other colored goods.

To Iron Linen.—The appearance of linen will be improved if it is ironed the same day it is washed and without hanging out to dry. Rinse thoroughly, wring dry, and roll the linen articles in a dry sheet. Let them lie for a time and iron dry with a hot iron. This saves the wear on fine linen of whipping on a clothesline, and gives an additional stiffness and luster, especially to cheap linens and well-worn articles.

To Do Up Handkerchiefs.—To save ironing, spread the handkerchief wet from rinsing water on a clean pane of glass or mirror. When dry, fold and lay away. Guests at summer hotels and persons who are boarding will find this plan very convenient. It is especially desirable for fine linen and delicate lace handkerchiefs, to save the wear and tear of the laundry.

Ironing Hints.—Table linen and handkerchiefs frequently show wear where the customary folds have been ironed in. To save wear press the article all over until perfectly dry, without folding. Then fold and press the folds lightly with a hot iron. The appearance will be the same as if the folds had been ironed separately, but the articles will wear longer.

Large tablecloths that are awkward to manage without folding may be rolled upon curtain poles as fast as they are ironed. When the entire cloth has been ironed it may be unrolled and folded with a light pressure.

The clothes wringer will smooth sheets, towels, pillowcases, and the like sufficiently without ironing, and upon occasion these articles may be folded and put away rough dry. Give handkerchiefs one fold less than is customary, leaving them oblong instead of square. The economy of time is small, but the handkerchiefs lie more conveniently in the drawer.

To Iron Embroidery.—Embroidered articles, as doilies, shirt waists, and the like, Hamburg trimmings, and other goods of similar texture may be ironed over a Turkish towel. This method raises the pattern clearly and beautifully. It may also be used for napkins, handkerchiefs, and tablecloths. The towel yields slightly, lessening the labor of ironing, and the process adds to the appearance of the article.

To Take Down Clothes.—Use care in wringing clothes and hanging them on the line. Lift tablecloths and similar large pieces by the middle from the last rinsing water, so as to straighten out the selvage edge, and wring by hand. Hang these carefully on the line so that they will dry straight and not draw on the bias. In hanging clothes, straighten the collars, raise the bands, and open the sleeves. Fold carefully when taken from the line, or, if too cold to fold outdoors, do so as soon as they are brought into the house and before the wrinkles caused by packing them in the basket have become set. In warm weather spread sheets, towels, and the like upon the tall grass. They will need very little pressing, and will be bleached by the sun.

TO DO UP SILKS, RIBBONS, AND WOOLENS

To Iron Silks.—Lift silks from the rinsing water, shake and snap them to remove as much water as possible without squeezing or wringing, and smooth them out on pieces of old cotton cloth or towels. Roll them up in these and iron as soon as possible without drying. Smooth pieces out while wet on the ironing board, lay over them a piece of thin white muslin, and iron on the wrong side with a moderate iron to prevent smutting. Now remove the cloth, iron perfectly dry on the wrong side, and smooth slightly, if desired, on the face with a warm, not hot, iron. The whole process of washing and ironing should be done as quickly as possible after the silk is wet, as the colors may be affected by lying in that condition.

To Iron Colored Silks.—Like other colored goods silk should not be allowed to dry, but should be ironed while still damp with a warm, not hot, iron. Place between two cloths and iron on the wrong side.

To Do Up Ribbons.—Wash same as other colored silks, and if stiffness is required, rinse in weak soapsuds containing a small amount of gum arabic. Now roll the ribbon about a glass bottle, or wind about a small rolling-pin, smoothing carefully, and dry in the shade.

Or smooth them out, face down, upon a piece of varnished wood. When dry they will require no ironing.

To Remove Wrinkles from Silk.—Wrinkled or creased ribbons and silks may be restored by laying them on a smooth surface and sponging them evenly with a sponge moistened in a weak solution of gum arabic. Smooth out while wet on a polished flat surface of wood, or roll about a rolling-pin and dry in the shade. Iron between two pieces of cloth, pressing on the wrong side with a warm, not hot, iron.

To Store Away Silks.—Do not wrap silks in white paper. The chloride of lime used to bleach the paper will attack the colors of the silk.

To Iron Flannel and Woolen Goods.—Iron flannels and woolens the same day they are washed, if possible, and before they become quite dry. Take from the line when still damp, roll up in a dry cloth, and press on the wrong side with an iron not too hot. If they become dry they should be dampened slightly by rolling up in a damp cloth to await their turn.

To Iron Blankets.—Iron blankets before they are quite dry, and air thoroughly before storing away.

TO DO UP LACES AND CURTAINS

To Starch Laces.—Good lace does not require starching. Enough white sugar dissolved in the last rinsing water to make it slightly sweet should give it the required stiffness.

Or boil 4 ounces of rice in 1 quart of water until the kernels break up. Strain through cheese cloth and dip the laces in the clear rice water.

Or use a thin solution of gum arabic.

Or mix 1 teaspoonful of cornstarch or wheat starch with cold water to the consistency of cream, beating and rubbing until all is wet evenly. Dilute to consistency of milk with cold water, add 5 or 6 drops of gum arabic, and thin with boiling water until nearly transparent. Boil for 5 or 6 minutes until well cooked. The poorer the lace the more stiffness will be required. Hence do not dilute too much for poor laces.

To Tint Laces.—For an écru tint add black coffee or powdered saffron to the rinsing water. Or add tea to give a stronger shade. Experiment with a small sample of the goods, adding a little more color at a time until the right shade is obtained.

To Iron Laces.—If laces are basted on cloth, and the cloth is thoroughly stretched, or if they are carefully wound about a bottle and stitched, they may not require any ironing. Lace wound about a bottle may be dipped into very thin starch or gum-arabic water without being removed, and may not need any ironing. Lace handkerchiefs may be pulled into shape while wet and carefully laid on a pane of glass, wrinkles being all smoothed out. When dry they will be ready for use.

Or dry small lace articles between two pieces of clean white blotting paper under a weight, with or without ironing. When starch is used, do not allow laces to dry, but roll them in a dry towel for half an hour or more, and press while still damp. Iron on the wrong side over a Turkish towel to bring up the pattern, protecting the articles from the iron with a piece of muslin or other thin white cloth. Use a warm, not hot, iron. Ironing pieces while damp greatly improves their appearance; ironing on a soft, rough surface both protects them and brings up the pattern, and ironing through a thin cloth makes it possible to bring out the points and pattern of the lace with the point of the iron without injury. New embroideries should be washed and ironed before using.

To Remove Wrinkles.—If lace becomes dry before ironing, or if it is desired to remove the wrinkles from clean lace without washing, hold it over the steam of the teakettle or a basin of steaming water until thoroughly moistened. While damp press it under a weight, with or without blotters, or iron it as above suggested.

To Starch Curtains. — Do not use much starch for lace curtains. This is a common mistake when curtains are done up at home. It is contrary to the essential delicacy of lace to make it stiff with starch. Moreover, the sun will rot lace which contains too much starch or other stiffening substances. Only the coarsest kind of lace can stand stiffening.

To Do Up Curtains. — Starch curtains the same as other laces with a thin boiled cornstarch or wheat starch containing a solution of gum arabic, and stretch them on suitable frames or otherwise to dry. If they are stretched properly, they will require no ironing or they may be pressed slightly when dry.

To Iron Curtains.—Lay the curtains while still damp on a folded flannel blanket and press on the wrong side with irons as hot as possible without scorching. This method brings out raised figures and designs.

To Prevent Scorch.—Wipe the iron on a cloth wet with kerosene.

To Remove Scorch.—Linen articles and other white goods slightly scorched by hot irons may be restored, if the fibers have not been destroyed, by simply exposing them to the heat of the sun or, on dark days, to the heat from an open oven. Moisten them at intervals by sponging lightly with clear water. If the stains are deeper, rub chlorine water into the spot with a sponge or linen rag.

Or run two onions through a meat cutter, squeeze out the juice through cheese cloth, and mix with half a pint of vinegar. Heat the mixture to a boil, and add a piece of hard white soap the size of an English walnut and two or three ounces of fuller's earth. Boil five minutes, cool, and pour over the scorched linen. Let it dry on, and afterwards remove by washing. Repeat if necessary.

TO MARK AND STORE LINEN

Linen Closet.—A special closet or wardrobe for linen is a great convenience. If this is not possible, and linen must be packed in chests or bureau drawers, the various articles will lie one upon another so that it is difficult to keep them in proper order. The shelves of the linen closet should be just wide enough apart to admit of piles of a dozen articles of each sort, and just deep enough to admit one row of articles. Numerous shallow shelves relatively close together make a more convenient arrangement than deeper shelves wider apart. A little care devoted to making the shelves tight, polishing them, and coating them with enamel paint or varnish to give them a smooth and shining surface will be more than compensated for by the beautiful appearance of the snowy linen reflected upon the shelves and the ease with which they may be kept in perfect order.

Comparatively few persons can afford a surplus of fine linen, but when possible, articles should be bought in half dozen or dozen lots and used in regular rotation. All fabrics will wear better if not used continually, but allowed to rest at intervals.

Place linen on the shelves in regular piles of one dozen each, and when it comes from the laundry sort it carefully and place the articles that have been just laundered at the bottom of the piles so that they will be used in regular rotation. It will assist you to do this and also to keep account of linen if the articles are numbered 1, 2, 3, 4, and so on, and piled in that way.

As linen and other articles are often mislaid or stolen when sent to laundries, and sometimes taken from the line or blown away when spread on the grass to bleach, it is advisable to make an inventory of the contents of the linen closet, a copy of which may be fastened with thumb tacks to the back of the closet door, and checked up each time the laundered articles are stored away. This will also assist in the preparation of a shopping list when articles that are worn require to be replaced.

While the term "linen closet" is used (and every housewife knows the good qualities of linen and would be glad to use it exclusively for many purposes), the same remarks apply to the disposition of cotton sheets, pillowcases, etc. These, if of good quality and well laundered, present almost as attractive an appearance as the linen itself, and will equally repay the same care and attention. A separate place should be set apart for those articles which have become worn past their original uses, and they should be laundered and stored in the linen closet until opportunity offers for making them up into covers for the ironing board, dishcloths, dish towels, and the many other uses mentioned elsewhere. Old linen is especially valuable for many purposes, and the discarded articles should be carefully stored in an orderly fashion instead of being thrust, as is too often the case, helter-skelter into the common ragbag.

When linen has been properly laundered, aired, and stored in the linen closet, nothing is required for the further care of articles in ordinary use except to preserve them from dampness and insects. The various essential oils and other perfume-bearing substances will assist in preserving linen from the attacks of insects. The use of thyme, mint, and lavender for this purpose by good housekeepers in colonial days and in England is proverbial. Bags containing any or all of the following may be employed for this purpose:

Spices, as powdered cloves, mace, nutmeg, and cinnamon.

Flowers of any sort, dried and mixed with spices.

Odorous leaves, as mint, balm, southernwood, laurel, geranium, sweet marjoram, rosemary, hyssop, and origanum.

Roots, as orris and angelica.

Perfumed woods, as sandalwood, rosewood, cassia, sassafras, rhodium.

Animal perfumes, as ambergris, musk, and civet.

Or essential oils extracted from any of these.

To Store Linens.—If linen articles are not in constant use they should be wrapped in brown, blue, or other dark-colored paper, as the bleaching powder and other forms of chlorine used in bleaching white and light-colored papers have a tendency to turn linen articles yellow, and so does exposure to air and sunlight.

To Prepare Linen for the Wash.—It will be found a matter of economy to examine the linen before it goes to the laundry and remove all stains, and also mend bracks, tears, and worn places before the articles are washed. Otherwise they may catch on the washboard or in the washing machine, or be whipped by the wind, caught by a flatiron, or otherwise made larger than is necessary. Here, as elsewhere, "a stitch in time saves nine."

Marking Linen.—A good stamping outfit may be obtained very cheaply and linen may be stamped with initials that can afterwards be worked over with embroidery. Large Gothic letters appear to be most approved for this purpose.

Or, by the use of a few cents' worth of carbon paper, which may be obtained of any stationer, linen may be stamped by tracing over any desired pattern. A paper pattern may be used for this purpose, or one article may be sent away to be marked and the initial afterwards transferred to the others by tracing over with carbon.

Before starting to work on any stamped linen, take a copy of the design on a piece of paper for duplicates, which may then be transferred, at very small expense of time and trouble, by means of carbon paper to other articles.

Or plain articles may be marked by tracing the initial with a soft lead pencil and going over the outline with the sewing machine, using any color of silk thread that may be desired.

Or apply marking ink with a steel pen or fine camel's-hair brush. For recipe, see under "Ink" elsewhere in this volume.

To Hem Table Linen. — Draw a thread at either end and cut straight across. Turn the hem through the narrow hemmer of an unthreaded sewing machine. This makes a narrower and more even hem than can be turned by hand.

The difficulty of drawing the thread

from linen is much lessened if a piece of castile or other hard white soap is first rubbed carefully over the threads.

Tablecloth Economics.—If a tablecloth wears around the edge by rubbing against the table, draw threads on either side of the worn place, cut straight across, and sew together with a perfectly flat, even seam. This will hardly be noticed, and the tablecloth will be almost like new.

When buying new tablecloths get a half yard extra material and from time to time take a narrow strip off one of the ends. This will bring the creases in different places and prevent the cloth from wearing where it is creased in the laundry. Ravelings taken from these strips will be found the best material with which to darn frayed places.

When a tablecloth is past its proper use it is still available for many purposes. The whole parts will make an excellent bread cloth and one or more tray cloths or napkins suitable for lunches and picnics, or for use particularly in the fruit season, when the best napkins often receive peach and other fruit stains that are so difficult to remove. The small pieces make the best of silver polishers, as they are so soft that they will not scratch the finest silver.

Or figured centerpieces may sometimes be embroidered, as for stamped linen, and made to do duty as doilies and lunch cloths.

Toweling.—Raw linen towels can be purchased at surprisingly low prices, and under proper care may be perfectly bleached in the laundry. Or remnants of tablecloth damask may be picked up, cut to the proper length, and hemstitched all around, or finished in drawn work and decorated with embroidered initials. For ordinary uses nothing is more satisfactory than wash crash toweling, which wears well, has a good appearance, and saves the wear of linen towels.

CHAPTER XIII

SWEEPING DAY

UTENSILS FOR SWEEPING—DUST AND DUSTING—HARD-WOOD FLOORS—RUGS—MATTING—OILCLOTH AND LINOLEUM

One day in the week, usually Friday, is set apart as sweeping day. At the top of the house, in the attic stairway, keep cleaning rags, brush, soap, dusters, and broom. Have a wastebasket in each of the rooms to receive bits of paper, rags, lint, burnt matches, and the like. Commence at the top of the house and clean each room as you go. Take up the dust from each room and put it in a tin bucket or other deep receptacle so that it will not be blown about. Never sweep the dirt from one room to another, and thence down the stairway to the front hall. This method covers the door lintels, window casings, and high shelves with a thick coating of dust which is blown about the room with every passing breeze.

Sweep the stairs with a short-handled brush or stiff whisk broom, holding a dust pan to catch the dust at each step. Triangular blocks, or brass fixtures made for this purpose, tacked into the corners of the stairways will assist in keeping them clean by preventing dust from accumulating.

After a room has been swept, open one or more windows, if possible, before beginning to dust.

UTENSILS FOR SWEEPING

Carpet Sweeper.—The ideal method of sweeping is by means of a carpet sweeper. This goes over the surface of the carpet with a light and even pressure, and takes up all dust and dirt with the least possible friction and consequent wear upon the carpet, and raises practically no dust at all. It saves strength and time, and probably saves money by outwearing the brooms that could be purchased for the same price. Hence a good carpet sweeper may be regarded as a necessity rather than a luxury in every household.

"The Ideal Method of Sweeping."

How to Sweep.—The old-fashioned brooms, however, are still commonly used, and are needed for some purposes in every household. To sweep well with a broom is an art that calls for quite a little skill and intelligence. There are wrong ways in sweeping as well as the right way, and the former are perhaps more often practiced than the latter.

It is wrong to lean on the broom, or dig into the carpet with great force, as if trying to dig down and get the dirt out of it. This cannot be done except by taking up the carpet and beating it. All the dust and dirt that can be removed is that which lies on the surface.

It is wrong to push the broom forward so as to drive a cloud of dust into the air.

It is wrong to sweep the whole length of the room toward the door in order to sweep the dirt into the next room. This carries the dirt over a larger surface of carpet than is necessary.

It is wrong to sweep always on one side of a broom so that it will get lopsided and have to be thrown away.

The right way to use a broom is to keep the handle always inclining forward and never allow it to come to the perpendicular; much less incline backward. The stroke should be rather long, the sweeper standing on the soiled portion of the carpet, reaching back, and drawing the dust and dirt forward as if pulling or dragging it over the surface. A skillful sweeper will lift the broom before it becomes perpendicular so as not to raise the slightest dust, and will tap it gently to shake the dirt out of it before reaching back for another stroke.

Begin in one corner, and work along the crack between the baseboard and carpet, as this is where moths and carpet bugs do their most destructive work. Work around the room, sweeping toward the center, and when that has been reached take up the dust with pan and brush. It is obvious that this process moves the dirt over a smaller surface than sweeping toward one of the doors. The practice of sweeping the dirt from one room into another, even if the latter room be the kitchen, is certainly inadvisable. Both brooms and carpets will wear much longer if sweeping is done in proper fashion, and the dust in furniture, draperies, and bric-a-brac will be reduced to a minimum.

Sweeping.—Before sweeping dip the broom in hot soapsuds, and have at hand a pailful of soapsuds in which to rinse the broom when it becomes dusty. Squeeze out the water so that the broom is damp but not wet. This practice toughens the straw, makes the broom last much longer, and softens it so that it does not cut the carpet. A damp broom also takes up the dirt better than a dry one and prevents the dust from rising in the air.

To prevent dust when sweeping wet a newspaper, tear it in small pieces, and scatter them over the carpet. Squeeze the paper so that it will not drip.

Or sprinkle the carpet with moist tea leaves, which may be saved daily for this purpose.

If a room is heated by hot air, a good deal of dust will come up through the register. To prevent this, place a fine wire screen or two or three thicknesses of cloth under the register, so that the hot air will be screened in passing through. When shaking down the furnace or removing the ashes sprinkle wet sawdust over the ashes. This will prevent filling the house with dust. When upholstered furniture, draperies, carpets, and Oriental rugs require dusting, lay over them large pieces of cheese cloth or outing flannel wrung out of cold water, and beat them with a stick or small carpet beater. As the dust arises it will adhere to the wet cloths, and these can be rinsed occasionally.

To Select Brooms.—Select a broom of light-green color and fine straw. It wears longer and gathers fine dirt that coarse straw would pass by. Choose a flat broom, not a round one. Shake the broom, and choose one which is not loose, otherwise the straw will fall out. Be sure that there is no stalk below the thread.

Care of Brooms.—Broom straw when dry is brittle and easily broken. It is also stiff and wears the carpets. Hence before using a new broom set it in a pail of boiling suds and let it stand until the water is cold. Hang it out of doors to dry.

When not in use a broom should always be hung upside down so that the straws will fall apart. This helps to keep it in shape. Have different brooms for different purposes. Use the newest for the finest carpets, the next older broom for kitchen use, and the oldest broom for the pavement and other rough places. When through sweeping pick all the lint from the broom, shake the dust out of it, and rinse in hot water before hanging it up.

Make a pocket in which to hang the broom upside down.

Or put two large clothes hooks facing each other, or two nails, and hang the head of the broom between these.

Or drive nails through two large spools to protect the straw.

Or put up a ring on the wall and thrust the broom handle through this.

Keep the broom in a dry, cool place, away from rats or mice. Too much heat makes it brittle, and rats and mice will gnaw it when they can. After a time the ends of a broom split and become sharp, and the broom gets out of shape. Wet it in hot suds, cut the split and broken ends straight across, and press it between weights to restore it to shape. A new broom sweeps clean because the straws are straight and the broom is square, hence a broom thus treated will sweep like new. When sweeping, sweep first with one side of the broom, then with the other, else it will get one-sided and have to be thrown away.

Care of Carpet Sweepers.—The carpet sweeper should be emptied every sweeping day, and never put away full of dirt. It may be opened over a newspaper. The brush should be taken out and freed from dust and lint with the fingers or a coarse comb, rinsed in soapsuds, and dried before being replaced.

When the rubber tires on the wheels become worn they may not assist the brush to revolve with sufficient strength to do good work. New tires may be obtained from the manufacturers, or thick rubber bands purchased from a stationer or rubber-goods dealer may be substituted. Remove the old tires and adjust the new ones with glue or cement. New brushes may be obtained from the manufacturer, and with care a good carpet sweeper should last a lifetime.

A toy carpet sweeper is a great convenience, as it may be kept at hand or easily carried from place to place. In the sewing room it is useful to catch all ravelings and small pieces from the floor without stooping. This may be done without rising from the chair. In the nursery it takes all bits of paper torn by children, about the dining-room table it catches crumbs, and all with little effort and without the need of using or even possessing a large-sized sweeper. The toy sweeper costs less than half a dollar and will save its price many times over.

DUST AND DUSTING

Dust is defined by the Century Dictionary as "earth or other matter in fine dry particles so attenuated that they can be raised and carried by the wind." The particles of earth and other mineral substances contained in dust are troublesome, but not especially harmful. In addition to this, dust contains three sorts of spores or germs, i. e., molds, yeasts, and bacteria. All of these are alive, or capable of life, and under suitable conditions multiply rapidly. They are invisible except under the microscope, and are exceedingly numerous. The conditions most favorable to their growth are darkness, warmth, and moisture. Direct sunlight kills them, and in the absence of moisture, they do not usually multiply.

All of these germs produce minute plant or vegetable organisms of which common mold or "mildew" and the yeast used in raising bread are familiar examples. A visible illustration of the spores or germs, that are the seeds of plants of this sort, is found in the common puff-ball or "smoke" ball, so familiar to country children. When broken, the contents escape as a cloud of dust.

These are the spores or seeds of the plant. The air is full of similar spores or germs, and while many of these are not harmful, others are the agents of decay and a few are the germs of contagious diseases. These are called bacteria. Their natural home is in moist soil. Thus they multiply rapidly in the soil of damp cellar floors, especially if decaying vegetable matter is present, and in the accumulation of dirt and grease beneath boarded-up sinks, and in the corners of rooms that are shut up and darkened. They are also very numerous about drains and cesspools. They sometimes find their way into the body by means of drinking water or by accidental contact with the body when the skin is cut or scratched. But more frequently they are dislodged from some moist locality and become dry. Then they are caught up by every passing breeze, and float in the air as dust, whence they are taken into the mouth and lungs in breathing.

The bacteria which cause disease find lodgment under certain conditions and grow in the body. They throw off in the process of growth certain poisonous substances called toxins. And these toxins are what produce the symptoms and conditions present in such diseases, and eventually, in many cases, produce death.

Spores or germs of mold that settle on carpets or other fabrics and on wood, books, or other objects where moisture is present, produce a crop of tiny plants, well known under the name of mildew. The yeast germs are less common and are relatively harmless. Knowledge of these facts emphasizes the dangers of dust, which may be avoided in three ways: by sterilization, by prevention, and by removal.

Sterilization of Dust.—The most efficient agent to sterilize dust, by killing germs that it contains, is direct sunlight. Like many other things that are plentiful and free, sunlight is not appreciated at its true value. In cities, buildings are crowded so closely together as to shade one another, and in the country too frequently direct sunshine is cut off from dwelling houses by thick masses of evergreen and other trees, shrubs or vines. Formerly it was the custom in many localities to keep the parlor and spare chambers closed by shut doors and drawn blinds. And rooms are still too often darkened to prevent carpets and other fabrics from fading. Happily, a change for the better is already apparent. Hardwood floors and Oriental rugs do not fade. It is much less customary than formerly to exclude light and air from spare rooms, to board up sinks and other plumbing, and otherwise to harbor breeding places for the germs of mildew, disease, and decay. In cities, boards of health are constantly studying these matters, and laws have been passed that tend to prevent unsanitary conditions. The resulting knowledge is being rapidly spread everywhere. And within recent years the death rate of most localities has been greatly diminished. There is little doubt that many deaths have been due to conditions that could have been prevented by a knowledge of the dust dangers.

But in the presence of direct sunshine, dust is rendered harmless. Hence choose furnishings that sunshine will not harm, and admit the sunlight freely to all parts of the house.

Preventing Dust. — A certain amount of dust, according to local conditions, is always floating in the outer air, and finds its way into dwellings through doors, windows, and other openings. This cannot usually be much lessened except by such means as oiling streets; sprinkling streets, lawns, and gardens; the prevention of smoke and the like. But the amount of dust formed within doors by the wear of fabrics, furniture, woodwork, and other objects, can be much lessened by the selection, when furnishing, of durable articles of all sorts, and by protecting floors, furniture, and other woodwork by suitable coatings of oil, wax, paint, or varnish. And, in addition, various means may be taken to prevent the distribution of dust when sweeping.

Removing Dust. — The ordinary means of removing dust is by sweeping, and afterwards wiping all exposed surfaces by means of a damp cloth, chamois, or other suitable duster. Good ventilation is also valuable as a means of removing dust, especially if the intake is screened so that the fresh air is pure when admitted. Carpet sweepers are especially valuable as dust removers. But the modern vacuum cleaners may be regarded as ideal for this purpose.

Vacuum Cleaners.—At present this method of cleaning is somewhat expensive, and is confined to localities where electric or other power is available. It is to be hoped, however, that vacuum-cleaning apparatus may be devised that can be run by cheap gasoline or alcohol motors at a price within the means of the average family. These cleaners, by producing a vacuum, cause suction powerful enough to draw dust, dirt, and other small objects out of the fiber of carpets and hangings, and from the surface of woodwork, furniture, and other objects. The dust is taken in through a suitable mouthpiece provided with a handle with which to guide it as desired, and carried, together with a current of air, through a tube into a receptacle containing water. This may afterwards be emptied, and all dust permanently removed from the premises. There is little doubt that some such means of cleaning will eventually take the place of the broom and carpet sweeper in ordinary households, and that thus the dust question will be finally and satisfactorily settled.

Dusters.—The object of dusting is, or should be, to remove the dust permanently from the room, and not merely to change its location from hangings, shelves, or furniture covering, whence it will be stirred by every footstep and carried by the first breeze back to its former resting place.

The old-fashioned feather duster is useful for moving the dust from one place to another, but for no other purpose. The feather duster doubtless owes its popularity to the long handle, which permits of dusting the lower parts of furniture without stooping, and also of dusting objects that would otherwise be out of reach. A substitute may be made on the same plan by using a short piece of broomstick, the handle of an old feather duster, or a child's broom, and fastening to the end with cord or wire in the same way that a whisk broom is wired, a deep double ruffle made of any suitable cloth and of any desired length and thickness.

A duster made in this way will retain the dust better than a feather duster, and it can be shaken out of the window. Cheese cloth is perhaps the best material for this form of duster, but almost any soft fabric may be employed.

Or hem squares of cheese cloth of any convenient size.

Or use the tops of old cotton or silk hose, either men's or women's. Cut these down the seam and whip them together with a loose seam.

Or for certain purposes, as dusting around baseboards, over windows, doors, and all woodwork that it is difficult to reach with a cloth, use a common dish mop. This is much superior to a feather duster, as it holds the dirt and can be easily cleaned. It will be improved for this purpose by wiring the upper end with a piece of wire taken from an old whisk broom.

Chamois leather slightly dampened is perhaps the best kind of duster, especially for polished furniture.

To Dust.—Begin in one corner of the room and dust thoroughly as you go. Commence with the highest articles, wiping but not brushing off the dust, the object being to cause all the dust to lodge on the cloth.

Shake the duster frequently out of the window. After using it wash it and hang it up.

Wing Dusters.—The wings of fowls, turkeys, geese, and chickens are useful to dig out the corners in washing windows, and also as brushes about the stove and hearth. Dip the bony ends in a bichloride solution to keep out moths and insects. Do not leave them where the cat can chew them.

To Freshen Carpets.—Before sweeping, scatter dry salt over the carpet. It brightens the colors and checks the ravages of moths.

Or, after sweeping, go over the carpet lightly with a broom dipped into half a pailful of hot water to which two teaspoonfuls of ammonia have been added. This freshens the colors of the carpet.

Or slightly moisten salt with kerosene. Sprinkle the carpet and sweep thoroughly. The dust will not rise, but will be thoroughly taken up by the mixture. The kerosene will leave no greasy effect, the odor will soon pass off, and the carpet will be wonderfully freshened. Corn meal may be substituted for salt. The same treatment may be applied to matting with equally good results.

Smooth Floors.—Smooth floors of hard wood, oilcloth, linoleum, or matting should not be swept in the usual way. Make a heavy canton or outing flannel bag with a draw string, large enough to hold the head of the broom. Or use for this purpose ticks that are becoming worn. Wring this bag out of hot water containing a little ammonia, slip the broom head into it, and draw the puckering string tight about the handle. This takes up all dust, lint, and bits of paper, and makes the room much fresher than ordinary sweeping. Cast-off flannel garments, such as nightshirts and the like, may be utilized in this manner.

Or stitch together loosely old cotton hose, crazy-quilt fashion.

HARD-WOOD FLOORS

Finish for Hard-wood Floors.—Rub down a new floor with sandpaper, and polish with pumice moistened with a little water. Wash clean, let dry, fill the nail holes with putty, and if the grain of the wood is open, apply a suitable filler. Avoid a cheap filler, based on plaster of Paris and the like, as these are not durable. The best filler consists of ground quartz mixed with linseed oil about as thick as white-lead paint. The particles of quartz are angular and adhere to the grain of the wood. When nearly dry, or as soon as it begins to " flat," go over it with a cloth or other polisher, and wipe clean all that will come off. Let stand a day or two and polish lightly with the finest grade of sandpaper. Wipe off the dust with a soft cloth and follow with two coats of the best quality of pure shellac. Avoid cheap shellac, as it is much less durable. This gives a high gloss. But if a dull finish is required, the shellac may be rubbed down by means of a piece of felt tacked over a flat surface as a block of wood, with pumice stone moistened with cold-drawn linseed oil or olive oil.

Or to refinish a hard-wood floor that has become defaced by age or wear, remove the previous finish by washing the floor with a strong solution of sal soda, or, if necessary, caustic potash or soda lye. Or if this does not remove the spots, apply turpentine. After the wood has been perfectly cleaned, proceed as above.

Wax for Hard-wood Floors.—Shellac alone makes a tough and durable finish, but on account of its high gloss it readily mars and scratches. And these defects are very apparent. Moreover, a shellac surface cannot be touched up in spots because the brush marks will show. When defaced, it must be refinished all over. Hence it is customary to follow the shellac with a protective coat of wax.

Or wood may be oiled with cold-drawn linseed or other clear fixed oil, and a coat of wax applied directly to the oiled surface without shellac. This last is the usual custom abroad.

A suitable wax properly applied gives a hard, glossy surface, is not sticky, and does not rub off. Scratches or mars on any part of the surface can be waxed over at any time, and the whole surface can be repolished frequently with a weighted brush. Floor oils, unless rubbed and polished with great care, tend to stain skirts, rugs, and draperies. Hence wax is the most satisfactory of all floor dressings.

To Wax Floors.—Apply, by means of a flannel cloth, beeswax thinned with turpentine and rub down with a weighted brush. This is a hard wax and difficult to apply without turpentine. But the turpentine quickly evaporates, and the wax then forms a very durable coating.

Or as a substitute for beeswax, use paraffin wax, which is cheaper, soft and easy to apply, but less durable. Paraffin is one of the petroleum products, and if not properly refined, tends to combine with the tannin of oak floors to form black petroleum stains, which are difficult to remove.

Or fasten together four or more common red bricks. Lay one or more thicknesses of felt over the largest surface, surround the whole with flannel or other soft cloth, sew it on and attach an old broom handle with which to push or drag it over the floor. This is equally as effective as a weighted brush and costs nothing.

Steel Wool for Waxed Floors.—To scour a hard-wood floor when scratched or marred, or to remove dirt that is ground in, use steel wool, which comes by the pound for this purpose. It can be used in the same fashion as cotton waste, and is a very effective scourer, which will not injure the finest surface.

Polish for Waxed Floors.—Substances recommended for polishing waxed floors are beeswax or rosin, thinned with turpentine, or paraffin wax. Stearin and even tallow candles are sometimes used for the purpose, but are much less suitable. Pure beeswax thinned with turpentine is the simplest and perhaps most desirable polish, but the following are recommended:

Rub through a coarse grater 6½ pounds of beeswax. Add 3 pounds of pearlash and a little water. Bring to a boil and stir well until they cease to effervesce. Now stir in 3 pounds of dry yellow ocher and pour all into a tin pail, having a tight cover, in which to preserve it for use. Thin when required for use with boiling water to the consistency of cream, and apply while hot with a soft cloth. Polish with a weighted brush and wipe up with a coarse flannel.

Or place in a tin pan 5 ounces of powdered rosin, 24 ounces of yellow beeswax, and rub through a coarse grater. Add 1 pint of turpentine, and place the pan in a larger pan, surrounded by boiling water. This should be done at a distance from a stove or open flame, and matches should not be lighted in the vicinity, as the turpentine gives off an inflammable gas. Stir until of a uniform consistency, and pour into glass fruit jars or tin pails having tight covers to preserve for future use. When required for use, thin with turpentine to the consistency of cream, and apply as above.

Spots on Waxed Floors.—Apply a little benzine or turpentine on a soft cloth to remove the wax. Rub clean with a dry cloth, and let the benzine or turpentine evaporate before waxing.

To remove dirt that is ground in, scour with steel wool. After the spot has been removed, rub over the spot and adjacent surface with a cloth moistened in a solution of wax and turpentine or other polisher. Rub dry with a weighted brush to a fine polish, otherwise it will be sticky. Avoid the use of water, as it will turn the wax white. Never use soft soap, sal soda, or other alkalies, as they tend to cut the oil in which the shellac is mixed, strike through and darken the floor beneath.

Oil for Floors.—Do not use crude petroleum oil on oak or similar hardwood floors. The crude petroleum contains a dyestuff which, with the addition of tannin, is the basis of black ink. All oak and some other hard woods contain tannin, which unites with certain constituents of crude oil and some other petroleum products to form in the fibers of the wood an insoluble black inky dye. Thus, in a short time the floor will be turned jet black, and its appearance ruined. To remove this stain, wash the floor with sal soda or caustic potash lye, rinse, dry, and apply a solution of 1 pound of oxalic acid dissolved in 10 or 12 quarts of warm water. Wet the floor with this solution and let it dry without rinsing. Let stand, if convenient, over night. But remember that oxalic acid is an active poison. Hence care must be taken to keep pets and children out of the room, and not to breathe in the dust that rises from the dry crystals. Pour out the rinsing water into a pit and cover it with earth. Oxalic acid will not injure shellac or interfere with any subsequent treatment.

Care of Hard-wood Floors. — To prevent furniture from scratching or marring hard-wood floors, get pieces

"And Rub Down with a Weighted Brush."

of thick felt or soft rubber or obtain from a cobbler a sheet of rubber soling. Cut these to the exact size of the table and chair feet. Cover them with glue, and when the glue becomes "tacky" lay them on. Put newspapers under the chairs to protect the floor until the glue is quite dry. The floor will be kept in much better condition if the members of the family wear rubber heels on their shoes.

To Restore Wax Floors.—Old wax may be removed from a hard-wood floor by mixing equal quantities of sal soda and slaked lime, and using about 1 pound of the mixture to a pailful of water. Apply this with a mop, and afterwards scrub the floor with sand soap and water. If necessary apply dilute sulphuric acid, 1 part of acid to 10 parts of water. Afterwards rinse in water containing a little ammonia and wipe dry.

Remove any remaining traces of wax by means of turpentine. Otherwise shellace will not adhere.

RUGS

Care of Rugs. — Before sweeping, rugs should be removed from the room and thoroughly cleaned before they are returned to the floor. If rugs are caught by the ends and shaken they soon tear out and unravel. A better way is to hang them on a line and beat them with a carpet beater.

Or lay the rug on a clean floor and sprinkle table salt over it. Sweep it hard with a broom until it is clean; turn it and sweep the other side the same way.

If rugs must be beaten indoors lay a damp cloth over them. If they are very much soiled, rinse the cloth in hot water and repeat until the rug is clean.

To Lay Rugs. — To prevent rugs from curling at the corners fasten under each corner a triangular bit of corrugated rubber. Let these extend 8 or 9 inches along the rug. Bore several small holes in the rubber and sew through holes in the fabric. This not only keeps the rugs in place but makes them last longer.

Or sew dress stays or whalebone under the corners to keep the rug from curling.

Or turn the rug upside down and apply a liberal coat of cold flour paste with a brush to the corners and edges. Let the rug dry flat on its face, and when dry turn it over, and the weight of the paste will keep it in position.

Care of Oriental Rugs.—Oriental rugs, if genuine, are in fast colors, and the top or right side is practically indestructible. The threads at the back, however, are very easily damaged. Hence Oriental rugs should always be beaten on the right side. When beaten they should be hung on the line or laid over grass or other soft surface.

If much soiled, they may be washed or scrubbed by means of a stiff brush with soap bark dissolved in boiling water, and afterwards wiped off with a clean sponge and dried with a dry cloth. In winter lay an Oriental rug on the porch or other flat surface out of doors, sprinkle it with snow, and brush it off with a stiff broom or heavy whisk broom.

To Brighten Colors.—Slightly moisten salt with kerosene. Sprinkle this over the rug and sweep it off. Kerosene will leave no greasy effect. The dirt will soon pass off and the colors will be freshened.

Or substitute corn meal for salt.

MATTING

To Clean Matting.—First sprinkle matting with bits of wet newspaper or similar substances, as with carpets, and sweep the way of the weave, but not across it. Wash with strong salt and water to strengthen the fibers.

Or wash with skim milk, rinse in warm water, and dry quickly with a coarse cloth.

To Brighten Matting. — If light-colored mattings become stained and faded, wash with strong soda water. This will give them a uniform solid cream color, harmonizing the different tints.

Or with a water-color brush apply suitable dyestuff to the pattern to revive and restore it.

OILCLOTH AND LINOLEUM

To Clean Oilcloth.—Oilcloth should not be scrubbed with a stiff brush or mop, or saturated with water, nor should sal soda or other strong washing compounds be used upon it. The surface is nothing but paint, and if it becomes soaked, especially with water containing strong soapsuds or washing compounds, it crumbles and quickly decays.

To use a large sponge with lukewarm water containing skim milk is the best way to wash oilcloth. A very little hard white or yellow soap may be used if necessary. A sponge is excellent, since it leaves no lint, and does not admit of scrubbing the floor hard enough to crack or peel off the surface.

After removing the dirt with skim milk and water, go over it a second time, rinsing with a sponge wrung out of clear warm water, and dry enough to take up nearly all of the moisture and admit of the floor drying quickly.

Or rub it over with a dry woolen cloth.

Finally go over the surface with a rag dipped in boiled linseed oil or crude petroleum oil. This is very cheap, costing only 8 or 10 cents a quart, and a cloth dipped in it will take up enough oil to go over the floor several times. After the cloth has been once saturated it will require but a small quantity of oil each time afterwards.

Or use buttermilk to wash the oilcloth. Afterwards rinse with a sponge dipped in clear water.

Table Oilcloths.—The thin oilcloths used on kitchen tables, shelves, etc., may be cleaned in the same manner as the floor oilcloth. Do not use either soap or hot water, but moisten the rag slightly in kerosene. Rub the oilcloth until it is perfectly clean, wring the cloth out of hot water, and dip again in kerosene when necessary. Afterwards rub dry with a flannel cloth.

Or wash with skimmed sweet milk or buttermilk, and rinse with a sponge and clear water.

Polish with a little linseed oil or a cloth slightly dampened with new milk.

To Wax Oilcloths and Linoleums.—First wash the floor as above and apply a thin coating of wax with a flannel cloth.

Or use a floor oil mixed with wax. This gives a hard, smooth surface, which is easily wiped up and kept clean.

To Remove Spots on Oilcloth.—Anything hot placed on oilcloth turns it white. To remove these spots rub with alcohol and polish with a dry cloth.

To Brighten Oilcloth.—Put a little salt in the water in which oilcloth is washed. This will brighten and freshen the colors with which it is painted.

CHAPTER XIV

HOUSE CLEANING

CLEANING THE CELLAR—CLEANING THE ATTIC AND CLOSETS—CLEANING THE CHAMBERS—TO CLEAN FLOOR COVERINGS—CLEANING AND REFINISHING WOOD FLOORS—CLEANING PAINT—WHITEWASHING—PAPER HANGING—CARE OF WALLS—WINDOWS, DOORS, ETC.—CLEANING AND CARE OF FURNITURE—CLEANING PICTURE FRAMES—CLEANING BRIC-A-BRAC AND MISCELLANEOUS OBJECTS—TO CLEAN MARBLE, BRICK, AND STONE — CLEANING KITCHEN STOVES AND OTHER METALS—PACKING

In addition to the daily and weekly routine of housework it is customary to give the house and its furnishings a thorough overhauling and renovating once or twice a year, usually in the spring and fall. But this custom varies in different parts of the country, and in cities is also quite different from what it is in rural neighborhoods. In cities, winter is the season when guests are received and most entertaining takes place; hence the fall house cleaning, as a preparation for the duties and festivities of the winter season, is likely to be the more important.

In rural neighborhoods, however, summer is the period of greatest activity, and the spring house cleaning is usually the more thorough and painstaking.

Spring House Cleaning. — Spring house cleaning should ordinarily be postponed until the weather has become sufficiently settled, so that winter underwear, draperies, carpets, etc., may be stored away if desired, and so that the health of the household need not suffer by reason of the open windows and dampness attendant upon scrubbing floors and walls, whitewashing, painting, and the like. Most women, after constant confinement during the winter months, are more or less run down in the spring, and the change from the bracing temperature of winter to the enervating warmth of the first spring days is likely to result in a lowering of tone that may expose them to serious mischief from overexertion. For these reasons there is a gradual change of sentiment in favor of making spring house cleaning a comparatively simple affair, putting off the heavy work until the fall. But the spring house cleaning must be sufficiently thorough to renovate and protect all woolens, furs, and feathers from the ravages of moths, to remove heavy hangings and draperies, and everything that impedes the free circulation of air during the heated term.

Plan of Campaign.—The work of house cleaning will be very much simplified by thinking out in advance a systematic plan of campaign. In a blank book make an inventory of the principal contents of each room. Measure the floors and the width and length of the window shades needed. Ascertain the number of yards of carpet or matting, the number of rolls of wall paper and the yards of border required for every room in the house, the amount of paint or stain needed for the various floors; also the size of the dining-room tablecloths, the length and width of sheets, and the size of pillow slips for different pillows. Divide the book in sections, assign a number of pages to each room in the house, take accurate measurements, note them down, and preserve the book for future use. Consult it to determine what changes shall be made in the rooms, what articles shall be stored away, and what, if any, need to be repaired. Provide in advance the requisite amount of materials of all sorts, and have them at hand when the work begins.

William Morris says: "Have nothing in your house that you do not know to be useful or believe to be beautiful." Hence before house cleaning go through the house and critically examine each object. Some of them may have passed their usefulness, or your tastes may have changed and you may no longer regard them as beautiful. Then remove them without question. The art of successful living consists in getting along with as few articles of furniture as possible, rather than in accumulating many different pieces. Remember that every additional one is an additional care. If you decide to retain an article, consider, if it is in order or not, if it can be put in order, and in that case whether it can be done at home. Gather up such pieces as you decide to repair and take them to the family workshop.

Consider the discarded articles to see if they can be given away, sold, or used for fuel, and if not, throw them together to make a bonfire to celebrate with when the house cleaning is finished.

Rules for House Cleaning.—It is a good rule in house cleaning to first clean the cellar, because it is the most difficult and often the most neglected part of the house. Afterwards begin with the attic and work down.

Another good rule is to clean thoroughly one room at a time, settling it as you go.

Preparations for House Cleaning.—Experienced housewives arrange for house cleaning by preparing food in advance, boiling ham, baking beans, pies, bread, and cake, so as to be spared as far as possible the labor of cooking while house cleaning is going on.

While house cleaning, dress appropriately for the work. Some housekeepers wear a divided skirt or bloomers made of four widths of heavy dark skirting. These are gathered into bands and buttoned about the ankles and waist. They are valuable protectors for skirts, and facilitate climbing stepladders, scrubbing floors, etc.

Pull the sleeves up as far as you want them to go, and put elastic bands on the arms over the sleeves. Trim the finger nails as short as can be borne with comfort. This prevents their being broken or torn when obliged to work without gloves. Wear a dust cap, a big apron, and loose gloves.

Half the disagreeableness of house cleaning is taken away by having a lotion to apply to parboiled and uncomfortable hands. Soak 2 or 3 ounces of quince seed over night, strain through cheese cloth, and add 2 quarts of water and 2 ounces each of glycerin, boracic acid, and witch-hazel. This is one of the best of lotions.

CLEANING THE CELLAR

To Clean Cellars.—Begin to clean house with the cellar. It is a hard job, and you may be inclined to neglect it if you wait till the rest of the work has been done. No part of the house cleaning is so important from the standpoint of sanitary cleanliness or, because it is out of sight, more likely to be neglected.

First sweep all dust and cobwebs from rafters and ceiling; sweep the shelves and wash them with strong suds or soda and water; remove, empty, and clean bins and barrels that have contained vegetables, and set them out of doors exposed directly to the air and sunlight. If the cellar admits of thorough drainage, wash down the ceilings, walls, and floor with a hose, or dash water on them from pails by means of a large dipper. Open the bulkhead windows and sweep the floor, especially digging out the corners. Remove everything that is not necessary. The fewer objects to accumulate dust and to get in the way when cleaning, the better.

Dissolve 2 pounds of copperas in 1 gallon of water, and sprinkle the walls and floor with this solution by means of an old whisk broom or watering pot having a fine spray. This is a good disinfectant and assists in driving away rats and other vermin.

Finally whitewash the walls with an old whitewash brush or old broom, and use plenty of whitewash, to which add copperas at the rate of ½ pound to 1 pound for each pailful.

Vegetable Cellars. — If vegetables are kept in barrels or bins in the house cellar, they should be examined from time to time and picked over as soon as they begin to rot. Leaves from cabbage heads, celery tops, and other vegetable stuff not wanted should be carefully removed before they begin to spoil. Decaying organic matter of any kind is the favorite breeding ground of the germs of typhoid fever, diphtheria, and other contagious filth diseases, and decay is much assisted by dampness. Hence unless the cellar is perfectly dry, clean and free from rotten vegetables, those who are responsible for its condition cannot in case of sickness have a clear conscience. An outbreak of black diphtheria which caused the death of five children in a single family was traced by a physician directly to some decayed vegetable matter on the cellar floor.

Or make an outdoor vegetable cellar by sinking a strong cask or box in the ground below the frost line. Knock out the bottom and let the vegetables rest on the ground. Provide a water-tight cover in two layers, with sawdust or charcoal between. Or throw over the top straw or hay. Thus cabbages, celery, and the like may be kept fresh in winter without danger of contaminating the air of the house.

To Keep Cellars Warm. — Make a flour paste containing a strong glue size, and with a whitewash brush apply one or more layers of building paper, brown paper, or even newspapers to the rafters of the ceiling, and let it come down over the sills and around the frames of windows to prevent draughts. The thicker the layer or layers of paper the better. This helps to keep the floors warm and to make the cellar frost proof.

Care of Casks. — Keep an empty cask bunged up tight to keep it sweet.

Tar casks slightly on the inside to assist in preserving salt meat.

To sweeten a sour cask that has held pickles, vinegar, or wine, wash it with lime water, or throw in hot charcoal and ashes. Add water and let the cask soak.

To remove must or other odors, wash with sulphuric acid and rinse with clear water, or whitewash with quicklime, or char the inside with a hot iron. In all cases rinse thoroughly with scalding water before using.

To Prevent Dampness in Cellars.— To avoid damp cellars furnish jets, gutters, and leaders to carry rain water from the roof to a cistern or away from the foundations of the house. Lay tile or other drains under the cellar floor to carry away water from springs or other natural moisture. Lay cellar walls in mortar made of water lime, and cover the cellar bottom and walls with hydraulic cement, water lime, or concrete made by melted asphaltum poured upon a surface of gravel and tamped hard while hot.

Or employ a layer of coal tar and asphaltum laid on a surface of gravel and covered with melted asphaltum applied hot. Finish with a layer of fine sand. Apply by means of a brush a thin layer of waterproof cement to the walls, floor, and sills.

If tile or other drains underly the cellar floor, let the floor slant slightly to an opening in the drain so that water coming in from freshet or otherwise may be carried off, and so that, if desired, the floor and walls may be flushed with water.

To Ventilate Cellars. — The upper part of the house being warmer than the cellar, the warm air of the upper rooms creates, by rising, a suction which draws the cellar air into the rooms above through cracks in the cellar door, or through the doorway whenever the door is open. By this means any impurities or germs of disease in the cellar are communicated freely to all parts of the house. Hence the importance of good ventilation in cellars.

Locate cellar windows, when possible, opposite one another so as to create a draught. Being placed near the ceiling, such windows afford good ventilation. But the best ventilator is a chimney reaching down to the cellar floor or resting on the foundation wall and communicating with the cellar by one or more good-sized openings.

Have the cellar windows open freely by means of rods or otherwise, and keep them open in clear weather whenever possible.

To Remove Dampness.—Place in the cellar a large open box or pan containing fresh lime. This will tend to dry and purify the air. Change the lime as fast as it becomes air-slaked.

Whitewash for Cellars. — Slake enough lime for a pailful of whitewash. Mix half a pint of flour with cold water to a smooth paste, thin with scalding water, and boil until it thickens. Pour this boiling hot into the whitewash and stir vigorously.

Or use boiled rice strained through cheese cloth. Add a teacupful of the strained rice to a pailful of slaked lime.

Cover cellar walls twice a year or oftener with whitewash, to which add copperas at the rate of 2 pounds to the gallon. Apply whitewash freely, especially in out-of-the-way corners, removing all shelves, etc., so as to cover the entire surface of the walls.

To Disinfect Cellars. — Close windows and other apertures and stuff the cracks with burlap. Burn a quantity of sulphur in a suitable receptacle on the cellar floor. An ordinary tin pie plate covered with earth or sand may be used. Place on this live coals, on which sprinkle flowers of sulphur or brimstone. Take precautions to escape quickly so as not to breathe the fumes.

To Prevent Dust in Cellars. — To minimize dust from furnaces, wet the ashes by throwing water on them from a dipper before taking them up. Or sprinkle them with water from a watering pot. Or sprinkle over them wet sawdust.

This also prevents dust from rising into the upper rooms through the registers.

Bins for Cellars.—Have all bins for use in the cellar small enough to be freely movable. Or use barrels, and place bins and barrels on planks turned on edge to lift them above the cellar bottom. Make a sufficient number of swinging shelves by tacking pieces of board to the rafters so as to project downward, and suspend shelves on these to hold canned preserves and other articles in place of having shelves on the walls. Keep the walls free to admit of complete whitewashing.

Pipes — To Prevent Frost. — Wrap exposed water pipes with bands of hay or straw twisted tight around them, or cover with the asbestos tubes that are on the market for this purpose.

Pumps—To Prevent Freezing.—Remove the lower valve and drive a tack into the under side of it, projecting in such a way that the valve cannot quite close. The pump will work as usual, but the water will gradually leak back into the well or cistern.

Or have at hand a suitable hook of stout wire by which to lift the valve and let the water out of the pipe at night.

To Thaw Pipes.—If the pipe is accessible, wrap woolen cloths, as old pieces of underwear, carpet, and the like, thickly about it and pour on boiling water. This holds the heat and melts the ice gradually.

Or, if possible, pour boiling water containing as much salt as it will dissolve into the pipe above the frozen part. This will settle and dissolve the ice.

To Clear Drainpipes. — Flush the pipe once a week with boiling water containing sal soda. Rinse the kitchen sink daily with strong soda water.

To Stop Leaks. — For cold-water pipes apply a thick paste of yellow soap and whiting mixed with a little water. Or, if the leak is too large, wrap the pipe tightly with a tarred cloth bandage, melt the tar, and spread it over strong duck canvas or burlap cloth three or four inches wide. Begin to wind the bandage several inches from the leak and lap it one half or more upon itself at each round.

For hot-water pipes mix iron filings with vinegar and sulphuric acid to a thick paste. Dry the pipe, fill the cracks with this mixture, and keep them dry until it sets. This is very durable.

To Protect Lead Pipes. — Coat the inside of the pipe with sulphide of lead. This is insoluble and cannot be acted upon by water. To effect this fill the pipes with a warm concentrated solution of sulphide of potassium, and let stand fifteen or twenty minutes. Then rinse it out. The sulphide coating will be formed by chemical action.

To Clean Boilers.—To prevent scale forming on the inside of the boiler put into it two or three white oak saplings. These will be entirely dissolved in three or four weeks, and the boiler will be clean.

CLEANING THE ATTIC AND CLOSETS

Closets and Drawers. — Choose a sunny day and empty the contents of bureau drawers, wardrobes, closets, and other storage places upon an old quilt or a sheet spread upon the lawn. Shake and dust these vigorously with a whisk broom, and sort them. Put in one pile ragged articles that are no longer useful except for carpet rags or to sell to the ragman; in another, those that are available for dusters, mops, dishcloths, and the like. Lay aside articles that need to be mended or renovated. Separate woolens and flannels, which require protection against moths, from cotton fabrics, which are moth proof. After removing with a whisk broom all traces of moths, hang the larger pieces on the line and leave the others out of doors exposed to direct sunshine.

Meantime apply suitable moth destroyers to the insides of the drawers, wardrobes, and boxes that have been emptied. Take off the wall paper in the closets, as behind the wall paper is where you will find the nests of moths and other vermin. Wash the floors and walls with moth destroyers, and apply suitable preventives to cracks and openings. Wash out the insides of the drawers, and take them out to dry in the sun.

Save fine towels that are too worn for further use and lay them in the bottom of the drawers, with lavender between the folds.

While the clothes on the line are airing, pack flannels, furs, feathers, etc., in moth-proof paper bags or boxes to be stored away in the attic, and before the dew falls at night return cotton and other fabrics required for summer use to the drawers and wardrobes that have been cleansed and aired.

Destroy with a hard heart every useless thing, and burn everything that you see no probability of needing in the near future. With the best of care odds and ends will accumulate, and the labor of handling and preserving them in the hope of finding use for them by and by is often more than they are worth.

But remember, if similar objects are classified and kept together, many uses may be found for them collectively. A lot of old stockings may be turned into a quilt. Old underwear is useful for dusters and many other purposes. Hence sort, classify, and arrange as much as you can, but when odds and ends are left over, throw them away.

Drawers that Stick. — Now is the time to remedy the bureau drawer that sticks. If it is not quite dry when returned to its place, you will discover the spot that in damp weather is likely to swell and make trouble. Take a piece of common yellow soap, moisten it, and rub freely the parts which are too tight. Also soap the under part of the drawer where it slides. Or apply a tallow candle. Or rub the parts freely with bacon rind. But the soap is likely to effect the more permanent cure.

Periodicals.—Each spring the attic will reveal a pile of magazines and papers. Some of these may be thrown away, but in others there will be one or more stories or articles of especial interest. Take out the wire fasteners and sort the contents into fiction,

"A Pile of Magazines."

travel, biography, history, and the like. Take out of each pile only what is really wanted. Thus, for example, the best short stories may be collected and made into a valuable book. To bind these articles together, cut strips of manila paper 1½ to 2 inches in width and the length of the magazines. Fold these lengthwise in the middle, and paste on either side. Slip the back edge of the printed pages into the crease thus formed, fastening it securely with paste. Now thread a needle with strong thread and sew the pages through and through to this reënforcement. Place as many of the separate stories as desired together, bore holes through them ½ inch from the back edge near the top, bottom, and in the middle, and lace them together with a strong cord. Draw over the outside of all a strong manila cover, pasting it liberally to the back.

Or the sheets may be sent to a bookbinder and at a slight expense made into an interesting and valuable book.

Or the periodicals will always be welcome at hospitals, schools, and other institutions, which in many cases will send for them if notified that they may be had at the expense of removal.

Curtains and Draperies. — Take down all curtains and draperies; launder, fold, and store them before the house cleaning begins. Thus they will be out of the way and ready to be put up when papering, painting, and whitewashing are finished.

How to Clean Rooms.—Clean one room at a time, doing everything thoroughly. Settle each room before going to another. This avoids upsetting the whole house, and is much better than cleaning by floors and having all the bedrooms or all the living rooms upset at the same time.

First take up the carpet and scrub the floor; then beat and clean the carpet and hang it on the line, so that both the carpet and the floor from which it is taken may have all day to dry and air.

Or, after the floor covering is taken up, the ceiling may be first cleaned, and papered or whitewashed, if necessary, and the walls papered before the floors are scrubbed, this being reserved for another day. Lastly, any necessary painting and varnishing may be done and the windows and woodwork cleaned.

In cleaning paint use but little soap, as the alkali tends to injure paint and varnish. If paint is kept in good condition by being rubbed occasionally with a cloth moistened in kerosene, it will need little scrubbing at house-cleaning time.

Last of all, stain or paint the floor, or relay the floor covering, and return furniture and pictures to their positions.

House-cleaning Hints.—Split open two short pieces of rubber hose and fasten them on the lower end of the stepladder. Turn them up on the sides of the supports, and nail them there. This prevents the stepladder from slipping on the bare floor.

Use a stiff bristle brush, preferably of wood fiber, to clean the cracks and crevices of woodwork, iron beds, and the like. Lay the brush when wet with the bristle side down. This prevents the water from soaking into the wood and loosening the bristles.

Or use a damp whisk broom that has served its time as a clothes brush to take dust from cracks and corners, carvings of furniture and woodwork, and to clean windows. If rinsed frequently it removes every particle of dust with little trouble and no injury.

Have at hand a small stick 3 or 4 feet long and 1 inch in diameter, with a screw hook screwed in one end. This is always handy to reach for articles that have fallen out of the window, behind furniture, or into the water pail or barrel, to hang or take down pictures, pull down escaped window shades, and for many other purposes.

CLEANING THE CHAMBERS

To Clean Bedrooms.—Take down all curtains and draperies, if not already removed, and carry them to the laundry. Put the bedding on the line, shake and beat it, and leave it to air. Take the mattress out of doors, and beat and air it.

If the bed spring is exposed and of metal, take it out of doors and turn the hose on it or dash water on it from a pail. Let it dry in the sun.

If the bedstead is of wood, wash it with water containing borax or ammonia, but do not use washing soda or soap, as the former will spoil the paint and the latter will leave a disagreeable odor.

If the bedstead is of metal, wipe it with a cloth dipped in kerosene. Or brush it over with gasoline and wipe off with a dry towel.

Rub the paint of wooden bedsteads with a cloth dipped in paraffin. This both cleans and freshens it.

Remove extra blankets and quilts to the laundry.

Take up carpets and rugs to be beaten and shaken, or if there is matting on the floor and it is not necessary to take it up, sprinkle dry salt over it and wipe with a cloth wrung out of warm water.

If the floor is of hard wood, wash it with gasoline as you would with water, and *ventilate thoroughly before admitting a light.* Polish with wax and suitable furniture polish.

If the floor covering is drugget, scatter moist bran over it and let remain several hours. When swept up the bran will take the dirt with it. Then scrub the drugget with hot water and ammonia by means of a stiff scrubbing brush, and afterwards wipe off with a soft cloth until the rinsing water is perfectly clear.

To Renovate Metal Beds.—If the enamel is worn from a white enameled bed, go over it with an additional coat of white enamel, or obtain gilt enamel

"Go Over It with Enamel."

and gild it. This gives the appearance of brass. The gilding wears better than white enamel and can be washed with gasoline.

Or, if desired, give the white bed that needs renovating a coat of black enamel.

Cotton Blankets.—In summer, cotton blankets and spreads, which are much cheaper than woolen ones, are to be preferred to woolen blankets or old-fashioned cotton quilts. They can be easily washed and are more sanitary. The aim should be in summer to have the bed coverings as light and easy to handle as possible.

Eiderdown. — With use an eiderdown quilt becomes compacted together and loses its elasticity. Take it out of doors, shake and brush it, and expose it to sunshine for several hours. Spread it on the lawn and work over it with a stiff whisk broom to loosen the nap. Thus its elasticity may be restored, and it will again feel soft and downy.

To Clean Mattresses. — Stains on mattresses may be removed by covering them with dry laundry starch and moistening this with enough soap or soap jelly (made by melting scraps of hard soap in about their own bulk of boiling water) to form a thin paste, which will dry on, but not soak through into the mattress. Let dry, and brush off with a stiff whisk broom. Repeat if necessary. Afterwards sponge with ammonia and water.

To Purify Feathers.—New feathers quickly become foul as the grease contained in the quills decays. Hence they require a thorough cleansing to remove the animal oils and other greasy substances. Old feather beds may also be renovated.

First, dry the feathers in the sunshine or by a fire, and put them in a sack. Moisten two sheets of burlap, lay the feathers between these, and beat them to loosen the dirt, which will adhere to the wet cloth.

Prepare a solution of limewater at the rate of ½ pound of quicklime to 1 gallon of water. Stir vigorously, allow to settle, and pour off the clear liquor. Soak the feathers in this for 3 or 4 days.

Or use instead cooking soda at the rate of 1 teaspoonful to 1 quart of water. Take a large piece of cheese cloth and pour the limewater or soda water and feathers upon this so that the water will pass through, leaving the feathers in the cloth. Now pour cold water over them and rinse them well.

Put on a wash boiler half full of water, and add a cupful of powdered borax. Put the feathers in this, bring them to a boil, and again pour them on cheese cloth. Drain and squeeze dry.

Tie the corners of the cheese cloth together and hang it over a clothesline, shaking occasionally until dry. Several days may be required to dry the feathers thoroughly. Do not use soap to wash feathers.

Care of Feather Beds.—Many feather beds are in use which have been slept on for more than one generation without being renovated. When the feathers have been properly cleaned and the ticks cared for, they perhaps do not need renovating oftener than once in two or three years, but at least once in three years the feathers should be passed into a fresh tick, the ticking washed, and the feathers renovated before they are returned to it.

After the tick has been washed, rub the inside with a mixture of equal parts of beeswax and turpentine and go over it with a warm iron. This will prevent the feathers from being soiled by perspiration or otherwise or from working through the tick.

Or, once a year, place the feather beds and pillows out of doors on the grass or on a clean, flat roof, and allow them to be thoroughly drenched by a warm summer rain.

Hang them to the limb of a tree to dry in the shade.

To Clean Feather Pillows.—Feather pillows may be washed without removing the feathers by boiling them in borax water to which a small quantity of ammonia has been added. Use half a teacupful of borax to a boilerful of water, and add a tablespoonful of ammonia. Boil fifteen or twenty minutes. After removing the pillow from the boiler, scrub the tick, if badly stained, by laying it on a washboard and applying suds with a stiff brush. Rinse in two or three waters and hang on the line in a shady place to dry. Shake the pillow and change ends two or three times a day. Bring the pillows into the house before the dew falls or if it should come on to rain, as it takes a long time to dry pillows at best. This process makes the feathers light, flaky, and sweet smelling.

Or, if you do not wish to wash the feathers, pass them into pillow covers and hang them on the line to air while the ticks are being washed.

Or put the pillows out of doors in a drenching rain storm. Afterwards squeeze as much water out of them as possible and hang them up to dry in a shady place.

To Mend Old Blankets.—To mend all breaks and tears in old blankets, cover both sides with cheese cloth. Tack all together with white or colored yarn, and thus make a light quilt superior to a comforter. Finish the edge by crocheting around all four sides.

To Store Bedding.—Line a large packing case with heavy wrapping paper by using brass tacks or by pasting paper to the inside of the case with flour paste and a whitewash brush. This will prevent moths from making their way through the cracks of the case and the folds of the paper. Air the bedclothes thoroughly, fold blankets in paper, and scatter freely among the folds hemlock or arborvitæ sprigs, dry sweet flags, lavender, or sachet powder. These are equally as effective as moth balls, and give the bedclothes an agreeable odor. Paste the ends of the paper together and paste wrapping paper over the top of the case in such a way as to leave no cracks through which moths can find an entrance. Nail down the lid.

Bedroom Ornaments.—Remove all unnecessary bric-a-brac from the bedrooms and take unnecessary articles from dressing tables. A room looks much daintier without useless little things.

To Clean the Bathroom.—Thoroughly wash down walls and floors, clean out the medicine closet, and throw away everything that is not likely to be used. Look over the shelves carefully for cracks and crevices which may give lodgment to vermin, and wash them with strong soap and water. Clean the porcelain tub and basin with a cloth wet with kerosene. Pour in kerosene, if necessary, and scrub with a whisk broom or fiber brush. Remove stains from porcelain with dilute muriatic acid (1 part of acid to 10 parts of water), applied by means of a cotton swab held in a cleft stick. Polish the metal work of faucets and pipes with a suitable cleaner.

Or clean the bathtub, washbowl, etc., with gasoline and flannel.

When painting the bathroom, if you wish the floor darker than the walls, without buying two shades of paint, get a light-colored paint, as lead color or light yellow, and after the walls are painted add to the remainder of the paint powdered burnt umber. This will give to the floor a darker color of the same general tone.

TO CLEAN FLOOR COVERINGS

Floors in Summer.—Take up carpets in the spring, beat and clean them, roll them up, protect them against moths, and, if desired, store them away until the fall house cleaning. Fill the floor cracks, if any, with a suitable wood filler, and paint or stain the floor, or cover with matting during summer. This plan saves time and labor in the care of floors, and prevents much dust from sweeping during the hot months. If carpets can be replaced by hard-wood floors and rugs, so much the better, and taking up carpets during the summer time is a step in the right direction. Or, if preferred, the carpets may, of course, be returned to the floors after cleaning.

When taking up large rugs and art squares for the summer, roll them on sticks and sew them in canvas or bed ticking. These may be tied with strong cords and slung on hooks attached to the wall or ceiling in the attic or storeroom. Thus they are well protected and out of the way.

To Take Up Carpets.—First draw the tacks and pick them up without moving the carpet. Then begin at one end of the room and roll the carpet carefully to the other end. Double the roll on itself or, if two persons can assist, take it up at both ends and carry it out of doors to be cleaned. Roll up papers or carpet lining carefully with the dust, and take them out of doors to be burned. If the papers are handled gently little or no dust will remain in the room, and the floor may be readily cleaned with soapsuds and a mop.

Or, if no lining-papers were used and the floors are covered with dust, sprinkle wet sawdust or bits of wet newspaper about the floor, and stir them gently with a broom to gather the dust. Sweep part of the room at a time, taking up the sweepings, and repeat with a fresh lot of sawdust or newspaper. Afterwards wash the floor with a mop.

To Put Down Carpets.—Use an ordinary carpenter's hammer, taking care to choose a tool which has a square, flat head, and not a hammer the head of which has grown round. One or two blows with such a tool will drive a tack, where a small tack hammer will require six or seven. The best and most convenient carpet stretcher is a pair of rubber overshoes. Tack the carpet down on one side, put on a pair of old rubbers, and scuff across the room. Repeat the process for the other three sides. If one person can stretch the carpet and another tack it as fast as it is stretched, it may be laid very quickly and with comparatively little effort.

Carpets—To Prevent Wear.—Before returning old carpets to the floor, rip up the seams and transpose the breadths, putting the least worn strips in place of those that are most worn; or turn the carpet end for end to change the wear.

Or, if the carpet is ingrain, turn and use wrong side up for a season.

Stair Carpets—To Prevent Wear.—Tack several thicknesses of newspaper or carpet lining or old carpet on the top of each step, having them deep enough to hang three of four inches over the edge. This pad prevents the stair carpet from wearing along the edge. It doubles the life of the stair carpet.

To Mend a Rag Carpet.—Holes in rag carpet caused by the breaking of the warp may be mended by sewing back and forth on the sewing machine. Large holes may be mended in this manner so as not to be noticeable.

When cutting out the good parts of an old rag carpet, sew across the rags back and forth before cutting. This prevents the carpet from raveling when cut, and the edges of the good pieces may be sewed together with the seam held down.

To Sweep Carpets.—Before taking up the carpet it should be well swept. The less dust it contains the quicker it can be beaten. Sprinkle with salt or corn meal, or with a mixture of salt and corn meal moistened with kerosene.

Or, if fresh clippings from a lawn mower can be had, sprinkle the carpet with them. Or, if the carpet is of a dark color, with wet tea leaves. Tea leaves may stain a light-colored carpet.

Or wring a newspaper out of cold water until it is damp, but not wet. Tear in small pieces and sprinkle with them. Sweep thoroughly before taking up the tacks.

To Beat Carpets.—If you have a clean green lawn, draw the carpet

"Use a Wire Beater."

over the grass for some distance, turn, and draw back on the other side. Beat the carpet while lying on the grass. Reverse the carpet so as to draw it over another spot, and beat on the other side. Then hang it over a line and beat until clean. Beat first thoroughly on the wrong side and afterwards more gently on the right.

To beat carpets, use preferably a wire beater made by bending a heavy piece of wire 8 or 10 feet long and ⅛ inch or more in thickness. Of this form a loop, and attach the ends to a convenient handle, as a broomstick.

Or use flexible hickory switches rather than heavy sticks, which may injure the warp of the carpet.

To Clean Carpets.—If a carpet is much soiled it may require washing or scouring after having been beaten. This may be done after the carpet has been laid on the floor. First remove stains and grease spots. Next wash, then, with a stiff bristle brush the size of a nailbrush, apply suds made with warm water and one of the following cleansing mixtures:

Have at hand a pail containing suds, another containing clear hot rinsing water, a stiff bristle brush, a large sponge, and a number of coarse porous cloths. Use as little water as possible. Take one breadth at a time and scrub what can be reached without moving. Rinse this section immediately with a sponge wrung out of clear water and dry with a coarse cloth before proceeding to the next. Soap soiled spots with any good hard white soap dipped in water. Take about 1½ yards at a time and work quickly, so that the water will not soak into the carpet.

Or pure soapsuds made by dissolving 1 bar of castile of other hard white soap in 2 gallons of water.

Or one bar of hard white soap, 1 tablespoonful each of borax, washing soda, fuller's earth, and salts of tartar. Cut the soap fine, mix the ingredients in a kettle, add 1 gallon of boiling water, and stir until all are dissolved.

Or 1 pint of ox gall dissolved in 1 quart of cold water. Apply with a scrubbing brush until a lather is formed. Rub pure ox gall on soiled places, rinse, and dry as above.

Or dissolve 1 bar of hard white soap in 1 gallon of water. Dissolve 4 ounces of borax and 4 ounces of sal soda in 4 gallons of water; mix, remove from the fire, and add ½ pint of alcohol, stirring well. Apply when cold.

Finally, open the windows and allow the carpet to thoroughly dry before the room is used. Kindling a fire, if convenient, will assist in drying.

Or ingrain carpets may be ripped into breadths and washed in the tub like other woolen goods with soap and water, or hung out on the line during a warm summer rain.

Any of these methods is suitable for all forms of carpets or rugs of similar materials, as Oriental, Smyrna, and domestic rugs, art squares, and the like.

To Clean Oriental and Other Rugs.—Oriental rugs and other rugs having fast colors may be scrubbed with soap and water, or any of the above cleansing mixtures. Tack the rug on a bare floor, as a porch or piazza, and proceed as with a carpet.

The following mixture is especially recommended for the best quality of rugs or carpets and other woolen fabrics: dissolve 8 ounces of good white soap in the same quantity of boiling water; add 10 ounces of aqua ammonia, 5 ounces of alcohol, 5 ounces of glycerin, and 4 ounces of ether or chloroform. Keep in a fruit jar or large glass bottle and cork tightly. Use 1 tablespoonful of this preparation to a pailful of warm water, and apply with a stiff brush. Or for obstinate stains use a stronger solution.

To Wash Goatskin Rugs. — Wash goatskin rugs in gasoline, or in a mixture of gasoline and pure soapsuds made of hard white soap.

To Freshen Faded Carpets.—After carpets have been cleaned and laid, the colors, if faded, may be freshened by sprinkling the carpet with strong salt water and sweeping hard.

Or dampen a cloth with ammonia

and rub over the surface of the carpet.

Or put ½ pint of turpentine in about 1½ gallons of water. Wring a cloth out of this solution and with it rub the carpet.

Or go over the carpet with a broom or whisk broom moistened with gasoline.

Or put 1 cupful of cold tea and 1 tablespoonful of turpentine in 2 quarts of warm water. Dip the broom in this before sweeping.

Or put 3 tablespoonfuls of turpentine and 4 of salt in 3 gallons of water, and moisten the broom with it.

Or put 1 gill of ox gall in 1 gallon of water and apply with a cloth wrung out so that it will not drip.

Or dissolve 1 teaspoonful of alum in 1 gallon of water.

Or apply to the patterns suitable dyestuffs or water colors mixed with gum arabic, following the outline of the design with a water-color brush.

Or any of the above may be applied with a clean mop if care is taken to wring it out so that it will be damp rather than wet. The above will not only brighten and set the colors of a carpet, restore faded colors, and prevent fresh colors from fading, but will also act as preventives against moths, and to some extent kill germs that may be present in the carpet.

To Clean Rag Carpets.—Shake and beat the carpet, drag it across the lawn a few times to remove dust by contact with the soft grass, and leave it spread on the grass or hung over a line during a gentle rain. Remove any grease spots with a suitable cleanser.

To Remove Grease from Carpets.—Substances recommended for taking grease out of a carpet are ammonia, saltpeter, ox gall, chloroform, ether, gasoline, fuller's earth, potter's clay, and various combinations of these.

To Remove Grease.—Apply gasoline, benzine, or naphtha with a sponge or stiff scrubbing brush.

Or, if the grease is fresh, cover the spot with a layer of French chalk or fuller's earth. Lay a piece of brown paper or blotting paper upon the chalk, and place on it a hot flatiron. Change the iron occasionally. The grease will be melted and absorbed by the chalk and powder.

Or apply pure ox gall with a stiff brush.

Or apply chloroform or ether with a toothbrush.

Or shave 2 ounces of hard white soap in 2 quarts of water. Add 2 ounces of aqua ammonia, 1 ounce of glycerin, and 1 ounce of ether; mix and apply with a stiff brush.

Or shave and dissolve 2 ounces of hard white soap in 1 quart of water. Add 2 ounces of ammonia and 1 teaspoonful of saltpeter and apply with a brush.

To Remove Ink Stains. — Cover quickly with dry salt or starch. Take this up with a spoon as it soaks up the ink, but do not rub or sweep it. It will take up the surplus and prevent the spot from spreading. Leave the spot covered with dry salt and test to see the kind of ink spilled. Put some of the ink on a piece of writing paper and allow it to dry. Or, better, take some writing made with the same ink that has stood several days and test that. First apply water, and if the ink runs, after having been thoroughly dried, it is probably stylographic ink, made of coal-tar products, eosin or nigrosine. In this case you must not use buttermilk or any acid. Use instead an alkali, as potash lye or sal soda, diluted with water. If the dry ink does not run when touched with water, it is probably an iron-gall ink or logwood ink with or without aniline dyes. For these inks use dilute sulphuric acid, 1 part of acid to 10 parts of water. If this takes out the color, restore it with aqua ammonia.

Or cover with fresh salt or starch, and moisten with buttermilk or salts of sorrel or tartaric acid, and let stand until dry. Repeat if necessary.

If the colors fade, apply aqua ammonia.

To Remove Kerosene.—To remove kerosene spilled on a carpet, cover the spot with blotting paper or brown paper and press with a hot iron. Repeat if necessary.

Or cover with corn meal, starch, or salt, and let stand until dry.

To Remove Whitewash.—Scrub with soapsuds applied with a brush, and renew the color by applying aqua ammonia, vinegar, or other acid.

To Remove Soot.—To remove soot which sometimes, in case of a defective flue or turning up a lamp too high, fills a room and falls on the carpet, sprinkle the floor liberally with corn meal and sweep carefully a little at a time, taking up the sweepings as you go and before they are trodden on. Continue to apply corn meal and sweep until the soot is all removed.

To Take Up Matting.—Take up the matting, roll it up, and shake as much dust from it as possible by jarring it on the floor. Unroll it on a green lawn and apply the hose to it, or dash pails of water on it until it is thoroughly clean. This should be done on a hot day, and the matting should be thoroughly dried in the open air as quickly as possible. Take it in before the dew falls and air it again the second day if it does not quite dry the first.

Or draw the matting over a table and apply moist corn meal with a scrubbing brush, thoroughly cleaning a section at a time.

Or scrub with bran water.

To Clean Matting on the Floor.—Matting should not be washed or scrubbed with soapy water, as dampness is injurious to it. It may be swept with a broom previously dipped in hot water, and afterwards gone over with a flannel cloth or sponge dipped in salt and water. The salt will freshen the colors and prevent the matting from turning yellow. It should be quickly dried with a second cloth before the water soaks in.

Or borax may be used in the water in place of salt. Afterwards, to give it a gloss and freshen the colors, it may be gone over with a cloth slightly moistened in fresh milk.

To Remove Stains from Matting.—Matting that has been badly stained may be cleaned by washing with a solution of oxalic acid in the proportion of 1 ounce of acid to 1 pint of water. Apply to the stain with a stiff brush, use as little of the solution as possible, and afterwards wipe off with a dry cloth. Care must be taken to throw out the water immediately after using, as oxalic acid is a *deadly poison.*

To Remove Grease Spots.—Cover with French chalk and moisten with turpentine. Let this stand for a few days, and then scrub off with a stiff brush.

To Lay Matting.—Before laying matting, cover the floor with several thicknesses of old newspapers. Matting is porous and lets the dust through. The paper catches this and admits of its being easily removed at house-cleaning time. Paper also protects the matting from the sharp and uneven edges of the boards.

Matting may be tacked down with ordinary carpet tacks or double-pointed brads.

Or the different breadths may be sewed together with strong linen or cotton thread, using loose buttonhole stitches an inch or an inch and a half apart. To prevent tacking, the edges may be fastened with flour paste.

Or, to avoid sewing, the edges of the several breadths may be pasted down.

Pieces of matting may also be used as rugs on hard-wood floors, especially for bedroom use in summer, by sewing the breadths together with buttonhole stitches and binding the cut ends with cotton braid or tape.

To Lay Oilcloths.—Oilcloths may be put down without the use of tacks by making a cooked paste of flour and water somewhat thicker than flour starch. Lay the oilcloth in place and apply a strip of paste about an inch wide first to the floor and afterwards to the edge of the oilcloth. Stand a heavy board edgewise over this strip until the oilcloth sticks.

Or, if conditions are right, merely

press the oilcloth down with the hands. The edges may be fastened to the floor in the same manner.

Thus the oilcloth can be taken up when necessary without the injury caused by tacks and with little difficulty.

To Repair a Smyrna Rug.—Shaking a Smyrna rug often ravels out the ends. Continue this raveling so as to expose two or three inches of the woolen filling. Tie and knot the loose threads to form a fringe. This will prevent additional raveling, and the fringe will stand as much wear as if new. Use the pattern as a guide, so as to make both ends uniform.

To Patch Rugs and Carpets.—A hole in a rug or carpet may be patched with the rubber mending tissue used for patching garments. Dampen a piece of the same material or of burlap, lay over this a piece of the rubber mending tissue, and place it directly under the hole. Over all lay a piece of brown paper and press with a hot iron. Clip off any frayed edges with scissors or darn them with the ravelings.

To Clean Sheepskin Rugs.—A sheepskin rug should never be immersed in water. The less the pelt side is wet the better. Hence tack the skin on a barrel, pelt side down, and apply hot soapsuds to the wool side with a stiff, clean scrubbing brush until it is clean. Rinse well by dashing cold water upon it, putting in the last water sufficient bluing to make the wool appear white, and leave it on the barrel to dry. This process does not expose the pelt to the rays of the sun, which would cause it to become dry and hard. After the wool is dry go over it carefully with a clean currycomb or other coarse comb to prevent the wool from matting. It will thus be left fluffy and white as snow.

Stair Carpets.—The better plan is to leave the stairs uncarpeted, but if a stair carpet is used the steps should be padded, especially over the edges, as otherwise the carpet will tend to wear along the edge. For this purpose use cotton batting or carpet felt or folded newspapers, tacking them at the back of each step and allowing them to fall two or three inches over the edge. This will also assist in deadening the sound of footsteps.

CLEANING AND REFINISHING WOOD FLOORS

Cracks in Floors.—Place in a saucepan 1 pound of pastry flour and rub up with a little cold water until free from lumps. Add 3 quarts of boiling water, place on the stove, bring to a boil, and stir in 1 tablespoonful of alum. Cut a quantity of newspaper into fine bits and stir it into this paste until it is about as thick as putty. Boil and stir until the mass is of a uniform consistency. Fill the cracks with this by means of a putty knife. Or a case knife with the point broken or filed square across will answer the purpose. Be sure to crowd it into the crack as deep as possible and finish level with the surface. This hardens like papier-maché, is of similar appearance and nearly as hard as the wood itself, and is very durable.

Or make a strong glue size of 1 ounce of glue to 16 ounces of water, and while boiling hot stir in bits of newspaper as above; or equal quantities of fine sawdust and prepared chalk; or plaster of Paris, and apply as above. Any of these may be mixed with coloring matter to match the boards.

Or cracks may be filled with putty. But this is not equally good, since with shellac or varnish it shows through, and is of a slightly different color than the wood.

Oil for Floors.—To oil floors, use linseed oil boiled. First remove all previous wax, paint, or varnish, wash the floor clean and let it dry. Apply the oil with a paint brush, keeping it at the boiling point by means of a small alcohol stove or otherwise.

One or two coats of oil, applied twice a year, will greatly improve kitchen or other rough wood floors, and the addition of a coat of wax will improve the finish and prevent the oil from soiling anything.

An oiled floor should be cared for in the same manner as a waxed floor, without the use of soap, washing powder, or an alkali.

To Color Floor Oil.—Add ½ tablespoonful of burnt umber to each quart of oil to darken it. Or an equal amount of yellow ocher to make it light.

Stains for Floors.—Ordinary oil and lead paints are not suitable for floors for two reasons: they tend to soften the wood, and also to crack, chip, and peel, or wear away in spots that are most trodden, so as to give the floor an uneven appearance. Hence suitable stains (which are the same colored pigments that are used in paints thinned with oils so as to penetrate into the fiber of the wood, but without lead) are better for this purpose.

Or the pigment may be applied in a vehicle of glue size.

Or various dyestuffs, as aniline and other dyes, may be applied, either dissolved in water or oil.

But the following will be found the most generally satisfactory:

For a floor 16 feet square, or approximately 250 square feet of floor space, one heavy or two thin coats, mix 2 quarts of cold-drawn linseed oil and 1 quart of turpentine, to which add 4 ounces of Japan dryer. Stir in about 2 heaping tablespoonfuls of any desired pigment or mixture of pigment, or enough to bring the whole to about the consistency of ordinary lead and oil paint, and bring to a boil over a slow fire. Dissolve with gentle heat 2 or 3 ounces of yellow beeswax in a little turpentine, taking care that the turpentine does not catch fire. Stir in the wax, remove from the fire, and when about lukewarm, thin with turpentine to about the consistency of new milk. Try the stain on a piece of the same kind of wood as the floor before using, to see if the color is right. Soft wood like pine will absorb more of the color than hard wood like maple. Hence it is important to thin the stain to the right consistency to get the desired effect. Take care to apply the stain evenly with the brush, as in painting, and lay it on freely the way of the grain, rather than against it. The addition of turpentine causes the stain to strike into the wood.

Or in place of cold-drawn linseed oil with turpentine, use boiled linseed oil mixed with any desired pigment, and apply boiling hot. Keep the oil at the boiling point by means of an alcohol stove or otherwise.

Or dissolve 3 ounces of glue in 2½ quarts of soft water. Remove from the stove and stir in 2 pounds of yellow ocher. Apply with a paint brush while hot, and follow with a coat of boiled linseed oil. Let stand over night before walking on it.

Or to give the floor a deep black like ebony, boil 1 pound of logwood chips in 2 quarts of water down to 1 quart, and apply one or two coats with a paint brush. When dry, follow with a strong solution of sulphate of iron in water. Afterwards, when dry, apply a thin coat of boiled linseed oil, wax, and polish.

Or to 6 quarts of caustic-potash lye made from wood ashes add 1 pound of copperas more or less, to give a light or dark oak shade as desired, and apply one or more coats with a brush. When dry, varnish the floor, wax, and polish.

Pigment for Stains.—Add any of the following pigments in the form of dry powder at the rate of about 2 heaping tablespoonfuls to the gallon of stain, to obtain the colors mentioned:

To imitate mahogany, use burnt sienna. For black walnut, burnt umber or Vandyke brown. For cherry, burnt sienna mixed with iron oxide. For yellow, raw sienna, yellow ocher, or raw umber. Or any of the above may be combined freely to form tints or shades as desired. Experiments may be made by adding the pigments a little at a time and testing the color from time to time on a piece of board of the same kind of wood as the floor is made of.

Varnish for Stained Floors. — Place in a 6-quart saucepan about 10 ounces of linseed oil. Bring to a boil over a brisk fire, stirring constantly, and stir in 2 ounces of pure white borate of manganese in very fine powder. Heat separately 8 pounds of linseed oil to the boiling point, and add it to the first solution in a thin stream, stirring constantly. Continue to heat the mixture as hot as possible without burning. Stir constantly and boil for half an hour. Take off the stove and strain through cheese cloth. Apply one or two coats while hot, and follow when dry with shellac or hard white copal varnish.

Or oil stains may be followed by ordinary shellac varnish with the addition of 4 ounces of cold-drawn linseed oil to each quart of varnish. One quart of varnish will be required for a floor 12 by 12 or about 150 square feet of surface.

To Clean Stained Floors.—Obtain a quantity of coarse sawdust of nonresinous wood free from dust or dirt, and store it in a bin where it will be kept dry and clean. Scatter this sawdust freely over the floor and scrub the floor with it by means of a stiff scrubbing brush, as if using water. The sawdust may then be swept up and burned, and the floor wiped up with a soft cloth drawn over the head of a broom. This is suitable treatment for unpainted, waxed, or varnished floors if much dirt has been tracked in upon them.

Or wring a mop out of kerosene oil and wipe up with this. Use about 1 quart for an ordinary floor. Use for this purpose only refined kerosene of the best quality, but do not use it freely on oak, as it tends to darken the wood.

Care of Oil-stained Floors. — An oil-stained floor will not soak up grease or show spots like a bare floor, and will not require scouring. It may be wiped up by means of a mop wrung out in clear warm water, but do not use soft soap, washing powders, or any alkali on an oiled surface, as the alkali will dissolve the oil. Oil-stained floors may be polished with wax or turpentine if desired.

Or the oil stain may be followed by one or more coats of hard white copal or shellac varnish before the wax is added.

To Clean Wood Floors.—Detergents recommended for cleaning kitchen floors and other coarse and unpainted woodwork are caustic potash and soda

"Clean a Small Section."

lyes, soft soap, sand, lime, chloride of lime, ammonia, kerosene, gasoline, and various mixtures of these.

To scrub a wood floor, first take up grease spots. Then apply hot soapsuds with a scrubbing brush or mop, rinse with clear water, and wipe dry. Clean and dry a small section of the floor at a time and change the water frequently.

Mops and Pails.—A strong pail fitted with a small wringer such as is used by janitors of large buildings will be found a great convenience. To save stooping, place this on a chair. Use two mops of soft woolen rags, one of small size for washing the floor, and a larger one for wiping dry.

Unpainted Floors.—An unpainted board floor, "white enough to eat off," as the homely saying goes, is very attractive, but requires a good deal of hard work. Our grandmothers used to cover unpainted floors with sand. Thus the family, in the process of walking to and fro, kept the floor boards scoured to a snowy whiteness. This is still a good way to whiten an unpainted board floor. Sprinkle the floor freely with clean

"A Pail with a Small Wringer."

white sand, and if there is no objection, let it remain a few days. Or the floor may be scoured with dry sand by means of a stiff scrubbing brush. The best sand for this purpose is obtained by purchasing marble clippings and heating them to redness in an old iron kettle or otherwise. When cold, they may be readily pulverized.

Or prepare a scouring mixture composed of 3 parts of sand, 2 parts of soft soap or soap jelly, and 1 part of lime. Apply with a stiff scrubbing brush, rinse with clear water, and rub dry with a flannel cloth. This has the additional advantage that it kills vermin.

Or mix equal parts of slaked lime and calcinated soda. Let stand about an hour and add eight times their weight of cold water. Place on the fire and bring to a boil. Wet the floor with this by means of a mop. Let stand over night to dry. Next morning scrub by means of a stiff brush with scouring sand and water.

Or moisten a thin flannel cloth with kerosene, draw it over the head of a broom, and wipe up the floor each day with this. It removes dust and grease, and thus obviates the necessity for scrubbing oftener than once every two or three weeks.

Or scatter sand over the floor and with an old whisk broom sprinkle upon the sand a solution of 1 pound of caustic potash or soda in 1 quart of water. Scrub with hot water and scrubbing brush, or mop, rinse, and dry.

Or apply soapsuds and sal soda.

Or dissolve unslaked lime in potash lye and apply with a mop.

Or add 1 tablespoonful of ammonia to a pail of water.

Or, for musty floors, use chloride of lime, ½ pound to a pailful of water.

Spots and Stains.—Scatter ground quartz-stone sand, or marble sand, over the stain. Pour over it a strong solution of caustic soda or potash at the rate of 1 pound to a pint of water, and scrub by means of a stiff bristle brush wet in soapsuds.

Or scour with a mixture of 1 part of chloride of lime and 3 parts of sand. This will bleach the boards and destroy vermin.

To remove whitewash, scrub with vinegar and water.

To remove mold, first scour with soap and sand, then sprinkle with chloride of lime. Pour on boiling water and scrub by means of a stiff brush.

To Remove Grease.—To prevent hot grease from sinking into the floor, sop cold water on it with a cloth to harden it. Scrape off what is on the surface with a dull knife. Remove the stain with a wet cloth sprinkled with baking soda.

Or mix equal parts of fuller's earth or pearlash to a paste with boiling water. Cover the grease spot, and let stand over night. Scour by means of a stiff brush with sand or other cleanser.

Or kill the grease by pouring turpentine over it and then scour as above.

Or cover the spot with slaked lime. Wet the lime and let it stand over night. Remove it and wash the spot with a cloth wet in soda and water.

Or sponge with gasoline, but take care not to work near a lighted stove. Greasy walls and other woodwork may first be rubbed with gasoline to kill the grease before washing them.

Or wash greasy paint with fresh slaked lime diluted to the consistency of milk. Let dry and rub off. Repeat if necessary.

Or sprinkle a grease spot with whiting, fuller's earth, or laundry starch. Lay blotting paper or brown paper over it and over that a hot flatiron. Let stand until cold. Repeat if necessary.

Or apply a paste of wood ashes and soap. Let stand over night, and wash off with soda and water. Repeat if necessary.

Or apply sand mixed with chloride of lime, and scrub with a stiff brush.

Or scrub with a mixture of powdered pumice stone and any strong washing powder.

To Remove Ink Spots from Floors.—If the ink contains coal-tar products, eosin or nigrosine, use a strong alkali, as caustic soda or potash; otherwise use a strong acid, as muriatic acid, vinegar, salts of lemon, or oxalic acid diluted with water.

Dissolve a solution of 1 part of oxalic acid and 10 parts of boiling water. Apply by means of a cloth, and afterwards rinse with water containing sal soda to neutralize the acid.

Or cover the ink spots with a paste of chloride of lime moistened with water.

Or scour out the ink spots with a solution of 1 part of sulphuric acid in 20 parts of water, applied by means of a stiff scrubbing brush with sand and water. Rinse with a strong solution of ammonia or sal soda in water.

CLEANING PAINT

To Clean Paint.—To clean paint and varnish, whiting, fuller's earth, cold tea, wood ashes, kerosene, soda, ammonia, turpentine, and bran water are all recommended. Do not use much soap or washing powders containing free alkali to clean paint, nor any soap at all to clean varnish. Soap tends to streak or to remove paint. Keep the water warm, but not hot, and change frequently. Use a flannel cloth or chamois, as cotton and similar goods leave lint, which sticks to the paint.

Or use outing flannel or flannelette.

Old underwear makes good wash cloths for woodwork. Moisture is good for woodwork, and hence it should be wiped off once a week with a damp cloth, and will be improved by a thorough washing several times a year. If woodwork is too dry, it tends to shrink. Hence it is important to wash woodwork for the sake of moisture as well as for the sake of cleanliness. Beware of recipes which call for soft soap, lye, and strong soapsuds to clean paint. They will remove the dirt, but in time will take the paint with it.

To Clean White Paint and Varnish.—To clean white and other delicate colored paints and varnish, moisten chamois or flannel cloth with warm water, dip it in whiting or fuller's earth, and rub over the surface gently. This will remove the dirt and leave the paint as bright as new. Rinse with clear water and dry with a soft cloth.

Fuller's earth is an excellent substitute for soap.

Or, for white paint, moisten a cloth in milk, dip it in whiting or fuller's earth, and apply.

Or, to wash varnish or delicate paint, use cold tea, with or without whiting or fuller's earth. Apply with flannel and rub until clean.

Or boil a pound of bran in a gallon of water and with it wash the paint. This will thoroughly clean the most delicate surfaces without injuring them.

To Clean Coarse Paint.—First go over it with a cloth dipped in kerosene to loosen the smoke and grime. Then rinse with ½ teacupful of kerosene in 1 gallon of water, and wipe dry with a soft cloth.

Or mix baking soda with water to form a thin paste. Smear the paint with this and wipe off with a cloth wrung out of clear warm water. Cover a small surface at a time and remove the soda before it dries.

Or wet a cloth in strong soda and water, wash the paint quickly, rinse with clear water, and dry at once. This should not be used on varnish or delicate paint. The cloth should be damp rather than wet.

Or mix 1 tablespoonful of ammonia with 1 quart or more of warm water for coarse or dirty woodwork. This saves labor and takes off the dirt, but should not be used on varnish or delicate painted surfaces.

Or dissolve 1 bar of hard white soap in 1 gallon of boiling water. Add 1 tablespoonful each of sal soda and saltpeter and 2 tablespoonfuls of ammonia. Bottle and cork tightly for future use.

Or mix 1 quart of sweet oil with 1 pint of turpentine and apply.

To Polish Woodwork.—Mix equal parts of lard oil and turpentine, or 2 parts of sweet oil to 1 part of turpentine, and rub the woodwork lightly with a cloth saturated with the mixture. This may be used on any painted surface after washing.

To Remove Smoke Stains.—To remove smoke stains, wet a cloth, dip it into very fine sifted wood or coal ashes, and scour the paint clean.

To Remove Match Stains.—To remove the marks left by scratching matches on paint, rub gently with a slice of fresh lemon and rinse with clear water, using a soft cloth.

To Remove Paint.—Detergents recommended for removing paint from woodwork are turpentine, benzine, gasoline, chloroform, oxalic acid, ether, alcohol, caustic potash, sal soda, and quicklime. When paint begins to check, it indicates that its ingredients were impure, and it must be removed.

To soften the paint, apply with a paint brush wood alcohol, spirits of turpentine, benzine, or a strong solution of equal parts of oxalic acid and water. Any of these will soften the paint so that it can be wiped off with a coarse cloth or scrubbed away. Repeat as often as necessary.

Or, if these do not soften the paint, apply chloroform, either alone or mixed with an equal quantity of spirits of ammonia. Moisten only a small surface, and scrape off the paint while moist before proceeding farther.

Or slake 3 pounds of quicklime, add 1 pound of potash, and dilute with water to the consistency of cream. Apply with a paint brush and let stand over night. Remove by washing the surface with a flannel cloth or mop dipped in a strong solution of sal soda and ammonia.

Or scrub with a stiff scrubbing brush.

Or dissolve a bar of hard yellow soap in twice its bulk of water. When cool, add 1 tablespoonful of potash lye and ½ cupful of kerosene. Before the mixture sets, apply to the woodwork with a paint brush. After 24 hours apply a strong solution of sal soda with a scrubbing brush.

Or paint may be burned off by going over the surface with a flat flame produced by a regular lamp made for that purpose, called a "paint burner."

Or apply a red-hot iron. Take care to remove the paint as soon as it is soft and before the wood is charred or burned.

To Remove Putty.—Go over the surface of the putty with a red-hot poker or other iron, taking care not to burn or char the woodwork. The putty can then be peeled off with a blunt knife blade.

Or with a brush apply a paste made of soap jelly containing caustic potash or soda.

Or apply dilute sulphuric, nitric, or muriatic acid with a brush. But if any of these soaks into the woodwork, it tends to rot the frames. Hence burning is the better method.

To Destroy the Odor of Paint.—Fill a pail partly full of hay and pour over it boiling water. Let it stand in the room which has been painted.

WHITEWASHING

Before applying whitewash, go over the wall or ceiling with a brush or dust cloth to remove dust, and wash with clear water. Fill all cracks and broken places with new plaster. Cut away the edges of broken places to make a square edge. Fill small cracks and breaks with plaster of Paris. Do not apply whitewash until the surface is quite dry. Give two or more coats as needed.

To Prepare Whitewash.—The principal ingredients in various kinds of whitewash are slaked lime, whiting, Paris white or sulphate of baryta, oxide and sulphate of zinc, alum, sugar, rice and wheat flour, and glue mixed with milk or water. These ingredients are used in various combinations. The addition of a little bluing will make a clearer white, and a small amount of salt assists by making the whitewash stick better.

The following mixtures are recommended:

Dissolve 2 ounces of fresh slaked lime in a small amount of milk to the consistency of cream. Add sufficient milk to make 2 quarts and stir in slowly 5 pounds of whiting. Mix the whole mass thoroughly by beating with a wooden spoon or an egg beater. For a clear white, add a little bluing. For a cream color, add a small amount of ocher, or tint with any other coloring matter as desired.

Or mix 4 pounds of Spanish whiting with cold water to the consistency of milk. Dissolve 2 ounces of pure white glue in hot water over a slow fire, and pour it into the whiting in a thin stream while hot, stirring thoroughly.

Or slake a sufficient amount of lime in water to make a pailful of whitewash, and while still hot stir in a pint of flour boiled with water to form a thin cooked starch. Stir well and dilute with hot water to the right consistency.

Or prepare a wash of slaked lime in a pail or tub and strain through cheese cloth. Mix 4 ounces of whiting or pulverized burnt alum, 2 pounds of sugar, and 2 quarts of rice flour with hot water and bring to a boil, stirring constantly. Add this mixture to 1 pailful of sifted lime wash. Add also 1 pound of best white glue dissolved in boiling water over a slow fire. This is a very brilliant and durable wash and will last for many years.

Or slake 8 quarts of lime, and add 1 pound of sulphate of zinc and ½ pound of common salt dissolved in water. This is a hard, firm wash that will not crack.

Or mix 6 pounds of Paris white with cold water to form a paste, and dilute with hot water to the consistency of milk. Stir in 4 ounces of the best white glue dissolved in boiling water over a slow fire. This is a cheap wash and gives a fine, brilliant surface.

To Color Whitewash.—For a fine clear white, add a little bluing.

For a reddish pink, add Spanish brown.

For a red stone color, mix common clay with Spanish brown.

For yellow, add yellow ocher (or chrome yellow, which goes farther and makes a better shade).

For gray or lead color, add lampblack.

For cream color, yellow ocher.

For stone color, 2 parts each of umber and lampblack.

For fawn color, 4 parts of umber, 2 parts of Indian red, and 1 part of lampblack.

Do not use green with whitewash.

The quantity of coloring matter required depends upon the amount of whitewash and the warmth of the tint desired, and must be determined by experiment, but approximately two or three pounds to a pailful of wash will be advisable.

Whitewash for Outdoor Use.—To make a good whitewash for fences, outbuildings, barns, stucco, and other surfaces exposed to the weather, slake 12 quarts of lime in a tight cask or barrel. Cover with canvas to keep in the steam. Strain through a large piece of cheese cloth or a fine sieve and add 2 quarts of coarse salt and 2 gallons of water. Bring this to a boil and skim off any impurities. Stir in 2 pounds of potash, 8 quarts of fine sand, and coloring matter as desired. This wash may be applied to wood, brick, or stone, looks as good as paint, and is weatherproof, fireproof, and very durable. It is an excellent preservative for shingle roofs and walls.

Or slake 8 quarts of lime in a tight cask or barrel, strain, and add 2 quarts of salt dissolved in hot water. Add boiling starch made of 2 pounds of rice flour. First mix the starch with cold water to a thin paste, dilute with hot water, and boil the mixture 15 minutes. Stir in while boiling hot. Then stir in 4 ounces of powdered whiting and 8 ounces of best white glue dissolved in hot water over a slow fire. Dilute with 3 gallons of hot water, stir vigorously, cover, and let stand 3 or 4 days. This mixture should cover 24 to 36 square yards of wood, brick, or stone. It may be used instead of oil paints, is much cheaper, and will last for years. It should be applied hot, which may be done by using a portable furnace or by suspending a kettle over a camp fire by means of three poles in the form of a tripod.

Or slake 8 quarts of lime, strain, and add 1 pound of dissolved glue and 1 or 2 quarts of boiled linseed oil. Dilute with water.

Or dissolve in hot water 4 quarts of water lime, 4 quarts of fresh-slaked lime, 4 pounds of powdered yellow ocher, and 4 pounds of burnt umber. This gives a rich cream color for fences, outhouses, and barns.

Wash for Bricks. — To make a wash for red brick walls, dissolve 2 ounces of glue in 1 gallon of water over a slow fire. Soaking the glue for a day or two beforehand will make it dissolve more quickly. Bring the glue to a boil and stir in 1 tablespoonful of powdered alum, ½ pound of Venetian red, and 1 pound of Spanish brown. Or vary these proportions according to taste. Mix and apply with a brush.

To Prepare Calcimine.—Dissolve with boiling water in separate kettles 10 pounds of Spanish whiting, 8 ounces of white glue, and 8 ounces of powdered alum. Use in each case enough water to make a thin cream. Pour together, stirring vigorously, strain through cheese cloth, and add 1 teaspoonful of bluing. Apply while warm. Add coloring matter to suit, and dilute with soap jelly to the right consistency. Remove paper, if any, wash off old calcimine or lime, fill holes or cracks with plaster of Paris, and apply a sizing of glue or shellac.

Mix calcimine with any coloring matter desired and apply the same as whitewash.

Blue Wash for Walls and Ceilings.—Dissolve 1 pound of blue vitriol and 8 ounces of whiting in 3 quarts of water. Boil with gentle heat 2 or 3 hours, stirring frequently. Remove from the fire, stir, and allow to cool. Pour the liquor from the sediment, mix the latter with 1 ounce of common glue dissolved in 1 gallon of water, and apply with a brush.

To Paint Frescoes.—To paint in fresco consists in applying colors not injured by lime to the fresh mortar, stucco, or plaster while still damp. The advantage of this sort of painting is that it incorporates with the mortar, dries with it, and is very durable. Frescoes may be applied in any design, free hand or by means of stencil. Or the walls may be painted in fresco with tints or solid colors.

Glazing for Frescoes.—To protect frescoes, dilute paraffin with benzol, and apply a thin coating with a brush.

PAPER HANGING

To Remove Wall Paper.—To prepare a wall for fresh treatment, whether by painting, calcimining, or hanging fresh paper, first remove any paper that may be on the walls. Never lay one paper over another. The germ of disease, eggs of vermin, and other obnoxious matter are not to be gotten rid of by this process. Wet the walls with boiling water applied with a whitewash brush, and remove the paper with a hand scraper or a large case knife or wide-bladed putty knife. Do not allow the scrapings to harden on the floor, as when dry they are very difficult to remove. After the paper is off, wash down the walls with pure water or strong soda water or vinegar and water applied with a large sponge or brush. Let them dry thoroughly before treating.

To Repair Plaster. — To repair cracks formed in plaster by the settling of new houses, the sagging of old houses, the decay of ceilings and floor timbers, and accidental breaks in the plaster, first cut away the edges of the cracks or breaks with a sharp knife. Make the edge straight or slightly slanting in. Then fill with plaster of Paris mixed with water, to which may be added vinegar, flour paste, or sand.

Or fill with paper pulp moistened with glue.

To mend small breaks, mix plaster of Paris with cold water and apply quickly with a case knife, smoothing the plaster as you apply it. Mix a small quantity at a time and work quickly, as the plaster hardens very fast.

Or to prevent plaster of Paris from hardening quickly, when repairing larger breaks that take more material and more time, mix 1 tablespoonful of plaster of Paris with 2 or 3 tablespoonfuls of fine sand and dilute with vinegar. The more vinegar used, the slower the plaster will set.

Or mix plaster of Paris with an equal quantity of cold flour paste.

Or to mend large cracks and breaks, soak bits of wall paper to a pulp with water, squeeze out the water, and mix to a stiff paste or jell with thin size or glue made by dissolving 1 ounce of good glue in 1 pint of hot water over a slow fire. Pour the whole on cheese cloth to remove the excess of water. Press the paper pulp into the cracks and holes in the plaster with a putty knife. But do not quite fill the crack to the surface of the plaster, as the pulp does not admit of a smooth surface. When nearly dry, smooth the surface with plaster of Paris and let dry before tinting or repapering. The paper pulp when hard is as strong as wood, and cracks filled in this manner will never reopen.

Size for Paper Hanging.—To prepare walls for paper hanging, first remove old paper, mend cracks and breaks, and wash down the walls with a cloth or sponge wet in warm water. Then apply with a whitewash brush a solution of 4 ounces of common glue dissolved in 1 gallon of boiling water over a slow fire. Or apply a good shellac size.

Paste for Paper Hanging. — See "Adhesives" elsewhere in this volume.

To Hang Wall Paper.—First trim close to the pattern the plain strip on one edge of the paper, but not the other. Next measure the height of the room by holding an end of the paper up to the ceiling and marking along the baseboard with any blunt instrument. Cut along this mark and use the first strip as a pattern. Cut a sufficient number of additional strips for the plain walls, making allowances for doors and windows. Lay the strips face down on a large table, or make a suitable bench by laying old boards

"Lay the Strips on a Table."

across a couple of chair backs or barrels. Apply the paste with a whitewash brush. If the paper is heavy, let it lie after pasting until it is slightly soaked with the paste, or until the surface is sticky rather than wet. Commence at a door or window and place the close-cut edge against the frame. First press the upper end against the ceiling and press downward with a clean cloth. Place the next strip so that the close-cut edge will overlie the half-inch strip left upon the first strip, and so proceed until the room is finished.

But remember that all heavy-weight papers in solid colors, as ingrain, duplex, or cartridge papers, and most cloth or fabric wall coverings, must be "butted" rather than overlapped. That is, the edges must be placed close enough together to cover the wall, but without overlapping each other.

To fit around doors, window casings, and other jogs, cut and paste a full strip, apply it to the wall at the ceiling, and press with a cloth down to the top of the door or window frame and along the side of the adjacent wall. Press carefully up to the frame and cut along the edge with a sharp knife to take out the section of paper which comes over the door or window. It will assist to clip diagonally with shears toward the corner of the opening, taking care not to clip too far, although the diagonal clipping, if it extends into the paper on the wall, may be concealed by carefully bringing the edges together.

To Paper a Rough Wall.—To paper old walls of boards, planks, or wainscoting without plaster, or sanded walls that have not been "skimmed" with plaster or lime, or other rough surfaces, it may be necessary to first hang a layer of cotton cloth to furnish a smooth surface on which to hang paper. The difficulty of hanging paper on a rough surface is that the paper, being stiff, does not yield to the depressions in the wall. Hence air spaces are left that cause the paper to blister and peel off. The advantages of using cloth are that it is flexible, that it takes up more paste than paper does, and hence that it adheres more closely to the wall. It affords a smooth and suitable surface on which to hang paper, and gives the final result a good appearance. First go over rough surfaces with sandpaper. Tack this to a large block of wood, into which, to avoid using a stepladder, insert an old broom handle.

Next apply liberally to the walls hot boiled flour or other suitable paste containing a tablespoonful of borax to each gallon of water. Cover with paste one strip at a time, and immediately hang on the wet wall any suitable cotton stuff. Unbleached cotton sheeting or cheese cloth answers this purpose; or old sheets, pillowcases, and the like may be utilized. After hanging the cloth, brush it down with a whitewash brush dipped in the hot paste, and allow it to dry. Then hang the wall paper in the usual manner.

To Paint Rough Walls.—To obtain a suitable surface for painting or tinting in colors on rough boards, sanded walls, stucco, or other rough surfaces, first apply a layer of cotton cloth as above and hang a cheap, light-colored wall paper. When dry, pare off with a potato knife the seams in the paper caused by overlapping the edges, running the sharp edge down the seam from top to bottom, or use carefully an old razor for this purpose. Apply two or three coats of paint and white varnish alternately, allowing one to dry before putting on the next. The varnish will prevent the paint from becoming soiled, and the surface will last a lifetime.

To Paint a Whitewashed Wall.—Scrape off the loose lime with any blunt-edged tool. A hoe is convenient. Go over the wall with sandpaper tacked to a large block of wood and fastened to a handle. Wash with a sponge to remove the lime and let dry. Fill cracks and breaks with plaster of Paris. They will be concealed by the paint. Do not use putty for this purpose, as that when dry would have a different-looking surface. Apply one or two coats of shellac or glue size, 3 or 4 ounces of either to a gallon of boiling water. Cover with any suitable paint and varnish.

CARE OF WALLS

To Clean Wall Paper.—Brush down the walls with a hairbrush or dust cloth, then cut a loaf of yeast bread two or three days old once vertically through the middle, and again crosswise. Hold these pieces by the crust and rub the wall downward with long, light strokes. Do not rub across the paper, or rub harder than is necessary. An ordinary coarse grater held in the left hand will be found convenient to rub off the surface of the bread as it becomes soiled. Clean thoroughly as you go.

Or make a stiff dough of rye flour and water and apply in the same manner. The dough should be stiff enough not to stick to the hands or to the paper. Take a piece as large as the fist, dip it in dry corn meal, and use until it becomes soiled. Change as often as necessary.

Or make a similar stiff dough of wheat flour and water. Afterwards brush down the walls with a clean soft brush or dust cloth to remove the crumbs.

To Remove Grease from Wall Paper.—To remove grease and oil stains from wall paper, fold a piece of blotting paper, and in the fold spread pipe clay or French chalk. Stitch or pin the edges together to keep the chalk from falling out. Lay this over the grease spot and apply a hot iron, taking care not to scorch the paper. Change the blotting paper occasionally, and, if necessary, repeat with a fresh iron.

Or make a thick paste of powdered pipe clay or French chalk and apply it to the spot with a brush. Let it remain until dry. Then brush off and repeat if necessary.

To Dust Walls.—To remove dust from walls, use a clean hairbrush or window brush with a suitable handle. Brush from the top downward.

Or make a bag to cover the head of the broom.

Or draw a sleeve or leg of a suit of old knit underwear over the head of the broom. Put the broom handle through the large part and draw it well down over the broom. The downward motion of the broom on the wall will hold the cloth tightly in place.

Or crumple an old paper bag in the hands, but without tearing it, and slip it over the head of the broom. This can be removed and burned after using.

Or insert into a clean mop handle a suitable dust cloth, as several thicknesses of cheese cloth or discarded cotton or woolen underwear, and sweep down the walls with this.

To Mend Wall Paper.—To patch a spot knocked out of the wall paper, or holes in exposed cracks or edges, take a piece of paper to match the pattern and expose to the sun until it fades to the same shade. Cut a patch an inch or two larger than the broken place, lay it face down on a piece of glass, moisten it with a suitable paste, and when moist scrape or pare the edge with a sharp knife or old razor to a very fine slant or bevel.

Lay on a fresh coat of paste, especially around the edge, and apply the patch so as to match the design. Rub the edges down with gentle strokes of a soft cloth, and if done skillfully the patch will not be noticeable.

Or, if spots are too small to patch, obtain, for a few cents, a child's box of water colors, mix the colors to obtain the right shade, and paint the spots with a small camel's-hair brush. A 25-cent box of colors will last a long time, and a little practice will enable anyone to match the colors and keep the wall paper in good order. Faded spots left on solid-colored wall papers by the removal of pictures may be renovated by painting them with dyestuff. Select a color as near that of the paper as possible, follow the directions that come with the dye, and apply to the wall with a brush. Care must be taken not to let the dye drip on floor coverings or furniture. When first applied, the painted spot will be darker than the rest, but it will quickly dry to its proper tint or shade.

To Clean Calcimined Walls.—Rub on corn meal with a coarse cloth, or moisten a soft cloth or sponge in aqua ammonia and rub spots very lightly.

To Renovate Blackened Walls.—A smoked or blackened ceiling or wall may be cleaned by means of a cloth wrung out of a strong solution of baking soda and water. Or use vinegar and water. If the stain is not all removed, dissolve gum shellac in alcohol to the consistency of milk or cream and with it cover the sooty parts. Paint or whitewash over the shellac. The black will not show through.

To Dry Walls that Are Damp.—If there is much dampness in a room that is not commonly heated, it may cause the walls to mold or mildew, besides being unhealthy. To absorb the dampness, place unslaked lime in flat, open vessels, as dripping pans, plates, or saucers. Lime has an affinity for dampness and also purifies the air. Renew the lime as fast as it becomes air-slaked and crumbles into a fine, dry powder.

Walls are often damp for no apparent cause. Brick and other porous walls may hold moisture, or it may work up from springs through the foundations of brick or stone houses. The causes should be sought and, if possible, removed.

To prepare damp walls for calcimine or paper, make a size of 1 ounce of glue to 1 gallon of water, and add 4 ounces of alum and 4 ounces of boiled linseed oil. Apply one or two coats and let dry before papering.

Or apply with a whitewash brush, during summer when the wall is dryer, a solution of 1 pound of castile or other hard white soap in 1 gallon of water. Let stand a day or two to dry. Follow with a second coat of ½ pound of alum in a pailful of water, and let dry before papering.

Or, if the walls are very damp, apply thin sheet lead or tin foil to the walls with a suitable cement. Or fasten with flat-headed copper tacks. These may be driven into the damp spots only or, if necessary, into the entire wall. Afterwards paper.

To Remove Mold from Walls.—To remove mold or mildew from walls or ceilings, apply with a whitewash brush a solution of 1 pound of chloride of lime dissolved in a pailful of water.

To prevent dampness when building, after the walls are a few feet above the ground lay a row of stone or brick with a mixture of tar pitch and fine sand in place of mortar.

WINDOWS, DOORS, ETC.

To Clean Windows.—Do not use soapsuds on windows. The soap adheres and requires a good deal of rinsing to remove. The easiest way to clean windows is with a chamois or clean cloth and clear water. Wring out the chamois or cloth so as to be wet but not dripping, and wash the windows clean. Afterwards wring dry and go over them again. Finally polish with a dry cloth or chamois. Rinse

"Clean Windows with a Chamois."

the cloth and change the water as often as necessary.

Or, if the windows are much soiled, use a little washing soda, but do not let water containing soda drip or stain the paint on the sash. Wash one pane at a time and wipe with a dry cloth. Or add a little gasoline to the water. This cleans quickly and gives a high polish.

Or add 1 tablespoonful of kerosene or ammonia to 1 quart of water.

Or, if the windows are not much soiled, wet them with a soft cloth dampened with kerosene or ammonia water, and wipe with a dry cloth.

Or mix a little dry starch with cold water to the consistency of cream, and wash the windows with this, leaving it to dry on. When dry, rub it off with a damp newspaper. This gives a high polish without lint or streaks.

To Remove Paint.—To remove paint spots from windows, soften them with hot, strong vinegar, and rub a copper or silver coin over them to loosen the paint.

To Remove Putty.—To remove putty, go over it with a red-hot poker or other hot iron, taking care not to touch the paint on the window sashes. When the putty is hot, slip a dull knife blade between it and the woodwork and it will readily come off. Any other method that will remove putty is likely to injure the paint on the sashes.

Or apply two or three coats of paraffin oil by means of a small brush, allowing each coat a half hour or more to penetrate before the next one is applied.

Or apply soft soap freely by means of a brush. In a short time the hardened linseed oil is dissolved, making the putty plastic, so that it can be readily removed.

Window Corners. — Use a whisk broom to dig out the corners of the window sash, or use wings of turkeys, geese, or chickens. These are also good to wash windows, as they are free from dust and lint.

Or use a piece of whalebone or a skewer to clean out the corners of the sash.

To Polish Windows. — Polish windows with dry chamois or tissue paper or an old newspaper slightly moistened.

Or apply with a moistened rag powdered indigo, pumice stone, or fuller's earth, and polish.

Or fold a piece of cheese cloth and put a quantity of pulverized pumice stone between the folds, stitching around the edge to keep the powder from spilling. Polish chimneys and window panes with this prepared cloth. It gives a high polish instantly, and will last a long time.

Or with a soft cloth rub a little vinegar on the glass. Rub dry and polish.

To Prevent Windows from Steaming. — After cleaning the glass, rub over it a rag slightly moistened with glycerin.

Windows—To Keep Out the Sun.— Make a paste of powdered gum tragacanth and white of egg. Beat with an egg beater and let it stand twenty-four hours. Apply with a soft brush and let dry.

To Clean Mirrors. — Mix a little powdered bluing, whiting, or pumice stone with alcohol to form a thin paste. Smear the surface of the mirror with this by means of a small sponge or soft rag, and before the alcohol evaporates rub it dry with a clean cloth. Afterwards polish with silk, chamois, or tissue paper.

Or wring a cloth or chamois out of clear water, dip in dry whiting, and apply. Rub with a dry cloth or chamois and polish.

Or apply whiting mixed with tea to form a thin paste. Use clear tea to remove stains.

Or wring a newspaper as you would a cloth out of cold water, so that it will be damp but not wet. Rub the glass with this, and afterwards dry with a fresh newspaper softened by crumpling it in the hands.

To Polish Mirrors. — Use a dry chamois or pumice bag, or a silk handkerchief, or tissue paper, or apply powdered chalk or whiting with any of these. Or use a dry cloth slightly moistened with a few drops of aqua ammonia.

To Support Window Sashes. — To support window sashes not provided with sash lines and pulleys, obtain a number of ordinary bottle corks and a bit or an auger of the same size. Bore three or four holes in the side of the sash and insert a piece of cork in each of these, letting it project just enough to rub against the groove of the window frame. The elasticity of the corks will admit of the window being raised, but the pressure will be sufficient to support the sash at any desired height. Renew the corks as often as necessary.

To Lubricate Window Sashes.—To lubricate a window sash that rubs or swells in damp weather so that it cannot be raised and lowered readily, slush freely with common yellow soap the edge of the sash and the groove in which it runs. This may be done by moistening the soap and rubbing it over the parts, or by dissolving the soap in its own bulk of water, and applying the soap jelly with a brush.

Or use a wax candle instead of soap.

To Prevent Window Sashes from Rattling.—A half of a clothespin will cure temporarily the rattling of a window sash.

To Restore Window Glass.—To restore the transparency of window glass that has become dingy by exposure to the elements, rub with dilute muriatic acid, 1 part of acid to 10 parts of water, and polish with a moist cloth dipped in whiting.

To Keep Doors Open.—Cover a common red brick with cretonne, carpet, or any suitable material to match the floor covering, and have a number of these weights about the house to place against the doors and keep them open.

To Prevent Doors from Creaking.—Dip a feather in oil and apply to the hinges.

Or rub on a piece of soap.

Or mix equal parts of soap, lard, and black lead, and apply with the point of a lead pencil or in melted form by means of a small brush.

Burglar-proof Lock. — Lock the door, leave the key in the lock, and keep it there by means of a heavy copper wire 11 inches long bent in the shape of a hairpin. Put this over the spindle back of the knob, with the ends down through the head of the key. The key cannot then be pushed out or turned by a burglar's tool or another key inserted from the outside. This is a convenient device for a traveler to use in hotels, where duplicate keys are often issued to servants and others.

Or one end of the wire may be fastened to the casement by means of a staple, and the other end formed into a hook to hold the key in position.

Or an ordinary hook may be used for this purpose.

Skeleton Key.—Obtain from a locksmith a skeleton key similar to the keys used by burglars and furnished to employees of hotels whose duties require them to have admission to all the rooms. This will be exceedingly convenient when other keys are lost or mislaid.

To Fit Keys.—To fit an old key or a blank to replace a key that has been lost, hold the key to be fitted in the flame of a candle until it is thoroughly blackened, insert it carefully in the lock, and turn it until it strikes the wards. Withdraw the key and file away the parts where the soot has been rubbed off by the wards.

CLEANING AND CARE OF FURNITURE

To Clean Furniture. — Furniture, like other woodwork, tends to shrink if it becomes too dry, and should be washed for the sake of moisture as well as for the sake of cleanliness. Hence furniture, besides being cleaned, when necessary, with suitable cleansing compounds, should be sponged occasionally with clear water and wiped dry.

But do not use soap or washing powders on painted or varnished furniture. Remove dirt, dust, and stains with other cleansing agents, and rinse by sponging with clear water. Wipe dry, oil, and polish. Detergents recommended for cleaning furniture, removing finger marks, white spots, and stains are olive, sweet, linseed, paraffin, and other oils; whiting, fuller's earth, cold tea, kerosene, turpentine, soda, essence of peppermint, camphor, asphaltum, vinegar, various acids, and combinations of these.

To Wash Furniture.—To wash furniture, use a large sponge, wipe dry, and polish dry as possible with a chamois skin wrung out of clear water, or with a soft flannel cloth. Do not use dry chamois on varnished wood or polished surfaces. Wipe always in one direction, preferably with the grain of the wood.

Wash carved wood with a stiff hair paint brush dipped in clear water.

Or wash with cold tea applied with a sponge or brush, wipe dry, oil, and polish.

Care of Furniture.—To keep polished or varnished furniture in good order, each article should be gone over lightly once a week on cleaning day with clear hot (not boiling) water without soap, or with cold tea, or any other suitable cleanser.

Or, if there is not time for this, after dusting the furniture, rub it over with a cloth moistened with kerosene, turpentine, cold tea, or cold-drawn linseed oil, or with a mixture of equal parts of these. This practice will assist in keeping it in good order.

To Remove Finger Marks.—Moisten a flannel cloth in olive, linseed, sweet, or paraffin oil to remove the spots. Wipe dry, and polish with flannel or a chamois skin wrung out of clear water. For oiled furniture use kerosene.

To Remove White Marks.—To remove white marks on furniture caused by heat or water, hold a hot iron near them, but not near enough to burn or scorch.

Or rub with a cloth moistened with kerosene.

Or with a cloth apply equal parts of linseed oil and alcohol.

Or, if the stain is obstinate, cover with baking soda and hold a hot iron close to the spot, taking care not to scorch or burn the wood. Repeat if necessary.

Or apply olive oil or sweet oil, and polish with a cloth moistened in alcohol.

Or apply essence of peppermint with a cloth. Wipe dry and polish.

Or use a mixture composed of equal parts of vinegar, sweet oil, and turpentine.

Or rub with a cloth wet in spirits of camphor or camphorated oil or turpentine.

Or use a cloth saturated with any of these.

After using any of the above, wipe the spot dry, apply furniture oil, and polish with damp chamois or silk or linen cloth. Do not allow alcohol, turpentine, camphor, or similar detergents to remain on a polished surface.

To Remove Ink Stains.—To remove ink stains, first test the ink by applying water to see if it contains coal-tar products, as eosin or nigrosine. If these are present the ink when wet will run. In that case use an alkali, as baking soda mixed with water to form a paste, and let it dry on. Repeat if necessary.

Or, if water does not cause the ink to run, it is probably an iron-gall or logwood ink; hence apply an acid, preferably oxalic acid, dissolved in an equal quantity of water. Saturate a cloth with the solution and lay it on the spot to soften the ink. Then wash with the solution until the ink disappears.

Or apply salts of lemon.

Or a mixture of 6 parts of spirits of salt (diluted hydrochloric acid) and 1 part of salts of lemon.

Or use 1 part of nitric, muriatic, or sulphuric acid diluted with 10 parts of water. Apply by dipping a cork in the mixture and touching the stain, or by means of a feather.

But remember that all of these acids are *poisonous,* and that all except oxalic acid will burn or blister the skin. Also, if used in too great strength, they will remove paint and varnish and themselves stain the surfaces they are applied to. Hence use no more acid than is necessary and immediately sponge off with clear water containing a little ammonia, wipe dry, oil, and polish.

To Remove Bruises from Furniture.—To renovate furniture that has been bruised or scratched without injuring the fiber of the wood, apply moisture and heat. Wet a cloth in warm water, not hot, and lay it over the parts. Hold near a hot iron, but not near enough to scorch or char the wood. Repeat until the bruise comes up. If the varnish is discolored, apply any of the above remedies.

Or use, instead of cloth, several thicknesses of brown paper moistened in water.

Or, if the bruise is small, omit the cloth or paper. Wet the spot and hold near it a hot iron. Then lay over the scratched or bruised surface a cloth dipped in linseed oil. Finally rub with a mixture of equal parts of turpentine and linseed oil, and polish.

Oils for Wood Furniture.—Furniture polish containing oil or wax will not be needed if the wood is washed occasionally with clear warm water, not hot, without soap, and rubbed dry with chamois or a soft cloth. But if furniture polish containing

"Oil Must Be Rubbed In."

fixed oils is used the furniture must be rubbed vigorously and kept in condition by daily rubbing to prevent oil accumulating so as to be felt or seen. Furniture oil should be sparingly used and the wood rubbed to a high polish or until it does not have any greasy feel.

Soap for Furniture.—Soap should not be used on wood finished with shellac or varnish or treated with furniture wax or oil. Soap has the property of destroying oily and resinous substances, and thus tends to eat away the coating, destroy the polish, and expose the wood.

To Remove Furniture Scratches.—Go over the articles with a soft rag dampened in kerosene oil. This will cause all light scratches or surface bruises to disappear.

Or, if the scratches or cracks are deep, melt a little beeswax, and thin out with turpentine to the consistency of sirup. Apply with a soft cloth, and polish with flannel or velveteen.

To Restore the Color of Furniture.—Apply raw linseed oil by means of a flannel cloth to restore the color, and let stand over night.

Or, for highly polished surfaces, as rosewood or mahogany, apply a cloth moistened with alcohol. Afterwards polish with a soft cloth moistened with turpentine.

Linseed Oil for Furniture.—Apply raw linseed oil as a restorer, with or without an equal quantity of turpentine.

Care of Piano.—The back of the piano should be protected by a dust cloth of denim or other suitable material tacked or pasted lightly to the frame. In moist climate the wires will be protected from rust by sprinkling them with unslaked lime. The keys should be wiped with alcohol once a week on cleaning day to prevent them from yellowing, and the varnish may be kept in good condition by wiping once a week with a chamois wrung out of cold or warm water, or by wiping with a cloth moistened with turpentine, kerosene, or cold-drawn linseed oil, or a mixture of these.

To Clean Pianos.—A careful inquiry by a dealer in pianos from the largest factories in the United States discloses the fact that there is no better means of cleaning a polished piano or any other highly polished furniture than to simply wash it in lukewarm water, drying each part perfectly by rubbing briskly as fast as it is washed. This method is as safe as it is simple. It leaves the polish absolutely uninjured.

To Clean Piano Keys.—Remove stains with oxalic acid and keep the keys white by rubbing with a soft piece of cloth wet with alcohol or with cologne water. Expose the keys to sunshine on bright, sunny days to bleach them.

Cleaner for Musical Instruments.—To clean guitars, violins, etc., mix equal quantities of linseed oil, turpentine, and water. Shake well before using to form an emulsion or cream. Rub the instrument with a cloth dampened in this cream, wipe dry, and polish with woolen cloth, chamois, or velveteen.

To Clean Cane Chairs and Wicker, Bamboo, and Rattan Furniture.—First blow the dust out of the crevices with a pair of bellows or a good-sized bellows or bicycle pump. This will greatly assist in cleaning. Make a suds by dissolving half a bar of white soap in a gallon or more of water and add half a cupful of common salt. This will prevent the cane from turning yellow. Apply the suds to the chair with a scrubbing brush, first one side and then the other, using plenty of water so that the cane may be thoroughly soaked. Place it out of doors to dry in a shady place. This will make the cane firm and tight and renew its elasticity.

To Bleach Willow Furniture.—To bleach willow furniture, make a suds as above and add 2 ounces of bleaching powder.

To Renovate Cane Chairs.—When the cane bottoms of chairs wear out, buy new cane and learn to weave cane seats. This is a simple art which may be easily learned by anyone, experimenting with the cane of an old chair and by a little practice.

CLEANING PICTURE FRAMES

To Protect Gilt Picture Frames.—Brush gilt frames with water in which onions have been boiled—three or four to a pint. Also wash the glass with it. Onion water will not injure the frames, and will prevent flies from lighting upon the picture.

Or, after dusting, go over the frames lightly with a soft flannel cloth moistened in kerosene.

Or give them a coat of clear parchment size. This will prevent the dirt from darkening the gilt. The size may be sponged with cold water or oil of turpentine, and left to dry without wiping.

Or give the frames when new a coat of white varnish. This may be washed with clear cold water.

Or wash soiled gilt frames with a gill of vinegar dissolved in a pint of cold water and applied with a soft brush.

Or stir into a quart of water enough powdered sulphur to give it a slightly yellow tinge, and in this water boil four or five sliced onions. Strain and apply with a soft brush to soiled gilt frames.

Or to 3 ounces of white of egg add 1 ounce of chloride of potassium or soda and beat up together. Dust the frame with a soft brush, and brush over them with the above mixture.

Or apply well-beaten white of egg with a camel's-hair brush and wipe off with a soft flannel cloth. But rub with the cloth very little and very lightly.

Or wash with alcohol or spirits of turpentine, using a soft sponge, and let dry without wiping.

All picture frames should be treated with one of the above preparations several times during the spring and summer.

Or cover the frames with oiled tarlatan, which may be obtained ready oiled for this purpose.

Or brush boiled linseed oil over ordinary tarlatan. This is excellent for keeping dust from books, bric-a-brac, and various other objects.

Apply alcohol to fly spots and other stains with a camel's-hair brush to soften them, and wipe off the frame with a soft chamois or flannel cloth. Do not use linen for this purpose, as it deadens the brightness of the gilding.

To Renovate Gilt Frames.—Apply gilt paint with a camel's-hair brush to spots where the gilding has come off so as to expose the wood.

Or if the bit of gilding that has come off can be found and is large enough, moisten the spot with glue and replace it, bringing it up to a level by means of putty if necessary. Let dry and go over it with gold paint.

To Clean Gilt Ornaments.—Make a strong solution of cyanide of potassium. But remember that this is a *deadly poison.* Apply with a stiff brush, or dip the articles in this solution. Afterwards rinse with water, using a soft brush, and dry in boxwood or other hard-wood shavings. These may be obtained of any jeweler. Store away gilt articles in boxwood shavings to keep them from tarnishing.

Or clean them with a lather of soft white soap, rinsing with clear water.

To Clean Silver Ornaments.—Make a suds by dissolving hard white soap in boiling water, immerse the articles, and boil for five minutes. Remove and scrub gently with a soft brush, rinse in clear boiling water, and wipe dry with a soft cloth. Lay them near the fire until the moisture has perfectly evaporated, or cover them with boxwood sawdust until fully dried.

To Preserve Oil Paintings.—Apply two or three coats of pure white-lead paint to the back of the canvas. This preserves the canvas from damp, mold, and mildew, and makes it practically indestructible. Many ancient canvases treated in this way have been preserved for centuries. The same process will strengthen a decaying canvas.

To Clean Oil Paintings.—To clean an oil painting, wash the surface gently with clear warm water, using a soft cloth or fine sponge, let dry, and rub gently with a soft flannel cloth moistened with pure olive oil. The water softens the accumulated smoke, dust, and dirt, and the oil assists in wiping it away.

Or wash with milk diluted with warm water, and dry without rinsing.

Or cut a potato in half and rub gently with the fresh surface, slicing off the soiled portions, until the whole is cleansed.

The practice of covering the surface of paintings with soft soap or other alkaline lyes is a very mischievous one. If the paintings are of any value, they should be cleaned only by an expert.

To Clean Prints.—Fasten the print to a board by means of thumb tacks, cover with fine common salt, and moisten the salt slightly with lemon juice. Turn the board at an angle and pour boiling water over the surface until the salt and lemon juice are washed off. Dry gradually in the shade.

Or, to remove yellow stains from engravings, dissolve hydrochloride of soda in water. Moisten a cloth with this solution and lay over the stain until it is removed. Rinse with clear water.

To Restore White in Oil Paintings.—To renovate old oil paintings in which the whites have become dark by the action of the air on paints containing carbonate of lead or other lead compounds, apply, by means of a soft brush, water charged with four or five volumes of oxygen. Afterwards let dry and go over the painting with copal varnish.

To Mend Gilt Frames.—To replace on gilt frames ornaments that have been broken off and lost, melt together with gentle heat 1 pound of rosin, ½ pint of linseed oil, and ½ gill of Venetian turpentine. Dissolve separately ½ pound of glue in 2 quarts of water and mix the two solutions. Boil and stir constantly until the water is evaporated, leaving a thick mass, to which add powdered whiting until the whole is of the consistency of putty. Mold to the desired shape while warm, and when cold it will set and harden. Color with gilt paint.

To Clean Wood Frames.—First dust with a soft brush, and afterwards wipe with flannel dipped in sweet oil.

To Renovate Old Gilt Frames.—Gilt frames that are past retouching with gilt paint may be renovated by removing the gilding with fine sandpaper or rubbing down the surface with a moistened cloth dipped in powdered pumice or rotten stone. Paint with black or other color of enamel paint or any desired stain, and afterwards apply a coat of copal or any hard white varnish.

CLEANING BRIC-A-BRAC AND MISCELLANEOUS OBJECTS

To Clean Brass Furniture.—Brass bedsteads and brass fittings on furniture may be cleaned by moistening a cloth in sweet oil and dipping it in powdered whiting or rotten stone pulverized finely and sifted through cheese cloth.

Or mix finely powdered tripoli with linseed oil. Apply with a sponge or rag, and polish with a piece of felt or velveteen.

Or moisten a cloth in ammonia and dip in powdered whiting.

To Clean Brass Inlaid Work.—Mix equal quantities of rotten stone, starch, and oxalic acid with water to a stiff paste and dilute with sweet oil. Apply with a piece of felt or velveteen, and polish with a flannel rag or moistened chamois.

To Clean Bric-a-Brac.—Brass ornaments on bric-a-brac may be cleaned with a piece of stale bread. Hold the bread by the crust and rub carefully, allowing the crumbs to fall with the dirt. Brass candlesticks, lamps, and the like may be cleaned with soap and water, but lacquered articles require careful treatment without soap.

To Clean Bronzes. — Genuine bronzes may be washed with good soapsuds and a sponge or rag, and wiped dry with a soft flannel cloth or chamois.

Or dirt and stains may first be removed with a flannel cloth moistened in sweet oil; afterwards polish with flannel or chamois.

To Clean Mother-of-Pearl.—Rub with a cheese-cloth bag containing dry pumice, or apply finely powdered pumice moistened with sweet oil, and polish with a piece of felt or velveteen.

To Clean Upholstered Furniture.—In cities the pneumatic cleaning machine removes all dust and dirt from upholstered furniture with little labor, but where this is not available take the furniture out of doors and freely apply gasoline or naphtha. Pour these on so as to saturate the upholstered parts, and rub vigorously with a soft hair brush, sponge, or flannel cloth dipped in warm gasoline until all spots and soiled places are fully cleaned. Keep the furniture out of doors in a draught until the cleanser evaporates. This process will also destroy moths.

To Clean Brick or Stone Work.—Mop with a solution of caustic potash or soda with oxalic acid dissolved in water. Or pour the mixture over the surfaces and scrub with a scrubbing brush, but do not dip the hands in this mixture and do not use it too strong.

To Clean Ivory.—For cleaning ivory, use prepared chalk, lime, brick dust, turpentine, lemon juice, salt and vinegar, lime, potash, and alum.

Ivory ornaments, brooches, card cases, bracelets, carvings, piano keys, and the like may be cleaned by painting them over with spirits of turpentine and, when possible, exposing them for two or three days to sunshine. Or articles that can be taken out of doors may be bleached by simply moistening them with water and exposing them to direct sunshine.

Or dissolve slaked lime in water to the consistency of milk. Cover the articles with this, or dip them in it if convenient, and steep as long as may be necessary. Remove them, allow the slaked lime to dry on, and when dry rub off and polish with a dry cloth.

Or apply salt and lemon juice. Polish with whiting. Apply with a moist cloth and rub with a chamois.

If small ivory articles are badly stained and discolored, first soak them for 24 hours or longer in a solution of 1 part of baking soda to 4 parts of water. Rinse, and immerse in a solution of 1 part of sulphite of soda to 3 parts of water for another day or 2. Finally add to the latter solution 1 ounce of hydrochloric acid diluted with 6 ounces of water, and allow the articles to stand in this for 2 or 3 days. Wash in clean water, dry, and polish.

To Clean Bric-a-Brac.—For deep, narrow-necked flower vases, rose bowls, or carafes, cut some potato parings in small squares and pour over them water in which baking soda has been dissolved. Put them into the glasses to be cleaned, let stand a few minutes, and shake well. Afterwards wash in soapsuds and polish.

Or use 3 tablespoonfuls of vinegar to 1 of rice. Shake well.

To polish, use fuller's earth finely powdered or whiting. Never use hot water for these articles. Allow the water to cool until it will bear the hands comfortably.

To Clean a Chandelier.—Apply pure vinegar with a small sponge; afterwards wash in soapsuds and polish with flannel or chamois.

To renovate tarnished metallic parts, paint black with the dull-black paint used for ebonizing. Or apply white, gilt, or any other enamel paint desired.

Glass Stoppers.—The glass stoppers of decanters or carafes and other bottles sometimes stick and are very difficult to remove. To obviate this, use a large glass marble, either of clear glass or containing fancy figures. This makes a good stopper for a decanter or water bottle and is easily removed.

To remove a stopper that sticks, first apply a few drops of sweet oil or salad oil to the neck of the stopper, and let stand a few minutes to soak in between the stopper and the neck of the bottle.

If this does not loosen the stopper, apply heat to the neck of the bottle on the outside. It is well known that heat expands all substances, and, if applied to the outside, the neck of the bottle will expand before the stopper does, and the stopper will become loosened. This may be done by putting a narrow strip of flannel about the neck of the bottle and drawing it back and forth rapidly to create friction. This will sometimes cause heat enough in a few minutes.

Or hold the hand about the neck of the bottle until the heat of the hand causes it to expand.

Or, if this is not sufficient, dip a rag in water as hot as the hands will bear and wrap it about the neck of the bottle. This must not be done, however, when the bottle is very cold, as it may be cracked by expanding too suddenly.

Or hold the neck of the bottle near a gas jet or an open flame, turning it constantly to prevent any part from becoming overheated.

Or wrap a piece of cloth about the stopper and with a light piece of wood tap it gently, first on one side, then on the other. Do not use a hammer or other metal tool or utensil for this purpose.

To Clean Clocks. — To clean a clock, saturate a cloth or pad of cotton with kerosene oil and lay it inside on a small dish that will prevent the woodwork from being saturated. As it evaporates, the fumes will loosen any foreign substance on the wheels of the clock and cause it to drop. Repeat as often as necessary. The fumes also tend to lubricate the works.

Or remove the works of alarm clocks and others which are made exclusively of metal, and place them in an earthenware jar or other clean vessel having a tight-fitting cover. Pour over them kerosene oil through a cloth strainer or filter paper to remove all sediment. Let stand until the grease and dirt have been entirely cut and removed. The clock may be returned to its case without waiting for the excess of oil to evaporate.

To Oil Clocks.—To oil a clock, obtain the purest olive oil and cleanse it by adding half a pint of lime water to each quart of oil. Shake well and let stand three or four days, when the pure oil may be carefully poured off the sediment and strained through silk or filter paper.

To Clean Metals. — Various acids are recommended for cleaning metals, as tartaric, oxalic, acetic, muriatic, and the like; also alcohol, turpentine, and petroleum products, and such materials as whiting, powdered pumice, rotten stone, bath brick, etc., mixed with water or oil.

Paste for Metals.—Mix 1 ounce of oxalic acid with 6 ounces of rotten stone, and dilute to a soft paste with equal parts of train oil and spirits of turpentine.

Or mix strong potash or soda lye with alcohol and apply to metals with a brush. Let dry, and polish with a soft cloth or moist chamois. This will remove verdigris and most other forms of rust or tarnish.

Brass — To Prevent Tarnishing. — Moisten powdered sal ammoniac with water and apply to the brass by means of a brush. Afterwards heat the article until the sal ammoniac is melted. Cool, and polish with dry whiting and soft cloth.

To Clean Brass.—Dissolve ½ ounce of oxalic acid in 1 pint of soft water and wash the brass, or moisten a cloth in sweet oil dipped in powdered whiting or rotten stone, and scour.

Or mix to a soft paste 1 ounce of starch, 12 ounces of rotten stone, 2 ounces of sweet oil, and 2 ounces of oxalic acid with water, and apply with a cloth or chamois.

Or, to clean brass inlaid work, mix tripoli with linseed oil, and apply by means of a piece of folded velveteen or other suitable polisher. Or use a good furniture paste. But if the wood has a very high polish, finish the cleaning by rubbing on dry starch with the palm of the hand.

Or mix 2 ounces of sulphuric acid, 1½ ounces of nitric acid, 1 dram of saltpeter, and 2 ounces of rain water, and let stand until the solution settles. Dip the articles in this, or go over them with a soft brush dipped in this mixture, rinse immediately with soft water, and wipe dry. Or dry in sawdust. To prevent future tarnishing, apply a good coat of brass lacquer.

To Clean Bronze.—To clean genuine bronze, apply hot soapsuds or boil the article in suds. Rinse and wipe dry with a soft cloth or chamois skin.

Or, for small articles, apply sweet oil with a brush and rub off with a flannel cloth.

Polish with dry whiting and chamois skin.

To Clean Nickel.—Mix equal quantities of alcohol and aqua ammonia and stir in whiting to the consistency of thin cream. Apply with a brush and soft cloth, let dry, and polish with a clean, dry cloth or chamois skin.

Or, to remove stains from nickel, dilute 1 part of sulphuric acid in 50 parts of alcohol, and dip the articles in the solution until the stains are removed, which should take not more than 5 or 10 seconds. Rinse in alcohol and afterwards in clear water, and polish with dry whiting and chamois. Repeat if necessary.

To Clean Gilt Metals.—Metals finished in gilt or lacquer should not be washed with strong soaps containing free alkali, but preferably with clear, soft warm water and a fine sponge.

Or a little castile soap or other fine white soap may be used if necessary.

Clean out the crevices in the ornamental parts with a soft brush, as an old toothbrush, but use no more force than is necessary to avoid injuring the gilding. Wipe dry with chamois or a piece of soft woolen cloth or silk.

Bronzed articles, not genuine bronze, require only dusting or wiping with a soft cloth. Washing will injure the bronzing.

Burnishing Powder.—To make a high polish for metals, mix 4 ounces of prepared chalk, 1½ ounces of pipe clay, 1 ounce of white lead, ½ ounce of carbonate of magnesia, and ½ ounce of jeweler's rouge.

TO CLEAN MARBLE, BRICK, AND STONE

To Clean Marble.—To clean marble mantels, table tops, tops of bureaus, washstands, and other polished marble surfaces, wipe them with a cloth moistened in kerosene.

Or mix 2 ounces of common soda, 1 ounce of pumice stone, and 1 ounce of fine common salt, and dilute with water to the consistency of cream. Pour this mixture over the marble and let stand until all stains are removed. Afterwards wash the marble with salt and water, rinse, and wipe dry.

Or mix soft soap and whiting to a thin paste, and apply to the marble by means of a soft brush. Let stand until fully dry, and wash off with lukewarm suds made of hard white or yellow soap.

Or give the marble a coating of mucilage made by boiling to the consistency of thick cream 4 ounces of gum arabic in 1 quart of water. Dilute with hot water if necessary. Apply with a brush and expose the article to the sun and air until the mucilage cracks and can be readily rubbed off, then wash with clear water and a soft cloth. Repeat if necessary.

Or stir into 1 pint of soft soap 1 teaspoonful of bluing and 2 teaspoonfuls of whiting, and bring to a boil. Apply hot, let dry, and rinse off the clear water.

Or make a paste of equal parts of whiting, soap, and sal soda with a small amount of bluing; apply with a piece of felt or velveteen and rinse with clear water. Wipe dry, and polish with a flannel cloth or chamois.

Or dissolve 1 pound of pipe clay in 1 quart of boiling water. Add 1 quart of beer and a few drops of bluing. Bring to a boil and stir. Apply this freely with a cloth, wipe dry, and polish.

To Remove Iron Rust from Marble.—To remove iron stains from marble, dilute 1 part of oxalic acid with 10 parts of alcohol, or 1 part of sulphuric acid with 25 to 50 parts of alcohol; cover the spot and let stand

15 minutes to a half hour. Wash off with water containing aqua ammonia to stop the action of the acid. Repeat if necessary.

Or cover the spot thickly with salt and moisten with lemon juice.

Or apply 1 part of nitric acid diluted with 25 parts of water, and rinse with aqua ammonia.

Or apply strong nitric acid direct to the stain by means of a small swab or cloth, or cotton on the end of a stick, and at once rinse off with aqua ammonia and water. Remember that the acid tends to eat and injure the marble if it is not immediately rinsed off; hence rinse well. If the surface of the marble is roughened by the acid, scour with a moist cloth dipped in rotten stone or powdered pumice.

Or cover the spot with salts of lemon, and add just enough water to dissolve the crystals.

Or mix equal quantities of salts of lemon and pumice stone, and rub the spot with a cloth dipped in this mixture. Continue until removed.

To Clean Marble Steps.—To clean coarse marbles, as doorsteps, monuments, and the like, mix equal quantities of quicklime and potash lye and dilute with water to a thin cream. Apply with a brush, let stand twenty-four hours or more, and wash off with hot soapsuds.

To Remove Stains from Marble.—Cut a lemon in half and rub with it, or apply a saturated solution of oxalic acid.

Or make a paste of equal parts of whiting and sal soda dissolved in water. Cover the stains, and let stand for several hours. Afterwards wash off with soapsuds.

To Remove Oil Stains from Marble.—Apply common clay, starch, whiting, or prepared chalk, and saturate with gasoline or other petroleum product. Should these injure the polish, scour with a moistened cloth dipped in pumice stone, and polish with whiting.

Or mix with boiling water 2 ounces of soft soap, 2 ounces of caustic potash, and 4 ounces of fuller's earth. Cover the spots thickly, and let stand for several hours. Rinse with clear water.

To Polish Marble. — For polishing marble, sandstone, sand and water, emery powder, putty powder, tripoli, and whiting are all recommended. But the coarser materials, such as sandstone and fine sand, should only be used on rough marble which has never been previously polished. Select material suitable to the condition of the marble, and follow with a finer one until the desired polish is obtained.

To polish a rough marble slab, use first a level block of fine sandstone for working down. Cover the surface with water and rub with the sandstone in a circular motion, working outward from the center until the whole surface shows a uniform texture. Next tack a piece of felt to a smooth block of wood and use a finer quality of sand or glass powder with water. Follow this with a fresh piece of felt mounted on a level block of wood, using fine emery powder with water, and lastly use putty powder or tripoli with water and a chamois skin mounted on a block of wood.

To Clean Brick and Stone Walks.—To remove the green fungous growth on brick or stone walks and walls exposed to moisture, pour over them boiling water in which potatoes or other vegetables have been cooked, provided that it does not contain grease of any kind. Repeat if necessary.

Or pour strong brine over the brick or stone, or scatter dry salt over it just before or after a rain. This will also kill any tufts of grass and weeds that come up between the bricks and stones, but care must be taken that it is not used in quantities sufficient to leach off into the soil and kill the adjacent grass of the lawn or the plants in flower beds. Hence use a small quantity of salt, and repeat if necessary.

To Polish Stucco Work.—Let the stucco dry, then rub it down with a flat block of pumice stone. Follow with whiting and polish with tripoli, using a piece of felt mounted on a block of wood. Wash down with soapsuds.

To Polish Mother-of-Pearl.—Polish with finely sifted pumice stone, followed by putty powder or tripoli mixed with water and applied with a piece of felt.

To Clean Alabaster.—Remove stains from alabaster by covering the spot with whiting and water, or with whitewash, or with salt and lemon juice. Or apply equal quantities of quicklime and soda made into a thin paste with water. Let stand until dry, then wipe off with a sponge or soft cloth and clear water. Repeat if necessary.

Or, to remove obstinate stains, apply a dilute solution of oxalic acid or spirits of salts, and rinse with aqua ammonia.

Or wash with castile soap and water. Cover with a coating of whiting mixed with water, let stand until dry, rinse with clear water, and polish.

To Polish Alabaster. — To polish alabaster, marble, or any similar mineral, first clean the articles, then take out scratches or other rough spots with finely powdered pumice stone or emery and water. Polish with putty powder and water by means of a piece of felt mounted on a block.

To Polish Glass.—A scratched window pane or a show-case top which has been roughened by use and partially lost its transparency may be polished by covering with a strong solution of potash lye applied by means of a brush. Let it dry, and polish with a moist cloth. Repeat if necessary.

Or, if this is not effectual, polish with putty powder and water by means of a piece of felt.

To Clean Papier-maché.—Wash with clean cold water, using a sponge or soft cloth. While still damp, cover it with dry flour and rub dry with a piece of woolen cloth or chamois.

To Clean Gutta Percha.—Dissolve with gentle heat a little hard white soap in an equal bulk of water, and stir into the soap jelly thus made an equal bulk of powdered charcoal. Scour the article with this, and polish with a dry cloth and finely powdered charcoal.

CLEANING KITCHEN STOVES AND OTHER METALS

To Clean Stoves.—First examine the stove or range to see if any parts need replacing. Make a note of these, and obtain new ones from the manufacturers or some local merchant. Remove

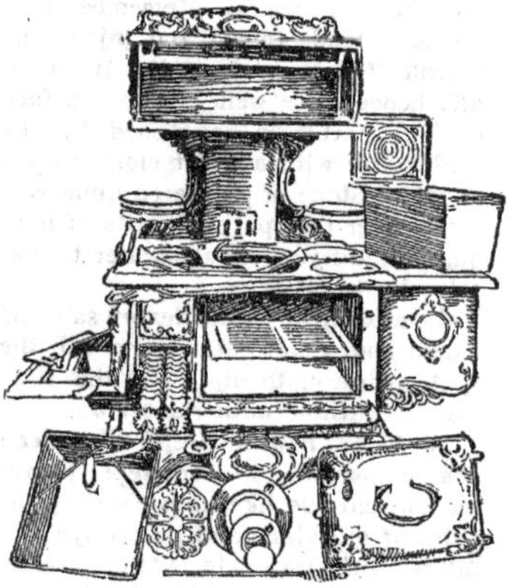

"See if Any Parts Are Needed."

clinkers, clean the grate, fireplace, spaces under and over the oven, flues, etc. Dust off the top of the stove, and wash the outside with very hot water and soda applied with a stiff brush or a coarse cloth, or both.

Suggestions for removing rust and polishing nickel and other ornaments, and for blacking and polishing the stove and preventing rust when not in use, will be found elsewhere.

To Make a Hearth.—Prepare mortar by mixing sifted wood ashes with salt and water in the proportion of 1 tablespoonful of salt to 1 gallon of ashes. Spread this over the hearth with a trowel, and tamp it down as hard as possible with the end of a log of wood, or otherwise. Level smoothly with the trowel.

Make a hot fire in the fireplace or

grate. If the mortar cracks, add more, tamping it into the cracks. This makes a hard, smooth white surface.

Or mix 2 parts of unslaked lime and 1 part of smith's black dust with water, and treat as above.

To Clean Grates.—Brush the dust from the grate with a stiff brush. Then mix 4 ounces of pure black lead with 1 pint of beer, add 2 ounces of hard white or yellow soap, bring all to a boil, and while hot apply this mixture with a paint brush. Allow it to cool, then polish with a hard brush or polishing mitten.

Or, if the grate is much rusted, allow the black lead to remain for a day or two. It will loosen the rust so that it can be scraped off. The grate may then be blacked and polished.

Or first scrub the grate with soap and water and apply rotten stone moistened with sweet oil. Black and polish.

To Black Grates.—Melt 2½ pounds of asphaltum and add 1 pound of boiled oil. Remove from the fire, and when cool add 2 quarts of spirits of turpentine, stirring vigorously. Apply with a brush.

Or melt 6½ pounds of asphaltum; add 1 pound of litharge and 1 gallon of boiled oil. Boil until the mixture falls in strings from the stirrer. To test, put a little on a glass plate. If on cooling it becomes quite hard, remove the mixture from the fire, and when cold, thin to any desired consistency by adding 3 or more gallons of spirits of turpentine.

To Prevent Rust.—Substances recommended for preventing rust are various animal fats, as lard, suet, and tallow, and oils, as linseed oil, olive oil, vaseline, etc.; also black lead, paraffin, collodion, quicklime, gutta percha, varnish, pitch-tar paint, and various mixtures of these. The object in all cases is to prevent contact of the metal with the oxygen of the air, especially where there is moisture.

The formation of rust is a process of combustion similar to that which takes place in breathing and in the burning of fuel and other combustibles. The oxygen of the air uniting with iron forms a compound called ferrous oxide, which is iron rust. This action is very much hastened by moisture. Hence a coating of any oily, greasy, or sticky substance which will adhere to the metal without injuring it will prevent rust. Which of the following recipes is best will depend upon the article to be protected, and whether or not it is to be used or stored away. Such substances as collodion, paraffin, and black lead mixed with lard or other animal fat, boiled linseed oil, etc., can be used on small polished articles, as steel tools, skates, and the like. They can be readily removed, when necessary, by washing.

Paraffin, collodion, boiled linseed oil, and copal varnish may be applied to tools and other articles which are in process of use, the excess being wiped off with a dry cloth. Pitch tar and paint can, of course, only be applied to coarser articles according to their several characters.

Stoves—To Prevent Rust.—To protect from rust stoves and stovepipes that are taken down in the spring and stored during the summer, apply kerosene with a brush or cloth. The crude oil is better for this purpose than the refined. It costs less and does not evaporate so quickly.

Or melt 3 parts of lard with 1 part of rosin, and apply with a brush while warm.

Or apply linseed oil, or a mixture of equal parts of linseed oil and kerosene.

Or a mixture of 4 parts of linseed oil, 4 parts of kerosene, and 1 part of turpentine.

Apply the above mixtures in a thin coat while slightly warm.

To Protect Stovepipes from Rust.—Shake the dirt and soot out of the inside of the stovepipe, then insert an old broom and brush out as clean as possible. Paint the outside of the stovepipe with a coat of black paint, or apply any of the above rust-proof mixtures.

Stovepipes rust on the inside as

well as on the outside. Hold the pipe with an open end toward a good light, or reflect a light inside by means of a mirror. Affix a brush to a long handle and cover the inside of the pipe

"Reflect a Light Inside."

as well as the outside with oil or other rust preventives.

To Keep Nickel Fittings from Rusting.—Remove the nickel fittings from the stove, cover them with any of the above preventives, wrap them in thin cloths, and lay them away until wanted.

Or cover them with unslaked lime.

Or, if badly rusted, go over the nickel fittings with aluminum paint.

To Prevent Rust.—To prevent rust on tin roofs and other exposed metal surfaces, bring to a boil 2 pounds of linseed-oil varnish. Stir into this a mixture of 2 ounces of black lead, 8 ounces of sulphide of lead, and 2 ounces of sulphide of zinc. Apply with a brush.

Or paint exposed metal surfaces with a paint consisting of 30 parts of pure white lead, 8 parts of crude linseed oil, 2 parts of boiled linseed oil, and 1 part of spirits of turpentine. Apply two or more coats as needed.

To Preserve Metals from Rust.—To preserve stoves, skates, sleigh runners, and other steel articles which are stored for a portion of the year, smear them with vaseline.

Or paint them with lampblack mixed with equal quantities of boiled linseed oil and copal varnish.

Or use powdered black lead and lard, melting the lard and stirring in the lead, and add a small piece of gum camphor. Apply while warm with a brush.

Or melt paraffin, and apply while warm with a brush, sponge, or cloth.

Or clean thoroughly and dust over with unslaked lime.

Or, plunge small articles into unslaked lime.

Or dip the articles in boiled linseed oil and allow it to dry on them.

Or apply a coat of copal varnish.

Or melt 5 pounds of beef or mutton suet, 1 pound of gutta percha, and 1 gallon of neat's-foot oil or rape oil until dissolved. Mix thoroughly and apply when cold.

Or coat with collodion dissolved in alcohol.

Or wrap in zinc foil or store in zinc-lined boxes.

Or mix 1 ounce of oil varnish with 4 ounces of rectified spirits of turpentine and apply with a sponge.

Or heat the articles and dip them in train oil.

To Prevent Rust on Tinware.—Rub new tinware with fresh lard, and heat in the oven before using. This tends to make it rust proof.

To Preserve Nails, etc., from Rust.—To preserve from rust nails, screws, hinges, and other hardware that will be exposed to water, heat them (but not enough to injure the temper) in an iron skillet over a fire and drop them into train oil. This will preserve them for many years.

Or mix ½ pound of quicklime in 1 quart of water and allow it to settle. Pour off the clear liquid and add to the lime sufficient olive oil to form a stiff paste. Apply with a brush to iron or steel articles to be stored.

Or, for rough castings and fence wire, mix mineral pitch, coal tar, and sand in the proportion of 1 pound each of coal tar and sand to 20 pounds of mineral pitch. Immerse the articles in the mixture, remove them, and let them stand a day or more to harden.

To Prevent Rust on Piano Wires.—Sprinkle piano wires with unslaked lime.

Steel Table Knives.—Fill a flower pot or other deep receptacle with quicklime and into it plunge the blades of the knives. Do not allow the lime to touch the handles.

To Remove Rust from Small Articles. — Substances recommended for removing rust are muriatic acid, kerosene, chloride of tin, and unslaked lime used with or without various abrasives, as sandpaper, emery paper, pumice stone, powdered brick, and the like.

First immerse the articles in a hot solution of sal soda or soapsuds to free them from oil or grease.

Or dilute muriatic acid with twice its own bulk of water and immerse the articles from a few minutes to several hours, according to the amount of rust. Remove and apply soap and water with a scrubbing brush. Repeat if necessary. Rinse, dry, and polish with oil and emery paper or other good abrasive.

Or immerse the articles in kerosene oil for several hours, or as long as may be necessary. This loosens the rust so that it may be rubbed off with sandpaper or emery paper.

But if the rust has etched deeply into the articles, they may have to be refinished.

Or soften rust with sweet oil and rub with sandpaper.

Or mix 2 parts of pumice stone with 1 part of sulphur. Moisten with sweet oil and apply with chamois.

Or use emery and oil.

Or immerse the articles in a saturated solution of chloride of tin over night, or as long as necessary. Rinse in clear water and polish with chamois.

Or immerse them in olive oil, and polish with whiting or slaked lime by moistening a cloth or chamois and dipping it into the dry powder.

To Clean Zinc.—Substances recommended for cleaning zinc are kerosene, soft soap, salt and vinegar, vinegar and alum, paraffin, coal ashes, sulphuric acid, turpentine, and various compounds of these. As zinc is not easily injured, these may all be used freely. Rub with a coarse cloth saturated with kerosene oil.

Or heat 2 ounces of salt or 2 ounces of alum in 1 quart of vinegar and apply hot. Wipe with a dry rag.

Or dip a cotton cloth in melted paraffin and rub until the dirt is removed. Rinse with clean water and wipe dry.

Or wet with cold vinegar, let stand for a few minutes, rinse, and wash.

Or make a soap jelly by dissolving hard soap with twice its own bulk in water. Mix with sifted coal ashes to a stiff paste. Apply with a moist cloth.

Or mix dilute sulphuric acid (1 part of acid to 10 parts of water) with glycerin.

Or mix 1 pint of linseed oil with 4 ounces of turpentine.

Or polish with bath brick.

To Clean Nickel.—Substances recommended for cleaning nickel are kerosene, jeweler's rouge, whiting, powdered borax, and alum. When not much soiled, use jeweler's rouge and vaseline mixed to a thin paste. Apply with flannel and polish with chamois.

Or dampen a rag and dip in powdered borax. Or, if the articles are small and movable, boil in alum and water.

Or rub with a cloth dipped in kerosene.

To Clean Brass.—Substances recommended for cleaning brass are vinegar and salt, lemon juice, citric acid, oxalic acid, rotten stone, turpentine, alum, ammonia, sulphuric, nitric, or muriatic acid, and various compounds of these.

To clean brass kettles and other utensils, dissolve a tablespoonful of salt in a teacupful of vinegar and bring to a boil. Apply as hot as possible to the brass with a scrubbing brush.

Or apply a solution of oxalic acid with a scrubbing brush or cloth, using equal parts of oxalic acid and water.

Or apply strong aqua ammonia with a scrubbing brush.

Or dissolve 1 ounce of alum in 1 pint of strong lye and apply with a scrubbing brush.

Or mix 6 ounces of rotten stone, 1 ounce of oxalic acid, 1 ounce of sweet oil, and ½ ounce of gum arabic, and dissolve to a thin paste with water. Apply with a cloth.

Or use rotten stone moistened with sweet oil. Apply with a cloth moistened in turpentine.

Or mix 1 ounce of bichromate of potash, 2 ounces of sulphuric acid, and 2 ounces of pure water. Do not touch this with the hands, but apply with a mop.

Or wet a cloth in water, dip in powdered sal ammoniac, and apply.

Or mix 4 ounces of rotten stone, 1 ounce of oxalic acid, and 1 ounce of sweet oil with turpentine to form a paste, and apply with a brush moistened in water.

Or dissolve 1 ounce of alum in 1 pint of strong potash or soda lye. Immerse the articles in this solution or apply hot with a scrubbing brush.

Or dissolve 1 ounce of alum in 8 ounces of water and apply hot with a scrubbing brush.

To Polish Brass. — After removing tarnish with any of the above cleansers, wash the article with warm soapsuds made of any good, hard white soap, dry with a cloth, and polish with dry chamois or any good silver polish, as whiting, or the like. Finish by rubbing the articles with a cloth slightly moistened with vaseline. This will prevent tarnishing.

Or coat with collodion dissolved in alcohol, or thin shellac applied by means of a camel's-hair brush.

PACKING

Packing — To Move. — Obtain plenty of barrels, and a relatively large number of small packing cases rather than a few large ones, a quantity of excelsior, burlap, and strong manila cord. Also a number of strong manila tags on which write, stamp, or print your name and the address to which the goods are to be shipped. Number these tags from 1 upward. Pack, as far as possible, by themselves articles from each separate room or part of the house, and note in a blank book the contents of each barrel, case, or package. For example, if numbers 1 to 5 are china, and numbers 5 to 10 are kitchen hardware, the packages can be delivered to the appropriate part of the house and unpacked as required without confusion.

To Pack China.—Pack china and other fragile articles, also small metallic objects, as lamps, kitchenware, bric-a-brac, etc., in barrels rather than packing cases. To pack such articles, first cover the bottom of the barrel with a layer 3 or 4 inches

"Nest Dishes Together and Pack on Edge."

deep of excelsior or fine hay slightly moistened. Wrap each article separately in newspaper or tissue paper. Select the larger and heavier pieces and lay a number of them side by side 2 or 3 inches apart. Stack plates and platters together, with just enough packing material between them to separate them ¼ of an inch or so, and stand them on edge. Nest together in the same way cups and saucers, sauce dishes, and other articles of similar shape and size, putting a little packing between, but handling the entire nest in packing as one solid article. Take special care to protect handles and other protuberances so that no strain will be likely to come upon them.

Surround these dishes with a layer of excelsior or hay 2 or 3 inches in thickness, crowding the packing material also between them, and finally cover them with a layer of equal thickness. On this lay a number of other articles of somewhat smaller size and less weight, surrounding, separating, and covering them with several inches of packing material, and pressing all so firmly together that they cannot be shaken out of place. Shake the barrel occasionally, and if any two pieces are not properly separated by the packing material, the fact can be detected by the sound of their contact.

Continue to add successive layers until the barrel is filled within 4 or 5 inches of the top. Fill in this space with packing material, heap it up, take off the top hoop, throw over the top a piece of burlap, replace the hoop, and tack it securely so as to hold the burlap in position. Fasten on the burlap near the top a tag containing your address on one side and on the other the words, "Fragile—This Side Up With Care."

To Pack Cut Glass.—Cut glass and delicate bric-a-brac, lamp shades, and the like may be packed in the same manner as china, or carefully wrapped in cloth and packed in barrels surrounded with pillows, or placed in trunks containing clothing, or in clothes baskets surrounded by pillows and covered with burlap. Barrels and baskets crated and marked "Fragile" will be handled with much more care than wooden cases, the lids of which are nailed or screwed on.

To Pack Pictures.—Pack small pictures face to face, with blankets or quilts or other folds of heavy cloth between, and lay them in bureau drawers, with thick layers of clothing above and below them.

Or place two large pictures face to face separated by a quilt, tie them with strong cord, and surround the whole with a crate of rough boards.

To Pack Mirrors.—Place two mirrors face to face, with several thicknesses of cloth between, and crate them.

To Pack Furniture.—Remove all movable parts from furniture, as the splasher racks from washstands, mirrors from bureaus, and the like. Remove the casters, tie together with stout cord those belonging to each article of furniture and attach them to some part of the article or drop them into a bureau drawer. Thus they can be found when wanted.

Pack the drawers with clothing and put small pictures, platters, and similar breakable articles between. Surround the whole with burlap sewed together at the corners, and crate with rough boards. Wrap the legs of chairs, serving tables, etc., with manila paper, newspapers, or cloth, and wind them with a stout cord secured so that it will not slip.

To Pack Books.—To pack a large quantity of books, use either a suitable number of small packing cases or barrels rather than a few large packing cases. Books are very heavy, and large packing cases are liable to burst open by their weight. Barrels are stronger, and if properly packed perhaps better than packing cases. To prepare books for packing, wrap up together, in packages of six or eight or more, those books that are most nearly of the same size. Have at least one thickness of paper between each binding and around the entire package. Tie the package together with a soft cord so that the books cannot rub against each other. To pack books in barrels, handle these packages the same as articles of china or bric-a-brac, surrounding them with excelsior, hay, straw, or other similar material, or with crumpled newspaper; except that not so much of the packing material need be used. The barrel may be headed up instead of covered with burlap, but care must be taken not to leave an inch of vacant space. Mark it "Books—Keep Dry."

To pack books in small packing cases, stand the parcels on end, with the edges next to the sides of the cases and the back of the bindings pointed inward, and pack between crumpled newspapers to ease the pressure on the round part of the books, which may otherwise be pressed flat. Line the case with wrapping paper. Lay a thickness of wrapping paper over the top, and fasten on the cover with screws in preference to nails. Or, if nails are used, take care to see that they do not slip and injure the contents.

Tools.—Pack in a hand satchel hammer, screw-driver, box opener, nails, tacks, and other necessary implements for unpacking and settling your goods, together with the book containing your inventory and list of packages. Then when the goods are unpacked, the movers can be directed to take each package to the proper room, and when any particular article is needed it can be readily located and unpacked as required. Also, if any case is missing or injured, the exact contents will be known, and a sworn statement can be made out as the basis of a claim for damages.

To Pack for Traveling.—To pack a trunk or satchel, first decide what to take with you. An old traveler describes his method of packing at short notice, without forgetting any necessary article, by saying that his method is "to commence with his feet and work up." The idea is to run over in mind the various articles of wearing apparel in that order. Thus, enumerate shoes, stockings, underwear, outer garments, linen, neckwear, etc. Determine what particular articles and how many of each to select. Get these all together and check them up to see that nothing has been omitted. Add, of course, toilet articles, night gear, medicines, etc. Pack first the heavy things or those the last to be needed. Fold each garment and lay it smoothly in the trunk. Do not attempt to roll garments into tight bundles in order to economize space. Folded articles laid flat will pack more tightly.

While packing, press down the contents occasionally to see that there are no lumps or other inequalities.

To Pack Men's Coats.—Spread out the coat on a flat surface with the outside up. Fold the sleeves back at the elbows and draw them straight down at the sides. Turn back the front laps of the coat over the sleeves, pull the collar out straight, take up the coat at the sleeve holes, and fold it wrong side out lengthwise. Thus the front flaps will be folded twice in.

To Pack a Plaited Skirt.—Pin each plait in its place at the bottom of the skirt. Lay the skirt on a flat surface and fold to just fit the largest part of the trunk or suit case. In other words, fold as little as possible.

To Pack Summer Gowns.—Remove the arm shields and fold the skirt in as few folds as possible. Fold the waist in the same fashion as a man's coat, stuff the sleeves and bust with tissue paper, put paper under ruffles, and surround the whole with tissue paper. But do not use white tissue for this purpose, as it is bleached with chloride of lime, which tends to turn white goods yellow. The blue tissue is therefore to be preferred.

Or put waists on coat hangers and stuff the sleeves and bust with tissue, or lay them flat in the tray or top of the trunk. When thus packed, they will neither lose shape nor wrinkle.

To Pack Hats.—Pin hats to the lids of hat boxes to prevent their moving around. Or improvise a hat box by laying the hat on the bottom of the trunk or tray, and cutting a strip of cardboard as high as the highest point of the trimming. Pin this together at the ends, thus inclosing the hat, and lay a piece of cardboard across the top. Surround this with other articles packed firmly to keep them from shifting, and the hat will receive no harm.

Miscellaneous Objects.—Pack bottles inside of shoes. Pack a chafing dish in the middle of the trunk and fill up with small articles. Lay pictures in the middle tray between folded garments and fill the tray with clean starched clothes. Put summer gowns or evening gowns at the top of the tray, which should not be packed quite full. Pack in the bottom of the trunk a child's toy washboard. You can then do up for yourself small pieces at hotels and summer resorts where laundry charges are high.

CHAPTER XV

HOUSEHOLD AND GARDEN PESTS

THE CLOTHES MOTH—CARPET BEETLE OR "BUFFALO MOTH"—THE HOUSE CENTIPEDE—THE COMMON COCKROACH OR CROTON BUG—THE BEDBUG—THE HOUSE FLEA—RATS AND MICE—BLACK AND RED ANTS—THE WHITE ANT—THE COMMON HOUSE FLY—THE MOSQUITO—ORCHARD, FARM, AND GARDEN PESTS

THE CLOTHES MOTH

History of Clothes Moths.—The life history of the clothes moth must be understood in order to fight intelligently against it and prevent its ravages. It is well worth while to give the necessary attention to this subject, since of all household pests the clothes moth stands in the most direct and obvious relation to the family pocketbook.

"A garment that is moth-eaten" has been mentioned in the Book of Job, hence the moth is known to be very ancient and it is distributed in all parts of the world. The destructive feeding habits of the larvæ have caused them to be very carefully observed and studied, and there is abundant information as to preventives and remedial measures against them.

Moths, as is well known, feed exclusively on animal substances, as woolens, silk, fur, and feathers, and as these are among the most expensive materials used as garments, floor coverings, draperies, and otherwise, the destruction of such articles in a single season by moths may and often does amount to many dollars. The three species of moths commonly found in the United States are the case-making species, universally distributed in the Northern States; the webbing species or Southern clothes moth, distributed through the Southern States as far north as or farther than the latitude of Washington, and the gallery species or tapestry moth, which is rare in the United States, and is found principally in barns and carriage houses, infesting horse blankets and the upholstery of carriages.

The eggs of the case-making species, which may be called the Northern moth, are laid but once a year, in the spring, the moths appearing from June to August. Professor Fernald states that the eggs are

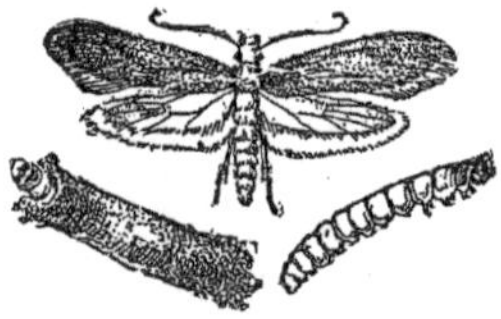

FIG. 1.—*Case-making Moth: Above, Adult; at Right, Larva; at Left, Larva in Case. Enlarged (from Riley).*

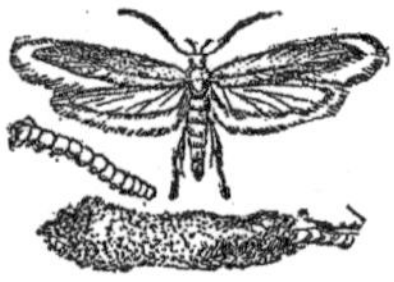

FIG. 2.—*Southern Clothes Moth: Moth, Larva, Cocoon, and Empty Pupa Skin. Enlarged (from Riley).*

FIG. 3.—*Tapestry Moth: Adult Moth. Enlarged (from Riley).*

never hatched in winter in the North, even in rooms that are heated night and day; but in the South this species appears from January to October, and breeds two or more times a year.

The webbing species or Southern clothes moth breeds twice a year, the first eggs being laid in May, and the second in August or September; hence in the North the moth is a summer problem, but in the South it must be fought the year round.

The adult moths do no damage except to deposit the eggs from which the injurious maggots or larvæ are hatched. Moths choose darkness rather than light, and select a quiet and secluded spot where they are not likely to be disturbed in which to deposit their eggs. They also appear to prefer garments or other articles which are soiled with spots of grease or other organic matter, and the larvæ appear to choose soiled spots or articles in preference to others. The eggs are very minute, and are usually deposited on woolens, feathers, furs, or other articles which are suitable food for the larvæ; but the latter have the ability to crawl from place to place, if necessary, to seek proper food. Hence they may be deposited in crevices of closets, trunks, etc., through which the larvæ may subsequently enter.

The larva of the moth is a dull white caterpillar. The larva of the case-making or Northern moth surrounds itself with a movable case or jacket, but that of the webbing or Southern moth merely spins a cobwebby path wherever it goes. When the larva of the case-making moth is mature it becomes quiescent and undergoes a transformation in its case. After about three weeks the moth appears. The larva of the Southern moth when mature weaves itself a cocoon in which it undergoes a similar transformation.

To Prevent Moths. — The facts above noted indicate the proper precautions to be preserved. In general, the moths must be prevented from laying their eggs on valuable woolens, silks, furs, or feathers, and the eggs themselves, or larvæ hatched from them, must be destroyed or removed before they can do serious damage. The measures necessary to effect these results are: (1) a thorough cleaning of all wardrobes and other receptacles liable to be infected by moths, and of the floors, especially the edges, on which woolen carpets are laid. (2) Treatment with suitable preventives, and the frequent beating and brushing of woolen and other articles, followed by exposure to outdoor air and sunshine. (3) Packing articles not required for immediate use in tight receptacles, after first removing from them all moths' eggs or larvæ with which they may be infested. Various moth-preventives and moth destroyers have been discovered, all of which will be carefully indicated.

Preventives Against Moths.—Preventives against moths are of various kinds, as repellents, poisons, and various mechanical methods. Experience indicates that moths are averse to strong odors; hence among repellents may be mentioned naphthaline, moth balls, camphor, and various essential oils and perfumed woods. Other repellents are pepper, tobacco, and the like. Various substances applied to wardrobes, floors, and other moth-haunted receptacles also act as repellents, but it must be clearly understood that they cannot be depended upon. They merely tend to discourage the visits of the moths, but they do not destroy the moths, their eggs, or their larvæ; hence if moths are present, and especially if the receptacle which contains them is tightly closed and undisturbed, they will deposit their eggs, and the young will hatch and feed practically the same in the presence of these repellents as otherwise. Hence other preventive measures are necessary to insure protection against them.

Repellents for Moths. — Among substances recommended as repellents against moths are paper dipped in melted paraffin, cedar chests, cloves, cloths saturated with gasoline, sprigs of cedar, pine, or other evergreens, tallow candles, wood soaked with carbolic acid, pieces of Russia leather, and lavender.

To Destroy Moths.—Chemicals and methods recommended for destroying moths are fumigation with hydrocyanic-acid gas or sulphurous-acid gas, the application of bisulphide of carbon, various petroleum products (especially gasoline and benzine), turpentine, solution of alum, corrosive sublimate, carbolic acid, chloroform, and the application of steam or hot water.

To Fight Moths.—In general, the following methods are recommended: in April or May, at the time of spring house cleaning, carry out of doors the contents of all wardrobes, bureau drawers, boxes, etc., containing woolens, furs, feathers, or other articles made of animal products, and empty them on a large quilt or sheet spread upon the grass. Choose for this purpose a clear, sunny day with a gentle breeze. Hang large articles on the line and beat them; afterwards brush them carefully with a stiff whisk broom, especially underneath the collars, lapels, and other similar places. Turn pockets inside out and brush them. Let them air in the sun as long as possible. Shake and brush thoroughly the smaller articles. Finally separate those that are likely to be used during the summer months, and lay aside all others to be packed in moth-tight receptacles and stored.

While these articles are airing, apply suitable moth destroyers to the inside of the empty wardrobes, chests of drawers, and boxes, and, if convenient, set them out of doors in the sun to air. Return to closets and chests of drawers the articles likely to be in constant use during the summer. Wrap those to be stored in newspapers or tar paper, carefully sealing the opening with flour paste, and label the packages. Or fold the articles in suitable paper, place them in pasteboard or wooden boxes, and paste strips of paper around the covers and joints and over all cracks so as to make the receptacles moth proof.

Adult moths cannot bite, hence they are unable to make their way through the thinnest layer of paper or other protective covering. The larvæ will not ordinarily chew wood, cotton, linen, or paper, especially newspaper, but both the moths and their larvæ will penetrate very minute cracks and crevices. Hence protection is to be found only in tightly closing all such openings with paper and paste. Put no dependence upon moth balls or other repellents.

To Protect Clothes Against Moths.—Clothing in closets, wardrobes, or chests of drawers not sealed may be protected against moths by tight bags or sacks of cotton or linen, or by wrapping in newspapers carefully pasted together at the edges; but at least once a week the contents of wardrobes and all articles of wool, fur, or feathers not sealed against moths should be carried to the open air, shaken or beaten, brushed thoroughly, and hung on a line to air during the heat of the day. This practice is also advisable on grounds of hygiene, personal cleanliness, and economy. Clothing thus cared for will last longer, present a fitter appearance, and be free from germs, mold, and other forms of impurity.

Substituting oiled or painted bare floors, and using rugs instead of carpets in summer time are effective measures against moths, but if carpets are used, care should be taken to sweep with especial thoroughness along the edges between the carpet and the baseboard.

To Repel Moths.—Line drawers and other receptacles with newspapers or wrap articles in newspapers. Moths do not like printer's ink.

Or place articles in unbleached cotton bags. Moths do not like cotton.

Or put gum camphor in and about

the articles. Or shavings of cedar wood or camphor wood inclosed in small cotton bags.

Or put allspice, black pepper, the seeds of the musk plant, tansy leaves, lavender flowers, juniper berries, or bits of sponge, paper, or linen moistened with turpentine, or Cayenne pepper or tobacco or, in fact, almost any substance or combination of substances which has a strong pungent and lasting odor, in and among the articles to be protected. Probably crystals of naphthaline are as effective as any repellent that can be mentioned.

Or place a vial containing chloroform, and having a small slit or hole in the cork through which it can slowly evaporate, where the fumes will penetrate the articles.

To Destroy Moths.—Fumigate with hydrocyanic-acid gas or sulphur or camphor.

Or brush out and dust the inside of closets, wardrobes, and chests of drawers, brush floors that have been or are to be covered by woolen carpets, and wash the woodwork, especially all cracks and crevices, with hot soapsuds. Then apply a strong solution of alum dissolved in boiling water (1 or 2 pounds to the gallon).

Or a strong solution of carbolic acid or spirits of turpentine, kerosene, benzine, or gasoline.

Or a solution of creolin in water.

Apply any of these by means of a brush or spring-bottom oil can or atomizer. Take care to work it into the cracks by means of a small brush, a long feather, or otherwise.

To Protect Carpets from Moths.—Sprinkle the floor with turpentine, benzine, gasoline, or petroleum, or scatter peppermint or other fragrant herbs upon it, before the carpet is laid.

Or, if a carpet becomes infested while on the floor, sponge the infested spots with a solution of 60 grains of corrosive sublimate dissolved in 1 pint of alcohol.

Or apply gasoline freely to the carpet by means of a sponge, brush, atomizer, or sprinkler.

Or apply turpentine freely. Any of these will destroy the eggs and larvæ.

Or sprinkle borax freely about the edges of the carpet and work it into the pile of the carpet beneath heavy pieces of furniture and other spots that cannot be easily swept.

Or spread a damp towel above the suspected places in the carpet and iron it dry with a very hot iron. Do the same round the edges of the carpet, under heavy furniture, and at other places not frequently swept. The hot steam destroys the eggs and larvæ.

Or, if necessary, take up the carpet, beat it as clean as possible, remove the grease spots, and sponge carefully on both sides with a mixture of 1 pint of turpentine to 1 gallon of water. Wash the floor with hot suds made of borax with the addition of turpentine, and apply around the edges a strong solution of alum, carbolic acid, or creolin.

To Protect Furs from Moths.—Beat the furs, using preferably a piece of rubber hose. This will not

"Beat Furs with Rubber Hose."

cut or tear them. Comb them over with a steel comb and expose them to direct sunshine in the open air. Shake and brush each piece carefully, wrap it separately in newspaper, paste the edges tightly, label it, and lay it away in a drawer, chest, or wooden box where the paper in which it is wrapped will not be broken.

Or, to prevent accidental breaking of the wrappers, lay the packages in pasteboard or wooden boxes and seal the joints with newspaper and paste. Cedar chests, moth balls, or other repellents are not necessary if all moths, eggs, and larvæ are first removed and the furs are packed tightly; but there can be no objection to sprinkling naphthaline crystals, red or black pepper, various essential oils, and other substances having strong odors among the furs, or to wrapping up in them pieces of gum camphor, tallow candle, etc.

Or, instead of newspapers, put the articles in tight pillow slips or unbleached cotton bags, tying these tightly at the tops. Moths will not penetrate cotton or newspaper.

Or furs may be washed in a solution of 12 grains of corrosive sublimate in 1 pint of warm water.

Cold Storage for Furs.—Many furriers and most of the large department stores in cities have arrangements for placing valuable furs in cold storage during the summer months. A temperature as low as 40° F. will prevent the depredations of moths, and many warehouses maintain as low a temperature as 20° F. These establishments insure furs against loss or damage.

Mixtures for Moths. — Dissolve 4 ounces of alum in 1 pint of water. Add 4 ounces of salt and ½ pint of spirits of turpentine.

Or dissolve 1 ounce of camphor and 1 ounce of carbolic acid in 1 pint of benzine.

Or dissolve 1 ounce of gum camphor and 1 ounce of red pepper in 8 ounces of alcohol.

Petroleum Products for Moths. — Gasoline, benzine, and naphtha may be freely applied to all woolen goods, garments, carpets, upholstered furniture, and the like by sprinkling or saturating the articles by means of a small watering pot having a fine spray, an atomizer, a sponge, brush, or rag.

Or they may be applied freely to floors, the inside of wardrobes, and other receptacles.

Or turpentine may be used in the same manner as petroleum products.

Corrosive Sublimate for Moths. — Mix in a glass bottle 1 ounce of corrosive sublimate and ½ pint of water. Let stand a day or two and shake occasionally. Then add ½ pint of alcohol. Apply to cracks in floors, wardrobes, drawers, and other receptacles, or other suspected places. The liquid soaks into the wood, leaving a thin powder of corrosive sublimate on the surface. Do not allow this mixture to touch brass or copper. It is *very poisonous* to human beings.

Camphor for Moths.—This is merely a repellent and does not destroy moths. Gum camphor may be wrapped up in articles to be stored, or placed in and about articles in wardrobes and chests, or it may be dissolved in alcohol and sprinkled upon them, but the former is the better method.

Tobacco for Moths.—Tobacco may be used in the form of snuff sprinkled on articles stored away, or in and about floors, wardrobes, etc. Or fine-cut tobacco may be sprinkled freely in the receptacles, or among the articles themselves, or about floors or under woolen carpets; or a strong infusion of tobacco steeped in water may be used to wash or sprinkle woodwork, or applied to cracks and crevices, etc.

Pepper for Moths.—Black or Cayenne pepper may be freely sprinkled in receptacles or among the articles themselves.

Borax for Moths.—Borax may be used with water to make suds to wash woodwork, or scattered dry about floors or the inside of receptacles.

To Trap Moth Millers. — A deep dish partly filled with sweetened milk, on which a candle is floated, supported by a piece of light wood or a cork, is said to form an effective trap for moth millers where they are very numerous.

To Store Furs and Woolens. — A cedar-wood chest, in which to store furs and woolens against moths, was formerly thought indispensable, but many substitutes are now in use that are cheaper and just as good. Empty lard cans which may be had of butchers and grocers are excellent. They are light, tight, and take up little room. Ordinary tin bread or cake boxes are good, but they must be wrapped up in paper or have paper pasted over the joints. Large paper flour sacks are excellent. The tops must be pasted together after the articles have been inserted.

Or pasteboard boxes that are used by dealers to deliver garments, or dry-goods boxes lined with newspapers or with tarred paper pasted carefully to the insides.

Or old trunks lined in the same manner.

Or a cask or barrel that has been used for whisky, wine, or alcohol, and still smells strongly of alcohol.

To Store Bedding.—Line a large dry-goods box with several thicknesses of newspapers pasted smoothly on the inside, or use one or more layers of tarred paper. Shake and air the articles, fold and pack them in this box, and paste papers on the cover in such a way that they will project several inches outside. Fold these edges downward and paste them to the sides of the box so as to make a tight joint, and finally tack down the lid.

Moths in Feathers.—Moths will not get into feather pillows, feather beds, etc., unless the ticks are ripped or torn, but should they infest feathers, the best remedy is to boil the feathers for half an hour or more, and afterwards wash and dry them.

Or soak feathers thoroughly with benzine or gasoline.

To Store Garments. — To protect winter garments, such as suits, overcoats, and the like, left hanging in closets or wardrobes during the summer, place one or more suits and overcoats on a good clothes hanger and prepare a bag of unbleached cotton or any old cotton cloth large enough to cover the whole while hanging in its natural shape. Draw this up over the garments and tie at the top with a hard knot.

A section of a barrel hoop covered with cotton cloth and having a piece of old broomstick fastened between the two ends of the crescent makes a good clothes hanger. A pair of trousers may be folded and hung over the rod, and coats and overcoats hung upon the convex side. A piece of stout twine or wire may be adjusted in the middle to hang by.

To Prepare Garments for Packing.—Wash or dry-clean all woolen garments before packing them away for the summer. Remove especially all grease spots, which are very attractive to moths, and by decaying tend to injure the fabrics. This takes time, but saves clothes and money.

To Clean Furs. — Before packing, clean dark furs by heating bran or oatmeal. Rub this thoroughly into the fur while warm. Remove by shaking and repeat if necessary. Beat the furs with a piece of rubber pipe and comb them with a steel comb.

Clean white furs by laying them on a flat surface and rubbing them with bran moistened in warm water. Apply the bran with a flannel, rub until dry, and afterwards apply dry bran. Shake clean, and apply magnesia against the grain of the fur. Shake, beat, and air well before packing.

To Pack Clothes.—Wash, dry-clean, shake, and air. Button coats and waists; fill sleeves and bodies with crushed newspapers. Place one upon another. Newspapers prevent creases. In folding skirts and trousers, place newspapers, not crushed, where the folds come and fold them inside the garments. Wrap loosely in newspapers separate articles when folded, and store them in boxes, trunks, or chests lined with newspaper or tarred paper. Label each package separately.

Wrap silk, linen, and other delicate articles in colored tissue papers. Chemicals used to bleach white paper will turn them yellow. Do not use newspapers.

To Remove Odors.—Musty and other unpleasant odors in goods packed and stored may be prevented by sprinkling charcoal in and about the articles, and putting lumps of charcoal in the receptacle in which they are stored.

To Store Silk.—To prevent silks or woolen goods from turning yellow when packed and stored, break up a few pieces of genuine white beeswax, fold loosely in cheese cloth, and place among the goods. Wrap up the articles in old white linen or cotton cloth. Do not use white paper. It will turn them yellow.

To Pack and Store Linen.—Wash linen articles, rinse without bluing or starch, and rough dry.

To Store Lace. — Cover lace with powdered magnesia to prevent its turning yellow.

Whitewash for Vermin.—Prepare whitewash as usual, and add to 1 gallon 4 ounces of corrosive sublimate or 2 ounces of powdered copperas previously dissolved in boiling water.

Alum Wash for Vermin.—Dissolve 1 or 2 pounds of alum to 1 gallon of water by boiling until dissolved. Apply with an oil can, a brush, or otherwise.

Benzine Wash for Vermin.—Make suds of hard white or yellow soap, using about ½ bar of soap to 1 pailful of water, and add 1 pint of benzine. Use to wash floors or woodwork. Apply with a brush, mop, or otherwise.

Phosphorus Paste for Vermin. — Mix 2 drams of phosphorus with 2 ounces of lard, and add 6 ounces of flour and 2 ounces of brown sugar, making the whole into a paste with a little water. Add to this for rats or mice a small quantity of cheese.

But remember that phosphorus is easily set on fire by friction, also that it must not be allowed to fall on the skin, as it burns the flesh, forming a dangerous ulcer. Hence pure phosphorus, which is a solid, is kept under water and handled by means of pincers or a sharp-pointed penknife.

To mix the above, place the phosphorus in a wide-mouthed glass bottle and pour over it an ounce or so of alcohol. Immerse the bottle in hot water until the phosphorus is melted. Cork it and shake vigorously until cold. Pour off the spirit, mix the phosphorus and lard, and add the other ingredients previously mixed together.

Salberg Vermin Wash. — Mix bichloride of mercury, 2 ounces; spirits of turpentine, 6 ounces; muriatic acid, 1 ounce; water, 100 ounces.

CARPET BEETLE OR "BUFFALO MOTH"

The destructive habits of these common and injurious pests are well known. The mischief is done by this insect in its larval stage, when it feeds upon woolen goods, particularly carpets. It is then rather less

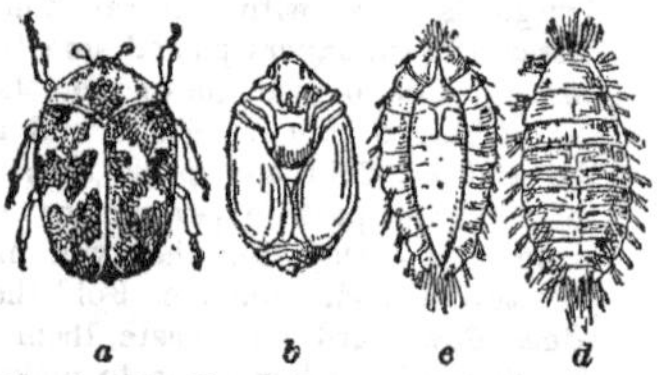

FIG. 1.—*The Carpet Beetle: a, Adult; b, Pupa, Ventral View; c, Pupa within Larval Skin; d, Larva, Dorsal View. All enlarged (from Riley).*

than a fourth of an inch in length, and is covered with stiff brown hair. It is often discovered working about the edges of carpets making irregular holes or following the line of a floor crack, and thus cutting the carpet in a long slit. It is most common in the northern and eastern portions of the United States, and most active in the summer months, although in well-heated houses it may continue its depredations the year round. The adult insect is a black and white beetle, having a red stripe down its back. It is rather less than one fourth of an inch in length.

The carpet beetle is rarely found in houses having polished floors with rugs, straw mattings, or oilcloth as floor coverings, and this fact suggests the most effective remedy. When the house has become infested with these insects, it is very difficult to eradicate them. Thorough house cleaning at least twice a year is advisable. And a special house cleaning toward the middle or latter part of the summer is particularly effective. Take up the carpets, beat them, spray with benzine, and hang on the line to air in the direct sunshine all day. Wash down floors and spray the floor and crevices about the baseboards with benzine or kerosene. Meantime open the windows and ventilate thoroughly before introducing a light. Fill all floor cracks and cracks about the baseboards with suitable crack-fillers, as elsewhere recommended, and, if possible, before relaying the carpet, cover the floor with a lining of tarred roofing paper. Tack the carpet loosely, and occasionally look under the edges to see if insects have put in an appearance. In that case lay a wet cloth over the spot and iron dry with a very hot iron. Steam until the insects are exterminated. Or fumigate the premises with sulphur or bisulphide of carbon or hydrocyanic-acid gas.

THE HOUSE CENTIPEDE

This insect is most commonly found in moist, warm localities, as in cellars, closets, and bathrooms. Its well-known appearance, rapid movements, and the fact that its bite is supposed to be poisonous, causes it to be an object of alarm. The centipede probably never bites human beings except in self-defense, but it is known to be carnivorous in its habits and feeds upon roaches, bedbugs, and other insects. The effect of its bite depends upon the susceptibility of the individual, but in the case of most persons, it is very slightly poisonous, causing an inflammation similar to that of a mosquito bite, which may be allayed by promptly treating it with aqua ammonia. This insect rarely occurs in sufficient numbers to make any special mode of treatment necessary. Open plumbing and care to avoid the accumulation of moisture in any part of the house are the best preventives. Bathrooms, closets, and other localities where they harbor may be inspected occasionally and the insect killed when they make their appearance by means of a wire or screen fly killer.

THE COMMON COCKROACH OR CROTON BUG

Exterminators of Cockroaches.— Substances recommended to kill or disperse cockroaches are fumes of hydrocyanic-acid gas, sulphur, pyrethrum, bichloride of mercury, borax, phosphorus, plaster of Paris, arsenic, pokeroot, chloride of lime, hellebore, and various mechanical means of trapping the insects.

To completely exterminate cockroaches in dwellings, warehouses, libraries, and stores, fumigate with sulphur or hydrocyanic-acid gas.

Or mix in a glass bottle 1 ounce of corrosive sublimate and ½ pint of water. Let stand a day or two and shake occasionally. Then add ½ pint of alcohol. Apply to cracks infested by cockroaches from an oil can or syringe. This liquid soaks into the wood and leaves a thin powder of corrosive sublimate covering the crevices. This is a deadly poison to cockroaches and other insects, but is also poisonous to human beings and must be handled with the utmost care. Do not allow this mixture to touch brass or copper.

Or mix equal quantities of grated sweet chocolate and powdered borax, or equal quantities of powdered sugar and powdered borax, and spread freely on shelves where cockroaches run, or spread on pieces of slightly moistened bread.

Or spread phosphorus paste on moist bread in their runways or under a damp dishcloth, towel, or mop.

Or mix in a saucer 1 part of plaster of Paris and 3 parts of flour, and place in the runways. Place near by another saucer containing pure water.

Lay thin pieces of cardboard from one to the other as bridges and float on the water bits of thin board touching the margin. The cockroaches eat the flour and plaster of Paris, become thirsty, and drink. The plaster then sets and kills them. This is an Australian method. It is simple, safe, and said to be very effective.

Or scatter pulverized hellebore on shelves, behind baseboards, about sinks, etc.

Or scatter hellebore on moistened bread, but remember that this is also poisonous to children and household pets. Cockroaches eat it freely.

Or mix hellebore with molasses, powdered sugar, or grated sweet chocolate.

Or mix arsenic with Indian meal or molasses. Spread on moistened bread. This also is a dangerous poison, and cockroaches will not take it as freely as other poisons.

Or mix in saucers chloride of lime with sweetened water and place in the runways, with bits of pasteboard leading up to the saucers and strips of wood floating on their surface touching the edge.

Or boil 2 ounces of pokewood in 1 pint of water 15 or 20 minutes. Strain through cheese cloth, mix with molasses, and spread on moistened bread or plates.

Or dust the cracks, shelves, etc., with powdered pyrethrum by means of a pair of bellows or otherwise. This is especially useful in libraries, but it stupefies and does not always kill the cockroaches; hence they must be swept up and burned.

Or scatter fresh cucumber peelings in their runways.

Or mix plaster of Paris, 1 part, oatmeal, 3 parts, powdered sugar or grated sweet chocolate, 1 part; scatter on moistened bread and place near to open water.

Or mix equal parts of carbolic acid and powdered camphor, and let stand until dissolved. Apply with a small paint brush to cracks and crevices haunted by them.

But of all the above, powdered borax, with or without flour, and powdered sugar, or both, is perhaps the safest and most useful remedy. It may be dusted freely on shelves, sinks, and kitchen floors, and also forced by means of bellows into cracks and crevices, about floors, baseboards, cupboards, sinks, etc. It is cheap, and harmless to children and household pets, and is far superior to any so-called "cockroach powder" upon the market.

To Trap Roaches.—Take any deep pasteboard or wooden box and substitute for the cover four pieces of window glass slanting toward the center. Put bread moistened with molasses in the trap and place it so that the cockroaches can easily get to the top. They fall from the glass into the box, and cannot get out. This is a well-known French device.

Another trap used in England consists of any suitable box of wood or pasteboard having a round hole in the lid fitted with a glass ring and baited with bread moistened with molasses or other sweetener.

Or take any deep china bowl or jar and put in it about a quart of stale beer or ale, of which cockroaches are especially fond, or water sweetened with molasses. Lean against this a number of pieces of pasteboard or any inclined surface bending over the top so as to project inside the vessel 2 or 3 inches. The cockroaches climb up the inclined plane, slip into the liquid, and cannot escape.

To Use Cockroach Traps.—Bait the traps freshly each night with any moist sweet substance, and destroy the catch of roaches each morning by fire or boiling water. Have traps always at hand, and they will keep down cockroaches so that it will not be necessary to use dangerous poisons more than perhaps once.

Crickets.—The celebrated story by Charles Dickens called "The Cricket on the Hearth," and the well-known superstition in regard to crickets, will perhaps prevent many persons from numbering these little insects among household pests. To exterminate them, if desired, scatter snuff about their haunts, pour boiling water into cracks and crevices from which they emerge, or put ginger cordial in open saucers where they can partake of it.

THE BEDBUG

To Keep Down Bedbugs. — Each week on cleaning day air the mattresses and turn them. Use, if possible, metal beds rather than wooden ones. Take down the bedsteads three or four times a year, especially at spring and fall house cleaning, and oil the joints with a mixture of kerosene and turpentine. At spring house cleaning in March or April apply bedbug exterminators thoroughly to kill the eggs that are laid at this time. Keep bedsteads dusted and cracks cleaned out at least once a week. Go over the bedstead inside and out with a cloth moistened in kerosene. Scatter wild thyme about the mattress and in the vicinity of the bed. The odor drives them away. Do not depend upon Persian insect powder.

Poisons for Bedbugs.—Poisons recommended for exterminating bedbugs are hydrocyanic-acid gas, sulphurous-acid gas, kerosene and other petroleum products, gasoline, benzine, naphtha, etc.; hot water, with or without alum, chloride of zinc; turpentine, camphor, corrosive sublimate dissolved in alcohol, and various combinations of these.

To thoroughly exterminate bedbugs, fumigate with hydrocyanic-acid gas or sulphurous-acid gas. This is the quickest and most effective method.

Or, if this is not convenient and the pests are numerous, take the paper off the walls, wash down the walls with boiling water containing sal soda and alum, apply one or more of the following eradicators, and repaper the walls. Take all bedding out of doors, beat and clean mattresses and other ticks, and apply gasoline to them freely with a sponge, cloth, or brush. Apply suitable poisons to all cracks in bedsteads and other furniture. Replace, if possible, wooden bedsteads with brass or iron ones, and carpet or matting with rugs.

Next to fumigation the best exterminator is kerosene or other petroleum products, as gasoline, benzine, or naphtha. Take down the bedsteads, dust the joints with a brush, and wash with soap and hot water. Boil cedar leaves in the water. While their scent lasts bedbugs will stay away. Thoroughly oil all joints and cracks with kerosene, benzine, or gasoline from a spring-bottom oil can or with a small paint brush or long feather. Gasoline and benzine do not leave any stains. Hence use these freely about baseboards and on bedsteads where kerosene might stain carpets or bedding, but remember that they are highly inflammable. Use them only during daylight, and before introducing a lamp or lighted match, air the room until all odor disappears.

Kerosene is less dangerous, and its stains will evaporate with time or may be taken up by such absorbents as whiting, prepared chalk, starch, and the like.

Or use an equal mixture of turpentine and kerosene.

Or fill all cracks after oiling with hard yellow soap or putty.

Or with a soft, small brush go over the bedstead, springs, and woodwork with a generous coating of hard oil varnish. Work this into all cracks and crevices, and your bedbug troubles will be over.

Or dissolve 2 pounds of alum in 3 or 4 quarts of boiling water, and apply hot from an oil can or with a brush to all crevices in furniture, walls, or floors where bedbugs harbor.

Or apply a weak solution of chloride of zinc.

Or apply with a brush equal parts of blue ointment and kerosene oil.

Or apply a mixture of 1 pint of benzine and ½ ounce of corrosive sublimate. Apply from oil can or with a brush.

Or ½ ounce of corrosive sublimate and ½ pint of alcohol.

Or ½ ounce of corrosive sublimate and ½ pint of turpentine.

Or 1 ounce of corrosive sublimate, 1 ounce of camphor, 4 ounces of spirits of turpentine, and ½ pint of wood alcohol. Apply from an oil can or with a brush.

But remember that corrosive sublimate is a *deadly poison.*

Enemies of Bedbugs.—The common house cockroach is an enemy of bedbugs, and the little red house ants also kill and eat them; but most persons would consider that to encourage such bedbug exterminators would prove a remedy as bad as the disease.

THE HOUSE FLEA

To Get Rid of Fleas.—The source of fleas is usually pet dogs or cats, but they may be brought into the house on clothing or otherwise. They do not breed freely in localities where their eggs are likely to be disturbed. Hence, contrary to the common supposition, they do not usually breed on cats and dogs. But the eggs are laid in floor cracks and other crevices, or they fall from the fur of cats or dogs, usually where they have their sleeping places. Hence carpets and mattings favor the spread of fleas by leaving their eggs undisturbed in the breeding places. Fleas breed very rapidly, especially in unoccupied houses. They are only to be kept down, when they get a foothold, by vigorous measures to insure cleanliness.

Methods recommended for preventing and eradicating fleas are the use of Persian insect powder, petroleum products, eucalyptus oil, oil of pennyroyal or sassafras: the leaves of pennyroyal or camomile flowers, and hot soapsuds; also washing animals with creolin, or, if necessary, fumigating the premises with hydrocyanic-acid gas or sulphurous-acid gas.

Dust Persian insect powder freely into the fur of domestic animals and into all cracks and crevices in the floor and walls about their sleeping places.

Or, if this is not sufficient, spray the entire carpet or matting and lower part of the walls and baseboards with benzine from a watering pot having a very fine nozzle or a spray-nozzle syringe. This must, of course, be done by daylight, and the room thoroughly aired before introducing any light.

Or, if necessary, remove all floor coverings, take them out of doors, and scrub them with gasoline or benzine. Wash the floors with hot soapsuds containing 1 or 2 pounds of alum dissolved in hot water to the pailful. If pets are kept, do this as a preventive measure when house cleaning, or before leaving the house when it is to be shut up for a long time.

Or wash down the floors with hot water containing 1 pint of creolin to the pailful. This method is sure. About once a week saturate in this mixture the bedding used by domestic animals, and let it drip dry in the open air.

If necessary, fumigate the premises with sulphurous-acid gas or hydrocyanic-acid gas.

Eucalyptus oil or the oil of pennyroyal rubbed on one's wrists and ankles will keep off fleas in localities or dwellings badly infested with them.

Or sprinkle either oil about sleeping places of domestic animals and on their fur. Mix with an equal quantity of alcohol and apply by means of an atomizer.

If beds and bedding become infested, spray them with this mixture.

Or place twigs and leaves of pennyroyal or camomile flowers in beds or kennels of cats and dogs or other infested localities. Substitute rugs for carpets in rooms frequented by domestic animals, also prevent the accumulation on the floor of litter of any kind, such as books, papers, and the like. No such accumulation should remain undisturbed more than a few days at a time. A good rule is, on cleaning day move everything.

Professor Gates, of Cornell University, has won international celebrity by a method of catching fleas in a badly infested building. He got the janitor to tie sheets of fly paper about his legs with the sticky side out, and to walk up and down the floor in the infested rooms. A large number of the fleas jumped for his ankles, as they were accustomed to do, and were caught by the fly paper.

Fleas on Domestic Animals.—To free domestic animals of fleas, sprinkle their fur liberally with insect powder, or wash them in a decoction of pennyroyal, sassafras, mint, or other strong vegetable perfume, or in a creolin wash composed for dogs, 4 teaspoonfuls of creolin, and for cats, 2 teaspoonfuls to 1 quart of water. Apply the wash with the hands or with a brush, or submerge the animals in it for about 5 minutes. If cats object to this process, place them in a bag composed of some strong washable material with a draw string, not too tight, about the neck, and immerse them for 5 minutes or more.

RATS AND MICE

To Destroy Rats and Mice.—Methods recommended for destroying rats and mice may be summed up as the use of poisons, traps, ferrets, fumigation, and the rat-proof construction of buildings. In addition, a bacteriological product has been discovered by the Pasteur Institute which communicates to rats and mice an infectious disease, not dangerous to man or other animals, by which they are completely exterminated. The loss to the United States from the brown or Norway rat alone is said to amount to several million dollars a year. These animals also spread the germs of infectious disease from house to house, and the bubonic plague or "black death" from city to city. An exhaustive list of the destructive agencies employed against rats and mice in historic times would more than fill this volume; but most of them are worthless, and only a limited number are necessary.

To Poison Rats.—Mix to a stiff dough 1 part of barium (carbonate of barytes) with 4 parts of corn meal, or 1 part of the barytes with 7 parts of water.

Or spread barytes on moistened bread and butter or toast. Scatter these preparations in small quantities in the rat runs. This poison is without taste or smell, and in the small quantities that suffice to poison rats or mice is harmless to domestic animals. It acts slowly, and the animals before dying will, if possible, leave the premises in search of water. Hence this is the safest poison to employ in dwellings. All receptacles containing water must be covered while this or any other poison is in use, and care must be taken that there are no leaky pipes or pools of water on or near the premises.

Or insert dry crystals of strychnine in small pieces of raw meat, sausage, or toasted cheese. Place these in the rat runs.

Or dissolve ½ ounce of strychnine sulphate in 1 pint of boiling water, add 1 pint of thick sugar sirup, and stir vigorously. Soak wheat or oatmeal in this strychnine sirup over night and spread it about the runs, but do not use strychnine in occupied dwellings, as it is an active poison, and the rats die in their holes before they can escape in search of water.

Or make a dough of phosphorous paste with corn meal, oatmeal, or flour and a little sugar, and add a few drops of oil of rhodium or aniseed. To make phosphorous paste, melt 1 pound of lard in a glass fruit jar, set it in boiling water, and when melted add ½ ounce of phosphorus and 1 pint of alcohol. Screw on the top and shake the jar vigorously to form a complete emulsion. Allow this to settle and pour off the spirits, which may be used again for the same purpose.

Or dissolve in a glass fruit jar ½ ounce of phosphorus in 10 ounces of warm water, and mix to form a stiff dough with 10 or 12 ounces of rye meal, 10 ounces of butter, and 8 ounces of sugar. Place small quantities of the dough in the rat runways.

But remember that phosphorus

readily ignites by friction, and the rats may carry it into their holes and set the place on fire; hence it is not as safe to use as barytes or strychnine.

To Stop Rat Holes.—Where the rat holes are visible, pour a little water into them at night, and after the ground about them becomes damp, sprinkle a thin layer of caustic potash or chloride of lime in and about the holes. The damp potash sticks to the rats' feet and produces sores. In attempting to lick these they communicate the sores to their mouths.

Rats caught in traps after the use of caustic potash are often found to have a mass of sores about the feet, tail, and mouth. They will usually leave the buildings before death. Hence where the holes can be found, this method is preferable to poison.

Or the holes may be coated with soft tar, or stuffed with burdock or cockle burs.

To Stop Mouse Holes.—Protect the bottoms of sideboards, cupboards, and the like with a layer of sheet tin; or cover mouse holes in plaster side walls with a piece of window glass set into the plaster and held in place by plaster of Paris. Filling the hole with plaster does no good, as the mice will gnaw through again.

Or place a little bag full of Cayenne pepper in the hole.

Or mix red pepper freely with the paste used to patch wall paper, and with it paste paper over mouse holes in the walls.

Or line cupboards with newspapers or wall paper, using a paste that contains red pepper.

Or plug mouse holes with newspapers soaked in a solution of red pepper.

Or hang a bag containing peppermint in infested cupboards, wardrobes, and the like.

Or scatter mint leaves about shelves and drawers infested by them.

Or mingle tartar emetic or nux vomica with suitable bait. This sickens mice without killing them, and discourages their visits.

Camphor placed in trunks or drawers will repel mice as well as moths. This is especially useful to preserve flower and garden seeds from mice. Mix gum camphor with the seeds freely. It will not harm them.

To Trap Rats.—Use preferably the thin flat rat trap of iron or steel having a coiled spring and wire fall released by a baited trigger. When rats are numerous, procure several of these and scatter them about the premises. The trap should be large enough and the bait adjusted the right distance from the mouth, so that the fall will strike the rat at about the back of the neck and kill it.

The French wire-cage traps are also useful, and many homemade devices are recommended. A common cask partly filled with water may be converted into a rat trap by taking out one end, cleating it, and replacing it, after rasping off enough of the wood around the edge of the head so that it will slip easily in and out of the barrel. Drive a couple of large wire nails at opposite sides of the head, and balance the head on them across the top of the barrel. Cut a notch on either side as sockets for the nails to prevent the head from slipping. Before using this trap, tack one or two shingle nails into the rim of the barrel so as to temporarily prevent the head from tipping, and place any suitable bait on the head of the barrel for a few days or a week, so that the rats will become accustomed to feeding there. Fasten pieces of raw meat to the head of the barrel by means of glue or tacks, taking care that it balances evenly, and remove the shingle nails. When the rats renew their visits, the first one to step on the edge will cause the head of the barrel to revolve on itself and drop him into the water beneath, when, if properly adjusted, the head will resume its place and be ready for the next comer.

Or the head of the cask may be

covered with stout wrapping paper and baited for a few nights. Then a couple of slits may be made crosswise in the middle of the wrapping paper and reënforced by means of pieces of whalebone glued to the paper and running along the cut edge

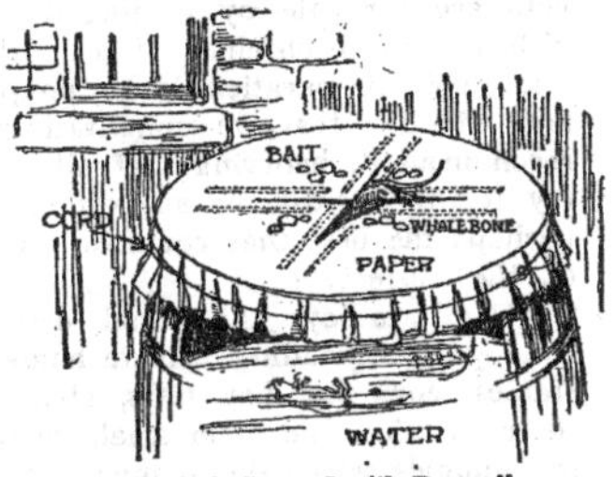

"A Cask Covered with Paper."

and on to the uncut margin. The rat walking to the middle of the sheet causes the paper to give way and drop him inside. The whalebones spring the paper back to place, in readiness for the next.

To Bait Traps. — Bait rat traps with pieces of bologna sausage, oatmeal, toasted cheese, buttered toast, sunflower seeds, or pumpkin seeds, or all of these used in succession. The bait must be changed frequently, as rats are very suspicious, and the location of the traps must be frequently changed. If wood or steel traps are used, insert a stick through the trap after baiting, light a bundle of paper, and smoke it thoroughly. This covers the scent of the hands.

Or place a few drops of oil of rhodium or aniseed on or about the trap. This covers the scent of the hands, and also seems to attract rats and mice.

Or, if wire rat traps are used, after catching one or two rats, do not release, but feed them. They thus act as decoys for others. When a number have been caught, place the trap in a tub of water to drown them.

A correspondent suggests releasing live rats after coating them with a mixture containing phosphorus. Mix with water to the consistency of milk 4 ounces of glue, 4 ounces of asafœtida, and 2 ounces of potash, and add ½ ounce of phosphorus dissolved in a little alcohol. Shake the whole to form a complete emulsion.

Catch one or more rats in a wire cage. Take a pronged stick having prongs about as long as the rat's neck is thick, wedge the fork just behind the animal's ears, and pin him firmly to the floor. He can be held in this position without risk or difficulty. Roll a bit of newspaper into a tight cylinder, set fire to one end, and with the lighted end singe the hair from his back. This can be done without burning the flesh. Fix a small paint brush on a long stick and after dark apply a coating of the phosphoric mixture, slightly warm, to the animal's back, and release him near his hole. Just what impression is produced by what seems to be the ghost of a departed rat reappearing in his old haunts would be hard to say, but those who have tried the experiment report that no rats remain in the vicinity to give an account of their sentiments.

Rats in Poultry Houses.—Traps or poison used to exterminate rats in poultry houses must be protected from fowl invasion. This can be done by inverting over the trap a wooden box or cheese box, with holes cut in the sides through which the rats can enter. As an additional precaution the poison may be placed under a smaller box having holes through which the rats can merely insert their noses without entering, and inverting the large box over the small one. This will prevent the poison from being scattered within the large box near enough to the openings to be reached by fowls. Tack these boxes to the floor on to stakes firmly driven into the ground so that they cannot be shoved about.

Dogs and Ferrets for Rats.—Ferrets in charge of an experienced person will drive rats out of their burrows so that dogs can capture them. The ferret is the rat's most deadly enemy, but ferrets in the hands of amateurs are not always a success. When rats attack a stack of grain, hay, or straw, or take refuge beneath it, they may be exterminated by building around the stack a temporary inclosure of fine mesh wire netting several feet high, and pitching the stack over the netting, to be relaid outside. One or more dogs or ferrets may be placed inside the inclosure to take care of the rats which endeavor to escape while the straw is being removed.

A similar method is employed to entrap the rats by natives in the rice fields of the far East. Temporary piles of brush and rice straw are built in which the rats accumulate. The straw is then removed and the rodents are destroyed.

Fumigation for Rats.—Rats which burrow in fields, levees, or rice-field dikes may be destroyed by saturating a wad of cotton in carbon bisulphide, pushing it into the opening of the burrow, and packing down the soil. Farm buildings are usually not tight enough to admit of fumigation with this or any gas.

Rat-proof Construction. — The use of concrete and cement in construction is the best means of abating the rat nuisance. All sorts of farm buildings and other structures are now being constructed of concrete. Edison predicts that dwelling houses will shortly be made of this material from cellar floor to chimney top. The foundations of all buildings and even whole cellars may be made rat proof by this means at very slight expense.

Fill rat holes with a mixture of cement, sand, and broken glass or sharp bits of stone. Line galleries, corn cribs, and poultry houses inside or outside with fine mesh wire netting. Or lay the floors and foundations in concrete, extending it up on the sills. Invert pans over the posts of corn cribs, but be sure to make these high enough so that the rats cannot jump from the ground on to the posts or sills. The posts should be at least 3½ feet high.

Ratite for Rats.—We make no apology for quoting in full the following extract from a circular of the Pasteur Vaccine Company, whose products are for sale by leading druggists or can be obtained of the makers. This preparation is so unique and effective that we unhesitatingly recommend it, believing that all who try it will regard the suggestion as perhaps the best that could be given on the subject:

"Until to-day, the usual means employed for ridding private houses, stables, corn and hay lofts, etc., of the rats, mice, and other small gnawing animals which do so much damage there, were various chemical products, of which the principal elements were arsenic, strychnine, nux vomica, etc., which destroyed them by poisoning.

"However, the desired result could only be thus obtained by each individual rat or mouse swallowing the bait, and this necessarily entailed a long time when the pests were numerous, and was even impracticable when large spaces required treating.

"Moreover, the use of these chemical products was not without danger for domestic animals, and hence could not be used in poultry yards, stables, kennels, pheasantries, farms, etc. Children have even been poisoned in this way when the necessary precautions were not taken to prevent them from touching the bait.

"Now, however, thanks to bacteriological science, which has made so much progress in the last few years, it has been established that certain microbes become pathogenic for small gnawing animals by giving them a disease peculiar to their species.

"This first fact thus made clear, we have undertaken to perfect the work already done in this direction, and have at last succeeded in preparing a product which we call 'Ratite' and which, when swallowed by rats and mice, gives them a disease not only fatal but contagious, while, being peculiar to their species, it is quite harmless to all other animals.

"'Ratite' thus possesses two big advantages over the means of destruction employed up to the present, viz.:

(1) "*It is absolutely harmless to man, domestic animals, and game of all kind* (feathered or otherwise). It can thus be utilized everywhere, in private houses, farms, stables, fowl runs, kennels, pheasantries, etc., without danger of any accident.

(2) "Not only does it act as simple poison by killing the rat or mouse which swallows it, but it continues its work by contagion, inasmuch as one of these rodents, having swallowed the 'Ratite,' not only catches the fatal disease but becomes an infecting agent among its companions, communicating it by simple contact.

"*Lastly.* The application of 'Ratite' being at once simple and without danger (see directions for use) in addition to its real efficacy, will insure its being preferred to all other systems of destruction employed up to the present.

"Directions for Use.—Pour out the virus in a clean basin, and cut up small cubes of bread (preferably crust) of about 1 c.c. Well soak the bread until it has thoroughly absorbed the liquid, taking care that the bread does not become too pulpy.

"Coarse oatmeal or 'Quaker Oats,' which readily absorb liquid, may be used instead of bread, and this vehicle is recommended for large areas.

"Both the preparation and distribution of bait should be carried out in the evening and spread about in places frequented by rodents—as far as possible in their holes. Six to eight days after distribution of the bait its effects will be apparent, but should any rodents remain after fifteen days, a second application should be made at once. The best results are obtained by one application of a given quantity of virus rather than by extending it gradually over a longer period.

"The virus should be used within twenty days of its preparation, which is marked on the bottle, and if not employed immediately should be kept in a dry, dark, and cool place (a cellar, for instance).

"It will be noticed that the bottles are not full, the empty space being necessary for its preparation.

"The odor of this virus is no sign of deterioration.

"The operator should have his hands free from cuts or sores, and wash them well after preparing and distributing the bait."

We would recommend that if other means prove ineffective "Ratite" be given a trial.

BLACK AND RED ANTS

Ants.—The means employed to keep the house free from ants are of three sorts: preventives, poisons, and mechanical methods.

To Get Rid of Ants.—Place lumps of gum camphor in their runways and near sweets infested by them.

Or scatter snuff in their runways, or branches of sweet fern or fresh green sage leaves or the leaves of green wormwood, or lumps of brimstone or flowers of sulphur or red pepper or powdered borax.

Or scrub shelves and drawers with strong carbolic soap.

Or inject diluted carbolic acid into crevices whence they issue.

Or inject gasoline.

Place any of these substances in their runways, and scatter it about shelves, pantries, and floors near where sweets are kept.

Or place preserves, cake, and other sweets attractive to ants in refrigerators, or small closets, boxes, or tables raised on legs set in pans of water. Add a tablespoonful of kerosene oil to the water to form a scum of oil over the top.

To Trap Ants.—Place near their runs a bit of raw meat or a bone with scraps of meat or a piece of bread moistened in molasses on a bit of board or wrapping paper. The ants will swarm on this, and may be lifted and dropped into the fire or a kettle of boiling water.

Or dip a good-sized sponge in a sirup made by dissolving borax and sugar in boiling water. Wring out the sponge nearly dry, attach a string to it, and lay it in their runways. Have ready a second sponge prepared in the same way. As soon as the first is infested with ants, lift it by the string and drop it into a vessel of boiling water and substitute the second. Meantime rinse the first, moisten it with sirup, and so continue until all are destroyed. Either of these plans will exhaust an ordinary colony of ants in a very few days. The sirup containing borax will also kill those which get away from the sponge and escape the boiling water.

To Destroy Ant Nests.—First locate the nest by placing coarse sugar where the ants can find it. Each ant will take up a load of this and go directly to the nest. The red ant often nests in the walls or floors of houses; hence is difficult to eradicate. Trace the ants to the crevice whence they emerged, and inject kerosene, gasoline, or, better, bisulphide of carbon into the opening. If this fails, the nest is probably some distance off, and it may be necessary to take up a few boards to locate it. When found, apply kerosene, gasoline, or carbon bisulphide.

The small black ant ordinarily makes its nest under stones in the yard. The large black or pavement ant also builds out of doors under pavements or flagstones in yards. To destroy these ants, locate their nests and drench them with boiling water or kerosene.

Or introduce carbon bisulphide into the ground near the nest. To do this, drive a hole into the ground with an iron bar, introduce an ounce or two of this substance, and cover it by immediately filling the hole solidly with earth.

Or dissolve 2 pounds of alum in 3 or 4 quarts of boiling water and pour this into the nests.

Or dissolve ½ ounce of cyanide of potassium in 1 pint of water. Pour this into the hole and saturate the ground about it. Plug the hole with cotton and saturate it with this mixture. But remember that it is a *deadly poison.*

Or pour into the hole a strong solution of carbolic acid in water.

To destroy the large mounds or ant-hills, make a number of holes in the mound with a bar or large stick, and pour an ounce or two of carbon bisulphide into each hole. This substance is not expensive and can be used freely. Close the hole immediately with the foot. The bisulphide will penetrate to all parts of the ant-hill and kill the whole colony.

THE WHITE ANT

This name is a misnomer, as the insect is not a member of the ant family, although its appearance and habits are similar. It is common throughout the United States, but most numerous and active in the Southern States, and in moist localities. The insects feed upon moistened or decayed vegetable matter, as the timber of buildings, books, papers, and the like. They burrow into the interior of these objects and sometimes riddle them through and through, so that they crumble into a mass of dust before any outward indication of their presence is observed.

Preventive Measures.—To prevent the ravages of the white ant, foundations of buildings, especially in warm climates and moist localities, should be of stone or cement, and should raise the walls well above contact with moisture from the soil. A clear space of gravel or asphalt next to the foundation, and the removal of decayed wood or vegetable substances, is helpful.

Or impregnate wood that comes in contact with the ground, or that is likely to be damp for any reason, with creosote.

Or use for such purposes California redwood, which is not eaten by these insects.

Destruction of White Ants.—The only certain remedy is the fumigation of the premises by hydrocyanic-acid gas. Frequent inspection of any accumulation of books and papers is advisable.

THE COMMON HOUSE FLY

To Banish Flies. — The preferred breeding place of the house fly is the manure pit of horse stables. The female lays about 120 eggs, which hatch in six or eight hours. The maggots or larvæ reach full growth in four or five days, and become adult flies in about five days more. Hence in the United States a single generation is bred in about ten days, and twelve to fifteen generations on an average every summer. Thus enormous numbers of flies may be hatched in a single manure pile.

The only effective means to prevent or reduce this nuisance is to board up a portion of the barn cellar, or build a lean-to against the horse stable having a tight trapdoor or screened window admitting to the stable, and a tight door to permit of removing the manure. Such precautions to prevent the entrance of flies, and thus to deprive them of their natural breeding place, have been proved by experience in Washington and other cities to greatly abate this nuisance.

In France the *Matin*, a Paris newspaper, offered a prize of 10,000 francs during the winter of 1905–6 for the best means of lessening this nuisance. The prize was awarded by scientific men for a proposal to use residuum oil in all cesspools and similar places.

For each square yard of the pit mix 2 quarts of the oil with water, and throw into the receptacle. This covers the surface with a scum which kills all larvæ, prevents flies from entering and laying their eggs, covers the contents, and also assists in preventing the development of the bacteria of germ diseases. The same substances may be mixed with earth, lime, or phosphates, and spread upon the manure in barnyards, stables, etc.

Or scatter about horse stables sawdust saturated with dilute carbolic acid, 1 part of the acid to 100 parts of water.

Disease from Flies.—The fact that flies carry the germs of typhoid and other filth diseases is now so well established that no one can have a clear conscience who is responsible for an open vault or drain or an exposed manure pile, if there is sickness in his household or neighborhood. In the country, farmhouses are usually far enough apart, so that the responsibility for the abatement of this nuisance rests upon the head of the family. But in towns and villages the responsibility rests upon the local board of health, who, upon complaint being made, have in most cases ample power to enforce sanitary measures.

To Destroy Flies. — The various household measures against flies are the use of screens, poisons, adhesive fly papers, traps, and various preventives.

Have screens for every window and door in the house. Removable wire screens on adjustable or other wood frames are, perhaps, most convenient. These may be inserted in the windows at will and removed when not wanted.

Or a wooden frame may be made the full size of the outer casing of the window and covered with wire or cloth netting. This may be inserted in the spring and removed in the fall, or, if desired, and wire net is used, may be left during the winter, especially in the upper rooms, to prevent children from falling out when the windows are open.

Or a cheap, handy way to screen against flies is to tack mosquito netting to the outer window casing so as to cover the whole window. This is always out of the way, will last one season, can be torn down in the fall, and replaced cheaply and easily in the spring. If there are children, have the screen door made in two sections, an upper and a lower, so that only the lower section opens when the children go in and out. The flies settle mostly on the upper part of the door. Hence this arrangement keeps out many flies. Adjust the two sections so that the whole door opens when pulled from above. Flies will come down the chimney even when there is a fire in the grate. Hence screen the chimney by means of wire netting across the top.

Have screens either half or full size made for each window on the same principle as a screen door, to fit into the outer frame and open outward. Hinge on the right side top and bottom, same as a door, and place hooks or bolts on the left side top and bottom to fasten in place. Use double hinges, and in the fall the screen can be lifted, leaving half of the hinge on the window frame. Protect this with suitable oil or paint, and the screen can be adjusted in the spring with little trouble.

Or tack wire or cloth screen to the outer frame of the window, to cover either the lower sash or the entire frame.

Or this may be done from the inside by tacking at the side first, then all around, and facing below.

Or, if the outside shutters are no longer in good repair, they may be converted into frames for screens. Cut out the shutters from the frames and replace with wire screen cloth. These are very convenient, as they cover the whole window, and when it is being washed, or it is otherwise desirable, the screens can be opened out of the way. In winter time they can be taken from the hinges and by varnishing the wire to prevent rust they can be preserved from year to year.

To Mend Screens.—To mend a wire window or door screen that has not become too rusty to work with, take a square piece large enough to reach firm wire on all sides of the damaged part. Ravel the edges of the patch, taking off two or more wires on each side to leave a fringe a quarter of an inch or more in width all around. Then, with the flat side of a pair of pincers, bend this fringe down at right angles. Place the patch in position and push the bent fringe through. Bend the fringe in toward the center, and place it in firmly by putting a small board against it and hammering it gently on the other side. The patch will hold, and flies cannot crawl under its edges.

Preventives Against Flies. — Flies are said to abhor sweet clover. Place in bags made of mosquito netting and hang them about the room.

Or sprinkle about the room oil of sassafras or oil of laurel. The latter has been used by the butchers of Geneva from time immemorial.

Or use oil of lavender or lavender buds.

Or soak houseleeks for five or six days in water, and wash pictures, furniture, and woodwork with the decoction.

Or boil onions in a quantity of water and wash picture frames, moldings, and delicate woodwork, using a soft cloth or a brush.

To prevent flies from settling on windows, wash them in water containing kerosene and wipe with a rag moistened in kerosene.

To Make Poisonous Fly Paper.—To make poisonous fly paper, dissolve 6 drams of chloride of cobalt and 2 ounces of brown sugar in 1 pint of boiling water. Saturate blotting paper with this solution and put a small square of the paper in a saucer of water, or use the solution itself, but remember that it is a *deadly poison.*

Or mix 1 teaspoonful of laudanum and ½ teaspoonful of brown sugar with 2 tablespoonfuls of water. Expose in saucers. Keep away from children and pets.

Or boil ½ ounce of quassia tips in 1 quart of water, and add 8 ounces of molasses or brown sugar.

Or dissolve 2 drams of mastic of quassia in ½ pint of water, and add 2 tablespoonfuls of molasses or brown sugar.

Or make strong green tea and sweeten with sugar.

Or mix ½ teaspoonful of black pepper and 1 teaspoonful of sugar with 2 tablespoonfuls of cream.

Or mix 1 tablespoonful of black pepper, 1 tablespoonful of molasses or brown sugar, and the yolk of 1 egg. Beat to a paste. Flies will eat freely any of the above if exposed where they congregate, and will be killed by them.

To Make Sticky Fly Paper.—Melt ½ pound of rosin, and dilute to the consistency of molasses with 4 ounces or more of sweet oil or lard oil. Spread this with a brush on two or more sheets of manila wrapping paper, leaving an inch or more margin all around. Place the sticky surfaces of each pair of sheets together, and when wanted pull them apart. This is also a useful preventive against ants and other insects.

THE MOSQUITO

Dangers from Mosquitoes. — A world-wide campaign is being carried on to exterminate the mosquito pest. The reason of this is found in the recent discovery that mosquitoes are the sole means whereby malaria and yellow fever are communicated to man, and the suspicion that they communicate other diseases. The fact that mosquitoes and malaria seem to go together has long been noted, and likewise the fact that malaria seems to be contracted after nightfall, but until recently the part played by mosquitoes in communicating malaria was not understood. The notion that the mists arising from swamps and stagnant water at nightfall convey the germs of malaria to man is now quite exploded. In 1880 Lavaren, a surgeon in the French army at Algiers, first identified the parasites of malaria in human blood. In 1898 two Englishmen, Manson and Ross, showed positively that malaria is transmitted by mosquitoes. In 1900 two English physicians, Sambon and Lowe, occupied a house in one of the most malarial districts in the world, the well-known Campagna in Rome. The house was screened against mosquitoes. The two men were quite free from malaria and chills, while people living near by in houses not screened were fever-ridden. Mosquitoes which had bitten malarial patients were sent to England and allowed to bite persons who had never had malaria or been exposed to it, but who thereupon developed typical cases of the disease.

Similar experiments made by a medical commission of the United States Army near Quamados, Cuba, prove that the mosquito also transmits yellow fever. The commission erected a small wooden building tightly sealed and screened against mosquitoes. For 63 days seven noncommune men occupied this building. They used unwashed bedding from the beds of genuine yellow-fever patients without contracting yellow fever.

In another experiment a house was built having two rooms separated by wire screens. The house was tightly screened against mosquitoes. Its entire contents were disinfected, and both rooms were occupied by persons not immune to yellow fever. Mosquitoes which had bitten yellow-fever patients were placed in one room, but not in the other. In the room containing no mosquitoes none had yellow fever, but in the other room six out of the seven that were bitten by mosquitoes developed genuine cases of the disease. These experiments led to scientific observations which have proved that a certain species of mosquito—the Anopheles—is present in all malarial and yellow-fever districts, but apparently not elsewhere; and also that the germs of malaria required for their development during a part of their life history occur as parasites in the bodies of the Anopheles mosquito.

These facts are stated at length to remove all doubts about the connection between malaria and yellow fever and the mosquito, and to impress the fact that such diseases are preventable. If they occur in any locality, the responsible heads of families cannot have a clear conscience until they have sought and removed the cause—namely, all near-by ponds or puddles of stagnant water in which mosquitoes breed.

Life History of Mosquitoes.—The mosquito passes through four distinct stages: egg, larva, pupa, and adult. The female deposits her eggs, from 75 to 300 in number, toward the latter part of the night or early morning on the surface of stagnant pools. She rarely deposits them on running water or pure water that is frequently stirred. The egg hatches in about twenty-four hours or more, according to temperature. It produces the larva or well-known wiggler or wiggletail which everyone may see in rain barrels or pools of stagnant water. The young larva rests just beneath the surface of the water, but breathes the outer air through a respiratory tube located at the tip of the abdomen. The larvæ cannot live more than a minute or two if unable to reach the surface to breathe, and to this fact is due the common method of destroying them by means of a film of petroleum on the surface of the water.

In five or six days the larvæ change into pupæ. In about two days more these assume the form of the ordinary adult mosquito. Hence in hot weather a generation of mosquitoes develops in from eight to ten days. Considering the number of eggs laid by a single female it will be readily seen that countless millions of these pests may breed in a single pool, pond, or swamp during one summer season.

To Destroy Mosquitoes. — Happily, the experiments of scientific observers seem to indicate that mosquitoes do not usually fly very far from the pools in which they were hatched. They require as breeding places pools of stagnant water that remain undisturbed for from ten days to two weeks, and they may be completely destroyed by covering the surface of these pools with a thin film of petroleum or kerosene oil. Hence the problem of exterminating mosquitoes is strictly a local one, and the means are quite within the reach of every responsible person. Farmhouses are often far apart, so that all the mosquitoes about the house and farm buildings are bred on the place. Consequently, the responsibility for exterminating them is purely an individual one.

Or a group of neighboring farmers can often be persuaded to act in harmony, or at least to permit an enterprising neighbor to take measures to prevent the breeding of mosquitoes in their vicinity.

School children may be encouraged to undertake the extermination of mosquitoes in an entire school district, or boards of health may be persuaded to take up the problem and appoint voluntary or paid representatives to wage a war of extermination through the entire community.

Kerosene for Mosquitoes.—To destroy mosquitoes, apply petroleum or kerosene oil to the surface of the pools, puddles, or marshes in which they breed. One ounce of kerosene is sufficient for 15 square feet of stagnant water. Thus a tank or pool 10 feet across would require about 1½ pints of the oil.

To apply the oil on small puddles, tanks, or pools, it is only necessary to pour it on the surface or scatter it to windward with a wide sweep of the arm. The oil will spread itself over the surface in a uniform film. But for larger ponds, marshes, and pools overgrown about the edges with grass or weeds which may prevent the oil from penetrating to every part, it is better to use an ordinary sprayer having a fine nozzle, such as is used for spraying fruit trees with Bordeaux mixture. This may be applied in pools by wading or from a raft or boat.

A single application of oil kills all eggs laid upon the surface and all wigglers previously hatched. The film of oil prevents their coming to the surface to breathe, hence they are suffocated or "drowned." The oil does not prevent the female mosquito from attempting to deposit her eggs on the surface, but destroys her in the act of doing so; consequently, until the oil evaporates, the breeding of mosquitoes is totally prevented. The film of oil, if undisturbed, will not evaporate for a week or more, and at least ten days will be required after it has evaporated for a generation of mosquitoes to mature. Hence in absolutely still water where there is no current to carry off the oil, two applications a month will be quite sufficient. In covered tanks, drains, and cesspools not exposed to the sun, one application a month should be enough. But those who are fighting mosquitoes must remember that after a rain an old tin can, the print of a cow's foot in the mud, or a puddle left in a wagon rut or hollow may breed enormous numbers of mosquitoes if it remains undisturbed for a period of ten days or more. Hence a few days after a rain the ubiquitous small boy should be sent abroad with a small waterpot having a fine nozzle and containing a gallon or more of kerosene, and he should be instructed to cover the surface of these pools with a layer of the oil. Tin cans before being thrown on the dump should have the bottoms knocked out or a few holes punched in them with a can opener. An ounce of prevention is better than a pound of cure.

To Destroy Mosquitoes by Drainage.—This needs little comment. Obviously, if swamps, pools, and the like have tile or other drains laid beneath their surface so that the water is entirely drawn off, mosquitoes cannot breed in them. But open drains are themselves favorite breeding places of mosquitoes. Hence these should be spread with oil, especially along the edges where grass and weeds make the current sluggish. If there is much current, they should be sprayed two or three times a month.

Rain barrels, buckets, and all other receptacles about the premises in which water collects should be emptied at least once a week or, if possible, permanently. Draining is the most satisfactory way to fight mosquitoes, as it is much easier to get people's interest in the subject thoroughly aroused by one concerted effort than it is to try keeping it up by spasmodic efforts from month to month and from year to year.

Screens for Mosquitoes. — Cover with fine wire screens rain barrels, cisterns, and all receptacles for drinking water that cannot be treated with kerosene or emptied frequently, and go over them occasionally with a cloth moistened in kerosene, taking care not to let any oil drip into the water. This will effectually prevent mosquitoes from squeezing through the screen to lay their eggs.

To Destroy Mosquitoes with Fish. —The small pools, marshes, swamps, and streams having shallow pools with stagnant edges which are used as watering places for stock, and hence cannot be covered with kerosene, should be stocked with small fish, as the top minnow and the sunfish (or "pumpkin seed"). Both these species feed on the wigglers and will quickly rid any infested waters of them. The pumpkin seed is preferable, as it is equipped with spine rays which protect it from the larger fish. But the top minnow is suitable for small pools and ponds where there are no pike or pickerel.

When depending upon fish to keep the watering places of stock clear from mosquitoes, be on the lookout against prints left by the hoofs of animals in the mud on margins of ponds, where, of course, the fish cannot approach. These must be treated occasionally with kerosene.

Household Remedies. — To screen all doors, windows, and other openings, including the entrance to the top of the chimney and to the cellar windows, against mosquitoes may be, in malarial and yellow-fever districts or during epidemics of contagious diseases, a matter of life and death, and is the best preventive at all times against the annoyance of the pests. An open porch or piazza fitted with movable screens or hinged screens that can be opened during the daytime if desired, is a great convenience and luxury in mosquito-ridden districts. If mosquitoes crawl through the screens, rub the latter just at twilight with a cloth moistened in kerosene, or, if preferred, one of the essential oils, as pennyroyal or other preventives.

Or burn Persian insect powder or pyrethrum in sitting or sleeping-rooms during the evening, moistening the powder with a little water and shaping it by hand to a rough cone about the size and shape of a chocolate drop. Place these cones in a pan and thoroughly dry them in the oven. When wanted, set fire to the top of one, which will smolder slowly and send up a thin column of pungent smoke, not harmful to man but stupefying to mosquitoes. Two or three of these cones burned during the evening will give much relief from mosquitoes in sitting rooms. The smoke does not, however, kill the insects, and is merely a palliative.

Or, to kill mosquitoes found in the evening on ceilings of sitting rooms or bedrooms, nail to the end of a broom handle or other suitable stick a shallow tin cup, such as the top of a blacking box, and wet the inside with kerosene. When this cup is placed under the mosquito, he drops or flies against the oily surface and is killed. The last two methods are recommended by the United States Department of Agriculture.

Or place a bit of camphor gum the size of a butternut on iron or tin and hold it over the flame of a lamp until it evaporates. Do not let it take fire. The smoke which fills the room will stupefy the mosquitoes.

Or scatter oil of pennyroyal about the room.

To Prevent Mosquito Bites. — Dilute oil of pennyroyal with water, or make an infusion of pennyroyal leaves and apply to the hands and face, or rub the bruised leaves on the skin.

Or apply camphorated spirits, or a mixture of 1 part of carbolic acid with 3 parts of sweet oil. Take care that this does not enter the eyes or mouth or any cuts or burns on the skin.

Or use a mixture of 3 ounces of sweet oil, ½ ounce of creosote, and ½ ounce of pennyroyal.

To Cure Mosquito Bites. — Apply aqua ammonia or salt and water or a decoction of tobacco or dilute carbolic acid.

Or crushed smartweed leaves put on with a bandage.

Or a mixture of 2 ounces of spermaceti, ½ ounce of white wax, 1 ounce of camphor, and 2 ounces of olive oil. Melt with gentle heat and stir vigorously. Preserve in covered jars for use.

Plant castor beans about the house. These are said to repel mosquitoes.

ORCHARD, FARM, AND GARDEN PESTS

Every farmer or family living in suburban or rural locations should invest in a good, practical spraying

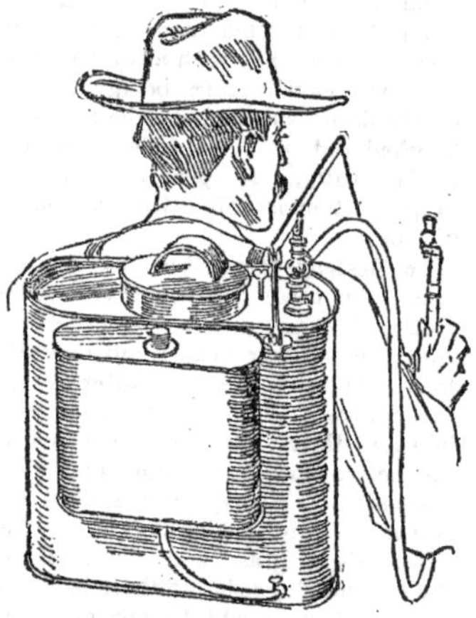

"The Compressed-air Sprayer."

outfit and have in readiness the necessary ingredients for the different kinds of solutions used for spraying quickly and conveniently. Such an outfit will save its cost many times over in the course of a year on any farm, or even in a vegetable garden, flower garden, or ordinary lawn with shade trees and shrubbery. We quote from Dr. Wilhelm Miller, editor of the *Garden Magazine*, as follows:

"The ideal way for you to insure yourself against all these troubles is to get a spraying outfit, costing about $7.50.

"I like best the compressed-air sprayers, because I am lazy, and pumping is hard work. With a dozen strokes of the plunger I can charge the machine in half a minute, and it will work automatically from six to fifteen minutes, according to the nozzle opening. It will spray three gallons with only two chargings. This is enough to cover a quarter of an acre of potatoes or strawberries.

"Seven dollars and a half may seem a lot of money, but a compressed-air sprayer saves its value the first year in the larger and better crops that you get. The outfits that cost less are generally more expensive of time or material, or both. Moreover, a good spraying outfit is invaluable if you keep chickens, because the best way to keep down lice is to spray the henhouse with kerosene. Also you can spray whitewash (an excellent vermin killer and disinfectant) in poultry houses and barns and on fences and walls much quicker than you can apply it with a brush. Also it is useful for watering plants, washing carriages, and applying shading material to hotbed sash or greenhouse glass.

"However, no one should plead poverty as an excuse for not controlling the San José scale on his premises, because anyone can spray a few bushes with the aid of a pail and an old whisk broom. Just get a quart of the prepared lime-sulphur-salt compound at any seed store for forty cents, and dilute it with forty quarts of water if you use it in November. From December to February you can use it twice as strong with safety.

"Many people buy these dollar squirt guns, which hold about a quart, but they are so slow and tire one so quickly that it is better economy to buy something that works faster and sprays farther.

"A bucket pump costs about $3.75 without the bucket, and this is the cheapest outfit I would recommend. But if you have any small trees to spray, you will want a pole with an extra seven feet of hose, which costs a dollar more. Then you will find that the liquid slops over unless you get a bucket with a cover that fastens down tight, and that may mean another dollar, or $5.75. By this time you will discover that it is very awkward to pump with one hand and hold up a seven-foot pole while spraying your fruit trees, and you will be willing to pay twenty-five cents more and get a compressed-air sprayer.

"Now, if you are willing to spend $6 for a sprayer, you might as well pay $7.50 and get the best there is, for that includes an anti-clogging device, like the 'auto-pop,' which will save you the most exasperating feature of spraying.

"Then you will have a brass tank, which cannot be corroded by chemicals or rusted like the tin and iron sprayers. It costs less than a knapsack sprayer, and you can carry it over your shoulder with the aid of a strap, for it weighs, when loaded, less than forty pounds. You can throw any kind of a spray, from a solid stream to a mist that will envelop a tree like a fog. And you have only one thing to think of—no pumping except once in ten or fifteen minutes."

Recipes for Spraying.—The standard preparations or solutions for spraying are as follows:

Bordeaux Mixture.—This consists of copper sulphate, quicklime, and water. The "Standard" formula is: copper sulphate, 6 pounds; quicklime, 4 pounds; water, 22 gallons.

The "Normal" formula is: copper sulphate, 6 pounds; quicklime, 4 pounds; water, 45 gallons. More recent experiments appear to favor a still more dilute solution.

We recommend for a strong solution: copper sulphate, 4 pounds; quicklime, 4 pounds; water, 50 gallons.

For a weaker solution we recommend: copper sulphate, 2 pounds; quicklime, 2 pounds; water, 50 gallons.

In compounding this mixture, first put the copper sulphate on a piece of cheese cloth, tying the ends together so it will not spill, and suspend it from a stick in a bucket of water. Fill the barrel or tank to contain the solution half full of water, carefully measuring the amount used. When the copper sulphate is fully dissolved, pour it into the receptacle. Thoroughly slake the lime and strain the milk of lime into the barrel. Then add sufficient water to make 50 gallons.

Stock Solution. — Weighing the copper and lime at the time of making the mixture is sometimes inconvenient, but as the mixture deteriorates if allowed to stand, it is not feasible to make it up in advance. It is, however, a good idea to make up stock preparations of sulphate of copper and of lime, and have them ready for mixing when required. The lime should be fresh quicklime and when slaked must be covered with water to keep out the air. Thus a stock mixture can be kept all summer without harm.

To prepare a stock solution of sulphate of copper, suspend some evening 50 pounds of copper sulphate in 25 gallons of water. The next morning, if the water is well stirred, each gallon of water will contain 2 pounds of sulphate. This will form the stock solution of copper sulphate. The undissolved sulphate must, of course, be removed.

Put in the spray barrel 2 gallons of this solution, which is equivalent to 4 pounds of copper sulphate. Fill the spray barrel half full of water before adding the lime. This is necessary, because if lime is added to a strong solution of sulphate of copper, the mixture will curdle. Now stir up the water in the lime barrel so as to make a dilute milk of lime, but do not let it get as thick as cream, otherwise lumps will form and clog the spray nozzle. To determine the amount of milk of lime necessary (which will depend upon the strength you desire), get from a drug store a vial of ferrocyanide of potassium (yellow prussiate of potash). Continue to add lime to the mixture as long as drops of the cyanide continue to change from a yellow to a brown color. When the change of color ceases, add another pail of milk of lime to make the necessary amount a sure thing. A little too much lime does not do any harm. The barrel can now be filled with water, and the Bordeaux mixture is ready for use.

This is the most generally useful treatment for fungous diseases.

The strong solution (third recipe) may be used on most plants, but for cherry trees, peach trees, and watermelon vines, the weaker solution (fourth recipe) is to be preferred.

Kerosene Emulsion.—Experiments seem to indicate that all soft-bodied sucking insects are destroyed by contact with kerosene. Pure kerosene may be applied to the hardier trees in winter when they are not growing. For application to growing trees and foliage in summer, a mixture called kerosene emulsion is recommended, as follows: hard, soft, or whale-oil soap, ½ pound; boiling soft water, 1 gallon; kerosene, 2 gallons.

The soap is first dissolved in the boiling water, then the kerosene is added and churned by the pump from five to ten minutes. Before using, this must be reduced with water from one fourth to one tenth its strength. A strong emulsion must be used for scale insects, as the San José scale.

For plant lice, thrips, red spiders, and mealy bugs, weaker solutions may be used. Soft-bodied insects and cabbage worms, currant worms, etc., can be destroyed by these. The emulsion should be made shortly before using.

Formula for San José Scale.—A special formula for San José scale is as follows: whale-oil soap, 1 pound; boiling soft water, 1 gallon; kerosene, 2 gallons. Mix, churn, and reduce with 6 times as much water as emulsion. Use this in summer to kill the young and tender scales.

Kerosene without Soap.—Kerosene and water, reduced as above, may be used instead of the emulsion with soap. This requires a pump with a kerosene attachment. Select for spraying a clear, windy day, so that the surplus mixture will evaporate rapidly.

Ammoniacal Copper Carbonate.—This mixture is cheap, but is not quite as good as the Bordeaux mixture. It is not much used except on fruit that is nearly ripe and on flowering plants, when it is preferred, because the Bordeaux mixture would stain them. This is a clear solution and leaves no stains. The formula is as follows: copper carbonate, 5 ounces; ammonia (26 per cent Beaumé), 3 pints; water, 45 gallons.

Mix the copper carbonate with a little water into a paste. Mix the ammonia with 7 or 8 times its amount of water. Put the paste into the diluted ammonia and stir until dissolved. Add enough water to make 45 gallons. When it has settled, use only the clear blue liquid.

Copper Sulphate Solution.—The same chemicals are used here as in the Bordeaux mixture. The formula is: copper sulphate, 1 pound; water, 15 to 25 gallons.

Dissolve the copper sulphate in the water and it is ready for use. For peaches and nectarines, use the weaker solution. This must never be applied to foliage, but must be used in winter and spring before the buds open. A very much weaker solution —1 pound to 250 gallons of water—can be used for trees in leaf in place of the ammoniacal copper carbonate. This solution may be combined with arsenical insecticides.

Potassium Sulphide.—This is expensive and is chiefly used for treating seed grain for smut. The formula is: potassium sulphide, 1½ pounds; water, 25 gallons. For spraying, use ¼ ounce to 1 gallon of water. This is a very powerful germ killer.

Corrosive Sublimate.—This is used on seed potatoes to prevent scab. The proper formula is: corrosive sublimate, 1 ounce; water, 7 gallons. This is also a disinfectant. It is very poisonous and corrodes metals.

Formalin or Formaldehyde.—This is naturally a gas, but is sold commercially in the form of a 40 per cent solution in water. It is not a poison, but the fumes are irritating to breathe. It is the best fungicide for prevention of smut in grain and scab in potatoes. For seed potatoes the formula is: formalin, ½ pint; water, 15 gallons. Immerse the potatoes for 2 hours in this solution.

The formula for seed wheat or oats is: formalin, 1 pound; water, 50 gallons. Immerse the seed for the same length of time.

Sulphur.—This is useful in preventing mildew on plants. Sprinkle dry powdered sulphur over the plants, or spray with the following solution: sulphur, 1 pound; water, 5 gallons.

The fumes of burning sulphur are powerful as a disinfectant, fungicide, and insecticide, but they kill the plants as well. Hence sulphur must not be burned in hotbeds or greenhouses.

Paris Green.—The active principle of this well-known insecticide is arsenic. It should be of a bright-green color, and should be bought of a reliable dealer, because it is often adulterated. The formula varies in strength according to the use intended. A general formula would be: Paris green, 1 pound; water, 100 to 250 gallons.

For fruit trees, add 1 pound of quicklime to prevent injury to the foliage. Paris green and Bordeaux mixture can be applied together with perfect safety, so as to spray for insects and fungous diseases at the same time. Add 4 to 12 ounces of Paris green to 50 gallons of Bordeaux mixture. This will kill all chewing insects.

Paris green may be dusted on foliage in a dry condition. The formula is: Paris green, 1 part; flour, dust, or ashes, 10 to 20 parts.

The proper solution for potato bugs is Paris green, 1 pound; water, 100 gallons.

For peaches and other tender-leaved plants, use Paris green, 1 pound; water, 200 gallons.

London Purple.—This contains arsenite of lime and may be dusted on plants dry, the same as Paris green. When used in solution, the proper formula is: London purple, 1 pound; water, 200 gallons.

This is more liable to cause injury than Paris green, and the latter is to be preferred.

Paragrene and Green Arsenoid.—These are patented preparations, and when of good quality are perhaps as effective as Paris green. They are said to require less mixing.

Paris green, London purple, and other arsenites above mentioned destroy injurious insects without danger to the foliage, and there is no good reason for buying these or other patented preparations that cost more and do not do the work any better.

Whale-oil Soap.—For San José scale on dormant trees in winter use whale-oil soap, 2 pounds; water, 1 gallon.

For scale or aphis in summer use: whale-oil soap, 1 pound; water, 5 to 7 gallons. This may be quickly dissolved by the use of hot water.

Kerosene Emulsion — Milk Formula. — Kerosene, 2 gallons; sour milk, 1 gallon. Agitate from 3 to 5 minutes with a pump. Add 15 or 20 times its amount of water, according to the plants to be sprayed.

Crude Petroleum.—This may be used in place of kerosene when it can be readily obtained. A crude petroleum emulsion is used on the Pacific Coast as follows: whale-oil soap, 1½ pounds; distillate petroleum, 5 gallons. Prepare as for kerosene emulsion, and add 12 to 15 times as much water.

Kerosene and crude petroleum in a mechanical mixture of about 25 per cent of the oil is about as effective as pure oil and much less injurious to foliage. Sometimes, however, injury results, and it is advisable to use the plain oil and water in winter, and the dilute kerosene emulsion in summer.

White Arsenic. — This is cheaper and of more uniform strength than Paris green. It may be used safely with Bordeaux mixture, or in connection with soda or lime, but it cannot be safely used alone.

Arsenite of Soda for Bordeaux Mixture. — Sal-soda crystals, 4 pounds; water, 1 gallon. Mix and dissolve. Add 1 pound of white arsenic and boil until dissolved. Add water to replace what has boiled away so as to leave 1 gallon of arsenite of soda. This is stock solution. Use 1 pint of this stock solution with 50 gallons of Bordeaux mixture.

Arsenite of Lime.—White arsenite if used alone may be prepared as follows; sal-soda crystals, 1 pound; water, 1 gallon. Mix and dissolve. White arsenic, 1 pound. Add this and boil until dissolved. Fresh slaked lime, 2 pounds. Add this and boil 20 minutes. Add 2 gallons of water to make stock solution. Use 1 quart of this stock solution to 50 gallons of water.

Arsenite of Lead or Disperene.—This preparation is very useful against beetles and similar insects, which are hard to poison. It can be applied in large quantities without harm to foliage, and adheres to the foliage a long time. This has been used almost exclusively by the Gypsy Moth Commission of Massachusetts, and is strongly recommended by them. It forms a whitish coating on foliage, so it is easy to see whether or not the arsenite has been sprayed and when it has been washed off by rain. For the potato bug it has been found a more effective insecticide than Paris green. It costs more than Paris green, but remains suspended longer in the water, and hence can be applied more evenly and goes farther. The formula is: arsenite of lead, 1 to 2 pounds; water, 50 gallons. It is ready for use as soon as the paste is mixed with the water.

Hellebore.—This poison is not so strong as Paris green and other arsenites, and loses its strength after being exposed to the air, hence it can be used to spray fruit a short time before ripening. It is in common use on currants, gooseberries, and other small fruits. It may be applied either dry or mixed with water. For a solution use fresh white hellebore, 1 ounce; water, 3 gallons. Apply when thoroughly mixed. This is for insects which chew, as turnip worms, gooseberry worms, currant worms, and sawflies.

Lime, Sulphur, and Salt Wash.—This mixture is commonly used on the Pacific Coast against the San José scale. The formula is: lime, 15 pounds; sulphur, 25 pounds; salt, 15 pounds. Water, sufficient to make 50 gallons after boiling.

This wash may be boiled in an iron kettle. Heat the water before adding the lime and sulphur. The sulphur must be thoroughly dissolved.

Pour the mixture through a strainer into the sprayer. The best results are obtained by applying this wash while warm. It must be applied only in the winter while the tree is dormant. This is used against the San José scale, apple and pear scab, and leaf curl.

Oregon Wash.—Same as lime, sulphur, and salt wash, but substitute blue vitriol for salt. Use in the same manner for the same purposes.

CHAPTER XVI

ADHESIVES, PAINTS, AND VARNISHES

ADHESIVES—PASTES—MUCILAGE—GLUE—CEMENT—SPECIAL ADHESIVES—SPECIAL PURPOSE CEMENTS—PAINTS AND PAINTING—USES OF PAINT—SPECIFICATIONS FOR PAINTING—CARE OF PAINTS AND BRUSHES—SPECIAL KINDS OF PAINT—VARNISHING—FIXED-OIL VARNISHES—SPIRIT OR LAC VARNISHES—VOLATILE-OIL VARNISHES—SPECIAL VARNISHES—SEALING WAX—OILS, LUBRICATORS, ETC.—FURNITURE POLISH—SOLDER AND SOLDERING

ADHESIVES

Adhesives.—Adhesives are a class of substances capable of attaching themselves to the surface of solid bodies, and thus, when interposed between them, of uniting such bodies. Various substances and compounds have adhesive or sticky properties. Among these are the gums arabic, tragacanth, and senegal; dextrin, gelatin or glue, isinglass or fish glue; various resins, as shellac, rosin, etc.; casein, from the curd of milk and cheese; India rubber, gutta percha, litharge, and other substances too numerous to mention.

Various preparations of these substances may be loosely classed according to their composition in the order of their adhesive power, as paste, mucilage, glue (either solid or liquid), and cement. But these terms hardly have a definite meaning.

Dextrin. — A substance formed from starch, rice flour, or cornstarch, also known as British gum or starch gum. It is used as a substitute for gum arabic, as a size for mucilage, and especially for the backs of postage stamps and sealing envelopes.

Gluten.—A substance believed to be produced by the action of a ferment. It is formed in flour by uniting or mixing it with cold water. Gluten is the substance which retains the carbonic-acid gas in bread making, and thus assists in the process of raising bread.

Gelatin.—Gelatin is produced from certain animal membranes by the action of hot water. Isinglass, calf's-foot jelly, and glue are chiefly composed of gelatin. It absorbs water, which causes it to swell, and may be dissolved in hot water or acetic and other acids. The addition of alcohol, corrosive sublimate, or tannic acid to a solution of gelatin in water causes the gelatin to be thrown down.

Glue.—The glue of commerce is dry gelatin having a more or less brownish color according to its purity. White or pale glue is the best. It is a hard, brittle, glossy substance which usually comes in thin sheets. Glue is obtained by cleansing scraps of hides, hoofs, and horns with lime, and boiling them until changed into gelatin.

Isinglass.—Dry gelatin is prepared from the air bladder of sturgeon and other fish, such as cod, weakfish, hake, etc. It is used in preparing jellies, blancmange, gum drops, etc.; in making court-plaster, as a size for delicate fabrics, and as an adhesive.

Fish Glue is an inferior isinglass made from the offal of fisheries.

To melt isinglass, beat up ½ teaspoonful of white of egg in 1 pint of water. Add 4 ounces of isinglass, and melt over a slow fire.

To detect adulteration by gelatin, drop a sample of the suspected isinglass into vinegar. Pure isinglass will swell like jelly, while gelatin will become hard.

Or put a sample in cold water. Pure isinglass becomes cloudy and white, and the adulteration becomes jellylike and clear.

Resins.—For the various resins having adhesive qualities including rosin, shellac, and the like, see under "Varnish."

Gutta Percha.—The hardened milky juice of a large tree growing in the East Indies. It is insoluble in water, slightly soluble in alcohol and ether, and readily dissolved in bisulphide of carbon, benzol, chloroform, and oil of turpentine. It deteriorates rapidly when exposed to the air, and becomes brittle and useless. It is chiefly used for coating submarine telegraph wires and other metallic articles under water.

Caoutchouc, gum elastic, or India rubber is the juice or sap of several tropical plants growing in the East Indies and South America. It is obtained by cutting the bark and drying the juice over smoky fires, which impart its black color. It is elastic and waterproof. When combined with about 25 per cent of sulphur and raised to a temperature of about 270° F., it is converted into soft vulcanized rubber; by the addition of 50 per cent of sulphur and heating to 300° F., it becomes hard vulcanized rubber or ebonite.

To Choose Adhesives.—An adhesive should be selected according to the nature of the substances to be united and the use to which they are to be put. If the right cement is employed, the hardest and smoothest surfaces, as glass and polished metals, may be united so firmly that they will break anywhere rather than where the parts are cemented.

To Use Adhesives.—The object of using adhesives is to bring two surfaces into such intimate contact as to make them practically one, and not to interpose between them any perishable layer or thickness of the adhesive itself. Most adhesives are more brittle than the substances which they unite; hence the best work is done when the adhesive penetrates into the pores of the materials on both sides and brings the particles of both surfaces closely together, so that the strength of the materials themselves is added to that of the adhesive in a union which may be stronger than the adjacent parts.

The presence of any foreign substance, as dirt, grease, or bubbles of air, hinders adhesion. Heating the surfaces to be joined promotes it by expanding the pores and thus enabling them to absorb more of the adhesive. Heating the adhesive itself also assists.

Moreover, heat tends to drive away the air. Hence the hotter one can handle the parts and the adhesive the closer they can be brought into contact and the less adhesive will be required.

To Use Glue.—To get the best results from glue, it should be thin and hot, and the parts should be at least warm enough to prevent the glue from being chilled by them. As glue is gummy and elastic, the parts, when possible, should be squeezed together by means of a vise or under clamps tightened by a screw, so as to squeeze out the excess of glue and bring the parts into intimate contact. The articles should be left in the vise until the glue is set.

To Use Cement.—Resinous cements which are used in a melted state will not do good work unless the adjacent parts are heated above the point at which the resins melt.

PASTES

Flour Paste. — Ordinary paste is made by mixing wheat flour or rice flour with water, with or without boiling. It may be improved by the addition of various other adhesives, as rosin, gum arabic, and glue, and also by the addition of alum.

To make simple cold flour paste

mix 1 tablespoonful of flour with 1 teacupful of cold water. Add a few drops of carbolic acid or other preservative.

Or, for library paste, dissolve ½ ounce of alum in 1 pint of warm water. Stir in flour to the consistency of cream, carefully breaking all lumps. Add 1 teaspoonful of powdered resin and 5 or 6 cloves, or a few drops of oil of cloves, and boil until it thickens. Thin, if necessary, with a little hot water. Put in an earthen or glass vessel, as a glass fruit jar tightly covered, and keep in a cool place. Soften when needed with warm water. This paste is suitable for scrapbooks and similar articles, and is better for such uses than a paste or mucilage containing gum arabic.

To soften library paste, add a few drops of water and melt the paste with gentle heat.

Or to 1 heaping teaspoonful of flour add ½ teaspoonful of pulverized alum. Rub smooth with a little cold water. Mix with boiling water to the consistency of cream and boil until it thickens.

To Preserve Flour Paste.—Add to each half pint of flour paste not containing alum 15 grains of corrosive sublimate. This prevents the formation of mold and preserves the paste from the attacks of insects and vermin. Add also a few drops of oil of lavender, rosemary, or cloves, or any of the essential oils, and a few drops of carbolic acid.

Paper Hanger's Paste. — Mix 4 pounds of flour, ¼ pound of powdered alum, and ¼ pound of pulverized rosin. Rub up this mixture with a small quantity of warm water until smooth and free from lumps. Mix with boiling water to the consistency of cream and boil until it thickens.

Or use cornstarch or wheat starch or rice flour instead of wheat flour.

To use this paste, spread it freely on the paper, then lay or fold the pasted sides lightly together. This assists in distributing the paste evenly and also in handling the paper. After the upper end has been attached, the lower part may be unfolded as it goes on the wall. The wall should first be coated with a thin glue size made of about 4 ounces of glue to 1 gallon of water.

Or make a glue size by dissolving 10 ounces of glue in 2½ gallons of water. Mix 9 pounds of bole, an earthy substance resembling clay, with water to the consistency of cream, and strain off the water through cheese cloth. Add the moistened bole to the glue size and stir in 2 pounds of gypsum. Strain through cheese cloth and dilute with boiling water. This is an excellent paste for old walls covered with one or more coatings of whitewash.

Rice Paste or Japanese Cement.—Mix powdered rice with a little cold water, rubbing it until smooth and free from lumps. Add boiling water and boil, stirring constantly, until it thickens. This is an excellent library paste, suitable for scrapbooks and all kinds of fancy paper work.

Or it may be used to paste strips of transparent paper used to mend tears in valuable books, as it is nearly transparent when dry. For all fine paper work, it is much superior to paste made of wheat flour.

Flour Cement.—A paste of wheat flour and cold water worked with the fingers into a stiff dough is a useful cement for attaching the metal tops to glass articles and other similar purposes. It requires two or three days to harden.

Flour Paste with Sugar.—The addition of 1 tablespoonful of sugar to 1 quart of flour paste increases its adhesiveness and tenacious quality.

MUCILAGE

Gum arabic and similar substances, as gum tragacanth, senegal, and the like, are readily soluble in water, and hence form the base of the liquid adhesives known as mucilage.

Gum-arabic Paste. — Dissolve 2½ ounces of gum acacia in 2 quarts of warm water. Stir in 1 pound of wheat flour to form a paste. Add 1½ ounces of sugar of lead and 1½ ounces of alum dissolved in water. Stir and bring to a boil with gentle heat. Remove the mixture from the fire, but before it boils, and cool for use. Thin, if necessary, with a solution of gum arabic in water.

Or dissolve 2 ounces of gum arabic in 1 pint of water. Add ½ ounce of laundry starch and ½ ounce of white sugar mixed with a little cold water to a thick paste free from lumps, and boil in a double boiler until the starch becomes clear. Add a few cloves or a few drops of any essential oil as a preservative.

Or mix 4 ounces of gum arabic, 3 ounces of starch, and 1 ounce of sugar in a dry mortar. Add cold water to make a paste as thick as melted glue. Bottle for use.

Or dissolve 1 ounce of gum arabic in 2 ounces of water and thicken to a paste with starch.

Gum-arabic Cement. — Dissolve ½ ounce of gum arabic in 2 tablespoonfuls of boiling water. Add plaster of Paris to make a thick paste. Apply with a brush to the broken edges of glass, china, and earthenware. Press or tie together, and let stand two or three days. The article cannot be broken again at the same place. The whiteness of this cement adds to its value.

Or dissolve 8 ounces of gum arabic to a thick mucilage with water, add 12 ounces of plaster of Paris and 2½ ounces of sifted lime. Mix well. Use to cement broken marble. Heat the cement and also the edges of the marble, and apply with a brush.

Gum arabic is also mixed with plaster of Paris and other substances to form pastes and cements.

Mucilage.—To make mucilage, put 3 ounces of gum arabic in a glass bottle with ½ pint of cold water. Let stand 24 hours and stir occasionally. Add a few whole cloves or a few drops of any of the essential oils to prevent molding.

Or mix 1½ ounces of gum arabic and 1½ ounces of gum tragacanth. Add ½ pint of water and dissolve. The solution may be made much more quickly by the use of gentle heat by means of a double boiler or otherwise.

Or mix 3 ounces of gum arabic or gum tragacanth, 3 ounces of distilled vinegar, and 1 ounce of white sugar.

Or 6 ounces of gum arabic, 1 ounce of acetic acid, 1 ounce of white sugar, and 5 ounces of water.

Botanical Mucilage.—Mix 5 ounces of gum arabic, 3 ounces of sugar, 2 ounces of starch, and 5 ounces of water. Boil and stir until very thick and white. Thin with hot water if necessary. Use for mounting pressed flowers and other botanical specimens.

Ivory Mucilage.—Mix 2 ounces of pulverized gum arabic and 1 ounce of calomel. Add water to make a thin paste. Use for gluing on ivory veneers, piano keys, and the like.

Label Mucilage.—Mix ½ ounce of gum arabic, 10 grains of sulphate of aluminum, and 5 ounces of water. This will attach labels to wood, tin, or metal, and will not become moldy. Before attaching the label, free tin or metal surfaces from grease by washing them with a dilute solution of caustic soda or potash by means of a rag or brush.

Or dissolve 2½ ounces of glue in 10 ounces of water. Add 5 ounces of rock candy and 1½ ounces of gum arabic. Brush this upon paper while lukewarm and allow it to dry. It keeps well without sticking, and when moistened will adhere firmly to clean glass or tin.

Dextrin Mucilage. — Dextrin and gelatin or glue treated with glycerin are also used to make mucilage.

Dissolve dextrin in hot water to the consistency of cream or honey. Add a few drops of any of the essential oils or alcohol as a preventive.

Dextrin mucilage is used on the backs of labels, envelopes, postage stamps, etc. To make the kind of mucilage used on the United States postage stamps, dissolve 2 ounces of dextrin in 5 ounces of water. Add 1 ounce of acetic acid, and when the dextrin is dissolved, add 1 ounce of alcohol as a preservative.

Or use gelatin in place of dextrin in the above.

To Preserve Mucilage.—Mucilage composed of gum arabic and dextrin is liable to become moldy and to decay. It may be preserved by the addition of alcohol or a few drops of any of the essential oils, as oil of cloves, lavender, etc.; or a few whole cloves, or a few drops of sulphuric acid, or carbolic acid or creosote in such quantity that the odor is just apparent; or corrosive sublimate, salicylic acid, or boracic acid.

If the use of these is objectionable, the addition of 10 or 12 grains of sulphate of quinine to ½ pint of mucilage is a good and safe preservative. Ordinary quinine pills dissolved in hot water may be used for this purpose.

GLUE

Liquid Glue.—Prepared or liquid glue is a solution of glue with water kept liquid by the addition of 1 fluid ounce of strong nitric acid to 1 pound of dry glue.

Or add 3 ounces of commercial acetic acid to 1 ounce of glue.

Or mix 2 ounces of glue, 2 ounces of vinegar, and 2 ounces of water; dissolve in a double boiler and add 1 ounce of alcohol.

Or dissolve ½ pound of the best pale glue in 1½ pints of water and add ½ pint of vinegar.

Or put any quantity of the best glue broken in small pieces in a glass fruit jar and cover with 1 part of vinegar or dilute acetic acid and 5 parts of water. Set the jar in a vessel of hot water, and let stand until the glue is melted. In all these cases the glue will dissolve more rapidly if allowed to stand a few days in cold water, which may be poured off when the glue is wanted.

Or dissolve in a double boiler 8 ounces of the best pale glue in ½ pint of water. Add slowly, stirring constantly, ½ ounce of pure nitric acid. Bottle and cork for use. This can be used cold for all ordinary purposes, and does not thicken, decay, or become moldy, but is not waterproof. This recipe has often been sold as a trade secret.

Other proportions recommended are equal parts by weight of glue and water and $\frac{1}{10}$ their combined weight of nitric acid; e. g., melt 10 ounces of glue in 10 ounces of water and add 2 ounces of nitric acid.

Or dissolve 10 ounces of glue in 20 ounces of water and add 1 ounce of nitric acid. Any of these is a powerful adhesive which is always ready for use.

Or dissolve 6 ounces of glue in 16 ounces of water and add 1 ounce of hydrochloric acid and 1½ ounces of sulphate of zinc. This is a permanent liquid glue which will not spoil under ordinary household conditions.

Or mix 1 ounce of clear gelatin, 1 ounce of glue, ¼ ounce of alcohol, and 1 tablespoonful of powdered alum. Add 2 ounces of commercial acetic acid. Melt in a double boiler. Bottle and cork for use.

Flexible Glue.—The addition to any of the above liquid glues of one fourth by weight of glycerin in proportion to the amount of glue employed, imparts a flexible quality which prevents the glue from cracking and is useful for all flexible surfaces, as leather, paper, bookbinding, and the like.

Photograph Glue.—Mix 3 ounces of chloral hydrate and 4½ ounces of gelatin and dissolve in 13 ounces of water. Let stand 2 or 3 days. Use for mounting photographs.

Waterproof Glue.—Dissolve in a double boiler ½ pound of best white glue in 1 quart of skimmed milk. Stir occasionally until the mixture has the consistency of glue. Apply with a brush. This hardens to a durable waterproof cement. The addition of a few drops of nitric acid converts this mixture into liquid glue or mucilage.

Portable Glue.—Melt in a double boiler 5 ounces of glue and 2 ounces of sugar with 8 ounces of water. Pour into small molds to dry. Dissolve when required in warm water.

Or dissolve ½ pound of best white glue in hot water, and strain through cheese cloth. Dissolve 2 ounces of best isinglass in water to the consistency of cream. Mix the two solutions in a glass vessel. Add 1 pound of pure brown sugar, put the vessel in boiling water, boil, and stir until it thickens. Pour off into small molds to harden. When cold this cement is solid and portable. When required for use it may be softened by holding it over steam for a moment, or wetting it with the tongue and rubbing it on the surfaces to be cemented. It is used for cementing paper, leather, and many other materials, and is doubly valuable on account of its convenience, being always ready for use.

Or mix 1 ounce of isinglass, 1 ounce of parchment, 2 drams of sugar candy, and 2 drams of gum tragacanth. Add 1 ounce of water and boil until dissolved. Pour into molds for use. This may be wet with the tongue or otherwise and rubbed on the edges of paper, silk, or leather to cement them. It is recommended for sealing letters.

Isinglass Adhesives. — Pure isinglass, which may be dissolved readily in water, is a very strong adhesive.

Isinglass is an animal tissue obtained chiefly from the air bladders of certain fish. The substance used in place of glass in stove windows, sometimes improperly called isinglass, is a stone or mineral, the correct name of which is mica.

Dissolve isinglass in hot water, using a double boiler, and apply with a brush to glass, china, or marble.

Or dissolve ½ ounce of isinglass in 1 or 2 ounces of alcohol and add a tablespoonful of water. Apply to the edges of broken glass or similar articles with gentle pressure, and the fracture will hardly be noticeable.

Or isinglass may be dissolved in about its own weight of brandy, gin, alcohol, or other spirits. This solution makes the best cement for glass and porcelain.

Or mix 2 ounces of isinglass and 1 ounce of gum arabic, cover with 95 per cent alcohol, cork loosely, and put the bottle in boiling water until dissolved. This is the best and most delicate cement. Used by opticians, jewelers, and others whose trades require the finest workmanship.

Spalding's Liquid Glue.—Dissolve in a double boiler 1 pound of pure isinglass in 1 pint of soft water. Add slowly, stirring constantly, 2 ounces of nitric acid. This is a permanent liquid glue, which is always ready for use and will not mold or putrefy. Bottle and cork to prevent evaporation. Used for wood, leather, paper, and, in the absence of special adhesives, for many other purposes.

CEMENT

Armenian or Diamond Cement.—Dissolve to the consistency of thin cream 6 lumps of gum mastic, each about the size of a large pea or about ½ dram each, in 3 drams of 95 per cent alcohol. Fill a 2-ounce vial loosely with isinglass broken in small pieces and cover with water. When the isinglass is slightly softened, pour off the water, cover with French brandy, and add two small lumps (10 grains) of gum ammoniacum powdered and dissolved in as little alcohol as possible. Mix the two solutions and dissolve with gentle heat in a double boiler. Keep in a glass bottle closely stoppered, and when required for use set the bottle in boiling water.

This celebrated adhesive has been used from time immemorial by the jewelers of Turkey, who are mostly Armenians. The formula was brought to England by a former British consul, and this preparation has been widely used with uniformly good results. It is employed in the Orient to ornament watch cases and other jewelry with diamonds and other precious stones by simply gluing or cementing them on. The stone is set in silver or gold, the lower part of the setting being shaped to correspond with the part to which it is to be fixed. The parts are then warmed slightly, the glue is applied, and the parts thus cemented never separate. This cement will unite polished steel with other metals or with glass. It is suitable for the finest work, and may be regarded as absolutely reliable. So-called Armenian cement as commonly found on the market is an inferior preparation and is usually sold at an exorbitant price.

Other proportions recommended for Armenian cement are as follows: isinglass, 1 ounce; acetic acid, 1 ounce; water, 5 ounces; alcohol, 2 ounces; gum ammoniacum, ½ ounce; gum mastic, ½ ounce. Mix and dissolve with gentle heat.

Or dissolve 1 ounce of isinglass in 6 ounces of water, and boil down to 3 ounces. Add 1¼ ounces of 95 per cent alcohol, boil two minutes, strain through silk, and add while hot ¼ ounce of milky emulsion of ammoniacum and 5 drams of tincture of gum mastic. Where instructions are carefully followed, this is a perfect cement.

Resin Cement.—A class of cements having valuable waterproof qualities is made of the gums amber, mastic, rosin, shellac, etc., dissolved in spirits or other solvents, and often combined for various purposes with other adhesives or solids, as plaster of Paris, clay, iron filings, etc. Beeswax is often combined with these resins to soften them and prevent excessive brittleness.

Shellac Cement for China and Glass.—Sealing wax, the principal ingredient of which is shellac, or powdered shellac itself, may be used as a cement by dusting the edges of chinaware or other articles with it, heating them until the shellac runs, and pressing them firmly together. Failure to get good results by this method is due to lack of sufficient heat or the use of too much of the material. Or dissolve white shellac in alcohol to the consistency of molasses, and apply to the edges of broken glassware or other glass surfaces to be joined. This sets quickly without heat and will stand all ordinary wear except heat equal to boiling water.

Or dissolve 2 ounces of white shellac and ¼ ounce of gum mastic in 1 ounce of pure sulphuric ether. Let the mixture stand for an hour and add 1 pint of 95 per cent alcohol. Bottle and cork tightly for use. Shake well before using. Heat the articles to be mended, apply the cement evenly with a soft brush, and hold the surface together until it sets.

Or, for so-called Chinese cement, put 4 ounces of pale-orange shellac in a glass bottle and pour over it 3 ounces of 95 per cent alcohol, and let stand in a warm place until dissolved. This will have the consistency of molasses. It is suitable for wood, glass, jewelry, ivory, and all fancy work. It is very strong.

Shellac Cement for Labeling on Metal.—Dissolve 1 ounce of pulverized borax and 5 ounces of gum shellac in 1 quart of boiling water. Boil until dissolved. Before applying, wash the metal with a dilute solution of caustic potash or soda and wipe dry with a clean cloth. Apply the cement warm. For inscriptions, size the metallic surface with this cement, and write the inscription with bronze powder by means of a brush. When dry, varnish over the bronze.

Shellac Cement for Rubber.—Soak in a glass fruit jar 1 ounce of gum shellac in 10 ounces of strong aqua ammonia. Let stand 3 or 4 weeks, or until the shellac is dissolved. Used to cement rubber to wood or metal. This cement softens the rubber, and after the ammonia evaporates, the union will be found to be both air-tight and water-tight.

Rosin Cement.—Melt together with gentle heat 8 ounces of rosin and 4 ounces of sulphur, and pour into molds for future use. When wanted, grind to powder 2 ounces of this mixture, and add ½ ounce of iron filings, fine sand, or brick dust. Fill the opening in the handle of a knife, fork, or other implement with this mixture, heat the stock, and force it into the handle while hot.

Or mix 4 ounces of rosin, 1 ounce of beeswax, and 1 ounce of fine brick dust. This cement is used by cutlers. Fill the openings in knife handles with this mixture, heat the stock of the knife, and force it into the handle. When cold it will be firmly set.

Or mix ½ pound of rosin and 1 pound of brick dust. Melt with gentle heat. Used by plumbers. Apply while hot to joints in lead pipe.

Or melt together 5 ounces of black rosin and 1 ounce of yellow wax, and stir in gradually 1 ounce of red ocher or Venetian red in fine, dry powder. Melt and apply warm. Used by instrument makers for cementing glass to metal.

Or melt 15 ounces of rosin and 1 ounce of wax, and add 4 ounces of whiting previously heated red hot and mixed while warm. Used by glass grinders to hold glass, stones, etc., while being polished or cut.

Rosin and Wax Cement or Bottle Wax.—Mix 4 ounces of rosin, 4 ounces of sealing wax, and 2 ounces of beeswax; melt together with gentle heat. When the mixture boils, stir it with a candle.

Or melt equal quantities of beeswax and rosin. Used to seal bottles. First insert a cork into the bottle, and then dip the cork and neck of the bottle in the melted wax.

Grafting Wax.—Melt together with gentle heat 1 pound of rosin, 3 ounces of tallow, and 5 ounces of beeswax. Stir continually while melting. Pour the mixture into cold water and let stand until cool. Then remove from the water and knead thoroughly to a homogeneous mass. This wax will last for years. It is not soft enough to run in hot weather not hard enough to crack in winter.

Amber or Varnish Cement.—Dissolve 2 ounces of amber in 3 ounces of sulphide of carbon. Apply with a brush and hold the surfaces firmly together until dry. This cement sets almost immediately.

White-of-egg Cement.—For crockery, white of egg mixed with prepared lime, or mixed with the same material (ground to powder) as the article to be mended, makes a firm and durable cement. Apply quickly to the edges and hold firmly together until the mixture sets. Do not mix more than is required, as it hardens very quickly and cannot be melted.

Or use for this purpose the white of an egg with plaster of Paris or prepared chalk or finely powdered oyster shells.

Or pound the lime or other solid to a fine powder and sift it through cheese cloth. Apply white of egg freely to the broken surfaces. Dust on the powder and hold the edges together firmly until united.

For glassware, grind a piece of flint glass to the finest powder, mix with white of egg, and apply.

To Mend Ironware.—Make a thin paste of finely sifted lime with the white of an egg and thicken with iron filings. Apply to the broken edges and hold them firmly together until the cement sets.

Casein Cement.—Grate 4 ounces of old cheese in ½ pint of milk. Let stand all day, stirring frequently. Stir in 4 ounces of unslaked lime reduced to fine powder and sifted through cheese cloth. Add the whites of 6 eggs and mix all thoroughly with an egg beater. This was long regarded as a trade secret in England for mending earthenware.

Or add ½ pint of vinegar to ½ pint of milk. Separate the curd from the whey and mix the whey with the whites of 4 or 5 eggs by means of an egg beater. Stir in powdered and sifted quicklime to the consistency of a thick paste. This cement is said to be fireproof and waterproof.

Or dissolve casein in a cold saturated solution of borax. This is a substitute for gum arabic and dextrin for envelopes, labels, and the like.

Or, to mend earthenware, place the pieces together and tie them firmly as possible by means of a string. If one piece of a set is broken, two other pieces of the same set may be placed one on each side of the broken article to assist in keeping the pieces together, but care must be taken to first wind string thickly around the broken plate or dish so as to separate it slightly from the others and permit liquid to flow around it. Then put it in a boiler or kettle, cover with cold sweet skimmed milk, and let stand for an hour or more to get an even temperature. Bring to a boil with gentle heat and let boil ten or fifteen minutes. Remove from the fire and let stand over night. Wash in warm water and let stand two or three days without using. The dish will be found to be as strong as new.

Rubber Cement. — The ordinary rubber mending tissue is a convenient article for repairing cloth, and also for flexible rubber surfaces, as hot-water bottles and the like. Use this mending tissue for umbrellas, raincoats, and similar articles requiring a tight waterproof joint. Lay the mending tissue over the break or tear. Place on the other side a piece of the same fabric and press lightly with a hot iron.

To mend a hot-water bottle, heat an artificial rubber band or a piece of pure rubber with hot iron, as a poker, until it becomes sticky, and lay it quickly over the hole or crack. Let dry before using. Rubber overshoes can be mended in the same way. But hot-water bottles will keep longer and not require mending if emptied, dried, blown up, and corked tightly before they are put away.

Or apply a patch of oiled silk by means of mending tissue and a hot iron, but do not use the iron hot enough to melt or injure the rubber.

Or dissolve 1 ounce of gutta percha in ½ pound of chloroform. Wash the parts to be cemented with a dilute solution of caustic potash or soda. Cover each freely with this gutta-percha solution and let dry for half an hour. Then warm each surface in the flame of a candle and let dry under pressure.

Or shave India rubber with a wet knife or shears to thin strings or shreds like yarn. Fill a glass fruit jar about one fourth full of these shreds and fill it up with high-grade benzine. Let stand, shaking occasionally, for four or five days or until completely dissolved. Thin with benzine, or add more rubber if necessary to make the mixture of the consistency of molasses.

Or dissolve India rubber in highly rectified spirits of turpentine.

Or dissolve 7 grains of India rubber in 1 ounce of chloroform, and add 2 drams of shellac varnish.

The above are suitable for patching boots and shoes, for cementing rubber and leather, and either of them to wood. Clean the parts to be cemented by washing with a dilute solution of caustic potash or soda, and apply two or three coats to each surface. Let dry under pressure.

Or melt together equal parts of gutta percha and pitch. Apply hot.

Or melt together ½ pound of gutta percha, 2 ounces of India rubber, 1 ounce of pitch, ½ ounce of shellac, and 2 ounces of boiled linseed oil.

Or heat 5 pounds of Venice turpentine, stir in 8 ounces of shellac and 2 ounces of India rubber cut to shreds, and stir over gentle heat until dissolved. When dissolved, add 10 ounces of liquid storax. Do not allow the mixture to boil or burn. Apply hot.

The above are suitable for cementing metals, leather, rubber, or cloth, especially flexible surfaces.

Or cut up 2 ounces of pure India rubber in 1 pound of bisulphate of carbon. Shake until dissolved. Add benzoin until the mixture is of the consistency of thick cream. Apply to both surfaces, warm the parts, and let dry under pressure.

This cement is used by shoemakers to put invisible patches on shoes, and is also suitable for mending harnesses, splicing leather straps, and the like.

To apply, shave the edges of the leather on a long bevel, lay over them a wet cloth, and press with a hot iron to take up any grease that may be present, but take care not to use an iron hot enough to burn or take the life out of the leather. Pour the cement on both surfaces quite thickly, and spread with a brush so as to fill the pores of the leather. Warm the parts over a flame for a few seconds until the cement becomes sticky, or "tacky," apply quickly, and hammer until firmly set. Keep the cement tightly corked in a cool place.

To fasten leather to iron or steel, spread over the metal a thin, hot solution of good glue, and soak the leather in a warm solution of gall-nuts before placing it on the metal. If fastened in this way the leather will tear before separating.

SPECIAL ADHESIVES

Marine Glue.—Dissolve 1 ounce of finely divided India rubber in 2½ pounds of crude naphtha. Let stand 2 or 3 weeks and shake frequently. Add 5 pounds of shellac, melt with gentle heat, and stir until evenly dissolved. Pour on a marble or stone slab to cool and break in pieces like glue for use. When required, melt with gentle heat, apply a thin coating to the edges to be joined, and press firmly together. This cement is used in foundries, for calking ships, joining blocks of marble and granite, joining wood to iron, etc. It is suitable for all heavy rough work exposed to the air.

Or dissolve in separate vessels by means of gentle heat 3 ounces of India rubber in rectified sulphuric ether free from alcohol. Mix the two solutions. When cool, bottle and cork tightly for use. This is suitable for fine work. Both of the above resist the action of hot and cold water, and of most acids and alkalies. Wood, leather, and other materials cemented by them will part almost anywhere except at the place mended. Thin this glue with ether and apply with a brush along the seams where leather is sewed, as the soles of shoes. This renders the seam air-tight and practically unbreakable. The last two cements are probably the strongest known.

To prepare the above in large quantities dissolve 1 pound of India rubber in 5 gallons of cold naphtha, and add to this solution an equal weight of shellac. Melt with gentle heat and stir while melting until thoroughly dissolved. This is extremely tenacious and is insoluble.

Lead and Oil Adhesives.—Linseed oil boiled to a varnish with litharge, and white lead ground in linseed oil, with or without various preparations of glue or other ingredients, make a class of adhesives which have valuable fireproof and waterproof qualities.

Mix 4 ounces of linseed oil with 4 ounces of slaked lime, and boil until stringy. Pour into tin molds and let dry indoors or in the shade. This will dissolve when wanted like glue. It will withstand fire and water.

Or boil 4 ounces of linseed oil with 4 ounces of litharge until the mixture is stringy, and add 8 ounces of melted glue of the consistency of molasses. Use this cement for leaders, the joints of wooden cisterns or casks, and similar places. It requires 3 or 4 days to harden, but renders wooden vessels air-tight and water-tight.

Or mix equal quantities by weight of linseed oil and litharge. Stir in porcelain clay or well-dried pipe clay to the consistency of stiff mortar. Thin, if desired, with oil or turpentine. Apply this substance to the outside of buildings.

Litharge Cements.—Mix 2 ounces of litharge, 1 ounce of unslaked lime, and 1 ounce of flint glass. Pulverize into fine powder, mix, and when required make into a stiff paste with boiled linseed oil.

Or pulverize brick or well-burnt clay to a fine powder. Mix 1 pound of litharge with 13 pounds of pulverized brick or clay, and add boiled linseed oil to make a stiff mortar. Dampen the surface to which this is to be applied and use as mortar.

The above are suitable for cementing stone, wood, or iron, filling leaks, mending cracks, and other similar purposes.

Or mix powdered litharge with glycerin to the consistency of putty. Used for fastening metal tops to glassware, mending holes in tinware, ironware, and the like.

Or mix 3 ounces of red lead, 3 ounces of white lead, 3 ounces of manganese, 3 ounces of silicate of soda, and 1 ounce of litharge. Use this cement for holes or cracks in steam or water pipes.

Or mix white lead ground in oil with powdered red lead to the consistency of putty.

Or mix equal weights of red lead and white lead with boiled linseed oil to the consistency of putty. Apply the cement to a washer of cloth or canvas and tighten up the joint. It dries like stone. This and the last are employed by engineers to make metallic joints.

Or use white lead mixed with oil to mend broken china and glassware, and to fill cracks in roofs, cisterns, and the like.

Plaster-of-Paris Cements. — There is a class of cements of which plaster of Paris or gypsum is the basis, in which the hardening is due to the union of the plaster with water, but they require the addition of various other ingredients to give them adhesive properties. For the use of gum arabic with plaster of Paris, see above under "Gum Arabic."

Or mix into a paste plaster of Paris and white of egg. Used for mending broken glass or china.

Or substitute oyster shells burnt in a stove or open fire and pulverized to powder.

Or melt 2 ounces of rosin and stir in 1 ounce of plaster of Paris.

Or melt 1 ounce each of rosin and beeswax, and stir in 1 ounce of plaster of Paris.

Or melt 8 ounces of rosin and 1 ounce of beeswax, and stir in 4 ounces of plaster of Paris. Apply these cements to alabaster, broken plaster casts, marble, porphyry, and similar materials.

Or mix equal quantities of pulverized alum and plaster of Paris, and add sufficient water to make a thin paste.

Or mix plaster of Paris with a saturated solution of alum, and bake in an iron vessel in an oven until dry. Pulverize this mixture to a fine powder, and when wanted mix to the consistency of paste with a solution of 1 ounce of alum in 12 ounces of water. This cement is suitable for attaching glass to metal.

Or boil 3 ounces of rosin, 1 ounce of caustic soda, and 5 ounces of water. Stir in 4½ ounces of plaster of Paris. This cement is especially recommended for fitting the brass work to kerosene-oil lamps, as it is not affected by petroleum products. It is a poor conductor of heat.

Or melt alum and use for the same purpose while melted. Kerosene does not penetrate this.

Or mix 1 pint each (dry measure) of litharge, plaster of Paris, and fine, dry white sand, and ½ pint of finely powdered rosin. Make into a stiff paste with boiled linseed oil and apply within 12 hours after mixing. This cement hardens under water and may be used for tanks, aquaria, water tanks for animals, and all similar purposes, as it contains nothing which is injurious to animals. Allow this cement to set 3 or 4 hours before wetting it.

Ironware Cements.—Mix 5 parts of powdered fire clay and 1 part of fine iron filings with enough boiled linseed oil to make a paste. This is not suitable for iron exposed to red heat, as a stove.

Or mix equal quantities of sifted wood ashes, powdered fire clay, and common salt. Moisten to a paste with water and fill cracks in stoves and other ironware.

Or use equal quantities of sifted wood ashes and common salt mixed to a paste with water, but without the clay. Let the mixture set before heating.

Or melt 2 ounces of sulphur in an iron pan, and stir in 1 ounce of fine black lead. Pour on a stone or an iron plate to cool. When cold, break in small pieces. An iron pot can be mended by soldering with this substance, using a hot soldering iron.

Or, to mend a small hole, insert a copper rivet or one of the brass brads used to fasten documents together, hammer smoothly on both sides, and cover with this cement.

Or melt 5 ounces of brimstone, and stir in 2 ounces of black lead and 2 ounces of cast-iron filings. Apply to leaks in cast-iron tanks, cisterns, etc., by drying the leak, heating it by means of red-hot iron, and pouring the melted cement from a ladle over the leak.

Or mix 4 ounces of barytes and 4 ounces of fine fire clay to a paste with soluble glass or a saturated solution of borax.

Or mix equal quantities of clay and powdered glass with soluble glass or a saturated solution of borax, and apply with a brush to cracks in iron stoves or furnaces.

Or mix 2 pounds of cast-iron filings with 1 ounce of sal ammoniac and ½ ounce of flowers of sulphur. Stir in enough water to form a paste. Mix this preparation in an iron vessel, as it becomes very hot from chemical action. Prepare when wanted and apply immediately, as it soon sets very hard.

Or mix 8 ounces of steel filings, 1½ ounces of sal ammoniac, and 1 ounce of flowers of sulphur. Preserve this mixture in dry form until wanted. When required, add 1 ounce of it to 15 ounces of iron filings, and mix with water acidulated with sulphuric acid to form a paste. Apply this cement to the joints of iron pipe and for similar purposes. Clean surfaces to be cemented with nitric or strong sulphuric acid. Use this cement for all iron and steel work. Or mix 10 ounces of powdered fire clay, 4 ounces of fresh iron filings free from rust, 2 ounces of peroxide of manganese, 1 ounce of sea salt, and 1 ounce of borax. Powder finely, mix to a paste with water, and apply immediately. Gradually bring the parts to a white heat. This cement is both fireproof and waterproof.

Or mix equal quantities of sifted peroxide of manganese and powdered zinc white, and make into a thin paste with soluble glass. Apply immediately.

Or mix 5 ounces of fire clay, 3 ounces of manganese, and 3 ounces of silicate of soda with water to the consistency of putty. Used to mend holes in castings and for similar purposes.

Or mix 10 ounces of clay, 3 ounces of manganese, 2 ounces of silicate of soda, and ½ ounce of asbestos. Grind to powder in a mortar, mix with water to make a paste, and use as mortar for lining stoves.

Compound Glues.—The number of pastes, glues, and cements that can be compounded by mixing various proportions of the above substances is, of course, numberless, but the following preparations are especially recommended as having given satisfaction:

For liquid glue, dissolve in a double boiler 8 ounces of white glue and 2 ounces of dry white lead in 1 pint of soft water. When dissolved, add 2 ounces of alcohol and stir briskly. Remove from the fire and bottle while hot.

SPECIAL PURPOSE CEMENTS

Wood Cement.—Mix 1 ounce of lime and 2 ounces of rye meal with boiled linseed oil to a stiff paste.

Or dissolve 1 ounce of glue in 16 ounces of water, and stir in sawdust or prepared chalk or both to make a paste.

Or thicken oil varnish with equal parts of white lead, red lead, litharge, and powdered chalk. Use these cements to fill cracks and defects in woodwork before painting.

Or mix 2 ounces of beeswax, 2 ounces of shellac, and 1 ounce of Indian red, and color with yellow ocher to the shade required. Use this cement to fill cracks, cover nail heads, and the like in mahogany furniture.

Cement for Glass.—Dissolve best white glue in as little water as possible, and add by bulk one half as much linseed oil varnish and one fourth as much pure turpentine. Boil together in a double boiler closely covered to keep in the steam. Apply to glass and metal joints, holding the two surfaces together with a vise if convenient or under weights for forty-eight hours until the cement sets.

Or, for the same purpose, melt together 5 ounces of rosin, 1 ounce of beeswax, 1 ounce of red ocher, and ½ tablespoonful of gypsum.

Leather Cement.—Dissolve in a double boiler 1 ounce of pure isinglass in ½ pint of ale. Add 2 ounces of common glue and dissolve with gentle heat. Stir in 1 ounce of boiled linseed oil until well mixed. This mixture will have the texture of India rubber. Bottle and cork tightly for future use. Dilute when required with fresh ale, and after shaving the surfaces of the leather apply hot with a brush to harness and other belts, bands, etc. Let stand in a vise or under pressure until it sets. This is waterproof and a very powerful adhesive.

Or dissolve in a double boiler equal quantities of glue and isinglass in pure tannin until the mixture assumes the appearance of white of egg. Shave the leather, rub the edges with sandpaper to roughen them, and apply the cement while hot. It will make a stronger joint if the surface is first moistened with a solution of gallnuts. A joint made of this cement will be as strong as any other part of the leather.

Or, to fasten leather and other fibrous material to metals, dissolve glue in hot vinegar and add one third by volume of hot white pine pitch.

Collodion Cement.—Collodion is a mixture of 1 ounce of gun cotton and 1 ounce of alcohol in about 1 pound of ether. When used as a cement or varnish to prevent rust or for other purposes, it easily cracks and peels. To prevent this, add to each 18 ounces of collodion 4 ounces of Venice turpentine and 2 ounces of castor oil.

Or, when using collodion for surgical purposes to dress cuts, etc., add to the ordinary collodion one eighth its volume of glycerin. This makes a varnish which adheres to the skin, but is elastic, and hence does not crack or crease.

Coppersmith's Cement. — Thicken fresh beef blood with powdered quicklime. Mix only as required and apply at once, as it sets rapidly. This is suitable for mending copper boilers, rivets, leaks in copper pipes, faucets, and the like. It is both cheap and durable.

Acid-proof Cement. — Mix in a double boiler 1½ pounds of rosin, 4 ounces of dry red ocher, 2 ounces of plaster of Paris, and 1 ounce of linseed oil. Dissolve with gentle heat. Mix and apply while warm. Use this for cementing troughs to hold acid. It will stand boiling sulphuric acid.

Parchment Glue.—Boil in a double boiler 1 pound of parchment in 6 quarts of water down to 1 quart. Strain through cheese cloth to remove the sediment, and with gentle heat evaporate the liquid slowly to the consistency of glue. Bottle and cork tightly for use. Use this for fine work with delicate white paper.

Peach-tree Gum.—The gum which

exudes from peach trees, when dissolved in alcohol and thinned with water, is a suitable cement for mending broken glassware, and is a good substitute for gum arabic, senegal, and the like.

To Mend Glass and China. — To take off grease or varnish, wash the pieces in ammonia and water, or apply alcohol or ether to the edges to be joined, but take care not to smooth off irregularities, as the rougher the surface the better the cement will hold. When the pieces are numerous it is best to unite them one at a time and let that harden before another is added. Select a quick-drying cement, heat the pieces, apply a thin coating of the cement to both surfaces, no more than will be partially absorbed, and bring the edges together before the cement sets. Hold them firmly until it hardens. After all the pieces have been thus united, let the article stand for several days or weeks before using.

Glue for Gilding.—Cut up rabbit skins as fine as possible, and boil them in water until the liquor on cooling is a firm gelatinous mass. Dilute with water, bring to a boil, and strain through a wire sieve.

Dissolve 1 part of alum and 3 parts of sulphate of zinc in boiling water, pour into the clear mixture, stir the whole while hot, and strain into a mold until it cools and jells. The mass will now be thick enough to remove from the mold and dry in the open air or with gentle heat.

PAINTS AND PAINTING

Paint, including painting and the care of paints, is an important subject. Both the inner and outer walls and the floors of houses and most articles of furniture are painted. Hence a knowledge of the nature and properties of paint, both before and after its application, enables it to be put to a thousand practical uses in the household. The uses of paint are twofold, i. e., to protect the wood and other materials to which it is applied, and also to decorate them. The ingredients of paint are of two sorts: the pigments or coloring matter, chosen mostly for decoration; and the vehicle chosen to hold the coloring matter in suspension, and also, when desired, to furnish the requisite protection.

Linseed Oil for Paints.—The best vehicle for paints used to protect woodwork and other surfaces from moisture and decay is linseed oil. This is one of the so-called drying oils which, on exposure to the air, absorb oxygen and form a resinous varnish that closes the pores and excludes the agents of destruction from all surfaces to which it is applied. Thus it holds the pigments in a firm waterproof varnish.

Linseed oil is of two sorts: raw and boiled. The raw oil is of two grades: the cold-drawn and the hot-pressed or ordinary quality. Raw linseed oil dries slowly, passing through a gummy or sticky stage before acquiring a hard, resinous surface. The object of boiling this oil with oxide of lead, peroxide of manganese, and borate or acetate of manganese is to cause it to dry more quickly. Boiling gives the oil a dark or high color. The raw oil is obtained from flaxseed by crushing the seed under great hydraulic pressure. When the seed is not heated, the oil is said to be cold-pressed or cold-drawn, and is of a light or pale color, but when the crushed seed is heated and pressed hot, the oil is darker. Much more oil can be extracted from the same quantity of seed by hot pressure. The cold-drawn oil is therefore more expensive, but it is of a better quality.

Pigments for Paint.—The pigments or coloring matter used in paints are prepared by grinding them in a mill and mixing them with a small quantity of raw linseed oil. They come in small packages and are prepared for use by mixing them with an additional quantity of raw or boiled linseed oil and one or more colored pigments, which are mixed together to produce any desired shade.

Thinners for Paints.—The various pigments mixed with oil alone would make too thick a coating; hence other ingredients known as thinners are employed to dilute them. These are oil of turpentine and benzine, which mix freely with linseed oil and various pigments, and reduce them to any desired consistency.

Dryers for Paints. — Even boiled linseed oil does not dry quickly enough; hence to hasten the union of oxygen with the paint, which transforms it into a dry, hard, resinous substance, it is usual to mix paints with certain substances known as dryers. Among these are sugar (acetate) of lead, red lead, verdigris, binoxide of manganese, sulphate of zinc, etc. The most powerful dryer is boric manganese, even the $\frac{1}{1000}$ part being enough to greatly hasten the drying of linseed oil. These and other dryers come ground in oil ready to mix with paint.

Ready-made Paints.—The materials used for paints for home use must be kept separate and not mixed until the paint is about to be used. Or, if mixed in advance, the paint must be covered with water and kept from the air. Otherwise the thinner will evaporate, the pigment will settle to the bottom, and the oil will become thick and ropy, forming a hard skin over the top which cannot be dissolved. Hence paints are now mixed in factories on a large scale by a process which forms an emulsion or permanent mixture of the pigment and the oil, and these can be had in any size cans, the contents of which are always ready for use. However, anyone can obtain the necessary ingredients, pigment, oils, thinner, and dryer, and mix paints for home use at less cost usually than he would have to pay for the ready-made article, and with the further advantage of knowing precisely the nature and purity of all the ingredients employed.

Water-color Paints.—Paints for interior work, walls, ceilings, pictures, maps, and the like, are sometimes prepared without oil by using as a vehicle glue or gum dissolved in water. After the water evaporates, the glue or gum is left, and this causes the pigments to adhere to the surface. The ingredients must not be mixed until ready for use, as glue or gum will not keep in solution for any length of time.

Calcimine is a paint of this character, being a mixture of prepared chalk with a solution of glue and various colored pigments.

Water colors can also be obtained in the form of cakes consisting of pigments and gum in solid form, which may be liquefied by dissolving in water or by rubbing them with a wet brush.

Paints — Other Ingredients. — Besides linseed oil, for finer kinds of work, as the preparation of artist's colors, other oils, as nut and poppy oils, are sometimes used.

Miscellaneous Ingredients. — Soluble glass, naphthas, tars, lime, and various other materials are sometimes employed for cheap paints or for special purposes. Poisonous substances are sometimes mixed with the paint used about salt water to prevent marine plants and animals from fastening to painted surfaces, and phosphorus is sometimes added when a luminous paint is desired.

USES OF PAINT

Quantity of Paint to Use.—To estimate the quantity of paint required, divide the number of square feet of surface by 200. The quotient is the number of gallons of paint required to give two coats.

Or divide the number of square feet of surface by 18. The quotient is the number of pounds of pure ground white lead required to give three coats.

Another rule is that new woodwork requires about 1 pound of paint to the square yard for three coats.

But the rules vary according to the nature of the surface and its condition, the temperature, and the like.

Old woodwork, especially if unpainted or if the paint has been allowed to wear off, will absorb more paint than new wood. Some kinds of wood take more paint than others, and surfaces of stone, brick, or metal may take less than wood.

Rules for House Painting. — The best time to paint houses, barns, and other surfaces exposed to the sun is in winter when the ground is frozen. In summer the heat of the sun opens the pores of wood and other materials, which causes the oil to soak in, leaving the pigments exposed on the surface. This may be prevented by first going over the surface with raw oil; but paint applied when the surface is contracted by cold in winter dries slowly, forms a hard, tough coat like glass, and will last twice as long as if applied at any other time of the year.

Another advantage of painting in cold weather is the absence of flies and other insects, and also the fact that there is much less dust. Painting may, of course, be done indoors at any time of the year, but it must be understood that a hot surface will absorb more paint than a cold one and should be first primed with a coat of raw linseed oil.

Buy, if possible, the best white lead and other pigments and the best oil, and mix the paint yourself.

To paint new wood for the first time requires four or five operations —knotting, priming, and two or three coats of paint. Old woodwork previously painted requires washing to remove the grease, and may require burning or other process to remove the paint, as well as refinishing the surface before the priming and fresh coats of paint are laid on.

Or it may be sufficient to wash the surface to remove all grease spots, and to lay a fresh coat over the old paint.

Keep up the paint on all surfaces that require painting. It is much cheaper after the original foundation has been laid to go over the woodwork with a thin coat of paint quite frequently, than to wait until the paint is all worn off in spots and the woodwork underneath is affected with dry rot.

Recoat standing woodwork at least once in two years, and go over window sills and sashes as often as they require it.

Prepare paint to suit the purpose for which it is intended. Do not attempt to make one kind of paint serve every purpose. One kind of paint is required for the outside of a house and another for the inside; and there are special paints for iron, stone, brick, and other surfaces.

Knotting. — The knots in pine boards and other resinous woods contain turpentine, and unless they are "killed" the turpentine will ooze out and destroy the paint. Hence to kill knots apply with a brush a mixture of red and white lead ground with water and mixed with a strong glue size consisting of 2 to 4 ounces of glue to 1 gallon of water. Apply while warm to the knots with a brush. Follow with a second coat composed of 3 parts of white lead ground in oil and 1 part of red lead or litharge. When bone-dry, rub down with pumice stone.

Priming.—After knotting, go over the surface with a very thin coat of priming, which consists of white lead with a very small quantity of dryer, as red lead or litharge, mixed with raw linseed oil. Use 1 pound of this priming for 18 or 20 square yards. Have no more oil than is necessary to make the lead work readily, but apply repeatedly and work the coating out thin with a brush.

Do not use a lot of thin priming.

First Coat.—When the priming is dry, put on a second coat. The work is now said to be "primed and one coat," and is ready for painting, which requires one or two coats more.

Second Coat.—Fill up all nail holes and the like, and lay on a regular coat of the desired color. Let dry for two or three days.

Third Coat.—Finally add the third

coat, if desired, of the same character as the second coat.

Or the third coat may be thin, with a larger proportion of turpentine than the second coat, giving the paint a dull surface and a delicate bloom. This is called flatting.

Painting Woodwork Indoors.— Careful landlords go over the inside woodwork of a house frequently with paint and varnish. This preserves the woodwork and saves labor, strength, and time. It is not economy to wait until the paint or varnish cracks or wears off. The more frequently it is painted the longer the woodwork lasts, and the easier it is to keep in good order.

If there is grease or soap on the woodwork the paint will not adhere. Hence, before painting, the surface should be cleaned by scrubbing with ammonia water or water containing kerosene or sal soda, and rinsed off thoroughly.

Apply a second coat, if necessary, to get a smooth, hard surface.

Window Sills and Sashes.—These should be "drawn" or painted frequently, as the rain outside and the steam inside collect on the glass and settle about the casings, causing them to rot unless kept in good order by fresh paint and varnish. If putty cracks or shows signs of decaying, it should be removed and new putty applied before painting.

To Apply Paint.— The proper stroke in painting is short, say 8 or 10 inches. The brush should strike the surface nearly at right angles and in the middle of the stroke; that is to say, the painter deposits the added load 4 or 5 inches in advance of the unpainted surface, and not at the end of the last stroke, and works the color back and forth with the brush.

The brush should be deep, so as to take up the paint through the hairs, and not merely on their ends, and the surface should be wiped so that it will not drip before using. But a brush should not be wiped on a cutting edge, or the bristles will be split and tend to curl backward. Hence paint should be taken from a pail or can having a wire fastened across the top or a smooth edge turned over to wipe the brush on.

SPECIFICATIONS FOR PAINTING

White Lead — Specifications for New Work Outside.—The following specifications were very carefully prepared by an architect of great experience for a leading manufacturer of pure white lead, and may be regarded as absolutely reliable:

Before Painting. — All woodwork must be thoroughly dry before any paint is applied. No painting is to be done when rain or snow is falling, or until after the dew or moisture which may be on the surface has completely disappeared.

Knot Killing.—Immediately after the woodwork is in place, all knots and sappy streaks shall be varnished with pure grain alcohol orange shellac varnish (knot killer).

It is very important that only the best grain alcohol shellac should be used, as preparations of wood alcohol (deadly poisonous), cheap shellacs, rosin, etc., are dangerous to health and apt to cause the knots to turn yellow after the work is completed, thus spoiling the appearance of the work.

Priming Coat. — One hundred pounds of pure white lead; 6 to 7 gallons of pure raw linseed oil; 1 gallon of pure turpentine; $1\frac{1}{2}$ pints of pure turpentine japan.

On white pine, poplar, and basswood (which more readily absorb oil) use 7 gallons of linseed oil.

On yellow pine, spruce, and hemlock use 6 gallons of linseed oil.

In winter and damp weather from $\frac{1}{4}$ pint to $\frac{1}{2}$ pint additional turpentine japan should be used.

A range of from 6 to 7 gallons of linseed oil has been specified to allow room for the painter's judgment; there may be circumstances where as much as 8 gallons of linseed oil to 100 pounds of white lead may be used to advantage, but they are rare, and as a rule 7 gallons may be taken as a safe maximum.

The painter may in some special cases find it advisable in the priming coat to increase the quantity of turpentine from ½ gallon to 1 gallon, but where this is done a corresponding decrease should be made in the specified amount of linseed oil.

Priming coats *should be thin*, and well brushed out, but it is a mistake to have them *too thin*.

Putty.—After the priming coat is thoroughly dry, putty up all nail holes, dents, cracks, and other defects in the surface with a pure linseed oil putty composed of equal parts of white lead and whiting.

Nearly all the putty sold at present is made of other oils than linseed (chiefly products of petroleum) and ground cliffstone sand. The use of such putty is the explanation of the yellow nail holes and cracks so often marring the appearance of what is otherwise good work.

The addition of 1 part of powdered litharge to 5 parts each of white lead and whiting in the composition of the white lead putty above specified is permissible and, where convenient, advised.

The addition of the litharge assists the drying and hardening of the putty.

Second Coat.—One hundred pounds of pure white lead; 4 to 5 gallons of pure raw linseed oil; ½ gallon of pure turpentine; 1 pint of pure turpentine japan.

In winter and damp weather from ¼ pint to ½ pint additional turpentine japan should be used.

Third Coat.—One hundred pounds of pure white lead; 4 to 4½ gallons of pure raw linseed oil; ½ gallon of pure turpentine; 1 pint of pure turpentine japan.

In winter and damp weather from ¼ pint to ½ pint additional turpentine japan should be used.

Specifications for New Work Inside.—*Before Painting.*—As above.

Knot Killing.—As above.

Priming Coat. — One hundred pounds of pure white lead; 5 to 6 gallons of pure raw linseed oil; 2 gallons of pure turpentine; 1½ pints of pure white turpentine japan.

On white pine, poplar, and basswood (which more readily absorb oil) use 6 gallons of linseed oil.

On yellow pine, spruce, and hemlock use 5 gallons of linseed oil.

In winter and damp weather from ¼ pint to ½ pint additional turpentine japan should be used:

A range of from 5 to 6 gallons of linseed oil has been specified to allow room for the painter's judgment; there may be circumstances where as much as 7 gallons of linseed oil to 100 pounds of white lead may be used to advantage, but they are rare, and as a rule 6 gallons may be taken as a safe maximum.

The painter may in some special cases find it advisable in the priming coat to increase the quantity of turpentine from ½ gallon to 1 gallon, but where this is done a corresponding decrease should be made in the specified amount of linseed oil.

Priming coats *should be thin*, and well brushed out, but it is a mistake to have them *too thin*.

Putty.—As above.

Second Coat—Gloss Finish.—One hundred pounds of pure white lead; 4 to 5 gallons of pure raw linseed oil; ½ gallon of pure turpentine; 1 pint of pure turpentine white dryer.

Third Coat—Gloss Finish.—One hundred pounds of pure white lead; 4 to 4½ gallons of pure raw linseed oil; ½ gallon of pure turpentine; 1 pint of pure turpentine white dryer.

Finishing Coat—Flat.—One hundred pounds of pure white lead; ½ gallon of pure raw linseed oil; 2 to 2½ gallons of pure turpentine; 1 pint of pure turpentine white dryer.

Finishing Coat — Eggshell Gloss. —One hundred pounds of pure white lead; 1 gallon of pure raw linseed oil; 2 gallons of pure turpentine; 1 pint of pure turpentine white dryer.

Specifications for Old Work Outside.—*Before Painting.*—As above.

Preparation of Surface.—All loose paint, scales, dirt, and dust must be entirely removed. If there are scales, a wire brush should be used. Where window frames, sashes, doors, piazzas, etc., show cracks or scales, a paint burner or patent paint remover must be used to make the surface ready for painting.

If new paint is applied over a surface that has cracked or scaled, a good job is impossible, as the rough surface will show through.

If the old coat is pure white lead, then there will be no scales or cracks, and gently sandpapering with No. ½ to No. 1 sandpaper, followed by a good dusting, will put the surface in good condition for repainting.

First or Priming Coat.—One hundred pounds of pure white lead; 4 to 5 gallons of pure raw linseed oil; 1 gallon of pure turpentine; 1½ pints of pure turpentine japan.

In winter and damp weather from ¼ pint to ½ pint additional turpentine japan should be used.

Putty.—As above.

Second or Finishing Coat. — One hundred pounds of pure white lead; 4 to 4½ gallons of pure raw linseed oil; ¼ gallon of pure turpentine; 1¼ pints of pure turpentine japan.

In winter and damp weather from ¼ pint to ½ pint additional turpentine japan should be used.

Specifications for Old Work Inside.—*Preparation of Surface.*—As above.

Priming.—One hundred pounds of pure white lead; 1 gallon of pure raw linseed oil; 2 gallons of pure turpentine; 1½ pints of pure white turpentine japan.

The painter may in some special cases find it advisable in the priming coat to increase the quantity of turpentine from ½ gallon to 1 gallon, but where this is done a corresponding decrease should be made in the specified amount of linseed oil.

Priming coats *should be thin,* and well brushed out, but it is a mistake to have them *too thin.*

Putty.—As above.

Finishing Coat—Gloss.—One hundred pounds of pure white lead; 4 to 5 gallons of pure raw linseed oil; ½ gallon of pure turpentine; 1 pint of pure turpentine white dryer.

Finishing Coat — Flat.—One hundred pounds of pure white lead; ½ gallon of pure raw linseed oil; 2 to 2½ gallons of pure turpentine; 1 pint of pure turpentine white dryer.

Finishing Coat—Eggshell Gloss.—One hundred pounds of pure white lead; 1 gallon of pure raw linseed oil; 2 gallons of pure turpentine; 1 pint of pure turpentine white dryer.

If painting is done white or light over a previous dark finish, three coats may be necessary. In such case put on a second coat mixed similar to first coat and finish as specified.

Specifications for Painting Brick, Stucco, and Concrete.—*Brickwork.*—If any mortar has become loose and washed out between the bricks, all such damaged places shall be repointed with mortar or Portland cement, before any paint is applied. After priming, correct small defects in surface with putty.

New brickwork shall not be primed except when thoroughly dry. At least two or three days of dry, clear weather shall precede painting. No painting shall be done in cold weather.

Stucco or Concrete Work.—Stucco or concrete work shall be allowed to dry and set at least two months before paint is applied.

The longer concrete work is allowed to dry out before painting, the better, even up to one year. If a longer time is available, specify it instead of the time given above.

Formulas.—The paint for all brick, stucco, or concrete shall be mixed according to the following formulas:

Priming Coat.—One hundred pounds of white lead; 9 gallons of pure boiled linseed oil (or 9 gallons of pure raw linseed oil and 1½ pints of turpentine dryer); 1 gallon of turpentine.

Body Coat.—One hundred pounds of pure white lead; 4 gallons of pure linseed oil, one third boiled, two thirds raw (or 4 gallons of pure raw linseed oil and 1 pint of turpentine dryer).

Finishing Coat. — One hundred pounds of pure white lead; 3½ gallons of pure linseed oil, one third boiled, two thirds raw (or 3½ gallons of pure raw linseed oil and 1 pint of turpentine dryer); 1 pint of turpentine.

Strictly kettle-boiled linseed oil should be used as specified whenever possible, especially on stucco and concrete, because it is less liable than raw oil to degenerate under the peculiar influence of lime, cement, etc. If strictly kettle-boiled oil is not available, use the alternative specifications for raw oil and a dryer.

Specifications for Painting Steel and Ironwork. — *Before erection.*— Before it leaves the shops, all steel and ironwork shall be thoroughly cleaned of all mill scale, dirt, rust, and oil, and receive one coat of red lead paint mixed according to the formula given below. Surfaces which will be inaccessible after structure is erected shall receive two coats of this paint before erection.

Formula.—Pure dry red lead, 30 to 33 pounds; pure raw linseed oil, 1 gallon.

These ingredients shall be thoroughly mixed no longer than twenty-four hours before being used.

After Erection. — All structural ironwork shall be cleaned after erection and all abrasions in first coat of paint brushed clean with a stiff wire brush and repainted. All surfaces shall then receive one additional coat of red lead paint prepared according to above formula.

All pipes, including automatic sprinklers, steam and hot-water radiators, conducting pipes, and interiorly exposed structural metal work shall receive two coats as above. Fire escapes, smokestacks, gutters, down spouts, and all other interior metal work shall receive three coats as above with 1 pound of pure lampblack, ground in oil, added to every 28 pounds of red lead used in the third coat.

Subsequent coats on exposed metal work shall be of strictly pure white lead and linseed oil, tinted according to the color scheme employed in the building.

Paint shall not be applied until previously applied paint is thoroughly dry.

No painting shall be done in wet or freezing weather.

Specifications for Painting Metal Roofs, Cornices, etc.—*New Work.*— All new metal, tin, galvanized iron, iron, or steel, used for roofing, cornices, valleys, gutters, down spouts, iron railings, gratings, etc., shall be painted according to the following specifications:

Before Painting.—All surfaces shall be carefully cleaned by scrubbing with sand soap and water, and thoroughly dried, before paint is applied. Only when this is done will the paint adhere properly to the metal. *This is very important.*

Formula. — Pure dry red lead, 30 pounds; pure boiled linseed oil, ⅓ gallon; pure raw linseed oil, ⅔ gallon; pure lampblack ground in oil, 4 ounces.

Mixing. — The materials must be thoroughly mixed before application. The mixture shall be of uniform consistency and stirred frequently while in use.

Application.—All surfaces shall receive two uniform coats, as above. When necessary to follow color scheme, finishing coats of pure white lead and linseed oil, tinted to suit, shall be applied over these coats. Each coat shall dry thoroughly before the next is applied. Paint on under side of roofing shall dry hard before roofing is laid.

Old Work.—Metal surfaces not new shall be thoroughly cleaned with wire brush, removing all loose paint and particles, and then painted as above.

Specifications for Painting with Zinc White.—*Outside.*—Any of the following combinations may be used at discretion:

Combination "A." — Primer, pure lead; second coat, pure lead; third coat, pure zinc.

The primer may be tinted with not

more than 1 per cent of pure lampblack, ocher, or umber in oil. This applies to all combinations, except where the final finish is to be white.

Combination "B."—Primer, pure lead; second coat, ⅓ zinc, ⅔ lead; third coat, pure zinc.

Combination "C."—Primer, pure lead; second coat, ½ zinc, ½ lead; third coat, ⅔ zinc, ⅓ lead.

Combination "D."—Primer, ½ zinc, ½ lead; second coat, ½ zinc, ½ lead; third coat, ½ zinc, ½ lead.

Combination "E"—Straight Zinc, Four-coat Work (White).—Primer, pure zinc with 1 pint of turpentine to the gallon of paint; second coat, pure zinc with ½ pint of turpentine to the gallon of paint; third coat, pure zinc with 1 gill of turpentine to the gallon of paint; fourth coat, pure zinc ground in pure linseed oil (without turpentine).

Combination "F"—Straight Zinc, Three-coat Work (White).—Primer, pure zinc, with ½ pint of turpentine to the gallon of paint; second coat, pure zinc with 1 gill of turpentine to the gallon of paint; third coat, pure zinc with all oil.

In all the foregoing, only a sufficient quantity of dryer to be used to insure work drying in five days.

Where tints are desired, add to the foregoing tints as desired, mixed with pure oil colors.

Inside Painting, Woodwork. — Where dark tones are required, the same combinations may be used as are specified on outside work.

Where light tones are required, combinations "B," "E," or "F" may be used; if white or very light, "E" or "F" should be used.

Where a flat surface is required, the proportion of turpentine should be increased and that of oil decreased to the point where a desired flatness is obtained.

Plaster Painting, Inside.—Make all plaster work perfectly smooth and clean by brushing and sandpapering and washing if necessary, to remove any discoloration which will show through or injure paint.

The specifications should be the same as the foregoing, except that another coat should be added. This coat should be the same as the primer if tone is dark and the same as final coat if tone is light.

If an extraordinarily good job is required, both the above primer and final coats should be repeated, making five coats in all.

Enamel Painting on Walls or on Woodwork. — First coat, primer of pure lead and linseed oil; second coat, ½ lead and ½ zinc; third coat, ⅓ lead and ⅔ zinc, with the addition of sufficient varnish to form a proper surface for final coat.

Or any of the foregoing formulas may be used with the addition of varnish to the third coat.

The above coats to be applied carefully and evenly, with brush marks showing as little as possible, and each coat to be lightly sandpapered so that final coat may be flowed on without showing any brush marks. *Final coat* to be a first grade of interior varnish with the addition of only sufficient zinc and color to produce the approved tint and to be carefully flowed on.

Good workmen can make a first-class job of the above, and a bad workman can, if so inclined, so stint the materials and workmanship that it may not be satisfactory, and another final coat may be necessary.

Should the bidding be public and the architects be unable to select painters of known reputation, a clause like the following may be added:

If, after the fourth coat, the work is not satisfactory, then the painter shall without extra charge do whatever is necessary to make the work perfectly satisfactory.

Stipple Wall Painting.—First coat, pure lead; second coat, ½ zinc and ½ lead (half turpentine and half oil); third coat shall be of stippling putty mixed with zinc and hard oil, and to be stippled evenly and lightly; fourth coat shall be of pure zinc in oil and turpentine (with such tint as required), to be applied perfectly even and to be only of sufficient thickness to give proper tint and show stippling.

CARE OF PAINTS AND BRUSHES

To Keep Paint Fresh.—Any paint left over after using must be sealed. Or it may be kept fresh in an open can or pail by merely filling up the vessel with water. When the paint is again needed the water may be poured off. But take care that the water does not evaporate, as in that case the paint will be ruined.

Care of Brushes. — Paint brushes should not be left in paint or allowed to rest on the bristles in such a way as to curve the bristles to one side. After using, they should be thoroughly cleaned with turpentine and dried. Or the bristles should be immersed in a slow-drying varnish, the handles being suspended so that the bristles wi'l not touch the bottom of the can, and the whole covered to keep out the air.

Or clean brushes first in linseed oil, then in warm soapsuds, and hang up to dry.

Or, if likely to be used again shortly, they may be suspended in water, oil, or varnish. But take care that these materials do not evaporate and allow the brush to get dry, as it may be ruined.

To preserve brushes for future use without cleaning, bore a hole through the handle, string them on a wire, and suspend in a covered can containing linseed oil or varnish sufficient to cover the bristles. Close the can tightly to prevent evaporation.

To Clean Paint Brushes. — When brushes become hard or gummed with oil and paint, soak the bristles in soft soap for two or three days, but do not immerse the head of the brush. Then soak out the paint in hot water.

To Paint Furniture. — Furniture, cabinetwork, carriages, and the like, which require a highly finished surface, should first have all old paints and varnish removed by means of burning or otherwise, and the surface refinished.

Or, if the old paint is not badly checked or cracked, it may be sufficient to wash the work quite clean and rub it down to a dead finish with a wet cloth and ground pumice powder, and again wash and dry before painting. This takes off all grease and oil, and provides a surface on which paint and varnish will lie smoothly and adhere.

Dryer for Paint.—Bring 6¼ pounds of water to a boil, and slowly stir in ¾ pound of shellac and ¼ pound of borax. Stir constantly until a complete emulsion is formed. This solution is a resinous varnish which, like paint, is waterproof and resists the action of the elements. To use this as a dryer, mix equal quantities of this solution with oil paints and thin slightly with turpentine, stirring to make a complete emulsion. Prepare this mixture only as wanted, since it dries in 10 to 20 minutes.

To Thin Oil Paint with Water.—Dissolve 1 pound of gum shellac in 3 pints of water, adding ½ pound of sal soda or a little more if necessary, and stir until all is dissolved. When cold, bottle for use. Instead of turpentine or benzine thinners, add to oil paints of any kind 1 pint of the gum shellac mixture to 2 quarts of oil paint. Afterwards thin with water to any desired consistency.

SPECIAL KINDS OF PAINT

Lime Paint.—A mixture combining the qualities of paint with those of whitewash may be made with slaked lime as a basis by the addition of various materials, as milk, whiting, salt, alum, copperas, potash, ashes, sand, and pitch, with or without a small proportion of white lead and linseed oil. These mixtures are more durable than whitewash, but have less finish than white lead and oil. The cost is intermediate between the two.

To prepare a lime paint, slake lime with water and let dry to the consistency of paste. Thin with skimmed milk to the proper thickness to lay on with a brush. Add coloring matter as desired.

Or slake 4 ounces of lime with water to the consistency of cream and stir into it 4 quarts of skimmed milk. Sprinkle on the surface through a sieve 5 pounds of whiting. Let this gradually sink, then stir and rub together thoroughly and add coloring matter as desired. The casein or curd of milk, by the action of caustic lime becomes insoluble and produces a paint of great tenacity suitable for farm buildings, cellars, walls, and all rough outdoor purposes Apply with a paint brush. Two or three coats will be necessary. The above quantity is sufficient for 100 square yards.

Or slake stone lime in a cask or barrel with boiling water. Cover it to keep in the steam. Sift 6 quarts through cheese cloth or a fine sieve, add 1 quart of coarse salt and 1 gallon of water. Boil and skim the mixture clear. While boiling, stir in for each 5 gallons of this mixture 1 pound of alum, ½ pound of copperas, ¾ pound of potash, and 4 quarts of finely sifted ashes or fine sand. Add these ingredients slowly and stir vigorously until all are incorporated. Remove from the fire and add any coloring matter desired.

Or slake 8 ounces of lime and let stand exposed to the air 24 hours. Mix with this 1 pint of milk. Stir in slowly 2 ounces of white pitch dissolved in 6 ounces of boiled linseed oil. Add 3 pints of skimmed milk and sift on top of this mixture 3 pounds of whiting, allowing this to sink of its own weight. Then stir and rub the whole together until thoroughly incorporated. Add coloring matter as desired. This quantity is sufficient to give two coats for 27 square yards.

Or mix 2 parts by bulk of fine ground water lime and 1 part of white lead ground in oil. Mix with boiled linseed oil and grind through a paint mill. Then mix with linseed oil to the proper consistency. Add coloring matter as desired. This is said to be more durable than ordinary paints based on lead alone.

Paint with Zinc. — Dissolve 4 pounds of crude sulphate of zinc in 1 gallon of hot soft water. Let the mixture settle, and turn off the clear solution from the sediment. Mix this solution with an equal amount of paint composed of lead and oil, and stir slowly until a perfect emulsion is formed, which will require 10 or 15 minutes. Thin, if necessary, with turpentine. This is a cheap paint, costing about 1 cent a pound, and is very durable. This recipe is said to have been sold for as much as $100 for painter's use.

Fireproof Paint. — Mix equal amounts of powdered iron filings, brick dust, and sifted ashes. Grind the whole to a fine powder. Prepare a warm glue size by dissolving 4 ounces of glue in 1 gallon of water. Stir into this the powdered mixture, to the proper consistency, and apply with a paint brush. Two or three coats will render woodwork fireproof.

Or slake stone lime in boiling water, covering it to keep in the steam. Reduce with water to the consistency of cream, and to each 5 gallons add 1 pound of powdered alum, 12 ounces of carbonate of potassium, and ½ pound of common salt. Stir in these ingredients in the order mentioned. Add coloring matter as desired. Mix well, bring to the boiling point, and apply while hot. This is a suitable paint for the roofs of farm buildings and the like.

Paint for Blackboards.—Dissolve 4 ounces of glue in 1½ pints of warm water; add 3 ounces of flour of emery and sufficient lampblack to make a mixture of the color and consistency of jet-black ink. Stir until free from lumps, and apply with the end of a roll of woolen cloth. Three coats will be necessary.

Or take 2 quarts of alcohol, and mix 3 ounces of rotten stone, 5 ounces of pumice stone, and 6 ounces of lampblack with enough of the alcohol to form a stiff paste. Grind this mixture in a paint mill. Dissolve 7 ounces of shellac in the remainder of the alcohol and mix the whole. Shake or stir before using. This quantity will give two coats on about 30 square yards of blackboard. Let the first coat dry thoroughly before applying the second.

To Imitate Stonework.—An imitation of a stone surface may be made either by mixing fine road dust or sand with paint, or by sprinkling a freshly painted surface with sand from a shaker having holes in the top similar to a pepper box. Mix 100 pounds of road dust, 25 pounds of white lead ground in oil, 50 pounds of whiting, 7 pounds of umber, and 3 gallons of lime water. Grind with linseed oil. This gives a solid stone color.

Or prepare an ordinary oil paint with white lead and suitable coloring matter, and while the surface is wet dust fine sand over it from a shaker. This imitates a stone surface.

Soluble Glass Paints.—Silicate of sodium or soluble glass may be used as a vehicle for coloring matter, especially for walls and ceilings, as it produces a very hard and durable surface. The coating of soluble glass containing coloring matter may be followed with a coating of clear soluble glass. This substance is much cheaper than the oil and lead paint, and has the advantage of being partially fireproof. It may be mixed with glycerin for flexible surfaces, as cloth, paper, etc.

Pigments suitable to use with soluble glass are terra di Sienna, green earth, ocher, red and yellow earth, Nuremberg green, chrome green, and ultramarine.

Acid-proof Paint.—Mix pulverized asbestos with a sirup solution of water glass to the consistency of paste until free from lumps. Thin with a solution of water glass as free from alkali as possible, and apply with a paint brush. This dries as hard as glass and resists the action of acid.

Barrel Paint.—Dissolve 8 pounds of rosin in 1 gallon of boiling linseed oil by boiling in a kettle and stirring until dissolved. This mixture is known as gloss oil. Use equal parts of gloss oil and benzine as a vehicle with lead, zinc, or anything you desire to use as a pigment. Stir well before using.

Glue Paint for Kitchen Floors.—Mix 3 pounds of spruce yellow with 2 pounds of dry white lead. Dissolve 2 ounces of glue in 1 quart of water with gentle heat. When nearly boiling, stir in the mixture and continue stirring until it thickens to the consistency of paste. Apply hot with a common paste brush.

To Mix Colored Paints.—The colored pigments used in mixing colored paints come ground in oil in the following colors: white, yellow, red, blue, green, brown, black. They also come in the form of powders. To prepare these for painting, it is only necessary to mix them with the proper amount of boiled linseed oil, with the addition of a thinner or dryer if desired. They are then ready to use.

Other tints and shades are prepared by mixing and blending the above colors. The following are among the principal pigments used in mixing colored paints:

White Paint.—White lead is usually the basis of white paint, but it is often adulterated with barytes, oxide of zinc, prepared chalk, whiting, lime, or road dust. All paint intended to show a pure white should have about ¼ ounce of Prussian blue mixed with every 2 pounds of white lead, otherwise the lead appears as a stone color and not white.

To mix white paint, use pure boiled linseed oil, and thin as desired according to conditions with oil of turpentine.

Yellow Paint.—The yellows are usually ochers, chromate of lead, and various adulterants.

To prepare chrome yellow pigment, dissolve in hot water 5 pounds of sugar of lead and 5 pounds of Paris white. Dissolve separately in hot water 6½ ounces of bichromate of potash. Add the bichromate solution to the former, mix, and let stand 24 hours. Strain through muslin and expose to the air to dry. Mix with boiled linseed oil.

To make a cheap yellow paint, take 60 pounds of whiting, 40 pounds of ocher, and 5 pounds of white lead ground in oil. Grind with raw linseed oil and mix with boiled linseed oil.

Red Paint.—The reds are usually red oxide of lead, ochers, oxides of iron, red oxide of copper, vermilion, bichromate of lead, carmine, and madder and other lakes. Mix any of the above with boiled linseed oil and apply.

Or, to make cheap red paint, mix Venetian red with skimmed milk and apply with a paint brush. This is suitable for gates, stone walls, and outbuildings.

Or use oxide of iron mixed with a little boiled linseed oil. This is cheap and gives a very durable stain.

Blue Paint.—The blues are usually Prussian blue, ultramarine, smalt. Thenard blue, verditer, etc.

To make Prussian blue pigment take 1 pint of nitric acid, and add slowly as much iron shavings from the lathe or iron filings heated, but not red hot, as the acid will dissolve. After the acid has dissolved all it can, add to it 1 quart of soft water, and continue to add iron shavings or filings as long as the acid dissolves them. Make a strong solution of prussiate of potash in hot water, and slowly add this to the iron and acid until the right tint is obtained. Strain through muslin, dry the sediment to powder, and grind or mix with boiled linseed oil.

Or dissolve separately equal quantities of sulphate of iron (copperas) and prussiate of potash. Mix the two solutions, strain through muslin, dry the sediment to powder, and mix or grind with oil.

Green Paint.—The greens are usually verdigris, Paris green, verditer, borate of copper, chromate of copper, oxide of chromium, cobalt green, and green lakes. The most common green paint is a mixture of chrome yellow and Prussian blue.

To make chrome green pigment, mix in the form of powder 6½ pounds of Paris white, 3½ pounds of sugar of lead, 3½ pounds of blue vitriol, 10½ ounces of alum, 3⅜ pounds of Prussian blue, and 3⅜ pounds of chrome yellow. Stir these powders slowly into 1 gallon of water. Let stand 4 hours, filter or strain through muslin, dry the sediment to powder, and mix or grind with boiled linseed oil.

Or dissolve separately chrome yellow and Prussian blue. Mix the two solutions to get the desired shade, and add spruce yellow to the proper consistency.

Or slake the best quality of stone lime with hot water, covering to keep in the steam. Strain through a fine sieve, let dry, and reduce the sediment to powder. Make this powder into a thick paste with a saturated solution of alum, and add, until the desired shade is produced, enough solution of bichromate of potash to produce a yellowish green, and solution of sulphate of copper to produce a bluish green.

Or mix thoroughly in powdered form 5 pounds of blue vitriol, 6¼ pounds of sugar of lead, 2½ pounds of arsenic, and 1½ ounces of bichromate of potash. Add 3 pints of water, mix, and let stand 4 hours. Strain or filter, dry the sediment to powder, and grind or mix with boiled linseed oil.

To make cheap green paint, dissolve 4 pounds of Roman vitriol in hot water. Add 2 pounds of pearlash and stir until dissolved. Add ¼ pound of powdered yellow arsenic. Mix and apply with a paint brush. Two or three coats will be necessary. A darker or a lighter shade may be produced by adding more or less of the yellow arsenic. This paint contains no oil. Hence, while it looks well, it does not protect wood as does an oil paint, but is suitable for stone walls and similar places.

Or mix powdered charcoal with linseed oil, and add litharge as a dryer, using 1 gill to 1 gallon of oil. Add ocher to produce the required shade of green.

Brown Paint.—The browns are usually umber, bole, terra di Sienna, bistre, sepia, etc.

To produce a brown pigment, make a solution of sulphate of copper in hot water, and separately a strong solution of prussiate of potash. Mix the two solutions to the desired shade. Filter or strain through muslin. Dry the sediment to a powder. Grind or mix with boiled linseed oil.

Black Paint.—The blacks are usually lampblack, bone black, anthracite, graphite, powdered charcoal, etc.

Lampblack is very commonly used both for black paint and also to modify the brightness of tone in other colors in producing various tints and shades.

To make a cheap black paint, mix powdered charcoal with linseed oil, and add as a dryer 1 gill of litharge to 1 gallon of oil.

Or take ivory or lampblack, 10 pounds; sifted road dust, 20 pounds; lime water, 2 gallons. Grind in raw linseed oil. Mix with boiled linseed oil.

Tints and Shades. — The various combinations of colors to produce tints and shades are innumerable, and can only be determined by experiment; but the following are the principal effects commonly desired, and indicate the lines along which the experiment should proceed.

Pigments should be thinned with boiled linseed oil before mixing, the most predominant color being taken as a base, the other colors being slowly added in a thin stream and stirre vigorously. The proportions must be determined by experiment and the taste of the painter. The predominant color stands first in the following list:

Ash color or gray, white lead and lampblack. Vary the quantity of lampblack to give the shade desired.

Lead color, white lead and indigo.

Drab, white lead, raw and burnt umber.

White oak, white lead and umber.

Flesh color, white lead, lake, or yellow ocher, or vermilion.

Pearl, white lead, black, and blue.

Buff, white lead and yellow ocher.

Straw color, white lead and a small amount of yellow ocher.

Fawn, white lead, yellow ocher, and red.

Chestnut, red, black, and yellow.

Walnut, white lead and burnt umber. Vein with the same, and touch the deepest spots with black.

Light willow green, white lead and verdigris.

Pea green, white lead and chrome green.

Grass green, yellow ocher and verdigris.

Olive, yellow ocher, blue, black, and white. Vein with burnt umber.

Bronze green, chrome green, black, and yellow.

Orange, yellow and red.

Brick color, red lead, yellow ocher, and white lead.

Brown, vermilion, black, and a little yellow.

Chocolate, raw umber, red, and black.

Violet, red lead, Prussian blue, and white lead.

Purple, same as violet, with more red and white.

Gold, white lead, stone ocher, and red lead.

Carnation, lake and pink.

Timber color, spruce ocher, white lead, and a little umber.

Chestnut color, red ocher, yellow ocher, and black.

Limestone, white lead, yellow ocher, lampblack, and red lead.

Freestone, red lead, lampblack, yellow ocher, and white lead.

Paint for Canvas.—Mix with boiled oil 24 pounds of ocher and 4 pounds of lampblack. Add 1 pound of soap dissolved in 2 pounds of water. Mix and apply with a paint brush two coats at intervals of 2 or 3 days. Allow to dry, and add a finishing coat of varnish formed of lampblack ground and thinned with boiled oil.

VARNISHING

Before varnishing, the surface should first be "flatted" either by mixing the last coat of paint with turpentine or by rubbing it down with a piece of felt moistened and dipped in pumice stone. For a level surface, tack the felt on a block of wood, or use thick woolen cloth or chamois tacked to a block of wood, or a smooth piece of pumice stone with water. Let dry and brush off the surface to remove the dust. Take care that the air is not full of dust when the varnish is applied.

For a fine quality of work, two to six coats may be spread on, one after the other. Do not lift too much varnish on the brush, but rather take up a small quantity, spread it on finely, and rub out well. Rub down the next to the last coat until the gloss is "flatted," and let the last be a flowing coat, heavy enough to flow out evenly of itself. For a cheaper grade of work, two or three coats are sufficient, the last coat being flowed on.

To finish varnish, rub down with very finely pulverized pumice stone, and wash off with clear water. Afterwards rub down with rotten stone and sweet oil, applied by means of the bare hands. Finally wipe and polish with chamois.

Killing Knots.—Use for this purpose only the best quality of pure grain alcohol orange shellac varnish or "knot killer." Apply over this with a brush equal parts of red and white lead ground with water, and mixed with hot glue size at the rate of 4 ounces of glue to a gallon of water. Apply before it cools. And for fine work, follow with a second coat of 3 parts of white lead ground in oil, and 1 part of red lead or litharge.

Or, for cabinetwork, cover the knot with an oil size and lay over it silver or gold leaf.

Or hold a hot iron against it until the pitch stews out so that it can be scraped off. Afterwards cover with gold or silver leaf.

Ingredients of Varnish. — Varnish is a solution of various gums, as the resins amber, copal, dragon's blood, mastic, lac, rosin, and sandarac, in various solvents, as alcohol, wood spirit, oil of turpentine, linseed, and other drying oils. It is used as a decoration to produce a hard, transparent, or glossy surface, and also as a protection against moisture and air.

Resins.—Resins in general are substances that occur in various plants, and which flow from trees of different species when the bark is cut. They are usually yellow and do not crystallize, but form in drops like gum. They are not, however, the same as gum, although the two words are often used interchangeably.

Amber. — A resin produced from certain extinct coniferous trees. It occurs as a fossil, usually of a pale yellow color, opaque, or transparent. It is mined the same as coal in various parts of the world, especially in the vicinity of the Baltic Sea. Small quantities are found in the United States. Amber was much prized by the ancients and was an object of commerce in prehistoric times. It is extensively used for ornaments, especially for the mouthpiece of pipes.

Anime.—A resin which exudes from a certain tree in Brazil. Used as a medicine and as incense. The name is also applied to a resin known in India as copal.

Copal. — This name is applied to several resins used in varnishes. It is a nearly colorless, translucent substance imported from tropical America, India, and eastern and western Africa. Zanzibar copal is said to be the best.

Lac.—A resinous substance caused to exude from certain trees in Asia by the bites of an insect about the size of a louse. The twig punctured by these insects becomes incrusted with lac, sometimes to the thickness of a quarter of an inch. It protects the eggs and supplies food for the young maggots. The mothers are often imprisoned and covered by the sticky fluid, imparting to it a lac dye similar to cochineal. The twigs are broken off before the maggots escape and are dried in the sun.

Stick-lac is the crude product or dry twigs. It is not soluble in water except the lac dye or red coloring matter, which washes out. It is partially soluble in alcohol, but not in linseed oil or turpentine.

Seed-lac is the resin removed from the twigs, and washed with water to remove the lac dye or coloring matter. It is coarsely pounded.

Lump-lac is seed-lac melted into lumps.

Shell-lac (or shellac) is prepared from seed-lac by melting and straining through cotton.

Lac Resin.—The essential principle of shellac may be obtained pure by refining shellac, which for this purpose is treated with cold alcohol, filtered, and distilled. It is a brown, translucent, hard, and brittle resin, and is very valuable. Shellac may be dissolved in alcohol, dilute hydrochloric and acetic acids, sal ammoniac, and alkalies. One part of borax dissolved in boiling water will dissolve five times its weight of shellac, making a solution which is as useful for many purposes as spirit varnish.

Shellac is much favored as a varnish, being harder than rosin and easily soluble in alcohol. It is also the principal ingredient of the best sealing wax. It is used as a size and has valuable waterproofing qualities.

Mastic.—A valuable gum resin produced from certain trees and shrubs in Barbary, the Levant, and China. It is used as an ingredient in many varnishes. Used by itself it is transparent, brilliant, tough, and delicate. It is also often employed in finishing maps and paintings, also in medicine, dentistry, and in mounting articles for the microscope. Mastic is used with other ingredients in varnish to impart a gloss.

Rosin or Colophony. — This substance is the residue obtained by distilling crude turpentine from pine trees, of which it comprises about 70 per cent to 90 per cent. It is largely manufactured together with oil of turpentine in North Carolina. In color it ranges, according to its purity, from transparent or straw color to a brownish yellow. It can be dissolved in alcohol, ether, wood spirit, linseed oil, or turpentine, partly in petroleum but not in water. It can also be dissolved by nitric acid and alkalies. It is largely used in varnishes and cements, in calking ships, in the preparation of plaster and ointments, in soldering metals, in making yellow soaps, and otherwise. A common use is for covering the bows of violins.

Sandarac is produced from a small coniferous tree in Barbary. It occurs in pale-yellow oblong grains or tears covered with a fine dust. It is transparent and brittle. It is used in pharmacy as an incense, and in varnishes, and also in powdered form it is rubbed on writing paper where erasures have been made in order to prevent the spread of ink. It is partly soluble in cold alcohol, and wholly in alcohol brought to the boiling point.

Gums.—Gums are substances which occur in plants and some animals, but which are neither oily nor resinous. They exude for the most part from various trees when the bark is cut. The principal gums are arabic, Senegal, mesquite, tragacanth, Bassora. They are principally employed in the manufacture of mucilage, also in medicine, pharmacy, confectionery, calico printing in the preparation of the inks, and also for sizes.

Gums Arabic and Senegal.—These gums exude from various trees in Africa and Asia, and are sold under various trade terms denoting the localities from which they come.

Gum Mesquite.—A substance similar to gum arabic, but produced in plants growing in the dry regions of Mexico and adjacent parts of the United States. It differs from the other gums in the fact that its principle is not precipitated by borax.

Gums arabic, Senegal, and mesquite are easily soluble in hot or cold water, forming mucilage. They can be separated from water by the addition of alcohol or subacetate of lead. They are coagulated by borax, except gum mesquite.

Gums tragacanth and Bassora swell, but do not perfectly dissolve, in water. They can, however, be rubbed with water into a very adhesive paste, which is not, strictly speaking, a solution.

Asphalt.—Asphalt occurs in nature in veins, beds, and lakes, usually beneath the surface of the ground. In the island of Trinidad, Venezuela, occur lakes of asphalts about three miles in circumference. It is a dry solid with a glossy black surface easily melted and very inflammable. It can be dissolved in alcohol, linseed oil, turpentine, or ether, also in benzol and bisulphide of carbon. With benzol it forms an intensely black solution called black varnish. It is used for varnish, insulation, waterproofing cement, roofing, and painting.

Kinds of Varnish.—The character of varnish is largely affected by the substance in which it is dissolved. Thus we have fixed-oil varnishes in which the principal solvent is turpentine; spirit varnishes or "lac varnishes," true solutions of resins in alcohol, wood spirit, acetone, benzine, etc.; volatile-oil varnishes, the principal solvents being oil of turpentine, and ether varnishes, being solutions of resin in ether. In addition to the above are various special varnishes of gutta percha, wax, and other substances.

FIXED-OIL VARNISHES

Solutions of resins in boiled linseed oil have the same durable quality as oil paint, with the addition of a high luster. As in paint, the linseed oil absorbs oxygen from the air, and is converted into a tough, elastic waterproof substance.

To prepare fixed-oil varnishes, melt the resins anime, amber, copal, etc., heat the boiled linseed oil to a high temperature, and pour it into the melted resin in a thin stream, stirring constantly. To test the proper amount of linseed oil to be added to the resin, take out a drop of the fluid now and then and let it cool on a glass plate. When the proportions of oil and resins are correct, the drop will be limpid like wax. If the drop becomes hard and brittle, more oil is required. When mixed, remove from the fire and allow the mixture to cool. Then dilute to the proper consistency by pouring in turpentine in a thin stream and stirring constantly.

But first boil the mixture of linseed oil and resin before adding the turpentine.

The best quality of linseed oil should be employed for a varnish.

The proper proportions for an ordinary oil varnish are about 10 parts by weight of resin, 5 to 25 parts of boiled linseed oil, and 15 to 25 parts of oil of turpentine. Varnishes of this character usually improve with age. The following are formulas for fixed-oil varnishes:

Amber Varnish.—Eight ounces of amber, 5 ounces of boiled linseed oil, and ½ pint of oil of turpentine. This varnish is very durable, but a slow dryer.

Or, for larger quantities, 6 pounds of amber, 2 gallons of hot linseed oil, and 4 gallons of oil of turpentine. Melt the amber, add the linseed oil hot, and boil until stringy. Cool and add the turpentine.

Or amber, 16 ounces; boiled linseed oil, 10 ounces; Venetian turpentine or gum lac, 2 ounces; oil of turpentine, 15 or 16 ounces.

Or melt 4 pounds of resin and ½ pound of beeswax. Add 1 gallon of boiled oil at a high temperature. Mix and boil until stringy. Cool and add 2 quarts of turpentine.

Or melt 1½ pounds of rosin, add 1 pound of Venetian turpentine, then stir in 1 gallon of boiled linseed oil at high temperature. Boil until stringy; cool and thin with 1 quart of turpentine. The above are ordinary oil varnishes suitable for common work.

Copal Varnish.—Fuse 2 ounces of African copal and add 4 ounces of best boiled linseed oil at a high temperature. Boil until stringy, cóol, and add 8 ounces of oil of turpentine. This is a transparent body varnish, hard, clear, and durable.

Or melt 4 ounces of copal, and add at a high temperature 2 ounces of boiled linseed oil. Stir and thin with 3¾ ounces of turpentine. To make a white copal varnish, color the above with the finest white lead.

Anime Varnishes.—Melt 4 pounds of gum anime and add at a high temperature 1½ gallons of boiled linseed oil. Boil until stringy. Stir in 2 ounces of camphor and 2 ounces of litharge, cool, and thin with 2¾ gallons of oil of turpentine. This is a good carriage or furniture varnish.

Or, for a finer grade of work, melt 4 pounds of gum anime; add at a high temperature 1½ gallons of clarified linseed oil, 2 ounces of litharge, 2 ounces of dry acetate of lead, and 2¾ gallons of turpentine.

Lac Varnishes.—Dissolve 1 pound of shellac, and add at a high temperature 2 quarts of boiled linseed oil. Stir in ½ pound of red lead, ½ pound of litharge, and 2 ounces of umber. Boil until stringy. This dries rapidly, and has a high gloss.

Waterproof Varnish.—Dissolve 1 pound of flowers of sulphur in 1 gallon of boiled linseed oil. Boil and stir until they form a perfect emulsion. This is a good waterproof varnish for woven goods.

Or cut India rubber in small pieces, put them in a glass bottle with benzine, and let stand four or five days, shaking frequently. Strain through cotton to remove the benzine, and thin with boiled linseed oil or turpentine.

Flexible or Balloon Varnish.—Cut 1 pound of India rubber into fine pieces and boil in 1 pound of linseed oil until dissolved. Cool, and add 1 pound of turpentine. Simmer with gentle heat and strain through cheese cloth.

Dissolve 8 ounces of birdlime in 8 ounces of boiled linseed oil. Boil until the birdlime ceases to crackle. Add 12 ounces of boiled oil and 2 ounces of litharge, and boil until it becomes stringy. Cool, and add 12 ounces of turpentine. Apply while warm.

Or dissolve ½ ounce of India rubber cut fine in 1 pound of mineral naphtha. Cover the vessel and melt with gentle heat until it dissolves. Strain through cheese cloth.

Or cut fine ½ ounce of India rubber, pour over this 1 pint of boiled linseed oil, and dissolve with gentle heat, stirring constantly. Strain through cheese cloth.

Or raise to a boil 2 quarts of boiled linseed oil, stirring in 1½ ounces of white copperas, 1½ ounces of sugar of lead, and 4 ounces of litharge. Boil until stringy. Allow to cool slowly and pour off the clear liquid.

Or take 1 gallon of boiled linseed oil, and dissolve 4 ounces of pure asphaltum with gentle heat in a small amount of the oil. Grind 3 ounces of burnt umber in a little of the oil. Add the remainder of the oil, boil until stringy, cool, and thin with oil of turpentine.

Black Asphalt Varnish for Ironwork.—Dissolve 3 pounds of asphalt in 4 pounds of boiled linseed oil. Remove from the fire and thin with 15 to 18 pounds of oil of turpentine.

Or boil 22½ pounds of foreign asphalt in 3 gallons of linseed oil. Add 3 pounds of litharge. Boil until stringy, then add 4 pounds of melted gum amber and 1 gallon of linseed oil. Bring to a boil, remove from the fire, and thin with 22 gallons of turpentine.

India rubber or gutta percha may be added to any common oil varnish if desired to impart additional flexibility.

Or melt 12 pounds of asphaltum, add 2½ gallons of boiled linseed oil, 2½ pounds of red lead, 2½ pounds of litharge, and 1 pound of dry and powdered white copperas. Boil 2 hours, add 2⅜ pounds of dark gum amber melted and ⅜ gallon of hot linseed oil. Boil 2 hours. To test, take out a few drops and allow to cool on a glass plate. When boiled sufficiently, it may be rolled into pills. Remove from the fire and thin with 10 gallons of oil of turpentine. This is suitable for varnishing the best grades of ironwork.

Or to ½ pint of boiled linseed oil add 6 ounces of powdered asphaltum. Bring to a boil and stir in 1 pound of melted amber. Cool, and add 1 pint of oil of turpentine.

Or dissolve 8 ounces of asphaltum and 4 ounces of rosin in 1 pint of oil of turpentine. Rub up 2 ounces of lampblack to a paste with boiled linseed oil and stir into the mixture. The above are suitable for iron fences or hinges exposed to the weather, or for iron shovels, tools, coal scuttles, and other sheet-iron or cast-iron surfaces to protect them from rust and to give them a good appearance.

Or melt 4 pounds of asphalt and add 1 quart of boiled linseed oil and 1 gallon of oil of turpentine. This is suitable for grates and other rough cast-iron surfaces.

Or melt 2½ pounds of asphaltum and add 1 gallon of turpentine. When cool, add 1 pint of copal varnish and 1 pint of boiled linseed oil. This is black varnish for wood or canvas.

SPIRIT OR LAC VARNISHES

These differ from fixed-oil varnishes in being true solutions of various resins, chiefly anime, mastic, shellac, and sandarac, in spirituous solvents, usually alcohol and wood spirit, or acetone, benzine, etc.

Sandarac is used to impart hardness, mastic to give a gloss. Venetian turpentine is frequently added to sandarac, or a little concentrated ammonia is often added to overcome the tendency of varnish to chill or crack and give a rough surface. Venetian turpentine is used with sandarac to prevent excessive brittleness.

To make spirit varnishes, first pulverize the resins and mix them with sand or broken glass to prevent their forming into lumps. Put them in a double boiler, cover with the spirit, which should be not less than 95 per cent pure, and dissolve with gentle heat. Afterwards filter, first through silk, then through filter paper.

Shellac Varnishes.—Shellac will be more soluble if powdered and exposed to the air as long as possible before using. To make cheap shellac, dissolve 1 ounce of borax in 8 ounces of boiling water. Add 5 ounces of pulverized shellac, stir, and boil until dissolved. If too thin, continue to boil until sufficient water has evaporated, or if too thick, thin with boiling water. This solution is equal to spirit varnishes for many purposes, and is much cheaper. When dry, weather has no effect upon it. Hence it is useful to dissolve water colors for calcimining and for other purposes.

Or India ink rubbed up in this solution may be used where an acid-proof labeling ink is required. It is not affected by the fumes of acids.

Or put in a glass fruit jar 8 ounces of water, 3 ounces of white shellac, and 1 ounce of sal ammoniac, and let stand over night. Place the fruit jar in a saucepan containing hot water, and boil, stirring constantly until the shellac is dissolved.

Or boil in an earthen vessel.

This solution may be used as a substitute for spirit varnish, is much cheaper, and has the advantage of being waterproof. Diluted with 10 or 12 parts of water and applied by means of a brush, it may be used for waterproofing cloth or making oilcloth. It may also be used for staining and waterproofing wood, as a stain paint or a varnish, according to consistency, and may be mixed with any water-color or oil pigments to produce any color that may be desired.

The above are not true spirit varnishes, but may be treated most conveniently in this place.

Or dissolve 10 ounces of white shellac in 1 quart of 95 per cent alcohol. This may be done without heat by pouring the alcohol over the shellac and letting it stand in a warm place until dissolved. Keep in a covered fruit jar or corked bottle to prevent evaporation. This is a good transparent varnish for furniture, woodwork, tools, and most other purposes. It dries rapidly. It is especially useful to coat woodwork that is exposed to the weather, as farming tools and other utensils that are frequently used or left out of doors. It is a very convenient and serviceable all-round varnish.

Or color the above by the addition of lampblack or asphaltum. This gives a glossy black varnish.

Or, to give a thicker coat of varnish, take 1 quart of 95 per cent alcohol, and add all the gum shellac it will cut. Strain out the excess through silk and filter paper. Add 2 ounces of Venetian turpentine. This gives a transparent gloss.

Or color with aniline dyes as desired.

Or, to make a hard shellac varnish for special purposes, as gunstocks and the like, dissolve 10 ounces of shellac, 1 ounce of sandarac, and 1 dram of Venetian turpentine in 1 gallon of 95 per cent alcohol. Put in a glass fruit jar or earthenware vessel, cover tightly, and let stand in a warm place until dissolved. Apply two or three coats, and finish, if desired, with one or two coats of still harder varnish, prepared as follows:

Dissolve 1 ounce of shellac, ½ ounce of sandarac, and ½ ounce of Venetian turpentine in 2 quarts of alcohol. This gives a high polish and requires less rubbing.

To Color Shellac.—Add 1 ounce of aniline dye to 1 pint of shellac varnish.

For mahogany, use aniline cardinal dye.

Other colors and coloring matters may be added freely to produce any colors desired.

Or mix equal weights of gum shellac and alcohol, and heat until the mixture becomes quite thick. Add any desired amount of aniline dyes dissolved in alcohol, and thin with about one fifth by weight of castor oil.

Lacquers.—Colored spirit varnishes are used to give a tinge of gold to articles made of brass or other base metals. The bases of these lacquers is a varnish consisting of 2 parts of seed-lac and 4 parts of sandarac or elemi dissolved in 40 parts of alcohol. To this, tinctures of annotto, coralline, dragon's blood, gamboge, gummigutta, Martius yellow, picric acid, or turmeric are added separately to give the required color.

To make a good gold lacquer for brass work, dissolve 3 ounces of seed-lac, 1 ounce of turmeric, and ¼ ounce of dragon's blood in 1 pint of alcohol. Put the solution in a glass fruit jar and let stand in a warm place, shaking frequently until dissolved. Filter through silk and filter paper.

Or, if deep gold is desired, dissolve ½ pound of ground turmeric, ¾ ounce of gamboge, 1¾ pounds of sandarac, and 6 ounces of shellac in 1 gallon of 95 per cent alcohol. Strain through silk and filter paper and add ½ pint of turpentine varnish.

Or, for deep red, dissolve 1½ pounds of annotto, ½ pound of dragon's blood, and 1¾ pounds of gum sandarac in 1 gallon of alcohol. Strain, filter, and add 1 pint of turpentine varnish.

Or, for pale gold, dissolve ½ ounce of gamboge, 1½ ounces of cape aloes, and ½ pound of white shellac in 1 gallon of alcohol.

Copal Varnishes.—Copal dissolved in alcohol forms a hard, durable varnish for fine cabinetwork and similar purposes, but it is more expensive than shellac and no better for ordinary purposes. To prepare ordinary copal varnish, first melt the resin with gentle heat in a double boiler. Then pulverize and mix it with sand. Finally dissolve it in strong alcohol and strain and filter. The addition of elemi resin or solution of turpentine softens it.

To make a transparent copal varnish, put 6 ounces of melted and pulverized copal and 6 ounces of 95 per cent alcohol in a glass bottle or fruit jar, cork it tightly, and set in a warm place until dissolved. Then add 4 ounces of turpentine and 1 ounce of ether.

Or dissolve 1 ounce of camphor in 1 quart of alcohol. Put this in a glass bottle or fruit jar with 4 ounces of melted and pulverized copal, and set in a warm place until dissolved. Strain, filter, and dry the sediment, if any, for future use.

Or dissolve 7 ounces of copal, 1 ounce of mastic, and ½ ounce of Venetian turpentine in 11 ounces of alcohol. First dissolve the copal in a small amount of alcohol with ½ ounce of camphor. Add the mastic and turpentine and thin with the remainder of the alcohol. This is a good varnish for articles frequently handled.

Colored Copal Varnish. — On account of its superior hardness, copal varnish is frequently used as a vehicle for various coloring matters for toys, picture frames, bric-a-brac, articles of furniture, and the like. Experiments may be made with any desired colors, but the following suggestions may be helpful:

For flaxen gray, mix ceruse with an equal quantity of English red or carminated lake. Add a little Prussian blue.

For yellow, use yellow oxide of lead or Naples or Montpellier. Mix in a glass vessel, and do not let it come in contact with iron or steel. Or use gummigutta, yellow ocher, or Dutch pink.

For violet, vermilion, blue, and white.

For purple, cochineal, carmine, and carminated lakes with ceruse. Or Prussian blue and vermilion.

For green, a mixture of verdigris with ceruse, white lead, or Spanish white. Or a mixture of yellow and blue.

For red, red oxide of lead, cinnabar, vermilion, red ocher, or Prussian red. These coloring matters may be used ground with boiled oil or in the form of powders, water colors, or aniline dyes.

Sandarac Varnishes.—Sandarac or lac varnishes containing a considerable amount of sandarac are very hard and brittle; hence they are liable to crack and their use is limited. They may be softened by the addition of gum elemi or Venetian turpentine. To make a hard white sandarac varnish, dissolve 1¼ pounds of sandarac in 1 quart of 95 per cent alcohol. Add ¼ pint of pale turpentine varnish. Mix and let stand 24 hours.

Or dissolve 3 ounces of sandarac, 1 ounce of shellac, and 2 ounces of resin in 16 ounces of 95 per cent alcohol. Add 2 ounces of oil of turpentine.

VOLATILE-OIL VARNISHES

These are solutions of various resins, principally gum copal, Canada balsam, resin, and others in oil of turpentine; are more durable and less brittle than spirit varnishes, but require more time in drying.

Like fixed-oil varnishes, they improve with age, whereas spirit varnishes deteriorate in quality. The resins may usually be dissolved in oil of turpentine without being previously melted. Seven pounds of oil of turpentine will usually dissolve about 5 pounds of resin.

To make ordinary turpentine varnish, dissolve with gentle heat ½ pound of powdered white resin in 1 pint of turpentine. Or other proportions recommended range from 3 to 5 pounds of resin in 1 gallon of turpentine.

Canada Balsam Varnish with Turpentine. — Mix equal parts of pure Canada balsam and pale oil of turpentine. Dissolve with gentle heat and shake occasionally. Let stand two or three days, strain, and filter. This varnish improves with age.

Copal Varnish with Turpentine.— Dissolve 3 ounces of copal in 1 pound of oil of turpentine.

Ether Varnishes.—These are a solution of various resins in ether. They are very little used.

To make an ethereal copal varnish, dissolve 5 ounces of copal and 2 ounces of ether. This is suitable for repairing jewelry, as, for example, broken enamel, for the setting of gems, and the like. It may be applied to wood by first rubbing the wood with a cloth moistened in oil of turpentine, wiping with a linen cloth, and then applying the varnish. This prevents the ether from evaporating too rapidly.

To make ethereal amber varnish, dissolve 4 grains of amber in 1 ounce of chloroform. Use this for varnishing photographs, maps, etc.

SPECIAL VARNISHES

Miscellaneous Varnishes.—In addition to the above, various miscellaneous varnishes are in use for different purposes, among which may be mentioned the following:

Map Varnish.—Dissolve 1 ounce of gutta percha in 5 ounces of oil of turpentine. Add 8 ounces of hot linseed oil.

Varnish for Oil Paintings. — Melt with gentle heat 1 pound of white wax. Add 1 pint of warm 95 per cent alcohol. Mix and pour on a cold porphyry slab. Grind to a smooth paste with a muller. Add sufficient water and beat up to the consistency of milk with an egg beater. Strain through cheese cloth. Spread this over the paint and allow it to dry. Afterwards go over it with a warm (not hot) iron to melt and diffuse it equally.

Zinc Varnish.—Dissolve equal parts of potassium chloride and copper sulphate in hot water. Immerse the zinc ten seconds. Dry, wash, and polish. This forms a solution of copper oxide having an indigo-blue color.

Varnish to Prevent Rust.—Melt 4 ounces of tallow and 2 ounces of rosin, strain through cheese cloth while hot, and stir in 1 ounce of finely pulverized black lead. Apply to tools and other metals with a brush.

Or melt paraffin and apply with a brush.

Or dissolve 4 ounces of mastic, 2 ounces of camphor, 6 ounces of sandarac, and 2 ounces of elemi in alcohol, and apply to fine tools and other metallic surfaces. This improves the appearance of the articles, and may be used on hardware exposed for sale.

Or dissolve 2 ounces of rosin, 3 ounces of sandarac, and 2 ounces of shellac in 3 ounces of alcohol. When cool add 2 ounces of turpentine. Strain, filter, and bottle for use.

Varnish from Sealing Wax.—Dissolve 1 ounce of any color of sealing wax in 4 ounces of alcohol, and apply while warm with a soft bristle brush. The principal ingredient of sealing wax is shellac.

Varnish for Window Glass.—Mix ½ ounce of gum tragacanth finely powdered with the whites of 2 eggs, and beat thoroughly with an egg beater. Let stand 24 hours and apply to window panes with a soft brush. When dry, this effectually prevents the sun's rays from passing through the glass.

Varnish for Leather. — Dissolve in water 3 ounces of gum arabic. Dissolve separately in brandy 3 ounces of isinglass. Mix and apply.

Tar Varnish.—Melt together 2 gallons of tar and 1 pound of tallow. Add 7 pounds of ocher ground in linseed oil. Thin with 6 pounds of oil of turpentine. Mix well. This is suitable for all rough outdoor work, protecting bulkheads, drains, water troughs, leaders, and woodwork in all localities exposed to much dampness.

Stone Varnish.—Melt 10 pounds of rosin, add 1 pound of linseed oil, and stir in 10 pounds of prepared chalk. Mix thoroughly. Add 4 ounces of native oxide of copper and 4 ounces of sulphuric acid. Mix well and apply hot with a brush. When dry, this is practically fireproof and is hard as stone.

Asphaltum Varnish.—Dissolve with gentle heat 2¼ pounds of pulverized asphaltum in 1 gallon of spirits of turpentine. This is a suitable varnish for all iron work, stoves, stovepipes, grates, coal scuttles, fly screens, wire netting, exposed hinges, and other hardware, and all iron or steel exposed to the weather or likely to suffer from rust.

Or to the above add 1 pint copal spirit varnish, and ½ pint boiled linseed oil. This is suitable for wood, iron, or leather.

Varnish for Paintings, Drawings, and Prints. — A number of special varnishes, including spirit or lac varnishes containing gum sandarac, mastic, and the like, turpentine varnishes with Canada balsam, and various special mixtures, are recommended for coating oil paintings, drawings, prints, and the like, to protect them from the effects of exposure.

Mastic Varnish.—To make the finest quality of pure varnish for oil paints and similar fine work, crush the mastic on a stone or marble with a knife blade or ivory paper cutter, and eject the soft part or tears. Put the hard grains into a glass bottle with rectified spirits of turpentine, and shake the bottle until the mastic dissolves without heat. Strain through a piece of muslin, cork the bottle, and stand it in direct sunlight for several weeks. A gummy sediment like mucilage will form in the bottom of the bottle. Reject this, pouring off only the clear liquor for use. To each ounce of this liquor add 2 ounces of alcohol, and thin, if desired, with rectified turpentine.

Or, for larger quantities, mix 2½ pounds of mastic with 1 pound of clean crushed glass and 1 gallon of rectified spirits of turpentine. Put the whole in a large jug or glass bottle, cork tightly, and shake or agitate the bottle until the gum is dissolved. Let the whole stand several months, the longer the better. Pour off the clear liquor from the top for use.

Mastic and Sandarac Varnish.—Mix equal quantities of gum sandarac and gum mastic dissolved in alcohol. Let stand forty-eight hours to settle, and strain through linen. Apply by means of a camel's-hair brush.

Or dissolve ¼ ounce of gum camphor in 3 pints of 95 per cent alcohol, and add 5 ounces of sandarac and 2 ounces of mastic. Cork tightly in a glass bottle, shake until dissolved, and let stand 48 hours or more in a warm place to settle. Pour off the clear liquor. This is suitable for drawings, prints, dry plants or flowers, and similar fine work.

Balsam Varnish.—Size colored designs, as water colors, maps, lithographs, and colored prints, with one or more coats of a solution of gum arabic or isinglass in water, or of boiled rice or wheat starch, and then apply a varnish composed of 2 parts of spirits of turpentine and 1 part of Canada balsam, or equal parts of each. Apply by means of a flat camel's-hair brush.

Or dissolve 3 ounces of Canada balsam, 3 ounces of white rosin, and 1 part of oil of turpentine.

Or, for a cheaper article, 6 ounces of pale-white rosin dissolved in 1 pint of turpentine.

Or dissolve 3 ounces of Canada balsam in ½ pint of turpentine, and add 3 ounces of pale copal varnish.

Shellac Varnish.—Heat in a suitable saucepan 5 ounces of clean animal charcoal, pour over this while warm 1 pint of 95 per cent alcohol, add 2½ ounces of pale shellac, and boil carefully over a slow fire, covering loosely to prevent too much evaporation.

Test the solution by filtering a sample, and if not colorless add a little more charcoal. When the liquor is colorless, strain through a piece of white silk and filter with filter paper. This gives a perfectly colorless liquor which dries quickly and does not chill or bloom. Apply by means of a camel's-hair brush at a temperature of at least 60° F. in an atmosphere free from dust. This is one of the best and purest of all varnishes, is commonly used by bookbinders, and may be applied to the finest oil paintings after the oil is thoroughly dried and hard, to drawings, prints, gilding, and all ornaments likely to be injured by damp, as it resists damp and prevents mildew.

Bookbinder's Varnish.—Dissolve in 1 quart of alcohol 2 ounces of shellac, ¾ ounce of benzoin, and ½ ounce of mastic. Shake until dissolved and add ⅛ ounce of oil of lavender.

Isinglass Size. — Put 4 ounces of isinglass shavings in a glass bottle with an equal quantity of water, and let stand 24 hours or more to soften. Add 1 pint of 95 per cent alcohol, and in this dissolve the isinglass in a double boiler with gentle heat. Cork the bottle to prevent evaporation, but not tightly enough to cause explosion. Apply two or three coats, letting each coat dry before the next is applied, and following with any of the above print varnishes.

Parchment Varnish. — Put white parchment cuttings with water in a glass or earthenware vessel, and boil in a double boiler until a clear jell or size is produced. Strain through cheese cloth. Apply one or more coats by means of a camel's-hair brush.

Varnish for Musical Instruments. —Dissolve together with gentle heat 2 ounces of gum sandaric, 1 ounce of seed-lac, ½ ounce of mastic, ½ ounce of benjamin in tears, and 1 ounce of Venetian turpentine in 16 ounces of pure alcohol. Stir in 2 ounces of pounded glass.

Or dissolve in 1 quart of 95 per cent alcohol 3 ounces of sandarac, 1½ ounces of mastic, and 1 gill of turpentine varnish. Mix together in a glass bottle and shake until dissolved. This may be thinned with additional turpentine varnish if desired.

SEALING WAX

Sealing wax is made of shellac, with the addition of turpentine to prevent brittleness and to make it melt evenly, and of earthy matters to increase the weight and to prevent its melting too quickly. Pale or bleached shellac is used for light-colored sealing wax, but common shellac is equally suitable for darker colors. Sealing wax is frequently adulterated with common rosin, beeswax, stearin, and similar materials. The addition of too much rosin or turpentine causes the wax to run in thin drops when melted. The addition of camphor or alcohol causes sealing wax to melt easily. The sealing wax of the Middle Ages consisted of beeswax mixed with turpentine and various coloring matters. The finest qualities of sealing wax are frequently perfumed with balsam of Peru, storax, or various essential oils and essences.

Colored Sealing Wax. — Various colors as desired may be imparted to sealing wax by the addition of cobalt blue, chrome yellow, bone black, vermilion, and other pigments such as are used in paints. These are added in powdered form to the melted wax.

To Make Best Red Sealing Wax.— Melt together with gentle heat 5 ounces of shellac, 1¼ ounces of turpentine, and 3¾ ounces of vermilion.

Or 3 ounces of shellac, 4 ounces of turpentine, 1½ ounces of chalk or magnesia, 1 ounce of gypsum or zinc white, and ¾ ounce of vermilion.

Or 3½ ounces of shellac, 3¾ ounces of turpentine, 1 ounce of chalk or magnesia, ½ ounce of sulphate of baryta, and 1¼ ounces of vermilion. Use Venetian turpentine preferably in these three. Melt together, stirring constantly, and when all the ingredients are fully incorporated let the mass cool, and while still soft roll it on a marble or other smooth slab and shape it into sticks, or pour it while fluid into suitable brass molds.

An inferior sealing wax may be made by substituting red oxide of iron in the place of vermilion, and common rosin or New Zealand rosin in place of shellac.

Or dissolve with gentle heat ½ ounce of gum camphor in 2 ounces of alcohol, taking care that the alcohol does not take fire. Add 8 ounces of gum shellac and stir until fully dissolved. Add 4 ounces of Venetian turpentine and sift in through a hair or other sieve 2½ ounces of vermilion, stirring constantly to avoid lumps. When the whole mass is mixed smoothly together, pour it into suitable molds, or let cool until of the consistency of soft wax. Roll to proper thickness and cut out with a suitable die like a biscuit cutter. Or weigh into soft balls of equal size, roll to the desired length, and flatten by pressure.

For commercial use, the sticks of sealing wax are polished by being held over a charcoal fire in an iron dish, and while hot rubbed with mutton suet or tallow and polished with chamois.

Or, for a larger quantity, melt together with gentle heat 2 pounds of shellac, 12 ounces of Venetian turpentine, 1½ pounds of fine cinnabar, and 2 ounces of Venetian red.

Other proportions recommended for fine sealing wax are:

Shellac, 6 parts; Venetian turpentine, 2 parts; coloring matter, 3 parts.

Shellac, 3 parts; Venetian turpentine, 1½ parts; vermilion, 3¾ parts.

For a cheaper grade of red sealing wax, melt together with gentle heat 2 ounces of rosin and 2 ounces of shellac; stir in 1½ ounces of Venetian turpentine; sift and stir in 1½ ounces of red lead.

Or melt together with gentle heat shellac, 2 ounces; yellow rosin, 1 ounce; Venetian turpentine, 1 ounce; vermilion, 3 ounces.

Or, for a still cheaper grade, substitute red oxide of iron in place of vermilion.

Yellow Sealing Wax. — Melt together with gentle heat 2 ounces of shellac, 2 ounces of yellow rosin, and 1 ounce of chrome yellow.

Or 4 ounces of pale shellac, 1½ ounces of yellow rosin, ¾ ounce of Venetian turpentine, and 1 ounce of sulphuret of arsenic.

Gold Sealing Wax.—Melt together bleached shellac, 1 ounce; Venetian turpentine, ¼ ounce. Stir in gold-colored talc to color.

Or bleached shellac, 3 ounces; Venetian turpentine, 1 ounce; Dutch leaf ground to powder or enough gold-colored mica spangles to color.

Blue Sealing Wax.—Melt together shellac, 2 ounces; yellow rosin, 2 ounces; smalts, 1 ounce.

Or, for a light blue, verditer in place of smalts.

Or a mixture of equal parts of smalts and verditer.

Or employ any of the above recipes for fine red sealing wax, including vermilion, but substitute in place of vermilion the same quantity of fine Prussian blue.

Green Sealing Wax.—Melt together shellac, 2 ounces; yellow rosin, 1 ounce; verdigris, 1 ounce.

Black Sealing Wax. — Follow any of the above recipes, but substitute finely powdered ivory black instead of other coloring matter, using only enough to give the required color.

Or, for a cheaper grade, use lampblack.

Or melt together 3 ounces of black rosin, ½ ounce of beeswax, and 1 ounce of ivory black.

Or 3 ounces of shellac, 1¼ ounces of Venetian turpentine, and 2 ounces of cinnabar.

White Sealing Wax.—Melt together 3 ounces of white wax, 2 ounces of stearin, and 1 ounce of mucilage.

Or 3 ounces of resin, 1 ounce of caustic soda, and 5 ounces of water. Add 4½ ounces of plaster of Paris. This mixture requires upward of an hour to set, but adheres very strongly and takes a good impression.

Soft Sealing Wax.—Melt together 1 ounce of yellow rosin, 4 ounces of beeswax, 1 ounce of lard, and 1 ounce of Venetian turpentine.

Or 8 ounces of beeswax, 5 ounces of olive oil, and 15 ounces of Venetian turpentine.

Or 11 ounces of beeswax, 3 ounces of turpentine, 1 ounce of olive oil, and 5 ounces of shellac. Any color may be given to the above by the use of suitable colored pigments, as vermilion, red lead, or red oxide of iron for red, verdigris for green, chrome for yellow, smalts or verditer for blue, and so on.

Marble Sealing Wax.—Melt in two or more different vessels equal quantities of uncolored sealing wax, and add to each the coloring matter desired. Allow these to slightly cool, and stir them all together to make any desired effect.

To Color Sealing Wax. — Add the coloring matter to sealing wax while in a fluid state on the fire by sifting in the pigments, in the form of a dry powder, through a hair or other fine sieve. To avoid lumps or spots, stir constantly until they are fully incorporated. Let the mass cool slightly before pouring into the molds, and continue stirring while it is being poured, otherwise the coloring matter will tend to settle as a sediment in the lower part of the mold or of the vessel in which it is melted.

To Perfume Sealing Wax.—Add to any of the above, when the mass has become slightly cooled, but before it sets, gum benzoin, storax, balsam of Peru, or any of the fragrant essential oils or essences. If added too soon, the heat will cause the perfumes to evaporate; if not added soon enough, it will be difficult to incorporate them perfectly with the mass.

OILS, LUBRICATORS, ETC.

Oils. — Oils exist ready made in nature, and may be divided into fixed oils, which are either of animal or vegetable origin, and essential or volatile oils, which are principally vegetable products.

Fixed oils are mostly liquid at ordinary temperatures, smooth to the touch, and on paper make a permanent greasy stain. Many of them have neither taste nor odor. They are not, as a rule, soluble in water, and are only slightly soluble in alcohol, but may be readily dissolved in ether. The chief characteristic of the fixed oils is their ability to unite with alkalies to form soap, setting free glycerin.

The volatile oils are not capable of saponification.

Fixed Vegetable Oils. — The fixed vegetable oils, including certain butterlike fats, as palm oil, cocoa oil, and the like, are usually found in plants: in the seeds, as linseed oil; in the pulp about the seeds, as olive oil, and more rarely in roots, as in the earth almond. They are procured by grinding and pressing the oil-producing parts, and are usually found associated with more or less gum and other impurities.

The fixed vegetable oils are of two sorts: the drying oils, as linseed oil, which oxidize when exposed to the air, and are transformed into a hard, resinous varnish; and the fatty or nondrying oils, as olive oil, which become rancid and thicken when exposed to the air, but do not dry up.

To Purify Vegetable Oils.—To purify crude vegetable oils, pour the oil in a lead-lined vat and add 2 or 3 per cent of concentrated sulphuric acid. Stir until the mixture takes on a greenish tint. Let stand 24 hours, add about 2 per cent its volume of water, hot but not boiling, and stir vigorously until the mixture takes on a milky color. Then let stand in a warm place for a few days to settle, and pour off the clear liquor through cheese cloth or filter paper.

To Prepare Drying Oils. — To improve the quality of drying oils, boil them with oxide of lead, binoxide of manganese, and borate or acetate of manganese. But this process gives the oil a high color. Hence, to make drying oils for colorless varnishes, prepare oleate of lead by adding oleic acid to oxide of lead or litharge, and add this to the oil when cold.

Or prepare a solution of sulphate of manganese, and add borax dissolved in water as long as a precipitate forms. Let this settle, turn off the liquor, wash the precipitate, and let it dry. This is manganese borate. Add 2 per cent of this substance to the oldest linseed oil obtainable, and mix with gentle heat in a double boiler. Stir constantly, lifting the oil and letting it run back into the boiler, to expose it as much as possible to the air. This gives a quick-drying oil of very high color.

A class of substances called dryers are added in painting to hasten the oxidation of the drying oils, but the rapidity of this process depends greatly upon atmospheric conditions, temperature, and the like.

Fixed Animal Oils. — These are compounds of glycerin with various fatty acids. They are very similar to the nondrying vegetable oils. Many of the animal oils have a peculiar odor, which in some of the fish oils is very offensive. Sperm oil is found in the head of the sperm whale mixed with spermaceti. This is the most valuable of the animal oils and also the highest in price.

Whale or train oil is found in the blubber of the right whale, the blackfish, and other species of whale. Various other marine animals produce oils having the same general characteristics, as the seal, shark, and sea calf. The menhadens are also used in large quantities for their oil.

To Purify Fish Oil.—Make for this purpose a bag of any coarse cloth, as burlap or canvas, line it with flannel, and put in between the bag and the lining a layer of charcoal ½ inch thick. The bag should be quilted to keep the charcoal in place. Pour the oil into this filter and let it run into a lead-lined vat containing water to the depth of 5 or 6 inches, slightly acidulated with blue vitriol. Let stand 3 or 4 days, and draw off the oil by means of a spigot fixed slightly above the level of the water. Repeat if necessary. Finally filter through cloth bags without charcoal into tanks or barrels for storage.

To Deodorize Putrid Fish Oil.—For each 100 pounds of oil, pulverize 1 pound of chloride of lime; rub to a stiff paste with a little cold water, and thin to the consistency of cream. Pour the oil into a lead-lined vat, stir in the chloride of lime, and let stand 3 or 4 hours, stirring frequently. Add 1 pound of sulphuric acid diluted in 25 times its volume of water, and boil in an iron kettle on a slow fire, stirring constantly. When the mixture is perfectly liquid and falls in drops from the stirrer, return to the vat, and when the oil has separated, draw off the water by means of a spigot.

To Preserve Animal Oils.—Add 1 dram of powdered slippery-elm bark to each pound of oil, and heat gently over a slow fire. When the bark settles. strain off the fat. This gives an agreeable odor to the oil and prevents it from becoming rancid.

To Restore Rancid Animal Oils.—Put the oil in a suitable kettle over a slow fire, and stir in clean lumps or grains of charcoal from which the dust has been removed by winnowing with fans.

Or prepare double bags of flannel containing a layer of charcoal between, and filter the oil through these.

Neat's-foot Oil.—This is a coarse animal oil obtained by boiling neat's feet, tripe, etc., in water. It is very emollient and is much used to soften leather. In the commercial process the feet are heated with steam until the hair, wool, and dirt can be removed, and afterwards boiled until the oil is extracted. The crude oil is of a grayish color, but when clarified by filtration is of a pale-lemon yellow. It is often adulterated.

To Purify Neat's-foot Oil. — Mix with gentle heat, stirring vigorously, equal parts of neat's-foot oil and rose water. When cool, the oil will rise to the surface and may be ladled off. Repeat if necessary. The refined oil is the basis of the best grades of cold cream.

Lubricants.—Lubricants are materials used to lessen the friction of working parts of machinery. All of the animal and vegetable nondrying oils are suitable; also the mineral oils, as petroleum products; and plumbago, graphite, or black lead, which is the only solid lubricant in common use. These substances are often mixed for lubricating purposes. Sperm oil is the best of lubricants, but is too expensive for ordinary use. Lard oil is cheap and good. Neat's-foot oil is also used. Olive oil, colza, and rape-seed oils are suitable.

Lubricants for Heavy Pressure. — Grind black lead with 4 times its weight of lard or tallow. Add, if desired, 7 per cent of gum camphor. This was formerly a trade secret.

Or mix pure black lead with tallow.

Or mix tallow with red or white lead, or substitute lard for tallow.

Or add a portion of heavy mineral oil to any of the above.

Axle Grease.—For axle grease, mix 3 pounds of tallow, 3 pounds of palm oil, ½ pound of caustic soda, and 1 gallon or more of water. Melt together and evaporate the water with gentle heat, but do not let the mixture boil.

Or boil up together 20 ounces of palm oil with 28 ounces of tallow. Remove from the fire and stir constantly until it cools to a blood heat. Strain through cheese cloth into a solution of 8 ounces of soda in 1 gill of water, mixing thoroughly. This mixture is suitable for summer heat. For cold weather, use 20 ounces of tallow to 28 ounces of palm oil. Or, for average temperatures, 20 ounces of each.

Lubricator for Drills. — For iron drills, use 4 ounces of soft soap to 1 quart of boiling water. This is cheap and effective.

Wood Lubricator.—Lubricate wooden bearings, as pulleys and the like, with common hard yellow soap or soft soap, taking care to evaporate with gentle heat any excess of water the latter may contain. Rub window casings, bureau drawers, and the like freely with hard yellow soap slightly moistened with water. This lubricates them permanently and prevents their sticking.

To Purify Lubricants.—The animal and vegetable oils of commerce, as neat's-foot oil, rape oil, and the like, often show traces of the acids used in purifying them, and these are likely to injure the works of clocks, watches, sewing machines, and other delicate machinery. Hence, to purify commercial oils for such uses, put them in a vessel containing a quantity of rusty iron and let stand for a few days, then strain through silk or cotton wool.

Or pour the best olive oil into a glass bottle, and add equal parts of zinc and lead shavings. Let stand in a cool place until the oil becomes transparent.

Or use lead shavings only and expose the oil to the sun for several weeks. A white precipitate will be formed, and the oil will become perfectly transparent. Strain through silk the pure liquor from the sediment and bottle for use. This oil will not injure the most delicate machinery.

Oil for Whetstones.—Use kerosene oil on whetstones, oilstones, or for mixing other abrasives. It keeps the stone in good condition, and also assists in the process of sharpening.

To Straighten Oilstones. — An oilstone, after having been used for some time, becomes concave and does not give a good edge. To face a worn oilstone, take a flat piece of iron or steel having a perfectly smooth face, back it with a wooden grip or handle, and rub down the face of the oilstone with a mixture of emery and powdered pumice stone in water. Finish with the finest emery or pumice and kerosene oil. This gives with very little effort a smooth, flat face.

FURNITURE POLISH

Holes in Furniture. — To fill up cracks or holes in furniture, make a thick glue size by boiling pure white glue with water to the consistency of milk or thin cream. Mix with fine sawdust from the same or similar wood to make a stiff paste. With this fill the holes and cover deep cuts and rough surfaces. When dry, thoroughly scrape down with an edge of broken glass and polish.

To Color Mahogany Furniture. — Use cold-drawn linseed oil colored with alkanet root or rose pink, or a mixture of equal parts of both. Put the coloring matter in an earthen vessel, cover with the oil, and let stand a day or two, stirring frequently. Rub on with a soft cloth, and let stand several hours before polishing.

French Polish. — This consists in rubbing shellac or other varnish on the surface of the wood with a cloth, instead of laying on a coating with a brush. The object is to get a very thin coating of varnish with a high polish and hard surface, not so liable to scratch as a thicker coat would be.

French polish is most suitable for hard woods. To prepare a porous or coarse-grained wood for French polish, give it a coat of clear glue size. Let dry, and smooth with very fine sandpaper, followed by a cloth moistened in water and dipped in fine dry pumice or rotten stone. This fills up the pores, and thus prevents a waste of time, polish, and labor.

To finish with a French polish any previous coating, all varnish should be removed and the surface given a smooth, dead finish with sandpaper, followed by a cloth moistened and dipped in fine pumice or rotten stone.

To apply the varnish, moisten a small square pad made of several thicknesses of flannel sewed or quilted together, and apply the middle of the cloth to the mouth of the bottle. Thus the pad will take up a small quantity of varnish, but sufficient to cover a considerable surface. Then lay the pad on a piece of soft linen cloth, double the whole back over the edges, and close it up at the back of the pad to form a handle. Apply a little raw linseed oil with the tip of the finger to the middle, place the work in a good light, and rub quickly and lightly over the surface with quick, light, circular strokes. Always work from the center outward. Continue until the varnish becomes nearly dry. Moisten the pad again, but without the oil, and give two additional coats. Moisten the pad slightly with oil, and finish with two additional coats of varnish. Lastly, wet the inside of the linen cloth with alcohol before taking up the varnish pad, and rub over the whole surface. Polish with oil and alcohol, without varnish, using a clean linen cloth. To give a fine French polish, soft clean linen must be used and the atmosphere must be entirely free from dust. Use no more varnish each time than can be rubbed to a high polish, and continue rubbing until the rag seems dry.

To Prepare French Polish.—Mix 4 ounces of shellac, 1 ounce of gum arabic, and ¼ ounce of gum copal. Bruise and mix the gums with 2 ounces of powdered glass. Cover them with 1 pint of alcohol and cork tightly. Let stand in a warm place, shaking frequently until dissolved. Strain through silk or muslin.

Or dissolve 1 ounce of gum shellac and ½ ounce of gum sandarac in 1 pint of alcohol.

Or dissolve 5½ ounces of shellac in 1 pint of naphtha.

Or mix 1 ounce of pale shellac with 2 drams of gum benzoin, and cover with 4 ounces of wood naphtha. Cork tightly and let stand in a warm place, shaking frequently until dissolved.

Or mix 1 pound of shellac with 1 quart of wood naphtha.

Or shellac, 8 ounces; mastic, ¼ ounce; sandarac, ¼ ounce; copal varnish, ½ gill; alcohol, 1 quart. Mix, cork tightly, and let stand until dissolved. Pour off the clear liquor.

To apply any of the above, moisten a pad of cotton wool with the polish by laying it on the mouth of the bottle and inverting the bottle. Cover with a linen rag, apply a drop of cold linseed oil with the finger to the center of the rag to keep it from sticking, and rub with light, firm strokes and uniform pressure in circles, working from the center. Finish with a few drops of alcohol or turpentine on a clean linen rag.

To Color French Polish.—Mix the coloring matter with the polish and let stand two or three days, stirring frequently, until all is fully incorporated. For red, use dragon's blood, alkanet root, or red sanderswood. For yellow, turmeric root or gum gamboge. For brown, seed-lac or brown shellac.

Or dip the pad of cotton wool used as a rubber in the color each time it is moistened with the polish. Then cover the rubber with a linen cloth, apply a drop of cold-drawn linseed oil, and polish. Use the ordinary coloring matters, as dragon's blood for red, chrome for yellow, ultramarine or indigo for blue, and ivory black or lampblack for black.

To Grain French Polish.—To grain any color with French polish, move the rubber when applying the color in irregular patterns. Streak, line, or mark the wood, according to taste. When dry, apply a coating of clear polish and finish as usual.

To Finish French Polish.—Dissolve 4 drams of shellac and 4 drams of gum benzoin in 1 pint of 95 per cent alcohol by corking tightly in a glass bottle and shaking occasionally until dissolved. Let cool and add 4 teaspoonfuls of white poppy oil. Shake well before using. Use for final coats to give an extra high finish.

To Polish Varnished Furniture.—First apply finely powdered pumice stone with a piece of flannel moistened with water. Rub the varnished surface with light, uniform strokes, working from the center with a circular motion. Follow with finely powdered tripoli, using a woolen cloth or chamois moistened with olive oil. Care must be taken not to use more strength than is necessary to give a smooth surface. Wipe off the tripoli with a soft cloth, let dry, and apply whiting with the palm of the hand.

To Wax Furniture.—Melt with gentle heat 2 ounces each of white wax and yellow wax, and add 4 ounces of best rectified turpentine. Remove from the fire and stir until cold. This gives a thin coat, as the oil penetrates the pores of the wood, brings out the grain and color, and causes the wax to adhere. When polished, it gives a luster equal to varnish.

Polishing.—To polish furniture or cabinetwork in general, work down the surface with sandpaper, smooth with glass paper, and polish with rotten stone, putty powder, and tripoli in the order mentioned. Apply pumice stone with a cloth moistened with water, and tripoli with a cloth moistened with olive oil or boiled linseed oil.

Wood Filler.—To fill the pores and other rough places as a foundation for varnish or French polish, apply, for cheap work, a thin glue size. Or, for a better grade, apply a thin coat of boiled linseed oil, sprinkle the surface with dry whiting, and rub it in with the palm of the hand, or a short, stiff paint brush. After filling the wood, let dry, give a coating of French polish or varnish, and rub down with very fine glass paper. This gives a foundation on which to lay the varnish or final coats of polish. Thus the whiting is absorbed by the oil, and the pores of the wood are filled with putty, which will last indefinitely and not be affected by damp air or water.

Or, for the best grades, mix plaster of Paris with whiting, and apply with a brush. Follow with a coating of tallow, and color with any desired coloring matter.

Or mix the whiting, tallow, and coloring matter together, and rub them into the work.

Or mix 1 gallon of plaster of Paris with ½ pint of flour, ½ ounce of powdered pumice stone, ½ ounce of prepared chalk, 1 quart of boiled linseed oil, and ½ gill of japan dryer.

One coat of varnish on such a foundation will give a better and more durable finish than three coats laid directly on the surface of the wood, as in the latter case the varnish enters the pores of the wood and does not dry smoothly.

To Color Wood Filler.—For black walnut, mix burnt umber with whiting; for cherry, Venetian red; for beech or maple, just a suspicion of Venetian red. Stir in just enough coloring matter to imitate the natural colors of the wood.

Or, if tallow is used, it may be colored with dragon's blood, gum gamboge, or otherwise if desired.

Fix circular articles in a lathe, and apply the filler with the hands or with a piece of velveteen or other stiff cloth.

To Polish Furniture.—Substances recommended for polishing furniture are kerosene, turpentine, olive oil, linseed oil, and paraffin oil, beeswax, white wax, castile soap, gum copal, gum arabic, shellac, and various combinations of these and similar substances.

To keep furniture at a high polish, go over it once a week on cleaning day with a clean cloth moistened in clear turpentine. This keeps the paint soft so that it will not crack, and it is not sticky after it has been polished.

Or use equal quantities of turpentine and linseed oil, or equal quantities of turpentine, linseed oil, and vinegar.

To improve the appearance of linseed oil, add 1 or 2 ounces of alkanet root to 1 pint of oil, boil gently, and strain through cheese cloth.

Or mix equal quantities of linseed oil and turpentine, and to each pint of the mixture add 1 teaspoonful of ammonia.

Or dissolve 1 ounce of hard white soap in ½ pint of water, and add 6 ounces of white wax dissolved in ½ pint of turpentine. Dissolve all with gentle heat, mix, and bottle for use.

Or melt ½ ounce of alkanet root with 8 ounces of beeswax, and simmer with gentle heat. Strain through cheese cloth and add 4 ounces each of linseed oil and spirits of turpentine.

Or melt 4 ounces of beeswax with gentle heat, and add while warm 8 ounces of spirits of turpentine. Stir until the mixture cools.

Or dissolve 1 ounce of beeswax and ½ ounce of castile soap in 1 pint of turpentine. Put in a quart bottle and let stand for a day or two, shaking occasionally. Fill the bottle with water, shake, and let stand for another day, when it should be of the consistency of cream. Apply with a flannel cloth or damp chamois.

Or dissolve ½ ounce each of pulverized rosin and gum shellac in 1 pint of pure alcohol. Add 1 pint of linseed oil, mix, and apply with a soft brush, a sponge, or a piece of flannel. Polish with moistened chamois or a bunch of tissue paper or soft newspaper.

Or add 1 pint of spirits of turpentine to the above.

Or dissolve 2 ounces of gum shellac in 1 pint of alcohol. Add 1 pint of linseed oil and ½ pint of spirits of turpentine. Mix and add 2 ounces of ammonia water and 2 ounces of sulphuric ether. Shake before using. Apply with a brush, sponge, or soft cloth.

Or mix equal quantities of gum shellac, kerosene, linseed oil, and turpentine. Shake before using, and apply with a sponge or brush. Afterwards polish.

Or dissolve in 1 pint of alcohol ½ ounce each of gum copal, gum arabic, and shellac. Apply with a sponge or brush. This is known as French polish.

Or paint the surface with a liberal application of olive oil, and let stand to soften the varnish. Then follow with a solution of 2 ounces of gum arabic dissolved in 1 pint of alcohol. Apply while warm. This is known as Italian polish.

Or mix 1 pound of linseed oil, 2 ounces of wax, 4 ounces of shellac varnish, and 1 ounce of alkanet root to color. Dissolve with gentle heat and stir while dissolving. Take off the fire after 15 or 20 minutes, strain through cheese cloth, and add 2 ounces of turpentine, mix, and let stand a few days, stirring occasionally. Shake well before using.

Or dissolve with gentle heat in 1 pound of boiled linseed oil 4 ounces of beeswax and 1 ounce of alkanet root. Strain through cheese cloth, and add 4 ounces of turpentine.

Or mix 4 ounces each of linseed oil and vinegar, add ½ ounce of alcohol, ¼ ounce of butter of antimony, and ¼ ounce of muriatic acid. Apply with a sponge, rag, or brush, wipe dry, and polish. Shake well before using. Apply this mixture to clean stained, greasy, or waxed substances.

Or mix 8 ounces of linseed oil, 4 ounces of vinegar, 2 ounces of black rosin, 2 ounces of spirits of niter, 1 ounce of spirits of salts, and 2 ounces of butter of antimony. First sponge the furniture with clear water or cold tea. Apply this mixture with a sponge or cloth. Oil, polish, and let dry. Then follow with a cloth slightly moistened in cold vinegar.

To Prepare Furniture Polish. — White wax, beeswax, gum copal, shellac, and other solid resinous substances may be cut or dissolved in turpentine, alcohol, or other spirits. This process may require several days if the ingredients are cold, but is much hastened by the use of heat, and also by pulverizing or shaving the solids as finely as possible. Hence, to prepare furniture polish containing these ingredients, shave or polish them as fine as possible, and pour over them turpentine, alcohol, or other spirits as required. Use for this purpose a glass fruit jar or a wide-mouthed glass bottle. Cork tightly and set the bottle in a warm spot until the solids are dissolved.

Or rest the bottle on straw or a folded cloth and put them in a saucepan. Fill the saucepan partly full of cold water, and bring to a boil with gentle heat. This is the best and quickest way to cut wax, gum, and other resinous substances with spirits, and also to melt glue and the like. The best results may be obtained by applying while warm furniture polish containing such substances; hence, before applying, the bottle may be heated by the method just given.

Gum arabic, on the contrary, cannot be dissolved in alcohol. Hence pulverize gum arabic as fine as possible, and dissolve with a little boiling water before mixing with other ingredients. Furniture polish containing gum arabic gives the best results when applied warm.

To Clean Furniture.—Dissolve 4 ounces of common salt in 1 quart of cold beer or vinegar. Add 1 tablespoonful of muriatic acid. Boil 15 minutes, bottle, and cork tightly. Warm and shake well before using. First sponge the furniture with clear water. Apply this mixture with a brush or sponge and polish with any of the above kinds of polish, using a flannel cloth or damp chamois.

Or dissolve in 1 quart of strong beer or vinegar 2 ounces of beeswax and 1 teaspoonful of sugar. First wash the furniture with clear water or cold tea. Apply this mixture with a sponge or brush. Oil, wipe dry, and polish.

To Polish Wood Carving.—The carvings of furniture may be filled, cleaned, and polished by means of brushes, using a stiff brush to clean out the dust, then a soft brush dipped in suitable polish, and finally a clean dry brush with medium hard bristles to give a polish.

Paste for Furniture.—For light wood, cover 8 ounces of beeswax scraped fine with 1 pint of turpentine, cork tightly, and let stand, shaking occasionally until dissolved.

Or cover 3 ounces of pearlash with 1 pint of water, and bring to a boil. Stir in 2 ounces of white wax scraped fine, and simmer with gentle heat 25 minutes. Let cool, and make into a soft paste with a little hot water.

Or mix 2 ounces of beeswax, 2 ounces of rectified turpentine, and 2 ounces of cold-drawn linseed oil.

Or dissolve in ½ pint of turpentine 6 ounces of white wax. Cork tightly and let stand in a warm place until dissolved, shaking frequently. Cover 1 ounce of castile soap with 2 gills of water, bring to a boil, and mix with the wax and turpentine. This is a standard commercial article.

Paste for Mahogany Furniture.—Moisten 2 ounces of beeswax shavings with turpentine, add ⅛ ounce of rosin, melt to a paste with gentle heat, and color with Venetian red.

Or pour over ½ ounce of alkanet root 1 pint of turpentine. Let stand 48 hours. Strain through muslin. Add 4 ounces of beeswax shavings, cork tightly, and let stand, shaking occasionally until dissolved.

Or mix and dissolve 4 ounces of beeswax shavings, 1 ounce of rosin, and 2 ounces of turpentine. Color with Venetian red.

SOLDER AND SOLDERING

To Mend Tinware.—Tin plate may be mended by covering small openings with melted solder (an alloy of tin with lead), or by soldering a suitable patch of sheet tin, tin plate, or zinc over larger openings. Before soldering, it is necessary to apply a solution of zinc in acid to the adjacent parts. This is known as soldering liquid.

To Make Soldering Liquid.—Put in a strong glass bottle or other vessel 2 ounces of muriatic acid. Cut scraps of sheet zinc into narrow strips and feed them into the liquor as fast as they will dissolve. The acid at first will unite with the zinc and generate considerable heat, which may burst the bottle. Hence do this preferably out of doors, and take care that the acid does not get on anything of value.

Or dissolve the zinc in an open vessel, and afterwards bottle for use.

When the acid ceases to dissolve the zinc, add 1 ounce of sal ammoniac and boil 10 minutes in an earthenware or copper vessel, but do not use any other metal for this purpose. Cork tightly. Apply this liquid with a feather to the parts to be soldered, or by wetting the cork of the bottle. A few drops are sufficient. Do not let it fall on the hands or clothing. This liquid causes the solder to flow freely and makes it adhere.

Soft Solder.—A solder suitable for the more fusible metals, as tin, pewter, Britannia ware, and zinc, is known generally as soft solder because it has the property of melting at very low temperature. The following proportions are recommended:

For tin—common solder, 1 lead; 1 tin. Or 1 lead; 1 tin; 2 bismuth. This solder is soft enough to melt in boiling water.

Coarse solder, 2 lead; 1 tin.

Fine solder, 1 lead; 2 tin.

For Britannia ware, 1 lead; 1 tin; ½ bismuth.

For zinc or lead, 1 or 2 lead; 1 tin.

For pewter, 1 tin; 1 lead; 1 or 2 bismuth.

To Make and Use Solder.—Melt the metals together in any of the above proportions with gentle heat. Apply soldering liquid to the parts with a pencil or with a feather; sprinkle the parts with powdered rosin. Apply the solder and smooth with a soldering iron. This is the usual method, but in the absence of a soldering iron a suitable solder may be made of shavings of solder melted in a large iron spoon, poured on the parts, and rubbed smooth before cooling with the bowl of the spoon.

Or, if necessary, a patch of zinc or sheet tin may be applied by covering the patch and the surface of the tin with soldering liquid and solder, and laying on the patch before the solder cools.

Or, in place of solder, tin foil may be used to apply patches or to solder two pieces of soft metal together. Cut a piece of tin foil the size of the surface to be soldered. Apply soldering liquid with a feather to both metal surfaces and place them in position with the tin foil between. Apply to the outer surface an iron hot enough to strike through and melt the foil.

Or, to apply a zinc or lead patch to soft metals, simply moisten both surfaces with soldering liquid, put the patch in place, and hold a kerosene or an alcohol lamp flame beneath it. This will cause the surfaces of the zinc or lead to run and fuse together.

To Mend Tin Pans Without Solder.—Use soft putty. Push it through the hole from the outside. Smooth on both sides with a knife after the manner of a rivet, and let stand until hard. This is not only a quick and easy way to make temporary repairs, but one that will withstand all ordinary treatment and may never need to be repeated.

CHAPTER XVII

LEATHER, INK, AND MISCELLANEOUS

TANNING LEATHER—TANNING AND CARE OF LEATHER—BOOTS AND SHOES — OVERSHOES — WATERPROOFING LEATHER — BLACKING LEATHER—WRITING INK—MARKING INKS—COLORED INKS—SPECIAL INKS—CARE OF INK—CARE OF JEWELRY —GLASS AND IVORY—GYPSUM, ALABASTER, ETC.

TANNING LEATHER

To Tan Sheepskins and Goatskins with the Hair on.—Clean the flesh side of fat and meat, mix ½ pound of alum and ½ pound of salt in 2 quarts of water, and soak the skins in this mixture 24 hours. Remove and nail to the sunny side of a building, flesh side out, until bone dry. Mix 2 pounds of pulverized alum, 1 pound of salt, and 1 quart of wheat bran with water to a thick paste, and apply evenly to the flesh side of the skin. Fold the skins in the middle with the flesh sides together, roll up, and put away for 6 or 8 days, protected from water and vermin. Then brush away the mixture, apply neat's-foot oil warm with a brush, and rub the skin between the hands until it is pliable.

Or wash the skins with strong suds and water to remove dirt from the wool, soak them over night in soap and water, and tack them, flesh side down, over a barrel to dry. When nearly dry, remove them, clean off any pieces of flesh or fat that remain, and rub prepared chalk over the skin until no more can be rubbed in. Then rub with powdered alum, and sprinkle alum thickly over the flesh side.

Or, instead of chalk and alum, rub the skins with a mixture of saltpeter and alum, afterwards fold the skins with the flesh sides together, roll them up tightly and lay them away for a week where they will be perfectly dry. Finally rub down the flesh side with a damp cloth dipped in pumice, or rotten stone to smooth and polish. This is a suitable treatment for coon, squirrel, and other skins used for caps, for sheepskins and goatskins used for rugs, for lambskins used for coats and vests, and for all similar purposes.

TANNING AND CARE OF LEATHER

Grain Side Black for Leather.—Throw into a tight tub or cask a quantity of old iron; fill it nearly full of salt water, and add 1 pint of sulphuric acid. Stir occasionally with a stick, and in a month or two it will be first-rate blacking for the grain side of leather. This is also suitable for boot, shoe, and harness edges.

Or dissolve 2 ounces of ground logwood and 12 ounces of bablah in 12½ pounds of water. Boil down to 6¼ pounds, and filter through cheese cloth, and add 1 ounce of powdered gum arabic, 1 ounce of sugar, and 3 ounces of copperas. Add also 1 or 2 drams of corrosive sublimate to prevent mold.

Or boil ¾ ounce of extract of logwood in 2 quarts of water 2 or 3 minutes. Remove from the fire, and add 96 grains of gum arabic, 48 grains of bichromate of potash, and 8 grains of prussiate of potash.

Or, to blacken tan leather, make a saturated solution of copperas in water and apply with a swab.

Care of Harness.—Wash harness frequently with a sponge or chamois and warm water, but without soap, and apply oil before the leather is fully dry. The use of varnishes should as a rule be omitted, but the harness should be frequently wiped over with a cloth moistened in a good harness oil, as neat's-foot or castor oil, or a combination of 1 part castor oil with 2 parts neat's-foot oil; or a mixture of 1 pint of neat's-foot oil, 2 ounces of beef tallow, and 1½ tablespoonfuls of lampblack. To this add 2 ounces of beeswax for summer use.

Care of Leather Furniture.—To restore leather furniture, first wash the leather with a sponge and warm water to remove the dirt. Or wash the leather with a cloth wrung out of hot milk, and varnish with the white of an egg.

Or apply a thin coating of cream, and rub off with a soft cloth.

Or rub with a small piece of prepared wax.

Or take 6 ounces of eggs, yolks and whites beaten together, 1 ounce of molasses, 1 ounce of isinglass, and 5 ounces of water. Dissolve the isinglass in the water with gentle heat, mix with the other ingredients, and color with lampblack.

Or beat together the yolks of 2 eggs and the white of 1, add 1 tablespoonful of alcohol and 1 teaspoonful of sugar, and thicken with ivory black. The two last, of course, apply only to black leather. They are suitable for leather belts, leather bags, and all black leather objects or articles.

To Remove Grease from Leather.—To remove grease and oil stains from leather, apply pipe clay powdered, and mixed with water to a thick cream. Let stand two or three hours, and repeat if necessary.

Or apply the white of an egg to the stain, and dry in the sun.

Or make a paste of boiled mealy potatoes, vinegar, and turpentine. Apply to the stain, let dry, and rub off.

Or sponge with a flannel cloth dipped in alcohol.

To remove mildew, apply vaseline with a flannel cloth.

To remove ink from leather, touch the spot with water to see if the ink runs. If it does, it is probably nigrosine or eosin or some other coal-tar ink. In that case apply a paste of baking soda in water; keep it moistened till the ink is absorbed. If it does not run, apply oxalic acid moistened with water. When the ink is absorbed, rinse with aqua ammonia and water to neutralize the acid.

BOOTS AND SHOES

Care of Boots and Shoes.—The great enemy of leather, especially patent leather, is heat. Extreme heat tends to rob the leather of its vitality and causes it to break and crack. Damp shoes should never be placed near a stove to dry, since if heated enough to give off the characteristic odor of leather they may be singed and ruined. Rubber overshoes also tend to destroy the strength of leather by retaining the animal heat. Hence they should not be worn more than is necessary.

To Dry Shoes.—Place damp shoes on their sides in a warm room, in a draught of dry air if possible, but not near a fire.

Or heat bran or sand and with this fill two old stockings, tying the tops tightly. Put the shoes on these as on shoe trees.

Or stuff the wet shoes full of dry crumpled newspaper.

To Restore Softness to Leather.—Rub boots or shoes, that have become hard from being wet, with neat's-foot oil or castor oil as warm as the hands will bear. Apply with a sponge and rub it in with the fingers.

To Preserve Boots and Shoes.—Pour a little boiled linseed oil in a tin pan or plate, and let the shoes stand in this until the soles are saturated. This oil dries rapidly and renders the soles tough and hard. But do not apply linseed oil to the upper leathers. Use neat's-foot oil or castor oil for this purpose, to render them soft and pliable. Apply to the seams a good waterproof varnish by means of a feather or pencil brush. Keep the upper leathers clean and oil occasionally before polishing. Go over the bottom and edges of the soles occasionally with one or two coats of hard white copal or other varnish. Boots and shoes treated in this way will last much longer than usual and be practically impervious to moisture.

To Clean Boots and Shoes.—Provide three good brushes, one hard to brush off the mud, another soft to apply blacking, and a third of medium hardness for polishing. If covered with mud, wash off the dirt with a damp sponge, dry, and rub with neat's-foot oil before polishing. Do not scrape off the mud with a knife. Use a stiff brush rather than a knife to clean mud from the seams.

Once a week rub leather shoes at night with milk. Polish next morning as usual. Milk freshens the leather. To clean upper leathers, mix 1 ounce of oxalic acid with 1 ounce of white vitriol, and dilute with 1½ pints of water. Wash the leather, apply this mixture with a sponge, and rinse with a sponge wet in a little clear water containing a teaspoonful of ammonia to neutralize the acid.

Or wash with clear water. When nearly dry, rub with kerosene or a mixture of equal parts of kerosene and glycerin.

Care of Boots and Shoes. — Have two or more pairs, and wear them alternately to let the leather dry and rest. When not in use, keep them on wooden shoe trees.

Or make homemade shoe trees by filling a pair of thick socks or stockings that fit the feet with fine, clean sawdust or bran, and tie the tops tightly. These shoe trees will absorb the perspiration and keep the shoes in perfect shape. The socks can be emptied, washed, and refilled when necessary. These shoe trees can be easily made and are a great aid in preserving shoes. On taking the shoes off, stretch out the wrinkles and bend the soles straight. Keep buttons sewed on and set back as far as is comfortable for the foot. If the heels become worn, have them straightened at once.

Shoe Cleaner. — A large, coarse scrubbing brush hanging near the kitchen door is a good and cheap shoe cleaner in muddy weather, especially when children are running in and out.

Or nail or screw a coarse-fibered scrubbing brush, bristle side up, to the edge of the doorstep.

Tight Shoes.—If the soles of shoes are of the right size, but the uppers do not quite fit the foot, put on the shoes and sponge the uppers with hot water, letting the shoes dry on the feet.

Or lay a folded cloth wet in hot water over the spot that pinches. Repeat several times if necessary.

Or press against the lining with the curve of a button hook so as to stretch the leather outward. Work thus over a circular spot outwardly from the point that seems to be tightest. This is often done by salesmen in large shoe stores.

Or, to ease a swollen joint, have a shoe repairer cut a slit in the leather an inch or two long close to and parallel with the sole on the inside of the shoe where the swollen joint comes. Stretch the shoe, and over the opening between the leather and the sole fit in a patch of soft leather to match the material of the shoe. Stitch the patch to the sole, but paste its upper edge over the upper leather of the shoe to avoid a ridge of stitches. Such a patch properly cemented is hardly discernible.

To draw on tight shoes, if a shoe horn is not convenient, use two or three thicknesses of newspaper or the inside of a towel. Warm a tight shoe slightly before trying it on.

To Stop Creaking in Boots and Shoes.—The creaking or squeaking of boots and shoes is caused by the rubbing against each other, while walking, of the two or more pieces of leather that make the sole. This is prevented in the finer grades of shoes by careful adjustment of the pieces, smoothing their surfaces, and the use of lubricants, prepared chalk, and the like.

If shoes squeak, saturate the soles with linseed oil, sweet oil, or melted lard. Let the shoes stand in one of these lubricants over night.

Or drive a few small pegs across the middle of the sole.

Or, if necessary, have a shoemaker take off the soles, and dust some powdered soapstone or French chalk between them.

Shoe Strings.—Pound the tin flats on the ends of new shoe strings before using them. They will not pull off so readily. If they come off, wax the end of the lace, and with a needleful of well-waxed thread begin an inch back from the end, take a back stitch, wind the thread around the lace twice, and stitch through the lace to the end and back. Beeswax stiffens the end, and the stitches keep the winding thread from unwinding. Wax the laces, especially for children, to prevent them from constantly getting untied.

Or wet the finger and place it on the knot part of the tie just before drawing it up tight.

Or tie a bow like an ordinary bowknot, but whip one loop in underneath the bow and the first knot. Pull it tightly together.

When a shoe string breaks and a new one is not available, sew the ends together instead of tying them in a knot.

For Nails in Shoes.—Cut an insole of thin pasteboard, as the side of a cracker box. The nails will not hurt the feet, and the pasteboard lasts a long time.

To Keep on Pumps.—Fasten a small piece of elastic two inches long across the heel inside. Attach the ends only. When the pump is drawn on, the elastic stretches tight over the ball of the heel and prevents its slipping off. Fasten other pieces of elastic on either side of the instep so as to be stretched when the pump is on. This prevents its gaping at the sides.

Or sew a piece of chamois to the lining inside the heel.

To Mend House Shoes.—When the soles of house shoes and slippers begin to wear, cut a piece of kid from the top of an old shoe and glue it over the worn sole. Go over the bottom and edges with hard white copal or other varnish applied warm.

Care of Kid Boots.—Kid tends to harden and crack. Hence it should be kept clean and rubbed once a week with castor oil.

Or, to soften kid, melt equal quantities of tallow and olive oil. First wash the kid with warm water, dry, and apply the mixture with a flannel cloth.

To restore the color to black kid, mix ink with the white of an egg and apply with a soft sponge.

White Kid.—Dip a clean white flannel cloth in a little ammonia and rub lightly over a cake of white soap. Rub the soiled spots gently, changing the cloth as soon as it became soiled. Or wet a clean white flannel cloth in benzine. Rub lightly, taking care not to rub the dirt in. Hang in the open air to dry. Remember benzine is inflammable.

To Clean White Canvas Shoes.—Place them on boot trees, or stuff the shoes full of newspapers rubbed between the hands until they are quite soft. Next scrub the shoes with good hard white soap and a little warm water. Then mix pipe clay with water to a stiff paste, apply with a clean white flannel cloth, and let dry. When dry, rub slightly with clean white flannel.

To Polish Tan Shoes.—Wash the shoes clean with a sponge and warm water. Wipe with a dry cloth and let dry. Then rub freely with the inside of a banana peel. Wipe carefully with a soft cloth and polish with cotton flannel. There is considcrable coloring matter and tannic acid in banana peel, and this polish is fully as satisfactory as any tan dressing on the market.

Orange juice is also excellent for the same purpose.

Or shave a tablespoonful of white soap in a little lukewarm water; add a pinch of powdered borax and two or three drops of ammonia. Apply this with a nailbrush, scrubbing vigorously, rinse with lukewarm water, and let dry.

To darken tan shoes, apply ammonia with a clean flannel cloth. Then polish as usual.

OVERSHOES

Box for Overshoes.—Take up the boards from the back doorstep, cleat and hinge them, and make a box underneath for the family rubbers.

Or make a shoe pocket to hang on the back of the outside door. Take a piece of any old waste material the width of the door, fold it upon itself about two thirds of the width, and stitch pockets on the sewing machine of a suitable width and number for the family overshoes. Turn a heading at the top, through which run a curtain stick, and attach brass rings to the top to hang it up by. Line the pockets, if desired, with oilcloth to facilitate washing.

Care of Overshoes.—Wash the dirt from rubber overshoes with a wet sponge. It will tend to rot them if left to dry on. After the newness has worn off, apply an ordinary paste polish, the same as for leather.

To Dry Rubber Boots.—If rubber boots become wet on the inside, heat oats or coarse sand or newspapers crumpled until they are quite soft. Fill the boots with any of these. Repeat if necessary.

To Mend Rubbers.—If shoes are allowed to run down at the heel, overshoes will quickly wear out in the heel. To prevent this, replace the heels of shoes promptly.

Or glue a little crumpled paper in the heel of the overshoe. If the heel wears out when the rest of the overshoe is good, it can be mended by a shoe repairer for about five cents a heel. Or anyone can mend it by means of rubber cement. Cut a patch from an old overshoe. Rub the patch and the shoe with sandpaper to get a clean surface. Apply rubber cement thickly to both patch and shoe and let the cement dry. Do this four or five times. Then apply a last coat and put on the patch while the cement is still tacky. Let dry under a weight.

WATERPROOFING LEATHER

To Oil Boots.—Sponge with warm water, and when nearly, but not quite, dry rub with kerosene oil or neat's-foot oil or castor oil.

Or dissolve 1 ounce of pure paraffin in 1 pint of the best lard oil by means of gentle heat.

Apply any of these with a sponge as warm as the hands will bear, and rub in with the palm and fingers. Let dry and repeat. Use plenty of elbow grease.

To Waterproof Leather. — Substances recommended for waterproofing leather are various animal fats and oils, as beef and mutton tallow, suet, neat's-foot oil, castor oil, wax, rosin, pitch, solution of India rubber, and various preparations of varnish. The animal fats and oils, and wax or paraffin, are preferable to the vegetable oils, except castor oil, rosin, or any form of varnish. A solution of India rubber is perhaps the best material to apply to the seams.

Linseed and other drying oils, especially boiled oils, should not be used for upper leather, as they dry rapidly and have a tendency to make the leather stiff and hard. Most forms of varnish have also the same tendency. With these thoughts in mind, selection may be made from the following recipes:

Melt together with gentle heat equal parts of beeswax and mutton tallow. Mix to a soft paste with neat's-foot oil or castor oil, and color, if desired, with ivory black. Apply hot.

Apply a mixture of equal parts of mutton suet and beeswax without other ingredients.

Or mix with gentle heat 4 ounces of beef suet, 2 ounces of beeswax, 1 ounce of rosin, 2 ounces of neat's-foot oil, and 1 ounce of lampblack, and apply hot.

Or mix with gentle heat raw linseed oil, 8 ounces; suet, 4 ounces; wax, 3 ounces; rosin, ½ ounce; turpentine, 2½ ounces, and apply hot.

Or mix ⅜ pound of boiled linseed oil, 1 ounce of rosin, 3 ounces of wax, and 4 ounces of dryer (litharge, red lead, or sugar of lead), and boil until the mixture becomes stringy. Thin with 1¼ pounds of oil of turpentine. Apply one or more coats with a brush while warm.

Or melt 1 pound of tallow and ½ pound of rosin, and apply hot with a brush all the leather will absorb. To polish, dissolve 1 ounce of wax in spirits of turpentine and add 1 ounce of lampblack. Apply this after the tallow and rosin mixture has thoroughly dried, thus producing a wax polish on the surface, but remember that this process tends to shrink the leather.

Or mix 2 ounces of mutton suet, 6 ounces of beeswax, 2 ounces of soft soap, 2½ ounces of lampblack, and ½ ounce of powdered indigo. Dissolve with gentle heat, stir well, and add ¼ pint of oil of turpentine.

Melt together with gentle heat 4 ounces of raw linseed oil, 5 ounces of boiled linseed oil, 4 ounces of suet, and 4 ounces of beeswax. Apply hot.

Or melt together with gentle heat 8 ounces of boiled linseed oil, 2 ounces of beeswax, 2 ounces of turpentine, and ½ ounce of Burgundy pitch. Apply hot, while the leather is warm and dry, until thoroughly saturated. Let dry before wearing.

Or melt together with gentle heat castor oil, 5 ounces; Burgundy pitch, 2 drams. When cold, add ½ ounce of spirits of turpentine.

India-rubber Mixtures. — Dissolve with gentle heat in ½ pint of neat's-foot oil as much India rubber from an old pair of rubber overshoes or rubber boots as the oil will contain. Tear out the cloth lining, cut the rubber up in shreds with a pair of shears, cover with the oil, and let stand two or three days on the stove until melted. It must not boil or burn. When melted, add 12 ounces of mutton tallow, 4 ounces of beeswax, and color with lampblack or ivory black if desired. Apply this mixture when warm to warm leather previously washed clean and nearly dry. Apply with a sponge and rub in with the hands until fully saturated. This composition thoroughly waterproofs leather boots and shoes.

Or melt together 4 ounces of neat's-foot oil, 4 ounces of beeswax, and 2 ounces of India rubber until thoroughly blended. Apply hot with a brush to warm, clean leather.

Or dissolve in ½ pint of camphene as much India rubber as possible. Pour off the clear liquor, and to this add Currier's oil, ½ pint; tallow, 3 pounds; lampblack, 1 ounce. Mix with gentle heat.

Shellac Varnish.—Put in a glass bottle or fruit jar 4 ounces of gum shellac. Cover with alcohol and let stand until dissolved. Add 1 ounce of gum camphor and ½ ounce of lampblack. Shake, and mix thoroughly until dissolved. Thin, if necessary, with alcohol, and apply with a brush. This covers the leather with a waterproof coating having a high polish, but is hard, brittle, and tends to crack.

Or mix 1 pint of alcohol, 3 ounces of white turpentine, 3 ounces of gum shellac, and ¼ ounce of Venetian turpentine in a glass fruit jar, and let stand in a warm place until dissolved. Add ½ ounce of sweet oil and ½ ounce of lampblack. This is a flexible varnish which will not check or crack.

Or mix 2 quarts of alcohol, ½ ounce of sulphuric acid, and 12 ounces of gum shellac. Let stand until dissolved and add 2 ounces of ivory black. Mix and let stand 24 hours. Pour off the top and apply with a brush.

French Varnish.—Dissolve in 2½ pints of white wine or best vinegar 3 ounces of loaf sugar and 4 ounces of powdered gum Senegal. Strain through cheese cloth and put over a slow fire, but do not let it come to a boil. Add 1 ounce of powdered galls, 2 ounces of green copperas, and ½ pint of alcohol. Stir for 5 minutes. Remove from the fire, and when nearly cool strain through cheese cloth and bottle. Apply with a brush.

Or melt with gentle heat in a double boiler ½ pint of alcohol, 1 ounce of gum benzoin, and ¼ ounce of gum sandarac or gum anime. Strain, and add ½ gill of poppy oil.

Or dissolve in 8 ounces of turpentine 3 ounces of copal varnish and ½ ounce of India rubber. Dissolve separately ½ ounce of beeswax in 8 ounces of boiled linseed oil. Mix and add 1½ ounces of litharge. Bring to a boil and bottle for use.

BLACKING LEATHER

Blacking for Leather.—The pigments chiefly used in making shoe and harness blackings are lampblack and ivory black. Logwood is sometimes used in liquid blackings, and indigo and Prussian blue are sometimes added in small quantities.

Lampblack is finely powdered carbon, resulting from the imperfect combustion of gases from substances containing carbon, as gas tar, wood tar, petroleum, and soft resinous woods. These substances are burned in a fireplace having a long flue, connecting with a series of chambers in which lampblack is deposited according to its fineness. The last chamber receives on a cloth screen the finest black of all. Hence lampblack varies in quality according to its degree of fineness. Crude lampblack contains some oily, tarry, and resinous matters which prevents its mixing freely with water. Hence, in preparing blacking for leather, it is customary to add a small amount of oil of vitriol or other acid, which chars and destroys these foreign substances, leaving the lampblack nearly pure carbon.

Ivory Black, bone black, or animal charcoal is produced by burning bones in close vessels. Various gases are driven off, leaving about one half the weight of the original bones in solid form. This is crushed and sifted, producing bone black, which varies in quality according to the degree of fineness.

Animal charcoal is a very powerful absorbent of gases and of various substances from solutions. Under the name "ivory black" it is much used as a pigment in the preparation of shoe and harness blackings on account of its property of absorbing other substances, and thus producing a smooth and uniform mixture. It is somewhat more expensive than lampblack, to which it is usually preferred.

Paste Blacking consists of a mixture of these pigments with molasses or sugar and various animal oils and fats or vegetable oils, more or less diluted with water, spirits, or vinegar, and with the addition of sulphuric acid or hydrochloric acid, or a mixture of these. The ordinary liquid blackings known as French polishes consist of the same pigments, with the addition of small quantities of gums or gelatin diluted with water, spirits, vinegar, or turpentine. Another class of liquid blackings, however, is formed of logwood, with the addition of small quantities of indigo or Prussian blue.

Paste Blacking.—Mix with gentle heat 1 pound of ivory black, 8 ounces of molasses, and 2 ounces of sweet oil. Dissolve separately 2 ounces of hydrochloric acid in 4 ounces of water, and 4 ounces of sulphuric acid in 8 ounces of water. Mix the solutions, and add the mixture in a thin stream to the other ingredients, stirring vigorously. This is the ordinary German paste blacking of commerce.

Mix 4 ounces of ivory black with

1 tablespoonful of alcohol. Stir in 1 fluid ounce of sweet oil and ½ pint of molasses. Add 1 ounce of hydrochloric acid and 1 ounce of sulphuric acid.

Or, to make large quantities for sale, mix 50 pounds of ivory black, 12 pounds of molasses, and 1 gallon of rape oil. Dilute 10½ pounds of oil of vitriol with 1 gallon of water, add this solution to the other substances in a thin stream, mixing thoroughly with a wooden shovel, and when stirred cover tightly, and let stand 24 hours.

Or mix 4 ounces of ivory black, 3 ounces of brown sugar, 1 tablespoonful of sweet oil, and 1 pint of beer.

Or mix 3 ounces of ivory black, 2 ounces of molasses, 1 ounce of sulphuric acid, 1 ounce of gum arabic dissolved in water, 1 tablespoonful of sweet oil, and ½ pint of vinegar.

Or mix 2 ounces of sulphuric acid with 4 ounces of tannin oil. Let stand 48 hours. Add 5 ounces of molasses and 1 pound of ivory black. This is a celebrated commercial article.

Or mix 8 ounces of ivory black and 8 ounces of molasses. Add ½ ounce of powdered alum, 1 dram of turpentine, 1 ounce of sulphuric acid, and 2 ounces of raw linseed oil.

Liquid Blacking.—Mix 4 ounces of ivory black with 1 tablespoonful of alcohol. Add 1 fluid ounce of sweet oil and ½ pint of molasses; mix, and add 1 ounce of hydrochloric acid and 1 ounce of sulphuric acid. Stir in 3 pints of vinegar.

Or mix 3 ounces of ivory black, 1 quart of molasses, and 1 pint of sweet oil. Add 12 ounces of sulphuric acid. Stir in 8 ounces of coarse brown sugar. Thin with stale beer.

Or 4 ounces of molasses, ½ ounce of lampblack, 1 teaspoonful of yeast, and 1 teaspoonful of oil of turpentine. Apply with a sponge.

Or 1 pound of ivory black, 4 ounces of brown sugar, and the whites of 6 eggs. Mix, dilute with beer, and simmer with gentle heat, but without boiling, for 10 minutes.

Dissolve in 2 quarts of water 1 ounce of best logwood extract. Bring the solution with gentle heat nearly to the boiling point, but do not boil. Add 1 dram of bichloride of potash and 1 dram of yellow prussiate of potash. Stir until the mixture turns to a deep blue. Stir in 1½ ounces of powdered borax until dissolved. Add 1 ounce of aqua ammonia and 8 ounces of shellac, and stir until all are dissolved. Bottle for use.

Or mix 1 pint of best vinegar with ½ pint of soft water. Add 2 ounces of pulverized blue, 4 ounces of logwood chips, 2 ounces of powdered indigo, 2 ounces of castile-soap jelly, and ⅛ ounce of isinglass. Boil 15 minutes and strain through cheese cloth. Cork tightly.

Or mix equal quantities of glycerin and black ink. Apply with a brush or swab.

Or dissolve 4 ounces of shellac in 3 pints of alcohol. Add 1 ounce of gum camphor, and when dissolved stir in 1 ounce of lampblack. Apply with a brush.

Care of Patent Leather.—Clean patent-leather shoes with a sponge and warm water. Warm the leather with gentle heat, but take care not to get it too hot, and apply sweet oil or olive oil with or without an equal quantity of turpentine. Apply the oil with a sponge or cloth, and rub with the palm of the hands while the leather is warm. Apply ordinary blacking to the edges of the sole, or liquid varnish blacking with a sponge or brush, but do not apply paste or liquid blackings to patent leather.

Or mix in 1 quart of water 4 ounces of molasses, ½ ounce of lampblack, ½ ounce of sweet oil, ½ ounce of gum arabic, and ½ ounce of isinglass. Stir together with gentle heat. Cool and add 1 ounce of alcohol and, if convenient, the gall of an ox.

Or, to replace the enamel when it becomes cracked or chipped, mix 2 ounces of Prussian blue, 1 ounce of ivory black, and 1 quart of linseed oil. Melt with gentle heat, grinding the pigments carefully in the oil. Apply two coats with a brush. Then add to the mixture 2 ounces of amber or copal varnish, and apply this as a last resort. When dry polish with a moist cloth dipped in powdered pumice.

To Clean Harness.—Never apply oil or blacking to leather which is dry or dirty. First wash the leather free from dirt or grease with soap and water. Then apply the oil, and finally blacken and polish. Prepare a tub full of soapsuds, hot but not boiling; take the harness to pieces, put these in the hot suds, and let them soak over night. Then remove the pieces, scrape them clean with a stiff brush, and rub dry with a coarse cloth.

Apply with a brush a black dye made by dissolving with gentle heat 1 ounce of extract of logwood and 12 grains of bichromate of potash in 2 quarts of water. Bottle and cork for use.

Let the harness stand under shade in a draught for three or four hours, and apply warm neat's-foot oil with a brush. Follow with a second coat of one third castor oil and two thirds neat's-foot oil mixed, and wipe dry with a woolen cloth.

Or mix neat's-foot oil with a small quantity of ivory black, but do not use lampblack, as it will rub off. A second oiling should usually be given. Treating a harness in this way three or four times a year will more than double its wear.

Or add to each quart of neat's-foot oil 1 ounce of beeswax. Simmer with gentle heat until dissolved, and add ½ pound of oil of tar. Stir until dissolved, and apply to clean, warm, slightly moist leather surfaces.

To make this waterproof, add 1 dram of India rubber dissolved in 1 ounce of naphtha; or mix with gentle heat 2 ounces of beeswax and 1 pint of neat's-foot oil. Dissolve 1 ounce of gum arabic in 1 gill of hot water. Shave fine 1 pound of castile soap, and dissolve in 1 gill of hot water. Mix all together and simmer with gentle heat to the right consistency. Apply to clean, warm, and slightly moist leather.

Or dissolve with gentle heat 2 ounces of white wax and 3 ounces of turpentine. Stir in 1 ounce of ivory black and 1 dram of indigo. Apply while warm a very thin coat with a brush, and polish with a soft brush or cloth. Apply to harness which has previously been washed and oiled.

Or dissolve with gentle heat in a double boiler 1½ pounds of stearin in 2¼ pounds of turpentine. Stir constantly while heating. When dissolved, stir in 1 ounce of ivory black; remove from the fire, and stir constantly until cold, otherwise it will crystallize and the ingredients will separate. Apply warm with a cloth a very thin coat and partially dry. Polish with silk or chamois. This gives a very high gloss and does not injure the leather.

Or cut fresh lard with kerosene oil, and add ivory black to color. Apply warm with a brush. This is cheap, handy, and generally useful.

Or melt 2 ounces of black rosin, and add 3 ounces of beeswax. Remove from the fire, and add ½ ounce of ivory black and ½ dram of Prussian blue. Rub up smoothly together and thin to soft paste with turpentine. Apply with a cloth and polish with a brush.

Or melt 2 ounces of mutton suet and 6 ounces of beeswax. Add 6 ounces of brown sugar, 2 ounces of castile-soap jelly, and 1 ounce of indigo. Melt with gentle heat, mix, and stir in 1 gill of turpentine. Apply with a sponge or cloth and polish with a brush.

Black Varnish Jet or Polish for Leather.—Dissolve with gentle heat 3 sticks of any color of sealing wax desired in 1 pint of 95 per cent alcohol, and apply warm with a sponge or brush. For carriage bodies, dashboards, and the like, apply first, to save extra coats, a dye of copperas water or logwood, and afterwards lay on the varnish.

Or to 1 gallon of alcohol add 1

ounce of sulphuric acid. Stir in 1½ pounds of gum shellac. Let stand 2 or 3 days or until dissolved, and add 4 ounces of ivory black. Let stand 24 hours and pour off the thin liquid from the top. This recipe is waterproof and is a suitable polish for all leather. It is a commercial article which sells on the market at about 25 cents an ounce.

Black Balls for Leather.—Melt together 2 ounces of lard, 8 ounces of neat's-foot oil, 2 ounces of wax, and 8 ounces of brown sugar in 8 ounces of water. Bring the whole to a boil, and stir in 10 ounces of ivory black. Remove from the fire and stir constantly until it cools, then roll into balls two inches in diameter.

Or melt 4 ounces of tallow and 2 pounds of beeswax, and add 4 ounces of lampblack mixed with 4 ounces of gum arabic. Stir together and roll into balls.

Melt together beeswax, 8 ounces; ivory black, 2 ounces; turpentine, 1 ounce; Prussian blue ground in oil, 1 ounce, and copal varnish, ½ ounce. Make into balls.

WRITING INK

Ink.—Inks are of several classes, as writing inks, marking or indelible inks, and printing inks. Writing inks may be black or colored. Black writing inks are chiefly nutgall iron inks, made from a solution of Aleppo nutgalls with copperas; chrome logwood inks, made by the addition of 1 part of potassium chromate to 1,000 parts of saturated solution of logwood; aniline inks, made of coal-tar products, as nigrosine, eosin, etc., and carbon inks, made of a resinous alkaline solution mixed with lampblack. Marking inks are chiefly lampblack, or nitrate of silver. Colored inks are now made chiefly of aniline coal-tar products. It is important to understand the nature of these different materials in order to choose the various kinds of ink required; to make them properly, if desirable, either for home use or for sale; to keep them properly, and to erase them when they produce any accidental stains. These points are the more important for the reason that since the use of coal-tar colors or aniline dyes, especially nigrosine, dating from about 1867, old-fashioned recipes for taking out ink stains have become untrustworthy. Unfortunately, a great many of these recipes taken from old books are still being published. Hence care must be taken not to be misled by instructions which were correct when they were first given, but can no longer be relied on.

To Make Black Ink. — Formerly black ink was usually made by exposing to the air a solution of green vitriol in an infusion of gallnuts in water containing dissolved gum, sugar, or mucilage. The result was a fine precipitate of tannate of iron held in suspension by the gum. Writing done with these inks was of a pale-brown color, which, however, turned black on the paper. They are still in use, and recipes for making them will be given; but they are open to the objections that they corrode steel pens, tend to settle on standing, and the writing fades to a yellow or brown tint with age. Many old letters dating from war times are in existence the writing of which is almost faded from the paper.

Modern inks of this sort are improved by the addition of a little free sulphuric acid, which prevents the tannate of iron from forming a precipitate or powder. Hence they are true solutions. The addition of a little indigo, carmine, or aniline blue is also an improvement. This is one of the reasons why modern inks cannot be removed by old-fashioned recipes, the acids which take out the stain of tannate of iron having no effeet on the modern coal-tar colors.

Inks of this class are made commercially from Aleppo nutgalls and copperas, or from green vitriol. The nutgalls contain 60 to 70 per cent tannic acid and 3 to 5 per cent gallic acid. The galls are crushed, steeped in hot, not boiling, water, and strained,

The infusion is mixed with a solution of copperas containing free sulphuric acid. Indigo and aniline blues are added, and also a solution of gum arabic, the last ingredient enabling the writer to make light strokes with the pen and to prevent the ink from spreading too quickly. An antiseptic, usually carbolic or salicylic acid, is added to prevent mold.

Some experiments will be required to make a good ink of this class, as the amount of tannin contained in nutgalls varies, and the amount extracted by inexperienced persons varies still more. Recipes will be given for the use of nutgalls, but for homemade inks it will be found more convenient, when possible, to buy tannic and gallic acids ready made than to extract them from nutgalls. We recommend for a good homemade ink the following:

Five ounces of tannin, 4 ounces of copperas, ½ ounce of indigo, carmine, or aniline blue, and 10 drops of sulphuric acid.

Or 5 ounces of gallic acid, 7½ ounces of copperas, ½ ounce of indigo, carmine, or aniline blue, and 12 drops of sulphuric acid. The latter formula gives a finer quality of ink than the former, but it does not turn black so quickly. Hence a still better formula is a mixture of the two.

Or 5 ounces of tannin, 5 ounces of gallic acid, 11½ ounces of copperas, 1 ounce of indigo, carmine, or aniline blue, and 20 drops of sulphuric acid; or, for smaller quantities, the same proportions by weight. This mixture will be found an excellent ink for schools, offices, and domestic purposes.

The following recipes will suggest interesting experiments in ink making: pulverized Aleppo galls, 3 pounds; gum arabic, 1 pound. Put these in an earthen jar and add 1 gallon of boiling water. Let stand in a warm place for 2 weeks, stirring frequently. Add 1 pound of green copperas dissolved in 1½ pints of water. Mix and let stand 2 or 3 weeks, stirring daily. The addition of 4 ounces of aniline blue and 2 ounces of sulphuric acid will improve this mixture.

Or mix 2 ounces of crushed gallnuts, 1 ounce of gum arabic, and 1 ounce of copperas with 16 ounces of soft water. Add 5 grains of corrosive sublimate to prevent mold. Let stand for 2 weeks, shaking frequently, before using.

A solution of logwood is often added to the nutgall inks to give a stronger black. Cover ¾ pound of Aleppo bruised galls with 1 gallon of soft water; let stand 3 weeks, stirring daily. Add 4 ounces of green copperas dissolved in 1 pint of water, 4 ounces of logwood chips, 6 ounces of gum arabic, and 2 ounces of alcohol. Stir, and let stand a week or 10 days before using.

Mix 4 ounces of bruised Aleppo galls, 2 ounces of thin logwood chips, and 3 quarts of soft water; boil down to 3 pints. Add 2 ounces of green copperas, 1½ ounces of powdered gum arabic, ½ ounce of blue vitriol, and ½ ounce of brown sugar. Stir until dissolved, let stand 24 hours, strain, and bottle for use.

Or mix 1 ounce of powdered copperas, 1 ounce of fine logwood chips, 3 ounces of crushed Aleppo galls, 1 ounce of gum arabic, and 6½ pounds of white wine or best vinegar.

Or boil 4 ounces of logwood chips in 6 quarts of water down to 3 quarts. Strain, and add 2 quarts of cold water. Add to this solution 1 pound of bruised Aleppo galls, 4 ounces of sulphate of iron, and ½ ounce of acetate of copper. Rub to a smooth paste with a little of the logwood liquor. Add also 3 ounces of coarse sugar and 6 ounces of gum arabic.

Chrome Logwood Inks.—These inks are prepared by the addition of 1 part of potassium chromate to 1,000 parts of saturated solution of logwood. Or boil the solution of logwood with chloride or acetate of chromium. Inks of this class have no sediment, do not corrode steel pens, and do not turn moldy. Writing done with them may be soaked in water without the ink running or washing off. They also have the advantage over iron-gall inks that they will not fade.

To make chrome logwood ink on a large scale, boil 22 pounds of logwood in 28 gallons of water down to 14 gallons; when cold, to 1,000 parts of this infusion add gradually 1 part of yellow chromate of potash, stirring constantly.

Or, for a small quantity, boil 1½ ounces of thin logwood chips in 3 pints of water down to 1 pint, and when cold add 17 grains of yellow chromate of potash, stirring thoroughly. Do not add gum or acid. To prevent mold, add a few drops of bichloride of mercury.

Copying Inks. — Copying inks are of the same composition as ordinary writing inks, but thicker. Gum, sugar, and other sticky ingredients are used in copying inks to keep them from soaking into the paper before it is brought in contact with the moist tissue paper of the copying press. The largest number of copies from one writing is obtained by means of a strong decoction of logwood extract with alum or chloride of aluminum, and by the use of sheets of tissue copying paper previously soaked in chromate of potash. A small amount of the logwood solution unites with the chromate salt in the tissue paper to form a black compound.

Or put 1 pound of powdered Aleppo galls in an earthen jar and cover with 2 gallons of rain water. Let stand 10 days. Add 4 ounces of clean copperas, 4 ounces of brown sugar, and 4 ounces of gum arabic dissolved with gentle heat in a little water. Put the whole in an iron kettle and boil down to 1 gallon.

Or put 2 ounces of logwood extract, 4 ounces of sal soda, and 18 ounces of soft water in an earthen vessel, and set it in the oven until the solution becomes a deep red and the ingredients are all dissolved. Remove from the oven, and stir in 2 ounces of glycerin, 30 grains of yellow chromate of potash dissolved in a little water, and ½ ounce of gum arabic dissolved in water. Strain through cheese cloth and boil down to one half with gentle heat.

Or add 1 teaspoonful of brown sugar to 1 pint of ordinary writing ink. To take a single copy from any of the above without a copying press, first let the ink dry, then moisten a sheet of tissue paper or unsized writing paper with water, but do not have it too wet. Lay it over the writing, and go over it with a warm flatiron.

MARKING INKS

Marking Inks.—On account of the resistance it offers to acids and other chemicals, carbon, in the form of lampblack, is often used as the basis of marking inks. But carbon cannot be dissolved. Hence it must be held in suspension in some gummy or resinous liquid, and is not suitable for use with ordinary steel pens. Carbon marking inks are usually applied by means of a brush or a marking pen having a special point for this purpose. To make a carbon marking ink, boil 2 ounces of shellac and 2 ounces of baking soda in 1 quart of soft water until the shellac is dissolved. Stir in fine lampblack to the proper consistency, and thin with water as desired.

Or dissolve 1 ounce of borax and 2 ounces of shellac in 1 quart of water with gentle heat. Add 1 ounce of mucilage, and stir in equal quantities of indigo and lampblack to the right color and consistency.

Or dissolve with gentle heat 25 grains of powdered copal in 3⅜ ounces of oil of lavender. Add 2½ grains of lampblack and ½ grain of indigo. Used for marking glass bottles and other vessels containing chemical substances of a corrosive nature.

India Ink.—India or China ink is finely divided carbon mixed with a solution of gum arabic or glue, dried in wooden molds, and coated with animal wax. It is applied with a wet brush or by diluting a small quantity in water.

To test India ink, draw a number of lines of different thicknesses on a piece of drawing paper. When bone dry, apply water with a sponge. If the ink runs, it is of poor quality.

To make a substitute for India ink, boil an old kid glove in water until it forms a thick size, which when cool is of a jellylike consistency. Hold a cold plate in the flame of a candle, and while it is still warm mix the lampblack which adheres to the plate with the size thus obtained. This mixture has all the qualities of a first-class India ink. This is a good dye with which to renovate black gloves that have become defaced.

Indelible Ink. — The old-fashioned nitrate-of-silver ink is still commonly used for marking linen and for similar purposes. To make an indelible ink, dissolve 1 ounce of nitrate of ilver in 2½ ounces of liquid ammonia. Dissolve separately with gentle heat 1¼ ounces of gum arabic and 1½ ounces of carbonate of soda crystals. Mix the two solutions and let stand in a warm place. Add a few drops of solution of magenta.

Or dissolve 1 ounce of nitrate of silver in 4 ounces of distilled water. Add strong liquid ammonia to dissolve the resulting sediment. Stir in ½ ounce of gum arabic and ½ ounce of sap green or powdered indigo.

The most convenient way to apply indelible inks to linen is to have a brass stencil cut with the family name or monogram. Lay this over the linen and with a soft brush apply the ink through the cut-out spaces. A little practice on a piece of old linen will enable anyone to do this work quickly and well. The above inks are ready to be applied.

Or another way of using marking inks is to first dip the linen in a solution called the mordant, and afterwards apply the ink, which then forms a chemical compound with the fibers of the fabric. To do this, first moisten the linen with a mordant composed of 2 ounces of baking soda and 1 ounce of gum arabic dissolved with gentle heat in 8 ounces of water. Dry with a warm flatiron, and apply an ink composed of 1 ounce of nitrate of silver, 14 ounces of distilled water, and 1 ounce of sap green. This must be applied with a quill pen, a gold pen, or a brush, as a steel pen will decompose the ink.

Black Stencil Ink. — Rub to a smooth paste 4 ounces of lampblack and 8 ounces of Prussian blue with a little glycerin. Add 6 ounces of gum arabic dissolved with gentle heat in a small amount of water, and thin with glycerin to the right consistency.

Or dissolve 1 ounce of aniline blue in 1 pint of water, and apply with a sponge.

Or dissolve 1 ounce of asphaltum in 4 ounces of turpentine, stir in lampblack to color, and thin with turpentine as required.

COLORED INKS

Colored Writing Inks.—Inks may be made of almost any color by the use of suitable dyestuffs. The variety and beauty of colored inks have been greatly increased by the discovery of the coal-tar products, known as aniline dyes. These are now in common use under various trade names.

Red Ink.—Red ink may be made out of cochineal or Brazil wood, or the coal-tar colors known as puchsin, magenta, or eosin. These are readily soluble in water, but should have a few drops of corrosive sublimate or other antiseptic added to prevent mold. Eosin inks copy freely, but fade if exposed to sunlight.

To make red ink, bring 1 gallon of the best vinegar to a boil with gentle heat, add 1 pound of Brazil wood, and simmer for half an hour. Stir in ¾ pound of powdered alum and strain through cheese cloth. Add ½ gill of fresh gall to each quart of the ink. Cork tightly in glass bottles.

Or boil for 1 hour 4 ounces of ground Brazil wood in 1 pint of diluted acetic acid (1 part pure acid to 10 parts water). Add ½ ounce of alum, strain, and add 1 ounce of gum arabic dissolved in a little hot water. Use copper or enamel ware for the above.

Or dissolve 10 grains of the best carmine lake in the least possible quantity of ammonia. Let stand 24 hours and dilute with 2½ fluid ounces of distilled water.

Or boil 2 ounces of powdered cochineal and 2 ounces of cream of tartar with 8 ounces of water until dissolved. Strain, and add 1 ounce or a little more of carbonate of potassium. Stir in 1 ounce of alum and 1 ounce of gum arabic dissolved in a little boiling water. Additional carbonate of potassium will darken the color of the ink.

Blue Ink.—Take 2 ounces of Prussian blue crystals and cover with hydrochloric acid. Stir or shake the mixture thoroughly, pour off the acid through a suitable strainer, and pour on water to rinse the blue completely free of the acid. Dry the crystals, mix with an equal quantity of oxalic acid in fine powder, and thin with distilled water to the color desired.

Or dissolve indigo carmine in water.

Or mix 2 ounces of ferrocyanide of iron and 2 ounces of strong hydrochloric acid. Dissolve and dilute with soft water.

Or mix 1 ounce of powdered Prussian blue with 1½ fluid ounces of muriatic acid. Dilute with water.

Violet Ink. — Dissolve with gentle heat 1 ounce of methyl-violet aniline in 1 gill of alcohol. Stir until thoroughly dissolved. Then add 1 gallon of boiling water. This is a vivid, beautiful violet, which flows smoothly and dries quickly, but will fade if exposed to sunlight. It is the common violet ink of commerce.

Green Ink. — Dissolve 1 ounce of iodine-green aniline in 1 gill of hot alcohol, and dilute with 2 quarts of soft water. This is a vivid and beautiful color which will yield several copies, and is very little faded by sunlight.

Or dissolve 2 ounces of verdigris and 1 ounce of cream of tartar in 8 ounces of soft water, and boil until the right shade is reached.

Or mix 1 ounce of crystallized acetate of copper with 1 pint of soft water.

Or rub together 3½ drams of soluble Prussian blue and 3 drams of gamboge with 2 ounces of mucilage, and dilute with ½ pint of soft water.

Yellow Ink. — Dissolve yellow or orange aniline colors in boiling water.

Or boil 1 pound of French berries with 2 ounces of alum in 1 gallon of water until the color is sufficiently strong. Strain, and add 4 ounces of gum arabic.

Show-card Inks.—Any of the above colored inks may be used for show cards if desired, or dissolve 1½ ounces of gum arabic in 8 ounces of water, and while hot strain through cheese cloth. Mix with this ordinary painters' colors, either dry or ground in oils, and apply with a brush. To make a show card permanent, brush it over with a thin glue size, lay on the ink with a brush, and finish with a hard, white varnish.

To mix various colors of ink for different tints, see under "Paints and Painting."

Gold, Silver, and Bronze Inks are prepared by grinding thin sheets of the metal on a glass plate with a little honey to reduce them to a fine powder. This powder is then laid on filter paper, washed with hot water to remove the honey, and dissolved in a solution of gum arabic for use.

The writing may be done with a nearly colorless glue size, and the fine bronze, gold, or silver powder may be dusted over it while the size is still wet.

SPECIAL INKS

Sympathetic Inks.—These inks are invisible until brought out by the effect of heat or some chemical. For an invisible ink, write with fresh milk, which will not show until the paper is gently heated.

Or write with a solution of sugar in water.

Or write with a mixture of 1 part of sulphuric acid and 20 parts of water, using a quill or gold pen. The acid will corrode an iron or steel pen. This is invisible until the paper is made warm enough to evaporate the water, when the acid will char the paper in black characters.

Or write with a solution of acetate of lead, and afterwards expose the writing to the fumes of a brimstone match.

Or write with a weak solution of nutgalls, and apply a solution of iron to the paper.

Or write with a solution of nitrate of silver, and apply a solution of common salt. These methods have often been used to conceal subjects of correspondence by writing letters with ordinary inks, and between the lines writing with invisible ink another message. The secret of the combination must, of course, be known to the person for whom the writing is intended.

Luminous Ink. — Dissolve 1 dram of phosphorus in 1 ounce of oil of cinnamon. Cork tightly, and put the bottle in hot water until dissolved. Letters written with this solution will be visible in the dark.

Hectograph Ink.—Mix 1 ounce of iodine-green or methyl-violet aniline colors with 1 ounce of glycerin, and dissolve the mixture in 10 ounces of distilled water. This is used in printing from a gelatin pad, usually called a hectograph. To make such a pad, cover 1 ounce of gelatin with cold water, and let stand over night. Put in a new tin dripping pan or other tin dish having low sides and square corners 12½ ounces of gelatin, and heat slowly, but do not let it boil. Stir in the soaked gelatin and let the mixture stand over a slow fire until the water is all evaporated. This will produce a solid pad of clear gelatin. Cover from dust and let stand over night. To use this pad, write with the above ink, let the ink dry, and moisten the pad slightly with water by means of a brush. When the pad is nearly dry, lay the writing, face down, on the pad, rubbing it down gently with a soft cloth. Let it stand a minute or more according to the number of copies required, remove the paper, and the pad is ready to print from. Use for this purpose soft unsized paper. Lay the paper on the pad, smoothing it with a cloth or roller, and remove immediately. Continue to take copies until the ink is exhausted. Then wash the pad with cold water and a sponge to remove the surplus ink. When dry, it is ready to be used again as before.

Rubber-stamp Ink. — Inking pads for rubber stamps may be re-inked by means of aniline dyes of suitable color mixed to the consistency of thin cream with glycerin.

Metal-label Ink.—Dissolve 1 ounce of copper in 10 ounces of nitric acid, and thin with 10 ounces of water.

Or mix 2 ounces of powdered sulphate of copper, 1 ounce of powdered sal ammoniac, and 4 ounces of acetic acid. Stir in lampblack or other pigment of any color desired.

Or dissolve equal quantities of verdigris and sal ammoniac in water, and add lampblack or other pigment to color. Mix the ingredients in earthenware with wooden paddles, as they will corrode metals. They are suitable for writing on steel, tin plate, or sheet zinc.

Mix 1 ounce of muriatic acid and ½ ounce of nitric acid. Cover the metal surface with beeswax, and when cold, write on it with any sharp-pointed instrument that will cut through to the wax. Apply the mixture with a small brush or feather, and let it lie for a few minutes according to the depth of etching desired. Then rinse off the wax and acid in hot water. Either of the acids alone will cut iron or steel, but the mixture is required for gold or silver. After rinsing off the acids, apply a little sweet oil or olive oil. The smoothness of the etching will depend upon the cleanness with which the wax is cut and removed from the metal in each letter. Hence a sharp-edged tool is the best.

CARE OF INK

To Prevent Mold in Ink.—The addition of a little alcohol or a few drops of any essential oil or a few cloves will prevent mold.

Or add a few drops of salicylic acid or corrosive sublimate or carbolic acid, but do not add metallic acids to inks containing aniline dyes.

To Prevent Ink from Thickening.—As inks thicken by the evaporation of the liquids with which they are diluted, the only way to protect them is to keep them covered from the air. Hence the use of inkstands with tapering funnels of glass or hard rubber is advisable. If the ink becomes too thick to write smoothly, or if, when a bottle has been exhausted, a residue of black sediment is left, it may be diluted with clear water or a small quantity of strong black coffee strained through silk or linen.

To Keep Ink from Freezing.—The addition of a small quantity of alcohol acts as a preventive.

To Restore Faded Ink. — Writing which has become partially illegible on account of age may be restored by applying carefully to the paper an infusion of galls, or a solution of prussiate of potash slightly acidulated with dilute sulphuric or muriatic acid. These substances have the property of turning iron-gall inks black.

To Remove Oiliness from Ink.—If the action of the air causes ink to become oily, ropy, or stringy, add a little oxgall or vinegar.

Printer's Ink is a carbon ink mixed with oils or resins. The carbon is usually lampblack or ivory black mixed with a little indigo or Prussian blue. The oil is usually boiled linseed oil or nut oil. Other ingredients are rosin, turpentine, balsam of copaiba, and yellow soap. Great care is required to produce the finest grades of ink, and printer's inks vary greatly in quality and price. The methods of preparation are trade secrets, and printers rarely attempt to make the better grades of ink for themselves.

Colored printing inks are made by using various colored pigments in place of carbon.

Bronze and other metallic effects are produced by printing with a nearly colorless glue size, and sprinkling the metallic powder on the surface while it is sticky.

Printing Ink. — Grind in a paint mill or with a marble mortar and pestle 9 ounces of balsam of copaiba, 4 ounces of finest lampblack, 1 ounce of powdered indigo, and 3 ounces of hard, dry yellow soap. Heat a quantity of linseed oil in an iron kettle until it begins to boil. Remove from the fire and kindle the escaping vapor. Allow it to burn until the oil becomes stringy when lifted with a stirrer. Then add to each quart of oil 1 pound of pulverized black rosin. Dissolve with gentle heat and stir in 4½ ounces of dry yellow-soap shavings to each quart. Melt these together with gentle heat. Measure for every pound of rosin employed 1 ounce of indigo, 1 ounce of Prussian blue, and 18 ounces of lampblack. Pour the melted mixture over these pigments, mix, and grind in a paint mill.

Dryers for Printer's Ink. — One ounce of beeswax, ¼ ounce of gum arabic dissolved to a thin mucilage with acetic acid, ¼ ounce of japan, and ½ ounce of asphaltum varnish. Add the above to 1 pound of printer's ink.

Lithographic Ink. — Melt together with gentle heat 3 ounces of shellac, 4 ounces of castile soap, 2 ounces of white wax, and 2 ounces of tallow. Add 3 tablespoonfuls of gum sandarac dissolved in 3 tablespoonfuls of alcohol, and stir in ivory black or the best lampblack to color.

To Remove Ink Stains.—The article to use depends entirely on the nature of the ink. For a logwood ink stain, use dilute muriatic acid, 1 part of acid to 10 parts of water. This removes the stain, first turning it red; but it converts the stain of red eosin ink to an insoluble brick-red substance, and a nigrosine ink stain to an indelible blue-black dye.

For an iron-gall ink, use oxgall or

mineral acids, as muriatic, sulphuric, and the like. These decompose the black tannate of iron, but have no effeet on the indigo and aniline blues which are added to most modern inks, especially the blue-black writing fluids.

Hence the first step is to find out what the ink contains. If convenient, this may be done by putting a few drops on a piece of cloth, and testing with that; meantime taking measures to prevent the stain from spreading. First dry the sample and attack it with water. If the ink contains nigrosine, it will dissolve in water and the stain will spread. In that case use an alkali, as baking soda, covering the stain thickly and moistening it with water. If the ink does not run, it is probably iron-gall or logwood ink, hence an acid may be tried, but if the acid does not succeed, try soda or other alkali.

On white fabrics, the best way to remove ink stains is to cover the spot with chloride of lime and moisten with dilute muriatic acid. This sets the chlorine free to attack the stain. Nitrate of silver stains may be removed by cyanide of potassium, but this must be used with great care, as it is very poisonous.

For colored fabrics pyrophosphate of soda may be tried. Fabrics should be immediately washed with clear water after the stain has been removed.

CARE OF JEWELRY

To Keep Jewelry at its best it should be properly stored when not in use and occasionally cleaned and polished, or recolored, when necessary, to restore its original luster. Most jewelry contains more or less alloy which will tarnish, and articles of silver are especially likely to tarnish by contact with substances containing silver, or by fumes of sulphur which are often present in the atmosphere. It should be remembered that 30 per cent to 50 per cent of rubber consists of sulphur; hence rubber bands and articles containing rubber should never be brought in close proximity to fine silver articles.

To Store Jewelry. — When not in use, jewelry may be covered with a thin film of collodion dissolved in ether or alcohol.

Or laid away in boxes covered with boxwood sawdust, which may be obtained from any jeweler.

To Clean Jewelry.—To clean articles of gold or silver, use castile soap and an old soft toothbrush or jeweler's brush, and wash carefully. Rinse in clear cold water, lay in a box of boxwood or other sawdust, and shake gently until dry. Rings containing gems should be removed when the hands are being washed, or their luster will be impaired.

To clean a gold or silver chain, put it in a small glass bottle with warm suds of castile soap and a little whiting or prepared chalk. Shake well, rinse with cold water, and dry in sawdust.

To Polish Jewelry.—To polish gold jewelry, make a paste of whiting with sal volatile, cover the article, and let dry. Then brush off with an old toothbrush or polish with chamois.

Or put in a glass vessel 2 ounces of sulphate of iron (green vitriol), and gradually add water, stirring with a glass rod until all is dissolved. Use no more water than is necessary. Add carbonate of ammonia gradually until all the iron falls as a sediment. Let the mixture settle and strain off the liquor through filter paper. Dry the pulverized iron by means of blotting paper. Place it in an earthenware cup or bowl or crucible, and heat it in a dark room until it glows softly. When cool, this is the best polishing powder that can be made.

Or take 2 ounces of hydrochloric acid and add iron filings, stirring with a glass rod until the acid has dissolved all it can. Add aqua ammonia until the iron is all precipitated from this solution. Dilute this solution with water and collect the sediment on filter paper, drying slowly in sunshine or with very gentle heat. To

3½ ounces of this substance add 1½ ounces of sal ammoniac. This mixture has been for many years a trade secret of German gold workers, and commands a high price on the market.

To Brighten Jewelry.—Heat to a boil ½ pint of soft water and pour it into a wide-mouthed glass bottle. Add 1 ounce of cyanide of potassium and shake until dissolved. When cold, add ½ fluid ounce of aqua ammonia and 1 fluid ounce of pure alcohol. This mixture is a deadly poison and must not touch any part of the skin. Even the fumes are most dangerous.

To clean jewelry, make a hoop of a bit of wire, and with this dip the articles in the solution for a few seconds, remove, and rinse in clear water. Then wash with soapsuds to thoroughly free from the cyanide, rinse, and dip in alcohol or benzine. To cause them to dry quickly, cover with sawdust. Cork the solution tightly for future use. Of course great care must be taken to keep this liquid out of the hands of children and careless persons. But if proper precautions are observed, it will be found to be one of the quickest ways to remove the tarnish from metallic articles and to give them their brightest luster.

To Color Gold. — Mix saltpeter, 3 ounces; green copperas, 1 ounce; white vitriol, 1 ounce; alum, 1 ounce. This mixture gives yellow gold a dark or reddish color. The addition of a little blue vitriol gives a darker shade.

To Clean Jet.—To clean jet articles, brush them free from dust with a soft camel's-hair brush, apply a little olive oil by means of a brush or bit of cotton wool, and polish with chamois. Great care must be used, as the carving usually makes jet articles very brittle.

GLASS AND IVORY

To Cut Glass.—To cut glass with a chisel, cover it with a solution of camphor gum dissolved in spirits of turpentine, and do the cutting while the glass is in the solution.

To Anneal Glass. — To anneal or season glass, as lamp chimneys and the like, so that they will be less likely to break, immerse the glass in a vessel of cold water and heat it very gradually to the boiling point. Boil for any length of time—the longer the better—and do not remove from the water until it is cold.

Or, if the glass is to be exposed to high temperatures, it may be more perfectly annealed by boiling in the same manner in oil.

To Imitate Stained Glass. — Cut a suitable pattern from leaves of colored tissue papers, and apply to the glass by any suitable paste or mucilage, as rice or wheat starch, with or without gum arabic. Cover with a coat of copal varnish.

To Soften Ivory.—Dissolve 2 ounces of spirits of niter in 10 ounces of soft water, and soak the ivory in this solution for 3 or 4 days, when it will be soft and flexible.

Or immerse the ivory in a solution of pure phosphoric acid until it becomes practically transparent. Wash with clean cold water and dry. It is then flexible, but hardens as it dries. Its flexibility may be restored by soaking in hot water. This process, if continued, will render the ivory transparent.

To Harden Ivory.—Wrap the ivory in tissue paper, cover with dry salt, and lay away a day or two. This will restore its natural hardness.

To Polish Ivory.—Moisten a piece of felt or velveteen, dip in putty powder or pumice stone, and polish.

Or fix the ivory on a nail or wheel and polish it by means of pumice stone and water, heat it by friction on a piece of coarse cloth, and while hot rub with whiting mixed with olive oil, followed by dry whiting and clean chamois. This gives a high luster.

Or rub first with fine sandpaper, next with a wet cloth dipped in pumice stone, then with a cloth wet in soapsuds and dipped in whiting. When changing from a coarse to a finer material, use clean cloths and rinse the article free from grit.

To Etch on Ivory.—Varnish the article with a mixture of white wax and mastic or with a thin coating of beeswax, and trace the required designs through the wax. Take care to protect all parts of the article except the design, and immerse it in a strong solution of nitrate of silver. After a sufficient length of time, to be determined by experiment, remove and wash in clear, hot water. The design will appear in black upon the ivory.

Or protect the article by a suitable varnish as above, and apply a solution of ½ ounce of sulphuric acid, ½ ounce of muriatic acid, and 10 ounces of water. The acids will eat away the exposed portions of the ivory, leaving the design engraved on its surface.

GYPSUM, ALABASTER, ETC.

Gypsum. — Gypsum is a mineral which is found in nature in several forms. Chemically it consists of bi-hydrated calcium sulphate. It occurs in translucent crystals, as selenite; in massive forms and opaque crystals, as gypsum; in fine-grained partially translucent masses, as alabaster, and in a fibrous form, as satin spar. When heated, gypsum gives off the water it contains and pulverizes into an opaque powder which, if moistened, quickly solidifies. This powder is known commercially as plaster of Paris. It is made by heating gypsum and grinding it to a fine powder. Gypsum is also used as a fertilizer, and in the manufacture of glass and porcelain. Plaster of Paris is chiefly used for making models and casts, and as a cement for marble and alabaster.

Among the most celebrated gypsum beds in the world are those of Montmartre near Paris, which have given plaster of Paris its name.

Alabaster. — This is a variety of gypsum of great beauty and easily carved on account of its softness; hence it is extensively employed for ornamental purposes.

To Use Plaster of Paris.—To use plaster of Paris, mix it with water to the consistency of thick cream and apply at once, as it sets quickly. No more should be mixed at a time than will be required for immediate use.

Or, if additional strength is desired, mix with a thin glue size, or a solution of 1 or 2 ounces of gum arabic in 1 pint of water. These not only harden the plaster but give its surface a desirable smoothness.

Or mix plaster of Paris with an equal weight of sulphate of potassium, and thin with 2 to 6 parts of water. This mixture sets very quickly and is harder than plaster of Paris alone.

To Prevent Plaster of Paris from Setting. — Mix 2 per cent of alum, sulphate of potash, or borax, with plaster of Paris before adding water, and it will be prevented from solidifying for 3 or 4 hours. Thus it can be handled much more readily. When dry, it will also be much harder than plaster of Paris alone.

Or mix with vinegar diluted with water. The more vinegar used the longer the plaster will require to set.

Molds for Plaster of Paris. — To make molds for casting plaster ornaments, mix 12 ounces of rosin, 8 ounces of tallow, and 6 ounces of beeswax.

Or use plaster of Paris itself.

Or mix equal quantities of clean white sand and pulverized limestone or marble dust, and to 14 pounds of this mixture add 1 pound of litharge and 4 pounds of linseed oil. Grind or rub up the litharge with the oil, heat the mixture of sand and limestone to dryness, stir into a stiff mortar, and pour in an oiled mold.

To Cast Plaster of Paris.—Oil the object to be copied and cover it to a sufficient depth with one of the above mixtures, so that when removed the mold will be strong enough to handle. If plaster of Paris is used to make the mold, the object to be copied must be moistened, but no drops must be allowed to stand on the surface.

The mold should be made in two parts, which may be done by molding first one side up to a given line, and then the other. Leave an opening through which to pour the plaster.

To make castings, it is only necessary to oil or moisten the inside of a mold. Lock the two parts of the mold together, oil the edges so that they can be readily separated, and pour the mold full of plaster from a funnel through the opening left for that purpose. After the plaster has set, the mold may be removed and used repeatedly.

To Harden Plaster-of-Paris Objects.—Put in an iron kettle 2 pounds of a solution of caustic potash. Add in shavings 2 ounces of stearin and 2 ounces of castile soap, and boil for half an hour, stirring constantly. Add 1 ounce of pearlash dissolved in a little soft water. Let the whole boil up, remove from the fire, and stir until cold. Now stir in cold potash lye until the mass becomes perfectly liquid and falls in drops from the stirrer. Let stand for several days tightly covered before using. This preparation will keep for years.

Clean the plaster-of-Paris casts and other objects free from dust and stains, and apply this mixture with a paint brush as long as the plaster of Paris will absorb it. Let dry and dust with a brush or chamois leather. Repeat, if necessary, until the casts take on a satisfactory polish.

To Make Artificial Marble. — Mix plaster of Paris with a solution of alum, put it in an oven, and bake until the water is completely evaporated. Afterwards grind to powder. Mix with water and stir in any desired coloring matter in powdered form to make clouds and veins. When dry, this mixture sets very hard and takes a high polish.

To Imitate Alabaster.—To imitate alabaster with objects made of plaster of Paris, warm the articles and suspend them by means of horsehair or fine wire in melted white wax of the best quality. Continue until the plaster of Paris has absorbed all it can. Hang up the articles to dry, and polish with a clean brush. Any pure white wax will answer this purpose. To harden these objects, suspend them in a clear solution of alum until crystals form upon the surface. Remove, and polish with a damp cloth.

To Clean Alabaster. — Wash with castile soap and water.

Or, to remove stains, cover with white fuller's earth or pipe clay. Let stand for a few hours and wash off.

Or, if much stained, wash with very dilute sulphuric acid, using about 1 ounce of sulphuric acid to 20 ounces of water.

Or rub with a cloth moistened with lemon juice and dipped in pumice stone. Rinse with clear water and polish with a dry chamois.

To Make Prepared Chalk.—Add a solution of carbonate of soda to a solution of muriate of lime as long as the chalk is precipitated. Strain through filter paper and then pour on clear water until the sediment is perfectly clean. Dry in direct sunshine.

Safety Matches.—To make safety matches, mix 6 ounces of chloride of potash, 2 ounces of bichromate of potash, 2 ounces of ferric oxide with 3 ounces of strong liquid glue. Mix thoroughly with gentle heat, taking care that it does not take fire, and dip the match heads in this. These matches will not kindle on sandpaper or by ordinary friction, but must be rubbed on a surface especially prepared for them as follows:

Mix 10 ounces of sulphide of antimony, 2 ounces of bichromate of potash, 2 ounces of oxide of iron, lead, or manganese, 1 ounce of glass powder, 2 ounces of strong glue or gum. This preparation is spread like paint while warm on suitable paper, which is fastened on the boxes containing the matches.

Or dissolve 4 ounces of gum arabic in just enough water to make thick mucilage or paste, and stir in 4 ounces of powdered peroxide of manganese, 2½ ounces of phosphorus, and place on the back of a closed stove, but do not heat above 130° F. or expose to an open flame. Stir until the phosphorus is melted, then add 3½ ounces of niter and stir the whole to a uniform paste. First dip the matches in melted brimstone, let dry, and afterwards dip the heads in this substance. This mixture may be perfumed by the addition of ½ ounce of gum benzoin. The lids of the boxes may be coated with the same mixture by means of a brush, or pieces of sandpaper may be coated in the same manner, and attached to match safes or boxes for convenience in lighting.

Ordinary Matches. — Dip the matches first in hot melted sulphur, let dry and steep in turpentine. Afterwards dip the heads in a mixture of 5 ounces of chloride of potash, 5 ounces of flowers of sulphur, 1 ounce of vermilion mixed to a paste with oil of turpentine.

Or dip the matches in hot melted sulphur, steep in turpentine, and dip the heads in a mixture of 4 ounces of melted glue, 1 ounce of phosphorus with the addition of whiting stirred in to make it of the right consistency, and vermilion or lampblack to color.

CHAPTER XVIII

THE TOILET AND BATH

THE SKIN—BATHS AND BATHING—KINDS OF BATHS—THE TOILET—TOILET SOAPS—MEDICATED SOAP—THE HANDS—MANICURING

THE SKIN

The Human Skin has two principal functions: to protect the body, and to remove, by perspiration, the results of certain bodily changes. The skin consists of two layers, as may be clearly seen when blisters form. The upper layer or outer skin shows a tendency to form cells of a horny substance, such appendages as the hair, nails, and corns being a continuation of this process. These horny substances have the property of absorbing a certain amount of water. This softens them and causes

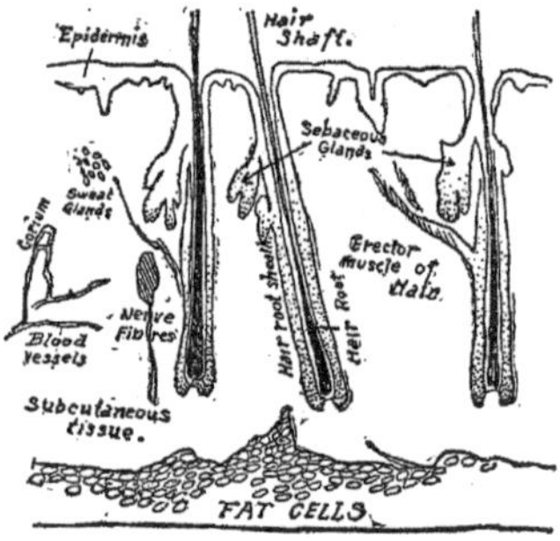

"The Anatomy of the Skin."

them to swell. It is well known that the skin becomes soft by immersion in a hot bath or by having the hands for a considerable time in suds or dishwater, and that this softening extends to the nails, corns, and calluses. After a warm bath a considerable quantity of the horny scales of the skin can be removed by the use of a rough towel. Nails, corns, and the like when wet can be readily cut or scraped off. A considerable amount of water remains in the skin after bathing, and unless care is exercised it tends by rapid evaporation to remove heat and to cause colds. But normally a certain amount of water should remain in the skin, and if too much of this evaporates, the skin chaps and cracks.

The permanent color of the skin is due to certain pigment granules found in its inner layer. The transient red color, as in blushing, depends upon the amount of blood in the blood vessels and the thickness of the epidermis or outer skin, most of the blood vessels themselves lying in the inner skin.

The skin contains sweat glands which secrete perspiration, and sebaceous glands, which secrete a fatty substance that tends to keep the skin smooth and to prevent it from drying by too great evaporation. This fatty substance also gives the hair its natural gloss. Obstruction of the sweat glands gives rise to pimples, blackheads, and the like. These are the principal facts regarding the anatomy of the skin, which should be understood by those who seek to improve its appearance.

There is a direct and reciprocal action between the condition of the skin and the general bodily health. The two watchwords in the campaign for the preservation or improvement of the complexion are, therefore, cleanliness and hygiene. Plenty of outdoor exercise, good ventilation, a well-regulated appetite, and a cheerful habit of mind are essential. As to diet, an excess of butter, fat meat, and greasy food should be avoided. All stimulants, as coffee, tea, wine, and spirits, should be given up or used with great moderation. Fruit and vegetables should be the staples of diet; sweets, cake, and pastry, and also pickles and acid foods, should be dispensed with. If these instructions, with those given under baths and bathing, are followed until they become the habits of a lifetime, the bloom of youth can be preserved far into old age.

Hardening the Skin.—The power of the skin to adjust itself to changes in temperature varies greatly. It can be increased by measures which improve the circulation of the blood, as nourishment and exercise; also by what is sometimes called the "hardening process." The skin may be hardened by living an out-of-door life, wearing light but sufficient clothing with woolen next the body, sleeping with open windows but avoiding draughts, and taking daily baths, first with warm, afterwards with cold water. These steps should be taken gradually, and increased in severity as the body becomes accustomed to them.

Nervous persons, especially children, may be overstimulated by these measures, which may thus lead to lifelong nervous difficulties. The danger is minimized by giving the warm bath first. Cold baths alone should not be taken except by persons of strong constitution. The air bath in various temperatures and currents of air is also a valuable means of hardening the skin. This hardening process tends to prevent colds and their consequences.

Diseases of the Skin.—No general treatment can be suggested that will apply to all diseases of the skin. Eruptions and rashes are often symptomatic of diseases of the blood and other grave conditions. When a strange eruption suddenly appears on the skin a physician should, as a rule, be promptly consulted. There are, however, a number of common disease conditions which yield to simple remedies. Among these are tan, sunburn, freckles, moth patches, pimples, blackheads or flesh worms, moles, etc.

Blackheads or "Flesh Worms."—The fatty substance which exudes from the sebaceous glands of the skin, if not removed by washing, sometimes hardens and corks up the gland itself. As the gland continues to secrete this substance it accumulates and causes a hard lump or swelling. When these blackheads are numerous, they become very unsightly. The best treatment is to press out the contents between the fingers or press the hollow end of a watch key over each speck. The entrance to these glands is in spiral form like a corkscrew. Hence the contents when pressed out have a vermiform appearance, and are supposed by many to be small animal creatures, hence called "flesh worms," but this is not the case.

A warm face bath twice a day, and gentle friction from a soft towel, as above directed, is the best preventive and remedy for this condition. Specifics for blackheads are the sulphate of zinc or of copper, or common potash properly diluted.

To use, mix 20 grains of sulphate of zinc or copper in 1 pint of distilled water or rose water, or mix 1 dram of fluid potash with 1 ounce of oil of sweet almonds. Then add 6 ounces of pure soft water. First press out the contents of the blackhead, rub with a rough towel, and apply this lotion with a camel's-hair brush or soft rag.

A face wash containing fluid potash, 1 ounce, cologne, 2 ounces, alcohol, 4 ounces, is also beneficial.

Freckles.—Freckles are discolorations formed in the deeper layers of the skin by the action of sunlight. Hence to affect them directly it is necessary to work through the outer layers of the skin with a remedy that will change the deposits of coloring matter. Freckles, accordingly, offer great resistance and are not amenable to ordinary treatment. Some authorities are of the opinion that indigestion may result in a deposit of carbonaceous or fatty matter beneath the skin, which, when acted upon by sunlight, will produce freckles. Hence, as a preventive, attention should be paid to diet and exercise to promote the normal secretions. The skin should be kept scrupulously clean by daily bathing, and the activity of the pores should be promoted by friction with a coarse towel. These methods are safer than the use of astringents or mineral emulsions, and the latter should never be employed without the advice of a competent physician. The only certain preventive is the wearing of a brown veil whenever the complexion is exposed to sunlight.

Moth Patches.—Apply a solution of common baking soda to the patches with a soft rag or camel's-hair brush several times a day for two or three days. Allow this to dry on. This treatment is usually sufficient. Afterwards cleanse the face with a bran bath and the skin will usually be found clear and brilliant.

Or keep alum at hand and rub occasionally on the moth patches. This will usually cause them to disappear.

Moles.—Depilatories advertised for sale for the removal of moles are dangerous and their use is not recommended. They frequently continue eating into the flesh until an ulcer is formed, and occasionally blood poison sets in. Some moles are of the nature of tumors, and too much care cannot be exercised in treating them. Concentrated acetic acid applied by means of a hair pencil will sometimes do the work. If this succeeds once it can be used again, but it will not prevent the blemish from returning. Care must be taken that the acid does not extend to surrounding parts.

Moles can sometimes be destroyed by the use of a burning glass. The patient must take his place in the clear, strong sunlight, and focus the burning glass on the affected part for about five minutes at a time daily, until the mole has been destroyed. Needless to say, this is a painful process, but it cannot be regarded as dangerous.

The electric needle in the hands of a competent physician is a thoroughly safe and reliable method of treatment.

Pimples.—The immediate cause of pimples is usually an excess of fatty matter in the skin. They are very common in young persons from fourteen to twenty years of age. They are often caused by constitutional conditions, and when very numerous are often persistent until the general health is restored. Exercise, attention to the diet, and general hygienic measures are recommended. A warm face bath with a heaping teaspoonful of borax in the water will be found helpful.

Scars.—Little scars are often left on the face after eruptions. A course of electric massage treatment soon effaces them. For home treatment, every night apply to the face a cold compress, keeping it on until the flesh becomes pink, then anoint the little spots with ointment of zinc oxide.

Ointment for Wrinkles or Relaxed Skin.—To 10 grains of camphor add 2 ounces of prepared lard and 1 fluid dram of rectified spirits of wine. Apply a little of the ointment at night, previously washing the face, and strengthen the body by means of tonics and nourishing diet.

Or bathe the parts where the wrinkles appear with alum and water. This will tighten the skin.

Or fresh butter, 2 drams; essence of turpentine, 2 drams; mastic, 1 dram.

BATHS AND BATHING

Historians say that the civilization of a community can be estimated by the quantity of soap it consumes.

Similarly the refinement of a family is indicated by the amount of water it uses.

Records of cities show that the amount used each day on an average by each person runs from seven or eight gallons among the poor, where there is only one faucet in the house, to about sixty gallons in the homes of wealthy persons. The average of an ordinary family in cities may be taken as about twenty gallons daily for each member. More water is used in the summer than in the winter—which is an argument in favor of a bathroom, even where there is no furnace in the house. About ten barrels of water would be required every day on this basis by a family of ten persons.

A humorist has said that mankind may be divided into two classes—those who take a full bath every day, and those who do not. Many folks would think this writer a snob, but the daily bath is common in households which enjoy all the modern conveniences. The daily "tub" of the English gentlemen is proverbial, and laughable stories are told of the efforts made by Englishmen to keep up this practice under difficulties. A great many English officers took folding bath tubs with them on baggage trains during the recent war in South Africa, and tried to enjoy their daily morning tub even under fire. This is extreme. But most families ought to approach nearer to this ideal than they ordinarily do.

The weekly bath, however, is customary in homes where there is no bathroom, but this custom might be even more generally observed. The habit of bathing grows, in most cases, out of regard for appearances rather than regard for health. The grimly facetious remark of a certain widower, who had been bereaved a number of times, that he was going to take a bath, because he always made it a point of doing so before being married, whether he needed it or not, hints at a habit of mind which is quite common.

Cleanliness is said to be next to godliness, and it is certain that the habit of church attendance is in many households a strong incentive to the custom of weekly bathing. The same remark applies to social gatherings, and such events as weddings, christenings, and funerals.

The bath is the foundation of the toilet. Most persons naturally take a bath preparatory to putting on their Sunday clothes or other holiday attire. If this were not the case we fear that consideration of the health, based on modern hygienic science, would not of itself be sufficient inducement to bathe. But when a person is half persuaded by custom to take a weekly bath, any knowledge he may have of its advantages to health will help him to decide in its favor.

In "Trilby" the Jew Svengali laughed immoderately at the two English gentlemen for bathing daily, when they "were not dirty." He overlooked the point that the proper function of the bath is not to make us clean, but to keep us so.

The human skin contains millions of pores. The business of these pores is to bring to the surface the waste materials of the body, which otherwise pass off principally through the kidneys. If the pores become clogged by the accumulation of effete matter they are unable to fulfill their proper functions, and the kidneys are obliged to do extra work, which may bring on chronic diseases of those organs.

Colds are caused by lack of proper contraction of the pores of the skin when the body is exposed from draughts or otherwise. As a result the blood is cooled too rapidly and has a tendency to chill and congest the internal organs, as the mucous surfaces of the head and nose, and also of the alimentary canal, the kidneys, etc. The resulting symptoms show in acute form the bad effects of neglect of bathing. In fact, frequent bathing is almost a sure preventive of colds. If the pores are kept clean they are active, and resist the chills which tend to produce cold. If they are not kept clean they are sluggish and inactive, and in no condition to offer normal resistance to sudden changes in temperature.

Certain portions of the body, as the armpits, the feet, and the groin, have many more pores to the square inch than the rest; hence these perspire more freely and should be cleansed often. The feet especially should be very frequently washed. There is no better practice from the health standpoint than a daily footbath.

The Bathroom.—Bathrooms are no longer a novelty in small towns and farmhouses. But it must be understood that to enjoy these in winter,

"No Longer a Novelty."

requires almost of necessity a range or furnace. Pipes in kitchens may be kept warm by stoves, and bathrooms adjoining the kitchen may be warmed by leaving the door open between or the bathroom may be over the kitchen, and a drum or smokepipe from the kitchen stove arranged so as to heat the pipes in the bathroom. But it is usually better not to have running water in the bathroom in winter until a furnace is put in. It pays, however, to partition off a bathroom near the kitchen and put in a bath tub, if there is running water or a hand pump in the bathroom, with drainpipes to carry away waste—even if it is necessary to carry cold water to the tub from the kitchen sink and hot water from the stove in pails. A good bath tub is not a luxury, but a necessity to comfort, cleanliness, and health.

If the bathroom is near the kitchen, the tub can be filled by bringing hot and cold water in pails; and if the tub is elevated slightly, the water can be drawn off in pails and carried to the drain after the bath; or, if a tub is used which does not have a faucet for drainage, the waste water can be easily removed by using a small piece of rubber tube as a siphon, or by a dipper and large bath sponge. Every household should be provided with a full-size tub, even if it is only of tin. Portable rubber tubs which can be folded and put away when not in use are also obtainable. But a cast-iron tub is preferable and not too expensive.

The entire cost of plumbing for a bathroom, including supply pipe, hot-water pipe, and all necessary fixtures, provided you have a water supply in the house, will not exceed $150. This sum can be reduced by doing some of the work yourself.

Even if there is no furnace, the bathroom can be used from early spring to late fall, and especially through the summer season, when it is above all essential to health and comfort. Every family should make the necessary sacrifices to put in and enjoy this great convenience.

To Paint an Iron Bath Tub.—Mix the paint to a proper consistency with best coachmaker's japan varnish. For white-lead paint, use half turpentine and half coachmaker's japan. It will not darken much. Venetian red is best for a first coat for any color but white.

Bathroom Conveniences. — Convenience has a great deal to do with the formation of habits; and parents, especially mothers, who desire to cultivate habits of personal cleanliness in the household, will find that a bathroom furnished with the necessary conveniences will largely solve this problem.

A closet should be constructed in one corner of the bathroom and stocked with the accessories of the bath and toilet.

A wire basket can be purchased for a few cents, or made by any ingenious member of the family, to hang on the edge of the bath tub and hold sponge, soap, etc. This will be found to be a great convenience.

A hamper or *laundry bag* makes a convenient receptacle for soiled body and household linen; or separate bags might be arranged—one for each kind.

A set time for each member of the family to take the weekly bath will also tend to promote the convenience of the household. Saturday night and Sunday morning are probably the best times for most persons. The weekly bath thus becomes a preparation for the Sunday morning toilet, which is ordinarily the most careful and elaborate of the week.

The following suggestions and recipes have been grouped about the idea of a thorough weekly personal "cleaning up" and toilet for "over Sunday." The reader will, of course, understand that these remarks and recipes apply equally well to the daily morning baths and those for special occasions; and in many cases specific recommendations for these occasions have been made.

Dont's for Bathers.—Don't take any kind of a bath within two hours after eating a hearty meal.

Don't neglect a daily bath of some kind. Don't neglect the daily sun and air bath.

Don't take a cold bath when fatigued; but take a bath in water as hot as can be borne. It will help to rest you.

Don't strip for a bath when the body is cooling after perspiration, but step into a warm bath while the body is heated.

Don't stay too long in the water. Get out before you begin to feel chilly.

Don't stand around on the bank or in boats after bathing until you get a chill.

Don't bathe early in the morning on an empty stomach unless you are vigorous and strong enough to stand it. The best time for you may be two or three hours after breakfast.

Don't neglect the weekly hot-water bath, followed by a change of clothing to keep the body clean and healthy.

Don't believe that you can get rid of wrinkles by filling them in with powder. Just before going to bed bathe your face in warm, then in cold water. And quit worrying. It will save you many a wrinkle.

Temperature of the Bath.—The temperature of the bath for cleanliness should be about 95° F. A cold shower bath or douche to follow the warm bath should be about 77° F. A cool bath should be about 77° F.,

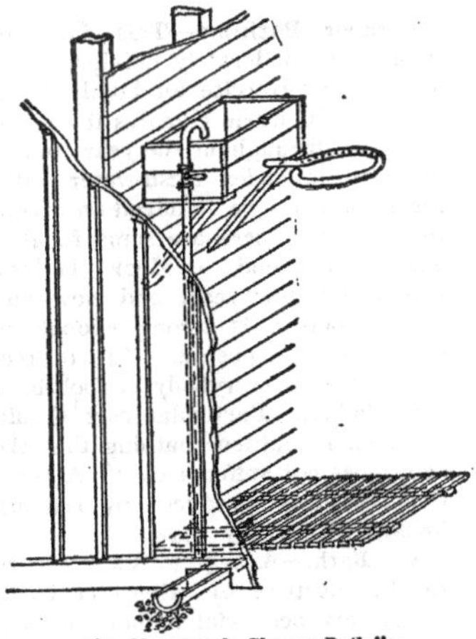

"A Homemade Shower Bath."

but the temperature at the start may be lowered for those who are accustomed to it.

The water for a person in ordinary health should be drawn about as hot as is agreeable; but care should be taken not to remain too long in a hot bath. This applies especially to persons who are thin-blooded, nervous, or neuralgic. After the body has been thoroughly cleansed, it is a good idea to gradually introduce cold water into the tub until a perceptible chill is felt.

If there is running water in the bathroom, a shower bath may be had by obtaining the detachable rubber tubes and fixtures used for this purpose, which come very cheap. The shower bath is the best means of cooling the body after a hot bath. When this is done, or after a cold bath, a reaction should be brought about by a vigorous rubbing with a Turkish towel until the body is in a warm glow. This practice would almost certainly prevent all colds and many fevers, with their fatal cousequences.

KINDS OF BATHS

Outdoor Bathing.—This form of bathing, if moderately indulged in, is an excellent exercise for bodily development. In warm climates it may be practiced throughout the year; but in northern latitudes fresh-water bathing should not be indulged in except in summer. There are some fanatics who recommend outdoor bathing throughout the year, and now and then a person is strong enough to endure such exposure. But to recommend it to everybody is foolish, if not criminal. Particular care should be taken in outdoor bathing that the body does not suffer a chill. A reaction should be produced by rubbing briskly with a dry towel.

Sea Bath.—A trip to the seashore for the purpose of salt-water bathing is very beneficial to persons in a run-down condition, with the exception of those suffering from nervous diseases, heart diseases, or consumption. Salt-water bathing is especially good for children who have scrofula, and for persons who have catarrh.

Salt water and salt air are stimulating and invigorating. The shock caused by the surf tends to produce a healthful fatigue which strengthens the bodily functions and promotes hunger and appetite. Bathers in salt water, especially invalids, should leave the water before they are chilled or overtired, dry the body thoroughly, and follow the bath by some mild exercise, as walking.

Air Bath.—After the bath all persons, especially children, should expose the body to the air for a considerable length of time. Benjamin Franklin says that every morning at daybreak he was accustomed to get out of bed, and pass more or less than an hour, according to the season, in writing or reading in his chamber without any clothes; and he adds that this custom was agreeable rather than otherwise. There is no doubt that light, especially direct sunlight, upon the skin is one of the most valuable agents for the preservation of health.

A complete change of clothing should be made after the bath. The contact of clothing with the skin greatly promotes its secretions, and this is very necessary to health. Flannel generates heat—hence opens the pores of the skin and allows the secretions to flow. It is therefore the proper clothing next the body.

If the effete matter thrown off by the skin in perspiration is retained by the clothing, the gravest consequences to health may result in addition to the discomforts of uncleanliness. Colds, fevers, and vermin of all sorts are merely human ignorance, laziness, and uncleanliness out on exhibition.

Cold Sponge Bath.—Many persons make a practice of taking a cold sponge bath every morning, followed by vigorous rubbing with a coarse towel or flesh brush. The best method of doing this is to fill a washbowl or basin with water and let it stand in the room over night, so as to acquire the same temperature as the air in the room. Rub with the bare hands rather than with a cloth or sponge, wetting only a small portion of the body at a time and rubbing that portion until a reaction is experienced. Washing the face and head, next the arms, the back, the lower portion of the chest, and the lower limbs, in the order mentioned, is a good rule for cold-water bathing. After the rub-down with a coarse towel, the skin should be pink, all in a tingle, and the whole surface of the body should be in a warm glow. Some persons cannot endure this regimen, although it is highly beneficial to others. A few days or weeks of experience will test its expediency. This is worth trying, because it often results in a life habit which is exceedingly beneficial. Those who are less robust may obtain some of the benefits of the cold sponge bath by a vigorous rubbing with a towel or flesh brush each morning when the bath is not taken. When bathing in winter, the shock from cold water is lessened by standing a minute in the cold air after removing the clothing and before applying the water.

Footbath. — This bath may be taken for cleansing purposes or for the purpose of drawing the blood from other parts of the body. Congestion of blood in the head may be relieved by a footbath in cold water. If convenient, the patient may walk for a few minutes in a brook or stream reaching about to the ankles. This may be followed by a brisk rubbing and some exercise, as walking. Or the patient may first put his feet in hot water for from three to five minutes and then plunge them for half a minute into cold water. Afterwards the feet should be rubbed dry and the person should take exercise by walking.

Salt-water Bath. — Add 4 or 5 pounds of sea salt, which can be purchased of any druggist, to a full bath at the temperature of 65° F. The patient should remain in this bath from 10 to 20 minutes, and afterwards should rest for half an hour in a recumbent position. Such baths are useful in general debility produced by wasting diseases, as scrofula and other diseases of the skin, anæmia, etc. Sea salt should not be used for children. It does not penetrate the skin, but acts as a stimulant.

Mustard Bath.—The addition of 3 or 4 tablespoonfuls of powdered mustard to a hot footbath in cases of chill is a preventive against taking cold, and is also useful in the early stages of colds to induce perspiration. The feet should be taken out of this bath as soon as the skin reddens and begins to smart. The parts bathed should be carefully cleansed, rinsed, and wiped dry. Great care should be exercised in giving mustard baths to children, else the skin may become badly blistered.

The Bran Bath.—Make a decoction of wheat bran by boiling 4 or 5 pounds of wheat bran in a linen bag. The juice extracted, and also the bran itself, should be put into the water. This is for a full bath at a temperature of about 90° F. This bath is of service in all skin affections accompanied by itching.

Cabinet Baths.—A number of special cabinets are devised for giving different kinds of baths for medicinal purposes. Purchasing one of these is usually not necessary unless there are one or more invalids in the family. In such cases the selection of a suitable cabinet should be made only upon the advice of the family physician. The following forms of bathing require the use of cabinets:

Stool Bath.—This is likewise known as the Russian bath. It consists in filling a room with steam at a temperature under low pressure of about 120° F. Stool baths are very little used, but the same effect is produced by a cabinet which has an opening for the head so that the patient is not obliged to breathe the steam. A steam bath for the face and head may be obtained by holding the face over a receptacle full of boiling water, and throwing a cloth or oilcloth over the head and shoulders so as to partly prevent the escape of the steam.

The Hot-air Bath.—In the Turkish bath, several connecting rooms are heated to different degrees of temperature, and the patient passes slowly from the coolest to the warmest room for the purpose of inducing perspiration. He is then given a cold shower or douche, rubbed dry, wrapped in blankets and permitted to rest. These baths are very enervating and should only be taken by persons of strong constitution. The hot-air bath, however, for the purpose of inducing perspiration, is superior to the steam bath. It should be so taken that the person's head will be outside of the cabinet and he will not be obliged to breathe the hot air. A temperature of 120° to 130° F. is sufficient. Great care should be taken that the air does not become superheated, as danger is likely to ensue from a temperature exceeding 140° F. The patient should not remain in the hot-air bath more than fifteen or twenty minutes, and should then be given a cool bath and rubbed down. If additional perspiration is desired, he should be wrapped in blankets.

Steam baths and hot-air baths should ordinarily be taken only by and with the advice of the family physician.

THE TOILET

The Complexion.—The object of attention to the complexion should be to preserve the skin in its normal condition of health, and to remove all abnormal effects and conditions. Among these may be mentioned excessive dryness or evaporation, by exposure to dry and biting winds, of the water normally contained in the skin; the opposite extreme of excessive perspiration; and the obstruction of the pores by dirt or grime or other causes, which is the parent of various eruptions and other skin diseases. These subjects are taken up in turn in the following pages, and the principal standard remedies are cited.

Many persons regard attention to these matters as evidence of vanity and light-headedness, and others go to the opposite extreme and give much more time and thought to the niceties of the toilet than is either wise or necessary. Doubtless the wise and sane course lies between these two extremes. The normal condition of the skin resulting in a firm, smooth, and soft texture and a clear pink-and-white complexion, not only contributes to personal attractiveness, but also to the sense of comfort, included in the general term "good health."

Women (and men, too) have a natural right to a good complexion. The contrary is evidence of some improper or diseased condition, and it is perfectly natural and proper to seek and apply suitable remedies.

Beauty Doctors.—On the other hand, we earnestly advise against the patronage of so-called "beauty doctors," many of whom are unquestionably quacks and charlatans, and we urge the use of homemade preparations. Many of the standard preparations widely advertised for sale contain the most injurious mineral drugs, such, for example, as mercury, arsenic, lead, bismuth, etc. These are freely used by many "beauty doctors," and we regret to say that recipes containing them have been published without caution in many books of household recipes which have had a wide circulation. All such preparations have been carefully excluded from this volume. Approved recipes have been given which will accomplish every desirable object without the possibility of any injurious consequences.

Homemade Toilet Preparations.—Many toilet preparations advertised for sale contain organic substances which deteriorate by decaying, and in this condition poison the skin. Moreover, most proprietary articles are very expensive. We feel safe in assuring the most careful and conservative mothers that the compounding at home and use of any of the preparations herein recommended will be a perfectly safe and innocent employment for their daughters or themselves. Any disposition to do so should, we think, be encouraged. A few vials of essential oils as perfumes, small quantities of almonds and other required ingredients, may be bought at the drug store for less than a single bottle of a proprietary article can be purchased, and all interested will have the satisfaction of knowing that the materials are fresh and of good quality, and that no harmful consequences from their use need be feared.

Country girls should have the best complexions in the world, but this is not always the case. Those who have not been favored by nature in this respect very often envy their city cousins' supposed advantages of easy access to "beauty doctors" and the large department stores and drug stores where toilet preparations of all sorts are for sale. The country girl has, in fact, a pronounced advantage over her city cousin if she has the wit to utilize it. Many of the most effective agents and remedies for the toilet are to be had in every farmhouse, and it is safe to say that the country girl can stock her dressing table with a full line of toilet preparations if she so desires, of better quality than her city cousin can purchase. And she can do so much more cheaply and conveniently.

To Preserve the Complexion.—To prevent the excessive evaporation of water normally present in the skin, it is well to rub a small quantity of cold cream over the face before going out in the hot sun or wind. Just enough should be used to cover the surface without its being noticeable. In hot climates the use of similar preparations to prevent the drying of the skin is practically universal.

A veil is also a desirable protection against bad weather. Chiffon or other material of the finest mesh should be preferred. Frenchwomen of the middle and upper classes never think of going out without a veil. Englishwomen and the inhabitants of warm climates generally carry parasols.

To Wash the Face.—When the face is red or dry from exposure to sun and air, or grimed with dirt or smoke, it is well to put on it a quantity of cold cream and rub thoroughly with a soft cloth. After the irritation has been somewhat lessened, the face should be thoroughly washed and cleansed. Fill a basin two thirds full of fresh soft water. If your source of water supply is hard water, put a teaspoonful of powdered borax into the basin. Dip the face in the water, and afterwards the hands. Soap the hands well, and rub with a gentle motion over the face. Dip the face a second time, rinse thoroughly, and wipe with a thick, soft towel. After the bath a slightly astringent lotion is very refreshing.

The use of a good cleansing cream before the face bath and a suitable lotion afterwards has a really wonderful effect in improving the complexion. The effect of a clean face, however, is itself altogether delightful. Such a bath tends to rest and refresh the bather and put her in a good temper. Many a bad complexion is due to neglect of a proper cleansing process. If more faces were kept really clean, a great improvement in the complexion would be noticed.

Face Cloth.—The hands themselves, in the judgment of many persons, are the most effective means of washing other portions of the body. To those who prefer face cloths we suggest scrim as the most sanitary material. Scrim is porous and free from lint, so that the air circulates through it freely. It is so thin that it can be quickly washed and dried.

The Toilet Sponge.—The wash rag and the sponge, while convenient and regarded by many as indispensable, are often sources of injury to the skin. Children, especially, are prone to take a sponge from dirty water and squeeze it dry without rinsing. The decaying organic matter caught in the pores of the sponge gives rise to certain acids and ferments very injurious to the complexion. Both the sponge and the wash rag should be thoroughly cleansed and rinsed after use. To clean a sour sponge, put 1 teaspoonful each of ammonia and borax into a basin of warm water, wash the sponge, rinse in clean soft water and hang in the air, exposed to sunshine if possible, until dry.

TOILET SOAPS

Soaps.—Pure soaps do not irritate the skin. There are two principal kinds of soaps: those containing free alkali in the form of potash or soda lye, and the so-called neutral or fatty soaps. The former increase the swelling and softening of the horny parts of the skin. When these are removed, they of course take the dirt with them. The latter are better adapted to persons of sensitive skin, although their detergent effects are not so marked. Among these are castile, glycerin, curd soaps, and the like. Medicated and highly colored or scented soaps should rarely be used, and we recommend purchasing for household use only well-known soaps which have an established reputation for purity and general satisfaction. It must be borne in mind that toilet preparations which may give good effects on one skin are sometimes injurious to another. Glycerin is said to burn some skins, and benzoin cannot be used by some persons. This shows how important it is for a woman to know what ingredients are used in making up her toilet preparations. It is not always safe to "try" some compound, the contents of which are unknown, because it is highly recommended by others.

On the other hand, the difference in results obtained by two women may often be attributed to the difference in the method of use. One woman will cleanse her face thoroughly as above indicated, while the other will merely apply a cream or lotion when the skin may be covered with grime and the pores filled with dirt. The result may be to still further clog the pores and produce an eruption of pimples and blackheads. No preparation can give satisfactory results in the absence of absolute cleanliness.

Toilet Soaps.—These soaps are distinguished by the purity of their ingredients, as almond oil, beef marrow, refined lard, and the like. They are usually saponified without heat, and may be perfumed according to taste. Any neutral hard white soap may be used as a foundation for toilet soaps if prepared as follows:

Shave the soap thin or run it through a meat cutter, and melt in a double boiler with rose water, orange-flower water, or other distilled water, and common salt, in the proportion of 6 pounds of soap to 1 pint each of rose water or orange-flower water and 2 ounces of salt.

After boiling, allow the mixture to cool. Cut it into small squares with a cord or wire, and dry without exposing to the sun. When dry, melt it again down with the same proportion of rose water or orange-flower water. Strain, cool, and dry thoroughly in a warm oven. Now reduce it to powder and expose it to the air under a screen. Coloring matter and perfume may be added according to taste. Other methods of purifying common household soaps and recipes for standard popular toilet soaps are given below.

Among the most popular toilet articles are honey, Windsor, borax, glycerin, and almond soaps, besides a multitude of soaps which derive their name from the various perfumes added, as cinnamon, orange flower, sandalwood, rose, musk, violet, citron, etc.

Perfumed Soaps.—Soaps may be perfumed by adding a few drops of any essential oil, or a proportionately larger quantity of essences or perfumed distilled waters to the saponified mass while cooling, but before hard soap has become cool enough to set. If perfumes are added while the soap is too hot they tend to volatilize and escape with the steam; if the soap is too cold they cannot be readily incorporated. Ordinary soap may be perfumed by cutting it with alcohol or other spirits and adding the perfume before the mixture hardens; or by melting up the soap in a small quantity of water, adding the perfume, and evaporating the excess of water by very gentle heat in a double boiler. Or the soap may be reduced to shavings, moistened slightly with distilled water, and the perfume incorporated by kneading or by the use of a mortar and pestle.

Honey Soap.—This is common yellow soap of good quality, to which has been added a certain proportion of pure strained honey and other ingredients. Shave and melt in a double boiler 2 pounds of yellow soap. Add 4 ounces of palm oil, 4 ounces of honey, and 1 ounce of oil of cinnamon or other perfume according to taste. Boil for 10 minutes. While cooling stir vigorously with an egg beater to thoroughly emulsify the ingredients. Cool. Ready for use as soon as hardened.

Windsor Soap.—This is a trade term which denotes merely a pure white soap, the base of which is 10 parts of any pure animal fat, as rectified suet or lard, and about 1 part of olive oil or bleached palm oil, to which are added any perfume, as the essential oil of bergamot.

Almond Soap.—Almond oil may be saponified with caustic soda by a process similar to that of making other hard soaps. About 1¼ pounds of caustic soda will be required to saponify 7 pounds of almond oil. Mix the soda, lye, and almond oil gradually, boiling hot. Boil and stir until saponification is complete, adding more oil or lye as may be necessary.

Or melt fine, pure, hard white soap, and add the essence of bitter almonds in the proportion of 1½ per cent by weight.

Borax Soap.—Dissolve 3 ounces of borax in 2 quarts of boiling water. Shave 2 pounds of pure white hard soap and add to the solution. Stir and simmer with gentle heat until the ingredients are thoroughly melted and mixed. When cold the soap is ready for use.

Soap from Corn Meal or Oatmeal.—Both of these articles are useful for the toilet, having the property of making the skin smooth, soft, and white. In summer mix 2 teacupfuls of corn meal with 1 tablespoonful of powdered borax, and use as a cleansing agent.

Or shave 12 ounces of neutral white hard soap, add enough water to keep it from burning, and melt with gentle heat. Stir in 4 ounces of cornstarch, and perfume according to taste.

Or melt together 12 ounces of hard white soap, 5 ounces of palm soap, and 3 ounces of cocoanut oil or marine soap; add 3 ounces of oatmeal or wheat bran. These ingredients should be incorporated with gentle heat in a double boiler. The soap will be improved if the mixture is thoroughly beaten with an egg beater to make a complete emulsion after it has been removed from the fire. Ready for use when cold and dry.

Or cut fine 1 pound of castile or other hard white soap, add enough water to prevent it from burning, and melt with gentle heat. Stir while melting to form a thick, smooth paste of the consistency desired. Put this in a bowl to cool. Perfume with any essential oil or perfumed water, incorporating the perfume with an egg beater. Now stir in Indian meal until the paste thickens. This must be kept in a fruit jar or other covered glass vessel, as it will spoil if exposed to the air.

Soft Soap for the Toilet.—A liquid soap may be made for the toilet of sweet oil saponified with caustic potash. Take of the sweet oil 7 parts; caustic potash, 1 part. Put these ingredients in a double boiler with a small quantity of rose water or other perfumed water. Beat the mixture with a spoon or an egg beater until a complete emulsion forms, and simmer until saponification takes place. Now add sufficient rose water to reduce the mixture to any desired consistency.

Marine or Salt-water Soap.—Dissolve 8 ounces of caustic soda in 3 quarts of boiling water to form a lye. Now melt with gentle heat 30 ounces of cocoanut oil or cocoanut lard. Gradually add the lye, stirring constantly until saponification takes place. One ounce of fused Glàuber's salts will cause the soap to harden.

Camphor Soap.—Dissolve in a double boiler 1 pound of neutral hard white soap in 8 fluid ounces of boiling water. Continue boiling until by evaporation the soap has the consistency of butter. Now add 6 fluid ounces of olive oil in which 1 dram of prepared camphor has been previously mingled. Take the mixture from the stove and beat up with an egg beater until a complete emulsion forms. This is a valuable remedy for chaps and scratches.

Citron Soap.—To 6 pounds of curd soap add ¾ pound of attar citron, ½ ounce of verbena (lemon grass), 4 ounces of attar bergamot, and 2 ounces of attar lemon.

Frangipani Soap.—To 7 pounds of light-brown curd soap add ¼ ounce of civet, ½ ounce of attar neroli, 1½ ounces of attar santal, ¼ ounce of attar rose, and ½ ounce of attar vitivert.

Cinnamon Soap.—Add 2 ounces of palm-oil soap to 3 ounces of tallow soap, ½ ounce of water, 7 ounces of essence cinnamon, 2 ounces of essence bergamot, and 1 ounce of essence sassafras. Stir in enough yellow ocher to color as desired.

Sandalwood Soap.—To 7 pounds of curd soap, add 2 ounces of attar bergamot and 7 ounces of attar santal.

Sand Soap.—To 7 pounds of curd soap, add 7 pounds of marine soap, 25 pounds of silver sand, 2 ounces of attar thyme, 2 ounces of attar cassia, 2 ounces of attar caraway, and 2 ounces of attar French lavender.

Soap à la Rose.—Take 30 pounds of castile soap, and add 20 pounds of tallow soap, sufficient water to melt, 3 ounces of attar rose, 1 ounce of essence cinnamon, 2½ ounces of essence bergamot, 1½ ounces of vermilion, and 1 ounce of essence cloves.

Musk Soap.—Add 26 pounds of palm-oil soap to 30 pounds of tallow soap, 4 ounces of essence bergamot, 5 ounces of powdered pale roses, 3¾ ounces of musk, and 4¼ ounces of brown ocher.

Tonquin Soap.—Take 5 pounds of light-brown curd soap and 1 ounce of attar bergamot, and add ¼ ounce of grain musk and 8 ounces of essence cloves.

Wash Balls.—Any good toilet soap may be made into balls of any desired size by a process similar to making butter balls, i. e., by using two wooden paddles. The addition of starch helps to give the soap the right consistency.

Melt 7 pounds of neutral white bar soap in distilled water or rose water sufficient to prevent burning. Add 1 ounce of powdered starch and more water, if necessary, to form a stiff paste. If too much water is added, continue the heat until the excess of water evaporates. Stir in 8 ounces of powdered wheat starch or cornstarch, and add essence of almonds according to taste. Remove from the fire, thoroughly incorporate the materials with an egg beater, mix or knead with the hands, and make into balls of any desired size.

MEDICATED SOAP

Soaps are frequently used as the vehicle for various remedial agents, as sulphur, iodine, tar, and the like, for diseases of the skin. Also for disinfectants, as carbolic acid, chlorine, and others. Any neutral white hard soap may be medicated by being dissolved in water. The following are especially recommended;

Sulphur Soap.—Shave 2 ounces of soft soap and add ¼ ounce of flowers of sulphur and 2 fluid drams of proof spirits, which may be perfumed and colored according to taste. Mix the ingredients thoroughly in an earthenware bowl or marble mortar. Sulphur is a valuable remedy in itch and other diseases of the skin.

Iodine Soap.—Dissolve 1 pound of white castile soap shaved fine in 3 fluid ounces of distilled water or rose water. Add 1 ounce of iodide of potassium. Put in a double boiler, melt, and mix by stirring. Iodine is a valuable remedy in scrofula and other diseases of the skin.

Juniper-tar Soap. — Dissolve 4 ounces of tar of the juniper tree in 1 pound of almond oil or olive oil. Put on the fire in a double boiler, and add gradually weak soda lye, stirring constantly until saponification takes place. Tar is a valuable remedy in all kinds of skin diseases. This soap is really an ointment. It should be applied at night and washed away next morning.

Carbolic-acid Soap. — Take 5 pounds of fresh cocoanut oil or marine soap, melt, and add 5 ounces of alcohol, 3 ounces of carbolic acid, 1 ounce of caustic potash, and ½ ounce of almond oil. Stir until the ingredients are thoroughly incorporated, and cool in molds.

Soap with Chlorine. — Shave 11 ounces of castile soap, dry in warm oven, and reduce to a powder. Add 1 ounce of fresh dry chloride of lime. Add a sufficient quantity of proof spirits to cut this mixture and reduce it to the consistency of dough. This soap must be kept from the air, which may be done by packing it in glass fruit jars with tight metal caps. It is especially valuable in the sick room and for nurses in contagious diseases. It also has the property of removing stains from the skin and making it white.

Soap with Arsenic. — This is a paste made by mixing 12 ounces of carbonate of potash with 4 ounces each of white arsenic, white soap, and air-slaked lime, with sufficient water to reduce to the required consistency. Powdered camphor, ¾ ounce, may also be added with advantage.

Or mix white soap, 8 ounces; powdered lime, 2 ounces; arsenious acid, 8 ounces; carbonate of potassa, 3 ounces, and gum camphor, 1¼ ounces. Reduce the ingredients separately to powder and mix. These two arsenical soaps are poisonous, and should be labeled accordingly and kept out of the way of children and household pets. They are used as preservatives in preparing the skins of birds and other animals, and to keep them free from the attacks of insects.

Bayberry Soap, or Myrtle Soap.—Dissolve 3½ ounces of white potash in 1 pint of water, and add 1 pound of melted myrtle wax or bayberry tallow. Boil slowly and stir until the mixture saponifies. Add 2 tablespoonfuls of cold water containing a pinch of salt, and boil 5 or 6 minutes longer. Remove from the fire and when it is cool, but before it sets, perfume by adding 5 or 6 drops of any essential oil or oils, according to taste. This soap is valuable for all toilet purposes, for shaving, chaps, and all diseased conditions of the skin. It should not be used until it is thoroughly seasoned. The longer it is allowed to dry and season the better it becomes.

Transparent Soap. — Any good white neutral soap may be rendered transparent by reducing it to shavings, adding one half its volume of alcohol, and setting the mixture in a warm place until the soap is dissolved. When allowed to cool it has somewhat the appearance of rock candy. It may be perfumed and scented according to taste.

Or shave 24 ounces of good hard yellow soap and add 1 pint of alcohol. Simmer with gentle heat until dissolved. Remove from the fire, add 1 ounce of almond or other essence, and stir vigorously with an egg beater to make a complete emulsion.

Pour into molds to cool. This gives a very cheap, pure soap of good appearance, as it is nearly transparent.

THE HANDS

Nothing betrays lack of daintiness in personal care more than neglect of the hands and nails. Of course it is more difficult for some women to keep their nails clean and their hands soft, white, and free from blemishes than for others. But in the care of the hands immaculate cleanliness is imperative. They should never be washed except when it can be done thoroughly. Constantly rinsing them in cold water grinds the dirt in and ruins the texture of the skin, making it rough, coarse, and red. When exposed to hard usage, as in the routine of housework, instead of frequently washing the hands in water, a few drops of oil should be rubbed into them. They should then be dusted over with talcum powder and wiped with a coarse towel. This will cleanse them and protect the flesh from growing callous. Lemon juice will remove stains.

The hands should always be washed in tepid water, and a good soap is an absolute necessity. It is also important that the water be soft. Avoid washing the hands frequently with cheap laundry soap, washing powders, soft soap, or other powerful detergents. They tend to roughen, redden, and chap the skin. The best soap is none too good for the toilet. There are many brands on the market which are known to be good, and it is better not to experiment with those that are new and untried. Any hard, white, pure or neutral soap is suitable for the toilet. Hence it is not necessary to purchase special toilet soaps, which are usually expensive, however desirable they may seem to be. To test soap for toilet purposes, apply the tongue to it. If it contains free alkali, it will have a caustic or burning taste and should be avoided. Otherwise it is not likely to be injurious.

In cold weather or when the hands are very dirty rub a little pure lard or cold cream over them, and afterwards wash them with soap and water in the usual way. This has a tendency to keep the skin from cracking or chapping. The use of gloves, especially when gardening, driving, or walking in sun or wind, helps to preserve the softness of the hands and keep them clean. Sprinkling the hands with orris root or talcum powder before drawing on the gloves will counteract excessive perspiration.

Redness and Burning. — These troubles are caused by defective circulation. Attention should be given to the general health, and as a preventive measure the hands should be protected from exposure to the weather—especially in the winter—by the use of a muff or by fur-lined gloves. Or two pairs of gloves may be worn, which will be found warmer than one pair lined. After the hands have been exposed to the cold they may be prevented from tingling by washing them in very warm water, and drying them carefully on a soft towel. The after effect will be a feeling of coolness, whereas the use of cold water causes a glow.

Moist Hands.—If the hands are constantly moist from too free perspiration, bathe them frequently either in salt water, which acts as a stimulant or tonic, or in a solution of vinegar or lemon juice, which acts as an astringent.

Or rub them with a mixture of powdered alum and tannic acid, both of which have astringent properties.

Or a little of this mixture may be dusted inside the gloves.

But care should be taken not to use acid or astringent cosmetics oftener than is necessary, as they tend to overwork the pores of the skin and to produce injurious after effects.

To Remove Stains from the Hands. — Substances recommended for removing stains from the hands are lemon juice, the juice of ripe tomatoes, sulphuric acid (oil of vitriol), chloride of lime, oxalic acid, fumes of sulphur, and various compounds of these. The following special directions may be noted:

To Use Sulphuric Acid.—Dilute a few drops in 20 times its volume of water, and apply to stains with a brush. Take care this does not touch a cut on the flesh or fall upon fabrics of woolen or cotton, as it will take out their color and eat holes in them.

To Use Oxalic Acid.—Make a weak solution of oxalic acid and water, and apply with a brush or rag. Take care this does not get into any sores and cuts, as it will inflame them. On healthy skin its action is as mild as lemon juice.

Or dampen the stain and hold it over the fumes of an old-fashioned sulphur match, freshly lighted. Or burn a small piece of sulphur out of doors and hold the stain in the fumes. Care must, of course, be taken not to burn the flesh or inhale the fumes of burning sulphur.

The above are specially useful for fruit stains.

To Remove Stubborn Stains.—Mix oxalic acid and cream of tartar in equal proportions, and keep the mixture in an old paper box among toilet articles. This box should be marked "Poison," and kept out of the reach of children. Wet the stain with warm water and sprinkle with this preparation, rubbing until the stain disappears. Then wash the hands with soap and rinse well. This will remove the most stubborn ink and dye stains.

To Soften the Hands.—Keep on the toilet stand near the soap a dish of oatmeal, and rub it freely on the hands after washing. This will cleanse and soften the skin.

Or use corn meal in the same manner.

Or keep at hand a quantity of clean white sand. The artificial sort, made by crushing quartz or flint stone and sold for filters, is preferable to sea sand or ordinary sand, since it has sharper edges. Mix a handful of sand with hot soapsuds, and wash and rub the hands with this mixture for several minutes. The sand may be cleansed by pouring fresh water over it and draining through a filter. It can be used again and again. This method softens and removes the calluses caused by housework. The hands may afterwards be rubbed with oatmeal or corn meal, as above, and treated with cold cream or some other simple lotion.

Or a pair of white kid gloves may be turned inside out and brushed over with cold cream or any melted mixture of wax, oil, lard, or other unguent. These gloves may then be drawn on the hands and worn at night.

Or the hands may be rubbed at night with cold cream, mutton tallow, or honey, and a large pair of gloves drawn on. In the morning the hands should be thoroughly washed with some good toilet soap, and rubbed with oatmeal or corn meal and any simple lotion. The following mixtures are recommended to use with gloves at night to soften and whiten the hands:

Put in a quart glass fruit jar ¼ pound of grated or shaved castile soap. Pour over this ½ pint of alcohol, and let stand in a warm place, shaking frequently until the soap is dissolved. Add 1 ounce of glycerin and oil of almonds, perfume with a few drops of any essential oil, and seal tightly.

Or put ½ pound of grated castile or other hard white soap in a double boiler; pour over it 1 gill of olive oil, and dissolve with gentle heat. Add 1½ ounces of mutton tallow, mix thoroughly, remove from the fire, and add 2 fluid ounces of alcohol and a few drops of any essential oil as perfume.

Or shave together in a flat glass dish or on a marble slab 1 ounce of spermaceti, 1 ounce of white wax, and 1 ounce of gum camphor. Mix with olive oil to a stiff paste.

Or mix 1 ounce of glycerin and ½ ounce of ammonia with ½ ounce of rose water.

Chapped Hands.—Substances recommended for chapped hands may be distinguished as follows: solid unguents, such as spermaceti and other forms of wax, lard, unsalted butter, mutton suet, tallow, and the like; liquid unguents, such as glycerin, yolk of egg, honey, almond oil, linseed oil, and olive oil; various substances which have specific soothing properties, as borax, bitter almonds, bran (decoction of), balsam of fir, camphor, sal soda, carbolic acid, quince seed, raisins, oatmeal; various flavoring and coloring extracts and perfumes.

The objects sought in using these substances are as follows:

The solid and liquid unguents are employed to hold the specific remedial agent in suspension, and to give consistency to the mass so as to make it easier to apply them; also to prevent their speedy evaporation. The various remedial agents are selected according to their several properties and the results desired. These vary in their effects with different individuals and also according to the condition of the skin. A little experience will indicate which to employ under given conditions. Coloring extracts and perfume may, of course, be used according to taste. With these thoughts in mind it is an easy matter to prepare a stock of emollients suited to one's ideas and experience, based upon a solid unguent if a paste or salve is desired, or upon a liquid unguent if a lotion is preferred, and containing such remedial agents, coloring matter, etc., as are desired.

Glycerin for the Hands.—Glycerin may be used pure or scented with any essential oil. Rub on the hands at night with the same motion as when washing them, either before or after the hands have been chapped, or apply immediately after they have been chilled by exposure. Soft chamois-skin gloves worn at night will prevent this and other preparations from making grease spots on bed linen.

To soften and whiten the hands, use a mixture of two thirds glycerin and one third rose water.

Or, to prepare glycerin paste for toilet use, put 1 ounce of any good transparent toilet soap in 4 ounces of soft water or rose water, and add 5 ounces of glycerin. Dissolve all with gentle heat, stir in 20 ounces of additional glycerin, pour into a glass fruit jar, and when nearly cold perfume with a few drops of any essential oil.

Or simmer with gentle heat in a double boiler 1 ounce of glycerin, 2 ounces of olive oil, and 2 drams of spermaceti. Apply to the hands night and morning.

Or mix 3 ounces of glycerin, 1 yolk of egg, and 30 grains of carbolic acid, and beat up to an emulsion with an egg beater. Rub into the skin several times daily.

Or simmer 1 dram of quince seed in ½ pint of boiling water for 10 or 15 minutes; strain out the quince mucilage through a piece of cheese cloth, and to it add 1 ounce of glycerin, 1 ounce of borax, and 6 ounces of soft water or rose water. Apply to the hands two or three times a day.

Bran for the Hands.—Boil a small quantity of bran in a linen bag. Put both the juice and the boiled bran in the washbowl, add warm or hot water, and wash the hands with or without soap. This is perhaps the best and simplest treatment for the redness, dryness, and roughness caused by housework and exposure. After washing, the hands may be rubbed with a few drops of honey or a lotion composed of ¼ pound of honey, ¼ pound of sal soda, and 1 pint of water. Mix well and heat without boiling.

Linseed Oil for the Hands.—This is good for chapped hands, and also for burns and sprains. It has the advantage of being cheap and almost always available.

Honey for the Hands.—This may be used when the skin is dry, hard, and rough. Moisten the hands and rub the honey in well. After a while wash them thoroughly in bran water or some other liquid preparation, and they will be perfectly clean and soft.

Camphor for Chapped Hands.—Camphor cakes or balls, to prevent chapped hands, may be made as follows:

Melt 3 drams of spermaceti and 4 drams of white wax. Add 1 ounce of almond oil. Moisten 3 drams of camphor with spirits of wine, and mix up all together. Run this into molds or make up into balls in the same manner as butter balls are made.

Or, for an ointment, melt together gum camphor, 3 drams; beeswax, 3 drams; olive oil, 2 ounces. Apply at night, and wear chamois-skin gloves.

Other Remedies for Chapped Hands.—Mix white wax, 4 drams; olive oil, 2 drams; spermaceti, 18 grains.

Or unsalted butter, ¼ pound; rose water, 1 wineglassful; yolks of eggs, 2; honey, 1 tablespoonful. Mix and stir in finely ground oatmeal to make a paste of the consistency of butter. Apply at night and wear gloves.

Or use almond paste instead of oatmeal in the last.

Or mix equal parts of white mutton tallow, unsalted butter, beeswax, and stoned raisins. Simmer until the raisins are dried up but not burned. Strain into molds to cool. This preparation smarts chapped hands, but quickly heals them.

Camphor Ice. — Oil of sweet almonds, 1 ounce; spermaceti, 2 ounces; white wax, 1 ounce; camphor, ¼ ounce. Melt these ingredients in a double boiler, and pour in molds of proper size and form.

Powder for the Hands.—Common starch reduced to powder by grinding with a knife or in a pestle is a good substitute for talcum powder for the hands. This is always at hand. When taking the hands out of suds or dishwater, or after washing them when they have been chilled by exposure, rinse them thoroughly, wipe them, and apply the starch while they are still damp, covering the whole surface. This is cheap, convenient, and easy to try.

MANICURING

Finger Nails. — The condition of the finger nails is one of the best tests of the care given to the toilet. Well-groomed finger nails are, as far as they go, a mark of refinement. Needless to say, the toilet for any social occasion is not complete until the nails have been thoroughly cleaned, trimmed, and, if possible, manicured. Young men are usually the worst offenders in this respect, and they would often have cause to blush if they should hear the comments caused by their appearances in society with finger nails "decorated in mourning."

Machinists and others whose work tends to cause the finger nails to become grimy will find it helpful to insert a little lard or cold cream under the nails each morning. Housewives will find this a good plan when blacking stoves.

The most useful article for use on the nails is a small orange stick, which can be obtained for a trifle at any drug store. With this the nails can be cleaned each time the hands are washed and the skin which adheres to the nails carefully pushed back. This may also be done with a dry towel. It will prevent the skin from cracking about the roots of the nails and forming hangnails. This method practiced daily will greatly improve the general appearance of the hands.

The nails should never be bitten. By this practice the appearance of the hands may be spoiled for life. To prevent children from biting their nails, rub a little bitter aloes on the tips of the fingers. If this does not effect a cure, tie glove tips upon them until the habit is given up.

Ingrowing Nails.—The finger nails do not often grow in, but when this happens a notch cut in the middle of the nail will have a tendency to draw it up from the sides.

Manicuring the Nails.—Special care and training must be bestowed upon the nails, as their condition in regard to shape, color, and texture of skin makes or mars the loveliest hand.

It is within the power of any woman possessed of average ability to become her own manicure. It takes only a few minutes each day to put the nails in perfect condition, and properly kept nails are indications of refinement. A manicure outfit will cost two or three dollars. Buy good instruments to begin with. You will need a flexible file, emery boards, buffer, orange sticks, cuticle knife, curved needle-pointed scissors, nail scissors, some red paste and white nail powder, and a good bleach of glycerin, rose water, and oxalic acid.

Begin by shaping the nail with the file. When you have finished one hand, the fingers should be dipped into a bowl of lukewarm water, into which has been poured a few drops of some pleasant antiseptic as listerine or peroxide of hydrogen. Let them remain in this some time to soften the cuticle, and then dry them with a soft towel.

With the point of the orange stick clean the nail, dipping the stick in the bleach if this is necessary. Loosen the skin around the nail with the cuticle knife. This skin should be lifted up, and not pushed down and back, as the latter movement cracks and splits the cuticle. Keep dipping the knife in the water, as it helps to lift up the cuticle, which must be well raised before it is cut. Now use the cuticle scissors, and try to trim the cuticle in one piece, otherwise you are likely to have ragged edges and hangnails.

Be extremely careful about this special part of the treatment, for the nail may be altogether spoiled by a too zealous use of the cuticle knife and scissors. Use your red paste sparingly, and rub it well into the nails with the palm of your hand. It is better to dip the fingers in the water again and dry thoroughly, as you cannot polish a wet nail. Cut off a hangnail with the nail scissors, and smooth the edge of the nail with the emery boards. Dip the buffer or polisher in the nail powder. Place the center of the buffer on the nail, and rub slightly.

In a short time you will find it very easy to manicure your own nails.

To Whiten the Nails. — First cleanse and soften the nails by soaking in soft water in which a little pure toilet soap has been dissolved, and then dip the fingers into a mixture composed of 2 drams of diluted sulphuric acid, 1 dram of tincture of myrrh, and 4 ounces of soft water. Rinse with clear water and polish.

Or, to remove stains and discolorations, moisten a chamois buffer or a piece of chamois in a mixture of lemon juice and water, or vinegar, and water. Dip it into powdered pumice stone or putty powder, and apply carefully until the stain is removed. But rub as little as possible, and do not use these substances oftener than is necessary, as their constant use tends to make the nails thick and coarse.

To Toughen the Nails.—Mix 8 grains of pure rectified tar with ½ ounce of cold cream, rectified lard, or suet. Apply liberally to the nails at night and draw on a pair of loose gloves.

To Polish the Nails.—Apply, with a chamois buffer, a mixture of 1 ounce each of finely powdered emery and cinnabar, softened with olive oil, almond oil, or the essential oil of bitter almonds.

Diseases of the Nails.—Splinters under the nails which cannot easily be drawn out by pincers may be removed by softening the nail with potash lye diluted with an equal quantity of water. Apply this with a brush, then scrape the nail until the splinter is laid bare and can be removed. To check the action of the lye when necessary rinse with clear water and apply vinegar or lemon juice. In all cases, however, when foreign bodies get under the nails, it is best to consult a physician.

The white spots which superstitious people, half in fun, sometimes say are produced by having told lies, are caused by air getting under the nails during their growth and being confined there.

CHAPTER XIX

TOILET PREPARATIONS

TOILET PREPARATIONS—SIMPLE HOME PREPARATIONS—ALMOND MILK CREAM AND PASTE—COLD CREAM—AROMATIC VINEGAR—TOILET POWDERS—ROUGE—ESSENCES AND PERFUMES

TOILET PREPARATIONS

Recipes for the Toilet.—The enormous array of mixtures of all sorts for the toilet evinces equally the popular interest in these recipes, and the whims, caprices, and vagaries of their makers. At first glance the number and variety of recipes recommended by standard authorities is bewildering. A careful study of these preparations, however, and their tabulation in the form of charts for comparison, discloses the fact that the number of remedial agents contained in them is relatively small. The various forms in which these recipes appear are merely so many attempts to attract the notice of the public, whether by appealing to its taste or its convenience. The same ingredients, for example, may be compounded so as to form washes, lotions, emulsions, creams, or pastes, according to the degree of dilution preferred by the individual user. Standard recipes differ also by varying the proportions of the same ingredients recommended. Very often these ingredients will be the same with the exception of the perfumes. Needless to say the latter may be varied to suit the preference of the user.

There are, of course, certain standard types of toilet preparations. These vary according to the different bases, remedial agents, and the kind and amount of liquids employed for diluting them. A few words on each of these subjects will assist the reader in making a satisfactory selection.

To Save Money.—Practical suggestions and instructions for preparing all kinds of toilet preparations are of universal interest and value. Many toilet preparations made according to recipes given in this section are widely advertised for sale. The cost of advertising these articles and placing them upon the market is usually from 50 to 80 per cent of their retail price. The purchaser has to pay all this in addition to the original cost of the ingredients and the labor of compounding. Moreover, it is impossible to tell what the ingredients are or whether they are of good quality. Very often they are injurious and even poisonous. Adulteration and substitution are very common. Anyone can save from 75 to 95 per cent on the cost of these by compounding them himself. He will know exactly what the preparations are composed of, and also that the ingredients are fresh and of good quality.

To Make Money. — Some persons, however, have little skill in compounding, or have not the time or the proper facilities for the work. While anyone can prepare these articles, it is, of course, true that a person may become very expert by giving special time and attention to them, and especially by the practice of making up prescriptions in fairly large quantities. Hence anyone who has an aptitude for work of this kind can make a good deal of money by preparing these articles in quantity, putting them up neatly in jars, bottles, boxes, etc., and affixing to them neat printed labels. These can be sold on shares at the local stores, or bought by friends and neighbors, or peddled from house to house by employing young people on a commission basis. Mail-order business can also be worked up for the sale of these preparations. The recipes are taken from the formulas of manufacturers of standard toilet articles. Such preparations also make a very popular bazaar at a church fair. The work of compounding them in such cases can be delegated to a committee.

Bases.—The standard bases for solid and semifluid preparations, as pastes, creams, and emulsions, are white wax, spermaceti, suet, lard, yolk or white of egg, and various soaps.

Animal fats, as lards, suet, and the like, must be specially refined and prepared for toilet purposes. This may be done at home by melting and simmering the fat slowly with gentle heat, and straining it through linen one or more times. On the farm these animal fats are easily obtained and consequently inexpensive, but unless alcohol or other preservatives are mixed with them they tend to become rancid. Hence small quantities at a time should be prepared, and care should be taken not to employ such preparations when they become in the least degree sour. The same caution applies to compounds containing the white or yolk of eggs and honey.

White wax, spermaceti, castile and other soaps as bases are free from these objections, and recipes containing them are to be preferred when such ingredients can conveniently be obtained. In compounding recipes having these solid unguents as bases they are first melted slowly with gentle heat, and while in a melted condition the other ingredients are added. They may also be "cut" or dissolved in alcohol and spirits.

Liquid Bases.—Certain toilet preparations, as emulsions, lotions, washes, and the like, omit the above solids or employ them only in small quantities, and in their place use certain oils and other liquids as bases. The principal liquid bases are almond oil, olive oil, glycerin, honey, and the like. These have a double value: they tend to soothe and also to feed the skin. They are, therefore, among the most deservedly popular of all ingredients.

Other Bases.—Gum arabic, quince seed, and white paste are also employed as bases when a certain degree of adhesiveness is desired, as in the preparation of bandoline and pomades for the hair and beard. The quince seeds are prepared by simmering them gently in rose water until they form a stiff jell. This must then be strained through a fine sieve to remove the hulls. Gum arabic may be dissolved in warm water.

Bases of Powders.—Wheat starch is the standard base for homemade toilet powders, but other materials often employed are fuller's earth, French chalk, and pearl white. Almond meal, like almond oil, has the double property of serving as a base and also as a remedial agent.

Remedial Agents.—This term is employed to describe certain ingredients used in toilet preparations which have specific curative properties. Some of the bases already mentioned, notably almonds, fall also under this heading. Among others of especial value may be noted substances which soothe and feed the skin, as the yolk of egg, honey, and cocoa butter; substances which are mildly astringent, as lemon juice, alum, spirits, and benzoin; and other specifics, as glycerin, camphor, and sulphur, whose action varies with different persons. These agents are in most cases of a harmless character except when otherwise stated.

Mineral Agents.—The use of mineral drugs in toilet preparations cannot be too earnestly deprecated. In many cases they are immediately harmful, and defeat the very object for which they are intended, as in the case of bismuth, which frequently blackens the skin. All compounds and preparations containing lead in any form are positively dangerous and sometimes give rise to blood poison. These mineral compounds are often recommended as heroic remedies, to be tried when other measures have failed; as, for example, for the removal of obstinate freckles, moles, pimples, and similar disfigurements. They are very common in hair dyes and pomades, and are too often employed under delusion, caused by the misleading statements of friends, beauty doctors, or others, and by publishers of otherwise reputable books.

Two statements we desire to earnestly make and stand by: first, mineral drugs in toilet preparations are dangerous; and, secondly, they are not necessary. The simple and harmless remedies hereinafter given, if patiently and skillfully applied according to directions, will, in due course of time, accomplish the results intended, and develop the most perfect complexion that the individual is capable of.

The use of mineral drugs, on the other hand, whatever the immediate benefits derived from them may appear to be, will in the end defeat its own object by producing after effects ruinous to the complexion, and the last state of the deluded individual who employs them will indeed be worse than the first.

Diluents or Vehicles.—Distilled water, various perfumed toilet waters, as rose water, together with alcohol, rectified spirits of wine, and other spirits, are the liquids most often recommended for diluting toilet preparations to the consistency of creams, lotions, washes, and the like.

Distilled water may be prepared at home by attaching a tube to the spout of the teakettle, immersing as much of its length as possible in a basin of water shielded from the fire and kept cold, if convenient, with ice, and collecting the condensed steam at the opposite end of the tube in a fruit jar or other receptacle. The object of this process is to remove all impurities held in suspension, as lime and other minerals which are found in hard water; also vegetable and animal matter and other impurities. In winter clean snow, melted, is equivalent to distilled water. Rain water collected in a clean vessel is a good substitute. The ordinary water supply, softened if necessary by means elsewhere recommended, will usually answer every purpose. Elder-flower water, orange-flower water, and other perfumed toilet waters are often recommended, but rose water or plain distilled or soft water may be used as a substitute, if preferred, in all cases.

Perfumes.—Substances used as perfumes commonly occur in several forms, i. e., the attar or essential oil, the essence, and the tincture or the "water," depending upon the degree of dilution. They can also be obtained in powdered form, as in sachets. The most convenient form in which to purchase perfumes is the otto or attar, i. e., the essential oil. This may be purchased in small quantity and employed according to taste, a few drops being sufficient to perfume most toilet preparations in quantities suitable for domestic use. The scent of these perfumes is familiar to most persons, but they can easily be inspected at a drug store and a selection can be made. It is not necessary, of course, to purchase or have on hand each and all the different perfumes recommended. In fact, perfumes are now used very much less than they were formerly, and a strong scent of cologne, musk, or other odor about an individual is regarded as a mark of vulgarity. Many ladies who enjoy perfumes compromise by selecting any particular odor they prefer, as violet, rose, lavender, or heliotrope, and employ this exclusively in the toilet. Any of the essential oils may be substituted freely for the others, and the quantity may be varied to suit the taste as determined by experiment.

Coloring Matters. — The standard coloring matters employed for lip salve, rouge, cold cream, and the like are as follows: for rose pink or red, alkanet root or dragon's blood; for yellow or orange, palm oil or annotto; for blue, finely powdered indigo; for green, spinach leaves. Other coloring matter, as the various lakes and other mineral substances, are intentionally omitted.

Utensils Required. — The utensils required in compounding the following recipes are usually at hand in every household. A small pair of druggist's scales or balances is a great convenience, and will be found useful in many ways. A graduate glass, marked for the measurement of fluid ounces, is also useful, and can be obtained of any druggist or dealer in photographic materials. A glass of the size of 4 or 8 ounces may be obtained at from 25 cents or less to 50 cents.

In addition to the above a small spatula or thin, broad-bladed, flexible knife, a small mortar and pestle, and one or two short pieces of glass tube or rod for stirring, will be found convenient. Ordinary porcelain-lined saucepans are the best receptacles in which to melt and mix the necessary ingredients. A double boiler is convenient, but if this cannot be had, a large saucepan may be partly filled with water, and a smaller one containing the ingredients to be melted placed within it so that the water will reach part way up the sides. A few nails or other solid objects placed in the bottom of the large saucepan will raise the small one so as to permit the water to circulate freely beneath it. In this way the ingredients may be melted without danger of burning or sticking to the pan. Care must be taken that the water in the outer saucepan does not all evaporate or boil up and flood the inner one.

Directions for Compounding. — First place the solid or liquid constituents used as a base in a double boiler or saucepan, as above suggested. Simmer with a gentle heat, but without boiling. When the solids are melted and the mass is warm enough to flow freely, first put in the coloring matter, if any, and simmer until the color has been fully incorporated. Next strain through linen while still hot.

Return the mixture to the double boiler, and while hot add such specific remedial agents as the oil of bitter almonds, honey, glycerin, benzoin, lemon juice, alum, etc.

If rose water or distilled water is to be added to form an emulsion, lotion, or wash, take the mixture off the fire and add the water gradually, stirring briskly with a spoon or egg beater to insure forming a perfect emulsion. The last ingredient to be added is always the perfume, and this should be done after the mixture has cooled somewhat, but before it sets. Perfumes are volatile, and if added to a heated mixture are likely to be wasted by evaporation.

Compounding of Pastes and Powders.—The above instructions apply especially to liquid compounds. The solid constituents of pastes may be rubbed together in a mortar, and kneaded with the hands or with a spatula on a marble or metal slab, a clean piece of zinc, or a kneading board. In some cases an egg beater can be employed if the consistency of the mixture will allow it. Almonds for pastes may be reduced in a mortar to the proper consistency by moistening them with rose water and grinding them with a pestle, or by heating them with water in a saucepan until the mass assumes a granular consistency, somewhat similar to cooked oatmeal. Both methods are employed, but the former is the more common. The materials for toilet powders may be compounded by simple mixture in a mortar or other suitable receptacle.

General Suggestions.—We would suggest to the novice that it will be well to first prepare a small quantity of some good toilet powder (preferably based on wheat starch), a good cold cream, and, if desired, one of the liquid emulsions or lotions as a wash for the face and hands.

Other preparations, as pastes, rouge, aromatic vinegar, and the like, may be made up as occasion demands. Persons experienced in these matters will, of course, need no suggestions.

Tables.—A number of tables have been prepared which contain practically all the standard recipes for the toilet in use by beauty doctors and others in all parts of the world. An exception to this statement has already been noted; all recipes containing preparations of lead and other injurious mineral drugs have been absolutely excluded. A list of the different ingredients is given at the left of the table, and the name of each preparation is quoted at the top. Under each name and opposite the names of the different ingredients will be found the amount of each to be employed. General directions for compounding the following recipes have already been given. Special directions follow each table when necessary.

SIMPLE HOME PREPARATIONS

The following simple homemade preparations are suggested in addition to the more elaborate receipts given later:

To Remove Freckles. — Preparations recommended for the removal of freckles are usually of an acid character containing alum, lemon juice, horse-radish, buttermilk, and the like; also mineral drugs, as salts of lead, mercury, bismuth, and others. It cannot be too clearly stated that all such preparations are distinctly injurious to the complexion, and their frequent use is not to be recommended. Most young persons of light complexion are annoyed by freckles, but these ordinarily pass away in later life, and the wisest possible course is to pay little attention to them and allow nature to effect a cure. The application of preparations advertised to remove freckles, the ingredients of which are unknown, should be avoided lest they contain bismuth, which is liable to blacken the skin, or lead or mercury, which are active mineral poisons. The following recipes, the active principles of which are principally animal or vegetable acids, are less injurions; but it must be borne in mind that all cosmetics of an astringent nature do their work by contracting the pores, which thus become weakened and in time are unable to discharge their natural functions. The result may be, in later life, wrinkles and sallowness, and the last state of the complexion may be distinctly worse than the first.

Grate a fresh horse-radish root very fine, cover with fresh buttermilk, and let stand over night. Strain through cheese cloth, and wash the face night and morning with the resulting liquor.

Or squeeze the juice of a lemon into half a tumbler of water, and use two or three times daily as a face wash.

Or dissolve in lemon juice as much sugar as it will hold, and apply with a soft brush frequently until the freckles disappear.

Or apply a lotion containing glycerin, but this is hardly a specific.

Or mix 2 ounces of lemon juice with 1 dram of confectioner's sugar or powdered rock candy and ½ dram of powdered borax. Let stand for 4 or 5 days, shaking occasionally, and apply with a camel's-hair brush two or three times a day.

Or to 1 pint of distilled soft water add 1 dram of sal ammoniac and ½ ounce of cologne. Rub on the face and hands two or three times daily.

Or dissolve in 4 drams of rose water 1 dram of muriate of ammonia, and apply two or three times a day with a camel's-hair brush.

Or put in a double boiler 1 ounce of grated Venice soap and 1 ounce of pure soft water (or distilled water); melt with gentle heat and continue the heating until the water is evaporated and only the melted soap remains. Remove from the fire, and stir in ½ ounce of lemon juice, ¼ ounce of oil of bitter almonds, ¼ ounce of deliquidated oil of tartar, and 3 drops of oil rhodium. This is said to be a recipe of the celebrated Mme. de Maintenon, the mistress of Louis XIV of France.

Or this mixture can be prepared by grating the soap, pouring over it the lemon juice and other ingredients, exposing it to direct sunlight, and shaking occasionally until it is of the right consistency. Apply to the face at night.

Or mix ¼ pint of tincture of tolu, ½ pint of tincture of benzoin, and ¼ ounce of oil of rosemary. Put a teaspoonful of this mixture in one fourth tumblerful of pure soft water, and apply to the face with a soft sponge two or three times a day.

Or put in a glass fruit jar or bottle 6 ounces of fresh oxgall. Add 2 ounces of rock candy, 2 ounces of rock salt, 1½ scruples of camphor, 1 dram of borax, and 1½ scruples of burned alum. (But remember that this is an heroic remedy.) Apply with a brush or sponge at night, and wash the face thoroughly next morning.

Or mix 2 ounces each of aqua ammonia, sweet oil, and limewater.

But none of these preparations can be regarded as desirable lotions for regular or frequent use.

Cucumber Milk. — Slice three or four large cucumbers with the skin on, add ½ pint of water, boil, stir to a soft pulp, cool, and strain. Mix 1½ ounces of this cucumber juice, 1½ ounces of 95 per cent alcohol, and ¼ ounce of grated castile soap. Let stand in a warm place over night; next day add 8 ounces more of the cucumber juice, 1 ounce of oil of sweet almonds, 20 drops of tincture of benzoin, and 5 grains of boracic acid. Shake well before using, and apply to the face two or three times a day with a soft cloth or sponge.

Milk for the Skin.—New milk, skimmed milk, and buttermilk each possess properties peculiar to itself, and they all make useful and simple washes having a general emollient action on the skin. If used daily they tend to make the skin soft, smooth, and white, and to preserve it from the effects of exposure to weather. Buttermilk is useful for freckles and acne, and relieves itching and local irritations of the skin. Pure, fresh cream is a simple and effective preventive of chapped hands and lips, and is excellent to cure these evils.

Milk as a cosmetic may be improved by infusing in it freshly grated horse-radish, or infusing in new milk or buttermilk a quantity of flowers of sulphur. These are useful remedies for freckles and other discolorations and slight eruptions of the skin.

Or mix flowers of sulphur with a little new milk and let stand an hour or two to settle. Pour off the milk from the sediment, and rub well into the skin before washing. This mixture is for immediate use only, and must be prepared daily. It may be prepared at night with evening milk and used the next morning, but not afterwards. Two or three tablespoonfuls are all that need be prepared at a time.

Or boil 1 cupful of fine Scotch oatmeal—not breakfast food—in 1 pint of boiling water until it forms a clear liquid. Use a double boiler, or place the saucepan containing the oatmeal in an open kettle or pan of boiling water to prevent sticking or burning. Strain the clear liquid through a cloth, boil again, and strain a second time. Add rose water, elder-flower water, or orange-flower water until the liquor has the consistency of milk. Add a few drops of your favorite perfume, and bottle for use.

Lemon Juice.—Dilute fresh lemon juice with five or six times its volume of pure soft water. This, however, should not be used too frequently on account of its acid quality and tendency to impair the work of the pores of the skin. It may, however, be used on occasion to relieve itching or local irritation.

Or mix equal parts of lemon juice, toilet water, and alcohol. Let stand over night, pour off the clear liquid, and strain through silk or linen.

Kalydor. — Dissolve 2 drams of tincture of benzoin in 1 pint of rose water, and use as a face wash for the complexion.

Magnesia Cream.—Mix fine powdered magnesia with rose water to a thin cream, dip the face in warm water to open the pores, apply a glycerin lotion, and afterwards apply the magnesia cream. Let dry and remove with a soft towel.

Or dissolve fuller's earth in water, stir well, then let it settle, and use once or twice daily.

Honey.—Honey is a favorite ingredient in various lotions under the name of "honey water," "balsam of honey," and the like. The term "honey water" is also applied to certain combinations of perfumes that do not, in fact, contain honey.

To prepare honey water from honey, put in a 2-quart fruit jar 4 ounces of pure white honey with ½ ounce of fresh grated lemon peel, ½ ounce each of calamayta, benzoin, and storax, ¼ ounce of cloves, and ¼ ounce of nutmeg. Add 2 ounces each of rose water and elder-flower water and 12 fluid ounces of 95 per cent alcohol. Let stand 3 or 4 days, shaking frequently, run through a filter, and bottle for use.

Or, for balsam of honey, mix with gentle heat 8 ounces of pure white honey and 2 ounces of best quality glycerin. Let stand until cool, stir in 2 fluid ounces of 95 per cent alcohol, and add 10 drops of the essence of ambergris.

Glycerin.—When pure, glycerin is a colorless viscid liquid, having a sweet taste and without odor. All the ordinary fats contain glycerin, which is produced by treating animal fats with alkalies, such as caustic soda or potash, as is done in the manufacture of soap. Glycerin is a by-product of soap factories. It may also be produced by treating fats with superheated steam, as is done in the manufacture of candles. Hence glycerin is also a by-product of candle factories.

Glycerin mixes freely with water, and pure glycerin absorbs about one half its own weight from the atmosphere. It is an excellent solvent, and is an important ingredient of pomades, toilet soaps, and cosmetics. Glycerin is recommended as a lotion for irritation of the skin and for itching; also as a preventive against sunburn, chaps, and redness from exposure to the weather. A preparation of 1 ounce of glycerin to 19 ounces of pure soft water is about right for regular use as a face wash, and is an excellent vehicle in which to dissolve various remedies.

Or 1 ounce of glycerin to 9 ounces of water may be used for chapped hands and lips, or whenever a strong solution is desired.

Borax.—Dissolve 5 drams of borax in 1 pint of pure soft or distilled water, and use as a wash for sore gums or nipples, boils, or any other irritation of the skin or mucous membrane.

Or combine borax with glycerin in the proportion of 6 drams of borax and 1½ ounces of pure glycerin; add 16 ounces of rose water. This may be used regularly as a face wash.

Or mix ¾ ounce of powdered borax with 1 ounce of pure glycerin and 16 ounces of camphor oil. Apply to the face with a soft cloth or sponge two or three times a day; let dry, and rinse with clear water.

Or to 1 ounce of glycerin add 2 ounces of fresh lemon juice, 1 pint of pure distilled water, and 1 pint of rose water. Apply to the face several times a day and let dry before rinsing.

Lotions for Tan or Sunburn.—These are based principally on oil of almonds, with the addition of castile soap and rock candy, and contain various remedial agents, including astringents, as alum and lemon juice, also benzoin, tincture of tolu, tartar oil, ox gall, and the like. They are diluted usually with alcohol or any perfumed toilet water, for which plain distilled or soft water may be substituted. And they may be perfumed with any essential oil or essence preferred. Apply any of these lotions to the face with a small sponge or a soft linen rag. Let it dry on without rubbing, and afterwards wash the face with soft warm water.

The following is a simple remedy for tan or sunburn: apply peroxide of hydrogen, pouring a teaspoonful or more in the palm of the hand, and applying it equally over the hands, arms, and face. Let it dry without rubbing. After it is thoroughly dry, apply any good lotion. This will rapidly bleach the skin without injuring the most delicate complexion.

bly the nut or kernel of the almond, of which there are two sorts: the sweet and the bitter. The almond is the fruit of a tree very similar to the peach tree. It is cultivated extensively in southern Europe, and is now grown largely in California. Almonds are much cheaper now than they were formerly, and are likely to become cheaper still. The almond contains two active principles: an odorless fixed oil of a light color, which is obtained by pressure; and the oil of bitter almonds, which is a volatile oil obtained by crushing bitter almonds in cold water and by distillation. This latter oil is colorless, limpid, and has the distinctive odor of bitter almonds, similar to that of prussic acid. It sometimes contains prussic acid, in which case, if taken internally even in minute quantities, it is a deadly poison.

The ordinary almonds of commerce are sweet almonds of the thin-shelled varieties. They contain about 50 per cent or more of almond oil, which may be extracted by boiling in water or by softening the kernels with water or other liquid, rubbing them in a mortar, and mixing the resulting mass with various other ingredients. Or the oils of commerce may be utilized. Preparations of almonds for toilet purposes are variously known as "milk of almonds," "almond cream," "almond paste," and the like. They are likewise

LOTIONS FOR TAN AND SUNBURN

Castile Soap					1 oz.		½ lb.					4 oz.
Ox Gall	1 lb.								1 oz.			
Borax	2 dr.					½ dr.				½ dr.		1 dr.
Almonds, Bitter			½ oz.						¼ oz.			8 oz.
" " Oil of					¼ oz.							
" Sweet "				1 oz.								
Rock Candy	½ oz.					1 dr.				1 dr.	8 oz.	
" Salt											2 oz.	
Camphor	1 dr.										1½ scr.	
Benzoin		1 pt.						1 pt.				2 dr.
Tinc. Tolu		½ pt.					½ oz.	½ pt.				
Alum	1 dr.										1½ scr.	
Lemon Juice					½ oz.	2 oz.			½ oz.	2 oz.		
Tartar Oil					¼ oz.				¼ oz.			
Limewater				1 oz.								
Alcohol (95%)							1 qt.					
Rose Water		¼ pt.	½ pt.				1 gal.	½ gill		2 qt.		1 qt.
Any Essential Oil		½ oz.			3 dr.		4 dr.	¼ oz.	3 dr.	20 m.		

ALMOND MILK CREAM AND PASTE

Almond Preparations.—The prime favorite among all ingredients of the various toilet preparations is probaknown as English, French, or other "milk of roses," and by similar fanciful titles, arising from the various added ingredients and the wishes of the different manufacturers.

Among the ingredients most often added to almonds in these preparations are solid unguents, as white wax, spermaceti, white paste, and the like; also liquid unguents, as glycerin, honey, the yolk of egg, and similar substances. Perfumed and distilled water, alcohol, and other spirits are often used as vehicles. And various specifics for the complexion, as benzoin, salts of tartar, alum, lemon juice, and other cosmetics, may be added. All recipes containing mineral substances, as salts of lead, mercury, bismuth, and the like, are here omitted.

The oil of almonds is a gentle emollient. It not only softens but also feeds the skin. Hence it is a specific for the complexion, and is especially useful for chaps, sunburn, redness, and other local irritations. The following are standard recipes for milk, cream, or paste of almonds, in the order mentioned. Among these are proprietary articles which are sold under various fanciful titles at exorbitant prices, but which can be readily prepared at home by anyone who cares to take the necessary pains, with the advantage of knowing that the materials are fresh and pure and that the mixture contains nothing injurious.

Milk of Almonds.—The principal object to be attained in preparing milk of almonds or milk of roses is to form a perfect emulsion which will not separate, or which, if it separates after standing, may be emulsified by shaking. Such substances as soap, gum, wax, and the like, are added for this purpose, and all such preparations will be improved by beating thoroughly with an egg beater or otherwise after all the ingredients have been incorporated.

The milk of roses varies from the milk of almonds merely in being perfumed with rose water or the essence or attar of roses. Other perfumes are frequently added, but in such limited quantities that the scent of roses predominates.

Rub up in a mortar 1 ounce of sweet blanched almonds by adding, a little at a time, ½ pint of distilled water or pure soft water, mixing and rubbing constantly until a smooth, homogeneous milky emulsion is formed. Finally strain the resulting mixture through a piece of net or gauze to remove the coarser particles. This is the common "milk of almonds" of perfumers, to which glycerin, various cosmetics, perfumes, and coloring matter may be added as desired.

Or mix in a mortar 5 drams of blanched almonds, 2 drams of white lump sugar or rock candy, and 1 dram of powdered gum arabic, and rub up the whole together in the same manner, adding distilled water, a little at a time, until 8 fluid ounces have been incorporated. This is an Irish formula, and is especially useful when it is desired to add oils, gums, or balsams.

Or milk of bitter almonds or emulsion of bitter almonds may be prepared in the same manner by substituting blanched bitter almonds for the sweet variety. The milk of bitter almonds is especially recommended to relieve itching and irritation (especially that caused by shaving), and as a remedy for freckles, but it develops prussic acid, a very active poison, and hence must not be swallowed or applied except in very minute quantities to a raw surface.

Or put in a mortar 5 ounces of blanched sweet almonds, and add slowly 1 pint of distilled water, rubbing up the almonds with the water until a complete emulsion is formed. Dissolve in a double boiler ½ ounce of spermaceti, ¼ ounce of white wax, and ¼ ounce of castile soap. Pour into this mixture in a fine stream the milk of almonds, stirring constantly. Remove from the fire, and stir in a mixture of 6 ounces of alcohol, 5 drops of oil of bitter almonds, and

1 dram of oil of bergamot. Strain through a piece of net or gauze and bottle for use.

Or mix in a mortar 1 ounce of sweet almonds and 3 ounces of bitter almonds, adding slowly 1 quart of pure soft or distilled water. Stir in 1½ pounds of sugar, and perfume with orange-flower water or otherwise, as desired. Strain and bottle for use.

Or rub up in a mortar 1½ ounces of sweet blanched almonds, adding slowly ¾ pint of rose water. Stir in 1 dram of finely powdered castile soap and 1 dram of oil of almonds, beating up with an egg beater or otherwise to form a complete emulsion; stir in a mixture of 2½ ounces of 95 per cent alcohol and ½ fluid dram of essence of roses. Add enough rose water to make 1 pint of the whole. Add, if desired, a few drops of the essential oil of bergamot or of lavender, or the attar of roses dissolved in the alcohol.

Or rub up gradually in a mortar 2 ounces of sweet blanched almonds and 12 ounces of rose water. Mix separately with gentle heat 2 drams each of white castile soap, white wax, and oil of almonds, to which add 1 dram of oil of bergamot, 15 drops of oil of lavender, and 8 drops of attar of roses. Add this mixture to the "milk of almonds," rub up thoroughly in a mortar, beat with an egg beater or otherwise to form a perfect emulsion, and strain through silk or linen.

Enough has been said to indicate the method of compounding these recipes. The following may be prepared in the same manner:

Blanched bitter almonds, 2 ounces; distilled water, 2 ounces; salt of tar-

ALMOND CREAM, MILK OF ROSES, ETC.

	Cream of Roses.	English Milk of Roses.	Almond Milk.	French Cream of Roses.	Commercial Milk of Roses.	Queen's Lotion.	Bernhardt Cream.	Italian Milk of Almond.	Bitter-almond Cream.	Barber's Almond Cream.	Bitter Almond.	German Milk of Roses.	Tartar Oil.
Almonds, Sweet...	16 oz.	1½ oz.	1 oz.		7 lb.	5 lb.	3 lb.	16 oz.		6 lb.			
Bitter...			3 oz.	5 oz.	16 oz.			1 oz.	8 oz.				
Oil......	1 oz.	1 dr.		5 d.		16 oz.	4 oz.				1 dr.		1 oz.
Milk....													
Paste...										3 dr.		3 dr.	
White Wax	7 dr.			¼ oz.			½ oz.	1 oz.					
Spermaceti	3 dr.			½ oz.			½ oz.	1 oz.					
Castile Soap...	1 oz.	1 dr.		¼ oz.		12 oz.	¼ lb.	1 oz.					
White Sug.			1½ lb.										
Alcohol....	1 pt.	2½ oz.		6 oz.	1 gal.	3 qts.	2 qts.			1 gal.	1 oz.		
RoseWater	7 pts.	¾ pt.	1 qt.	1 pt.	5 gal.	q. s.	10 qts.	1 qt.	8 oz.	3 gal.	1 pt.	½ pt.	4 oz.
Rosemary Water...		½ pt.											
Elder-Fl. Water...			1 oz.						6 oz.				
Lavender Water...													
Tin. Storax									2 dr.				
Tinc. Benzoin.....	½ dr.										1 dr.	½ fl. oz.	
Pearlash...						8 oz.	2 oz.						
Oil of Rose		6 m.			60 m.	20 m.				20 m.			
Oil of Lavender...	½ dr.				1 oz.	4 dr.	½ oz.			1 oz.			
Oil of Tartar......				1 dr.					20 m.				20 m.
Oil of Bergamot...													
Balsam of Peru....											20 m.		

tar, ¼ dram; tincture benzoin, ½ dram. Rub up together in a mortar, beat to an emulsion, and strain.

Or blanched sweet almonds, 1 ounce; grated castile soap, 1 ounce; oil of almonds, 1 ounce; white wax, 6 drams; spermaceti, 3 drams; oil of bergamot, ½ dram; oil of lavender, ½ dram; rose water, 3 quarts; alcohol, 1 pint.

Complexion Paste.—The principal ingredients in standard pastes for the complexion consist of solid and liquid unguents, as spermaceti, wax, paste, suet, various soaps, and the like; soothing substances, as almond oil and honey; mild astringents, as lemon juice and alum; rose water and alcohol for mixing purposes, and varions perfumes.

As in other toilet preparations, the solid unguents give substance to the compound and hold the various remedial agents in suspension. Yolk of egg, almonds, honey, and the like, feed the skin, and other ingredients are used for convenience in compounding, perfuming, etc.

Any of these pastes may be colored by adding coloring matter in the process of preparation while the mixture is in a liquid state. Rich rose, pink, or red may be obtained by dissolving ½ dram of alkanet root or dragon's blood in about 8 ounces of melted fat. For orange or yellow, use palm oil or annotto. For blue, use finely powdered indigo. For green, steep spinach leaves in oil, and strain before using.

If coloring matter is not used, these pastes will be of a pure white or a slightly tinted yellow from the yolk of egg.

In compounding the above mixtures, a small marble mortar and pestle will be found convenient.

White of egg may be boiled in rose water or plain soft or distilled water. Where pulverized almonds are required, it is better to obtain the fresh nuts and pulverize them shortly before using. The nuts may be first crushed by a rolling-pin, and afterwards pulverized in a mortar. A few drops of rose water or almond oil added in the mortar will assist by softening them. An egg beater will be found convenient in thoroughly blending all the ingredients in these mixtures. Perfumes must be added while the material is in a liquid state. When oil is used, perfume may be first mingled with the oil. Spermaceti, white and other soaps, may be first reduced to liquid form by melting. Where alkanet root or other solid substances are used, the paste may be improved by straining while in a liquid condition through a linen cloth. The milk of pistachio nuts may be obtained by distilling fresh peeled nuts in an equal quantity of rose water. Simmer over a slow fire, and when melted form an emulsion with the egg beater.

With a little attention to the above instructions anyone may compound a paste for himself, and have the satisfaction of knowing that the materials are fresh and that no harmful ingredients have been used.

Almond Paste may be prepared in two ways: either in the cold or by cooking the almonds. To prepare almond paste in the cold, pound the dry kernels of sweet almonds to a fine powder in an earthenware or marble mortar. This will require time and patience. When the almonds are sufficiently fine, add just enough elder-flower, rose, or orange-flower water to make a paste of the desired consistency and perfume with some essential oil—as the attar of roses, bergamot, neroli, or any other desired. Preserve in covered glass jars.

Or, to prepare paste of bitter almonds, take equal parts of bitter and sweet almonds and proceed as before. It is not necessary to add perfumes, as the scent of the bitter almonds is sufficient.

Or add to either of the above 2 ounces of powdered spermaceti or 1 ounce of grated castile soap for each pound of almonds.

Or the white of 1 egg to each pound of almonds.

ALMOND PASTE FOR THE COMPLEXION

	Mme. de Vestus.	Amadine.	Royale.	Regia.	Amaryllis.	German.	Hunter's.	Hungarian.	Anglin's.	Hebe Liquid.	Countess.	Amandine.	Mme. de Maintenon.
White Wax						4 oz.	2 oz.						
Spermaceti			1 oz.	1 oz.		2 oz.		2 dr.					
Suet							14 oz.						
Castile Soap		1 oz.						½ oz.				3 oz.	
White Paste					8 oz.								
Simple Sirup		4 oz.											
Gum Arabic											2 oz.	2 oz.	
Honey					8 oz.						8 oz.	6 oz.	
Yolk of Egg					3							5	
White of Egg	4		1	1									1
Almonds, Sweet			8 oz.	4 oz.				2 oz.	4 lb.	4 oz.			3 oz.
" Bitter		1 oz.		4 oz.				2 oz.	1 lb.	4 oz.			4 oz.
" Oil of	½ oz.	7 lb.			16 oz.	½ pt.		½ oz.		1 oz.		2 oz.	3 oz.
" Attar of						1 dr.	1 dr.					1½ dr.	
Milk of Pistachio												8 oz.	
Alcohol										1 oz.			q. s.
Lemon Juice										6 oz.			3 oz.
Alum	½ oz.												
Rose Water			q. s.	q. s.					q. s.	2 oz.	q. s.		
Oil of Bergamot		1 oz.						12 m.					
" Cloves		½ oz.				½ dr.	½ dr.						
" Mace													
" Roses								12 m.					
Orris Powder									4 oz.				

Or, to prepare almond paste by cooking, chop or grind 24 ounces of blanched bitter almonds, which may be done by passing them through a meat cutter, cover with 8 ounces of elder-flower or orange-flower water, and cook over a slow fire, stirring constantly until the almond kernels burst and assume the consistency of paste. If the fire is too brisk or the mass is not constantly stirred, the almonds will burn and the quality of the paste will be impaired. It must be borne in mind that much of the oil of bitter almonds is volatilized by heat, and care must be taken not to breathe the fumes, which are poisonous. Before removing from the fire, stir in 4 ounces more of orange-flower or elder-flower water, and rub up the paste in a mortar to the proper consistency, adding 16 ounces of alcohol and 3 ounces of attar of roses or any other essential oil desired. Rub through a hair or other fine sieve and bottle for use.

Or, for honey-almond paste, heat in a double boiler 4 ounces of pure white honey, strain through cheese cloth, and add 4 ounces of bitter white paste, 8 ounces of expressed oil of bitter almonds, and 2½ yolks of eggs. Add the egg and the oil gradually, and beat vigorously with an egg beater or otherwise, as in preparing mayonnaise.

Or rub up together in a mortar 2 ounces of sweet and bitter almonds with 1½ ounces of oil of almonds, and add ½ ounce of ground castile soap. Stir in 12 drops of attar of roses and oil of bergamot.

Or rub up to a smooth paste in a mortar 4 ounces of bleached sweet almonds; add the white of 1 egg and equal quantities of rose water and alcohol to make a paste of the right consistency.

Or rub to a smooth paste 4 pounds of bitter almonds with elder-flower or lavender water, and beat up with this 1 pound of pure strained honey, 4 ounces of fine orris powder, 8 ounces of almond powder, and 2 ounces of oil of jasmine.

Or rub up in a mortar 4 ounces of

powdered almonds, and beat into these 3 ounces of oil of almonds and 3 ounces of lemon juice, and dilute with equal parts of alcohol and rose water to make a paste of the right consistency.

Or cover the whites of 4 eggs with rose water and bring to a boil, stirring in ½ ounce of alum and ½ ounce of oil of almonds. Evaporate the water with gentle heat, and stir constantly until the paste is of the right consistency.

COLD CREAM

Cold Creams.—The basis of most cold creams is either white wax or spermaceti or both, with almond oil or rectified animal fats, as lard, suet, and the like, to which may be added various specifics for the complexion, and distilled waters, essences, or essential oils to perfume as desired.

Cold cream is among the most useful of all toilet preparations, both as a preventive and as a remedy for sunburn and reddening of the skin by exposure, chapped hands and lips, frostbite, and other local irritations. It is also useful for whitening the hands and to prevent wrinkles. For this purpose it should be applied at night and thoroughly washed off in the morning. The hands may be protected at night by a loose pair of kid or chamois gloves.

To prepare cold cream, melt in a double boiler 2 drams of white wax, 1 ounce of spermaceti, and 3½ ounces of oil of sweet almonds. Remove from the fire and add in a thin stream 2 fluid ounces of rose water, and stir constantly until cold. Those who can use glycerin with safety may add ½ ounce to 1 ounce before the mixture sets.

Or, for a medicated cold cream, melt with gentle heat in a double boiler ½ ounce of white wax, ½ ounce of spermaceti, and 4 ounces of almond oil. Mix separately ¼ fluid ounce each of the tinctures of balsam of Peru, tolu, and benzola, to which add in a thin stream 2 fluid ounces of elder-flower water. Beat in the mean time with an egg beater or otherwise to form a complete emulsion. Pour this emulsion in a thin stream into the melted wax and oil, meantime beating with an egg beater until all the ingredients are fully incorporated. When cold, this compound will set as a permanent

COLD CREAM

	Rose Cream.	Crème de Cathay.	Wax Cream.	Cream of Roses.	Chrystalline.	French Cream.	Quince Cream.	Hudson's Cream.	Sultana Cream.	English Cream.	Georgia Cream.	Farmer's Cream.	Oriental Cream.
White Wax...	4 oz.	½ oz.	½ oz.	10 dr.	½ oz.	5 dr.		1 oz.	½ oz.	4 dr.			
Spermaceti.....		½ oz.		10 dr.	½ oz.	5 dr.		1 oz.	½ oz.	6 dr.		3 oz.	1 oz.
Lard.........				8 oz.							2 lb.	16 oz.	10 oz.
Suet..........											1 lb.		2 oz.
Quince Seed Mucilage.....							20 oz.						
Cocoa Butter...													
Almond Oil...	16 oz.	4 oz.	2 oz.		2 oz.	10 oz.		8 oz.	¼ lb.	8 oz.			4 oz.
" Soap....							½ oz.						
Glycerin......							1 oz.		¼ lb.				
Borax.........										20 gr.			
Stearic Acid....							5 oz.						
Sub. Carbonate Potash......				15 gr.									
Alcohol........				2 oz.									
Rose Water...	12 oz.	2 oz.	2 oz.	4 oz.		3½ oz.		5 oz.	2 dr.	8 oz	4 oz.		3 oz.
Any Essential Oil.........		10 m.		10 m.		15 m.			12 m.		30 m.	10 m.	15 m.

cold cream which is highly recommended as a cosmetic.

Or melt together in a double boiler with gentle heat 2 ounces of spermaceti and 1 ounce of oil of almonds. Stir in 3 ounces of pure glycerin, and ½ ounce of balsam of Peru. Remove from the fire and beat with an egg beater until cool enough to stir.

AROMATIC VINEGAR

Aromatic Vinegar, or Toilet Vinegar, is a toilet preparation, the active principle of which is acetic acid—in the form of glacial acetic acid, white wine or other vinegar, or the like. It may be perfumed according to taste and may serve as a vehicle for various cosmetics. To compound toilet vinegar, first dissolve the essential oils or other perfumes in the spirits, next add the vinegar or acetic acid, and lastly the distilled or toilet water.

Or, if no spirits are used, mix the ingredients in a glass fruit jar or other tightly stoppered vessel, and let stand for several days, shaking frequently.

The following recipes are recommended:

Dissolve in ½ pint of pale rum 1 dram each of the essences of bergamot, rosemary, and marjoram. Add ½ pint of pure white-wine vinegar and 1 pint of elder-flower or rose water. Filter and cork tightly for use.

Or dissolve in ½ pint of glacial acetic acid 1 ounce of camphor. Add 5 grains of pure oil of lavender and 12 grains of oil of cinnamon.

Or put in a close vessel 4 ounces of dried red-rose leaves, and pour over them 1 quart of white-wine vinegar; add ½ pint of strong essence of rose. Seal and let stand 2 or 3 weeks, shaking frequently; filter and preserve in a tightly stoppered glass vessel.

Or to 1 pint of cologne add ½ ounce of glacial acetic acid.

Or to 1 pint of white-wine vinegar add ½ pint of essence of rose, ¼ pint of extract of cassia, and ¼ pint of extract of orris.

Or dissolve in 1 quart of rectified alcohol 1 dram of attar neroli, ½ dram of attar cloves, 1 ounce of balsam of Peru, and 3 ounces of gum benzoin. Add 1 ounce of glacial acetic acid.

TOILET POWDERS

The bases of most toilet powders are compounds of magnesia, including talc or talcum—which chemically is magnesium silicate, and which is mined in large quantities in various parts of the world — and French chalk, which is not chalk but ground soapstone; fuller's earth, a greenish clay found in many parts of England and on the continent of Europe; and starch, especially rice and wheat starch, which is sometimes adulterated with cornstarch, potato starch, etc. These preparations usually contain pulverized perfumed woods, as orris root, sandalwood, and other perfumes. In addition, it is quite customary to use in face powder metallic bismuth, preparations of mercury, and other mineral drugs—all of which are distinctly harmful, and the use of which is therefore never advisable. No recipes of this sort are included in the present volume.

The following are standard preparations which contain no injurious ingredients:

For plain face powder without perfume, pure white starch can hardly be improved upon.

Or mix together equal quantities of rice flour, fuller's earth, and white starch, and perfume with any essential oil—rose, violet, or any other preferred.

Or, for violet powder, mix 3 ounces of white starch with 1 ounce of powdered orris root, rub up together in water, and perfume with the essential oils of lemon, bergamot, and cloves, using about double the amount of lemon as of the two others.

Or, for a rose face powder, mix 8

ounces of pulverized rose leaves with 4 ounces of pulverized sandalwood, and add 1 dram of the attar of roses.

Or to 3½ pounds of powdered rose or white starch, add ¼ dram of rose pink and 1 dram each of rose oil and santal oil.

ROUGE

Rouge Paste and Powder. — The base of rouge for the lips and cheeks is usually French chalk, almond oil, or other animal fat, or oil, or one of the gums, as gum tragacanth, colored with cochineal, carmine, vermilion, alkanet, or other red coloring matter, and perfumed to taste. To this may be added a mild astringent, as alum, acetic acid, and the like.

For carmine rouge, raise to a boil in an aluminum or copper vessel 1 quart of distilled water, to which add 1 ounce of the best pulverized cochineal. After 5 or 6 minutes stir in carefully 30 grains of powdered Roman alum. Continue boiling 3 to 5 minutes and set aside to cool. When lukewarm, but before the mixture settles, pour off the clear liquor from the sediment through a piece of white silk or chiffon into a glass fruit jar. Let stand 3 or 4 days and again pour off through white silk into another vessel. Allow the resulting liquor to settle; pour off the clear liquor from the top, and dry the sediment carefully in a cool, shady place. The result is a very finely divided powder, making a rouge of the best quality.

Or finely powdered carmine can be used by taking a piece of fine unscented pomatum about the size of a pea, and placing on it a bit of carmine the size of a pin head. Mix the two together and apply with a bit of cotton.

Or mix 4 ounces of powdered French chalk with 2 drams of oil of almonds and 1 dram of powdered carmine.

Or powdered French chalk, 4 ounces; rectified lard, 4 ounces; powdered carmine, 1 ounce. Perfume with essential oils as desired.

Or the rouge ordinarily used for theatrical purposes may be prepared by mixing fine French chalk with any quantity of powdered carmine necessary to give the required color.

Or the so-called Turkish rouge may be prepared by putting 1 ounce of alkanet in a glass fruit jar and pouring over it 1 ounce of alcohol. Let stand for a week or 10 days, shaking frequently; strain and bottle for use.

Or vinegar rouge may be prepared by mixing together 1½ drams each of powdered cochineal and carmine lake and 3 drams of alcohol. Pour over these ½ pint of alcohol and let stand 2 or 3 weeks; afterwards strain and bottle for use. Perfume with essential oils according to taste.

Or, for another vinegar rouge, dissolve 25 grains of balsam of Peru in 12 ounces of alcohol; dissolve separately 15 grains of alum in 6 ounces of rose water; mix the two solutions and add 2 drams of acetic acid; let stand 3 or 4 hours, shaking occasionally; and finally add 1 dram of the finest quality of powdered carmine dissolved in ½ dram of aqua ammonia. Shake well, allow to settle for 10 or 15 minutes, and pour off the clear liquor.

Or dissolve ½ ounce of gum tragacanth in hot water and color with vermilion; add a few drops of almond oil, and evaporate the excess of moisture with gentle heat.

Liquid Rouge. — Rouge in liquid form is variously known as "bloom of youth," "bloom of roses," "almond bloom," "Turkish bloom," etc. These various preparations are based upon distilled water and alcohol, or other spirit, as vehicles, and are colored with Brazil wood, red sanders, cochineal, and various other red coloring matter. In some instances they contain an adhesive ingredient, as isinglass, and various specifics, as benzoin, alum, borax, and the like.

Put in a glass fruit jar 2 drams of dragon's blood, 2 ounces of red sanders, and 1½ ounces of gum benzoin; pour over these 2 ounces of 90 per cent alcohol and 4 ounces of pure soft water. Seal the jar and let stand a week or 10 days, shaking frequently; filter and bottle for use.

Or put in a glass fruit jar 4 ounces of finely powdered cochineal; add 4 fluid ounces of distilled water and the same amount of aqua ammonia; cover with a wet cloth and let simmer 3 or 4 hours in a double boiler. This preparation is ready for use as soon as it is cool.

Or, for a larger quantity, put in a 2-gallon glass fruit jar 1 pound of gum benzoin, 2½ ounces of dragon's blood, and 1¼ pounds of red sanders. Cover with 1 gallon of alcohol; let stand 2 weeks or more, shaking frequently; strain or filter for use.

Or put 1 ounce of Brazil wood in a double boiler; cover with 1 ounce of pure soft water, and let boil 15 or 20 minutes. Strain through cheese cloth; return to the fire; add ½ ounce of borax, ¼ ounce of cochineal, 1 ounce of alum, and ¾ ounce of isinglass. Dissolve with gentle heat, stirring constantly, and strain or filter for use.

Or put in a fruit jar with tight rubber ring ¼ ounce of finely pulverized carmine, and add 1 ounce of pure, fresh aqua ammonia. Seal tightly and let stand 3 or 4 days, shaking frequently. Add 1 pint of rose water, ½ fluid ounce of essence of roses, and ½ ounce of 90 per cent alcohol. Seal; let stand a few days, shaking frequently; pour off the liquor and bottle for use.

Or put in a gallon glass bottle 1 ounce of powdered Brazil wood and ¼ ounce of cochineal; pour over this 2 quarts of boiling hot soft water; let stand for 3 or 4 days, shaking frequently; strain through cheese cloth, and add 2 drams each of isinglass and gum arabic, and 2 ounces of 95 per cent alcohol. Perfume with essential oils or essences as desired.

Or put in a quart fruit jar 1½ ounces of red-rose leaves, dried and pulverized. Add 1 pint of pure soft water, boiling hot; simmer with gentle heat in a double boiler for 2 or 3 hours, taking care that the water does not approach the boiling point. Strain the liquor, and add the strained juice of 2 or 3 large lemons; let stand 24 hours, filter, and add 4 fluid ounces of 95 per cent alcohol as a preservative.

Circassian Cream.—Put in a glass fruit jar 4 ounces of fresh suet, 6 ounces of olive oil, 1½ ounces of powdered gum benzoin, and ½ ounce of alkanet root. Place the jar in a double boiler and simmer with gentle heat for several hours. Let stand 24 hours more; heat, and strain through cheese cloth, and when cold perfume with ½ dram of essence of ambergris, ½ dram of oil of lavender, or any other essential oil preferred.

Chapped Lips.—Preparations recommended for chapped lips are usually based upon white wax, spermaceti, or beeswax, with the addition of almond oil and such specifics as benzoin, honey, unsalted butter, and the like, adding perfumes and coloring matter according to taste.

Melt together with gentle heat 2 ounces of white wax and 1 ounce of spermaceti; add 2 ounces of pure strained honey, and continue to heat and stir until fully incorporated. Add in a thin stream 4 ounces of oil of almonds; remove from the fire and continue stirring until the mixture is nearly cold; finally perfume with any essential oil according to taste.

Or cover with rose water in a glass fruit jar 4 ounces of unsalted butter divided into small pieces; seal, and set aside in a cellar or other cool place for 4 or 5 days. Drain off the rose water, and put the butter in a porcelain double boiler; melt with gentle heat, and stir in 1 ounce each of spermaceti and grated beeswax, ½ ounce of powdered alkanet root, 1 ounce of powdered borax, ½ ounce of confectioner's sugar, 2 drams of powdered gum benzoin, and a double spoonful of strained lemon juice. Beat into an emulsion with an egg beater, and set over a slow fire, stirring constantly. Just before it comes to a boil remove from the fire; cool, strain, and bottle for use.

Or put in a clean double boiler 4 ounces of unsalted butter and 2 ounces of grated beeswax; squeeze in through a piece of cloth the juice of a bunch of ripe grapes; add the pulp of the grapes and a large apple, chopped fine. Simmer with gentle heat, and when all dissolved add ¼ ounce each of benjamin and storax, also ½ ounce of alkanet root. Mix until all are incorporated; strain through a piece of fine linen; remelt and pour into jars or molds for use.

Or use pure clarified honey. Perfume as desired.

Or mix equal quantities of white sugar candy, white wax, oil of almonds, and spermaceti, melting all together with gentle heat.

ESSENCES AND PERFUMES

Perfumes. — The subject of perfumery is perhaps not so important as it was formerly, because the use of strong perfumes appears to be going out of fashion. The natural fragrance of flowers, spices, and perfumed woods—the sources of the ingredients used in perfumery—is, however, so delightful that those substances are likely always to be employed to a certain extent in the toilet.

The various forms in which perfumes are placed upon the market are, according to the degree of dilution, the attar or essential oil, the essence or extract, and the perfumed toilet water. Innumerable compounds are sold under various fanciful titles, as colognes, scents, spirits, (French *esprit*), and the like. The substances from which these perfumes are obtained may also in some cases be purchased, as the dry leaves or flowers of plants, various kinds of wood or roots, ambergris (supposed to be a morbid secretion of the sperm whale), and the like.

Perfumes are also used in the form of sachets or dry powder, to be placed among garments or linen, either in sachet bags or scattered loosely in chests and drawers. They are likewise employed to perfume the atmosphere of a room by putting them in open jars, or burning them in the form of pastilles and incense.

Generally speaking, the most convenient form in which to obtain perfumes is the attar, otto, or essential oil. A few drops of these concentrated substances, usually about 5 or 6 drops to the pint or pound, will yield any desired odor. When the essence, the perfumed water, or the original substances themselves are prescribed in recipes, the essential oil can be substituted in most cases by a little careful experimenting. The process of extracting essences and essential oils, however, is not difficult, and can be carried on at home by anyone who is interested enough to procure suitable apparatus. Several methods of preparing homemade extracts are given below which can be employed successfully by anyone.

Volatile Oils. — These are found naturally in plants, and are usually obtained by distillation. They are distinguished by their pungent odor and also by the fact that they are not capable of uniting with alkalies to form soaps. They are used principally in perfumery, with the exception of turpentine, which is employed in mixing paints and varnishes. This oil is obtained from various cone-bearing trees, and exudes from the bark mixed with rosin and other vegetable juices, from which it is extracted by distillation.

The volatile oils upon being exposed to air absorb oxygen and crystallize into substances having the appearance of rosin, balsam, or gum camphor. The perfumed oils, if not tightly corked, gradually lose their delicate scent. Most volatile oils are obtained by distillation in the presence of water or alcohol, but others are obtained by mechanical processes without heat. The essential oils in solution with water are known as essences, as essence of pennyroyal or of mint, and the like. These are often prepared by distillation with water, forming the distilled perfumed waters of commerce. The bath in which perfume-bearing substances are distilled should be slightly acidulated with sulphuric acid. Use a few drops only—just enough to give a sour taste to the tongue. All the essential oils are soluble in alcohol and ether.

To Test Essential Oils.—As many of the essential oils are expensive, they are frequently adulterated. Obtain a drop of the pure oil and determine the presence of substitutes by placing a drop of each on separate pieces of paper and comparing them carefully. The attar of roses is often adulterated with the oils of rhodium, sandalwood, camphor, spermaceti, etc. The pure article has a sweet, smooth taste. A bitter taste indicates the oil of rhodium or sandalwood; a pungent flavor, the oil of geranium or camphor; a greasy stain on paper, spermaceti.

Or mix a drop of the attar of roses with a drop of sulphuric acid. The pure attar will not be affected, but the adulterated article will become dark colored, and the characteristic odors of the different substances with which it may have been adulterated can easily be discerned.

Or, to test for adulteration with fixed oils, place a drop of the suspected oil on paper and evaporate it with gentle heat. The presence of a fixed oil will be detected by a permanent greasy stain.

Or distill off the volatile oil with gentle heat. The fixed oil will be left behind.

Or add three or four times its volume of 80 per cent alcohol. The fixed oil will not be dissolved.

Or, to test for alcohol, dilute the suspected oil with water. If the quantity of alcohol is large, the mixture will become roily or turbid.

To test for oil of turpentine—which is often used to adulterate the oils of orange, lemon, neroli, and the like—set a little of the oil on fire, blow it out, and the presence of turpentine may be detected by its characteristic odor.

Odor of Perfumes.—The odor of the volatile oils is probably caused by their gradual oxidation or chemical union with the oxygen of the air. This is the same process as that which takes place in the rusting of iron, and is similarly promoted by moisture. When treated chemically so as to be perfectly pure and free from oxygen and moisture, the most powerful perfumes are odorless. Exposure to moist air restores their odor. Perfume-bearing flowers are much more fragrant when moistened, as with dew. Roses and other fragrant blossoms are nearly scentless in dry climates. Rose jars and other mixtures of dry perfume-bearing substances give off very much more perfume when slightly moistened.

Individual Perfumes.—Many persons prefer to have a perfume of their own different from those which are on the market or used by others among their acquaintances. This is not especially difficult, although the perfumes that are usually employed, such as heliotrope, violet, white rose, and the like, may, of course, be obtained by anyone. An individual perfume may be secured by experimenting with two or more essential oils, mixing and blending a few drops at a time until a new and agreeable fragrance is obtained. This is, in fact, the way in which colognes and similar preparations are compounded for the market. One celebrated "German cologne" of the past generation is said to have contained no fewer than thirty different kinds of ingredients, the result being a pungent perfume of a peculiarly agreeable odor. The proportion in which the various ingredients should be blended is entirely a matter of individual preference, to be determined by experiment.

PERFUMES—COLOGNE

	Eau de Cologne.	Cologne Water.	Superior Cologne Water.	Cologne Water.	Do.	Cologne Water.	Eau de Cologne.	Cologne Water.	Best Cologne Water.	Cologne Water.	Farina Cologne.	Portugal Cologne.	Eau de Bouquet.
Oil Bergamot...		1 oz.	1 dr.	1 dr.		⅛ oz.		30 d	2 oz.	1 oz.	1 oz.	1 oz.	
" Cedrat.....		2 dr.								2 dr.			
" Cinnamon..				8 d.		8 d.			1 d.				
" Cloves......				8 d.		15 d.							¾ oz.
" Jasmine....									½ oz.				
" Lemon.....		2 dr.	1 dr.			¼ oz.		30 d				2 oz.	
" Lavender...	40 d.		2 dr.	1 dr.		⅛ oz.		30 d	2 dr.				
" Neroli......							50 d.		2 dr.		3 dr.		
" Orange.....			1 dr.							1 oz.	½ oz.	8 oz.	
" Roses......			10 d.			15 d.				6 d.		2 dr.	
" Rosemary..	2 d.	1 dr.	1½ dr.	2 dr.		¼ oz.				1 dr.		2 dr.	
Tinct. Benjamin	1 dr.												
" Benzoin..									3 oz.				
Ess. Bergamot..	1½ dr.				5 dr.		50 d.		2 oz.				
" Cedrat.....							50 d.						
" Ambergris..													1 dr.
" Citron......					5 dr.								
" Cardamoms......							2 dr.						
" Lemon.....	1½ dr.			2 dr.	4 dr.								
" Or. Flower.	1½ dr.				3 d.								
" Musk......			2 dr.	50 d.					½ oz.				1 dr.
" Neroli.....	2 oz.												6 dr
" Jasmine....													8 oz.
" Rosemary..					2½ dr.		50 d.						
Distilled Water.											1 pt.		
Orange-flower Water.......								30 d		32 oz.			
Rose Water....									2 pt.				
Scented Honey Water.......													1 pt.
Alcohol (95%)..	1½ pt.	5 oz.	1 pt.	1 pt.	1 qt.	2 qt.	1 gal.	½ pt.	1 gal.	1 gal.	3 pt.	1 gal.	3 pt.
Calamus Aramaticus.....													4 oz.

Sachet Powders.—Various solid perfume-bearing substances, to which may be added small quantities of the essential oils, are used in powdered form and sprinkled between layers of absorbent cotton or otherwise to perfume garments laid away in chests or drawers. To prepare the various sachet powders, it is only necessary to finely pulverize the solids in a mortar, add the essential oils drop by drop, and mix the whole thoroughly together. When not required for use, sachet powder should be kept in tightly sealed boxes, jars, or bottles, so that the volatile perfumes will not be lost by evaporation.

Incense—Pastilles.—Several perfume-bearing substances may be utilized in solid form by mixing them with combustibles, such as charcoal, niter, and various gums, and setting them on fire to perfume apartments. The table on page 478 embraces a number of recipes for incense pastilles. In all cases first reduce the solids separately to powder in a mortar. This may be done by beating the ingredients together in an earthenware bowl, or by mixing them on a marble slab or plate of glass with an ordinary knife or a palette knife having a thin, broad blade. If gum tragacanth is used, it should be dissolved in water to the consistency of mucilage. The essential oils and other liquid perfumes are then to be added and thoroughly worked into the mass, the whole formed into small cones like chocolate drops, and thoroughly dried either in a very slow oven or by the heat of the sun. When required for use, one or more of these cones may be placed on any hot surface or set on fire at the tip and allowed to gradually smolder, when they will give off an agreeable perfume.

Or, where niter and charcoal are both employed, dissolve the niter in sufficient soft water to make a soft paste with the charcoal. Dry this paste thoroughly, and pour over it the liquid perfumes. If other solid ingredients are added, they should be in powdered form. Mix the whole with gum tragacanth dissolved as above. Dry and use as above.

be free from all foreign substances. They are then placed in a large earthen pot or a wooden vessel, covered with pure soft or distilled water, and exposed to sunshine. The vessel should be taken indoors at night, kept covered, and placed preferably in a warm spot. The attar or essential oil of the rose petals rises on the surface in the form of a scum. This may be carefully taken up by a small piece of absorbent cotton on the end of a stick. The oil may then be squeezed from the cotton into a very

PERFUMES—SACHET

Caraway							¼ oz.				
Cassia			1 oz.	1 oz.						½ lb.	
Cedar		1 oz.									
Cloves		1 oz.	1 oz.	1 oz.			¼ oz.				
Coriander Seed			1 oz.	1 oz.	1 oz.						
Black Currant Leaves										1 lb.	
Arom. Calamus					1 oz.						
Gum Benzoin										½ lb.	
Tonka Beans						¼ lb.					
Dried Lemon Peel								1 lb.			
Lemon Geranium Leaves								4 oz.			
Lavender Flowers			8 oz.	1 oz.			½ lb.		½ oz.		
Rose Leaves			8 oz.	1 oz.	1 oz.	1 lb.			1½ oz.	1 lb.	1 lb.
Orris Root	1 lb.		1 oz.	1 oz.	1 oz.	1 lb.			2 oz.	2 lb.	
Mint							½ oz.				
Rhubarb Wood		1 oz.									
Santal Wood						¼ lb.					½ lb.
Salt							1 oz.				
Thyme							½ oz.				
Vanilla Beans									½ dr.		
Musk	12 gr.				5 gr.	1 dr.			4 gr.	1 dr.	
Oil Bergamot								1 oz.			
" Almonds										¼ dr.	
" Lemon								4 dr.			
" Neroli						1 dr.			6 m.		
" Lemon Grass								1 dr.			
" Rhodium					¼ dr.						
" Rose						½ dr.			10 m.	¼ dr.	¼ oz.
" Santal									20 m.		
Ess. Ambergris	1 dr.										
" Bergamot	½ dr.										
" Jasmine									2 dr.		
" Lavender	1 dr.										
" Lemon	½ dr.										

Rose Perfume.—One of the most universally popular odors is the perfume of the rose. Most persons can obtain rose petals in any quantity during the month of June, and their fragrance may be extracted and stored for future enjoyment.

Attar of Rose.—This costly perfume is prepared principally in the Orient and imported to America, but the process of preparation is simplicity itself and can be tried by anyone. A large quantity of petals of the rose are picked carefully so as to

small vial with a glass or rubber stopper and preserved for use. The process should be continued until the scum no longer rises. The vessel in which the roses are steeped should be covered during the day with a fine screen; otherwise it is likely to become a breeding place for mosquitoes. Needless to say, it should be kept as free as possible from dust and dirt. Or put dried rose petals in an earthenware or glass vessel, cover with olive oil, and simmer with very gentle heat until the oil has

PERFUMES—PASTILLES—INCENSE

	Pastilles for Burning.	Perfumed Fumigating Pastilles.	Pressi's Pastilles.	Pastilles of Or. Flower.	Pastilles of Rose.	Pastilles à la Vanilla.	Pastilles for Perfuming Sick Room.	Incense.	Do.	Do.
Niter	1½ dr.	2 oz.	¾ oz.		2½ oz	5 oz				
Charcoal	6 oz.	1¼ lb.	½ lb.	17 oz.		23 oz.	2 lb.			
Gum Galbanum				3¼ oz.		5 oz.				
" Frankincense							1 lb.	2½ oz.		
" Benzoin	4 dr.	2 oz.			3 oz		1 lb.	12 oz.	1 oz.	2 oz.
" Tragacanth	q. s.	¾ oz.	q. s.	½ oz	½ oz.			1½ oz.		
" Storax		1 oz.	11 parts	3 oz.		5 oz.		2½ oz.		
Oil Bitter Almond							2 oz.			
" Caraway			½ dr.							
" Cloves			½ dr.			5 oz.				
" Neroli				¼ oz.						
" Lavender			½ dr.							
" Rose			½ dr.							
" Santal			½ dr.							
" Olibanum	2 dr.	1½ oz.	12 parts	3 oz		5 oz.			2 oz.	7 oz.
" Styrax	2 dr.									
" Thyme			½ dr.							
Ess. Ambergris							2 oz.			
Benzoic Acid			6 oz.				6 oz.			
Clear Sirup							4 oz.			
Ess. Musk							4 oz.	15 gr.		
" Rose					¼ oz.					
Alcohol						2½ oz.				
Orange-flower Water				4 oz.						
Rose Water		q. s	½ pt.	4 oz.	6 oz			q. s.		
Cascarilla Bark	8 dr.	¾ oz.						1 part	1 oz.	1 oz.
Burnt Sugar								½ oz.		
Orange Powder				4 oz.						
Powder of Rose					4 oz					
Yellow Sanderswood	2 dr.									
Vanilla Bean						7 oz.				

fully extracted both the odor and the color of the flowers. Or the essential oil of roses or of any flower which has an agreeable fragrance may be extracted as follows: procure a quantity of the petals of any flower or flowers desired, a roll of absorbent cotton in thin layers, a wide-mouthed glass bottle or earthen vessel, and a small quantity of high-grade olive oil. Put a layer of petals in the empty bottle, sprinkle over them a small quantity of fine salt, and cover with a layer of absorbent cotton dipped in olive oil. So continue until the bottle is filled. Close it tightly with a glass stopper, a piece of bladder, parchment, or rubber cloth, and expose to the sun. In from ten to twenty days squeeze out the oil, which will be found nearly equal to the commercial article.

Or arrange the flowers in the same manner in an earthen jar and simmer with gentle heat by means of a double boiler, changing the flowers occasionally until the odor is satisfactory. Rectified spirits may be added, and the whole squeezed and strained for use.

Rose Jar. — Many artistic vases with suitable lids can be purchased for this purpose, and these make very acceptable holiday gifts; or an earthenware or glass vessel, such as a fruit jar which can be tightly closed, may be employed.

Gather fresh roses on a clear day when the petals are dry. Place these petals in the rose jar in layers, covering each with a thin layer of common salt. Then add two or three handfuls each of lavender flowers, rosemary leaves, and sweet marjoram. Other flowers may be added if desired, or a jar may be filled entirely with rose petals. Add 4 ounces of pulverized bay salt and 1 ounce each of various spices, as cloves, cinnamon, grated nutmeg, and the like, also orris root, storax, or indeed any other perfumes that may be preferred. The jar is to be kept closely covered, except when perfume is desired. Then the lid may be removed and the contents slightly moistened.

Potpourri.—This is a mixture of dried flowers and spices not ground. To make it, take dried lavender flowers, 1 pound; dried rose leaves, 1 pound; crushed orris root, ½ pound; crushed cloves, 2 ounces; crushed cinnamon, 2 ounces; crushed allspice, 2 ounces; table salt, 1 pound.

To Prepare Tinctures.—A tincture of flowers having strong perfume, as the tuberose, jasmine, violet, jonquil, and heliotrope, may be prepared by crowding the fresh blossoms into a fruit jar and covering them with alcohol. After they have stood for a few days, the mixture may be strained through a linen cloth, the flowers squeezed to extract as much of the essence as possible, and fresh flowers added.

Or glycerin may be scented for the toilet and bath with any desired odor by the same method.

Or put half-inch layers of any flowers in an earthen pot or glass jar with layers of fine salt between. Screw the top on tightly and place the jar in a cellar or other dark, cool place. This process requires from one to two months. At the end of this time strain and squeeze the liquor through a cloth, put it into a glass bottle, and let it stand in the sun to clarify.

Or place dry rose or other petals in a large bottle or fruit jar, cover with alcohol or other rectified spirits, close tightly, and preserve for use. A few drops of this tincture sprinkled about a room will give it a delicious perfume.

Geranium Perfume. — A perfume which is very agreeable to many may be made by either of the above methods from the leaves of any of the sweet-smelling geraniums. The tincture, obtained by packing the leaves in a fruit jar, filling it with alcohol and allowing it to stand for a few weeks, is perhaps the easiest to prepare. The leaves may be renewed, if desired, to strengthen the perfume.

To Distill Essences.—A common glass retort, such as is used by chemists, may be used for distilling perfumes. This consists of a round glass vessel with a wide mouth that can be closed by a cork or glass stopper. A glass tube passes through this cork to a receiver placed upon the table. This tube should be long enough to allow the steam forming in the retort to condense before escaping. To facilitate condensation, a cloth kept wet with cold water may be wrapped about the tube. A small alcohol lamp is kept burning under the retort, care being taken to keep the lamp at just the right distance, so that the liquor will not run over but pass over gently, drop by drop. Perfumes are essentially volatile; and by this process they pass off with the steam condensed in the tube, and thus become thoroughly amalgamated with the distilled liquor. Special appliances called stills can be purchased for the manufacture of perfumes, but this method is entirely practical for home use. The bath in which perfumes are distilled should be slightly acidulated with sulphuric acid.

Smelling Salts.—The base of the best quality of smelling salts is the true neutral carbonate of ammonia. This is a volatile salt which keeps its pungency as long as it lasts. The portion exposed to the air as it volatilizes separates into carbonic-acid gas and gaseous ammonia. Care should be taken in ordering to procure the true carbonate of ammonia and not the sesquicarbonate, which does not possess an equally strong, agreeable, or lasting pungency.

Smelling salts may be prepared by putting the carbonate of ammonia in a suitable glass bottle with a stopper of ground glass, and adding any desired perfume, as 8 parts of carbonate of ammonia to 1 part of oil of lavender, or a suitable quantity of other essential oils, as bergamot, cloves, cassia, verbena, and the like.

Or put equal quantities of slaked lime and carbonate of ammonia in a glass-stoppered bottle, cover with aqua ammonia, and add 12 to 20 drops of any desired essential oil or oils.

Or put in a glass-stoppered bottle absorbent cotton or a small sponge cut up into fine pieces. Fill with common liquid ammonia, and add 5 or 6 drops each of various essential oils according to taste.

Perfumed Toilet Waters. — These preparations are the product of distillation. The perfume-yielding ingredients are placed in a glass retort or a still, with water or spirits, and subjected to heat. The perfume is volatilized and passes with the steam into the receiver, the distilled water thus becoming thoroughly impregnated. Distillation is usually conducted on a large scale, and the proportions recommended are often for manufacturers' use. Most persons prefer to purchase perfumed waters rather than to go to the expense and trouble of obtaining a retort and conducting the operation. Anyone, however, who wishes to make this experiment for amusement or to make money by the sale of these preparations may readily reduce the proportions to suit his apparatus.

To distill with water, put the perfume-bearing substances in the retort in the proportion of about 1 part by bulk to 8 parts of water. Continue the distillation as long as the distilled water carried over continues to yield the desired odor. Additional water may be added if necessary. The less water used, the stronger the perfumes. The quality can be greatly improved by distilling a second or third time.

To distill with spirits, put the ingredients in a flask, and cover with just enough spirits to thoroughly moisten them. The receptacle at the end of the tube should be a corked flask or bottle through which a tube should pass to within an inch of the bottom of the flask. This receptacle should be placed in a basin of iced water. The principal substances from which perfumed waters are distilled are lavender flowers, rosemary tops, orange flowers, rose leaves, myrtle flowers, marjoram, orange peel, lemon peel, laurel leaves, bitter almonds, and elder flowers. These are distilled separately, and the distillate is, of course, named accordingly.

Perfumed Waters. — A substitute for rose water and other distilled waters may be quickly prepared by dropping the essential oil or attar of rose or other substances into distilled boiling water. The water should be taken off the fire at a boil, the oil dropped in, and stirred vigorously while cooling.

Rose Water.—Dissolve 1 dram of attar of rose, or a proportionate quantity of other essential oils, in 1 pint of rectified spirits; while hot place in a 2-gallon jug and add 1¾ gallons of pure distilled water, heated, but not quite to the boiling point—say 190°. Cork the jug and shake, cautiously at first but thoroughly afterwards, until cold. This form of rose water will be found equal to the commercial article.

Or drop 12 drops of attar of rose on a half ounce of cube sugar. Add 2 drams of carbonate of magnesia. Put in a fruit jar and pour in gradually 1 quart of water, stirring briskly. Add 2 ounces of rectified spirits. Place a funnel of filtering paper in another fruit jar, and pour through the funnel to filter. The effect of the magnesia is to break up the oil globules and assist in forming an emulsion with water. The magnesia is removed by filtering. Other perfumed waters may be prepared in a similar manner.

Violet Water.—Put 1 pint of alcohol or proof spirits in a quart fruit jar. Add 1 pound of orris root, cover, and shake. Let stand on the dregs for a week or 10 days. Filter through filter paper to remove the orris root.

Or mix deodorized alcohol, 15 ounces; rose water, 2 ounces; extract of cassia, 1 ounce; and extract of violet, 2 ounces. Mix, shake, and filter.

Or mix 1 pint of alcohol and 1 ounce each of neroli and essence of violets.

Lavender Water.—A favorite article for the toilet is the oil of lavender diluted with rectified alcohol, to which various other perfumes may be added according to taste. To prepare lavender water, it is only necessary to first mix the oil of lavender and other essential oils (if any) with a little of the alcohol; then add the remaining alcohol in a thin stream, stirring constantly. Finally stir in the other ingredients. The whole should be placed in a glass fruit jar with rubber rings, or other closely stoppered vessel, and allowed to stand for several months before using. It should be shaken frequently. The longer it can be allowed to stand before being opened the better the quality will be. The English oil of lavender is the best.

Other perfumed toilet waters may be prepared by substituting any of the essential oils, according to taste, in the following table.

Perfumed Toilet Waters. — The number of possible combinations of perfumes diluted with distilled or soft water, which form the perfumed toilet waters of commerce, is, of course, unlimited. The following examples illustrate the method of combining these, and may be recommended to be as desirable as any:

Put in a pint glass bottle or fruit jar ½ ounce of oil of rosemary and 1 dram of essence of ambergris; add 1 pint of 95 per cent alcohol. Shake well, remove the cork, and let stand 24 hours. Then cork tightly and let stand a month or 6 weeks, shaking frequently, after which put in a tightly stoppered bottle until ready for use. This is the well-known "Hungary water."

Or put in a 2-quart fruit jar 1 ounce of oil of bergamot, ½ ounce of tincture of benzoin, 1 dram of oil of cinnamon, and cover with 1 quart of

LAVENDER TOILET WATER

	Princess.	Hoyt's.	Fragrant.	Elegant.	Queen's.	Plain.	Old Virginia.	Princess.	Bachelor's.	Old Colony.
Alcohol (95%)	6 oz.	1 pt.	2 pt.	1 pt.	1 pt.	1 gal.	½ gal.	½ gal.	2½ qt.	20 oz.
Rose Water	1 oz.		4 oz.				1 pt.			
Oil Lavender	4 dr.	1 oz.		½ oz.	3 dr.	2 oz.	1½ oz.	2 oz.	2 oz.	6 dr.
" Cloves	½ dr.		1 oz.		6 m.					
" Roses					6 m.					
" Bergamot				½ oz.	3 dr.			½ oz.	6 dr.	
" Rosemary					¾ dr.					
" Lemon							3 dr.			
" Sage							½ dr.			
" Orange							1 dr.			
" Thyme							4 dr.			
" Nutmeg							1 dr.			10 m.
" Rose Geranium										2 dr.
Essence Ambergris		2½ dr.						½ oz.	1 dr.	4 m.
" Musk					¾ dr.			1 oz.		4 m.
" Roses					2 oz.					
Tinct. Orris Root			1 oz.							
" Musk			2 dr.	6 dr.			½ oz.			
Honey					1 oz.					
Benzoic Acid					½ dr.					
Tinct. Benzoin							1 oz.			

95 per cent alcohol. Let stand a month or 6 weeks, shake frequently, filter, and put in a tightly stoppered glass bottle. This is a standard recipe for "Florida water."

Or, for a cheaper grade of "Florida water," put in a 2-quart fruit jar ¼ ounce of oil of bergamot, ½ ounce of lavender. Cover this with 1 pint of oil of lemon, and ¼ ounce of oil of 95 per cent alcohol. Shake well and add ½ dram each of oil of cloves and oil of cinnamon. Let stand 24 hours, add 1 quart of pure soft or distilled water, filter, and bottle for use.

Or, for a simple "Florida water," put in a corked fruit jar ¼ ounce of oil of bergamot, ¼ ounce of tincture of benzoin, and ¼ pint of 95 per cent alcohol. Dilute with pure soft or distilled water to the extent desired.

Or, to illustrate the great variety of ingredients that may be employed in this manner, the following recipes will be stated without comment. Any of these, while more expensive than the above, will be found to be of most excellent quality.

Mix ½ pint of tincture of cedar wood, ¼ pint of tincture of myrrh, and ¼ pint of tincture of krameria, and add 6 drops of oil of rose.

Or put in a glass fruit jar 1 dram each of oils of lemon, lavender, and bergamot, ½ dram of oil of neroli, ½ dram of tincture of turmeric, 16 drops of oil of balm, and 6 drops of attar of rose. Cover with 1 pint of pure alcohol and let stand a week or 10 days, shaking frequently.

Or mix ½ pint each of the essence of rose, jasmine, orange flower, and clove gillyflower. Add 1 pint of deodorized alcohol, ½ ounce each of essence of vanilla and musk, ¼ ounce of red sanderswood, and ½ pint each of orange-flower water and rose water.

Or put in a 2-quart fruit jar ¼ ounce each of essence of cloves and balsam of Peru, ½ ounce each of musk and bergamot, ¼ ounce each of essence of neroli and thyme, and ½ pint of orange-flower water, and pour over all 1 quart of deodorized 95 per cent alcohol. This is the so-called "balsam of a thousand flowers."

Or mix 2 ounces each of extract of violet, orange flower, and tuberose, ½ ounce of tincture of musk, 1 dram of essence of cedrat, 6 drops of attar of rose, ¼ dram of oil of bitter almonds, and 1 ounce each of rose water and orange-flower water. Cover all with 1½ pints of deodorized 95 per cent alcohol, and let stand a week or 10 days, shaking frequently, after which filter and preserve in tightly stoppered bottles.

CHAPTER XX

HAIRDRESSING BOTH FOR MEN AND WOMEN

DANDRUFF AND SHAMPOOING—HAIR WASHES—HAIR TONICS—HAIR OILS—HAIR DYES—OTHER HAIR TOPICS—THE BEARD, MUSTACHE, AND SHAVING—TOILET PREPARATIONS FOR MEN

Hairdressing. — The subject of hairdressing, while of interest to both sexes, is especially important to women, both because the mass and length of their hair render it difficult to handle and keep clean, and also because any peculiarities it may have are very conspicuous. This subject is not only of interest to every woman for herself, but it may also be mentioned among the many methods of earning pin money in small communities. In neighborhoods where there is no professional hairdresser any woman with natural deftness and taste can earn a good many dollars by caring for ladies' and children's hair, doing up ladies' hair in proper style for parties, and also by teaching inexperienced persons, for a small fee, how to do up their own hair in the latest style of coiffure. The information contained in the following paragraphs can thus be put to practical use and turned into dollars and cents. The attention of neighbors can be called to a woman's willingness to serve them in this manner by having a few business cards printed and giving them to one's friends to distribute among their acquaintances, or by means of a reading notice or business card in a local paper, which may be paid for by services to the wife or family of the editor.

Nature of the Hair.—The hair, like the nails, is formed of the same horny substance as that which appears on the outer surface of the skin when it becomes callous. Each hair, on the other hand, has a well-developed root which runs deep into the skin. The pigments which give the hair its color are present in light hair as well as dark, except that gray hairs may not contain them. Sometimes gray hairs are produced by the splitting of the hair in such a way as to admit the air. The daily growth of the hair is about one twentieth of an inch. It normally continues to grow for several years, and reaches from 18 inches to 1 yard in length. The hair is subject to varions diseases, and may be affected by the constitutional results of wasting and infectious ailments, such as typhoid fever, and also by severe emotions, such as fright, grief, and the like. Many preparations are advertised which claim that they will infallibly promote the growth of the hair. It cannot be too strongly emphasized that all such claims are humbugs.

Care of the Hair. — The proper care of the hair under normal conditions is very simple. The objects to be kept in mind are to preserve its natural luster, and texture by means of absolute cleanliness, and to massage the scalp sufficiently to remove any scurf or dandruff that may adhere to it, and thereby promote the active circulation of the blood. All this must be done without injury to the scalp or the hair by pulling, scratching, or tearing. Cutting the hair frequently has a tendency, especially in youth, to thicken the individual hairs and promote their growth. Neither this nor any other known process, however, tends to increase the actual number of hairs. All claims to the contrary are the pretensions of charlatans.

Professional hairdressers do not advocate shampooing the hair oftener than once a month. A thorough brushing once or twice a week is regarded by them as sufficient for cleanliness and as much more beneficial to the hair and scalp.

Much contradictory advice has been given on the subject of brushing the hair, some persons saying that stiff brushes should be used and the scalp and hair brushed by means of them with a good deal of vigor; others recommending soft brushes and a very moderate amount of friction. These differences are probably due to different views of the objects to be obtained by brushing. One object is to promote the health of the scalp and hence to give strength and vigor to the hair. For this purpose brushes with hard, stiff bristles may be used with considerable vigor, provided the skin is not injured. The other object is to smooth the hair and free it from dust. For this purpose brushes may be soft and used with a very moderate pressure.

Care should be taken, on the one hand, not to scratch the scalp, tear the roots of the hair, or cause it to split; and on the other, not to neglect the stimulating effects of massaging the scalp and removing dandruff. In other words, a vigorous brushing should be directed to the head or scalp, the gentler stroke being employed in brushing the hair itself.

The general opinion is that it is feasible to brush the hair free from dust each night before retiring. Applications of tonics and restoratives should also be made at this time, as they have the best opportunity of doing their work during sleep and especially while the blood is circulating freely as the result of brushing. The care of the hair must be governed by common sense, and general rules must be adapted to individual conditions. Some persons find it necessary to wash the hair as often as twice a month, and with others once a month is sufficient. When the hair is oily it should not be brushed as freely or frequently as otherwise. When it is dry and harsh the application of lanolin or other pomades may be necessary.

An analogy may be found in the grooming of horses. Every good groom knows by experience that plenty of combing and brushing not only produces a fine coat but promotes the health and vitality of the animal. Hence brushes with moderately stiff bristles should be chosen.

For men the so-called military or broad double brushes, one for each hand, are to be preferred.

To Dry-clean the Hair.—To thoroughly cleanse the hair it should be brushed successively from partings made in all directions upon the scalp, the utmost care being taken that foreign matter accumulated on the brush is removed and not returned by the next stroke to the hair.

Professional hairdressers when giving the hair a dry cleaning run a comb through the brush each time the latter is drawn through the hair, and afterwards wipe the comb clean on a towel. The object of this process is to remove dirt and dandruff and bring about the additional softness resulting from perfect cleanliness. If this is not done, the natural oil of the hair mixing with foreign substances merely makes the hair sticky.

Care of Hairbrushes. — Brushes should be cleaned very often and thoroughly, as a surprising amount of dust and dirt gathers in the hair. This quickly accumulates in the brushes and fills them. Hence the brush should be cleaned immediately after using.

Substances recommended for this

purpose are gasoline, ammonia, borax, and sal soda, of which the last is least desirable. It is also a good plan to disinfect the brush by putting a few drops of carbolic acid in the water. Neither hot water nor soap should be used, and the bristles should be allowed to dry thoroughly before using them. The effect of hot water and soap is to soften the bristles and also the glue with which they are commonly fastened into the brush, and when soft, the bristles are likely to split and break off or fall out.

To Clean a Hairbrush. — First comb out the loose hair with a coarse comb. Turn the brush downward and strike the bristles on a smooth, solid surface to loosen the dust and dandruff. Then rub the bristles over a Turkish or other coarse towel to wipe off as much of the loosened dust as possible.

To Wash a Brush. — Take two bowls of cold water in which to wash and to rinse the brush respectively. In one put about 1 tablespoonful of ammonia to 1 pint of water, and introduce the bristles in this without immersing the back of the brush. Rub the bristles back and forth with the hand in the water until they are clean.

Or, to assist in cleaning them, remove the brush from the water and brush the dust and dirt out of it with a clean, stiff whisk broom which will work down into the bristles. Afterwards rinse in clear water in the same way.

Or add about 2 or 3 teaspoonfuls of alum to 1 pint of water, and rinse the bristles in this to toughen them. Wipe the bristles back and forth on a clean, dry towel, and hang up the brush by the handle to dry, or better still, lay it down in the draught with the bristles down. Never lay a wet brush down on the back, as this permits the water to run down the bristles and soak the glue with which they are fastened to the back. Do not expose a wet brush to direct sunshine or other drying heat, as too rapid drying has a tendency to warp or crack the back of the brush.

Or first moisten the bristles in clear warm water and sprinkle them with powdered borax, after which wash and rinse as above.

Or dissolve 1 tablespoonful of sal soda in 1 quart of boiling water and let stand until it is cold. Wash and rinse the brush as above.

To Clean Combs.—A wire brush or whisk broom is the best means to clean gutta-percha combs, and is preferable to soaking them in water.

Or they may be washed in either of the solutions recommended above for washing brushes.

DANDRUFF AND SHAMPOOING

Dandruff. — Dandruff is a very common disease. It is caused by the formation of a scurf on the scalp which becomes detached in fine, dry scales. Unless these scales are removed from the hair by frequent brushing they give it a dry and lusterless appearance. They also tend to accumulate on clothing and to give the impression of uncleanliness. Advertised preparations for the cure of dandruff are not only usually of no avail, contrary to the claims which are so persistently advertised in their favor, but are often positively injurious.

Among the causes of dandruff may be mentioned weakness of the scalp from infectious diseases or otherwise, pressure of heavy and close hats and caps or of the hair matted upon the scalp, excessive use of hair oils and dyes, and other causes. These conditions should be avoided as much as possible, and the scalp should be kept perfectly clean, with due attention to instructions already given for its care. Hygienic measures for the improvement of the general health are also very important. Substances which are especially recommended for dandruff are yolks of eggs with chloroform, borax with or without camphor, carbolic acid, soda, and chlorate of potash.

Add 10 drops of chloroform to the yolk of an egg, and beat with an egg beater to a stiff consistency. Rub the size of an English walnut of this mixture into the scalp with the tips of the fingers, taking care to rub it thoroughly into the roots of the hair. Afterwards wash the scalp with castile or lanolin soap, and dry thoroughly with a soft towel. Some physicians claim that this is the only remedy for dandruff that is at once harmless and efficacious.

Or pulverize 1 ounce of borax and ½ ounce of camphor, and dissolve in 1 quart of boiling water. Use this solution cold. Moisten the hair frequently. Some of the camphor will sink to the bottom of the vessel, but enough will remain in solution to be effective. After using, rub a little neat's-foot oil into the scalp.

Or dissolve 1 ounce of flowers of sulphur in 1 quart of water. Shake frequently while dissolving. Allow the solution to stand until it settles, and saturate the hair with the clear liquor night and morning.

Or put a lump of fresh quicklime the size of a butternut in 1 pint of water. Let it stand 12 hours. Strain through a linen cloth and add ¼ pint of white-wine vinegar. Rub this mixture into the roots of the hair with the finger tips. If white-wine vinegar is not obtainable, the best that you have will do.

Or mix 2 ounces of glycerin with ½ dram of carbolic acid and 1 dram of oil of bergamot or other perfume. Rub this mixture into the roots of the hair with the finger tips and afterwards use bay rum. This tends to keep the hair and scalp in good condition and to prevent the formation of dandruff.

Or dissolve 1 thimbleful of powdered borax in 1 teacupful of water. Rub this mixture into the scalp with the fingers, and follow with a brisk brushing. Where the dandruff is plentiful, use this mixture daily for a week. Afterwards use twice a week until a cure is effected.

To Shampoo the Hair.—Shampooing is a word which means cleansing the head and hair. The base of the best shampoo mixtures is undoubtedly yolk of egg. Castile soap, however, is highly recommended. Borax, ammonia, sal soda, and salts of tartar are added on account of their cleansing properties; alcohol or bay rum to cut the oily substances and as preservatives; distilled water and rose water for convenience of application.

Perhaps the best of all shampoos is the yolk of an egg beaten up with a pint of soft warm water. Apply at once, and rinse off with warm water and castile or other hard white soap.

Or add 6 drops of chloroform to the above.

Or salts of tartar may be used for this purpose and is commonly employed by barbers. Dissolve ½ ounce of salts of tartar in 1 pint of soft water; apply freely and rub to a lather. Wash with soft warm water and castile soap.

Or dissolve 1 ounce of salts of tartar in 1½ pints of soft water. Add 1 ounce of castile soap in shavings and 4 ounces of bay rum. The salts of tartar will remove dandruff, and the soap will cleanse the hair and scalp.

Or mix 1 pint of soft water, 1 ounce of sal soda, and ¼ ounce of cream of tartar.

Or mix ½ ounce of alcohol, ½ ounce of glycerin, ½ ounce of sulphuric ether, ½ dram of aqua ammonia, ½ ounce of castile soap in shavings, and 1 pint of soft water.

After using a shampoo mixture, a little vaseline, oil, or pomade should be rubbed into the hair to take the place of the natural oil which is washed out in the shampooing.

Or pea flour or almond meal is recommended for cleansing the hair and scalp. The hair should first be washed with cold water, and a small handful of pea flour or almond meal, as preferred, rubbed into it for five or ten minutes. Fresh water should be added from time to time until a perfect lather forms. The whole head should then be rinsed clean, dried with a soft towel, and brushed thoroughly. This process thoroughly cleanses the hair and tends to give it a soft, silky texture. It is also said to be invigorating to the scalp.

To Compound Shampoos.—When yolk of egg is employed it should be beaten stiff with an egg beater, other dry materials added, and the whole diluted by adding distilled water slowly, and stirring briskly with an egg beater or otherwise to form an emulsion or thin paste. For the ideal egg shampoo, however, see above under "Dandruff."

For other remedies, bring distilled water to a boil, take it off the stove, dissolve in it such substances as castile soap, sal soda, borax, etc., add bay rum and spirits if desired, strain through linen, and allow to cool before perfumes are added.

To Apply Shampoo Mixtures.—Apply about a tablespoonful of a good shampoo mixture, rubbing it into the scalp with the tips of the fingers and working it in thoroughly. Massage with the hands until a fine lather is produced. Afterwards rinse with clear soft water, first hot then cold, dry the hair with a coarse towel, and apply a little oil or pomatum, if desired, to take the place of the natural oil which has been removed from the hair by this process.

Dry-hair Shampoo.—Mix 4 ounces of powdered orris root with 1 ounce of talcum powder, and sprinkle freely through the hair. This absorbs the superfluous oil and gives the hair a very thick and fluffy appearance. It is especially useful to persons whose hair is heavy and oily. It is also cooling and cleansing to the scalp.

HAIR WASHES

The solid and semisolid bases commonly found in toilet preparations are naturally to a great degree absent from those given here. The base of these washes is usually soft water, rose water, eau de cologne, or some form of spirits in which the remedial agencies and perfumes are held in solution. Preparations containing alcohol and other spirits should be used with caution, as by evaporation they tend to dry the scalp and also to deprive the hair of its natural oil, which gives normally a perfect luster.

Such substances as castile soap, ammonia, sal soda, salts of tartar, borax, and the like are often added for their cleansing properties. The principal remedial agents recommended are such substances as cantharides, arnica, camphor, sulphur, iron sulphate, and the like, and various vegetable infusions. These are employed for certain specific properties beneficial to the scalp. As in other similar toilet preparations, rose, elder-flower, orange-flower, rosemary, and other waters may be used, according to taste, and the same may be said of the various perfumes.

Nothing, perhaps, is better to cleanse the hair than diluted ammonia water—1 part of aqua ammonia to 10 parts of water. The hair and scalp should afterwards be well rinsed with clear warm water.

Or pour 1 pint of boiling water on a handful of rosemary leaves, and add ½ tablespoonful of carbonate of ammonia. Cork tightly and let stand over night, shake well, and strain through cheese cloth. Preserve in a tightly stoppered bottle.

Or mix 2 ounces of sal soda and 1 ounce of cream of tartar. Dilute with soft water to any desired consistency.

Or dissolve 1 tablespoonful of aqua ammonia and 1 teaspoonful of borax in 1 quart of soft water. Wash the hair thoroughly and rub dry with a towel.

Or dissolve 20 grains of salts of tartar in 1 pint of soft water, and add 1½ ounces of glycerin.

Or dissolve ½ ounce of camphor and 1 ounce of borax in powdered form in 1 quart of boiling water. Put in a tightly stoppered bottle and let stand over night. Shake well before using.

Or dissolve 1 dram of pearlash in ¼ pint of alcohol; dilute with 2 quarts of soft water.

Or boil 1 ounce of sassafras wood and 1 quart of soft water or diluted water, and add ¼ pint of alcohol and ¼ pint of pearlash.

Care, however, should be taken not to use these preparations too frequently. Once or twice a month is often enough to wash the hair in this manner unless it is unusually oily, and it should be borne in mind that the use of hair washes, by depriving the hair of its natural oil, has a tendency to make it harsh and dry, and hence tends to split it. After the use of washes of this sort a little vaseline, hair oil, or pomatum may be rubbed into the hair to replace the natural oil.

for fifteen or twenty minutes to make a strong infusion. Next strain, add such solids as castile soap (in shavings), borax, sal soda, and the like while the liquor is warm enough to dissolve them, and reserve the perfumes until it becomes cool.

HAIR TONICS

Loosening and Falling Out of the Hair.—This often takes place as the result of infectious diseases, on account of the weakening of the scalp. Contrary to common belief, it is probably never due to results of dissipation and excesses. Hygienic measures to improve the general health come first in importance. The use of tar soap and the yolk of egg is beneficial. To plunge the head

HAIR PREPARATIONS, WASHES, ETC.

	Tartar Wash.	Myrrh.	Colonial.	Athenian.	Rondeletia.	Rosemary.	Ammonia.	Barber's Cheap.	Spanish.	Lavender.	Rosemary.	Camphor.	Pearlash.
Borax								2 oz.				1 oz.	
Castile Soap					¼ oz.				1 dr.	¼ oz.			
Camphor												½ oz.	
Cream of Tartar	1 oz.												
Pearlash				1 oz.									2 dr.
Salts of Tartar	15 dr.												
Glycerin	1½ oz.	2 oz.											
Ammonia						2 oz.	2 dr.	2 oz.					
Tinct. Cantharides		¼ oz.	1 oz.										
Alcohol				¼ pt	¼ pt.								½ pt.
Sherry Wine								½ pt.					
Lavender Oil			½ dr.							1 oz.			
Rosemary Oil			½ dr.								2 oz.		
Eau de Cologne		1 oz.	8 oz.		1 qt.								
Tinct. Myrrh		1 oz.											
Ext. Rondeletia					⅛ pt.								
Water (Soft)	1 pt.	24 oz.		1 qt.		2 qt.	½ pt.	1 qt.	4 pt.	2 qt.	2 qt.	1 qt.	1 gal.
Box Leaves									6 oz.				
Hay Saffron					¼ dr.								
Hazel Bark											2 oz.		
Maidenhair											2 oz.		
Myrtle Berries											2 oz.		
Rosemary Leaves						6 oz.			2 oz.	1 lb.			
Southernwood									2 oz.		2 oz.		

Compounding Hair Washes. — When the solid substances, as rosemary or bay leaves, saffron wood, southernwood, and the like are recommended, they are prepared by boiling in the water or other liquid

into cold water night and morning, and afterwards to dry the hair, brushing the scalp briskly to a warm glow, is beneficial for men so affected. The recipes for various tonics and lotions will be given containing all the known specific remedial agents, and persons threatened with baldness are earnestly advised to compound their own remedies and not purchase advertised nostrums.

Dry and Harsh Hair.—This condition of the hair may be improved by shampooing the scalp with yolk of egg, as recommended for dandruff, or the scalp may be washed with a weak solution of green tea applied cold, or with an emulsion of castile soap containing a small quantity of tannin. Alcohol in any form is highly objectionable, as it tends by rapid evaporation to increase the dryness of the scalp. Shampooing the scalp occasionally with a good shampoo mixture is also useful. This condition may occur from too frequent washing of the scalp with soap or other substances that deprive it of its natural oils.

Baldness.—Absolute baldness is a condition in which the follicles or roots of the hair have lost their vitality. It is absolutely incurable. Hence preventive measures should be taken as soon as there is any indication of a tendency to baldness, as shown by the falling out or loosening of the hair. The bases of most hair invigorators and restorers is some form of cantharides or quinine. A number of simple household remedies have been recommended which are harmless and may be tried by anyone, among these being sage tea, Jamaica rum, lemon juice, vinegar, salt water, lobelia, onion juice, boxwood, and ammonia.

Instructions for the use of these homemade remedies are as follows:

Mix 1 pint of strong sage tea, 1 pint of bay rum, and 1 or 2 ounces, more or less, of glycerin, depending upon the amount of natural oil in the hair; or substitute neat's-foot oil for glycerin if the latter does not suit the skin. Shake the mixture well and apply with the finger tips to the scalp, rubbing thoroughly into the roots of the hair every night. This tends to prevent the hair from turning gray.

Or wash the head daily with good old Jamaica rum.

Or rub the pulp of a lemon on the scalp.

Or pour boiling water on rock salt or sea salt, using 2 heaping tablespoonfuls to 1 quart of water, and allow it to cool before using. Use as a wash daily.

Or 1 teaspoonful of ammonia in 1 quart of warm water. Use as a wash.

Or fill a jar or bottle with powdered lobelia. Mix brandy and sweet oil in equal parts, and add as much of the mixture as the powdered lobelia will take up. Mix and allow the compound to stand three or four days. Apply to the roots of the hair by rubbing with the finger tips daily.

Or cut a small onion in half and rub the scalp with it just before retiring. The onion juice is said to stimulate the skin and invigorate the roots of the hair. Rinse well with soft water and castile soap in the morning.

Or steep in a covered saucepan for 15 or 20 minutes 4 large handfuls of the leaves of the common box, such as is used for garden borders. Let the decoction stand over night. Strain through a linen cloth and add ½ ounce of cologne or lavender water. Use as a wash daily.

Hair Tonics.—The principal remedial agents in proprietary articles usually known as invigorators or restoratives for the hair are the various preparations of cantharides (usually the vinegar or tincture), quinine (either in the form of cinchona bark or quinine sulphate), carbonate of ammonia, tincture of arnica, an infusion of the tendrils of the grapevine, and various astringent substances. These preparations may be based on solid unguents, as lard, white wax, spermaceti, or beef marrow; or on liquid unguents, as sweet, olive, cocoanut, or other oil, especially castor oil, which is thought to be a specific for promoting the growth of the hair; and diluted with various vehicles, as alcohol, eau de cologne, rose water, distilled water, and the like. Jamaica rum, with or without the oil of bay, and sherry wine are thought to have tonic properties. And various cleansing agents, as borax and ammonia, are frequently added. All of these preparations may be perfumed with the various essential oils according to taste. They require only mixing. Hence it is sufficient to give the formulas in the following table. The ingredients should be shaken well before using and applied daily, being well rubbed into the roots of the hair until it stops falling out, or is otherwise in a satisfactory condition.

The following is an especially recommended recipe: put in a glass bottle 8 ounces of 95 per cent alcohol; add ½ ounce of glycerin, 8 grains of sulphate of quinine, 1½ grains of tincture cantharides, 2½ drams of tincture rhotany, and ½ ounce of essence of lavender. Mix and shake well before using.

HAIR TONICS, INVIGORATORS, AND RESTORATIVES

	Cantharides Tonic.	Wilson's Lotion.	Arnica Tonic.	Owen's Invigorator.	Balsam Tolu.	Chili Tonic.	West Indian Invigorator.	Kilner's Tonic.	Spanish Wash.	Cheap Tonic.	Lavender Tonic.	Bay Rum.	Capsicum Tonic.	Jamaica Tonic.	Chinese Tonic.
Lard......					2 oz.										
White Wax					3 oz.										
Castor Oil..				4 oz.		3 oz.	½ oz.	½ oz.			1 qt.	1 oz.		1 oz.	
Glycerin...	1 oz.												1 oz.		3 oz.
Sweet Oil..										1 pt.				1 pt.	
Aromatic Sp. Am .			1 dr.												
Aqua Am..						4 dr.									
Tinc. of Arnica..			⅓ oz.												
Tinc, of Canthar-ides.....	2 dr.	1 oz.				2 dr.	½ oz.	1 oz.			½ oz.	1 oz.	2 dr.	1 oz.	½ oz.
Ving. of Canthar-ides									1 oz.						
Capsicum .													1 dr.		
Carb. Am..							¼ oz.			1 oz.		½ oz.			
Cinchona Bark....								½ dr.					3 oz.		
Black Tea.															2 oz.
Tannic Acid....													½ dr.		
Alcohol....						1½ pt.	½ pt.	7½ oz.			1 qt.	1 pt.		1 pt.	
Bay Rum.				8 oz.			1 pt.					2 pt.	1 oz.	1 qt.	1 qt.
Sherry Wine....			½ pt.												
Water.....	3 oz.		½ pt.						1 oz.						1 gal.
Balsam of Tolu....					2 dr.										
Oil of Bergamot..					30 d.	3 oz.					½ oz.				
Eau de Cologne.									1 oz.				9 oz.		
Oil of Lavender...		½ dr.		30 m.		10 m.					½ oz.				
Oil of Cloves,..						15 dr.									
Tinc. of Myrrh..								½ oz.							
Oil of Rose				10 m.											
Oil of Rosemary...		½ dr.													
Thyme (white) .								¼ oz.							

Compounding Hair Tonics.—In compounding the various hair tonics in the preceding table the solids, as black tea, bay leaves, and the like, must be boiled fifteen or twenty minutes to produce an infusion, and then strained through a linen cloth. Cinchona bark and jaborandi should be first reduced in a mortar to a fine powder before boiling. Solid unguents must be melted with gentle heat, oils cut in alcohol or other spirits, and remedial agents added while the mixture is still hot enough to dissolve them readily. The whole should then be removed from the fire, thoroughly mixed by beating with an egg beater or otherwise, and strained through a linen cloth to remove the dregs. The essential oils and other volatile perfumes, if any, should be reserved until the liquor is nearly cold, to prevent loss by evaporation.

HAIR OILS

Use of Hair Oils.—The natural luster of the hair is often destroyed by the excessive use of hair oils and similar preparations. The sebaceous glands which secrete an oily substance are attached closely to the roots of the hair, and normally supply it with sufficient oily matter to keep it in good condition. To promote the activity of these glands and to distribute the natural oil evenly to the extremities of the hair is one of the principal objects of brushing. This is why a person whose hair is naturally too oily should refrain from brushing the hair more than is necessary for cleanliness. A multitude of hair oils and similar preparations are on the market, and various preposterous claims are set forth by their venders. Many of these contain minerals and other injurious ingredients, and none of them are equal to the simple preparations which may be compounded at home from the following recipes. We earnestly advise against the use of any preparation the ingredients of which are kept a secret, and the quality and condition of which cannot be definitely ascertained by the user.

The hair is liable to certain abnormal conditions, as premature grayness, falling out, dryness and harshness caused by the absence of its natural oils, and partial or total baldness. Certain special methods of treatment and remedial agents may properly be employed in such cases, and recipes for compounding these are given below.

Hair Oils.—Preparations recommended to replace the natural oil of the hair when that is, for any reason, deficient, are based upon various fixed oils, with the addition of essential oils as perfumes and various remedial agents. The best quality of hair oil is, perhaps, that based on the oil of ben (which is colorless, odorless, does not become rancid, and therefore requires less perfume than others), olive oil, the oil of sweet almouds, and castor oil. Cotton-seed oil is employed for the cheaper varieties. As specific remedial agents they frequently contain cantharides. Alcohol and other spirits are used to cut oils, and also as preservatives.

Bear's grease was formerly in high approval for this purpose, but marrow oil from beef marrow is equally good and much less expensive, besides being free from the objectionable odor of bear's grease. In fact, the latter is not usually obtainable, as substances sold under that name are largely diluted with various other animal fats. These preparations require only mixing and the addition of a few drops of essential oil or other perfumes according to taste. The extent to which they should be used will, of course, depend upon the condition of the hair and the tastes and preferences of the individual. Their principal use is in cases of unusual dryness or harshness of the hair, or when the natural oil of the hair has been temporarily removed by shampooing.

To Compound Hair Oils.—Oils prescribed in these compounds should be

HAIR OILS

	Cheap Oil.	Cocaine.	Jasmine Oil.	Cheap Barber's Oil.	N. Y. Barber Oil.	Colorless Oil.	Hickory-nut Oil.	Olive Oil.	Manon Oil.	Star Oil.	Macassar Oil.	Acme Oil.	Castor Oil.
Beef Marrow.....						1 pt.			4 oz.	1 pt.			
Oil of Ben.......			1 pt.										
Castor Oil.......		15 oz.			6½ pt.						4 oz.	4 oz.	1 qt.
Cocoanut Oil ...										1 pt.			
Cotton-seed Oil...	1 qt.			1 gal.			1 gal.						
Olive Oil.........						1 pt.		3 oz.					
Tinc. of Cantharides ...											1 lb.		
Vinegar of Cantharides....													
Glycerin.........		2 oz.											
Alcohol..........		2 oz.			1½ pt.							1 pt.	½ pt.
Oil of Bergamot..		20 dr.								10 d.		10 m.	½ oz.
" Cinnamon..													¼ oz.
" Citronella..					½ oz.								
" Civet......			3 gr.										
" Cloves.....				¼ oz.			¼ oz.						
" Fennel.....							2½ oz.						
" Jasmine....			3 oz.										
" Lavender .				1 oz.	¼ oz.		¼ oz.	1 m.					
" Myrbane...	½ oz.	2 dr.											
" Nutmeg ...								6 d.	12 d.				
" Origanum..											1 m.		
" Rose			3 d.										
" Rosemary .							½ oz.		½ oz.		1½ d.		
" Sassafras..							½ oz.						
" Thyme....				½ oz.			¼ oz.						

first melted together with gentle heat. Next add coloring matter, if any is desired. Now put in remedial agents, add spirits, if any, mix while warm, and allow to cool before adding perfumes.

To Color Hair Oil.—Any desired color may be imparted to oils for the hair by treating the fixed oil used as a base before the other ingredients are added. To accomplish this the olive, cotton-seed, or other oil which is used in the largest quantity in the mixture should be warmed with gentle heat, the coloring matter added, and the whole simmered without boiling, until the desired color or a little stronger tint is obtained. This may require from one to two hours. The oil should then be poured into a closed vessel and kept in a warm place for a day or two so that it may be evenly tinged with color. Finally it should be warmed and strained through coarse linen to remove the dregs and to give it brilliancy and luster.

For red, pink, or rose, use alkanet root—about 2 drams to a pint. The trouble of straining the oil may be avoided by putting the alkanet root in a muslin bag and suspending it in the oil, but the former method is to be preferred.

For yellow or orange, use a little annotto or palm oil.

For green, use a little green parsley, or lavender in the same manner, or dissolve 2 or 3 drams of gum guaiacum in each pint of oil as above directed.

Perfumes for Hair Oils.—Instead of taking the trouble to measure the exact quantities of different perfumes directed to be used in various recipes, many persons select a particular perfume for their own use, or blend two or more essential oils to produce an individual perfume suited to their taste. The combinations of essential oils that may be made up are, of course, countless; but the ones recommended elsewhere will serve as suggestions to those interested. An ounce or two of any of these perfumes added to a pint of rectified spirits produces an agreeable perfume or "cologne" for personal use.

HAIR DYES

Dyeing as a means of changing the normal color of the hair is now very little resorted to, except by a small number of thoughtless girls and women who are misled by ignorant or interested persons. This practice is regarded by all intelligent persons as an unmistakable mark of vulgarity. Even the young men themselves, who are supposed, if any are, to be deceived and attracted by this process, have coined the expression "chemical blonde" and "peroxide blonde" to define a woman who has been deluded into following this silly fad, and boast themselves able to recognize such an individual at sight.

There is more justification for the use of hair dyes in case of premature grayness and especially in those peculiar cases where irregular patches of gray hair make their appearance. The causes of these conditions are not fully understood. It is well known that the hair may turn gray suddenly as a consequence of extreme emotion, fright, pain, and the like. Patches of gray hair are sometimes attributed to fungous growths at the roots. Even in these cases, however, it is usually better to avoid taking a plunge into the unknown. The difficulties connected with dyeing the hair are many, and the injurious consequences are inevitable. Such a substance as a harmless hair dye is not known, all claims to the contrary notwithstanding. Neither is it possible to deceive anyone. The natural color of the hair is subtly blended by nature with the tints and shades of the complexion, and any change in the color of the hair will produce an unnatural disparity which the practiced eye readily detects. Men might perhaps be deceived, but women never. And the man or woman who adopts the use of hair dyes speedily becomes the subject of more or less invidious gossip and ridicule. The practice is usually begun with the idea that a single application will be sufficient. This is not the case. The hair grows at the rate of about one twentieth of an inch each day; hence in a few days a new growth appears and a fresh application of the dye becomes necessary. Meantime the dye has injured the hair and in many cases the scalp, brain, and nervous system. All preparations of lead, silver, and other mineral substances are distinctly and often fatally injurious. We have excluded from this book all preparations of this character, but in deference to the wishes of those who have a legitimate reason for wishing to darken the color of the hair, we give a number of recipes which are as efficacious as any that can be recommended with safety.

Hair Dyes.—A careful examination of more than 100 counted recipes for hair dyes recommended in otherwise reputable books of household recipes discloses none which do not contain injurious mineral substances, except those we give below.

Recent chemical analysis of widely advertised hair dyes and washes for bleaching, darkening, or otherwise changing the color of the hair discloses the presence of these mineral agents in practically every instance, notwithstanding the fact that in all cases the proprietors announce that the preparations are "harmless.". Among the injurious substances recommended are the following:

Nitric, muriatic, and sulphuric acids; bismuth; lead, as litharge and the acetate or sugar of lead, etc.; antimony, silver (usually the nitrate), potassium, baryta, iron, tin, copper, etc. These metals are recommended in the form of various salts, as sulphates, acetates, chlorides, and the like. They are each and all vicious in principle and injurious in practice, and those who knowingly or unknowingly recommend them should be regarded with suspicion.

To Prevent Gray Hair. — A preventive against grayness of the hair has already been mentioned, i. e., the yolk of egg. Preparations containing neat's-foot oil are also beneficial for darkening the hair. The action of hair dyes in pomades is necessarily slow, and they must be used daily or frequently until the proper results have been secured. Compounds containing vegetable ingredients are better than those containing mineral ones. Among materials which are relatively harmless are stains from walnut shells and green walnuts, which gradually dye light hair to dark-brown shades. These have to be used constantly, as the color is not durable. These stains cannot be used in the form of pomades. Henna and indigo powders produce various shades from yellow to dark brown, and other compounds and substances are mentioned below. "Chemical blondes" wash the hair with greatly diluted hydrogen peroxide. When dyes are applied to the hair it should first be thoroughly cleansed of its natural oils and other foreign substances. This may be done by washing the hair with a mixture containing one fourth part of chloroform and three fourths of alcohol. Gloves should be worn, and the dye worked into the hair with a comb and a clean toothbrush.

Or mix 1 part of bay rum, 3 parts of neat's-foot oil, and 1 part of French brandy by measure. Use this as a hair wash daily. Shake well before applying.

Or into 1 gallon of new milk put 2 quarts of the green tendrils of the grapevine. Add 2 pounds of honey and a handful of rosemary. Simmer slowly until the bulk is reduced about one half. Strain through a linen cloth and apply to the hair frequently.

An excess of lime in the system is said to have a tendency to make the hair brittle and cause it to split and crack. This, by admitting air to the hair, is the most common cause of grayness. Hence hard water for drinking purposes should be avoided, or softened by means elsewhere recommended.

Walnut Hair Dye.—Press the juice from the bark or shells of green walnuts. Add a small quantity of rectified alcohol and a little allspice or a few cloves. Let the mixture stand for a week or ten days and shake occasionally. Filter through a linen cloth and add a small amount of common salt as a preservative. Keep in a cool, dark place.

Yellow Hair Dye. — Boil 1 or 2 ounces of pure annotto in 1 pint of soft or distilled water, adding a pinch of baking soda. This gives the hair a golden yellow, which, however, varies according to its strength and the original color of the hair. Washing the hair in a solution of alum water deepens the color. The application of a solution of lemon juice or vinegar after the use of this dye reddens the hair or gives it an orange color.

Black or Brown Hair Dye.—Boil 2 ounces of black tea in 1 gallon of water. Strain through a linen cloth. Add 2 or 3 ounces of glycerin, ½ ounce of tincture of cantharides, and 1 quart of bay rum. Let the mixture stand 48 hours, shaking occasionally, and perfume with any essential oil preferred.

Black Hair Dye.—Mix juice of green walnuts as above described with neat's-foot oil, using about 1 part of the oil to 4 parts of walnut juice according to the amount of natural oil present in the hair.

Red Hair Dye.—Make a strong decoction of safflowers or of alkanet by boiling either in water to which a small amount of baking soda has been added. This gives the hair a bright-red or reddish-yellow color, according to its strength. When the hair is dry after this application, wash with a solution of lemon juice or vinegar mixed with an equal quantity of water.

Or, to darken red hair, mix 1 dram each of oil of nutmeg and rosemary, 1 ounce of castor oil, 2 drams of tincture of cantharides, and 8 ounces of French brandy. Work a teaspoonful or more of this into the hair each day with a moderately stiff brush, brushing 12 to 20 minutes.

OTHER HAIR TOPICS

Superfluous Hair. — There is no known method which is entirely satisfactory for removing superfluous hairs. Among the various methods recommended are shaving, plucking out the hairs with tweezers, the use of the electric needle, and various depilatories. The active principle in these compounds is usually chloride of lime, quicklime, or sulphide of arsenic. These cause the hair shafts to fall out, but do not affect the root of the hair, and hence must be frequently repeated. These substances are strong irritants and unless handled intelligently may create ugly ulcers.

Shaving stimulates the growth of the hair and by thickening it increases the discoloration caused by the ends of the hair shafts showing through the skin. Plucking the hairs perseveringly by the roots, the skin having been previously softened and prepared by the application of a suitable toilet emulsion, is perhaps the most satisfactory method.

A competent operator supplied with the proper apparatus can remove superfluous hair permanently by means of the electric needle. The electrode from the positive pole of the battery is attached to the back of the patient's neck or other convenient spot. A three-cornered electric needle with sharp cutting edges is attached to the negative pole of the battery. This is inserted into the skin, alongside the hair, care being taken not to penetrate too deeply. When the current is applied the needle becomes hot and causes bubbles of froth to appear at the point where it is inserted. The needle is then turned so that the sharp corners scrape the adjacent surfaces, and the process is continued until the hair is loosened and destroyed. The resulting scar is so slight as to be hardly noticeable, and if the operation is properly conducted the results are sure and permanent. The following are standard recipes for depilatories. These are severe remedies, and should be employed only with caution and due regard to what has been said above.

Spread equal quantities of galbanum and pitch plaster on a piece of soft chamois leather. Lay it smoothly on the superfluous hair and let it remain three or four minutes. It may then be pulled off, hair and all. The inflamed skin may then be rubbed with olive oil.

Or pulverize finely in a mortar 1 ounce of fresh limestone and 1 dram of pure potassa. Soak the parts for 10 minutes in warm water, so as to soften the superfluous hairs. Form a paste of the above powder with warm water, apply with a brush, and remove after 5 or 6 minutes or as soon as the skin begins to be inflamed. To remove this paste, wash it away with vinegar. This softens the skin and neutralizes the alkali.

Or mix equal quantities of sulphuret of calcium and quicklime pulverized to a fine powder. Apply precisely as for the preceding. The action is quicker. Hence it should be removed after two or three minutes in the same manner as the last.

To Curl the Hair.—Preparations recommended for curling the hair are usually based upon various more or less adhesive substances, as gum arabic, quince mucilage, beeswax, spermaceti, and the like, mixed with various oils and diluted with alcohol or water. They may be perfumed according to taste. Specific curling properties are claimed for beeswax, oil of origanum, mastic, and carbonate of potassium.

It is also said that when the hair is clipped, as is sometimes done with children or after a serious illness, if the head is shaved "against the grain" the hair will come in curly or wavy. The use of the egg shampoo elsewhere recommended also has the same tendency.

The following recipes are recommended:

Put in a double boiler 1 ounce of oil of sweet almonds, 1 dram of spermaceti, white wax, or beeswax, and dissolve with very gentle heat. Remove from the fire, stir in 3 drams of tincture of mastic. Bottle and cork tightly until wanted. Apply a small quantity and arrange the hair loosely. This is a French preparation and a commercial article of considerable reputation.

Or mix 12 ounces of olive oil, 1 dram of origanum, and 1 dram of oil of rosemary. Bottle and cork tightly until wanted. Apply every other day.

Or melt a piece of white beeswax about the size of a hickory nut in 1 ounce of olive oil, and perfume with a few drops of oil of neroli. This is simple and effective.

Or beat up the yolk of an egg, rub it into the hair, and let dry. Rinse off with clear warm water and apply a little bandoline or pomade when arranging the curls.

To Compound Curling Fluids.— Put the above solids or oils in a saucepan and simmer with gentle heat. When solids are melted or oil is well warmed, add other ingredients, except perfume. Strain, cool, and add perfume when nearly cold.

Hair Powders.—The basis of powders for the hair was formerly wheat starch, but potato farina is now more commonly used, as it is whiter and more lustrous. This is the ordinary plain hair powder of commerce, to which may be added for a black powder powdered charcoal or ivory black, or, for a sparkling effect, white frosting. Various perfumes are used according to taste. These may be used as a dry powder in the form of sachet, or they may be dropped on loaf sugar, which is afterwards pulverized in a mortar.

The following preparations are recommended:

Mix and sift together through a fine hair or other sieve 8 ounces of powdered wheat bran and 1 ounce of powdered orris root.

Or mix 8 ounces of starch powder with 2 ounces of rose sachet.

Or, for musk hair powder, mix 1 scruple of musk with 3 pounds of wheat starch or farina.

Or mix 12 ounces of starch or farina with 3 ounces of powdered ambergris; or 12 ounces of starch or farina with 3 ounces of violet sachet.

Or, for a blond hair powder, mix 4 ounces each of powdered starch or farina and powdered orris root; add 1 ounce of powdered yellow ocher.

Or, for a black hair powder, mix 4 ounces each of powdered starch or farina and powdered orris root, and add ½ ounce each of powdered charcoal and ivory black.

Or, for a sparkling effect, grind white frostings to a powder in a mortar.

Compounding Hair Powders. — These powders are merely mechanical mixtures. The ingredients should be thoroughly mixed in a mortar or other suitable receptacle, or sifted through a fine hair or wire sieve.

THE BEARD, MUSTACHE, AND SHAVING

Care of the Beard.—Unless properly cared for a full beard may seriously interfere with cleanliness. The beard should be frequently washed with soap, thoroughly dried, and treated with some simple preparation. The object of care of the beard, as in the case of the hair, is to keep it clean and to preserve its normal luster. Lotions which have alcohol or other spirits as a base may be used once or twice a week to cleanse the beard of oily or fatty materials that may have accumulated, and to clean the skin. These may be applied with a wash cloth and the beard afterwards rubbed dry with a towel. Frequent cutting or shaving of the beard has a tendency to make the individual hairs thick and short.

It does not increase their number. Singeing is harmful unless the hair is treated with oil or grease. Otherwise singeing tends to split the hair at the ends and to make it dry and brittle. Lanolin soap is perhaps the best soap for use on the hair and beard.

How to Raise a Mustache.—Stimulate the circulation by the application of hot towels, followed by rubbing briskly with a rough towel, and apply one of the following mixtures:

Alcohol, ½ pint; castor oil, ½ dram; tincture of cantharides, 1 ounce. Perfume with 20 to 40 drops of any of the essential oils, as cloves or bergamot, and 1 ounce of cologne or other essence.

Or dissolve in 5 ounces of alcohol 1 dram of compound tincture of benzoin, 1 dram of tincture of Spanish flies, and 3 ounces of castor oil, and perfume with 10 to 20 drops of any of the essential oils. Do not use this mixture too frequently as it may inflame the skin.

Or melt with gentle heat 1 ounce of white wax or spermaceti, and stir in while hot 15 drops of saturated tincture of cantharides. Remove from the fire, and when nearly cool perfume with 10 or 12 drops of any of the essential oils. This is a powerful stimulant, but must not be employed oftener than once or twice a week, as otherwise it may inflame the skin.

Mustache Pomade.—Melt 4 ounces of white wax, and add 2 ounces of pure white vaseline and ¼ ounce of Canada balsam. When nearly cold add about 30 drops of any essential oil or mixture according to taste. For coloring matters, see under "Hair Oils."

Or dissolve ½ pound of white wax, ¼ pound of lanolin soap, ¼ pound of gum arabic, and ½ pint of rose water. Melt and mix all together with gentle heat, and when cool perfume by adding 12 to 20 drops of essential oils according to taste. Color as recommended under "Hair Oils."

Shaving.—Those who snave should make it a practice to do so daily, or at least every other day. Some men complain that this practice makes the skin sore, but this will not be the case if a good razor is used, if it is kept in good order, and if the razor strokes are always in the same direction, never against the grain of the beard. The use of a good lotion after shaving is another preventive of soreness. A good toilet soap for shaving is indispensable. Shaving sticks or cream which can be rubbed on the face without the use of the shaving mug are a great convenience, especially to those who travel. It should be borne in mind that the skin and hair absorb warm water freely, and swell and soften under its influence, and that this effect is greatly promoted by the use of soap. The more time spent in softening the face by the application of lather the better. The razor should be dipped in hot water before using.

Safety Razors.—The modern custom of using safety razors is most commendable. These convenient little implements have now been so perfected as to give entire satisfaction. A number of separate blades are sold with each razor, and additional blades can be had at a very low price. These blades can be stropped by means of a special device, or returned by mail to the manufacturer to be honed, or thrown away when they become dulled by use. The luxury of having a set of seven razors—one for each day in the week—has often been suggested in books and otherwise to persons who have felt that they were hardly able to afford it. But the safety razor is a means of bringing this luxury within the reach of all. It is always ready without honing or stropping, can be used without the best of light, is entirely safe, is economical, and has made a multitude of friends for itself within recent years. Millions of these little implements are being manufactured, and the problems of how to get a good razor and how to keep it in good condition have thereby been greatly simplified. It is advisable to buy only the best-known make of safety razor, patronizing the makers who advertise most extensively in leading periodicals, so as to insure obtaining a thoroughly satisfactory article.

To Strop Razors.—Comparatively few persons seem to understand the theory of stropping a razor. The cutting edge of a razor should be in the form of a V, the sides of the V being perfectly flat and not round. The object of honing to produce this angle, and that of stropping, is to keep the edge perfect in overcoming its tendency to become round as a result of wear. The strop, therefore, should be held in such a way that the leather will bear with equal pressure on every part of the straight sides of the V which terminates in the edge. Barbers are able by constant practice to hold a loose strop in such a way as to accomplish this purpose with little apparent effort, but novices are very apt to allow the strop to move and to strike it with the razor in such a way as to round the edge, and do more harm by stropping than good. Hence a novice will usually accomplish the best results by means of a strop glued flat on a piece of wood. The razor should be stropped carefully both before and after using until it will cut a hair held loosely in the fingers, and before it is put away in its case it should be wiped dry with a clean, dry towel. If any moisture is left on the edge the steel will rust and may be ruined.

Much of the satisfaction of the use of an ordinary razor depends upon the strop and its condition. If the strop is purchased, only the best quality should be obtained, and it is better to prepare a paste for the strop than to buy a preparation for this purpose, as many of those advertised for sale are entirely unreliable.

Razor Strop.—A good razor strop may be made at home by anyone having a little ingenuity which will give at least as good satisfaction as the purchased article. Take a piece of hard wood about 15 inches long, 1½ inches wide, and ½ inch thick. Allow 3 inches or more for handle. Select a piece of horsehide or calfskin the width of the wood, and notch the wood to the depth of the leather at about ½ inch from the handle, so that the leather can be set in flush with the surface of the wood. Attach a piece of canvas to the other side, and the strop is done. The razor should be stropped first on the canvas and afterwards on the leather.

To Keep a Razor Strop in Order.—Various methods of keeping a strop in order are recommended. Fine mutton tallow or a few drops of sweet oil rubbed into the surface of the strop and a little very finely powdered emery dusted over the surface is perhaps the most satisfactory dressing. The snuffings of candle wicks in place of the emery are also recommended. Other recipes for razor paste are suggested below.

Preparations for Razor Strops.—The articles used for giving an edge to a razor are flour of emery, ground coke, and oxide of tin or prepared putty. Any of the following will be found more satisfactory than most preparations on sale, and a great deal cheaper:

Mix fine flour of emery with mutton tallow or white wax or beeswax. If the emery is not fine enough, pound and grind it in a mortar. Put the whole into a large open-mouthed bottle, fill it two thirds full of water, cork, and shake. Allow it to come to rest, and when the coarser particles have fallen to the bottom, turn off the water with the finer particles into a shallow pan. When the water has evaporated, the emery dust remaining will be found of suitable fineness.

Or collect the grit from a fine grindstone as it gathers in the form of paste on the blade of an ax or scythe. Shake in water, and treat as above suggested for emery. If the quality of the grindstone is suitable, this will prove an excellent razor paste.

Or mix 1 ounce of levigated oxide of tin or prepared putty with a saturated solution of oxalic acid to form a thick paste. If convenient, add 20 grains of gum arabic dissolved in water. Rub this composition evenly over the strop and let it dry. Dampen slightly before using. Oxalic acid has a strong affinity for iron, which is, of course, increased by moisture, and very slight friction with this preparation will give a razor a good edge.

Or coke prepared as above recommended for emery is said to be the true "diamond dust" for sharpening purposes. The above preparations, the materials of which cost practically nothing, are often sold at from twenty-five to fifty cents a box.

Or melt together equal parts of good tallow and lard, thicken with finely powdered charcoal, make into cakes, wrap in tinfoil, and sell for ten cents. To color red and to thicken, use princess metallic, such as painters use.

To improve the quality, get a little olive oil and thicken it with the metallic in one box. In another box put a little of the oil and thicken with charcoal. Put the red on one side of the strop and the black on the other side. First strop on the black side, then finish on the red side.

Barber's Itch.—This disease is supposed to be caused by a microscopic fungus, the trichophyton. The symptoms are the appearance of small red pimples with yellow tops, each of which is pierced by a hair. The disease often takes a chronic form and sometimes causes the skin to become hard and covered with crusts. There is another type which is not caused by the presence of the trichophyton, but it is difficult to tell one from the other. It is desirable in this disease to keep the beard shaved, wash thoroughly with soap, and use simple ointments and soothing solutions. The disease is very obstinate, and it is always advisable to consult a physician.

Lewis's Toilet Water for Shaving.—The following is recommended as a cheap and agreeable toilet water to use as a face wash after shaving:

Fill any size bottle you wish with 95 per cent alcohol, and add as much boracic acid as the alcohol will cut, usually about 15 per cent. If a little of the boracic acid is not dissolved and settles at the bottom of the mixture, it will not do any harm. Add a few drops of any of the essential oils, or perfume with cologne or otherwise according to taste. This mixture is not only soothing and refreshing, but it also assists in healing any local irritation caused by shaving. It is especially useful to those who shave every day.

TOILET PREPARATIONS FOR MEN

Shaving Creams. — The base of creams, pastes, or soap for shaving is usually a good, hard white castile or other soap mixed with white wax or spermaceti, and with the addition of almond, olive, etc., or palm oil, honey, and various cosmetics, as benzoin, glycerin, etc. Substances having cleansing properties, as carbonate potassa and borax, are sometimes included. Alcohol or other spirits are employed to cut the oils, and various perfumes are added later.

To Compound Shaving Creams.—These compounds are all prepared by dissolving the solids with gentle heat in a double boiler, adding the soap in shavings, stirring in the almond oil and various remedial agents while hot, and when nearly cold adding volatile substances, such as spirits of turpentine, and any of the essential oils to perfume according to taste. Solid soaps used as a base of these compounds should be exposed to the air until dry, then reduced to fine shavings or powder. Or, if alcohol is used, the soap may first be cut in the alcohol. The whole mixture, after being removed from the fire, should be thoroughly beaten with an egg beater or otherwise until it has a

SHAVING CREAMS

	Tartar Cream.	French Cream.	Palm Cream.	Yankee Liquid.	Jelly Cream.	Barber's Cream.	Soda Cream.	German Cream.	English Paste.	Honey Cream.	Russian Cream.	Honey Paste.	Owen's Cream.
White Wax..		½ oz.				1 dr.		2 oz.		½ oz.			
Spermaceti...		½ oz.						2 oz.		½ oz.			
Hard White Soap......	3 oz.	2 oz.	3 lb.	3 lb		2 oz.	2 oz.	2 oz.	2 oz.			2 oz.	3 lb.
Castile Soap.				1 lb.					4 oz.		1 oz.	4 oz.	1 lb.
Soap Jelly...					1 lb.	4 oz.					3 oz.		
Almond Oil..		½ oz.					2 oz.			½ oz.			
Olive Oil.....						1 oz.		2 oz.					
Palm Oil.....			1 lb.										
Honey......									1 oz.	4 oz.		1 oz.	
Alcohol......	8 oz.				1½ pt.								
Rose Water...	4 oz.	q. s.	12 oz.	1 qt.		4 oz.	1 oz.	q. s.	q. s.	q. s.			12 oz.
Sal. Soda....			1 oz.			2 dr.	1 oz.	2 oz.					
Carb. Potassa	1 dr.												
Sp. Turp....				1 gill									
Beef's Gall...				½ pt.									1 oz.
Any Essential Oil....	10 m.		120 m.				q. s.	20 m.	30 m.	10 m.	10 m.	18 m.	100 m.

perfectly smooth and uniform consistency. A small quantity of any of these shaving creams may be rubbed on the face and worked up to a lather with a wet shaving brush. If properly prepared they will give a good lather with either hot or cold water, that will not dry during the time required for shaving.

Bay Rum.—This fragrant liquid is obtained by distilling with rum the leaves of a number of large trees of the myrtle family, growing in Jamaica and the West Indian islands. It is not only very refreshing but it acts as a tonic and tends to prevent taking cold. Bay rum may be prepared from the oil of bay diluted with rum or other spirit, and with the addition of various cosmetics and perfumes as desired.

For a cheap bay rum, take ¼ pound of carbonated magnesia in lumps, and pour the spirit on it drop by drop until it is all saturated. Now crush the lumps on a marble slab or a piece of clean zinc with a rolling pin or otherwise. Put this in a filter and pour over equal parts of water and alcohol until the desired quantity and strength of bay rum is obtained,

Or dissolve 5 cents' worth of powdered magnesia in 1 quart of 50 per cent alcohol, and add 1 ounce of oil of bay. Put in a filter, bottle, and cork tightly until needed. Dilute with soft water as desired.

Or add 6 ounces of extract of bay to 1 gallon of 50 per cent alcohol.

Or mix 1½ fluid drams of oil of bay, ¼ fluid dram of oil of pimento, ¼ ounce of acetic ether, and 1 dram of castile soap in shavings with 3 pints of alcohol. Add 2 pints of soft or distilled water. This is a standard preparation for barbers' use.

Or, dissolve in ½ pint of 95 per cent alcohol ½ dram of oil of bay, 3 drops of oil of nutmeg, and ¼ dram of oil of orange. Add 2 ounces of Jamaica rum and sufficient water to make of the whole 1 quart.

To Compound Bay Rum.—These are for the most part simple mixtures. Magnesia should be first dissolved in soft water and the other ingredients added. The solution may afterwards be filtered by means of filter paper or fine linen. It is desirable, when convenient, to allow these mixtures to stand for two or three weeks before filtering. If they can be shaken occasionally during the period, so much the better.

Bandoline.—These preparations are employed to adjust the hair and keep it in place. Hence they are based upon substances which have a slightly adhesive character, including gum tragacanth, paste of quince seed, isinglass, Irish moss, and the like.

Bring to a boil in a double boiler ½ pint of soft or distilled water; stir in 1 tablespoonful of cold-drawn linseed oil, and boil for 5 minutes. Let cool, add any desired perfume, and put in a glass fruit jar until required for use.

Or place in a quart fruit jar 1½ ounces of gum tragacanth, and add 1 quart of rose water. Let stand 2 or 3 days, shaking frequently, and squeeze through a coarse white linen cloth. Let stand 2 or 3 days more and repeat. Finally add 10 or 12 drops of attar of rose, and tint with an infusion of alkanet wood, cochineal, or other red coloring matter.

Or boil ¼ ounce of clean Irish moss in 1 quart of water until it thickens; add 4 ounces of 95 per cent alcohol as a preservative.

Or boil ½ ounce of quince seed until it thickens. Strain through a piece of cheese cloth, put in a double boiler; add 1 pint of soft water, bring to a boil, and stir in 1 tablespoonful of linseed oil. Let boil 5 minutes, remove, and add 10 drops of the oil of bitter almonds or other essential oil to perfume.

Brilliantine.—These preparations are employed to give luster to the hair and beard when the natural oils are deficient or are temporarily removed by shampooing.

Put in a glass bottle 2 ounces of alcohol, 1 ounce of pure honey, and ½ ounce of glycerin. Shake well and perfume with any of the essential oils or essences.

Or dissolve ½ ounce of castor oil in 2 ounces of cologne. Or mix equal parts of cologne and glycerin. Or dissolve 1 ounce of honey and 2 ounces of alcohol.

Or put in a glass bottle 6 ounces of castor oil; add 2 ounces of 95 per cent alcohol, and ⅛ ounce of ammonia. Shake well and perfume with any essential oil according to taste. This is the celebrated French "lustral."

Compounding Brilliantine and Bandoline.—Such substances as gum tragacanth, quince seed, isinglass, and Irish moss may be dissolved by boiling in hot water until sufficiently thick. They should be allowed to stand on the dregs from twenty-four to forty-eight hours, squeezed through a coarse linen cloth, melted, and perfumed after cooling but before they have finally set. Boil linseed oil in water for five or six minutes. Perfume when cool.

Melt Burgundy pitch with white wax, cool slightly, mix in the spirits, replace on the fire, and bring to a boil. Remove, and strain through linen.

Eyebrows and Eyelashes.—In general the less attention paid to these features the better. The practice of attempting to deepen the color of the eyes by darkening the lids or lashes is a dangerous one, and many of the preparations advertised for sale for this purpose contain lead or other poisonous ingredients. Any preparation which is good for the hair is also good for the eyebrows and may be applied to them at the same time.

A simple lotion consists of sulphate of quinine, 5 grains; alcohol, 1 ounce. Preparations containing cantharides are also of assistance.

Clipping the eyelashes is, on the whole, a dangerous practice, as it tends to thicken them and cause them to become stiff like bristles. The presence of superfluous hairs causing the eyebrows to run together calls for remedies given elsewhere.

A stick of India ink is perhaps the best method of darkening the eyelashes if that is thought desirable.

Or burnt cork is sometimes employed.

Or cloves charred to a crisp in an open flame.

CHAPTER XXI

THE TEETH

THE TEETH—DENTIFRICES—THE BREATH—TOOTHACHE—TOOTHACHE REMEDIES

THE TEETH

Good Teeth.—Modern dentistry has greatly assisted in causing the public to realize the value of a set of good teeth, but much still remains to be done in this direction. Medical inspectors in the public schools of large cities report that a very large percentage of school children have poor teeth due to the ignorance or neglect of parents. Good teeth are necessary to health, speech, and beauty.

From the standpoint of health, it must be remembered that the process of digestion begins in the mouth. This fact is the basis of the system of hygiene known as Fletcherism. The originator of this system, after having become a chronic dyspeptic, cured himself at an advanced age by attention to two principles: never eating when not hungry, and chewing food until all the taste is chewed out of it and it disappears without conscious effort of swallowing. The importance of this last is due to the fact that the saliva of the mouth has the property of converting starchy foods into sugar, thus aiding digestion. And the further fact that food finely divided by proper chewing is more readily acted upon by the gastric juice of the stomach. Good teeth are, of course, necessary to good chewing. If any of the teeth are lost, part of the food is likely to be swallowed without being properly chewed, and the ill effects are no less certain because they are not always immediately noticed or attributed to the true source.

The teeth play an important part in pronunciation, and their loss often causes a difficulty in speech which, in the case of children, at the age when they are learning to pronounce their words, may have the effect of retarding the child's mental development.

Apertures caused by the loss of teeth, or irregularities due to the permanent teeth coming in unevenly, are life-long disfigurements. For all of these reasons, intelligent and painstaking attention to the teeth is perhaps the most important single subject in connection with the toilet.

Bad Teeth.—Decayed teeth showing cavities in the crown, or having decayed roots, are not only painful, offensive in appearance and in contaminating the breath, but frequently are the direct causes of serious disturbances of digestion. The temperature of the mouth is about 96° F. or considerably above that of ordinary summer weather. The humidity of the mouth is, of course, high. Under these conditions, experience teaches that fresh meat and other organic matter will decay very rapidly. Hence, particles of food lodged in cavities or between the teeth, if not removed, decay and afford breeding places for the bacteria of filth diseases. These are swallowed with food and upon occasion of any irritation of the digestive tract, find lodgment and give rise to indigestion and other troubles. These substances also contaminate the breath and become highly offensive to others. So that absolute cleanliness is an imperative duty that everyone owes to himself and also to his neighbor.

Moreover, if any of the teeth are unsound and painful the adjacent teeth are not likely to be used in the process of chewing, and the consequence is imperfect digestion. The remedy for these conditions is twofold: personal cleanliness and other hygienic measures, and prompt treatment by a good dentist as soon as the first symptoms of decay appear.

Structure of the Teeth.—The outer structure of the tooth consists of three parts: the *root*, which is contained in the bony substance of the jaw; the *neck*, which is contained in the gum, and the *crown*, which is the exposed portion. In the interior of each tooth is a cavity which contains the *pulp*, a pale-red soft substance composed of nerves and blood vessels. The surface of the root of the tooth is covered by a thin membrane called the *periosteum*, which, when the teeth decay, frequently becomes inflamed and is one of the causes of toothache.

Infant's Teeth.—Fasten a bit of absorbent cotton on the point of an orange stick or a piece of soft pine wood. Dip it in a 5 per cent solution of boric acid, and with this cleanse the milk teeth of children as soon as they appear.

Or wind a piece of cotton around the finger and dip it in a 5 per cent solution of boric acid or a dilute solution of listerine.

As soon as the full set of milk teeth, consisting of twenty teeth, or five on each half of each jaw, have all come in, a soft toothbrush should be used daily. Otherwise the milk, which forms such an important part of a child's diet, will be deposited between the teeth and become transformed into lactic acid. This tends to destroy the enamel and cause decay.

Two important facts regarding children's teeth are often overlooked, and much mischief results. One is that the first permanent teeth usually appear about the sixth or seventh year. The other is that several of the milk teeth are retained until about the twelfth year. This overlapping of the two sets of teeth makes early and constant care imperative. The first permanent teeth must, of course, have attention if they are to be preserved, and the milk teeth that are retained must be kept in good order to insure proper digestion during the period of most rapid growth of the child.

Teeth of Children.—One of the most common causes of trouble with the teeth in after life is the mistaken notion that children's teeth do not require very much attention because they will soon be lost and replaced by others. Children, on the contrary, should be taught to clean their teeth at a very early age, partly because they will thus acquire a habit which it will afterwards be more difficult to teach them, but more especially because the lack of proper development or decay of the milk teeth has a direct effect upon the health of the child, and an indirect effect upon the permanent teeth themselves.

The appearance of the milk teeth about the seventh month is a signal that the child should commence to have solid food and should no longer be fed exclusively on milk and other soft foods. And during the entire period when the milk teeth are coming in, children should be encouraged to eat crackers and dry bread, and not allowed to discard the crusts. The resistance of coarse food increases the circulation of the blood and gives the necessary exercise to develop the gums and the jaw muscles that are necessary to proper chewing. All of this has a direct influence in improving the quality of the permanent teeth. If the milk teeth show black spots or other evidence of decay, they should be at once treated, and filled, if necessary, with the same care as the permanent teeth. If they are suffered to decay, the permanent teeth coming in their place will be likely to decay also.

Care of the Teeth.—There are two cardinal rules in the care of the teeth: keep them clean and consult a good dentist. Few professions have arrived at a degree of proficiency equal to that of modern dentistry. In fact, the public does not generally realize what dentistry can and ought to do. The notion is far too prevalent that the business of a dentist is to fill decayed teeth, or to pull them, and make false teeth, crowns, or bridges to take their place. A very important part of the duty of a modern dentist is to prevent the teeth from decaying. Hence it is most unwise to postpone visiting a dentist until one's teeth commence to ache. On the contrary, a dentist should be consulted at least twice a year and oftener if necessary, and children, especially, should be taken to a dentist quite frequently during the period when the milk teeth are being lost and the permanent teeth are coming in.

An honest dentist will make no exorbitant charges or attempt to do work that is unnecessary. On the other hand, by keeping the teeth clean, filling small cavities when they first appear, correcting any malformation of the teeth and giving advice as to suitable mouth washes and other treatment when abnormal conditions are present, a positive saving in future dentist's bills will be effected; toothache and the pain of pulling teeth and other dental work will be avoided, and the teeth themselves will be, as a rule, preserved intact with all of the attendant benefits.

Tartar on the Teeth.—The accumulation of tartar in the form of a yellowish incrustation, which is usually most plentiful on the inner side of the lower jaw, is almost universal. But the deposit is much more pronounced in some cases than in others. Tartar is not only objectionable in appearance, but also tends to push the gum away from the neck of the tooth, and thus expose the soft dentine between the root and the harder enamel of the crown. In the course of years, the gum will recede so far as to allow the tooth to fall out, even if it is kept perfectly clean and is thus protected from decay. The accumulation of tartar cannot always be prevented by brushing the teeth, although the use of suitable tooth powders, pastes, or mouth washes will assist, but in all cases where the tartar is plentiful, the teeth should be thoroughly cleaned by a competent dentist three or four times a year, and an astringent lotion, as a 5 per cent solution of chloride of zinc or a solution of alum in soft water, should be rubbed on the gums daily.

Aside from the advice and services of a dentist, the teeth should be thoroughly brushed and cleaned at least once a day, or better still when possible after each meal, and especially before retiring at night. And the teeth of small children should be cleaned for them before they are themselves old enough to form the habit of caring for them.

Permanent Teeth are thirty-two in number, or eight on each half of each jaw. Two in the front center of the jaw are called *incisors* or cutting teeth, and appear in the eighth or ninth year. One, next in order, the *canine* or dog tooth, appears between the eleventh and fifteenth year. Two next, called *premolars*, appear between the tenth and fifteenth year. Three last in the back part of the mouth are called *molars*, of which the first (as has already been mentioned) appears about the seventh year, the second between the thirteenth and sixteenth year, and the third, which is called the "wisdom" tooth, between the eighteenth and twenty-sixth year.

Care of the Permanent Teeth.—Chewing dry toast, crackers, hard bread or other coarse food, greatly assists in keeping the permanent teeth in good condition. But for the purpose of dislodging particles of food, removing tartar and other substances a good toothbrush is indispensable. A toothbrush having medium soft bristles is preferable to one having stiff bristles, which may tend to injure or inflame the gum. The shape of the brush is not particularly important, although the so-called "prophylactic" brush assists in dislodging food from the teeth in the back part of the mouth. What is more important is the manner in which the brush is handled. In addition to the sidewise strokes, the brush should also be worked up and down so as to remove from between the teeth particles of food that would

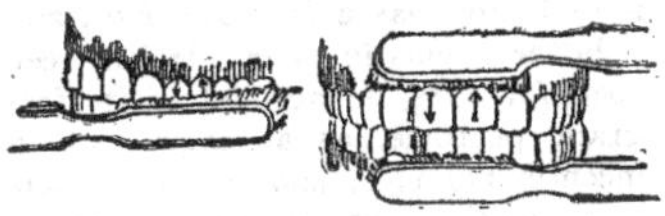

"The Way the Brush is Handled."

only be crowded in more tightly by rubbing back and forth. This is very important. The inner surface of the teeth should be brushed in the same manner, care being taken to cover, in brushing, every portion of the teeth that can be reached. The strokes of the brush should also cover the adjacent gums. This may cause them to bleed slightly at first, but in time they will harden and become strengthened. By promoting the circulation of blood, this will greatly improve the nutrition of the teeth and insure their permanency.

Toothpicks.—Etiquette forbids the use of the toothpick in public. But a supply of quills or wooden toothpicks of good quality should always be kept at hand at the toilet table. These should be used as frequently as possible after meals to remove particles of food that cannot be dislodged by the use of the brush. When, as sometimes happens, the formation of the teeth is such that a toothpick cannot be used to advantage, a piece of silk thread, such as is used by dentists, can be procured at a drug store or dentist's office. This will be found very useful for this purpose. After the use of the toothpick or thread, the mouth should be thoroughly rinsed, preferably with warm water, which has the property of dissolving foreign substances to a greater extent than cold water would do. And, if possible, a good antiseptic mouth wash, such as peroxide of hydrogen, should be used. Or use a strong solution of table salt in warm water.

Care of the Toothbrush. — After using a toothbrush, rinse it carefully, wipe it dry on a clean towel and hang it up where it will be exposed to sunlight and a draught of air. Never keep a toothbrush in a closed box or hang it up in a closet. Never lay down a wet toothbrush to dry, especially on the back, as this allows the moisture to run along the bristles into the back of the brush, softens the glue with which they are fastened in, and causes them to decay and fall out. It is hardly necessary to say that no two persons should ever use the same toothbrush.

DENTIFRICES

This is a general term including all tooth powders, pastes, and washes for the teeth. The principal ingredients of these preparations are various substances in powdered form that are capable of exerting a gentle friction on the teeth and also have antacid, absorbent, or other useful properties, as chalk, Armenian bole, cuttlefish bone, charcoal, orris root, and Peruvian bark. To these may be added mild alkalies, and other substances having cleansing properties, as borax, bicarbonate of soda, and castile soap; astringent substances as alum and tannic acid; and agreeable vehicles as powdered sugar, rock candy, honey, sirup, and sugar of milk. Any of these mixtures may be perfumed with a few drops of any of the essential oils or essences, or colored by the addition of finely pulverized red coral, rose pink, cochineal, dragon's blood, or red sanders for red; ocher for yellow; indigo for blue or violet. Various other substances having specific properties too numerous to mention may be added.

Prepared Chalk is the most universally popular ingredient in tooth powders, as it is cheap, safe, and effective, and tends to neutralize any acids that may be present in the mouth.

Bole is an earthy substance similar to clay, which is found in veins and fissures of basalt and other rocks in various parts of the world. It has a greasy feeling when rubbed between the fingers, and is slightly sticky on the tongue. There are several kinds of bole found in different localities, of which the Armenian bole has a red tint and is used in tooth powders to impart that color and also because of its absorbent and astringent properties.

Magnesia. — Carbonate of magnesia or "magnesia alba" is a white powder which is valuable because of its absorbent qualities and its power to neutralize acids that may be present in the mouth. It is used in medicine for acid dyspepsia. Hence it is entirely safe and a very effective ingredient in tooth powder.

Charcoal is a form of carbon obtained by charring wood or by heating it in close vessels. Charcoal varies according to the method by which it is produced. The best charcoal for toilet purposes is areca-nut charcoal, but this is expensive and often adulterated. Next best is the sort of charcoal used as an ingredient of gunpowder made of hard, nonresinous wood, or soft wood such as willow and poplar, by roasting in iron cylinders. Charcoal has an extraordinary capacity for absorbing gases. It cannot be melted or dissolved in acids, will not decay, and is not affected by ordinary temperatures. It is a very poor conductor of heat. On account of its property of absorbing gases, it is used in medicine in certain forms of dyspepsia, also to preserve flesh or sweeten it when tainted. As an ingredient of tooth powders, it tends to sweeten and purify the breath.

Cuttlefish Bone.—This substance is the shell of a mollusk of world-wide distribution. It is sold in powdered form under the name of "pounce" for tooth powder and other purposes. It has some value in neutralizing acids, but is less valuable for this purpose than chalk or magnesia. It is also harsher in its scouring effect, for which reason it is, in small quantities, a valuable ingredient in tooth powders. It must, however, be finely powdered and used with caution.

Myrrh.—This is a reddish-brown brittle substance obtained from the juice of a small tree growing in Arabia and vicinity. It occurs in resinous lumps, has a fragrant odor, and a bitter aromatic taste. It has been used for ages, on account of its fragrant perfume, as an ingredient in incense, perfume, and salve. It acts as a tonic on the mucous membranes and hence is much used in mouth washes to harden and strengthen the gums and is good for sore throat and canker.

Cinchona Bark, or Peruvian Bark, is obtained from a fragrant evergreen tree growing in South America which produces the alkaloid quinine of so much value in medicine. Quinine is an indispensable tonic in the cure of intermittent fevers and debilitating diseases. It is used in medicine principally in the form of the sulphate. And the bark itself is much less used than formerly. The pulverized bark has valuable tonic and astringent properties.

Iris or Orris Root.—This substance is a pulverized root of the common species of lily known as the *flower de luce* which is cultivated in the neighborhood of Florence for this substance. It is particularly valuable for its violet-scented perfume.

Coral.—This substance is a carbonate of lime obtained by grinding up the hard skeleton of the coral polyp which produces the Coral Islands. In ground form it has a quality similar to chalk, but as an ingredient for tooth powder is valued principally for its color.

Other Ingredients.—In addition to the standard recipes for dentifrices given in the following tables, a number of simple remedies may be mentioned which are always at hand.

Salt water in strong solution is a useful mouth wash, and dry salt may also be applied by means of a brush to cleanse the teeth.

Borax is also useful and tends to remove the smell of tobacco and other unpleasant odors from the breath. Dissolve 2 to 4 ounces of borax in a pint of hot water and flavor, if convenient, with half a teaspoonful of tincture of myrrh or spirits of camphor.

Castile **Soap**, or other neutral hard white soap, is good for the teeth. It may be applied by rubbing the cake of soap with a wet toothbrush, which may afterwards be dipped into a scented tooth powder to cover the slightly unpleasant taste. But the taste of castile soap is not objectionable to those who have become accustomed to it.

To Whiten the Teeth.—Salt combined with peroxide of hydrogen is a powerful bleach. Apply by wetting the brush with the pure peroxide and sprinkle with dry salt, but do not use this oftener than is necessary.

Tooth powders containing charcoal assist in whitening the teeth. A little dry charcoal powder may be rubbed gently into the crevices between the teeth on retiring at night, and brushed or rinsed out thoroughly in the morning. The use of bicarbonate of soda as a tooth powder has the same property.

Mix 1 ounce of chloride of lime, 10 ounces of prepared chalk, ½ ounce of Peruvian bark, 1 teaspoonful of tincture of myrrh. Use once a day until the teeth are sufficiently whitened. Afterwards use an ordinary tooth powder.

The juice of the common strawberry is said to be a natural dentifrice which has the property of dissolving tartar and sweetening the breath.

Or, to remove tartar, dip the brush in powdered magnesia.

Tooth Powder. — A good tooth powder is a very necessary toilet article, as it not only increases the efficiency of the brush, but also makes the operation of cleansing the teeth more agreeable, and hence tends to strengthen the habit.

Standard tooth powders are based mainly upon some carbonate having a slightly alkaline quality. But care must be taken not to use the stronger alkalies, as they tend to irritate the gums and mucuous surfaces of the mouth. Many of the tooth powders of commerce, especially the cheaper sorts, contain substances that if used with hard water produce free alkali. This may have a very injurious effect upon the gums. Hence it is much better to buy the ingredients and make up a tooth powder for yourself, or have a recipe made up for you by a local druggist. Thus you will know exactly what ingredients it contains. The powders used in tooth powders must be very finely pulverized and free from gritty particles. Such substances as ground oyster shells, pumice, cuttlefish bone, cigar ashes, and the like, unless ground very fine indeed, are unnecessarily coarse and gritty. Tooth powders may be colored at will, as the coloring matter does not affect their efficiency one way or the other. The addition of some agreeable perfume, as the oil of wintergreen, sassafras, or the like, may have a decided advantage in making children and others take more kindly to the frequent use of tooth powder. A word of caution is especially needed against the use of commercial tooth powders that rapidly remove tartar and quickly give the teeth a snowy whiteness. To accomplish these results they contain strong acids that will injure the enamel and make the last state of the teeth much worse than the first.

To Compound Tooth Powders.—If charcoal or cuttlefish bone are used, they should be reduced to a very fine powder in a mortar, and may be improved by mixing with water and allowing the coarser and heavier particles to settle. The finer particles that settle more slowly may then be poured off without disturbing the sediment. The water may then be permitted to evaporate, thus leaving a resulting powder of the best quality.

TOOTH POWDERS

	Camphorated Powders.	Safe Tooth Powder.	Violet Tooth Powder.	Orris Powder.	Cocoa Soap.	Tooth Powder.	Premium Powder.	Qunia Powder.	Beal's Tooth Powder.	Parisian Tooth Powder.	Excellent Tooth Powder.	Antiscorbutic Tooth Powder.	Peruvian Tooth Powder.
Bole		1 part	2 oz.		1 lb.					8 oz.	4 oz.		4 oz.
Chalk	3 oz.	4 parts	6 oz.	1 lb.	1 lb.	1 lb.	6 oz.	½ lb.	12 oz.		4 oz.	2 oz.	4 oz.
Charcoal											4 oz.	4 oz.	
Cuttlefish Bone			3 oz.			½ lb.				8 oz.	4 oz.		
Pulverized Sugar					½ lb.	1 lb.							
Alum										1 lb.			
Borax	2 dr.			8 oz.		2 lb.							
Carb. of Magnesia.		1 part			1 lb.	10 oz.		4 oz		½ lb.			
Cream of Tartar				4 oz.						2½ lb.			
Castile Soap											6 oz.		
Bicarbonate of Soda			2 dr.						2 oz.				
Pul. Camphor	1 oz.										4 oz.		
Sulphate Quinine								½ dr.					
Myrrh	2 dr.			4 oz									2 oz.
Orris Root		1 part	1½ oz	4 oz.			1 oz.	4 oz.	2 oz.	12 oz.		1 oz.	4 oz.
Cassia Powder							½ oz.			¾ oz.			2 oz.
Peruvian Bark	½ oz.	1 part			½ dr.							1 oz.	2 oz.
Any Essential Oils					¼ oz.					1¼ dr.		2 oz.	1 dr.
Any Essences			3 oz.										
Rose Pink						10 oz.			2 oz.	3 oz			

TOOTH PASTES

	Violet.	French Paste.	Ward's Tooth Paste.	Tooth Paste.	Quinine Paste.	Camphor Paste.	Rose Paste.	Lloyd's Aromatic Areca.	Carbon Paste.	Do.	Charcoal Paste.	Do.	Coral Paste.
Honey (white)	q. s.	½ gal.	3 oz.	8 oz	4 oz.	q. s.	3 oz.	q. s	5 oz.	4 oz.	1 oz.	1 oz.	10 oz.
Chalk			2 oz.	8 oz.		1 oz.	2 oz.		4 oz	1 oz			
Charcoal								4 dr.	2 oz	3 oz.	2 oz.	2 oz.	
Cuttlefish Bone	3 oz.	4 oz.	½ oz.		1 oz.		1 oz.	2 dr.		1 oz.			1 oz.
Pow. Sugar	2 oz.												
Castile Soap											eq. parts		
Cream of Tar.		1 oz.											2 oz.
Bicar. of Soda.													
Burnt Alum		1 oz.											½ dr.
Sal Ammoniac.						1 oz.							
Chlor. Potassa.											1 dr	½ dr.	
Camphor						4 dr.					eq. parts		
Disulphate Quinine					½ dr.								
Tinc. Opium				1¾ dr.									
Myrrh		2 oz.	1 oz.	1¾ dr.	1 dr.	1 dr.							
Orris Root	1 oz		¼ oz.	8 oz.		2 dr.							
Any Essential Oils				1 dr.			10 d.	2 dr.	1½ dr.			q. s	
Any Essences				½ dr.				3 dr.		2 dr.			
Drop Lake	½ oz.	2 oz.											
Rose Pink													
Red Coral					3 oz.								4 oz.
Cochineal							½ dr.		1½ dr.				1 oz.
Alcohol					3 fl. dr.		2 fl. dr.		q. s.		1 oz.	½ oz.	

Or, after the ingredients have been rubbed up together in the mortar as finely as possible, the whole may be rubbed through a very fine gauze sieve to remove the coarser particles. As tooth powders contain absorbent substances, they should be kept in tightly closed wide-mouthed bottles when not in use.

Tooth Pastes.—Any of the ordinary tooth powders may be put up in the form of pastes by reducing them to a very fine powder and mixing them with a little clarified honey or almond cream or simple sirup to a moderately stiff paste. Sufficient essential oils or alcohol to act as a preservative should be added, otherwise they are likely to ferment or effervesce.

Or the ingredients may be mixed with cologne or lavender water or other perfumed toilet waters to the desired consistency. They should be tightly covered to exclude the air.

To compound tooth pastes, first rub up the dry materials to a very fine powder in a mortar, moisten slightly with alcohol or perfumed toilet water, and add slowly enough honey or sirup to form a paste of the right consistency, beating all the time with an egg beater or otherwise to thoroughly incorporate the materials. Or mix the mass on a piece of glass or marble or other smooth hard surface. Let stand twenty-four hours before sealing.

Mouth Washes.—The use of an antiseptic and scented mouth wash is very agreeable and is to be recommended especially after the use of a silk thread, toothpick, or toothbrush for cleansing the teeth. But it must be carefully observed that the use of a mouth wash does not take the place of these mechanical agencies, all claims to the contrary by manufacturers of various proprietary washes notwithstanding. A mouth wash

WASHES FOR THE MOUTH AND GUMS

	Miahle's Rational.	Pelleties's Quinine.	Sozodont.	Fragrant Sozodont.	Van Buskirk's Sozodont.	Superior Mouth Wash.	Mouth Washes.	Do.	Do.	Kirkland's Tooth Lotion.	Cleveland Wash.	Violet.
Cuttlefish Bone	1 oz.											
Borax							1 oz.					
Bitartrate of Potassa			½ oz.									
Tannic Acid	3 dr.											
Camphor							½ oz.					
Alum								¼ m.				
Disulphate Quinine		15 gr.										
Honey			4 oz.			1 oz.						
Glycerin				½ oz.	1½ dr.							
Castile Soap					1½ dr.	2 dr.						
Tinc. of Soap Bark				2 oz.								
Aqua Ammonia	1 oz.									½ oz.	1 dr	
Mucilage												
Saltpeter								⅛ m.				
Sugar of Milk	3 oz.											
Orris Root											1 fl. oz.	tinct. ½ pt.
Myrrh		1 dr.		tinct. 1 dr.			2 oz.	1 oz.	½ oz.	1 oz.	1 fl. oz.	
Peruvian Bark									2 oz.		1 fl. oz.	
Red Lake	1 dr.											
Red Coral		3 oz.		q. s.								
Water			10 oz	1¼ oz.	4 oz.		8 oz.		q. s.	2 oz.	½ pt.	
Alcohol			2 oz		1 oz.	3 oz.		½ pt.				½ pt.
Any Essential Oils			q. s.		q. s.						q. s.	5 d.
Any Essences				20 d.		4 oz.	1 pt.					½ pt.

should be agreeable and antiseptic in taste and odor, and should contain nothing injurious to the general health.

Mouth washes are used with several objects in view, and the ingredients recommended vary accordingly. Among these may be mentioned hardening and strengthening the gums, cleansing the teeth, neutralizing the effects of acids and bacteria present in decayed teeth or particles of food, and sweetening and purifying the breath. Substances recommended for these various purposes are astringents, such as burnt alum, tannin, chloride of zinc, and lemon juice, which tend to harden the gums and prevent the bad effects of accumulation of tartar and scurvy; antiseptics, such as carbolic acid, peroxide of hydrogen, and salt; bleaching substances, as chloride of soda and peroxide of hydrogen; cleansing agents, as castile soap, salts of tartar, and borax; perfume substances, as the various essences and toilet waters.

These preparations are simple mixtures. Hence it is only necessary to give the various recipes in the table given on page 509.

Peroxide of Hydrogen.—Peroxide of hydrogen is perhaps the most generally efficient and satisfactory all-around mouth wash that can be used. If the peroxide is too active in its effects and causes the sensation described by athletes as "spitting cotton," it may be followed by a solution of baking soda in water, which will neutralize its effects. This is a chemical substance consisting of dioxide of hydrogen diluted with water. It is a limpid, colorless liquid having a slightly acid taste. It is similar in composition to water charged with oxygen, which is readily set free when in contact with any substance for which it has an affinity. Thus when applied to the mucous membrane, oxygen is set free, which actively attacks any foreign organic matter that may be present. It is used as a deodorant and an antiseptic. Peroxide of hydrogen is also used for restoring paintings that have become dim by the effects of sulphur on the white lead contained in the original paints; as a hair bleach and for bleaching ostrich feathers, ivory, silk, wool, and cotton. It is used in medicine for the treatment of sores, sore throat, diphtheria, and as a mouth wash for bleaching the teeth and cleansing the gums and other mucous surfaces. It is at once the safest and most active substance known in medical science for these purposes, and its general use is to be highly recommended.

THE BREATH

Foul breath is most often caused by decayed teeth, inflammation of the gums, or neglect to use the toothbrush. It may also be caused by catarrh or various diseases of the throat and stomach or other internal organs.

Substances recommended for purifying the breath are essence of camphor, chloride of lime, tincture of myrrh, chloride of soda, chloride of potash, carbolic acid, and various substances designed to heal and strengthen diseased gums. In addition, various perfumes are made up into pastilles to perfume the breath, but these are rarely effective in overcoming foul breath, are in themselves offensive to many, and their use may be obviated by suitable means to remove the cause.

One of the most effective remedies for foul breath is a mouth wash composed of a teaspoonful of concentrated solution of chloride of soda in a tumbler of water. This should be used as a gargle and also forced back and forth between the teeth. Or, if foul breath is caused by stomach troubles, take 8 drops of the solution of chloride of soda in half a tumbler of soft water before breakfast.

Or dilute a small quantity of bromochloralum with ten times its own bulk in water and use as a gargle.

Or mix 20 drops of carbolic acid, 2

drams of alcohol, 6 ounces of salt water. Apply by moistening the toothbrush and afterwards dipping it into any good tooth powder. Rinse well with salt and water or other mouth wash.

Or use any good mouth wash containing chloride of potash, tannin or tannic acid, myrrh or Peruvian bark. All of these are good for the gums and tend to prevent foul breath and like conditions.

Or chlorine water obtained from a druggist and employed as a wash or gargle is helpful. Use a tablespoonful to half a tumbler of water.

Or use as a mouth wash 2 drops of concentrated solution of permanganate of potash in a glass of water, or moisten a bit of cotton with this solution and insert it in the cavity of the tooth.

Or to 4 ounces of fresh prepared limewater add 1 dram of Peruvian bark and use as a mouth wash night and morning.

Or swallow half a teaspoonful of powdered charcoal mixed with a little cold water. Or two or three charcoal tablets after each meal.

Or use a tooth powder containing charcoal and one of the mouth washes mentioned above. If these are not efficacious, there is probably some organic disease, and a physician should be consulted.

Loose teeth or looseness of the teeth may be due to the effects of tartar, to diseases of the gum, old age, or other causes. Use as a remedy an astringent mouth wash of a teaspoonful of alum dissolved in a quart of soft water or any mouth wash containing myrrh, tannic acid, and similar substances.

To Remove the Odor of Onions.—A cup of black coffee tends to remove the odor of onions from the breath.

Or parsley with vinegar is useful for this purpose.

Or 4 or 5 drops of the concentrated solution of chloride of soda taken in 2 tablespoonfuls of cold water.

Mouth Pastilles to Perfume the Breath.—Mix 6 drams each of powdered chocolate and pulverized coffee with 4 drams of prepared charcoal, 4 drams of pulverized lump sugar previously saturated with 4 drops of extract of vanilla, and make into lozenges with gum tragacanth dissolved in water. This may be used freely to purify the breath.

Or extract of licorice, 6 ounces; oil of cloves, 3 drams; oil of cinnamon, ½ dram. Mix and divide into 2-grain pills and coat them.

Or place in a double boiler 1½ ounces of extract of licorice, 1½ ounces of water. When dissolved, stir in ½ ounce of catechu, ½ ounce of gum arabic. Continue a gentle heat, stirring constantly until all the ingredients are dissolved, then add 15 drops each of mastic, cascarilla, charcoal, and orris, all in powdered form. Beat the whole with an egg beater or otherwise until thoroughly mixed. Remove from the fire and when nearly cold perfume with 10 drops each of oil of peppermint, oil of wintergreen, and 5 drops of essence of ambergris. Form into lozenges. These are used by smokers to perfume the breath.

TOOTHACHE

This may arise from several causes. Either the crown or root of the tooth may partly or wholly decay, the gum may recede so as to expose the soft dentine of the neck of the tooth, or the membrane covering the outer surface of the root of the tooth may be inflamed. All of the conditions that give rise to toothache are a serious menace to the general health, and should have the early attention of a competent dentist. Toothache is a warning that these conditions are present, and if attended to in time will certainly be a means of avoiding graver consequences. When the enamel of the tooth becomes broken, the bone decays in all directions until the pulp or nerve of the tooth becomes affected. Often a very small orifice in the enamel, which is hardly noticeable, may lead to the decay of the whole interior of the tooth. And this condition may not be suspected until the crown happens to be chipped or broken. Hence, if the teeth are sensitive to cold or to the touch, or if they ache or "grumble" more or less from time to time, a dentist should be immediately consulted, so that the cavity may be filled before the nerve is affected. Otherwise the roots of the nerve may decay and produce ulcers, which will work their way through the bones of the jaw and the gums and discharge into the mouth. During these conditions the process of chewing is much affected, tartar accumulates on the teeth, and general bad conditions prevail.

Hence the use of toothache remedies is only advisable when for any reason it is not possible to consult a dentist. And the fact that they allay the pain, and thus seem to effect a temporary cure, should not be allowed to cause the sufferer to lose sight of the danger signal that means trouble ahead unless the cause of the pain is permanently removed.

Treatment of Toothache.—This depends upon the cause. And the only permanent cure is the removal of the cause, if possible, by the aid of a good dentist.

Toothache caused by cavities which expose the dentine, but do not affect the nerve, is usually due to local irritations caused by acids, sweets, or salt taken into the mouth, by the presence of acid in the saliva due to indigestion, by the use of the toothbrush, or by exposure to cold. In such cases a dentist should be consulted and the tooth filled as soon as possible. But in the mean time varions pain-killers mentioned below may be used to relieve or deaden the pain. Filling the cavities will almost always give immediate relief. If the neck of the tooth is exposed, mouth washes should be used containing such substances as bicarbonate of soda, carbonate of magnesia, and other alkalies, to neutralize the acid that may be present in the saliva, and suitable washes should be used to strengthen the gums.

Among substances recommended to give temporary relief in toothache are counterirritants, such as oil of cloves or cinnamon, alum, carbolic acid, ammonia; and various anæsthetics, as opium, belladonna, ether, sulphate of morphia, chloral hydrate, laudanum, and the like. Many of these are powerful and dangerous drugs and should be used only with the most intelligent caution. They should never be used when it is possible to consult a dentist, and they must not be expected to effect a permanent cure.

First cleanse the cavity, if possible, with a bit of cotton on the point of a toothpick dipped in peroxide of hydrogen or a solution of baking soda in warm water, or a solution of boric acid, listerine, or other antiseptic. Rinse out the cavity with the same solution by means of a medicine dropper or small syringe, or by using it as a mouth wash. In using the following powerful substances be careful that they do not fall into the mouth so as to be swallowed.

TOOTHACHE REMEDIES

Use the oil of cloves or equal parts of the oil of cloves and chloroform. Saturate a bit of cotton with this and crowd into the cavity. Renew frequently. But if the tooth is ulcerated, saturate the cotton and place it on the gum. Meantime soak a small piece of absorbent cotton in chloroform and insert it loosely in the ear on the affected side. Renew from time to time. Care, of course, must be taken not to be overcome by the fumes of the chloroform.

Or mix 1 dram of finely powdered alum with 3 drams of nitrous spirit of ether. Apply to the cavity on a piece of cotton.

Or mix equal parts of salt and alum with just enough water to dissolve them, saturate a bit of cotton and insert in the cavity. Renew frequently.

Or place ½ ounce of carbolic acid in a glass bottle and melt by placing the bottle in hot water. Add ½ ounce of collodium, saturate a bit of cotton and insert in the cavity, but do not let this come in contact with the inside of the mouth, as the carbolic acid will burn wherever it touches.

Or mix 5 grains of opium, 5 grains of extract of henbane, 3 drams of oil of cloves, 10 grains of extract of belladonna with powdered pellitory into a stiff paste and fill the cavity with this.

Or saturate a bit of cotton with a solution of ammonia and insert. Or insert cotton saturated with camphor dissolved in turpentine.

Or, with great care, touch the inside of the cavity with the point of a pencil of lunar caustic. Protect all but the point of the caustic by means of a cloth or otherwise, and carefully hold the lips and face away from the parts while the application is being made.

Or mix 4½ ounces of alcohol, 2 drams of camphor, 2 scruples of opium, 3 drams of oil of cloves, ¾ ounce of bruised pellitory. Let stand a week or 10 days and strain. Rub on the outside of the face or in very small quantities on the gum, or insert in the cavity on cotton.

Or mix 1 ounce each of ginger, cloves, and camphor. Grind to powder in a mortar, add 4 ounces of tincture of opium, 16 ounces of pure soft water, let stand a week or 10 days and strain. Apply as above.

Or dissolve in alcohol 5 grains of opium, 5 grains of camphor, 1 dram of oil of cloves, 1 dram of oil of cajeput. Apply to the cavity on cotton.

Or place in a glass bottle 1 ounce of creosote and add ½ dram of sulphate of morphia. Let stand until the solution is clear, then add 3 ounces of chloroform. Apply to the cavity on cotton.

Or rub to powder in a mortar ½ dram of chlorate hydrate, 1 grain of sulphate of morphia, 8 drams of camphor until they liquefy. Add 1 dram of oil of peppermint. Apply on cotton.

Or mix 10 drops each of camphorated oil, carbolic acid, creosote, chloroform, oil of peppermint, oil of cloves. Apply to the cavity on cotton.

In addition to the above, toothache will usually be relieved by applying to the face any poultice having the property of retaining heat, or resting the face on a hot-water bottle, soapstone, or common red brick covered with flannel.

Dental Work.—Teeth should never be pulled unless it is absolutely necessary. And this will not often be the case if the warning given by sensitiveness of the tooth, or by toothache, is heeded in season. The loss of the tooth usually renders the corresponding tooth on the opposite jaw useless for chewing. It also impairs proper pronunciation in speech.

Always consult the best dentists available and do not put too much confidence in the men who advertise cheap or painless dentistry. When the pulp or nerve of the tooth is affected it should be deadened and completely removed, and the root canal should be thoroughly cleaned out. This cannot be done properly without some pain. And if the operation is painless there is ground for suspicion that it may not have been thorough. Once the cavity and roots have been thoroughly cleaned and filled by a competent dentist, all trouble with that tooth will be at an end. The judgment of a dentist should be taken as to what sort of filling should be employed in any tooth. But all cavities should be filled promptly and properly, otherwise stomach troubles are sure to follow.

Artificial Teeth.—The progress of modern dentistry is nowhere more apparent than in the cheapness and perfection with which lost teeth can be replaced. Sometimes when the crown of the tooth is broken, it can be covered with an artificial crown, and the loss of one or more teeth can sometimes be repaired by a bridge consisting of several crowns anchored to two or three adjacent roots. All lost teeth, whether in the front or back part of the mouth, should be, on the ground of health, replaced at the earliest possible moment. Artificial teeth should be kept perfectly clean. And plates should be removed at night and placed in an antiseptic solution, such as listerine or boric acid.

Temporary Filling for Teeth.— First cleanse the cavity by using a bit of cotton at the end of a toothpick. Dip this in an antiseptic solution, as boric acid in water. Rinse out the cavity with the same, or a solution of peroxide of hydrogen, by means of a small glass or rubber syringe. Drop a small piece of gutta-percha into boiling water. Cut off with a penknife sufficient to fill the cavity and press it in the tooth with an orange stick or a piece of soft pine wood whittled to convenient size and shape. After filling the cavity, remove carefully any gutta-percha that may adhere to the outside of the tooth; and fill the mouth with cold water several times until the gutta-percha hardens.

Or melt a small piece of gutta-percha at the end of a wire by moistening in boiling water or holding over a hot stove or other heated surface, and insert while warm.

Dentists' Amalgam for Filling Teeth.—Gold, 1 part, mercury, 8 parts, melted together with gentle heat and poured while melted into cold water.

Or dissolve 2¼ parts of powdered mastic in 1 part of ether and mix to a stiff paste with powdered alum.

Or melt together equal quantities of tin foil and mercury and when cold enough to bear the hands, knead a small quantity with the fingers and insert quickly before it hardens.

Or melt together 1 part of cadmium, 2 parts of tin. Allow the resulting alloy to harden, reduce to filings and add sufficient mercury with gentle heat to make a fluid amalgam. Squeeze out any excess of mercury through leather. Knead up the solid remnant with the fingers and fill the cavity with this.

Or make a fluid amalgam of either gold or silver with mercury. Squeeze out the excess of mercury through leather and use the residue.

Or for a quick, cheap, and handy amalgam, mix when required for use 20 grains of fine zinc filings, 40 grains of mercury.

Or amalgamate with quicksilver 6 parts of zinc, 21 parts of tin, 73 parts of silver.

Or melt together 1 part of powdered gold, 3 parts of silver; add 2 parts of tin, allow to cool and harden; reduce to fine filings and mix with an equal quantity of pure mercury when required for use.

Or make into a paste with equal parts of quickly drying copal and mastic varnish 1 part of gypsum, 1 part of powdered porcelain, 1 part of iron filings.

Or amalgamate 2 parts of steel filings with 4 parts of quicksilver.

Dentists' Nerve Paste.—The substance used by dentists to kill the nerve is arsenic in very minute quantities.

Mix 1 part of arsenic with 2 parts of rose pink and apply on a bit of cotton moistened with creosote. Remove after 3 or 4 hours and wash out the cavity with water containing an antiseptic, as boric acid.

Mix 15 grains of arsenious acid and 10 grains of sulphate of morphia with creosote to a paste, and apply on cotton; but this should never be done without having the nerve immediately removed by a competent dentist. Otherwise the nerve pulp in the roots of the tooth will decay and will form an ulcer, which will work through the gum and sometimes through the face and continue to discharge until properly treated. Hence work of this sort should be intrusted only to a competent dentist.

CHAPTER XXII

FOOD VALUES AND ADULTERATIONS

HUMAN NUTRITION—DIETARY STANDARDS—KINDS OF NUTRIENTS—PROBLEMS OF DIET—MEAT IN THE DIET—FISH AS FOOD—POULTRY AND DAIRY PRODUCTS—SOURCES OF CARBOHYDRATES—FOOD ADULTERATIONS—CANNED VEGETABLES AND FRUITS—FLAVORING EXTRACTS AND CONDIMENTS—BAKING CHEMICALS—TEA AND COFFEE—DAIRY AND MEAT PRODUCTS

The choice, preparation, service and care of food are topics of vital importance in every home. Until quite recently experience—as represented by the traditions of the best housekeepers—has been about the only source of information on these subjects. And such experience is still in many respects the best and safest guide. But of late a great many scientific investigations as to food values and adulterations have been made—notably under the direction of the United States Department of Agriculture—and very practical results have been secured. The most essential facts and principles are here condensed for ready reference. In many respects the result of scientific study has been to confirm popular impressions derived from everyday experience. Yet it has been shown that certain very widespread beliefs are wholly groundless. All the conclusions here stated have been abundantly confirmed by practical experiments and may be accepted without hesitation. Such knowledge is valuable because it dispels doubt and uncertainty. It confirms good practices. It also draws attention to mistakes and shows how they may be corrected.

HUMAN NUTRITION

The human body has often been likened to a steam engine in which the food we eat takes the part of fuel. This comparison is partly true but is inadequate. A steam engine gradually wears out with use. Then the worn or broken parts must be replaced from some source without itself. The human body also wears away, but—unlike the steam engine—it has the power of rebuilding its own parts from the fuel (food) which it consumes. It can also bring about certain chemical changes whereby its fuel (food) is converted into new forms either for immediate use or for storage within the body against future needs. Hence the value of food depends in part upon its capacity to produce needed heat and energy, and in part upon its capacity to supply material for growth and repair of bodily waste.

Food Wastes. — The relation between the cost of food and its actual value to supply bodily needs is affected by at least three different kinds of wastes. These differ greatly in different kinds of food. They are among the things which should be most jealously watched and studied by the housewife. There is considerable loss between some kinds of foods as purchased and as cooked or served. Familiar examples are the shells of eggs, skins and seeds of fruit and vegetables, bones and offal of meat, bran of cereals and the like. These are commonly known as refuse. Some are of no value since they are wholly indigestible (for example egg shells). Others may be utilized in various ways as meat bones, which may be used for soup stock.

A second kind of waste is that caused by cooking. This is less important since, in most cases, it cannot be helped. But with some of the more expensive kinds of food, the choice among methods of cookery may be affected by the fact that some ways are more economical than others.

A third waste is due to the fact that a part of the food actually eaten is not taken up into the lymph and blood channels but passes through the digestive tract and is excreted from the body. This is said not to be "available" to digestion.

The net product which finally gets into the blood is called nutritive material, or nutrients.

Nutrients in Food.—Formerly a great many scientific terms were used in discussing the nutritive value of foods. This made the subject uninteresting to most persons because difficult to understand. With the increase of popular interest, efforts were made to simplify the language of science. It was found that all nutrients may be classed under five heads and referred to by means of terms, all but two of which are in every-day use. These unusual terms are "proteid" and "carbohydrate." Of these the former is indispensable. There is no other word which can take its place. It refers to that part of foods which contains (among other things) the element nitrogen. These include, chiefly, the lean of meat; the gluten of wheat and other cereals; the curd (casein) of milk; and the white (albumen) of eggs. The two words sugar and starch can be used in place of the term "carbohydrate" as the word refers chiefly to these two substances. These and other carbohydrates are so called because they contain the element hydrogen in the same proportions in which it occurs in water but combined with the element carbon; hence the name. Good examples of carbohydrates are potato or corn starch, and cane, grape, or milk sugar.

The names of the other three classes of nutrients are in common use. These are water, fat and ash. Water occurs in varying percentages in nearly all foods, even those which we are accustomed to think of as entirely dry, such as wheat and other dry grains, or dried peas and beans. Common examples of fat are lard, suet, butter and olive oil. The ash in foods consists of various kinds of mineral matter which are left as a residue when the foods are burned. The only kind of mineral matter usually added to foods in cookery is common salt.

In addition to these five kinds of nutrients, there is another class of substances in food which is of some value in cookery, although it is not believed that they furnish fuel or contribute to the growth of bodily tissue. They are called "extractives." They include various volatile oils and similar flavors which are "extracted" from foods in the process of cookery, whence the name. They give to certain foods the characteristic taste and odor which "make the mouth water." They aid digestion by stimulating the palate and promoting the flow of the saliva, gastric juice and other secretions which are necessary to good digestion. An example is the well known meat extract used for bouillon. This is not a food but merely an appetizing condiment.

Interest in the subject of food values centers in the three classes of nutrients—proteid, carbohydrate, and fat. Water is plentiful in every diet and is usually taken freely to satisfy thirst. Ash or mineral matter represents only about 1 per cent of most foods and is thought to be abundant in the ordinary diet. It is most plentiful in the natural food of the young, as in milk and eggs, and is of special importance to furnish material for bony structures during the period of growth and also in some diseased conditions. The housekeeper's problem is thus narrowed to the supply of sufficient proteid, carbohydrate and fat in the right proportions, as cheaply as possible, and in readily available, that is easily digestible, forms.

Uses of Nutrients in the Body.—The three principal classes of nutrients—proteid, fat and carbohydrate, all serve as fuel to yield energy in the forms of heat and muscular power. But the chief source of fuel is fat. Hence the Eskimo eats freely of tallow and blubber to keep up the bodily heat in winter. Any excess of fat may be stored in the body against future needs. Thus the bear lives on his fat during his long winter's sleep, and comes out lean in the spring. The carbohydrates—sugar and starch—may be immediately consumed as fuel, or they may be converted into and stored as fat. The proteids may also be consumed as fuel. But this does not ordinarily happen unless there is a deficiency of fat and carbohydrate in the diet. The normal use of proteid is in the growth and repair of the bodily tissues. The importance of this class of nutrients in food is due to the fact that none of the others can take its place. This explains why an infant fed wholly on condensed milk—which is rich in sugar and fat, but deficient in proteid (curds), may be fat but not strong. Roughly speaking, fat and carbohydrate supply heat and energy, and proteid forms tissue. This broad distinction is very serviceable and should be kept clearly in mind.

DIETARY STANDARDS

Balanced Diet.—A diet is said to be balanced when it contains available proteid, carbohydrate and fat in the right proportions. A great many experiments have been made to determine the ratio which the different classes of nutrients should sustain to one another in human food. In American publications the conclusions of Atwater and Chittenden are most often taken as standards. The Atwater standard, for a man with light exercise, is 100 parts (by weight) of proteid, 100 parts of fat and 360 parts of carbohydrate. The Chittenden standard is that for every 100 food units about 10 should be proteid, 30 fat, and 60 carbohydrate. These figures are interesting chiefly as showing that there can be no universal rule of proportion fixed by science. So-called standards are merely attempts to arrive at a general average on the basis of experience. In practice it will be sufficient if each of the principal nutrients are present in the dietary in sufficient quantities and without marked excess or deficiency of either. If this is the case the normal appetite will ordinarily select a well balanced diet.

The Graphic Method of Diet Calculations. — Prof. Irving Fisher has devised a method of making "food maps" which show the proportions of proteid, fat, and carbohydrate in graphic form. He says: "Any food is represented on the food map by a point the relative distance of which from the three sides of the triangle represents the proteid, fat and carbohydrate. Fatty foods are represented by points near the fat corner, F; starchy and sugary foods by points near the carbohydrate corner, C; and proteids by a point near the proteid corner, P. A food devoid of proteid is evidently located on the base line CF. A food devoid of fat on the side, CP, and a food devoid of carbohydrates on FP. . . . In each case the position of the point relative to the sides of the triangle represents the proportions of proteid, fat and carbohydrate and the number opposite each name represents the weight in ounces of a 'standard portion.'"

The accompanying food maps prepared by Dr. Fisher are a much more convenient means of comparing the values of different foods than tables of percentages. If carefully

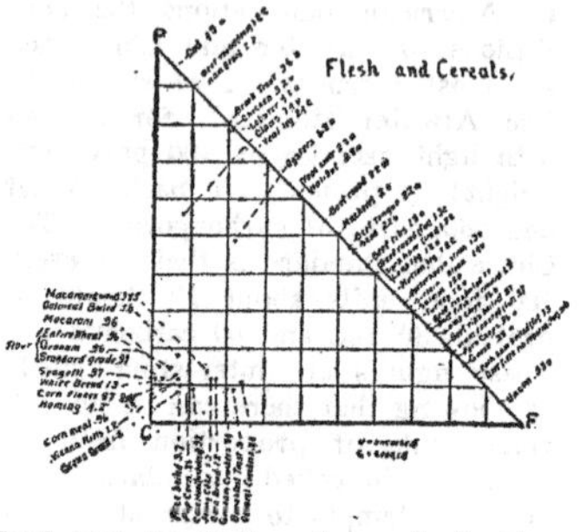

Food map for flesh and cereals by Dr. Irving Fisher.

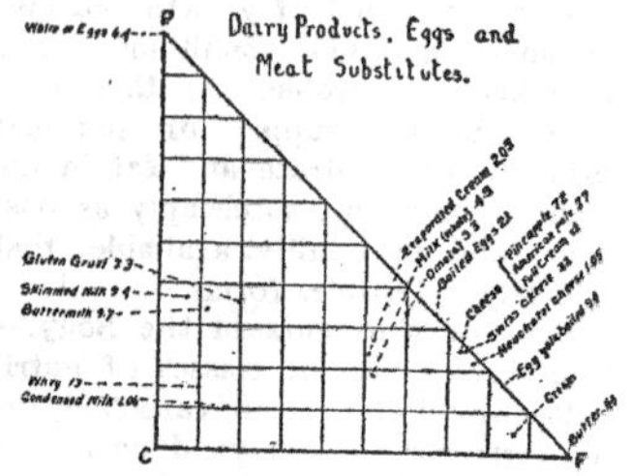

Food map for dairy products, eggs, and meat substitutes by Dr. Irving Fisher.

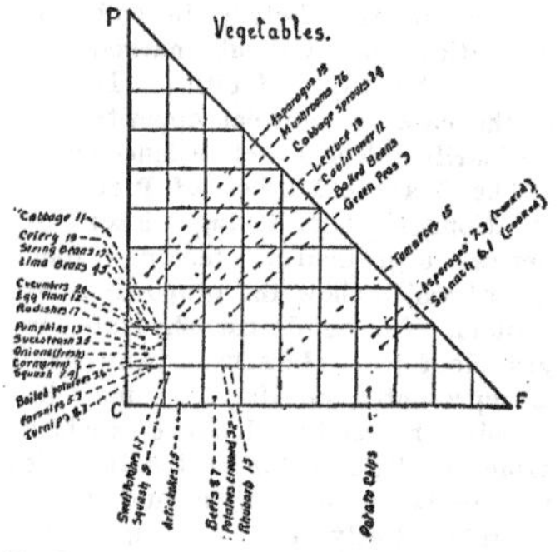

Food map for vegetables by Dr. Irving Fisher.

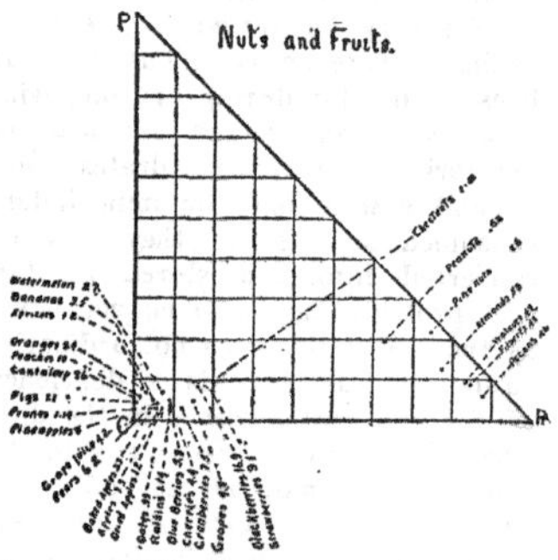

Food map for nuts and fruits by Dr. Irving Fisher.

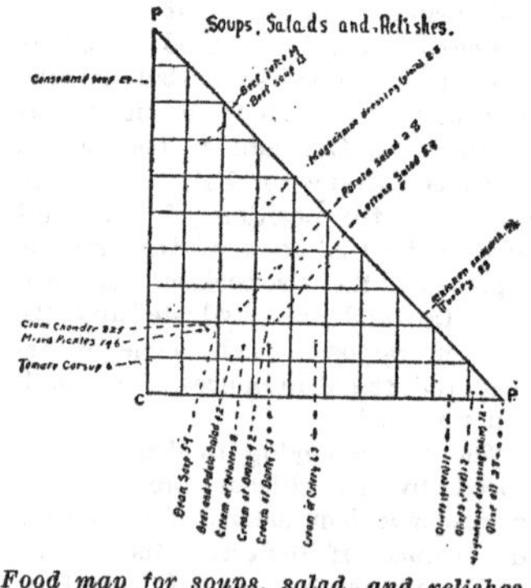

Food map for soups, salad, and relishes by Dr. Irving Fisher.

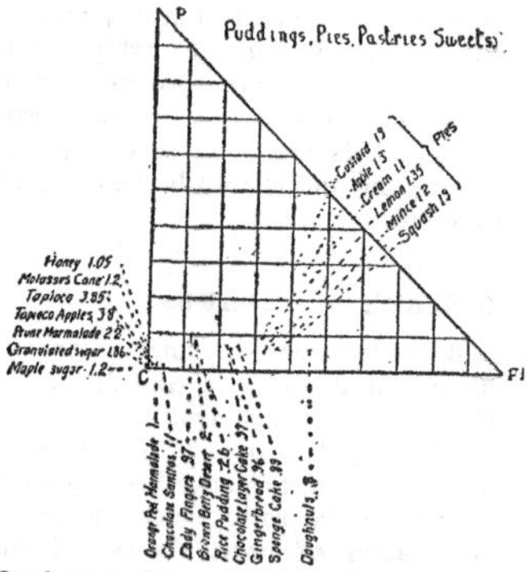

Food map for puddings, pies and pastries by Dr. Irving Fisher.

studied they will be found to contain about as much information as most persons would be apt to need or use. Roughly speaking, a balaneed ration should contain one or more foods from each of the three corners of this triangle. To take an extreme illustration, butter, white of egg and sugar combined in standard

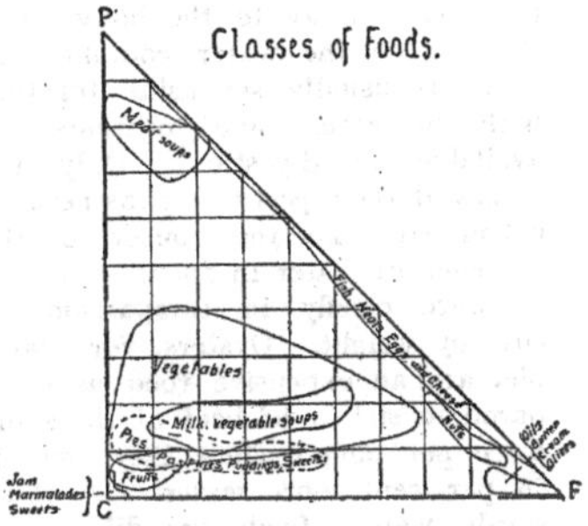

Food map for classes of foods by Dr. Irving Fisher.

proportions—if such a combination were possible in cookery—would give an example of a well balanced ration because they consist of almost pure fat, proteid and carbohydrate respectively. Or, a food located near either corner of the triangle may be balanced by one which is about equidistant between the opposite corners. The food map "Flesh and Cereals" affords many good illustrations of this principle. The different kinds of flesh are seen to contain both fat and proteid, but practically no starch or sugar. But the cereals are nearly all carbohydrate. For example, beef tongue and brown bread make a well balanced ration. Observe that brown bread is shown by the food map to be near the carbohydrate corner. Its food values are practically all sugar or starch. Beef tongue is about half way between the fat and proteid corners. Its food values are about equally divided between these two kinds of nutrients.

The foods that are represented on or near one of the side lines of the triangle show absence or marked deficiency of the kind of nutrient represented at the opposite corner. Those at or near one of the corners show absence or deficiency of the kinds of nutrients represented at *both* the opposite corners. The foods appearing at or near the center of the triangle contain each of the three classes of nutrients and, according to their position, afford a naturally more or less well balanced ration.

By reference to the standards given on page 618 it will be seen that the body requires, according to Chittenden, about one part proteid to three parts fat and six parts carbohydrate. Hence foods constituting a naturally well balanced ration appear toward the bottom of the food map. Here they fall within what is called the "normal rectangle" shown in the accompanying illustration. The position of all possible combinations of food can be worked out upon the

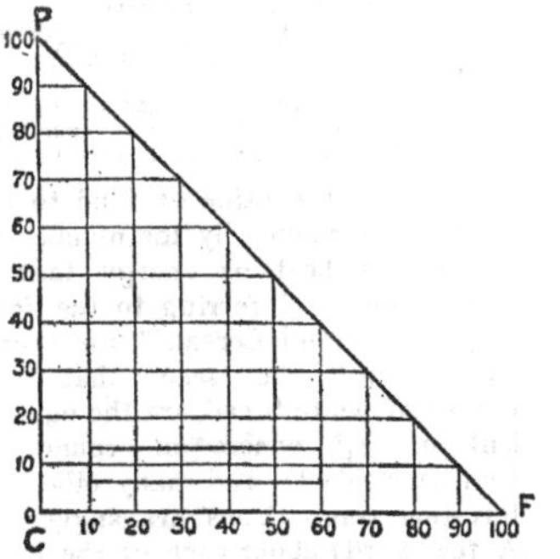

Food map showing normal rectangle for a balanced diet, Chittenden's standard. (Dr. Irving Fisher.)

food map and thus a perfectly balanced diet can be calculated. But the process is too complex for the ordinary person.*

Standard Portions. — Dr. Fischer has adopted for the purpose of calculating food values, a unit which he

* Those who wish to give the subject further study should send 10 cents to the American School of Home Economics, Chicago, for its bulletin, "Food Values."

calls the "standard portion." This is a quantity of each kind of food which will produce 100 calories of energy. The "calory" is the unit of measurement of heat, just as the pound is the unit of weight, or the acre the unit of land measure. A calory is approximately the amount of heat that is required to raise the temperature of one pound of water 4° F. The figures after the names on the food maps give the weight of "standard portions" in ounces. They are useful as a means of comparing the values of different kinds of

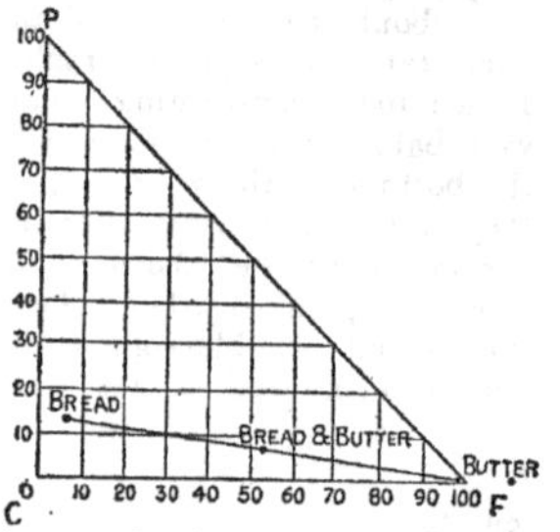

Food map showing combination of one "portion" of bread and one "portion" of butter. (Dr. Irving Fisher.)

foods, since the value of food to the body is determined by the number of calories of heat or energy that it can produce. Referring to the food map "Flesh and Cereals," for example, it will be seen that $1\frac{3}{10}$ ounces of white bread are the equivalent of $2\frac{2}{10}$ ounces of round of beef (uncooked), and many other interesting comparisons are suggested. A few words about each of the principal kinds of nutrients and a brief discussion of each of the chief classes of food from which they may be obtained—with the aid of the food maps for purposes of comparison—will enable any housewife to provide a reasonably well balanced diet.

KINDS OF NUTRIENTS

Water.—Water makes up a very large part of many kinds of food, such as milk, fresh meat, and fresh fruits and vegetables. It is present in practically all food products. Roughly speaking, over one-half of fresh lean meat and fish, and about three-fourths of fresh fruit and vegetables are water. It forms over 60 per cent by weight of the average human body and is a component part of all the tissues. It is thus an important constituent of our food. But it cannot be burned and hence does not yield energy to the body. For this reason the water contained in foods is usually set aside together with the refuse and nutrients not available to digestion. Only the values of the digestible solids need be calculated. To the housewife, the presence of water in foods is of importance chiefly in comparison of cost by weight. Oysters, for example, are an expensive food as compared to sirloin of beef at the same price per pound, since they contain 36 per cent more water. In other words, watery foods are dilute and bulky and must be paid for and eaten in far larger quantities to yield an equal amount of nutrient.

Mineral Matter or Ash. — When food or body material is burned, a small residue of mineral matter remains as ash. This constitutes some 5 per cent or 6 per cent of the body by weight. It is found principally in the bones and teeth. It is, however, present in other tissues and in solution in the various fluids. Mineral matter yields little or no energy, yet is indispensable to life and health. The average of mineral matter in the various kinds of food is not far from 1 per cent, but the proportion ranges to over 2 per cent in some cereals. It is most plentiful in the hulls (as the bran of wheat found in whole wheat flour) and in dried legumes (peas and beans); these contain about 4 per cent of mineral matter. Fresh vegetables, especially lettuce, are esteemed —especially in certain kinds of diseases—for the mineral salts they contain.

Proteid.—The proteid compounds form about 18 per cent by weight of the average human body. They include the white of egg, the lean of meat, the curd of milk and the gluten of wheat. They also occur to some extent in animals in the tendons, skin and bones. They are most important constituents of our food since they make the basis of bone, muscle and other tissues. They may also be used as fuel or even, to some extent, transformed into fat and stored in the body, especially if there is a deficiency of fats or carbohydrates. The chief sources of proteid are animal foods — meat, fish, eggs and dairy products. Butter and lard are exceptions; they represent only the fat of milk and meat.

The proportion of proteid present in meats and fish varies greatly with the kind and cut. In beef, veal, and mutton it composes between 14 and 26 per cent of the edible portion. It is somewhat less abundant in the flesh of fish, because the latter is more watery than meat. The fatter the meat, the smaller is the proportion of proteid. Lean pork has less than beef and mutton, and fat pork almost none. It is very abundant in cheese (28-38 per cent) and likewise in dried beans and peas (18-25 per cent). Proteid makes up, roughly speaking, from 7 to 15 per cent of the cereals, being least abundant in rye and buckwheat and most abnudant in oats. Wheat flour averages not far from 11 per cent and bread not far from 9 per cent of proteid. Fresh vegetables and fruits contain almost no proteid, seldom if ever more than 5 and often only 1 per cent or less.

Fats.—These form about 15 per cent by weight of the body of an average man, but the amount varies greatly with food, exercise, age and other conditions. As a general rule any excess of the diet tends to be converted into fat and stored in the body. But the tendency to fatness or leanness cannot be controlled by the diet alone. It depends also on individual peculiarities which are not well understood. Fats occur chiefly in animal foods, as meat and dairy products. They are also abundant in some vegetable products, such as olives and cottonseed. From these they are expressed as oil. They occur to a less extent in some cereals, as oatmeal and corn, and also in all common edible nuts.

Fats may be stored in various parts of the body in masses, or may be scattered through the tissues in minute particles. The quantities present in meat vary from less than 10 per cent in some cuts of beef and veal, to over 40 per cent in a side of pork, or over 80 per cent in fat salt pork. Lean fish, like cod and haddock, contains a small amount, but fatter kinds, like shad, mackerel, and notably salmon, often contain from 5 per cent to 10 per cent and sometimes as high as 15 per cent of fat. The chemical composition of salmon is not unlike that of lean meat. Milk averages about 4 per cent of fat. Butter is nearly pure fat, and cheese contains from 25 per cent to 40 per cent of fat, according to the richness of the cream or milk from which it is made. Vegetable foods are as a rule very deficient in fats. The principal exceptions have been noted.

Carbohydrates. — The carbohydrates form only a very small part of the body, less than 1 per cent, They are either immediately consumed as fuel or transformed in the body as fat. They include such compounds as starches, different kinds of sugar and the fiber of plants or cellulose. They are very abundant in vegetable foods like cereals, green vegetables and potatoes, but unlike the fats, are almost entirely absent from the animal foods except milk. Carbohydrates make up from 70 per cent to 80 per cent of the cereals, 60 per cent to 70 per cent of the dry legumes (peas and beans) and the bulk of the nutrients of fresh fruits and vegetables. Sugar, molasses, honey and the like are almost entirely carbohydrates. Milk also contains a considerable amount of carbohydrates in the form of milk sugar. They are a very important portion of the diet, because they are an excellent source of energy and are easily digested.

Atwater says:

"In brief then, the chief source of proteid is animal foods, legumes and cereals; of fats, animal foods; and of carbohydrates, vegetable products and milk. Mineral matters are found in all food materials. Refuse and water are most abundant in meats, fish, eggs, milk, fresh vegetables and fruit. The fuel value varies within wide limits, being greatest in those materials which contain the most fat and the least water.

"The ingredients of food and the ways they are used in the body may be briefly summarized in the following schematic manner:

stomach could be observed or removed at will. Beaumont's table giving the average time required for the stomach to digest various articles of diet has been frequently published. More recent experiments show that his conclusions are by no means a safe guide. The process of digestion is not confined to the stomach. It continues in the intestine. The digestibility of foods is also affected by the quantity taken, its mechanical condition, and other causes.

As a general rule the less attention given by housewives to this question the better. Recent experiments seem to indicate that all well-cooked ordinary foods are about equally well digested by normally healthy persons. The question of modification of diet

NUTRITIVE INGREDIENTS (OR NUTRIENTS) OF FOOD

Food as purchased contains—	Edible portion..................... e. g., flesh of meat, yolk and white of eggs, wheat, flour, etc.	Water.	
		Nutrients....	Proteid. Fats. Carbohydrates. Mineral matters.
	Refuse. e. g., bones, entrails, shells, bran, etc.		

USES OF NUTRIENTS IN THE BODY

Proteid.......................... e. g., white (albumen) of eggs, curd (casein) of milk, lean meat, gluten of wheat, etc.	Forms tissue.............	All serve as fuel to yield energy in the forms of heat and muscular power.
Fats............................ e. g., fat of meat, butter, olive oil, oils of corn and wheat, etc.	Are stored as fat.........	
Carbohydrates...................... e. g., sugar, starch, etc.	Are transformed into fat ...	
Mineral matters (ash)............... e. g., phosphates of lime, potash, soda, etc.	Share in forming bone, assist in digestion, etc.	

PROBLEMS OF THE DIET

Digestibility. — Many experiments have been made to learn the comparative value of different kinds of food as affected by their digestibility and by various processes of cookery. Some of the earliest and most famous of these were made by Dr. Wm. Beaumont, U. S. A., between 1825-33. His subject was a French-Canadian trapper, a man whose stomach had been torn open by a gunshot wound but had healed, leaving an opening closed only by a valve which developed over it. By pressing this valve inward the contents of the

on the grounds of digestibility, is of importance only in some kinds of disease. It should then be referred to the attending physician. It is true that some kinds of foods do not agree with certain individuals. But this is a matter which does not admit of general rules. It can be settled in each case only on the basis of experience. Each person must learn what kinds of food yield him nourishment with the least discomfort and must avoid those which do not agree with him.

The value to persons in good health of special diets consisting exclusively of vegetables, fruits and nuts, or of an exclusive diet of uncooked foods is often grossly exaggerated. The ordinary mixed diet has been shown by scientific tests to be by far the most wholesome and economical. As general rules, however, it may be said that carbohydrates—especially in the form of sugar—are more completely digested than proteids and fats; and that the proteid of animal foods—as meat, fish, milk and eggs—is more digestible than that of vegetable foods.

Economy in Diet.—The needs of individuals differ, but it has been estimated that an average man at moderately active labor—as a farmer, carpenter or mason—should have about one-fourth of a pound of available proteid each day, and sufficient fats and carbohydrates, in addition, to bring the total fuel value of the whole diet up to about 3000 calories. A man at sedentary employment would require only one-fifth of a pound of proteid, and other nutrients enough to produce a total of only 2700 calories of energy. A woman under similar conditions would need about eight-tenths as much food as a man. Children require lesser amounts, varying with their ages. The proportions usually stated are about seven-tenths for a boy from the ages of 12 to 14; six-tenths from 10 to 12; five-tenths from 6 to 9, and four-tenths from 2 to 5 years of age. Girls require slightly less nutrient than boys of the same age, but in practice the difference is negligible.

The cost of the amounts of different nutrients required varies greatly with the different kinds of food at ordinary prices. For example, one-fourth of a pound of proteid from a sirloin of beef at 25 cents a pound would cost 40 cents. The same amount from a shoulder clod of beef at 12 cents a pound would cost 19 cents, and from a piece of beef stew meat at 5 cents a pound only 9 cents; yet the actual value of each in the diet would be identical. The table on the next page of the comparative cost of digestible nutrients and energy in different food materials at average prices, prepared by the Department of Agriculture, is very useful and suggests many similar comparisons.

The most common errors in food economy are (1) the needless waste of expensive foods, (2) the use of a one-sided diet, (3) waste of food from over-eating, (4) table waste, and (5) neglect of the value of refuse. Many housekeepers buy the more expensive kinds of meat and pay higher prices for vegetables and eggs out of season, from a mistaken belief that such foods are enough more nutritious to be worth what they cost. In point of fact equal amounts of nutriment could be obtained from other foods at very much lower price. The result is a great waste of money. The maxim that "the best is the cheapest," as popularly understood to apply to high prices, is not true of food. The larger part of the price of the costlier foods is paid for appearance, flavor or rarity. While often more pleasing to the palate and sometimes more easily cooked or of finer flavor, the dearer articles are no more digestible or nutritious than the cheaper ones. The plain, substantial standard food materials—like the cheaper cuts of meat and fish, milk, flour, cornmeal, oatmeal, beans and potatoes—are as digestible and nutritious and as well fitted for the nourishment of persons in good health as are any of the costly materials.

A one-sided or badly balanced diet is one in which either proteid or fuel ingredients are in excess. If we eat too much meat and too few vegetables, the diet will be too rich in proteid and may be harmful. Or, if we eat too much pastry and other food rich in fats and sweets, the diet furnishes too much energy and too little building material. The result is injurious to health as well as false economy. Waste from over-eating is perhaps not common except among persons of sedentary occupations—brain workers, as distinguished from hand workers—but table waste is al-

COMPARATIVE COST OF DIGESTIBLE NUTRIENTS AND ENERGY IN DIFFERENT FOOD MATERIALS AT AVERAGE PRICES

[It is estimated that a man at light to moderate muscular work requires about 0.23 pound of proteid and 3,050 calories of energy per day.]

Kind of food material	Price per pound	Cost of 1 pound proteid *a*	Cost of 1,000 calories energy (*a*)	Amounts for 10 cents.				
				Total weight of food material	Proteid	Fat	Carbohydrates	Energy
	Cents	*Dollars*	*Cents*	*Pounds*	*Pound*	*Pound*	*Pounds*	*Calories*
Beef, sirloin	25	1.60	25	0.40	0.06	0.06	......	410
Do	20	1.28	20	.50	.08	.08	......	515
Do	15	.96	15	.67	.10	.11	......	685
Beef, round	16	.87	18	.63	.11	.08	......	560
Do	14	.76	16	.71	.13	.09	......	630
Do	12	.65	13	.83	.15	.10	......	740
Beef, shoulder clod	12	.75	17	.83	.13	.08	......	595
Do	9	.57	13	1.11	.18	.10	......	795
Beef, stew meat	5	.35	7	2	.29	.23	......	1,530
Beef, dried, chipped	25	.98	32	.40	.10	.03	......	315
Mutton chops, loin	16	1.22	11	.63	.08	.17	......	890
Mutton, leg	20	1.37	22	.50	.07	.07	......	445
Do	16	1.10	18	.63	.09	.09	......	560
Roast pork, loin	12	.92	10	.83	.11	.19	......	1,035
Pork, smoked ham	22	1.60	13	.45	.06	.14	......	735
Do	18	1.30	11	.56	.08	.18	......	915
Pork, fat salt	12	6.67	3	.83	.02	.68	......	2,950
Codfish, dressed, fresh	10	.93	46	1	.11	......	......	220
Halibut, fresh	18	1.22	38	.56	.08	.02	......	265
Cod, salt	7	.45	22	1.43	.22	.01	......	465
Mackerel, salt, dressed	10	.74	9	1	.13	.20	......	1,135
Salmon, canned	12	.57	13	.83	.18	.10	......	760
Oysters, solids, 50 cents per quart	25	4 30	111	.40	.02	......	.01	90
Oysters, solids, 35 cents per quart	18	3.10	80	.56	.03	.01	.02	125
Lobster, canned	18	1.02	46	.56	.10	.01	......	225
Butter	20	20.00	6	.50	.01	.40	......	1,705
Do	25	25.00	7	.40	......	.32	......	1,365
Do	30	30.00	9	.33	......	.27	......	1,125
Eggs, 36 cents per dozen	24	2.09	39	.42	.05	.04	......	260
Eggs, 24 cents per dozen	16	1.39	26	.63	.07	.06	......	385
Eggs, 12 cents per dozen	8	.70	13	1.25	.14	.11	......	770
Cheese	16	.64	8	.63	.16	.20	.02	1,185
Milk, 7 cents per quart	3½	1.09	11	2.85	.09	.11	.14	885
Milk, 6 cents per quart	3	.94	10	3.33	.11	.13	.17	1,030
Wheat flour	3	.31	2	3.33	.32	.03	2.45	5,440
Do	2½	.26	2	4	.39	.04	2.94	6,540
Corn meal, granular	2½	.32	2	4	.31	.07	2.96	6,540
Wheat breakfast food	7½	.73	4	1.33	.13	.02	.98	2,235
Oat breakfast food	7½	.53	4	1.33	.19	.09	.86	2,395
Oatmeal	4	.29	2	2.50	.34	.16	1.66	4,500
Rice	8	1.18	5	1.25	.08	......	.97	2,025
Wheat bread	6	.77	5	1.67	.13	.02	.87	2,000
Do	5	.64	4	2	.16	.02	1.04	2,400
Do	4	.51	3	2.50	.20	.03	1.30	3,000
Rye bread	5	.65	4	2	.15	.01	1.04	2,340
Beans, white, dried	5	.29	3	2	.35	.03	1.16	3,040
Cabbage	2½	2.08	22	4	.05	.01	.18	460
Celery	5	6.65	77	2	.02	......	.05	130
Corn, canned	10	4.21	23	1	.02	.01	.18	430
Potatoes, 90 cents per bushel	1½	1.00	5	6.67	.10	.01	.93	1,970
Potatoes, 60 cents per bushel	1	.67	3	10	.15	.01	1.40	2,950
Potatoes, 45 cents per bushel	¾	.50	3	13.33	.20	.01	1.87	3,935
Turnips	1	1.33	8	10	.08	.01	.54	1,200
Apples	1½	5.00	8	6.67	.02	.02	.65	1,270
Bananas	7	10.00	27	1.43	.01	.01	.18	370
Oranges	6	12.00	40	1.67	.01	......	.13	250
Strawberries	7	8.75	47	1.43	.01	.01	.09	215
Sugar	6	......	3	1.67	......	......	1.67	2,920

a The cost of 1 pound of proteid means the cost of enough of the given material to furnish 1 pound of proteid, without regard to the amounts of the other nutrients present. Likewise the cost of energy means the cost of enough material to furnish 1,000 calories, without reference to the kinds and proportions of nutrients in which the energy is supplied. These estimates of the cost of proteid and energy are thus incorrect in that neither gives credit for the value of the other.

most universal in America. In many families it is a matter of pride to furnish more food than is needed. The waste in the preparation of food materials for consumption is also considerable. This is especially the case with animal foods which are the most expensive. The trimmings of meat left with the butcher or thrown away in the kitchen often represent one-eighth of its value. Much of this might be saved by its use in soups, stews and the like. But persons who wish to get the most nutriment for their money should avoid such cuts as loin of beef, rib chops of lamb, and others, one-fifth or more of which are bone, and buy more economical cuts in which there is less waste. The common remark that "the average American family wastes as much food as a French family would live upon" is greatly exaggerated. Yet it contains considerable truth. Tests have shown that the waste in private families is often as high as twenty per cent. A study of the information here given is important for both health and purse.

MEATS IN THE DIET

Reference to the food map will show that the nutritive part of meat contains no carbohydrate but consists of proteid and fat in varying proportions. It is possible to live on animal food alone. And this is done in the arctic regions where vegetable food is lacking. But the diet is better and more wholesome if the proteid and fat of meat are balanced by the sugar and starch contained in vegetables. Meat is an expensive source of proteid as compared to some foods of vegetable origin, but is to be preferred upon the ground that it is more easily digested. Meats are more similar in composition to the tissues of the human body than foods of vegetable origin. Hence they require less change in the body to make them available to digestion.

A comparison of the nutrients in the different cuts of meat shows that they vary chiefly in the amounts of fat and water which they contain, but that there is very little difference in the proportion of proteid. Langworthy says, in substance, that for every day purposes the proportion and net value of the proteid obtained from a given weight of meat differs very little either with the kind of meat or the cut, with the exception of fat salt pork or bacon. This makes it easy for the housekeeper to be sure that her family is getting enough of this nutrient.

The total amount of proteid needed each day for a man at moderate labor is estimated at 3½ ounces. Of this, one-half is usually taken in the form of animal food, including milk, eggs, poultry and fish, as well as meat. The remainder is taken in the form of bread and other cereal foods, or beans and other vegetables. An ordinary helping of three to five ounces of lean meat may be considered to contain about one-half of the required proteid. An egg or a glass of milk contains about one-twelfth of the needed daily supply. Hence the housekeeper who gives each adult member of her family a helping of three to five ounces of cooked meat each day with eggs, milk or cheese—together with puddings or other dishes which contain eggs or milk—can feel sure that she is supplying sufficient proteid. The remainder necessary will be supplied by bread, cereals and other vegetable foods.

Langworthy says further, that there is practically no difference between the various cuts of meat, or the meats from different animals, with respect to either the thoroughness or the ease with which they are digested. Red meat is equally as digestible as white meat, pork is as digestible as beef, and the cheaper cuts are equally as digestible as the tenderest steak. Meats of all kinds and cuts are therefore to be classed as easily digested foods. Those who wish to use the cheaper cuts need not feel that, in so doing, their families are less well nourished than by the more expensive meats. It is, however, true that some kinds of meat—as roast chicken, or veal, tenderloin of steak and lamb chops cooked rare—are tender, easily masticated, well flavored and appetizing. Hence so far as stomach or gastric digestion is concerned, they are somewhat more easily and rapidly digested than others. In other words, they pass quickly out of the stomach and into the intestine where the principal work of digestion actually takes place. This agrees with the practice of using so-called white meats in diets for the sick room. It remains true, however, that nearly all of the proteid and about 95 per cent of the fat of all sorts of meat are digested by the average person.

Cuts of Meat.—The method of cutting sides of beef, veal, mutton and pork into parts for sale, and the terms used for the different "cuts" as these parts are commonly called, vary in different localities. The standard adopted by the U. S. Department of Agriculture is shown in the accompanying illustrations both for the live animal and the dressed carcass. Elsewhere the principal cuts are illustrated as they appear on the butcher's table. Both the lines of the different cuts and the names vary more or less in different parts of the country. The best way to learn the cuts of meat, as sold in your local market, is to ask the butcher to allow you to watch him cut up one or more sides of the different kinds of meat. Ask him to give you the names of the parts and also to give you his own ideas concerning them. In this way a great deal of valuable information can be obtained. Too many housekeepers are in the habit of buying only two or three of the highest priced cuts of meat. They do not realize that by proper methods of cookery equally as much nutriment can be obtained from cheaper cuts at from one-half to one-tenth the cost. The characteristics of the different cuts are described by Woods, in substance, as follows:

Cuts of Beef.—The diagram shows the general method of cutting up a side of beef. The neck piece is sometimes cut so as to include more of the chuck than is here shown. The shoulder clod is usually cut without

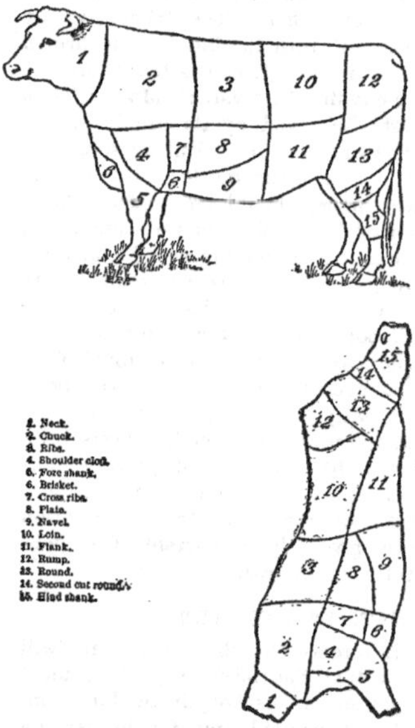

Diagrams of cuts of beef.
(Chas. D. Woods.)

bone, and hence is an economical cut, being free from refuse. The shoulder (not indicated in the diagram) includes more or less of the shoulder blade and the upper end of the foreshank. Shoulder steak is cut from the chuck. The blade is sometimes made to include all the parts of the forequarter here shown as brisket, cross ribs, blade and navel. The different portions of the blade as thus cut are then spoken of as the "brisket" end of the blade, or "navel" end of the blade. This part of the animal is largely used for corning. The ribs may also be divided into first, second and third cuts. The latter lying nearest the chuck are slightly less desirable than the former. The chuck may also be divided in a similar way, the third cut being nearest the neck.

The names applied to different portions of the loin vary considerably. The part nearest the ribs is often called "small end of loin" or "short steak." The other end is called "hip sirloin" or "sirloin". Between the "short" and the "sirloin" is a portion quite generally called the "tenderloin" for the reason that the real tenderloin—the very tenderest strip of meat lying in the tenderloin—is found most fully developed in this cut. "Porterhouse steak" is the term usually applied to either the short steak or the tenderloin. The flank may be cut to include more of the loin, in which case the upper portion is called "flank steak". The larger part of the flank is, however, very often corned, as is also the case with the rump. Or the rump may be cut so as to include a portion of the loin, which is then sold as "rump steak". The portion of the round on the inside of the leg is frequently preferred to the outside as more tender than the latter. As the leg lies upon the butcher's table, this inside of the round is usually the upper or top side and is therefore called "top round". Sometimes the blade is called the "rattle".

Cuts of Veal.—A side of veal cuts up into fewer parts and otherwise quite differently than a side of beef. The chuck is smaller and is often cut off with the neck. Or the chuck may be so cut as to take in part of the shoulder—more nearly like the chuck of beef. The shoulder of veal, as usually cut, includes the larger part of what is classed as chuck in the full grown animal. The under part of the forequarter, corresponding to the blade in beef, is often called the "breast" in veal. The part of the veal corresponding to the rump of beef is most often cut with the loin, but may be cut to form part of the leg. The fore and hind shanks of veal are sometimes called "knuckles".

Cuts of Lamb and Mutton.—These number but six, three in each quarter. The chuck includes the ribs to the end of the shoulder blades. Beyond this comes the loin. The flank is made to include all the underside of the animal. Some butchers however include part of the "loin" and "chuck" in a cut known as the

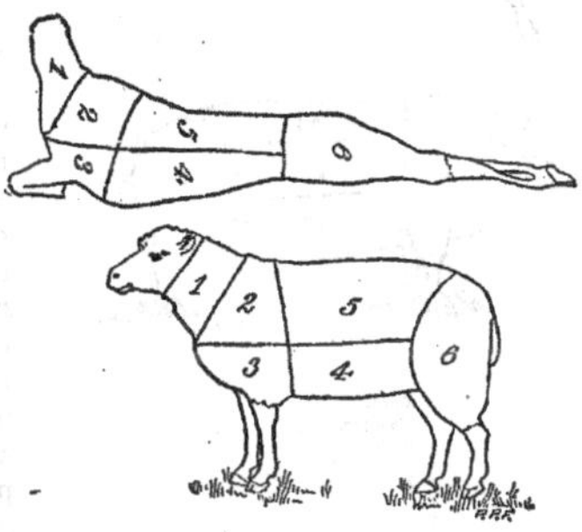

1. Neck.
2. Chuck.
3. Shoulder.
4. Flank.
5. Loin.
6. Leg.

Diagrams of cuts of lamb and mutton. (Chas. D. Woods.)

"ribs" and part of the flank and shoulder in a cut known as "brisket". The term "chops" is applied to parts of the loin, rib, chuck or shoulder, cut or chopped by the butcher into pieces for frying or boiling. The chuck and ribs are sometimes called the "rack".

Cuts of Pork.—A large portion of the carcass of a dressed pig is almost clear fat. This is used for salt pork and bacon. The cut designated as "back" is almost clear fat used for salting and pickling. The "middle" cut is used for bacon or for lean ends of salt pork. The "belly" is salted, pickled or made into sausages. Beneath the "back" are the ribs and loins. They furnish the "spareribs", "chops" and roasting pieces, here shown by dotted lines. The hams or shoulders may be cured or sold fresh as "pork steak". The tenderloin proper is a very small strip of comparatively lean meat lying under the bones of the loin. It usually weighs a fraction of a pound. Some fat is usually trimmed from the hams and shoulders. This is called "ham and

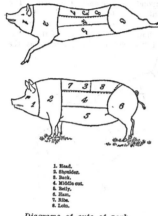

1. Head.
2. Shoulder.
3. Back.
4. Middle cut.
5. Belly.
6. Ham.
7. Ribs.
8. Loin.

Diagrams of cuts of pork.
(Chas. D. Woods.)

shoulder fat" and is often used for sausages. The kidney fat from the inside of the back is often called "leaf lard".

Cost of Different Cuts.—The table below is useful as showing the proportion of bone or other waste in the different kinds of cuts and the effect of this waste in the actual, as compared with the apparent cost of meat.

Langworthy says: "The relative retail prices of various cuts usually bear a direct relation to the favor with which they are regarded by the majority of persons. The juicy, tender cuts, of good flavor, sell for the higher prices. When porterhouse steak sells for 25 cents a pound, it may be assumed that in town or village markets round steak would ordinarily sell for about 15 cents, and chuck ribs, one of the best cuts of the forequarter, for 10 cents. This makes it appear that the chuck ribs are less than half as expensive as porterhouse steak and two-thirds as expensive as the round. But apparent economy is not always real economy. In this case the bones in the three cuts should be taken into account. Of the chuck ribs, more than one-half is bone or other materials usually classed under the head of 'waste' or 'refuse'. Of the round,

NET COST OF EDIBLE PORTION OF DIFFERENT CUTS AS COMPARED WITH ASSUMED MARKET PRICE (*a*) PER POUND

Kind of meat	Proportion of bone or waste in cut	Proportion of edible material in cut	Assumed market price per pound	Net price per pound of edible portion
BEEF:	*Per cent*	*Per cent*	*Cents*	*Cents*
Brisket	23.3	76.7	7.0	9.0
Rump	19.0	81.0	10.0	12.5
Flank	5.5	99.5	7.0	7.5
Chuck rib	53.8	46.2	10.0	22.0
Porterhouse	12.7	87.3	20.0	23.0
Neck	31.2	68.8	7.0	10.0
Ribs	20.1	79.9	15.0	20.0
Round	8.5	91.5	15.0	16.0
Shin	38.3	61.7	3.0	5.0
Heart	5.9	94.1	5.0	5.3
Tongue	26.5	73.5	22.0	29.8
VEAL:				
Cutlets	3.4	96.6	20.0	21.0
Breast	24.5	75.5	12.5	17.0
MUTTON:				
Leg	17.7	82.3	15.0	18.0
Chops	14.8	85.2	15.0	17.5
Forequarter cut for stewing	21.2	78.8	12.5	20.0
PORK:				
Loin	19.3	80.7	15.0	20.0
Salt pork	8.1	91.9	12.5	13.0
Bacon	8.7	91.3	20.0	22.0
Ham	12.2	87.8	20.0	23.0

a Prices vary greatly in different parts of the country. These prices are assumed for the purpose one-twelfth is waste, and of the porterhouse, one-eighth. In buying the chuck, then, the housewife gets, at the prices assumed, less than one-half pound of food for 10 cents. This makes the net price of the edible portion 22 cents a pound. In buying round, she gets eleven-twelfths of a pound for 15 cents. This makes the net value about 16½ cents. In buying porterhouse, she gets seven-eighths of a pound for 25 cents. This makes the net value about 28½ cents a pound. The relative prices, therefore, of the edible portions are 22, 16½ and 28½ cents. Or to put it in a different way, a dollar at the prices assumed will buy 4½ pounds of solid meat from the cut known as chuck, 6 pounds of such meat from the round, and only 3½ pounds of such meat from the porterhouse."

Owing to the extremely high price of meats in recent years a special study has been made by the United States Government on the economical use of meat in the home. The conclusion has been reached that the expense for meat can be reduced in a number of different ways. Among these may be mentioned lessening of the amount of meat used as food; buying meat in quantity for home use; utilizing the fat, bone and trimmings and the left-over cold meats; extending the flavor of meats to various vegetables and cereals by means of mixed dishes; utilizing the cheaper cuts; and developing and improving the flavor by proper methods of cookery, including use of herbs, spices, sauces and the like.

To accomplish these results a number of valuable recipes have been prepared by Miss Caroline L. Hunt, an expert in nutrition, under the supervision of Dr. C. F. Langworthy, who has been in charge of this investigation, all of which are so valuable as to merit reproduction elsewhere in this volume.

In general, it is suggested that most American families eat too much meat and that the simplest way to reduce the meat bill would be to serve meat once only, instead of two or three times a day, or to use less meat at a time. One good meat dish a day will furnish sufficient proteid, provided other and cheaper substitutes such as eggs, milk, cheese and beans are used instead. Fish might well be substituted for meat for the sake of variety as well as of economy, wherever it can be obtained fresh and cheap. Canned or salt fish also makes a useful and economical variation of the diet.

FISH AS FOOD

The flesh of fish is included with that of other animals on the food map on page 619. This shows that fish is similar in composition to meat and occupies much the same place in the diet. It contains practically no carbohydrate but consists almost wholly of proteid and fat in varying proportions. Some fish such as fat mackerel, shad and salmon, contain a high percentage of fat. And these are believed to be less easily and readily digestible than the leaner kinds such as cod, haddock, perch, pike, bluefish and others. The ash or mineral matter in fish does not vary greatly in quantity or value from other foods. The notion that fish are richer in phosphorus, and hence more valuable as a brain food for students and other sedentary workers, has no scientific foundation. Experiments do not indicate that fish contain a larger percentage of phosphorus than other kinds of flesh used as food, nor that phosphorus is any more essential to the brain than nitrogen, potassium or other elements. The percentage of available nutrients per pound is somewhat less in fish than in most kinds of meat because fish contains a much larger proportion of water. But this difference is offset by the difference in cost under ordinary conditions and prices.

A careful comparative study of different sources of proteid shows that shell fish are the most expensive and the cheaper meats, fish and cereals less expensive in the order mentioned. As sources of energy, shell fish are higher in price than common fish. The ordinary kinds of meats and the cereals are most economical. Both fish and the leaner kinds of meat are deficient in materials which yield muscular power. But when supplemented by bread, potatoes and the like, they are the more important parts of a well-balanced diet.

Cautions Concerning Fish.—Avoid fish which is not perfectly fresh and especially that which has been frozen and kept for a time after thawing and before being cooked. Such fish is liable to rapid decomposition with the forming of ptomaine poisons. As a general rule fish are unfit for food if the eyes are dull, the ball of the eye clouded, the gills pale and frothy, the scales dry and easily loosened, or the meat so soft that it can be dented with the finger like putty. To test fish about which you are in doubt, lay them in water. If they sink they are probably good. But if they float they are certainly unfit for food. Remove canned fish promptly from the can and use at once. If left in the can there is danger of poisoning from metallic oxides formed by the action of the air on the inside of the can. Moreover, canned fish deteriorates very rapidly after being opened.

Do not buy or use clams in the shell unless they are alive. That is, use only clams which close the shell when taken out of water. Also avoid oysters which are not perfectly fresh. Oysters dead in the shell and even slightly decomposed may be extremely poisonous. When removed from water good oysters close the shell, move when touched, are of normal size and color and have a clear fluid inside the shell. In the case of dead oysters the shells remain open. The oysters in a short time become discolored and very soft. They have a stale odor and show blackish rings inside the shell. Oysters are sometimes "floated" or "fattened" in water contaminated with sewage, and death sometimes results from eating them from typhoid fever and other diseases. The only safeguard against such conditions is to buy oysters only from the most reliable dealers.

POULTRY AND DAIRY PRODUCTS

In addition to meat and fish, the chief sources of proteid in the ordinary mixed diet are poultry and dairy products. Poultry differs very little in composition from other kinds of flesh used as food and is but slightly more digestible than beef, pork or mutton. The difference in digestibility between the different kinds of poultry depends chiefly upon the amount of fat present. Fat birds such as fat geese are least easily digested. Tenderness assists digestion; hence young birds are more easily digested than old. The less used muscles such as those of the breast are also more digestible than the much used muscular tissues of the thighs or "drumsticks." Experiments indicate that there is very little difference in digestibility between the white fleshed and dark fleshed birds, or between the white and dark meat of the same species.

From the standpoint of economy, home-grown chickens fed chiefly upon table scraps, sour milk and other by-products are among the cheapest and most wholesome kinds of food. Reckoning the cost of the actual nutrients, chicken as purchased in city markets at low or average prices is the cheapest kind of poultry. It then compares favorably in economy with the cheaper cuts of beef and pork. Turkey and goose may be compared in value and economy to sirloin of beef and leg of lamb. Out-of-season chicken and turkey, capon, duck and green goose are more expensive. Squab, pheasant and quail are so dear as to be luxuries. Their place can be filled, however, in most localities at little or no expense by trapping the ordinary English sparrow by methods elsewhere recommended. These birds are equally as fine as game birds in flavor. They are especially valuable as delicacies in sickness, either broiled or used as the basis of stews or broths. The chief value of game and poultry to invalids is found in the extractives they contain. These under proper methods of cookery give the characteristic flavor which makes the patient's "mouth water", i. e., they start the digestive juices flowing and stimulate the appetite.

Eggs are a very important part of the average dietary. They furnish a light, easily-digested food, rich in proteid and especially suitable for breakfast or other light meals and useful for persons of sedentary habits. It is the practice of many families of moderate means to serve fresh meat for only one meal a day—i. e., dinner. They use for breakfast such foods as bacon, dried beef, cod fish or left-over meats. For lunch or supper, they have bread and butter, with cold meats and other left-overs, and perhaps the addition of cooked, fresh or preserved fruits. It is not sound economy to omit eggs from such a diet. At ordinary prices they are among the cheapest sources of proteid and should be used freely as meat substitutes. Eggs at 25 cents a dozen are cheaper than meat, especially if one egg is sufficient to satisfy each person or if the average is less than two eggs per person, as will usually prove to be the case. Even at high prices the occasional use of eggs in the place of meat need not be regarded as a luxury.

Milk and Skim Milk.—While milk is universally recognized as the standard food of infancy and childhood its value as a food for adults is often underestimated. Milk is most commonly thought of merely as a beverage like coffee, tea or water. It is taken or not according to taste—or to satisfy thirst—rather than as a substitute for meat or other substantial portion of the diet. Yet a single glass of milk contains about as much of the nutritive value of a meal as a quarter of a loaf of bread or a good slice of roast beef. A quart of fresh milk contains nutrients equivalent to three-fourths of a pound of meat or 6 ounces of bread.

On the other hand milk is sometimes spoken of as the only perfect food. This is perhaps true in the sense that it is possible to sustain life indefinitely upon an exclusive milk diet. Such a diet is sometimes prescribed in the treatment of rheumatism and in some other diseases. Persons doing ordinary sedentary or light work can take sufficient milk to sustain themselves in good health and to furnish normal energy for periods of several months. Such a diet is not advisable for adults under ordinary conditions for the reason—among others—that to secure the required amount of carbohydrate it is necessary to take a much larger amount of proteid than is necessary. Yet these facts indicate that milk should be regarded as a substantial food.

Skim milk is often regarded on the farm as having little food value. It may be purchased in cities at a very low rate, usually about 2 or 3 cents a quart. Yet even after the bulk of the butter fat has been removed from milk by skimming, the solid nutrients make up nearly one-tenth of its entire weight and it affords one of the cheapest sources of proteid generally available. A lunch or meal of bread and skim milk is very nutritious in proportion to its cost and convenience. Eight ounces of bread eaten with a pint of skim milk will furnish very nearly one-third of the proteid required for a day's nutriment at a cost of 5 cents. As compared with the ordinary mixed diet of meat and potatoes, bread and skim milk make a better balanced and equally wholesome ration.

Many housewives hesitate to remove the cream from whole milk in the belief that they are thus robbing members of their family, and especially growing children, of a necessary kind of nutriment. But this is not the case. The fuel value of the butter fat removed in cream can be supplied in the ordinary diet more cheaply by the use of butter, meat, sweets and other carbohydrates. And the skim milk is rich in carbohydrates and proteid. Many families in moderate circumstances who are in the habit of drinking whole milk and buying cream, would be quite as well off if the top of the milk for 2 or 3 inches were poured into the cream pitcher. And there would be a marked saving in the cost of cream.

Growing children will ordinarily drink freely of skim milk, if it is available, and nothing could be more wholesome for them. But since the older members of the family may not take kindly to skim milk as a food, it is an excellent plan to use it freely in cookery. Skim milk should be preferred to water for making bread and all other recipes for which it is available.

Milk soups furnish an excellent means of increasing the food value of a meal or using up superfluous milk. Milk may be mixed with stock made from meat, or used as a basis of vegetable purées, such as bean, pea, potato, corn and celery soups, or tomato bisque and the like. Oyster stew made of milk owes its food value to the milk more than to the oysters.

Milk "white" or "cream" sauces are also very useful. They are nutritious and are a convenient and economical way of using up left-overs. Numerous recipes found elsewhere in this volume for puddings, desserts, blancmange, ice cream and junket, illustrate the many ways in which surplus milk may be used up in the ordinary mixed diet. Among ordinary by-products of milk may be mentioned —junket, cottage cheese, butter milk, whey, sour milk or clabber, and koumiss. All of these may profitably be employed to give variety.

Cheese.—One of the most important among dairy products is cheese. This has been a common article of diet among civilized people since the earliest times. Yet, oddly enough, its food value is not fully appreciated and it labors under what seems to be an unfounded prejudice, being supposed to cause certain digestive disturbances. Cheese is among the best of all meat substitutes and, at ordinary prices, is one of the cheapest sources of proteid. Its flavor is so pronounced that there may be one or more members of a family who do not relish it. And from lack of experience most housekeepers are unskillful in the use of cheese in cookery. Yet when properly cooked and relished it may fill an important place in the diet.

A series of careful experiments under the auspices of the Department of Agriculture have led to the conclusion that cheese, when used by normal healthy persons in sufficient quantity to be a substitute for meat, is not indigestible. Nor does it seem to cause any digestive disturbances. While there are persons with whom cheese does not agree, the same is true with many other articles of diet. If it should have a tendency to produce constipation, this may be offset by adding fruits and fruit juices to the diet. Bread and cheese taken with fruit is a thoroughly well balanced and very economical ration. A number of suggestive bills of fare and recipes for the use of cheese, prepared under the supervision of the Department of Agriculture, are given elsewhere. (See Appendix.)

SOURCES OF CARBOHYDRATES

Sugar as Food.—Sugar, on account of its pleasant flavor and high nutritive value, is among the most deservedly popular of all food products. It occurs in several forms of which the best known are cane sugar —the ordinary granulated sugar and other well known kinds used in cookery—glucose, made from starch; milk sugar, grape sugar and honey. Sugar is also produced in large quantities from the sugar beet. And maple sugar is an important article of commerce. Roughly speaking, sugar is the equivalent of starch after the latter has been digested and made soluble. Thus a mealy potato is very nearly akin to sugar, but—like all forms of starchy food—it must be turned into a kind of sugar by the digestive juices before it can be absorbed by the system. This process is started by a ferment contained in the saliva. It is continued and completed in the intestine. Sugar in proper quantity is very fully and rapidly digestible and is one of the most important sources of heat and energy in the diet. For this reason men employed at hard labor—especially in cold climates, as lumbermen in the northern forests—use large quantities of sugar in the form of molasses. And, for similar reasons, it is relished by children to supply the energy required by their active habits.

Sugar, like starch, is fattening since, when taken in excess, it may be transformed into fat and stored as reserve fuel. On this account sugar should be used sparingly by persons who tend to become corpnlent.

Sugar, confectionery, and the various sweet table sirups and molasses are not luxuries. They are not only valuable as flavors. They have high food value and may properly be regarded as economical sources of heat and energy. Well-to-do families in our country consume about 2 pounds of sugar per week per person. Most of the bad effects sometimes ascribed to sugar are due to its use in excess. Sugar is not any more harmful to the teeth than other foods. If allowed to cling to the teeth after eating it rapidly ferments and forms acids that may be injurious. But this is true of all starchy foods. The remedy is to be found in proper care of the teeth as elsewhere recommended. Neither does sugar produce gout; although it may be injurious in large quantities in certain classes of illness.

In addition to being used as a flavor in cooked foods and otherwise, considerable quantities of sugar are taken in fresh fruits—of which it sometimes forms one-tenth or more—and dried fruits such as figs, dates and raisins, of which as much as 50 per cent may be sugar.

Large quantities of sugar are also taken as confectionery. Cheap candies are made largely from glucose. This is no longer considered an injurions adulterant, although it is not quite so digestible as sugar. It may, therefore, overload the stomach more easily. The best authorities seem to agree that, while sugar is a valuable food for growing children, it should be withheld from infants under two years of age. Nor should it be used for older children to sweeten cereal foods which form their staple food. Mush, porridge, and similar preparations of wheat or other grain, should be eaten only with milk or cream. They are then in the same class as bread and milk and form the simple, wholesome basis of a meal. Sugar should preferably be given afterward in a simple pudding, or dessert, or in the form of lump sugar or homemade candy. Indeed, the best manner and time for giving candy to children is in the form of a few bonbons for dessert rather than at all hours of the day between meals.

Cereals.—Wheat bread and loaves of corn, rye or other cereal products, together with the cereal breakfast foods, form a very essential part of the ordinary mixed diet. The varions cereals are similar in chemical composition. They contain little fat, but consist, on an average, of 10 per cent proteid and from 60 to 80 per cent carbohydrate with varying proportions of water and ash. The cereals rank with milk and other dairy products as among the cheapest sources of nutriment. An average man at moderately active work requires about ¼ of a pound of proteid with enough fats and carbohydrates daily to make a total of 3,000 calories of available energy. Milk contains all three classes of nutrients but not in the proper proportions for healthy adults. Meats and cheese are rich in proteid and fat. Vegetables are especially rich in carbohydrates. Cereals contain both proteid and carbohydrates but in such proportions that, in order to get the requisite amount of proteid from bread alone, one would have to take more carbohydrate than would otherwise be necessary. Hence, the combination of bread with such foods as meat, milk or cheese, which are rich in proteid, makes a much better balanced ration.

All of the cereals contain an inner kernel surrounded by one or more outer hulls. These hulls are ordinarily removed in the process of milling and sold as bran which is fed to stock. The popular opinion that bread made from the entire grain is more wholesome is not sustained by scientific experiments. The bran contains a large proportion of cellulose, or woody fiber, which is wholly indigestible. This substance may have some value as a laxative in cases of constipation, since, by mechanical action it stimulates the peristaltic action of the bowel. But it adds very little nutritive value to the loaf. On the contrary, experiments indicate that its presence somewhat lessens the digestibility of the finer portion of the grain. On the whole it may be taken for granted that the ordinary white bread is not only more palatable, and preferable for appearance sake, but is actually a more economical source of nutriment. However, all kinds of bread are nutritious and are to be recommended for the sake of variety. This is equally as important in bread as in meats, vegetables and puddings.

The cheaper grades of flour are about as nutritious as the more expensive and may be used without hesitancy if economy is required. Crackers, macaroni, and the various kinds of cake made from white flour have practically the same nutritive value as bread and are equally well digested by healthy adults. Hot bread in the form of rolls and biscuit is also found to be digestible, if properly masticated. The value of toast for invalids and others is due to several changes produced by heating. A portion of the carbohydrates becomes more soluble and hence more easily digested. If the heating is strong enough any ferments and bacteria present may be killed. Toast, on account of its dryness, is likely to be well masticated. And partial caramelization gives a crispness and flavor which stimulate the digestive juices. Bread made with skim milk makes a better balanced ration than that made with water alone and is preferable since it does not materially increase the cost. The common custom of eating butter or some other fat with bread is justified by the fact that the cereals, with the exception of corn, have little or no fat content.

Breakfast Foods.—Careful studies in large numbers of American families show that the various cereals furnish over one-fifth of the total food, about one-third of the total proteid and considerably over one-half of the total carbohydrates of the average dietary. Of these about 2 per cent are furnished by the modern cereal breakfast foods. Notwithstanding that the percentage is small, the total quantity of such foods consumed is very great. And the millions of dollars expended in advertising the claims of superiority made for these foods by their manufacturers give the subject popular interest. A careful study of the principal breakfast foods, made under the supervision of the Department of Agriculture, indicates that their nutritive value and digestibility are practically the same as the old-fashioned porridge and similar dishes. The ready-to-eat cereals economize time and, to some extent, fuel. This advantage may justify the difference in their cost under certain conditions in the household. The process of preparation in most cases is thoroughly cleanly and sanitary. And the small pasteboard packages in which these products are put up protect the contents from all possible contamination. They also afford a convenient means of storage in the pantry. In general it was found that the less expensive kinds of raw cereal breakfast foods selling for about 4 cents a pound in bulk were as economical as flour, meal, or other forms of cereals with which they may be properly compared. The higher prices of ready-to-eat brands, however, do not yield any additional nutriment. Their advantage, if any, lies in their convenience and the pleasant variety they afford. Some of these are excessively high in price, the maximum being about 15 cents per pound, or nearly four times as much as their nutritive value would justify.

The so-called malted foods and others said to be predigested, are perhaps the most objectionable of any. The claims made for them are largely fraudulent. The addition of malt and similar processes are designed to transform the starch content of such foods into sugar and other soluble forms. Experiment with most of the advertised foods shows that this has really not been done to any appreciable extent. Moreover, healthy adults are more likely to be injured than benefited by the use of predigested foods. Nor should they be used by invalids except upon the advice of a competent physician. Hence, while these foods are really more wholesome than they would be if actually predigested, they are sold under misrepresentation, and at excessively high prices which are in no way justifiable.

Coffee Substitutes. — Cereal products as coffee substitutes appear to be made of parched barley, wheat and other grain, sometimes mixed with pea hulls, corn cobs or bran. Such grain parched with a little molasses in an ordinary oven makes something undistinguishable in flavor from the cereal coffees on the market. The claim of the manufacturers that these substitutes yield more nourishment than coffee is entirely unfounded. They contain little or no nutriment, skim milk being about twenty times as nutritive. If strict economy is necessary it will be found equally as satisfactory to use old-fashioned "crust coffee" made by toasting broken crusts of white, brown, or preferably "rye and Indian" bread, steeping them in hot water and straining until comparatively clear. Or parched corn, rye sweet potato or other old-fashioned coffee substitutes may be used.

Vegetables in the Diet.—In addition to the cereals, vegetable foods may be classified as legumes, tubers, roots and bulbs, green vegetables and fruits. The principal legumes used as food are peas, beans, cow-peas and lentils. While about one-half of these consists of carbohydrate in the form of starch, they also contain about one-fourth proteid. The remainder is chiefly water and refuse, since the proportion of fat which they contain is small. The dried legumes are so rich in proteid and comparatively so cheap a source of this most important nutrient, that they may well be used for the sake of both economy and variety, as substitutes for meat in the daily dietary. The lack of fat in legumes suggests the addition of butter or other suitable fat, as salt pork, in the process of cooking. Dietary studies and experiments with legumes indicate that, when properly cooked and combined with other foods in the ordinary mixed diet, they are well digested. Their tendency to cause flatulence may be corrected by soaking in soda and water and parboiling to remove the skin. Also by the addition of soda and salt in cooking. There can be no doubt that such foods as baked beans, purée of peas, and the like, are a valuable and economical part of the diet, especially for men employed at muscular work and for growing children. In view of their low cost, high nutritive value and wholesomeness, they may profitably be used to a much greater extent than they are at present.

The potato, among roots and tubers, is most commonly used as food. This and other root crops contain from 70 to 90 per cent of water. Hence the digestible nutrients present are somewhat less than 10 to 30 per cent. The greater part of the solid matter consists of carbohydrate. The amount of proteid and fat furnished by root crops is negligible. Hence, potatoes and other roots must be balanced in the diet by meat, milk, butter and similar sources of fat and proteid. Mashed potato, prepared with milk and butter, is for this reason more wholesome and palatable than plain boiled potato.

Use preferably young potatoes of the early varieties, of medium size, smooth and regular in shape and with comparatively few eyes. Avoid old potatoes especially about the time they begin to sprout and become soft and watery. Discard, especially in the case of old potatoes, any which have been turned green by the sun. The green portion contains solanin, a virulent acid poison. The danger from this increases the longer the potato is kept before being used. Potatoes rank next to bread stuffs as a source of carbohydrate in the diet.

The sweet potato resembles the white potato in composition although it contains a larger proportion of sugar and there are some other differences. It is equally as wholesome. While slightly more expensive it is to be recommended, at ordinary prices, as a substitute for the white potato for the sake of variety.

Succulent roots, tubers and bulbs such as beets, carrots, parsnips, turnips, onions and the like are much less important as source of nutrients than the cereal foods, or the starchy roots and tubers such as the potato. Their chief value lies in their flavors as aids to digestion. They also supply the body with mineral salts and by their bulk and the proportion of cellulose which they contain stimulate the peristaltic action of the bowel.

Fresh fruits are similar to green vegetables in composition, but they often contain considerable percentages of sugar. They are very dilute foods and usually contain 80 per cent or more of water. With the notable exception of the olive, fruits contain very little fat, nor do they have any importance as sources of proteid. They have some nutritive value as sources of carbohydrate, chiefly in the form of sugar, the percentage of which in common fruits ranges from 1 to as high as 15 per cent. But like green vegetables their value is chiefly in their flavors and mineral salts as aids to digestion and in their laxative effect.

Experiments have shown that persons living on an exclusive fruit and nut diet may apparently maintain their health and strength for a considerable length of time. The cost of such diet, however, does not differ greatly from that of an ordinary mixed diet. Nor is there anything to show that it is in other respects equal or superior. Dried and preserved fruits form an especially important part of the diet since they may contain 50 per cent or more of available carbohydrates in the form of sugar, in addition to many characteristics of fresh fruit. In short fruits are a valuable part of a well-balanced diet and may well be eaten in larger quantities than at present.

FOOD ADULTERATIONS

A preservative added to a food is an adulteration, because it is a foreign substance and neither a food nor a condiment. It is an entirely different question whether the food thus preserved is wholesome. A commercial sausage may contain a considerable amount of starch, which is added in order to allow the use of more fat or water to the product. This is not injurious, but the customer buys the product at a high price believing that he is getting a genuine sausage and nothing else.

On account of the frequent use of

adulterants, some simple tests are here given. These can be performed without any special chemical knowledge by carefully following the directions given. Any hou‑ekeeper or teacher can do the work. These instructions were compiled by E. H. S. Bailey, Ph. D., for the Kansas State Board of Health. The complete details of many of the processes are given in the recent article by Bigelow and Howard, in Bulletin No. 100, United States Department of Agri-

"Is It Any Wonder I Am Getting the Reputation of Being a Dyspeptic?"

culture, Bureau of Chemistry. From this excellent publication many of the following tests are taken.

Kitchen Tests.—In addition to the ordinary kitchen dishes and utensils the following will be required: One glass funnel, three inches in diameter; white cut filter-papers, five inches in diameter; and one medicine-dropper. The chemicals required are: One four-ounce bottle of strong hydrochloric (muriatic) acid; one four-ounce bottle of aqua ammonia; one eight-ounce bottle of chloroform; one four-ounce bottle of alcohol; one one-quarter pound bottle of hydrogen peroxide; one one-ounce bottle of tincture of iodine; one-quarter of an ounce of ferric alum; one-half an ounce of logwood chips; one-quarter of a pound of fuller's earth; a few pieces of sheet zinc; a few square inches of turmeric-paper.

All of the above can be readily obtained at any drug store. If it is proposed to have the chemicals about the house, the bottles should be provided with poison labels by the druggist.

CANNED VEGETABLES

Vegetables put up by reputable manufacturers who think it worth while to keep a good brand on the market are usually of good quality and wholesome. Sometimes, however, coloring matter and preservatives are present. Notice the appearance of the tin can containing canned vegetables or fruit. If it is convex instead of concave at the ends, and if when water is poured on the end of the can and the can is punctured, bubbles of gas come out through the water, the contents have begun to ferment and are not fit for use.

Copper.—The only artificial coloring matter usually found in canned vegetables is copper. This is added to produce a natural green color. This is most likely to be found in peas and string-beans. It has also been frequently used in pickles.

To test for copper: Mash two heaping tablespoonfuls of the sample with a stiff spoon, and put the pulp in a teacup, with three times as much water. With a medicine-dropper add thirty drops of hydrochloric acid, and set the cup in a pan of boiling water on the stove. Drop a bright two-penny nail in the mixture, and keep the water in the pan boiling for about twenty minutes. Take care to stir the solution occasionally with a splinter. Pour out the contents of the cup, rinse off the nail and examine it. If any appreciable quantity of copper is present in the food the nail will be plated red.

PRESERVATIVES

The preservatives most commonly used in canned vegetables are borax, sodium benzoate and salicylic acid. Sodium sulphite is also sometimes added both to bleach the product and to act as a preservative. Saccharin, which acts very slightly as a preservative, is used with such vegetables as sweet corn and in tomato catsup, as a sweetening agent.

Borax.—To detect borax or boric acid, mash a sample, as for copper, with a tumbler used as a pestle in a tea saucer, add a few teaspoonfuls of water, and strain through a cloth, putting the wet, folded cloth in the funnel. Collect about a teaspoonful of the liquid that comes through the filter in a sauce-dish, and add to this four drops of hydrochloric acid. Dip into this solution a piece of yellow turmeric-paper about an inch square. Then dry the paper by placing it in a clean saucer over a teakettle of boiling water. If borax is present, the yellow paper will become cherry-red when dry. If a drop or two of ammonia be put upon it, when cold, the color will change to a greenish black.

Benzoic and Salicylic Acid.—To detect sodium benzoate or benzoic acid and salicylic acid, macerate and filter a sample as above. By gently squeezing the bag or cloth containing the sample, obtain two ounces of the liquid. Place this solution in a narrow bottle holding about five ounces. The ordinary quinine bottle of the druggist is convenient. Add a quarter of a teaspoonful of cream of tartar and about three tablespoonfuls of chloroform, and mix thoroughly with a splinter. Do not shake too vigorously or the chloroform will not separate readily from the rest of the liquid. Pour the mixture into a tumbler, and after the chloroform layer has settled to the bottom of the tumbler, take out with a medicine-dropper all the clear chloroform possible and divide it into two parts, A and B.

Place one-half of the chloroform solution (A) in a glass sauce-dish. Set the dish on the outside of a window-ledge close to the window, and allow the chloroform to evaporate. In cold weather the sauce-dish should be placed in a pan of hot water before being placed on the window-ledge. When the chloroform has evaporated, if the quantity of benzoic acid is sufficient it will be seen in the bottom of the dish in small flat crystals. If the dish is warmed slightly the odor of gum benzoin may be recognized. A better confirmatory test, however, is, without warming the residue left after the evaporation of the chloroform, to add to it a half teaspoonful of strong ammonia water and three teaspoonfuls of strong hydrogen peroxide, as obtained at the drug store, and let the solution stand over night. The next day pour the liquid remaining in the sauce-dish into one of the tall bottles used above, add a piece of turmeric-paper and then hydrochloric acid, drop by drop, stirring with a splinter, until the turmeric-paper changes from a brown to a clear yellow color, then add chloroform as in the first part of the test, and after stirring thoroughly take out the chloroform with the dropper and allow it to evaporate on the window-ledge. Finally treat the residue remaining in the sauce-dish for salicylic acid as noted below. The treatment with ammonia and hydrogen peroxide was for the purpose of changing the benzoic acid to salicylic acid.

To test the other half of the solution (B) for salicylic acid, pour it into a tall five-ounce bottle containing a tablespoonful of water, and add to the solution a piece of iron alum about as large as the head of a pin.

Shake the mixture and allow the chloroform to again settle to the bottom of the bottle. If salicylic acid is present, the upper layer of the liquid, or the line separating the two liquids, will be of purple color.

Sulphites.—To detect sulphites, in food, as for instance in jelly or in sirups, place about an ounce of the material, with the addition of some water—if necessary—to make a thin liquid, in a tumbler, add a dozen small pieces of zinc, and about fifty drops of hydrochloric acid. Cover the tumbler with a sauce-dish, and allow to stand for a few minutes in a warm place. In the presence of sulphites the gas, hydrogen sulphide, which has a disagreeable odor like rotten eggs, can be recognized in the tumbler by the sense of smell.

If the hydrogen sulphide cannot be detected by its odor, it can often be found by proceeding as follows: Stick, by means of sealing wax, a clean, bright ten-cent piece on a splinter of wood so that it will hold the silver coin above the liquid in the cup. Place the stick and coin in the tumbler and let it stand covered in a warm place for from thirty minutes to an hour or so, if the color does not appear before. If the coin is stained brown to black, sulphites are indicated; the greater the quantity, the darker the stain.

Saccharin.—Saccharin is used in the place of sugar to sweeten various food products. It is made from coal-tar and is about 500 times as sweet as ordinary sugar. To detect this substance, the sample of food is extracted with chloroform as described in the method for detecting sodium benzoate, and the chloroform solution is allowed to evaporate in a glass dish in the open air. If a considerable amount of saccharin is present the residue left in the dish will have an intensely sweet taste.

CANNED FRUIT AND PRESERVES

There is very little excuse for the use of preservatives, and not any at all for the use of artificial coloring matters in canned fruits. The preservatives mentioned under canned vegetables are those more commonly used, and the methods for their detection given in the previous section may also be applied to canned fruits.

Jams, Jellies and Preserves.—There is no class of food products, with the exception of spices, so commonly adulterated as jams and jellies. The basis for the cheap jellies is often the pomace or refuse from the cider-mill, the sweetening is glucose or corn sirup, the coloring matter is a coal-tar dye. Hence the use of a preservative is almost always necessary. Starch is often used as a filler or gelatinizing agent.

Dyeing Test.—To detect a coal-tar or anilin dye, mix a few teaspoonfuls of the jam or jelly with some water and filter first through cloth and afterwards through filter-paper. The filter-paper should be folded across the middle, and again at a right angle to this fold. Place in the funnel so that there shall be three thicknesses on one side and one on the other. Moisten the paper with water to hold it in place. Add a few drops of hydrochloric acid to the filtered solution of the jelly, and place it in a teacup in a pan of boiling water on the stove. Boil a small piece (about an inch square) of white woolen cloth or nun's veiling with a little soap, and, after rinsing, place it in the colored solution to be tested. After heating for ten minutes, take out the cloth and rinse in clear water. If the cloth is not colored, the experiment may be discontinued.

If, however, the cloth is colored, to confirm the test, heat the cloth in a teacup in clear water containing about a teaspoonful of ammonia. This will dissolve the anilin color out of the cloth, but will have little effect on a natural fruit color. Take the piece of cloth and add enough hydrochloric acid to the contents of the cup so that the solution will not smell of ammonia. Put into this solution a new piece of washed woolen cloth and heat again in a pan of water. If an anilin dye is present, the cloth will be dyed, and after heating a short time, may be taken out and rinsed in clear water. This method of testing may also be applied to tomato catsup, which is frequently artificially colored.

Starch.—If considerable starch paste has been added to a jelly, it may be detected by adding to the cold filtered solution a few drops of

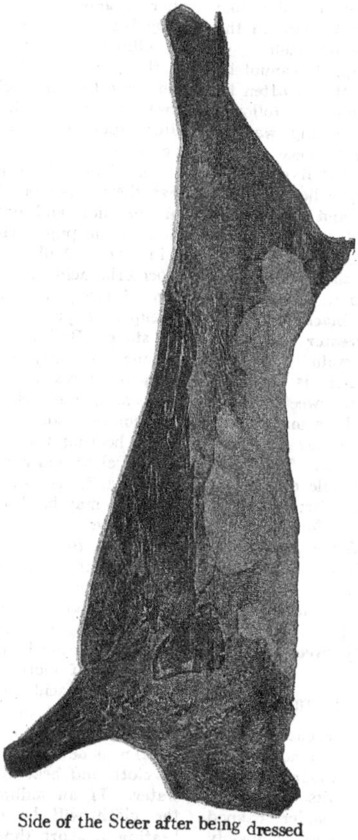

Side of the Steer after being dressed

tincture of iodin. The production of an intense blue color indicates starch. Observe that this color may be modified by any dye that is present in the sample examined.

FLAVORING EXTRACTS AND CONDIMENTS

Lemon Extract.—The extracts in most common use are those of lemon and vanilla. Extract of lemon, according to the United States Pharmacopœia, should contain 5 per cent of oil of lemon. About 85 per cent of alcohol is required to keep this in solution. Much of the extract of lemon on the market contains so little oil of lemon that it can with difficulty be measured. The oil is also often replaced by some other essential oil, as that of lemon grass. To hold the small quantity of oil of lemon in solution, a 25 or 30 per cent alcohol is often used. The yellow color of this product is produced by the use of a yellow anilin dye. As oil of lemon is held in solution by alcohol, to test the character of the extract, add to a teaspoonful of the sample, in a tumbler, three times as much water. If the liquid does not become milky the sample is not genuine. If the solution remains perfectly clear on the addition of the water, or is slightly turbid only, the extract is of very poor quality. When buying lemon extract, shake vigorously. If the foam does not disappear immediately the extract is not genuine.

Vanilla Extract.—Extract of vanilla, if genuine, is made by exhausting vanilla beans with alcohol. Frequently Tonka beans are in part or wholly substituted for the vanilla beans. The coloring matter in the artificial extract is usually caramel, burnt sugar, or prune juice, and artificial vanillin is added to strengthen the ordinary product. To detect caramel, shake the bottle containing the extract, and observe the foam on the top of the liquid. If the extract is pure the foam is colorless and persists; but if caramel has been added, there is a brownish color at the point of contact of the bubbles until the last bubble disappears.

As pure extract of vanilla contains considerable resin, which is held in solution by the alcohol, a test may be made for this as follows: Evaporate about two tablespoonfuls of the extract in a sauce-dish placed over a teakettle of boiling water. When one-third of the liquid has evaporated off, pour the residue into a tumbler and dilute with water to the original volume. If the liquid is turbid, and the resin separates as a brownish substance, the extract is probably genuine. If, on the other hand, the liquid remains clear after dilution, though of course of a brown color, this indicates that it is artificial.

Vinegar.—Vinegar is usually made from cider, wine, malt, or spirits. Much of the so-called "white wine vinegar" is made from spirits of alcohol. One method of detecting the source of a vinegar is to rinse out a tumbler with the sample and allow it to stand over night. The odor of the residue will enable one who is accustomed to these odors to detect the source of the vinegar. Another method is to evaporate some of the vinegar in a tea saucer over a teakettle of boiling water. The odor and taste of the residue left in the saucer are characteristic. From spirit vinegar the residue is very small in quantity and practically odorless.

To detect the addition of caramel to vinegar, add about two teaspoonfuls of fuller's earth to two ounces of vinegar, in a tall bottle of about five ounces' capacity. Shake vigorously, allow to stand a half hour, and filter. The first part of the filtrate should be poured through the filter a second time. Compare the color of this filtrate with the color of a sample of the vinegar which has not been filtered. This may be conveniently poured into another bottle of the same size as that containing the filtered sample. If the coloring matter is largely removed by filtration, this indicates that the sample has been colored with caramel.

Sulphuric acid has often been used as an adulterant of vinegar. To detect it, moisten a lump of sugar with the suspected vinegar and place on a saucer. Place a second piece of sugar moistened with water on a second saucer, and put the two into a warm (not hot) oven. If the sugar moistened with the vinegar becomes brown to black after a short time, while the second piece remains white, the presence of sulphuric acid is indicated.

Sugar; Honey.—Artificial honey is sometimes made by the use of common sugar and glucose, which is flavored to resemble the natural product. To detect the latter, add to a somewhat dilute solution of honey at least an equal volume of alcohol and stir. The production of a white precipitate of dextrose, which finally settles to the bottom of the glass, indicates the presence of glucose. This test may also be applied to a solution of candy. Glucose is not, however, properly considered an adulterant in candy.

To detect starch in candy, boil some of the solution, and after cooling add a few drops of a tincture of iodine. The production of an intense blue color indicates starch. White sugar, especially granulated, before the passage of the pure food laws, usually contained a little blue coloring matter, such as ultramarine. This may be detected by making a strong solution of sugar in a tumbler and allowing it to stand for several days. The blue coloring matter will finally settle to the bottom of the glass. If saccharin is added to candy or a food product, it may be detected by the test given under "Canned Vegetables."

Spices and Condiments. — Spices, especially those which are ground, are very often adulterated. If a sample has not a strong spicy odor and taste, this is an indication of adulteration. Cocoanut shells, prune pits and inert materials are often used as adulterants, but starchy substances are also extensively used. But observe that many spices also naturally contain starch. This is not the case, however, with cloves, mustard, and cayenne. Hence these may be tested for starch as follows: Stir a half-teaspoonful of the spice into half a cup of boiling water, and heat in a pan of water on the stove for a few minutes. Cool the mixture, and dilute with water so that the solution shall not be very strongly colored. Add a few drops of tincture of iodine. The production of a blue color indicates starch.

To test for turmeric—a vegetable coloring matter in ground mustard—digest some of the sample with alcohol, and after a short time dip a piece of white filter-paper in the mixture. If the paper is colored a bright yellow turmeric is probably present.

BAKING CHEMICALS

Baking Powder.—As the statement that appears on the label of a baking powder can is often deceptive, it may be of interest to prove whether a sample contains alum or not. To test for alum, make a fresh extract of logwood, either from the chips or the solid extract, by treating with water and pouring away the first and second extracts. Use the third extract obtained and allow it to settle. Place two teaspoonfuls of baking powder in a teacup and add to it four teaspoonfuls of cold water. With a medicine-dropper add twenty drops of extract of logwood to the mixture and stir with a splinter. Place the teacup in a pan of hot water on the stove and examine the color after two hours. If the baking powder contains alum, or a compound of aluminum, a distinct lavender color will be produced, but if this substance is not present in the sample, only a dirty brown or pink color will appear. It is well to make a test at first on samples of known composition, so as to recognize the colors accurately.

Cream of Tartar.—The cream of tartar on the market is frequently adulterated with acid calcium phosphate, alum, and even plaster, and starch. A simple test to determine the purity of the sample is to stir one level teaspoonful of it into a cupful of boiling water. Pure cream of tartar will dissolve completely, but many of the adulterants will only partially dissolve. The solution may then be poured into a tumbler that has been previously warmed. When cold, the cream of tartar will crystallize out in very characteristic crystals. To detect starch, add to a little of the cooled solution a few drops of tincture of iodine. The production of a blue color indicates that starch or flour is present.

TEA AND COFFEE

There is hardly any adulterated tea on the market, although there are some very poor grades and there may be too much "tea siftings" in the sample. Ground coffee is very often adulterated. Some simple tests for adulterants may be made. If ground coffee is dropped into a glass of cold water, the genuine coffee will float, and will not discolor the water for several minutes. Most of the adulterants sink to the bottom and leave a brown trail in the water. But little coffee is contained in the so-called "coffee substitutes." The proportion of coffee in a sample may be ascertained approximately by dropping it into cold water, as very few coffee substitutes will float.

Many of the substitutes are of a starchy nature. Starch may be tested for in the ordinary infusion prepared for the table, when cold, by diluting it until it is not too strongly colored, and then testing by tincture of iodine. (See test under "Sugar.")

DAIRY PRODUCTS

Milk, butter, ice cream and cheese are frequently adulterated. Milk is adulterated by adding water, coloring matters and preservatives. When water is added to milk, it changes the natural color, and the milk becomes bluish-white. If a yellow coal-tar dye has been added to the milk to restore the natural color when watered, this may be detected by adding an equal quantity of strong hydrochloric acid to a sample of the milk and afterwards heating. A pink coloration indicates the presence of the dye.

Another test is to allow the milk to stand in a tumbler for about twelve hours, or until the cream rises, and notice the color of the cream and of the milk layer. If the lower layer is of a yellow color, about the same as that of the cream, an artificial color is indicated.

To detect annatto, a yellow coloring matter, stir some washing soda into the milk, and after standing a few minutes filter through filter paper. Then wash the milk off the paper, and if annatto is present the paper is colored yellow to orange.

If the milk does not turn sour in the usual time, the presence of a preservative is indicated. Baking soda is sometimes added to correct the acid of the milk. If an appreciable quantity of this substance has been used, the milk, after standing a few hours, will have a slightly alkaline reaction; that is, it will change a piece of yellow turmeric paper to an orange-red color.

Formaldehyde. — Other preservatives are sometimes used, but that which is the most common is formaldehyde or formalin, because a little goes a long way as a preservative. To detect this substance, place four tablespoonfuls of the sample in a teacup, with an equal quantity of strong hydrochloric acid and a piece of ferric alum about the size of the head of a pin. After mixing, by giving the contents of the cup a rotary motion, place the cup in a pan of boiling water on the stove, and allow to stand for five minutes. If formaldehyde is present, the mixture will be of a purple color. A similar test may be made for formaldehyde in ice cream, although if starch is present in the cream this may modify the shade of the purple.

Butter.—The substitutes for genuine butter are "process" or "renovated" butter, and oleomargarin or "butterine." Process butter is made by treating old or rancid butter by melting, skimming and allowing the brine and curd to sink to the bottom, whence it is drawn off. Air is then blown through the melted butter-fat, and the product is churned with milk or cream. Oleomargarin is made from various mixtures of oleo-oil, cottonseed-oil, neutral lard and milk or butter. It should always be sold under its true name.

The spoon test may be used to distinguish fresh butter from renovated butter and oleomargarin. A lump of butter the size of a hickory nut is placed on a large iron spoon and heated over the flame of a small kerosene or alcohol lamp or over a gas flame. Fresh butter will melt quietly, with many small bubbles throughout the mass, which produce much foam; oleomargarin or process butter will splutter and crackle, like hot fat containing water, and produce but little foam.

To make the "milk test", as it is called, place about two ounces of sweet milk in a wide-mouthed bottle, which is set in a pan of boiling water on the stove. When the milk is hot, add a teaspoonful of butter, and stir with a splinter until the fat is melted. Place the bottle in a pan of ice water and stir continually while the fat is solidifying. If the sample is butter, either fresh or renovated, it will solidify in a granular condition and be distributed through the milk in small granular particles. If, on the other hand, the sample is oleomargarin, it solidifies practically in a single lump, so that it may be lifted from the bottle with a stirrer.

Eggs.—Probably the best method for testing the freshness of eggs is the time-honored one of candling. The egg is held between the eye and a bright light. A fresh egg shows a perfectly uniform rose-colored tint, while if not fresh there will be numerous dark spots.

In packed eggs there is a tendency for the white and yolk to slightly intermingle along the line of contact. Packed eggs also are apt to adhere to the shell on one side. If eggs have been in a nest for any length of time they are smooth and glossy and the appearance is entirely different from the dull, rough surface of fresh eggs.

MEAT PRODUCTS

The preservatives most commonly used in meat products are borax, boric acid and sodium sulphite. The latter chemical also develops a bright red color in the meat in imitation of the natural red of fresh cut meat. If the meat keeps an exceptionally long time without a tendency to spoil, or if it retains its red color, the presence of preservatives may be suspected.

The method of testing for borax, which has already been described under "Canned Vegetables", may be used in testing meat products. The meat must be finely divided, and should be warmed with water for some time, then the liquid which is filtered off should be tested. To test for sulphites, see process described under "Canned Vegetables."

Sausages.—The principal adulteration of sausages, in addition to the introduction of inedible meats into the product, is the addition of starch. This is added as a "filler" to allow the incorporation of more fat and water and on the ground that it prevents shrinkage when fried. It should be remembered in this connection, however, that starch is cheaper than

meat. To detect this adulteration boil the sausage in water, pour the resulting liquid into a teacup and allow it to cool thoroughly. Then take out some of the liquid below the fat with a dropper, and test with tincture of iodine for starch as described under "Jams and Jellies".

CHAPTER XXIII

PRESERVING AND CANNING FRUIT AND VEGETABLES

CANNED GOODS FOR THE MARKET—UTENSILS AND MATERIALS—THE PROCESS—PRESERVES AND PRESERVING—SMALL FRUITS—LARGE FRUITS—PURÉES AND MARMALADE—JELLY MAKING—CANNING VEGETABLES

The art of preserving and canning fruit and fresh vegetables is much more important than is usually realized. Preserved fruit is, perhaps, most often classed with candy and other sweetmeats as an expensive luxury. But fruit, properly put up, is not necessarily expensive and may be regarded as a very essential part of the diet in winter. The value of fruit as food can hardly be overestimated. The fruit juices have a peculiarly wholesome effect upon the digestive organs and tend to keep the blood in good condition. They also, to a large extent, prevent the necessity for cathartic medicines. Fresh fruit in season should, of course, have the preference, but in winter properly canned fruit and preserves may take their place with almost equally good effect.

The art of canning fresh vegetables in the kitchen has now been so perfected that most kinds of garden truck may be canned without expense other than for jars, labor and fuel. All housewives who have not yet attempted this newly devised process will be delighted to discover that they can easily preserve such garden vegetables as early peas, sweet corn, and others, and serve them in midwinter with all their original delicacy of texture and flavor. The value of such a contribution to the winter diet is apparent. It not only adds to the palatability, æsthetic value and wholesomeness of the diet. It is also an important measure of economy, since by this means any surplus of garden products, which would have little or no value in summer, may be preserved for use during the period of greatest scarcity and consequent high prices.

Preserving and Canning.—These terms are used somewhat loosely, but the word preserves more properly applies to the old-fashioned method of our grandmothers, which consisted in boiling the fruit in sirup after the time-honored recipe of "pound for pound." This process, to be entirely successful, is difficult and tedious. It is also expensive on account of the amount of sugar required. The old-fashioned preserves are still favored by some, but the easier, quicker and cheaper method of canning has largely deposed them. The term "preserves" also covers jams, or purées, and marmalade, which are fruit, or mixtures of fruit, stewed to a smooth paste.

CANNED GOODS FOR MARKET

Money in Preserving Fruit.—In addition to the importance of preserving fruit and vegetables for home use there is a large and constantly increasing market both locally and in the large cities for a fine grade of homemade canned products. Prices ranging from seventy-five cents to $1.50 per quart, at retail, for a high grade domestic article are not infrequent. After deducting the cost of fruit, or vegetables, sugar and other materials including jars, rings, bottle wax, labels, the cost of packing and transportation, and the labor cost (at a nominal figure, say, ten or fifteen cents an hour) for all time actually engaged in picking the fruit, preserving and packing it, there should be a profit of at least 100 per cent clear to the maker. And after a reputation has been established for a product of uniformly high quality, even better prices can be realized. This is not only a practical way for any housekeeper to earn extra pin money. In many localities it is the only feasible method of marketing the fruit and truck crop.

Ordinarily so much produce ripens at about the same time in villages and rural communities, that there is no sale for it at any price. And the comparatively small amount grown by one family, together with the distance to the nearest market, often makes it unprofitable to pack and ship the produce as it ripens to a commission merchant. But the smallest quantities can be gathered and canned from day to day during the season. Thus a sufficient quantity can be accumulated to justify the time and cost of packing and shipping by freight to the nearest city.

Or if the quantity is large enough, it may be worth while to make a trip in person, taking a sample of the product, in order to make an advantageous sale to some large consumer. Commission merchants and wholesale grocery houses are usually glad to buy, at fair prices, all the homemade goods of this sort they can obtain. But the stewards of the finest hotels and clubs, such as the country clubs that are springing up all over the United States, will often pay fancy prices for an especially fine article.

Even local merchants have a considerable demand for these goods and will sometimes make a special effort to sell them for a good customer. Or orders can be secured from neighbors by means of an advertisement in the local paper or by tactful solicitation.

The principal difficulty met in the sale of homemade goods is the common belief among merchants and others that they may not be of uniformly high quality. Factory-made goods are nowadays done up with scientific care and accuracy. The jars are carefully inspected and the contents very rarely mold or sour.

Unless one is willing, therefore, to take every step with the most rigid and painstaking thoroughness, it is useless to attempt to compete with the factory product. But once a well-deserved reputation has been built up, a demand will have been created for all that one will ordinarily wish to supply.

Many women earn a living for themselves or contribute largely to the family income by thus creating a market for all the produce that their husbands can grow. Many others find it profitable to buy fruit and vegetables from their neighbors, employ and carefully train assistants and put up hundreds of dollars' worth annually.

To Pack Canned Goods for Market.—Use only the best quality of all-glass jars. Do not attempt to economize on labels, but obtain the most attractive that money will buy. A distinctive label is an immensely important point in promoting sales and building up a reputation for one's product. Cement the labels neatly and securely in a uniform position on the jars. Wrap each jar in stout colored wrapping paper, fold and seal top and bottom with mucilage, or by means of a label gummed over all, and place a label on the outside of the wrapper in addition to that on the jar itself.

The best method of packing is to obtain from a dealer cylinders of the proper size which are made for this purpose of corrugated cardboard. Obtain also a supply of the same cardboard to place between the layers of jars. If your annual output is large enough, suitable cases to hold a quarter gross or half gross of jars can be made at home, or for a trifle by a local carpenter. These will be returned by the purchaser on request.

Or the jars may be packed in stout packing cases or barrels and surrounded with excelsior, straw or hay. An excellent method is to place between two sheets of thick manila paper a layer of excelsior and stitch or quilt the whole together at intervals with long stitches such as are used in basting. The whole may then be cut with shears to proper lengths, between the rows of basting. In these wrap up the separate jars. Also line the box or barrel with them and place one or more thicknesses between the different layers of jars. In addition crowd excelsior between the jars so that no two jars can come into contact.

If packing cases are used, the excelsior must be crowded in at the top so that the contents cannot move, and the lids securely nailed on. It is easy to ascertain by shaking it vigorously whether the case has been solidly packed. If any rattling is heard, it should be opened and repacked.

If barrels are used, it is sufficient to take off the top hoop and cover the top with a piece of canvas or burlap. Replace the hoop over the cloth and put on the top a stout label marked "Glass, This Side Up, With Care." Better care is given a package thus left without a head than to a sealed box or barrel. Place even dozens in each package, and be sure to make an accurate count. Have a printed billhead and promptly notify the consignee of the time of shipment by mailing the bill with a courteous note.

To Fix a Price on Canned Goods.—Keep account of all time taken in picking, preserving or packing the produce and figure out what it would cost you to hire the work done by ordinary day labor. Usually ten or fifteen cents an hour is a fair figure. Add to this the cost of the produce and sugar actually consumed, jars and all accessories, including packing material, labor, etc. When you have thus arrived at the actual cost including labor, double this amount to allow yourself 100 per cent profit. If at first you are unable to sell your goods at this price or better, it is probably because you are inexperienced. Either you are not taking advantage of the work, or others are taking advantage of you in the price you are paying for labor or material. But 100 per cent profit is the ideal you should have in view, and some persons making homemade canned goods realize two or three times as much on their investment.

Storing Preserves.—Canned vegetables, fruits and preserves should be stored in a cool, dark, dry place. The cellar is not the best place unless it is dry and well ventilated. A storeroom partitioned off from the cellar and built of concrete is an ideal apartment for this purpose. In houses that are heated in winter, a dark, airy closet in the upper part of the house is a good place. But of course, they must not be placed where they will freeze in cold weather. If it is necessary to store them in an ordinary cellar to prevent freezing, a swinging shelf should be constructed for this purpose. The jars should be allowed to become stone cold before being stored away. They will keep much better if carefully wrapped in dark-colored paper folded and pasted top and bottom, and labeled on the outside so that it will not be necessary to disturb the wrappers until they are required for use.

UTENSILS AND MATERIALS

Utensils for Canning.—The most useful utensil for canning in considcrable quantities is an ordinary tin wash boiler, such as is used in the laundry, cut down to convenient size. As this utensil will not ordinarily have a great deal of wear, a cheap tin wash boiler may be purchased, or an old wash boiler that has been discarded may, by means of patches and solder, be put into sufficiently good order to answer this purpose. Measure from the bottom of the wash boiler to a point four or five inches higher than the top of an ordinary quart fruit jar, mark a line all around at this point, and have a tinsmith cut it off on this line. Or you can cut it off yourself with a chisel and hammer by inserting the end of a block of wood and striking against this. But it is better to have this work done by a tinsmith, and have

"A Utensil for the Ordinary Range."

him turn over the sharp edge so that you will not cut yourself on it. Now have a gridiron of wooden slats or wires fitted into the bottom in the inside. This is to keep the jars off the bottom on the principle of the double boiler. The result is a utensil of the right size for use on an ordinary range or on two burners of a gas or alcohol stove, and of convenient depth for sterilizing jars as well as canning the produce.

Or use an ordinary wash boiler fitted with a suitable false bottom. This has the same advantages, except that it is less convenient to reach into its steaming depths when removing the jars.

A large porcelain preserving kettle holding ten or twelve quarts, a porcelain skimmer and ladle and a long-

"A Large Porcelain Kettle."

handled stirring spoon of wood are also necessary. A pair of scales and suitable measuring cup should always be at hand in the kitchen. The old-fashioned Mason jar is still in use, but the so-called lightning jar is preferable. Have on hand a sufficient quantity of new rubber rings. Never attempt to use old rings, as rubber decays very rapidly, and the old ring is almost certain to admit the air into the jar, causing the contents to spoil before it is used. Old rings also harbor bacteria that cause fermentation. With clean jars and new rubber rings, the battle is already half over. Other useful devices in canning, preserving and jelly making are the sugar gauge, fruit pricker, ordinary wooden vegetable masher, wire sieve or colander and wire basket such as are shown in the accompanying illustrations.

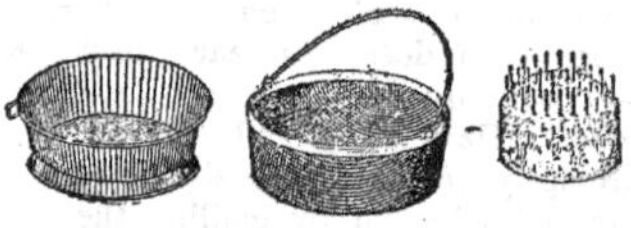

a b c

(a) Wire sieve; (b) wire basket; (c) fruit pricker.

To make a fruit pricker cut a piece one-half inch deep from a broad cork, press through this a dozen or more coarse darning needles and tack the cork on a piece of board. One stroke on this bed of needles punctures the fruit with a dozen holes. But be sure to use large, strong needles and take care that none of the points are broken off and remain in the fruit. Remove the cork from the board, and wash and dry thoroughly after using. A little olive or sweet oil on the needles will prevent rusting.

The sirup gauge and glass cylinder are essential to uniform success in making jelly. These may be obtained from any druggist at a cost of about 75 cents. A cylinder with a lip as illustrated and holding a

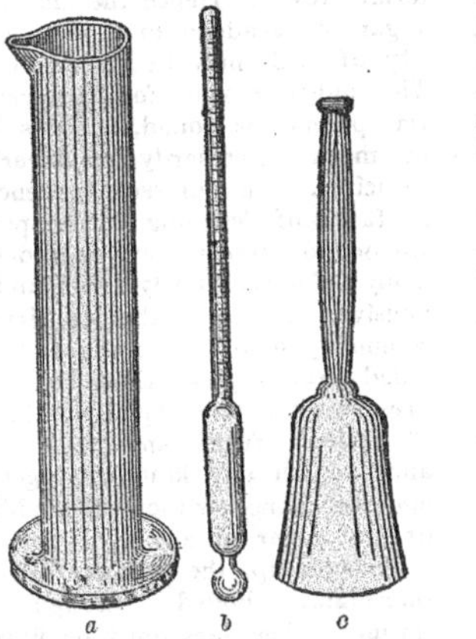

(a) Glass cylinder; (b) sirup gauge; (c) wooden vegetable masher. (Maria Parloa.)

little over a gill is the best size. The sirup gauge is a glass tube with a weighted bulb so graduated as to register 0° to 50°. To use the sirup gauge, fill the glass cylinder to about two-thirds of its height with a sample of the liquid to be tested. Insert the gauge and the quantity of sugar present, if any, will be registered. In pure water the bulb will rest on the bottom. The more sirup is dissolved in the water the higher the gauge will rise. When testing hot liquids, the gauge and cylinder must be heated gradually to avoid breaking. The fruit juice or sirup either for canning, preserving or making jellies may thus be tested at any stage. The sirup may be made heavier by adding sugar or lighter by adding water as the case demands.

Alcohol Stove.—A proper stove is a very important consideration. Produce is ordinarily ready for canning in sultry weather, and the heat of a cook stove or range is so unbearable that the process rarely receives the quality of skill and the degree of attention that the best results demand. A tired and overheated housekeeper is in no mood to closely observe the delicate points that contribute to the perfection of a high grade product. Housekeepers fortunate enough to enjoy the use of gas will need no suggestion to use a gas range for canning fruit, and at a time when the oven burners are not lighted. But where there is no available supply of gas a two-burner stove consuming denatured alcohol is especially recommended. This is self-contained and portable. Thus the whole apparatus for canning fruit can be moved into a large, cool room, into an outhouse, or if desired in still, clear, or sultry weather, out of doors on the veranda, or in the shade of a tree on the lawn. At all events, an effort should be made to "keep cool" in both senses, if one is ambitious to obtain the best possible results.

Materials for Canning and Preserving.—The materials used for canning and preserving should invariably be of the finest quality. Only the best grade of white granulated sugar should be used. And this should be clarified as described under candy making. Fresh, ripe fruit and vegetables of the best quality should be selected and carefully picked over. All bruised, specked, or wormeaten specimens should be discarded. Small fruits, as raspberries and strawberries, and all vegetables, should be canned if possible the morning they are picked. Great care should be taken in handling produce to avoid bruising it. A silver paring knife should be used for fruit as an iron or steel knife tends to darken it. The fruit when pared should be instantly dropped into a vessel of clear cold water, care being taken that it is not bruised in falling. This prevents the fruit from "rusting" or turning dark by exposure to the air. All hard portions should be removed as they resist the effects of heat. And all "specks" or decayed portions since they injure the flavor and color.

The best quality of canned fruit is obtained by heating fruit in the jars as hereafter described. This method avoids bruising the fruit by stirring, lifting, or pouring it from one vessel to another. Particular attention and care when preparing all canned goods will be amply repaid in the improved quality of the product. If fruit is pared, the work should be done thoroughly and no particles of skin allowed to remain. If the cores, pits, or stones are removed at all, the work should be done in a painstaking manner. Especially if the goods are offered for sale, a small fraction of additional labor at the start will add largely to the price and salability of the product. For similar reasons only the best quality of spices, brandy, or other condiments should be used.

PROCESS OF CANNING AND PRESERVING

Nature of the Process.—Canning or preserving is a process of killing, by means of heat, the germs that cause decay and preventing the contact of other germs by covering the produce with boiling sirup and sealing it hermetically so as to exclude the air. The reason that boiling is necessary, is that the germs of decay may be already present in the substance of the produce itself. Hence it must be boiled until the heat has penetrated every part and effectually destroyed the germs. And the reason that air must be excluded is that the microscopic germs that cause putrefaction float in the air in very large numbers. Hence if a bubble of air remains among the fruit, or if air is admitted through a crevice as fine as a needle point in the rubber ring or metal top of the jar, putrefaction will certainly result.

Other substances such as clear water or fruit juices exclude the air as well as sugar sirup. Sugar is added partly because it makes the product more palatable and nutritious, and partly because the presence of sugar is unfavorable to bacterial growth. Hence the amount of sugar to be added to a given quantity of fruit may be varied at will. The old-time rule for "preserving" was pound for pound, but this is by no means necessarily an invariable principle. The present tendency is in favor of "canning." The pound-for-pound preserves are regarded by many as unnecessarily sweet and expensive. A much thinner sirup is commonly used in canning and, provided proper precautions are taken, preserves the fruit equally well. Or, if desired, fruits and fruit juices and in fact any kind of vegetable, may be canned without the addition of any sugar at all.

To sum up, the produce must be thoroughly boiled through and through. The jars must be filled to overflowing with boiling hot sirup or other liquid so that all bubbles of

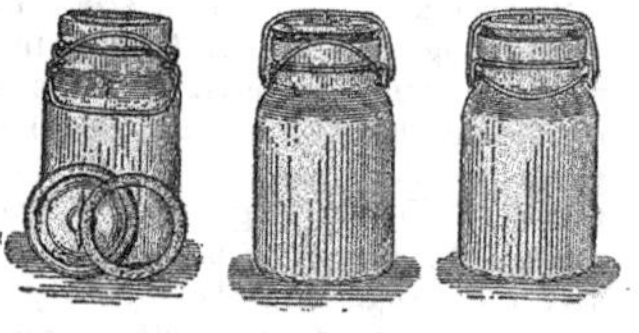

a b c

(a) Spring-top jar; (b) position of spring during sterilizing; (c) position of spring after sterilizing.

air will be excluded. Then they must be instantly sealed, else the contents will cool slightly and leave a space filled with bacteria-laden air between the top and the jar cover. The jar must be provided with a tight ring of new rubber or other substance that will absolutely exclude the air or the bacteria that it contains. Such substances as blotting paper and cotton batting are sometimes used for the reason that they have the property of screening or filtering the air so as to prevent bacteria from passing through.

Methods of Canning and Preserving Fruit.—There are two different ways of canning or preserving fruit, either of which will give satisfactory results: (1) boiling the fruit in the jars or cans, or (2) boiling it in a preserving kettle. The old-time method of "preserving" consisted in boiling the fruit in a suitable preserving kettle, in sugar sirup, lifting it from the sirup when sufficiently boiled, packing it into jars or cans and pouring the boiling sirup over it. This method is still preferred by many.

The modern method of "canning" consists in packing the fruit in the cans or jars without sugar, or with sugar sprinkled between the different layers at the rate of about one tablespoonful to each pound of fruit, placing the jars on the stove in a suitable receptacle surrounded by water, bringing the whole to a boil and finally filling the cans with boiling sugar sirup and sealing them.

Canning is somewhat slower unless a large receptacle is provided in which to place a considerable number of fruit jars while boiling. But the process is easier and is likely to give a more satisfactory result. All bubbles of air are driven out of the fruit while boiling. And the jar itself is uniformly heated, so that when boiling sirup is added to fill it to the brim, it does not shrink by cooling in the moment of time required to clap on the cover and seal. Then, too, the fruit is undisturbed, and its shape, color, and texture are not injured.

Preserving Day.—Many housekeepers prefer, when putting up fruits for home use, to prepare a jar or two each day, selecting the finest fruits as they ripen. Thus the labor is distributed over the season and associated with other cooking from day to day so as to be hardly realized. But it is of some advantage, when a considerable quantity of fruit is to be preserved, to get everything in readiness at one time and make a day of it.

To Test Jars.—The contents of several jars may be saved in the course of a season by testing the

"Testing the Jars before Using."

jars before using. To this end, fill them with warm water, put on the new rubber rings that are to be used, seal them and stand them upside down on a large sheet of blotting paper. Or butcher's brown paper, or an ordinary folded newspaper, will answer. If there is the slightest leak, the water will trickle out and be seen on the absorbent paper. Thus defective rubber rings, or uneven, nicked, or cracked jar tops can be discarded and assurance can be had that no valuable material and labor will be wasted. Similarly, it is a good plan to turn the filled jars upside down on absorbent paper and let them stand overnight before storing them away. If by chance a defective ring or jar has been used it will be detected and the contents can be transferred to another jar.

To Sterilize Jars.—The first step is to place in the special boiler above mentioned, or in a preserving kettle, the jars that are to be used, with about one tablespoonful of borax to twelve quarts of cold water, and bring them to a boil over a slow fire. The tops and rubber rings should be put in place and boiled with the jars themselves. They are unfit for use if they will not stand this process. Jars having glass tops should invariably be given the preference. This will effectually kill all germs, free the jars from dust and dirt, and also toughen them so that, if properly handled, they will not crack in the process of canning. After they have boiled fifteen minutes or so, pour off the borax water and pour over them hot water to rinse them. Care must, of course, be taken not to pour cold water over hot jars, or expose them to a draught of cold air while hot, or they may be cracked and broken.

Canning Fruit.—After the jars have been thus rinsed and sterilized, replace them on the stove in the above-mentioned boiler or other suitable receptacle, surround them with hot water, and pack in the fruit, either without sugar, or with sugar sprinkled among the layers of fruit at the rate of one tablespoonful to a pound of fruit up to a teacupful to each can, more or less, as desired. Boil until the fruit is soft enough so that a straw can be run through it. The time required will vary according to the fruit, from a few minutes in the case of small fruits, as raspberries, strawberries, and others, to an hour or more in the case of hard pears, quinces, and the like. But observe that the latter cannot be cooked properly in the cans. They must be done up in the preserving kettle in the old-fashioned way. And there is the less objection as their firmer texture protects them from being injured by handling.

Berries and small fruits of soft and delicate texture, undoubtedly present a better appearance and have a finer flavor and color if cooked in the can. These include cherries, strawberries, raspberries, huckleberries or blueberries, ripe peaches, summer pears, and ripe plums.

Some fruits cooked in the can with sugar, shrink and leave the can only partly full. Do not attempt to crowd the cans when first filled as this will crush the fruit and injure its appearance. Remove one can and gently pour its contents into the tops of the others until all are full. Finally, when sufficiently boiled, remove the jars one by one, wrapping a towel about each; pour boiling sirup on top until it runs over and instantly seal before the contents cool, and air is admitted. Place the jars in a warm place and out of a draught, as otherwise they may crack in the process of cooling.

Sirup for Canning and Preserving.—The strength of the sirup to be used in filling jars after the fruit has been cooked in them is a matter of individual preference. It also depends upon the amount of sugar, if any, that has been sprinkled in the fruit while cooking.

The old time pound-for-pound rule called for ½ a pint of water more or less, for each pound of sugar and pound of fruit, according to the amount of juice in the fruit. But a larger amount of water is more commonly used at present. To prepare sirup, place the sugar in a small preserving kettle, pour the required amount of cold water over it and stir until the sugar is fully dissolved before placing on the fire. The sirup will be clarified and improved by the addition of a little gum arabic or white of egg. The scum, as fast as it rises, may then be removed with a skimmer, taking all impurities with it. This sirup may be poured over the fruit after it has been cooked in the can.

Or according to the earlier method, the fruit may be dropped into the clarified sirup while at a boiling point, cooked until it is tender, removed with a skimmer, packed in the jars and the boiling sirup added until they are filled to overflowing.

PRESERVES AND PRESERVING

Preserving Fruit.—The process of preserving is a very simple one, although it takes a large amount of time and great care. However, any housekeeper can accomplish it. The principal secret of success is that the fruit should be put up and sealed while hot and the jars filled to the brim. It is usually the custom to place the fruit in the kettle, a layer of fruit and a layer of sugar, pound for pound or measure for measure and to let the whole come to a boil at once.

Or place the fruit in a vessel without the sugar. Put just enough water over it to keep it from scorching, and allow it to boil until the scum rises. Carefully skim away the scum while it continues to rise before adding the sugar. Many seem to think that the scum rises entirely from the sugar, but the experience of those who have used the above-mentioned method is that an equal amount of scum comes from the boiling fruit.

Or weigh the sugar and the fruit, pound for pound, then place the sugar in the kettle without the fruit. Put in just enough water to dissolve the sugar and stir until it is dissolved. Now place on the fire and let come to a boil. Continue to simmer for half an hour or so before dipping in the fruit, being careful to skim away the scum as it rises. Then place the fruit in the boiling liquid and let it continue to simmer on the back of the stove until the fruit becomes thoroughly impregnated with the sirup.

When about half done lift the fruit from the boiling sirup, place it in large porcelain or other vessels, being careful not to allow any sirup to come with it, and place it in the sun for an hour or more to bleach. After this, again drop the fruit into the sirup and let it boil until tender enough to allow a straw to run through it.

When the fruit is thoroughly done, if the sirup is not as thick as desired, it may continuously simmer until the desired thickness is reached. Then place the fruit in glass jars that have been previously heated and sterilized by boiling in water containing a little borax and rinsing in hot water. After filling the jar with fruit as full as you conveniently can, pour in the boiling sirup until it fills up all the crevices between the fruit, excluding all the air possible. While performing this process, place the jar in a pan filled with hot water. This will prevent cracking the jar.

CANNING SMALL FRUITS

The method of canning such small fruits as raspberries, blackberries, currants, gooseberries and blueberries, is substantially the same except for the proportions of berries, sugar and water required. Select fruit just before it is perfectly ripe—choose an underripe rather than overripe fruit—and can promptly while freshly picked. Discard all imperfect fruit. Gnarled, broken or otherwise defective specimens not decayed, may be used for marmalade or jellies. Avoid berries having a large proportion of seeds to pulp and if no other can be obtained—as may happen during a dry season—remove the seeds by rubbing through a sieve and preserve the strained pulp as marmalade or purée. Pick over the berries, hull and stem them and drop the perfect fruit in small quantities into a colander. Rinse in cold water and turn them on a sieve to drain. Do this quickly so that the fruit will not absorb too much water.

Have ready two bowls, one for sugar and one for fruit. Observe how much of each will be required to fill the preserving kettle or the number of jars desired. Measure the fruit into the proper bowl as fast as it is picked over and washed, and for each measure of fruit add to the other bowl the proportionate amount of sugar. When the required quantity of fruit and sugar has been measured, put both into the preserving kettle, add the required amount of water, if any, and while the first kettle is cooking prepare the fruit and sugar for another. Fruit designed to be served as sauce may have any proportion of sugar cooked with it according to taste, or if intended for beverages or cooking purposes, it may be canned without the addition of sugar. Juicy fruits require little or no water, except when cooked in a heavy sirup. The above are general rules which require to be modified for particular fruits as follows:

For raspberries and blackberries use 2 quarts of sugar to 12 quarts of fruit. First express the juice from 2 quarts of the fruit by heating it slowly on the stove in the preserving kettle, crushing with a wooden vegetable masher and squeezing through cheese cloth. Rinse the preserving kettle, pour into it the strained juice, add the sugar, heat and stir until the sugar is dissolved. Let the sirup come to a boil, add the remaining 10 quarts of berries and heat slowly. Boil ten minutes from the time it begins to bubble and skim carefully while boiling. Can and seal as above directed.

For currants the process is the same as for raspberries and blackberries, but the proportions are different, namely: 4 quarts of sugar to 12 of fruit. For raspberries and currants combined use 2½ quarts of sugar to 3 quarts of currants and 10 quarts of raspberries. First express the juice from the currants as above directed, then proceed as for raspberries.

For green gooseberries use 1½ quarts of sugar and 1 pint of water to 6 quarts of fruit. Dissolve the sugar in the water, add the fruit and cook fifteen minutes. Or can the same as rhubarb. For ripe gooseberries use only one-half as much water.

For blueberries use 1 quart of sugar and 1 pint of water to 12 quarts of berries. Put all together in the preserving kettle and heat slowly. Boil fifteen minutes from the time the mixture begins to bubble.

For cherries use 1½ quarts of sugar and ½ pint of water to 6 quarts of fruit. Measure after stemming. Stone or not as preferred, but if the stones are removed, take care to save the juice. First stir the sugar into the water over the fire until dissolved, then add the cherries and bring slowly to a boil. Let boil ten minutes, skimming carefully.

For grapes use 1 quart of sugar and 1 gill of water to 6 quarts of fruit. First squeeze the pulp from the skins. Cook it five minutes and rub through a fine sieve to remove the seeds. Now bring the water, skins and pulp slowly to a boil. Skim, stir in the sugar and boil fifteen minutes. If the grapes are sweeter or more sour than ordinary, use more or less sugar, according to taste.

Rhubarb may be cooked and canned with sugar in the same manner as gooseberries, or either rhubarb or gooseberries may be canned without heat as follows: Cut the rhubarb when young and tender, wash thoroughly, pare and divide into pieces about two inches long. Pack in sterilized jars, fill to overflowing with cold water and let stand ten minutes. Drain off the water and once more fill to overflowing with fresh cold water. Seal with sterilized rings and covers. When the cans are opened the rhubarb may be used in all respects the same as if fresh.

CANNING LARGE FRUIT

Such large fruit as apples, pears, peaches and quinces must usually be pared and cored before canning. Select first class fruit just before it is ripe—preferably underripe rather than overripe—and discard all imperfect specimens. It is better not to can or preserve spotted or bruised fruit, but if such are used, all decayed or bruised spots must be freely cut out. Measure the fruit as soon as it is pared and cored into a large bowl containing cold water made slightly acid with lemon juice at the rate of one tablespoonful to the quart. This will keep the fruit from turning brown. For each measure add the proportionate quantity of sugar into another bowl until the amount of fruit and sugar needed to fill the preserving kettle or required number of jars is at hand.

To peel peaches, plums or tomatoes, have ready a deep kettle a little more than half full of boiling water. Fill a wire basket or colander with the fruit and suspend it by means of a string through the handles, or otherwise, in the boiling water for three minutes. Now remove and plunge the basket for a moment into a pan of cold water. Let drain a few moments and peel. The process of canning in general is much the same for all fruits, but the following special modifications for particular fruits may be observed:

For peaches and ripe pears use 1 quart of sugar and 3 quarts of water to 8 quarts of fruit. Prepare the fruit either whole or in halves as desired. If the latter, remove all the pits except a few in each jar which retain for the sake of their flavor. Stir the sugar into the water over the fire until dissolved and bring slowly to a boil. Skim carefully and let stand where it will remain hot but not boil. Put only a single layer of the prepared fruit in the preserving kettle at a time and cover with some of the hot sirup. Bring slowly to a boil, skim carefully, boil gently for ten minutes, or longer if not fully ripe, can and seal. The fruit is not done until it can be readily pierced with a straw or a silver fork. Unripe or hard pears will require much longer boiling.

For quinces use 1½ quarts of sugar and 2 quarts of water to 4 quarts of fruit. Rub the fruit hard with a coarse crash towel. Then wash and drain. Pare, quarter and core and drop the pieces into cold water acidulated with lemon juice. Cover the fruit in the preserving kettle with plenty of cold water, bring slowly to a boil and let simmer until tender. Remove the pieces one by one as soon as they can readily be pierced with a silver fork and let drain on a platter. Now strain the water in which the fruit was cooked through cheese cloth and put 2 quarts of the strained liquid over the fire. Stir in the sugar until dissolved, bring slowly to a boil, skim well, add the cooked fruit and boil gently for about twenty minutes.

For crab-apples use 1½ quarts of sugar and 2 quarts of water to 6 quarts of apples. A part of the stem may be left on the fruit if desired, but wash carefully and especially rub well the blossom end. Stir the sugar into the water over the fire until dissolved, bring slowly to a boil, skim, add the fruit and cook gently from twenty to fifty minutes, or until tender, depending upon the kind of fruit.

For plums use 2 quarts of sugar and 1 pint of water to 8 quarts of fruit. Wash and drain the fruit and remove the skins if desired as above suggested. Or if they are left on, prick them thoroughly with a fruit pricker to prevent bursting. Stir the sugar into the water over the fire until dissolved, bring to a boil and carefully skim. Add the fruit in small quantities one or two layers at a time, cook five minutes, can and seal and so continue, adding more sirup from time to time if necessary.

FRUIT PRESERVING

While the modern method of canning fruits with small quantities of sugar or none at all is to be preferred in most cases, there are a few fruits which make preserves of such excellent quality that their use may be recommended for special occasions. These are strawberries, sour cherries, sour plums and quinces. They should be put up preferably in tumblers or small jars.

For strawberries use equal weights of sugar and fruit. Put a layer of berries in the bottom of the preserving kettle and sprinkle over it a layer of sugar. So continue until the fruit and sugar are about four inches deep. Bring slowly to a boil, skim carefully and boil ten minutes from the time it begins to bubble. Now pour upon platters to a depth of about two or three inches and place these in a sunny window in an unused room for three or four days, when the preserve will thicken to a jelly-like consistency. Put the cold preserve into jars or tumblers and seal. The large proportion of sugar present in this and other preserves is unfavorable to the growth of bacteria and thus prevents them from spoiling.

For white currants select large firm fruit, remove the stems and proceed as for strawberries.

For cherries select the sour varieties such as Early Richmonds and Montmorency. Remove stems and stones and proceed as for strawberries. Or cherries may be preserved with currant juice. Use for this purpose 2 quarts of sugar to 3 quarts of currants by heating in a preserving kettle, crushing them as they boil up and straining through cheese cloth. Stem and stone the cherries taking care to save all the juice. Add the cherries to the fruit juice, stir in the sugar over the fire, bring to a boil slowly and carefully skim. Boil twenty minutes. Put in sterilized jars or tumblers and seal. This gives an acid preserve. The quantity of sugar may be doubled if desired.

For plum preserve use 2 quarts of sugar to 1 pint of water and 4 quarts of greengage or other plums. If the skins are left on, prick the fruit and cover with plenty of cold water. Bring slowly to a boil and let boil gently for five minutes. Drain well. Now stir the sugar into the water over the fire until dissolved and boil five minutes, skimming well. Add the drained fruit and cook gently twenty minutes. Put in sterilized jars. Remove the skins from the white varieties.

For quince preserve use 2 quarts of sugar to 1 quart of water and 4 quarts of fruit. Pare, quarter and core the quinces. Boil in clear water until tender, skim and drain. Now stir the sugar into the water until dissolved, bring slowly to a boil, skim well and boil for twenty minutes. Pour one-half the sirup into another kettle. Put one-half the cooked and drained fruit into each kettle, simmer gently half an hour and put in sterilized jars. Preserve the water in which the fruit is boiled and add to it the parings, cores and gnarly fruit to make jelly.

Purées and Marmalades.—These preserves are merely crushed fruit pulp cooked with sugar. Purées differ from marmalades in being cooked with a small quantity of water and not cooked so long. They retain more of the natural fruit flavor. This process is especially useful for preserving small seedy fruits for frozen desserts, cake and puddings. Pick over and remove leaves, stems and decayed portions, or peach, plum and cherry pits. Rub through a purée sieve and add to each quart of strained fruit a pint of sugar. Pack in sterilized jars, put the covers on loosely and place on the rack in the boiler. Put enough cold water in the boiler to come half way up the sides of the jars. Bring slowly to a boil and boil thirty minutes from the time the water begins to bubble. Remove the jars from the boiler one by one, place in a pan of hot water, fill with hot sirup and seal.

For marmalade pick over berries with great care and rub through a fine sieve to remove the seeds. Remove all cherry, plum or peach pits. Wash, pare, core and quarter large fruit. Allow 1 pint of sugar to each quart of fruit. Rinse the preserving kettle with cold water leaving a slight coat of moisture on the sides and bottom. Put in a layer of fruit, sprinkle with a layer of sugar and so continue until all the fruit and sugar are used. Heat slowly and stir very frequently so as to break up the fruit as much as possible. Cook for about two hours and put in small sterilized jars.

Fruit Preserved in Grape Juice.—Any kind of fruit can be preserved by this method without the use of sugar, but it is particularly recommended for apples, pears and sweet plums. Boil 6 quarts of grape juice in an open preserving kettle down to 4 quarts. Have the fruit washed and pared and large fruit quartered and cored. Cover the prepared fruit with boiled grape juice, boil gently until tender and put in sterilized jars.

Boiled Cider.—Choose cider that is perfectly fresh and sweet. Fill an open preserving kettle not over two-thirds full and boil down one-half, skimming frequently. Put in bottles or stone jugs and use to improve mince meat or make cider apple sauce.

Cider Apple or Pear Sauce.—Use 5 quarts of boiled cider to 8 quarts of pared, quartered and cored fruit. Cover the prepared fruit with boiled cider and cook for two or three hours, or until clear and tender. Place the kettle on an iron tripod or ring to prevent burning. But if necessary to stir the sauce take care to break the fruit as little as possible.

JELLY MAKING

All fruit when ripe or nearly so contains a substance called pectin which has properties somewhat similar to starch. All housekeepers know that starch when boiled in water cools in a jelly-like mass. A similar property in pectin causes fruit juices, when properly boiled, to jell. But if fruits become overripe, or if fruit juices ferment or are cooked too long, the pectin undergoes a change and loses this power. Experience has shown that a definite amount of sugar dissolved in the fruit juice—namely, 25 degrees as registered by the sirup gauge—is exactly right for combining with pectin to make jelly. Any excess of sugar tends to form crystals and the presence of these tends to cause the whole mass to crystallize. Moreover, if the sirup boils so rapidly that some of it rises on the sides of the preserving kettle, such particles will form crystals and these, if stirred into the sirup, may crystallize the whole. Hence the three chief secrets of jelly making are: (1) The selection of fruit which is just ripe, or slightly underripe; (2) the use of the sirup gauge; and (3) slow and careful boiling with especial care not to boil too long. The sirup gauge should register 25 degrees for every kind of fruit without exception.

Housewives are often perplexed because one lot of jelly crystallizes or refuses to harden, whereas another prepared by the same recipe and treated under apparently similar conditions is entirely satisfactory. The difference may be due to either of several causes. One lot of fruit may be overripe or may contain a greater or less proportion of fruit sugar than another. Or the difference may be caused by too rapid or prolonged boiling. Fruit picked during a cold, wet season or immediately after a rain will contain a good deal more water and consequently a less proportion of sugar than if picked after a prolonged period of heat and sunshine. Hence if the proportion of sugar is determined solely by measurement, somewhat less than a pint of sugar will be required for a pint of juice during wet seasons and vice versa. For the same reason small fruits should be washed quickly and thoroughly drained to prevent their absorbing much water. But the use of the sirup gauge will obviate all such difficulties. It measures the exact amount of sugar present, including both the natural fruit sugar and cane sugar added in the process of preserving.

Hence, in general, select for jelly making juicy fruit picked during a period of sunshine, or at least preferably not immediately after rain. Wash quickly, drain, express the juice, add to the clear juice about 1 pint more or less of granulated sugar to the pint of juice, boil, skim and pour into tumblers or small jars.

Acid fruits make the best jelly and the following are to be preferred in the order given: Currant, crab-apple, apple, quince, grape, blackberry, raspberry, peach. Wild raspberries, blackberries, barberries, grapes and beech-plums all make delicious jellies. Take care to choose barberries that are fresh and not overripe. Sweet fruits, such as apples, make a very mild jelly, but may be flavored with fruits, flowers or spices, but with the sour varieties this will not be necessary. Some fruits, such as the strawberry, contain very little pectin and are difficult to jell without the addition of some other fruit juice, such as the currant, when a pleasant jelly will result.

Currant Jelly. — To make good jelly from currants, raspberries, blackberries, ripe grapes and plums, proceed as follows: Pick over the fruit and remove all leaves, large stems and the like. Wash quickly, drain, and put fruit over the fire in a preserving kettle. Crush with a wooden vegetable masher or spoon enough to start the juice, heat slowly and stir frequently. When hot crush thoroughly with the vegetable masher. Express the juice into a large bowl through two thicknesses of cheese cloth spread over a hair or wire sieve. Let the juice drip without pressure, merely moving the pulp about by lifting the corners of the cheese cloth and slightly shaking the contents until all the free juice has been obtained. Use this to make the best quality of jelly either as it is or after first passing it through a flannel or woolen cloth or jelly bag. This will make a somewhat more transparent jell. Now remove the sieve to another bowl, twist the corners of the cheese cloth and squeeze out as much more juice as can be obtained. Use this to make jelly of a lower grade.

Measure the juice into a clean preserving kettle and stir in a pint of granulated sugar for every pint of juice until the sugar is dissolved. Place over the fire and bring to a boil slowly. Observe carefully the moment it begins to boil, withdraw from the fire and skim. Again bring to a boil, remove and skim a second and third time. Then pour into hot sterilized glasses and place these on a hot sunny window-sill covered preferably with panes of glass. When cool and firm seal and store in a dark, cool place.

Or jelly may be prepared directly from the strained juice without boiling by dissolving the required amount of sugar in the cold juice, pouring it into warm sterilized glasses and otherwise treating as before. Such jelly is more delicate but does not keep quite so well.

Other good jellies may be made by the same process from a mixture of equal parts of currants and raspberries, or a mixture of 10 quarts of strawberries with 2 quarts of currants, but the last mentioned must be boiled fifteen minutes.

For ripe grape jelly choose an acid grape, as the sweet varieties contain too much sugar, or use half ripe fruit or equal portions of nearly ripe and green grapes. Wild grapes are excellent.

For plum jelly use an underripe acid plum. Wash, stem and cook gently in 1 quart of water for each peck of fruit. Strain the juice and proceed as for currant jelly.

Apple and Crab-apple Jelly.— Large fruits such as apples, peaches and pears must be boiled in water to extract the pectin and flavoring matter they contain. As a rule 4 quarts of water added to 8 quarts of fruit will produce 3 quarts of strained juice, but juicy peaches and plums may require only 3 or 3½ quarts of water. Boil down the juice if necessary to 3 quarts. Stem and wash the fruit. Wipe dry and clean carefully the blossom end, and cut in quarters. Add 4 quarts of water to 8 of fruit and cook gently until soft and clear. Strain the juice, boil down to 3 quarts if necessary and proceed as for currant jelly. The quality of the jelly will depend upon the natural flavor of the fruit. Hence choose preferably a fine flavored acid apple and make the jelly at any time of the year when the fruit chosen is at its prime. Apple jelly made in the spring may be improved by the addition of the juice of a lemon to every pint of apple juice.

To make cider apple jelly, use cider fresh from the press instead of water.

Quince Jelly.—Rub the quinces with a coarse crash towel. Cut out the blossom end, rinse and drain. Wash and pare the fruit, quarter and cut out the cores, and keep them by themselves. Drop the best pieces of fruit into a bowl half full of water containing lemon juice, to be preserved or canned. Run the parings and imperfect parts through a meat chopper or chop finely. Add a quart of water to every 2 quarts of chopped fruits and parings and cook gently for two hours. Strain and proceed as for apple jelly. Put the cores into another kettle, cover with plenty of water and cook two hours.

Now, to make a second grade of jelly, add the chopped parings and fruit from which the juice has been extracted, mix and strain. Return the clear juice to the preserving kettle, stir in a pint of sugar for each pint of juice and boil ten minutes.

Covering Jelly.—Cut out some discs of any thick white paper, preferably paraffin or butter paper, the size of the top of the jelly glass. A simple way to make a pattern of the exact size is by means of a small compass or pair of dividers. When the jelly is hard and firm, brush over the top with brandy or alcohol to kill any spores of mold that may be present. Dip a disc of paper in the spirits and let it rest on the jelly. Now put on the covers.

Or tie a disc of cotton batting over the top of the glass.

Or cut discs of paper about half an inch in diameter larger than the top of the glass, wet them in a mixture of the white of an egg beaten together with a tablespoonful of cold water and press down the sides until they stick.

Or cut covers about an inch in diameter larger than the top of the glass, dip in olive oil and tie on the glass with string.

Or pour melted paraffin in the top of the glass over a piece of paper dipped in brandy or alcohol. Set the paraffin in a cup surrounded by warm water and heat gently until melted. Make a layer at least one-fourth of an inch thick.

Fruit Juices. — These may be canned or bottled with or without sugar as desired. Use preferably self-sealing bottles such as pop or beer bottles with care to sterilize both bottles and corks.

For grape juice wash the grapes, pick them over and remove the stems and all defective specimens. To express the juice crush slightly in the preserving kettle, heat slowly and boil gently for half an hour. Crush the fruit and express the juice as for jelly making, except that all the juice may be preserved together. Bring the strained juice to a boil in a clean preserving kettle, remove and skim. Do this a second time. Then stir in the sugar until dissolved, boil five minutes, skim and put into hot sterilized bottles or jars. Set these in pans of boiling water in a moderate oven for ten minutes. Now fill up with boiling juice, seal and place on boards to cool protected from drafts. For grapes use about 1 gill of sugar to a quart of juice.

For raspberries, blackberries and strawberries, use ½ pint of sugar to each quart of juice and for currants a full pint, otherwise proceed as for grape juice.

For cherry, plum and peach juices add ½ pint of sugar to each quart of juice.

Fruit Sirups.—Proceed in all respects as for fruit juices, but use at least one-half as much sugar as fruit juice. Use fruit sirups to flavor ice creams and water ices, also for beverages at the rate of two or three spoonfuls to the glass of ice water.

Preserving Powders.—Avoid all so-called "preserving powders" whether advertised under various trade names or put up and sold by druggists or peddlers. Any antiseptics that will prevent the decay of fruits and vegetables are injurious to health regardless of all claims by interested persons to the contrary. Nothing of the sort is necessary if sound ripe fruit is selected and sterilized by means of heat in the proper manner. And since the necessary care to do good work adds little or nothing to the cost of preserving fruits and vegetables, the so-called "preserving powders" serve no useful purpose. On the contrary they tend to encourage unclean and slovenly work and to conceal the effects of using decaying fruits and vegetables.

CANNING VEGETABLES

Some vegetables are more difficult to preserve properly than fruits and fruit juices, since they contain a considerable proportion of the element nitrogen, the presence of which makes any substance a good culture medium for the bacteria, spores and molds which cause decomposition. Moreover, the addition of sugar to fruits and fruit juices helps to produce a condition which is unfavorable to the growth of these injurious organisms. But the addition of sugar to most vegetables would not be desirable. Hence, a considerably longer and more heroic treatment for canning vegetables is required. The process, however, is simple and is so similar to the ordinary methods of canning fruit that it can be readily carried out by any housekeeper if the following suggestions are observed:

The secret of canning vegetables lies in the fact that whereas bacteria may be readily killed at the temperature of boiling water, the spores or seeds of certain kinds may retain their vitality unless they are kept at the temperature of boiling water for a long time—about five hours—or preferably boiled for about one hour upon two or three successive days. The latter is the method employed by scientific men and is the one here recommended. The first day's boiling kills all the molds and most of the bacteria but does not kill their spores or seeds. These start to grow as soon as the contents of the jar is cool. The second boiling kills the crop of bacteria thus formed before they have time to develop spores. The third boiling is not always necessary, but is advised to make assurance doubly sure. This process is called by scientists "fractional sterilization." It is the whole secret of canning meat, fruits or vegetables and anyone who will bear it in mind may be sure of satisfactory results.

Observe, however, that the air must be excluded at all times after the first boiling. Otherwise a new crop of bacteria, spores and molds will be deposited from the air and the work of sterilization will be undone. Cooking for three short periods in a closed container at a comparatively low temperature instead of cooking for one short period at a high temperature, or for one long period in an open vessel makes the vital difference and insures a freshness of flavor and color such that the difference between the product and the fresh vegetables can hardly be detected. After the jars have been sterilized and tested keep them in the dark, or wrap them closely in dark colored paper, as sunlight will soon destroy the color.

Canning Corn. — All housewives will be glad to know that corn is one of the easiest vegetables to can if proper precautions are observed. Select preferably the sweetest and most delicate varieties. Experiment has proved that the amount of sugar in sweet corn diminishes very rapidly after the ear is pulled from the stalk. Hence endeavor to get the kernels into the can within an hour after the corn is picked. If this can be done the result will be far superior to the ordinary commercial product. Select ears with full grains, just before they begin to harden, since the corn is then sweetest. Husk the ears and remove the silks with a stiff brush. Sheer off the grain with a sharp knife, pack the jar full and salt to taste, usually at the rate of one teaspoonful to the quart. Fill up the jar to the top with clear cold water, put on the rubber ring and place the glass top on loosely but without depressing the spring. Now place the jars upon a false bottom in a wash boiler and separate

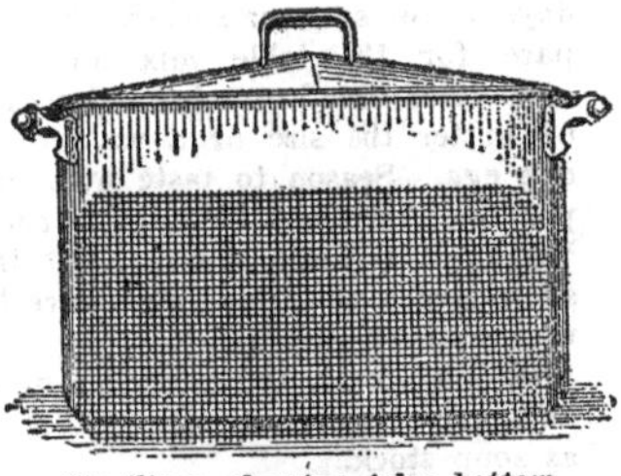

Sterilizer, showing false bottom. (J. F. Breazeale.)

them by means of rags or cotton rope, such as an old clothesline, so that they cannot strike one another when the water begins to boil. Pour in about three inches of cold water or enough to fill the boiler with steam. More than enough to prevent the boiler from going dry is not necessary as the steam will do the cooking. Cover the boiler tightly, bring to a boil and let boil for a full hour. Now remove the cover and allow the steam to escape. Press down the spring to prevent air from entering. Remove the jars to cool, or let them stand in the boiler until the next day.

On the second day raise the spring as before and again boil for one hour. Once more clamp down the top and let stand until the following day. Then repeat the operation. Observe that the jars when hot must be carefully shielded from drafts of cold air or the sudden change of temperature will crack them.

After the third boiling clamp on the top and let stand two or three days. Then test each jar by releasing the spring and picking up the jar by the glass top. If the top does not come off the contents are reasonably sure to keep unless there should chance to be one or more anaerobic bacteria present which may cause trouble later on. Should this happen increase the length of boiling for the next lot to 1½ hours.

If the tops come off when the can is tested, decomposition has begun to take place and gases have been formed which offset the atmospheric pressure on the outside of the jar. In this case it is best to reject the contents and to cleanse and refill the jar.

The above directions apply only to pint and quart jars. Increase the time of boiling for half gallon jars to one and a half hours. A little practice may be required at first to secure perfect results by this method; hence do not try too many jars the first time. Make a few experiments in the early part of the season until you fully understand the directions and learn to follow them properly. After that there will be no difficulty and the benefits of fresh vegetables from the kitchen garden will be extended to every season of the year.

The same general process applies to canning other vegetables except for the mode of preparing them, as to which the following suggestions are offered:

Stringbeans. — Pick these when young and tender, string, break into short lengths, pack firmly in the jar, cover with cold water and add a teaspoonful of salt to each quart. Otherwise proceed as for corn. Add a small bit of red pepper in the bottom of each jar, if desired.

Eggplant. — Pare, cut in thin slices and drop into boiling water for fifteen or twenty minutes. Drain and pack in jars. Proceed as for corn. Remove in slices when required and fry in bread crumbs, or make into puddings and bake.

Beets.—Pull while young and tender. Cut off the tops, wash and drop in boiling water for one and a half hours, or until thoroughly cooked. Skin, slice and pack in jars. Proceed as for corn. To pickle, cover with equal parts of water and good vinegar and sweeten to taste.

Okra or Gumbo.—Pick the pods while young and tender, wash, cut in short lengths and sterilize as above. Use for soups and stews.

Summer Squash.—Cut into small blocks, pack, cover with water, add salt and sterilize as above. Or skin, boil or steam until well cooked, mash, pack and sterilize. But in this case steam for an hour and a half each day as the heat penetrates the jar more slowly. Each jar will contain about twice as much of the cooked vegetable as if uncooked.

English Peas. — Choose young sweet peas and proceed as for corn. This product has all the delicate flavor of the fresh vegetable.

Asparagus.—Can the tips only, the same as for corn.

Cauliflower.—Prepare in summer the same as for serving at table. Pack in jars and sterilize.

Carrots and Parsnips.—Gather in early summer when the young plants are tender and sweet. Prepare as for serving at table and sterilize as for corn.

Turnips and Kohl-Rabi.—Prepare as for the table, pack and sterilize.

Lima Beans. — Pick before the pods begin to harden and treat as for corn.

Pumpkin or Winter Squash.—Preserve these in their natural condition in a suitable storeroom as long as possible. But should they show signs of decay, steam and can the same as summer squash. By this time the jars which have been emptied of other vegetables will be available and may thus be made to do double service.

Succotash. — Gather fresh corn and beans early in the morning. Prepare and sterilize as above. This is one of the most difficult things to can, hence boil an hour and a half each day as for summer squash.

Vegetable Roast. — Prepare corn, lima beans, tomatoes, stringbeans, okra, squash and eggplant as for canning separately. Mix in any desired proportions but let the corn and lima beans predominate. Add two or three medium sized onions to each quart and run through a food chopper to mix thoroughly. Pack into jars and sterilize by boiling an hour and a half each day for three days as for summer squash. To prepare for the table mix an equal amount of bread crumbs, add a piece of butter the size of a walnut and one egg. Season to taste with pepper and salt and bake in a round baking dish until brown. Cut into slices like a meat loaf and serve hot with drawn-butter sauce.

Or corn, okra and tomatoes mixed in equal proportions may be canned as soup stock.

Stewed Tomatoes. — These keep very easily even in the common screw-top jar. Hence such jars may be set aside for tomatoes and the more modern styles used for canning other vegetables. In this case observe that the tops and rubbers must first be sterilized by placing them in cold water. Bring to a boil and boil for ten minutes. Handle as little as possible, especially the inside of the top or inner edge of the rubber. Fill the jar with the cooked tomatoes while steaming hot, put on the rubber, screw the top down firmly, invert it and let it stand in that position until cold. To prepare the tomatoes, wash and plunge them in boiling water for five minutes. Now dip for a moment in cold water, pare, slice and place them in a preserving kettle over an iron ring or tripod. Heat slowly and stir frequently from the bottom. Bring to a boil and then boil thirty minutes. Put in sterilized jars and seal.

Whole Tomatoes.—Use 8 quarts of medium sized whole tomatoes and 4 quarts of sliced tomatoes. Prepare the sliced tomatoes as for stewed tomatoes. Boil twenty minutes, rub through a strainer and return to the fire. Now pare the whole tomatoes and put them in sterilized jars. Pour over them the stewed and strained tomatoes until the jar is full. Put the uncovered jars in a moderate oven on a pad of asbestos, or in a shallow pan of hot water and cook for half an hour. Remove, fill to overflowing with boiling hot strained tomatoes and seal. Any strained tomatoes left over may be canned for sauces.

How to Open a Jar.—Run a thin knife blade under the rubber next to the jar and press against the jar firmly. If this does not let in enough air to release the pressure on the top, place the jar in a deep saucepan of water, bring to a boil and keep boiling a few minutes. It will then open easily.

CHAPTER XXIV

VINEGAR, PICKLES, AND PICKLING

SPECIAL VINEGARS—PICKLES AND PICKLING—MIXED PICKLES—PICKLED VEGETABLES, NUTS, AND FRUITS

All vinegar, of which there are several kinds, consists of a dilute solution of acetic acid in water with a small amount of sugar and other organic matter. Vinegar is the result of the action of the oxygen of the air, in the presence of a particular kind of yeast or ferment, upon a solution of alcohol. The alcoholic liquors from which vinegar is made may be produced by the fermentation of almost any vegetable or fruit juices. The principal kinds of vinegar are, accordingly, wine vinegar, produced from grapes; malt vinegar, from barley; cider vinegar, from apples; sugar and molasses vinegar, from cane sugar products; corn vinegar; beet vinegar; etc. The alcoholic fluid, or "wash," as it is called, should contain not over 4 per cent to 12 per cent of alcohol. And for the best results the temperature should be from 70 per cent to 85 per cent Fahrenheit. Plenty of air to introduce the oxygen required by the process must be supplied and mixed with the alcoholic solution. The changing of alcohol to acetic acid by the action of oxygen produces heat and increases the weight of the liquid.

Commercial vinegar is made on the Continent of Europe principally from cheap grades of wine, in England from malt and sour beer, in the United States from cider and cheap grades of alcoholic liquors, as whisky and the like.

Methods of Making Vinegar. — There are two principal ways of making vinegar — the slow and the quick process. In the former the alcoholic solution is placed in a barrel or vat containing a little old vinegar or mother, which supplies the necessary yeast, or in the case of wine vinegar, old wine lees, either exposed to the sun or placed in a warm room. Air is admitted through the bung of the casks or otherwise, and the liquid is allowed to stand until it turns to vinegar. This takes two weeks or more in summer, and a month or more in cold weather. The process is similar to that of making cheap vinegar from molasses and yeast, or making ordinary cider vinegar.

Or to make vinegar by the quick, or German process, prepare a special contrivance as follows:

Supply a large vinegar cask with a false bottom about a foot from the true bottom perforated with a large number of ¼ inch gimlet holes. If a fine quality of vinegar is desired, cover this with one or more thicknesses of white flannel cloth, and an inch layer of clean white sand on top. Bore, around the outside of the barrel an inch below the false bottom, a row of ½ inch auger holes slanting downward from without 2 or 3 inches apart. These are necessary to admit the air. Fill the barrel from the false bottom to within 4 or 5 inches of the top with maple, beech, or basswood chips previously soaked for three or four days in first-class vinegar.

Now cut another cask of somewhat smaller size in halves. Bore the bottom of one half barrel full of gimlet holes the size of a goose quill or about ⅛ inch in diameter. Cover this with cotton batting or yarn, and place it on top of the barrel resting on cross slats or upon the chips.

Insert a spigot into the cask below the false bottom, slanting downward to the bottom of the cask but having

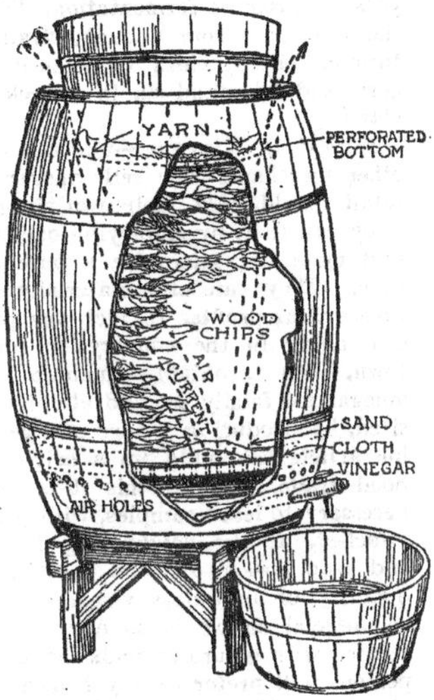

"Vinegar by the Quick or German Process."

its opening just below the level of the row of air holes, and place beneath the spigot the other half barrel, protected by a wooden cover from dust and dirt.

The alcoholic liquor poured into the upper half barrel causes the yarn or cotton in the bottom to swell and fill the gimlet holes, whence the liquor drops through upon the chips. The process of fermentation produces heat, which causes a current of air to rise through the openings for that purpose below the false bottom, and to meet the alcoholic liquor as it percolates drop by drop through the chips. The air current escapes between the bottom of the upper half barrel and the top edges of the large cask. Thus the action of the oxygen in the air in turning the alcohol into acetic acid is made very rapid.

The vinegar, after passing through the sand and flannel strainer, and the false bottom, accumulates in the bottom of the barrel but cannot escape through the spigot until it reaches the level of its mouth, or a depth of 8 or 10 inches. It is then first drawn from the bottom where its strength is greatest. And the strong vinegar thus accumulated assists in the process of fermentation.

To use this apparatus, pour in about 4 gallons of alcoholic liquor or "wash" every hour with the addition of 1 quart to make up for the waste. And withdraw every hour about 4 gallons of vinegar from the bottom. The first product must be ladled back into the upper half barrel, run through again and again, when it will be converted into vinegar in three or four days. It must then be poured into a clean tank or cask, and one or two quarts of molasses added to it each day, until the molasses settles in a bed 3 or 4 inches thick. This improves the flavor of the vinegar and gives it a fine color. This process is the quickest and most satisfactory that has ever been devised. And as the apparatus is inexpensive, and the product is more salable than ordinary vinegar, there would seem to be no reason why it could not be utilized by grocers and other dealers in vinegar, or by private families or individuals either for domestic use or for sale.

Water for Vinegar.—Pure soft or distilled water ought to be used for the manufacture of good vinegar, and if the water is not pure it should be purified by filtering through charcoal.

Wash or Liquors for Vinegar.—The commonest alcoholic liquor used for commercial vinegar in this country consists of about 3 gallons of corn whisky, 4 gallons of good commercial vinegar, and 33 gallons of pure water.

Or 50 gallons of 60 per cent whisky and 37 gallons of beer or maltwort.

Or 2 gallons of brandy, 4 gallons of vinegar, and 12 gallons of water, with the addition, to promote fermentation, of about 1 gallon of an infusion of equal parts bran and rye meal.

Or use 1½ pounds of sugar to each gallon of pure water.

Or ½ gallon of water to 2 gallons of cider. Add to the above in all cases 2 quarts of yeast to every barrel of the liquor.

To Ferment Vinegar.—The process of making vinegar requires the presence of the minute vegetable organisms called yeast, and is greatly hastened by conditions favorable to their growth. This is the reason that vinegar is made more rapidly in hot than in cold weather, and that the temperature of 75° to 80° F. hastens the process. The germs of yeast are, of course, present in large numbers in the lees and mother of old vinegar and also in the vinegar which is soaked into the fiber of the cask. Hence an old vinegar barrel, if sound, is preferable to a new one. The germs of yeast are also present in ordinary vinegar, and if 1 gallon of sound vinegar can be added to each 3 or 5 gallons of cider or other alcoholic liquor or "wash" from which vinegar is to be made, no other yeast will be necessary.

Or good brewers' yeast may be added to the alcoholic liquor at the rate of about ¾ of a pint to each 12 gallons.

Or homemade hop yeast at the rate of 1½ pints to 12 gallons. The "wash" should be at a temperature of about 75° or 80° F. when the yeast is added, and should be kept at or near that temperature while the vinegar is being made. Yeast must not be scalded as a temperature above 140° F. kills it. When old vinegar barrels are employed, or ordinary vinegar is put into new casks to hasten fermentation, care must be taken that the vinegar formerly made in the casks, or used for this purpose, is of the same kind and of at least equally good quality to the desired product. That is, if a fine quality of cider vinegar is desired, only casks that have been used in making pure cider vinegar, or the best grade of cider vinegar itself should be used in the process.

Or boil until tender 1½ pints of shelled corn to each gallon of the "wash" and add this in place of yeast to promote fermentation. When the vinegar is sour enough, strain it through cheese cloth to remove the corn and let stand another week to clarify.

Money in Vinegar.—Grocers and other merchants who sell vinegar at retail should make their own vinegar. They can thus, by employing only the best materials, guarantee a pure article. They can also materially increase their profits. In fact, any person living in the country or small town, can profitably manufacture vinegar for family use and also, if desired, by producing a pure and genuine article can build up a neighborhood trade. To do this it is only necessary to leave samples, with price attached, at the neighboring houses and keep always on hand a sufficient quantity of first-class vinegar. The commercial article is so often adulterated with injurious acids that most persons will prefer to buy homemade vinegar at the market rates or better and a satisfactory profit will be assured.

Cheap Molasses Vinegar.—To make vinegar by the slow process, fill a large jug, keg, or cask with a mixture consisting of 1 quart of best New Orleans molasses, 1 pint of yeast to each 3 gallons of warm rain water. Tie a piece of cheese cloth over the bung to keep out dust and insects, but to admit the air. Place the receptacle out of doors in the sun during hot weather. Or in cold weather let it stand near the kitchen stove. It will be converted into vinegar in from three weeks to a month. When it gets low, draw off a supply for family use, leaving more or less old vinegar with the mother and lees in the bottom of the cask. Fill up with new liquid in the same proportions, and let stand until converted into vinegar as before.

Or dissolve ½ a pound of light-brown "A" or coffee sugar in 2 gallons of soft warm water. Add 3 pints of homemade hop yeast or 1½ pints of good brewers' yeast to each 12 gallons. Pour all into a suitable keg or cask.

Or a firkin may be used if fitted with a tight cover having one or more auger holes to admit air through it. Fill the receptacle about two thirds full, or a little more, so as to expose as large a surface as possible to the air. Cover the openings with cheese cloth and let stand in a warm place. Where the conditions are favorable it will be converted into vinegar in about two weeks or a month.

Or for a somewhat better quality, take 5 gallons of water to 1 gallon of molasses, and add a quart of yeast. The addition of a gallon of good vinegar will hasten the process. Odds and ends of sirup, as rinsings from fruit jars, molasses cans, and the like, may be added to the liquor from time to time.

Or for a cheaper quality, take 25 gallons of warm rain water, 4 gallons of molasses, and 1 gallon of brewers' yeast.

To Manufacture Vinegar for Sale.—Grocers and other merchants who sell vinegar at retail may keep themselves supplied with vinegar in the following manner:

Have on hand three or more barrels in multiples of three, and use them in rotation. If less than a barrel of vinegar is sold each week, three barrels will be sufficient, as the process will be completed in three weeks or less. Commence with a barrel of good commercial vinegar. Before it is quite empty draw off and pour into each of the other two barrels 2 or 3 gallons of vinegar. Now fill up the vinegar barrel with a fresh liquor in the proportion of 1 gallon of molasses to 5 gallons more or less of warm rain water according to the quality of vinegar desired, and about 1 quart of yeast for each 12 gallons of the mixture.

Fill up the other two barrels with the same liquor. The first or old vinegar barrel containing more or less lees and mother will turn to vinegar very quickly, and may be sold first, and refilled when it gets low. By that time the second will be ready to use, or nearly so. After the three barrels are once started, if filled up when nearly emptied, they will furnish a constant supply.

Or if upward of two barrels are sold each week, six casks may be kept going in the same manner. A good-sized bunghole should be kept open to admit the air, but they should have two or three thicknesses of cheese cloth tacked over them to keep out dust and insects.

Or to manufacture vinegar on a large scale summer and winter alike, it is necessary either to have a large cellar equipped with suitable vats or casks, or a building which is well ventilated, and can be warmed in winter by means of a furnace or otherwise. In addition to suitable arrangements for storing ordinary casks in tiers, and the necessary apparatus for leaching the wash through beechwood shavings by the quick or German process, an important part of the equipment is one or more large ripening casks or vats capable of holding 500 to 1,000 gallons and upward. The cider or other "wash," after having been turned into vinegar by either the slow or quick process and run off into smaller casks, should be transferred at intervals to these large casks so that the output of the establishment will be of a uniform flavor. Care must, of course, be taken that the casks, vats, and other apparatus used to produce a particular kind or grade of vinegar should not be used for any other purpose, if the object is to build up a trade for a particular brand or quality.

Malt Vinegar.—In the vicinity of breweries, where wort can be procured at a reasonable price, malt vinegar can be made very cheaply. Add to each 25 gallons of wort 1 gallon of beer yeast. Ferment for about thirty-five or forty hours, and draw off the liquor into casks about two thirds full. Let them stand at a temperature of 70° to 75° F. Keep the bungs out to admit plenty of air.

Sugar Vinegar.—To make sugar vinegar for domestic use, add ¼ pint of yeast to a solution of 1½ pounds of sugar in 1 gallon of water. Let the mixture ferment for about three days in a large earthenware jar or other receptacle, placed where the temperature will be at least 80° F. Then draw off the clear liquor from the sediment into a clean cask and add 1 ounce of cream of tartar and 1 ounce of bruised raisins. Let stand until sufficiently sour, clarify, bottle and cork for use.

Or boil any quantity of coarse brown sugar with filtered rain water at the rate of 2 pounds of sugar to the gallon and with a skimmer remove the scum as fast as it appears. Now add a quart of cold water for every gallon of hot. Let cool, and add about a pint of yeast for each 6 gallons of the liquor. Run into a cask. Cover the bunghole with wire gauze or several thicknesses of cheese cloth, and place it out in the sun. If this vinegar is made in the early spring and exposed to summer heat it will be ready for use by midsummer. In winter six months will be required.

Cider Vinegar.—The best quality of vinegar is undoubtedly that made from cider, providing the apples used are sound, ripe, sweet fruit. As the best grades of cider vinegar bring a fancy price, it is advisable to separate ripe, sweet windfalls from small, unripe, or defective fruit, and use the best fruit for an A 1 grade of cider. The usual careless method of making cider is merely to fill a cask to its capacity with cider and let it stand four to six months to sour. But, with proper care and attention, a better grade of cider can be made in a much quicker time. The better way is to place the cider in a hogshead or large tank. Lay the ripening casks, with the bungholes open, on their sides, exposed to the heat of the sun or in a warm cellar, and fill them at first only about a quarter full of cider. After about two weeks, add another quarter, making the barrel half full, and after two weeks more do the same, leaving the cask about three quarters full. Thus a considerable flat surface inside is left exposed to the air. Once a day for the first few weeks draw from the spigot a gallon or more of cider and pour it from a considerable height through a funnel into the bunghole. This keeps the cider full of air. Also, put into each barrel a pound or more of bread dough, prepared as for making ordinary wheat bread, in the state in which it is ready to be put into the oven.

Other methods recommended for hastening the process of fermentation are the addition of a quart or more of molasses to each cask, 2 ounces of brown sugar to each gallon of cider, or brown paper dipped in New Orleans molasses. But the bread dough is perhaps to be preferred. The ordinary skunk-cabbage balls, which occur plentifully in swamps and meadows in many localities, are also employed for this purpose.

Or the mother of vinegar from an old cider barrel will greatly hasten the process.

Cheap Cider Vinegar.—Save the pomace from which cider is made, or buy pomace from the cider mill. Put it into tight casks or hogsheads with the head knocked out of one end and a spigot near the bottom, and cover with filtered rain water. Tack over the top two or three thicknesses of cheese cloth to keep out insects and dust. Draw off the liquor from the bottom as fast as it ferments, and use it to dilute pure cider. Thus nearly two barrels of vinegar can be made from one of cider.

To Make Cider Vinegar Quickly.—Fill a jar or jug with cider and add for each gallon of cider a pint of New Orleans molasses and a cupful of good yeast. Take out the cork of the jug or leave the cover of the jar tilted slightly to admit the air,

The cider will commence to ferment at once and will be turned into vinegar in about a week. Pour off the clear into demijohns or bottles and cork tightly for use. Leave the lees or mother, and fill up the original receptacle with fresh cider to repeat the process.

To Preserve Vinegar.—To preserve vinegar after it has ripened to perfection, draw it off from the mother into a clean cask and drive in the bung to exclude the air.

Or clarify and bottle it in tightly stoppered bottles and store at a low temperature. If it again thickens and shows traces of mother, it must be once more drawn off into a clean vessel.

Grape Vinegar.—The juice of the grapes must first be extracted in a wine press and allowed to ferment. Wine when a year old usually furnishes the best vinegar, as with greater age the wine loses a part of its organic matter and becomes unsuitable for vinegar. To make vinegar from wine it is first poured into a cask containing wine lees. It is then placed in cloth sacks in an ironbound vat or cask and squeezed through the cloth by means of weights from above. It is then placed in upright casks having a bunghole at the top and allowed to sour, same as cider vinegar. If casks are exposed to the summer sun, the contents turn to vinegar in about two weeks. But in winter the process in a warm room requires a month or more. The temperature should be 75° to 86° F. The wine is next drawn off into barrels containing beech-wood chips, to clarify for about two weeks. It is then ready for use. The original cask, containing the residue of mother, is used without cleansing to ferment additional wine.

In making the best qualities of vinegar the wine is first clarified by running it into casks or vats containing beech shavings. The ripening casks are then filled about a quarter full of boiling vinegar, which is allowed to stand for three or four days, after which the wine is gradually added at the rate of about a gallon at a time until the casks are filled. After about two or three weeks the wine is turned to vinegar. One half is then drawn off and bottled or stored for use, and the cask is refilled as before. This process is sometimes continued for ten years, without the casks ever becoming more than half empty, but after that length of time it is necessary to remove the accumulated sediment.

White-Wine Vinegar. — Crush 2 pounds of clean juicy raisins. Add a gallon of filtered rain water, place in a 2-gallon jug uncorked, and let it stand in a warm place. In about a month it will be converted into pure white-wine vinegar.

Pour out the clear vinegar through a cheese-cloth strainer, leaving the raisins and sediment in the jug; add ½ pound of raisins in another gallon of water, and repeat the process.

Corn Vinegar.—Boil in a gallon of rain water a pint of shelled Indian corn until the kernels burst. Pour the whole into a 2-gallon stone jug and add filtered rain water to supply that lost by evaporation, making a gallon all told. Dissolve ½ pound of granulated sugar in ½ pound of soft water by bringing it to a boil. Pour into the jug; shake well. Cover the mouth of the jug with two or three thicknesses of cheese cloth. Let stand in a warm place at a temperature of 75° or 80° F. It will be converted into vinegar in about a month. Pour off this vinegar into another jug, leaving about half the mother, and repeat the process.

To preserve this vinegar, cover the mouth of the jug with a piece of cloth and store it in a dry, warm place. This recipe makes vinegar about as cheaply as it can be made, and gives a quality that is preferred by many to ordinary cider vinegar. It is worth trying.

To Clarify Vinegar.—To clarify vinegar for bottling, draw it off into a clean cask or other vessel and throw into it a handful more or less of shredded isinglass. Let it stand for a few days and filter through a cheese cloth.

Distilled Vinegar.—Vinegar is distilled by heating in an ordinary retort by means of a sand bath, about 7 pints being carried over from each gallon. No lead or pewter can be used in any part of the retort or condenser, as the acetic acid acting upon these metals produces a poisonous compound. Distilled vinegar is weaker than the ordinary commercial article for the reason that water boils at a lower temperature than acetic acid. Hence more water than acetic acid is carried over. Distilled vinegar is used principally by druggists.

To Decolorize Vinegar. — Substances recommended for this purpose are ivory black, bone black or ordinary charcoal, all of which have the property of absorbing the various coloring matters so as to reduce ordinary cider, red wine, or other highly colored vinegar to a limpid and transparent whiteness.

Mix with each gallon of red wine or cider vinegar about 6 ounces of pure bone charcoal, from which, by means of a coarse sieve, all loose dust and small grains have been removed. Place the whole in a glass or earthenware vessel and shake or stir from time to time until the color has been removed.

Or the charcoal, in the same proportion, can be thrown into an ordinary cask, and the contents stirred occasionally.

Or if the cask is bunged up, the cask may be rolled or rocked, or ended up from time to time, to bring the charcoal in contact with all parts of the vinegar.

Or a double bag of any desired size may be made of coarse linen and lined with a layer of charcoal 2 or 3 inches in thickness. This should be quilted sufficiently to prevent the charcoal from settling or bunching up. Vinegar may be decolorized by straining through this.

Strength of Vinegar.—The strength of vinegar or the amount of acetic acid which is contained in different specimens, differs greatly. To determine the proportion of acetic acid, suspend 4 or 5 ounces, by weight, of broken pieces of fine marble in 16 ounces, by weight, of vinegar. The acetic acid will attack the marble and will be gradually neutralized. Let stand overnight. Remove the marble, rinse it in cold water, dry it thoroughly with gentle heat on top of the stove (but take care not to melt it), and weigh it carefully, $\frac{5}{8}$ of its loss in weight is the quantity of actual acetic acid contained in the sample. And from this amount the proportion of acetic acid can be readily obtained.

Good vinegar should contain about 5 per cent of absolute acetic acid. The commercial test is the number of grains of pure carbonate of potassium that will exactly neutralize 1 fluid ounce of vinegar. If 20 grains of carbonate of potassium are required, the sample is known as 20 grains' strength.

Purity of Vinegar.—Various mineral acids, as sulphuric, nitric, hydrochloric and others, are sometimes added to vinegar as adulterants to increase its acidity, and for other purposes. Red pepper, mustard, and other acrid substances are also used, and traces of copper and lead are sometimes derived from the vats or kettles in which the vinegar is prepared.

Test for Sulphuric Acid.—Stir into a sample of suspected vinegar a small quantity of potato starch and bring to a boil. Remove from the fire and let stand until entirely cold. Add slowly, drop by drop, a solution of iodine. If the vinegar is pure, the iodine solution will produce the blue color of iodide of starch, but if sulphuric acid is present the starch will have been converted by boiling into dextrin, and the blue color will not appear.

Or dip a piece of writing paper in the vinegar and heat it over the stove; if the vinegar is pure, the paper will not be charred, but the presence of 2 per cent or more of sulphuric acid will char it.

Or a more delicate test consists in bringing to a boil a solution of ½ ounce of sugar in 16 ounces of water and when it reaches the boiling point dipping into it a china cup or saucer. If a drop of vinegar is let fall on this china surface while moistened with sirup at the temperature of boiling water (212° F.) if pure it will produce no perceptible effect. But if it contains the slightest trace of sulphuric acid it will produce a spot of color ranging from pale green to a darker brown or black in proportion to the quantity of free sulphuric acid present.

Test for Hydrochloric Acid.—To test for hydrochloric acid use the boiled potato-starch and solution-of-iodine test for sulphuric acid; the reaction will be the same.

Or add to the suspected sample a little silver nitrate, which, if hydrochloric acid is present, will produce a white precipitate.

Test for Nitric Acid.—To test for nitric acid, add a solution of indigo to the sample of vinegar and bring to a boil. The nitric acid can be detected by a yellow color.

Tests for Other Adulterants.—To discover the presence of red pepper, mustard, etc., boil down the vinegar until all the water it contains has been evaporated, when, if these substances are present, the resulting extract will have a sharp, biting taste.

To test for copper, add potassium ferrocyanide, which will give a brown precipitate.

To test for lead, add hydrogen sulphide, which will give a black precipitate, or potassium iodine, which will produce a yellow precipitate.

To Strengthen Vinegar. — To strengthen a quantity of weak vinegar, boil down a gallon of good vinegar to 2 quarts, and let it stand in the sun for a week or ten days. Add this to about six times its own bulk of weak vinegar. The whole will be strengthened and given an agreeable flavor.

SPECIAL VINEGARS

Aromatic Vinegar.—This is a mixture or compound of strong acetic acid or ordinary vinegar with various essential oils. It is a volatile and powerful perfume having a pungent odor and is snuffed in the nostrils as a stimulant in languor, faintness, nervous debility, etc.

To produce the best qualities of aromatic vinegar, a glacial or crystallizable acetic acid is combined with various essential oils at the rate of 6 drops, more or less, of the oils of clove, lavender, rosemary, calamus, etc., to 1 ounce of glacial acetic acid.

Aromatic vinegar must be kept tightly corked. For use it may be dropped on a sponge or snuffed from a vinaigrette. It may also be used as a caustic for warts, corns, and other callouses. But on account of its caustic properties it must be carefully kept from clothing and the skin. Treat accidental burns with cooking soda.

Imitation of Aromatic Vinegar.—Common vinegar may be boiled down with very gentle heat until 90 per cent to 95 per cent of its bulk has been lost by evaporation, and the remainder will be almost pure acetic acid. To this the essential oils may be added in the above proportions, and a fairly good grade of aromatic vinegar obtained.

Fruit Vinegars. — The juices of most ordinary fruits, as raspberries, currants, gooseberries, and the like, contain sufficient sugar to ferment and produce an alcoholic liquor from which vinegar can be made, either with or without the addition of sugar sirup or molasses.

To make vinegar from fruits, extract the juice by boiling the fruit with about its own quantity of water. Squeeze out the juice through several thicknesses of cheese cloth. This may be done by inserting sticks at either end and twisting them. To each gallon of fruit juice add about a quarter pint of good yeast, and let stand in an open jug or jar with the cover slightly tilted at a temperature of 70° or 80° F.

Or the boiled fruit juice may be allowed to stand for two or three days, to ferment before straining. And the yeast may be added after the fermented liquor has been freed from the fruit pulp.

Vinegar made from fruit juices is of better quality and keeps better than that made from malt liquors. These juices are often prepared in much the same manner before they are fully turned into vinegar and used as cooling drinks. And ordinary vinegar is frequently flavored with fruit juices for table use. The following include miscellaneous recipes of these kinds:

Raspberry Vinegar.—Pick over 1½ pints of fresh raspberries. Place them in an earthenware jar or jug, and pour over them 3 pints of pure vinegar. After twenty-four hours strain out the liquor, discard the fruit pulp, clean the jar, place in it 1½ pints of fresh raspberries, and pour the liquor over them. After another twenty-four hours repeat the process for the third time, thus using, all told, 4½ pints of fresh raspberries. Decant the clear liquor through two or three thicknesses of cheese cloth, without squeezing, into a double boiler of graniteware, porcelain, or tin. But do not use a graniteware kettle that is chipped so as to expose the iron. Stir in until dissolved 1 pound of crushed loaf sugar for each pint of liquor. Boil for one hour, taking off the scum with a skimmer as fast as it appears. Bottle, cork, and seal.

Gooseberry Vinegar.—Mash in a suitable vessel half a bushel of ripe gooseberries. Using for this purpose the end of a stick of hard wood. Add 6 gallons of lukewarm rain water, and let stand twenty-four hours. Strain through several thicknesses of cheese cloth, stir in 12 pounds of coarse brown sugar, and pour the whole into a 9-gallon cask, filling it up with warm rain water. Let stand three or four days, stirring several times a day to dissolve the sugar, which settles at the bottom. Head up the cask, pack two or three thicknesses of cheese cloth over the bung-hole, and place the cask in a warm place, near the kitchen stove indoors, but not in the sun. It will be turned into vinegar in from nine to twelve months. It may then be strained and bottled for use. When so made gooseberry vinegar is superior to the best white-wine vinegar, and will make a better quality of pickles than the most expensive vinegar of commerce, preserving the ingredients better, whereas the cost is next to nothing.

Or for each quart of ripe gooseberries, add 3 quarts of water, ferment forty-eight hours, strain, stir in 1½ pounds of sugar, and let stand in a warm place ten months or more, when it will be ready for use.

Raspberry, corn, and other fruit vinegars may be made by the same plan, and substantially the same proportions may be observed.

Horse-Radish Vinegar. — Mix 1½ ounces of horse-radish, ½ ounce of minced shallot, ½ ounce of Cayenne pepper or paprika, and pour over it a pint of vinegar. Let stand a week or ten days, strain through cheese cloth and bottle for use.

Cucumber Vinegar. — Place in a large stone jar about 1½ dozen large cucumbers, pared and sliced, 4 large onions, pared and sliced, 2 or 3 pieces of garlic and shallots, 2 tablespoonfuls of salt, 3 tablespoonfuls of black or white pepper, and ½ teaspoonful of paprika or Cayenne. Let stand four or five days, bring to a boil, cool and strain, or filter through linen cloth or filter paper, and bottle for table use.

Chili Vinegar.—Chop fine 25 chili peppers and pour over them ½ pint or more of pure vinegar. Let stand about ten days or two weeks, strain through cheese cloth and preserve in small bottles tightly corked for table use.

Cayenne Vinegar.—Place ½ ounce of Cayenne pepper or paprika in a glass bottle and pour over it a pint of pure vinegar. Let stand a month or more, shaking frequently. Strain into small bottles and cork tightly.

Shallot Vinegar.—Chop fine ½ dozen shallots, put them in a glass bottle, pour over them a pint of pure vinegar. Cork tightly. Let stand a month or more, strain and preserve in small bottles tightly corked.

Camp Vinegar.—Chop together ½ dozen anchovies, 1 shallot, 1 clove of garlic, and stir in ½ saltspoonful of Cayenne and 2 ounces of walnut catsup. Place in a glass bottle and pour over it ½ pint pure vinegar. Let stand a week or ten days, strain and bottle for use.

Garlic Vinegar.—Place in a glass bottle 1 ounce of finely chopped garlic, pour over it a pint of strong vinegar. Let stand ten days, shaking frequently, strain and bottle for use.

Curry Vinegar.—Place 3 ounces of curry powder in a glass bottle, add 3 pints of strong vinegar. Let stand a week or ten days in a warm place, strain and bottle for use.

PICKLES AND PICKLING

Pickling Vegetables. — Almost every sort of esculent may be preserved for table use by means of spiced vinegar. The objects to be obtained are to secure firmness or hardness of texture, to impart a fine bright green or other color, to kill all germs of decay that may be present, and to protect from the air.

Firmness of texture is secured by steeping the vegetable in strong brine for a number of days, and by picking them over at intervals to discard all doubtful specimens. This may be done by lifting them from the brine, rinsing them and after they have been picked over, covering them with brine that is freshly made. The excess of brine may then be removed by freshening them in pure salt water for twenty-four hours or more.

A fine green is imparted by lining a kettle with fresh vine leaves and packing the pickles with these in alternate layers. The addition of powdered alum sprinkled among the layers assists in setting or fixing the color. They are then covered with cold water and boiled for two hours or more until the color is satisfac-

"Pickles and Pickling."

tory. Cooking, of course, softens them, but their freshness may be restored by dropping them into iced water for an hour or two.

Finally, scalding hot pickling liquid is poured over them both to kill the germs of decay and exclude the air. And this process may be repeated by pouring off the pickling liquid, bringing it to a boil and again pouring it over them at intervals of every two or three days for a fortnight. The jars may then be sealed, or a layer of cotton batting tied over them to exclude the germs that float in the air, and thus they may be preserved for years.

To Select Cucumbers for Pickling. —Plant for pickles a variety of cucumbers that bears a large number of small cucumbers, only 2 or 3 inches long when ripe. These are small, compact, and make firm, crisp pickles that are preferred by most persons to the large cucumber pickles, which, when ripe, are 5 to 7 inches long, 2 to 3 inches thick, and full of seeds.

Or use the small, unripe specimens of the large varieties. Cut the cucumbers from the vines carefully. Leave part of the stem on. And take care to handle them gently. If bruised they will become soft and decay. Pick the vines clean each morning of all that are of a suitable size. This keeps the vines bearing. Pick them over carefully. Throw out any that are bruised or spotted in any way. And, if an A1 quality of pickles is desired, either for home use or for sale, sort them into lots of uniform size and shape.

To Preserve Cucumbers for Pickles.—Have ready two or more stout wooden tubs or earthenware jars, and in these each morning as fast as they are gathered pack the pickles in layers. First put on the bottom of the vessel a layer of salt ½ inch thick, then a layer of cucumbers. Over them put a layer of salt about ¼ inch thick. When about 30 cucumbers have been packed in this way, add a large cupful of water. This will dissolve the salt and make brine enough to cover the cucumbers. Put a stout board, with a stone on top, over the cucumbers to press them down in the brine. Continue to add more cucumbers from time to time as they are ready, picking them if possible in the morning before the dew is off. Add salt and water until the keg is full. Weigh down the cucumbers securely under the brine and until ready to do them up store the keg in a cold cellar. Look at them now and then to be sure that they are kept under the brine, and add more brine, if necessary, to replace the water lost by evaporation. Let stand in brine ten days to two weeks, or until they become yellow. But they will not be injured if allowed to stand longer, provided the brine covers them.

Or after standing in cold brine for one week, lift them carefully from the brine with the hands, so as not to bruise them. Place the brine over the fire and bring it to a boil. Immerse the cucumbers in the brine while boiling hot.

Or some authorities recommend that the brine be poured off, heated, and again poured over the pickles each day for a week or more, or every two or three days. But the better opinion seems to be in favor of steeping or immersing them in cold brine for a longer period to draw out the rank juices that occur in all crude fruit rather than to pour scalding brine over them. Scalding is thought by many to be unnecessary, and to tend to make the pickles soft.

To Store Pickles.—Wooden tubs or casks are to be preferred for storing pickles in large quantities, or glass bottles or fruit jars for the finer qualities. There is an advantage in small bottles, crocks, or jars as only a small quantity need be opened at a time.

Porcelain, graniteware, aluminum, or new tinware are the most suitable vessels in which to heat the vinegar and the brine. Anything that has held grease will spoil pickles.

If packed in wide-mouthed glass bottles or fruit jars, seal tightly, or cork and cover the corks with melted paraffin or other bottle wax. But if the pickles are laid down in jars or kegs they should be looked over occasionally, and if any of them are soft they should be removed, the vinegar turned out, scalded, and again poured over the pickles. There must be sufficient vinegar to cover the pickles thoroughly, and it must be of at least medium strength. If the vinegar becomes weak, pour out and replace with fresh vinegar scalding hot. The addition of a little sugar when the pickles are looked over helps to keep them and improves their flavor. By the blending of the flavors of the various ingredients, pickles, if properly laid down, should improve with age.

Store pickles in a cold place, as if they are kept too warm they may be attacked by the small fly so familiar in autumn.

Or to lay down pickles permanently in brine, cover them with boiling water and let stand until they are cold. Drain thoroughly. Put a layer of dry salt in the bottom of the barrel, put down a layer of pickles, cover with dry salt, and so continue. Add no water. Put a weight above them and their juice will furnish the necessary moisture to dissolve the salt and make sufficient brine to cover them. A small quantity can be freshened from time to time and freshly pickled as required for use. But this method of laying down pickles is not the one commonly preferred.

To Freshen Cucumbers. — After cucumbers have been steeped in brine until they are entirely yellow, and about three days before they are to be done up, lift them carefully from the brine into a clean vessel, cover them with clean cold water and let stand three or four days, changing the water each day or oftener to freshen them.

To Pickle Cucumbers.—Pack the freshened cucumbers in wide-mouthed bottles or jars and pour over them either pure vinegar boiling hot or any desired pickle of spiced vinegar and seal.

Or first pour over them pure vinegar scalding hot and let stand in a warm place until they become green. Every two or three days pour off the vinegar, reheat it and again pour it over the cucumbers scalding hot; when the color is satisfactory pour off the pure vinegar and cover them with the spiced pickle if desired. But while the above is recommended as a thorough method designed to prepare a high-grade quality of pickles, recommendations of authorities differ very widely and good practice doubtless varies equally as much or more. One authority recommends merely washing cucumbers in salt and water, and immediately bottling and covering them with boiling hot pickle. Another, scalding fresh-picked cucumbers with boiling brine, and when cold draining and at once covering them with boiling vinegar. Another would cover fresh-picked cucumbers at once with boiling vinegar containing a handful of salt, reheating the vinegar every two or three days until they become green, then pickling and sealing. Hence it may be inferred that preserving in brine before pickling is not necesssary, but we prefer to recommend it for reasons already stated.

Authorities also differ as to whether the brine should be cold or heated, and the length of time the cucumbers should be immersed in brine, and also as to whether it is sufficient to cover the cucumbers with scalding vinegar and immediately seal, or preferable to let them stand, reheating the vinegar occasionally to green them. All of these questions must be decided by each person for himself according to the grade of pickles desired, and his willingness to take the necessary pains. In general, it is believed that the slower and more painstaking the process, the better will be the quality of the product.

Utensils for Pickling.—It was formerly customary to make pickles in kettles of brass or bell metal in order to give them a bright green color, and also to add more or less alum for the same purpose. But the action of the acetic acid contained in vinegar upon brass and similar metals is to produce a poisonous compound, especially if the pickles are allowed to stand in them until they become cold. The use of alum is also injurious, and for the same reason cheap earthenware, which is frequently glazed with lead, should not be employed.

Many people have a prejudice against deep green pickles found on the market, on account of the fear that poisonous substances may have been used in the manufacture. Hence homemade pickles of a good color and flavor usually find a ready and profitable local market.

To Test Pickles for Copper.—To find out if pickles are poisonous from having been cooked in brass or copper kettles, chop a sample of the pickle fine, place it in a glass bottle with a few drams of liquid ammonia diluted with about half as much water. Shake thoroughly, and if there are any traces of copper in the pickles the contents will be of a deep blue color.

Vinegar for Pickles.—White-wine or sugar vinegar is perhaps the most suitable for a fine grade of pickles. But any good quality of vinegar that is fully ripened and has been previously clarified may be used. The vinegar should be boiled and freed from mother or sediment that would cause the pickles to ferment.

To Clarify Vinegar.—Throw an ounce or so of shredded isinglass into each gallon of vinegar and let stand a few days to clear. Strain through cheese cloth.

To Keep Vinegar Free from Mold.—Lay a small bag of thin muslin containing mustard on top of the pickles. If the vinegar has been properly boiled and clarified, it will tend to prevent the formation of mold.

To Strengthen Weak Vinegar.—Pour it off the pickles, bring it to a boil, pour it back over them and add about ¼ teaspoonful of alum and spread over the top layer a piece of brown paper soaked in New Orleans molasses.

Or boil down the vinegar with very gentle heat so as to allow it to lose its surplus water by evaporation.

Or allow it to freeze, and remove the ice before it melts. Acetic acid does not readily freeze. Hence the quantity of acid in proportion to the bulk of water becomes greater.

Spiced Pickle.—The following recipes are recommended for pickling liquids for cucumbers and other vegetables, mixed pickles, etc., including mushrooms, onions, walnuts, cucumbers, cauliflowers, samphires, green gooseberries, barberries, radish pods, melons, French beans, tomatoes, lemons, peaches, garlic, peas, codlins, beet root, and red cabbage without brine and with cold vinegar. The smaller and more delicate vegetables should not be soaked in brine as long as the larger and the coarser sorts, and may in some cases be pickled cold by pouring over them strong pickling vinegar without scalding. Spices for pickles should not be ground, and should be slightly bruised or crushed in a mortar, which may be improvised by using a wooden bowl and a potato masher as a pestle, or the end of a hard piece of wood. When ground spices are used they should be tied up in bags of thin muslin. To make spiced pickle add to 1 gallon of vinegar 1 cup of salt, 1 cup of sugar, 1 handful of horse-radish, 2 tablespoonfuls of mustard, 1 green pepper.

Or to every 2 quarts of vinegar add ½ ounce of mace, 1 ounce of ginger sliced, 1 dozen cloves, 1 ounce of black pepper, 1 handful of salt. Boil all together for not more than five minutes, and pour over the pickles scalding hot.

Or add to the above if desired 3 or 4 cloves of garlic and shallots.

Or to 3 quarts of pure white-wine or other strong vinegar add 2 ounces of ginger, ½ ounce of mace, ½ pound of salt, ½ tablespoonful of Cayenne pepper, 1 ounce of white or black pepper unground, 1 ounce of mustard seed, 4 ounces of shallots. Boil together not more than five minutes and pour over cucumbers and other hard, firm vegetables scalding hot, or over small and delicate vegetables cold.

Or crush together in a mortar 4 ounces of unground black pepper, 2 ounces of ginger root, 1 ounce of allspice and 4 ounces of salt. Cayenne, paprika, or garlic may be added in small quantities if desired. Place a quart of vinegar in an enameled saucepan, and bring to a boil. Stir in these spices. Let boil not more than five minutes and pour over the pickles scalding hot for cucumbers, walnuts, and the like, or cold for cabbage or fancy mixed pickles.

Or place these spices in a glass bottle or stone jar, cover with a quart of green vinegar, seal and let stand in a warm place three or four days, shaking frequently. Pour over the pickles either hot or cold.

Or to 1 gallon of vinegar add 6 ounces of salt, 1 ounce of spice, 1 ounce of mustard, ½ ounce of mace, ½ ounce of cloves, ½ ounce of nutmeg, 2 ounces of sliced horse-radish. Bruise these spices in water, mix, cover with cold water and boil not over five minutes. Pour over the pickles hot or cold, and if desired, after letting them stand twenty-four hours, place the whole in a porcelain saucepan and simmer until the color is satisfactory. Bottle and seal.

Or to every 2 quarts of vinegar add 1 teaspoonful of black pepper, 1 teaspoonful of mace, ½ cupful of sugar. Let the mixture boil up not to exceed five minutes. They may be bottled hot or cold and will be at once ready for use.

Or heat the vinegar and pour it boiling hot over the pickles.

Or place in a porcelain kettle 100 small cucumbers previously soaked in brine and freshened, cover with vinegar, add a handful of pepper corns, a handful of horse-radish, 1 ounce of cloves, 1 ounce of white mustard seed, a small quantity of Cayenne or paprika, and let the whole boil not to exceed five minutes.

Or heat the vinegar and spice and pour it hot over the pickles. The addition of horse-radish helps to keep the pickles sweet and sound. Old-time housewives used often to add to the pickles a little dill from the herb bed.

Or to each gallon of vinegar add 1 pound of good quality brown sugar, 1 tablespoonful of olive oil, 1 tablespoonful of mustard seed, 1 tablespoonful of green pepper pods, 2 ounces of horse-radish, ½ ounce of cloves, ½ ounce of mace, 1 ounce of ginger, 1 ounce of allspice.

To Pickle Large Cucumbers.—Pare 7 pounds of large cucumbers, remove the seeds and cut into inch pieces. Cover with vinegar and water, half and half, and add a large pinch of salt. Boil until clear but not overdone. Drain in a colander.

To one pint of good vinegar add 3½ pounds of brown sugar; as soon as it comes to the boiling point put the cucumbers back into the kettle and let the whole boil up. Again drain through the colander, and when cold put them in layers in a jar, sprinkle between the layers stick cinnamon, cloves, allspice, a few kernels of black pepper, a little mace, and a handful of raisins. Cover with the pickling liquid and seal.

Or cut a piece from the large end of each cucumber, leaving it attached by a piece of the skin. Scoop out the seeds and steep in strong brine for a week until entirely yellow. Stuff with equal parts mustard seed, ground ginger, and pepper, with the addition of small onions, shallots, or garlic if desired. Sew on the tops and cover with pickling liquid as for gherkins.

To Pickle Melons and Mangoes.—Prepare as for large cucumbers, cutting off the top and stuffing the inside with the same mixture. Or pickle as for gherkins. First steep in strong brine for a week or more, then freshen in clear water and pickle in pure vinegar or spiced pickling liquid, as preferred.

Sweet Pickles — Cucumbers and Melons.—Prepare as for gherkins by steeping in strong brine for a week or more. Quarter them, take out the seed and pulp, freshen in clear water for three or four days, and cover with a sirup prepared of sugar, ginger, and lemon as follows:

Dip 1 pound of loaf sugar lump by lump in clear, soft water and place dripping wet in a porcelain saucepan. Stir in ½ ounce of bruised ginger and boil to the thread, stirring in the juice and grated rind of one lemon. Pour over the melons cold.

To Green Pickles.—If fresh grapevine leaves are obtainable, line a kettle with these and pack into it the cucumbers, etc., in alternate layers with vine leaves, and put a thick layer of vine leaves on top. In addition, sprinkle powdered alum, if desired, among the layers and over the top. Fill up the kettle with cold water and cook or steam the contents over a slow fire for two hours, or until the color is satisfactory. Drain off the hot water through a colander, immerse the vegetables immediately in iced water, and let stand for an hour or more to harden. Then pack in a suitable vessel and pour scalding hot pickling liquid over them.

Or the vine leaves may be used without the alum and will assist in giving a fine green color to the pickles.

MIXED PICKLES

To make cheap mixed pickles have at hand a keg containing vinegar and put into it from time to time odds and ends of vegetables, as small green beans, young cucumbers, small onions, radish pods, bits of cauliflower, and the like, adding vinegar from time to time to keep the vegetables covered. Thus any odd vegetables can be preserved without expense except for the vinegar, spice, etc., and with very little trouble. When the keg is nearly full place the contents in a suitable kettle with vine leaves and boil them about two hours.

Drain off the hot vinegar, immerse the vegetables in cold water for an hour or more to harden, add spices to the vinegar, boil for five minutes, drain the vegetables thoroughly, place them in a suitable keg or jar and pour the scalding hot pickling liquid over them.

Or take any assortment of succulent vegetables, as small French beans of uniform size, small select gherkins 2 or 3 inches long, small cucumbers sliced, and prepare them as for ordinary cucumber pickles.

Prepare separately such vegetables as broccoli, cauliflower stripped into branches, small pickling onions peeled, small red peppers, capsicums, radish pods, small fruit, white and red cabbage, celery, nasturtium seeds and the like by steeping for a short time, say two or three days, in brine and slightly freshening them. Now pack the gherkins and sliced cucumbers with the other vegetables in wide-mouthed glass bottles or jars in such a way as to show the greatest variety of color and display the contents to the best advantage. Much of the attractiveness and consequent salability of mixed pickles is due to skillful packing. Cover with any of the above spiced liquids recommended for cucumber pickles.

Or prepare a special pickle containing turmeric, which will improve the color. For each gallon of vinegar mix 4 ounces of ginger, 4 ounces of turmeric, 2 ounces of white pepper, 2 ounces of chili pepper, 2 ounces of allspice, 1 ounce of garlic, ½ ounce of shallots, ½ pound of bay salt. Bruise together in a mortar and boil in the vinegar not to exceed five minutes. Pour this liquid scalding hot over the vegetables and when cold slice in ¼ pound of horse-radish and stir in 1 pound of mustard seed.

Or for each gallon of vinegar mix 3 ounces of bay salt, ½ pound of mustard, 2 ounces of turmeric, 3 ounces of ginger, 1 ounce of cloves, ½ ounce of black pepper, Cayenne, or paprika to taste. Bruise the spices in a mortar, mix all together and boil in the vinegar not more than five minutes.

Mustard Pickles.—Steep in a weak brine for twenty-four hours about 2 quarts of gherkins, 1 quart of pickling onions, 2 quarts of small green tomatoes, 1 small cabbage head chopped fine, or one large cauliflower pulled into branches with 3 or 4 green peppers and boil. Then stir together in a mixing bowl 1 cup of flour, 6 tablespoonfuls of mustard, 1 heaping teaspoonful of turmeric, 1 quart of sugar. Rub up with a little cold vinegar and stir in the additional vinegar to make 2 quarts in all. Cook over a brisk fire, stirring constantly until it thickens. Pour over the pickles scalding hot and seal.

Cut into small pieces 1 quart of large green cucumbers, 1 quart of very small gherkins, 2 inches in length or less, 1 quart of white button onions, 1 quart of green tomatoes sliced and cut in cubes, 1 large cauliflower pulled into tiny flowerets, and 4 peppers sliced and cut into cubes. Do not chop the ingredients, but cut into cubes or chunks ¼ to ½ inch in thickness. Soak for twenty-four hours in a weak brine of about 1 cupful of salt in a gallon of water.

Place the whole on the fire, bring to a boil and pour into a colander to drain. Mix together in a bowl 6 tablespoonfuls of ground mustard, 1 of turmeric, 1 cupful of flour, 1 cupful of brown sugar, mix dry, rub into a smooth cream with a little vinegar, and dilute with additional vinegar, 2 quarts being used in all. Pour the mixture into a preserving kettle and let it boil until it thickens, then stir in the pickles, let them boil up. Pour into suitable cans or jars, and seal.

Or for sweet chowchow, cut into inch cubes 2 dozen small cucumbers, 6 green peppers, or 3 green and 3 red peppers, and 2 quarts of green tomatoes. Add 2 quarts of small button onions, 2 heads of cauliflower picked into pieces. Place these in a preserving kettle, and pour over them a sauce composed as follows:

Mix together in a bowl 4 teaspoonfuls of celery seed, 1 cupful of mustard, ½ ounce of turmeric, 4 cupfuls of sugar. Rub to a smooth paste with a little of the vinegar and dilute with the remainder of the vinegar, using 2 quarts in all. Pour over the strained pickles, bring them to a boil, pour out and seal.

India Pickle. — Chop together 1 peck of green tomatoes, 1 small head of cabbage, 6 or 8 large green peppers and 8 large onions. Mix and cover with vinegar and boil until they are tender. Salt to taste. Drain in a colander. Add a dressing composed of ½ pound of mustard with 2 tablespoonfuls of curry powder stirred to the consistency of cream with vinegar. Mix well and seal in glass jars or wide-mouthed bottles.

Spanish Peppers.—Steep in brine for three days ½ dozen good-sized cucumbers. On the second day slice ½ dozen onions and chop fine ½ peck of green tomatoes and 2 heads of cabbage. Sprinkle these with salt and let stand overnight. Now drain the cucumbers from the brine, cut in slices, place all in a preserving kettle and cover with vinegar. Add 2 ounces of white mustard seed, ½ ounce of celery seed, 1 heaping tablespoonful of turmeric, ½ cup of mustard, 1 pound of brown sugar. Mix and simmer with gentle heat for half an hour. Pour into wide-mouthed glass bottles or jars, seal, and keep in a cool place.

Piccalilli, or Indian Pickle.—This consists of a great variety of succulent vegetables (the more varied the better) mixed and pickled together. To make piccalilli slice 1 hard white cabbage head, remove the outer leaves, pull to pieces 2 cauliflowers, add 20 selected French beans, 1 root of horseradish, sliced fine, 2 dozen pickling onions, 1 dozen green gherkins of uniform size. Let stand in brine three or four days, drain through a colander, and place in a preserving kettle. Add 2 ounces of curry powder, 1 ounce of garlic, 1 ounce of ginger, 1 ounce of white mustard seed, ½ ounce of capsicum or paprika. Cover with vinegar and bring to a boil. Preserve in glasses tightly sealed.

Or pull apart the branches of a large head of cauliflower, cut a hard white cabbage head in quarters, remove the outer leaves, chop it fine or shred it as for cold slaw. Slice a number of cucumbers and pickling onions, French beans, radish pods, nasturtiums, samphire, and any other vegetables at hand. Place these in a large sieve, sprinkle them with salt and lay them out in the sun for three or four days to dry. Now place them in a preserving kettle, cover with cold vinegar, and bring to a boil. Let them boil up once. Pack in glass and seal.

Or if it is desired to make an extra quality, keep all the ingredients separate and scald them separately in hot vinegar, but do not put them together until they are cold. Bruise together in a mortar 4 ounces of ginger, 2 ounces of whole white pepper, 2 ounces of allspice, ½ ounce of chilis, 4 ounces of turmeric. Add ½ pound of shallots, 1 ounce of garlic, ½ pound of bay salt. Cover with 1 gallon of vinegar and boil thirty minutes. Strain through cheese cloth and add 1 pound of mustard rubbed up free from lumps with a small quantity of cold vinegar. Then dilute with more vinegar to the consistency of milk and stir into the pickling liquid. When the pickling liquid is cold pour it over the pickles. Mix well and pack in glass bottles or a large jar corked or sealed to exclude the air.

Piccalilli if well prepared should improve with age.

Chowchow.—Chowchow is the Chinese name for a kind of mixed pickles originally imported from that country and similar to piccalilli or Indian pickle, except that the ingredients are minced fine and mixed together. Chowchow is frequently used to stuff pickled peppers. It is sometimes known as English chowchow on account of its popularity in that country. French chowchow is a name sometimes applied to mustard pickles.

To make Chinese or "English" chowchow chop fine 2 medium-sized heads of firm, white cabbage, ½ peck of green tomatoes, 2 quarts of firm ripe tomatoes, ½ dozen of green peppers, and 2 red peppers. Mix all together and pack in a bag of coarse burlap or linen in layers of 2 or 3 inches deep, mixed between with layers of salt. Improvise a rack of slats of wood laid over the top of the barrel or keg into which it can drain. Place the chowchow on this and put over it a heavy weight. Let stand twenty-four hours under this pressure. Remove, pour out into a large pan and add 1½ pints of sugar, ½ cupful of grated horse-radish, ½ teaspoonful of ground mustard, 1 ounce of white mustard seed, 1 ounce of celery seed, 1 tablespoonful of mace, 1 gill of Dutch mustard. Stir well, pack in glass or wood and seal.

Or for another sort of chowchow slice or chop fine, as preferred, ½ peck of tomatoes, 1 quart of green peppers, 2 quarts of onions, 1 medium-sized cabbage head shredded as for cold slaw, and 1 quart of white mustard seed. Keep these ingredients separate and pack in layers in a jar or tub, first tomatoes, next peppers, next onions, next cabbage. Sprinkle over this part of the mustard seed, and so continue, repeating the layers again and again until all has been packed. Pour over this any strong liquid desired, scalding hot. Let stand twenty-four hours, pour the whole into the preserving kettle, bring to a boil and let boil not more than five minutes. Pack down in suitable jars or tubs and seal.

Bengal Chutney. — To make this celebrated Indian condiment, mix together 1 pound of tamarind pulp, 1 pound of sultana raisins, 1 pound of ripe tomato pulp, 1 pound of sweet apples minced fine; extract and add the juice of 12 lemons, grate and stir in the rinds; add 4 ounces of garlic, 6 onions chopped fine, ½ pound of red chilis, 12 ounces of powdered ginger, 1 pound of brown sugar. Place all together in a tub or jar, cover with a gallon of strong vinegar, and let stand for a month or more in a warm place, stirring occasionally until it is well fermented. Pack in small, wide-mouthed glass bottles and seal tightly.

Cucumber and Onion Pickles.—Cut into thick slices 3 large onions to each dozen cucumbers. Place in a colander or sieve, sprinkle with salt and let stand twenty-four hours. Place in a suitable keg or jar, cover with boiling vinegar. Cover tightly and let stand overnight. Boil up the vinegar each day, pour over them scalding hot, and at once cover tightly to exclude the air. When the color is satisfactory pour over them spiced pickling liquid and seal.

PICKLED VEGETABLES, NUTS, AND FRUITS

To Pickle Tomatoes.—Slice ½ peck green tomatoes, bring to a boil ½ gallon of any good spiced pickling liquid, and put the tomatoes to boil in this for a quarter of an hour. When cold pack away in tubs or jars and seal.

Or slice 1 peck of green tomatoes; sprinkle with salt. Let stand two days. Slice and salt separately 12 medium-sized onions. Mix in a bowl

4 ounces of mustard, ½ ounce of mustard seed, 1 ounce of cloves, 2 ounces of turmeric, and add garlic, capsicum, or paprika to flavor if desired. Put in a preserving kettle a layer of onions, sprinkle with mixed spice, then a layer of tomatoes and spice, and so on. When all are packed pour over them boiling vinegar and simmer for about two hours until the color is satisfactory.

Or slice green pickles and place them in a colander. Steam in a kettle of boiling water until they are soft, place in jars, cover with any good pickling liquid cold. Let stand twenty-four hours, draw off the liquor, bring it to a boil and pour over the pickles scalding hot.

Or gather the tomatoes when they are turning red, but before they are dead ripe. Pack them in jars whole and without peeling, sprinkle mixed spices with a little bay salt at the rate of about a cupful to a gallon. Pour over them cold cider vinegar and seal.

Or pour over 1 bushel of whole tomatoes a quantity of boiling water. Let stand until cold, pour off the water, skin the tomatoes, place them in a preserving kettle and boil until they are soft. Stir in mixed spices. Lay down the tomatoes in jars and seal to exclude the air.

Pickled Onions.—To prepare onions for pickling, "top and tail" them, remove the outer skins and steep them in brine for a period of two or three days, to two weeks or more. Afterwards freshen them in clear water for a period of one to three days.

Or if preferred, boil them in clear water or brine for ten or fifteen minutes. Afterwards pack them in wide-mouthed glass bottles or jars, and cover with pure vinegar or spiced pickling liquid scalding hot or cold. When cold seal for use. The addition of a spoonful of olive oil to each bottle is said to keep the onions white. Cork tightly and cover the corks with bottle wax or melted paraffin. Seal with cotton batting.

To Select Pickling Onions.—Choose for pickling small silver-skin button onions, preferably of uniform size. Gather them when they are quite dry and ripe and pick them over carefully, rejecting any that are soft, unripe, or spotted.

To Pickle Onions Cold.—Place the onions in a clean, dry glass bottle or jar, cover them with cold vinegar and add mixed spices as preferred. Add a little mustard seed, mace, and capsicum, or allspice and black pepper unground or grated, or sliced horseradish or garlic, capsicum and paprika, if desired. Seal the bottle and let stand two or three weeks before using. Onions are very easily pickled in this way and have an exquisite flavor, but will not keep more than about six or eight months.

To Pickle Onions with Brine.—Cover the onions with cold brine and let stand two weeks or more, or steep in strong brine for one week, then heat the brine and pour it over them scalding hot.

Or pour over them at once strong and hot brine and let stand two or three days. After steeping in brine drain through a colander, freshen in clear water for twenty-four hours, pour off the water and lay them on a dry cloth to drain. Pack them in jars or bottles and cover with spiced pickling liquid boiling hot. Cork tightly and seal.

Or pour over them cold pickling liquid or cold vinegar and seal.

Pickled Cabbage.—Select firm, ripe heads of either white or red cabbage, or mix the two. Quarter them, remove the outside leaves, and let them dry. Shred them as for cold slaw and lay them down in a suitable jar between layers of salt. Cover with strong spiced pickling liquid and seal.

Or shred the cabbage, place it in a preserving kettle or suitable jars, and cover with boiling water. Let stand until cold. Drain. Add mixed spices and cover with cold vinegar, or cover with spiced pickling liquid.

Or boil the cabbage in salted water

until it is tender. The pickling liquid may be poured on cold or scalding hot. In the latter case let stand until perfectly cold. Seal air tight and store in a cool, dry place.

Or if the jars are not air tight, after a few days open them, fill up with vinegar and again seal.

Pickled Cauliflower.—Cut the cauliflowers on a dry, hot day, after the dew has evaporated and before they are fully blown. Slice and sprinkle them with salt, and let stand for two or three days.

Or boil in salt and water until they are tender. Drain off the water or juices, spread upon a dry cloth, covering with another cloth, and let stand in a warm place for twenty-four hours. Pack in jars, cover with cold spiced pickling liquid and seal.

Or place the cauliflowers in cold salt and water at the rate of 4 ounces of salt to 1 quart of water, and bring to a boil over a slow fire. Remove immediately and cover with cold spiced vinegar.

Pickled Green Corn.—Pull the ears of corn when slightly overripe but not too hard. Take off the outer husks, leaving the corn well covered with the inner husks, and tie the latter tightly at the top end. Pack the ears of corn thus prepared in a clean firkin or cask and cover with strong brine. When wanted for use soak in fresh water twelve hours or more, changing the water occasionally.

Pickled Walnuts.—Pick small green walnuts about the first week in July or before the middle of the month, after which they are likely to become hard and woody. Test them by thrusting a strong pin through them, and discard all that are too old and hard. Scald them slightly in boiling water. Rub off the outer skin between cloths (or this may be omitted if preferred), and put them into cold brine strong enough to bear up an egg. Thrusting a pin through them also allows the pickle to penetrate more thoroughly and quickly than would otherwise be the case. Let them stand a week or two, changing the brine every two or three days. Pour them out in a sieve or into a cloth strainer to dry and let them stand a day or two or until they turn black. Pack them in bottles or jars and pour over them spiced pickling liquid scalding hot. Let stand until cold and seal.

Or if they are not to be sealed air tight, pour off the pickle each day for three or four days, bring it to a boil, take off the scum and pour over the walnuts scalding hot.

Or instead of steeping in cold brine, place the walnuts in a strong brine and simmer for an hour or two. Expose in a sieve or cloth strainer twenty-four hours or more, or until they turn black. Pack and cover with scalding hot spiced pickling liquid. Two to six months will be required before they are fit to eat. During this time they must be kept covered from the air either by sealing the jars or keeping them covered with vinegar.

To Pickle White Walnuts.—Pick small green walnuts as above and pare them very thin, or until the whites appear. Place in cold brine strong enough to bear up an egg and simmer for five or ten minutes, but do not let them come to a boil. Drain and cover them with cold brine for twenty-four hours or more. Pour out in a sieve or cloth strainer, cover them with a cloth, dry them carefully between clean, soft pieces of cloth and pack them down with blades of mace, nutmeg, and horse-radish. Cover with cold or hot vinegar and when cold seal tightly to exclude the air.

Pickled Lemons. — Slice ½ dozen lemons, sprinkle them with salt, lay them down in a large glass jar and sprinkle among them 2 ounces of spice, 2 ounces of white pepper, ¼ ounce of mace, ¼ ounce of cloves, all bruised together in a mortar with ¼ ounce of Cayenne, 2 ounces of horse-radish, 2 ounces of mustard seed. Pour over them 2 quarts of vinegar scalding hot. This pickle is for immediate use, and will be ready in three days to a week. Red peppers, paprika, or garlic and shallots may be added if desired.

Or cut ½ dozen lemons into six or eight pieces, cover with the mixed spices, as in the first recipe, place in a preserving kettle, cover with 2 quarts of vinegar and boil a quarter of an hour.

Or pack the lemons in a jar, set the jar in boiling water and boil for fifteen or twenty minutes. Let the jar stand in a warm place stirring daily for several weeks. Finally, bring to a boil, pack in small jars or bottles and seal.

Or to pickle whole lemons, select small fruit and slit the rinds as if to take off the peel in quarters, but do not cut through the pulp. Cover the lemons with salt, and pack it down hard to fill these slits. Pack them on end in a dripping pan three or four days, or until the salt melts, and let them stand, turning them end for end in the liquor two or three times a day until the rinds are tender. To this liquor add sufficient spiced vinegar to cover the lemons. Pack them in jars with mustard seed and garlic. Cover with any prepared pickling liquid and seal.

Or pare a dozen lemons very thin, taking off so little of the outer portion of the rind that the white will not be seen. Cut a gash in each end and rub them thoroughly with salt, rubbing it into the gashes. Cover with salt and let stand for three or four days. As the salt dissolves rub more into them and especially fill the gashes at the end. Now cover with dry salt, place them in a very slow oven with a dozen cloves of garlic and half a teacupful of scraped horseradish, and let them dry, taking care that they are not burned, or even browned. They should be thoroughly dried out—as dry as paper. Now pour over them a gallon of spiced pickling liquid cold. Place the whole in a suitable jar, and let stand in a warm place for two or three weeks, stirring or shaking frequently. Shake well and strain off a little of the liquid from time to time for table use in soups and sauces. Shred the lemons fine when required for made dishes, soups, sauces, etc.

Pickled Peaches.—Look over the peaches carefully, selecting the ripe fruit and discarding all that are soft or specked. Rub clean with a soft, dry cloth and stick into each large peach 4 or 5 cloves without the heads, and into each small one 2 or 3 cloves. Place in a preserving kettle 1 gallon of vinegar. Stir in 6 pounds of brown sugar and bring to a boil, removing the scum as fast as it appears. Pack the peaches in suitable bottles or jars. Pour the boiling sirup over them scalding hot and cover tightly. Let stand overnight, pour off the sirup once more, bring to a boil and again pour over the peaches. Do this for three or four days. Finally, pack in cans or bottles and seal while hot.

Or for sweet-pickled peaches, allow ½ pound of sugar by weight to each pound of fruit. Put the sugar and peaches in layers in a preserving kettle and bring to a boil. Add for each 6 pounds of fruit a pint of vinegar and in the vinegar place a thin muslin bag containing a tablespoonful each of cinnamon, cloves, and mace. Pour the spiced vinegar into the peaches and sirup with the bag of spices, and boil for not more than five minutes. Take out the peaches with a skimmer, lay them on blotters to cool and continue boiling the sirup until it thickens. Pack the peaches in jars, fill to overflowing with boiling sirup, and seal at once.

Or for sour pickled peaches, select full-grown peaches before they are ripe. Salt them in strong brine for a week or two, change the brine every two or three days, dry them on a cloth strainer, wipe them with a cloth and cover with hot, spiced, pickling liquid containing garlic, mustard, ginger, cloves, and the like. Seal and store for four or five months before bringing them to the table.

Pickled Pears.—The above recipes for pickled peaches may also be applied to pickled pears.

Or pack in a preserving kettle in

alternate layers 10 pounds of ripe pears and 3 pounds of coffee sugar. Pour over them 1 quart of vinegar containing, in a thin muslin bag, 1 ounce of cinnamon, 1 ounce of cloves, ¼ ounce of mace. Slice and stir in 4 ounces of citron and boil until the pears are tender. Take out the pears with a skimmer, boil the sirup half an hour or more until it is thick. Fill the jars or cans to overflowing and seal at once.

Or prepare a sirup of 1½ pints of vinegar and 3 pounds of fine sugar. Bring this to a boil. Place in a preserving kettle a peck of ripe fruit, peeled and cored, pour the sirup over it and boil until the fruit is tender, but not soft. Remove the fruit with the skimmer and pack it in jars. Preserve the sirup, which may be used again, and prepare a fresh sirup of 1½ pints of vinegar and 2 pounds of coffee sugar. Place in this sirup a thin muslin bag containing an ounce each of any kind of mixed spices preferred. Bring to a boil, fill the jars to overflowing, and seal.

Pickled Cherries. — Fill a wide-mouthed glass bottle or jar with nice firm and medium ripe cherries. Add 2 tablespoonfuls of salt, and fill the jars with cold vinegar. Seal and let stand six or eight weeks before using.

Pickled Peppers.—Soak fresh bell peppers, either green or red, in strong brine for a week or two, changing every two or three days. Pack in suitable jars and cover with cold vinegar. The seeds tend to make the peppers very strong, and may be removed if less strength is desired. A few peppers added to pickled cucumbers improves them very much, as the heat of the peppers is taken out by the vinegar and becomes blended with the cucumbers, giving them an agreeable flavor.

Pickled Beets. — Select small red beets having the roots on and wash them carefully so as not to break the roots or the skin. Place in a large kettle, cover with plenty of water and boil three or four hours. Take them up carefully with a skimmer so as not to break the skins. Place them on a cloth strainer to cool and dry. When cold, quarter them or pack them in suitable jars, cover with pure or pickled cold vinegar, and seal so as to exclude the air. If not sealed it will be necessary to pour off the vinegar occasionally, bring it to a boil and pour it scalding hot over the beets.

Or after the beets have been boiled, pack them in jars and cover with hot brine strong enough to float an egg. When cool put the jars in a saucepan full of cold water, place it on the stove, and boil half an hour or more. Seal air tight while hot and store in a cool place.

Nasturtiums. — Collect the seeds while young and tender. Place them in a double boiler, cover with strong cold brine. Let stand for an hour, then place on the stove and bring to a boil. When they boil up take them out of the skimmer, put them into a suitable jar, and cover them with boiling hot spiced pickling liquid.

Or have at hand a jar of sweetened spice vinegar and into this drop nasturtium seeds picked as they accumulate during the season before they become hard and woody. They make an excellent substitute for capers and an agreeable addition to salads or sandwiches.

Pickled Barberries.—To pickle barberries for a garnish, especially for cold meats, salads, and the like, select the large, firm bunches of berries of a fine deep red. Remove the leaves and the discolored berries. Place them in jars and cover with brine strong enough to float an egg. Seal to exclude the air, or cover with paraffin or waxed paper. If any scum or mold appears upon the surface pour out the barberries on a cloth strainer, dry them between two cloths, and cover them with fresh brine.

To Pickle Mushrooms. — Select small button mushrooms, remove the stems, rub off the skins with a piece of flannel moistened in salt water and throw them into weak brine of about a cupful of salt to a gallon of water. Let stand three or four hours. Pour them out on a cloth strainer to drain and dry.

Or after cleaning them with salt and water, put them over a slow fire until the juice from them has dissolved the salt. Then pour them out to drain on a cloth strainer. Finally, pack in suitable jars or bottles and cover with spiced pickling liquid, scalding hot, or place the mushrooms in the spiced liquid and boil for ten minutes. Pack in bottles, cover with the scalding liquid. Let stand until cold, and seal.

Pickled Melons.—Take hard muskmelons that are late in ripening, cut out a circular piece around the stem about 3 inches across and through this opening remove the seeds and scrape out any part that may be soft or ripe. Pack the melons in a wooden tub, fill them inside, and cover them with salt and let stand until the salt is melted. Remove them from the salt, rinse with pure water and fill with a mixture of chopped peppers and onions with a few shallots, a little garlic, and a quantity of bruised mustard seed. Close the opening with the plug, and fasten it with thread or with skewers made of toothpicks. Pack the melons in a tub or earthen jar and cover with spiced pickling liquid boiling hot. Remove and scald the spiced liquid every day for four or five days, pour it back over the melons, and finally seal up the jars.

Or stuff the melons with a piccalilli or chowchow or any sort of mixed pickles, as desired.

Pickled Citron. — Cut the citron into inch cubes, cover with weak brine. Let stand twenty-four hours and pour out on a cloth strainer to dry. For every gallon of spiced vinegar add 4 ounces of coffee sugar, bring to a boil and pour over the citron boiling hot. Let stand three or four days, each day pouring off the pickling liquid from the citron, scalding it and pouring it back. Finally, bring the whole to a boil and cook until the citron is very tender. Pack in suitable jars. Seal and store in a cool, dry place.

Peach Mangoes.—Select large freestone peaches and take out the stone through a slit in the side. Cover with weak brine scalding hot. Let stand until cool enough to handle. Lift out the peaches on a cloth strainer, and wipe dry with a clean, soft cloth. Now fill the cavity with mixed spices to taste, as white mustard seed, cloves, mace, cinnamon, grated horse-radish, ginger root, etc., softened by placing all together in a thin muslin bag and immersing for a few minutes in boiling water. Remove the bag from the water, let the spices drip dry, fill the peaches, sew them up, pack them in jars, and fill to overflowing with a scalding hot sirup made of 1 pint of sugar in 3 pints of vinegar. Seal while hot. Let stand a week or two before bringing to the table.

Tomato Catsup. — Wash ½ bushel fine ripe red tomatoes. Quarter them, place them in a preserving kettle, and bring them to a boil. Remove from the fire and let cool until they will bear the hands. Then rub them through a wire sieve and add to the strained juice 2 teacupfuls of salt, 2 teacupfuls of mixed spices, 1 quart of vinegar. Boil over a slow fire for an hour or more, stirring constantly to prevent burning. Fill the bottles to overflowing with the hot liquid and seal at once. Thin for use, if necessary, with a little vinegar. Wrap in colored paper to exclude the light.

Or boil the tomatoes until they are soft. Squeeze them through a fine sieve, and to the juice add 1 pint of salt, 1 ounce of Cayenne pepper, a few cloves of garlic or shallots. Mix and boil until reduced one half. Bottle and seal.

Or cut up the tomatoes, place them in a preserving kettle in layers sprinkled with salt, using about 2 teacupfuls of salt to ½ bushel of fruit. Let stand three or four hours before boiling. Strain and add to the juice horse-radish, onions, or garlic, mustard seed, and mixed spices. Let stand twenty-four hours or more. Boil down to the right consistency. Bottle and seal.

Select firm, ripe tomatoes, gash them on two or three sides and place them in a porcelain saucepan. Boil them to a pulp. Rub the pulp through a colander or coarse sieve, and afterwards through a hair or other fine sieve, and for each peck of fruit add 1 ounce of salt, 1 tablespoonful of black pepper, 1 teaspoonful of Cayenne, 1 ounce of mace, 1 ounce of ground cloves, 6 ounces of ground mustard and 1 ounce each of celery seed and mustard seed tied in a cheese-cloth bag. Boil the whole for four or five hours, stirring frequently, especially toward the last. When the catsup is of the right consistency, remove from the fire and let stand overnight to cool. For each peck of fruit stir in 1 pint of pure white wine or cider vinegar. Remove the bag of celery and mustard seed. Bottle and cork tightly. Store in a cool, dark place.

Or cut the tomatoes in half and boil to a pulp. Press through a coarse, and afterwards a fine sieve, and for each peck of fruit add seasoning as follows: $\frac{1}{8}$ ounce of Cayenne pepper, $\frac{1}{4}$ ounce of black pepper, $\frac{1}{2}$ ounce each of mace, allspice, cloves, 2 ounces of mustard. Salt to taste and add ginger or essence of celery if desired. Boil as above. When cool, stir in 1 pint of vinegar for each peck of fruit. Bottle and seal as above.

Or cut the tomatoes into quarters, place them in a porcelain saucepan and boil to a pulp. Run through a coarse, and afterwards a fine sieve, and boil down for three or four hours, or until as thick as jelly, stirring constantly especially toward the last to prevent burning. Stir in for each peck of fruit, 3 ounces of salt, 3 drams of allspice, $\frac{3}{4}$ ounce of yellow mustard, $1\frac{1}{2}$ ounces of black pepper, 4 drams of cloves, $\frac{1}{4}$ ounce of Cayenne pepper, 2 quarts of pure white-wine or cider vinegar. Stir in the ground spices and the vinegar. Bring the whole to a boil for not more than five minutes and bottle when cold.

Canning Tomatoes. — Select firm, ripe tomatoes, place them in a colander and dip them into boiling water just long enough to loosen the skin. Remove from the water, place them where they will drain, and carefully pull off the skin without injuring the fruit. Once more place in colander to drain and pack carefully in large glass jars or cans as full as they will hold. Place these in hot water, bring to a boil and seal.

Or if tin cans are used, first apply with a soft brush fresh butter or unsalted lard to the inside of the can and its cover. This will prevent the fruit acid from attacking the tin and forming a poisonous compound. Seal with a bit of solder or putty, or lay over the top a cloth dampened with alcohol, run paraffin over this and draw over the top a piece of cotton batting.

Currant Catsup.—Pick over carefully 2 pounds of ripe red currants and place them in a preserving kettle with $\frac{3}{4}$ of a pound of granulated sugar. Cook until of the consistency of thick cream. Boil in a separate saucepan for not more than five minutes $\frac{3}{4}$ of a pint of vinegar, in which place a muslin bag containing $\frac{1}{2}$ tablespoonful of ground pepper, and any other spices desired. Pour the spiced vinegar into the currants and sugar and bottle for use.

Mushroom Catsup. — There is a prejudice against mushrooms due to the existence of certain poisonous species. Those who are not thoroughly conversant with the difference between the edible and poisonous varieties should buy mushrooms from a reliable dealer or buy the spawn and grow the mushrooms rather than attempt to gather the native varieties growing wild. As there is a possibility that poisonous mushrooms may be offered for sale by careless or ignorant persons, we give the following rules for distinguishing mushrooms from poisonous toadstools. The greatest caution should, however, be used where there is the slightest doubt, as no matter how good a rule may be, there can be no assurance that it will be understood or intelligently applied by an inexperienced person.

As a rule, the false mushrooms grow in tufts or clusters in woods or on the stumps of trees. They are likely to have a cap covered with warts or fragments of membrane growing on the upper surface, and to be heavy and irregular in shape. They have a disagreeable taste, like alum, turn blue when cut, are moist on top and usually of a rose or orange color.

The true mushroom, on the other hand, has under parts or gills of a pinky red, changing to a liver color. The flesh is pure white, and the stem is long, white, and round.

The best rule is to sprinkle a little salt on the spongy parts or gills of one of the mushrooms and let it stand for some minutes. Be sure to allow plenty of time. If it turns yellow the mushrooms are poisonous. If black, they are edible.

To make mushroom catsup pack 2 pounds of mushrooms in layers with 1 pound of salt in a saucepan, and let stand until the salt is fully dissolved. Squeeze through cheese cloth and add to the juice 3 ounces of white pepper, ½ ounce of cloves, or any other mixed spices desired. Boil with gentle heat to the consistency desired. Strain and bottle for use. Add more salt to the mushrooms from which the juice has been strained, and if sufficient juice has been left in them to dissolve the salt it may be used to make an inferior quality of catsup.

Or add to each pound of mushrooms ½ pound of salt. Let them stand for four days stirring them occasionally. Pour them into a colander to drain and preserve the juice. Now add a little cold water to the mushrooms and let them boil half an hour or more over a slow fire. Squeeze them through cheese cloth. Now mix both liquors. Add any desired mixture of spices. Boil not over five minutes. Seal and bottle for use.

Or squeeze out the juice in a press and to each gallon of juice add 1 pound of salt, 1½ ounces of shallots, and any desired mixture of spices to the amount of four to six ounces all told. Boil for one hour or until of the desired consistency. Strain and bottle for use.

To preserve mushroom catsup in its full strength it is necessary to reboil it at intervals of a month or six weeks, adding fresh spices. By these means it can be kept good and fresh the year round.

To Preserve Mushrooms. — Select small mushrooms, trim them and rub them clean with a soft flannel cloth. Drop them immediately into cold water to preserve their color. Place them in a saucepan and to each quart of mushrooms add 3 ounces of butter, 2 teaspoonfuls of salt, ¼ teaspoonful of Cayenne, ¼ teaspoonful of mace, and cook until tender. Pour them into a colander to drain. When cold, pack them in glass jelly tumblers or fruit jars and pour clarified mutton suet or butter over them. Lay over this a thickness of cloth dipped in alcohol and tie over the top a layer of cotton batting.

Or trim and clean the mushrooms, peel off the skin and dry them in a slow oven. Tie up tightly in paper bags and hang up in a dry place. They will resume their natural size when cooked.

Or season mushrooms with onion, cloves, pepper, mace, or otherwise to taste. Slice, and dry in a slow oven. Rub to a powder and preserve in tightly stoppered jars or bottles.

Preserving Olives.—After opening a bottle of olives, if the remainder are not required for immediate use, pour off the liquid and cover with olive oil. This will keep the olives good and fresh for several weeks.

Walnut Catsup.—Pick young green walnuts about the first week in July, as for pickled walnuts, and squeeze the juice out of them under a press. Or run them through two or three times with a hatpin. Crush them with a wooden mallet, place in a keg or jar throwing in a handful of salt for each two dozen walnuts. Cover with water and let stand two weeks or more, stirring frequently. Squeeze out the liquor through cheese cloth into a preserving kettle. Moisten the walnuts with boiling hot vinegar and mash them to a pulpy mass. Pour on additional hot vinegar to cover them. Mix and squeeze out the vinegar into the juice and brine in a preserving kettle. Add to each gallon of juice 12 or 14 ounces of mixed spices as desired, bruising the whole spices in a mortar, or placing the ground spices in a thin muslin bag. Flavor with Cayenne, paprika, garlic, or shallots as desired, and boil one hour or more, or until reduced about one half. Bottle and seal when cold.

Or bring the walnut juice to a boil and skim until it is clear. For each quart of walnut juice add ½ pound of anchovies, ½ pound of shallots and 1 or 2 ounces of mixed spices. Flavor with garlic, Cayenne, paprika, celery, etc., as desired. Simmer over a slow fire about twenty minutes, salt to taste. Strain through cheese cloth. Bottle and seal when cold. This catsup will keep indefinitely and will not be at its best under one year after it has been made.

Or crush the green walnut shells and to each ½ peck of shells, dry measure, add 1 quart of salt. Mix and let stand a week or ten days. Squeeze out the juice. Add to each gallon of juice about 12 ounces of mixed spices, flavoring with garlic, etc., if desired, and boil down about one half. Bottle when cold.

Or take 1 gallon of spiced vinegar in which walnuts have been pickled for six months or a year. Add ½ pound of anchovies, 1 teaspoonful of Cayenne. Boil down one half and bottle when cold. Thus the spiced vinegar from the pickled walnuts may be turned into good catsup after the walnuts have been used.

Camp Catsup. — A catsup mixed with stale beer and various spices is often put up and sold under this name for sea stores or persons going on exploring and other expeditions and likely to be gone a long time. It will keep under all conditions for many years.

To 1 gallon of strong stale beer add 1 pound of anchovies washed and cleaned, 1 quart of mushrooms, first rubbing off the skins with salt and water, 1 pound of shallots, and 8 or 10 ounces of mixed spices. Boil down one half over a slow fire. Strain through cheese cloth and bottle when cold.

Or to 1 gallon of strong stale beer add 3 quarts of vinegar, 1½ pounds of cleaned and washed anchovies, 1½ pound of shallots, 8 or 10 ounces of mixed spices, and 2 quarts of mushrooms. Boil down one half and bottle when cold.

Or mix 2 quarts of stale beer to 1 quart of white wine or white-wine vinegar. Add ½ pound of anchovies, 4 ounces of peeled shallots, 4 ounces of mixed spices. Let stand in a warm place two or three weeks, stirring constantly. Bring to a boil and bottle when cold.

Oyster Catsup.—Squeeze through a sieve 1 pint of oysters with the juice. Add 1 pint of white wine or sherry, and salt to taste. Add 2 or 3 ounces of mixed spices. Flavor with garlic, celery, etc., as desired. Simmer fifteen or twenty minutes. Strain and bottle when cold.

Pepper Catsup.—Place in a preserving kettle about 25 large red bell peppers without removing the seeds. Add 1 pint of vinegar and boil until tender, stirring constantly. Rub the whole through a sieve. Set aside the juice. Pour over the pulp another pint of vinegar with 2 tablespoonfuls of brown sugar, and 2 or 3 ounces of mixed spices. Stir all together and boil down one half. Strain through cheese cloth and bottle when cold.

Gooseberry Catsup.—Select gooseberries that are ripe but not soft, pick them over carefully, and remove the stems and blossoms with a pair of small scissors. To each quart of gooseberries add 1 pound of brown sugar and 1 ounce of mixed spices,

Place in a preserving kettle and boil to a soft pulp or for about 2 or 3 hours stirring constantly. Add for each quart of gooseberries ¼ pint of vinegar. Bring to a boil. Fill bottles to overflowing and seal while scalding hot.

Grape Catsup.—Take grapes that are ripe but not soft. Pick them over carefully and add ½ by weight of sugar and to 5 pound of grapes 1 pint of vinegar, 2 or 3 ounces of mixed spices, and salt to taste. Boil until it thickens. Bottle when cold.

To Preserve Horse-Radish.—Slice the horse-radish in November and December about $\frac{1}{16}$ of an inch thick. Place it in a tin pan, cover and set it in a warm place near the stove to dry; but do not heat it too much, as otherwise it will lose its flavor. When bone dry grind it in a mortar, place it in suitable jars or bottles, and seal for use.

Or grate the green roots, cover with strong vinegar. Bottle, seal, and store in a cool place.

To Preserve Tomatoes for Soup.—Select all the small cracked or faulty-shaped ripe tomatoes that are unmarketable, wash, trim, and cut them up unpeeled in a preserving kettle. Stew them well, grind them through a flour sieve so as to remove the seeds and skins, reheat and can for soup stock.

Or take the large, sound, ripe tomatoes, wash and drain, halve them crosswise, and pack them with the cut side up between layers of salt in a jar or wooden firkin. Let stand twenty-four hours or until the salt melts. Now pour off and discard the brine and seeds that escape with it. Boil the tomatoes to a pulp, and rub through a flour sieve. Season with Cayenne pepper or paprika, salt to taste and boil to the consistency of cream, stirring briskly. Pour out to a depth of about ½ inch on large platters, and let dry in the sun or a slow oven. Before it dries mark in 3-inch squares with a sharp knife and when fully dry pack tightly in hot, dry glass jars. Seal closely to exclude the air, and store in a dry place. One of these squares will season 2 or 3 quarts of soup, or enough for a large family.

Or the squares may be soaked in warm water and stewed with bread crumbs as tomato sauce.

Or peel large, ripe tomatoes, remove the seeds, pack them in a preserving can with pepper and salt. Let stand twenty-four hours or until the salt is melted, and boil for an hour or more, stirring frequently. Pour into small jars or bottles, as it will not keep well after being opened, and seal when cold.

Curry Powder. — To make curry powder mix together the required spices, which should be of the best quality, and well dried in a slow oven. Grind them to powder in a mortar. Pack in small bottles, and seal for use.

Or if preferred, the required spices may be mixed whole in the small pepper grinders which are to be had for table use, and the powder may be freshly ground as required.

To use curry powder, mix 1 tablespoonful of the powder with 1 of flour. Add 1 cupful of fresh milk. Season with salt and lemon juice, and pour into soup or stews and the like fifteen or twenty minutes before serving.

The following proportions are recommended: 4 ounces of turmeric, 4 ounces of coriander, 4 ounces of black pepper, 3 ounces of fenugreek, 2 ounces of ginger, 1 ounce of cummin seed, 1 ounce of ground rice, ½ ounce of cardemoms, ½ ounce of paprika.

Or 4 ounces of turmeric, 4 ounces of coriander seed, 2½ ounces of pimento, 1 ounce of ginger, ½ ounce of cinnamon, ½ ounce of mace, ½ ounce of cloves, 2 drams of cummin seed, 1 ounce of cardemom, 1 ounce of Cayenne.

Or 2 ounces of turmeric, 5 ounces of coriander, ½ ounce of paprika, 2 ounces of pimento, ¼ ounce of cloves, 2 ounces of cinnamon, 1 ounce of ginger, 1½ ounces of cummin, 1 ounce of shallots.

CHAPTER XXV

PRESERVATION OF MEAT AND VEGETABLES

FERMENTATION—FRESH MEAT AND FISH—SALTING AND PICKLING MEAT—CURING HAMS, TONGUES, AND BACON—MAKING AND KEEPING SAUSAGE—PRESERVATION OF COOKED MEAT—TRYING OUT AND STORING LARD—PRESERVING, TESTING, AND PACKING EGGS—STORING AND PRESERVING VEGETABLES, FRUIT, NUTS, AND HERBS

FERMENTATION

Fermentation in the widest sense of the term includes all forms of decomposition in both vegetable and animal substances when exposed to air and moisture at temperatures between the freezing and boiling point of water. But in common language, the word fermentation is more often confined to those processes by which vegetable juices are transformed into alcoholic liquors. These processes, however, are entirely similar to putrefaction, or the decomposition of organic matter which sets free foul-smelling gases; and decay, or the change by which without moisture, the trunk of a tree molders into dust. Fermentation does not ordinarily take place much below 32° F. or much above 140° F. It usually causes liquids to rise in temperature and to give off gases with considerable internal motion, to become turbid, to form a scum and to deposit a sediment.

Among the useful results of fermentation are the raising of bread with yeast; the preparation of alcoholic beverages and certain food products, as sauerkraut; the curdling of milk by means of rennet to form cheese; the manufacture of vinegar, etc.

Among the injurious results of fermentation are the souring of milk and vegetables, the putrefaction of meat, the becoming rancid of fats and the decay of articles of wood or textile fabrics.

Fermentation is caused by the vital action of microscopic plants, the germs of which may be present in the fermenting substance, or may be deposited on their surface from the air or from contact with water or other substances containing them. Or they may be introduced intentionally, as when yeast is used for brewing, or for making vinegar or bread. These small plants feed upon fermentable substances and bring about various chemical changes. Thus the subject of fermentation has two phases: i.e., (1) how to induce those forms of fermentation that are useful, and (2) how to prevent those that are injurious.

The promotion of fermentation falls under such various subjects as fermented beverages, the making of vinegar, cheese, bread, etc. The prevention of fermentation falls under such subjects as the preservation of food, the preservation of timber, etc.

As fermentation occurs from the presence and development of germs, it is evident that its prevention depends upon the destruction of any germs that are present, and keeping away others, or the removal of conditions favorable to germ life. Hence, in general, fermentation and putrefaction may be prevented by drying heat; by cooling below the point at which fermentation takes place; by heating or cooking substances to a point sufficient to kill the germs present, and then hermetically sealing them to exclude others; and by the employment of various antiseptics, as alcohol, common salt, saltpeter, sugar, sirup, smoke, borax, and many other substances.

Putrefaction. — This change is a decomposition of animal or vegetable substances with the liberation of ill-smelling gases. It can only take place at a temperature between the freezing point of water (32° F. and 140° F.), in the presence of moisture and after exposure to the air. Generally speaking, the more moisture and the greater warmth present, the more rapid is the process. The germs of the bacteria which cause putrefaction are heavier than the germs of yeast and mold, and hence do not float in equal numbers, as dust in dry air. They are more often communicated by contact with water or moist surfaces. For this reason in dry climates meats and vegetables may be preserved simply by drying or curing them by exposure to sunlight. But it is well known that if these substances are left out after the dew falls, and allowed to become moistened, they may be covered with a coating of mold. Most of the bacteria that cause putrefaction are killed by exposure to a temperature of 140° F. for a number of hours; to a temperature of 212° F., the boiling point of water, for ten to fifteen minutes; or to a temperature of 215° F. for 4 or 5 minutes. The activity of these bacteria ceases at the freezing point, but they cannot be killed by freezing, and again become active when warmed to a temperature of 40° F. Hence, in general terms, boiling in water kills bacteria and freezing suspends their activity.

FRESH MEAT AND FISH

To Keep Fresh Meat.—Refrigeration in a dry, well-ventilated air chamber cooled to a temperature of 40° F. or lower by means of ice, is the best means of preserving fresh meat in summer or in warm climates. For this purpose ice may be stored in northern climates in homemade ice houses, and utilized by means of homemade refrigerators as elsewhere recommended.

If ice houses are not available, fresh meat may be kept for several days by the use of sour milk, vinegar, charcoal, or borax, or by immersing it in cold running water, or by means of a mixture of salt, sugar, and saltpeter.

Or hang up joints of meat, if not required for immediate use in any dry, shady place where there is good ventilation. They will keep fresh from 2 to 4 days, and will become more tender and digestible by hanging. But in all cases, hang them with the cut end up and knuckle downward, or the reverse of the usual way. Thus the blood remains in the meat and keeps it sweet and juicy. In summer, if the weather is dry, lamb and veal will keep 2 days, and beef and mutton 3 to 4 days. In cold weather, mutton may be kept for twice that length of time.

Or if running water is available from a spring or otherwise, provide a covered box or tub in a shady place, into and out of which the water can flow. Immerse the meat in this. If fresh it will sink of its own weight. Look at it two or three times a day and as soon as it commences to rise from the bottom, it must be used. The outside will be somewhat whitened, but the flavor will be uninjured. The meat will be sound and tender after 3 or 4 days in hot summer weather, and may then be boiled or roasted.

Or pieces of fresh meat may be placed in large stone jars and covered with skimmed milk, sour milk, or buttermilk. They must be weighted with a clean stone to keep the meat under the surface of the liquid, and the jar placed in a cold cellar or in the running water from a spring. It is not necessary to remove the bone or fat. Thus fresh meat can be preserved for a week or 10 days. The milk can afterwards be fed to pigs. Before cooking, the meat should be washed thoroughly in clear water and afterwards soaked 3 to 5 minutes in water containing about one tablespoonful of cooking soda to the gallon. This neutralizes the acid of the milk and makes the meat more tender.

Or fresh meat may be preserved by soaking it for 3 to 5 minutes in a solution of one tablespoonful of borax to a gallon of water, or by rubbing it with powdered borax dry. Rinse with clear water when required for use.

Or trim the meat carefully with a knife, removing any parts that seem likely to taint, and wrap it up with a cloth moistened with vinegar, or equal parts of vinegar and water. The acid vapor drives away flies and the moisture, by evaporation, keeps it cold.

Or rub meat thoroughly with fresh powdered charcoal, which has powerful antiseptic properties. It can be readily rinsed off with clear water.

Or cut the meat in pieces, not exceeding 2 or 3 pounds in weight, and pack them down between layers of dry corn meal or bran. Or cover with corn meal or bran as thickly as possible and hang in some shady place where there is a free circulation of air.

Or when meat can no longer be preserved by any of these methods and more is on hand than can be immediately consumed, cook it all, and each day place it on the stove and bring it to a temperature equal to the boiling point of water. Thus the germs of putrefaction will be killed and the process will be arrested from day to day.

Or fresh meat may be preserved in the following manner: by laying it down in an earthenware jar and sprinkling with a mixture of salt, sugar, and saltpeter. If the meat is fresh killed, first hang it up or lay it on slats overnight to drain it free from blood. Then cut it up in readiness for the frying pan or the table, separating and trimming chops, steaks, scollops, etc. For every pound of meat, measure 1½ teaspoonfuls each of salt and sugar, ½ teaspoonful of saltpeter, and ¼ teaspoonful of black or white pepper. These should be dry, mixed, and reduced to powder in a mortar. Now sprinkle the bottom of the jar with a thin layer of this mixture and lay down a layer of steak or chops of uniform thickness, packing tightly to cover the bottom of the jar. Sprinkle over this the mixture of antiseptics so as to cover the surface lightly or about the same as when seasoning for the table. Add another layer of meat, and so on, until the jar is full. Cover the top of the jar with a layer of cotton batting wet in a solution of the same mixture of antiseptics in water. Put on the lid of the jar tightly and set it in a cellar, spring house, or other cold place. When the meat is required for use, rinse and scald it. Soak the cotton batting in the covering solution of antiseptics and pack it down closely over the meat as before.

Or the top of the jar may be covered with a layer of melted tallow, lard, or paraffin to keep out the air.

To Preserve Meat from Flies.—In addition to the germs that cause putrefaction, fresh meat is liable to be visited by flies and other insects for the purpose of depositing their eggs, and these will, in warm weather, quickly hatch and produce maggots. A cloth moistened with vinegar prevents the approach of insects.

Or the meat may be rubbed with ground pepper or ginger. It may also be protected by a coating of waxed paper. To prepare this paper, melt with gentle heat 5 ounces of stearic acid. Stir in 2 ounces of carbolic acid and add, in a thin stream, 5 ounces of melted paraffin, stirring constantly. Remove from the fire and continue to stir until the mixture sets. Again melt with gentle heat, and apply with a brush to suitable paper. Wrap up the meat in the paper and seal.

To Preserve Fish.—To keep fish fresh without ice for any length of time is very difficult. But if ice is not available, wash inside and out with a solution of equal parts of vinegar and water. Lay the fish on an earthenware platter on a stone floor. Place in the inside of each fish a cheese-cloth bag containing fresh charcoal in small lumps, about the size of small peas or large gravel stones, and wrap in a cloth moistened with vinegar, or equal parts of vinegar and water. In very hot weather remove the cloth and bag of charcoal two or three times a day and dip the fish into cold salt water. Afterwards wrap up as before.

Or if the fish shows signs of decay, immerse in a pickle of vinegar and water.

To Sweeten Tainted Meat.—Apply a solution of chloride of soda by means of a soft clean brush or sponge. With this quickly wash over the tainted portions and rinse immediately with fresh water. Afterwards broil or roast the meat so as to expose the tainted portions to a high temperature and char them with the heat.

Or if they are to be boiled, place half a dozen lumps of charcoal, the size of an egg, in the water.

Or place a quantity of pulverized charcoal in a cheese-cloth bag, and place these in the kettle. All odors will be absorbed by the charcoal and the meat will be sweet and clean.

Or hang the meat on a nail in a box, or suspended inside of an inverted barrel. Place beneath half a teacupful of table salt in an earthenware bowl and add by degrees 2 ounces of sulphuric acid at the rate of ½ ounce each 15 or 20 minutes, until all has been added. The resulting fumes will disinfect anything with which they come in contact. But care must be taken not to breathe them. Afterwards rinse the meat well with a solution of 1 tablespoonful of baking soda or borax to a gallon of water.

To Keep Frozen Meat.—In cold climates and in winter, meat may be preserved indefinitely by allowing it to freeze. But it must not be permitted to freeze and thaw frequently, and must not be thawed out too quickly when required for use. To preserve meat by freezing, first expose it to the weather until thoroughly frozen through and through. Wrap in waxed paper or cover with a cloth coated with shellac or other varnish and pack in an ordinary flour barrel between layers of hay, straw, or excelsior, pressing the whole as tightly and solidly as possible. Place the barrel in a bin or packing case, and surround it with a layer of 5 or 6 inches of dry sawdust.

To thaw frozen meat when required for use, place it in a moderately warm room at a distance from the fire, and allow it to thaw gradually.

Or better still, soak it 2 or 3 hours in cold water.

If thawed too quickly it will be unfit for use.

SALTING AND PICKLING MEAT

Curing Meat.—Among the various methods of preserving beef, pork, mutton, and other meats for considerable periods of time, are drying, canning, pickling, and smoking. Drying meat is practiced chiefly in hot climates and in localities where the air is free from moisture. It is accomplished by cutting the meat into convenient pieces and exposing it to direct sunlight on suitable drying forms so arranged as to admit of a free circulation of air. The canning of meat is similar in principle to the process of canning fruit and vegetables. It consists in cooking the meat until tender, placing it while at the boiling point in sterilized jars, and sealing while hot so as to exclude the air. In addition, it is customary to pour over the meat the gravy or meat jelly in which it has been cooked, in the same manner that sirup is poured over canned fruits. Pickling consists, in immersing the meat in a solution of antiseptics, usually salt, sugar, and saltpeter with soda or potash. Smoking is accomplished by suspending the meat in a suitable chamber, exposed to the fumes of smoldering corncobs, hickory or beech chips, sawdust, or other substances. The antiseptic effect of smoking is due to impregnation with pyroligneous acid, an impure acetic acid which, together with tarry matter is contained in the smoke. The effect of smoking is therefore similar to that of rubbing fresh meat with vinegar, except that the admixture of tarry matter prevents the acetic acid from escaping by evaporation.

Pickling Meat.—The points to be observed in pickling are cleanliness and sterilization. That is, all foreign matter, as blood, dirt, and the like, should be removed from the meat, and the tubs or casks in which it is packed should be sterilized. In addition, of course, the pickle must be sufficiently strong, and the meat fully covered with it and heavily weighted. If these precautions are observed, there is no reason why meat cannot be kept sweet the year round.

Preparation of Meat for Pickling.—The beef, pork, or mutton carcass to be pickled should be carefully cut into strips of equal thickness, so that it can be packed tightly in tubs or casks in uniform layers. The carcass should be cut up as soon as the animal heat is out of it, and the pieces to be pickled rubbed thoroughly with fine salt or powdered saltpeter or a mixture of these dried in a slow oven. After the salt and saltpeter have been well rubbed over the surface of the meat, sprinkle the pieces lightly with the same, and lay them on slats or boards slanted so that the blood will drain off, and let them stand from 24 to 48 hours. This will remove all the surface blood and leave the meat fresh and clean. When the necessary tubs or casks and pickling liquid are in readiness, rinse off the meat by dashing cold water over it from a dipper or pail. Wipe dry with a clean cloth. It will then be perfectly clean and ready to pack.

Pickling Liquid for Meat.—A full barrel, if properly packed, will contain about 200 pounds of meat and will require from 6 to 8 gallons of pickle. The proportions of salt, saltpeter, and sugar recommended are about as numerous as the various authorities. But as these antiseptics do their work separately, the proportion is not essential, provided the pickle is strong enough. To prepare a standard pickling liquid, place in a large kettle 8 gallons of pure soft cold water, to which add 14 to 16 pounds of pure salt, 4 to 6 ounces of saltpe-

"Pour Over it the Pickling Liquid."

ter, about 6 pounds of good brown sugar, or about 3 pounds of the sugar and an equal bulk of good New Orleans molasses. To which may be added 2 to 6 ounces of pure baking soda. Place the whole over a slow fire and bring to a boil with very gentle heat, removing the scum as it rises so as to have the liquid clear before it boils. After the pickle has been clarified, remove from the fire. Cover to keep out the dust and let stand until it becomes cold.

To Pack Meat.—Scald thoroughly the inside of the tubs or barrels by pouring into them boiling water and washing down the sides with a swab of clean cloth tied to the end of a stick or clean mop handle. Cover the bottom of the cask with common salt ½ inch or more in depth. Pack the meat in layers as tightly as possible with common salt sprinkled between them and, when packed, pour over it the cold pickling liquid through cheese cloth until the barrel is full. Place on top a loose cover of wood, previously scalded, small enough to slip inside of the barrel and rest on the meat. Lay on this a stone or other heavy weight, to keep it below the surface of the pickle, and be sure that the pickle does not evaporate so as to leave the meat exposed to the air. Otherwise it will rust. The above is a general method to which the following favorite recipes may be added to show the manner in which the proportions may be changed according to the experience of different individuals. But all of these are tested recipes.

Pickle for Beef.—Dissolve in 8 gallons of soft water 20 pounds of coarse fine salt, 8 ounces of saltpeter, and 4 pounds of coarse brown sugar. Bring to a boil with very gentle heat, skimming constantly. This quantity is sufficient for one full barrel, or 200 pounds of beef, if properly packed.

Or prepare in a similar manner a pickle containing 14 pounds of coarse fine salt, 2 ounces of saltpeter, 2 ounces of Cayenne pepper, 3 pints of New Orleans molasses, 2 pounds of brown sugar, and 12 gallons of soft water.

Or 10 pounds of salt, 1 ounce of saltpeter, 2 pounds of brown sugar, and 6 gallons of soft water.

Or 12 pounds of salt, 4 pounds of brown sugar, 4 ounces of saltpeter, 8 gallons of soft water, and 4 ounces of potash.

Or 2 quarts of coarse fine salt 3½ quarts of molasses, 2 teaspoonfuls of saltpeter, and 8 gallons of soft water.

Pickle for Beef.—Any of the above pickles may be used.

Or for a full barrel of beef, or 200 pounds, dissolve in 8 gallons of pure soft water 10 ounces of coarse fine salt, 4 ounces of saltpeter, 3 pints of New Orleans molasses, and 2 pounds of brown sugar. Place over a slow fire and bring to a boil, skimming constantly.

Or 15 pounds of salt, 2 pounds of sugar, 6 ounces of saltpeter, and 2 ounces of baking soda in 8 gallons of soft water.

Salting Meat.—Another method of curing meat is to rub or pack it with a mixture of salt, sugar, and saltpeter, but without water, thus allowing the meat to form a brine by means of its own juices. If the brine which forms is allowed to drain from the meat, it is said to be dry-salted. Or if the meat is packed in a tight receptacle, and the brine is allowed to remain over it, it is said to be wet-salted.

To salt beef or pork, first remove all bones. Rub the pieces, especially the cut surfaces, with a mixture of 1 pound of salt, 1 ounce of saltpeter, and 1 ounce of sugar. Use pressure enough to rub the salt thoroughly into the grain of the meat. Let stand 24 to 48 hours. Again rub with the same mixture, sprinkling common salt freely between the layers. Cover also the top thickly with salt, and put over all a heavy weight—the heavier the better.

Or for ½ a barrel, or 100 pounds of beef, prepare a mixture of 4 quarts of coarse fine salt, 4 pounds of brown sugar, and 4 ounces of saltpeter. Rub thoroughly into the meat. Let stand 48 hours to drain, turning occasionally, and pack in layers under a heavy weight, sprinkling the above mixture between but without the addition of water. If a scum rises it should be taken off with a skimmer and a little fine salt sprinkled over the surface.

Or for the same quantity of beef, prepare a mixture of 6 quarts of coarse fine salt, 4 pounds of light "A". or coffee sugar, 6 ounces of soda, and 4 ounces of saltpeter. Cure in all respects as above.

Rusty or Tainted Meat.—If meat has been properly drained to free it from blood, the pickle boiled and clarified, the barrels scalded, and the meat kept under the pickle by means of a suitable weight, it should keep indefinitely. But it is quite customary, as a precaution, to pour off the pickling liquid on the approach of summer, say in April, in temperate climates. Again bring it to a boil, with the addition of about ½ pound of salt to each gallon of pickling liquid, and when cold, once more pour it over the meat through a cheesecloth strainer. But this is said to harden the beef and injure its flavor. It is believed that if the meat is properly cured, this will not usually be found necessary.

If the meat should become tainted, pour off the tainted pickle and discard it. Rinse the meat with clear water and wash out the barrel with a strong solution of lime water or wood ashes. If the barrel is much tainted, it may be well to fill it with this solution and let stand overnight. Afterwards scald with boiling water.

Rub the meat in a mixture of saltpeter and sugar, and pack it between layers of charcoal. Finally, pour over it fresh pickling liquid, prepared as above, strong enough to float an egg.

Or mix 12 pounds of powdered charcoal, 10 pounds of common salt, and 4 pounds of saltpeter. Cover the bottom of the cask with a layer of this mixture, rub each piece with the same, and sprinkle it freely between the layers of meat. By either of these methods all traces of taint can be removed. The charcoal can be rinsed off with clear water.

Red Pickling Liquid for Meat.—To impart a fine red color to meat and to improve its flavor, dissolve in 8 gallons of pure soft water 8 pounds of bay salt, 8 pounds of common salt, 6 pounds of brown sugar, 1 pound of saltpeter, 8 ounces of bruised pimento, 5 ounces of bruised black pepper, and 2 ounces of grated nutmeg.

To Improve Corned Beef. — The quality of corned beef can be improved by immersing the pieces for half a minute by the watch, in boiling water before pickling. This is in accordance with the well-known practice of immersing beef that is to be boiled for the table in hot water in order to harden the surface, and cause the meat to retain its natural juices. Similarly this method tends to make corned beef more tender and juicy than otherwise. To effect this result first drain the meat to free it from blood, rinse it in clear water. Bring to a boil a solution of 2 ounces of saltpeter in 4 gallons of water and with a large fork having a long wooden handle, or a piece of wire having a hook at the end, immerse the pieces of meat for half a minute each in the boiling solution.

Or the same result may be obtained by pouring the pickling liquid while scalding hot over the meat; but the former method is to be preferred.

CURING HAMS, TONGUES, AND BACON

Pickling Mutton Hams.—First rub the hams with a mixture of 1 pound of salt, 1 ounce of saltpeter, and 1 ounce of sugar. Hang up for 24 or 48 hours to drain. Cover with a solution of about ½ pound of salt to 2 gallons of water, and let stand for 2 or 3 weeks. Pack closely in tubs or barrels and for each ½ barrel, or 100 pounds, prepare a pickle by dissolving 6 pounds of coarse fine salt, 2 ounces of saltpeter, 2 ounces of soda, 1 pint of molasses, and 1 pound of brown sugar in 6 gallons of pure soft water.

Pickling Tongues. — After trimming off the roots, with the exception of a little of the fat, rub the cut surface with a mixture of 1 pound of salt and 1 ounce of saltpeter. Sprinkle with the same and let drain for 48 hours. Now prepare a pickle by dissolving in 1 gallon of soft water 2½ pounds of bay salt, 2 ounces of saltpeter, and 1 pound of brown sugar. Bring to a boil over a slow fire, skimming constantly, and immerse the tongues in this.

Or mix 1 tablespoonful of salt, 1

tablespoonful of brown sugar and 2 tablespoonfuls of saltpeter to each tongue. Rub this well into the tongues twice a day for a week and let them stand in the brine. At the end of this time, add 1 additional tablespoonful of salt for each tongue and rub the pickle into them once a day for a week or 10 days.

Curing Pork Hams. — Pork hams may be cured either by dry- or wet-salting or pickling. It is then customary to smoke them, both to impart a smoky flavor and as a protection against insects. And they may be further protected by wrapping or scaling in cloth or paper cases.

To dry-salt hams for smoking, but without pickle, which is the English method, rub the fleshy parts thoroughly each day with fine table salt and hang up the hams for 3 or 4 days where they can drain. On the fourth day, rub well into the hams, using plenty of "elbow grease," a mixture of 1 pound of common salt, 1 pound of bay salt, 4 ounces of saltpeter, and ½ pound of brown sugar. Lay the hams on a board or shelf, rind side down, and each day apply to the fleshy side with a soft brush, a mixture of 1 pound of brown sugar and 1 pound of molasses. At the end of a fortnight, smoke with hickory wood or corncobs.

Or for each 100 pounds of pork, mix 1½ ounces of saltpeter, 1 ounce of black pepper, 5 ounces of brown sugar and 1 quart of common or bay salt. Add just enough hot water to dissolve. Mix all together and rub thoroughly into the meat. A woman's hands are not heavy enough to do this work properly. It is advisable to take out the bone and rub the inside of the ham where the bone is removed in the same manner. But if this is not done, the bone may be loosened slightly with a knife and the mixture forced into the cut for a few inches. Lay the hams with the fleshy side up and rub them over with this mixture every day for 10 days or 2 weeks, after which smoke them with hickory chips or corncobs.

Or for a wet-salting process, mix 1 pound of common salt, 1 pound of bay salt, 3 ounces of saltpeter, and ½ pound of brown sugar. Dissolve the saltpeter in a little boiling water, using no more than is necessary to dissolve it. Mix the other ingredients and rub the whole thoroughly into the fleshy side of the ham. Place them in a firkin or other tight receptacle and add for each ham 2 tablespoonfuls of pure vinegar. Each day turn the hams, and rub the brine into them thoroughly for a week or 10 days. Then let stand 3 or 4 days in the pickle, basting them occasionally with a large wooden spoon.

Or for each ham of 16 or 18 pounds' weight, mix 2 tablespoonfuls of saltpeter, and 4 ounces of brown sugar and rub it thoroughly into the fleshy side. After which cover the fleshy side with a layer of fine salt ½ inch thick, and lay the hams down in the tubs for 4 or 5 weeks.

Or mix 1 pound of bay salt, ¼ pound of saltpeter, ¼ pound of common salt, and ¼ pound of brown sugar. Heat to dryness, and rub well into the fleshy side of the ham. Lay it in a tub, barrel, or firkin, the rind side down. Cover the fleshy parts with a layer of this mixture and each day turn the hams, and rub the brine into them for a week or 10 days. Afterwards let stand for a month basting the pickle over them daily with a large wooden spoon. Hang up to dry for 2 or 3 days and smoke.

Or protect against insects, and store without smoking. A small ham will require about 2 weeks, and a large one 3 to 4 weeks to cure by the above method. A tongue will require about 12 days. They may then be used at once without drying, or may be dried and smoked.

Or if the weather is hot, and the hams show signs of rusting, make a pickle of common salt and water strong enough to float an egg, and pour it over them.

Or to pickle pork hams, first rub them with a mixture of 1 pound of pure salt and 1 ounce of saltpeter. Sprinkle with same and let them drain on slats for 48 hours. Rub into each ham a mixture of ½ teaspoonful of saltpeter, ½ teaspoonful of brown sugar, and 1 salt spoon of Cayenne pepper. Scald a suitable tub or barrel. Cover the bottom with a layer of pure salt. Pack the hams in this, rind side down, sprinkling salt freely over the fleshy side of each, and let stand for a week. Prepare a pickling liquid by dissolving in 6 gallons of soft water 10 pounds of salt, 4 pounds of brown sugar, 4 ounces of saltpeter, and 2 ounces of soda. Bring to a boil with very gentle heat, skimming constantly. Set aside until cool, and pour into the cask through a cheese-cloth strainer. The hams should remain in this pickle from 6 weeks to 3 months, according to their size.

Or for 100 pounds of meat, dissolve in 4 gallons of soft water, 8 pounds of coarse fine salt, 1 ounce of baking soda, 2 ounces of saltpeter, and 2 pounds of brown sugar. Prepare in all respects as above.

Or for 100 pounds of meat, dissolve in 4 gallons of soft water 7 pounds of coarse fine salt, 2½ pounds of brown sugar, 2 ounces of saltpeter, and 2 ounces of soda. Immerse the hams and pickle for 2 or 3 months, according to their size.

Or rub the hams with a mixture of 1 pound of salt, 1 ounce of saltpeter, and let drain 3 or 4 days. Immerse in brine strong enough to float an egg, and for each ½ barrel or 100 pounds of meat, add 2 quarts of molasses, 4 ounces of saltpeter, 2 ounces of baking soda, and pickle 6 to 8 weeks.

Smoking Pork Hams.—Remove the hams from the pickling liquid and hang them up to drain and dry. When they have drained sufficiently, wipe them carefully with a sponge or clean cloth, and rub thoroughly into the fleshy side a mixture of equal parts of Cayenne and black pepper, especially about the bone and hock. This will prevent flies lighting upon them. Now sew up each ham in a bag of cheese cloth or scrim to protect it from soot, and hang up in the smoke house under a barrel or any suitable receptacle and smoke—the longer the better. Chips or sawdust from hickory or beech wood or corncobs are the most suitable fuel with which to smoke hams. After being lighted they must be kept smoldering by sprinkling them lightly with water

"Hang up Under a Barrel."

whenever they commence to blaze. And the process may be continued for 8 or 10 hours or for several weeks, according to convenience or the quality desired. Some persons who burn wood exclusively as fuel, smoke hams by sewing them up in a coarse cloth and hanging them up in the chimney, but this method is not suitable if coal is used as fuel in any part of the house. When hams are smoked properly the pyroligneous acid of the smoke permeates the meat. It also dries slowly at the same time. Quick smoking merely coats the outside of the ham, but does not penetrate its fiber.

Or an imitation of smoking may be had by immersing the ham in diluted pyroligneous acid for 2 or 3 hours, or giving it 2 or 3 coatings with a brush. But this method tends to harden and toughen the meat and is therefore not to be recommended for domestic use.

To Store Smoked Ham.—After removing hams from the smoke house, they may be rinsed in cold water, or better still, immersed for 2 or 3 minutes in boiling water, the effect of which is to cover them with a coating of grease and also to kill any germs or eggs of insects that may be present. Next, coat them with flour paste prepared by rubbing up 2 teaspoonfuls of flour in a little cold water, bringing to a boil, and stirring in 1 teaspoonful or more of Cayenne pepper. Cover the hams thickly with this paste by means of a soft brush, and hang them up in the direct sunlight until the paste dries. When dry, sew them up in coarse cloth, and give the cloth a coating of shellac or other varnish.

Or suspend them in a loose bag surrounded by finely chopped straw to the thickness of 2 or 3 inches.

Or place them in ordinary paper flour sacks. Tie tightly to exclude the air and insects and hang up in a cool, dark, well-ventilated place.

Or wrap each ham in ordinary brown butcher's wrapping paper, seal with paste containing Cayenne pepper, and tie with twine. Pack in packing cases or barrels in finely chopped straw. A coating of pyroligneous acid, if carefully applied, so as to cover the entire surface and penetrate all crevices, will effectually prevent contamination of insects.

Curing Bacon. — The process of curing bacon is similar to dry-smoking pork hams. Rub the flitches of bacon with 1 ounce of common salt, 1 ounce of saltpeter, and 1 ounce of brown sugar. Lay them on slats or slanting boards to drain for 48 hours, turning frequently. Next lay the flitches in a deep dripping pan, and cover with the same mixture. Turn and rub the pickle into them 2 or 3 times a day for a week or 10 days. Let stand in the pickle for about 3 weeks in all, basting them frequently with a large wooden spoon. Remove and smoke as for hams. Place in paper flour sacks and tie tightly to exclude the air and preserve from insects.

MAKING AND KEEPING SAUSAGE

Sausage. — Fresh pork, beef, and other meats may be preserved in the same manner as sausage meat by seasoning them highly with spices and packing them in air-tight cases, or in earthenware or other tight receptacles, and running over them a layer of melted lard or tallow to exclude the air.

Intestine Cases for Sausage. — Remove from the pig's intestines the loose fat and outer membranes. Turn them inside out and cleanse them thoroughly in borax water. Bleach by letting them soak for 24 hours or more in water containing 1 ounce of chloride of lime to the gallon. Rinse thoroughly in clear soft water and scrape or tear off a part of the inner lining until they are as thin as may be without tearing or puncturing them. Finally, wash them thoroughly several times in warm water.

Seasoning for Sausage.—Salt, pepper, and sage, according to taste, are ordinarily used for seasoning sausage. Summer savory is also frequently used, and other spices, as allspice, cloves, ginger, etc., are sometimes recommended. But, as a rule, salt, pepper, and sage are sufficient, and will be preferred by most persons. The proportion of seasoning recommended varies, and it is a good plan in mixing sausage meat, to fry a little of the meat after seasoning and add more of the ground meat or seasoning, as desired, until the flavor is satisfactory. The following are all tested recipes, and by comparison, a selection may be made according to whether it is desired to have the sausage highly seasoned or not:

For 10 pounds of ground sausage

meat, use 4 ounces of salt, ½ ounce of pepper, and ¾ ounce of sage.

Or for the same quantity, 5 tablespoonfuls of sage, 4 tablespoonfuls of salt, and 2 tablespoonfuls of pepper.

Or for each pound of meat, 1 heaping teaspoonful of salt, 1 of pepper, and 1 of sage, with the addition to each 3 pounds of meat, if desired, 1 teaspoonful each of allspice, ginger, and summer savory.

Or for over 25 pounds of meat, 12 ounces of salt, 2 ounces of sage, and 2 ounces of pepper.

Or for 10 pounds of meat, 4 ounces of salt, 1 ounce of sage, and 1 ounce of pepper.

Grinding Sausage Meat. — The trimmings of the hog's carcass are ordinarily ground into sausage meat, the proportion of fat and lean being varied according to taste. Some prefer ⅓ fat meat to ⅔ lean. Others ¼ fat to ¾ lean.

To Prepare Sausage.—To prepare good sausage, it is desirable to have a sausage grinder or suitable meat cutter, although the sausage meat can be chopped in a wooden tray with a

"A Coat of Melted Lard."

chopping knife or on a block by means of a heavy knife or cleaver. It will be found easier in mixing the spices thoroughly into the meat to dry and pulverize them as finely as possible, cut the meat into rather small pieces and sprinkle the spices over it before it is ground. It will thus become thoroughly incorporated with the meat in grinding. The sausage grinder is ordinarily fitted with a device for filling the cases. If link sausage is to be made, care must be taken not to fill the sausage cases too full, but to pinch and twist them at intervals to make them link properly.

Or sausages may be packed in cases of muslin or other clean white goods about 2½ or 3 inches thick, forced in by means of a clean round stick of hard wood, laid down in jars, and covered with brine or melted lard.

Or the cloth cases may be dipped in melted lard and hung up to dry, care being taken that they have a uniform coating of lard to exclude the air.

Or the sausage meat may be laid down in earthenware pans 4 or 5 inches deep, and a coat of melted lard ¼ to ½ inch deep poured over them to exclude the air. As long as the coating of lard is not broken, the sausage meat will keep indefinitely. Or if the dish is not too large, it will usually keep after being opened until required for family use. Or after slices have been removed for use, the open end can be covered with a coating of melted lard until more is needed.

Or large earthenware jars may be used for this purpose, although, in most cases, they are not as convenient.

To Improve Sausage Meat.—The addition of about $\frac{1}{10}$ by weight of ground beef to pork sausage, is preferred by many, as it makes the sausage less greasy and firmer in texture.

Or for immediate use, powdered bread crumbs at the same rate may be added for this purpose. But this should not be used if the sausage meat is to be laid down for a long time as it will not keep so well.

Bologna Sausage. — The so-called bologna sausage is a mixture of approximately equal parts of pork and beef or other meats highly seasoned and packed in large cases, 3 to 6 inches in diameter, obtained from the intestines of beeves. The following mixtures are recommended:

Grind up together in a sausage machine or meat cutter 4 pounds of beef and 2 pounds of pork free from fat or gristle, to which add 6 pounds of fresh fat pork cut in thin strips and chopped on a block by means of a heavy knife or cleaver into pieces about ¼ of an inch square or less. Season this quantity with 8 ounces of salt, ⅛ ounce of saltpeter, 8 ounces of coffee sugar, and ½ ounce of bruised pimento. To exclude the air, the cases must be packed with as much pressure as they will stand without bursting, and this may be done by tying them at the bottom and pressing in the meat with a round block of wood or pestle, nearly but not quite large enough to fill the inside of the case. If the meat is not packed tightly enough, the sausage will not keep.

Rub the outside of the cases with salt butter. Tie them tightly at both ends and hang up to dry for 3 weeks, then smoke as for hams or bacon.

Or cut into small pieces an inch or two square 3 pounds of pork, 1½ pounds of beef free from fat or gristle, and 1 pound of clean fresh beef suet. Sprinkle with a mixture of spices consisting of 3 ounces of salt, 3 tablespoonfuls of black pepper, 2 teaspoonfuls of Cayenne, 1 teaspoonful each of cloves and allspice, and a small onion chopped fine. If the meat cutter is coarse, run through a second time and pack tightly in cases 4 or 5 inches in diameter. Knot both ends and cover with strong brine for a week or 10 days. Change the brine and let stand another week. After which dry and smoke them as for hams or bacon. Rub the cases with butter and store them in a cool dark place.

Mixed Sausage. — Cut in small pieces equal parts of fat pork, lean pork, lean veal, and beef suet. For each 6 pounds of meat add the rind of a lemon grated, a small nutmeg grated, ½ ounce of powdered sage, 2 teaspoonfuls of butter, 4 teaspoonfuls of salt, and 1 teaspoonful of summer savory. Pack in cases or lay down in jars and cover with lard.

Beef Sausage.—In summer, when fresh pork is not obtainable, raw beef may be ground up with beef suet in the proportion of about 1 part of suet, 2 parts of lean beef, and the whole seasoned with 1 teaspoonful each of pepper, salt, sage, and summer savory ground through the meat cutter or sausage grinder, and made into cakes to be fried, or laid down in earthenware pans under a coating of lard until required for use.

Pickled Tripe.—Empty the paunch by turning it wrong side out, taking care not to let any of the contents get on the outside. Rinse with cold water. Tie or sew up the openings tightly with strong cord so that the lime water cannot get inside, and immerse it in a tub of cold fresh slaked lime about as thick as whitewash. Let it stand 15 or 20 minutes, or until the dark outside skin is loosened and can be readily pulled off. Pass through 3 or 4 rinsing waters. Tack up on a board and with a dull knife scrape off the dark surface until it looks clean and has no offensive odor. Soak for half an hour in hot water, then scrape with a dull knife and repeat until perfectly white and clean. Immerse in strong brine and let stand 3 or 4 days, changing the water each day. Cut into pieces a foot long and 6 inches wide, and immerse in buttermilk for 3 or 4 days to whiten. Rinse and lay down in a suitable cask. Cover with pure white wine or cider vinegar, or spiced pickling liquid as preferred.

PRESERVATION OF COOKED MEAT

In addition to the preservation of fresh meat in various ways, cooked or partially cooked meats may be preserved for considerable periods of time by canning or taking other means to exclude the air. Meats to be canned are first cut into suitable pieces, boiled until tender and packed in glass jars surrounded by boiling water. The meat jelly, or "aspic," in which they have been cooked, is then seasoned to taste and poured over them, boiling hot, until the jar is filled to the brim, and they are then sealed while hot. The addition of the aspic, which is, of course, melted when the cans are sealed, but which solidifies on cooling, not only assists in preserving the meat, but also improves its flavor.

Or suitable tin cans may be used. The cans, surrounded with hot water, are packed with the cooked meat, and the meat jelly poured over them. The cover is then soldered in place, a small hole is punctured in it and the water surrounding the can is boiled until steam escapes from the aperture. The opening is then closed with solder. The condensation of the steam inside the can on cooling produces a vacuum by which the sides of the can are made slightly concave. And if at any time this concavity disappears, or the sides of the can swell so as to become convex, it is a sure indication that the contents were not properly preserved and have become putrid.

Or to preserve pork chops or sliced ham for summer frying, pickle fresh pork about 10 days or 2 weeks and fry it until about half done.

Or remove the hams from the brine in April, slice, trim, and fry them until half done. Pack the chops or hams separately in solid layers in stone jars. Let them cool, and when entirely cold, pour over them their own fat with the addition of a little melted lard, so as to cover the surface with a layer ½ inch or more thick. Place over the top of the jar a layer of cotton batting. Put on the lid tightly and store in a cool place until required for use. After taking out a portion of the meat for use, remelt the lard and pour back over the meat to exclude the air. Lamb or veal chops, beefsteak or sausage meat may be laid down in the same manner.

Preserving Cooked Sausage.—Pack sausage in cases, or sausage meat, into a small crock or bean pot about ⅔ full. Place in a baking oven and bake about fifteen minutes for each pound of sausage, i. e., for 6 pounds of sausage bake an hour and a half. Remove from the oven and set aside to cool. When cold, fill the crock with melted lard. Throw over the top a layer of cotton batting, put on the lid, and store in a dark, cool place until required for use.

Or fried sausage can be laid down in the same manner and covered with its own grease.

Or for cooked bologna sausage, grind together 2 pounds each of pork, bacon, beef, and veal free from fat or gristle, and 2 pounds of beef suet. First cut in small pieces and sprinkle over it before grinding 4 ounces of salt, 6 tablespoonfuls of black pepper, 1 tablespoonful of Cayenne, and pack tightly into beef cases 4 or 5 inches in diameter. Form links about 12 or 15 inches in length, tying at both ends. Prick the skins and boil for about an hour. Hang up to dry for 2 or 3 days and afterwards smoke with hickory wood or corncobs.

Or grind up together with suitable seasoning equal quantities of ham, veal, or pork; or ⅓ pork and ⅔ beef. Cook and smoke as above.

Potted Beef.—Cut 3 pounds of lean beef into pieces weighing about ¾ of a pound each and sprinkle over them a mixture of ½ pound of table salt and ½ ounce of powdered saltpeter. Let the beef lie in this pickle 2 or 3 days, turning the pieces occasionally. Remove the meat from the pickle, place it in a stone jar or pan covered, if convenient, with a little beef gravy or just enough cold water to prevent burning. Put an earthenware plate over it and bake in a slow oven for about 4 hours, or until the meat is very tender and falls away from the bones. Remove the meat from the gravy. Shred or chop it fine, moisten it with the gravy and pound it in a marble mortar or otherwise with a little fresh butter to a very fine paste. Season to taste with pepper, allspice, nutmeg, mace, or cloves. Or add, if desired, Cayenne, Tabasco, curry powder, or anchovies, mustard, or other condiment, according to taste. Press tightly in small crocks or jars, or in fruit jars. When cold, pour over the tops of the jars melted lard or butter to a thickness of ¼ inch, and cover with a layer of cotton batting tied tightly on any cover that will exclude the air.

Pressed Beef.—Or select about 5 pounds of cheap beef that would otherwise be too tough to cook, including about ¾ of a pound of beef fat. Cover with a mixture of ¾ pound of salt and ½ ounce of saltpeter and let stand for a couple of days turning it now and then, and rubbing brine into it. Rinse in clear water and boil until it falls from the bones, taking care that when boiled down, the gravy will be as thick as possible. Remove the beef from the gravy with a skimmer and chop fine. Allow the gravy to cool. Take off the cake of fat, and dissolve ½ ounce of gelatin in the gravy with gentle heat. Spice to taste. Stir in the chopped meat. Pack in jars under a weight and pour melted lard or butter over the top to the depth of ¼ inch or more. If carefully preserved from the air, this will keep for a considerable time at ordinary temperatures, and may be sliced and eaten cold without further cooking.

TRYING OUT AND STORING LARD

Lard.—The leaf fat which adheres to the ribs and belly of the hog make the so-called "leaf lard," which is of the best quality. Hence it is a good plan to try out the leaves separately. But any part of the hog fat not used for other purposes may be tried out to make an ordinary quality of lard. A set kettle, or other large kettle, held over a camp fire by means of a tripod out of doors on a clear, calm day, is the best utensil for this purpose. Cut the fat into small pieces 1 or 2 inches square, and add 1 ounce of soda for each 25 pounds of meat. Stir frequently as soon as the fat melts and the scraps begin to brown. Melt with very gentle heat, taking care not to allow the fat to smoke or burn. Toward the last, the lard must be stirred constantly to prevent burning. The lard will be done when the steam ceases to rise. When the scraps are brown and shriveled, throw in a little salt to settle the sediment, and strain through a cheese-cloth strainer into tubs or jars. Tie over the tops a layer of cotton batting to exclude the air. Lard will keep better in small jars than in large ones. Good lard should be white and solid without any offensive odor. Store in a cool, dry place. The lard from the intestines will not keep as well as leaf lard, hence should be rendered separately. It will keep better if soaked for 3 or 4 days in strong brine changed each day.

Bleaching Lard.—The addition of about 1 pint of boiled white lye from hickory ashes, strained through cheese cloth into the fat before boiling, tends to bleach it.

Adulteration of Lard with Water.—The addition of 3 to 5 per cent milk of lime, allows about 25 per cent of water to be mixed with lard while cooling, thus greatly increasing its weight and volume. The presence of water may be perceived by the sputtering made in melting the lard. Also, the water will collect in the bottom of the vessel and the lard will float on its surface. This test will often show that the purchaser is paying for a considerable percentage of water instead of lard.

Cod Fat.—The suet taken from the beef flank is called cod fat. It makes a much softer and better fat than the common suet. Obtain the best looking pieces of cod fat from the butcher, free them from veins or spots and melt with very gentle heat. Pour the melted suet into clear cold water, iced water, if convenient, to harden. Pour off the water, remove all dampness with a clean dry cloth. Wrap up the fat in waxed paper and store in a cool, dry place.

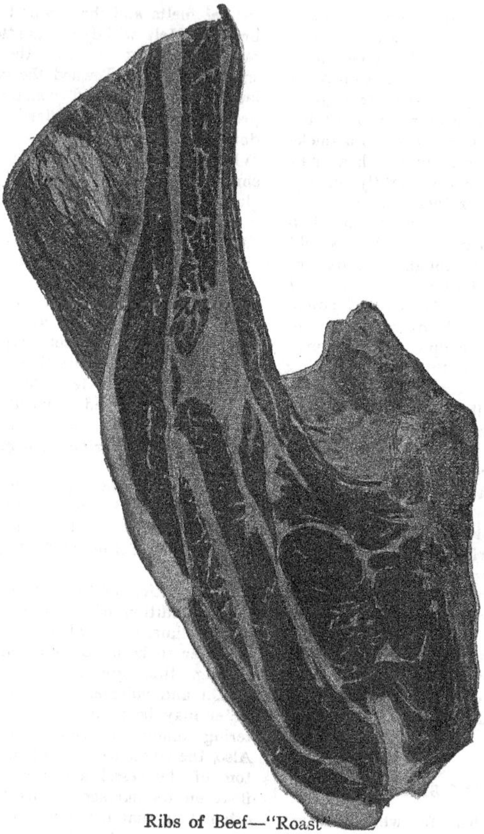

Ribs of Beef—"Roast"

Cottolene. — This substitute for lard or suet consists of 6 parts cotton oil, 4 parts oleostearine. Melt together with very gentle heat and run through a filter in jars. This is preferred by many to animal fat, being purer as well as cheaper.

PRESERVING, TESTING, AND PACKING EGGS

Preservation of Eggs.—More hens' eggs are laid during the months of March, April, May, and June than during the other 8 months of the year. Hence the bulk of the consumption of eggs during the fall and winter months is of eggs that are not fresh laid. The commercial method of preserving eggs is by means of cold storage in vaults kept at a temperature of 40° F. or less. Eggs are collected all over the United States and stored in the largest cities, whence they are distributed at wholesale and often times sold in the winter months to farmers and others who keep hens, but who are not, at that season, getting enough eggs for their own consumption. The wholesale market recognizes seventeen grades of eggs according to their size, weight, and freshness and the localities from which they come. But the ordinary buyer of eggs is unable to distinguish among them, and often gets a very much cheaper grade of cold-storage egg than she pays for. Hence on all grounds, it is much better and cheaper for those who keep chickens to preserve, in the season when eggs are plentiful, all that are not required for immediate use. If care is taken, eggs if perfectly fresh when preserved will be nearly, if not quite equal to new. But at all events, home-stored eggs, if properly preserved, will be superior to cold-storage ones, which are often far from fresh when gathered and placed in storage.

Testing Eggs.—Eggshells are porous or perforated right through by minute holes for the admission of air needed by the chick for breathing. Hence in time a part of the liquid contents of the egg evaporates. The white and yolk shrink and the resulting emptied space is filled with air. This space is normally at the broad end. And this is the reason why, in

"Look Through them at the Light."

storing eggs, the point should always be downward. To test eggs take a candle or electric light or lamp in an otherwise dark room and fit it with a candling chimney, which may be obtained at any poultry store or may be readily made from a piece of cardboard. This is merely a cylinder of cardboard large enough to surround the candle or the lamp chimney, and having a tube inserted at right angles somewhat smaller in diameter than an ordinary egg, and about the level of the flame. Through this the egg can be observed against the light.

To test eggs, hold each one up against the opening of this cylinder, broad end upward, and look through them at the light. If the contents do not fill the shell, the egg is not perfectly fresh, and the larger the air space the older is the egg. The yolk should be perfectly clear and round in outline. If, besides the air space, there is a dark haze or cloud in the egg, it has become spoiled. If the cloud contains a black spot, the egg is bad. All storage eggs show some shrinkage, and eggs shipped by freight from distant points to a wholesale market, will shrink on the way even if not afterwards preserved in cold storage.

Methods of Preserving Eggs.—The object to be secured in preserving eggs is to prevent the evaporation of their contents, and thus prevent the air coming in to fill the space. This may be accomplished by any method of filling the pores of the shell so as to effectually prevent the passage of air. Among the substances recommended for this purpose are mucilage made of gum arabic or gum tragacanth dissolved in water; albumen, or the white of egg; collodion, linseed oil, paraffin; shellac, or other varnish; saltpeter, lard, sugar sirup; finely powdered gypsum, or plaster of Paris, dry salt, and various solutions, as lime, soda, saltpeter, salt, etc., in water.

As the object of all these methods is the same, it becomes merely a question of selecting whatever substance is most readily obtainable and whatever method is most convenient under the circumstances. Hence to preserve eggs, dissolve with gentle heat 1 ounce of gum arabic or gum tragacanth in 1 pint of water, and if too thick, thin with boiling water to the consistency of common mucilage. Remove the mucilage from the fire, allow it to cool and apply it with a soft brush. Have at hand large sheets of blotting paper or a bed of dry sand on which to rest the eggs while the mucilage is drying. If laid on wood or any other hard substance, the mucilage will cause them to stick and they cannot be removed without chipping the shell. After laying down the eggs take care to cover the finger marks where the egg was held. When dry, pack, with the small ends down, in pails, tubs, or cases in dry bran, meal, or flour. Do not use salt with gum arabic or tragacanth as, by attracting moisture, it may cause them to dissolve. If a little of the blotting paper or sand adheres to the egg it will do no harm. When the eggs are required for use, the mucilage can be removed with cold water, taking any foreign substances with it.

Or beat up the white of an egg with a saltspoonful of salt, and apply in the same manner.

Or apply shellac or copal varnish.

Or apply by the same method a thick coating of collodion dissolved in alcohol, or a coating of paraffin or of linseed oil.

Or place in the palm of the hand a little salt butter or pure salted lard, and turn the egg about until every portion of the surface has been covered with the grease. Thus a small amount of lard or butter will cover a large number of eggs. Pack with the small ends down in bran or other substance as described above.

Or pack eggs, greased with salted lard or butter, between layers of common salt. Take care to store in a perfectly dry, well-ventilated place where the eggs will not freeze. Eggs thus stored can be preserved for several months.

Or for home use, dip the egg for 10 or 20 seconds into boiling water. This forms a thin coating of albumen inside of the shell that partially closes the pores. Remove from the boiling water and dip into a thin sugar sirup made by dissolving 5 pounds of brown sugar in a gallon of water, and set aside to dry. Small quantities of eggs may be dipped in these liquids by means of a colander or suspended in a wire or wicker basket. But take care to shake them slightly so that every part of the shell will be exposed to the solutions. When dry, pack as above.

Or to preserve eggs for a longer period of time, they may be immersed in a solution of lime with other substances, in water. The celebrated English patent of Jayne consisted in slaking fresh stone lime in a wooden tub or barrel with just enough water to dissolve it, and afterwards thinning with cold water to a point that will just float a fresh egg. Then, for each bushel of lime, stir in 2 pounds of salt and ½ pound of cream of tartar. Immerse the eggs and keep them below the surface by means of a floating cover of wood weighted just enough to rest upon the eggs without crushing them.

Or for a small quantity of eggs, the same recipe would require about 1 ounce of salt, ¼ ounce of cream of tartar, and 1 quart of lime.

Or a standard American recipe consists in packing the eggs with the small ends down, in a crock or firkin, and covering them with a cold solution of 1 pound of lime, 2 ounces of salt, and ½ ounce of saltpeter, dissolved by stirring in boiling water and allowed to stand overnight before using.

Or to 3 gallons of water, add 1 pint of fresh slaked lime, ½ pint of common salt, and 2 ounces of saltpeter.

Or a more elaborate recipe calls for 4 pounds of fresh stone lime to be slaked in 12 gallons of water. Stir in 2 pounds of salt and let stand for 24 hours. Decant the pure lime water without disturbing the sediment. Dissolve separately in one gallon of boiling water 2½ ounces of soda, 2½ ounces of cream of tartar, 2½ ounces of saltpeter, 2½ ounces of borax, and 1 ounce of alum. Mix this solution with 10 gallons of the pure lime water. Pack the eggs, point down, in suitable tubs or casks, and cover with this liquid. They must be kept below the surface by means of a cloth or wooden cover and suitable weights. This quantity is sufficient for about 75 dozen eggs. The same proportions may be observed for smaller quantities.

Or pack the eggs in stone crocks, points down, and pour over them melted lard as cool as it will blow, or just before it sets, and allow it to harden about them.

Packing Eggs.—To pack eggs for transportation, layers of newspaper or any soft, cheap paper that may be available will be found safer than oats or bran. Crumple a number of newspapers, and lay them in the bottom of the box or basket, and bring them up well around the sides. Pack the eggs close together so that they cannot roll against each other. Lay over them 2 or 3 thicknesses of paper, on this another layer of eggs, and so on. Throw over the top 2 or 3 thicknesses of coarse burlap and fasten it around the outside of the package with cord. Eggs packed in this way in a clothes basket may be driven in a wagon over the roughest roads without breaking.

Or to pack for market, obtain an egg case, manufactured for this purpose, which will serve as a model for making cases at home. Or they can be made at trifling expense by the local carpenter. It will be found that the cost of these cases will be more than repaid in convenience and in preventing breakage.

Pickling Eggs.—Prepare a spiced pickling liquid the same as for spiced cucumber or other pickles.

Or boil in a cheese-cloth bag for 15 or 20 minutes in 1 quart of white wine or pure cider vinegar, 1 ounce of raw ginger, 1 ounce of allspice, 2 blades of mace, 1 ounce of pepper, 1 ounce of salt, 3 or 4 cloves of garlic, and 1 ounce of mustard seed. Boil for this quantity of pickle, a dozen eggs for 10 minutes. Place to cool in a pan of cold water. Remove the shells, pack them in a crock, and when perfectly cold, pour the pickling liquid over them. Lay over the top a folded cloth to keep the eggs under the pickling liquid, and tie over the top of the jar a thickness of cotton batting. They will be ready to use in about 4 weeks.

Dried Eggs.—Break any quantity of eggs in a suitable receptacle, and beat them well with an egg beater. Spread out in a thin layer on a clean earthenware platter, and let them dry into a paste. Pack closely in glass jars and seal.

Or pour the beaten eggs into glass jars and set the jar in a pan of hot water at about a temperature of 125° F. until the moisture is evaporated and the egg becomes hard. Seal until required for use. They can then be dissolved with about 3 times their own bulk of cold water, and beaten up together, when they will be found to have retained much of their original flavor.

STORING AND PRESERVING VEGETABLES, FRUIT, NUTS, AND HERBS

Conditions that cause vegetables to decay are moisture and heat, or frequent and extreme changes of temperature, as alternate freezing and thawing. These conditions are also favorable to the attacks of insects. Cold storage in a dry vault, with a temperature near or below the freezing point, is, of course, the best method. Coöperative cold storage plants, both large and small, the benefits of which may be shared by a group of neighbors or an entire community, are likely in time to come to be very numerous. But if cold storage is out of the question, a cool, dry place, where the temperature is likely to be as even as possible, should be sought for most vegetables.

Vegetable Pits.—To preserve root crops—as beets, turnips, and parsnips, also cabbages—dig a trench on the north side of a sandy slope or ridge where the drainage is as perfeet as possible, so that after a storm no water will stand in the trench. Dig a trench two or three feet deep about the same in width, and any desired length. Pack the vegetables carefully in this. Pile them up in a pyramid like the ridge of the roof of a house. Cover with a layer about a foot thick of meadow hay or straw and throw enough earth lightly over the straw to keep it in place. After the first frosts in the fall cover with a layer of earth 5 or 6 inches thick, and in the latter part of November or about the 1st of December, cover solidly with earth to the depth of a foot or more. Remove the vegetables from one end as required for use and cover the opening with hay or straw and keep it in place with boards, or shovel snow over it.

Ventilate these pits by means of 6-inch tile drains or square boxes of 6-inch boards nailed together. Insert these ventilators at intervals of 25 or 50 feet in large pits and plug the opening with loose straw to keep out the frost. Otherwise there is danger of decay from moisture in the event of an early thaw.

Or pull root crops, as turnips, beets, and the like on a hot, dry day and let them lie in the sun until all dirt can be shaken from the roots. Twist off the tops, leaving the tap root on. Pack them in clean, dry barrels or bins and fill with fine dry sand or road dust, shaking it down around them until the box or barrel is full. Root crops should not be packed on the floors of cellars, as dampness is likely to cause them tc decay and furnish breeding places for bacteria that cause filth diseases.

To Keep Celery.—In the latter part of October dig a trench 18 inches deep and 12 to 15 inches wide on a dry, well-drained ridge. Loosen the earth about the roots of the celery and draw out the stalks without shaking off the soil that adheres to them. Stand them upright close together in the trench inclining slightly toward the middle, and draw the earth around them up to the tips. Cover with a thick layer of leaves, straw, or meadow hay, put a board across the top and weight with stones or otherwise. If there is any danger of standing water from rains or melting snow, in winter, dig a ditch deeper than the celery trench for drainage.

Vegetable Cellar. — To preserve small quantities of vegetables for domestic use, sink a half hogshead, cask, or large dry-goods box about two-thirds of its depth into the ground and slope the earth around it on all sides to the top. Knock the bottom out, and line the space with loose brick laid on the earth side by side or with a layer of loose stone. Fit it with a water-tight cover coming down over the edge.

Pack in this such vegetables as cabbage, celery, beets, turnips, etc. They will keep fresh all winter.

When cold weather comes on, throw over the top a large bag of burlap or potato sacking made like a mattress

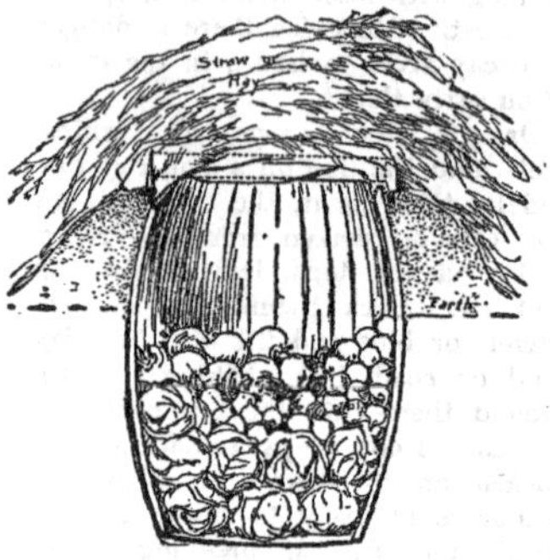

"Sink a Cask in the Earth."

and filled loosely with hay or straw. This can readily be removed to allow access and replaced after required vegetables have been taken out for use.

To Store Onions.—Pull the onions and let them lie in the field until the tops are withered. Spread them under cover on an open floor or on slats until they are bone dry.

The best receptacles for onions are slat boxes having solid heads of inch pine stuff, with sides and bottoms of rough laths, the width of one lath open between every two. These should be made to hold a bushel or half a bushel. Stack them one above the other, with pieces of inch pine stuff between to admit of free cirenlation of air. Pack these in a cool cellar on a platform raised 8 or 10 inches from the cellar bottom.

Or stack them in a shed or outhouse. Make a bin around them of rough boards about 6 inches from the outside of the crates, and fill the space with chopped straw, chaff, or sawdust. Cover over the top with sand and throw over the whole any old burlap, carpet, or canvas that may be at hand. Thus protected it will do no harm if the onions freeze, as chaff or straw is a nonconducting material, and they will not thaw out until spring, and then very slowly. The same would be true in an ordinary cellar.

Or small quantities may be packed in barrels or boxes in chaff or sawdust, and stored in a dry attic which is not heated in winter.

To Keep Parsnips.—Parsnips may be left in the ground all winter in temperate climates, or in very severe climates they may be buried in a deep pit in the garden.

Or pull them late in the fall, leave the tips on, and lay them side by side in rows and cover with 6 or 8 inches of coarse straw, leaves, or chaff. Freezing tends to improve their quality.

Salsify.—Like parsnips, salsify is improved by freezing and hence may be preserved in the same manner.

Turnips.—Turnips are not injured by freezing. Hence they may be packed in small crates, boxes, or barrels placed in an outhouse and covered with straw to exclude the light and to prevent their thawing readily. Or they may be buried in trenches or packed in boxes or barrels between layers of fine earth and allowed to freeze.

Beets.—Beets may be stored as for onions, but should be kept in a dry place and at as uniform a temperature as possible. In small quantities they may be stored in any suitable receptacle in sand or dry moss.

Squashes and Pumpkins. — These vegetables are very susceptible to frost and moisture. Hence they should not be placed in cellars or outhouses. Hung by the stem from the ceiling in a warm, dry storeroom the hard-shelled varieties will keep practically all winter.

To Store Tomatoes. — Pack green tomatoes in lath crates and store in a cool, dry storeroom away from the frost.

To Store Potatoes.—Potatoes are usually stored in bins or barrels in a dark cellar. They should not be left in the field any longer than is necessary to dry them after being dug, as they are injured by exposure to direct sunshine. It is advisable to cover the bottom of the bin or barrel with a layer of fine, dry sand, throw over the top a piece of burlap and place a layer of sand on this. They should be examined once or twice a month during the winter, and if they commence to rot should be picked over, care being taken to handle them carefully so as not to bruise them.

To Keep Potatoes from Sprouting. To keep old potatoes not intended for seed from withering and sprouting, place them in a sack or handled basket and lower them into boiling water for a minute or two, moving them about so that the water will reach all parts of the surface. Lay them out on a flat surface to dry thoroughly before storing them away. The boiling water kills the germs.

Potatoes thus treated will continue practically as good as new until new potatoes come in. By this process old potatoes can be held over until the market price is at its height.

Or they can be preserved for domestic use when there are only new potatoes at high prices on the market.

To Store Sweet Potatoes.—Pack in boxes or barrels on a very hot day in summer in clean, dry sand. Take care that the potatoes do not touch one another, and place in a dry storeroom where the temperature will range between 40° and 60° F. Care must be taken not to bruise them, and they must be bone dry when packed. Small quantities procured from dealers in winter may be kept in sand near the kitchen stove, or in any warm, dry place.

To Store Cabbage.—Cabbages are not injured by frost, but wither and wilt in a drying heat. Hence they should be kept in a cool, dark, and moist place, but must not be kept in standing water, as it injures their flavor, or packed together, else they will heat and rot.

Cut them before the severe fall frosts, leaving about 2 inches or more of the stem attached. Let the outside leaves remain on. Tie a strong cord about the stalks, and hang them from the timbers of the ceiling of a cool, dry cellar, heads downward. Several cabbages may be suspended on one cord one above another, and in this way a large number can be stored in an ordinary cellar, just enough space being left among them to admit of a circulation of air.

Or pack in sawdust in large casks or packing cases. Take care to have a layer of several inches of sawdust between the cabbages and the box. Put them in any outhouse and let them freeze. Sawdust being a non-conductor, they will not thaw out until spring, and will not be injured.

Or cabbages may be stored out of doors by loosening the earth about the roots and pulling them up without shaking off the dirt which adheres. Now set them out in furrows, burying the roots just as they grow up to the head in soil. Let the heads touch. Drive posts in the ground, build a shed roof over them of rough boards or poles high enough so that there will be circulation of air between the roof and the cabbages, and cover the roof with corn fodder or straw. Pack straw or meadow hay around the sides to keep out the snow, and let them freeze. They will keep green and fresh all winter.

Sauerkraut. — Sauerkraut consists of sliced cabbage laid down between layers of common salt—at the rate of about one pint of salt to a barrel of cabbage—in a wooden tub or firkin, and with the addition of black pepper, anise, mustard, caraway, or celery seed if desired.

Thoroughly scald the tub, firkin, or cask. Remove the outer leaves of the cabbage and use them to line the cask. Slice the heart of the cabbage fine by means of a slaw cutter or sharp knife. Place a layer of clean leaves on the bottom of the cask. Sprinkle over them a small handful of salt and put in a layer of sliced cabbage about 6 inches in depth, using the outer leaves as a lining to keep the sliced cabbage from the sides of the cask. Sprinkle over the cabbage a small handful of salt, and by means of a wooden beetle or the end of a round stick of hard wood, pound the cabbage until it is a solid mass, or until the juice just makes its appearance, but do not pound or salt the cabbage too much. Now add another layer of cabbage and another handful of salt, and so continue pounding down each layer solidly until the cask is nearly full.

Cover the top over with the loose outer leaves, and lay over these several thicknesses of cheese cloth. Lay on a loose cover of boards and on this a weight of stone equal to 25 or 30 pounds. Let the cask stand in a warm place for three or four weeks, during which it will ferment and give off at first a very disagreeable odor. After forty-eight hours, if brine has not been formed, add a little salt water, about as salt as tears, to cover the cabbage. After two days more, add more salt water, if necessary, until brine forms over the top of the board cover and a scum appears. Remove the cloth cover, taking the brine with it, rinse thoroughly in cold water, wring dry, and return to its place. Continue to do this every few days until it ceases to ferment. This will require four or five weeks. It is then ready for use and may be stored in any cool, dark place.

Sauerkraut is usually made in the fall for winter use, but if it is desired to keep what is left for use in summer, squeeze out the brine through cheese cloth. Select a suitable earthenware jar, sprinkle the bottom with salt and pack the sauerkraut in this. Make a brine by dissolving 1 tablespoonful of salt to a quart of cold water. Bring to a boil over a slow fire removing the scum as it rises. Set aside to cool and pour over the sauerkraut. Lay over the top several thicknesses of cheese cloth, and tie over the jar a piece of cotton batting. This will keep until the hottest days of summer.

Cauliflower. — In a well-drained part of the garden dig a ditch 12 or 15 inches deep and 12 inches wide. Pack the cauliflowers in this with the roots down and cover with earth up to the heads. Fill the trench with hay or straw 6 or 8 inches thick, and weight it down with stone, earth, or boards.

Or pack the cauliflowers on the cellar bottom, burying the roots and stalks in earth. In this way they can be kept until the 1st of March or later.

To Store Green Beans.—Pack down green string beans in glass jars between layers of salt. Seal the jars. When required for use, freshen in clear water for several hours, changing the water frequently.

To Store Green Peas. — Select shelled peas that are full grown but not hard and dry them in a dripping pan in a very slow oven or on the back of the stove. Let them dry slowly, stirring them frequently, and do not have them too thick in the pan. Continue the heat until they are hard and dry as bone. Pack in glass or stone jars. Seal and keep in a dry place. Let soak overnight in cold water before boiling.

To Store Dry Beans.—Dry shelled beans should be stored in a dry, cool place, and will not require protection unless they become infested with bugs. In that case place the beans in a coarse sack or basket and dip them in boiling water for a minute or two. Hang up to drip dry and they will not only be free from insects but will also keep better.

To Store Lima Beans.—Gather lima beans before they ripen, and while they are still tender and green. Spread them on cloths in the sun to dry.

To Dry Peas.—Pick over the peas and remove any pods that are mildewed or spotted. Spread the pods to dry on cloths in the sun.

To Store Peas.—Store shelled peas in any dry place. They will keep unless they become infested with weevils. In that case put them in a tin dripping pan, cover, place in a slow oven and heat until the weevils are killed.

To Dry Corn.—Cut the corn raw from the cob and dry it thoroughly in pans in an oven. This gives a finer flavor than when it is partly boiled.

Or dip green corn on the ear in boiling water, remove, and hang up the ears until dry in a room where there is a free circulation of air.

Or husk and clean the silk from the corn. Place the ears in a colander over a kettle of steaming water, and steam a half hour or more. Split the kernels with a sharp knife, scrape out the pulp and dry it on clean tins or earthenware platters. Care must be taken not to scorch or brown it.

Or husk and clean the corn, shave off the kernels with a sharp knife, scrape the remaining pulp from the cobs, and lay on earthenware platters. Sprinkle ½ teacupful of sugar to each 3 quarts of corn, stir well and place in a medium hot oven for ten minutes, but do not scorch or brown it. Remove and spread to dry in a drying rack or under a hotbed sash. It should be dried as quickly as possible as it deteriorates with exposure. Store in tight jars or boxes in a dry place. When required for use soak it in lukewarm water.

Preserving Green Peas.—Shell and pick over the peas. Cover them with cold water and bring to a boil. Pour them into a sieve or colander to drain. Crush the pea pods in a saucepan or run them through a meat cutter, and pour over them a little of the water in which the peas were boiled. Pack the peas into glass jars. Salt the juice from the pea pods to taste, pour it boiling hot over the peas and seal.

Or shell and pick over the peas, place them in a kettle of cold water and bring to a boil for two or three minutes only. Remove from the boiling water and let them drip dry. Now spread them out on a cloth on a table or other smooth surface. Lay over them another dry cloth to remove all moisture. Pack them in jelly tumblers or fruit jars, and pour over them clarified butter or mutton suet to the depth of an inch. Tie over the top a piece of cotton batting and store in a cool place until required for use.

Or shell and pick over the peas when full grown, but not hard, and dry them in shallow earthenware plates in a slow oven. Stir frequently and let them dry slowly. When they are hard, set them aside to cool and pack them in stone jars covered with cotton batting. Soak in cold water when required for use.

To Dry Pumpkins. — Prepare the ripe fruit, cut into cubes about as large as the rind is thick, discarding the inner pulp and seeds. Cook until soft and squeeze through a colander. Dry in a slow oven with the doors open, on earthenware plates covered to the depth of about an inch. This will require eight or ten hours. Store the sheets in a dry place and soak overnight in milk when required for use.

To Dry Rhubarb. — To dry the stalks of rhubarb, first strip off the outer skin with a sharp knife. This is a painstaking process, but it pays as the rhubarb dries more quickly and thoroughly. Spread on cloths in the sun, preferably under a hotbed sash, and dry as quickly as possible.

To Cure Rhubarb Root.—Pull up the roots from the old rhubarb bed when a new bed has been set out. Brush off the earth with a dry brush, and cut the roots into squares 2 inches long. Take off the skin with a sharp knife. Bore a hole through the middle and run a string through them, knotting it so as to keep each piece of root separate from the others. String these between suitable posts or pegs upon the ground, and expose to the sun to dry. Take them indoors at night or when it rains, as dampness is apt to cause mold.

To Dry Parsley.—To have bright, crisp parsley, pick it in dry weather. Spread it thinly on a platter and bake it in a moderate oven with the doors open, turning frequently. If the oven is not too hot, the leaves will become dry and brittle without losing their green color. Take care that the heat is not sufficient to turn the leaves brown or they will be spoiled. Now rub it to powder between the palms of the hands, pick out the stalks, sift the powder through a coarse sieve, place it in a glass bottle or jar and cork tightly. Keep in a dry place. A peck or more of the parsley should be gathered, as it is reduced very much in bulk by drying. The dry powder is suitable for most purposes for which fresh parsley is employed, and is much more convenient.

To Dry Herbs.—Herbs should be gathered in dry weather, carefully picked over and dried as quickly as possible, either in a slow oven or under a hotbed sash. They should be spread out thin on sheets of blotting paper and turned occasionally. Fresh herbs are, of course, to be preferred, but as they are not obtainable in winter it is necessary to preserve them by drying.

The season at which herbs are best fit to be preserved by drying varies with different species. Orange flowers, elder flowers, parsley and chervil in May, June, and July; burnet and tarragon in June, July, and August; knotted marjoram and mint in July; summer savory, July and August; basil, winter savory, and lemon thyme, the end of July and August.

The aromatic herbs must not be exposed to too great heat, as otherwise the essential oils which give them their flavor will be volatilized. After being dried, the herbs should be screened through a large sieve to remove dust and other impurities, the stems removed, and the leaves stored in glass bottles. All of the above herbs will be found useful condiments in cookery, and several of them have medicinal qualities. These and many others can also be obtained of druggists and other dealers.

To Gather Roots.—Most medicinal and other roots should be gathered in the spring and are, as a rule, better in the fresh than in the dry state. To dry them it is only necessary to brush off the dust with a dry brush, rinse the roots in cold water, string them together and expose them to the heat of the sun or in a slow oven until bone dry.

Lath Boxes for Vegetables and Fruit.—Cut end pieces of inch thick pine stuff 14 inches long and 12 inches deep. Cut laths $17\frac{1}{2}$ inches long which will give two pieces for each lath. Tack these laths to the end pieces to form two sides and the bottom, having the thickness of one lath between every two. Cut holes about $3\frac{1}{2}$ inches long and 1 inch or more deep in the two ends about 3 or 4 inches from the top as handles, and use these boxes for picking up apples, potatoes, onions, and other vegetables, and storing them for winter use.

Packing Fruit. — Carefully pick over the fruit and discard all windfalls, and specked or wormy specimens. For an extra fine quality, wrap each fruit in tissue paper. Pack in clean, dry, flour barrels and pour over the top dry sand or road dust, shaking it down until the barrel is full. Place the barrels in a cellar or other cool place where they will not freeze.

Evaporated Apples. — To dry or evaporate apples, peel and core them and cut across in thin slices. Let the slices fall into cold water to prevent their rusting. When all are sliced, and in readiness, lay the slices on a large piece of cheese cloth and baste them to this by means of a darning needle and suitable cotton thread, taking a stitch through each slice, so that it will lie flat and keep in place. Suspend the cheese cloth out of doors by the four corners to suitable stakes, high enough to be out of the reach of small animals, spread another thickness of cheese cloth over the fruit and expose to direct sunlight. Be sure to take them in before dew falls. When sufficiently dry store them in a dark place. This is the cheapest and most convenient way to dry apples, and the color will be nearly equal to that of the commercial article.

Or thin trays or slats about $\frac{1}{4}$ of an

inch in width may be tacked together, the apples spread on these and covered with cheese cloth to prevent the fruit turning dark.

Storing Nuts. — Pack walnuts in jars, boxes, or casks between layers of fine dry sand. If they have become shriveled, let them stand overnight in skimmed milk or a solution of milk and water. Chestnuts and filberts may also be stored in the same manner.

Almonds. — Buy for domestic use the sweet almond, as the bitter almond contains prussic acid which is a deadly poison. To freshen almonds place them while still in the shells in a colander set in a basin of cold water and bring to a boil. Lift them out, peel them as quickly as possible and drop the kernels into cold water. Never leave almonds in boiling water to cool as it is likely to make them bitter.

To roast almonds for salting or bonbons, put them in an ordinary corn popper and shake them over a brisk fire.

CHAPTER XXVI

CANDIES AND CANDY MAKING

KINDS OF CANDIES—BOILING SIRUP FOR CANDY—THE SEVEN DEGREES—CREAM OR FONDANT—CREAM CANDIES—FRUIT AND NUT CREAMS—BONBONS—TAFFY AND MOLASSES CANDY FOR CANDY PULLS—SIRUP CANDIES—PASTILS OR CANDY DROPS—CANDIED FRUITS, FRUIT AND NUT CANDIES—CARAMELS—KISSES AND MARSHMALLOWS—NOUGATS—POPCORN CANDY—LOZENGES—COUGH CANDIES—TO COLOR AND FLAVOR CANDY—ICES AND ICING—HONEY AND BEESWAX

Candy Making should be taught and acquired as one of the most useful of womanly accomplishments. Like every other art that calls for skill and intelligence, it has an educational value. And the universal fondness for sweets renders the candy maker a popular favorite. Thus the mother who can make good candy and is fond of practicing her skill, or teaches and encourages her daughters to do so, will not only make her home attractive to her own family, but will also acquire an enviable reputation as an entertainer. Then, too, there is a good market in all parts of the country for first class homemade candies. Even in cities where the large confectioners' shops seem capable of supplying every demand, good homemade candies are given preference at the highest prices; while in small towns and rural districts, where cheap candies are the rule, the homemade article, if of good quality, will always find a ready sale. Children may offer a few pounds of homemade candies for sale at a small booth or table placed, in summer weather, on the lawn, and in many localities can thus earn a good many dollars from passers-by. Or after a reputation for the quality of the product has been acquired, orders may be obtained from local merchants or from neighbors. When any considerable amount of candy is made, the best materials will not cost over 15 cents a pound, and prices ranging from 50 cents to $1 a pound are the rule for a high grade domestic article. A candy booth, always providing the contents are of the best quality, is usually one of the most profitable features at church fairs, lawn parties, and other entertainments for the purpose of raising money.

Utensils for Candy Making.—The entire outfit of a professional candy maker can be afforded by anyone. First in order is a suitable surface on which to pour and work fondant and other candies. A flat or shallow box or tray, 3 or 4 inches deep and of any convenient size, lined with tin or zinc, is used by many confectioners. But a marble slab, such as the top of an old-fashioned center table or bureau, is ideal for this purpose. It should be used wrong side up. A couple of candy scrapers or toy hoes like garden hoes are needed to work cream candy. Or have a carpenter make a spatula or flat scoop of hard wood, 12 or 15 inches long, shaped like a snow shovel, but having a very thin beveled edge, as shown in the illustration. This is used to lift and scrape the fondant. A good granite or porcelain double-boiler, a broad, thin-bladed palette knife, a quantity of waxed paper, a two-tined

"The Entire Outfit of a Candy Maker."

fork with which to dip creams and bonbons; these complete the necessary outfit. A good pair of scales, a suitable measuring cup or graduated glass should be at hand in the kitchen. And a small stock of fancy molds or starch prints will be found convenient.

Ingredients for Candy.—These are of three sorts: sugar, fruit, nuts and the like, perfume or flavoring, and coloring matter. As to sugar, that known as Confectioners' XXX is the best and is used by confectioners for the finest grades of uncooked candies. Confectioners' "A" sugar is not as good, but is sometimes used for cooked candies. Pure granulated or loaf sugar properly clarified, forms a satisfactory substitute. But if adulterated sugar is used it will not be possible to get satisfactory results. The ordinary powdered sugar sold by grocers is not usually properly refined, and in many cases is adulterated. If the scum which rises is dirty or if the melted sirup has a brownish or purplish tinge, it is not fit for the finest grades of candy. And even the best granulated sugar or ordinary powdered sugar is not suitable for uncooked candies. Hence, if you expect to make candy for sale or are ambitious to secure the best results, ask your grocer to make a special order for Confectioners' XXX sugar, which can be procured of any large dealer in candy or wholesale grocery house at a slightly higher price than ordinary powdered sugar, and use this for uncooked fondant, icing, and the better grades of creams and bonbons.

White sugar must be used for all light-colored candies. But coffee or dark-brown sugar may be used for caramel, dark-colored nut candies, taffy or molasses candy that is to be pulled; or for any candy that is to be colored in dark shades.

Measurements for Candy. — One pint Confectioners' "A" sugar, Confectioners' XXX or "powdered" sugar equals $\frac{3}{4}$ of a pound.

One teacup or tumbler equals $\frac{1}{2}$ a pound.

One pint of brown sugar equals 14 or 15 ounces; 1 teacup of brown sugar equals about 9 or 10 ounces.

Two tablespoonfuls equal 1 ounce, or 32 tablespoonfuls 1 pound.

These measures are approximate, but are sufficiently accurate for practical purposes.

KINDS OF CANDIES

Among the many sorts of candy turned out by professional confectioners, certain standard makes or kinds may be noted which admit of a general description. One important distinction is between the cooked candies, the basis of which is the clarified sirup boiled to the required degree, and the uncooked candies.

The secret of uncooked candy consists in using Confectioners' XXX or other very finely powdered sugar. Ordinary powdered sugar is not suitable for this purpose, as it will be found if tested between the thumb and finger to have a rough grain, whereas the Confectioners' XXX sugar is as fine as starch. Uncooked candies may be made equal to the finest French cream. They should be allowed to stand twenty-four hours or more before being eaten.

Among the standard sorts of cooked candies are fondant or cream, which may be clarified sirup boiled to the soft-ball degree and creamed by dipping or working with a wooden spoon or paddle, or by beating up Confectioners' XXX sugar with white of egg and water or milk. These fondants are the foundation of chocolate and other cream candies, and many others.

Bonbon is a general name for fancy candies, the heart or center of which may be made of nuts, fruits, or any sort of sweetmeats, and afterwards dipped in melted fondant either of plain white sugar sirup, or sirup containing chocolate, coffee, or other flavoring matter, and tinted with various coloring matters according to taste.

Creams and cream candies are made of simple fondant with the addition of nuts, fruits, or sweetmeats stirred in, or having the fondant poured over them, or otherwise.

Molasses Candy consists of molasses in place of sugar sirup boiled down with or without a mixture of sugar or glucose.

Butter-scotch and Taffy may consist of either molasses or sugar sirup with the addition of butter and flavoring matter.

Pastils or Drop Candy usually consist of simple clarified sirup with a small quantity of water and flavoring extract.

Kisses and Marshmallows are simple sirup beaten up with the white of egg or gum arabic.

Fruit and Nut candies are mixtures of various sweetmeats with simple fondant.

Macaroons and Ratafias consist of almonds beaten up with simple sirup and white of egg.

Pralines or candied almonds are blanched almonds coated by immersion in boiling sirup.

Candied Fruit and other sweetmeats are made by pouring over them the clarified sirup boiled to the feather degree. This is afterwards withdrawn, leaving the sweetmeats coated with sugar in a form which crystallizes after a while.

Caramels are made of hard-baked candy with the addition of various sweetmeats and flavoring extracts.

Degrees for Kinds of Candy.—The following are general rules as to the state or degree of sugar boiling best adapted to the different sorts of candy, but these may be varied more or less by particular recipes which should, of course, be carefully observed.

Ordinary Fondant or French Cream is boiled to the soft ball.

Sugar, Cream, or Molasses Candy for a "candy pull" to the snap or crack.

Taffy and Butter-scotch the same.

Pastils or Drop Candy.—Boil as little as possible; the candy should merely be dissolved.

Kisses, Marshmallows, and Macaroons are not boiled (except French kisses, which are boiled to the thread), but are beaten up with white of egg and browned in a baking oven.

Sirup for Candied Sweetmeats boiled to the feather or flake.

Pralines boiled to the pearl.

Caramels boiled to the caramel or hard-baked degree.

BOILING SIRUP FOR CANDY

To Clarify Sugar.—To make good candy it is first advisable to clarify the sugar by boiling it to a thin sirup with half its own bulk or more of water and the addition of the white of egg, gum arabic, or gelatin. This precaution will cause the impurities to rise in a scum, which may be removed with a skimmer. The resulting clarified sirup is the basis of all high-grade candies.

Similarly to clarify brown or yellow sugar, add white of egg or a solution of gelatin, isinglass, or gum arabic with water, and boil until the impurities rise to the surface. Dissolve 4 cupfuls of sugar in 1 of warm water and add the white of 1 egg beaten up with 1 cupful of cold water. Boil with gentle heat, removing the scum as fast as it appears.

Or dissolve 4 cupfuls of sugar in 1 cupful of warm water; simmer with gentle heat, and add ½ ounce of gum arabic dissolved in a little boiling water. Remove the scum with a skimmer as fast as it appears.

For white sugars, less of the white of egg is required, but the same quantity of water should be used.

To clarify loaf sugar, 1 white of egg to every 6 pounds of sugar is all that will be required. But add, when boiling loaf sugar, 1 tablespoonful of lemon juice or vinegar to prevent it from graining. As the sirup boils, add a little cold water to prevent it boiling over, and skim as the froth subsides. Do this three or four times, and strain the whole through cheese cloth. Add flavoring matter, if desired, after the purified sugar has been removed from the fire.

To Clarify Molasses.—To make a fine grade of molasses candy or to purify molasses so that it may be used in place of sugar for candies, cooking, and other purposes, take equal parts of molasses and water, and ¼ part of coarse broken charcoal; as, 24 pounds of molasses, 24 pounds of water, and 6 pounds of charcoal. Mix and boil for half an hour over a slow fire. Pour into a large flat pan or vat and let stand until the charcoal settles to the bottom. Strain off the clear molasses through a piece of cheese cloth and simmer with gentle heat until the water is all evaporated and the molasses has returned to its proper consistency. Molasses will lose nothing in bulk by this process, as 24 pounds of molasses will give 24 pounds of clarified sirup, from which the finer grades of molasses candy can be made.

To Clarify Maple Sugar. — To weigh, melt, and clarify maple sugar, break up the cakes and add enough water according to the condition of the sugar — whether hard or soft grain—to dissolve. Place over a slow fire and stir while melting. If the sugar was of a soft grain, add 15 pounds of granulated sugar. Or, if a hard grain, add 15 pounds of best light coffee sugar. Boil to a medium ball. Test by pouring a little in a porcelain-lined saucepan until the grain is cloudy. Leave a little of the grained sirup in the saucepan from the last stirring to make the next grain quicker. Pour in buttered molds, or set the kettle into a tub of ice water to cool and harden. But observe that maple sugar thus mixed with cane sugar must not be offered for sale without a statement of the fact that it has been thus treated.

To Boil or to Candy Sugar.—The art of candy making is very ancient, and the process of boiling sugar for candy has been observed and studied for many generations. Thus it has been observed that the clarified sirup, as it gradually loses moisture by evaporation in the course of boiling down, assumes certain stages in which it is best adapted for use in making different kinds of candies. For convenience in preparing recipes these stages have been named and carefully defined, so that with a little attention they may be noted by anyone. When once observed they will always be recognized at a glance, and the process of candy making will become almost as easy for the amateur as it is for the professional confectioner.

Seven different states or degrees are noted, three of which fall into two different stages. These are called respectively (1) the *lisse* or the thread, which may be large or small; (2) the *perle* or pearl, either large or small; (3) the *souffle* or the blow; (4) the *plume* or feather; (5) the *boulet* or ball, large or small; (6) the *cassé* or the crack or snap; and (7) the *caramel* or hard baked.

To Test Sirup.—The method practiced by professional confectioners to test the state or "degree" of boiling sirup is to dip the tip of the forefinger and thumb of the right hand into iced water, then into the boiling sirup, and quickly back into the iced water again. The operation is much like that of testing a hot flatiron with a wet finger. If the test is made quickly enough, the ice water will prevent the hot sirup from burning the fingers. There is, of course, a knack in doing this, but with a little practice it can be readily acquired. The thumb and forefinger are brought together in the iced water, to prevent the sirup from running off, and quickly withdrawn, holding a pinch of sirup between the forefinger and the thumb. By spreading them, the state or degree of the boiling sirup can be ascertained.

Another method of testing, which may perhaps be preferred by the beginner in candy making, is to take out a little of the sirup with a spoon, lower it in a cup of cold water, and let a drop fall from the edge on the tip of the forefinger.

Or, to dip the forefinger and thumb in iced water, take out a little of the hot sirup on a small stick or skewer, and test a drop between the thumb and finger.

Candies that are to be pulled may be tested by pouring a spoonful of sirup into cold water and observing if it is brittle enough to break without bending, like a pipestem, otherwise the boiling must be continued.

THE SEVEN DEGREES

To make the experiment of noting the seven degrees in sugar boiling, crush 1 pound of fine loaf sugar, add 3 gills of water and put it on or boil in a clean saucepan over a sharp fire. Have at hand a bowl full of iced water, a suitable skimmer and if desired a small stick or skewer. Remove the scum as fast as it rises to the surface, and after about 2 minutes by the watch make the first test as above suggested either by dipping the thumb and forefinger, first into the iced water, then into the boiling sugar, and back into the iced water again, or by means of a spoon or skewer. Take great care that the sirup does not boil over, and stir frequently so that it may not burn.

The Lisse or Thread.—If on separating the thumb and forefinger with a pinch of sirup between them, a thin, short thread is formed which quickly snaps, the sugar is in the state known as the "small thread." In a few seconds more, when the thread can be drawn out to double its former length without snapping, its state is known as the "large thread."

The Perle or Pearl.—After another minute or two longer, the sugar in boiling will form small round bubbles or globules that look like large pearls. This state is known as the "small pearl." Soon the pearls will cover the entire surface of the sirup, and this state is known as the "large pearl." In the pearl state a pinch of sirup may be drawn out to the full extension of the finger and thumb without breaking. This is the proper degree for most kinds of candy making.

The Soufflé or Blow.—After another minute or two, dip the skimmer in the sirup and jar it sharply by striking it on the edge of the pan. Blow through the holes, and if the sirup forms small bubbles or globules on the reverse side, the sirup is in the state known as the "blow."

The Plume or Feather.—Again dip in the skimmer, and shake it so as to flirt the sirup from the edges. If it threads and flies from the skimmer in flakes or hangs from the edge in strings it is in the state known as the "feather."

The Boulet or Ball.—Make the next test with the thumb and finger, or by dropping a little sirup into cold water. If it can be rolled between the finger and thumb into a soft, creamy, but not sticky ball, the state is known as the "soft ball." After a few seconds' more boiling, on testing in the same manner, it will be found to be in the state known as the "hard ball."

The Cassé or the Crack or Snap.—The next test is made with the thumb and finger, and if the pinch of sirup is brittle enough to crack or snap, leaving the parts attached to the thumb and finger dry and hard, it is in the state known as the "crack." In this state it does not stick to the teeth, and a spoonful dropped into cold water will be hard and very brittle. This is the state in which candy is ready to be pulled.

The Caramel or Hard Baked.—When the sirup begins to brown, it is in the state known as "caramel" or "hard baked." It will then give off a pungent odor and brown rapidly, when it must be at once removed from the fire, as otherwise it will burn to a black cinder.

In this state, if a little sirup is dropped into cold water it will crackle and snap like glass. Care must always be taken not to allow the fire to burn up against the sides of the saucepan, or the sugar may be burned and discolored.

The above are the definitions of the different degrees in sugar boiling noted by French confectioners, who are considered the best in the world.

By others the distinctions between the little and great thread, the small and great pearl, and the soft and hard ball are less noted; the blow and the feather, or the feather and the ball are often regarded as identical.

Sirup for Candied Sweetmeats.—Boil down clarified sirup to the feather degree, or 35 degrees by a sirup tester. Quickly remove the pan from the fire and set it into a dish of cold water, iced water, if possible, coming up all around the sides so as to cool it as quickly as possible. Lay over the top of the sugar a piece of waxed paper cut to fit the inside of the saucepan. When entirely cold, stir the sirup over the sweetmeats to be candied. A special utensil can be obtained for this purpose, having corrugated tubes at the bottom from which the sirup may be drained off.

Or the sweetmeats may be placed in a small basket strainer and put in the sirup, which may be placed in an earthenware or other round-bottomed vessel slightly larger in size than the strainer. The whole should be covered tightly and placed in a refrigerator, cellar, or the coldest place attainable. A temperature below the freezing point is desirable.

After standing over night, or about eighteen hours in this temperature, the strainer containing sweetmeats should be lifted from the sirup (which should be drained off), and without being removed from the strainer should be placed in a clean vessel and allowed to dry and complete the crystallization.

Sirup for Molds.—To prepare a sirup for lead molds or starch prints, boil together to the soft ball 2 cupfuls of sugar, 1 large tablespoonful of glucose, ½ cupful of water.

Or test by tangling a yard or more of fine wire in a mass of loops, dip this in the sirup, lift and blow through them, when, if the sirup is done, bubbles will be formed and the sirup will be feathery and fly off in flakes. Now pour on a moistened molding board or on a marble slab to cool. When lukewarm, cream with a wooden paddle and set away in an earthenware bowl covered with several folds of wet cloth. Let stand twenty-four hours or more before using. To use this fondant set the required quantity in an earthenware bowl in a double boiler over a dying fire and stir constantly until melted. But do not let the fire burn up or the sirup approach the boiling point, as if it simmers or boils it will grain. At this stage add any desired flavoring or coloring matter.

Sirup for Crystals. — Boil 1½ pounds of sugar with ½ pint of water to the fine thread, for small crystals, or to the great thread for larger crystals. Remove from the fire and let stand until nearly cold. Sprinkle over the top a little water to dissolve the film which gathers on it. Lay the sweetmeats to be crystallized in shallow pie tins inclined at a slight angle, and pour over them sirup from a ladle until they are covered. Lay on the top of the sweetmeats two or three folds of damp cloth, to prevent a crust from forming, and let stand until the sirup crystallizes, which may require several hours. Drain off the sirup, which may be done by laying on top of the cloth another pan of similar size to keep the candies in place, and tilting the vessel to let the sirup escape at the edge. Lay away the candies to dry, leaving the cloth over them, and sprinkling it with water until it is quite damp. The remaining sirup may be preserved and used again for other sweetmeats.

When the candies are dry, hold a cloth tightly to the edges of the pan, turn it upside down on a smooth surface, and the candies will drop out on the cloth. They may then be separated and wrapped in paper or boxed. They must be kept in a cool, dry place.

CREAM OR FONDANT

To prepare fondant or cream, which is the foundation of the justly celebrated French creams and bonbons, the sirup must be removed from the fire at the soft-ball degree, or just before it is ready to produce taffy or hard candy.

The sure way to determine the right state is by means of the sugar thermometer. The "soft ball" occurs at 238 degrees. The beginner who has mastered the art of making good cream or fondant is in possession of the principal secret of professional candy making, and may turn his or her skill to good account by making saleable sweetmeats. There are, of course, many recipes for making fondant both with and without glucose. The latter makes a somewhat cheaper candy, and if it is readily obtainable, of good quality, its use in homemade candy is not objectionable.

To Boil Fondant. — To prepare fondant in general, boil the sirup rapidly over a quick fire to the soft-ball degree. Do not stir the sirup while boiling, as this would cause it to grain. When a drop of the sirup cooled in cold water can be rolled into a soft creamy, but not sticky, ball it is done and should be removed immediately from the fire. If on rubbing a little of the sirup with a wooden spoon against the sides of the pan it seems soft and creamy it should be allowed to stand until lukewarm and then creamed, but if by chance it has been boiled too hard, add a little boiling water, return to the fire, and make a new test.

Cautions on Making Fondant.— Never attempt to make fondant when the air is humid, as in rain or foggy weather, or when there is a high wind. Select a clear day with a cloudless sky and still air or a gentle breeze. Sirup tends to grain in windy weather, and fondant cannot be worked properly in wet weather, since the slightest moisture affects it.

Do not add more moisture to the fondant in the form of flavoring matter or otherwise than is absolutely necessary.

After mixing the sugar and water for fondant, stir until the sugar is thoroughly dissolved, but do not stir after it is placed on the stove to boil, otherwise the fondant will grain and it will be necessary to melt it over again. Do not be discouraged if you do not at first succeed.

If the sirup grains or is too soft, add boiling water, stir until it is dissolved, place it back on the stove and boil as before. This may be done a dozen times if necessary. Thus experiment with your first batch of fondant until you acquire the necessary skill or knack. After that the art of candy making will come more easily.

Oil slightly with pure olive oil the marble slab, or other surface on which you work. But use as little oil as possible.

Do not let the fondant become too cold or hard before commencing to work it. Pour it out on the slab in a rather thin layer so that it will settle in uniform thickness. As soon as it hardens enough on the edges to be lifted and rolled, commence to work from the edges in toward the center of the mass. Do not give the fondant time to harden, but work very briskly, turning the edges in with the scraper or spatula, or working the hoes back and forth until the whole gathers into a solid mass which cannot be readily divided. Then knead with the hands like bread. Work hard until the fondant acquires the proper consistency.

Store fondant in tightly sealed glass fruit jars. Thus it may be kept indefinitely. Or to keep it for a few days only, place in an earthenware bowl and cover with two or three layers of cloths wrung out so as to be moist but not wet.

Let fondant stand twenty-four hours or more before making centers for creams or bonbons and let the centers themselves stand for twenty-four hours or more before dipping. Otherwise they will be melted when dipping into the hot chocolate or other fondant. Again, let the candies stand a day or two to set before they are packed for use or sale.

Do not use more coloring or flavoring matter than is necessary—just enough so that the tint or flavor can be readily distinguished, is a good rule. Do not add flavoring matter to fondant until it has been removed from the fire and is nearly cool. Sprinkle the flavoring over the surface in the process of creaming and it will be thoroughly worked into the mass by kneading.

To Roll Fondant. — Cut off as many pounds of fondant, at least 24 hours old, as you need to make candy. Measure ½ teaspoonful of flavoring extract or less to each pound of candy and add to the flavoring extract 1 drop of the appropriate coloring matter. Roll the fondant out thin on the slab, sprinkle the coloring matter over it and thoroughly incorporate it by kneading, the same as when working over bread. Have ready prepared sheets of waxed paper. And have at hand nuts, fruit, or decorations for the candies you are about to make. Cut the fondant into small pieces and roll into the desired shape with the fingers or palms. If fruit or nuts are to be used, add them at once while the cream is moist. Or if the centers are to be dipped, set them in order on waxed paper and let stand twenty-four hours more to harden.

To Dip Fondant.—If the chocolate for dipping fondants becomes too thick, add to it a little cocoanut oil. This is the natural oil of chocolate, and is, hence, the most appropriate substance with which to thin it. Do not attempt to thin it with hot water, as it will immediately cause the chocolate to grain.

Or use fresh, unsalted butter or olive oil. To dip the centers, use a slender two-tined fork, turn the conical point of the chocolate to the right, downward, dip under in a half circle, remove it point first and hold it upright over the chocolate for a moment or two to drip. Then set it down gently on the waxed paper. Add nuts, fruit, or decorations, if any, while the chocolate is still damp. Dip bonbons in the same manner.

To Cream Fondant. — When the sirup is done set it away from the fire and let it stand until about lukewarm. Now commence to stir with a wooden paddle. Commence to stir round and round, always in the same direction; keep the sirup away from the sides of the kettle so that it will not grain or form in lumps. Presently the edges will commence to show white and dry. The mass must now be laid on a marble slab or a kneading board, which may be dusted with fine flour, cornstarch, or Confectioners' XXX sugar, and kneaded with the hands in the same manner as bread dough until it is of a uniform soft and creamy consistency.

Place the mass of fondant if not required for use in an earthenware bowl and cover it with several folds of a cloth wrung out so as to be moist but not wet. It may thus be kept for a number of days, and will only require to be warmed at the fire or by setting the bowl in a vessel of boiling water or on a hot soapstone, or on two or three common bricks previously heated in the oven, to be ready for immediate use. Any remnant of the fondant which becomes hard and dry, or a batch of fondant which has been cooked too much, may be softened with hot water and reboiled to the proper degree.

Confectioners' Fondant.—The following recipe is that of a professional confectioner, and the full quantities are given for the benefit of dealers in candy, grocers, or persons desiring to make candy in large quantities for sale at a fair, church bazaar, or otherwise. The quantity of candy here described will require a large kneading board or vat with low sides; but any smooth surface, as a clean kitchen table, will answer. As the mass will be too large to be worked with the hands it is better to take a small garden hoe with a short handle, which should, of course, be scoured clean for the purpose.

Boil down 20 pounds of fine granulated sugar with 2½ quarts of water to the stiff ball. Remove from the fire and sprinkle on top 6 pounds of glucose, but do not stir it in. Set back on the fire and let it boil until the scum boils in.

Note that the glucose must not be added until the sugar is boiled to the hard ball, and must not be stirred, but allowed to boil in of itself. Dust the vat or molding board with Confectioners' XXX sugar, pour out the mass on this as soon as the scum has boiled in, and let it cool until you can lay your hand on it. But it is better to begin a little sooner than to let it get too cold. Take two short garden hoes or cream scrapers, work it flat and sprinkle over it rather less than ¼ pint of glycerin. Cream thoroughly with the hoes or scrapers, and let stand over night before using.

When this fondant is first made it will be rather rough and coarse in texture, but standing twelve hours or more will give it a uniform fine texture and it improves with age, never graining or turning stale. If this recipe is carefully followed, a fine quality of cream for chocolate drops, cream candies, and other fondants can be made at a very satisfactory profit.

Fondant without Glucose.—Boil rapidly over a quick fire to the soft-ball degree 6 cupfuls of fine granulated sugar, 2 cupfuls of water, and ¼ teaspoonful of cream of tartar.

Or 3 pounds of granulated sugar, 1 pint of water, and ½ teaspoonful of cream of tartar. The addition of cream of tartar prevents the sirup from graining. Remove from the fire as soon as done, let the mass cool until lukewarm, and proceed as before.

Chocolate Fondant. — Instead of pure melted chocolate, a fondant containing 2 tablespoonfuls of grated chocolate to each pound of cream may be used. Place in a bowl, set in a vessel of hot water, 2 tablespoonfuls of chocolate and when melted add a cupful of clarified sirup and 1 pound of melted fondant. Stir and mix well. In this chocolate fondant dip the hearts or centers of creams or bonbons by transfixing them with a fork or hatpin and dropping them on waxed or buttered paper or sheets of tin to harden. Fruits, as cherries, figs, and the like, are very delicious coated in this way, or mixed nuts dipped and rolled with French cream and thus coated are also excellent.

Bonbon Fondant. — Prepare any ordinary fondant, but cream it with a wooden paddle, and do not knead it as for ordinary fondant. Let it stand twenty-four hours or more in an earthenware bowl covered with several thicknesses of wet cloth. To dip bonbons heat the fondant by setting it on a soapstone or in a pan of hot water over the stove and stirring constantly, but do not allow it to boil. A double boiler may be used for this purpose. Dip the centers by transfixing them with a fork or hatpin, and set them to cool on sheets of waxed paper. This recipe is suitable for all sorts of nuts, fruits, and other sweetmeat centers. The fondant may be tinted or colored as desired.

Uncooked Fondant.—Beat up the white of egg and mix with the same amount of water by bulk in an earthenware bowl. Whip in Confectioners' XXX sugar to a stiff paste, which will stand when molded with the fingers to any desired shape. Flavor and tint as desired. After molding let the pieces stand several hours to harden, but make up no more fondant than is required for immediate use, as it soon hardens. This fondant may be used as centers for chocolate creams, or for nut or fruit sweetmeats in place of any of the cooked fondants as desired.

CREAM CANDIES

Chocolate Creams.—Mold French cream or any of the fondants into cone-shaped balls with the hands or fingers. Let them stand over night on waxed paper or a marble slab, or until they are thoroughly hardened. If they are allowed to stand twenty-four hours or more all the better.

Coating for Chocolate Creams.—Melt a cake of chocolate in a double boiler, but do not let it boil. When melted add a lump of paraffin as big as a small walnut, half as much butter, and a few drops of vanilla.

Or melt in a double boiler a piece of paraffin the size of a hickory nut, a teaspoonful of lard, and add ½ pound of chocolate. Stir until melted. If a thicker coat of chocolate is desired, add to the melted chocolate to thicken it a little glycerin or a few drops of linseed oil.

Do not attempt to thin dipping chocolate with water or else it will immediately grain and harden.

To Coat Chocolate Creams.—Place the pan of melted chocolate in a larger pan of boiling water on a very hot soapstone. This keeps the chocolate melted. Place the creams on waxed paper at the left, and a sheet of waxed paper to receive the coated chocolates at the right. Take up the creams by thrusting them through with a fork or a hatpin, dip them quickly in the chocolate, and slip them off on the waxed paper.

Or, holding the cream on a fork or

"Dip Them Quickly in the Chocolate."

hatpin, pour the melted chocolate over them from a teaspoon. Let the creams stand twenty-four hours or more to harden.

Chocolate-cream Candy.—Melt together in a double boiler ½ ounce of chocolate scraped fine, 3 ounces of powdered loaf sugar, 1 pint of sweet cream. Bring these nearly to a boil but remove before they simmer and beat them up with an egg beater. Let cool, adding the whites of 4 or 5 eggs. Again beat up the whole with an egg beater, remove the froth with a sieve, and serve in glasses decorated with the froth on top.

Or dissolve in 6 glasses of fresh milk 1 ounce of grated chocolate and 3 ounces of white sugar. Beat up the yolks of 3 eggs and stir into these the milk and chocolate, stirring slowly one way. Add a few drops of vanilla boiled with milk. Mix well, place in cups in a pan of water, and boil for an hour. Serve cold.

French Cream.—Place in a clean saucepan 2 cupfuls of white sugar, ½ cupful of hot water. Boil 8 minutes without stirring. When done it should fall in threads from the stirrer, and when rubbed against the side of the pan should be of a creamy consistency. A few drops in cold water should roll into a soft ball between the fingers.

It is better to remove from the fire

too soon than to cook too much, as if necessary it can be returned to the fire and the cooking continued.

When done pour into a bowl and beat with an egg beater. When cool add any desired flavoring matter. This is a fondant which may be molded or cut into any desired shape, tinted and colored as desired, or made into bonbons by molding into various shapes and decorating with almonds or other nuts pressed into the top or side. Place the pan containing the cream in hot water or on a warm soapstone while molding it to prevent its getting too cold.

Or place in a clean saucepan 2 cupfuls of granulated sugar, ½ cupful of milk. Bring to a boil over a slow fire and boil for 5 minutes. Remove and set the saucepan in a pan of cold water. Beat up with an egg beater until it creams. Mold into balls with the hands, and arrange in layers with figs, dates, or nuts between, and cut into squares.

Or mold into any desired shape and place the nuts on top. This is suitable fondant for chocolate creams.

French Cream, with Glucose.— Pour over 2 tablespoonfuls of glucose ¾ cupful of boiling water. Stir in Confectioners' XXX sugar to make a stiff paste. After standing half an hour knead thoroughly with the hands. Color and flavor to taste.

French Vanilla Cream.—Take the whites of any desired number of eggs and an equal quantity of cold water or milk. Stir in Confectioners' XXX sugar to make a stiff paste, tint and flavor to taste. Form in fancy shapes and place on waxed paper to dry. This is suitable fondant for all bonbons and chocolate drops. About 1½ pounds of confectioners' sugar will be required for the white of 1 egg.

Cream Candy.— Boil together to the hard snap 1 pound of white sugar, 1 cupful of water, ½ teaspoonful of cream of tartar, 2 teaspoonfuls of best white vinegar, 2 teaspoonfuls of vanilla, butter the size of an egg. When it hardens on being dropped in water pour into a buttered pan and when nearly cold pull.

Or boil to the hard snap, or about half an hour over a slow fire, 3 pounds of loaf sugar, ½ pint of water, add 1 teaspoonful of fine pickled gum arabic dissolved in 2 tablespoonfuls of boiling water and 1 tablespoonful of vinegar. Boil until it hardens on being dropped in water, remove and flavor as desired. Rub the hands with unsalted butter and pull until the candy is white. Twist or break it, stretch into ribbons, cut to any desired size, and lay on buttered plates or waxed paper to harden.

Maple Creams.—Beat up together with an egg beater or otherwise the white of 1 egg and 1 cup of pure maple sirup. Stir in Confectioners' XXX sugar to make a stiff paste, mold to any desired shape, and coat with chocolate or fondant.

Or boil to the soft-ball state 1 pound of maple sugar with ⅛ teaspoonful of cream of tartar and ½ cup of water. Let stand in the saucepan until nearly cold, and stir until it clouds or becomes creamy. Pour into a shallow tin greased with oil of sweet almonds or unsalted butter to cool. When cold cut to any desired shape.

Or mix grated maple sugar with French cream, and stir in dry confectioners' sugar to make a stiff paste.

Peppermint Creams. — Flavor French cream freely with essence of peppermint and shape into round, flat creams.

Wintergreen Creams. — Flavor French cream freely with wintergreen essence and color pink. Shape into round, flat forms or mold as desired.

Neapolitan Creams. — Divide French cream into a number of parts. Tint and flavor these differently, and arrange on waxed paper or a marble slab in the same fashion as layer cake or marble cake. Roll out the mass with a rolling pin or by pressure with the hand to any desired thickness, and the parts will be found to keep their relative positions. Cut to any desired shape.

FRUIT AND NUT CREAMS

Fruit Creams.—Chop up any desired fruit as citron, currants, figs, or seedless raisins very fine and mix with French cream while the sugar is being stirred in. Roll the mass on a suitable slab with a rolling pin, and cut or mold to any desired shape.

Fig Creams.—Quarter small figs with a sharp knife so as to leave the quarters connected at the stem. Color and flavor French cream or fondant as desired, roll flat, cut into strips of the thickness of the little finger, cut off pieces somewhat shorter than the fig and place one in each fig, closing the quarters about it. Dip the whole in French cream or fondant.

Or cut dry figs in strips and wrap the inner seed side around a piece of fondant. Cut to any desired shape. Chop any desired nut or mixture of nuts very fine, and stir with the sugar into French cream. Mold to fancy shapes and tint or flavor as desired.

Date Creams. — Remove the pits from the dates, split open the end, insert a ball of cream with a clove stuck in the end.

Almond Creams. — Chop the almonds fine and stir with the sugar into French cream, or mold the French cream to fancy shapes and press the almond meat into the side.

English Walnut Creams. — Mold French cream in any desired size and place half an English walnut meat on the top or on either side.

Walnut Creams.—Boil to the hard snap stage 1 cupful of grated chocolate, 1 cupful of brown sugar, 1 cupful of molasses, ½ cupful of sweet milk. When it hardens on being dropped in water stir in butter the size of an egg, 1 cupful of chopped walnuts, or add, in place of milk, pure cream.

Or boil together to the hard snap 4 cupfuls of granulated sugar, 3 tablespoonfuls of glucose, 1 cupful of boiling water. Now add a cupful of cream, ½ cupful of butter, and stir until done; before removing from the fire add 2 cupfuls of finely chopped hickory nuts, stir thoroughly, and pour out to cool. Other nut caramels can be prepared from the same recipe.

BONBONS

To prepare bonbons it is necessary to have suitable lead molds oiled with the oil of sweet almonds, or starch prints of various shapes and sizes. These are filled by means of a suitable funnel with sirup in the state known as the blow.

To test the sugar, dip the skimmer, strike it against the sides of the pan, and blow through the holes. If small bubbles and gleams of light may be seen, it is in the right condition. Add a few drops of any desired flavoring matter, and if coloring matter is desired add the color just as the sugar is taken from the fire. If the bonbons are to be white, let the sugar cool a little, and stir it in the pan until it grains and shines on the surface.

Allow the molds to cool, and let stand two or three days. As soon as the molds are cold remove the bonbons on waxed paper, and let stand two or three days to dry.

Chocolate and Vanilla Cream Bonbons. — Strain through a piece of muslin 1 ounce of fine picked gum arabic, soaked in ½ gill of hot water. Add a few drops essence of vanilla, and stir in as much icing sugar as it will take, working it into a stiff but soft and yielding paste. About 1 pound of sugar will be required. Dissolve 2 ounces of French chocolate with a tablespoonful of water in an oven. Beat up the mixture, and work smooth, and add to it the white of 1 egg beaten as for icing.

Mold suitable drops of vanilla cream fondant; place these on a sheet of waxed paper or plain paper brushed with fine sugar, and let stand until hard. Dip these creams in the chocolate coating in the usual way.

Almond Bonbons. — Mold almond paste into any desired shape, and dip them into melted fondant.

Cocoanut Marshmallow Bonbons. —Cut fresh marshmallows into quarters or any desired shape, dip in melted fondant, roll in grated cocoanut, and set on waxed paper to harden. The fondant may be of various tints and flavors for variety. Use if possible fresh coarsely grated cocoanut, as if too fine it will not adhere well to the fondant. Or desiccated cocoanut may be used, if necessary, but is not equally good.

Cocoanut Maple Bonbons.—Grate fine 1 fresh cocoanut and stir it into a pound of soft maple cream or fondant. Mix the mass with the hands until thoroughly incorporated. Roll and cut out with a small candy cutter, roll into round balls with the palms, let stand to harden slightly, and dip in cream fondant or chocolate as preferred.

Cocoanut Strawberry Bonbons.—To 1 freshly grated cocoanut add about four times as much, by bulk, stiff fondant, mix thoroughly with the hands, and mold into conical shapes the size of strawberries. When dry dip into melted fondant flavored with strawberry and tinted pink. Afterwards roll in red sugar sand.

Maple Bonbons.—Use maple sugar instead of granulated to make a cream or fondant in the usual manner.

Or use part maple sugar and part granulated sugar. Form this fondant, when of a soft and creamy consistency, into any desired shape, let stand to harden, dip in melted cream or fondant, and place on waxed paper to harden.

Jelly Cream Bonbons.—Obtain a starch tray having molds with two sections, one smaller than the other. Cook a suitable quantity of apple jelly to a stiff consistency, and with this by means of a funnel fill one half of the mold. Let cool and fill the remainder of the mold with the melted fondant of the consistency of ordinary cream. A variety of different tints and flavors and molds of different shapes and sizes may be used to produce different effects.

Pineapple Bonbons.—Dip in melted fondant pineapples cut into fancy shapes and place on waxed paper to harden.

Walnut Bonbons.—Mix equal parts of chopped black walnuts with a soft fondant, mold to any desired shape, dip in chocolate, maple or cream fondant and arrange on waxed paper to harden.

TAFFY AND MOLASSES CANDY FOR CANDY PULLS

Taffy is a simple candy, which may be made of either granulated, light- or dark-brown sugar or molasses. Or both sugar and molasses, with the addition of butter and vinegar, lemon juice or other flavoring substance, as desired.

The ingredients may be boiled together, or the butter may be added when the sirup is nearly done. Lemon juice or other flavoring matter should not be added until the boiling is nearly finished, as otherwise the flavor will be partly lost. Taffy is a good candy for children to make, as it is simple and easily handled. It may also be worked into various designs, twisted, braided, formed into horseshoes, baskets, and the like. Two or more strands of different colors may be braided together. Baskets in different shapes may be formed by winding strands around the bottom or outside of cups or other dishes, which should be buttered on the outside, adding a suitable handle and setting the whole away to cool. When cold it may be easily removed.

Candy canes may be rolled and twisted on a sheet of waxed paper; or strips of party-colored taffy may be twisted or braided and cut into sticks with scissors. The work must be done quickly as soon as the candy is cool enough to bear the hands, as after it sets it cannot be worked to advantage. When taffy is poured from the kettle use only the quantity that will run freely. Keep the scrapings by themselves, as if they are added to the candy they may cause it to harden and grain.

Molasses Taffy.—Boil in a buttered kettle for 3 hours over a slow fire, or until the sirup ceases to boil, 1 quart of Porto Rico molasses and ½ pound of light-brown sugar. Stir frequently to prevent burning or boiling over. When nearly done stir in the juice of a large lemon. When it hardens in water pour into buttered pans.

Or boil over a slow fire to the ball 1 quart of Porto Rico molasses and 1 gill of cold water. Now stir in 1 tablespoonful of butter, 1 teaspoonful of brown sugar. Boil until it hardens in water and pour in a buttered pan to cool.

Or boil together 1 cupful of molasses, 1 cupful of sugar, butter the size of an egg, until it will harden in cold water. Cool in a buttered pan.

Everton Taffy.—To make this celebrated taffy extract the juice of a large lemon and grate ½ the rind. Mix 1½ pounds of coffee sugar, 3½ ounces of butter, 1¼ cupfuls of water, and the grated lemon rind. Boil together over a quick fire, stirring constantly until it becomes hard and brittle in cold water. Remove from the fire, stir in the lemon juice and pour in buttered tins to cool.

Buttercups. — Make any desired quantity of taffy and pour out about ¼ inch deep to cool on a smooth buttered surface. Warm a similar quantity of stiff fondant, and work it near the fire until it is creamy and soft. Pull the taffy as soon as it will bear the hands until it is white, stretch it out in broad, flat strips, lay a roll of fondant in the center of each strip, roll the fondant in the taffy and cut the strips crosswise with a sharp scissors to any desired length.

To Pull Candy.—The best way to pull candy is to grease the hands thoroughly with butter to prevent sticking, or they may be covered with flour. The work should commence as soon as the candy is cool enough to bear the hands. Work with the tips of the fingers until it grows cool.

"Pull Smartly."

Continue to pull until it is of a light golden color, or white, according to the recipe. Pull smartly, either by the help of another person or over a hook. Finally, draw out in sticks on waxed paper, or other smooth surface, which may be dusted with flour and cut with shears into sticks.

Pulled Taffy for a Taffy Pull.—Either sugar or molasses taffy may be pulled. For sugar taffy, boil together to the soft ball 3 cupfuls of granulated sugar, ½ cupful of vinegar, ½ cupful of water; now add 1 tablespoonful of butter stirred in quickly, and boil until it hardens and becomes brittle in cold water. Add any flavoring extract desired just before removing from the fire. Pour on a buttered platter to cool, turn in the edges as fast as it cools, and when cold enough to handle pull until white and brittle.

Or for molasses taffy boil to the soft ball 1 quart of New Orleans molasses, 1 tablespoonful of granulated sugar. Now stir in 2 tablespoonfuls of vinegar, ¼ pound of butter, and boil until it becomes hard and brittle in cold water. Just before removing from the fire stir in ¼ teaspoonful of soda dissolved in hot water and pull.

Or boil together to the hard snap 2 cupfuls of brown sugar, 1 cupful of molasses, ½ cupful of water, 1 tablespoonful of vinegar. Just before removing from the fire stir in ½ teaspoonful of soda dissolved in hot water. Test in cold water. Add flavoring matter and pull until the color becomes a rich gold.

To Make Molasses Candy. — The simplest way to make old-fashioned molasses candy for a candy pull is to boil the best Porto Rico molasses over a slow fire until it is done, which will require 2 hours or more. Butter a large saucepan which will hold about four times the quantity of molasses to be used. Stir frequently, especially when nearly done, to keep it from burning or boiling over. To test it, pour a spoonful into cold water; if it is hard, brittle, and snaps like a pipestem without bending, it is done, otherwise the boiling must continue. It is, however, quite customary to mix with molasses about ½ as much brown sugar to make it boil more quickly, and some persons add a little butter or glycerin to make it pull easier. Others stir in ½ teaspoonful of baking soda dissolved in an equal amount of water or a little vinegar when the candy is nearly done to make it more brittle. The flavoring matter, if any, should be added just before the candy is taken from the fire and may be quickly stirred in or merely dropped on the top of the mass. Nuts of all kinds may be stirred into the candy just before removing it from the stove, or they may be placed in the buttered pan and the candy poured over them. The flavoring matter will be worked in when the candy is pulled. When done it should be poured out on a large buttered platter or pan so as to be about ½ inch thick to cool. As the edges cool they should be turned in and as soon as it will bear the hands the pulling should commence.

Or boil together in a buttered saucepan over a slow fire for 2 hours, stirring frequently, 1 quart of molasses and 1½ pounds of light-brown sugar. Now stir in the juice of a large lemon and 12 drops oil of lemon, and continue the heat until the sirup ceases to boil. Test by dropping a little in water, when, if done, it should be crisp and brittle. Pour in a buttered pan to cool.

Or 2 quarts of Porto Rico molasses, 1 pound of brown sugar, the juice of 2 large lemons or a teaspoonful of strong essence of lemon.

Or 2 cupfuls of molasses, 1 cupful of sugar, butter the size of an egg, 1 tablespoonful of glycerin. Test by letting a few drops fall in cold water. If they keep their shape and are brittle it is done, but do not boil too much. Stir in 1 teaspoonful cream of tartar or soda just before removing from the fire.

Butter-scotch. — To make butter-scotch the ingredients may all be boiled together, or the butter and flavoring matter may be added to the sirup after it has boiled about twenty minutes, or when nearly ready to take from the fire. The sirup should boil to the hard-snap stage. To test when it is done, either use the confectioners' test with the fingers, or test by dropping in cold water or on a cold plate, when it will harden if boiled sufficiently.

The following recipes are recommended:

Boil to a hard snap ½ cupful of sugar, ½ cupful of molasses, ¼ cupful of butter, ½ tablespoonful of vinegar, ⅓ teaspoonful of soda, stirring sufficiently to prevent burning.

Flavor to taste, after removing from the fire. Butter a tin and pour out the sirup in a thin layer, which may be checked off in any desired shape when nearly cold with a sharp knife. Wrap in a piece of waxed paper. This is among the best recipes and very easy to make.

Or boil 1 pound of sugar in 1 pint of water to the soft ball, stir in 1 tablespoonful of butter, boil to the hard snap, remove from the fire and flavor to taste.

Boil to the soft ball 2 pounds of light-brown sugar, 2 pints of water. When done it should be crisp and not hard when dropped in water. Now stir in 2 tablespoonfuls of butter, boil to the hard snap, remove and flavor to taste.

Boil to the soft ball 1 pound of "soft A" or "coffee" sugar, 1 teacupful of water, stir in 2 ounces of butter, boil to the hard snap and flavor with lemon juice and oil of lemon or otherwise, as desired.

Or boil about 20 minutes or to the hard-snap stage 1 cupful of brown sugar, ½ cupful of water, 1 teaspoonful of vinegar, and a piece of butter the size of a walnut. When it will harden in water pour out to cool.

SIRUP CANDIES

Sirup candies may be made of any desired flavor by boiling a sirup the same as for molasses candy. Clarify it by adding a little carefully picked gum arabic dissolved in hot water. The impurities which are taken up by the gum rise to the surface and can be removed with the skimmer. Continue to boil and skim until the sirup becomes perfectly clear and is hard and brittle when dropped into cold water. This will require half an hour or more steady boiling over a slow fire. Remove from the fire and as soon as the boiling subsides stir in vanilla, wintergreen, hoarhound, peppermint, rose, or any other flavoring matter as desired. Pour out in buttered tins to cool, and when nearly cold mark into squares or any desired shape with a sharp knife.

The following recipes are recommended:

To 3 pounds of dark-brown sugar add 1½ pints of water and ½ ounce of gum arabic dissolved in a little hot water.

Or boil together 1 quart of sirup, 1 pound of granulated sugar, 1 teaspoonful of butter, 1 tablespoonful of glycerin.

Or 2 pounds of granulated sugar, ⅔ cupful of water, ⅓ cupful of vinegar, butter the size of an egg, 1 tablespoonful of glycerin. Just before taking from the fire stir in 1 level teaspoonful of soda and pour 2 teaspoonfuls of vanilla, wintergreen, or any other flavoring matter over the top. Pull until white and glistening, and cut to any desired shape with sharp scissors.

Maple Sirup Candy.—Boil down any desired quantity of maple sirup until it will harden and crack if dropped into cold water. When it is done, and just before removing from the fire, stir in a teaspoonful of butter for each cupful of sirup. This gives a hard candy.

Or it may be made soft and waxy by less boiling.

Or melt down 2 pounds of maple sugar in rather less than a pint of warm water. Boil until it hardens in cold water, and stir in 3 or 4 tablespoonfuls of pure cider vinegar. In both cases pour in buttered pans to the depth of about ¼ inch to cool.

Twist Candy.—Boil without skimming over a slow fire 1½ pounds of granulated sugar and ½ pint of water, for half an hour. Remove from the fire and as soon as the hands will bear it pull it the same as molasses candy until it is white and glossy. Work it into fancy shapes and cut it to any desired size with a sharp scissors.

Sugar Candy.—Boil together without stirring 2 cupfuls of white coffee sugar, ⅓ cupful of good cider vinegar, and ⅔ cupful of water, until it hardens in cold water. Pour over it any desired flavoring matter, cool on a smooth buttered surface and pull until it is white and glossy, but without twisting. Do not use butter on the hands, but have them clean and dry.

To make nut candy, place the nuts or popcorn in the dish, and pour this fondant over them.

Rock Candy.—A special kettle is required to make fine rock candy. This kettle should be broad and shallow, the width being three or four times the depth. Place in the bottom of the kettle a circular rim of smooth tin about 2 inches high and closely fitting to the inside of the kettle all around. Near the top of this make ten or twelve holes in a circle all around at equal distances from each other, and string across threads from one side to the other on which the candy may crystallize.

Prepare the sirup in a separate vessel, and when it is done pour it into the kettle so that it will reach an inch above the threads. Place the kettle on the stove at a moderate heat and leave it to crystallize, shaking it from time to time. It will require about six days. When the crystals have formed pour off the remaining sirup and dash in a little cold water to clean the crystals from the sediment left in the bottom of the kettle. Remove the rim with the rock candy adhering to the threads, and set it in a clean vessel in a hot oven until it is dry and fit for use.

To prepare the sirup clarify refined granulated sugar, filter and boil until it is ready to crystallize, which will be at 35 degrees on the sirup test.

PASTILS OR CANDY DROPS

Special utensils are required for this purpose—namely, a round-bottom sugar boiler with pointed spout and a large piece of wrought iron or other metal with a hole in the center large enough to receive the bottom of the sugar boiler. The object is to prevent the heat from reaching the sides of the boiler and burning or discoloring the paste. The sugar for drop candy is not boiled but heated or baked, hence only a very small quantity of water is to be used.

As a general rule, 2 ounces of water with the necessary liquid flavoring will take up about 15 ounces of sugar, or 2 ounces of fruit juice or pulp will be required for 15 ounces of sugar without the addition of any other liquid. Small quantities only should be made at a time, to facilitate making the whole into drops before it hardens.

Pound the best quality of lump sugar and sift first through coarse and afterwards through a fine sieve. Place a little over 3¼ ounces of sugar in an earthen vessel and add ½ ounce of water, to which the necessary flavoring matter has been added. If the sirup is too liquid, the drops will not form properly, and if too thick the sirup will not pour easily. Mix the sugar to a stiff paste and place it over a moderate fire. As soon as the sides begin to bubble, showing that the sirup is melting on the bottom, stir it a minute or two in the middle, and the moment it will run remove it from the fire, stirring constantly, and drop pastils the size of large peas in close rows upon a sheet of tin. To cut off the pastils the right size, hold the pan in the left hand and use a curved wire similar in shape to a hairpin.

Let stand for two hours, then hold the sheet over the stove, moving it back and forth to finish drying. But do not have the heat strong enough to remelt the candy, and remove them as soon as they are hard and brilliant, as otherwise they will lose their flavor.

Or pastils may be dropped on a sheet of stiff paper and left two hours to set firmly. Then the paper may be turned over a sieve and the bottom moistened with a soft brush dipped in water. Loosen the drops if necessary with a knife, and let them fall in the sieve. Then move the sieve gently back and forth, over a slow fire, until they are dry. Pastils may be kept in closely stoppered glass bottles or fruit jars to exclude air and moisture. Use the above directions for all of the following recipes:

Peppermint Pastils.—Four drops of essence of peppermint, ½ ounce of water, 3¼ ounces of sugar.

Raspberry Pastils.—Half an ounce of raspberry juice, 3½ ounces of sugar. Or a little less of the raspberry juice may be found sufficient in some cases.

Currant Pastils. — Half an ounce of red currant juice, 4 ounces of sugar.

Rose Pastils. — Four drops of essence of roses, 4 drops of prepared cochineal, ½ ounce of water, 3½ ounces of sugar.

Orange Pastils.—The juice of 2 oranges strained, ½ ounce of orange sugar, 3½ ounces of sugar.

Ginger Pastils. — One teaspoonful Jamaica ginger, ½ ounce of lemon juice, 3½ ounces of sugar.

Clove Pastils.—Four ounces of oil of cloves, ½ ounce of water, ¾ ounce of sugar.

Candy Drops.—In addition to the regular pastils, the following recipes for candy drops are recommended:

Orange Drops.—Extract and strain the juice of 1 orange, grate up the rind, stir in a pinch of tartaric acid and thicken with confectioners' sugar to a stiff paste; roll into balls the size of marbles. These may be coated with chocolate if desired.

Acid Drops. — To 8 ounces of pounded and sifted sugar add 2½ ounces of water. Place in pastil sugar boiler and proceed as for pastil drops. When ready to remove from the fire stir in ¼ ounce of tartaric acid. As soon as this is stirred in form into drops as for pastils.

Cinnamon Drops.—Four drops of oil of cinnamon, ½ ounce of water, 3½ ounces of sifted sugar. Add a few drops of prepared cochineal to color rose pink.

Coffee Pastils. — Extract the strength of 1 ounce of coffee by boiling down in ½ pint of water for 6 minutes, strain and use ½ ounce of this liquid to 3½ ounces of sugar.

Cocoanut Drops.—Beat up 1 pound of fresh grated cocoanut and ½ pound of white sugar with the whites of 6 or more eggs to a stiff froth. There must be sufficient white of egg to moisten the whole. Drop on buttered plates in pieces the size of macaroons.

Currant and Raspberry Paste Drops.—Use 1 pound of currants or raspberries, or equal parts of each, boil and sift the pulp. Add an equal bulk of coarse sifted sugar. Boil down until it will harden in water. Drop on clean tin from a pastil sugar boiler in wafers the size of macaroons. Let sand for 2 hours to dry, and wrap up each piece in waxed paper, or pack between layers of paper and keep in a dry place.

Ginger Drops.—Pound and sift Chinese ginger and stir in ½ ounce of water in quantity according to taste. To this add 3½ ounces of sifted sugar and make into pastils.

Lemon Cream Drops.—Extract and strain the juice of 1 lemon and grate the rind. Stir in a pinch of tartaric acid, thicken with confectioners' sugar to a stiff paste, and form into balls as large as marbles.

CANDIED FRUITS, FRUIT AND NUT CANDIES

To Candy Fruits. — Use for this purpose fine white loaf sugar in any quantity desired. Dip each lump into clear soft water and drop the moistened lumps into a porcelain or other saucepan. Boil to the caramel state, removing the scum as fast as it appears. Remove the saucepan from the fire and place it in a vessel of hot water. As soon as the sirup ceases to boil, dip the fruit to be candied, one by one, into the hot sirup, and place it to dry and harden in a cool place. Almost any kind of ripe fruit may be candied in this manner, as ripe grapes, plums, cherries, sections of orange, lemon, or pineapple, etc.

Or make a sirup of 3½ pounds of granulated sugar and 1 pint of soft water or distilled water by boiling 3 to 5 minutes. Remove from the fire, immerse the fruit, and let stand 2 or 3 hours. Strain off the sirup, which may be used for other candies, and let the fruit stand in front of a baking oven with the door open until the moisture is dried out, when the sugar will crystallize.

Candied Peel.—To candy orange or lemon peel, first soak peel in salt and water 4 or 5 days, changing the water frequently as it becomes bitter. When the bitterness has been removed, rinse them in clear warm water and boil in soft water until they are tender. Make a sirup at the rate of 3 pounds of loaf sugar to a pint of water, stir in the peels and boil to the caramel stage. Put them to drain in a sieve, powder them with Confectioners' XXX sugar, and let them dry on the edge of a cool oven with the door open. Store in a cool place to harden.

Candied Orange Marmalade.—Remove the juice and pulp of sweet Florida or navel oranges, taking care to pick out the seeds and inside skin. For bitter marmalade, boil the rinds at once until they become tender. Or, if the bitterness is not desired, use peels that have been soaked four or five days in advance in salt water, but the pulp must be freshly extracted.

Finally, in either case boil the peel until it is tender. Chop or crush it fine, stir in the pulp and juice, add double the weight of moist loaf sugar and boil over a slow fire to the caramel stage, which will take about half an hour. Preserve in small jars covered with waxed paper.

Fruit Sweetmeats.—Make a clarified sirup of ½ pound of coffee or brown sugar by stirring in the white of an egg and skimming it out as the sirup boils. Stir in 1 pound of sliced fruit, as peaches, pears, or sweet apples, etc., and boil to the thickness of jelly. Or, if desired, place the whole peaches in cold water without peeling them, and bring them to a boil. Remove and dry them on a towel, and immerse them in boiling sirup.

Or dip small fruit, as cherries, raspberries, plums, etc., in white of egg, place them in a sieve, dust with XXX powdered sugar, and shake until well coated.

Orange Straws.—Boil orange peel in soft water in a large saucepan until it is tender, using plenty of water, and changing it frequently as it grows bitter. Place in a sieve to drain, and when cold enough to handle cut into narrow strips with a sharp, thin knife blade. Boil in sirup to the caramel stage and dry in a warm place.

Fig Candy.—Boil to the hard ball over a slow fire 1 pound of graunlated sugar in 1 pint of water. Stir in ½ teaspoonful of vinegar, a lump of butter the size of an English walnut, and pour over split figs previously prepared in a buttered pan.

Date Candy. — Remove the pits from any desired quantity of dates, and lay them in rows side by side in the bottom of a buttered pan about ¼ inch apart. Pour over these a sirup prepared as for fig candy. Let stand until cold. When nearly cold mark between the rows of dates with a sharp knife blade. When the candy is set cut along these lines and wrap the bars in waxed or buttered paper.

Raisin Candy.—Prepare the sirup as for fig and date candy, cover the bottom of a buttered pan with a layer of seeded raisins, pour on this a thin layer of sirup, add more raisins, and so continue until the candy is of any desired thickness. Mark in squares when nearly cold.

Fig Bars.—Boil to the soft thread 4 cupfuls of granulated sugar and 1 cupful of water to which ¼ teaspoonful of cream of tartar has been added. Now stir in a pound of finely chopped figs, boil to the hard thread, take off the fire and sift in a half cupful of powdered sugar. Work the whole with a wooden spoon or paddle to a thick, smooth mass, using additional sugar, if necessary. Pour out on a smooth surface, lay over it a sheet of waxed paper and press down smooth with the bottom of a tin pan or any smooth, hard surface. Melt with gentle heat 1 pound of fondant in an earthenware bowl, set on a hot soapstone or in a pan of boiling water. Flavor to taste. Remove the waxed paper from the fig paste, pour over it a layer of the fondant, let the whole harden, reverse if desired, and pour a layer of fondant on the other side, and when hard cut it into bars and wrap in waxed tissue paper.

Ginger Candy.—Boil over a quick fire 1 pound of granulated sugar with ½ pint of spring water. When dissolved mix a spoonful of finely powdered Chinese ginger with 2 or 3 ounces of the sirup and stir it into the whole. Boil to the blow and at this stage stir in the rind of a large lemon, grated, and continue to stir until a spoonful dropped on a cold plate remains stiff without falling. Remove at once and drop from a pan having a lip or spout, on buttered tins in pieces the size of macaroons.

Fruit Rolls.—Mix seeded raisins, lemons, figs, dates, citron, or any desired sweetmeats, and chop them together. Knead the whole with enough fondant to give consistency to the mass, which should be very rich and nearly all fruit. Roll this on a molding board dusted with flour or confectioners' sugar into a roll ½ inch thick and 1 inch or more in width. Roll out plain white fondant ¼ inch thick and 4 inches in width, and roll up the fruit roll in the plain fondant as a cover. Let stand over night to harden, cut into 4-inch lengths, cover with melted chocolate, and lay on waxed paper to cool.

Jelly Rolls. — Make crab-apple, currant, or any other jelly as stiff as possible, and pour out on a buttered tin pan to the depth of ¼ inch. Roll out on a molding board dusted with Confectioners' XXX sugar, cornstarch, or flour a layer of plain French cream or fondant ¼ inch thick, turn over the pan so that the sheet of jelly will lie upon this, and roll up the two in the same fashion as jelly cake. Let stand to harden, cut into slices.

Fruit Tarts.—Lay ripe small fruit, as raspberries, cherries, plums, and the like, in glass fruit jars and cover each pound of fruit with 6 ounces of powdered loaf sugar. Seal the jar, set it in boiling water up to the neck, and boil for 3 hours. The jars must be kept sealed until required for use.

Fruit Lozenges.—Place any small fruits, as currants, raspberries, cherries, and plums, in glass or earthenware jars set in boiling water. Scald and strain the fruit through a sieve. Add to each pint of juice an equal weight of finely sifted sugar and the white of an egg. Whip the whole to a stiff froth, drop on buttered paper, and place in a slow oven. As soon as they will loosen from the paper turn them and let stand in the oven until quite dry. Cut to any desired shape, pack between waxed papers, and keep in a dry place.

Macaroons. — These popular confections are usually made of sweet or bitter almonds with sugar and the white of eggs, but sometimes with other substances, as nuts, flavoring matter, and the like. To make macaroons blanch and pulverize a pound of almonds, adding a little rose water to form a moist elastic mass. Beat to a stiff froth the whites of 7 eggs, stir in the almonds and a pound of Confectioners' XXX sugar. Drop the macaroons in the desired size on buttered paper from a spoon, and brown on tin plates in a slow baking oven. Set them aside in the pan in which they were baked until cold.

Or pound 4 ounces of blanched sweet almonds with 4 tablespoonfuls of orange flower or rose water. Beat up the whites of 4 eggs to a stiff froth and stir all together with 1 pound of Confectioners' XXX sugar. Brown in a slow oven.

Or to 1 pound of sweet almonds, blanched and bruised with a little water, add 1½ pounds of sugar, the whites of 6 eggs and 2 grated lemon peels. Brown in a slow oven.

Or, for pistachio macaroons, beat

up with the whites of 2 eggs 4 ounces of pounded bitter almonds, 12 ounces of Confectioners' XXX sugar, 6 ounces of shelled pistachio kernels, 1 tablespoonful of orange or vanilla sugar. Brown in a slow oven.

Ratafias.—Scald 4 ounces of Jordan almonds in a colander with boiling water. Remove the skins, rinse with cold water, and dry on a napkin. Prepare also 2 ounces of bitter almonds in the same manner. Place the whole in a sieve and dry thoroughly by moving backward and forward over the fire. Pound the almonds very fine with a little water and whip in the whites of 2 eggs to form a stiff froth. To this add ¾ pound of Confectioners' XXX sugar and work the whole to a firm paste. Drop these on buttered paper in a tin pan, moisten the surface slightly with water and brown lightly in a very slow oven.

Cocoanut Candies.—To make the best quality of cocoanut candy the fresh grated cocoanuts should be used, but where these are not available place the desiccated cocoanut in a sieve or colander and steam a few minutes over a saucepan of boiling water so as to soften the cocoanut slightly before it is stirred in. Prepare a fondant or French cream and stir into the melted fondant ⅓ by bulk of freshly grated or desiccated cocoanut, mixing thoroughly. Roll the mixture into round rolls 1½ or 2 inches in diameter, cut off into pieces of the same length, and roll into balls. Sprinkle these with freshly grated or desiccated cocoanut until well covered, and let stand to harden and cool.

Cocoanut Squares. — Bring to a boil a pound of sugar with ½ cupful of water and stir in a small freshly grated cocoanut. Boil to the hard thread, remove from the fire, add a drop of blue to give a clearer white, and cream with a wooden spoon or paddle against the sides of the saucepan. Pour out in a tin pan dusted with powdered sugar, and when cold cut into blocks with a sharp knife.

Or to ¾ pound of white sugar add ¼ cupful of fresh milk. Bring to a boil and stir in ½ a small cocoanut freshly grated. Boil to the soft ball and pour out in a tin pan dusted with confectioners' sugar. When cold cut into squares.

Nut Loaf Candy.—Boil to the soft ball 1 pint of light coffee sugar with ½ pint of sweet fresh milk or cream and a lump of butter the size of an English walnut. Stir in 1 teacupful of assorted nut meats, and pour into a small cake tin or other mold.

Nut Cups.—Lay a pound of fondant on a warm soapstone or in an earthenware bowl, set in a pan of boiling water. When it is sufficiently warm stir in a cupful of finely chopped hickory-nut meats, which can be assorted or of any single kind desired, and work the whole with a wooden paddle until the fondant becomes soft and warm. Pour on a molding board with Confectioners' XXX sugar, and roll into a strip ½ inch or more in thickness and ½ to 2 inches in width. Lay this aside in a warm place. Meantime boil to a hard crack 2 pounds of granulated sugar, 2 tablespoonfuls of glucose, 1 pint of water, and pour into a tin buttered dish. Pull this taffy over a hook and roll out in a wide, flat sheet, and in this roll up the fondant. Let cool and cut crosswise into small pieces or bars as desired.

Chocolate Walnuts. — Dip half meats of English walnuts in melted sweet chocolate and lay aside on paraffin paper to dry.

Cream Walnuts.—Boil to the medium thread 2 cupfuls of sugar, ⅔ cupful of hot water, 1 tablespoonful of glucose, ⅛ spoonful of cream of tartar. Remove from the fire, beat up until it thickens, stir in chopped walnut meats, and pour into a buttered tin.

Sugared Almonds.—These bonbons are of two sorts: burnt almonds, sometimes called pralines, and sugared almonds, sometimes called dragees. They consist of whole almonds coated with sugar, which is often colored in various delicate tints.

To make burnt almonds, bring to a boil over a moderate fire ½ pound of finely granulated sugar in ¼ pint of water in a round-bottomed vessel, stirring constantly with a wooden spoon until dissolved. Then throw in 1 pound of fine Jordan almonds shelled and sifted, to remove dust and dirt. Stir in the almonds gently in the sirup until they are heard to crackle slightly. Take them off the fire and stir vigorously so that the sugar grains and becomes almost a powder, and each almond has a complete coat. Pick out the almonds, shake them gently in a coarse sieve to remove the loose sugar, and cover them with a folded flannel cloth to keep them warm. Replace the sugar, add ½ pound of Confectioners' XXX sugar and ½ pint of water with a teaspoonful of any desired coloring matter.

Boil to the soft ball, remove from the fire and stir in the almonds as before. Again sift out the loose sugar and repeat the process until the candies are of the desired size.

Or blanch any desired quantity of almonds and fry them to a light-brown color in butter. Roll them in a napkin to remove the excess of butter, and pour over them a sirup of white sugar boiled to a thread, stirring until they are quite cold. This is a celebrated Indian sweetmeat.

To Gloss Burnt Almonds.—Dissolve 2 tablespoonfuls of gum arabic in 4 tablespoonfuls of water in a double boiler. Drop the burnt almonds in this after they have become cold and hardened, stir them gently and turn them out in a sieve. After the gummed water has dripped away shake the sieve gently over a slow fire until they are dry.

Or pour over a little clean white gum shellac sufficient alcohol to cover it, and let stand over night. Pour off the clear solution from the sediment, dilute with alcohol, and apply to the burnt almonds with a brush.

CARAMELS

To make caramels in general boil clarified sugar until it is very brittle or to the point where it begins to gain more or less color and give off an acrid smell. But care must be taken not to burn the sugar or darken it beyond a light-brown shade. Then pour the sirup on an oiled marble slab or tin, let cool until nearly hard, mark in small squares or cut out with a mold and lay away on waxed paper to harden.

If no suitable mold is at hand mark off the slab ¼ inch deep or more with the back of a case knife and sprinkle slightly with powdered sugar to keep the marks open.

Chocolate Caramels.—Boil in a double boiler 1 cupful of grated chocolate, 1 cupful of brown sugar, 1 cupful of molasses, ½ cupful of sweet milk, until it hardens when dropped in cold water. Now stir in a piece of butter as large as an egg and 1 cupful of chopped nuts of any kind, or any desired mixture of nuts. Pour into a buttered tin pan and cut into squares or mold when nearly cold.

Or boil 1 pound of sugar to the hard snap and stir in 4 ounces of grated chocolate dissolved in a tablespoonful of hot water. Boil until the sirup caramels.

Or boil over a hot fire, stirring constantly, 4 ounces of grated chocolate, 1½ pounds of dark-brown sugar, 6 ounces of butter, and ½ teacupful of milk. Remove from the fire as soon as it becomes hard on being dropped in water, and if wanted hard, pour immediately into buttered dishes. Or stir for a few minutes to give a sugary consistency. Flavor after removal from the fire with lemon, orange, or vanilla either in the form of essences or grated lemon or orange peel.

Coffee Caramels.—Boil to the hard snap 1 pound of sugar, stir in black coffee made from 2 ounces of coffee with as little water as possible. Strain through cheese cloth. Continue to boil until the sirup caramels.

Maple Caramels.—Boil together in a double boiler or buttered saucepan ½ cupful of boiling water, 3 cupfuls of pure maple sirup, 2 cupfuls of coffee sugar, 3 tablespoonfuls of glucose, until the sirup threads or hardens in cold water. Then stir in a cupful of pure cream, ½ cupful of butter, and boil until it caramels. When it hardens on dropping in cold water pour out to cool.

Lemon Caramels. — Stir into the boiled sirup at the hard-snap stage the yellow rind of a lemon grated and mixed with a lump of sugar dissolved in lemon juice and water. Stir well until the mixture hardens in water, then pour out to cool.

Strawberry Caramels.—Boil to the hard-snap stage 2 cupfuls of graunlated sugar, 2 tablespoonfuls of glucose, ½ cupful of boiling water, stirring constantly. Now stir in a cupful of cream and butter the size of an egg. Stir well until it hardens in water, pour out to cool, and while hot sprinkle thickly with grated cocoanut. When cold cut to any desired size. Use for this purpose preferably freshly grated cocoanut, but desiccated cocoanut may be used if necessary.

KISSES AND MARSHMALLOWS

These are made of Confectioners' XXX or powdered sugar, stiffened with the white of egg or gum arabic and browned in a baking oven. Baking powder or cream of tartar is sometimes added to make them lighter. To make plain kisses, beat the whites of 4 eggs to a stiff broth and whip in ½ pound of powdered sugar. The harder the mass is beaten the stiffer the candy will be. Lay on wet paper on a piece of hard wood and bake in a moderate oven.

Cocoanut Kisses.—Beat up together the whites of 3 eggs and whip in 2 cupfuls of powdered sugar, 2 cupfuls of freshly grated cocoanut, and 2 teaspoonfuls of baking powder. Brown slightly in a quick oven.

Chocolate Kisses. — Beat up 2 whites of eggs and whip in 2 ounces of grated chocolate, 1 pound of Confectioners' XXX sugar. Bake in a slow oven on wet or buttered paper spread on a piece of hard wood.

French Kisses.—Dissolve 3 cupfuls of granulated sugar in water, using no more water than is necessary, and add a pinch of cream of tartar. Bring to a boil, stir in a freshly grated cocoanut of medium size and boil to the thread. Add a drop or two of blue color and work to a cream with a wooden spoon or paddle. Drop the kisses upon sheets of clean tin from a pan having a lip or spout, cutting them to the size of macaroons with a sharp knife or wire.

Nut Kisses.—Beat up the white of 3 eggs and whip in 30 teaspoonfuls of pulverized sugar, 3 tablespoonfuls of brandy, and 1½ cupfuls of finely chopped nuts. Flavor as desired. Beat all together to a stiff mass and drop on wet or buttered paper the size of large macaroons. Brown in a moderate oven.

Wintergreen Kisses.—Beat up the whites of 3 eggs to a stiff froth and whip in gradually ½ pound of Confectioners' XXX sugar, and flavor with essence of wintergreen to taste. Beat the whole very light, drop on wet or buttered paper, and bake on a piece of hard wood in a moderate oven to a light-brown color.

Psyche's Kisses.—Boil the sugar to the crack, stir in 2 ounces of apple juice while boiling, remove from the fire and stir in gradually about ¼ its bulk of fruit juice, coffee, diluted chocolate, or any kind of liqueur or flavoring matter desired, and set aside to cool. When cool beat up with a wooden paddle, stirring the mass vigorously from the sides and bottom until it becomes soft and elastic. This will be hard work at first, but gradually becomes easier. The longer it is worked the better the kisses will be. Let stand over night and warm with gentle heat 3 or 4 ounces at a time in a sugar boiler with a spout, such as is used for pastils. Stir carefully and avoid burning or overheating. When the mass will pour readily drop from the spout on wet or buttered paper in pieces the size of macaroons.

Marshmallows. — Cover an ounce of carefully picked gum arabic with 4 tablespoonfuls of water, and let stand for an hour. Heat the gum in a double boiler until it is dissolved. Strain through cheese cloth and whip in about 3½ ounces of Confectioners' XXX sugar. Place on a moderate fire and beat for ¾ of an hour, or until it comes to a stiff froth. Remove from the fire, beat 2 or 3 minutes while cooling and stir in ½ teaspoonful of vanilla. Dust a tin pan with cornstarch, pour in the marshmallow, dust cornstarch over the top and set aside to cool. When cold cut into squares with a knife dipped in cornstarch, roll the squares in the starch and pack away in tin or other tight boxes.

NOUGATS

Nougats. — Nougat is made by melting in a copper sugar boiler granulated sugar with the addition of lemon juice at the rate of a dessertspoonful to each pound of sugar and twice the weight of the sugar in almonds or other nuts, as filberts, pistachios, and the like, with a little sweet liqueur. The almonds and other nuts should be blanched, drained, and skinned, and allowed to stand for some hours before being used. They should then be placed just inside the oven door to heat them thoroughly, as they must be hot when put into the sirup. Nougat is used either to line molds or in the form of bars protected by layers of white wafer. For lining molds the nougat should be pressed into the mold with a lemon until the inside is covered, and the edge of the mold should be trimmed with a sharp knife before it hardens, as it will then be brittle and likely to break. The mold should be oiled slightly and the nougat turned out as soon as it hardens.

To Make Ordinary Nougat. — Blanch, drain, and skin 1 pound of almonds, and let stand until thoroughly dry before chopping or shredding them. Place the shredded almonds on a pie plate just inside an open oven door and dissolve in a copper sugar boiler 10 ounces of grannlated sugar, stirring with a wooden spoon until it begins to melt. Stir constantly until the sugar comes to the pearl degree. Now add the almonds and stir them in. Have ready suitable molds oiled thinly with olive oil by means of a camel's-hair brush and pressing small pieces of the nougat into the mold with a piece of lemon until they are well coated. Trim the edge of the mold with a sharp knife. Turn out the nougat as soon as it hardens.

Marseilles Nougat.—Melt 8 ounces of honey and remove the scum with a skimmer as fast as it appears. Boil to the crack degree 8 ounces of granulated sugar, stir in the melted honey and ½ gill of orange-flower water, have ready in an egg bowl the whites of 3 eggs beaten to a stiff froth and pour into the egg bowl in a thin stream the melted honey and sirup, stirring constantly. Place the mixture over a slow fire and continue to stir.

While the paste is baking, which will require about 3 hours' constant attention, test by dropping a spoonful of the paste in cold water. If it is brittle enough to be broken across without bending, it is done. Now stir in the almonds, lay out the white wafer on a molding board, and on this spread the nougat about 1 inch deep. Cover with additional sheets of white wafer, lay a clean piece of white paper on top, and on this place a weight having a smooth surface, as a large weighted pan, to level it up. Let stand to cool and harden. Cut into any desired size, strips or bars, for use.

Parisian Nougats. — Boil to the crack 6 ounces of granulated sugar, stir in 8 ounces of chopped pistachio kernels, a few drops of cochineal, and coloring and flavoring matter as desired. Spread out on a sheet of waxed paper, and while hot cut to any desired shapes and sizes with a sharp knife. This nougat may be dusted with granite sugar and cleaned currants if desired.

Peanut Nougat.—Boil to the crack 1 pound of granulated sugar, and stir in 1 quart of peanuts shelled, screened, and chopped fine, and sprinkled with $\frac{1}{3}$ teaspoonful of salt. Pour out on waxed paper or in a buttered tin and cut into bars for use.

POPCORN CANDY

Popcorn is used as an ingredient of candies in several forms, including the ordinary popcorn balls, popcorn cakes, bars, or nougats, and crystallized popcorn.

Choose for this purpose a quality of popcorn which pops light and tender, and select only the kernels that are fully open, discarding burned or partially opened kernels. Shake the corn in a coarse sieve to free it from dust and chaff. It will be found a great aid in popping corn to swing a wire from a hook in the ceiling having a loop at the right height above the stove through which the handle of the popper can be passed. Thus the popper may be held over an open coal fire with less labor.

To roll popcorn balls, dip the hands into very cold water before forming each ball and work quickly before the candy hardens. To improve the appearance of the balls, and also to prevent them sticking to the fingers, cut out a piece of tissue or waxed paper in circular form by cutting around the edge of a large pie plate, lay the ball on this, bring the edges together and twist them up at the top. Store popcorn balls in a cold place to prevent the popcorn from becoming tough.

To Make Popcorn Balls.—Boil to the thread about $2\frac{1}{2}$ pounds of sugar with $\frac{3}{4}$ pound of glucose and 1 pint of water. Place the popcorn in an earthenware bowl, pour the sirup over it, mix with 2 wooden paddles and form into balls with the wet hands.

Or boil $\frac{1}{3}$ pint of molasses about 12 minutes to the stiff-ball degree. Place 2 quarts of popcorn in a wet earthenware bowl, pour the boiling molasses over it, mix with paddles, and roll with the wet hands.

Or for a better quality of popcorn balls for home use, add to the above a good-sized piece of butter and flavor with lemon extract or otherwise as desired.

Or boil to the hard snap 1 pint of sugar, $\frac{1}{2}$ teaspoonful of butter, 1 tablespoonful of vinegar with about $\frac{1}{4}$ teacupful of soft water. Have ready about 1 peck of freshly popped corn in a wet pan or tub, dip the boiling sirup over it, mix with wooden paddles, roll with the wet hands.

Popcorn Cakes. — Prepare sirup according to any of the above rules, but crush the corn with a rolling-pin. Stir the corn into the kettle when the sirup is at the hard-snap stage, and pour into buttered tins. Lay over the top a piece of buttered or waxed paper, and let stand under pressure to harden. When cold and hard cut into cakes with a thin, sharp knife blade.

Crystallized Popcorn.—Place in an iron kettle or frying pan 1 teacupful of granulated sugar, 1 tablespoonful of butter, or less, 3 tablespoonfuls of water. Boil to the hard snap, stir in 2 or 3 quarts of popcorn and continue stirring until it is entirely dry. This amount of sirup will give a heavy coating of sugar to 2 quarts, or a lighter coat to 3 quarts. A beginner is apt to think that the sirup is not sufficient for the quantity of corn, but with constant stirring it will come out all right. Continue to stir until the corn is dry, but take care that the fire is not hot enough to scorch it. Nuts may be crystallized in a similar way.

LOZENGES

Peppermint Lozenges. — Place 1 ounce of picked gum tragacanth in an earthenware vessel covered with 5 ounces of warm water and let stand over night. Squeeze it through a cheese cloth, pour it out on a marble or other hard, smooth surface, and knead it with the palms of the hands until it becomes white and springy. Knead in gradually enough Confectioners' XXX sugar to make a stiff paste. About 1½ pounds will be required. Hollow the top of the mass, sprinkle over it ½ teaspoonful of essence of peppermint and 2 or 3 drops of strong cobalt blue to make a brilliant white. Knead this in thoroughly, flatten out the mass, sprinkle top and bottom with Confectioners' XXX sugar, and roll out to ⅛ inch or less in thickness. Stamp out the lozenges with a suitable cutter, and place them on sheets of paper dusted with confectioners' sugar to dry and harden.

Or stir together ½ pound of pure starch, 3½ pounds of Confectioners' XXX sugar, and flavor with oil of peppermint. Mix to a stiff paste with dissolved gum arabic. Roll out and cut to any desired shape.

Licorice Lozenges. — Stir up 2 pounds of Confectioners' XXX sugar with 1 pound of pure concentrated extract of licorice, knead to a stiff paste with the aid of a little dissolved gum arabic, and mold or stamp to any desired shape.

Or mix 10 ounces of Confectioners' XXX sugar, 3 ounces of powdered gum tragacanth, with 10 ounces of pure concentrated essence of licorice. Knead to a stiff paste with the aid of a little rose water, and form into drops or lozenges. The refined extract of licorice comes in solid form and after being dried for a few days in a warm place can be easily reduced to powder and mixed with the other ingredients.

Ginger Lozenges.—Place ½ ounce of gum arabic in an earthenware bowl, pour over it 1 gill of hot water, and let stand to cool. Stir to a stiff paste with Confectioners' XXX sugar, of which about 14 ounces will be required, and flavor with ½ spoonful of powdered ginger. Knead to a stiff paste, roll out, and cut or mold to any desired form.

Sweet Almond Lozenges.—Knead together to a stiff paste 1½ pounds of Confectioners' XXX sugar, ½ pound of wheat or cornstarch, 1 pound of powdered blanched almonds. Flavor with essence of orange or lemon if desired.

COUGH CANDIES

Hoarhound Candy.—Boil the hoarhound in a little water until the juice is extracted, and strain through cheese cloth. Boil any desired quantity of sugar with just enough water to dissolve it and stir in the juice. Work the sugar with a spoon against the sides of the pan until it grows thick and creamy. Pour out in a buttered pan. When nearly cold mark into squares and let dry.

Or boil the sugar until candied and stir in dry and powdered hoarhound. Pour out in buttered tins to cool.

Pine-tree Tar Cough Candy.—To 10 pounds of granulated sugar add 3 pints of water. Boil to the hard snap, pour out and while cooling spread on top 10 drops of tar (made by dissolving 1 tablespoonful of tar in 2 tablespoonfuls of alcohol), 1 tablespoonful of oil of capsicum, 1½ tablespoonfuls of oil of wintergreen. Work together with the hands or a wooden paddle until these substances are thoroughly worked in, keeping the mass warm before the fire, or by means of a soapstone. Roll into round sticks and keep rolling until cold.

TO COLOR AND FLAVOR CANDY

Colorings for Candy. — Coloring matter for candies can be purchased in small jars for a few cents each. These are so intense that a drop will tint a pound of candy. Hence they will last a long time. Red, yellow, orange, light green, violet, maraschino, constitute a good assortment. Some knowledge of color is necessary to a tasteful effect. White cream may, of course, be coated with any other color, but colored cream should be coated only with tints or shades of the same color. Otherwise the center will show through and produce an unsatisfactory effect. The center should usually be of a lighter tint than the coating. A good rule when coating bonbons is, after having formed the centers, to set the fondant away for twenty-four hours. Then melt it with a little added coloring matter to give a deeper shade and coat the centers in this. Thus maple cream may be coated with maple fondant, chocolate cream with chocolate fondant, and the like.

It is customary with confectioners to associate certain coloring with certain flavoring. Almond or pistachio cream are usually tinted green. Orange or lemon flavoring are tinted with those colors. Rose is tinted pink. A good way to obtain suggestions for producing tasteful and artistic effects is to study the display in a good candy shop and imitate what you like best.

To Color Confectionery. — Care must, of course, be taken in coloring confectionery not to use aniline dyes, mineral pigments, lakes, or any other substance of a poisonous nature. The animal and vegetable dyestuffs are usually harmless in small quantities, but the following combinations are especially recommended:

To Color Red.—Cover 1 ounce of cochineal with ½ pint of boiling water and boil about 5 minutes. Stir in 1 ounce of cream of tartar, ½ ounce of powdered alum, and continue boiling about 10 minutes. Test by letting a few drops fall on a piece of clean white paper. If the color is not sufficiently clear and bright, boil a little longer. When done, stir in 2 ounces of granulated sugar and put up in a stoppered glass bottle for use.

To Color Blue.—Dissolve a little indigo stone in warm water and test with a few drops on a piece of white paper. Continue to add more indigo until the color is bright and clear.

To Color Yellow.—Dissolve a little gamboge in warm water, or the heart of a yellow lily with warm water, until the bright tint is produced.

Or steep ½ ounce of saffron in soft water for 24 hours or more until the proper tint is obtained.

Or for small quantities, a good pinch of saffron in a spoonful of water may be boiled until the water is nearly evaporated. Squeeze out the juice through cheese cloth. This color is an orange yellow, and a few drops will go a long way.

To Color Green.—Cover fresh spinach leaves with boiling water and let stand two or three minutes, or until the color is as strong as desired. Cork tightly to exclude the air.

Or steep ½ ounce of saffron in soft water for 24 hours and steep separately ¼ ounce of indigo carmine for the same length of time. Mix the two for use. This mixture can be preserved for a considerable time by adding clarified sirup and preserving in a closely stoppered glass vessel.

Or for a larger quantity, wash a peck of fresh green spinach very carefully in several waters to remove all grit, and while dripping wet pound it with a suitable mallet or any piece of hard wood, to a soft pulp. Place this pulp in several thicknesses of cheese cloth and wring out the juice, which may be done by twisting the ends of the cloth by means of short sticks or rods. Place the juice over a gentle fire until it begins to curdle or thicken. Strain off the water through a piece of cheese cloth, leaving the thick part of the spinach juice on the cloth. This is the vegetable green or spinach green for confectioners. Care must be taken in drying substances colored with this material, as if the heat is too strong it is likely to take on a yellowish cast.

To Color Pink.—Use a little carmine moistened with rose water.

Granite Sugar.—Crush by cracking it with a hammer a pound of fine loaf sugar into small lumps. Place these on a hard, smooth surface and break them up fine with a wooden mallet or any smooth piece of hard wood. Shake first through a coarse sieve to remove the lumps, and afterwards through a very fine sieve to remove the powdered sugar. The result will be in grains of intermediate size, like coarse sand or gravel, known by confectioners as granite sugar.

To Color Granite Sugar.—Any of the above coloring matters may be used to tint granite sugar to any desired stage. Pour a few drops of the coloring matter on a plate, spread the sugar over this, and dry on a screen with very moderate heat. While drying, rub the sugar frequently between the hands to prevent the corners sticking together. Preserve in a closely stoppered glass bottle in a warm, dry place for use.

Flavorings for Candy.—Buy only the most expensive grades of flavoring extracts for candies. Every first-class dealer has the better qualities or can obtain them on request. This is important for two reasons: the flavor of the candy will be improved and a few drops only will be required. The less moisture added to fondant the easier it is to work.

Or buy the essential oils of rose, wintergreen, peppermint, cloves, and others, drop them on lump sugar, pulverize the sugar with a rolling-pin and carefully preserve in tightly stoppered bottles until required for use.

To Flavor Sugar.—As a matter of convenience in flavoring candies, it is customary with confectioners to flavor in advance a quantity of loaf or other sugar and have it in readiness to be mixed with sirup to impart any flavoring that may be desired. Flavoring matter should not be added to sirup until the process of boiling is at an end and the sirup is ready to be taken from the fire, otherwise the flavor, which is usually imparted by one of the volatile essential oils, will be evaporated and lost.

To Flavor Orange.—Grate the rind of 1 or more oranges on a suitable quantity of lump sugar and place the whole in a tightly stoppered bottle until the sugar has been thoroughly impregnated and the rind dries and can be readily scraped off. Remove the rind and preserve the sugar for future use.

To Prepare Lemon Sugar.—Grate the rind of 1 or more lemons and prepare in the same manner as orange sugar.

Cinnamon Sugar.—Dry ½ ounce of cinnamon and pulverize with ½ pound of loaf sugar by grinding in a mortar or with a suitable piece of hard wood. Cork tightly and preserve for use.

Clove Sugar.—Pulverize 1 ounce of cloves to ½ pound of loaf sugar and preserve in the same manner as cinnamon sugar.

Ginger Sugar.—Preserve ½ ounce of pulverized ginger in the manner described above for cinnamon sugar.

Vanilla Sugar.—Pulverize 4 sticks of vanilla with ½ pound of loaf sugar and preserve for use.

ICES AND ICING

Icings for Candy and Cake. — Icing, as ordinarily made, consists of powdered sugar beaten up to a stiff froth with white of egg. Gum arabic is frequently used to give additional stiffness. The addition of butter or cream improves the flavor and prevents the icing from drying rapidly or cracking when cut, and various flavoring and coloring matters are added as desired. Icing may be of two sorts, either boiled or uncooked.

Uncooked Icing. — Beat up the whites of any required number of eggs to a stiff froth and whip into them Confectioners' XXX sugar until the icing is of the desired consistency. Generally speaking, the white of 1 egg will make sufficient icing for a small cake or 2 eggs for a large one. And the white of 1 egg will require ¼ pound of sugar, more or less. Some prefer to add the sugar gradually, while the white of egg is being beaten. The addition of a little lemon juice, while beating, will improve the color and flavor. The following recipe is recommended:

Beat up the whites of 2 eggs to a stiff froth, whip in ¾ pound of Confectioners' XXX or powdered sugar, ½ tablespoonful of starch, ⅛ ounce of pulverized gum arabic or less, and 1 teaspoonful of lemon juice. Mix the sugar, starch, and gum arabic together, and sift them into the white of egg. The longer the mixture is whipped or beaten the better the icing will be.

Boiled Icing.—For an ordinary cake, boil a cupful of sugar to the thread. Beat in the white of 1 egg, 1 tablespoonful of cream or 1 teaspoonful of butter. Now stir in, if convenient, 3 or 4 marshmallows and ¼ teaspoonful of cream of tartar. Beat the whole until cold.

To Apply Icing.—To ice the top of a cake, but not the sides, dust the top with a little flour to kill the grease, which prevents the icing from running, brush, blow, or dust off the excess of flour and cut a band of white paper long enough to go around the cake and 1½ inches wide, grease the inside with butter, dust it with flour, and pin it around the cake so that the upper edge will be ½ inch or more above the top. Pour on the frosting evenly, when if thin enough it will settle in a perfectly smooth and even surface. Let stand until it hardens, run a thin-bladed knife between the cake and the paper, and take off the paper.

Or, after dusting the cake with flour, spread the icing with a broad knife blade or thin wooden paddle dipped in iced water, and set it on the edge of an oven to harden, taking care that the oven is not hot enough to brown it.

Or a second coat of fresh icing may be added the following day or after the first layer is hardened. Any ornamentation must be added while the icing is wet, as otherwise it will not adhere.

To Ornament Icing.—For this purpose prepare a special icing by beating slightly the white of 1 egg and stirring in gradually 2 cups of Confectioners' XXX sugar. Add the juice of ½ a lemon and beat the whole until the mixture is stiff and elastic. Now make a paper cone of stiff white writing paper, pinning the side and clipping off the point, so that the icing can come through in a pencil or point of any desired thickness. Small tin cones are provided which may be used for this purpose, but the paper cone will answer. Fill this with the icing ½ or ⅔ full, fold in the top and press on it with the thumbs to force the icing through the small end of the funnel.

Ice the cake as above, let it stand for fifteen or twenty minutes until the icing is "tacky" but not hard, trace the design on the cake lightly with a lead pencil and follow it with the icing forced through the paper funnel. The icing may be flavored and tinted as desired.

Chocolate Icing.—A quick way to make chocolate icing for cake is to place a few good chocolate creams in a saucepan, add a tablespoonful or less of hot water or milk, and place it in a pan of hot water or over the steam of a teakettle until the chocolates are dissolved. Stir thoroughly and apply.

Or add to 1 pint of boiled icing prepared in the usual way 1 ounce of grated chocolates and the yolks of 2 eggs. Mix and apply.

Or beat up the white of an egg in a bowl, dissolve ¼ pound of grated chocolate in 1 cup of milk in a double boiler, stir in a cupful of powdered sugar and 1 teaspoonful of vanilla. Pour the mixture over the white of egg and beat to a stiff froth.

Coffee Icing.—To 1 pint of icing prepared in the usual way add 2 ounces of strong black coffee, ½ ounce of confectioners' sugar, and the yolks of 2 eggs.

HONEY AND BEESWAX

Honey.—Honey is not, as some suppose, produced by bees, but is the sweet material collected from flowers by the honeybee and stored by them as food for themselves and their progeny, hence the aroma and flavor of honey varies with its source, that from white clover or buckwheat usually being regarded as the best. In Turkey and some other countries honey produced by certain plants is poisonous, and that of others is injurions to health. Honey is frequently adulterated with glycerin and glucose, and various imitations of honey can be made of other materials suitably flavored with various essential oils.

Honey is deposited by bees in wax cells known as honeycomb. When pure it consists partly of a sirup of sugar that will not crystallize, and partly of crystallized grains somewhat like grape sugar. The finest quality, called virgin honey, is that which drips freely from the comb. The ordinary quality is obtained by melting the comb and extracting the honey by pressure. It should be noted that if honey is heated in iron or copper utensils it takes on a darker color, hence porcelain, earthenware, or tinware should be employed for this purpose. The proper proportion of water to be added in extracting or purifying honey is equal parts by weight.

To Extract Honey.—First strain the comb through a sieve to free the honey from the wax. Melt it with gentle heat in a double boiler and take off the scum with a skimmer as fast as it appears. Let cool, pour into jars and seal with paraffin, waxed tops, or otherwise, so as to be air-tight.

To Preserve Honey in the Comb.—Set aside for this purpose combs that do not contain pollen, stand them edgewise in earthenware jars or tin cans, and cover them with extracted honey. Cover the tops with paraffin or otherwise to exclude the air.

To Clarify Honey.—Melt down the pure honey in a double boiler of porcelain or earthenware, and strain while hot through a flannel cloth dipped in hot water. This dissolves the crystals and converts the honey into a uniform thick sirup. The test is not as acceptable, but the honey keeps better and is more wholesome.

Or beat up the white of an egg to a stiff froth and whip it into 4 or 5 pounds of honey. Stir in pure water to make a sirup of the consistency of cream, and boil until the white of egg can be removed with a skimmer. Pour out the honey into a milk can or other receptacle having a spigot or faucet at the bottom, and let stand for about a month. Then draw off the clarified honey from the spigot.

Or melt down the honey in a double boiler with clear water to a sirup of the consistency of cream, and stir in 6 ounces of purified animal charcoal to 8 pounds of honey. Simmer with gentle heat for 20 minutes. If the sirup is sour, stir in a little prepared chalk to sweeten it, strain through a flannel cloth dipped in hot water, and let stand over a slow fire until the excess of water it contains is removed by evaporation.

Or dissolve the honey with water in a double boiler, and let it boil up briskly, stirring four or five times at intervals, but not skimming. Remove from the fire, let cool and pour on cloth strainers covered with an inch or more of fresh white sand. After the honey has run through, pour on gradually clear water, to rinse the strainer, and finally with gentle heat evaporate the excess of water from the honey.

Or to clarify on a large scale, mix 9 large fresh eggs with 2½ gallons of water for each half barrel of honey, in a tin-lined vat. Simmer with gentle heat, skim and filter through strong linen strainers covered with about 1 inch of clear white sand. Afterwards evaporate the excess of water with gentle heat.

To Make Artificial Honey.—The cost of pure honey is so great that various artificial preparations are manufactured, and these may be put up if desired for home use in place of honey and maple sirup at less expense.

Dissolve in 1 pint of boiling water ⅛ ounce of alum. Remove from the fire, stir in 4 pounds of granulated sugar, bring to a boil and stir until dissolved. Remove quickly, strain through cheese cloth, and when nearly cool stir in 1 teaspoonful of artificial honey-flavoring extract composed as follows:

To ½ pint of 98 per cent alcohol add ½ ounce of Jamaica ginger, 3 drops of attar of roses and shake well before using. This extract must be prepared in small quantities only as required for use. This was formerly closely guarded as a trade secret, and a great deal of artificial honey made from this recipe has been placed upon the market.

Or to make so-called French honey, break into a bowl 4 large fresh eggs and add the yolks of 2 more. Stir in 1 pound of granulated sugar, add the juice of 4 lemons and the grated rind of 2, and stir in ¼ pound of butter. Melt over a slow fire to the consistency of honey.

In addition to the above are numerous recipes for diluting or adulterating pure honey with sugar sirup and various flavoring substances.

Dissolve 8 pounds of white sugar in 2 quarts of water, boil 4 minutes, stir in 1 pound of pure honey and while hot strain through a flannel cloth dipped in hot water. When nearly cool add 1 or 2 drops of oil of peppermint and a drop of attar of roses.

A standard recipe consists of a mixture of 5 pounds of clear light-brown or coffee sugar, 1¼ pounds of bee-bred honey, 1½ pounds of soft water, 20 grains of pure cream of tartar, 1½ ounces of gum arabic. Boil these ingredients in a porcelain or tinware utensil for 5 minutes. Then add an infusion of 1 teaspoonful of pulverized slippery elm bark in 8 ounces of water, straining it into the mixture through a piece of cheese cloth.

Now stir in the whites of 2 eggs beaten to a stiff froth, boil 2 minutes, remove the white of egg with a skimmer as it rises, remove and when lukewarm flavor with 1 drop of attar of roses, 6 drops of oil of peppermint, and add ½ pound or more of pure honey. This is an old standard recipe that perhaps can hardly be improved upon. The decoction of slippery elm should, however, be omitted in warm weather, as otherwise it will ferment and cause a scum on the surface. The larger the quantity of pure honey the better will be the flavor and value of the product.

Or 1 pound of honey will impart its natural flavor to about double the weight of pure white sugar, thus making a useful sirup for domestic purposes, nearly equal in value to the pure honey, and less likely to disagree with those who are unable to use the pure article. To make this sirup dissolve 2 pounds of pure granulated sugar in about 12 or 15 ounces of boiling water, and add 1 ounce of gum arabic dissolved in a little boiling water, or the white of 1 egg. Bring to a boil and remove the scum with a skimmer as it appears. Remove this clarified sugar sirup from the fire and stir in 8 ounces of pure bee honey. When partially cool, stir in 4 ounces more, and when lukewarm stir in the remaining 4 ounces, making 1 pound all told. Flavor when nearly cold with a few drops of essence of peppermint and a drop or two of attar of roses. The quality can be improved by the use of a little less water and the addition of a somewhat larger proportion of honey.

To Prepare Beeswax.—To prepare beeswax melt the honeycomb in boiling water. Let cool, when the wax will form a cake on the surface. Remove the cake, scrape off any impurities from the bottom, and repeat if necessary.

To Refine Beeswax.—Add about 5 per cent water to crude beeswax and melt with gentle heat. Raise to a boil, let boil for a few minutes, and add about 1 per cent concentrated nitric acid. Use for this purpose an earthenware vessel set in boiling water, and continue to boil until the fumes of the acid cease to be evolved.

Or when the melted wax has boiled for a few minutes scatter 5 or 6 per cent of sulphuric acid over the surface of the melted wax. It must be done with care. If the vessel is not sufficiently deep the wax will froth up and run over the sides. After adding the acid cover the mixture, remove it from the fire, and before it is quite cool skim it off with a heated ladle. Take care not to disturb the sediment. Scrape the impurities from the inside of the cake. Remelt and strain through cheese cloth. The addition of a little annotto will improve the color of the wax.

To Whiten Beeswax.—Melt up the wax with gentle heat and dip into it thin hard-wood boards, plates, or any suitable flat articles previously dipped in water to prevent the wax sticking. When these are removed they will be covered with a thin plate of wax. Loosen this film of wax with a knife and strip it off. Spread these thin sheets upon a white cloth upon the grass and expose them to the sun and air to bleach. Afterwards remelt and form into cakes.

Or melt the wax with hot water and squeeze through a fine linen cloth. Pour in shallow molds and when hard expose to the air, sprinkling frequently with water and turning from time to time until quite white.

To Color Beeswax.—To color beeswax, add bright palm oil. Or as a sufficient quantity of palm oil to color adulterates the wax, color with annotto in the proportion of about 4 ounces to 100 pounds of wax, according to the color required. Shave the annotto in 3 to 4 quarts of soft water, to which add about 1 pound of wax, let boil until the water is evaporated and the wax is of a deep-orange color. Melt the remainder of the wax, and stir in the colored wax until the proper shade is produced. Test from time to time by cooling a little on a glass plate.

Bottle Wax.—To make wax for sealing corked bottles and similar purposes, melt together 6½ ounces of black rosin, ½ ounce of beeswax, and 1½ ounces of fine ivory black.

Or for red wax, substitute 1½ ounces of Venetian red or red lead for the ivory black.

Or mix 1 pound of beeswax, 1 pound of rosin, ½ pound of tallow. Color with red or yellow ocher or other coloring matter. Melt and stir together.

Or for white wax, substitute bleached wax for beeswax and color with Spanish white.

To Test Adulterated Wax.—Beeswax is sometimes adulterated with spermaceti or Japanese wax. To test for Japanese wax, cover a sample with concentrated solution of borax and bring it to a boil. Beeswax is insoluble in this solution, but Japanese wax dissolves and forms on cooling a milky-white sticky coating.

Imitation of Beeswax.—Melt together 14 pounds of yellow rosin, 7 pounds of suet, 1 pound of turmeric, 2 pounds of potato flour and mix and form into cakes before it cools. If the color is too bright, add a little ivory black. Rub each cake when cold with flour.

Or 8 pounds of yellow rosin, 4 pounds of pure mutton tallow or stearin, and 1½ pounds of palm oil.

Or substitute ½ pound of turmeric in place of palm oil.

Or place 1 ounce of pure annotto in 1 quart of water. Bring to a boil, stir in 5 pounds of mutton suet or stearin, 10 pounds of yellow rosin, stir and boil until well mixed and colored. Pour into molds to cool. Dust the cakes when cold with cornstarch.

CHAPTER XXVII

WEIGHTS AND MEASURES

WEIGHTS AND MEASURES—LINEAR OR LONG MEASURE—SQUARE OR SUPERFICIAL MEASURE—SURVEYORS' AND LAND MEASURE—CUBIC OR CAPACITY MEASURE—WOOD, LUMBER AND BOARD MEASURE—MEASUREMENT OF STONE AND BRICK—DRY AND LIQUID MEASURE—MEASURES OF WEIGHT—COOKS' TABLE OF PROPORTIONS—CIRCULAR MEASURE—LONGITUDE AND TIME—MEASURES OF VALUE—UNITED STATES MONEY—ENGLISH OR STERLING MONEY—METRIC SYSTEM OF WEIGHTS AND MEASURES.

WEIGHTS AND MEASURES

There are four principal classes of weights and measures, namely: Measures of Length, of Surface, of Volume, and of Weight. In addition to these are measures of value as applied to money and coinage—measurement of time, temperature, and others. The principle underlying the use of weights and measures is that of reference to an agreed unit as standard. Some distinct means of determining quantity is essential to the most primitive forms of human society. Hence, the use of weights and measures is very ancient. As the applications of this principle have increased in number and importance with advancing civilization, a great variety of different units as standards of measurement, adapted to different purposes, have been introduced. The result is a great degree of confusion in the common mind on this subject which entails enormous loss and expense in all commercial business. An attempt has been made by scientific men to remedy this condition by the introduction of the metric system, but thus far this system has not come into general use in the English-speaking world.

At present the units in general use in the United States are as follows: of measures of length, the unit for carpentry and mechanics is the foot. This is subdivided into inches and lines, or inches, halves, quarters, and so on. The unit for textile fabrics is the yard divided into quarters and nails. For field surveying, the chain divided into links and decimals. For road measure, the mile divided into furlongs and rods. The units of square or superficial measure are the squares of these with the addition as a unit for land measure of the acre. Of capacity measures, the units for liquids are the gallon, quart, pint, and gill. For cereals and other dry substances, the bushel and peck. For fire wood, the cord. The unit of weight for ordinary commerce is the avoirdupois pound, divided into halves, quarters, and so on; or, for large masses, into the quarter, hundred, and ton. The unit for bullion, plate, and coin, or jewelers' measure, is the pound troy which is irregularly divided. The unit for drugs and medicines, or apothecaries' measure, is a pound equal to the pound troy but differently subdivided. Jewelers also make use of a unit for the measurement of gems called the carat.

Origin of Standards.—The derivation of the original units of linear measurement appears to have been from comparison with various parts of the human body. The use of the foot seems to have originated in

Greece, the standard, according to tradition, having been taken from the foot of Hercules. The natural mode of measuring various distances by counting one's steps, which is still occasionally made use of for rough measures, early gave rise to the pace as a unit or standard. Hence, the Roman *mille passuum*, 1,000 paces, from which has been derived the mile of the present day. The ancient cubit is taken from the length of the forearm. This is still a standard of measurement in many Eastern countries.[1] The ell, a term used in Europe down to our own time for cloth measure, is also derived from the forearm. The English yard, from an old English term meaning to gird, signifies the girdle or circumference of the body. The fathom is from an old English word meaning to embrace and signifies the length of two arms. The breadth of the hand or palm is still used as a standard in the measurement of the height of horses. The nail and the thumb's breadth have also been frequently made use of.

Measurements of weight were a much later introduction. The wheat-corn or grain of wheat, required by law to be taken from the middle of the ear, was used in England as a standard of weight until within modern times. With the introduction of modern science, the length of a pendulum measuring seconds under certain prescribed conditions has been taken as a linear standard. And the weight of a prescribed quantity of water under certain conditions has been taken as a standard of weight. The standard of solid measure has also been similarly determined.

The unit of the metric system is the meter, intended to be one ten millionth of the distance from the equator to the pole. This unit has been agreed upon as a standard by the principal European nations and has been accepted by Great Britain and the United States, although its use is not compulsory in either of those countries. The standard units employed by the United States Government at Washington are themselves corrected by reference to the international meter. Hence, the metric system is actually the ultimate standard in the United States. It is to be very much regretted that the use of the metric system has not become universal. At present, it is employed by somewhat more than half the population of the civilized world.

[1] Among the Israelites the cubit was divided into two spans, the spans into three palms, the palms into four digits, the order of nature being adhered to throughout.

LINEAR OR LONG MEASURE

Linear Measure.—The standard of linear, or long measure, is the length of a pendulum that will vibrate in a vacuum, at the sea level in London, at 62° F., once in a second. Scientists have determined that such a pendulum is nearly 39.1393 inches in length; $\frac{36}{39}$ of this is taken as a standard yard. The standard yard of the United States is a metal bar kept at Washington. It is identical with the English imperial yard. Subdivisions and multiples of this are shown in the following table:

12	inches	1 foot.
3	feet	1 yard.
$5\frac{1}{2}$	yards	1 rod, pole, or perch.
40	poles	1 furlong.
8	furlongs	1 mile.
320	rods	1 mile.
1760	yards	1 mile.
5280	feet	1 mile.
3	miles	1 league.
$69\frac{1}{15}$	miles	1 degree of a great circle of the earth

The mile is commonly divided into halves, fourths, eighths, etc. The furlong ($\frac{1}{8}$ of a mile) is seldom used.

A league is 3 miles, but its length is variable, for it is, strictly speaking, a nautical term, and should be 3 geographical miles, equal to 3.45 statute miles; but when used on land, 3 statute miles are said to be a league.

The length of a degree of latitude varies; 69.16 miles is the average length, and is that adopted by the United States Coast Survey.

Less Common Linear Measures.—Additional linear measures less commonly used are the following:

48	hair's breadths	1 inch.
3	barley corns	1 inch.
3	inches	1 palm.
4	inches	1 hand.
18	inches	1 English cubit.
21.888	inches	1 Bible cubit.
$2\frac{1}{2}$	feet	1 military pace.
3	feet	1 common pace.
3.28	feet	1 meter.
11	feet	1 great cubit.

In biblical and other old measurements, the term span is sometimes used, which is a length of 9 inches.

The sacred cubit of the Jews was 24.024 inches in length.

The common cubit of the Jews was 21.704 inches in length.

Horses are measured directly over the forefeet, and the standard of measure is 4 inches—called a hand.

Subdivisions of the Inch.—Tool cutters and other machinists engaged in fine metal work, scientists, revenue officers, and some others, divide the inch decimally, i. e., into tenths, hundredths, etc. Carpenters and mechanics engaged in rough work divide the inch into eighths or sixteenths.

The former custom of dividing the inch into twelve parts, called lines, has gone out of use.

Following are equivalents of the decimal parts of a foot in inches:

Decimal value in feet.	Fractions of a foot in inches.	Decimal value in feet.	Fractions of a foot in inches.
.01041	$\frac{1}{8}$	.25	3
.02083	$\frac{1}{4}$	.3333	4
.03125	$\frac{3}{8}$	.4166	5
.04166	$\frac{1}{2}$	.5	6
.05208	$\frac{5}{8}$	.5833	7
.0625	$\frac{3}{4}$	.6666	8
.07291	$\frac{7}{8}$	.75	9
.0833	1	.8333	10
.1666	2	.9166	11

Nautical Measure.—In addition to the above a distinct table of measurements is used by geographers and mariners as follows:

6	feet	1 fathom.
110	fathoms, or 660 feet	1 furlong.
120	fathoms	1 cable's length.
6086.7	feet	1 nautical mile.
3	nautical miles	1 league.
20	lea., or 60 naut. miles	1 degree.
360	degrees	The earth's circumference = $24,855\frac{1}{2}$ miles nearly.

The nautical mile is also called the geographical mile or for brevity the knot. It is $795\frac{4}{5}$ feet longer than the common mile.

Cloth Measure.—Another mode of measurement formerly much used by merchants on the continent of Europe and in colonial times in this country is as follows:

$2\frac{1}{4}$	inches	1 nail.
4	nails	1 quarter of a yd.
4	quarters	1 yard.
1	aunze	$1\frac{1}{2}$ yard.

Foreign Cloth Measure

$2\frac{1}{2}$	quarters	1 ell Hamburg.
3	quarters	1 ell Flemish.
5	quarters	1 ell English.
6	quarters	1 ell French.
$4\frac{1}{18}$	quarters	1 ell Scotch.

An Amsterdam ell is equal to 26.796 inches.
A Trieste ell is equal to 25.284 inches.
A Brabant ell is equal to 27.116 inches.

In measuring cloth, ribbon, etc., the width is not considered, and the yard is now usually divided into halves, fourths, eighths, and sixteenths. In the United States custom house the yard is divided into tenths and hundredths.

Scales for Linear Measure.—The many occasions that a standard of linear measure is required suggest the utility of having always at hand a scale from which a yardstick or other measure can be constructed. Carpenters, mechanics, and farmers frequently make it a practice to carry a jointed yardstick in the pocket. It is convenient to glue a yard measure on the edge of a carpenter's bench or a sewing table, or to indicate the division into inches or fractions of an inch by means of small brass brads driven in flush with the surface and rubbed to a polish with emery paper. Sailors not infrequently tattoo a yard measure on the outer side of the left arm beginning at the point of the little finger, the subdivisions being pricked into the skin in India ink. This device will be found useful to farmers, mechanics, and others. Builders, paper hangers, and others, engaged in the building trades, find a narrow steel measure, a rod or more in length, winding up in a suitable circular case by means of a spring or crank, a very convenient contrivance.

SQUARE OR SUPERFICIAL MEASURE

Square Measure.—Square or superficial measure is employed by carpenters, masons, and others, in the building trades, in house furnishing and decoration, and notably in surveying and the measurement of land.

The ordinary square measure for carpenters, masons, and others is as follows:

144	sq. inches	1 sq. foot.
9	sq. feet, or 1,296 sq. inches	1 sq. yard.
100	sq. feet	1 sq. of flooring, roofing, etc.
36	sq. yards	1 rood of building

Carpenters, architects, and mechanics often write 8″ for 8 inches, and 5′ for 5 feet. They also use sq.″ and sq.′ for square inches and square feet.

Plastering, ceiling, etc., are commonly estimated by the square yard; paving, glazing, and stone cutting by the square foot; roofing, flooring, and slating by the square 100 feet.

Cost of Lathing.—Laths are 4 feet long, 1½ inches wide, and are laid ⅜ inch apart at the sides, and close together at the ends. A bunch of lath contains 100 pieces, and is estimated to cover 5 square yards of surface.

Cost of Clapboarding and Shingling.—Clapboards are usually cut 4 feet long and 6 inches wide, and are put up in bundles of twenty-five each.

Shingles are estimated at 9 shingles, laid 4 inches to the weather, to the square foot. Allowing for waste and defects, 1,000 shingles are estimated to cover 100 square feet, called a square. In practice, 1,000 shingles of the best quality will cover 125 square feet.

Or to find the number of shingles required in a roof: multiply the number of square feet in the roof by 9 if the shingles are exposed 4 inches, by 8 if exposed 4½ inches, or by 7⅕ if exposed 5 inches.

To find the number of square feet, multiply the length of the roof by twice the length of the rafters.

To find the length of the rafters at ¼ pitch, multiply the width of the building by .56 (hundredths); at ⅓ pitch by .6 (tenths); at ⅖ pitch by .64 (hundredths); at ½ pitch by .71 (hundredths). This gives the length of the rafters from the apex to the end of the wall, and whatever they are to project must be taken into consideration.

By ¼ or ⅓ pitch is meant that the apex or comb of the roof is to be ¼ to ⅓ the width of the building higher than the walls or base of the rafters.

Measurement of Wall Surfaces.—A common application of square measure in the household is in estimating material and labor for the treatment of wall surfaces by paper hanging, plastering, painting, or calcimining. All of these are usually computed by the square yard.

Wall paper is sold by the roll, which is usually 18 inches wide and 8 yards in length. Or in double rolls of the same width, 16 yards long. These are counted as 2 rolls each. They economize waste in cutting.

These are the dimensions of most wall papers made in America, and may be taken for granted unless otherwise specified. Imported papers differ as to the length and width of the roll.

Borders or friezes are sold by the yard. They vary in width from 3 inches upward.

Cost of Hanging Wall Paper.—It is not possible, as a rule, to find in advance the exact cost of papering a room. The measurement of the room will, however, assist in making an estimate of the number of rolls required. The actual number to be paid for can be determined only after the papering has been done. Then all rolls that have been cut must be paid for, the uncut rolls being, as a rule, allowed to be returned.

When estimating the number of rolls of paper required for papering a room of ordinary height (i. e., if the distance from the baseboard to the border is not more than 8 feet), first measure around the room, leaving out the widths of the doors and windows; then allow one double roll or two single rolls for every 7 feet.

Or by another method, measure around the room in yards. The number of strips required will be just about double the number of yards. Find how many strips can be cut from a roll and divide the number of strips required to go around the room by the number that can be cut from a roll. The result will be the number of rolls.

Cost of Plastering, Papering, and Calcimining. — These are measured by the square yard. Allowances are sometimes made either in whole or part for the area of openings, for baseboards, and the like. But there is no uniform rule respecting these allowances. Custom varies so greatly that it is better to make a written contract to govern the final settlement. The surfaces of the walls of a room may be found by multiplying the sum of the lengths of the four sides changed to square units by the height.

Cost of Carpeting Rooms.—Carpeting and matting is in various widths, commonly 1 yard or ¾ of a yard in width, and is sold by the yard. Oilcloth and linoleum come in various widths and are sold by the square yard.

The number of yards of carpeting required for a room depends on the size of the room, the directions in which the strips run, and the loss caused by matching the figures. Hence it is necessary to decide first whether the strips shall run lengthwise or across the room; next, how much will be wasted in matching the pattern; and finally the number of strips required. The number of yards in a strip, including the waste in matching the pattern, multiplied by the number of strips, will give the number of yards required. In large carpet stores, loss in matching the figures is sometimes avoided by cutting strips from different rolls. Waste may also occur from turning under carpets that are too wide, and from borders. If borders are put all around the carpet, the corners must be counted twice, because one half of each corner is wasted in the making.

SURVEYORS' AND LAND MEASURE

Land Measure. — The same table with certain additions as follows is

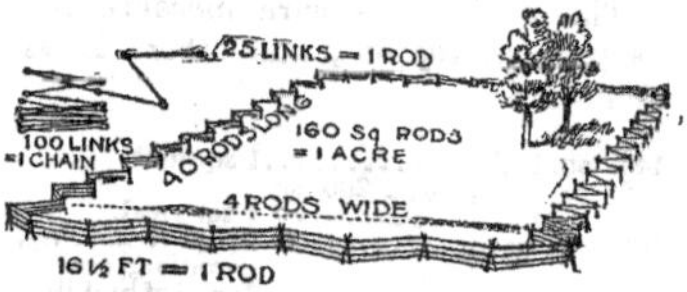

"Ordinary Land Measure."

used for ordinary land or surface measure:

144	sq. inches	1 sq. foot.
9	sq. feet	1 sq. yard.
30¼	sq. yards	1 sq. rod or perch.
40	sq. perches	1 rood.
4	roods	1 acre.
640	acres	1 sq. mile.

Surveyors' Measure.—In addition, the following table based upon Gunter's Chain, which is 4 rods or 66 feet, is employed for land surveying. An engineer's chain, used by civil engineers, is 100 feet long, and consists of 100 links.

7.92	inches	1 link.
25	links	1 rod.
100	links	1 chain.
66	feet	1 chain.
4	rods	1 chain.
10	sq. chains—160 sq. rods	1 acre.
80	chains	1 mile.
640	acres	1 sq. mile.
625	sq. links	1 sq. pole.
16	sq. poles	1 sq. chain.
10	sq. chains	1 acre.

sq. mi. A. sq. rd. sq. yd. sq. ft.
1 = 640 = 102400 = 3097600 = 27878400
sq. in.
4014489600

Scale.—640, 160, 30¼, 9, 144.

The term perch or pole is sometimes used instead of square rod. The rood, 40 perches, or ¼ acre, is found in old title deeds and surveys.

Rules for Land Measure.—The following rules and suggestions may be of assistance in measuring land.

Measure 209 feet on each side and the result will be a square acre within an inch.

To find the number of acres in any plot of land when the number of rods is given, divide the number of rods by 8, multiply the quotient by 5, and remove the decimal point two places to the left. To find how many rods in length will make an acre when the width in rods is given, divide 160 by the width in rods and the quotient will be the answer.

To find the number of acres in a body of land having square corners and parallel sides, ascertain the length and the width in rods, multiply these numbers and divide the product by 160, the number of square rods in an acre. If there is a remainder, carry out to two decimal places. The result will be the answer in acres and hundredths. If opposite sides of a piece of land are of unequal length add them together and take ½ as the mean length or width.

To measure a triangular field, multiply the length of the longest side in rods by the greatest width in rods; take ½ the product and divide by 160. To measure any field of irregular outline, provided the sides are straight, divide the field into triangles and measure each triangle by this rule. But if the sides are crooked make a number of parallel measurements across the field at places equal distances apart, add them, and divide the total by the number of measurements made; this will give the mean length; similar measurements in the opposite direction will give the mean width. Multiply the two results and divide by 160.

To find the surface of a circular field, measure the diameter in rods, multiply the diameter by itself and the result by 7.854 and divide by 160.

To Lay Out an Acre.—An acre of land contains 160 square rods or 43,560 square feet. To lay out an acre at right angles, i. e., square corners, one side being known, divide the square contents of an acre by the length of the known side, taking care that both are expressed in the same kind of units. For example: if one side is known to be 4 rods, divide 160, the number of square rods in an acre, by 4 and the quotient will be 40 rods or the depth of the acre plot.

Or, if the length of the known side is 180 feet, divide 43,560, the number of square feet in an acre, by 180 and the result will be 242 or the depth of the acre plot in feet.

The following table will be found convenient for reference:

A.	R.	Rds.	Sq. Yds.	Sq. Ft.	Sq. In.
1 =	4 =	160 =	4840 =	43560 =	6272640
	1 =	40 =	1210 =	10890 =	1568160
		1 =	30¼ =	272¼ =	39204
			1 =	9 =	1296
				1 =	144

Estimate of Waste Land. — A standard English mile, which is the measure that we use, is 5,280 feet in length, 1,760 yards, or 320 rods. A strip 1 rod wide and 1 mile long is 2 acres. By this it is easy to calculate the quantity of land taken up by roads, and also how much is wasted by fences.

United States Government Land Measure. — Government surveys in this country are made with references to a principal meridian running north and south, of which there are 24 in the United States. A base line is run east and west at right angles with the meridian. The land is then divided by means of lines running parallel with these into sections 6 miles on each side. These are called townships. A line of townships running north and south is called a range. It is designated by a number east or west from the principal meridian. Each township is divided into 36 sections. These are each 1 mile square and contain 640 acres. The sections are all numbered from 1 to 36, commencing at the northeast corner. They are further subdivided into quarters, which are named by the cardinal points, and the quarters are again subdivided in the same way. The following table will be found convenient for reference:

1 township, 6 miles square........ 36 sections.
1 section, 1 mile square..........640 acres.
1 quarter section, ½ mile square . . 160 acres.
1 eighth section, ½ mile long,
north and south, ¼ mile wide... 80 acres.
1/16 section, ¼ mile square......... 40 acres.

Most of the Western States have been laid out on this plan by the Government. All titles, except city lots, are established under this survey.

Comparative Land Measure.—The standard acre varies in the different countries of the world and allowance must be made for this difference in statements of the products of the land per acre in various countries. The same land measure is used in this country as in England. The comparative size of the different units of land measure of different countries, in square yards, is given as follows:

English acre............... 4,840 sq. yards.
Scotch acre................ 6,150 sq. yards.
Irish acre.................. 7,840 sq. yards.
Hamburg acre.............11,545 sq. yards.
Amsterdam acre............ 9,722 sq. yards.
Dantzic acre............... 6,650 sq. yards.
France (hectare) acre.......11,960 sq. yards.
Prussia (morgen) acre...... 3,053 sq. yards.

This difference should be borne in mind in reading of the products per acre in different countries. Our land measure is that of England.

In Texas, New Mexico, and other Spanish sections of the United States, the Spanish land measures are still in use. The unit of length is the vara, equal in Texas to 33⅓ inches, in California to 33 inches, and in Mexico to 32.9927 inches. Counting 33⅓ inches to the vara, 108 varas = 100 yards, and 1900.8 varas = 1 mile.

Land is measured in square varas, labors, and square leagues.

1,000,000 sq. varas = 1 labor = 177.136 acres.
25 labors = 1 sq.lea. = 4428.4 acres.
1 acre = 5645.376 sq. varas.

Dimensions of Acre Plots.—The following are approximate measures of an acre plot:

3 by 53⅓ rods is....................1 acre.
4 by 40 rods is....................1 acre.
5 by 32 rods is....................1 acre.
6 by 26⅔ rods is....................1 acre.
7 by 22⅚ rods is....................1 acre.
8 by 20 rods is....................1 acre.
9 by 17⅞ rods is....................1 acre.
10 by 16 rods is....................1 acre.
11 by 14 6/11 rods is....................1 acre.
12 by 13⅓ rods is....................1 acre.

Twelve rods 10 feet and 8½ inches square make an acre.

Dimensions of Small Lots.—The following are approximate measures of plots less than an acre:

Fraction of an acre.	Square feet.	Feet square.
1/16	2722½	52¼
⅛	5445	73¾
¼	10890	104⅓
⅓	14520	120½
½	21780	147½
1	43560	208¾
2	87120	295¼

CUBIC OR CAPACITY MEASURE

Capacity Measure.—Measures of capacity are principally of three sorts: solid, liquid, and dry measure. In practical application of capacity measure, however, a number of different units are employed for different purposes. Among these is cubic measure used by scientists and also in the building trades for the measurement of stone, lumber, and for many other purposes. The ultimate unit is the cube of the standard yard with the cubes of its subdivisions into feet and inches. Other common units are the cord and the cord foot used in the measurement of wood for fuel, and the perch used in the measurement of stone for masonry. The bushel with its subdivisions is the unit of dry measure and is used for grain, vegetables, and the like; but there is an

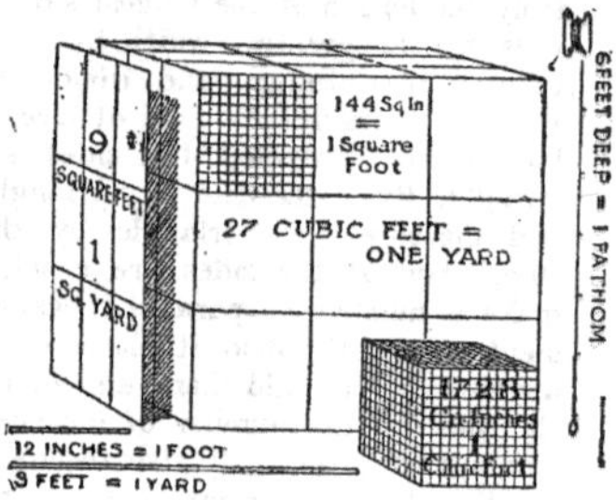

"The Ultimate Measure is the Yard."

increasing tendency to determine the measurement of these articles by weight. The gallon is the unit of measurement for liquids, with the exception of medicine, for which a special unit is provided. The following is a table of solid or cubic measure:

1728 cu. inches	1 cu. foot.
27 cu. feet	1 cu. yard.
40 cu. feet of round timber or 50 cu. feet of hewn timber	1 ton or load.
42 cu. feet	1 ton shipping.
16 cu. feet	1 cord-foot of wood.
8 cord feet	1 cord of wood.
128 cu. feet	1 cord of wood.
24¾ cu. feet	1 perch of stone or masonry.
2150.42 cu. inches	1 standard bushel.
268.8 cu. inches	1 standard gallon.
1 cu. foot	⅘ bushel.

A perch of stone or masonry is 16½ feet long, 1½ feet thick, and 1 foot high, and contains 24¾ cubic feet.

A cubic yard of earth is considered a load.

WOOD, LUMBER AND BOARD MEASURE

Measurement of Wood and Lumber.—Among the most frequent applications of cubic or capacity measure is the measurement of cord wood for fuel and of round timber or sawed lumber for building and other purposes.

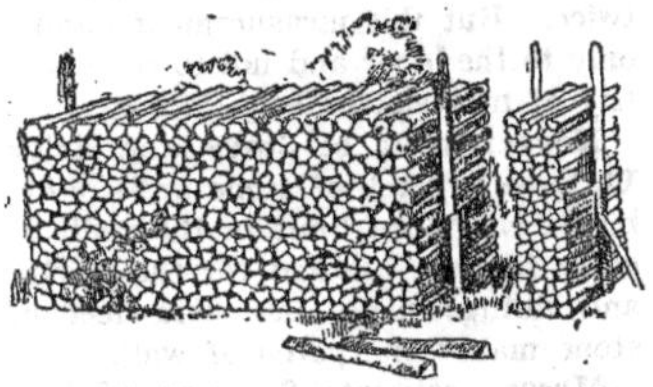

"A Cord-Foot is One-eight of this Pile."

Wood is usually cut for fuel into 4 feet sticks. A cord of wood is a pile 8 feet long, 4 feet wide, and 4 feet high. It contains 128 cubic feet. A cord-foot is ⅛ of this pile or a pile of wood 4 feet long, 4 feet high, and 1 foot wide.

To obtain the number of cords in a pile of wood, multiply the length of the wood by the height of the pile expressed in feet and that result by the length of the pile in feet. Divide the product by 128 and the quotient will be the number of cords.

Board Measure.—Lumber is sold at so much " per M," meaning per thousand feet B. M. or board measure. Board measure is used in measuring lumber sawed into boards, planks, joists, scantling, etc. The unit of board measure is the board foot, which is 1 foot long, 1 foot wide, and 1 inch thick, and hence is equal to $\frac{1}{12}$ of a cubic foot. Hence to find the number of board feet in a board or other piece of lumber having square edges and parallel sides, first find the surface of the board in square feet and multiply the product by the thickness in inches. Boards 1 inch in thickness or less are sold by the square foot, surface measure.

Thus a board 1 foot wide and 16 feet long, if 1 inch or less in thickness, would contain 16 square feet or 16 feet board measure. A board 18 feet long, 6 inches wide, and 1 inch or less thick would contain $18 \times \frac{1}{2}$ foot B. M. or 9 feet B. M. A joist 12 feet $\times$ 6 inches $\times$ 2 inches contains $12 \times 2 \times \frac{1}{2}$ feet B. M. or 12 feet B. M.

The width of a board that tapers uniformly is averaged by taking one half the sum of the two ends, or, in practice, by measuring across the middle. In practice the width of a board is reckoned to the next smaller half inch. Thus, a width of 6⅜ inches is taken as 6 inches, and the width of 6¾ inches is taken as 6½ inches.

To Measure Inch Boards.—Multiply the length in feet by the width in inches, and divide the product by 12. The quotient will be the contents in feet. For lumber 1¼ inches thick, add ¼ to the quotient. If 1½ inches thick, add ½. If 1¾ inches thick, add ¾. If 2 inches thick, divide by 6 instead of by 12. If 2¼ inches thick, add ¼ to the quotient and so on. If 3 inches thick, divide by 4. If 4 inches thick, divide by 3. Or to ascertain the contents (board measure) of timber, including scantling, joist, planks, sills, rafters, etc., multiply the width in inches by the thickness in inches, and that by the length in feet and divide the product by 12. The result will be the number of feet.

The measurement of round logs is intended to give the amount of lumber in board measure that can be sawed from them. Logs not over 15 feet in length are measured by means of a table stamped on calipers, the length and diameter of the small end being given. In the case of logs over 16 feet in length, the average diameter is taken.

Or to measure round timber take the girth in inches at both the large and the small ends, add them, and divide by 2, which gives the mean girth. The square of $\frac{1}{4}$ of the mean girth multiplied by the length of the timber in feet will give the contents in cubic feet. This is the common practice based on the estimate that round timber when squared loses $\frac{1}{5}$. The result gives $\frac{4}{5}$ of the actual contents, the remaining $\frac{1}{5}$ being allowed for waste in sawing.

Or, by another rule, subtract 4 from the diameter of the log in inches, multiply the square of $\frac{1}{4}$ the remainder by the length of the log in feet. These two rules should give approximately the same result.

Or to find how many solid feet a round stick of timber, if of the same thickness throughout, will contain when squared, square half the diameter in inches, multiply by 2 and multiply this product by the length in feet. Finally, divide by 144; the result will be the contents of the squared timber in solid feet.

Or to find the number of feet in timber having the bark on, square $\frac{1}{5}$ of the circumference in inches and multiply the product by twice the length in feet. Then divide by 144. Subtract $\frac{1}{10}$ to $\frac{1}{15}$ of the total, according to the thickness of the bark. As a general rule, to find the solid contents of sawn lumber multiply the depth in inches by the breadth in inches and multiply the product by the length in feet and divide by 144.

To determine how large a tree must be cut to get out a stick of timber a given number of inches square, divide the side of the required square by .225. The quotient will be the circumference of the timber required.

MEASUREMENT OF STONE AND BRICK

Cost of Brick and Stone Work.—A common application of capacity measure is in preparing estimates for brick and stone work. Masons commonly measure stone work by the perch, $16\frac{1}{2}$ feet long, $1\frac{1}{2}$ feet wide, and 1 foot thick, or $24\frac{3}{4}$ cubic feet. Brick work is commonly estimated by the thousand bricks. It is, however, customary in many localities to reckon stone work by the cubic foot instead of by the perch. Usually a deduction is made by bricklayers, masons, and joiners, for one half of all openings. But this should be clearly established in each case in the contract.

In computing the capacity of walls of cellars and buildings, masons and bricklayers multiply the entire distance around the outside of the wall (the girth) by the height and thickness. Thus the corners are measured twice. But this measurement applies only to the labor and not to the quantity of material to be paid for.

Measurement of Stone and Brick Walls.—A perch of stone is 24.75 cubic feet. When built in the wall, $2\frac{3}{4}$ cubic feet are allowed for the mortar and filling; hence 22 cubic feet of stone makes one perch of wall.

Masons estimate 3 pecks of lime and 4 bushels of sand to a perch of wall.

To find the number of perches of stone in a wall, multiply together the length, height, and thickness in feet and divide by 22.

Measurement of Brick Work.—The size of bricks varies, and rules for estimating the number of bricks required must be modified accordingly. Bricks are now usually made 8 inches long, 4 inches wide, and 2 inches thick. Hence 27 bricks are required to make a cubic foot without mortar. But it is assumed that mortar fills ⅛ of the space. The first step is to find the number of cubic feet in the wall by multiplying the length, height, and thickness together in feet, and if the bricks are of this size multiply the number of cubic feet by 22½.

Formerly, however, and to some extent at the present time, bricks were made of two sorts and sizes—common brick, 7¾ inches to 8 inches long by 4¼ inches wide and 2½ inches thick, and front brick, ¼ inch longer and wider. Of common brick 20 are required to lay one cubic foot or 15 common brick will lay one square foot of wall 8 inches thick. Hence to estimate the number of bricks required for a wall 12 inches or more in thickness, multiply together the length, height, and thickness in feet, and that product by 20; or for an 8-inch wall multiply the length by the height and that by 15. An allowance of one half should be made for doors, windows, and other openings. Multiply their length by their width and that by the thickness of the wall in feet. Deduct one half the result from the cubic contents of the wall before multiplying by 20 or by 15, as above.

DRY AND LIQUID MEASURE

Dry Measure.—The standard unit of dry measure is the English or Winchester bushel, containing 2150.42 cubic inches or 77.627 pounds avoirdupois of distilled water at its greatest density. The standard measure is circular in form, its diameter inside being 18½ inches, and its depth 8 inches. Dry measure is used in measuring grain, coal, fruit, vegetables, etc. The following is a table of dry measure commonly used in the United States:

4 gills	1 pt.	= 34⅔ cu. in. nearly.
2 pints	1 qt.	= 69½ cu. in.
4 quarts	1 gal.	= 277¼ cu. in.
8 quarts	1 pk.	
2 gallons	1 pk.	= 554½ cu. in.
4 pks. or 8 gal.	1 bu.	= 2150½ cu. in.
8 bushels	1 qr.	= 10¼ cu. ft. nearly.
36 bushels	1 chaldron.	

When articles usually measured by the above table are sold by weight, the bushel is taken as the unit. The number of avoirdupois pounds in a bushel varies in different States and with different articles.

In measuring grain, seeds, or small fruit, the measure must be even or "stricken." In measuring large fruits or coarse vegetables, corn in the ear, etc., and also meal and bran, the measure should be heaped at least 6 inches.

Five stricken bushels are considered equal to 4 heaped bushels. The stricken bushel is now little used, except to ascertain capacities.

All the denominations are used in trade, the peck being the least in use.

	Cu. in. in one gal.	Cu. in. in one qt.	Cu. in. in one pt.	Cu. in. in one gi.
Liquid Meas.	231	57¾	28⅞	7 7/32
Dry Measure	268⅘	67⅕	33⅗	8⅖

English Dry Measure.—In addition to the above the following terms for units of dry measure are still customary to some extent in the British Empire:

2 quarts	1 pottle.
2 bushels	1 strike.
2 strikes	1 coomb.
2 coombs	1 quarter.
5 quarters	1 load.
3 bushels	1 sack.
36 bushels	1 chaldron.

Thirty-two British or Imperial bushels are equal to 38 of our bushels.

Capacity of Boxes, Cribs, Wagon Bodies, etc.—The most convenient mode of ascertaining the capacity of boxes, bins, cribs, and the like, and also of measuring their contents, is by ascertaining the number of cubic feet which they contain; ⅘ of this amount will be the number of bushels, 1 cubic foot being ⅘ of a bushel nearly. Hence, to find the number of bushels in any receptacle which has parallel sides and square corners, first find the number of cubic feet by multiplying the height, length, and width in feet and deduct ⅕; the result will be the contents in bushels. Or for an approximate answer multiply the number of cubic feet by 8 and point off one decimal place.

These rules will give the number of bushels of apples, potatoes, and other vegetables or the capacity of any size bin or crib or wagon body.

In estimating corn on the cob, its quality and condition must be taken into account. Corn shrinks considerably during the winter and spring months. But, as a general rule, 2 heaping bushels of corn on the cob at the time it is put into the crib will make from 1 to $1\frac{1}{2}$ struck bushels of shelled corn. In buying or selling it is advisable to make a test from a fair sample taken from the crib at the time of sale. To measure corn in the crib, multiply together the length, width, and height of the crib in inches, divide by 2,748, and the result will be the number of heaped bushels of ears. Or divide by 2,150 for the number of struck bushels. The quotient in each case will be the corresponding number of bushels contained in the bin.

If the sides of the crib flare, ascertain the mean width by measuring the width at both top and bottom, add the two amounts and divide by 2.

Or, it is estimated that 2 cubic feet of sound dry corn on the ear will make 1 bushel shelled. Hence multiply together the length, breadth, and height of the crib in feet and divide by 2. This should give the number of bushels of shelled corn in the crib. The corn should, of course, be uniformly level so as to be of equal depth throughout.

Capacity of Boxes.—The following is a table showing the principal units of dry measurement with the inside dimensions of boxes or bins having square corners and parallel sides that will contain the quantities stated.

One convenient form of making boxes in small sizes for the storage of vegetables and numerous other purposes about the household, farm, and garden, is to cut the two ends of inch pine stuff to the proper size and form the bottom and two sides of laths. Saw these to the right length and tack them to the ends, with the thickness of a lath between each two. Such boxes are light, strong, and serviceable. Larger bins or crates of heavier materials can be prepared on the same principle.

Capacity.	Length.	Breadth.	Depth.
1 pint.....	3 in.	3 in.	$3\frac{3}{4}$ in.
1 quart...	4 in.	4 in.	$4\frac{1}{4}$ in.
$\frac{1}{2}$ gallon...	7 in.	7 in.	$2\frac{3}{4}$ in.
Gallon....	8 in.	8 in.	$4\frac{1}{4}$ in.
1 peck....	$8\frac{3}{8}$ in.	8 in.	8 in.
$\frac{1}{2}$ bushel...	12 in.	$11\frac{1}{2}$ in.	9 in.
1 bushel...	26 in.	$15\frac{1}{2}$ in.	8 in.
1 barrel...	24 in.	$16\frac{1}{2}$ in.	28 in.
20 bushels..	4 ft. 8 in.	2 ft. 4 in.	2 ft. 4 in.
24 bushels..	5 ft.	3 ft.	2 ft.
36 bushels..	5 ft.	3 ft.	3 ft.
48 bushels..	5 ft.	3 ft.	4 ft.
100 bushels..	7 ft.	5 ft.	3 ft. 9 in.
216 bushels..	9 ft.	6 ft.	5 ft.
500 bushels..	13 ft.	8 ft.	6 ft.

Liquid Measure.—The measurement of wine and other liquors, molasses, vinegar, and the like, has been the occasion of great confusion due to vari-

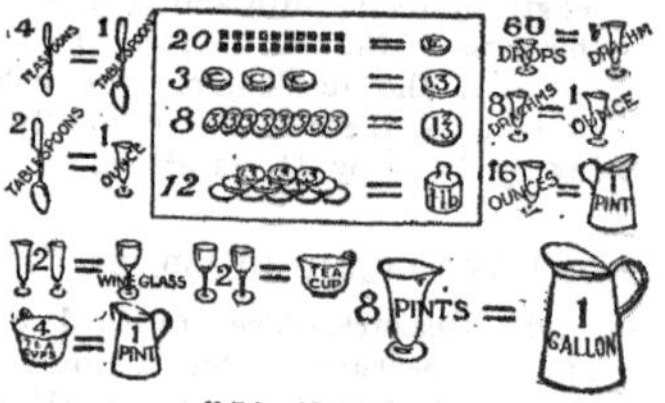

"Liquid Measure."

ations of the standard unit of liquid capacity, the gallon. The gallon was originally a standard unit of weight. But as an equal bulk of various substances differs in weight, early usage led to the adoption of two different gallons, wet and dry, and the gallon is still used as a unit of both wet and dry measure in Great Britain. The gallon at present the standard in the United States had its origin in an English statute passed shortly after the discovery of America by Columbus. A new standard gallon measure was constructed capable of holding 8 pounds of wheat of 12 ounces troy each. This was afterwards determined by statute to contain 268.8 cubic inches of water at a temperature of 62° F. The Winchester gallon, as this standard was called, having been generally adopted in the United States, it became ultimately necessary to establish a national standard for customhouse purposes. Accordingly, by resolution of the United States Senate, on May 1, 1830, the Secretary of the Treasury procured the construction of a set of uniform standard weights and measures to be supplied to all the customhouses. For this purpose a Winchester gallon of water, at a temperature of 39.83° F., was taken as the standard, and this was afterwards legalized by Congress. Hence the legal capacity of the gallon, the present United States standard, was fixed at 231 cubic inches of water. As a result there is a considerable discrepancy between the British Winchester and the so-called American Winchester gallon, the present United States standard.

In the meantime, by an act of English Parliament, which went into effect January 1, 1826, the capacity of the British gallon was made such as to contain 10 pounds avoirdupois of distilled water at the temperature of 62° F. or 277¼ cubic inches nearly. This is the so-called Imperial gallon, and since its introduction has been the only legal gallon in Great Britain for either wet or dry measure.

The reason that it is necessary to state these facts in detail is that works of reference in the English language circulate quite generally through all English-speaking countries, and it is quite customary to copy reference tables from one to another on the assumption that standard units of weights and measures are invariable. This, however, as has been seen, is not the case. Hence it is necessary in making use of any published recipes or similar information where great accuracy is required, to ascertain whether the British Winchester, the American Winchester, or the British Imperial gallon is referred to. The only standards that are of universal application throughout the civilized world are those of the metric system.

Tables of Liquid Measure.—The following is the United States standard of liquid or wine measure:

4	gills..............	1 pint (pt.) 28⅞ cu. in.
2	pints..............	1 quart (qt.) 57¾ cu. in.
4	quarts..........	1 gallon (gal.) 231 cu. in.
31½	gallons..........	1 barrel (bbl.)
2	barrels..........	1 hogshead (hhd.)
63	gallons..........	1 hogshead (hhd.)
2	hogsheads......	1 pipe or butt (pi.)
2	pipes..............	1 tun.
282	cu. in..........	1 beer gallon.
36	beer gallons....	1 barrel.

The following is a table of the measure of capacity based upon the British Imperial gallon, which is in general use throughout the British Empire:

Measure of Capacity for All Liquids.

5 ounces avoirdupois of water make 1 gill.

4	gills.........1 pint = 34⅔ cu. in. nearly.	
2	pints.........1 quart = 69⅓ cu. in. nearly.	
4	quarts.......1 gallon = 277¼ cu. in. nearly.	
31½	gallons....................	1 barrel.
42	gallons....................	1 tierce.
63	gallons or 2 bbls..........	1 hogshead.
2	hogsheads................	1 pipe or butt.
2	pipes........................	1 tun.

The British Imperial gallon must contain exactly 10 pounds avoirdupois of pure water at a temperature of 62° F., the barometer being at 30 inches. It is the standard unit of measure of capacity for liquids and dry goods of every description, and is ⅕ larger than the old wine measure, $\frac{1}{32}$ larger than the old dry measure, and $\frac{1}{60}$ less than the old ale measure.

The following are terms in wine measure — more frequently used in England than in this country—with comparative capacity in British and American gallons:

18	U. S. gallons..................	1 rundlet.
25	Eng. gallons or 42 U. S. gallons..................	1 tierce.
2	tierces..........................	1 puncheon.
62¼	Eng. gollons or 63 U. S. gallons..................	1 hogshead.
2	hogsheads....................	1 pipe.
2	pipes............................	1 tun.
7½	Eng. gallons..................	1 firkin of beer.
4	firkins..........................	1 barrel of beer.

Comparison of Liquid and Dry Measure.—The capacity of bins for grain is usually measured in bushels, and the capacity of casks, cisterns, and the like, in gallons or barrels. In determining the capacity of cisterns and reservoirs, 31½ gallons are considered a barrel, and 2 barrels or 63 gallons a hogshead.

In commerce the size of casks for liquids is variable, barrels being made to contain from 30 to 40 gallons or more. Casks of large size called tierces, pipes, butts, tuns, etc., do not now hold any fixed quantity. Their capacity is usually marked upon them. While the standard liquid gallon contains 231 cubic inches in approximate measurements, 7½ gallons are allowed to the cubic foot. As compared with the weight of water, a gallon will hold a little over 8⅓ pounds, which is near enough for practical purposes.

In comparison with dry measure, the United States standard bushel contains 2150.4 cubic inches, the liquid gallon 231 cubic inches, and the dry gallon (the former British Winchester standard—⅛ bushel) 268.8 cubic inches. Hence 6 dry gallons equal nearly 7 liquid gallons. The British Imperial gallon contains 277.274 cubic inches or 10 pounds of distilled water, temperature 62° F., barometer 30 inches. The beer gallon contains 282 cubic inches, but it is not now in use. Hence the following rules to find the capacity of bins, cisterns, etc.

To find the number of bushels, divide the volume in cubic inches by 2150.4. To find the number of gallons, divide the volume in cubic inches by 231.

Apothecaries' Fluid Measure.—In addition to the above is the apothecaries' fluid measure, used in compounding medicines which are in fluid form as follows:

60 drops (gtt.) or minims (♏)	= 1 fluid dram (f ʒ)
8 fluid drams	= 1 fluid ounce (f ℥)
16 fluid ounces	= 1 pint .... (f O)
8 pints	= 1 gallon .... Cong.

Cong. 1 = O8 = f ℥ 128 = f ʒ 1024 = ♏ 61440.
Scale: 8, 16, 8, 60.

(1) Cong., from the Latin *congius*, means gallon.

(2) O, from the Latin *octarius*, means ⅛.

(3) The minim is about equal to a drop of water.

Comparison of the Measures of Capacity.—The following is a comparison of measures of capacity:

1 gal. or 4 qt. wine measure contains 231 cu. in.
⅛ pk. or 4 qt. dry measure contains 268⅘ cu. in.
1 gal. or 4 qt. beer measure contains 282 cu. in.

The gallon containing 231 cubic inches is the standard unit of wine measure. The British gallon called the Imperial gallon contains 277.274 cubic inches.

Measurement of Tanks, Casks, and Cisterns.—To find the capacity of cylindrical tanks of any size in United States gallons, multiply the square of the diameter in inches by the length in inches and that product by .0034; the result will be the contents or capacity in wine gallons and decimals of a gallon. For beer gallons, multiply by .0028 instead of .0034. To ascertain the diameter, measure at the bung and also at the head; add together and divide the same by 2 for the mean diameter. To ascertain the actual contents if the cask is only partially filled, multiply the height of the liquid in inches instead of the height of the cask.

To ascertain the contents of a square cistern or watering trough, multiply together the length, width, and depth in inches and divide by 231, the number of cubic inches in a gallon. This will give the contents in gallons.

To ascertain the contents of a circular cistern, multiply the square of the diameter in feet by the depth in feet, and that product by 5⅞. The result will be the contents in gallons.

MEASURES OF WEIGHT

Origin of Standards.—The use of weights depends upon the principle of balance. Hence they were probably not introduced until some time after measures of length, surface, and capacity. The first English statute on the subject founded measures of weight upon a given quantity of wheat corns. The language of the ancient statute is interesting and suggestive.

"An English penny, called a sterling, round and without any clipping, shall weigh 32 wheat corns in the midst of the ear, and 20 pence do make an ounce, and 12 ounces 1 pound, and 8 pounds do make a gallon of wine, and 8 gallons of wine do make a London bushel, which is the eighth part of a quarter."

The pound weight provided by this statute known as the tower pound, or the easterling or sterling pound (whence our word sterling as applied to silverware and otherwise), continued in use until about the time of Columbus, when the pound troy was substituted in its place. By a later statute a brass 1-pound weight was established as the imperial standard troy pound. It was declared to contain 12 ounces of 20 pennyweights, each pennyweight containing 24 grains, so that 5,760 such grains shall be a troy pound, and 7,000 such grains a pound avoirdupois. It was further provided that 1 cubic inch of water weighed by brass weights in air, at a temperature of 62° F., and 30 inches barometic pressure, is the equivalent of 252.458 grains. This standard became quite generally adopted in the United States, and in 1836 the Secretary of the Treasury caused a uniform set of weights to be delivered to the governor of each State for local use. Thus a pound is practically the same in all parts of the English-speaking world. There is still, however, great confusion in comparisons between weight and capacity measures, and the legislation of different States and countries in defining the number of pounds in a bushel of various grains, fruits, and vegetables, differs widely.

Systems of Weight. — There are three principal systems of weights in general use: avoirdupois weight, the universal standard, except as to the weight of the precious metals, jewels, and drugs; troy weight used in coinage and by jewelers (who also make use of a standard unit in weighing jewels called the carat); and apothecaries' weight, used by druggists and physicians. Avoirdupois weight, so called from the Norman *Avon du poids*, "goods of weight," is derived from the imperial standard pound above mentioned, equal to 700 troy grains. The grain is the same in both avoirdupois and troy weight. Formerly the ton consisted of 2,240 pounds, and the hundredweight of 112 pounds, divided into four quarters of 28 pounds each. And this practice continues in Great Britain and in the United States customhouse. In the ordinary commerce of the United States, however, it has become customary, as a matter of convenience, to reckon 100 pounds to the hundredweight, and 2,000 pounds to the ton; and this practice has been legalized in some of the States. By act of Congress, however, when not specified to the contrary, the ton is to be construed as meaning 2,240

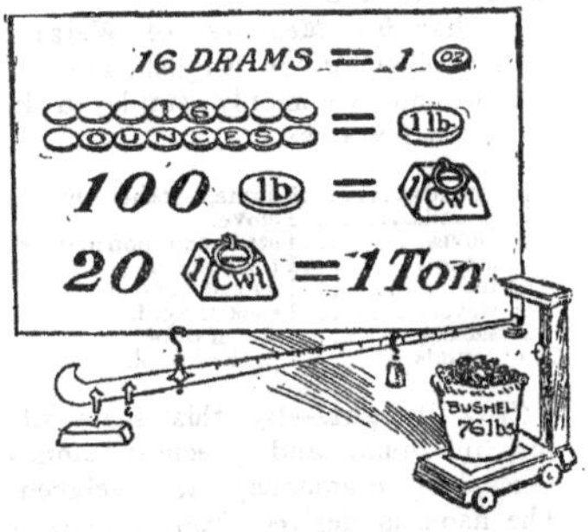

"American Avoirdupois Weight."

pounds. This is commonly called the long ton; that of 2,000 pounds the short ton. The long ton is most often used for weighing coal and iron at the mines, and for plaster, and in some other wholesale transactions in mining products. The shipping ton is 40 cubic feet, known as actual tonnage. The registered shipping ton is 100 cubic feet. The word ton is supposed to have been derived from the tun, an old British liquid measure for ale or beer. A tun of water weighs a little over 2,200 pounds. Hence the ton weight seems to have been taken from the tun measure, of which it is a rough equivalent.

Avoirdupois Weight.—The following are English and American avoirdupois tables:

American

16	drams	1 ounce (oz.).
16	ounces	1 pound (lb.).
25	pounds	1 quarter (qr.).
4	quarters	1 hundred (cwt.).
20	hundred	1 ton (T.).

English

27 11/32	grains	1 dram (dr.).
16	drams	1 ounce (oz.).
16	ounces	1 pound (lb.).
28	pounds	1 quarter (qr.).
4	quarters	1 hundred (cwt.).
20	hundred	1 ton (T.).

The weight of 22.79+ cubic inches of distilled water at its greatest density, with the barometer at 30 inches, is equal nearly to 1 pound troy. This is taken as a standard by which to find any number of greater or less units of weight.

English Old Measures of Weight.—The following are English units of weights not commonly employed in the United States:

3	pounds	1 stone, butchers' meat.
7	pounds	1 clove.
2	cloves	1 stone common articles.
2	stone	1 tod of wool.
6½	tods	1 wey of wool.
2	weys	1 sack of wool.
12	sacks	1 last of wool.
240	pounds	1 pack of wool.

Troy Weight.—By this scale silver, platinum, and precious stones (excepting diamonds) are weighed. The name is derived from Troyes, a town in France, where this weight was first used in Europe. It was introduced from Cairo, Egypt, during the crusades of the twelfth century. The term grain originated in the use of grains of wheat to determine the pennyweight or weight of the old silver penny of England. At first 32, and afterwards 24, grains of wheat were called a pennyweight. The symbol oz. is from the Spanish word *onza* meaning ounce; lb. is from the Latin *libra* meaning pound.

As a unit of measure the troy pound of 5,760 grains is equal to 22.794422 cubic inches of distilled water at the temperature of 39.8, 30″ barometic pressure. The following is the table of troy weight:

20	mites	1 gram.
24	grains (gr.)	1 pennyweight (pwt., dwt.).
20	dwt.	1 ounce (oz.).
12	oz.	1 pound (lb.).
3⅙	grains	1 carat (diamond wt.) (k.).

The avoirdupois pound contains 7,000 grains, the troy pound 5,760 grains. Therefore 1 pound of iron is heavier than 1 pound of gold. The troy pound is accordingly less than the avoirdupois pound in the proportion of 14 to 17 nearly. The troy ounce is greater than the avoirdupois ounce in the proportion of 79 to 72 nearly.

Carat Weight.—The term carat is used in two ways: as a unit of weight used by jewelers in weighing diamonds, the carat in the United States is 3⅙ grains troy nearly, a carat grain being ¼ of this. In assaying gold the term is equivalent to 1/24 part. Its use is to designate the proportion of pure gold in an alloy. Pure gold is said to be 24 carats fine; 18 carats gold contains 18 parts of pure gold and six parts of alloy, and so on.

Apothecaries' Weight.—The units of weight in use by physicians in prescribing, and by druggists in mixing and compounding medicines, are the same as the troy weight as to the pound, ounce, and grain. The ounce, however, is differently divided. They are shown by the following table:

20 grains (gr. xx)	1 scruple (sc.) ℈.
3 scruples (sc. iij)	1 dram (dr.) ʒ.
8 drams (ʒ viij)	1 ounce troy (oz.) ℥.
12 ounces (℥ xij)	1 pound troy (lb.) ℔.
1 lb. avoirdupois	7,000 gr.
1 oz. avoirdupois	437½ gr.
1 lb. troy and apothecaries'	5,760 gr.
1 oz. troy and apothecaries'	480 gr.

Physicians in writing prescriptions use Roman numerals (the small letters only) instead of figures. They write j for i when it terminates a number. They also employ the symbols above indicated writing the symbol first, thus ℥vij, meaning 7 ounces. This practice is a survival of the mediæval custom of surrounding all knowledge of drugs and medicines with an air of mystery. Hence the names of medicines written in Latin and arbitrary symbols employed to express quantity. These symbols have been thought by some to be modifications of the figure 3 (derived from the fact that there are three scruples in the dram), but it is more probable that they are inherited from ancient Egypt. There is an increasing tendency among physicians to do away with this air of mystery, and it is not improbable that prescriptions in time to come may be written in English and quantities expressed in ordinary fashion.

Medicines are bought and sold by avoirdupois weight, apothecaries' weight being used only in mixing and compounding them.

Druggists' Abbreviations. — The following are abbreviations frequently used by druggists and physicians, and freely made use of in this volume, especially in the department of toilet recipes:

℞	is an	abbreviation	for	recipe, or take.
P	"	"	"	particula, or little part.
Q. s.	"	"	"	quantity sufficient.
P. æ.	"	"	"	equal parts.
Q. p.	"	"	"	as much as you please.
Gr.	"	"	"	grain.
Ss.	"	"	"	semi.
A, āā	"	"	"	equal quantities.
II	"	"	"	2.
Gt.	"	"	"	drop.
Cong.	"	"	"	*congius*, the Latin for gallon.
O	"	"	"	pint from *octarius*, Latin for ⅛.

♏, minim, equal to a drop of water.

Comparison of Measures.—The following table of comparative weights will be found convenient for reference:

1 U. S. lb. troy	5,760	grs. troy.
1 Eng. lb. troy	5,760	grs. troy.
1 lb. apoth	5,760	grs. troy.
1 U. S. lb. av	7,000	grs. troy.
1 Eng. lb. av	7,000	grs. troy.
144 lb. av	175	lb. troy.
1 French gram	15.433	grs. troy.
1 U. S. yard	36	inches.
1 Eng. yard	36	inches.
1 French meter	39.368+	inches.
1 U. S. bushel	2,150.42 +	cu. in.
1 Eng. bushel	2,218.19 +	cu. in.
1 U. S. gallon	231	cu. in.
1 Eng. gallon	277.26 +	cu. in.
1 French liter	91.533+	cu. in.
1 French are	119.664	sq. yds.

Weight of Cattle.—To estimate the weight of live cattle or carcasses undressed, first measure in inches the girth behind the shoulders, next the length from the forepart or point of the shoulder blade along the back to the bone at the tail in a vertical line with the buttocks. Multiply the girth in inches by the length in inches, and divide the product by 144. This will give the number of superficial feet. If the girth of the animal is from 3 to 5 feet, multiply the number of superficial feet by 16; the result will be the animal's weight. Or if the girth is from 5 to 7 feet, multiply by 23. If from 7 to 9 feet, multiply by 31. If less than 3 feet, as in the case of small calves, hogs, sheep, etc., multiply by 11. Of course, individual animals will vary. But these rules will give approximate results.

Or multiply the square of the girth in feet by 5 times the length in feet. For average stock divide the product by 1.5; for fat cattle by 1.425; for lean by 1.575. The quotient will be the dressed weight of the quarters, or net weight of the steer after dressing.

Or for a short method, multiply the square of the animal's girth by 17.5, which will give the weight of the animal nearly.

In estimating the weight and price of hogs, it is usually considered that about ⅕ is lost in dressing the animal. Hence the gross weight diminished by ⅕, or by 20 per cent, gives the net weight. Or the net weight increased by ¼, or 25 per cent of itself, gives the gross weight.

Measurement of Hay.—Hay is ordinarily and properly sold by weight, and this is the only exact mode of measurement. But experience has shown the following rules to be sufficiently correct for ordinary practical purposes. If the hay is loosely packed, as in windrows, multiply the length, breadth, and height in yards, and divide the product by 25. The quotient will be the number of tons in the windrow. If the hay has been recently placed in the mow, or if the mow is shallow, multiply together the length, height, and width in yards, and divide by 18. Or if the hay is well packed, divide by 15 or divide by any number between 15 and 18, according to the way in which the hay is packed or settled in the mow.

Or if the hay is in square or long stacks with flat tops, well settled, multiply the length of the base in yards by the width in yards, and that product by ½ the height in yards, and divide by 15.

Or if the hay is in a load, multiply the length, width, and height in yards, and divide the product by 20.

Or, by another method, it is estimated that old hay well packed in a mow will run about 520 cubic feet to the ton, clover 720 cubic feet, timothy and clover mixed 600 cubic feet. Hence ascertain the number of cubic feet in the mow and divide by one of these figures, according to the quality of the hay.

Or to ascertain the number of cubic feet in a round pointed stack, multiply the area of the base in square feet by ⅓ of the height in feet. This will give the number of cubic feet in a stack, or if the stack is built up square with pointed eaves, like a house, first measure the height from the ground to the eaves and to this add ½ of the height from the eaves to the top. Take this figure as the mean height, and multiply together the mean height, length, and breadth in feet, and divide the result by 520, 600, or 720, according to the quality of the hay.

To ascertain the value of a given amount of hay, straw, or other commodity sold by the ton, when the price per ton is given, multiply the number of pounds by ½ the price per ton and point off three figures from the right. The result will be the price of the article.

Weights of Trade Packages.—The following is a table showing the style of package in use in ordinary commercial practice in the sale of various kinds of commodities, and the corresponding weight as ordinarily recognized in the trade:

Article.	Package.	Weight.
Beef	Barrel,	200 lbs.
Butter	Firkin,	50 or 100 lbs.
Corn	Barrel,[1]	
Corn	Barrel,[2]	
Cotton	Bale,[3]	400 lbs.
Cotton, Sea Island	Sack,	300 lbs.
Feathers	Bale,	100 lbs.
Fish, dry	Quintal,	100 lbs.
Fish in brine	Barrel,	200 lbs.
Flour	Barrel,	196 lbs.
Flour	Cental,	100 lbs.
Grain	Cental,	100 lbs.
Hay	Bale,	300 lbs.
Hay	Load,	36 trusses.
Hay	Truss,	60 lbs., new.
Hay	Truss,	50 lbs., old.
Honey	Gallon,	12 lbs.
Iron	Stone,	14 lbs.
Lead	Stone,	14 lbs.
Meat	Stone,	80 lbs.
Molasses	Hogshead,	130 to 150 gal.
Nails	Keg,	100 lbs.
Pork	Barrel,	200 lbs.
Powder	Barrel,	25 lbs.
Raisins	Barrel,	112 lbs.
Raisins	Cask,	100 lbs.
Rice	Barrel,	600 lbs.
Salt	Barrel, (at N.Y. works)	280 lbs.
Soap	Barrel,	256 lbs.
Soap	Box,	56 lbs.
Straw	Truss,	40 lbs.
Sugar	Barrel,	200 to 250 lbs.
Tea	Chest,	60 to 84 lbs.
Tobacco	Hogshead,	168 lbs.
Wood	Tod,	28 lbs.
Wool	Pack,	17 stone.
Wool	Sack,	22 stone.
Wool	Pack load for a horse,	240 lbs.

[1] As bought and sold at New Orleans, a flour barrel full of ears.

[2] As bought and sold in Kentucky and Tennessee, 5 bu. of shelled corn.

[3] Varies in different States from 280 to 720 lbs.

Comparative Table of Weight of Commodities per Bushel.—While the standard units of weight and of capacity are now practically uniform throughout the United States, legislation in the various States differs widely as to the standard of weight for a bushel of various kinds of produce. The law in each State usually specifies the weight of a bushel, requiring it to weigh at least the amount specified. The following table shows the range in the standard weights as prescribed by statute in the various States, and also the standard or minimum prescribed by the laws of the United States and in effect wherever there is no State statute to the contrary. The majority of the States have adopted the United States standard, and there is an increasing tendency in this direction. Eventually, it is to be hoped that uniformity will prevail throughout the country:

Article.	Range in different States Lbs. per bu.	U. S. standard. Lbs. per bu.
Apples, dried	22–28	26
Apples, green	50–56	
Barley	43–50	48
Beans, castor		46
Beans, white	60–70	60
Beets	50–60	
Bran		20
Buckwheat	40–56	48
Carrots	50–55	
Charcoal (hardwood)	22–30	
Clover seed	60–64	60
Coal, anthracite	76–80	80
Corn, Indian (in car)	68–72	70
Corn meal	48–50	48
Corn, shelled	52–60	56
Cranberries	33	
Flax seed	44–56	56
Grass seed (blue)		44
Grass seed (Hungarian)	45–50	50
Grass seed (timothy)	42–60	45
Hemp seed		44
Hickory nuts	60	
Lime, quick	80	
Malt	34–38	34
Millet seed	45–50	50
Oats	26–36	32
Onions	48–57	57
Peaches, dried	28–33	33
Peas	46–60	60
Peas, ground		24
Peas, in pod	32	
Plastering hair, dry	8	
Popcorn	70	
Pototoes	46–56	55
Potatoes, Irish	56–60	60
Rye	32–56	56
Rye, meal	50–56	
Salt, coarse	50–85	
Salt, fine	55–56	
Turnips	42–60	55
Wheat		60

Weight of Commodities by State Law.—The following are the exceptions to the United States standard:

Barley, 48 lb., except in Oregon, 46 lb.; in Alabama, Georgia, Kentucky, Pennsylvania, 47 lb.; in California, 50 lb.; in Louisiana, 32 lb.

Beans, 60 lb., except in Maine, 62 lb.: in Massachusetts, 70 lb.

Buckwheat, 52 lb., except in California, 40 lb.; in Connecticut, Maine, Massachusetts, Michigan, Mississippi, New York, Pennsylvania, Vermont, Wisconsin, 48 lb.; in Idaho, North Dakota, Oklahoma, Oregon, South Dakota, Texas, Washington, 42 lb.; in Kansas, Minnesota, New Jersey, North Carolina, Ohio, Tennessee, 50 lb.; in Kentucky, 56 lb.

Clover seed, 60 lb., except in New Jersey, 64 lb.

Coal, 80 lb., except in Kentucky. Pennsylvania, 76 lb.

Corn in the ear, 70 lb., except in Mississippi, 72 lb.; in Ohio, 68 lb.; in Indiana after December 1st, and in Kentucky after May 1st, following the time of husking it, 68 lb.

Corn meal, 50 lb., except in Alabama, Arkansas, Georgia, Illinois, Mississippi, North Carolina, Tennessee, 48 lb.

Corn, shelled, 56 lb., except in California, 52 lb.

Grass seed, 45 lb., except in Arkansas, 60 lb.; in North Dakota, South Dakota, 42 lb.

Oats, 32 lb., except in Louisiana and Oregon, 36 lb.; in Maryland, 26 lb.; in New Jersey and Virginia, 30 lb.

Potatoes, 60 lb., except in Maryland, Pennsylvania, Virginia, 56 lb.

Rye, 56 lb., except in California, 54 lb.: in Louisiana, 32 lb.

Table of Weight of Commodities per Cubic Foot.—The following is a table of the weight per cubic foot of various metals and other commodities:

Brass	534¾ lbs.
Bricks	125 lbs.
Charcoal (hardwood)	18½ lbs.
Charcoal (pinewood)	18 lbs.
Clay	135 lbs.
Clay and stones	160 lbs.
Coal, anthracite	50 to 55 lbs.
Coal, bituminous	45 to 55 lbs.
Copper	555 lbs.
Cork	15 lbs.
Earth, loose	95 lbs.
Granite	165 lbs.
Iron, wrought	486¾ lbs.
Lead	708¾ lbs.
Marble	171 lbs.
Sea water	64 3/10 lbs.
Soil, common	124 lbs.
Soil, strong	127 lbs.
Tallow	59 lbs.
Water	1,000 oz.
Wood, oak	55 lbs.
Wood, red pine	42 lbs.
Wood, white pine	30 lbs.

To find the weight of any of these commodities, arrange loose materials in square bins, or pack such commodities as bricks in piles having straight sides and square corners; multiply the length, width, and depth together in feet and multiply this result by the number of cubic pounds in a cubic foot, as shown by the above table. The result can then be turned into quarters, hundredweight, or tons by reference to the table of cubic measure.

Household Weights and Measures.—The uniform accuracy of results obtained by professional cooks, bakers, and caterers is due, in great degree, to the fact that the measurement of ingredients called for by their recipes is accurately determined by weight, and the temperature of their ovens is definitely ascertained by means of the thermometer. Thus the conditions surrounding each batch of food cooked are made identical, and uniformity in the product necessarily follows. Any cook can obtain similar results by like means, and a good pair of scales in the kitchen may be regarded as one of the marks of a good housekeeper. There are numerous occasions when the use of scales is necessary, and there is no question but that measurement by weight could be advantageously made use of far oftener than is usually done at present.

Capacity measures, or measurement by bulk, in comparison to measurement by weight, is always more or less inaccurate. But steps can and should be taken to insure as great a degree of accuracy as possible. Hence all dry ingredients, such as flour, meal, confectioners' and powdered sugar, should be sifted before using. Mustard, baking powder, cream of tartar, soda, salt, and spices should be stirred before measuring to lighten and free them from lumps. To dip a measuring cup into flour or other dry material in order to fill it and to then shake the cup to level its contents, condenses or packs the flour and causes the cup to contain more than the recipe calls for. Instead, the sifted material should be lifted into the measuring cup by spoonfuls, the contents rounded slightly, and leveled with the back of a case knife, care being taken not to shake the cup.

A cupful is measured level with the brim; a heaping cupful rounding, not as much as will stand upon the cup; a scant cupful level, with two tablespoonfuls taken out.

All ingredients, measured by the tablespoonful or teaspoonful, are measured level unless otherwise stated. To measure a spoonful, fill the spoon and level it with the back of a case knife. For a half spoonful, first measure a spoonful, then divide it in halves, lengthwise, with a thin knife blade. To measure a quarter spoonful, first measure a half spoonful and divide it crosswise, a little nearer the back than the point of the spoon, to allow for its curvature. This is equivalent to one saltspoonful. A speck is a little less than one half a saltspoonful or one eighth of a teaspoonful. Butter, lard, and other solid fats are measured by packing them solidly into the spoon or cup and leveling with a knife. Butter should be measured before melting, unless melted butter is stated in the recipe, in which case it should be measured after melting.

The ordinary coffee cup, which holds half a pint, is the common standard of domestic measure. A common-sized tumbler holds the same amount. Cups and tumblers, however, vary more or less in the size, and are not well adapted for use as measures on account of their curvature. A cup is smaller at the bottom than at the top. Hence to measure half a cupful in a coffee cup it must be filled a little more than halfway up. The ideal utensil for this purpose is a standard measuring cup, having straight sides divided into fourths and thirds, and containing half a pint. Measuring cups of glass are the most convenient, as it is easier with them to see when the measurements of small quantities are level. Also they do not rust and can be more easily kept clean. A common tin measuring cup is, however, useful and convenient. Either of these can be obtained at any good 5- and 10-cent store or mail-order establishment.

Spoons also vary in size. Hence it is well to use the same spoon in measuring or to use the small measuring scoop spoons, which are obtainable in different sizes. The use of the same spoon throughout in making up any recipe will keep the proportions correct. A heaping spoonful is all the spoon will hold. To get a rounded spoonful, fill the spoon and shake it until it is slightly rounded on top.

Tables of Domestic Measure.—The following are tables of domestic liquid and dry measure with comparative measurements by spoonfuls, cupfuls, and the weight of distilled water. It will be noted that a tablespoonful, liquid measure, is divided into four teaspoonfuls, but that the tablespoonful, dry measure, is divided into three teaspoonfuls only:

Domestic Liquid Measure

10 drops	1 saltspoon.
4 saltspoons	1 teaspoon.
4 teaspoons	1 tablespoon.
4 tablespoons	1 basting spoon.
2 basting spoons	1 gill.
2 gills	1 cup.
2 cups	1 pint.
2 pints	1 quart.
4 quarts	1 gallon.

Domestic Dry Measure

4 saltspoons	1 teaspoon.
3 teaspoons	1 tablespoon.
12 tablespoons	1 cup.
8 tablespoons, heaping	1 cup.

Measurement by Water

⅙ oz.	1 teaspoon.
½ oz.	1 tablespoon.
2 oz.	1 basting spoon.
4 oz.	1 gill.
8 oz.	1 pint.
16 oz.	1 quart.

Measurement by Spoons

10 drops	1 saltspoon.
4 saltspoons	1 teaspoon.
4 teaspoons	1 tablespoon.
½ oz. water	1 tablespoon.
1 basting spoon	4 tablespoons.
1 gill	8 tablespoons.
1 gill	32 teaspoons.
1 cup	64 teaspoons.
1 cup	16 tablespoons.
1 cup	4 basting spoons

Measurement by Coffee Cup or Common Tumbler

64 teaspoons	1 cup.
16 tablespoons	1 cup.
4 basting spoons	1 cup.
2 gills	1 cup.
½ pint	1 cup.
8 fluid oz	1 cup.
1 pint	2 cups.
1 quart	4 cups.

Weight of Food Stuffs Used in Cookery.—The following is a comparative list of the bulk and weight of different articles of common domestic use. These will be found to vary slightly, but are as accurate as can be given and have been proved by universal experience to be sufficiently correct for all practical purposes:

Article.	Quantity.	Weight.
Almonds, shelled	1 cup,	7 oz.
Barley	1 tablespoon, heaped.	½ oz.
Barley	1 cup,	4 oz.
Bread crumbs, grated	1 cup,	2 oz.
Bread crumbs	1 breakfast cup, well pressed, abt.	4 oz.
Butter	1 tablespoon, rounded,	1 oz.
Butter, hard	1 cup, even,	7 oz.
Butter, melted	1 cup,	7 oz.
Butter, packed	2 cups, scant,	1 lb.
Butter, soft	size of an egg,	2 oz.
Butter, soft	1 quart,	1 lb.
Butter, soft, well packed	2 cups,	1 lb.
Citron, chopped	1 cup,	7 oz.
Coffee	2 tablespoons, rounded,	1 oz.
Coffee	1 cup,	4 oz.
Coffee, ground	2 tablespoons, heaped,	1 oz.
Coffee, ground	4 cups,	1 lb.
Corn meal	1 tablespoon, heaped,	½ oz.
Corn meal	1 cup, even,	4½ oz.
Corn meal	3 cups,	1 lb.
Corn meal	1 quart,	1 lb. 2 oz.
Cream	1 cup (½ pint).	7 oz.
Currants, cleaned and dried	1 cup,	6 oz.
Dates	1 cup,	½ lb.
Eggs	white of,	about 1 oz.
Eggs	yolk of,	about 1 oz.
Eggs, average size	10,	1 lb.
Eggs, large	9,	1 lb.
Figs	1 cup,	½ lb.
Flour	1 teaspoon, heaped.	½ oz.
Flour	1 tablespoon, heaped,	1 oz.
Flour	2 tablespoons,	1 oz.
Flour	1 cup, level,	4 oz.
Flour	1 cup, heaped,	6 oz.
Flour	4 cups,	1 lb.
Flour	4 cups,	1 quart.
Flour, dry	4 cups, even,	1 lb.
Flour, well sifted	1 quart, heaped,	1 lb.
Juice of an ordinary lemon		about 1 tablespoon.
Lard	1 tablespoon, rounded,	1 oz.
Lard	size of an egg,	2 oz.

Article.	Quantity.	Weight.
Lard	2 cups	1 lb.
Lard, hard	1 cup, even,	7 oz.
Lard, melted	1 cup, even,	7 oz.
Lard, soft	1 quart,	1 lb.
Liquid	1 generous pint,	1 lb.
Meal, Indian	3 cups, even,	1 lb.
Meat, chopped	1 cup, solid,	8 oz.
Meat, chopped fine, well packed	1 pint,	1 lb.
Milk	1 tablespoon,	½ oz.
Milk	1 cup (½ pint),	8 oz.
Milk	2 cups,	1 lb.
Molasses	1 cup (½ pint),	12 oz.
Nutmegs	5 medium sized,	1 oz.
Prunes	1 cup,	½ lb.
Raisins	1 cup,	8 oz.
Raisins, stoned	1 breakfast cup, heaped,	½ lb.
Rice	1 tablespoon, heaped,	½ oz.
Rice	1 cup, heaped,	8 oz.
Sago	1 tablespoon, heaped,	1 oz.
Sago	1 cup,	8 oz.
Spice, ground	1 tablespoon, heaped,	½ oz.
Sugar, brown	1 tablespoon, well heaped,	1 oz.
Sugar, brown	1 cup, heaped,	½ lb.
Sugar, brown	2½ teacups, level,	1 lb.
Sugar, coffee, A	2 teacups, well heaped,	1 lb.
Sugar, granulated	1 tablespoon, heaped,	1 oz.
Sugar, granulated	1 tablespoon, well heaped,	1 oz.
Sugar, granulated	2 teacups, level,	1 lb.
Sugar, granulated	1 pint, heaped,	14 oz.
Sugar, powdered	2 tablespoons, heaped,	1 oz.
Sugar, powdered	2 tablespoons,	1 oz.
Sugar, powdered	1⅓ pints,	1 lb.
Sugar, powdered	2½ cups, even,	1 lb.
Sugar, powdered	2½ cups,	1 lb.
Sugar, powdered	2¾ cups, level,	1 lb.
Tea	1 tablespoon, heaped,	¼ oz.
Tea	1 teaspoon, heaped	⅛ oz.
Tea	1 cup, heaped,	2 oz.
Vinegar	1 cup (½ pint),	8 oz.
Walnuts, shelled	1 cup,	7 oz.
Water	1 cup (½ pint),	8 oz.
Water	2 cups,	1 lb.

Cooks' Complete Time Table.—The question which is frequently asked by housekeepers, How long is it necessary to cook this article or that? is not easily answered. Several factors enter into the calculation. Among these are size, especially as to thickness; age, as effecting the tenderness or toughness of meat and the softness or hardness of vegetables; temperature, and others. Closely allied questions are the degrees of temperature at which different substances cook, temperature produced by different kinds of fuel, time required to digest different articles of food, and the like. It is not possible to answer all these questions exactly without a knowledge of all the conditions surrounding the individual case. Hence it is always necessary for the housekeeper to use good judgment. But the following table is based upon the practical experience of the best cooks and other authorities, and will at least afford a basis of comparison. The various conditions likely to be met with in practical experience are, as far as possible, indicated:

Article.	How Cooked.	Time.
Artichokes, globe	Boiled,[1]	30 m.–1 h.
Artichokes, Jerusalem	Boiled,[2]	15 m.–30 m.
Asparagus	Boiled,	15 m.–25 m.
Au Gratin dishes	Baked,[2]	10 m.–20 m.
Bacon	Boiled gently,	15 m.
Bacon	Broiled,	4 m.–8 m.
Bacon	Fried,	3 m.–5 m.
Bacon	Fried (in its own fat),	2 m.–3 m.
Beans	Baked,[3]	8–10 h.
Beans, Lima	Boiled,	30 m.–40 m.
Beans, old	Boiled,	2 h.–4 h.
Beans, string	Boiled,[1]	1 h.–3 h.
Beans, with pork	Baked.	6 h.–8 h.

ARTICLE.	HOW COOKED.	TIME.
Beans, young	Boiled,	about 1 h.
Beef, brisket of	Boiled gently,	about 30 m.
Beef, corned	Boiled gently,	about 31 m.
Beef, corned, fancy brisket	Boiled,	5 h.–8 h.
Beef, corned, rib or flank	Boiled,	4 h.–6 h.
Beef, fillet of	Rare,	20 m.–30 m.
Beef, fillet of	Rare,[3]	45 m.–1 h.
Beef, fresh	Boiled,	4 h.–6 h.
Beef, long or short fillet of	Baked,	20 m.–30 m.
Beef, rib roast, rolled	Rare,[3]	10 m.
Beef, ribs or loin	Rare,	8 m.–10 m.
Beef, ribs or loin	Well done,	12 m.–16 m.
Beef, rolled rib or rump	Baked,	12 m.–15 m.
Beef, sirloin	Baked (rare),	8 m.–10 m.
Beef, sirloin	Roasted (rare),	9 m.
Beef, sirloin	Baked (well done),	12 m.–15 m.
Beets, new	Boiled,	45 m.–1 h.
Beets, old	Boiled,	4 h.–6 h.
Biscuit	Baked,	10 m.–20 m.
Bread, brick loaf	Baked,	40 m.–1 h.
Brocoli	Boiled,	about 30 m.
Brown bread	Steamed,	3 h.
Brussels sprouts	Boiled,	15 m.–25 m.
Brussels sprouts	Boiled,	10 m.–20 m.
Cabbage	Boiled,	30 m.–80 m
Cabbage, sliced	Boiled,	40 m.
Cabbage, winter	Boiled,	1 h. or more
Cabbage, young, quartered	Boiled,	30 m.–45 m.
Cake, fruit	Baked,	2 h.–3 h.
Cake, layer	Baked,	15 m.–20 m.
Cake, loaf, plain	Baked,	30 m.–1½ h.
Cake, sponge, loaf	Baked,[2]	45 m.–1 h.
Cake, thick	Baked,	30 m.–40 m.
Cake, thin	Baked,	15 m.–20 m.
Carrots, old	Boiled,	1 h. or more
Carrots, young	Boiled,	20 m.–30 m.
Cauliflower	Boiled,	15 m.–35 m.
Celery	Boiled,	20 m.–30 m.
Chicken	Broiled,	20 m.
Chicken	Roasted (in oven),	20 m.
Chicken, fall	Boiled,	1 h.–1½ h.
Chicken, prairie	Broiled,	4 m.–6 m.
Chicken, spring	Boiled gently,	20 m.
Chicken 3 to 4 lbs	Baked,	1 h.–1½ h.
Chops	Broiled,	8 m.
Chops, breaded	Fried,	4 m.–10 m.
Chops, lamb	Broiled,	8 m.–10 m.
Chops, mutton	Broiled,	8 m.–10 m.
Clams	Boiled,	3 m.–5 m.
Cookies	Baked,	10 m.–15 m.
Corn	Boiled,	10 m.–20 m.
Corn, green	Boiled,	20 m.–25 m.
Croquettes	Fried,	1 m.–2 m.
Cucumbers	Boiled,	12 m.–15 m.
Custards	Baked,[3]	20 m.–30 m.
Doughnuts	Fried,	3 m.–5 m.
Duck	Baked,[4]	20 m.–30 m.
Duck, domestic	Roasted,	1 h. or more.
Duck, full growth	Roasted,	45 m.–1 h.
Duck, tame	Baked,	40 m.–1 h.
Duck, wild	Roasted,	12 m.
Duckling	Roasted,	25 m.–35 m.
Endive	Stewed,	5 m.–10 m.
Fish	Broiled,	5 m.–15 m.
Fish balls	Fried,	1 m.
Fish, bass	Boiled,	10 m.
Fish, blue	Boiled,	10 m.
Fish, blue	Broiled,	15 m.–20 m.
Fish, cod	Boiled,	10 m.
Fish, fillets of	Fried,	4 m.–6 m.
Fish, haddock	Boiled,	10 m.
Fish, halibut, whole or thick piece	Boiled,	15 m.
Fish, salmon, whole or thick piece	Boiled,	10 m.–20 m.
Fish, shad	Broiled,	15 m.–30 m.
Fish, slices of	Broiled,	12 m.–15 m.
Fish, small	Fried,	1 m.–3 m.
Fish, small	Boiled,	6 m.–8 m.
Fish, small and fillets	Baked,	20 m.–30 m.
Fish, smelts	Fried,	1 m.
Fish, whole	Baked,	10 m.
Fish, 6 to 8 lbs	Baked.	1 h.

Article.	How Cooked.	Time.
Fowl, old	Boiled gently,	20 m.–30 m.
Fowl, old	Roasted,	20 m.–30 m.
Fowl, tender	Boiled,	15 m.
Fritters	Fried,	3 m.–5 m.
Gingerbread	Baked,	20 m.–30 m.
Goose	Roasted,[2]	1 h.–1¾ h.
Goose, 8 to 10 lbs	Roasted,	2 h. or more.
Graham gems	Baked,	30 m.
Grouse	Roasted (in oven),	30 m.–35 m.
Grouse	Roasted,	25 m.–30 m.
Ham	Boiled gently,	20 m.
Ham	Boiled,	4 h.–6 h.
Ham	Roasted,	15 m.
Kohl-rabi	Boiled,	15 m.–20 m.
Lamb	Roasted (well done),	15 m.–18 m.
Lamb	Baked (well done),	15 m.
Lentils	Boiled,	2 h. or more.
Lettuce	Steamed,	10 m.–15 m.
Liver	Broiled,	4 m.–8 m.
Liver	Roasted[3] (well done),	2 h. in all.
Liver, whole	Baked,	12 m.
Loaf bread	Baked,	40 m.–1 h.
Lobster	Boiled,	30 m.–40 m.
Macaroni	Boiled,	20 m.–50 m.
Meat, for bouillon	Simmer gently,	35 m.
Muffins	Fried,	3 m.–5 m.
Muffins, baking-powder	Baked,	20 m.–25 m.
Muffins, yeast	Baked,	about 50 m.
Mushrooms	Stewed,	about 15 m.
Mutton	Boiled,	15 m.
Mutton	Baked (rare),	10 m.
Mutton	Baked (well done),	16 m.
Mutton, leg of	Roasted (rare),	10 m.
Mutton, leg of	Boiled gently,	17 m.
Mutton, leg of	Roasted (well done),	15 m.
Mutton, loin of	Roasted (rare),	9 m.
Mutton, saddle of	Roasted (rare),	10 m.
Mutton, shoulder, stuffed	Roasted,	15 m.–25 m.
Mutton, shoulder, stuffed	Roasted (well done),	16 m.
Okra	Boiled,	30 m. or more.
Onions	Boiled,	45 m.–2 h.
Onions, old	Boiled,	2 h. or more.
Onions, young	Boiled,	30 m.–1 h.
Oyster plant	Boiled,	45 m.–1 h.
Oysters	Boiled,	3 m.–5 m.
Parsnips	Boiled,	30 m.–45 m.
Parsnips, large	Boiled,	1 h.–1½ h.
Parsnips, small	Boiled,	30 m.–1 h.
Partridge	Roasted,	35 m.–40 m.
Peas	Boiled,	20 m.–50 m.
Peas, green	Boiled[1],	15 m. or more.
Pie crust	Baked,	30 m.–45 m.
Pies	Baked,	30 m.–45 m.
Pigeons	Roasted,	20 m.–30 m.
Pork	Baked (well done),	30 m.
Pork	Roasted (well done),	20 m.
Pork, leg of	Roasted[5] (well done),	20 m.
Pork, loin of	Roasted[5] (well done),	18 m.
Pork, shoulder of	Roasted[5] (well done),	20 m.
Potatoes	Baked,	30 m.–45 m.
Potatoes	Baked,	45 m.–1 h.
Potatoes	Baked,	25 m.–40 m.
Potatoes	Boiled,	20 m.–30 m.
Potatoes	Boiled,	25 m.–35 m.
Potatoes	Fried,	2 m.–5 m.
Potatoes, sweet	Baked,	1 h.–1¼ h.
Potatoes, sweet	Boiled,	15 m.–25 m.
Potatoes, sweet	Boiled,	45 m.–1 h.
Pudding, 1 quart or more	Steamed,	2 h.–3 h.
Puddings, bread	Baked,	45 m.–1 h.
Puddings, plum	Baked,	2 h.–3 h.
Puddings, rice	Baked,	45 m.–1 h.
Puddings, tapioca	Baked,	45 m.–1 h.
Pumpkin	Stewed,	4 h.–5 h.
Quail	Broiled,	10 m.–15 m.
Quail, in paper cases	Broiled,	10 m.–12 m.
Rabbit	Roasted (in oven),	30 m.–45 m.
Rice	Boiled,	20 m.–30 m.
Rice	Steamed,	40 m.–1 h.
Rolls	Baked,	10 m.–15 m.
Rolls, biscuits	Baked,	10 m.–30 m.

Article.	How Cooked.	Time.
Salsify	Boiled,	about 1 h.
Scalloped dishes	Baked,[2]	10 m.–20 m.
Sea kale	Boiled,	15 m.–20 m.
Sorrel	Scalded,	10 m.–15 m.
Spinach	Boiled,	20 m.–30 m.
Spinach, covered closely	Boiled,	about 1 h.
Squabs	Broiled,	10 m.–15 m.
Squash	Boiled,	20 m.–30 m.
Steak	Broiled,	4 m.–8 m.
Steak, 1 inch thick	Broiled,	8 m.–12 m.
Steak, 1½ inch thick	Broiled,	9 m.–15 m.
Timbales	Baked,	about 20 m.
Tomatoes	Baked,	30 m.–45 m.
Tomatoes	Stewed,	15 m.–20 m.
Tomatoes	Stewed,	30 m.–45 m.
Tongue, corned	Boiled,	3 h.–4 h.
Tongue, salted	Boiled,	3 h.–4 h.
Tripe	Boiled gently,	20 m.
Turkey	Boiled,	15 m.–18 m.
Turkey	Boiled gently,	20 m.
Turkey, 8 lbs	Roasted (in oven),	3 h.
Turkey, 8 lbs	Baked,	3 h.
Turkey, 8 to 10 lbs	Roasted,	12 m.
Turnips	Boiled,	35 m.–45 m.
Turnips, old	Boiled,	45 m.–75 m.
Turnips, young	Boiled,	15 m.–20 m.
Veal	Baked (well done),	20 m.
Veal	Roasted (well done),	18 m.–20 m.
Veal, fillet of	Roasted[5] (well done),	20 m.
Veal, loin of	Roasted[5] (well done),	17 m.
Veal, shoulder, stuffed	Roasted[5] (well done),	20 m.
Venison	Roasted (rare),	10 m.
Venison, haunch of	Roasted (rare),	10 m.
Venison, saddle of	Roasted (rare),	10 m.

[1] According to age. [2] According to size. [3] In moderate oven. [4] In hot oven. [5] In slow oven.

COOKS' TABLE OF PROPORTIONS

Baking powder, for bread	1 teaspoon to 1 cup flour.
Baking powder, for cake	1 teaspoon to 2 cups flour.
Batters	1 scant cup liquid to 1 cup flour.
Bread	1 scant cup liquid to 3 cups flour.
Bread	1 teaspoon baking powder to 1 cup flour.
Bread	4 teaspoons baking powder, (even) to 1 quart flour.
Cake	1 saltspoon spice to 1 loaf.
Cake, plain[1]	1 teaspoon baking powder to 2 cups flour.
Cake, plain	1 teaspoon extract to 1 loaf.
Cake, plain	1 saltspoon salt to 1 loaf.
Cloves, for soup	4 to 1 quart soup.
Cream tartar	2 teaspoons to 1 teaspoon soda (level).
Custard	1 teaspoon extract to 1 quart.
Custard	1 saltspoon salt to 4 cups milk.
Extract, for cake	1 teaspoon to 1 loaf.
Extract, for custard	1 teaspoon to 1 quart.
Flour	2 quarts to 1 teaspoon salt.
Flour, for batter	1 cup to 1 scant cup liquid.
Flour, for bread	3 cups to 1 scant cup liquid.
Flour, for bread	1 cup to 1 teaspoon baking powder.
Flour, for bread	1 quart to 4 teaspoons baking powder (even).
Flour, for cake	2 cups to 1 teaspoon baking powder.
Flour, for muffins	2 full cups to 1 scant cup liquid.
Herbs, mixed, for soup, each	1 teaspoon to 1 quart soup.
Liquid, for batter	1 scant cup to 1 cup flour.
Liquid, for bread	1 scant cup to 3 cups flour (full).
Liquid, for custard	1 quart to 1 teaspoon extract.
Liquid, for muffins	1 scant cup to 2 full cups flour.
Liquid, for soup stock	1 quart for each pound of meat and bone.
Liquid, for yeast	1 cup to ¼ cake, compressed.
Meat	1 quart water to 1 lb. meat and bone.
Milk, for custard	4 cups to 1 saltspoon salt.
Milk, sour	2 cups to 1 teaspoon soda.
Molasses	1 cup to 1 teaspoon soda.
Muffins	1 scant cup liquid to 2 full cups flour.
Pepper (white) for soup	1 saltspoon to 1 quart soup.
Pepper corns for soup	4 to 1 quart soup.
Salt	1 teaspoon to 2 quarts flour.
Salt, for cake	1 saltspoon to 1 loaf.
Salt, for custard	1 saltspoon to 4 cups milk.
Salt, for soup	1 teaspoon to 1 quart soup.

Soda	1 teaspoon (level) to 2 teaspoons cream tartar.
Soda	1 teaspoon to 2 cups milk (sour).
Soda	1 teaspoon to 1 cup molasses.
Soda	1 teaspoon (even) to 2 teaspoons cream tartar.
Soup stock	1 teaspoon mixed herbs to 1 quart.
Soup stock	1 teaspoon salt to 1 quart.
Soup stock	1 saltspoon pepper (white) to 1 quart.
Soup stock	4 pepper corns (black) to 1 quart.
Soup stock	4 cloves to 1 quart.
Soup stock	1 tablespoon vegetables, chopped, to 1 quart.
Spice	1 saltspoon to 1 loaf of cake.
Vegetables, for soup	1 tablespoon, chopped, each to 1 quart stock.
Yeast	1 cup (liquid) to ½ cake (compressed).

[1] Cake, made light with eggs needs less.

Paper Measure.—The mode of measurement by counting and otherwise employed by paper manufacturers and dealers, printers, and the book and stationery trade is a source of confusion to many persons. Paper, like other commodities, can be most accurately measured by weight, and it is accordingly bought and sold at wholesale by the pound.

Paper can be made to order in any desired size, and with large orders this is customary, to avoid waste. For convenience, however, in deference to custom, paper is ordinarily kept in stock by wholesale dealers, cut to various convenient sizes, and sold by count according to the following table:

24 sheets	1 quire.
20 quires	1 ream.
2 reams	1 bundle.
5 bundles	1 bale.
1 bale contains	200 quires or 4,800 sheets.
480 sheets	1 ream.

A somewhat different table of measurement is used between printers and paper manufacturers (on account of the waste of paper from soiled sheets and otherwise in printing) as follows:

24 sheets	1 quire.
20 sheets	1 quire, outsides.
25 sheets	1 quire. printers'.
20 quires	1 ream.
21½ quires	1 ream, printers'.
2 reams	1 bundle.
4 reams	1 bundle, printers'.
10 reams	1 bale.
60 skins	1 roll of parchment.

Now, for convenience in counting, 500 sheets are more often called a ream, and the word quire is used only for the folded note paper, other paper being usually sold by the pound.

Quotations are ordinarily made in cents per pound. But the number of pounds in a given ream of paper is determined by the thickness of the individual sheets, and the weight in turn determines the price per ream. Hence it is customary in the paper trade to refer to paper as 40 pound, 80 pound, or 100 pound stock, meaning the number of pounds required to make a ream of a known sized sheet of the stock in question. A bill for paper properly expresses all of these particulars. For example: 32 × 45 /500/105 @ 5 cts., $5.25, signifies that the sheets in question are 32″ × 45″ in size, that 1 ream, containing 500 such sheets, will weigh 105 pounds, which, at 5 cts. per pound, would amount to $5.25 a ream.

Stock Sizes of Paper.—The following sizes of various grades of paper were formerly recognized generally by the trade and kept on hand in most wholesale printing houses. This is still the case to some extent; but the sizes recognized by these trade terms vary considerably, and the present tendency in the trade appears to be in favor of dropping the use of these trade terms, and in buying or selling to quote, in all cases, the size of the sheet only:

Writing Papers—Flat Cap

Name.	Inches.
Law blank	13 x 16
Flat cap	14 x 17
Crown	15 x 19
Demy	16 x 21
Folio post	17 x 22
Check folio	17 x 24
Double cap	17 x 28
Medium	18 x 23
Extra size folio	19 x 23
Royal	19 x 24
Superroyal	20 x 28
Imperial	22 x 30
Elephant	22½ x 27¾
Columbia	23 x 33¼
Atlas	26 x 33
Double elephant	26 x 40

Printing Paper

(Used in Printing Newspapers and Books)

NAME.	INCHES.
Medium	19 x 24
Royal	20 x 25
Superroyal	22 x 28
Imperial	22 x 32
Medium-and-half	24 x 30
Small double medium	24 x 36
Double medium	24 x 38
Double royal	26 x 40
Double superroyal	28 x 42
Also sometimes	29 x 43
Broad twelves	23 x 41
Double imperial	32 x 46
Also sometimes	32 x 44

Writing Papers—Folded

NAME.	INCHES.
Billet note	6 x 8
Octavo note	7 x 9
Commercial note	8 x 10
Packet note	9 x 11
Bath note	8½ x 14
Letter	10 x 16
Commercial letter	11 x 17
Packet post	11½ x 18
Ex. packet post	11½ x 18½
Foolscap	12½ x 16

Classifying Books. — Books are printed on sheets of paper of varying sizes, which are afterwards folded and trimmed to the size of book desired. One sheet of paper thus folded is called by printers a "signature." The marks sometimes found at intervals at the bottom of pages as a, b, c, 1, 2, 3, 1a, 2a, etc., are what printers call "signature marks." They are placed on the first page of each signature to indicate the order of the signatures for the convenience of binders in folding and gathering the sheets. These are less commonly used than formerly. In the early days of the printing industry book papers were practically of the same size. Hence the number of times a sheet was folded to make one signature of a book was an accurate means of classifying book sizes. A sheet of paper folded once into 2 leaves making 4 pages was then called a folio; 1 folded twice into 4 leaves making 8 pages a quarto, and so on, according to the following table:

2 leaves	folio,	4 pp.
4 leaves	quarto, 4to,	8 pp.
8 leaves	octavo, 8vo,	16 pp.
12 leaves	duodecimo, 12mo,	24 pp.
16 leaves	16mo,	32 pp.
18 leaves	18mo,	36 pp.
24 leaves	24mo,	48 pp.
32 leaves	32mo,	64 pp.

These terms, in deference to custom, are still retained; but on account of the extent to which paper is manufactured to order in a great variety of shapes and sizes, these terms are no longer accurate. They may be applied without regard to the sizes of the sheet folded, which may vary widely. Hence publishers apply them rather loosely, according to the approximate size of the volume compared to the earlier standards. The following table indicates roughly the most usual sizes:

SIZE.	INCHES.
32mo	4 x 5½
24mo	4½ x 5¾
18mo	4½ x 6
16mo	5 x 7
12mo	5½ x 7½
Crown octavo	5½ x 8
Octavo	6 x 9
Royal octavo	7 x 10
4to or quarto	10 x 12½
Folio	13 x 15

Or a more accurate subdivision of the principal sizes of book papers gives the following approximate book sizes:

NAME.	INCHES.
Royal folio	12 x 12
Demy folio	18 x 11
Super imperial quarto—4to	15½ x 13
Royal 4to	12½ x 10
Demy 4to	11½ x 8½
Crown 4to	11 x 8
Royal octavo	10½ x 6½
Medium 8vo	9½ x 6
Demy 8vo	9 x 5½
Crown 8vo	7½ x 4½
Foolscap 8vo	7 x 4
12mo	7 x 4
16mo	6½ x 4
Square 16mo	4½ x 3½
Royal 24mo	5½ x 3½
Demy 24mo	5 x 2¾
Royal 32mo	5 x 3
Post 32mo	4 x 2½
Demy 48mo	3¾ x 2½

Counting in Groups.—The units indicated by the following table are in frequent use for counting in various trades and otherwise:

2 things	1 pair.
6 things	1 set.
20 things	1 score.
12 units	1 dozen.
12 dozen	1 gross.
12 gross	1 great gross.

Copying.—A mode of counting occasionally made use of in copying manuscripts, taking evidence in courts of law, and otherwise, is as follows:

72 words make 1 folio or sheet of common law.
90 words make 1 folio in chancery.

CIRCULAR MEASURE

Circular measure is used in measuring arcs of circles, and angles, and in estimating latitude and longitude. It is also called angular measure.

The denominations are seconds (″), minutes (′), degrees (°), signs (s), and circumferences (cir.).

TABLE

60 seconds (″)	= 1 minute	′
60 minutes	= 1 degree	°
360 degrees	= 1 circumference	cir.

Cir.	°	′	″
1 =	360 =	21,600 =	1,296,000.

Scale: 360, 60, 60.

Circular measure is used by surveyors in surveying land; by navigators in determining latitude and longitude at sea; and by astronomers in measuring the motion of the heavenly bodies, and in computing difference in time.

The curved line which bounds a circle is its circumference. Any portion of a circumference is an arc. Every circumference may be divided into 360 equal parts, called degrees.

One half of a circumference is a semicircumference; one fourth, a quadrant; one sixth, a sextant; and one twelfth, a sign. A semicircumference contains 180°; a quadrant, 90°; a sextant, 60°; and a sign, 30°.

Since every circumference contains 360 degrees, the length of a degree depends upon the size of the circle. A degree of the earth's surface at the equator contains 69⅙ statute miles, or 60 geographical miles—a minute of space being a geographical or natural mile.

The size of an angle is the same whether the arc included between its sides be a portion of a large or small circle. Hence the measure of an angle is definite whatever be the length of a degree of the included arc.

That part of the circumference which is included between the lines which form the angle is the measure of the angle.

LONGITUDE AND TIME

Longitude is distance east or west from a given meridian. It is measured by degrees, minutes, and seconds. Thus, 15° 24′ 40″ east longitude denotes a position 15° 24′ 40″ east of the meridian from which longitude is reckoned.

A meridian is an imaginary line passing on the earth's surface from pole to pole.

Each nation selects some meridian of longitude as its standard from which to reckon, but the two in principal use throughout the English-speaking world are that of England which passes through Greenwich and that of the United States which passes through Washington. The meridian of Greenwich is most commonly employed as an international standard.

All meridian lines run north and south, and when the rays of the sun are vertical at any point of a given meridian, it is midday or noon at all places on this meridian which are then lighted by the sun. One half of every meridian circle is in light and the other half in darkness.

The rotation of the earth on its axis gives the unit of time, called a day. The day is divided into twenty-four equal parts, called hours. Since the earth rotates on its axis from west to east, the sun appears to revolve around the earth from east to west, and its rays move westward at the same rate over the earth's surface. Hence when it is noon, or twelve o'clock, at any place, it is past noon at all places east of its meridian, and before noon at all places west of its meridian. When, for example, it is noon at Cincinnati, it is later than noon at New York, and before noon at St. Louis.

Measurement of Time.—Formerly, when traveling was slow, time could be adequately measured for practical purposes by reference to the sun and by means of sundials and hourglasses. But the introduction of modern means of rapid communication and the invention of clocks and watches have enormously increased the importance of the accurate measurement of time. Hence an outline of the present mode of measuring time is of general interest.

The standards afforded by nature are the revolution of the earth about the sun, constituting the year; the revolution of the moon about the earth, the month; and the rotation of the earth upon its axis, the day. Of these the longest which can be determined by direct observation is the year. The length of the year may be established by observation in two ways, which give rise respectively to the "solar" and the "sidereal" year. The solar year may be defined as the mean interval between two returns of the sun to the vernal equinox. This takes place about March 21st. This is the year upon which the change of the seasons depends. The sidereal year is the mean interval between two returns of the sun to the same star. This is the true time of the earth's revolution, but is slightly longer than the solar year. Since, however, the change of seasons is what marks the length of the year for the practical purposes of life, the solar year is universally recognized as the standard.

The lunar month or the interval between two new moons is the next shorter unit of time. It does not, however, consist of an even number of days, nor is it an even fraction of the solar or sidereal year. Hence it has given place to an arbitrary division of time called the calendar month.

The most accurate and useful measure of all is the day, both because of the practical importance of the alternation of day and night, and because, so far as can be ascertained, the time of the earth's revolution on its axis does not change by as much as $\frac{1}{1000}$ of a second in a century. As in the case of the year, there are two ways of determining the duration of the day, giving rise respectively to the sidereal and the solar days. The sidereal day is the interval between two passages of a star across the meridian. The solar day is the interval between two passages of the sun over the meridian. Hence astronomers have set aside the use of the sidereal year and sidereal day, and the lunar month and year, as standards, and have based the measurement of time for practical purposes on the solar day and year, which are determined by the passage of the sun over the meridian.

Accepting this as the basis of the measurement of time, it remains to distinguish between "apparent solar time," "mean solar time," "local time," and "standard time," of which the first is determined by the order of nature and the rest by agreement among authorities for the convenience of civilization.

Apparent solar time is, to speak exactly, the moment at which the meridian of any place passes under the sun as the earth revolves. On account of the facts that the path of the earth about the sun is an ellipse, that the earth is accordingly farther from the sun at certain seasons of the year than others, and hence that it travels faster at one time than another (and for other reasons) the interval between two passages of the sun over the meridian at a given place, i. e., a solar day varies slightly from day to day. Hence, as a matter of convenience, an average is struck.

Mean solar time, as this average is called, is determined by the motion of an imaginary sun called the "mean sun," conceived as moving with perfect uniformity. The hours as thus determined are those measured by an accurate timepiece. Hence *apparent solar time* is set aside and *mean solar time* becomes the universal standard.

Local time is the mean solar time of any place; that is, the moment at which the place passes under the "mean sun" as the earth revolves. This moment is called noon. The sun at noon passes around the earth at the rate of four minutes for each degree of longitude. It takes about three hours to pass from New York to San Francisco. Hence at noon in New York it is later than noon on the side toward London, east; and earlier on the side toward San Francisco, west.

After the introduction of railroads and steamships the use of local time became a source of great confusion. The traveler's watch would vary from the local time four minutes for every degree of longitude traversed with the added modification caused by the time occupied in the journey. Prior to the year 1883 each railway system adopted its own standard of local time. Hence the traveler could not determine the time of the arrival of trains without adjusting his watch to the local time of each railway system he patronized.

Standard Time.—The introduction of standard time in 1883 was intended to lessen this confusion. It is based upon the selection of certain meridians, the mean solar local time of which differs by exactly one hour

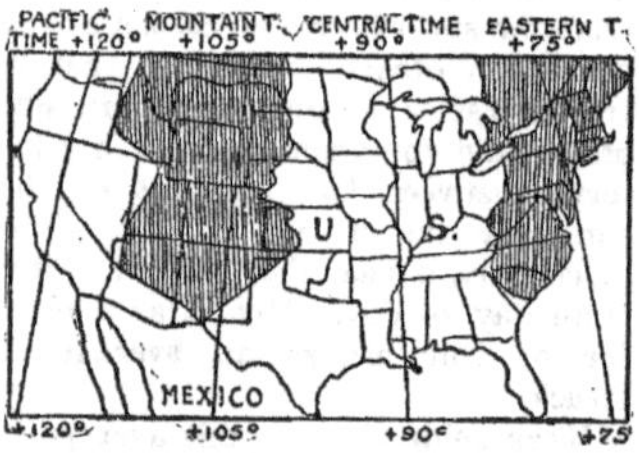

Map of Standard Time.

or multiples of one hour, and the agreement among railway authorities and others to adopt the local time of these meridians as a standard for intervening sections. The first of these meridians passes through Philadelphia, the second near New Orleans, St. Louis, and Davenport, the third near Denver, the fourth near Sacramento and Stockton. The moment that the sun crosses these meridians is taken for noon in all places not more than half an hour distant from it either east or west. Hence these meridians give rise to four belts governed by four different standards of time; namely, Eastern, Central, Mountain, and Pacific time, respectively. The lines dividing these are approximately halfway between the meridians of Philadelphia, St. Louis, Denver, and Sacramento, respectively. In each of these belts railway time is uniform, and this is practically adopted by the entire population. The traveler in passing from one belt to another merely changes his watch one hour to conform to the local time. The division into minutes remains unaltered.

In practice the lines adopted for the demarcation of the time belts are not true meridians but conform to the location of centers of population and other local conditions. The first section, *Eastern time*, includes all the territory between the Atlantic Coast and a broken line drawn from Detroit to Charleston, S. C.; which is the most southern point. The second section, *Central time*, includes the territory between this eastern line and a broken line running from Bismarck, N. D., to the mouth of the Rio Grande. The third section, *Mountain time*, includes the territory between this central line and a line representing nearly the western borders of Idaho, Utah, and Arizona. The fourth section, *Pacific time*, runs thence to the Pacific Coast. Standard time is uniform inside each of these sections and the time of each section differs from that next to it by exactly one hour. Thus, at 12 noon in New York City, Eastern time, at Chicago, Central time, it is 11 A.M.; at Denver, Mountain time, 10 A.M.; at San Francisco, Pacific time, 9 A.M.

Standard time at Boston is 16 minutes earlier than mean solar local time; at New York, 4 minutes earlier; at Washington, 8 minutes faster; at Charleston, 19 minutes faster; at Detroit, 28 minutes slower; at Kansas City, 18 minutes faster; at Chicago, 10 minutes slower; at St. Louis, 1 minute faster; at Salt Lake City, 28 minutes faster; at San Francisco, 10 minutes faster.

This difference between standard and mean solar local time causes some inconvenience. At some points, sunrise, noon, or sunset may vary from standard time as much as half an hour. The variation, however, cannot be greater than this, and in some localities is very slight. This difference may affect such matters as the hour for meals and the time given in the almanac (which is based on mean solar local time) as the hour of sunrise or sunset. Proper adjustments can be made, however, by estimating the difference in time between the meridian of the place and the standard meridian at the rate of four minutes to each degree of longitude. Standard time is now in use practically throughout the civilized world. The difference in time between two places can be easily determined by observing on a map their distance apart in degrees of longitude and allowing four minutes to each degree based on the following calculation:

1440 minutes....................1 day, or revolution of the earth.
1 revolution of the earth is 360 degrees.
Therefore, 1 degree..............4 minutes.

The following is a table of the standard for the measurement of time:

60 seconds	1 minute.
60 minutes	1 hour.
24 hours	1 day.
7 days	1 week.
4 weeks	1 lunar month.
28 days	1 lunar month.
30 days (in computing interest)	1 month.
28, 29, 30, or 31 days	1 cal. month.
12 calendar months	1 year.
13 lun. mo., 1 day, 6 hours	1 Julian year.
365 days	1 com. year.
366 days	1 leap year.
365¼ days	1 Julian year.
52 weeks and 1 day (12 cal. mo.)	1 year.
365 d., 5 h., 48 m., 49 s.	1 solar year.
365 d., 6 h., 9 m., 12 s.	1 sidereal year.
100 solar years	1 century.

The Calendar.—The following jingle will be found convenient to recall the variations in the calendar months:

Thirty days hath September,
April, June, and November;
All the rest have thirty-one
Except the second month alone
Which has but twenty-eight, in fine,
'Til leap year gives it twenty-nine.

The common year has 365 days, or 52 weeks and 1 day; the leap year 366 days.

The length of the solar year 1880 was 365 da., 5 hr., 48 m., 47⅓ sec., which is nearly one quarter of a day longer than the common year. On the supposition that 365¼ days was the true solar year, Julius Cæsar introduced a calendar in which every year exactly divisible by 4 (every fourth year) included 366 days, called leap year. The error of the Julian calendar amounts to 3,1142 days in four centuries. To correct the error, Pope Gregory XIII, in 1582, modified the Julian calendar by making three of the centennial years in every four centuries common years and one a leap year. Hence every year that is divisible by 4 and is not a centennial year is a leap year, and every centennial year that is divisable by 400 is a leap year. The year 1900 will be a common year, and the year 2000 a leap year.

Pendulum.—Any weight suspended so as to swing freely under the action of gravity is called a pendulum. Scientific investigation of the swing of the pendulum has proved that the time of the vibration of the pendulum is in proportion to the square root of its length; that is, a pendulum which vibrates once in a second must be four times as long as one which vibrates once in half a second, sixteen times as long as one which vibrates in one fourth of a second, and so on. It has been further shown that the time of the vibration is independent of the length of the arc, or the distance through which the pendulum swings, so long as the arc is comparatively small. This is what gave rise to the application of the pendulum to the regulation of timepieces.

The attraction of gravity which causes the vibration of the pendulum depends upon the distance of a body from the center of the earth. The earth being flattened at the poles, this distance is greater at the equator and less at the poles. Hence the same pendulum will vibrate faster at the poles than at the equator. Hence the pendulum is used to determine the force of gravity at various points on the earth's surface. And the length of a pendulum vibrating secouds under stated conditions is now the accepted standard of length in Great Britain and the United States. In the vicinity of New York a pendulum vibrating once in a second is $39\frac{1}{10}$ inches long.

To shorten the pendulum of a clock makes it run faster; to lengthen it makes it run slower.

Measuring Temperature.—We commonly use a thermometer known as Fahrenheit's.

In scientific work the centigrade (a word meaning "100 degrees") is used. Because there are just 100° between the freezing and boiling points of water, on the centigrade thermometer, and the freezing point is at 0°, that would be easier than the Fahrenheit to work with if we were used to it.

	FAHRENHEIT	CENTIGRADE
Water Boils	212° —	100°
Blood Heat	98° —	
Water Freezes	32°—	0°
	0°—	

Specific Gravity. — The specific gravity of any substance is the number of times its weight contains the weight of an equal volume of water. Since the weight of a cubic foot of water at its greatest density is 1,000 oz., or $62\frac{1}{2}$ lb., the weight of a cubic foot of any substance is found by multiplying 1,000 oz. avoirdupois by its specific gravity.

MEASURES OF VALUE

The common measure of value is money.

It is also called currency, and is of two kinds, viz.: coin and paper money.

Stamped pieces of metal having a value fixed by law are coin and specie.

Notes and bills issued by the Government and banks, and authorized to be used as money, are paper money.

All money which, if offered, legally satisfy a debt are a legal tender.

UNITED STATES MONEY

The unit of United States or Federal money is the dollar.

TABLE.

10 mills (m.)	= 1 cent	ct.
10 cents	= 1 dime	d.
10 dimes	= 1 dollar	$
10 dollars	= 1 eagle	e.

Scale: decimal.

The dollar mark is probably a combination of U. S., the initials of the words "United States."

The coins of the United States are:

Gold.—The double eagle, eagle, half eagle, quarter eagle, and one-dollar piece.

Silver.—The dollar, half dollar, quarter dollar, and ten-cent piece.

Nickel.—The five-cent piece.

Bronze.—The one-cent piece.

There are various other coins of the United States in circulation, but they are not coined now. The denominations dimes and eagles are rarely used, the dimes being regarded as cents and the eagles as dollars.

The unit of value is the dollar. Its standard weight in gold is 25.8 gr. The standard purity of the gold and silver coins is by weight, 9 parts of pure metal and 1 part alloy. The alloy of gold coins consists of silver and copper; the silver, by law, is not to exceed one tenth of the alloy. The alloy of silver coins is pure copper. The nickel coins consist of one fourth nickel and three fourths copper. The cent is composed of 95 parts copper and 5 parts tin and zinc.

All gold coins are a legal tender for any amount; silver coins less than $1 are legal tender for any amount not exceeding $10 in any one payment; nickel and bronze coins, for any amount not exceeding 25 cents in any one payment.

Aliquot Parts of a Dollar.—When the price of an article is an aliquot part of a dollar, the cost of any number of such articles may be found more readily than by multiplying.

The aliquot parts of a dollar commonly used in business are:

50 cts.	= $\frac{1}{2}$ of \$1	$12\frac{1}{2}$ cts.	= $\frac{1}{8}$ of \$1
25 "	= $\frac{1}{4}$ " 1	$6\frac{1}{4}$ "	= $\frac{1}{16}$ " 1
20 "	= $\frac{1}{5}$ " 1	$33\frac{1}{3}$ "	= $\frac{1}{3}$ " 1
10 "	= $\frac{1}{10}$ " 1	$16\frac{2}{3}$ "	= $\frac{1}{6}$ " 1

The following aliquot parts of a dollar are also used:

25 cts.	= $\frac{1}{2}$ of 50 cts.	$16\frac{2}{3}$ cts.	= $\frac{1}{2}$ of $33\frac{1}{3}$ cts.
$12\frac{1}{2}$ "	= $\frac{1}{4}$ " 50 "	$12\frac{1}{2}$ "	= $\frac{1}{2}$ " 25 "
$6\frac{1}{4}$ "	= $\frac{1}{8}$ " 50 "	$6\frac{1}{4}$ "	= $\frac{1}{4}$ " 25 "

ENGLISH OR STERLING MONEY

English money is the currency of Great Britain. The unit is the pound or sovereign.

TABLE.

4 farthings (far.)	= 1 penny	d.
12 pence	= 1 shilling	s.
20 shillings	= 1 pound, or 1 sovereign	£

£ s. d. far.
1 = 20 = 240 = 960.
Scale: 20, 12, 4.

Farthings are commonly written as fractions of a penny. Thus, 7 pence 3 farthings is written $7\frac{3}{4}$d.; 5 pence 1 farthing, $5\frac{1}{4}$d.

The value of £1 or sovereign is \$4.8665 in American gold, and the other coins have their proportionate values.

The coins of Great Britain in general use are:

Gold.—Sovereign, half sovereign, and guinea, which is equal to 21 shillings.

Silver.—The crown (equal to 5 shillings), half crown, florin (equal to 2 shillings), shilling, sixpenny and threepenny pieces.

Copper.—Penny and halfpenny.

METRIC SYSTEM OF WEIGHTS AND MEASURES

The metric system has been adopted by Mexico, Brazil, Chili, Peru, etc., and except Russia and Great Britain, where it is permissive, by all European nations. Various names of the preceding systems are, however, frequently used: In Germany, $\frac{1}{2}$ kilogram = 1 pound; in Switzerland, $\frac{3}{10}$ of a meter = 1 foot, etc. If the first letters of the prefixes *deka, hecto, kilo, myria,* from the Greek, and *deci, centi, mili,* from the Latin, are used in preference to our plain English, 10, 100, etc., it is best to employ capital letters for the multiples and small letters for the subdivisions, to avoid ambiguities in abbreviations: 1 dekameter or 10 meters = 1 dm.; 1 decimeter or $\frac{1}{10}$ of a meter = 1 dm.

The meter, unit of length, is nearly the ten-millionth part of a quadrant of a meridian, of the distance between equator and pole. The International Standard Meter is, practically, nothing else but a length defined by the distance between two lines on a platinum-iridium bar at 0° Centigrade, deposited at the International Bureau of Weights and Measures, Paris, France.

The liter, unit of capacity, is derived from the weight of one kilogram pure water at greatest density, a cube whose edge is one tenth of a meter and, therefore, the one-thousandth part of a metric ton.

The gram, unit of weight, is a cube of pure water at greatest density, whose edge is one hundredth of a meter, and, therefore, the one-thousandth part of a kilogram, and the one-millionth part of a metric ton.

The metric system was legalized in the United States on July 28, 1866, when Congress enacted as follows:

"The tables in the schedule hereto annexed shall be recognized in the construction of contracts, and in all legal proceedings, as establishing, in terms of the weights and measures now in use in the United States, the equivalents of the weights and measures expressed therein in terms of the metric system, and the tables may lawfully be used for computing, determining, and expressing in customary weights and measures the weights and measures of the metric system."

Approximate Equivalents.—A meter is about a yard; a kilo is about 2 pounds; a liter is about a quart; a centimeter is about $\frac{1}{2}$ inch; a metric ton is about same as a ton; a kilometer is about $\frac{5}{8}$ mile; a cubic centimeter is about a thimbleful; a nickel weighs about 5 grams.

The following are the tables:

Measures of Length

Metric Denominations and Values.		Equivalents in Denominations in Use.
Myriameter	10,000 meters.	6.2137 miles.
Kilometer	1,000 meters.	0.62137 mile, or 3,280 feet 10 inches.
Hectometer	100 meters.	328 feet 1 inch.
Dekameter	10 meters.	393.7 inches.
Meter	1 meter.	39.37 inches.
Decimeter	$\frac{1}{10}$ of a meter.	3.937 inches.
Centimeter	$\frac{1}{100}$ of a meter.	0.3937 inch.
Millimeter	$\frac{1}{1000}$ of a meter.	0.0394 inch.

Measures of Surface

Metric Denominations and Values.		Equivalents in Denominations in Use.
Hectare	10,000 square meters.	2.471 acres.
Are	100 square meters.	119.6 square yards.
Centare	1 square meter.	1,550 square inches.

Measures of Capacity

Metric Denominations and Values.			Equivalents in Denominations in Use.	
Names.	Number of Liters.	Cubic Measure.	Dry Measure.	Liquid or Wine Measure.
Kiloliter or stere	1,000	1 cubic meter	1.308 cubic yards	264.17 gallons.
Hectoliter	100	$\frac{1}{10}$ of a cubic meter	2 bush. and 3.35 pecks	26.417 gallons.
Dekaliter	10	10 cubic decimeters	9.08 quarts	2.6417 gallons.
Liter	1	1 cubic decimeter	0.908 quart	1.0567 quarts.
Deciliter	$\frac{1}{10}$	$\frac{1}{10}$ of a cu. decimeter	6.1022 cubic inches	0.845 gill.
Centiliter	$\frac{1}{100}$	10 cubic centimeters	0.6102 cubic inch	0.338 fluid oz.
Milliliter	$\frac{1}{1000}$	1 cubic centimeter	0.061 cubic inch	0.27 fluid dr.

Weights

Metric Denominations and Values.			Equivalents in Denominations in Use.
Names.	Number of Grams.	Weight of What Quantity of Water at Maximum Density.	Avoirdupois Weight.
Millier or tonneau	1,000,000	1 cubic meter	2204.6 pounds.
Quintal	100,000	1 hectoliter	220.46 pounds.
Myriagram	10,000	10 liters	22.046 pounds.
Kilogram or kilo	1,000	1 liter	2.2046 pounds.
Hectogram	100	1 deciliter	3.5274 ounces.
Dekagram	10	10 cubic centimeters	0.3527 ounce.
Gram	1	1 cubic centimeter	15.432 grains.
Decigram	$\frac{1}{10}$	$\frac{1}{10}$ of a cubic centimeter	1.5432 grains.
Centigram	$\frac{1}{100}$	10 cubic millimeters	0.1543 grain.
Milligram	$\frac{1}{1000}$	1 cubic millimeter	0.0154 grain.

APPROXIMATE EQUIVALENTS

A meter is about a yard; a kilo is about 2 pounds; a liter is about a quart; a centimeter is about ⅓ inch, a metric ton is about same as a ton; a kilometer is about ⅝ mile; a cubic centimeter is about a thimbleful; a nickel weighs about 5 grams.

Precise Equivalents.

1 acre	= .40	hectare	.4047
1 bushel	= 35	liters	35.24
1 centimeter	= .39	inch	.3937
1 cubic centimeter	= .061	cubic inch	.0610
1 cubic foot	= .028	cubic meter	.0283
1 cubic inch	= 16	cubic centimeters†	16.39
1 cubic meter	= 35	cubic feet	35.31
1 cubic meter	= 1.3	cubic yards	1.308
1 cubic yard	= .76	cubic meter	.7645
1 foot	= 30	centimeters	30.48
1 gallon	= 3.8	liters	3.785
1 grain	= .065	gram	.0648
1 gram	= 15	grains	15.43
1 hectare	= 2.5	acres	2.471
1 inch	= 25	millimeters	25.40
1 kilo	= 2.2	pounds	2.205
1 kilometer	= .62	mile	.6214
1 liter	= .91	quart (dry)	.9081
1 liter	= 1.1	quarts (liquid)	1.057
1 meter	= 3.3	feet	3.281
1 mile	= 1.6	kilometers	1.609
1 millimeter	= .039	inch	.0394
1 ounce (avoirdupois)	= 28	grams	28.35
1 ounce (troy)	= 31	grams	31.10
1 peck	= 8.8	liters	8.809
1 pint	= .47	liter	.4732
1 pound	= .45	kilo	.4536
1 quart (dry)	= 1.1	liters	1.101
1 quart (liquid)	= .95	liter	.9464
1 sq. centimeter	= .15	sq. inch	.1550
1 sq. foot	= .093	sq. meter	.0929
1 sq. inch	= 6.5	sq. centimeters	6.452
1 sq. meter	= 1.2	sq. yards	1.196
1 sq. meter	= 11	sq. feet	10.76
1 sq. yard	= .84	sq. meter	.8361
1 ton (2,000 lbs.)	= .91	metric ton	.9072
1 ton (2,240 lbs.)	= 1	metric ton	1.017
1 ton (metric)	= 1.1	ton (2,000 lbs.)	1.102
1 ton (metric)	= .98	ton (2,240 lbs.)	.9842
1 yard	= .91	meter	.9144

Courtesy, The Kellogg Fruit Co.

MRS. CURTIS'S COOK BOOK

Revised Edition

A MANUAL *of* INSTRUCTION *IN THE* ART *of* EVERYDAY COOKERY

By

ISABEL GORDON CURTIS

Author of

"Leftovers Made Palatable"
"The Everyday Cook Book"
"The Making of a Housewife"
"The Progress of a Housekeeper"

SUCCESS COMPANY'S
BRANCH OFFICES

PETERSBURG, N. Y. TOLEDO, OHIO
DANVILLE, ILLS.
OKLAHOMA CITY, OKLA. SAN JOSE, CAL.

PREFACE

This book is designed for the use of the home cook, who is interested in the best way to do her work, and who strives to set an attractive table as well as to practice economy. Although this compilation contains a number of recipes for what are termed "fancy dishes," the greater part of its teaching deals with the plain food, which is served three times a day on the table of an everyday American family. It teaches every detail about how to make good bread, how to cook vegetables, fish, meat, eggs, cereals, and other wholesome foods in the most tempting way possible. It also teaches how to utilize all sorts of left-overs—daintily and economically. I believe that every woman should know how to cook, whether she is compelled to use that knowledge or not. The knowing how is not unlike being able to swim: you may spend nearly all your life upon dry land, then suddenly comes a crucial moment when swimming means life or death. In the career of nearly every housekeeper there comes at some time a crucial moment, when the knowledge of cookery means life or death, for a steady course of unwholesome, badly cooked food is certainly death. Cookery may seem to the novice at first distasteful and hard work, but when one begins to master the principles it is an art that grows in interest. To-day instead of looking upon domestic tasks as menial labor, the woman of sense and dignity sees in a thorough and scientific mastery of such labor a step toward the higher education.

Isabel Gordon Curtis.

INTRODUCTION

WHEN the query was recently put to Isabel Gordon Curtis, "Where and how did you learn to cook?" she went back to the days of her childhood, which were spent in Scotland.

"If I was eager for one thing," she confesses, "it was to get into the kitchen on baking days. Baking day in a Scottish kitchen is very different from that in America. No yeast-raised bread is made, no cakes, cookies, pies, or doughnuts. Twice a week a Scotch housewife piles a tray full of crisp oatcakes. They are baked on a griddle, then dried on a little hanging shelf in front of a red peat fire. There is a batch of puffy scones, also griddle-baked, but no sweet stuff. The stoves are long ranges built into the wall; they never fire up enough to bake anything that needs more heat than a milk pudding. Then Scotch women do not know the secret of bread-making, for 'loaf-bread,' as it is called, comes from the bakeshops. For me there was no fascination of watching bread rise or the mysterious process of kneading. Only I loved to roll out my own little oatcakes and scones and bake the tiny batch on the edge of the griddle—that was if the cook was good-natured enough to let me hang around. When I read American stories, which told of baking days in a farmhouse kitchen, and luscious things coming from a brick oven, I longed to be in the thick of it, not so much to eat as to cook.

"I tried to make American bread—just once. Some Canadian cousins visited us and I listened eagerly to their description of baking pie, bread, and cake. The housewife of the party was a fine cook, and while she described the processes of bread-making I took it all in. My mother left with them for a few days of sight-seeing, and in her absence I determined to make bread. I took two shillings from my bank and at the bakeshop bought ten pounds of flour and a cup of yeast, 'barm' as it is called in Scotland. I rose very early next morning, and mixed the dough, kneading it till my arms ached; then I laid it into round pans. If the rising process had been described I missed it. The pans were popped straight into an oven as hot as I could make it. The loaves baked and baked and baked, while I stood right by the stove keeping it at a roaring heat. They never rose as I supposed bread ought to do and my hopes fell. Hours later I took the loaves from the oven; they were heavy and dark, with a crust you could not have broken with an axe. They looked like curling stones more than anything I can think of. The perplexing question was where to put them, for I wanted nobody to know of my failure. If I had buried them in the garden they might be dug up. Our wash house in the yard had a queer little attic which nobody entered, because the only entrance it had was a hole opening from the wide chimney. I climbed on the rough cobble stones of the wall and rolled my loaves into the dimmest recess of the attic. Years after, when I had utterly forgotten them, the wash house was demolished by a windstorm and among the débris were found my loaves. They were a curiosity to the neighbors, for I never told my secret. One old man declared they were meteorites, and his theory was looked upon as a possibility.

"In these days there were no cooking schools in Scotland, though in school we studied a text-book on domestic economy, only of what use was a text-book without practise? My mother sent me into a caterer's kitchen where many girls were taught something of cookery. There I learned how to make shortbread, the famous hot mutton pies of Scotland, gingerbread, pound cake, sponge cake, and Bath buns. We did not make bread; that was a bakery product. I had lessons, though, on how to turn out a magnificently upholstered christening or wedding cake, which shows what an impracticable course it was.

"A few years later we sailed for America. From a friendship made in this new country, I look back on the beginning of an ideal and also the beginning of a definite ambition. My ideal was one of the most gracious, accomplished, and capable women I have ever known. As I came to know her well, I realized that a woman may occupy the highest social position with charming dignity and lose none of that dignity by being a thoroughly capable housewife. She could cook, sew, or even do the work in her own kitchen, when necessity demanded it, with a perfection that is seldom found in hired help. From this woman I had my first lessons in housewifery; she taught me not only how to do work of all sorts as well as it can be done, but that it was work every woman ought to know how to do and she should be proud of that knowledge. Twenty years later, when a dedication was required for the first book I wrote on housekeeping, I gave it to the woman who at just the crucial point in my life instilled a belief that there is no higher accomplishment than to know how to live well, yet economically, making a home healthful, attractive, and happy.

"Years after, when I drifted into newspaper work and edited the woman's department of a farm paper as well as that of a city weekly, I found the knowledge I had gained of housewifery no small value. Later I married, and that knowledge was put to practical use. I began then to make domestic economy a regular study, for each day there came a new problem that demanded something more than the information in cook books. Experience and experiment prove valuable teachers.

"Ten years ago, I was called to the editorial staff of *Good Housekeeping.* That required even more extended study; a course in a cooking school and constant reading. No wider experience can be gained than in answering the questions that come from housekeepers to a home magazine. In learning how to solve problems for other people, you absorb a multiplicity of knowledge that cannot be achieved in one home. The cookery of America is cosmopolitan, its housewifery is conducted after the customs of many nations, and the woman who answers questions on a magazine cannot help but learn much that is not found in books. Following *Good Housekeeping* came similar work on *Collier's Weekly*, the *Delineator*, then on *Success Magazine.* One thing I am learning from it is, that as wide as our continent is interest in the betterment of homes, in the moral influence of wholesome, well-cooked food, in simpler living, and in household economy. It means a steady development of the American woman toward the highest ideals of housewifery."

THE PUBLISHERS.

CHAPTER XXVIII

BEVERAGES

WHEN we speak of beverages, it includes such daily drinks as tea, coffee, and cocoa, also the delicious fruit punches, which are easy to make and, in hot weather, as cooling to the blood as they are palatable. In preparing all hot beverages, freshly boiled water is a necessity, for after water has boiled five minutes it

loses a sort of sparkle that makes all the difference between a poor cup of tea and one that is stimulating and fragrant. As to coffee, there are varions methods of making it, but in boiled coffee, which is the common, everyday way of making it, we have probably the quickest and most economical method. To have coffee at its best, the water and coffee should be carefully measured, carefully watched and timed in the cooking, and the coffeepot kept scrupulously clean. Don't buy poor, cheap tea and coffee; it is simply impossible to make them fit to drink; better a small quantity of decent quality.

The majority of fruit punches, as a rule, have one base—a sirup of equal quantities of water and sugar. This is a much better way to prepare such drinks than by melting sugar, which can only be half dissolved in cold water. After the sirup for such a beverage is prepared, its flavoring is limited only by the variety of fruit on hand. The ever-handy lemon gives it necessary tartness, and to add to the deliciousness anything may be added, even a left-over of sirup from canned fruit or a cup of cold tea.

French Coffee.

1 cupful finely ground coffee,
6 cupfuls boiling water.

There are a number of pots on the market for making French coffee; any of them are suitable, provided they contain a fine strainer, which holds the coffee and prevents the grounds from getting into the infusion. To make coffee in this fashion, put the coffee into the strainer, which is generally set into the mouth of the pot; place the pot on the stove and slowly pour the water over the grounds, allowing it to filter through. If you wish to have the coffee stronger, pour out the infusion and pour it a second time over the grounds, but do not allow it to cool.

Boiled Coffee.

4 heaping tablespoonfuls ground coffee,
1 quart freshly boiling water,
½ white of egg.

Mix the white of egg with 3 tablespoonfuls cold water, beating with a fork; add the coffee and stir till wet. Scald coffeepot, put in prepared coffee, pour in boiling water, cover the spout, and boil five minutes. Pour in quickly ¼ cupful cold water; stand three minutes to settle. Strain into a hot pot or have strainer on table.

Tea.

Water for tea should be used when it has just reached the boiling point. Teas are of differing strengths, but a safe rule is 1 teaspoonful dry tea to ½ pint boiling water. Scald the pot, put in dry tea, and cover one minute. Add boiling water and cover closely. Let stand three to six minutes and strain off into another hot pot. A wadded cozy keeps the tea hot for a long time.

Cocoa.

In a tablespoonful of boiling water dissolve a small teaspoonful of Runkel's cocoa powder, then add a cupful of boiling milk, and boil together for five minutes, stirring continually. When served, sweeten to taste. This is for one cup; for larger quantities, follow the same proportions. Use only earthen or porcelain vessels, as tin spoils the flavor of cocoa.

Afternoon Chocolate.

1 quart milk,
3 squares Runkel's chocolate,
3 tablespoonfuls boiling water,
2 tablespoonfuls sugar.

Put the chocolate in a double boiler. When it melts, add the sugar and stir thoroughly till both are dissolved. Add the boiling water and beat it smooth, then pour over it the scalded milk. With an egg beater, whip the beverage till it foams, keeping it over the fire. Serve from a chocolate pot, sweetening to taste and putting into each cupful a tablespoonful of whipped cream. If you desire the chocolate delicately thickened, add ½ tablespoonful cornstarch dissolved in cold milk during the cooking process.

Piazza Punch.

Juice 2 lemons,
Juice 1 orange,
1 cupful sugar,
2 cupfuls grape juice,
2 cupfuls water.

Mix together the juice of the lemons and orange, add sugar, grape juice, and water. Place a small cake of ice in the bottom of a punch bowl or in a tall glass pitcher and pour in the liquid.

Lime Punch.

½ cupful lime juice,
2½ cupfuls sugar sirup,
2 cupfuls pineapple juice,
¾ cupful orange.

Mix together the lime juice and sirup; then add the pineapple juice and orange. When ready to serve, put in glasses half filled with crushed ice and add a few Maraschino cherries.

Pineapple Punch.

1 cupful grated pineapple,
2 cupfuls water,
2 cupfuls sugar,
½ cupful fresh-made tea,
Juice 3 oranges,
Juice 3 lemons,
1 cupful grape juice,
2½ quarts water.

Put the pineapple and 2 cupfuls water to boil for fifteen minutes. Strain through cheese cloth, pressing out all the juice. Add 1 pint of water to the sugar, which has been boiled ten minutes, then add the tea, juice of the oranges and lemons, grape juice, and the balance of the water. Put in a punch bowl with a large lump of ice. Serve perfectly chilled in sherbet glasses.

Fruit Punch.

Juice 6 lemons,
2 cupfuls water,
1 pound sugar,
Chopped rind 1 lemon,

2 bananas,
1 grated pineapple,
½ bottle Maraschino cherries and their liquor,
2 quarts Apollinaris.

Put the water, sugar, and rind of lemon on to boil; boil five minutes, strain, and while hot slice into it the bananas, pineapple, cherries and their liquor. When ready to serve, put in the center of punch bowl a square block of ice; pour over it the Apollinaris; add to the fruit the juice of the lemons and put it all into the bowl.

Mulled Cider.

1 quart cider,
1 teaspoonful whole allspice,
½ teaspoonful cassia buds,
3 eggs.

Put the cider with the spices in it in a saucepan and boil three minutes. Pour it carefully over the eggs, which habe been beaten thoroughly, and serve hot.

Raspberry and Currant Punch.

A pleasant drink is made of raspberries and currants—a pint of the former to a quart of the latter. Bruise the fruit in a preserving kettle with a potato masher and pour over it 2 quarts cold water. Put the kettle over a moderate fire, where it will heat gradually. After it begins to boil, remove the kettle from the fire; pour the contents into a jelly bag and let it drain through the bag into a large bowl. When it is clear and cool, ice and sweeten it and serve in little glasses.

Tea Punch.

1 quart boiling water,
4 tablespoonfuls tea,
1 cupful granulated sugar,
Juice 4 lemons,
½ pint Apollinaris.

Pour the boiling water over the tea; cover and leave for five minutes; strain off and cool. Half fill the punch bowl with cracked ice, add the sugar and strained juice of the lemons. Pour the tea over these, and, as it goes to table, add the Apollinaris. Strew a handful of mint sprays on the surface and serve at once.

Cocoa Nibs or "Shells."

Wet 2 ounces cocoa shells with a little cold water and stir into them a quart of boiling water. Boil steadily for an hour and a half; strain, stir in a quart of fresh milk, bring almost to the scalding point, and serve. Sweeten in the cups.

Raspberry Vinegar.

Mash the berries and, when reduced to a pulp, add enough vinegar to cover them. Set close by the stove for twelve hours, stirring often. Strain and press; add as many raspberries (mashed) to the vinegar as before; cover and leave in the hot sun for six hours. Now strain, and measure the juice; add half as much water as you have juice, and stir into this 5 pounds granulated sugar for every 3 pints of liquid. Bring slowly to a boil, let it boil up once, and strain. Bottle, cork, and seal.—MARION HARLAND.

Ginger Beer.

6 ounces bruised ginger,
6 quarts water,
5 pounds loaf sugar,
1 gill lemon juice,
¼ pound honey,
17 quarts cold water,
1 egg,
2 teaspoonfuls essence lemon.

Boil the ginger and water for half an hour; then add the sugar, lemon juice, honey, the balance of the water, and strain through a cloth. When cold, put in the egg and essence of lemon. After standing three or four days it may be bottled.

Ginger Pop.

2 gallons lukewarm water,
2 pounds white sugar,
2 lemons,

1 tablespoonful cream of tartar,
1 cupful yeast,
2 ounces white ginger root, bruised and boiled.

Pour this mixture into a stone jar and stand in a warm place for twenty-four hours; then bottle. The next day it will be ready to "pop."—Marion Harland.

Cream Soda.

1 pound loaf sugar,
2 cupfuls rich cream,
1 quart water,
1 tablespoonful McIlhenny's Mexican vanilla,
½ ounce tartaric acid.

Mix the ingredients and bring slowly to a boil; then put in jars. Use a tablespoonful of this and a third of a teaspoonful of soda to a glass of iced water.

Portable Lemonade.

Rasp the rind of a large and not too-ripe lemon on ¼ pound loaf sugar, reduce it to powder, and mix with the strained juice of the fruit. Stir well together, and when thoroughly mixed, press tightly into a small jar, cork, and tie over with waxed paper. When required for use, dissolve a tablespoonful of the paste in a glass of water with a lump of ice. This paste will keep good for months. If too sweet, a slight amount of citric acid will give it the necessary sharpness.

Egg Lemonade.

2 cupfuls sugar,
3 cupfuls water,
Grated rind 1 lemon,
Juice 3 lemons,
1 egg,
1 bottle effervescent water.

Boil together the sugar and water for ten minutes; add the grated rind and juice of the lemons. Allow this to cool, and at time of serving add the egg, beaten until very light and creamy, and the effervescent water, poured from some height in order that the mixture may foam. Serve with cracked ice in glasses.

Chocolate Cream Nectar.

4 tablespoonfuls hot coffee,
2 squares Runkel's chocolate,
1½ cupfuls sugar,
3 cupfuls water,
1 teaspoonful McIlhenny's Mexican vanilla.
Whipped cream.

Melt the chocolate in the hot coffee; add the sugar and water; boil clear and strain. There should be 1 quart of the liquid. When cold, add the vanilla, then pour it into glasses in which you have placed 1 tablespoonful whipped cream and a little shaved ice. Stir before drinking. This is good hot, if a portion of milk is added to the chocolate sirup, and the whipped cream placed on top.

Iced Coffee with Orange Flavor.

1 quart strong coffee,
2 cupfuls sugar.

Boil the ingredients ten minutes. Allow this to cool and add to each cup or glass 1 tablespoonful orange sirup and the same amount of cream partially whipped. The orange sirup may be obtained at a drug store or made by allowing cut oranges to stand in sugar and straining off the juice.

Black-Currant Cup.

To 1 quart weak green tea add ½ pint black-currant juice; sweeten to taste and chill thoroughly before serving.

Ching Ching.

Fill a glass two thirds full of shaved ice; add 3 or 4 lumps of sugar, the juice of a large orange, and a few drops of essence of cloves or peppermint.

Fruit Cup.

Juice ½ lemon,
1 teaspoonful lime juice,

1 teaspoonful pineapple juice,
4 ounces sugar,
2 ounces shaved ice.

Fill up the glass with rich milk, shake until foamy, and drink at once.

Pineapple Lemonade.

1 pineapple,
Juice 4 lemons,
1 pound sugar,
1 pint water.

Pare, eye, and grate the pineapple; add the strained juice of the lemons and a sirup made by boiling together for four minutes the sugar and water. When cold, add 1 quart water; strain and ice.

Fruit Beverage.

12 lemons,
2½ pounds sugar,
1 quart ripe raspberries,
1 pineapple.

Peel the lemons very thin; squeeze the juice over the peel and let stand two hours; then add 1 pound sugar; mash the raspberries with ½ pound sugar, strain the lemon juice and mash the raspberries through a coarse sieve, then the pineapple, and mix all together, adding 3 quarts cold water. Stir until the sugar is dissolved; strain, and serve with a little of the fruit in each glass.

Picnic Lemonade.

1 quart water,
2 figs,
Peel and juice of 2 lemons,
1 tablespoonful honey.

Put the water into a stewpan to boil; add the figs cut in two; let the water and figs boil a quarter of an hour; add the lemon peel cut in thin slices; boil ten minutes longer; pour into a jug; cover closely with paper until cold; pass through a sieve and add the honey and lemon juice. Sugar can be used in place of honey.

Russian Tea.

4 teaspoonfuls tea,
1 quart boiling water,
1 teaspoonful sugar,
½ slice lemon,
1 Maraschino cherry.

Pour the boiling water over the tea, and allow it to stand for five minutes. Into each cup put the lemon, cherry, and sugar, and pour the tea over them.

Raspberry Shrub.

For every cupful raspberry juice take ½ cupful white-wine vinegar and 2 cupfuls sugar. Put the fruit juice, sugar, and vinegar over the fire, stir until the sugar dissolves and boil to a thick sirup; strain and bottle. All fruit juices are used in the same manner. When served, allow ¼ cupful sirup to ¾ cupful ice water.

Elderblossom Wine.

1 quart elderberry blossoms,
9 pounds sugar,
1 yeast cake,
3 gallons water,
3 pounds raisins,
½ cupful lemon juice.

The blossoms should be picked carefully from the stems and the quart measure packed full. Put the sugar and water together over the fire, stir until the sugar is dissolved, then let it boil without stirring. Boil five minutes, skim, and add the blossoms. As soon as the blossoms are stirred in, take from the fire and cool. When lukewarm, add the dissolved yeast and lemon juice. Put in an earthen jar for six days, stirring thoroughly three times daily. The blossoms must be stirred from the bottom of the jar each time. On the seventh day strain through a cloth and add the raisins, seeded. Put in glass preserve jars and cover tightly. Do not bottle until January.

Mint Fizzle.

Cut the rind of 1 lemon thin, then into small strips. Squeeze juice of ½ lemon in each glass; add 1 teaspoonful sugar; stir until dissolved; fill half up with shaved ice; pour in half ginger pop and half grape juice; place 3 sprigs of mint and 2 pieces of peel in each glass and serve with straws.

Red-Currant Punch.

Boil for five minutes 1 cupful sugar and 3 quarts water. Remove from the fire, and, while the sirup is still hot, dissolve in it 1 pint red-currant jelly. Add 3 lemons and 3 oranges, sliced thin. Set on ice until chilled and serve in glasses partly filled with crushed ice.

Tutti-Frutti Punch.

2 quarts water,
1 pound sugar,
Grated rind 2 lemons,
Grated rind 4 oranges,
Juice from the lemons and oranges,
24 Malaga grapes,
2 slices tangerine oranges,
4 slices pineapple,
1 banana,
1 pint Maraschino cherries.

The special characteristic of the above recipe is found in the Maraschino cherries, which give a peculiar zest to the punch. Boil five minutes 1 quart of the water and sugar; add the grated rinds of the lemons and oranges and continue boiling for ten minutes longer. Strain the sirup through cheese cloth and add 1 quart cold water. Extract the juice from the lemons and oranges, strain, and mix with the grapes, cut in half and seeded, oranges, pineapple, sliced banana, and the Maraschino cherries with their liquor, the cherries being halved. Serve from a punch bowl in which a cube of ice has been placed.

Sparkling Lemonade.

36 lemons,
3 pounds granulated sugar,
6 oranges,
1 pineapple,
1 box strawberries,
4 quarts carbonic water.

Squeeze the juice from the lemons and remove the pips. Put it into the punch bowl with the sugar and stir until dissolved. Slice the oranges, shred the pineapple, hull and wash the berries; then add them all to the lemon juice. Put a large cube of ice in the punch bowl. Just before serving, add the carbonic water, which has previously been chilled.

Cider Eggnog.

To each quart of cider allow 4 eggs. Beat the yolks until they assume the consistency of cream. Beat the whites to a stiff froth. Stir together the cider and beaten yolks and sweeten to taste. Stir in half the beaten whites and season slightly with grated nutmeg. Stand on ice until cold. Serve in punch glasses with a teaspoonful of the meringue on top of each glass.

Mint Ale.

Juice 5 lemons,
1½ cupfuls sugar,
½ dozen stalks and leaves of bruised mint,

2 bottles ginger ale.

Mix the lemons and sugar together; when melted, place in a punch bowl with the bruised mint, and when the bowl has been half filled with cracked ice, add the ginger ale.

Chocolate Sirup.

To use in emergency for making cool drinks.

2 ounces Runkel's chocolate,
2 cupfuls boiling water,
2 pounds sugar,
2 tablespoonfuls McIlhenny's Mexican vanilla.

Put the chocolate in a double boiler and let it melt gradually, stirring occasionally. Add the sugar and water. When thoroughly dissolved, strain and add the vanilla. Bottle and keep in a cool place until wanted. A tablespoonful added to a glass of iced water or charged water makes a delicious cool drink in a moment or two. Or pour a few spoonfuls of it in a cocktail glass over shaved ice and cover with sweetened whipped cream for an afternoon-tea delicacy. With boiling water and whipped cream it makes a cupful of hot chocolate without a moment's delay.

Old Colonial Mint Cup.

1 bunch fresh mint,
6 oranges,
2 lemons,
½ ounce pulverized gum arabic,
½ cupful cold water,
1 cupful sugar,
Whites of 2 eggs.

Steep mint in sufficient hot water to extract the flavor, adding the juice of the oranges and lemons. Dissolve over hot water the gum arabic, soaked in cold water for twenty minutes, add the sugar and cook until it spins a thread; pour this boiling hot upon the stiffly beaten whites of eggs, beating until cold and smooth. Stir in the strained mint flavoring and fruit juice. Dilute to the required strength with carbonated water and serve in tumblers containing finely cracked ice, garnishing each portion with lemon peel and sprigs of mint.

Lemonade.

2 cupfuls sugar,
1 quart water,
¾ cupful lemon juice.

Boil the sugar and water fifteen minutes, then add the fruit juice. Cool and, if too strong, add a piece of ice to dilute it.

Ginger Punch.

2 cupfuls sugar,
2 quarts water,
1 pound Canton ginger,
1 cupful orange juice,
1 cupful lemon juice.

Pour the water over the sugar and add the ginger, which has been cut coarsely in a meat chopper. Boil for twenty minutes, add the fruit juice, and strain. Allow it to cool, then pour over a piece of ice in a punch bowl.

CHAPTER XXIX

BREAD

First in every household is demanded good bread. Not hit-and-miss bread—fair at one baking, poor at another—but a sweet, wholesome, nutty-flavored loaf, beautiful chestnut brown all over, and so perfectly baked as to be palatable when ten days old.

The very best flour is the cheapest; it makes the finest bread, it contains the largest amount of nutrition, and it produces twice the quantity of wholesome bread that cheap flour does. In nearly every pantry you find two brands of flour; usually we call them bread flour and pastry flour. It is possible to make fair pastry and good cake from bread flour, but it is hard to make good bread from pastry flour. You can apply three tests to flour to discover whether it will make good bread; first, it should be of a creamy color; second, it will cake slightly when gathered up into the hand, falling apart in a gritty sort of way when the fingers are released; third, its wetting capacity is very different from poor flour, one quart of first-class bread flour absorbing about one and a half cupfuls of water. Before purchasing a barrel, or even a half-barrel, of flour, buy a bagful, try one sort after another, use the same yeast, and the same care with the mixing, raising, and baking. Presently you will discover with what flour you have the best success; then stick to that brand. As for yeast; none is better than compressed yeast, which can be found fresh every day even in the smallest village. If it has been kept too long, it will begin to show dark streaks, have a strong odor, and it will not break clean. Let us stop for a minute to study the properties of yeast and its action when mixed with flour and liquid, then it will be much easier to understand what is happening during the process of bread making. If you could look at a drop of yeast under a microscope, you would see a mass of tiny, rounded cells. You can imagine how tiny they are when I tell you there are fifty billion cells in a two-cent yeast cake.

Each cell is a minute sac filled with watery matter, and while you watch, you may see new cells budding out of the old ones. Yeast is the same fungus which finds its way into cans of fruit that have not been hermetically sealed, and into maple sirup or any sweet liquid which is not properly protected from the air. Then, given a warm temperature and sugar for the creation of oxygen, it begins to work, as every housewife knows to her sorrow. The same working process is what we invite when we set bread with yeast. It will not begin its work until it has been given sugar, heat, and moisture. It thrives best at 78°; you can make it work more quickly by raising the temperature, but when it reaches 130° it is blighted, just as a plant dies in an overheated room. Now you know what happens when you set your bread near a hot stove or register—the "yeast has been killed." It is almost impossible, however, to kill yeast with cold. I have thawed it very gradually more than once and made excellent bread from it. You know how slowly bread rises after it has been chilled by a cold night.

Still it will rise, for the growth of the yeast was simply brought to a standstill.

In chemistry a name which means sugar fungus has been given to yeast. It needs, you remember, air as well as moisture to make it grow, and when sugar is at hand, it will supply itself with some of the oxygen contained in it. Oxygen is what is required to raise every dough or batter; so frequently bread recipes call for a tablespoonful of sugar. Sugar is not a necessity, however, because yeast changes the starch in flour into sugar. It is needed only when the yeast is none too lively and requires a bit of help. Immediately when yeast goes into batter, which is the first step in bread making, a chemical change, which we call fermentation, begins to take place. We help the yeast to begin work by hard beating of the batter, then by kneading the dough, for both of these processes tend not only to mix the ingredients thoroughly, but also to inclose air; the longer the beating and kneading the more air is inclosed, and the spongier becomes your bread.

The first step in bread making, as in cookery, is to get together everything necessary in utensils and materials. The utensils we need are a bread pan with a close-fitting, ventilated cover, a measuring cup, a wire spoon for beating the batter, a slitted wooden spoon to stir with, and a molding cloth. The molding cloth is a square yard of heavy duck or sail cloth; it is much superior to the smooth surface of a wooden molding board, because considerable flour can be sifted into the rough surface of the fabric. It holds the flour and there is no sticking of soft dough. As the flour works into the dough, sift in more, rubbing it into the cloth with your hand. When you have finished work, shake it, fold the cloth, and lay it away until needed again. It can be used a number of times before being washed; when it has to go to the laundry, soak it for an hour in cold water, and rinse several times before putting in the suds; hot water would turn the flour into dough; then it would be no easy task to get it clean.

Sift into a pan four or five quarts of flour, and set it either over the register or in a moderate oven to warm, unless you are working in midsummer. Cold flour will always retard the raising of bread. Scald one pint of milk and pour it into the bread pan over two teaspoonfuls of salt. Add a pint of cold water, then one yeast cake dissolved in half a cupful of lukewarm water. To this liquid add seven or eight cupfuls of warm flour, and beat the batter thoroughly with a wire spoon. Do not stop beating until the batter is a mass of bubbles. Then take the slitted spoon and begin adding more flour till you have a soft dough. When it becomes too stiff to stir, dust plenty of flour into the molding cloth, rubbing it into the fabric till it will hold no more. Gather the dough into a ball and drop it on the cloth. Now begin to knead, folding the edge of the dough farthest from you toward the center, pressing it away with the palms, gently yet quickly. The process of kneading has more to do with good bread than almost anything else. In a cooking school I have seen pieces of the same dough, raised in the same temperature, baked in the same oven, yield two entirely different qualities of bread. One loaf was molded by an energetic, strong-muscled girl whose kneading was so strenuous that all the life had been banged out of it. The other loaf was kneaded by a girl whose every movement was grace; she used her hands deftly, lightly, and briskly. Her bread was as fine as bread could be made, a spongy, delicious, well-shaped loaf. So remember that it is not brute force that tells in kneading; it is steady, light, springy, dexterous movements, which distribute the yeast plant evenly through the dough and inclose all the air it is possible to get. As you work you can see how the air is doing its duty, for the dough becomes full of little bubbles and blisters. When it is smooth as satin, elastic, does not stick, and is so spongy that it rises quickly after denting it with your finger, it is ready to set to rise. Wash the bread pan and grease it well, even inside the lid; this makes the dough slip out clean after the next raising. Put on the cover and set the pan in a warm place. When it has doubled in bulk, drop it again on the floured molding cloth, and shape into loaves.

As soon as the dough has doubled in bulk, turn it out on a slightly floured molding cloth and knead into loaves. This second kneading is a slight one, only enough to prepare it for the pans and get rid of any large air bubbles which, if left in, would mean holes in the bread. Have the pans greased, using a butter brush which penetrates to every corner. Always make small loaves; generally the right size can be guessed at by having each pan half full of dough. I like bread baked in the French or round bread pans. The crust of it is exceedingly good, the loaf cuts into neat slices, not a bit of the bread being wasted, and it bakes to a nicety without any danger of burning. In rectangular pans the dough in the corner does not have room to fully expand. When large brick-shaped loaves are made, it is almost impossible to bake them to the heart unless the crust gets very thick and hard. If heat does not penetrate to the center of a loaf, yeast may remain alive, and when it ferments in the stomach there is good cause for serious indigestion.

After the bread is in the pans we have to find a place for it to rise. In the summer I set it in the window, which, of course, is closed, for a draught on rising bread hurts it. During the winter the bread goes on a shelf close to the kitchen chimney, behind the stove. The shelf is covered with white oilcloth and just wide enough for four pans. When set to rise, the loaves are covered with cloths made from old table linen. These are kept laundered and never used except on baking days. A question I am often asked is: "How do you know when bread is raised enough to be put in the oven?" This is one of the most important points about bread making. I might tell you to let it rise for an hour, only time depends so much upon temperature. I might suggest that it be allowed to become doubled in bulk, but even that is not a sure test. The only one I ever use is to keep "hefting" it, as a New England cook would say. The loaf will keep on for an hour or so being of quite good weight, then all of a sudden it feels light. Pop it in a hot oven. Strange as it may seem, a row of pans filled with bread at the same time, which have stood in the same temperature, will seldom "heft" light at the same minute. I have seen half an hour of difference between the time three or four pans were ready to go in the oven.

Nearly every cookbook gives a different test for the proper heat of the oven. It ought to register 360°, but as few cooks use a thermometer, you may go by this test: Sprinkle a teaspoonful of flour on the oven bottom, and if it browns in five minutes the oven is just right for the bread. If it grows chestnut brown in that time, cool the oven or your bread will crust too quickly. When the loaves are in, watch them; if you see one throwing up an awkward ridge or hump anywhere, you may know that corner of the oven is too hot and the bread is rising faster than it ought to do. Do not let one loaf touch another; the dough will run together if they do. Then when they are pulled apart, there is not only an unsightly loaf, but a heavy streak in the bread. If the oven is just right, it will begin to brown in fifteen minutes; it will not rise farther. Then cool the oven slightly; if you are using a gas stove, turn out one of the burners, and let the baking go on moderately till the bread has been in for an hour. Take out the well-browned loaves, turn them immediately out of the pans, brush over the crust with a buttered brush, and set them to cool on a wire stand. If loaves are set flat, the bottom will become moist; if they are wrapped in a cloth, there is a soft, steamy crust. In summer if the steam is not allowed to evaporate from bread, there is danger of it molding, so it must never be put away until perfectly cool. The best place to store it is in a small, shelved closet of japanned ware, with a door that closes tight. This is a better and handier receptacle than the wooden tub or stone jar used in some households. Never keep bread in a cellar; it is a horribly unwholesome custom.

Little Notes About Bread Making

Some cooks prefer to set a sponge when making bread, allowing it to rise in the shape of a well-beaten batter before adding flour enough to do the kneading. "Sponging" makes a fine-grained bread, but it lengthens the time required for making, as two risings are needed after the sponge is light.

Bread may be made from water alone instead of "half and half," as milk and water bread is called. Water bread is tougher and sweeter and keeps better than that made from all milk.

A good test of whether bread has been kneaded enough is to leave it on the board or molding cloth for a few minutes. When you take it up again, if it does not stick it is ready to put in the bread pan.

If you want to make bread in a hurry, simply double the amount of yeast, that is, if you are using compressed yeast. It gives no yeasty flavor, although brewers' and home-made yeast do leave a slight taste when more than the prescribed quantity is used. Should the oven be too hot, set a pan of cold water in it for a few minutes.

Don't use potatoes or potato water in bread. The liquid in which potatoes have been boiled contains a poisonous alkaloid and it tends to darken the bread as well as giving it a

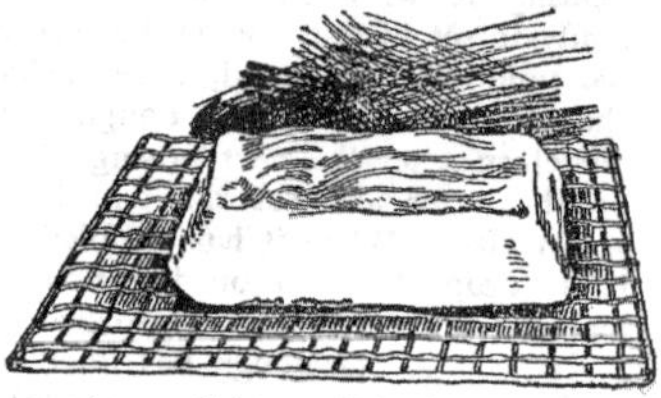

Cake on a Wire Cooler.

peculiar flavor. Years ago, before milling had been brought to perfection, there might have been reason for adding mashed potatoes to bread; now, with our fine flour, there is no necessity for it.

The best way to care for a bread box is to wash it in hot water, then close it, and dry it on the cool end of a stove. This ought to be done between each baking to keep it fresh and sweet.

Milk bread browns more quickly than water bread; so do not imagine because your loaf is a nice chestnut brown that it is baked. Give it time enough, which is from fifty to sixty minutes for brick loaves four inches thick.

If you are detained from getting bread into the pans when it has risen sufficiently, take a knife and cut down the dough till you are ready to attend to it. This allows the gas to escape and there is no danger of souring if you cannot return to it for half an hour.

It is best to have your fire in such condition that it will need no replenishing while bread baking is in progress.

Yeast may be kept perfectly fresh for at least a week or ten days by immersing the cake in cold water. The particles of yeast settle at the bottom and water acts as a seal from the air. Cover the glass in which yeast is dissolved and keep it in a cellar or refrigerator. Occasionally pour off the water that covers it and add fresh water.

If you do not own a covered bread pan, raise the dough in a large, clean bowl or basin, only keep it well covered with a towel. A paper tightly tied down is better still, for it prevents air from entering.

When a recipe calls for one compressed yeast cake and nothing can be obtained but liquid yeast, use one cupful of it instead.

If you don't have a wire stand for cooling bread, simply turn up a couple of bread tins and stand the loaves against their edges. The idea is to let the steam escape, so that your bread will neither be heavy nor moist.

If you want to hurry bread slightly, add one tablespoonful of sugar to four quarts of flour. The yeast plant begins to grow quicker when there is sugar to feed on. When there is no sugar, the yeast has to change some of the starch to sugar, and, of course, this takes time.

Pricking the top of a loaf with a fork before it is put in the oven tends to make it rise and bake evenly.

Do not try setting bread over night either in midsummer or midwinter. In cold weather bread is likely to be chilled, in summer it may sour. There is plenty of time to raise and bake bread in the daytime, when one can watch it and give the careful consideration it requires above any other cooking.

If you live in a region where the water is very hard, boil it, and let it grow lukewarm before mixing with flour, for soft water is better than hard in the bread-making process.

Flour is almost as sensitive to odors as is milk; therefore it should be kept in a perfectly clean, wholesome, dry place. Always raise the barrel off the floor, either on two strips of wood or on one of the handy little contrivances which will swing it out and in to a cupboard. Never use flour for anything without sifting it first—it may be perfectly free from any foreign substance and it may not.

Water Bread.

4 cupfuls boiling water,
4 tablespoonfuls lard,
1 tablespoonful sugar,
1½ teaspoonfuls salt,
1 yeast cake dissolved in ½ cupful lukewarm water,
3 quarts sifted flour.

Put the lard, sugar, and salt in a bread raiser; pour on boiling water; when lukewarm, add dissolved yeast cake and 5 cupfuls flour; then stir until thoroughly mixed. Add remaining flour, mix, and knead. Return to bowl; let rise over night. In the morning cut down, knead, shape into loaves or biscuits, place in greased pans, having pans nearly half full. Cover, let raise again, and bake.

Entire-Wheat Bread.

4 cupfuls scalded milk,
½ cupful brown sugar,
1½ teaspoonfuls salt,
1 yeast cake,
9 cupfuls entire-wheat flour.

Put sugar and salt in a bread raiser and pour the hot milk over them; when cool, add the flour and yeast cake, beat hard with a wooden spoon for five minutes, cover the pan and set in a warm place till the batter doubles its bulk. Beat it down, turn into greased bread pans, having each half full. Let the batter rise nearly to the top, then bake.

Caraway Bread (German recipe).

Follow the recipe for entire-wheat bread, substituting rye flour for entire-wheat flour and adding 2 tablespoonfuls sugar. Make the bread as directed at the first kneading, working in a tablespoonful of caraway seeds. Shape into loaves, raise, and bake.

Graham Bread.

1 quart Graham flour,
1 quart white flour,
1 yeast cake,
1½ teaspoonfuls salt,
½ cupful brown sugar,
1 quart milk.

Scald the milk and pour it over the sugar and salt; when lukewarm, stir in the flour and the yeast, which has been dissolved in warm water. Beat hard and let it rise in the pan till spongy. This is a dough which is not stiff enough to knead; it simply requires a thorough stirring and beating. Put it into greased pans, raise, and bake in an oven which is hot at first, but cool during the later part of the baking process. This dough may be used to drop into greased gem pans and bake as muffins.

Rye Bread.

2 quarts rye flour,
1 quart wheat flour,
1 yeast cake,
3 pints warm water,
2 teaspoonfuls salt,
3 tablespoonfuls sugar.

Sift the flour with the sugar and salt, stir in the warm water and dissolved yeast. When thoroughly mixed, begin to work it with your hands; it will be sticky, but the dough must be kept very soft. When thoroughly beaten, pour it into well-buttered pans and set it in a warm place. Let it rise to twice its bulk and bake an hour in an oven which is a little slower than for white bread. Rub the crust over with butter to soften it as soon as it is taken from the oven.

Cornmeal Bread.

2 cupfuls flour,
¾ cupful cornmeal,
2 cupfuls milk,
2 cupfuls water,
1 teaspoonful salt,
1 yeast cake.

Put the milk and water in a double boiler, and let it get scalding hot; then stir in the cornmeal and allow it to cook slowly for half an hour. Pour it into a bread raiser and when lukewarm add the salt and yeast. Gradually beat in the flour. Put on a cover and set in a warm place to raise. When it doubles its bulk, add more flour if necessary and work with a wooden spoon until it can be handled. Turn out on a floured baking board and knead thoroughly. Mold into loaves, put into greased bread pans, and set it to rise in a warm place. When light bake in a moderate oven for three quarters of an hour.

Squash Bread (German recipe).

2 cupfuls squash,
¼ cupful sugar,
3 cupfuls scalded milk,
2 tablespoonfuls butter,
1 yeast cake,
Flour enough to knead.

Press the stewed squash through a potato ricer, stir it with the sugar, salt, and butter into the hot milk; when cool, pour in the dissolved yeast and as much flour as will make a dough that can be handled. Turn out on a baking board and knead for fifteen minutes. Return to the bread raiser and let it double its bulk. Knead again, shape into loaves, raise, and bake.

Oatmeal Bread.

½ cupful rolled oats,
1½ cupfuls flour,
2 cupfuls boiling water,
1 yeast cake,
½ tablespoonful salt,
1 tablespoonful butter,
½ cupful molasses.

Put the oatmeal into a bread raiser, pour the boiling water over and let stand until lukewarm; then add salt, butter, dissolved yeast cake, and molasses; stir in the flour, beat thoroughly, and set it to raise in buttered bread pans. When it has almost doubled its bulk, bake.

Nut Bread.

1 cupful entire-wheat flour,
1 cupful white flour,
½ cake yeast,
1 cupful milk,
2 tablespoonfuls brown sugar,
1 teaspoonful salt,
¼ pound shelled hickory nuts.

Set a sponge of the wheat flour, white flour, yeast, and milk; when light, add sugar, salt, hickory nuts, and enough entire-wheat flour to make as stiff as can be stirred with spoon. Put in the pan, raise, and bake one hour.

Rye and Indian Bread.

2 cupfuls yellow cornmeal,
½ cupful yeast,
½ cupful molasses,
1 teaspoonful salt,
½ teaspoonful soda,
2 cupfuls rye meal.

Put the cornmeal into a mixing bowl and scald with boiling water; after ten minutes mix to a soft batter with cold water. When lukewarm, add the yeast, molasses, salt, soda, and 2 cupfuls rye meal. Beat thoroughly, cover with a pan, and set in a warm place to rise over night. When the surface cracks open, stir it down, then grease and flour a pan, turn in the dough, smooth over the top, and sprinkle evenly with flour to prevent crust from forming. Let it rise again until cracks appear, then bake it in a moderate oven from two to three hours, covering with a tin lid after the first hour.

Fruit Bread.

2 cupfuls sweet milk,
2 cakes yeast,
½ teaspoonful salt,
4 tablespoonfuls lard,
4 tablespoonfuls sugar,
1½ cupfuls fruit, cut fine,
Flour.

Scald milk and cool to lukewarm; strain in the yeast dissolved in one quarter cupful lukewarm water. Sift salt with three cupfuls of flour, beat vigorously into liquid, and let sponge rise. Cream the lard, butter, and sugar; dredge the fruit with flour and add to the sponge. Add sufficient flour to make a soft dough. Knead thoroughly and set to rise. When light, divide, form into loaves, put in bread pans, and when ready, bake in slightly cooler oven than is required for plain bread. For the fruit in this bread, use either raisins, currants, citron, dates, figs, or prunelles.

Bread Made with Dry Yeast.

2 quarts flour,
2½ cupfuls warm water,
2 tablespoonfuls lard,
1 yeast cake,
1 tablespoonful sugar,
1 teaspoonful salt.

Sift the flour in the bread pan; break up the yeast cake and put in a quart bowl; then add a gill of water, and mash with a spoon until the yeast and water are well mixed. Beat in 1 gill of flour. Cover the bowl and set in a warm place for two hours. At the end of that time the batter should be a perfect sponge. Add to the sponge a pint of warm water, half the lard, also salt and sugar. Stir this mixture into the flour and mix with a spoon. Sprinkle the board with flour, turn out the dough, knead twenty minutes, using as little flour as possible. At the end of this time the ball of dough should be soft, smooth, and elastic. Place the dough in the bowl and rub the second spoonful of butter or lard over it. Cover with a towel, then a tin cover. Set the bowl in a warm place and let it raise over night. In the morning the dough will have increased to three times its original volume and be a perfect sponge. Knead it in the bowl for five minutes—do not use flour—then shape into three small loaves. Put these in deep pans, and with a sharp knife cut lengthwise through the center of each loaf. Put the pans in a warm place and cover with a towel. Let the loaves rise to twice their size, then bake fifty minutes.

Sweet-Potato Bread.

1 cake yeast,
¼ cupful lukewarm water,
1 cupful scalded milk,
1 tablespoonful salt,
½ cupful sugar,
1 cupful sweet mashed potatoes,
3 tablespoonfuls melted butter.

Dissolve the yeast in the lukewarm water, add the milk, salt, sugar, and potatoes (roasted, scraped from the skins, and worked to a cream with the melted butter), then allow to cool. Beat all together until light, then stir in with a wooden spoon enough flour to make a soft dough. Throw a cloth over the bread bowl and set in a warm place until well raised. Make into small loaves; let them rise for an hour and bake in a brisk oven.

Salt-Rising Bread.

2 cupfuls hot water,
1½ teaspoonfuls salt,
1 pint lukewarm milk,
Flour.

Dissolve ½ teaspoonful salt in hot water, and beat in gradually enough flour to make a very soft dough. Beat for ten minutes, cover, and set in a warm place for eight hours. Stir the salt into the milk and add enough flour to make a stiff batter before working it into the raised dough; mix thoroughly, cover, and set again in a warm place to rise until very light. Knead in enough flour to make the batter of the consistency of ordinary bread dough. Make into loaves and set them to rise; when light, bake.

SMALL BREADS MADE FROM YEAST

Stockholm Bread (Swedish recipe).

6½ cupfuls flour,
1 yeast cake,
2½ cupfuls scalded milk,
⅓ cupful melted butter,
1 egg,
⅜ cupful sugar,
½ teaspoonful salt,
1 teaspoonful cinnamon.

Scald 1 cupful milk; when lukewarm, dissolve the yeast cake in it. Beat in 1 cupful flour and let the sponge rise till light; add the rest of the milk with 4 cupfuls flour, beat again and allow it to rise. Then add the butter, sugar, cinnamon, salt, and the egg beaten to a froth, also the remainder of the flour. Mix and knead on a floured baking board. Cover and raise. Roll the dough into coils about an inch and a half thick and twelve inches long. Braid them, pinch the ends together, set in a greased pan to rise, and bake in a moderate oven. Cool slightly, then brush with powdered sugar moistened with boiling water and slightly flavored with cinnamon.

Federal Bread.

1 quart milk,
1 teaspoonful salt,
1 yeast cake,
1 tablespoonful melted butter,
3 eggs.

Scald the milk and add to it the butter and salt; when cool, pour in the dissolved yeast cake and beat in enough flour to make a dough that is softer than for bread. Pour into a shallow pan and raise over night; bake in the morning. When taken from the oven, split it shortcake fashion, butter generously, and serve hot. This is an excellent hot bread to make for breakfast, because, unless the weather is unusually warm, the cook will find it just in proper condition to bake when breakfast is required.

Rice Bread.

½ pound boiled rice,
2 quarts flour,
½ yeast cake,
2 cupfuls milk,
1 teaspoonful salt,
3 teaspoonfuls sugar.

Mash the rice while hot and rub it into the flour with the tips of the fingers. Add the salt and sugar, warm milk, and dissolved yeast. Make it into a dough just soft enough to handle, knead well, and bake in a shallow pan. Let it double its bulk, and bake in a hot oven.

Parker House Rolls.

7 cupfuls flour,
1 teaspoonful salt,
1 tablespoonful sugar,
3 tablespoonfuls butter,
1 pint milk,
1 yeast cake.

Put 4 cupfuls flour into a mixing bowl with the salt, sugar, and butter; pour on the milk, scalding hot, and beat thoroughly; allow it to cool, then add the dissolved yeast and let the sponge raise till frothy; put in the rest of the flour, mix thoroughly, and knead. Raise again, then turn out on a baking board and shape into Parker House rolls. The way to make these rolls is to cut off a small ball of dough and roll it flat and thin. Brush over the top with melted butter, cut across the middle, but not quite through the dough, with the back of a silver knife. Fold over and lay nearly double then press down to make the dough adhere; allow them to rise. Bake fifteen minutes in a hot oven, and brush with melted butter.

Swiss Rolls.

2 cupfuls milk,
2 tablespoonfuls sugar,
¼ cupful butter,
1 cake yeast,
1½ quarts flour,
1 teaspoonful salt.

Scald the milk and melt the sugar and butter; when lukewarm, add the dissolved yeast. Stir in the flour and set in a warm place to raise. Turn out on a floured bread board, roll till an inch thick, brush the top over with melted butter, and roll up the sheet of dough like a rolled jelly cake. Press it lightly into shape and cut from the end slices about an inch thick; put the slices, cut side up, into a greased pan and let rise until they have doubled in height. Bake in a hot oven twenty minutes, and brush over with melted butter.

Hot Cross Buns.

1 pint milk,
½ cupful butter,
½ cupful sugar,
3 eggs,
½ teaspoonful salt,
1 yeast cake,
Flour.

Scald the milk and pour it over the butter and salt; when lukewarm, add the dissolved yeast and eggs well beaten, then sift in flour enough to make a thin batter, and beat with a wire whisk ten minutes; when full of bubbles, add flour enough to make a dough; knead it hard and raise. When it has doubled its bulk, turn it out, knead it and cut into buns. Place them in a greased pan to rise, brush them over when ready to go into the oven with a sirup made of 1 tablespoonful cream and 2 tablespoonfuls sugar boiled together for a minute. Dust with cinnamon and just before putting in the oven cut two gashes in the top with a sharp knife. By adding raisins or currants to this recipe you can have very nice fruit buns. If you wish to transform them into prune kringles, chop 6 or 8 meaty prunes, which have been cooked and sweetened, add to the dough, let rise, and, instead of baking them bun shape, cut into sticks.

Yorkshire Sally Lunn (English recipe).

2 quarts flour,
1 yeast cake,
2 eggs,
1 cupful butter,
1 tablespoonful sugar,
⅓ teaspoonful salt,
2 cupfuls milk.

Warm the flour, add the milk lukewarm, the melted butter, beaten eggs, sugar and salt, then the dissolved yeast cake. Beat thoroughly. This makes a very soft dough, but it must be kneaded; therefore, add a little more flour, as it is difficult to handle. Cut into small balls; drop each one into a greased muffin pan, raise, brush over with white of egg, and bake till delicately brown. When taken from the oven, brush with a sirup made from milk and sugar. Serve hot.

Apple Cake (Dutch recipe).

1 cupful milk,
⅓ cupful sugar,
⅓ cupful butter,
½ teaspoonful salt,
1 yeast cake,
2 eggs,
Flour,
5 apples,
4 tablespoonfuls sugar,
½ teaspoonful cinnamon.

Scald the milk, pour it over the butter, sugar, and salt; when lukewarm, add the eggs, dissolved yeast cake, and enough flour to make a soft dough. Beat it thoroughly and set in a warm place to raise. Beat again and let it rise a second time. Then pour into a shallow greased pan, spread the dough out thin with a palette knife, and brush over the top with melted butter. Pare the apples, core, and cut into eighths. Lay them thickly on top of the dough in straight rows. Dust sugar and cinnamon over them, cover with a towel, set in a warm place, and let the dough raise again. Bake in a moderate oven half an hour, cut into squares and serve hot, with whipped, sweetened cream.

Entire-Buckwheat Cakes.

2 cupfuls warm milk,
½ cake yeast,
1 teaspoonful salt,
Buckwheat flour,
1 teaspoonful soda,
½ cupful boiling water,
1 tablespoonful molasses.

The general idea is that you have to mix buckwheat with white flour to make good cakes, but they are excellent made with buckwheat alone. Pour the milk into a mixing bowl, add the dissolved yeast, and stir in as much buckwheat flour as will make a medium batter, then add the salt and molasses, and leave the batter to stand over night. In the morning, when ready to bake, dissolve the soda in boiling water, stir it in, beat for a few minutes, then make your cakes. Turn them just once.

Luncheon Rolls.

2 cupfuls sifted flour,
½ cupful milk,
1 tablespoonful butter,
1 teaspoonful salt,
2 teaspoonfuls sugar,
1 cake yeast.

Dissolve the yeast in lukewarm milk, add sugar and salt, then add the butter, melted. Stir milk into flour gradually. Give the dough a hard kneading, adding sufficient flour to make it soft. Cut and form into rolls, place in buttered biscuit pans, set in a warm place to rise, and bake in a brisk oven.

Buckwheat Cakes.

1 cake yeast,
2 cupfuls lukewarm milk,
1 tablespoonful wheat flour,
1 tablespoonful molasses,
½ teaspoonful salt,
1 quart buckwheat flour.

Dissolve the yeast in the milk. Rub together the flour, molasses, and salt; add to this the milk containing the yeast, and rub until perfectly smooth, then stir in two cupfuls lukewarm milk or water. To this add sufficient buckwheat flour to make thin batter, which should be rubbed perfectly smooth. Set the batter in a moderately warm place to rise over night. In the morning thin. if necessary, and fry on well-greased griddle.

Raised Batter Cakes.

1 cake yeast,
2 cupfuls milk,
2 cupfuls flour,

4 tablespoonfuls melted lard,
4 tablespoonfuls sirup,
Dash salt.

Dissolve the yeast in lukewarm milk. Put into mixing bowl the flour melted with lard, then add sirup, salt, and milk. Add the yeast, and mix until a smooth batter is produced. Set in a moderately warm place, cover with a cloth, and let it raise over night. In the morning beat well, and fry on well-greased griddle.

English Bath Buns.

4 cupfuls flour,
½ cupful butter,
4 eggs,
5 tablespoonfuls granulated sugar,
½ cupful milk,
1 cake yeast.

Put flour in bowl, make well in center, break eggs in whole, then add butter, milk, and, last, the yeast, which has been previously dissolved in a little warm water. Mix thoroughly and raise. If it is put in a moderately warm place, it will be light in an hour. Turn it out on a well-floured board, and with the tips of the fingers lightly work in 5 tablespoonfuls sugar and add the flavoring. Drop by tablespoonfuls on a buttered baking pan, raise for ten minutes, and bake twenty minutes in a hot oven. Sultanas or chopped almonds may be added.

Lancashire Tea Cakes.

6 cupfuls flour,
½ cupful butter,
2 cupfuls milk,
1 yeast cake,
1 cupful currants,
2 ounces candied lemon,
2 eggs,
2 tablespoonfuls sugar,
A little grated nutmeg.

Put the sugar and the currants with the flour; melt the butter in the milk; when cool, mix with the beaten eggs and yeast. Add the dry ingredients, beating well, and set to raise. When light, put in cake pans to double its bulk. Bake in a moderately hot oven. These are delicious when fresh, and equally good split and toasted the second day.

Swedish Rolls.

1 yeast cake,
2 cupfuls milk, scalded,
½ cupful butter,
¼ cupful sugar,
1 scant teaspoonful salt,
Whites of 2 eggs,
7 or 8 cupfuls flour.

Melt the butter, dissolve the sugar and salt in the hot milk; when lukewarm, add the yeast and beaten whites. Mix in flour to make a drop batter. In the morning add the remainder of the flour and knead twenty minutes. Raise till light; then knead again slightly and roll half an inch thick. Have the edges as straight as possible. Spread all over with a thin layer of soft butter, a sprinkling of sugar, cinnamon, grated lemon rind, and currants. Roll like a jelly roll, cut off slices an inch wide, lay them with the cut side down on greased pans, and when raised bake in a hot oven fifteen or twenty minutes. Glaze with sugar dissolved in milk.

Currant Squares.

1 cupful cream,
½ cupful melted butter,
3 eggs,
1 cupful sugar,
½ cake yeast,
2 tablespoonfuls water,
4 cupfuls flour,
1 teaspoonful powdered mace,
1 teaspoonful powdered cinnamon,
1 cupful currants.

Heat the cream in a double boiler, then stir in the butter, well-beaten eggs, and sugar. Add the yeast dissolved in a little water, the flour sifted with the spices, then the currants dredged with flour. Beat hard for fifteen minutes. Pour into a shallow baking pan and raise until it is almost doubled in bulk. Bake in a quick oven; when done, sprinkle with powdered sugar and cinnamon. Let the cake cool slightly, then cut into squares with a sharp knife.

Raised Wheat Muffins.

2 cupfuls flour,
1 cupful milk,
1 tablespoonful butter,
½ tablespoonful sugar,
½ teaspoonful salt,
1 egg,
⅛ yeast cake.

Pour the flour, salt, and sugar in a bowl; boil the milk and add the butter to it. Let the mixture stand till lukewarm, add the milk, butter, and yeast to the flour, and beat well. Cover the bowl and set in a cool place over night. In the morning the batter will be a light sponge. Beat the egg and add to this sponge. Half fill buttered muffin pans with the batter; cover, and let the muffins raise in a warm place. Bake for half an hour in a moderately quick oven.

Raised Wheat Waffles.

2 cupfuls flour,
1½ cupfuls milk,
½ yeast cake,
1 tablespoonful sugar,
2 tablespoonfuls butter,
½ teaspoonful salt,
1 egg.

Boil the milk and, after adding the butter to it, cool the mixture. Put the flour, sugar, and salt in a bowl, add the milk and yeast, and beat well. Raise the batter over night. In the morning add the well-beaten egg. Have the waffle irons hot and greased. Cook the cakes quickly.

Broiché (French recipe).

4 cupfuls flour,
½ yeast cake,
1 teaspoonful salt,
2 tablespoonfuls sugar,
7 eggs,
1 cupful butter,
Warm water.

Sift the flour; into 1 cupful of it pour the dissolved yeast with just enough warm water to make a batter. Set it to raise. When it has doubled its bulk, put in the salt, sugar, melted butter, and 4 eggs. Beat five minutes, add another egg, beat again, and so on until all have been used; keep beating until the paste leaves the side of the bowl, then set in a warm place for four hours. Turn it out on a floured board, roll in a long piece half an inch thick, spread with softened butter, and fold one end over the center, then the other end over that, until you have three layers. Cut off pieces about an inch wide, lay them on the board to raise, and cover with a towel. When puffy, take each strip between the fingers and thumbs, twist in different directions, coil pyramid shape, letting one point come on top. Set to raise on a greased pan, bake twenty minutes, and brush over with powdered sugar, moisten with water, and flavor with cinnamon.

Kreuznach Horns (German recipe).

4 cupfuls flour,
1 yeast cake,
2 tablespoonfuls sugar,
2 eggs,
⅛ cupful water,
1 cupful milk,
½ teaspoonful salt.

Set a sponge with 2 cupfuls flour with the yeast cake and milk. When it rises, make into a dough with the rest of the flour, adding the butter, sugar, eggs, and salt. Let it rise again. Roll it out into pieces six inches square and quite thin. Cut each square into four triangles, brush with melted butter, dust lightly with flour, roll up from the wide side, letting the point of the triangle come on top and bend around in the form of a horseshoe. Put them to rise in a greased pan when ready to bake, brush over with milk, and bake in a hot oven.

Raised Doughnuts.

2 cupfuls bread dough,
1 cupful sugar,
1 tablespoonful melted butter,
½ teaspoonful nutmeg,
2 eggs,
Flour.

When the dough for a baking of bread rises the last time in the pan and is kneaded out on the board, cut off a piece large enough to fill a pint measure, put in a bowl, add all the ingredients called for in the recipe and work them into the spongy mass, sifting in flour as needed to make it of a consistency that can be rolled. When thoroughly blended, turn it out on the board, sift with flour, and roll about three quarters of an inch thick. Cut into fingers or rings with a doughnut cutter and spread them out on the board to rise. When puffy, fry in boiling fat, turning so they will be browned all over. Drain from the kettle and toss immediately in powdered sugar. A favorite breakfast in New England is the bread dough, taken without any addition of sugar, eggs, or spices, cut into strips, raised, and fried like doughnuts, then eaten hot with maple sirup.

German Coffee Cake.

1 egg,
1 cupful milk,
2 tablespoonfuls butter,
3 tablespoonfuls sugar,
¼ yeast cake,
¼ teaspoonful salt,
½ teaspoonful cinnamon,
½ cupful raisins,
¼ cupful shaved citron,
Flour.

Scald the milk, pour it over the butter, sugar, and salt. When lukewarm, add the dissolved yeast and enough flour to make a soft dough; beat the mixture hard; let it rise over night. In the morning add the beaten egg and the fruit, also a little more flour if necessary, and knead for a few minutes. Shape the dough into a ring, put in a greased pie plate, and set to rise. Before putting into the oven, brush the top with melted butter, and sprinkle with cinnamon and sugar. Bake half an hour.

CHAPTER XXX

BAKING-POWDER BREADS

Baking-Powder Biscuits.

2 cupfuls flour,
2 tablespoonfuls lard,
1 cupful milk,
½ teaspoonful salt,
2 teaspoonfuls Calumet baking powder.

Sift the salt, baking powder, and flour together, rub in the lard, add the milk, and beat to a soft dough. Turn out on a floured baking board, roll out about an inch thick, and cut into biscuits. Lay in a baking pan, brush the tops with milk, and bake in a quick oven.

Drop Biscuits.

3 cupfuls flour,
2 tablespoonfuls butter,
3 teaspoonfuls Calumet baking powder,
½ teaspoonful salt,
1½ cupfuls milk.

Sift the baking powder, salt, and flour together, rub in the butter with the tips of the fingers, then add the milk, and beat to a soft dough. Grease a baking pan, lift a level tablespoonful of the dough and drop it into the pan, having each biscuit an inch apart, and bake in a hot oven. This is an excellent recipe to use when one is in a hurry and there is not time to make a biscuit which has to be rolled out and cut.

Flannel Cakes.

1 tablespoonful butter,
2 cupfuls milk,
2 eggs,
1 teaspoonful salt,
2 teaspoonfuls Calumet baking powder.

Warm the butter in the milk, pour over the well-beaten yolks of the eggs, add sufficient flour to make it pour, then the salt and baking powder. Beat the whole thoroughly, fold in the whipped whites of the eggs, and bake on a hot griddle.

Batter Bread.

2 eggs,
1 cupful cornmeal,
1 cupful milk,
1 tablespoonful butter, melted,
½ cupful white flour,
½ teaspoonful salt,
1 teaspoonful Calumet baking powder.

Melt the butter over hot water; separate the eggs; beat the yolks slightly; add the milk, butter, cornmeal, flour, and salt. Beat thoroughly, add the baking powder, beat again, and fold in, carefully, the whites of the eggs beaten to a stiff froth. Bake in greased shallow baking pan in a moderate oven thirty-five minutes. Cut into squares, and serve warm.

Shortcake.

2 cupfuls flour,
½ teaspoonful salt,
2 tablespoonfuls sugar,
2 teaspoonfuls Calumet baking powder,
4 tablespoonfuls butter,
1 cupful milk.

Sift together all the dry ingredients, rub in the butter with the tips of the fingers, then wet with the milk to a soft dough. Drop it on a floured baking board and, handling it just as little as possible, roll and pat into two round cakes, which will fill a deep pie plate. Drop in one cake of the dough, brush with melted butter, and lay the other one on top of it. Bake until crisp, brown, and puffy. Split and between the cake and on top spread any fruit which is in season. Strawberries, of course, make a most delicious shortcake. Besides this, peaches can be used, red raspberries, cherries, fresh apricots, oranges, or a blend of oranges and bananas, while a shortcake filled with stewed prunes or well-seasoned apple sauce is not to be despised. Chipped pineapple mixed with bananas and oranges makes a delicious filling. In every case, have it juicy by leaving the fruit covered with sugar to stand for an hour in a cool place before it is served.

Graham Biscuits.

2 tablespoonfuls butter,
2 cupfuls Graham flour,
1 cupful white flour,
1 teaspoonful salt,
1 teaspoonful sugar,
3 teaspoonfuls Calumet baking powder,
2 cupfuls milk.

Mix thoroughly, and chop into the mixture 2 tablespoonfuls butter. Add the milk, and if the mixture is then too stiff to handle, add enough water to make it a soft dough. Turn upon a floured board, roll out and cut into biscuits, handling as little and as lightly as possible. Bake in a steady oven.

Waffles.

2 eggs,
1 cupful milk,
1¾ cupfuls flour,
1 tablespoonful melted butter,
½ teaspoonful salt,
2 teaspoonfuls Calumet baking powder.

Beat the yolks of the eggs light; add alternately, and beating in well, the milk and flour. When these ingredients are mixed, add the butter, baking powder, salt, and whipped whites of the eggs.

Sally Lunn.

2 tablespoonfuls butter,
2 cupfuls sweet milk,
3 eggs,
6 cupfuls flour,
3 teaspoonfuls Calumet baking powder,
1 teaspoonful salt,
1 tablespoonful sugar.

Warm the butter in the milk; pour over the eggs, beaten light; then stir in a little at a time, and beating continuously, the flour, with which has been sifted the baking powder, salt, and sugar. Turn into a greased cake mold, and bake in a steady oven.

Egg Biscuits.

3 cupfuls flour,
1 teaspoonful salt,
2 eggs,
1 tablespoonful lard,
1 cupful sweet milk,
1½ teaspoonfuls Calumet baking powder.

Sift the flour, add the salt, sugar, eggs (beaten well), lard, milk, and baking powder. Work to a smooth dough, roll half an inch thick, cut in large biscuits, rub over with sweet milk, lay on buttered tins, and bake brown in a quick oven.

Corn Cakes.

2 cupfuls cornmeal,
1 teaspoonful salt,
3 eggs,
1 cupful sweet milk,
1 teaspoonful Calumet baking powder.

Put the meal in a bowl, mix with salt, and pour over it enough boiling water to moisten the mass; cover for five minutes or an hour, as convenient. Beat the eggs separately, add a cup of sweet milk to the yolks, and pour over the scalded meal; mix well, add the baking powder and the beaten whites of the eggs. Grease a griddle with bacon drippings, and fry.

Vienna Biscuits.

2 teaspoonfuls Calumet baking powder.
½ teaspoonful salt,
4 cupfuls flour,
1 tablespoonful butter,
1 tablespoonful lard,
1½ cupfuls milk.

Sift the baking powder and salt with the flour; mix thoroughly with the butter and lard; wet with the milk; turn out on a floured bread board, and knead smooth; roll into a sheet half an inch thick, and cut with a biscuit cutter. Bake at once in a quick oven.

Ground-Rice Muffins.

4 cupfuls ground rice,
2 tablespoonfuls butter,
1 teaspoonful sugar,
Dash salt,
3 eggs,
1 tablespoonful Calumet baking powder.

Cream together the butter and sugar. Pour on enough boiling water to moisten the rice, stirring all the time. Cool and add the yolks of the eggs, well beaten, creamed butter and sugar; then enough sweet milk to form a batter, beating thoroughly; add the baking powder and salt, and, last, fold in the whites of the eggs, well beaten. Bake in gem pans in a quick oven.

Twin-Mountain Muffins.

¼ cupful butter,
¼ cupful sugar,
1 egg,
¾ cupful milk,
2 cupfuls flour,
3 teaspoonfuls Calumet baking powder.

Cream the butter; add the sugar and egg, well beaten; sift baking powder with flour, and add to the first mixture, alternating with milk. Bake in buttered gem pans twenty-five minutes.

Rye Gems.

1⅔ cupfuls rye flour,
1⅓ cupfuls white flour,
4 teaspoonfuls Calumet baking powder.
1 teaspoonful salt,
2 eggs,
¼ cupful molasses,
1¼ cupfuls milk,
3 tablespoonfuls melted butter.

Sift the dry ingredients, add molasses, milk, eggs, well beaten, and

a Oval Muffin Pans; b, Oblong Muffin Pans; c, Round Popover Pans.

butter. Bake in hot oven in buttered gem pan twenty-five minutes.

Nut Biscuits.

2 cupfuls flour,
½ teaspoonful salt,
1 tablespoonful butter,
1 cupful chopped nuts,
2 tablespoonfuls butter,
2 teaspoonfuls Calumet baking powder,
2 tablespoonfuls sugar,
¾ cupful milk.

Sift together the flour, salt, and baking powder; rub in the butter, add the nuts—English walnuts, hickory nuts, or almonds—and sugar; mix to a soft dough with milk. Mold with the hands into small balls, place well apart on greased pans, brush each with milk, put a pinch of chopped nuts on top, and bake in a hot oven.

Corn Muffins.

2 cupfuls cornmeal,
2 cupfuls flour,
1 tablespoonful sugar,
1 teaspoonful salt,
2 teaspoonfuls Calumet baking powder,
1 tablespoonful butter or lard,
2 eggs,
2 cupfuls milk.

Sift together cornmeal, flour, sugar, salt, and powder; rub in the shortening, add eggs, beaten, and milk; mix into batter of consistency of cup cake; fill muffin pans, well greased, two thirds full. Bake in a hot oven.

Berry Muffins.

2 cupfuls flour,
1 teaspoonful salt,
2 tablespoonfuls melted butter,
¼ cupful sugar,
2 teaspoonfuls Calumet baking powder,
1 egg,
1 cupful milk,
1 cupful berries.

Mix as for plain muffins; add berries last, dusting them with a little flour. Bake in muffin pans in a hot oven.

Graham Muffins.

1 quart Graham flour,
1 tablespoonful brown sugar,
1 teaspoonful salt,
2 teaspoonfuls Calumet baking powder,
1 egg,
2 cupfuls milk.

Sift together Graham flour, sugar, salt, and powder; add beaten egg and milk; mix into batter. Bake in a hot oven fifteen minutes in greased muffin pans.

Slappers.

2 cupfuls Indian cornmeal,
½ teaspoonful salt,
2 tablespoonfuls butter,
3 eggs,
1 cupful milk,
1 cupful wheat flour,
2 teaspoonfuls Calumet baking powder.

Mix together meal, salt, and butter; pour on slowly sufficient boiling water to thoroughly moisten the meal. Cover; let stand over night. Add the eggs, well beaten, milk, flour—the first half-cupful of flour being mixed with the baking powder—to make a very thick drop batter. Drop by spoonfuls on a hot greased griddle, cook slowly till brown, turn and brown on other side.

No-Egg Wheat Cakes.

3 cupfuls flour,
3 teaspoonfuls Calumet baking powder,
½ teaspoonful salt,
2 cupfuls milk.

Sift dry ingredients; add milk to make a soft batter, and beat hard. Bake immediately on hot griddle. Serve with butter and maple sirup.

Jam Griddle Cakes.

3 cupfuls flour,
4 tablespoonfuls sugar,
½ teaspoonful salt,
1½ teaspoonfuls Calumet baking powder,
2 tablespoonfuls butter,
2 eggs,
2 cupfuls milk.

Rub butter and sugar to a cream; add yolks of eggs, one at a time. Sift flour, salt, and powder together; add to butter with milk and whites of eggs whipped to dry froth; mix to a batter. Bake in small cakes; as fast as browned, lay each cake on a plate and spread raspberry jam over it, then bake more, lay on other already done; repeat this until you have used jam twice, then bake another batch.

Blueberry Griddlecakes.

1 cupful blueberries,
2 cupfuls flour,

1 teaspoonful salt,
1 tablespoonful brown sugar,
2 teaspoonfuls Calumet baking powder,
2 eggs,
2 cupfuls milk.

Sift together flour, sugar, salt, and baking powder; add beaten eggs, milk, and berries. Mix into a batter. Have griddle hot enough to form a crust as soon as the batter touches it. In order to confine the juice of berries, turn quickly to form a crust on the other side.

Griddled Muffins.

1 cupful flour,
1 teaspoonful butter,
1 egg,
2 teaspoonfuls Calumet baking powder,
½ cupful milk.

Mix the flour, butter, baking powder, and egg with the milk. Place small muffin rings on a hot griddle, put a little fat into each ring, fill them half full with the batter, and bake over a moderate fire till light brown. Turn with a pancake turner, and bake the same on the other side.

French Pancakes.

3 eggs,
2 cupfuls milk,
2 teaspoonfuls Calumet baking powder,
A pinch of salt,
2 cupfuls flour.

Beat the yolks of the eggs light; pour over them the milk; add gradually the baking powder, salt, and flour; fold in lightly the whipped whites of the eggs. Bake by large spoonfuls on a hot griddle. Spread each cake as soon as baked with jam, and shape into a roll.

Bannocks (Irish recipe).

4 cupfuls flour,
½ cupful butter,
1½ cupfuls milk,
½ teaspoonful salt,
3 teaspoonfuls Calumet baking powder.

Mix the ingredients to a soft dough; roll an inch thick, shape into cakes, six inches across, with a large cooky cutter, and bake on a hot griddle. Before taking from the fire, be sure they are baked to the heart. Split in two, butter, and serve hot.

One-Egg Griddlecakes.

3 cupfuls flour,
3 teaspoonfuls Calumet baking powder,
1 teaspoonful salt,
1 egg,
2 tablespoonfuls melted butter,
2 cupfuls milk.

Sift the dry ingredients, separate the egg, and add to flour the milk and beaten yolk. Beat thoroughly, add the melted butter and white of egg, beaten to a stiff froth. Bake at once.

Whole-Wheat Griddlecakes.

1½ cupfuls white flour,
¾ cupful whole-wheat flour,
½ teaspoonful salt,
4 tablespoonfuls sugar,
4 teaspoonfuls Calumet baking powder,
1¾ cupfuls milk,
2 tablespoonfuls melted butter.

Sift the flour, baking powder, salt, and sugar; stir into a batter with the milk, the beaten egg and butter. Bake at once.

Indian Griddlecakes.

1 cupful Indian meal,
1 cupful flour,
2 eggs,
1 teaspoonful butter,
½ teaspoonful salt,
2 teaspoonfuls Calumet baking powder,
Milk.

Put Indian meal into a mixing bowl and pour over it enough scalding milk to make a thick mush. When it cools, add the flour and enough cold milk to make a thick batter, add the eggs, well beaten, the butter, melted, the salt, and baking powder. Beat till full of bubbles, then bake on a hot griddle.

Hominy Gems.

2 cupfuls cold hominy,
3 eggs,
2 cupfuls milk,
1 cupful cornmeal,
1 teaspoonful salt,
1 tablespoonful sugar,
2 teaspoonfuls Calumet baking powder,
1 tablespoonful melted butter.

Put the cornmeal in a mixing bowl, pour over it the scalded milk, beat thoroughly, and when cool add the hominy. Stir in the eggs, whip to a froth, add salt, sugar, baking powder, and butter, beat hard, pour into greased gem pans, and bake in a hot oven. This recipe when thinned with more milk makes delicious griddlecakes.

Graham Griddlecakes.

1½ cupfuls Graham flour,
½ cupful white flour,
2 teaspoonfuls Calumet baking powder,
2 cupfuls milk,
1 egg,
1 tablespoonful melted butter.

Sift the dry ingredients, then beat into a batter with egg, milk, and butter; bake on a griddle.

Egg Biscuits.

4 cupfuls flour,
2 teaspoonfuls Calumet baking powder,
¾ cupful butter,
2 eggs,
1½ cupfuls milk,
2 teaspoonfuls sugar,
½ teaspoonful salt.

Sift the dry ingredients, rub in the butter, and make into a dough with the beaten egg and milk. Turn out on a baking board, roll into a sheet and mold into biscuits, as directed for Parker House rolls. Bake fifteen minutes in a quick oven.

Pitcaithley Scones (Scotch recipe).

4 cupfuls flour,
3 teaspoonfuls Calumet baking powder,
2 tablespoonfuls butter,
1½ cupfuls milk,
½ teaspoonful salt.

Sift together the dry ingredients, rub in the butter, and mix to a soft dough with the milk. Turn out on a floured baking board and roll into rounds. Dust the griddle thinly with flour, slip on the round of dough, and cut into quarters. Bake slowly and do not turn until the top is beginning to show bubbles. Scones ought to be turned only once. Serve hot.

Maryland Biscuits.

1 quart flour,
1 cupful milk and water mixed,
1 tablespoonful shortening,
1 teaspoonful salt.

Rub the shortening into the flour and add the salt; mix the milk and water, and add them slowly to the flour, stirring all the while, until you have a hard, almost dry, dough. Put the dough out on a floured board and knead continuously for fifteen minutes, until it is soft and elastic. Then beat it, constantly folding, for twenty minutes longer. Roll out, cut in biscuits; prick the tops with a fork, stand in a pan so that they will not touch each other, and bake in a moderate oven for thirty minutes. The sides of these biscuits should be white but cooked, the tops and bottoms brown.—MRS. S. T. RORER.

Popovers.

1 cupful sifted flour,
¼ teaspoonful salt,
1 cupful milk,
1 egg.

Sift together the flour and salt, then gradually beat in the milk and egg. Beat two minutes with a Dover beater and bake about half an hour in gem pans, buttered, in a fast oven.

Oat Cakes (Scotch recipe).

- 2 cupfuls Canadian oatmeal,
- 1 teaspoonful lard,
- ½ teaspoonful salt,
- Water.

Put oatmeal in a mixing bowl; rub in the salt and shortening, add enough water to make a stiff dough, dust the bread board with oatmeal and roll out thin; cut the cake into a round big enough to fit a griddle and slip it carefully on to the hot iron. Before it begins to bake, cut the round into quarters. Bake until crisp and delicately brown, and if they do not seem quite hard enough, set the cakes in the oven until thoroughly dried out.

BREADS MADE FROM SOUR MILK

Milk or cream used for baking is best when it sours quickly and does not separate, but remains thick and smooth. The usual measurement to use in every recipe where lightness is desired is 1 level teaspoonful soda to 2 cupfuls sour milk or 1 cupful molasses. Sometimes the milk is sour, but not loppered; then use it in gingerbread or brown bread, where there is molasses enough to complete the acidity, or let it stand for a few hours in a warm place to lopper. The more acid the milk is, the more soda it will require. Never use milk which has turned bitter or moldy. If you are lucky enough to possess sour cream, cut down in each recipe 2 tablespoonfuls butter to 1 cupful sour milk, else the mixture will be too rich.

Woodlawn Brown Bread.

- 2 cupfuls sour milk,
- 1 egg,
- 3 cupfuls Graham flour,
- 1 teaspoonful soda,
- ½ cupful molasses,
- ½ teaspoonful salt.

If the Graham flour is very coarse, sift it and throw away the bran. Add the salt, pour in the molasses, milk, beaten egg, and the soda dissolved in a little water. If you desire bread that is not very dark or sweet, use 2 tablespoonfuls molasses and 1 teaspoonful sugar. Steam for two and a half-hours in pound baking-powder can. Give it three hours if steamed in a quart pail.

Sunday-Morning Loaf.

- 2 cupfuls Graham flour,
- 1 cupful wheat flour,
- 1 cupful Indian meal,
- 1 teaspoonful salt,
- 1 cupful molasses,
- 1½ teaspoonfuls soda,
- ½ cupful cold water,
- 1 tablespoonful melted lard,
- 1 cupful sour milk,
- 1½ cupfuls sweet milk.

Sift the dry materials together, add the molasses, lard, soda melted in water, and milk. Beat thoroughly; pour into a buttered mold, and steam for three hours. This makes two medium-sized loaves. In New England these are called Sunday-Morning loaves, because they are generally made Saturday night and put in the oven for half an hour next morning to serve with the traditional baked beans. They keep for one or two weeks and may be heated for use at any time.

Steamed Graham Loaf.

- 3 cupfuls of Graham flour,
- 1 cupful wheat flour,
- 1 teaspoonful soda,
- 1 teaspoonful salt,
- 1 cupful molasses,
- 2½ cupfuls sour milk.

Sift dry ingredients, add molasses and milk, beat well and turn into a buttered mold. Steam three and a half hours. This mixture, cooked in pound baking-powder cans, will make four loaves, which can be reheated when required. Place the can on a frame in a kettle containing boiling water.

Whole-Wheat Muffins.

1 cupful whole-wheat meal,
1 cupful flour,
2 tablespoonfuls sugar,
½ teaspoonful salt,
¾ teaspoonful soda,
1¼ cupfuls sour milk,
2 tablespoonfuls melted butter,
1 egg.

Sift the dry ingredients together, mix with the beaten egg, milk, and butter. Bake in hot gem pans.

Spider Corn Cake.

¾ cupful cornmeal,
¼ cupful flour,
1 tablespoonful sugar,
½ teaspoonful salt,
½ teaspoonful soda,
1 egg,
½ cupful sour milk,
½ cupful sweet milk.

Sift the dry ingredients together and mix them with the well-beaten egg and milk. Beat thoroughly. Melt 2 tablespoonfuls butter in an iron spider and pour the mixture into it. Pour ½ cupful sweet milk over the top of the batter and set it very carefully into a hot oven. Bake for twenty minutes.

Rice or Hominy Griddlecakes or Muffins.

1 cupful sour milk,
1 cupful cold rice or fine hominy,
½ teaspoonful salt,
¾ teaspoonful soda,
1 egg,
1 teaspoonful melted butter,
Flour to make a batter.

Heat the rice or hominy over hot water and moisten gradually with the milk till free from lumps. Add salt and soda, stir in the beaten egg yolk, then the melted butter, then flour to make a soft batter, lastly the white of egg beaten stiff. This is for griddlecakes. For muffins, use flour enough to make a stiff batter.

Corn Bread.

2 cupfuls sour milk,
3 eggs,
2 cupfuls Indian meal (white),
1 teaspoonful soda,
1 teaspoonful sugar.

Beat the eggs separately, sift the soda twice through the meal, and add the salt. Beat the ingredients well together, adding the whites last of all. Bake in a moderate oven in muffin rings, with a large spoonful of the batter to each, until golden brown.

Batter Cakes.

1½ teaspoonfuls soda,
3 cupfuls sour milk,
3 eggs,
3½ cupfuls flour.

Beat thoroughly the soda with the sour milk. Beat the yolks of three eggs and add to the milk, then stir in the flour and a little salt, making the batter of the consistency of cake. Then beat the whites to a stiff froth, fold in, and bake.

Biscuits.

1 quart flour,
4 tablespoonfuls lard,
1 teaspoonful salt,
1 teaspoonful soda.

Sift the flour, add the lard, salt, soda, and enough sour milk to make soft dough; roll thin, cut into biscuits, and bake in a very quick oven.

Entire-Wheat Gems.

2 cupfuls sour milk,
2 tablespoonfuls brown sugar,
1 saltspoonful salt,
1 teaspoonful soda.

Stir them all together, add sufficient flour to make a batter that will drop without spreading. Bake in gem pans.

Spoon Biscuit.

4 cupfuls sour milk,
2 teaspoonfuls soda,
1 saltspoonful salt,
2 tablespoonfuls melted butter.

To the sour milk add the soda, salt, butter, and sifted flour to form a batter that will drop from a spoon. Drop into a hot greased pan, and bake in a quick oven.

Sour-Milk Graham Bread.

1 egg,
2 tablespoonfuls sugar,
2 tablespoonfuls melted butter,
1 teaspoonful soda,
2 cupfuls sour milk,
1½ cupfuls Graham flour,
1½ cupfuls white flour.

Beat the egg with the sugar, put in the melted butter; dissolve the soda in 2 spoonfuls hot water, and add the sour milk. Stir up with the flour and bake slowly one hour.

Griddlecakes.

1 pint sour milk,
2 cupfuls flour,
½ teaspoonful salt,
1 egg,
1 teaspoonful soda.

Mix thoroughly the flour, salt, and beaten eggs; add more flour if needed to make a good batter. Last of all add 1 teaspoonful soda dissolved in 1 tablespoonful hot water. Bake at once on a hot griddle.

Sour-Milk Doughnuts.

2 cupfuls flour,
¾ teaspoonful salt,
1 scant teaspoonful soda,
1 scant teaspoonful cream of tartar,
Grating of nutmeg,
½ tablespoonful butter,
1 egg,
½ cupful sugar,
½ cupful sour milk.

Sift together the dry ingredients, rub the butter into the flour with the finger tips, add the sugar, well-beaten egg, and milk; beat thoroughly and toss the dough on a floured board. It ought to be a soft dough and it is not easy to handle. Use a knife in turning it over if you have any difficulty. Knead lightly and roll into a sheet. Cut the doughnuts with a ring cutter and fry in boiling fat, putting only about four in the kettle at once. If more are fried at a time, the fat will cool and the doughnuts become greasy.

RECIPES FOR CORN BREAD

Indian corn is a native of the new world and is one of the chief sources of national wealth. It is so commonly used as an article of food, both in an unripe state, as green corn, and as a dry grain, crushed or ground as hominy, or as corn meal, and cooked in various forms that it may almost be regarded as the national food of America. In addition to corn meal mush, the well known hasty pudding of our grandmothers, it forms the basis of many of the appetizing modern breakfast foods. In New England it takes the form best known as the Rhode Island Johnny Cake. In the South it forms the celebrated Hoe Cake or Corn Pone. In all parts of the country corn meal bread, muffins, and batter cakes are cooked and served according to a great variety of recipes. The following have been selected as typical of the various corn meal breads in use in different parts of the United States as recorded by the foremost writers on cookery. This selection has been made with great care and is believed to be one of the most complete and satisfactory in existence.

RHODE ISLAND JOHNNY CAKE

Any kind of corn meal can be substituted in the following recipe, but the flavor of the true Rhode Island Johnny Cake cannot be realized without meal made from well seasoned white (not yellow) corn ground nearly as fine as flour. This is known to the trade as bolted white Indian meal. It is packed in small cloth bags by certain manufacturers and can be obtained from grocers in most parts of the United States if specially requested. The process of making Johnny Cakes is most simple. Measure in a mixing bowl a quantity of meal sufficient for the needs of the family, which can be determined only by experience, and add boiling water in a thin stream, stirring vigorously until the dough is nearly, but not quite, soft enough to pour. It should be very wet but firm. Stir in salt to taste and fry with butter, or any suitable fat, on a hot griddle until a crisp brown crust is formed on both sides. The cakes are usually formed of a single mixing spoonful of dough and flattened so as to be about three or four inches across and an inch or less in thickness. They are best relished by most persons when the crust is firm and brittle and the interior soft and moist. A little experience will enable any one to make Johnny Cake dough of the right consistency. Some cooks prefer to use no more hot water than is necessary to thoroughly scald the meal and then thin the dough to the desired consistency with fresh or skimmed milk. Made by either recipe Rhode Island Johnny Cakes are most wholesome and delicious.

Southern Johnny Cake.

Stir together 3 cupfuls of Indian meal, 1 of flour, ⅓ of molasses and a little salt, with enough sour or buttermilk to make a stiff batter. Stir in 1 teaspoonful of soda and bake in a hot oven. (Wm. H. Lee.)

Mrs. Jake's Hoe Cakes.

Take 1 pint of white corn meal, ½ teaspoonful salt, and 1 teaspoonful of sugar. Mix well and add sufficient boiling milk or water to scald. (Add 2 eggs, or not, as desired.) The batter should be thick enough not to spread when put on the griddle. Grease the griddle with bacon-fat or lard, and drop the batter upon it from spoon. Flatten the cakes until about ½ inch in thickness. Cook slowly but do not burn. When of a brown color on underside turn over and brown other side. Spread a little butter on each cake. Serve immediately when done. (Wm. H. Lee.)

Southern Corn Pone.

Sift a quart of white corn meal, add a teaspoonful of salt. Pour on enough cold water to make a mixture which will squeeze easily through the fingers. Work it to a soft dough. Mold it into oblong cakes an inch thick at the ends and a little thicker in the center. Slap them down on the pan and press them a little. These cakes they say must show the marks of the fingers. The pan must be hot and sprinkled with the bran sifted from the meal. Bake in a hot oven for about 20 minutes. (Mary Roland.)

Southern Hoe Cake No. 1.

Make the same mixture as for pone. Spread it on the greased hoe, or a griddle, making a round cake ¼ of an inch thick. Bake it on the top of the range, turning and baking it brown on both sides. (Mary Roland.)

Southern Hoe Cake No. 2.

Use for these cakes if possible coarse water-ground white meal. Add to a quart of meal a teaspoonful of salt; pour over it enough boiling water to make a soft dough. Add also a little milk to make it brown better. Let it stand an hour or longer then work it together with the hand. Form it into little cakes an inch thick and bake on a greased griddle till brown on both sides. Serve very hot. They are split and spread with butter when eaten. (Mary Roland.)

Genuine Johnny Cake.

Eight heaping tablespoonfuls fine sifted corn meal, 1 teaspoonful sugar. Stir in enough sweet milk to make a thin batter. Bake in smoking hot iron gem pan, in very hot oven, until "golden brown." (Mary Lewis.)

Aunt Anne's Hoe Cake.
Take a large cupful of corn meal, sift it in a bowl, a pinch of salt. Mix it with a little boiling water. Let it get cold. Make some small round cakes, pinch them on top. Put in a pan to bake in the oven. (Celestine Eustis.)

Corn Pone.
Corn pone is highly recommended as a breakfast dish. Take a heaping coffee-cupful of boiled hominy, heat it and thin in a tablespoonful of butter, 3 eggs and nearly 1 pint of sweet milk. As much corn meal may be added as will serve to thicken this till it is like the batter for "Johnny Cakes." Bake in a quick oven and serve. (Celestine Eustis.)

White House Corn Bread.
Two cups of sifted meal, half a cup of flour, 2 cups of sour milk, 2 well-beaten eggs, ½ cup of molasses or sugar, a teaspoonful of salt, 2 tablespoonfuls of melted butter. Mix the meal and flour smoothly and gradually with the milk, then the butter, molasses and salt, then the beaten eggs, and lastly dissolve a level teaspoonful of baking soda in a little milk and beat thoroughly together. Bake nearly an hour in well-buttered tins, not very shallow. (Hugo Zieman and Mrs. F. L. Gillette.)

Favorite Corn Bread.
Scald 1 quart of Indian meal with one quart of boiling water; when cooked, add one pint of Graham flour, 1 pint of wheat flour, half cupful of yeast, half cupful of molasses, 1 teaspoonful of salt, 1 tablespoonful of shortening. Dissolve and fill the cup half full with warm water. Make it as thick as can be stirred with a spoon. Bake in a milk pan or deep dish, letting it rise first. (Mrs. Grace Townsend.)

Gold Medal Corn Bread.
One pint yellow meal, ½ pint flour, 1 teaspoonful salt, 2 teaspoonfuls baking-powder, all sifted together; 1 tablespoonful sugar, 3 tablespoonfuls melted butter, 3 eggs, 1 pint sweet milk. Beat long and hard and bake in a large round loaf. The oven must not be too hot.

Economical Corn Bread.
Take 1 quart of sweet milk, corn meal enough to thicken, 3 eggs, half a cup of butter, 2 tablespoonfuls of brown sugar, 1 teaspoonful of soda and 2 of cream of tartar. Bake in a moderate oven. (Mrs. Jane Warren.)

RECIPES FOR CORN BREAD

Boston Corn Bread.

1½ cupfuls Graham flour,
1 cupful Indian meal,
½ tablespoonful soda,
1 saltspoonful salt,
½ cupful molasses,
1⅔ cupfuls milk.
(Fannie Merritt Farmer.)

Southern Batter Bread or Egg Bread.
Beat two eggs light; stir half a cupful of cold boiled rice into a pint of milk and add to the eggs, rice and milk a tablespoonful of melted butter. Sift a teaspoonful of salt into two cups of Indian meal; stir all together and bake in shallow pans. Eat hot. (Marion Harland.)

Corn Meal Loaf.
1 pint milk,
1 level teaspoonful salt,
1 pint white flour,
1 pint water,
1 compressed yeast cake,
Corn meal.
(Sarah Tyson Rorer.)

CHAPTER XXXI

STALE BREAD

A CAREFUL housewife plans to keep in stock the smallest amount possible of stale bread, and of that stock not a morsel is consigned to the garbage pail. There is economy in adopting the English fashion of bread cutting, placing the loaf on a wooden trencher with a keen knife, and cutting at the table each slice as it is required.

Look carefully to the stale-bread remains of each day. Keep a wire basket, set in a tin pan in the pantry, to receive all scraps left on plates, toast crusts, or morsels from the bread jar. Never put them in a covered pail or jar; they will mold. Save all soft inside parts of a loaf to be used as soon as possible for crontons or croustades, slices or cubes for toast and toast points, and soft scraps for meat and fish dressings, puddings, omelets, scalloped dishes, griddlecakes, soufflés, croquettes, and the numerous dishes for which stale bread may be utilized.

For stuffing for poultry, fish, spareribs, veal, or game it is often possible to use dry "heels" and crusts by soaking and adding to them a portion of dry crumbs. The scraps which can be used in no other way may be saved for crumbing. When the basket becomes full, put the bread in a pan and set in a moderate oven with the door open. Never allow these crusts to grow more than a golden brown. The browner crumbs are, which are used as a covering for croquettes, etc., the less frying they will stand. Before a croquette rolled in very brown crumbs is heated to the heart, it will appear almost burned. When the scraps of bread are thoroughly dry, roll them on a board or put through the meat chopper, using the finest knife.

If there are children in the family who like "rusk," the old-fashioned New England name for browned crumbs sprinkled into cold milk, reserve the coarser crumbs for this purpose. Sift through a fine sieve, and the crumbs, no larger than cornmeal, may be put away to be used for crumbing purposes. Save the rusk in the same way, keeping it always uncovered. If the air is not allowed free circulation into the can, the crumbs will spoil. When rusk is used, heat it slightly in the oven. After croquettes have been crumbed, scrape together all the fine crumbs left on the board and sift, returning what is dry to the can.

Bread crumbs are always preferable to cracker crumbs in covering anything which has been dipped in egg. Cracker crumbs do not brown well. In the recipes following, stale bread and crumbs are spoken of in a distinctive fashion. Dried bread crumbs are those which are rolled and sifted, suitable for crumbing, but not for use in puddings or scallops, for they would absorb too much moisture. Stale crumbs are made from odds and ends of stale bread, rubbed on a grater or crumbled fine. They must be used at once or they will mold.

Stale bread that is broken and unsightly can be used for brewis, bread puddings, or in scallops. Toast or steam all that can possibly be used in such a way. Remove crusts before toasting. It makes a dish more sightly, and the crusts can be dried for crumbs or worked into a dressing. Slices of bread too ragged to be toasted may be trimmed into diamonds, fingers, oblongs, rounds, or triangles for canapes. Cut smaller pieces in dice, narrow strips, or squares for croutons. Fry forty seconds in hot fat, or butter lightly and brown in the oven. They are an attractive accompaniment for thick soups.

Toast that will cut into vandykes or long points can be utilized for surrounding dishes of spinach, Brussels sprouts, asparagus, or green vegetables served in a mold. Dishes *au gratin* will use any of the dry bread crumbs. Instead of dotting the crusts with morsels of butter, melt the butter in an omelet pan, 2 tablespoonfuls butter to ½ cupful crumbs, and toss lightly with a fork till every morsel is buttered. Brewis, steamed bread, and toasts of a large variety are some of the changes to ring in the daily menu, and they can be made so appetizing that a family has no suspicion it is aiding to keep the bread jar in good condition.

Brown-Bread Brewis.

2 cupfuls stale brown bread,
1 cupful stale white bread,
1 tablespoonful butter,
2¼ cupfuls milk.

For this dish use the smallest odds and ends of the bread, crumbling the larger portions into inch pieces. Put the butter in a spider. Allow it to melt, but not brown, and put in the bread. Pour the milk over it and simmer, stirring occasionally to keep the bread from sticking to the pan. Season with a dash of salt and white pepper. Serve hot.

Steamed Bread.

Into the middle of a large steamer with a close-fitting lid set a cup or bowl inverted and around it arrange slices of stale bread you wish to steam. Do not allow them to touch the side of the steamer or they will become water-soaked. Fit the steamer tightly into the mouth of a kettle of boiling water. The bread will be ready in a few minutes. In taking it out, turn the lid over instantly to prevent water dripping on the bread. Butter each slice and arrange on a hot plate with a napkin over them. Stale biscuit or rolls may be steamed in the same fashion, or sprinkled with cold water and set for a few minutes into a hot oven.

Toasted Sandwiches.

Often after a picnic or entertainment a housewife has a number of bread-and-butter sandwiches left, too stale to serve. They may form the basis of a bread pudding or they make an attractive dish for breakfast, luncheon, or supper in the shape of toasted sandwiches. Do not take them apart, lay them between the wires of a toaster, and hold over a clear, red fire. The butter will melt and the inside be left soft, warm, and buttered, with the outside a crisp, golden brown.

Toast.

Trim the crust from stale slices you wish to toast and move it carefully over a clear, red fire for two minutes. Then turn it over and let all the moisture be drawn out of the bread. Butter and serve immediately. Toast may be utilized, especially for breakfast, in all sorts of ways. Plain toast is a favorite in most households; then there are milk toast, cream toast, dropped eggs on toast, water toast, and the excellent dish of bread soaked in egg and milk which has all sorts of names, French, Spanish, German, and Scotch toast, but more properly egged toast. At the luncheon and dinner table toast appears in all forms—under chicken and with such vegetables as asparagus and spinach; under minced meats, fricassees, and creamed mixtures, or in the delicate canape.

Spider Browned Toast.

Take several slices of stale bread cut rather thick, cut off the crust and butter them on both sides. Lay them in a dry, hot spider over a rather slow fire and cover with a tight lid. When one side has browned delicately, turn and brown the other. They will be crisp outside, yet soft inside.

Sandwiches in Cream Sauce.

Sandwiches left over are not usually inviting, but they may be made so by this method. Toast them delicately in the oven, and to every four sandwiches made from chicken, veal, or tongue makes a white sauce with 1 tablespoonful flour, ½ teaspoonful salt, a dash of pepper, and 1 cupful milk cooked until thick. Then add the yolk of 1 egg, well beaten. Pour this over the sandwiches and serve at once.

White-Bread Brewis.

Heat a pint of milk in a double boiler. Stir into it enough bits of stale wheat bread to absorb all the milk. Season with a little butter and salt. It should not be pasty or sloppy, but should be a light, dry porridge. It is a favorite with children, especially if served on a small, pretty saucer and dotted with bits of bright jelly. Serve hot.

Bread-Crumb Buckwheat Cakes.

½ cupful stale bread crumbs,
2 cupfuls milk,
½ teaspoonful salt,
¼ cake yeast,
¾ cupfuls buckwheat flour,
1 tablespoonful molasses,
¼ teaspoonful soda.

Scald the milk and soak the crumbs for half an hour. Add the salt, yeast, and buckwheat flour, and let it stand over night. In the morning stir in the molasses and soda melted in a spoonful of warm water. Beat briskly for a few minutes and bake on a hot, greased griddle.

Brown-Bread Cream Toast with Cheese.

2 tablespoonfuls butter,
1 tablespoonful flour,
1 cupful milk,
¾ cupful grated cheese,
1 egg,
1 cupful cheese.

Make a white sauce from the milk, butter, and flour; when it boils, add the grated cheese and well-beaten egg. Cook slowly until mixed, then add a cupful of cheese, cut into small cubes. Season with salt and cayenne, and pour over slices of toasted brown bread.

Fried Bread.

3 slices stale bread,
1 egg,
6 tablespoonfuls milk,
2 tablespoonfuls oil (olive).

Cut the bread into fingers three inches wide and the length of the slice. Beat the egg slightly, add the milk. Dip the bread in the mixture. Put the oil in a spider and allow it to grow hot. Drop the bread in and sauté till brown. Drain on soft paper. Arrange log-cabin fashion, and serve with a sweet liquid sauce or maple sirup.

Milk Toast.

6 slices stale bread,
2 cupfuls milk,
2 teaspoonfuls cornstarch,
2 tablespoonfuls butter.

Dry the bread thoroughly in the oven, then toast over a clear fire to a golden brown. Heat the milk in the double boiler, add the butter, and when scalding hot, the cornstarch moistened in cold milk. It ought to be like a milk sauce. Lay the toast on a hot platter and baste each slice with the sauce. Serve very hot.

Brown-Bread Sauté.

Cut the crusts off around slices of Boston brown bread with a large cooky cutter. Fry bacon in a spider and put it on a hot platter when crisp. Then lay the bread in the bacon fat, and sauté on both sides. Serve a crisp curled slice of bacon on each brown round.

Tomato Toast.

1½ cupfuls strained tomato,
½ cupful scalded milk,
¼ teaspoonful soda;
3 tablespoonfuls butter,
3 tablespoonfuls flour,
½ teaspoonful salt,
6 slices toast.

Make a tomato sauce from the butter, flour, and tomato, add the soda and salt, then the milk. Dip the toast in the sauce. Serve hot.

Bread Griddlecakes.

1½ cupfuls scalded milk,
1½ cupfuls stale bread crumbs,
2 tablespoonfuls butter,
2 eggs,
½ cupful flour,
½ teaspoonful salt,
3½ teaspoonfuls Calumet baking powder.

Pour the hot milk and the melted butter over the crumbs and soak until they are soft. Add the well-beaten eggs, flour, salt, and baking powder. Cook on a griddle like cakes.

Bread Roulettes.

1 cupful stale bread crumbs,
½ cupful milk,
1 egg,
Dash salt.

Soak the bread crumbs in the milk. Mix with the egg and seasonings. Form into tiny balls, flour, egg, crumb, and fry in hot fat.

Bread Sauce.

½ cupful stale bread crumbs,
1½ cupfuls scalded milk,
1 tablespoonful butter,
Pepper and salt,
½ cupful browned crumbs.

Pour the hot milk over the stale crumbs and cook in a double boiler for twenty minutes. Add the butter, pepper, and salt. Put 1 tablespoonful butter in an omelet pan and in it brown ½ cupful dry crumbs. Pour the sauce about game, timbales, or anything you wish to serve with it, and on top sprinkle browned hot crumbs.

Bread Croquettes.

2 cupfuls stale bread crumbs,
1 cupful hot milk,
Grated rind 1 lemon,
½ cupful currants,
½ teaspoonful cinnamon,
Yolks 2 eggs.

Boil the bread crumbs for two minutes in the hot milk. Add the lemon, currants, cinnamon, and remove from the fire. Beat in the yolks of the eggs. Cool, form into croquettes, crumb, and fry in hot fat.

Beignets of Buns.

2 stale buns,
1 egg,
½ gill milk,
1½ tablespoonfuls flour,
Dash salt.

Soak the buns five minutes in the milk. Mix the yolk of the egg with milk, add the flour, salt, and beaten white. Dip the buns into batter, fry in half lard and half butter, light brown on both sides. Dust with sugar, and serve with jelly or preserved fruit.

CHAPTER XXXII

SANDWICHES

The old-fashioned sandwich—two thick wedges of bread, erratically buttered, hard of crust, exuding mustard, and with frills of ham or corned beef about the edge—has been relegated to the past by the arrival of the meat chopper. The sandwiches of the past were of a half-dozen varieties; the filling of a modern sandwich is limited only by what you have on hand. Fish, flesh, fowl, vegetables, eggs, nuts, olives, fruit, cheese, and pickles may be utilized alone, or combined, and the result, when prepared by a skillful cook, is a dainty and delicious morsel.

If many sandwiches are required, as for a reception or picnic, bake the bread specially for them; there is less waste and the work is much easier. Keep on hand plenty of baking-powder cans, pound and half-pound sizes, also a few oblong tins which have held one pound of cocoa. Nothing can excel these as molds for baking bread for picnic sandwiches; it is tender, almost crustless, it needs no trimming to make two slices accord in size, and it bakes or steams much more quickly than in larger tins. Make the bread twenty-four hours before it is required and try to have it fine grained. Fill the cans half full of dough and set to raise. When almost at the top of the tins, put to bake with the lids off. Fill three quarters full of brown-bread mixture; it does not raise so much as bread which has yeast in it. Slip the small loaves out of the tins as soon as taken from the oven or steamer and set on a wire stand to cool; then wrap in towels and put away in the bread box until required.

The next consideration is butter. Put a pound of butter (if you have many sandwiches to make) in a mixing bowl and with a slitted wooden spoon beat it to a fine, light cream, exactly as for cake making. The butter is much easier to spread, it is more economical, then it is ready to divide into portions and blend with anything to make what is called a flavored butter, the most delicious of all fillings.

Before preparing sandwiches, if they are to be used at a luncheon or entertainment where other dishes accompany them, be careful that the flavoring is different from the salad with which they are served. It is really in better taste to offer nothing with a salad or cold meat except plain bread and butter; still, fashion seems to demand a flavored nibble as a salad accompaniment. Fish, lobster, or shrimp salads are most appetizing with sandwiches of Boston brown bread holding a tender lettuce leaf or a sprig of watercress dipped in mayonnaise. Serve sandwiches of mild cheese, flavored by mustard or tarragon, with green salads. White-bread sandwiches holding tender young nasturtium leaves between the buttered folds go well with salads of meat or fish. Garnish a plateful of this variety with a few nasturtium leaves and blossoms. Finely cut peppergrass, chives, endive or celery are all fitting accompaniments to sandwiches which are offered with a meat or chicken salad. Cucumbers and tomatoes thinly sliced and spread with mayonnaise make a delicious bite between buttered bread. Cut with a small cooky cutter rounds of bread slightly larger than a slice of tomato or cucumber, and put the vegetable between them. These, as well as herb sandwiches, must not be made until immediately before serving.

Cheese, which is generally the first course in a sandwich menu, may be spread between folds of white, Graham, or entire-wheat bread, or delicate crackers. Roquefort, fromage de Brie, or any of the stronger cheeses should be flavored with finely chopped olives or parsley and creamed butter. Combine with a milder cheese chopped olives, walnut meats, anchovy essence, and a dash of mustard, McIlhenny's Tabasco Sauce, and salt. Grate hard cheese and mash soft cheese with a spoon, afterwards rub to a paste with mayonnaise or butter and flavoring. The delicious little cream or Neufchâtel cheeses may be blended with chopped walnuts, given a bit of seasoning by Parmesan cheese, also a hint of lemon juice and paprika.

Under the head of savory sandwiches is a long list of possibilities. They include meat, fish, egg, as well as fillings obtained from chopped olives and pickles, or some strong seasoning, curry, caviare, or anchovy. For all sorts of meat, use a chopper, grinding with the finest knife. It provides a paste which, blended with mayonnaise, is as easy to spread on bread as butter. Scores of recipes might be offered to direct this blending process, but the clever cook, with her own palate as criterion, can easily adapt a few suggestions to the materials on hand. Chicken combines well with celery, chopped nuts, and olives. The most delicate chicken sandwich is seasoned with celery salt and moistened with thick whipped cream instead of mayonnaise. Ham paste is blended with mayonnaise, mustard, chopped olives, and gherkins. Veal paste may be seasoned like chicken—indeed one can scarcely tell the difference between the two fillings. Roast beef, corn beef, lamb, and poultry paste make good sandwiches. If you have not enough of one meat, add to it another which harmonizes in flavor; for instance, veal goes well with any sort of poultry, while tongue and ham make a good mixture. If remains of roast beef, lamb, or corn beef are small, chop and blend each separately; nothing seems to assimilate well with red-blooded meats. Use mustard, a few drops of onion extract, and chopped pickles as flavoring. They are better moistened with creamed butter than with mayonnaise. Put lobster, shrimp, or crab meat through the chopper. Cold fish or canned salmon is better delicately

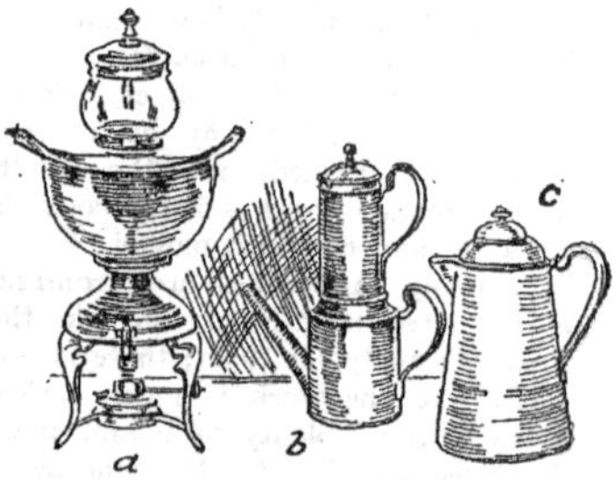

a, French Coffeepot; b, Filter Coffeepot; c, Everyday Pot for Boiled Coffee.

picked to flakes with a fork. Sardines, anchovies, and salt fish make tasty picnic sandwiches. Pound to a paste, and give a touch of acidity by lemon juice or chopped pickle. Eggs should be hard-boiled; allow to become thoroughly cold, then put through a chopper, mix with mayonnaise or butter, and season well.

When one comes to sweet sandwiches, the variety is almost unlimited. Figs, dates, prunes, raisins, nuts, preserved ginger, and candied peel may be chopped, sweetened, moistened with whipped cream, lemon, orange, or pineapple juice and spread between folds of white bread. When preparing them for an entertainment cut heart, diamond, or club shaped, and on top of each lay something which suggests the filling—an English walnut meat, a shred of green citron peel, or half a Maraschino cherry, dipped in icing to make them stick. When you wish to roll sandwiches, use fresh bread, spread very lightly with the filling, and pin into shape with a toothpick.

It is easy to keep sandwiches fresh some hours before they are required. Wring a napkin as dry as possible from hot water—a good plan is to put it through the wringer—wrap the sandwiches in it, then cover in a stone jar or something which will exclude air.

Lamb Sandwiches.

Mince cold roast lamb, season with salt, pepper, and a dash of McIlhenny's Tabasco Sauce. Add minced olives and a chopped pimento, then make into a paste with mayonnaise dressing. Spread between slices of white bread.

Sweetbread Sandwiches.

Cut cold boiled sweetbreads in a meat chopper, moisten with whipped cream, season with salt, cayenne, and lemon juice. Spread between thin slices of buttered bread.

Hot-Ham Sandwiches.

Butter thin slices of bread. Broil thin slices of ham, put between slices of white bread, and eat hot. Bacon may be served in the same fashion.

Chicken and Celery Sandwiches.

1 cupful cold chicken,
1 cupful celery,
4 tablespoonfuls mayonnaise.

Put chicken through the finest knife of a meat chopper, add celery cut fine and mayonnaise. Butter white bread and spread with the chicken mixture.

Tongue Sandwiches.

Make a dressing of one part mustard and six parts butter, add salt, pepper, and a dash of McIlhenny's Tabasco Sauce. Butter the bread with this mixture and lay between thin slices of cold tongue.

Oak-Hill Sandwiches.

⅓ cupful butter,
1 cupful finely chopped cold boiled ham,
1 cupful cold chicken,
Dash of salt and paprika.

Cream butter, add ham and chicken, then salt and paprika. Spread the mixture between thin slices of white bread.

Rare-Beef Sandwiches.

Chop rare cold roast beef fine. Sprinkle with salt, pepper, a dash of horse-radish, and a few drops of McIlhenny's Tabasco Sauce. Make into sandwiches with thinly sliced Graham bread.

Club Sandwich.

Toast a slice of bread and butter it. On one half put, first, a thin slice of bacon which has been broiled till dry and tender, next a slice of the white meat of either turkey or chicken. Over one half of this place a circle cut from a ripe tomato and over the other half a tender leaf of lettuce. Cover with a generous layer of mayonnaise, and complete this delicious "wholemeal" sandwich with the remaining piece of toast.—A. W.

Lobster Sandwiches.

Blend with the chopped lobster meat a dash of McIlhenny's Tabasco Sauce, lemon juice, salt, pepper, and oil. Spread the mixture between slices of thinly buttered bread.

Crab Sandwich.

1 hard-boiled egg,
1 tablespoonful softened butter,
½ can deviled crab,
1 tablespoonful lemon juice.

Moisten the sifted yolk of egg with butter, add chopped crab, and lemon juice mixed to a paste. Spread it between thin slices of buttered bread, put two together, press with a bread knife, and cut into fingers, triangles, or small squares.

Salmon Sandwiches.

1 can salmon,
Yolks 6 hard-boiled eggs,
Dash McIlhenny's Tabasco Sauce,
2 tablespoonfuls lemon juice,
2 tablespoonfuls parsley,
½ cupful boiled salad dressing,
½ teaspoonful salt.

Drain the oil from salmon, remove the skin and bones, and mash fish fine. Add eggs, press through potato ricer, then salt, lemon juice, chopped parsley, Tabasco, and salad dressing. Spread between folds of white or entire-wheat bread.

Mock-Crab Sandwiches.

½ cupful grated cheese,
4 tablespoonfuls creamed butter,
½ teaspoonful salt,
½ teaspoonful paprika,
½ teaspoonful mustard,
1 teaspoonful anchovy paste,
1 teaspoonful vinegar,
2 tablespoonfuls chopped olives.

To cheese add butter, salt, paprika, mustard, paste, vinegar, and chopped olives. Spread between rounds of white bread.—STELLA A. DOWNING.

Cheese Sandwiches.

½ cupful grated cheese,
½ cupful Roquefort cheese,
½ cupful cream,
Dash McIlhenny's Tabasco Sauce.

To the grated cheese add Roquefort cheese rubbed to a paste; add sauce and cream. Beat till smooth and spread between slices of Graham bread.

Walnut-and-Cheese Sandwiches.

½ cupful walnut meats,
½ cupful Neufchâtel cheese,
Dash pepper and salt.

Chop walnuts fine and mix with cheese; add pepper and salt. Spread between slices of white bread. If desired, this sandwich may be further improved by putting between the folds a crisp lettuce leaf.

Anchovy-Cheese Sandwich.

1 cottage cheese,
1 teaspoonful anchovy essence,
1 teaspoonful paprika,
2 tablespoonfuls chopped parsley.

To the cheese add anchovy essence, paprika, and parsley. Spread between slices of entire-wheat bread.

Boston Sandwiches.

Slice Boston brown bread thin, butter lightly, and spread with Neufchâtel or cottage cheese. Dip crisp lettuce leaves in French dressing, then lay on the brown bread. Press another slice of buttered brown bread on top.

Cheese-and-Olive Sandwiches.

Work a cream cheese until smooth and creamy; add half the quantity of olives finely chopped; moisten with mayonnaise dressing. The mixture may be slightly moistened with cream and seasoned with salt and cayenne. Spread between crackers.

Walnut Sandwiches.

Blanch and chop English walnuts. To each tablespoonful of nuts allow ½ tablespoonful cream cheese. Beat together and spread between thin slices of Graham bread.

Peanut Sandwiches.

Skin freshly roasted peanuts and reduce them to a powder in a meat chopper. Add salt, and mix the crushed nuts with fresh cream cheese. Spread the paste between slices of unbuttered Graham bread.

Water-Cress Sandwiches.

Chop cress coarsely and season with salt, pepper, and a few drops of vinegar. Blend with cottage cheese and spread between slices of white bread.

Tomato Sandwiches.

Slice Graham or whole-wheat bread thin, pare off the crust, butter on one side, spread with minced ripe tomatoes, drain off superfluous juice, and sprinkle with salt, pepper, and sugar. Serve at once. The tomatoes should be ice cold and minced quickly.—Marion Harland.

Onion Sandwiches.

Cut bread very thin, removing the crust. Spread between each slice Bermuda or Spanish onions, chopped fine and mixed with a mayonnaise dressing.

Cucumber Sandwiches.

Chop 2 cucumbers fine, drain off the liquor, add a little onion juice, a dash of red pepper, and mix with a well-seasoned mayonnaise. Spread between white bread.

Pimento Sandwiches.

Cut bread thin, spread sparingly with thick mayonnaise dressing. Place on it a slice of scarlet pimento, then more salad dressing, and cover with the upper piece of bread. Serve with a leaf of lettuce. Trim neatly either round, long, or square, cutting through lettuce and all.

CHAPTER XXXIII

CEREALS AND FLOUR PASTE

Cereals include the grain foods from cultivated grasses, containing every variety from oatmeal to macaroni, which is a paste made of wheat flour rich in gluten. Among them are most valuable foods—rice, for instance, which is the staff of life for certain nations. In what we call breakfast cereals we have a number of foods that are unusually rich in nitrogenous matter and mineral substances, therefore making an excellent morning meal with no further addition than milk or cream, for all cereals are lacking in fat. Unless cereals can be subjected to the long, slow cooking which is necessary, they had better not be eaten, for nothing is so indigestible as half-raw oatmeal. Twenty years ago, when most of our oatmeal was the old-fashioned steel-cut oats, it needed interminable cooking—ten hours was none too long for it; to-day most of the cereals put up in packages, so the directions say, can be cooked in half an hour. That is not possible; few of them, except the fine-grained wheat foods, are fit to eat till they have had at least one hour's cooking in a double boiler. If they can have longer, they are so much the better. Always add the proper amount of salt to a cereal—1 teaspoonful to a quart of water—and let it dissolve before the grains are put in, so it will flavor the whole mass. The best way to cook any rough-grained cereal is to drop it slowly into water which is boiling briskly in the upper part of a double boiler. After cooking for a few minutes on the stove, set it over the water and allow the grains to swell slowly so the food is stiff enough to be chewed. Cornmeal demands a long time for cooking—at least six hours—and it swells so it should have six times the same measurement of water. Granular cereals, farina, for instance, should be mixed with a little cold water and stirred smooth before being added to the necessary amount of boiling water; this prevents it from becoming lumpy. Never stir any cereal after it has been put to cook, until just before it is turned out. This treatment makes oatmeal pasty and sticky. Store cereals in glass cans with tight-fitting lids instead of the pasteboard boxes in which they are sold. It keeps them fresher and safe from the invasion of moths or mice.

Cereal with Fruit.

¾ cupful wheat germ,
¾ cupful cold water,
2 cupfuls boiling water,
1 teaspoonful salt,
½ pound dates, stoned and cut in pieces.

Mix cereal, salt, and cold water; add to boiling water in a saucepan. Boil five minutes, steam in double boiler thirty minutes; stir in dates, and serve with cream. Serve for breakfast or as a simple dessert.—Fannie M. Farmer.

Hasty Pudding.

1 cupful cornmeal,
2 tablespoonfuls flour,
1 teaspoonful salt,
1 cupful milk,
2 cupfuls boiling water.

Mix the meal, flour, and salt with the milk; when smooth, stir in the boiling water. Cook in a double boiler one hour or more; or over direct heat one half hour. Serve with cream and sugar, or turn into tins to cool if wanted for sautéing. Cut into slices, dip in flour, and sauté in drippings or butter.

Hominy Mush.

½ cupful fine hominy,
½ teaspoonful salt,
3 cupfuls boiling water.

Put all together in a double boiler, and cook three hours. Add more water if mush seems stiff; all preparations of corn absorb a great deal of water in cooking, and hominy usually needs a little more than four times its bulk.

Oatmeal Porridge.

1 cupful granulated oatmeal,
1 teaspoonful salt,
1 scant quart boiling water.

Put the oatmeal and salt in a double boiler, pour on the boiling water, and cook three or four hours. Remove the cover just before serving and stir with a fork to let the steam escape. If the water in the boiler be strongly salted, the oatmeal will cook more quickly.

Rolled Oats.

1 cupful rolled oats,
2⅔ cupfuls boiling water,
½ teaspoonful salt.

Mix ingredients, and cook in double boiler one hour.

Steamed Rice.

1 cupful rice,
1 teaspoonful salt,
3 cupfuls boiling water.

Pick over the rice and wash in three or four waters. Put it with the salt and boiling water in upper part of double boiler. Cook over boiling water. Do not stir while cooking. Steam until the grains are tender.

Boiled Rice.

¼ cupful rice,
1 teaspoonful salt,
4 cupfuls boiling water.

Wash rice thoroughly and gradually add to boiling water, care being taken that the water does not stop boiling. Cover and cook twenty minutes, or until grains are soft. Turn into a strainer and drain, put in oven a few moments to dry, with oven door open.

Turkish Pilaf.

½ cupful rice,
¾ cupful tomatoes, stewed and strained,
1 cupful brown stock, lightly seasoned,
3 tablespoonfuls butter.

Add tomato to stock, and heat to boiling point; add rice, and steam till soft; stir in butter with a fork, and keep uncovered that steam may escape. Serve in place of a vegetable, or as a border for curried or fricasseed meat.—FANNIE M. FARMER.

Rice Timbales.

1 cupful rice,
½ teaspoonful salt,
1 egg,
1 teaspoonful butter.

Place the rice in a double boiler over the fire, cover with cold water, boil five minutes, then drain it on a sieve, rinse off with cold water, return to saucepan again, cover with ½ pint water, add the salt and boil till tender; add the egg and butter to the mixture, fill the rice in small timbale forms, set them in a pan of water so the water reaches halfway up the forms, place the pan in a hot oven, and bake ten minutes. Unmold and set the timbales in a circle.

Rice à la Creole (Southern recipe).

1 onion,
1 slice cooked ham,

1 tablespoonful butter,
1 cupful cooked rice,
1 can tomatoes,
1 teaspoonful salt,
Dash of McIlhenny's Tabasco Sauce.

Chop the onion and ham fine; put in a saucepan with the butter; add the rice and tomatoes, salt, and paprika. Mix and heat thoroughly. Then put in a baking dish, cover with bread crumbs, and put in the oven for fifteen minutes. The tomatoes should be stewed until thick before mixing.

Manana Land (Mexican recipe).

1 tablespoonful olive oil,
1 sliced onion,
8 green peppers,
1 cupful uncooked rice,
½ can tomatoes.

Fry in the olive oil the onion and green peppers, chopped fine; to this add the uncooked rice, and stir constantly until the rice is nicely browned; then put in the tomatoes, fill up the skillet with rich soup stock, and cook slowly, without stirring for an hour.—May E. Southworth.

Rice Milanaise Fashion.

1 cupful rice,
2 tablespoonfuls butter,
1 onion,
1 quart stock,
1 teaspoonful salt,
2 tablespoonfuls butter,
½ cupful grated cheese.

Cook the rice in a quart of cold water, stir until the boiling point is reached, and let boil three or four minutes, then drain and rinse in cold water and turn on a cloth to dry for a few minutes. Put the butter into a stewpan; cook in it until softened and slightly yellowed, a slice of onion chopped fine; then add the rice and stock and salt; cook until the rice is tender and the liquid absorbed; add the butter and grated cheese. Lift the rice with two forks to mix the butter and cheese evenly. Vary the dish occasionally by adding a cup of strained tomato with the broth and two tablespoonfuls chopped green pepper with onion.

Spaghetti à la Italien (Neapolitan recipe).

½ cupful dried mushrooms,
1 tablespoonful butter,
1 onion,
1 clove garlic,
1 pound chuck steak,
2 slices bacon,
1 cupful tomatoes,
Salt,
Paprika,
Pepper,
1 package spaghetti.

Soak the mushrooms in a cup of tepid water for fifteen minutes; put the butter into a frying pan; when melted, add the onion and garlic, cut fine. Let this cook to a straw color, then add the meat and bacon, cut into finger lengths. Let this cook about five minutes, add the tomatoes and simmer slowly for about fifteen minutes. Then add the mushrooms, together with the water in which they have been soaked. Season very lightly with salt, pepper, and paprika. Let this simmer slowly for an hour and a half. During this time cook the spaghetti in about 2 quarts boiling water to which 2 tablespoonfuls salt have been added. Cook twenty minutes, then pour in a colander and blanch with warm water. When the sauce has cooked sufficiently, take a large platter, spread half of the spaghetti upon it, and pour over it some of the sauce. Now sprinkle upon this grated cheese. Add the remainder of the spaghetti, finish with sauce and cheese, and serve.

Macaroni Siciliana (Italian recipe).

1 onion,
1 carrot,
1 tablespoonful butter,
2 pounds beef,
1 quart tomatoes,

Bay leaf,
3 cloves,
1 pound macaroni,
1 pound grated Swiss cheese.

Slice very thin the onion and carrot; put in a pot with the butter and let it fry, then put in the beef that has been cut in thick slices. Stir until it has browned nicely, add the tomatoes, bay leaf, cloves, salt, and peppers to taste. Stew slowly for two hours or more, till the sauce gets thick. Strain through a sieve until the sauce is free from the meat. Take the macaroni and boil for twenty minutes, salt to taste. Drain off the water, and put it in a large, deep dish; pour over it the sauce and put in grated cheese. Mix all thoroughly, and serve hot.

Macaroni Ravioli (Italian recipe).

½ package macaroni,
½ Parmesan cheese,
2 tablespoonfuls butter,
12 chicken livers (parboil),
2 stalks celery,
1 onion,
½ carrot,
½ turnip,
Pepper and salt.

Mince the livers and vegetables fine, and put them in a saucepan to cook in a little butter. Blanch the macaroni; add pepper and salt and let it drain. Lay some macaroni in a baking dish, then a layer of the liver and vegetables, then the cheese, and so on till the dish is full enough. End with a layer of cheese. Set the dish in the oven and let it cook for a few minutes. Brown on top and serve very hot.

Macaroni à la Napolitaine (Italian recipe).

1 pound macaroni,
1 tablespoonful butter,
1 onion,
4 tablespoonfuls grated Parmesan cheese,
Pepper and salt,
1 cupful cream.

Put the macaroni into boiling water, add butter, salt, and onion stuck with cloves. Boil for three quarters of an hour; then drain the macaroni and put into a saucepan with cheese, nutmeg, salt, and cream. Let stew gently a few minutes, and serve very hot.

Macaroni with Tomatoes.

Break half a pound of macaroni into inch lengths and boil in salted water until tender. Drain, and put a layer of the macaroni in the bottom of a greased pudding dish, sprinkle with pepper, salt, onion juice, and grated cheese. Cover all with a layer of stewed and strained tomatoes that have been previously seasoned to taste. On these goes another layer of macaroni, and so on till the dish is full. The topmost layer must be of tomatoes sprinkled with crumbs and good-sized bits of butter. Set in hot oven, covered, for twenty minutes, then bake, uncovered, until the crumbs are brown.—MARION HARLAND.

Spaghetti with Cheese.

½ pound spaghetti,
½ cupful Swiss cheese,
3 tablespoonfuls melted butter,
Dash McIlhenny's Tabasco Sauce.

Break the spaghetti into bits and boil in salted water. Grate the cheese and turn into a saucepan with the butter. Stir well, add the hot spaghetti; just long enough to melt the cheese; add tabasco, and serve very hot.

Spaghetti with Chicken.

½ package spaghetti,
2 cupfuls chicken stock,
1 tablespoonful flour,
1 tablespoonful butter,
1 cupful cold chicken,
1 egg.

Boil the spaghetti until tender; drain, drop in cold water, and drain again. Cut into half-inch pieces.

Thicken the stock with flour and butter. Stir in the chicken chopped fine and macaroni. Beat in the egg, whipped, remove from the fire, season to taste, turn into a buttered dish, sprinkle crumbs over the top, and bake half an hour.

Spaghetti Piquante.

½ pound spaghetti,
1 teaspoonful butter,
1 teaspoonful flour,
2 cupfuls beef stock,
4 tablespoonfuls tomato catsup,
6 drops McIlhenny's Tabasco Sauce,
1 teaspoonful kitchen bouquet,
Pinch salt,
Dash paprika.

Break spaghetti into small bits. Boil until tender, in salted water. Drain and keep hot while you make the following sauce: Cook together the butter and flour; when blended pour the stock and stir until smooth, then add the catsup, tabasco, kitchen bouquet, salt, and paprika. Turn the spaghetti into this sauce, stir and pour the mixture into a dish. Sprinkle buttered crumbs and grated cheese over the top, and bake till brown.

Entrades (Mexican recipe).

¼ cupful olive oil,
2 tablespoonfuls butter,
2 green onions,
1 spray parsley,
1 stalk celery,
1 leek,
½ garlic,
1 green pepper,
1 teaspoonful salt,
1 tablespoonful Spanish sausage,
½ cupful stock,
½ package macaroni,
Edam cheese.

Make a sauce of olive oil and butter heated together; in this fry the onion, parsley, celery, leek, garlic, pepper, all chopped fine. Season with salt and the sausage. After it is well cooked down, add the stock. Boil the macaroni until tender, then plunge in cold water to blanch. Place on a large platter, strain the hot sauce over it, and cover the top with grated cheese.—May E. Southworth.

Baked Macaroni.

½ pound macaroni,
1 quart stock,
1 tablespoonful butter.

Break the macaroni into inch lengths. Boil till tender in stock. Drain, put the macaroni in a dish; pour over it ½ cupful stock in which it was cooked, add the butter, in small pieces, here and there through it. Sift over it fine bread crumbs and grated cheese. Dot with bits of butter and brown.

Oatmeal.

½ teaspoonful salt,
1 cupful oatmeal,
4 cupfuls water.

Put the boiling water in a granite pan, salt it, then scatter in the oatmeal. Allow it to cook six minutes, stirring steadily. Into the fireless cooker saucepan set the oatmeal dish, cover with a plate, and pour in boiling water to surround it till it almost reaches the top of dish. Cover, set on the stove and let the water boil five minutes, then place in the fireless cooker and leave there for five hours, or if required for breakfast, till morning. If it is not quite hot enough, set the cooker saucepan on the stove and let the water in the other vessel boil for a few minutes; then serve.

Quaker Oats.

2½ cupfuls boiling water,
1 teaspoonful salt,
1 cupful Quaker oats.

Cook in exactly the same way as oatmeal.

Cream of Wheat.

2¼ cupfuls water,
½ teaspoonful salt,
½ cupful cream of wheat.

Prepare after the same fashion as oatmeal, and give four hours in the fireless cooker.

Cracked Wheat.

4 cupfuls cold water,
1 cupful cracked wheat,
1 teaspoonful salt.

Pour the cold water over the wheat and let it stand six hours. Put it in a granite pan as used for oatmeal and set it on an asbestos mat over the fire, allowing it to cook and swell for two hours, stirring occasionally. Cover closely, set into the fireless-cooker saucepan, pour boiling water around it, let it boil up, then put into the cooker and allow it to stand over night.

Indian Meal.

3½ cupfuls water,
1 teaspoonful salt,
1 cupful cornmeal.

Bring the water to a boil, stir the meal slowly into it, being careful that it does not lump. Boil half an hour, stirring frequently, set into the saucepan of cooker with water around it and leave it over night.

Fine Hominy.

4 cupfuls water,
1 cupful hominy,
1 teaspoonful salt.

Treat this cereal in the same fashion as others, leaving in the cooker over night.

CHAPTER XXXIV

CEREAL LEFT-OVERS

THE appetizing dishes which may be evolved from a small left-over of any cereal are many. Even a few spoonfuls of well-cooked cereal can be utilized in gems or griddlecakes, or can be fried in butter and eaten hot with maple sirup. Set it away carefully, covering tightly. An excellent plan is to keep three baking-powder tins—a quarter, half, and pound size for this purpose. The variety in size will fit the amount of the left-over. Brush the can inside with butter, pack in the cereal while hot, and cover. When needed, slip it out of the can, cut in half-inch slices, and roll in flour to dry. Dip in egg and crumbs and fry in smoking hot fat. Eat with maple sirup. Cream of wheat, mush, hominy, wheatena, Quaker oats, flaked rice, farina, Pettijohn, Ralston's food, wheatlet—indeed, any of the large variety of cooked breakfast foods can be made palatable in this way. If the left-over only amounts to a cupful, combine it with flour as given in oatmeal muffins and you will have a most satisfactory hot breakfast bread. Served with bacon these second-day preparations of cereals form a very nice relish. The uses of cold rice cannot be enumerated. There are so many methods of transforming it into attractive dishes that many housewives while preparing hot rice for the table, cook a double portion and reserve it for various uses. A cupful of rice is a pleasant addition to many hot breakfast breads. It may be made into delicious puddings, fritters, pancakes; mixed with a cupful of cold tomato or even left-over tomato soup, well seasoned, sprinkled with cheese and buttered bread crumbs and baked till brown, when it appears as a palatable entrée. It can be utilized for croquettes, drop cakes, for a thickening to soup and stews; it may be curried, worked into left-over meat dishes, and even changed into ice cream. Macaroni and spaghetti left-overs make good *réchauffés.* With the addition of a few spoonfuls of milk and water, cold macaroni cooked in white sauce or spaghetti, which made its first appearance in tomato sauce, may be reheated in the double boiler, a spoonful of each put in a ramequin dish, then covered with grated cheese and baked.

Rice with Cheese Crust.

2 cupfuls boiled rice,
1 cupful milk,
2 eggs,
Pepper,
Salt,
1 cupful grated cheese,
1 tablespoonful butter.

Put the rice in a double boiler and cook it in the milk till smooth and soft. If there are any lumps in the rice, beat with a wire whisk. Add the well-beaten eggs and the salt and pepper. Pour into a shallow baking pan, sprinkle the cheese lightly over the top, dot with morsels of butter, and bake till the top is delicately brown. This makes a nice entrée.

Rice with Cheese.

3 cupfuls cold rice,
1 tablespoonful butter,
Dash cayenne and salt,

1 cupful grated cheese,
1 cupful milk,
½ cupful buttered cracker crumbs.

Reheat the rice in a double boiler. Butter a pudding dish and cover the bottom of it with rice; dot with scraps of butter; sprinkle with grated cheese, cayenne, and salt, and repeat until the rice and the cheese are used up. Add the milk, cover with buttered cracker crumbs, and bake twenty minutes.

Rice Griddlecakes.

½ cupful cold rice,
2 cupfuls flour,
3 teaspoonfuls Calumet baking powder,
½ teaspoonful salt,
4 tablespoonfuls sugar,
1½ cupfuls milk,
1 egg,
2 tablespoonfuls melted butter.

Sift together the dry ingredients; work in the rice with the tips of the fingers. Add the well-beaten egg, milk, and butter; beat well; cook on a griddle.

Rice with Date Sauce.

Take cold rice, put it in a double boiler with a little milk, and let steam till the milk is absorbed. Sweeten to taste and add a dash of nutmeg. Press the rice into buttered cups. Turn out and serve hot, individually, with a lemon sauce in which cut dates have been stewed for a few minutes. This makes a nice dessert.

Rice Waffles.

1¾ cupfuls flour,
¾ cupful cold rice,
1½ cupfuls milk,
2 teaspoonfuls Calumet baking powder,
½ teaspoonful salt,
1 tablespoonful melted butter,
1 egg.

Sift the flour, sugar, baking powder, and salt. Work the rice with the tips of the fingers. Add the yolk of the egg, well beaten, milk, butter, and, last of all, the white of egg, beaten stiff. Cook on hot waffle irons.

Rice Gems.

1 egg,
1 cupful milk,
1 tablespoonful melted butter,
1 cupful cold rice,
1 cupful flour,
2 teaspoonfuls Calumet baking powder,
½ teaspoonful salt.

Beat the eggs till light, add the milk and butter. Beat the rice with this until smooth, then sift in the salt, flour, and baking powder. Bake twenty minutes in hot gem pans.

Rice Bread.

2 eggs,
1 tablespoonful melted butter,
1 cupful cold rice,
1 cupful cornmeal,
½ cupful flour,
1 teaspoonful Calumet baking powder,
½ teaspoonful salt,
1½ cupfuls milk.

To the yolks of the eggs, beaten well, add the milk and butter, rice, corn, and flour. Whip thoroughly, add the salt and baking powder, and last the whites of the eggs beaten to a stiff froth. Pour into shallow pans; allow the batter to spread only an inch thick. Bake in a moderate oven for half an hour. Cut into squares when baked, and serve hot.

Rice and Cornmeal Muffins.

½ cupful white cornmeal,
½ cupful flour,
1 teaspoonful salt,
2 teaspoonfuls Calumet baking powder,
1 cupful cold rice,
1½ cupfuls milk,
2 eggs,
2 tablespoonfuls butter.

Sift the dry ingredients together, rub the rice in lightly with the tips of the fingers till every grain is separated. Beat the yolks of eggs till thick, mix with the milk, pour over the dry ingredients, and beat well. Add the melted butter, and last the whites of the eggs beaten to a dry froth. Bake in hot oven.

Cream Rice Pudding.

2 tablespoonfuls cold boiled rice,
3 tablespoonfuls sugar,
Yolk 1 egg,
3 tablespoonfuls cornstarch,
2 cupfuls milk,
½ teaspoonful McIlhenny's Mexican vanilla.

Put the milk with the cold rice in a double boiler, add the sugar and salt. When it boils, add the cornstarch wet in a few tablespoonfuls cold milk. Just before it is ready to take from the fire, add the egg and flavoring. Eat cold with whipped cream.

Rice Croquettes.

1½ cupfuls cold rice,
½ teaspoonful salt,
Yolks 2 eggs,
1 tablespoonful butter.

Put the rice in a double boiler with a little milk and let it cook until the rice has absorbed the milk. Remove from the fire, add the beaten egg yolks and butter, and spread on a plate. Shape into balls, roll in crumbs, then dent with the finger till the croquette is like a small nest. Dip in egg, then in crumbs again, fry in deep fat, and drain. Serve hot with a cube of jelly in each nest.

Oatmeal Muffins.

¾ cupful scalded milk,
4 tablespoonfuls sugar,
½ teaspoonful salt,
¼ yeast cake dissolved in
¼ cupful warm water,
1 cupful cold oatmeal,
2½ cupfuls flour.

Scald the milk and add it to the sugar and salt; as soon as it grows lukewarm, add the yeast. Work the flour into the oatmeal with the tips of the fingers and add to the milk. Beat thoroughly, cover, and allow it to raise over night. In the morning pour into greased iron gem pans and set in a warm place to raise. Bake half an hour.

Farina Muffins.

1 cupful cold farina,
2 cupfuls flour,
3 eggs,
½ teaspoonful salt,
1 teaspoonful sugar,
2 tablespoonfuls melted butter,
2 teaspoonfuls Calumet baking powder,
¾ cupfuls milk.

Sift the dry ingredients together and work in the farina. Add the butter, milk, and yolks of the eggs; at the last minute the beaten whites of the eggs. Pour into greased gem pans. Bake twenty minutes in a hot oven.

Fried Mush and Bacon.

Cook slices of bacon in the spider. Lift them out and lay on a hot platter. Cut cold mush in neat slices, dip in flour, egg, and crumbs. Fry in hot fat till brown and crisp on both sides. Drain on soft paper and serve with the bacon. This makes a delicious breakfast dish.

Fried Mush.

If there is any cornmeal mush left from breakfast, do not scrape it in cold spoonfuls into a bowl; reheat and allow it to become smooth, then pour into a square cake tin; calculate the amount of mush to the size of the tin, so it will make a cake two inches in depth. Cover when it cools and set in the refrigerator. When it is needed for breakfast or supper, cut into squares about four inches in size and roll them in flour until dry. Drop into smoking hot fat and fry brown. Drain, and serve hot with maple sirup.

Raised Hominy Muffins.

1 cupful cold hominy,
4 tablespoonfuls butter,
1 cupful scalded milk,
3 tablespoonfuls sugar,
½ teaspoonful salt,
⅓ yeast cake dissolved in
¼ cupful lukewarm water.

Warm the hominy in a double boiler and break it into grains in a mixing bowl. Add the butter, milk, sugar, and salt. When it is lukewarm, stir in the yeast and enough flour to make a thick batter. Let it stand over night. In the morning fill gem pans two thirds full, set to raise in a warm place, and bake in a moderate oven.

Hominy in Cream Sauce.

2 cupfuls cream sauce,
2 cupfuls cold hominy.

Make a cream sauce and into it stir the hominy. Reheat in a double boiler and serve very hot instead of potato.

Hominy Griddlecakes.

½ cupful cold hominy,
2 eggs,
2 cupfuls sour milk,
1¼ teaspoonfuls soda,
2 cupfuls flour,
½ teaspoonful salt.

Warm the hominy and mix with it the well-beaten eggs. Sift in the flour and salt, alternating with ½ cupful milk till the mixture is ready to beat; at last stir in the soda dissolved in a tablespoonful warm water. Bake on a hot greased griddle. Eat with maple sirup.

Macaroni and Celery.

1 cupful boiled macaroni,
1 cupful celery,
1 cupful white sauce,
½ cupful buttered bread crumbs,
Salt and pepper,
½ cupful grated cheese.

Cut the celery into inch pieces and boil for ten minutes in salted water. Drain and lay in a dish with the macaroni stirred lightly through it. Over it pour the white sauce; season with salt and pepper. Sprinkle over the top buttered crumbs and grated cheese. Bake till the top is delicate brown.

Savory Macaroni.

2 cupfuls cold macaroni,
2 tablespoonfuls butter,
Pepper,
Salt,
Paprika.

Melt the butter in an omelet pan. Put in the macaroni, dust with pepper, salt, and paprika. Let it brown slightly, tossing it with a fork while it cooks. Serve very hot as a side dish; sprinkle with grated cheese.

Creamed Macaroni on Toast.

1½ tablespoonfuls butter,
1 tablespoonful flour,
1 cupful milk or cream,
Salt and pepper,
1 cupful cold macaroni,
½ cupful grated cheese,
6 slices toast.

Make a white sauce from the butter, flour, and milk. Chop coarsely the macaroni, add to it the white sauce, and allow it to cook for ten minutes. Pour over the buttered toast, and dust liberally with grated cheese. Set on the top shelf of the oven for a few minutes, and serve very hot.

Macaroni and Chicken.

1½ cupfuls cold chicken,
1½ cupfuls macaroni,
1½ cupfuls cold tomato sauce,
½ cupful buttered crumbs.

Butter a baking dish, put in a layer of macaroni, then a layer of cold chicken cut in small strips, then a few spoonfuls of tomato sauce. Repeat in the same order till the dish is full, making the top layer macaroni. Cover with crumbs and bake till the top is brown and crusty. No seasoning is given in this recipe, because usually tomato sauce is well flavored.

Macaroni Croquettes.

2 tablespoonfuls butter,
4 tablespoonfuls flour,
1 cupful milk,
Yolk 1 egg,
2 cupfuls chopped macaroni,
2 tablespoonfuls cheese,
Pepper and salt.

If the macaroni is the remainder of a dish of tomato and macaroni or a well-seasoned cheese dish, it will be the more tasty. Make a thick sauce from the flour, butter, and milk, beat in the egg and cheese. Mix thoroughly, spread to cool, flour, egg, crumb, and fry. Serve very hot with tomato sauce.

CHAPTER XXXV

EGGS

WHEN we consider that nine eggs are equal in nutritive value to a pound of meat, we realize they are not only capable of forming a most important item in everyday diet, but also an economical food during the season when eggs are cheap. Even when eggs are expensive, it is economy to use only the best grade. Eggs

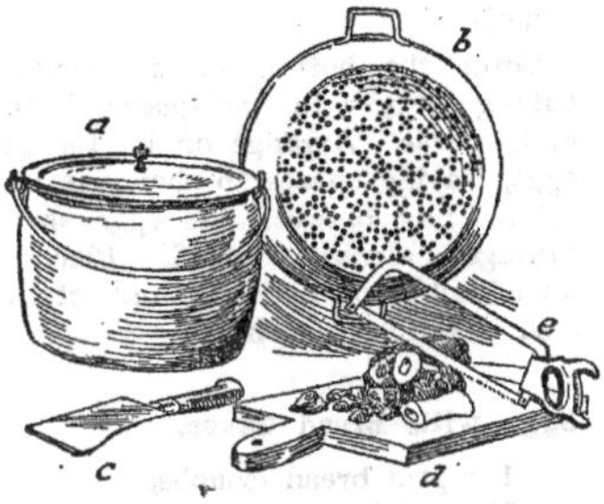

a, Soup Pot; b, Colander; c, Meat Cleaver; d, Meat Board with Handle to Hang By; e, Meat Saw.

that cost fifty cents a dozen are cheaper than eggs at twenty-five cents where half of the dozen may be stale or worse. There are a number of household tests of the freshness of eggs. The most reliable is to candle them. Hold the egg in the hand with the fingers wrapped about it and look through it against a bright light; in a perfectly fresh egg, you can see the yolk like a golden ball and the white about it clear as water. Or you may drop an egg into a basin of water; if perfectly fresh, it will sink and rest on its side. If it rolls around standing on its end, it is comparatively fresh; if it floats, you had better discard it unopened. When an egg is perfectly fresh it has a porous, dull surface; if shiny, it is pretty sure to be at least stale. There are three ways in which eggs are generally used for breakfast or luncheon dishes; in a soft-boiled condition as in a poached egg, hard boiled as in a salad, or with the yolk and white separated and beaten to a froth as in an omelet. Eggs are most digestible in the soft-boiled stage, but to many difficult of digestion when hard boiled. They are deficient in fat; therefore we find them served with bacon, with an oil mayonnaise in salad, or with bread and butter. Indeed, their highly concentrated, nutritive properties demand always an accompaniment of some starchy food, such as potatoes or bread.

Poached Eggs.

A deep spider is the best utensil in which to poach eggs. Fill it nearly full of boiling water which has been slightly salted. Add a few tablespoonfuls of vinegar, which will preserve the color of the white of the egg, break in a saucer, and drop into boiling water, cooking slowly, until the whites are like jelly.

Poached Eggs Ball-Shaped.

Have a shallow saucepan half full of water; add salt and a few tablespoonfuls of vinegar. When the water is boiling, stir with a wooden spoon until you start a sort of whirlpool, then into the center of it drop an egg from a cup. The egg will cook in a rounded form. When the white is set and before the yolk is cooked, lift it from the water and set it on a slice of toast.

Eggs Poached in Milk.

Instead of using water to poach eggs, drop them into boiling milk; as soon as the egg is set, lay it on a slice of toast. Thicken the milk with a little cornstarch, add butter, salt, pepper, and a dash of celery salt; pour it over the eggs and around the toast.

Frizzled Beef with Poached Eggs.

½ pound finely chipped beef,
1 cupful milk,
1 tablespoonful butter,
1 tablespoonful flour.

Put the butter to melt in a saucepan, add the flour and stir it to a paste, then put in the milk, scalding hot, and beat with a wire whisk until creamy. Add the beef and stir for a few minutes. Turn into a deep platter and cover the top with poached eggs.

Eggs in Ramequins.

Butter small ramequins and drop a raw egg into each one, being careful that it remains whole. Set the ramequins in a pan of boiling water and put it in a hot oven until the eggs are set. Put a dab of butter on each one and a dust of pepper and salt before taking from the oven.

Eggs Baked in Tomatoes.

Pick out several well-shaped tomatoes, cut off the stem ends, and with a spoon lift out enough of the pulp so that each shell will hold an egg. Drop it in carefully, sprinkle with pepper and salt, put a dab of butter on top of each; place the tomatoes in a baking dish and pour the water around them. Cook until the eggs are set and the tomatoes soft. Lift each one on a slice of buttered toast, and serve.

Eggs Baked in Green Peppers.

Cut off the stems of green peppers, scoop out the seeds and ribs, and parboil until tender. Break an egg into each one. Set them in a baking pan with ½ cupful boiling water poured around. In fifteen minutes the eggs should be firm. Set each one on a slice of buttered toast and, if you wish, pour white sauce or tomato sauce about them.

Eggs in Tomato Sauce (Spanish recipe).

Cover the bottom of an earthen baking dish with well-seasoned tomato *purée*. Arrange on it poached eggs, leaving spaces to show the red color. Lay between the eggs small sausages, already cooked. Place a bit of butter on each egg and set the dish in the oven to heat.

Eggs with Bread Sauce.

1 cupful bread crumbs,
1½ cupfuls milk,
½ teaspoonful salt,
½ teaspoonful onion juice,
6 eggs.

Put the bread crumbs in a saucepan, then add the milk, salt, a dash of cayenne, and the onion juice. Simmer slowly till thick and smooth, beating several times with a spoon. Pour the sauce into a broad, shallow dish and break the eggs carefully over it. Place in a hot oven until they are set.

Eggs on Rice.

Butter a baking dish, fill it half full with well-seasoned boiled rice; make as many depressions in the rice as there are people to be served; break an egg into each one, sprinkle with salt and strew with bits of butter. Bake until the eggs are set.

Eggs and Mushrooms.

½ cupful milk,
1 pound mushrooms,

1 tablespoonful butter,
6 poached eggs,
Dash McIlhenny's Tabasco Sauce.

Peel and wash the mushrooms; place them in a saucepan and cook gently, with the butter, milk, a pinch of salt and tabasco. Cook ten minutes, thicken with flour, let come to a boil, then pour on a hot platter. Have your poached eggs ready; serve on top of the sauce, the mushrooms being in the middle.

Cheesed Eggs.

Place in a serving dish a tablespoonful butter and several slices rich cheese. When it is melted, break whole eggs into it; put the dish into the oven or before the fire. When the white sets, sprinkle grated cheese and pepper on them. Brown on top, and serve.

Eggs à la Bonne Femme (French recipe).

Cut an onion in dice; fry with a tablespoonful butter; add a tablespoonful vinegar; then butter a dish lightly, spread the onions over it, break in the eggs, and put the dish in the oven. When the eggs are done, strew over them fried bread crumbs, and serve hot.

Eggs in Nests.

Separate as many eggs as are needed for this dish and beat the whites to a stiff froth. Drop irregularly on a flat buttered baking dish, dust with pepper and salt here and there, in the middle of the white, slide in carefully the raw yolks. Put a tiny bit of butter on each yolk. Place the dish in a hot oven for eight minutes. Serve immediately. If desired, the froth may be piled into individual dishes with the yolk in the center of each and baked as described.

Boiled Eggs.

If the eggs have been set in a refrigerator, drop them in warm water for a few minutes before boiling, as the sudden change of temperature is liable to crack the shells. Put them into a saucepan where the water is boiling, and if you wish them soft, cook gently for three and a half minutes.

Poached Eggs with Greens.

For this dish use outer leaves of lettuce; wash them thoroughly and boil until tender in salted water. Drain, chop fine, and season with salt, pepper, and butter. Toast a few slices of bread, butter them, cover with the chopped greens, and on top of each drop a poached egg.

Fried Eggs.

Fry thin slices of bacon to a crisp, lift them out and lay on a hot platter. Break into the pan as many eggs as you need; let them cook until the white is set, and baste with hot fat till a film forms over the yolk. If you like them turned, run a knife under each and reverse quickly. Cut off the ragged edges and serve on a platter with the crisp bacon.

Fried Eggs with Brown Sauce.

Fry eggs in butter in a spider, lift them and keep hot over boiling water. If there is not enough gravy in the pan, put in a little more butter, 1 tablespoonful vinegar, a dash of onion juice, salt, pepper, and a few drops of McIlhenny's Tabasco. Thicken slightly with flour, beat till creamy, and strain the brown gravy over eggs.

Baked Soufflé of Eggs.

6 eggs,
1 cupful milk,
1 tablespoonful butter,
Pepper and salt.

Scald the milk in a double boiler, add to it the yolks of eggs, beaten till thick, also the butter and seasonings. When the mixture begins to thicken like a custard, stir in the whites of eggs, beaten to a stiff froth. Pour into a deep buttered baking dish and bake in a moderate oven till puffy and brown. Serve immediately.

Scrambled Eggs.

4 eggs,
½ teaspoonful salt,
Dash pepper,
3 tablespoonfuls milk.

Whip the eggs just enough to break them up; they do not need to be light or frothy. Put the butter into an omelet pan, and when it is brown pour in the egg. Scrape the cooked eggs from the bottom of the pan, tipping it so the uncooked egg will run down on the hot iron. Double it over before it begins to get brown, and serve very hot.

Deviled Eggs.

5 hard-boiled eggs,
½ cupful white sauce,
Salt and pepper,
Dash McIlhenny's Tabasco Sauce,
2 tablespoonfuls grated cheese.

Chop the eggs coarsely, sprinkle the cheese through them, and toss the mixture together with a fork. Add the seasonings, then stir in the sauce. Put in a saucepan, simmer gently for a few minutes, and serve on slices of buttered toast.

Eggs Farci (French recipe).

6 hard-boiled eggs,
½ teaspoonful onion juice,
Pepper and salt,
4 tablespoonfuls stale bread crumbs,
2 tablespoonfuls chopped parsley,
Dash McIlhenny's Tabasco Sauce.

Shell the eggs, cut them in halves lengthwise, remove the yolks and mash them. Add the bread crumbs, soften with a little milk, the seasonings, and parsley. Mash the yolk and bread mixture together till pasty, fill it into the whites of the eggs, and with what is left make a small mound in a baking dish; set the stuffed eggs on top, pour a white sauce over them, and set in the oven till piping hot.

Curry of Eggs.

6 hard-boiled eggs,
1 tablespoonful flour,
1 tablespoonful butter,
1 tablespoonful curry powder,
½ teaspoonful onion juice,
Pepper and salt,
1 cupful veal or chicken stock.

Melt the butter in a saucepan, blend with the flour, put in the stock and seasoning, and beat the sauce till creamy. Lay on eggs cut in slices, cook to the boiling point, and serve hot on buttered toast.

Eggs Lucanian (Italian recipe).

5 eggs,
1 cupful macaroni,
½ cupful grated cheese,
1½ cupfuls white sauce.

Boil the eggs hard, cutting in eighths, lengthwise, then add the macaroni, cheese, and sauce; season with salt, paprika, onion juice, and anchovy essence. Turn into a buttered baking dish, cover with buttered crumbs, and set in the oven long enough to brown the crumbs.

Eggs à la Cuba (Spanish recipe).

4 tablespoonfuls sausage meat,
1 teaspoonful minced onion,
8 eggs.

Cook the sausage meat and minced onion for five minutes over a hot fire. Beat the eggs until light and add to the meat and onion; season with salt and pepper; stir until the eggs become thick. Serve on slices of hot, buttered toast.

Egg Croquettes.

6 eggs,
½ can mushrooms,
2 cupfuls milk,
1 tablespoonful butter,
2 tablespoonfuls flour,

Boil the eggs hard; chop the whites and add the mushrooms (which should be drained from liquor). Mash the yolks of the eggs through a press. Scald the milk; rub together until smooth the flour and butter; add to the milk and stir until it thickens; add the yolk of one raw egg, the whites and yolks of the boiled eggs, mushrooms, and salt and pepper to taste. Stir quickly, take from the fire, and put away to cool. When thoroughly cold, form into croquettes; dip in egg and bread crumbs and fry in smoking hot fat. Garnish with parsley, and serve.

Omelet Rudolph (German recipe).

2 tablespoonfuls butter,
1 raw onion,
1 tablespoonful salt pork,
1 tablespoonful roast beef,
2 mushrooms,
1 tablespoonful tomato sauce,
1 tablespoonful grated bread crumbs,
Dash McIlhenny's Tabasco Sauce.

Into a saucepan put the butter and raw onion chopped very fine; add the salt pork, which has been slightly cooked, the beef, mushrooms, a pinch of salt, chopped parsley and tabasco, then stir in the tomato sauce and bread crumbs. Make a plain omelet; when cooked, spread with the above mixture and turn over carefully.

Plain Omelet.

4 eggs,
4 tablespoonfuls hot water,
1 tablespoonful butter,
Pepper and salt.

Separate the whites from the yolks, beat the yolks with an egg beater till thick, and whip the whites on a platter with a wire whisk until you have a stiff froth. Add the seasonings and hot water. Last of all blend in the beaten whites. Heat an omelet pan and grease with butter, pour in the egg mixture, tip till the eggs set evenly, then set it where it will cook slowly, turning the pan around that it may brown all over. When puffed and delicately browned on the bottom, take it from the fire and set on the top grate of the oven for a few minutes to cook to the heart. Press it with your finger; if none of the egg mixture clings, it is cooked. Score lightly down the center, and turn out on a hot platter.

Omelet Chassi (French recipe).

Make an omelet as described above. Before folding, spread a cupful of creamed chicken over the top, then double and turn over on a platter. Put on the top some thick, well-seasoned tomato sauce.

Bread Omelet.

6 eggs,
3 tablespoonfuls stale bread crumbs,
1 cupful milk,
Pepper and salt,
1½ tablespoonfuls butter.

Scald the milk, pour over the crumbs and allow it to soak, beat the whites and yolks separately until very light. Stir the crumb mixture into the yolks, add the seasoning, then cut in with a palette knife the whites beaten to a stiff froth. Pour into a deep buttered baking dish and bake in a hot oven till browned on top.

Oyster Omelet.

12 oysters,
3 tablespoonfuls cream,
3 tablespoonfuls strained oyster liquor,
Pepper and salt,
1 tablespoonful butter,
1 tablespoonful flour.

For this dish, prepare the oyster filling before beginning to cook the omelet. Strain the oysters and cut them with a scissors into small pieces. Make a white sauce from the butter, flour, oyster liquor, cream, and seasonings. When hot and creamy, put in the chopped oysters and cook a few minutes. Set the sauce over boiling water to keep hot while making the omelet. When ready, pour over the oyster mixture, fold, and serve immediately.

Cheese Omelet.

Over an omelet, when ready to fold, sprinkle grated cheese with a little seasoning. Slip out on a hot platter and sprinkle again with cheese. Set in a hot oven for a few minutes before serving.

Ham Omelet.

Over the top of an omelet, before the egg begins to set, sprinkle ½ teacupful minced ham; let it cook for a minute or two longer, then set in the oven as directed, and serve hot.

Bismarck Omelet (German recipe).

¼ pound bacon,
8 eggs.

Fry the bacon cut in dice; beat the eggs with pepper and salt; add to the bacon, and fry all together. Stir until it gets thick, and turn out on a dish.

Parsley Omelet (Scotch recipe).

½ cupful cream,
6 eggs,
1 tablespoonful butter,
1 tablespoonful minced parsley.

Beat the yolks of the eggs with a little cayenne and salt; add a small piece of shallot and parsley shredded fine; mix; whip the whites of the eggs and stir into the omelet, melt the butter in a frying pan, and pour in the eggs. Cook five minutes; serve very hot.

Eggs Fricasseed.

Put a piece of butter in a stewpan with some finely minced parsley and minced onion, 1 teacupful stock and 1 tablespoonful flour. Boil eggs hard, cut in slices, and put them in with a little salt and pepper. Beat up the yolk of an egg in ½ cupful cream; add this with the juice of half a lemon. Mix well, make very hot, and serve with sippets of toasted or fried bread.

CHAPTER XXXVI

SOUPS

Soup making is as much of an art as turning out fine cake or pastry, still the American housewife devotes twice as much study to the making of sweet dishes as to soup. The French woman makes a trifle of something sweet serve as dessert, while her soups are famous the world over. It is economy to be able to provide a soup which will often take the place of the *pièce de resistance* in a dinner, for a fine bisque or smooth, creamy soup is a meal in itself. Then there are the stimulating thin soups which make a proper beginning to a dinner. Soup is divided into several classes—soups with stock and soups without—and the variations which can be wrought by a clever housewife on these are numberless. With a pot of stock on hand and the assistance of vegetables for stockless soups, even in a frugal home there may be a soup for everyday in the year. Besides, we have excellent soups made from fish, and satisfying chowders with the addition of potatoes which makes the dish a full meal.

In recipes for making stock, the list of ingredients for seasoning seem endless. Still, a good cook keeps on hand everything that tends to fine flavoring. Spices such as mace, bay leaves, peppers, etc., are very cheap, so are the winter vegetables that most recipes call for and they may be kept constantly on hand. In a large family where there is a roast or meat dish once, perhaps twice, a day, little fresh meat is required for the stock pot if all bones and scraps are saved and utilized. Every morsel of a stew, roast with its gravy, chop and steak bones, carcasses of chicken or game, and the trimmings from meat, which a housewife pays for and should insist on having, are all grist for the soup pot. The meats to avoid using are bits of raw lamb or mutton with fat on them, which gives a disagreeable flavor, also smoked or corned meat. Scraps of bacon, cold ham, or even calf's liver may be added; they give a touch of good flavoring. Several utensils are a necessity for soup making. First there is a sharp meat knife, a hard-wood board, a strong *purée* strainer, a soup pot with a tight lid, and a strainer with a slide, which allows it to be placed across the tureen.

A soup pot need not do a continuous performance on the back of a stove from Monday to Saturday. It is too handy for all sorts of fag-ends to be thrown in without being critically looked over; besides, the stock which is constantly at the boil, or very near it, does not extract the nourishment from meat and bones that cold water does. If you would have fine-flavored, good-colored soup, save all the scraps and keep in a scrupulously clean jar in the refrigerator. Make soup twice a week; three times if the weather is too hot for meat remains to keep, or if they accumulate very fast. Never add a morsel of anything that has the slightest taint; it will spoil the whole potful. Break bones thoroughly. If you would extract all the flavor from bits of meat, put them through a chopper. With a skewer pick marrow from the bones. Lay the bones at the bottom of the pot.

If there are any left-overs in the refrigerator of such vegetables as onions, celery, tomatoes, carrots, parsnips, or peas, chop fine and add, but do not put in too much of one thing; it gives too strong a flavor to the soup. If there are no left-over vegetables on hand, chop ½ cupful each of carrot, turnip, and celery, and add for flavoring, with ½ teaspoonful peppercorns, 1 bay leaf, sprig of parsley, 6 cloves, and 1 chopped onion. Do not add salt till the stock is half cooked.

Cover the bones with cold water and set far back on the stove where it will come to the boil slowly. Let it simmer five or six hours, strain through a fine sieve, and cool as quickly as possible. Do not remove the cake of fat from the top of the soup until you are ready to use it, then run a thin knife around the edge to loosen it. Cut into quarters and lift each piece carefully. If there are any grains of fat left on the top of the jellied stock, dampen a bit of cheese cloth and carefully wipe over the top. Floating globules of grease will ruin the finest-flavored soup.

For an everyday family soup in which nourishment is the first consideration, it does not require clearing. In the sediment there is considerable nutriment. If it is to be cleared, set the strained, skimmed soup over the fire, mix with the white and crushed shell of one egg, a dash of celery seed, the chopped rind and juice of half a lemon, and pepper and salt if required. Mix thoroughly, heat, and boil ten minutes. Just before taking from the fire, pour in ½ cupful cold water. Pour through the finest strainer, and heat again to the boiling point before using.

Mutton Broth.

4 pounds neck mutton,
2 quarts water,
1 onion,
3 stalks celery,
1 small carrot,
Bay leaf,
Few peppercorns.

Wash the mutton thoroughly, cut it up and place it in the vessel of fireless cooker with water, allow it to boil, then skim and boil slowly fifteen minutes. Add the flavoring and vegetables. Cook ten minutes longer without raising the lid, set it into the cooker five hours.

Mock-Turtle Soup.

1 calf's liver,
1 calf's heart,
Small knuckle veal,
2 quarts water,
1 onion,
Salt and pepper,
½ teaspoonful ground cloves,
2 tablespoonfuls brown flour,
Yolks 4 hard-boiled eggs.

Put the liver, heart, and veal into the saucepan of the cooker, cover with water and boil fifteen minutes. Put into the cooker for six hours. When soup is lifted out, strain it, chop the meat fine, add the chopped onion, seasonings, thicken with brown flour, and cook for a few minutes. After pouring into the tureen, add the yolks of the eggs cut in pieces, also some fine cubes of lemon. An excellent way to make this soup, as well as many others, is to leave it in the cooker over night, then strain, skim off any fat that may rise, allow it to cool, and prepare when needed for the table.

Bean Soup.

1 quart white beans,
3 pints boiling water,
1 teaspoonful salt,
1 slice salt pork.

Wash the beans and soak over night; in the morning put them in the fireless vessel, add the pork and salt, boil ten minutes, then set into the cooker for five hours. Strain, thicken, and serve.

Creole Soup.

1 quart brown soup stock,
1 pint tomatoes,
3 tablespoonfuls chopped green peppers,

2 tablespoonfuls chopped onion,
¼ cupful butter,
⅓ cupful flour,
Salt,
Pepper,
Cayenne,
2 tablespoonfuls grated horse-radish,
1 teaspoonful vinegar,
½ cupful macaroni rings.

Cook pepper and onion in butter five minutes. Add flour, stock, and tomatoes, and simmer fifteen minutes. Strain, rub through sieve, and season highly with salt, pepper, and cayenne. Just before serving, add horse-radish, vinegar, and macaroni previously cooked and cut in rings. —Fannie Merritt Farmer.

Veal Soup.

2 pounds veal,
2 quarts cold water,
1 cupful chopped ham,
1 onion,
1 tablespoonful parsley,
Pepper and salt,
1 pint cream,
3 slices carrot.

Cook veal in water slowly for two or three hours. Take out the veal and add to the boiling stock ham, onion, parsley, and carrot. Let this simmer slowly for an hour, strain, then add the cream, season with salt and pepper, and serve with croutons.

Consommé.

3 pounds lean beef,
1 carrot,
1 turnip,
1 parsnip,
1 onion,
1 red pepper,
1 tablespoonful whole cloves,
1 tablespoonful chopped parsley,
4 stalks celery,
3 quarts water.

Cover the meat with water, and simmer four hours. Add the other ingredients, and cook one hour longer. Strain and stand over night. Next day skim off the grease, add the white and shell of one egg to clear it, boil up, strain again, and serve with imperial sticks.

Brown Stock.

10 pounds shin beef,
3 slices bacon,
4 onions,
3 carrots,
1 turnip,
1 bunch celery,
1 sprig parsley,
1 sprig thyme,
12 cloves,
2 tablespoonfuls butter,
2 tablespoonfuls salt,
1 teaspoonful pepper,
7 quarts cold water.

Cut in rather small pieces all the meat from a shin of beef; break the bone in pieces, and put into a large pot with bacon, onions, carrots, turnip, celery, parsley, thyme, salt, cloves, pepper, butter, and a cupful cold water. Set it over a brisk fire, stirring frequently to prevent burning. Cook until the juice from the meat and vegetables begins to thicken. Then add cold water, set it back on the fire, where it will simmer slowly for six hours, skimming very often. Strain carefully through a fine sieve, not bruising the vegetables. Next morning skim off the fat. You can make a variety of soups from this stock by adding to it macaroni, Italian paste, or finely cut vegetables.

Tomato Soup.

2 tablespoonfuls butter,
2 tablespoonfuls onion,
1 bay leaf,
10 peppers,
1 tablespoonful chopped ham,
1 tablespoonful flour,
1 can tomatoes,
3 cupfuls stock,
1 teaspoonful salt,
Dash McIlhenny's Tabasco Sauce.

Place a saucepan, with butter and fine-chopped onion, over the fire;

cook five minutes; add bay leaf, peppers, ham, and flour; stir and cook two minutes; add the tomatoes; stir and cook five minutes; add salt, stock, and tabasco; cook ten minutes, then press the soup through a sieve and serve with toasted bread cut into dice.

Soup à la Reine (French recipe).

1 fowl,
Small knuckle veal,
4 quarts cold water,
1 tablespoonful salt,
2 leeks,
2 onions,
3 sprigs parsley,
2 blades mace,
4 tablespoonfuls butter,
1 pint cream,
Yolks 4 eggs.

Place in a soup kettle the fowl, cut up knuckle of veal, and cold water; as soon as it boils, add salt, leeks, onions, parsley, and mace; cover and boil slowly; when the chicken is done, take it out, remove the meat, chop the bones, return them with the skin to the soup kettle and boil half an hour longer. Strain through a sieve, remove the fat, return 2½ quarts soup to the kettle and place it over the fire; melt butter in a saucepan, add flour, stir until the flour has absorbed all the butter; pour in slowly 1 pint stock, and stir until smooth; then add it to the soup; boil fifteen minutes; mix the yolks of 4 eggs with 1 pint cream; season to taste with salt; draw the soup kettle to side of stove; add a little of the soup to the cream and yolks; mix well; then pour it into the soup; place the fine-cut chicken meat from the breast in tureen, pour the soup over, and serve.

Vegetable Mutton Soup.

1 turnip,
1 carrot,
1 onion,
2 tablespoonfuls butter,
½ cupful chopped celery,
1½ quarts mutton broth.

One hour before serving, cut the vegetables into slices, put in saucepan with butter and celery. Stir over the fire six minutes, then add the mutton broth, cover and cook till done, season to taste and serve.

Potato Cream Soup.

1 tablespoonful butter,
1 onion,
3 stalks celery,
1 teaspoonful salt,
1 meat bone,
2 quarts cold water,
2 large potatoes,
½ cupful milk,
1 teaspoonful chopped parsley.

Place a saucepan with butter, onion, and celery over the fire; cook and stir five minutes, add salt, small meat bone, and water. Cover and cook slowly one hour, then strain the broth into another saucepan. Boil potatoes, drain and mash them fine, add with butter and milk, to the broth, cook a few minutes, season to taste, garnish with chopped parsley and serve.

Soup Bègue (Southern recipe).

3 pounds fowl,
3 tablespoonfuls butter,
2 quarts cold water,
1 teaspoonful salt,
1 cupful green lima beans (parboiled),
1 cupful sweet corn,
1 cupful diced celery,
½ cupful stewed tomatoes,
Pepper,
1 cupful cream.

Choose a young fowl, with yellow legs; after disjointing it and dividing the large pieces, brown it carefully in butter, then place in the soup kettle with water and salt, and simmer until tender. Remove the chicken, carefully skim the grease from the broth, and add to it lima beans, sweet corn, celery and tomato, with salt and pepper to taste. Simmer until the vegetables are perfectly cooked, then the choice chicken meat may be cut in small pieces and added to the soup, and, lastly, the cream.

Soup à la Menestra (French recipe).

2½ pints mutton broth,
1 carrot,
1 onion,
1 stalk celery,
1 cupful fine-cut cabbage,
2 tablespoonfuls butter,
1 tablespoonful rice,
Dash pepper.

Cut fine the carrot, onion, celery, and cabbage; place a saucepan with butter over the fire, add the vegetables, and cook ten minutes, then add the rice, mutton broth, salt, and pepper; boil slowly, well covered for one hour; serve with grated cheese.

Du Barry Soup (French recipe).

1 cupful rice,
2 quarts chicken stock,
1 cupful cold cauliflower,
Pepper and salt,
2 cupfuls cream.

Boil rice in the stock, add cauliflower pressed through a potato ricer. Season with white pepper and salt, add cream and bring again to the boil. Serve in bouillon cups; garnish with small flowerets of cauliflower.

Oxtail Soup à la Tabasco.

1 oxtail,
2 onions,
1 tablespoonful parsley,
Garlic,
1 tablespoonful McIlhenny's Tabasco Sauce,
6 cloves,
6 allspice berries,
2 hard-boiled eggs,
1 lemon.

Cut the oxtail into small pieces, chop the other ingredients, and rub into a tablespoonful lard and a tablespoonful sifted flour. Mix thoroughly and brown without burning. Add cloves, allspice, and salt to taste. Fry ten minutes, stirring often. Add hot water enough to make the soup. Cook from three to four hours. Put into a tureen the eggs and lemon sliced in small pieces. Pour the soup into this through a strainer, and serve.

Fish Chowder.

4 pounds fish,
½ pound pork,
2 onions,
1 quart potato cubes parboiled,
1½ quarts water,
2 tablespoonfuls flour,
2 tablespoonfuls McIlhenny's Tabasco Sauce,
1 cupful tomatoes.

Skin the fish and cut the flesh from the bones. Put the bones on to cook in the water and boil ten minutes. Fry the pork, then add the onions, cut into slices. Cover and cook five minutes; add the flour, cook ten minutes longer. To this add the water in which the fish bones were cooked and boil for five minutes; then strain all on the potatoes and fish. Add salt and tabasco and let it simmer fifteen minutes. Add tomatoes, let it boil up once, and serve.

White Soup Stock.

3 pounds knuckle veal,
1 pound lean beef,
3 quarts boiling water,
1 onion,
6 slices carrot,
1 large stalk celery,
½ teaspoonful peppercorns,
½ bayleaf,
2 sprigs thyme,
2 cloves.

Wipe veal, remove from bone, and cut in small pieces; cut beef in pieces, put bone and meat in soup kettle, cover with cold water, and bring quickly to boiling point; drain, throw away the water. Wash thoroughly bones and meat in cold water; return to kettle, add vegetables, seasonings, and 3 quarts boiling water. Boil three or four hours; the stock should be reduced one half.—Fannie M. Farmer.

Purée de Lentilles (French recipe).

Take 6 heads celery, 3 onions, 2 turnips, and 4 carrots; put them into a stewpan with 1 pound lentils, a slice of ham, 4 tablespoonfuls butter; set it upon a stove to stew slowly for an hour, then add 2 quarts stock; let it stew for two hours; strain the soup into a dish, rub vegetables through a sieve; put again in the stewpan with salt and pepper; let it simmer for quarter of an hour longer, and serve.

Chicken Soup.

Carcass roast chicken,
2 quarts cold water,
1 pound lean veal,
2 tablespoonfuls chopped bacon,
1 bay leaf,
1 slice onion,
1 stalk celery,
2 tablespoonfuls cornstarch,
1½ teaspoonfuls salt,
¼ teaspoonful pepper,
1 tablespoonful flour,
2 tablespoonfuls butter,
Yolks 2 eggs,
1 cupful cream.

Slice the best meat from fowl, leaving only wings and carcass, with skin removed from meat as well. Break bones, put them into the soup kettle with cold water and the uncooked neck and feet, scalded and cleaned. Cut veal in dice, dust with flour and pepper, and brown in finely chopped bacon; add 1 cupful hot water, simmer for a few minutes, cool, and pour into the soup kettle. Cook slowly for one hour, then add bay leaf, onion, and celery; cook half an hour longer, strain, and cool. Mix together in a saucepan cornstarch, salt, pepper, flour, and butter. Add gradually 1 pint hot stock and cook until thickened, then add 1½ cupfuls hot stock, mix well and add yolks of eggs beaten and diluted with cream. Do not boil after egg is added, but keep hot until egg has thickened. Serve in bouillon cups, with or without a spoonful of whipped cream on top of each.

Mullagatawny Soup.

3 quarts chicken stock,
4 onions,
1 carrot,
2 turnips,
6 stalks celery,
1 tablespoonful curry powder.

Chop the vegetables, add to the stock, and put them in a saucepan over a hot fire until it begins to boil, then set aside to simmer for twenty minutes. Add curry powder and flour. Mix well, boil three minutes, and strain. In serving, add some pieces of the white meat of the chicken chopped.

Soup à la Flamande (French recipe).

Take 2 quarts veal stock, put in 1 cupful cooked spinach and 1 cupful sorrel, and let it boil till tender; season with salt and while it is boiling, but about two minutes before serving stir into it a pint of cream previously mixed with the yolks of 2 eggs.

Barley Broth (Scotch recipe).

1 neck mutton,
3 carrots,
3 turnips,
2 onions,
1 celery head,
4 tablespoonfuls barley,
2 quarts water.

Soak the mutton in water an hour; cut off the scrag, and put it into a stewpot with 2 quarts water; as soon as it boils, skim it well; let it simmer for an hour and a half, then take the best end of the mutton, divide in cutlets, trim off some of the fat, and add as many to the soup as you wish; skim the moment the fresh meat boils up, and every quarter of an hour after; then add the carrots, onions, turnips, celery, cut, but not too small; and barley previously washed in cold water. The broth should stew for three hours before serving; some chopped parsley may be added, and season to taste.

Mutton Broth (Irish recipe).

2½ pounds mutton,
1 quart water,
3 turnips,
3 carrots,
2 leeks or onions,
3 mutton chops,
1 head lettuce,
3 spoonfuls barley.

Boil the mutton with a little barley, slowly, for three or four hours; strain it off and remove the fat; add turnips, carrots, and leeks, cut fine; put them, with mutton chops, into the broth, and boil till tender; when nearly done, add some lettuce, previously blanched and drained; boil for ten minutes, season with salt, and serve. The vegetables should be quite thick in the broth, but cut very small.

Sheep's-Head Broth (Scotch recipe).

Take a cupful of barley, sheep's head and trotters, and, if the broth should be wanted stronger, a neck of mutton; put them into a pot with 2 quarts cold water; as soon as it comes to the boil, skim it well. Chop 2 carrots and 2 turnips small, a sprig of parsley and 2 onions; before you add the roots, skim it again. Boil slowly till the head is tender; take the pot off the fire and stand it near, covered closely, for a quarter of an hour before serving. The head and trotters should be served separately with whole carrots and turnips.

To Prepare the Head and Trotters.

They should be well singed, which is best done at the blacksmith's. Split the head down the middle of the skull; take out the brains, lay the head and trotters to soak in water all night, scrape and wash well before using. Sheep's head is excellent eaten cold.

Cock-a-Leekie (Scotch recipe).

1 fowl,
4 pounds beef,
12 leeks,
Dash pepper,
1 tablespoonful salt,
5 quarts water.

Truss a fowl as for boiling, put it into a stewpan with a piece of lean beef, leeks cut in pieces an inch long, rejecting the coarser green part, a little pepper and salt, and water. Cover the stewpan closely and allow its contents to stew slowly four hours; then place the fowl in a tureen; remove the beef, pour the soup and leeks over it, and serve.

Friar's Chicken (French recipe).

1 knuckle veal,
2 turnips,
2 carrots,
3 onions,
4 sprigs sweet herbs,
1 quart cream,
6 yolks eggs,
2 chickens.

Boil veal, carrots, turnips, onions, and a few sweet herbs to a good stock and strain it. Have ready the chickens, boiled tender and cut in pieces, cream and yolks of eggs beaten together; add these to the broth, heat them up together, and send it to table. A little minced parsley may be added just before serving.

Rabbit Soup (English recipe).

1 rabbit,
1 carrot,
1 head celery,
3 onions,
1 ounce peppercorns,
1 bunch herbs,
1 tablespoonful ground rice.

When the rabbit is skinned, take care to save all the blood. Cut in pieces and put into a dish with the water required for soup. Let it stand an hour; then add the blood of the rabbit, strain it through a sieve into a soup pot, and put all on the fire; stir constantly till it boils, to prevent its curdling, and skim it a little; put in carrot, celery, onions, peppercorns tied up in a bit of muslin, herbs, salt, and chopped onion. Boil for three hours; take it off an hour before dinner; strain through a sieve; take out the onions, carrot, pepper, etc., and put in some of the best pieces of the rabbit; return it to the saucepan, and let it boil. Stir the ground rice dissolved in water into the soup; continue stirring till removed from the fire.

Tomato Bouillon with Oysters.

1 can tomatoes,
1½ quarts brown stock,
1 chopped onion,
½ bay leaf,
6 cloves,
1 teaspoonful peppercorns,
1 pint parboiled oysters,
Pepper and salt,
Dash McIlhenny's Tabasco Sauce.

Boil together the stock, tomatoes, bay leaf, cloves, tabasco and peppercorns. Cook twenty minutes. Strain, cool and clear, then strain into cups over parboiled oysters. When cooked, clear it as if you were making a plain, clear soup. Beat the white of 1 egg lightly, just enough to separate it, and add to it the eggshell broken up. When the stock has cooled, add this and set it where it will come slowly to the boil, stirring constantly. The egg will attract all particles of tomatoes and everything solid. Let it boil two minutes, then strain through two thicknesses of cheese cloth. It will be perfectly clear, but with the red-tomato coloring. If it were left to cool, it would become a solid jelly.—Stella A. Downing.

Okra Gumbo (Southern recipe).

1 chicken,
1 onion,
½ pod red pepper without the seeds,
2 pints okra, or about 50 pods,
2 slices ham,
1 bay leaf,
1 sprig thyme or parsley,
1 tablespoonful each lard and butter,
Salt and cayenne to taste.

Clean and cut up the chicken. Cut the ham into small squares or dice, and chop the onion, parsley, and thyme. Skin the tomatoes and chop fine, saving the juice. Wash and stem the okras and slice into thin layers of half an inch each. Put the lard and butter into the soup kettle; when hot, add the chicken and ham. Cover closely and let it simmer ten minutes. Then add the chopped onions, parsley, thyme, and tomatoes, stirring frequently to prevent scorching. Add the okras, and when well browned, the juice of the tomatoes. The okra is very delicate and is liable to scorch if not stirred frequently. When well fried and browned, add about 3 quarts boiling water and set on the back of the stove to simmer for an hour longer. Serve hot with boiled rice.

Beef Gumbo (Southern recipe).

Another recipe for gumbo, which is similar to the preceding one, the manipulation being practically the same, calls for the following ingredients:

1 quart tomatoes sliced,
2 pounds beef cut in small pieces,
2 quarts okras sliced,
4 tablespoonfuls butter,
½ pound corned ham or pork, cut up,
Small piece red pepper without seeds,
Spray parsley.

Cream-of-Celery Soup.

1 head celery,
1 slice onion,
2 cupfuls milk,
3 tablespoonfuls cornstarch,
3 tablespoonfuls butter.

Clean outside stalks and white leaves of celery. Cut into small pieces and cook until tender in 3 cupfuls water. Scald onion in milk in double boiler. Rub the celery, when soft, through a sieve. Blend together cornstarch with butter, cook for a few minutes, lifting from fire, beating and cooking in turn. Season with salt and white pepper to taste, gradually add the strained, scalded milk, cook thoroughly, then add the strained celery stock, and reheat. Serve with croutons, bread sticks, or toasted wafers.

Cream-of-Corn Soup.

1 can corn,
2 cupfuls boiling water,
1 teaspoonful salt,
¼ teaspoonful celery salt,
¼ teaspoonful onion juice,
2½ tablespoonfuls cornstarch,
3 tablespoonfuls butter,
2 cupfuls milk,
1 cupful whipped cream.

Rub corn through sieve into a saucepan, add water, salt, celery salt, and white pepper to taste. Blend together in a saucepan cornstarch, with butter, gradually add the milk, and cook together five minutes, stirring constantly. Just before serving add beaten cream. Serve with crisp wafers.

Leek Soup.

3 quarts boiling water,
2 cupfuls leeks cut fine,
4 cupfuls potatoes cut in dice,
2 tablespoonfuls butter,
3 teaspoonfuls salt,
½ teaspoonful pepper,
4 slices stale bread cut in small pieces,
4 tablespoonfuls minced onion.

Wash the leeks and cut off the roots. Cut the white part in thin slices. Pare the potatoes and cut in dice, put them in a bowl of cold water. Put the butter, leeks, and onion in the soup pot and on the fire. Cook slowly twenty minutes, stirring frequently, then add the hot water, potatoes, and seasoning, and cook at least half an hour longer. Serve very hot. If it is convenient and liked, cook with the leeks and butter the white stalks of 4 or 5 cibols, or 1 shallot may be cut fine and cooked with the leeks.—Maria Parloa.

Hotchpotch (Scotch recipe).

2 pounds lean beef,
2½ quarts stock,
1 cupful beans (green),
2 carrots,
2 onions,
2 stalks celery,
2 turnips,
1 small cauliflower,
4 tablespoonfuls butter,
1 tablespoonful flour,
Dash McIlhenny's Tabasco Sauce.

Mince the beef in chopper, and place in a stewpan with stock and beans. When these come to a boil, add chopped carrots, onions, celery, turnips, and cauliflower; cover, and boil gently for three hours. Melt butter and mix with it the flour; let it brown, dilute with a little broth, and add to the stew. Season with salt, pepper, and tabasco.

Cream-of-Onion Soup.

2 large onions,
3 tablespoonfuls butter,
4 tablespoonfuls cornstarch,
1 tablespoonful flour,
1 teaspoonful salt,
¼ teaspoonful white pepper,
2 cupfuls boiling water,
1 quart milk,
1 cupful mashed potatoes,
1 cupful croutons.

Slice the onions and fry until lightly brown in butter, then add cornstarch, flour, salt, and pepper. Stir until slightly browned, but do not allow to burn. Pour in gradually boiling water, and cook until smooth. Keep hot. Scald milk, pour it gradually on mashed potatoes. Combine the mixtures. Simmer and stir for a few minutes, add croutons, cover, and let stand a moment before serving.

Soup Normandie (French recipe).

1 onion,
2 tablespoonfuls butter,
2 cans tomatoes,
1 quart cold water,
1 tablespoonful cornstarch,
12 cloves,
1 tablespoonful sugar,
Dash McIlhenny's Tabasco Sauce,
Salt and pepper.

Fry the onion in butter (do not let brown), add tomatoes and water. Boil twenty minutes. Strain through a colander, set back on stove, and add cornstarch dissolved in water, cloves, salt, and sugar. Let boil five minutes, then season with tabasco. Serve with croutons.

Dried-Bean Soup.

2 cupfuls dried beans,
4 quarts water,
1 large onion minced fine,
4 tablespoonfuls butter,
3 tablespoonfuls flour,
1 tablespoonful minced celery or a few dried celery leaves,
½ teaspoonful peppers,
2 teaspoonfuls salt.

Wash the beans and soak them over night in cold water. In the morning pour off the water and put them in the soup pot with 3 quarts cold water. Place on the fire, and when the water comes to the boiling point, pour it off. Add 4 quarts boiling water to the beans and place the soup pot where the contents will simmer for four hours. Add the celery the last hour of cooking. Cook the onion and drippings slowly in a stewpan for half an hour. Drain the water from the beans (save this water) and put them in the stewpan with the onions and drippings. Then add the flour and cook half an hour, stirring often. At the end of this time mash fine and gradually add the water in which the beans were boiled until the soup is like thick cream. Then rub through a sieve and return to the fire; add the salt and pepper, and cook twenty minutes or more. Any kind of beans may be used for this soup; Lima beans give the most delicate soup, but the large or small white beans are very satisfactory and are less expensive than Limas. In cold weather the quantities of beans and flavorings may be doubled, but only 6 quarts water are used. The resulting thick soup can be kept in a cold place and a portion boiled up as required and thinned with meat stock or milk.—MARIA PARLOA.

Bouillabaise (English recipe).

Take 3 pounds cod, cut in pieces from 2 ounces to ¼ pound each. Slice 2 good-sized onions and place them in a stewpan large enough to contain all the fish at the bottom. Add 2 tablespoonfuls olive oil; fry the onions light brown; put in the fish with as much warm water as will cover it well, a teaspoonful salt, dash pepper, half bay leaf, peeled lemon cut in dice, 2 tomatoes cut in slices, a few peppercorns, and ½ clove garlic. Boil till the liquor is reduced to one third. Then add a tablespoonful chopped parsley, let it boil one minute longer, and pour into a tureen over crontons. This is also good made from any white fleshed fish; the garlic may be omitted, if preferred.

Oxtail Soup.

1 small oxtail,
6 cupfuls brown stock,
½ cupful carrot cut in fancy shapes,
½ cupful turnip cut in fancy shapes,
½ cupful onion cut in small pieces,
½ cupful celery cut in small pieces,
½ teaspoonful salt,
Few grains cayenne,
1 teaspoonful Worcestershire Sauce,
1 teaspoonful lemon juice.

Cut oxtail in small pieces, wash, drain, sprinkle with salt and pepper, dredge with flour, and fry in butter ten minutes. Add to brown stock, and simmer one hour. Then add vegetables, which have been parboiled twenty minutes; simmer until vegetables are soft; add cayenne, Worcestershire sauce, and lemon juice.—FANNIE M. FARMER.

Asparagus Cream Soup.

1 bunch asparagus,
3 cupfuls milk,
1 cupful veal stock,
3 tablespoonfuls flour,
3 tablespoonfuls butter,
Salt and pepper.

Cook the asparagus in boiling, salted water for thirty minutes. Take from water, cut off tips, and put into soup tureen. Press pulp from stalks through sieve. Scald milk, add stock. Mix flour with butter in a saucepan over the fire, adding gradually portion of scalded milk to make very smooth. When thoroughly done, add remainder of milk and asparagus pulp. Season with salt and pepper. Stir till boiling, then strain into the tureen.

Soup Maigre (French recipe).

6 cucumbers,
4 heads lettuce,
2 onions, blanched,
1 cupful spinach,
Sprig mint,
1 pint green peas,
Small piece ham,
4 tablespoonfuls butter.

Put ham and vegetables into 2 quarts water and boil four hours, then pass all through a sieve. When cooked to a *purée,* strain, put in 1 pint parboiled green peas, and a few slices of cucumber.

Purée of Celeriac.

1 quart celeriac cut in dice,
2 tablespoonfuls butter,
1 tablespoonful flour,
1 teaspoonful salt,
¾ cupful stock or cream.

Cook the celeriac thirty minutes in boiling water, rinse in cold water, then press through a *purée* sieve. Put the butter in a saucepan on the fire. When hot, add the flour and stir until smooth and frothy, then add the strained celeriac, and cook five minutes, stirring frequently. Add the salt and stock, or cream, and cook five minutes longer.—MARIA PARLOA.

Split-Pea Soup.

1 cupful split peas,
1½ quarts stock,
1 teaspoonful salt,
2 tablespoonfuls minced onion,
3 tablespoonfuls chopped celery,
1 carrot.

Place a saucepan with split peas and stock over the fire; when it boils, add salt, onion, celery, and carrot; cover, and boil slowly until done; press the soup through the sieve; if too thick, add a little more water, season to taste with salt and pepper, and serve with small squares of fried bread.

Green-Pea Soup.

1 quart shelled peas,
3 pints water,
1 quart milk,
1 onion,
2 tablespoonfuls butter,
1 tablespoonful flour,
3 level teaspoonfuls salt,
½ teaspoonful pepper.

Put the peas in a stewpan with the boiling water and onion, and cook until tender, which will be about half an hour. Pour off the water, saving for use later. Mash the peas fine, then add the water in which they were boiled, and rub through a *purée* sieve. Return to the saucepan, add flour and butter, beaten together, and the salt and pepper. Now gradually add the milk, which must be boiling hot. Beat well and cook ten minutes, stirring frequently.—MARIA PARLOA.

Winter Okra Soup (a New Orleans recipe).

1 can okra,
1 can tomatoes,
2 onions,
2 tablespoonfuls butter,
1 dozen oysters,
3 tablespoonfuls rice,
1 red pepper pod without the seeds.

Chop the onions and fry them in the butter. Wash the rice well, stew the onions, tomatoes, and pepper together in about 3 quarts water and 1 pint oyster water for about three hours, stirring frequently. Ten minutes before serving, add the okra and let it come to a boil. Then drop in the oysters, boil up once, and serve.

Oyster Bisque.

1 quart oysters,
1 quart milk,
½ cupful bread crumbs,
½ bay leaf,
1 sprig parsley,
1 slice onion,
1 quart thin cream,
2 tablespoonfuls butter,
4 yolks eggs.

Parboil oysters in their own liquor until the edges curl. Drain and separate the hard part from the soft, chop the hard parts fine. Put the chopped oysters into a double boiler with milk, bread crumbs, bay leaf, parsley, and onion, and let cook half an hour. Rub through a *purée* strainer and return to fire with cream. Cream together butter and flour, and add gradually some of the hot soup. Add the soft parts of the oysters, season with pepper and salt, and pour into the tureen over the well-beaten yolks of eggs. Serve with crisp crackers, browned.

Lobster Bisque.

2 pounds lobster,
2 cupfuls cold water,
4 cupfuls milk,
¼ cupful butter,
¼ cupful flour,
1½ teaspoonfuls salt,
Few grains cayenne.

Remove meat from lobster shell. Add cold water to body bones and tough end of claws, cut in pieces; bring slowly to boiling point, and cook twenty minutes. Drain, reserve liquor, and thicken with butter and flour cooked together. Scald milk with tail meat of lobster, finely chopped; strain and add to liquor. Season with salt and cayenne; then add tender claw meat, cut in dice, and body meat. When coral is found in lobster, wash, wipe, force through fine strainer, put in a mortar with butter, work until well blended, then add flour, and stir into soup. If a richer soup is desired, white stock may be used in place of water.—Fannie Merritt Farmer.

Corn Chowder.

1 can corn,
1 quart potato cubes (parboiled),
1 tablespoonful chopped fat pork,
1 sliced onion,
1 quart scalded milk,
3 tablespoonfuls butter,
Salt and pepper.

Put the corn through a meat chopper, fry the onion and the pork a light brown, strain the fat into a stewpan, add the corn, potato cubes, the milk, seasoning, and butter, thicken with a little flour, and pour over split crackers.

Lobster Chowder.

1 pound lobster,
1 quart milk,
3 crackers,
¼ cupful butter,
1 teaspoonful salt,
½ teaspoonful white pepper,
¼ teaspoonful cayenne pepper.

Boil 1 quart milk. Roll 3 crackers fine; mix with them ¼ cupful butter, and the green fat of the lobster.

Season with 1 scant teaspoonful salt, ½ teaspoonful white pepper, and ¼ teaspoonful cayenne pepper. Pour the boiling milk gradually over the paste. Put it back in the double boiler; add the lobster meat cut into dice; let it boil up once, and serve.—MARY J. LINCOLN.

Sorrel Soup (French recipe).

3 pints boiling water,
3 tablespoonfuls butter,
½ cupful shredded sorrel,
3 tablespoonfuls milk,
1 teaspoonful salt,
Yolk 2 eggs,
½ cupful bread cut in dice and dried in the oven or fried in butter.

Tear the tender green parts from the midribs of the cultivated sorrel; wash in cold water and shred very fine. Put half the butter in a stewpan and add the shredded sorrel. Place on the fire and cook five minutes, stirring frequently. Now add the boiling water and salt, and boil ten minutes. Beat the yolks of eggs well, add the milk, pour into the soup tureen, and add the remaining half of the butter cut into bits. Gradually pour the boiling hot soup in the tureen, stirring all the while to combine the hot mixture with the egg yolk. Add the bread dice, and serve. —MARIA PARLOA.

Black-Bean Soup.

1 pint black beans,
2 quarts cold water,
1 small onion,
2 stalks celery or ¼ teaspoonful celery salt,
½ tablespoonful salt,
⅛ teaspoonful pepper,
¼ teaspoonful mustard,
Few grains cayenne,
3 tablespoonfuls butter,
1½ tablespoonfuls flour,
2 hard-boiled eggs,
1 lemon.

Soak beans over night; in the morning, drain and add cold water. Slice onion, and cook five minutes with half the butter, adding to the beans, with celery stalks broken in pieces. Simmer three or four hours, or until beans are soft; add more water as it boils away. Rub through a sieve, reheat to the boiling point, and add salt, pepper, mustard, and cayenne well mixed. Bind with remaining butter and flour cooked together. Cut eggs in thin slices, also lemon, removing seeds. Put in tureen, and strain the soup over them. —FANNIE MERRITT FARMER.

Chicken Chowder.

Take the remains of a stewed chicken, cut the meat off the bones and with a scissors clip it into small pieces; put the bones in a kettle with cold water, adding any left-over chicken gravy, and let them stew till all the good is out of the meat. Strain, add 1 quart milk to each quart chicken stock, a tablespoonful minced onion, fried with a tablespoonful salt pork, 2 cupfuls parboiled potato cubes, 2 tablespoonfuls butter, the cut-up chicken, and flour enough to thicken slightly; salt and pepper to taste.

Clam Soup.

½ peck clams in shells,
Salt to taste,
1 teaspoonful pepper,
¼ teaspoonful cayenne pepper,
1 tablespoonful chopped onion,
1 tablespoonful chopped parsley,
1 tablespoonful butter,
2 tablespoonfuls flour,
2 cupfuls milk or cream.

Prepare the clams by boiling in the shells, and cutting as directed for clam chowder, keeping the soft part separate from the hard. Pour off 1 quart clam liquor after it settles, being careful not to take any of the sediment; put it on to boil, and remove the scum. Add 1 pint hot water, and season to taste with salt, pepper, cayenne, onion, and parsley. Put in the hard part of the clams. Simmer fifteen minutes, strain, and boil again, and when boiling thicken with flour cooked in the butter. Add the hot milk or cream and the soft part of the clams; serve at once.

Another method of preparing clam soup, if needed quickly, is to heat the clam broth to a boiling point, add the clams cut fine, season, and pour into the tureen over 2 eggs beaten up with boiling milk.—Mary J. Lincoln.

Onion Chowder.

3 quarts boiling water,
2 cupfuls minced onion,
1 quart potatoes cut in dice,
8 teaspoonfuls salt,
½ teaspoonful pepper,
3 tablespoonfuls butter,
1 tablespoonful fine herbs.

Cook the onion and butter together for half an hour, but slowly, so the onion will not brown. At the end of this time, add the boiling water, potatoes, salt, and pepper, and cook one hour longer, then add the fine herbs, and serve.—Maria Parloa.

Sportsman's Broth (English recipe).

Take grouse, partridge, or any other game you have; cut in small joints, put them into a pot with water and plenty of vegetables whole. Let it stew slowly four or five hours; then take the best pieces you have saved out, season them and toss in a little flour; brown over a quick fire, and add to the strained stock with 12 small onions, 2 heads celery, sliced, and half a cabbage shredded fine, to stew slowly till tender. Half an hour before serving, add 6 potatoes cut in slices.

Clam Chowder.

½ peck clams in shells,
1 quart potatoes sliced thin,
A 2-inch cube fat salt pork,
1 teaspoonful salt,
½ teaspoonful white pepper,
1 tablespoonful butter,
1 quart milk,
6 butter crackers.

Wash clams with a small brush, and put in a kettle with ½ cupful water. When the clams at the top have opened, take them out with a skimmer, and when cool enough to handle, take the clams from the shells; remove the thin skin; cut off all the black end (cut the "leather straps" into small pieces), leaving the soft part whole. Let the clam liquor set, and pour it off carefully. Use half water and half clam liquor. Fry the pork and onion; add the potatoes, which have been soaked and scalded, and boiling water to cover. When the potatoes are soft, add the clam liquor, seasoning, and clams; when warmed through, add the hot milk, and turn into the tureen over broken crackers.—Mary J. Lincoln.

Old-Fashioned Bean Soup (New England recipe).

2 cupfuls white beans,
3 pints cold water,
4 ounces lean salt pork,
½ cupful chopped celery,
½ carrot,
1 onion.

Soak beans for several hours in cold water; then drain and put them with the pork over the fire; wash and scald in boiling water; add to the beans as soon as they boil celery, carrot, and onion; cover and cook till the beans are tender; then strain the soup, season to taste with salt, and serve with small pieces of toasted bread. This soup may be served without being strained—some people prefer to have the beans whole in the soup. A little beef extract and ½ cupful cream is always an improvement, but the soup is very nice without them.

Herb Soup.

1 cupful finely shredded spinach,
½ cupful shredded sorrel,
½ blanched and sliced leek,
White heart leaves head lettuce,
4 potatoes,
3 teaspoonfuls salt,

4 tablespoonfuls butter,
1 tablespoonful chervil,
2 quarts boiling water,
½ pint croutons.

Have the sorrel, spinach, and lettuce fresh, tender, and free from tough midribs. Wash and shred. Cut the washed leek into thin slices. Put in the stewpan with the butter and cook fifteen minutes, being careful not to brown. Now add the potatoes, salt, and boiling water. When the soup begins to boil, draw the stewpan back where the contents will cook gently for one hour. At the end of this time, crush the potatoes with a fork, add the chervil, and simmer five minutes longer. Turn into the soup tureen, add the croutons, and serve. If preferred, the soup may be rubbed through a *purée* sieve, returned to the fire, and when boiling hot be poured on the yolks of 2 eggs which have been beaten with 2 tablespoonfuls milk. This soup may be varied indefinitely. Any number of green vegetables can be employed in making it, care being taken to use only a small quantity of those of pronounced flavor.—MARIA PARLOA.

CHAPTER XXXVII

FISH

I CAN think of no better lesson on how to choose fish than this: if it is possible in your neighborhood, or while vacationing, go to see a fish boat empty its gleaming cargo on the wharf. Learn to know the earmarks —not only those left by St. Peter on a haddock, but the signs of perfect freshness on all fish. Do not be afraid of touching them; fresh smelts have the fragrance of violets, and every fish has a wholesome smell. Turn them over, examine them closely. "An eye like a dead fish" refers to a fish which has lain for weeks in cold storage, not to one just from the water. It will have eyes as full and almost as clear as any live creature. Notice the gills; they will be beautifully red, the fins will be stiff, the scales shining, and the flesh so firm that it springs back after the finger has been pressed into it. One cannot expect, especially if your home is some distance from the ocean or the great lakes, to find in the market fish as superlatively fresh as when lifted straight from the net. Still, to be fit for human food, they should not have lost much of their beauty. The signs to avoid are limp fins, dull eyes, pale, liver-colored gills, flesh in which you leave a dent by an impression of the finger, streaks of gray or yellow in the skin and flesh, and the slightest symptom of a disagreeable odor. If you have to make the choice between salt cod and a fish of this description, choose salt cod; it is infinitely more healthful; it does not contain a possibility of ptomaine poisoning.

When purchasing halibut or swordfish, where the head and fins have been removed, the test is pearly white or shining gray skin, firm flesh, and a good odor. It is an excellent rule never to buy fish which is out of season. If you want bluefish in February or shad in November, you can probably obtain it—a fish dealer will produce almost anything from his refrigerator at any time of the year—but you may rest assured it has seen a repose of months in cold storage. If not really dangerous to eat, it will be flabby, it will go to pieces before it is cooked, and be lacking in flavor. It is an excellent plan to post oneself thoroughly on the fish which is in season all the year round and purchase according to the month. A dealer will assure one that fish which has been packed in ice ten days is in as excellent condition as when fresh caught. I should say seven or eight days is the limit. After that time it will begin to lose its beautiful mother-of-pearl sheen.

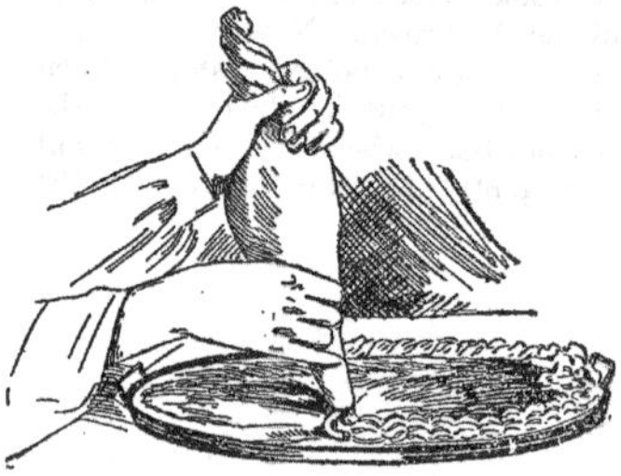

Garnishing a Planked Fish with Mashed Potato Squeezed Through Pastry Bag.

Although the old theory that fish is brain food has been exploded, the brain worker will find what he most requires in a bountiful diet of fish. It is digestible food, which is not overstimulating or overnutritive. Both the poet and preacher will do better work on a dinner of broiled bluefish than on rare roast beef. Salmon, mackerel, and eels, which are exceedingly oily, are an exception to the digestible rule. They should be severely let alone by people of weak stomachs, while white fish may be classed as the most digestible of all fish.

The shimmering array on the market stall is alluring and confusing, and the fish dealer is apt to be persuasive. It is no economy to be inveigled into buying a 5-pound bluefish when 2 pounds of halibut would have fed your family. Fish left over can be utilized nicely in many ways, but it is better not to have any; in summer, cold fish has not remarkable keeping qualities. Decide when you order a fish how you will cook it. The fish dealer can prepare it for planking or broiling better than you can. The cheapest fish is not always the most economical. Five pounds of cod contains about 2 pounds of waste in the shape of skin, head, tail, and bone, while 2 pounds of halibut is solid fish with scarcely an ounce of waste.

The cooking of fish depends largely on taste, for various methods apply frequently and most appetizingly to the same fish. Take halibut, for instance. It may be baked, broiled, fried or boiled, and be quite as delicious in one way as another. This rule is also true of cod, haddock, and nearly every kind of white-fleshed fish. What a cook or a fish dealer calls oily fish—this class contains bluefish, mackerel, herring, salmon, eels, and shad—are best suited for broiling, baking, or planking. They contain so much oil distributed through the flesh that it requires a dry, intense heat to make them palatable. Salmon is an exception to this rule, being at its best when boiled. An old saying declares, "Small fish should swim twice—once in water, once in oil." It is a good proverb for the cook to remember, because it applies well to every tiny fish; smelts, brook trout, perch, whitebait, catfish, sunfish, bullheads, and everything in small finny things. Sometimes these small fish are sautéd, but they are not so good nor so wholesome as when they "swim in oil."

The fish which plank to perfection are shad, whitefish, mackerel, bluefish, red snapper, and pompano. There are a number of real advantages to this method of cooking; it is so easy, it may be done in the hot oven of any coal or gas stove, the wood imparts a flavor to the fish, which can be obtained in no other way. Then there is no difficult task of sliding it from a broiler or bake pan to the platter, because it is the proper thing to send the plank straight to the table laid on a folded towel. If you have to prepare a fish for planking, remember it must be cut down the back instead of the stomach, the thin portion of the flesh being folded on the middle of the plank.

Improvise a fish kettle if you haven't one. Line a wire basket with a napkin, allowing the linen to fall over the edges, put in the fish, coiling it slightly if it is large, and drop the basket in a kettle of boiling water. This is an easier method for lifting it out whole than if set right in the kettle.

An oily fish, such as mackerel or bluefish, needs no enrichment of fat before broiling; a white-fleshed fish does. If it is cut in steaks, dip it in oil or melted butter and a good seasoning of pepper and salt, then put between the wires of the broiler. Lay the thickest end in the center of the broiler over the hottest part of the fire, skin side up. Let it get perfectly crisp and brown on the flesh side before turning. Broil the skin side carefully; it is apt to burn. Set it in a hot oven for five minutes to thoroughly finish cooking.

Fish of all sorts requires the accompaniment of a starch food to make a well-balanced meal; it may be bread, rice, potatoes, or macaroni.

An iron fish sheet, with rings at each end for handles, may be made by any tinsmith for twenty-five cents. Grease it well before setting the fish to cook and lay under it strips of salt pork, then set in a baking pan. You will find it easy to slip a baked fish from this sheet on a platter.

When baking halibut, pour milk over and around it before setting in the oven. It keeps the fish moist, improves the flavor, and makes it brown more thoroughly.

In spite of careful watching, a fish will occasionally break in the boiling. Do not try to patch it together into an unsightly heap of skin, bones, and meat. Flake it quickly and lay in good-sized portions on a large platter. Garnish with roses of mashed potatoes squeezed from a pastry bag, and over the fish pour a sauce. This transforms an almost hopeless failure into a most attractive dish.

The same general rules for various methods of cooking fish apply to all kinds; they may be boiled, fried, sautéd, planked, broiled, or baked. Of course, after cooking by any process, a dish may be varied by one of the sauces which are to be found in a following chapter.

For highly flavored fish, such as shad or salmon, use the simplest sauce; drawn butter or egg sauce is much more appetizing than a rich herb-seasoned, stock sauce, which is apt to destroy the fine flavor of fish. There are certain fresh-water fish, as well as several white-fleshed varieties, cod, halibut, and haddock, for instance, that are improved by a certain amount of seasoning, only it must be done very carefully and with an educated palate as criterion.

The following methods for cooking fish can be applied to anything that swims, though the table appended will serve as a guide:

Methods for Cooking Fish

Bass	May be baked, boiled, or broiled.
Bluefish	May be planked, baked, or broiled.
Butterfish	May be fried or sautéd.
Cod	May be boiled, broiled, or baked.
Eels	May be fried or broiled.
Flounder	May be baked, fried, or sautéd.
Haddock	May be baked, broiled, planked, or boiled.
Halibut	May be baked, boiled, fried, broiled, or planked.
Herring	May be baked or broiled.
Kingfish	May be broiled.
Blackfish	May be baked or broiled.
Mackerel	May be baked, broiled, or planked.
Perch	May be fried or broiled.
Pickerel	May be baked.
Pompano	May be broiled.
Red Snapper	May be fried or boiled.
Salmon	May be boiled, broiled, or baked.
Shad	May be broiled, baked, or planked.
Sheepshead	May be boiled or baked.
Smelts	May be sautéd, baked, or fried.
Trout	May be baked, broiled, or sautéd.
Muskellunge	May be baked.
Turbot	May be boiled.
Whitefish	May be planked, baked, or broiled.
Sturgeon	May be roasted, broiled, baked after being parboiled.
Carp	May be boiled or baked.
Scrod	May be broiled.
Swordfish	May be baked, broiled, or boiled.
Mullet	May be baked.
Pike	May be boiled.
Whitebait	May be fried.
Porgies	May be planked, broiled, or baked.
Catfish	May be fried.
Alewives	May be baked.

How to Plank Fish.

Heat and oil an oak plank made for the purpose; spread upon this, skin side down, a fish, dressed and cleaned and split down the under side; brush over with butter or oil, and set in the dripping pan in the lower gas oven, at first near the burners; after cooking a few minutes, remove to the floor of the oven to finish cooking. Cook about twenty-five minutes, basting often. Set the plank upon a platter. Spread over the fish 3 tablespoonfuls butter, creamed and mixed with salt, pepper, and a tablespoonful lemon juice. Garnish the edge of the plank with mashed potatoes, slices of lemon and parsley.

How to Sauté Fish.

Fish may be fried in oil, salt pork fat, lard, or clarified drippings. Whatever fat is used, it should be deep enough to cover the fish and hot enough to brown a piece of bread in thirty seconds. The pork fat is obtained by trying out thin slices of fat salt pork, being careful not to let it burn. Pork gives the fish a flavor not to be obtained by any other oil or fat. When pork fat is used, salt should be added sparingly. Fried fish should be seasoned while cooking. After wiping dry, fish should be rolled in Indian meal, flour, or sifted crumbs before frying. If the fish has been on ice, or is very cold, do not put it in the fat fast enough to cool it perceptibly. Watch carefully while cooking; don't break or mutilate in turning; cook brown, drain on a sieve, colander, or paper, and serve hot on a napkin. Unless fish are very small, they should be notched on each side before rolling in meal previous to frying.

How to Broil Fish.

Broiling is probably the simplest as well as the best method of cooking many kinds of fish, the flavor and juices being better preserved. Salt pork is the best thing to use. The double broiler is the best utensil, though they may be cooked on a griddle or a spider. Heat and butter well before laying in the fish, the flesh side first; when that is perfectly browned, turn and finish cooking. Serve on a hot platter, spread with butter or cream or both, and season to taste. A fish may be broiled in a dripping pan, and if the oven is hot it will cook nicely. Baste once or twice with butter or cream while cooking.

How to Boil Fish.

Boiling is the most insipid way of cooking fish, yet there are certain varieties that are better cooked this way if accompanied by a rich sauce. Fish, if boiled in a common kettle, should first be wrapped in cheese cloth, to preserve its shape. The head is the best part of a boiled fish, and the nearer the head the better the portions. Boiled fish should be served on a napkin and the sauce in a tureen. A fish of 6 pounds should boil or steam in thirty or thirty-five minutes. The water should always be salted. A boiled fish may be stuffed if desired.

How to Bake Fish.

A baked fish presents a more attractive appearance when served in an upright position on the platter; it also cooks better. To keep it upright, press it down enough to flatten the under side, then, if necessary, brace with skewers or potatoes placed against it until it is well under way for cooking, then it will keep its position until cooked and dished. Sometimes it is advisable to bend the fish half-moon shape and cook it that way, or if the fish is long and slender, the tail may be tied to the mouth, either of which methods will keep the fish in upright position.

How to Fry Fish.

Small fish may be broiled, but in nearly every case they are better sautéd or fried. There are tiny fish, smelts for instance, which cannot be treated in any other way. Lard may

Courtesy, The Kellogg Fruit Co

be used as a frying material; a mixture of suet and lard is better, but best of all, if it can be afforded, is a clear frying oil, which leaves no greasy taste. To prepare a fish for frying, such as perch, brook trout, catfish, smelts, or tiny mackerel, wash in cold water, clean thoroughly, and wipe dry inside and out. Small fish must be gently handled; they are tender and the flesh bruises easily. Roll them in flour, then in beaten egg, to which a tablespoonful water has been added, and roll again in finely sifted bread crumbs. Have the oil boiling hot, put 4 fish at a time into the frying basket, and cook five or seven minutes. Do not allow them to get dark brown. Drop on absorbent paper and drain off as much of the fat as possible. Lay on a folded napkin on a hot platter, garnish with parsley and points of lemon. When smelts are very tiny, run a skewer through the heads of three or four of them and fry in bunches. Fish which is sliced, then cut in fillets, can be cooked in the same fashion. The easiest way to prepare it is to roll each fillet and fasten with a toothpick.

Baked Red Snapper.

1 5-pound red snapper,
1 beaten egg,
½ cupful powdered crackers,
1 cupful oysters,
1 teaspoonful onion juice,
1 tablespoonful butter,
1 teaspoonful salt,
⅛ teaspoonful paprika,
1 tablespoonful minced parsley.

Draw, clean, and wipe the fish; rub inside and out with salad oil and lemon. Make a stuffing of egg, cracker, oysters (drained and chopped), onion juice, butter, salt, paprika, and parsley; moisten with cream and oyster liquor. Fill the fish and sew it up. Put a layer of minced fat pork on the covered roaster, lay a few slices of tomato and onion on the pork, then the fish on this. Dredge with salt and flour, and put on more minced pork. Place in a hot oven, add a cupful boiling water, and cover. Baste frequently. Bake one hour. Serve with Sauce Hollandaise.

Baked Fresh Cod with Cheese Sauce.

Lay a slice of cod in salt and water for half an hour; wipe dry and rub with melted butter and lemon juice. In the bottom of the baking pan, under the grating and not touching the fish, have a cupful veal stock. Pepper and salt the fish, cover and bake ten minutes to the pound. Take up on a hot platter and sift fine crumbs over it. Put dots of butter on these. Set in the oven to brown while you strain the gravy from the pan, thicken with browned flour, add the juice of ½ lemon, 4 tablespoonfuls grated Parmesan cheese, and a little onion juice. Boil one minute, pour a few spoonfuls carefully over the crumb crust of the fish, the rest into a boat.—Marion Harland.

Baked Bluefish.

This recipe will answer for all sorts of fish. Have the fish opened at the gills, and the intestines drawn out through the opening. Make a stuffing of ½ pint bread crumbs, a tablespoonful melted butter, a teaspoonful salt, and a dash pepper. Mix the ingredients, fill the fish, and sew the head down firmly. If you use pork, cut the fish into gashes two inches apart and all the way across on one side down to the bone; fill the gashes with larding pork, dust the fish thickly with bread crumbs, baste it with a little melted butter, put ½ cupful water in the pan, and bake in a quick oven about an hour, basting frequently. Dish the fish carefully, garnish with parsley and lemon, and serve with brown or tomato sauce.—Mrs. Rorer.

Bluefish Baked with Tomato Sauce.

Prepare a fish of about 4 pounds, put in a buttered pan, cover with tomato pulp, sprinkle liberally with bread crumbs, and dot with bits of butter. Place in oven forty minutes, until the flesh begins to separate from the back bone.

Cod Steaks à la Cardinal (French recipe).

Cut 3 pounds fresh cod into slices an inch thick; sprinkle with salt, pepper, and lemon juice, fasten each slice with a toothpick to give it a neat shape. Brush the fish with warmed butter, lay it on the bottom of a large saucepan, pour over it a cupful white stock, and cover closely, first with buttered paper, then with the pan lid. Simmer gently for twenty to twenty-five minutes, take skewers and arrange the fish neatly on a hot dish; pour over it tomato sauce, flavored with essence of anchovy; garnish round the edge with sprigs of fresh parsley and slices of lemon.

Fillets of Flounder à la Normandy.

Prepare the fillets and lay in a buttered baking pan, season with salt and pepper, dredge with flour, moisten with brown stock, adding a teaspoonful lemon juice; lay the fillets on serving dish, and pour over them Normandy sauce, garnish with slices of lemon.

Baked Haddock.

Stuff with a dressing, baste the fish with butter, put a cupful water into the pan, and bake in a moderate oven one hour, basting often; just before taking up, sprinkle a tablespoonful cracker crumbs over the fish and let it remain in the oven long enough to brown delicately. Put the fish on a warm platter, add water and thickening to the gravy, serve in a gravy tureen, garnish with parsley and sliced lemon.

Fish Timbales.

½ pound halibut or other white fish,
Whites 5 eggs,
1 teaspoonful salt,
1 cupful soft bread crumbs,
½ cupful milk,
6 tablespoonfuls cream,
1 saltspoonful white pepper.

Put the uncooked fish through the meat chopper. Boil together, until you have a smooth paste, the milk and bread crumbs. When cold, add it gradually to the fish and press through a sieve; add the cream, salt, and pepper, and fold in carefully the well-beaten whites of the eggs. Grease small timbale molds with butter, and line the bottoms with paper; garnish with chopped truffle, mushrooms, or green peas, or they may be used plain. Fill in the mixture; stand in a baking pan half filled with boiling water; cover the top with greased paper, and bake in a moderate oven twenty minutes. Serve with lobster, shrimp, or oyster crab sauce. —Mrs. Rorer.

Baked Halibut.

Take a square piece of fish, weighing 5 pounds, wash, wipe dry, and place in the dripping pan with a few thin slices of salt pork on top. Bake one hour; baste with melted butter and water. Stir into the gravy 1 tablespoonful Worcestershire Sauce, juice of 1 lemon, seasoning to taste, and thicken. Serve the gravy separately; garnish with slices of hard-boiled eggs.

Baked Smelts.

Dip in beaten egg, roll in cracker crumbs, season with salt, pepper, and a little nutmeg, lay on a sheet of buttered paper in a buttered baking pan, put a piece of butter on each fish and bake delicately brown; serve on a hot dish, garnished with slices of lemon and parsley.

Baked Salmon Trout with Cream.

Wipe dry and lay in a pan with enough water to keep from scorching. Bake slowly an hour, basting with butter and water. Into a cupful cream stir 3 or 4 tablespoonfuls boiling water, add 2 tablespoonfuls melted butter and a little chopped parsley; add it to the gravy from the dripping pan in which fish was baked; lay the trout on a hot platter and let the gravy boil up once, then pour over the fish; garnish with sprigs of parsley.

Baked Shad.

Stuff with a dressing; rub the fish with flour, lay in a pan with a few thin slices of pork on top. Bake a medium-sized fish forty minutes; add a little hot water, butter, pepper, and salt to the gravy; boil up and serve in gravy tureen. Garnish the fish with sprigs of parsley. A tablespoonful anchovy sauce is a decided improvement in making the gravy.

Brochet of Smelts (French recipe).

Spread melted butter in bottom of shallow baking dish, dredge with raspings of bread, season with salt, pepper, chopped parsley, and shallots; put in fish and pour over it a teaspoonful anchovy sauce; cover with melted butter and bread raspings, and bake fifteen minutes. Serve hot; arrange the fish on a napkin, heads to heads, in center of dish, or lay them all one way in rows, each overlapping the next. Garnish with quartered lemon and fried parsley.

Broiled Turbot (English recipe).

Soak the fish in salted water to take off slime; do not cut off fins; make an incision down the middle of the back to prevent skin on the other side from cracking; rub it with lemon and lay in a kettle of cold water; let it boil slowly; when done, drain, and lay on hot napkin; rub a little lobster coral through a sieve, sprinkle it over fish, garnish with sprigs of parsley and sliced lemon. Serve with lobster or shrimp sauce, or plain drawn butter.

Baked Whitefish (Point Shirley style).

Split the fish and lay open with the meat side up. Season with salt and pepper, and place in a baking pan on a bed of chopped salt pork. Bake in a quick oven, brushing it over with beaten egg and milk while cooking. Just before sending to the table, cover with crisp brown crumbs, made by frying grated bread crumbs in butter. Serve with oyster sauce.

Crimped Fish.

Cut uncooked fish into long strips, roll them around the finger, and fasten each roll with a wooden toothpick. Put into boiling salted water with 2 tablespoonfuls vinegar, and boil fifteen minutes. Drain, arrange on a platter, and serve hot with oyster or lobster sauce poured into cavities.

Codfish Soused in Oyster Sauce.

Boil 3 slices fish; drain and dress upon a dish; blanch 3 dozen oysters by putting them into a stewpan with their juice; move them around occasionally, but do not let them boil. As soon as they become firm, place a sieve over a basin, pour in the oysters, beard and throw them into their liquor. Put them into a stewpan. When boiling, add 2 cloves, ½ blade mace, 6 peppercorns and 2 ounces butter, to which you have added a tablespoonful flour. Stir, season with salt, cayenne pepper, and essence of anchovies. Add a gill of cream, and pour the sauce over it.

To Roast Sturgeon.

Take the tail part, skin and bone it; fill the part where the bone comes from with stuffing, as for a fillet of veal; put buttered paper around it, and tie up like a fillet of veal. Roast, and serve with melted butter.

Flounders Souchet (French recipe).

Take 4 or 6 flounders, trim and cut in halves; put ½ pint water in a sauté pan with a little scraped horseradish, pepper, salt, and sprigs of parsley; place over the fire, boil a minute, then add the flounders, stew ten minutes; take them out and place in a dish, reduce the liquor they were stewed in, pour over and serve.

Hampton Court Perch (English recipe).

Clean the fish, dry well, and make an incision upon each side with a knife. Put 2 tablespoonfuls butter in a sauté pan over a slow fire, lay in the fish, season with salt, and sauté gently. When done, serve with the following sauce: Put 6 spoonfuls melted butter in a stewpan with a little salt and the juice of a lemon; when boiling, stir in the yolk of an egg mixed with a tablespoonful cream. Add small pieces of lemon rind and shredded parsley to the sauce, pour it over the fish, and serve.

Baked Shad Roe.

Skin two large roes, sprinkle with salt, and stand half an hour. In the bottom of a baking pan put a layer of fine bread crumbs mixed with a chopped onion, chopped parsley, 6 chopped mushrooms, melted butter, and a little lemon juice. Lay the roes on the crumbs, sprinkle with more crumbs seasoned and dressed like those in the pan. Over all pour a cupful white stock. Bake half an hour, drain off the liquid, sprinkle the roes with bread crumbs moistened with melted butter, put back in the oven for fifteen minutes to finish cooking and brown. Thicken the liquid that was poured off with flour blended with melted butter, and pour over the roes.

Broiled Brook Trout.

Wash and clean the fish, split and remove the backbone. Put a thin strip of bacon in each fish where the backbone was, fold the fish together, brush with melted butter, and broil over a clear fire. Garnish with fried parsley.

Fish Dressing.

Either of the following recipes may be used to prepare a stuffing for any fish: 2 cupfuls bread or cracker crumbs, 1 cupful mashed potatoes, 1 well-beaten egg, 2 tablespoonfuls butter, teaspoonful sage and savory, or a little thyme, and 1 dozen chopped clams or oysters; moisten with milk, salt, and pepper to taste.

For a plainer dressing, use 1 pint bread crumbs, 2 tablespoonfuls melted butter, 1 raw egg, pepper, salt, and 1 tablespoonful celery seed.

CHAPTER XXXVIII

FISH LEFT-OVERS

For fish *réchauffés* it is absolutely necessary to have a thorough knowledge of sauces. Stews and fricassees are foods that have been cooked in a sauce, and they are excellent methods for reheating fish. When fish left-overs come from the table, pick them over carefully before they cool and become gelatinized. Reject every bone, layers of fat or dark meat, and flake the eatable portions neatly. Put in a bowl, cover closely, and set in the refrigerator till required. Generally a fish *réchauffé* with a sauce calls for a small amount of fish stock. To obtain this, put the bones and poor pieces of fish—not the skin or fat—into a small saucepan, cover with cold water, allow to simmer slowly for a few minutes, then strain and cool. Never add salt to any fish without tasting, as it is very easy to over-season it. Croquettes are an excellent method for using up scraps of fish, especially salmon or any white-fleshed fish. When heated in a sauce, it can be served in ramequins or large scallop shells which are sold by the dozen in crockery stores. With a crust of brown crumbs, these individual dishes are very attractive. Delicious curries, soups, and deviled dishes may be prepared from cold fish. It can be combined with mashed potatoes and crumbs in a pie; it makes a tempting *soufflé* or excellent timbales, and may be used with cold potatoes for a relishing hash. Save even a few spoonfuls of any sauce accompanying fish. Half a cupful egg, tomato, shrimp, oyster, or plain white sauce adds much to the flavor of fresh sauce used for reheating a dish. If the amount of fish is scant, add 2 or 3 hard-boiled eggs, using them as a garnish or cutting the white in rings and squeezing the yolk through a potato ricer and sifting it over the top of the dish. Sometimes there are small left-overs of cooked oysters or clams. If the oysters are in a milk stew, strain off the liquor and save it. It may be enriched by a spoonful of butter or ½ cupful cream. Season well and heat in the double boiler, then add the oysters, but only just long enough to heat them. More than a minute will overcook them. Oysters or clams which have been cooked in any way may be deviled, curried, or used in rissoles or chops. Chop coarsely a cupful cold scalloped oysters with a well-beaten egg and shape into croquettes. Flour, egg, crumb, and fry. Lobster meat can be utilized in almost any receipt that calls for that excellent shellfish, or converted into delicate lobster soup. The smallest amount of fish or shellfish can be utilized for a sauce to accompany baked fish, lobster, oyster, and shrimp being most suitable.

Fish Bisque.

2 cupfuls cold fish,
1 tablespoonful butter,
1 teaspoonful parsley,
1 teaspoonful Worcestershire Sauce,
1 quart white or chicken stock,
1 tablespoonful butter,
1 tablespoonful flour,
2 cupfuls hot milk,
2 tablespoonfuls cracker crumbs,
½ teaspoonful salt,
Dash cayenne.

Mince the fish, add to it the butter, chopped parsley, Worcestershire Sauce, and stock. Bind with the butter and flour cooked together. Add the milk, cracker crumbs and seasonings.

Salmon Loaf.

2 cupfuls salmon,
1 cupful stale bread crumbs,
1 teaspoonful onion juice,
1 teaspoonful chopped parsley,
3 eggs.

Flake the salmon fine, mix with the bread crumbs and seasonings, and moisten with the well-beaten eggs. Pack into a buttered mold and steam for two hours. Serve hot. Any leftover of this dish may be broken into small pieces, then served with mayonnaise; it makes a palatable salad.

Halibut Boudins.

½ cupful cold mashed potato,
1 cupful cold halibut,
½ cupful soft bread crumbs,
½ teaspoonful pepper,
1 teaspoonful salt,
1 egg,
½ teaspoonful onion juice.

Mash the halibut, mix well with the other ingredients, and press through a potato ricer. Moisten with the beaten egg. Butter Dario molds and dust them with fine bread crumbs. Fill each mold with the fish mixture, set them in a pan of hot water, and bake twenty minutes in a moderate oven. Serve on a hot platter, pour a white sauce over them, and garnish with slices of hard-boiled egg.

Kedgeree.

1 cupful cold rice,
1 cupful cold flaked fish,
1 tablespoonful butter,
1 egg,
Salt and pepper.

Into a double boiler put the rice and fish and let them grow quite hot, stirring lightly so the fish may not break and the mixture grow pasty. When hot, add the butter, the egg unbeaten, salt, and pepper. Stir till well blended, and serve.

Halibut Ramequins.

2 tablespoonfuls butter,
1 tablespoonful flour,
½ cupful cream,
½ cupful fish stock,
2 cupfuls cold flaked halibut,
Yolk 1 egg.

Make a white sauce from the butter, flour, cream, and fish stock. Pepper and salt to taste. Add the flaked fish and egg beaten thick. Pour into ramequins and cover the top with buttered crumbs. On top lay a ring of hard-boiled white of egg, and inside each a sprig of water cress.

Fish Friandises.

2 tablespoonfuls butter,
2 tablespoonfuls flour,
1 cupful scalded milk,
1 egg,
2 cupfuls cold fish,
1½ cupfuls buttered crumbs.

Make a sauce of the butter, flour, and milk. When it thickens, add the well-beaten egg. Take the remains of cold baked or boiled white-fleshed fish and separate it into flakes. Put a thin layer of butter crumbs into the bottom of a baking dish, cover with the flaked fish, sprinkle with salt, paprika, and nutmeg. Pour in a layer of sauce, then fish. Alternate in this fashion till the dish is filled; and cover with buttered crumbs. Bake for twenty minutes.

Curried Salmon.

½ onion,
1 tablespoonful butter,
1 teaspoonful curry powder,
1 cupful hot water,
½ tablespoonful flour,
½ tablespoonful tomato catsup,
Salt and pepper to taste,
1 cupful cold salmon.

Fry the onion brown in the butter, sift in the curry and flour, pour the water in slowly, and stir till smooth. Add the seasoning, and last the salmon. Serve hot with toast.

Salmon Croquettes.

3 cupfuls cold salmon,
1 cupful cream,
2 tablespoonfuls butter,
1 tablespoonful flour,
1 egg,
Pepper and salt.

Chop the salmon well, and make a white sauce from the butter, flour, and cream. Cook and beat till smooth and creamy, then add the salmon and seasonings. Just before taking from the fire, add 1 well-beaten egg, and spread on a buttered plate. When quite cool, roll into small croquettes with flattened ends, flour, egg, crumb, and fry in deep boiling lard.

Lobster Croquettes.

1 cupful chopped lobster,
¼ teaspoonful salt,
½ teaspoonful mustard,
Dash McIlhenny's Tabasco Sauce,
½ cupful cream sauce.

Stir the lobster and seasonings into the hot cream sauce and spread on a plate to cool. Shape into tiny pyramids. Into the small end of each croquette stick a few inches of macaroni or a lobster claw. Fry in deep fat. Garnish with parsley or water cress.

Fish Puff Balls.

1 cupful cold flaked fish,
1 tablespoonful butter,
¾ cupful flour,
1 cupful boiling milk,
2 eggs,
Pepper and salt.

Make a white sauce with the milk, flour, and butter. Season with pepper and salt. When it has thickened, stir in the fish, then the well-beaten eggs. Fry a tablespoonful at a time in smoking hot fat, fritter fashion.

Bluefish Salad.

3 cupfuls cold flaked bluefish,
½ teaspoonful salt,
¾ teaspoonful white pepper,
¾ cupful olive oil,
1 tablespoonful vinegar.

Flake the bluefish neatly and marinate for an hour with a French dressing made from the oil, vinegar, and seasonings. Arrange on a nest of lettuce, and serve with mayonnaise garnished with chopped olives.

Clam Salad.

2 cupfuls cold clams,
1 cupful shredded lettuce.

Use for this salad cold steamed clams or left-overs from a Rhode Island bake. Take off the black heads and remove the skins. Serve in a nest of shredded lettuce. Marinate for ten minutes with French dressing, then serve.

Halibut Salad.

2 cupfuls cold halibut,
1 cupful shredded lettuce,
½ cupful cold boiled potatoes.

Flake halibut into small pieces. Shred the lettuce with scissors. Cut the potato into half-inch cubes. Mix fish and potato lightly. Lay in a nest of lettuce, and pour over it French dressing.

Salmon Salad Molds.

1 cupful cold salmon,
½ tablespoonful lemon juice,
½ teaspoonful parsley,
2 drops McIlhenny's Tabasco Sauce,
1 tablespoonful gelatin.

Mix the salmon, lemon, parsley, tabasco, and gelatin, dissolved in a little water, with enough salad dressing to moisten. Wet ½ dozen Dario molds. Fill with salmon, level the top of each one, place on ice, and turn out on lettuce leaves. Serve with a mayonnaise.

Spiced Fish.

Cold salmon, halibut, or shad makes tasty dishes when flaked and covered with hot spiced vinegar and left a day before serving. Cold fried fish is excellent served very cold. Spanish mackerel is nice in this way. Any kind of catsup or salad dressing may be served with it, but it is quite palatable with bread and butter, and makes a change from cold meat.

HOW TO COOK SALT FISH

Stuffed Salt Mackerel.

Freshen 2 fish by soaking six or eight hours, wipe, dry, and squeeze lemon juice over the flesh side. Lay 1 fish in the bottom of a baking pan, and cover with a thick dressing made of bread crumbs well seasoned with parsley, pepper, salt, butter, and bits of thin lemon peel. Lay the other fish on this dressing and baste with melted butter and hot water. Bake until brown, remove to a hot platter without disturbing the layers, and cover the top with bread crumbs moistened in melted butter and baked brown. Garnish with parsley.

Baked Salt Mackerel.

Soak the mackerel in cold water over night, placing the split side down. Cut off the fins and tail. Wash and put in a baking pan with the split side up. Mix a teaspoonful flour with a little milk and stir into ½ pint milk. Pour this over the mackerel, and bake in a moderate oven for half an hour. Just before the fish is done, add a teaspoonful butter.

Boiled Salt Mackerel.

Soak the mackerel over night; wash and put in a flat saucepan; cover with hot water, and cook slowly twenty minutes. Serve with cream, butter, egg, tomato, brown, or parsley sauce.

Broiled Salt Mackerel.

Soak over night; wash and wipe. Broil over clear coals for twelve minutes. Put the split side over fire first. Season with butter, and serve hot.

Broiled Salt Salmon or Halibut.

If fish is very salt, freshen for an hour or two in cold water; if merely smoked and slightly salted, wash and cut in small pieces about an inch thick. Season well with pepper and salt, and wrap each slice in tough paper well buttered. Twist the ends so the fish is inside a paper bag. Put in a broiler, and move over a clear fire for about eight minutes. Take the fish from the paper cases and pour egg sauce over it.

Codfish Fritters.

Cut the codfish into strips about the size of a finger, freshen by soaking over night in cold water; in the morning, dry between towels. Dip each piece in fritter batter, and fry delicately brown in hot fat.

Codfish and Potato Omelet.

Make a potato-and-fish mixture exactly as if for fishballs, but leave out the egg. Try out some salt pork in a spider, and in the dripping put the fish and potato to cook. When well browned, fold in omelet fashion, and turn out on a hot platter.

Creamed Salt Codfish.

Pick salt codfish in pieces (there should be ¾ cupful) and soak in lukewarm water. Drain, and add 1 cupful white sauce. Garnish with slices of hard-boiled eggs.

Salt Codfish (Creole style).

- 1 pound boneless codfish,
- ½ cupful rice,
- 2 tablespoonfuls butter,
- 1 can tomatoes,
- 1 onion,
- ½ teaspoonful salt,
- 1 saltspoonful pepper.

Wash and soak the codfish over night. When ready to serve, put the butter and onion in a saucepan; cover and cook on the back part of the stove until the onion is soft, not brown. Drain the codfish, add it and the rice, which has been boiled for twenty minutes; pour over the tomatoes strained; cover the saucepan, and cook gently twenty minutes. When ready to serve, add salt and pepper, push the rice aside and dish the fish first; put on top of it the rice, and pour over the sauce.—MRS. RORER.

Salt Fish (Nantucket style).

Freshen cod for twenty-four hours, changing water four or five times. Place in a kettle with cold water; as soon as it boils, remove to back of range and simmer forty-five minutes. Serve on a warm dish, with generous lumps of butter (melted by heat of fish) and boiled potatoes.

Salt-Codfish Chowder.

2 cupfuls milk,
1 cupful shredded codfish,
1½ cupfuls potato cubes,
3 ounces salt pork,
2 tablespoonfuls minced onion,
¼ teaspoonful pepper,
1 tablespoonful flour,
Salt,
3 Boston crackers.

Wash the fish and cut in two-inch lengths. Tear these in pieces, and, covering with cold water, soak for three or four hours. Slice the pork, and cook in the frying pan for ten minutes. Add the onion, and cook ten minutes. Now add the flour, and stir until smooth; afterwards stir in 1 gill water. Put the potatoes in a stewpan and pour the mixture in the frying pan over them. Season with pepper and ½ teaspoonful salt. Place on the fire, and cook for ten minutes; then take out the slices of pork and add the fish, milk, and split crackers. Cook gently for half an hour, being careful to let the chowder only bubble at one side of the stewpan. At the end of the half hour, taste before serving, to be sure to have it salt enough.—MISS PARLOA.

Codfish Balls.

1 cupful salt codfish,
2½ cupfuls potato cubes,
1 tablespoonful butter,
Dash pepper,
1 egg.

Cut the fish in small pieces, put in a saucepan with the raw potato, and cover with boiling water. Let them cook until the potatoes are nearly soft. Drain thoroughly and put through the meat chopper. Stir in the butter, the well-beaten egg, and pepper, beat with a fork until light

Waffle Iron and Waffles on Plate.

and fluffy, roll into balls. Dip in flour, fry in deep fat, and drain on brown paper.

Soufflé Codfish.

2 cupfuls hot mashed potatoes,
1 pound salt codfish,
2 eggs,
Dash pepper.

Soak the codfish over night; in the morning, pick into thin fine flakes, drain, and dry in a towel; add to it the beaten potatoes, pepper, and yolks of eggs well beaten. Whip the mixture until light, then blend in the whites of the eggs beaten to a stiff froth. Pile in a mound on a platter, and bake until delicately brown.

Codfish with Macaroni.

2 ounces macaroni,
1 cupful strained potatoes,
1 tablespoonful butter,

½ teaspoonful salt,
½ pound salt cod,
1 tablespoonful onion juice,
1 tablespoonful flour,
1 saltspoonful pepper.

Break macaroni in two-inch lengths, put in boiling water, boil rapidly for thirty minutes, drain, throw in cold water, and blanch fifteen minutes, then cut into pieces about half an inch long. Wash the codfish, cut it into blocks. It is better to have it soaked over night. If you wish to use it in a hurry, cover with cold water, bring to boiling point, drain, throwing away the water, and cover again. Do this three times, and it will be sufficiently fresh. Rub the butter and flour together, add the tomato, stir until boiling, then add the macaroni, fish, onion juice, salt, and pepper. Mix until boiling; stand over the teakettle or in hot water for thirty minutes, and it is ready to serve. —Mrs. Rorer.

Toasted Codfish.

Cut the fish in thin strips and freshen it. Dry, put between the wires of a broiler, and toast till delicately brown. Lay on a hot platter, and spread well with butter.

Broiled Haddie (Scotch recipe).

Select a small haddie, as they are more delicate than large ones. Put the fish in a dripping pan, skin side up, and bring slowly to the boiling point; drain, wipe dry, rub over with soft butter, salt, and lemon juice.

Creamed Haddie (Scotch recipe).

Trim the fins from a thick finnan haddie, cover with cold water, and let stand on the back of a range an hour, simmering slightly at the last. Drain carefully and set into a baking dish; pour over it a cupful milk; cover and set in the oven; cook ten minutes. Remove the fish to a serving dish and pour over the milk. Garnish with slices of lemon and pickles.

Shredded Haddie.

Braise 2 cupfuls finnan haddie that has been picked fine in a lump of butter the size of a walnut. Add 1 cupful cream into which 1 tablespoonful flour has been rubbed smooth. Let it come to a boil and when cooled a little add 1 large tablespoonful grated cheese, a dash pepper, and, just before serving, the beaten yolk of an egg. Serve on toast.

Finnan Haddie à la Delmonico.

Cut fish in strips (there should be 1 cupful, put in baking pan, cover with cold water, place on back of range, and allow water to heat to boiling point. Stand on range, keeping water below boiling point for twenty-five minutes, drain, and rinse thoroughly. Separate fish into flakes, add ½ cupful heavy cream and 4 hard-boiled eggs thinly sliced. Season with cayenne, add 1 tablespoonful butter, and sprinkle with finely chopped parsley.—Fannie M. Farmer.

Baked Salt Herring.

Soak the herrings over night, roll in flour and butter, place in a dripping pan with a very little water over them; season with pepper, and after putting in the oven, baste frequently.

CHAPTER XXXIX

SHELLFISH

Fried Clams.

Select plump clams, dry them on a towel, roll in cracker crumbs, dip in egg, again in crumbs, and fry in hot fat; lay a sheet of paper in a colander and put the clams on this as fast as taken up; serve on a napkin.

Clam Fritters.

Either whole clams or chopped ones may be used. Prepare a fritter batter, stir in the clams, using considerable clam liquor in making the batter. If whole clams are used, the large ones are best, having one in each fritter; when chopped clams are used, the fritters may be made any size. Drain, and serve on a napkin.

Quahog Cocktail (an individual service).

6 tiny quahogs,
1 tablespoonful clam liquor,
Speck cayenne,
1 teaspoonful ground celery,
1 teaspoonful tomato catsup,
1 teaspoonful vinegar,
Dash McIlhenny's Tabasco Sauce,
1 teaspoonful Worcestershire Sauce.

Put the quahogs in a glass with clam liquor, add cayenne, celery, tomato catsup, vinegar, Tabasco and Worcestershire Sauce. Stir thoroughly with fork.

Roast Clams.

Wash the clam shells thoroughly and drain in a colander. Spread them in a dripping pan and put in a hot oven. The shells will begin to open in five or eight minutes. Take from the oven, and, holding the shell over a warm dish, let the clam and juice drop out. Season with butter, salt, and pepper; serve very hot with thin slices of buttered brown bread.

Clams à la Newburg.

25 soft-shelled clams,
1 tablespoonful butter,
1 tablespoonful flour,
Yolks 2 eggs,
1 cupful cream.

Put butter into a saucepan; stir until heated; add the flour, and cook until it thickens. Add the beaten yolks of the eggs with cream; beat well and pour over the clams; stir thoroughly until heated and cooked, but do not boil.

Clams (Boston style).

12 soft clams,
⅛ pound salt pork.

Cut pork in pieces size of dice, and fry crisp. Add clams, freed from the tough part, and sauté them in the pork fat. Serve on Boston brown bread.

Clams in Vienna Rolls.

Take a large Vienna roll, cut out a piece of the crust the size of a half dollar, and remove the soft bread from the inside. Open as many little-neck clams as will fill the roll, replace the small piece of crust, and place in the oven for ten minutes. Take the juice from the clams, make a thickening of flour and the juice, mix with it paprika, black pepper, Worcestershire Sauce, a dash McIlhenny's Tabasco Sauce, and heat. Remove the baked roll from the oven and pour sauce over it.

Escalloped Clams.

25 clams,
1 cupful cracker crumbs,
½ cupful milk,
¼ cupful clam liquor,
2 eggs (well beaten),
1 tablespoonful melted butter,
Salt and pepper.

Season the clams highly, mix with crumbs moistened with milk and clam liquor; add eggs and melted butter and the clams chopped. Fill each shell, sprinkle with bread crumbs, and brown. This fills twelve shells.

Sautéd Oysters.

Put 2 tablespoonfuls butter into a sauté pan; when it is hot add as many drained oysters as will make 2 cupfuls. Add a little salt and pepper and a tablespoonful lemon juice. Shake them in the pan until the gills are curled, then add a tablespoonful parsley chopped fine. Serve on slices of toasted bread on a hot platter.

Fried Oysters with Cold Slaw.

Lay the oysters on a cloth to dry. Roll in cracker dust, then in egg diluted with a little milk, season with pepper and salt, again cover with cracker dust. Lay in a frying basket and fry in smoking hot fat long enough to give them a light-brown color. Oysters toughen if cooked too long. Prepare only 4 at a time; more lower the temperature of the fat too much, and if they are rolled before the moment of frying, they moisten the cracker dust. Place them on a paper in the oven until they are done. Fold a napkin and place it in the center of a platter. Pile the oysters on the napkin, and make a wreath around them of cold slaw.

Oysters à la Newburg.

25 large oysters,
1½ tablespoonfuls butter,
1 tablespoonful lemon juice,
Pepper and salt,
½ cupful mushrooms,
Yolks 4 eggs,
1 cupful cream.

Place the oysters in a saucepan with the butter, lemon juice, pepper, and salt. Cook until the oysters are plump, then add the mushrooms cut in quarters. Beat the yolks of the egg into the cream, turn it into the oyster mixture, let it get hot and a little thickened, without boiling. Turn it into a hot dish, and garnish with croutons.—Mary Ronald.

Oysters à la George Trimble Davidson.

Melt butter the size of 2 eggs, then pour in a quart oysters and the strained liquor, flavor with salt and pepper, a teaspoonful paprika, and a dash McIlhenny's Tabasco. Cut up celery, put in 2 tablespoonfuls, and squeeze in the juice of ½ lemon. Cook four minutes, and serve on hot toast. A pint of rich cream added to the broth of the oysters makes the dish richer.—Deschler Welsh.

Oyster Rarebit.

Clean and remove the hard muscles from a cupful oysters; parboil in their own liquor until the edges curl, and remove to a hot bowl. Put 1 tablespoonful butter, ½ pound cheese (broken in small bits), 1 saltspoonful each salt and mustard, and a few grains cayenne into the chafing dish; while the cheese is melting, beat 2 eggs slightly, and add them to the oyster liquor; mix this gradually with the melted cheese, add the oysters, and pour over hot toast.

Oysters Encoquille (French recipe).

Clean large oyster shells, into each put a couple of small oysters, and sprinkle with bread crumbs which have been peppered and salted and tossed in melted butter. Set the shells closely together in a baking pan, put in a hot oven, and bake till the crumbs are delicately browned. Serve a shell to each person on a small plate. Garnish with ¼ lemon and a sprig of parsley.

Pigs in Blankets.

Dust large, plump oysters with pepper and salt, wrap each inside a thin slice of bacon and skewer together with a toothpick. Lay in a hot spider, cook till oysters begin to curl and the bacon crisps. Take out the toothpicks, and serve three or four on a slice of toast to each person.

Broiled Oysters.

Drain large oysters from the liquor, dip each in melted butter, dust with pepper and salt, then roll in sifted cracker crumbs. Grease the wires of an oyster broiler, lay the oysters in closely, and broil over a clear fire until the juice begins to flow. Serve on toast.

Roasted Oysters in the Shell.

Scrub the oyster shells thoroughly, lay them in a large roasting pan with the round side down, so they retain the juices as they cook. They may be roasted in a hot oven, on top of the stove, in a steamer, or under a blaze of a gas stove. When the shells open, remove the upper shell and serve the lower shells, as many as will go on a hot plate, each one with a hot oyster in its own juice. Dust with pepper and salt and squeeze a dash of lemon juice over each. Serve immediately. If desired, they may be slipped from the shells upon slices of buttered toast and the juice poured over.

Scalloped Oysters.

1 pint oysters,
¼ cupful melted butter,
Pepper and salt,
Dash McIlhenny's Tabasco Sauce,
1 cupful stale bread crumbs,
½ cupful milk.

Cover the bottom of a baking dish with bread crumbs, and lay carefully over it the oysters lifted from the liquor. Cover with another layer of crumbs dusted with pepper and salt; then more oysters, and make the top layer crumbs. Strain the oyster liquor, add to it the tabasco, melted butter, and the milk scalding hot. Pour it over the dish. Sprinkle over the top a layer of crumbs moistened with melted butter. Set it in the oven, and bake till the crumbs are brown.

Creamed Oysters.

1 cupful cream sauce,
1 pint oysters.

Make a cupful cream sauce, season with salt, pepper, paprika, and celery salt. Pick over the oysters, and parboil in their own liquor until they begin to curl. Drain and add to the sauce. Serve on slices of buttered toast, in puff-paste patties, in *vol-au-vent*, or in croustade boxes.

Oyster Pie.

Line a deep dish with good puff paste, not too rich, roll out the upper crust and lay cn a plate just the size of pie dish, set it on top of the dish and put into the oven, so the crust may be nearly cooked before the oysters are put in, for they require less cooking than the crust. While the crust is baking, strain the liquor from the oysters and thicken. Add 2 tablespoonfuls butter and the same of cracker crumbs, season with salt, pepper, nutmeg, or mace. Let the liquor boil, slip in the oysters, boil it up once, stir, remove plate with the crust, pour the oysters and hot liquor into the pie dish, put the top crust on, and return to the oven for five minutes.

Curry of Lobster.

¾ cupful lobster meat,
1 cupful meat stock,
2 tablespoonfuls butter,
1 tablespoonful flour,
1 teaspoonful salt,
Dash McIlhenny's Tabasco Sauce,
⅛ teaspoonful white pepper,
1 teaspoonful curry powder,
1 tablespoonful minced onion,
3 slices toast.

Cut the lobster into small pieces and season with half the salt and pepper. Put the butter and onion on the fire in a frying pan, and cook until the onion turns straw color; then add the flour and curry powder and stir until brown. Gradually add the stock to this, stirring all the while. Season, and cook for three minutes. Strain this into a saucepan, and add the lobster. Cook for five minutes. Cut the slices of toast in strips and lay in a warm dish. Pour the lobster over these, and serve at once.

Breaded Lobster.

1 large lobster,
1 egg,
1 teaspoonful salt,
⅛ teaspoonful pepper,
Dried bread crumbs,
Fat for frying.

Split the claws and tail and set aside. Take the meat from the large joints and body and chop fine. Mix with this ¼ teaspoonful salt and 2 tablespoonfuls tomalley. Shape into three small, flat cakes. Season the lobster with salt and pepper. Beat the egg in a soup plate. Dip the pieces of lobster and the little cakes, one at a time, into the egg; then roll in crumbs, and, after arranging on a plate, put in a cool place. Put the breaded lobster in the frying basket, and cook in fat until crisp and brown. Serve with Sauce Tartare.

Lobster (French style).

Chop an onion and put it in a stewpan with 2 ounces butter; fry light brown; mix with it a tablespoonful flour; add ½ pint milk, a teaspoonful salt, a little pepper and cayenne, nutmeg, and chopped parsley. Boil till rather thick; put in lobster meat cut in pieces. Let it boil up, add yolk of an egg, and a little cream, mix quickly; fill the shells, egg and bread-crumb them; put in the oven for ten minutes; brown, and serve.

Creamed Lobster.

1 cupful lobster meat,
1 tablespoonful butter,
1 teaspoonful grated onion,
1 tablespoonful flour,
1 cupful stock,
1 tablespoonful lemon juice,
½ cupful cream,
Yolk 1 egg.

Cut the lobster meat into inch dice. Put the butter in a saucepan with the grated onion, let them cook a minute, then add the flour. Stir for a few minutes, and add, slowly, the stock and lemon juice. When this thickens, add the lobster meat, turning carefully so as not to break it. When the meat is heated, remove from the fire and mix cream with the yolk of an egg beaten in it. Replace on the fire for a minute, and serve on toast or in timbales.

Rissoles of Lobster.

Mince the meat from a boiled lobster, season with pepper, salt, and a little mace. Add 3 tablespoonfuls melted butter and some bread crumbs; roll into balls, dip in yolk of beaten egg, put more crumbs over them, and fry brown.

Langosta à la Catalana (Mexican recipe).

Remove lobster meat from the shell, lay it in a bowl so as to save all the liquor, and cut in quarters. Chop 4 large onions and a bunch of parsley, mash 4 cloves of garlic, and fry together in ½ cupful olive oil until nearly brown. Season with salt and cayenne; add the lobster with the juice, a cupful washed rice, and a tablespoonful of capers. Cook until the rice is done. When serving, put whole pimentoes on top.—May E. Southworth.

Lobster à la Newburg.

2 hard-boiled eggs,
½ pint cream or milk,
2 tablespoonfuls flour,
2 tablespoonfuls butter.

Put butter in saucepan, and when melted, add flour gradually, then cream or milk. Mash yolks of eggs and moisten with 2 tablespoonfuls milk then add to ingredients in saucepan. Add salt and cayenne, and stir until thick and smooth. Add a cupful boiled lobster and the whites of the eggs cut in strips.

Cangrejueloe (Mexican recipe).

1 teaspoonful butter,
½ pound ham,
1 onion,
Dash salt,
Dash chili powder,
1 pint picked shrimps,
½ pint washed rice,
1 bay leaf, thyme, and parsley.

Put the butter in a saucepan; when hot, add the ham, chopped fine, onion, salt, and chili powder. When these are well browned, add the shrimps and stir until hot; then put in the washed rice and parsley. Cover and simmer with sufficient water added to cook the rice until each grain stands out alone.

Scalloped Scallops.

Cut scallops into small pieces and mix with cracker crumbs, beaten egg, and a little milk or cream, seasoning to taste. Fill shells, washed for the purpose, cover with crumbs, put a bit of butter on each, and bake delicately brown.

Fried Scallops.

Marinate the scallops in a mixture of oil, lemon juice, salt, and pepper. Roll in cracker dust, then in egg, and again in cracker dust or white bread crumbs. Fry in smoking-hot fat to a golden color.

Scallops on the Shell.

Cut scallops into quarters, if large. Place them in the scallop shells. Dredge with salt, pepper, and chopped parsley, cover with chopped mushrooms, some bits of butter, a teaspoonful lemon juice for each shell, and bread crumbs moistened with butter. Place in a hot oven for ten or fifteen minutes.

Soft-Shell Crabs.

To prepare them for cooking, lift the shell at both edges and remove the gray, spongy substance, which can be plainly seen, then pull up the little triangular apronlike piece on under side of shell, wash and wipe the crabs dry, dip in milk, roll in flour, and fry in hot fat; or dip in beaten egg, roll in crumbs, and either fry or broil.

Partan Pies (a Scotch dish).

Pick the meat, after boiling from hard-shell crabs, clean the shells, mix the meat with a little pepper, a bit of butter, and bread crumbs; add 3 spoonfuls vinegar and put into the shells again; strew bread crumbs over, and set them in the oven. Serve when brown on top.

Crabs à la Creole (Southern recipe).

2 tablespoonfuls butter,
1 onion,
1 sweet Spanish pepper minced,
1 cupful strained tomato pulp,
½ cupful chicken broth,
4 soft crabs.

Melt the butter, and cook for five minutes the onion and pepper; stir while frying, then add the tomato pulp, chicken broth, and the crabs cleaned and cut in two. Use celery salt in the seasoning, and simmer seven minutes.

CHAPTER XL

MEATS

In regard to meat more than any other food, it pays the housewife to do her own marketing. A study of the cuts laid out on a butcher's stall often reveals something good and cheap, which would not have been thought of if one were giving her orders to a clerk or over the telephone. During the past ten years meat has risen so steadily in price that roasts, chops, and steaks, on which the average housekeeper was wont to rely, make a food bill appallingly high. But there are other pieces which produce very savory dishes by careful cooking.

The good marketer ought, first of all, to know at a glance not only the various cuts but the appearance of good, wholesome meat. When first killed, a side of beef is reddish purple, but it changes fast to a bright-red tint, while the fat is a creamy-white color, not in chunks by itself but threaded, as it were, through the red. It ought to have a fresh, juicy appearance that tells it has hung long enough to become well ripened and fit for human food.

Before beginning to consider cuts of meat, their price, their tenderness or toughness, try to imagine the animal on its feet wandering about a grassy field in search of food. Like every other creature, it has a wonderful network of muscles. Some of these muscles work overtime, others get little usage. Therefore we find the tenderest portions where the body has had little exercise—the flesh on top of the back, that long strip we call the tenderloin lying alongside of the spine, the porterhouse, the seven prime ribs, as a butcher calls the thick sirloin, all cuts which are best adapted for broiling or roasting. Near the neck are the chuck ribs and shoulder, besides the tail and rump; then we come down to the round and the leg, portions of all creatures that abound in muscle. Where sinews are abundant and the flesh has a coarse-grained appearance, different methods of cooking must be resorted to; if it were broiled or roasted, it would be almost impossible to chew. It should be subjected to slow cooking, such as braising, pot roasting, or simmering just below the boiling point or to the moderate heat of a casserole. The nearer one approaches the hoof of the animal, the better is the meat adapted for soup making. The tendons of the shin are rich in gelatin, and when dissolved by long, slow cooking, give flavor and consistency to a soup.

Beginning at the hoof of a creature, there is a piece which makes excellent soup. As we go farther up the loin, the meat begins to be of better flavor and the bone contains finer marrow. Then comes the round; from the top of it can be cut a really good steak. With a slight amount of pounding and marinating, it can be made almost as tender as a more expensive cut. By marinating is meant laying it in a mixture of oil and vinegar in the coldest corner of the refrigerator. Next comes the rump, from which stews and roasts are cut. Then the sirloin, which contains the best steaks and roasts. From this portion is cut the tenderloin, a fine strip of tender meat that lies inside the bone. This bit of the creature does not receive the slightest exercise. It is a delicate morsel, which sells from fifty to eighty cents a pound, according to the demand for it. I have bought it in country places as cheap as twenty-five cents a pound, while in New York it often brings ninety cents. Although deliciously tender, it does not possess the flavor and nourishment of a cheaper piece of steak.

Now we come to the forequarter, which begins at the five prime ribs for roasting. Close to them lie the five chuck ribs, excellent cuts for stews and small steaks. The neck is generally converted into Hamburg steak, while the under part of the animal, which includes the flank, plate, navel, and brisket, are corned. Here also is the shoulder clod; no cut can excel it in juiciness and flavor when a pot roast or beef à la mode is desired. For the housewife anxious to have a small income provide the best food possible, there are any number of pieces that make a savory dish, only they must be cooked in the way which best fits them. A cut from the top of the round marinated, as I suggested, and broiled gives an excellent steak. A cheaper piece of round, from farther down the leg, may be put through the chopper; when broiled, it is good as Hamburg steak; baked, it makes a savory cannelon. A cut from the rump may be braised and is as appetizing hot as cold. A pound or two of rump is the base for a nourishing stew, while a braised or boiled tongue affords one hot meal and several lunch dishes. An ox tail is delicious fricasseed or in soup. Pot roasting converts a number of cheap cuts into excellent dishes. Among these are the juicy, lean cross ribs, or a solid piece from the lower part of the round or face of the rump. Two pounds of flank, which costs ten or twelve cents a pound, is very good when cooked *à la Milanaise.* Roll the meat, sauté it brown, season well, and braise slowly for two hours with enough water to make a good gravy.

A sheep's liver is as highly esteemed in England as calf's liver is here. In American markets it is almost given away. If liver looks cloudy, or a heart and kidney have a streaky, spotted appearance, you may be sure they are diseased and will make dangerous food. When cut from a well-nourished, healthy animal, they are smooth, red, and juicy. A calf's heart is a most appetizing dish larded, stuffed with a well-seasoned dressing, roasted, and served with rich, brown gravy.

There is a knack in picking out a soup bone as well as in knowing how to cook it. It ought to be two thirds meat, one third bone and fat. If one has a large family, the best method to follow in winter when making soup, is to purchase two pieces of shin, one heavy with meat, the other bone and gristle. It must be cooked very slowly. When tender, take the meat, separating it from the bone and gristle, which may be left to cook until all the good is out of it. The meat makes a good hash or stew and is not to be despised for croquettes. Fifty cents' worth of shin (when there is no waste) yields several nourishing meals in the shape of stew, hash, galantine, and soup.

It will pay a housewife who caters to a large family to purchase a set of butcher's tools. They cost several dollars, but within a year she can save the price of them by getting pieces of meat, during the winter at least, big enough to make a number of meals. Of course cold-storage room is a necessity. For instance in the course of two weeks, a quarter of mutton can be utilized in a good-sized household. The first part to be used is the flank, because its keeping qualities are not so good as other parts of the quarter. Cut off the small end of the ribs, leaving the loin chops and the rib quite short. The loin can then be hung in a cold pantry. The flank will make several quarts of fine mutton stock as well as a stew. In this way, one may have at a moderate cost the chops for which a butcher charges fancy prices, besides a number of other cuts, which, although not quite as choice, make excellent dishes when cooked properly. Beef, pork, and veal in large cuts may be purchased during the winter and cut by the housewife to suit her needs. An accommodating butcher will generally be willing to give his customer a lesson on how to divide meat, and with sharp tools any woman can accomplish it.

Roast Beef.

Use, if possible, a covered roaster for cooking any sort of meat. The result is much more savory roast and less shrinkage. Wipe the meat, set it in a dripping pan, skin side down, rub with salt and pepper, then dredge with flour. Have the oven as hot as possible when it is put in, so the outside will sear quickly and prevent the escape of the meat juice. As soon as the flour in the pan is brown, reduce the heat and baste with the fat, which has flowed from the roast. When the meat is half done, turn it on the other side and dredge with flour. Should there be the slightest appearance of flour in the pan turning black, add a little water and baste every fifteen minutes until done, allowing one hour for each five pounds if the meat is desired rare. An hour and twenty minutes is needed if you wish it well done.

Roast-Beef Gravy.

Pour out the largest part of the fat, set the pan on top of the stove, add ¼ cupful flour, and stir it through the dripping until well browned. Pepper and salt to taste. Add gradually from 1 to 2 cupfuls boiling water, and beat the gravy smooth with a wire spoon; if it is not rich enough in coloring, brown with ½ teaspoonful kitchen bouquet.

Casserole of Beefsteak.

Sauté 3 sliced onions in a tablespoonful butter; put them into the casserole. Cut a steak, from the upper side of the round, into pieces suitable for one portion. Put them in the sauté pan and sear on all sides, then in the casserole. Add a tablespoonful flour to the sauté pan, let it brown, add 1½ cupfuls water, and stir until thickened, season with salt, pepper, and a tablespoonful chopped parsley. Add a little Worcestershire Sauce and mushroom catsup. The sauce will be richer if stock is used instead of water. Pour the sauce over the meat, cover the casserole, set in the oven, and cook slowly until the meat is tender, then cover the top with parboiled, sliced potatoes, and return to the oven to finish cooking the potatoes. Serve in the casserole.

To Broil a Steak.

Have the coals glowing hot, without flame or smoke. Grease a broiler with beef fat, place the steak in it, and hold it over the fire while counting ten slowly. Turn the broiler and hold the other side down for the same length of time. Turn the meat once in ten seconds for about one minute, or until it is well seared; then hold it farther from the fire, turning occasionally until the surface is brown. Just before taking it from the fire, sprinkle with salt and pepper, turning each side once more to the heat to cook the seasoning. When the steak is cooked, lay it on the platter, and spread both sides with butter.

Braised Beef.

3 pounds beef,
2 ounces fat salt pork,
2 tablespoonfuls flour,
3 teaspoonfuls salt,
½ teaspoonful pepper,
1½ pints water,
2 tablespoonfuls minced onion,
2 tablespoonfuls minced carrot,
2 whole cloves,
1 sprig parsley.

Cut the pork into thin slices and fry until brown and crisp. Take out the pork, putting the vegetables in the fat remaining in the pan, and cook slowly fifteen minutes. Rub half the pepper and 2 teaspoonfuls salt into the piece of meat, and place it in a deep graniteware pan. When the vegetables are cooked, put them with the meat, first pressing from them as much fat as possible. Into the fat remaining in the pan put the flour, and stir until it becomes brown. Add the water gradually, stirring all the while. Season this gravy with the remainder of the salt and pepper, and boil for five minutes; then pour over the meat in the pan. Add the cloves and parsley. Cover the pan and set in a very moderate oven. Cook for five hours, basting every half hour with the gravy in the pan. The oven must never be so hot that the gravy will bubble.—Maria Parloa.

Beef Stew with Dumplings.

2 pounds upper part of round steak with the bone,
3 pints boiling water,
1 turnip,
1 carrot,
1 onion,
½ tablespoonful salt,
⅛ tablespoonful pepper,
½ bay leaf,
⅓ cupful flour for thickening.

Cut meat in one-and-a-half inch pieces, wipe with a damp cloth, and sprinkle with a little salt and flour. Put some of the fat in a hot frying pan, and when tried out, add meat, turning often, till well browned. Then put in a kettle with the bones, add boiling water, rinsing out frying pan with some of it, that none of the goodness of the meat be wasted. Let meat boil for five minutes; then set back on the stove where water will just bubble, and cook slowly for two hours. Then add onion, carrot, and turnip which have been cut in half-inch cubes, and cook for another hour. Twelve minutes before the stew is done, put dumplings on a perforated tin pie plate, or in a steamer, cover closely, and do not lift the cover until stew is cooked.

Corned Beef and Cabbage.

Wash and, if very salt, soak in cold water for an hour a piece of corned beef weighing 5 or 6 pounds. Put in a kettle with cold water to cover, place on stove, heat slowly, taking off scum as it rises to the top of the water. Cook slowly for three or four hours, or till very tender. Take out the meat, and in the liquor cook a cabbage which has been prepared according to directions given in chapter on vegetables; also some potatoes that have been washed and pared. If beets are to be used, cook them in boiling water in a kettle by themselves. When cabbage and potatoes are tender, take out with skimmer and serve with the meat. Save the fat that rises to the top.

Fillet of Beef.

Trim into shape, lard the upper side, dredge with salt, pepper, and flour. Put several pieces of pork in the pan under the meat, bake in a hot oven twenty or thirty minutes. Serve with mushroom sauce. Or brush the fillet with beaten egg, sprinkle seasoned and buttered crumbs all over it, and bake thirty minutes. Or stuff the incisions left by the removal of the veins and tendons with any stuffing or forcemeat. Dredge with salt and flour, and bake. —Mary J. Lincoln.

Hamburg Steak.

Two pounds round beef chopped fine; press it into a flat steak, sprinkle with salt and pepper and a little onion juice; flour lightly, and broil as beefsteak. Make a brown gravy with a little soup stock, thicken with flour, and pour around the steak.

Steak à la Bordelaise (French recipe).

1 sirloin steak,
2 tablespoonfuls butter,
2 tablespoonfuls flour,
2 cupfuls beef stock,

2 tablespoonfuls chopped raw ham,
½ bay leaf,
1 tablespoonful chopped onion,
Salt and pepper to taste,
1 tablespoonful tomato catsup,
½ cupful finely chopped mushrooms.

Brown the butter and flour, stir in the stock; when thick and smooth, add the ham, bay leaf, and onion. Cover and simmer gently for an hour, then strain. Add salt, pepper, catsup, and mushrooms, and keep hot at the side of the fire. Broil a sirloin steak, arrange on a hot platter, and pour this sauce around it.

Beefsteak and Onions.

Broil the steak over the fire, being careful to turn it often; after it is cooked, place on a hot platter and set in the oven with dabs of butter on it. Put a little finely chopped suet in a frying pan and fry light brown; into that place 3 onions sliced fine. Cover the pan and cook until tender, remove the cover and continue cooking until the onions are light brown. In serving, pour the onions and gravy over the steak.

Beefsteak Pie.

3 pounds lean steak,
Sweet thyme and parsley chopped fine,
Peppers,
2 onions,
1 teaspoonful Worcestershire Sauce,
6 hard-boiled eggs,
Salt.

Cut the steak in strips four inches thick; put it to stew in sufficient boiling water so it does not cover the meat. After cooking slowly half an hour, add the thyme, parsley, pepper, and onions, cut in thin slices. When seasoning is added, continue stewing until the meat is tender. Add cornstarch to make the gravy as thick as cream, also season with salt and sauce. Have ready the hard-boiled eggs, and place them in alternate layers with the meat in a pie dish; pour the gravy over all, cover with pastry, and bake.

Beef Omelet.

½ pound raw beef,
3 crackers,
½ teaspoonful Calumet baking powder,
2 well-beaten eggs,
½ teaspoonful herbs.

Chop the beef fine; roll in the cracker dust, with which has been mixed the baking powder. Add the eggs and mix with salt, pepper, and powdered herbs; put a lump of butter in a baking dish, let it melt, then put it in the mixture. Bake half an hour. Turn out on a hot platter, fold over as you would an omelet, and pour a meat sauce around it.

Steak à la Victor Hugo (French recipe).

1 porterhouse steak,
½ teaspoonful finely chopped shallot,
1 tablespoonful tarragon vinegar,
½ cupful butter,
Yolks 2 eggs,
1 teaspoonful lemon juice,
1 teaspoonful meat extract,
½ teaspoonful horse-radish.

Wipe a porterhouse steak, broil, and serve with Victor Hugo sauce made as follows: Cook shallot in vinegar five minutes. Wash ½ cupful butter and divide in thirds. Add 1 piece butter to mixture with yolks of eggs, lemon juice, and meat extract. Cook over hot water, stirring constantly; as soon as the butter is melted, add second piece, then a third piece. When the mixture thickens, add horse-radish. The time for broiling the steak, depends, of course, on how you like it; if it is wished rare, five minutes over a hot fire or under the flame of a gas stove will cook it sufficiently. When you wish the steak well done, give it from six to eight minutes.—Stella A. Downing.

Steak Savory (Hungarian recipe).

1 pound round steak,
1 teaspoonful butter,
½ teaspoonful salt,
¼ teaspoonful pepper,
½ cupful chopped beef fat,
2 onions.

Cut the steak into four parts. Place a frying pan over the fire with enough suet to grease the pan. When very hot, put in the meat and fry over a quick fire until light brown on both sides. Remove to a hot dish. Mix butter, salt, and pepper. Spread this over both sides of the steak and set in a warm place. Put chopped beef fat in the pan and fry to straw color; remove the bits of fat, leaving the liquid fat in the pan. Add to this the onions cut in slices, season with salt, cover, and cook five minutes, stirring them occasionally. Lay them over the steak, and serve.

London Meat Pie (English recipe).

1 pound steak,
¼ pound kidney,
2 cupfuls flour,
6 tablespoonfuls butter,
2 teaspoonfuls Calumet baking powder,
Pinch salt,
1 cupful milk.

Cut the steak and kidney in thin slices, and sprinkle over it flour, pepper, and salt. Put in a pie dish with a little hot water. Put the flour in a basin with the baking powder and salt, rub in the butter, and add milk. Turn on a floured board, and roll a quarter of an inch in thickness. Wet the edges of the pie dish, and line it with strips of pastry, then cover, brush over with egg, make a hole in the center, and bake for an hour and a half in a moderately hot oven.

Steak Pudding (English recipe).

2 cupfuls flour,
3 ounces suet,
1 teaspoonful Calumet baking powder,
1 cupful milk,
Salt and pepper,
1 pound steak,
½ cupful hot water,
Seasoning.

Cut the meat in slices, and dip each piece in seasoning. Cover with hot water, and let stand while making the pastry. Mix the flour with the suet finely chopped, the baking powder and salt, and make into a stiff paste with milk. Drop on a floured board, and roll. Line a greased pudding basin with the pastry, reserving a piece for the top. Put in the meat and water, wet the edges, and cover with the remainder of the pastry. Tie over the top a floured pudding cloth. Put into a saucepan of boiling water to boil two hours.

Beef Bouilli (French recipe).

Short ribs beef,
1 turnip,
1 carrot,
1 onion,
3 stalks celery,
1 clove garlic,
Pepper and salt,
1 tablespoonful vinegar,
1 teaspoonful mushroom catsup.

Put the beef on to stew with turnip, carrot, onion, celery, garlic, salt and pepper. Cover with boiling water, and simmer till the meat is tender as possible. For sauce, add vinegar, mushroom catsup, salt, and pepper. Simmer a few minutes. Serve the sauce about the meat.

Beef à la Mode.

4 pounds beef,
2 tablespoonfuls butter,
2 tablespoonfuls flour,
3 pints boiling water,
1 bay leaf,
1 sprig celery,
1 sprig parsley,
1 onion,
2 carrots,
1 turnip,
1 tablespoonful salt,
Dash pepper.

Put the butter in a stewpan over a hot fire; when it melts, brown the meat on both sides. Remove the meat temporarily and add flour to butter; let it brown and thicken, then add water, bay leaf, celery, parsley, and onion with clove stuck in it, carrots, turnip, salt, and pepper. Replace the meat in this liquid and simmer

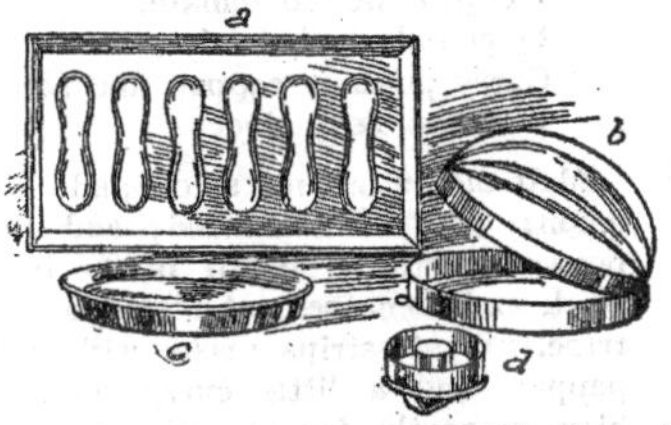

a, Mold for Lady's Fingers; b, Mold for Steamed Puddings, Brown Bread, or Parfait; c, Layer-Cake Tin; d, Doughnut Cutter.

six hours. Turn the meat over and stir occasionally. Place the meat on a platter, strain the gravy over it, and garnish with sliced boiled carrots and parsley.

Beef Goulash (Hungarian recipe).

- 3 pounds round steak cut in inch cubes,
- 3 onions sliced,
- 3 potatoes diced,
- ¼ cupful butter,
- ½ cupful water,
- 1 cupful cream,
- 1 teaspoonful beef extract,
- 1 teaspoonful salt,
- ⅛ teaspoonful black pepper,
- ½ teaspoonful paprika.

Put the butter in a kettle, set it on the range, and fry the onions, add the meat, cook until brown. Dissolve the beef extract in water, and add it to the contents of the kettle. Cover closely, and cook slowly until the meat is tender, then add the seasonings, and place the potatoes in the kettle on top of the meat. Cover and cook until the potatoes are tender, add the cream, and simmer five minutes.

Flank à la Milanaise (French recipe).

- 2 pounds flank,
- 1 tablespoonful salt,
- ½ teaspoonful pepper,
- ½ cupful chopped onion,
- 1 tablespoonful butter,
- 2 ounces suet,
- 1 cupful water,
- 2 slices carrot,
- 1 tablespoonful cornstarch.

Season flank with salt and pepper. Place a saucepan with onion and butter over the fire, add a small piece of bruised garlic, cook five minutes. When cold, spread this over the meat, roll, tie at each end and in the center with a string. Set a saucepan with suet over the fire, fry until the suet is fried out; then put in the meat; cook and turn till the meat becomes a light brown, add water, carrot, and onion; cover and cook till done, which will take about two hours, adding more water if necessary, but only ½ cupful at a time. Shortly before serving, lay the meat on a hot dish, take off the strings, skim the fat from the gravy, mix cornstarch with cold water, add it to the gravy, stir, and cook two minutes; add sufficient boiling water to make a creamy sauce, cook five minutes, strain, and serve.

Beef Ragout (French recipe).

- 2 pounds lean beef,
- 1 teaspoonful salt,
- ½ teaspoonful pepper,
- 1 tablespoonful butter,
- 2 onions.

Cut the beef into one-and-a-half-inch pieces, season with salt and pepper. Place a saucepan with butter and onions over the fire, cook a few minutes, add the meat and seasoning, cover, and cook over a slow fire two and a half hours, adding a little boiling water if the gravy gets too brown. When the meat is tender, dust with 1 tablespoonful flour, add cupful boiling water, and cook slowly ten minutes.

Hot Collops (Scotch recipe).

Mince 1½ pounds round steak fine and season highly. An onion can be added if liked, chopped very fine. Melt a tablespoonful butter in a stewpan, put in the mince, and stir frequently to keep from getting into lumps. Dredge flour over it, and pour on a little stock. Let simmer a few minutes, serve very hot on slices of toast.

Boiled Tongue.

Bend the tip of the tongue around and tie it to the root. Put it in cold water and place over the fire. When it boils, pour off the water, and put it on again in cold water. Boil until tender. Remove the skin, roots, and fat, and serve cold. Tongues may also be braised and served cold.—MARY J. LINCOLN.

Sweetbreads and Macaroni Sauce.

2 beef sweetbreads,
12 sticks macaroni,
2 tablespoonfuls butter,
2 tablespoonfuls flour,
1 cupful cream,
Salt and pepper.

Parboil the sweetbreads; cut into small pieces. Boil the macaroni; when tender, cut it in tiny pieces, making little rings. Into a saucepan put butter and flour; stir, add the cream; when smooth, add the macaroni and sweetbreads. Season with salt and pepper. Boil up and serve.

Tripe à la Creole (Southern recipe).

2 tablespoonfuls butter,
12 peppercorns,
2 cloves,
1 blade mace,
1 onion chopped fine,
2 tablespoonfuls flour,
1¼ cupfuls strained tomato,
½ pound boiled tripe.

Put into a saucepan the butter, peppercorns, cloves, mace, and onion chopped fine. Cook slowly until the butter is light brown; add the flour, and brown again. Strain, and return to the fire. Season to taste; add the boiled tripe, cut into inch strips; cover, and simmer gently for twenty minutes.

Curried Tripe (Southern recipe).

1 tablespoonful butter,
1 finely chopped onion,
1 tablespoonful flour,
1 cupful stewed tomato,
1½ pounds boiled tripe,
Curry powder, pepper, and salt,
1 cupful beef stock.

Melt the butter in a spider; add the onion; cook until colored; add the flour and brown it; stir in the beef stock and tomatoes. Add the boiled tripe, cut into strips, season with salt, pepper, and a little curry powder. Simmer gently for ten minutes, and serve.

Tripe Lyonnaise (French recipe).

2 pounds tripe,
1 tablespoonful butter,
Slice onion,
Salt and pepper.

Cut the tripe in thin strips. Put the butter in a frying pan; when hot, add the onion, and fry light brown. Turn in the tripe, add a little salt and pepper. Cook gently until tender. Thicken the gravy with flour.

Tripe à l'Espagnole (French recipe).

3 tablespoonfuls oil,
½ cupful finely chopped onion,
½ finely chopped green pepper,
1 bruised clove garlic,
½ cupful finely chopped mushrooms,
1½ pounds tripe,
1 teaspoonful salt,
¼ teaspoonful pepper,
2 finely cut tomatoes,
1 teaspoonful flour,
1 cupful boiling water,
1 teaspoonful beef extract,
1 teaspoonful finely chopped parsley.

Place the oil in a saucepan over the fire, add the onion, pepper, and garlic; cook five minutes without browning. Wash and cut the tripe into inch-sized pieces, season with salt and pepper; mix the tripe with the seasoning; add it to vegetables in the saucepan, cover, and cook ten minutes; add the tomatoes, seasoning and mushrooms, cook five minutes; dust with flour, add boiling water and beef extract, cook a few minutes longer. Serve, sprinkled with parsley.

Stewed Tripe and Tomato Sauce.

1 pound tripe,
1 onion cut in slices,
2 cupfuls tomatoes,
2 tablespoonfuls flour,
½ cupful cold water,
Salt and pepper.

Wash the tripe, cover with hot water; add the onion, cover the saucepan, and cook slowly half an hour. In another saucepan put the tomatoes, cook ten minutes; strain through a sieve and return to the pan. Wet the flour with the water; add it to the strained tomatoes, stirring all the time. Add salt and pepper to taste. Place the tripe on a hot platter and pour the sauce over.

Tripe with Oysters.

Simmer ½ pound tripe for three quarters of an hour in slightly salted water; take out the tripe; add to the water in which the tripe was cooked a little butter, flour, salt, and pepper. Return the tripe and a dozen oysters, simmer until the oysters are cooked, and serve.

Tripe and Onions (English recipe).

1 pound tripe,
2 onions,
1 cupful milk,
½ tablespoonful flour,
Pepper and salt.

Parboil the tripe, and cut into small pieces. Parboil the onions, and cut in rings. Put them both in a saucepan with boiling water and a little salt. Simmer gently from an hour and a half to two hours. Mix the flour and milk smoothly; when the tripe is tender, pour it in. Let it come to the boil, and serve very hot.

Beef Heart Sauté.

Soak a beef heart in cold water an hour, changing the water several times to draw out all the blood. Cover with boiling water, add 1 teaspoonful salt, and simmer gently two hours. Set aside until cold. Cut into half-inch slices and take out the tough muscle in the center. Dip each slice in slightly beaten egg, with which has been mixed salt and pepper, ½ teaspoonful onion juice, and 2 teaspoonfuls warm water; roll in dry bread crumbs, and stand ten minutes. Fry golden brown in deep fat. In a frying pan melt 1 tablespoonful butter; when brown, add 1 tablespoonful flour, and brown again. Add gradually ¾ cupful water in which the heart was cooked, ½ cupful vinegar from piccalilli, and 1 tablespoonful pickle chopped fine; salt and pepper to taste. Simmer two or three minutes.

Stewed Beef's Heart (English recipe).

1 beef heart,
1 cupful bread crumbs,
3 slices salt pork minced,
Salt and pepper,
1 teaspoonful chopped parsley,
½ teaspoonful sweet marjoram,
½ teaspoonful chopped onion,
2 teaspoonfuls melted butter,
1 tablespoonful browned flour,
½ lemon.

Wash the heart thoroughly and soak two hours in cold water slightly salted. Stuff with forcemeat made of bread crumbs, salt pork, salt, pepper, parsley, sweet marjoram, and onion. Moisten with melted butter. Fill the heart with this, sew up the opening, and tie firmly in a piece of cloth. Put in a saucepan, nearly cover with boiling water, and stew gently for three hours. The water should by this time be reduced to a pint. Take out the heart, remove cloth and dish.

Set aside a cup of gravy and thicken what is left in the saucepan with butter rubbed smooth in browned flour. Salt and pepper to taste. After taking from the fire, add the lemon juice, and pour over the meat. Carve in slices across the top.

Beef Kidney à la Baden-Baden (German recipe).

1 beef kidney,
2 tablespoonfuls butter,
1 tablespoonful salt,
1 teaspoonful pepper,
2 tablespoonfuls finely cut mushrooms,
Yolks 2 eggs,
1 cupful sweet cream.

Split the kidney in half; remove the white fat and all stringy parts; cut the kidney in four-inch squares. Place a saucepan over the fire, add the butter, and as soon as hot, put in the kidney; season with salt and pepper, stir, and cook five minutes; add the mushrooms, cook six minutes. Mix the yolks of the eggs with the cream; add to the kidneys; stir and beat till nearly boiling; add a little cayenne pepper, and serve.

Hungarian Kidney.

1 beef kidney,
1½ tablespoonfuls butter,
½ teaspoonful salt,
⅛ teaspoonful white pepper,
4 tablespoonfuls beef stock,
1 tablespoonful chopped mushrooms,
Yolks 2 eggs,
⅔ cupful milk.

Wash the kidney, and with a sharp knife cut off the outer part of each lobe, rejecting the purplish portion and tubes. In a saucepan put the butter, salt, and pepper. When hot, add the kidney; shake, and cook for five minutes; add the beef stock and mushrooms; simmer for ten minutes; mix the eggs and milk, add to the contents of the saucepan, stir until the sauce begins to thicken; then take from the fire, and serve in a hot dish.

Broiled Kidneys (Scotch recipe).

Cut the kidneys in slices, soak an hour in salted water, wipe them dry, dip in beaten egg, then in crumbs, and broil over a hot fire.

Frizzled Dried Beef.

Cover dried beef with hot water to take out the salt; throw this water away, and put the beef into a saucepan with a few tablespoonfuls boiling water; let it simmer; add a little butter, put the beef on slices of toast and pour a thin tomato sauce over them.

Fricassee of Oxtails.

Wash and clean 2 small oxtails, cut them in pieces two inches long, put them into stock, and simmer until tender. Do this the day before they are to be used. Dip them in beaten eggs and crumbs, season with salt and pepper, and fry light brown. For the sauce, thicken the stock the oxtails were cooked in with flour, pour over the meat, and serve.

Savory Oxtail (Mexican recipe).

2 oxtails,
8 onions,
Clove bruised garlic,
1 tablespoonful salt,
1 teaspoonful pepper,
1 carrot,
2 turnips,
2 sweet potatoes,
4 potatoes,
1 cupful Lima beans,
5 tablespoonfuls butter.

Cut oxtails into pieces, scald in boiling water and cool in cold water; place a saucepan with butter over the fire, add onions and garlic; cook three minutes; drain the meat and season with salt and pepper; stir, and cook six minutes; then cover with boiling water and cook two hours. Add carrot, turnips, sweet potatoes, onions, and potatoes; cover, and cook till nearly done; then add the Lima beans described below: Soak 1 cupful Lima beans in cold water over night, place them over the fire with cold water, add a little salt, and boil till tender; melt 1 tablespoonful butter in a small saucepan, stir, and cook two minutes; add 1 pint broth, cook a few minutes; then add to the stew; cook a few minutes, and serve. In place of butter, the Spanish people use oil.

Creamed Frankforts (German recipe).

1½ tablespoonfuls butter,
1½ tablespoonfuls flour,
1 cupful milk,
Pepper and salt,
4 Frankfort sausages.

Make a cream sauce of butter, flour, and milk. Season with salt and pepper. Skin Frankfort sausages, cut into pieces an inch long, and bring to a boiling point in the sauce.—STELLA A. DOWNING.

CHAPTER XLI

LEFT-OVERS OF BEEF

A ROAST of meat goes on the table in some households day after day in the same style, with the carver doing his best at each meal to leave it as sightly as possible. Its last appearance is calculated to take away the appetite of an entire family. The careful housewife, whose aim is economy and a healthful, attractive table, on the second day studies the cold roast with a keen eye. It comes from the refrigerator on a clean plate, and with it a bowl of brown gravy to which has been added every drop of the meat juices left in the platter on which the roast was served. Probably for luncheon she plans cold meat, cut in neat slices from the choicest bits of the roast, rare slices and well done, to appeal to various tastes. The meat is not cut until almost ready to put on the table. It is nicely arranged on a small platter with a garnish of parsley, cress, or cubes of aspic. She does not reheat the gravy to serve on cold plates. Worcestershire, tomato, or some cold homemade sauce makes a more fitting accompaniment. Then she carves the roast and plans for future meals. The tough outside pieces are laid away to be chopped, the fat to be rendered down for drippings, the tender bits of meat to be deviled, used for pie, ragout, or warmed up in the gravy, while the bones and gristle go to the soup kettle. Not a morsel of the meat is wasted in such a kitchen, and the daintily served, appetizing meals that follow the roast at intervals do not hint to the uninitiated of *réchauffés.*

To make warmed-up meats appetizing, there are various commodities which ought always to occupy a place in the pantry. Have a small jar of onion butter, a bottle of caramel, a glass can filled with browned flour, a jar of finely rolled bread crumbs, Worcestershire Sauce, celery salt, mace, bay leaves, a bottle of McIlhenny's Tabasco Sauce, cayenne, curry, catsup, canned mushrooms, paprika, kitchen bouquet, and horseradish. The secret of appetizing food is good flavoring, and a frequent varying of flavor has more to do with a tempting table than a large butcher bill.

Meat Minced with Poached Eggs.

2 cupfuls cold meat,
1 cupful gravy or stock,
Pepper,
Salt,
1 teaspoonful butter.

Chop a pint of meat coarsely, season well, heat in a cupful of left-over gravy or stock. Do not allow it to boil, merely to come to a simmer. Serve on diamonds of toast with a poached egg on top of each slice.

Bubble and Squeak.

4 cupfuls cold corned beef or beef left from a pot roast,
3 tablespoonfuls butter,
2 cupfuls cold boiled cabbage,
Salt and pepper.

Cut the cold meat into small strips and sauté them in a tablespoonful butter. Chop the cabbage and 2 tablespoonfuls butter in an omelet pan. Pepper and salt it, then stir over the fire till it begins to brown. Arrange on a hot platter as a border and into the middle put the hot meat. Serve with boiled potatoes.

Grilled Slices with Creole Sauce.

Cut from roast beef 6 slices of rarest meat, broil for five minutes over a clear fire, put on a hot plate, and serve with a sauce made as follows: In a saucepan put 2 tablespoonfuls butter, 2 tablespoonfuls chopped onion, and 1 tablespoonful chopped green pepper. Fry light brown, stirring constantly. Add 2 tablespoonfuls flour and stir to a paste; then put in a pint brown stock, 2 teaspoonfuls Worcestershire Sauce, a teaspoonful dry mustard, and 2 teaspoonfuls vinegar. Salt and pepper to taste. Cook over a slow fire, beating the sauce smooth. Add a teaspoonful chopped parsley and ½ can mushrooms cut in halves. Let the sauce come to a boil, then pour over the grilled meat.

Deviled Beef.

Take slices of rare roast beef and spread with butter on each side, as if you were buttering bread. Over this scrape a mustard made by mixing a tablespoonful vinegar with 3 tablespoonfuls mustard and a dash salt and pepper. Lay on a smoking-hot iron spider and fry till the slices begin to curl over.

Mock Terrapin.

6 hard-boiled eggs,
2 cupfuls brown stock,
4 cupfuls cold beef,
2 tablespoonfuls flour,
2 tablespoonfuls butter,
⅔ cupful cider.

Put the butter and flour in a saucepan, and when blended, pour in the soup, and beat till smooth. Let it come to the boil, then add the meat cut in inch pieces, and draw to a cooler place on the stove where it can simmer half an hour. If you cannot watch it, pour it in a double boiler, for the success of this dish depends on the steeping of the meat at just below boiling point. Season with salt, pepper, and the cider when the dish is ready to take from the fire. Boil 6 eggs hard and lay in cold water to make the shells come off easily. Pour the mock terrapin on a large platter, garnish with eggs sliced, split gherkins, and points of lemon.

Roast-Beef Pillau.

Cook for five minutes 1 tablespoonful butter and a small onion chopped fine. Before it begins to brown, add 2 cupfuls cold beef cut in fine dice, seasoned with ½ teaspoonful salt and ¼ teaspoonful pepper. Simmer slowly for ten minutes. While it is cooking, cover ½ cupful rice with cold water and set it over the fire to boil. When it has cooked for five minutes drain and let cold water run through it till every grain separates. Add the rice to the beef, pour over it 1½ cupfuls canned tomatoes. Pour in a cupful boiling water, and cook slowly till the rice is perfectly soft.

Beef Fricassee.

3 cupfuls cold beef cut in thin slices,
2 cupfuls brown stock,
3 tablespoonfuls butter,
2 tablespoonfuls flour,
⅛ teaspoonful pepper,
1 teaspoonful onion butter,
1 teaspoonful salt.

Season the meat with salt and pepper. Melt the butter in a spider, add the flour, and stir to a brown paste. Pour in the stock and beat smooth with a wire whisk. Season with pepper, salt, and onion butter, and cook ten minutes. Add the cold meat, simmer a few minutes, and serve on a deep platter with a border of rice, mashed potatoes, or points of toast.

Beef Ragout with Tomato.

3 cupfuls cold roast beef,
1½ cupfuls tomato pulp,
1 tablespoonful butter,
1 teaspoonful onion juice,
Salt and pepper.

Cut the beef into half-inch cubes, cook the tomatoes half an hour, and push through a potato ricer. Reheat the tomatoes, adding butter and seasonings, at the last the beef. Let it simply heat, not boil, then serve.

Creamed Corned Beef au Gratin.

2 tablespoonfuls flour,
2 tablespoonfuls butter,
1 cupful milk,
1 sliced onion,
1 stalk chopped celery,
Pepper,
2 cupfuls cold corned beef,
½ cupful buttered cracker crumbs.

Put the celery, cut in inch lengths, and the onion in the milk; scald in a double boiler. Strain when boiling and convert the milk into a white sauce with the butter and flour. When thick, add the corned beef, cut into small neat cubes, and a dash of pepper. Pour into a shallow dish, cover with buttered cracker crumbs, and brown. Garnish with blanched leaves of celery.

Beef Hash.

Use for beef hash the tough part of the roast thoroughly freed from fat and gristle. Chop and mix 1 cupful meat with 2 cupfuls chopped potatoes. In an iron spider put 2 tablespoonfuls butter and ½ cupful stock, or a spoon of gravy added to enough hot water to half fill a cup. Boil up, then add the meat and potatoes seasoned with pepper and salt. Stir occasionally with a fork. Let the water evaporate from the hash, leaving it dry but not pasty.

Fatherland Farm Meat Loaf.

Butter a long, narrow cake tin and line with cold mashed potatoes, smoothing with a spatula into a layer an inch thick. Inside this put a filling of roast beef, chopped coarsely, seasoned with pepper, salt, and a few drops of onion juice, and moistened with gravy. Smooth this filling till within one inch of the top of the tin, and cover with mashed potatoes. Bake in a hot oven for half an hour and turn out on a long platter. It will look like a finely crusted loaf, and may be cut in neat slices. This makes a delicious luncheon or tea dish.—Mrs. S. B. Forbes.

Papas Rellenas (Cuban recipe).

3 large potatoes,
1 cupful cold roast beef,
1 tablespoonful butter,
2 tablespoonfuls cooked tomato,
2 eggs,
1 tablespoonful flour,
3 olives,
Pepper, salt, cayenne.

Boil the potatoes, and cut in halves lengthwise. Scoop out the inside with a spoon, leaving the potato shell half an inch thick. Make a "piccadillo" to stuff them with. Chop the beef, put it in a spider with the butter and tomato. Cook till the mixture begins to look dry, add 1 well-beaten egg, a dust cayenne, salt, and pepper and 3 olives chopped. Stuff the potato halves with this mixture. Beat 1 egg light, add 1 teaspoonful flour, and in this batter dip the half potatoes. Fry in boiling lard as you would croquettes.

The Remains of a Boiled Dinner.

Winter squash can be served in a pie, sifting and seasoning it as if boiled for the purpose. Cold cabbage may be put into hot spiced vinegar, served cold with vinegar, or heated with a little butter and pepper, salt, if needed, and just a suspicion of vinegar. Cut it fine, and heat thoroughly. Beets make good pickles. Turnips, carrots, and parsnips can be warmed up. A favorite dish with many people is "red-flannel hash," plain hash containing a little chopped beet. Look over the meat, cutting out all the gristle and soft fat. Chop it fine with some of the hard fat. Mince potatoes which have been boiled in pot liquor. Use three times as much potatoes as meat. Chop with the potatoes a small quantity of the cabbage and some of the beets: For 2 quarts potatoes use ½ pint cabbage and 1 large beet. Mix thoroughly with the meat. Pour some milk into a frying pan and turn in the hash, using enough to moisten thoroughly. Add 2 tablespoonfuls butter and season with pepper and salt if necessary. Be sure it is heated through. Serve with brown bread and pickles.—H. ANNETTE POOLE.

Tongue Sandwiches.

1 cupful finely chopped tongue,
1 teaspoonful made mustard,
1 tablespoonful soft butter,
¼ teaspoonful paprika,
Yolk 1 hard-boiled egg,
Juice ½ lemon,
Dash nutmeg.

Chop the tongue fine, and mix thoroughly with the other ingredients. Spread between thin slices of bread.

Beef Rissoles.

Roll pie crust as thin as possible and cut into rounds with a large biscuit cutter. Mince cold beef or steak, season with salt and paprika, and moisten with stock or gravy to make the meat stick together. Put a spoonful of this mixture into each round of paste, pinching the edges together carefully so that not a particle of the meat may escape. Brush egg over the outside, and fry like doughnuts in deep lard. They will take eight minutes to brown. Drain on thick paper, and serve hot in a folded napkin.

CHAPTER XLII

LAMB AND MUTTON

Mutton Stew (Irish recipe).

1½ pounds neck mutton,
2 quarts potatoes,
4 onions,
2 cupfuls boiling water,
Pepper and salt.

Cut the mutton in pieces, and put in saucepan with the onions cut in rings, also the hot water and salt. Let it boil, then simmer gently for two hours. Parboil the potatoes, cut them in halves, put in the saucepan with the meat, about half an hour before it is done. In serving, put the potatoes round the dish, with the meat and onions in the center, and pour the gravy over.

Roast Lamb.

Wipe the meat with a damp towel, place in a baking pan, dredge with pepper, salt, and flour. Add a cupful boiling water and a teaspoonful salt to the pan. Baste every ten minutes, and bake fifteen minutes to the pound in a hot oven. When done set the meat on a platter, and serve with mint sauce and green peas.

Boiled Leg of Lamb.

Choose a hind leg, put into a kettle, and cover with boiling water. Set over the fire, let come to a boil, pour in a pint cold water and simmer gently until done. Take the meat up on a hot dish, and serve with caper sauce.

Stuffed Shoulder of Lamb.

Bone a shoulder of lamb, leave the knuckle, and fill the cavity with rich bread stuffing; tie neatly in shape and wrap in a buttered paper. Lay in a deep pan with 4 tablespoonfuls butter, a sliced carrot and turnip, an onion stuck with cloves, and a bunch sweet herbs. Pour on sufficient stock to cover the bottom of the pan. Set over a slow fire and simmer gently; baste every ten minutes. When nearly done, lift from the pan, remove the paper; brush the meat with melted glaze and set in the oven to brown. Take up the shoulder on a heated dish. Strain the gravy, and pour around it. Garnish with *purée* of green peas, and serve with maitre d'hôtel sauce.—Eliza Parker.

Pressed Lamb.

Put a shoulder of lamb on to boil, with water to cover; when tender, season with salt and pepper. Boil until tender, when the juice will be nearly boiled out. Chop the meat, and season. Put it in a bowl with a plate on top and press out all the juice; set in a cool place to harden. Slice thin when serving. Soup can be made of the broth.

Broiled Breast of Lamb.

Trim a breast of lamb and put it in a saucepan, cover with stock, add a bunch sweet herbs, a slice onion, a piece mace, and 2 or 3 cloves; simmer gently until tender. Take up, dredge with salt and pepper, brush over with beaten egg and grated cracker, and broil over a clear fire until brown on both sides. Take up on a heated dish, pour over a little melted butter and garnish with asparagus tips.

Imitation Barbecue of Mutton.

Remove the skin from a leg of mutton, sprinkle with salt, and dredge with flour. Place in the pan and roast. Allow the meat twenty minutes to the pound. One hour before serving, prepare the following mixture:

- $\frac{1}{3}$ cupful Worcestershire Sauce,
- $\frac{1}{3}$ cupful tomato catsup,
- $\frac{1}{3}$ cupful vinegar,
- $\frac{1}{4}$ teaspoonful pepper,
- 2 teaspoonfuls mustard.

Stick the meat all over with a sharp-pointed knife, pull the cuts open and fill with this hot mixture. Baste with the liquor which gathers in the pan, and pour it over the meat before sending it to the table.

Army Stew.

- 1 tablespoonful chopped parsley,
- 2 pounds forequarter lamb,
- 1 teaspoonful pepper,
- 1 tablespoonful salt,
- 4 onions,
- 2 turnips,
- 2 carrots,
- 4 potatoes,
- $\frac{1}{2}$ cupful milk,
- 2 teaspoonfuls Calumet baking powder,
- 1 egg,
- 2 cupfuls flour.

Cut lamb in pieces, place in a saucepan, cover with boiling water, cook two minutes, remove, drain and plunge into cold water, drain and return the meat to the saucepan. Cover again with boiling water, add salt, pepper, and onions, boil an hour and a half, add turnips, peeled and cut into quarters, carrots and potatoes, cut into quarters; boil till done. Ten minutes before serving, mix flour with baking powder, egg and milk, cut with teaspoonful small portions from the mixture and drop them in the stew; cover, and cook five minutes; then remove the saucepan to side of stove, where it stops boiling, otherwise the dumplings will become heavy; add parsley, and serve.

Haricot Mutton (English recipe).

- $1\frac{1}{2}$ pounds neck mutton,
- 1 onion,
- 1 carrot,
- 1 turnip,
- 4 tablespoonfuls butter,
- 2 tablespoonfuls flour,
- Pepper and salt to taste,
- 2 cupfuls hot water.

Divide the meat into small joints, and cut the vegetables in small square pieces. Put the butter in a saucepan, add the meat, and fry brown with the onions. Pour off the fat, add the vegetables, flour, water, and a little salt. Let it boil; then simmer gently from one and a half to two hours. In serving, put the meat on a hot dish, pile the vegetables on top, and pour the gravy round about.

Breaded Chops.

- 4 loin chops,
- 1 egg,
- 1 cupful bread crumbs,
- 1 teaspoonful salt,
- Dash pepper,
- 1 tablespoonful chopped parsley.

Cut chops three quarters of an inch thick. Dip each in beaten egg and lay on a meat board. Mix bread crumbs with salt and pepper, minced parsley, and a little grated nutmeg. Roll the chops in the bread crumbs and fry in boiling fat until light brown. Garnish with slices of lemon and sprigs of parsley.

Curry of Lamb (Southern recipe).

- Breast lamb,
- 2 onions,
- 1 carrot,
- Bunch parsley,
- 1 bay leaf,
- 4 tablespoonfuls butter,
- 3 tablespoonfuls curry powder,
- 2 dozen sweet potatoes,
- 2 tablespoonfuls flour,
- 3 tablespoonfuls grated cocoanut,
- 3 dashes McIlhenny's Tabasco Sauce.

Cut lamb in inch squares, trim, and put on fire with enough water to cover; add onion, carrot, parsley, and bay leaf; cook half an hour. Prepare butter in saucepan with curry powder, simmer five minutes, add flour, moisten with stock of lamb strained; add pieces of lamb, also sweet potatoes, cocoanut, salt, and tabasco. Cook fifteen minutes, and serve with garnishing of boiled rice. Chicken, veal, or mutton may be prepared in the same way.

Lamb Chops à la Boulangère (French recipe).

10 or 12 cutlets,
2 tablespoonfuls butter,
½ cupful cream,
Salt, pepper, and cayenne,
1 tablespoonful chopped chervil,
1 lemon.

Trim the cutlets, season with salt, pepper, and a little cayenne, dip in olive oil, then in flour. Broil over a slow fire. While they are cooking, put cream in a stewpan, and when boiling add butter, chervil, the juice of ½ lemon, and a little pepper and salt; stir quickly till it forms a smooth sauce; pour it over the cutlets when done, and serve quickly. Fillets of veal or rabbit are good cooked in this way.

Mutton Chops à la Cleveland.

8 mutton chops,
3 tablespoonfuls sweet oil,
3 tablespoonfuls butter,
1 onion,
1 pint mushrooms,
½ pint strained tomatoes,
Dash McIlhenny's Tabasco Sauce,
Salt,
Chopped parsley.

Fry the chops in the oil and butter. Put them on a hot platter while you make the sauce. Chop the onion and mushrooms fine; put them in a saucepan with a little butter and fry until brown. Add the tomatoes, and boil five minutes; add the tabasco, salt, pepper, and parsley. Lay the chops in a circle; pour the sauce in the center, and garnish with points of toast.

Broiled Lamb Chops.

Have the chops cut thick, dust with salt and pepper; broil over a quick fire; pile neatly on a hot platter, and put a small bit of butter on each one.

Stuffed Mutton Chops.

10 mutton chops,
1 tablespoonful butter,
1 tablespoonful chopped onion,
½ cupful chopped mushrooms,
1 teaspoonful salt,
Pinch pepper,
1 tablespoonful flour,
2 tablespoonfuls stock.

Trim the chops, which have been cut very thick. With a sharp knife split each chop in two, without separating the meat from the bone. Put the butter in a pan, add the onion, and cook five minutes; add to this the chopped mushrooms, salt, and pepper, and cook five minutes longer. Add the flour and stock. Cook for a few minutes; stuff each chop with this mixture after it has cooled; press them tightly together, and broil.

a, Brown-Bread or Pudding Mold; b, Waffle Iron; c, Patty Pans.

Mutton Cutlets with Mushrooms.

Take the bones from mutton chops, and use the round, lean portions. Brush with melted butter and broil. Serve them on rounds of toasted bread, with mushroom sauce poured over. Sauce.—Peel 1 pint mushrooms, cut in pieces, season, and cook in cream sauce for ten minutes.

Lamb Fricassee (German recipe).

2 breasts lamb,
2 ounces butter,
2 tablespoonfuls chopped onion,
2 teaspoonfuls salt,
½ tablespoonful butter,
2 tablespoonfuls flour.

Dip the lamb breasts into boiling water, then instantly into cold water; cut the meat into two-inch pieces. Melt the butter in a saucepan, add the onions, and cook five minutes without browning; season the meat with the salt; add it to the saucepan; cook ten minutes, cover with boiling water, put on the lid, and cook until done. Shortly before serving, melt ½ tablespoonful butter, add the flour, stir, and cook a few minutes; add it to the fricassee, and boil a few minutes longer.—Gesine Lemcke.

Deviled Kidneys (German recipe).

6 lamb kidneys,
1 ounce butter,
2 tablespoonfuls chopped onions,
½ bruised clove garlic,
1 teaspoonful salt,
1 cupful stock,
Yolks 3 eggs,
1 teaspoonful chopped parsley,
Cayenne pepper.

Split the kidneys, remove the white part in center and chop fine. Place the butter in a saucepan, add the onions, and cook three minutes; add the kidneys and salt; stir, and cook three minutes; then add the stock, and cook three minutes longer. Remove from the fire, add the eggs, parsley, and a little pepper. Fill this mixture into 6 ramequins, sprinkle over each ½ tablespoonful fresh grated bread crumbs and a little melted butter. Place the ramequins in a tin pan, set it in a hot oven, and bake brown.—Gesine Lemcke.

Kidneys à la Maître d'hôtel (French recipe).

Split and cut in two, lengthwise, lamb's kidneys. Run a skewer through to keep them flat. Dip in melted butter and fine bread crumbs; season with salt and pepper. Broil five minutes. Serve with maître d'hôtel butter.

Lamb-Heart Stew (French recipe).

3 lambs' hearts,
1 tablespoonful butter,
½ peeled lemon,
½ bay leaf,
Salt,
Pepper.

Wash the hearts and slice, cutting across the grain of the meat. Dry slightly and dust with flour. Put the butter in a stewpan and when hot add the meat; stir and cook about ten minutes. Add enough water to nearly cover the meat, the lemon cut in slices, and bay leaf. Cover the kettle, and cook gently half an hour, stirring often and adding more water, if needed; add salt and pepper; remove the bay leaf and lemon, thicken, and serve.

Lamb's Liver Curried.

1 lamb's liver,
1 onion,
Few slices pork,
½ teaspoonful curry powder.

Cut the lamb's liver in slices, soak in salted water for five minutes, take from the water, and dry in a cloth. Slice the onion and fry with pork. Take out the pork and fry the liver. Brown well, add the curry powder to the sauce, stir smooth, and serve.

CHAPTER XLIII

LAMB LEFT-OVERS

Lamb can be used in nearly every recipe given for beef. It is especially good for croquettes and makes a savory stew. Save every drop of gravy or liquid from the platter when setting a roast of lamb away. It requires all the enriching it can have and always plenty of seasoning.

Potatoes with Lamb Stuffing.

8 large baked potatoes,
1 cupful cold chopped lamb,
4 tablespoonfuls chopped ham,
½ cupful thin white sauce,
2 tablespoonfuls cream,
White 1 egg,
Salt and pepper.

Bake 8 large, perfect potatoes. While they are cooking, chop the lamb and ham, mix lightly together, add the seasonings, and moisten with white sauce. When the potatoes are soft, cut a thin slice from the end of each and scoop out the inside. Put it at once through a potato ricer and set away to keep warm. Fill the potato skins almost to the top with the meat mixture. Add to a cup of the mashed potato the cream and beaten white of the egg. Pepper and salt, and on the top of each potato put a spoonful, leaving it in a small, rocky mound. Bake till the top is a delicate brown. Serve the potatoes piled on their ends in a shallow dish, with a plentiful garnish of parsley.

Mound of Lamb with Peas.

2 cupfuls cold chopped lamb,
1 small onion,
1 cupful cold potatoes,
Pepper and salt,
3 tablespoonfuls stock,
¾ cupful buttered crumbs,
1 cupful green peas.

Mix lightly with a fork the chopped meat, potato, onion, and seasonings. Heap it in a mound in the middle of a shallow baking dish. Cover with buttered crumbs and bake till brown. When ready to serve, pour around it a cup of green peas drained and seasoned.

Lamb-and-Rice Croquettes.

2 cupfuls chopped lamb,
1 cupful cold rice,
1 tablespoonful lemon juice,
1 tablespoonful chopped parsley,
Pepper and salt,
1 cupful white sauce.

Mix the lamb and rice with the seasonings and stir into a hot, thick, white sauce. Cool. Roll into cone-shaped croquettes. Flour, egg, and crumb. Fry in deep fat. Garnish with parsley.

Lamb in Savory Stew.

1½ cupfuls cold lamb,
4 tablespoonfuls butter,
1 tablespoonful flour,
½ onion,
1 cupful gravy or brown stock,
2 cucumber pickles,
Pepper, salt, cayenne.

Into a granite saucepan put the butter, onion, and flour, and rub to a paste. When it grows light brown, add the gravy or stock, salt and pepper, and allow to simmer for two minutes. Cut the pickles in small pieces, add to the sauce and the lamb cut in neat slices. Let it heat through, then serve in a deep platter surrounded by a ring of hot boiled rice or mashed potatoes.

CHAPTER XLIV

VEAL

Roast Breast of Veal.

1 cupful stale bread,
3 tablespoonfuls butter,
2 tablespoonfuls minced onion,
½ teaspoonful salt,
½ teaspoonful thyme,
1 egg,
Small breast veal (about 3 pounds),
½ tablespoonful cornstarch.

Soak stale bread in cold water; when soft, put it in a towel, press out the water, place butter with minced onion over the fire, stir and cook five minutes without browning, then add the bread, stir five minutes longer, season with salt, pepper, thyme, and 1 egg, and mix. Have the butcher prepare the veal for filling, wash and wipe the meat dry, season inside and out with 1 tablespoonful salt and ½ teaspoonful pepper, then stuff the breast, sew it up, lay the meat in a roasting pan, with slices of pork under it, spread over with butter, and lay a few slices of pork on top. Place the pan in hot oven, roast until the meat becomes light brown, basting frequently with its own gravy, add 1 cupful boiling water, roast about two hours longer, basting frequently until done; add more water should the gravy brown too much. Ten minutes before serving, lay the meat on a platter, remove the fat from the gravy, mix cornstarch with ½ cupful cold water, add to it the sauce, stir, and cook three minutes, then strain, pour a little of the sauce over the meat, and serve the remainder in a gravy boat.

Veal Roasted with Mushrooms.

Bone a loin of veal. Remove the kidneys and fat, and lay them, after splitting in two, inside the loin. Season inside with pepper and salt, and fold over the flap to inclose the kidneys. Roll and tie securely with string, making the roast oblong shape. Cover the bottom of the roasting pan with thin slices of fat pork, a sliced onion, and chopped parsley. Lay the meat on top, and moisten with a little cream. Have the oven rather slow at first, basting the veal frequently with a little cream. When nearly done, sprinkle with fine bread crumbs, moisten with melted butter, and let it brown. Take out the veal, untie, sprinkle Parmesan cheese over it, set in a very hot oven, surround with broiled mushrooms, and pour over the strained liquid left in the roasting pan.

Veal Savory (French recipe).

1½ pounds ham,
3 pounds raw veal,
6 hard-boiled eggs,
1 tablespoonful butter,
1 tablespoonful flour.

Cut the veal and ham into small pieces. Cut eggs in slices, lay part of them in the bottom of a well-buttered earthenware dish, sprinkle with minced parsley, then put in a layer of veal and ham, with salt and pepper to season. Proceed with these alternate layers until all is used, then add just enough water to cover it, with butter rolled in flour and divided into tiny portions dotted over the top. Tie a buttered paper over the dish, and bake one hour in a hot oven. Remove the paper, lay a plate over the meat with a weight to keep it in place, and let it remain another hour in a slow oven. When cold, turn out and garnish with small lettuce leaves filled with cold peas dressed with a little mayonnaise.

Veal Loaf.

4 pounds raw lean veal,
¼ pound ham,
¼ pound salt pork,
1 cupful stale bread crumbs,
¼ cupful melted butter,
1 teaspoonful salt,
1 teaspoonful paprika,
1 teaspoonful onion juice,
¼ teaspoonful allspice,
¼ teaspoonful nutmeg,
¼ teaspoonful cloves,
1 lemon, juice and rind,
2 eggs.

Chop very fine the veal, ham, and salt pork. Mix with meat the bread crumbs soaked in milk, butter, seasonings, and well-beaten eggs. Press into a buttered bread pan, cover the top with lardoons of salt pork; bake one hour. Cut when cold into thin slices.

Curried Veal Cutlets.

Trim cutlets into uniform shape and size; dip in the beaten yolks of eggs, and cover with grated bread crumbs that have been mixed with 2 tablespoonfuls curry powder and a tablespoonful salt. Fry in butter till brown. Take out of the spider, and in it melt and brown a little butter and flour, add a cupful water, and pour over the cutlets.

Veal Hearts (Spanish recipe).

4 slices bacon,
1 sliced onion,
4 veal hearts,
1 cupful stock,
½ minced pimento,
1 teaspoonful salt,
½ bay leaf.

Fry bacon to a crisp, remove from the spider, and crisp the sliced onion in the hot fat. Trim and wash hearts, slice them, roll in flour, and fry in hot fat. Add to the fat in the pan the stock, pimento, salt, and bay leaf. Pour the mixture over the hearts, and cook two hours. Five minutes before serving, add the bacon.

Brown Stew.

2 pounds veal,
2 tablespoonfuls butter,
2 tablespoonfuls flour,
1 pint water,
1 teaspoonful salt,
Dash pepper,
Slice onion,
1 teaspoonful kitchen bouquet.
1 bay leaf.

Cut the veal into cubes and roll in flour. Put 2 tablespoonfuls butter into a pan; when hot, add the meat, and stir constantly until browned. Dust with the flour, mix, add the water; stir, add the salt and pepper, onion, kitchen bouquet, and bay leaf. Cover, and simmer gently for an hour.

Veal Cutlets.

Divide the cutlet into pieces about four inches square; dip in egg, then in crumbs; fry for five minutes. Add ½ cupful boiling water, and let simmer for an hour. Dish, and serve with bits of lemon.

Ragout of Veal.

Cut the meat in thin slices, put 2 tablespoonfuls butter in a pan, dredge with flour, and fry light brown. Take out the meat and put into the pan a cupful cold stock or gravy, season with salt and pepper and a tablespoonful tomato catsup. Lay a few slices of cold ham in the gravy, also the veal. Serve very hot.

Veal Oysters.

Cut 1½ pounds veal cutlets into pieces the size of large oysters; season with 1 tablespoonful salt, dust with flour, dip into beaten egg, roll in bread crumbs, and fry light brown on both sides. Serve on a hot dish; garnish with lemon quarters.

Veal Birds (English recipe).

Cut thin slices of veal into pieces two and a half by four inches. Chop the trimmings of the meat fine with one small slice of fat salt pork and half as much cracker crumbs as there is meat. Season highly with salt, cayenne, and onion juice, moisten with beaten egg and a little hot water. Spread each slice of veal with this mixture and roll tightly; fasten with a toothpick. Dredge with flour, pepper, and salt, and fry slowly in hot butter. Add ½ cupful cream, and simmer twenty minutes. Remove the fastenings, put the birds on toast, pour the cream over them, garnish with points of lemon, and serve.

Wiener Schnitzel (German recipe).

2 pounds veal steak,
1 egg,
2 tablespoonfuls butter,
1 tablespoonful lard,
½ teaspoonful capers,
6 anchovies,
Lemon.

Cut the veal in slices half an inch thick and three inches square; pare the corners round; beat lightly to flatten; season with salt and dust with flour; dip each cutlet in egg, cover with fine crumbs, and pat smooth with a knife. Fifteen minutes before serving, place a pan with the butter and lard over the fire; as soon as hot, put in the cutlets, fry light brown. Arrange on a warm dish; lay in the center of each schnitzel ½ teaspoonful capers. Soak the anchovies in cold water; remove the skin and bones; divide in halves, roll them up; place 2 of these rolls on each schnitzel with ¼ lemon cut in two. Garnish with water cress or parsley, and serve.

Smothered Veal.

Place in the bottom of a baking pan 2 slices salt pork cut fine, a layer of sliced potatoes, a little chopped onion, a layer of finely chopped uncooked veal, pepper, and salt. Continue until the dish is full. Spread over the top bits of butter. Bake forty-five minutes.

Veal Stew.

3 pounds breast veal,
3 tablespoonfuls butter,
2 tablespoonfuls flour,
Bunch parsley,
2 carrots,
2 cupfuls cooked green peas.

Cut up the veal and fry light brown in a pan with the butter; drain off most of the butter; sprinkle the flour over the meat; mix well and fry a little longer, add 1 pint water and let boil; take out the meat, put it in another pan, strain the sauce over it. Add the parsley chopped fine, carrots cut fine, and peas. Boil up again, and serve.

Veal Collops (Scotch recipe).

1½ pounds veal,
2 tablespoonfuls butter,
1 tablespoonful chopped onion,
2 cupfuls stock,
1 can green peas,
Salt and pepper.

Trim off skin and fat from the veal and put through a meat chopper. Melt the butter and brown the onion, then add the stock; season to taste and simmer five minutes. Fry the chopped raw meat in a spider. Stir until the butter is absorbed; strain over it the stock in the saucepan; cover, simmer for twenty minutes, stirring occasionally. Place the peas in a saucepan with butter, salt, and pepper, and heat. When the meat has absorbed the liquor, turn it into the center of a hot platter; sprinkle with finely chopped parsley and surround with the peas.

Calves' Tongue with Tomato Sauce.

2 calves' tongues,
1 tablespoonful flour,
1 cupful water,
4 tablespoonfuls vinegar,
1 bunch parsley,
1 onion,
3 cloves.

Soak the tongues in warm water an hour; drain and parboil, cool, pare, and scrape off the white skin. Put the flour in a saucepan, stir into it gradually the water. When it boils, add the tongues with vinegar, parsley, onion, and cloves. Cover and cook slowly an hour. Serve with tomato sauce.

Stewed Calf's Liver.

1 calf's liver,
1 turnip,
1 carrot,
1 stalk celery,
1 onion,
1 tablespoonful butter,
1 tablespoonful browned flour.

Wash and cut the liver in slices. In a saucepan put the turnip, carrot, celery, and onion (all sliced); lay the liver on top of the vegetables; sprinkle salt and pepper over it, and pour on a pint boiling water; cover, and let stew until the liver is tender. When done, take out the liver and put on a hot platter; thicken the gravy with butter and flour; strain, and pour over the meat.

Broiled Liver.

Cut calf's liver into half inch slices, cover with boiling water, let stand five or six minutes, drain, and wipe dry. Sprinkle with salt and pepper and broil in a greased broiler five minutes. Put on a hot platter and spread with bits of butter. Serve very hot.

Braised Calf's Liver.

1 calf's liver,
1 onion,
2 ounces bacon,
3 tablespoonfuls flour,
1 sliced carrot,
½ bay leaf,
1 teaspoonful salt,
1 cupful stock,
½ cupful strained tomatoes.

In the liver make many small slits with a paring knife and insert slices of onion and bits of sliced bacon. Heat in a spider 3 tablespoonfuls bacon drippings and add flour to the fat. Brown the flour in the fat, then add the liver, and roll it on all sides until it is seared in the fat and covered with fat and flour. Place the liver in the heated casserole, add carrot, bay leaf, salt, stock, and tomatoes. Bake two hours and a half.

Calf's Liver and Bacon.

Sauté calf's liver in bacon fat, and when done, make a gravy from it with flour and hot water. Heat a pan, and drop in slices of bacon. If the pan is very hot, they will curl into rolls and brown in a few minutes. Arrange the liver, and garnish with parsley.

Veal Kidney Omelet.

1 veal kidney,
1 tablespoonful butter,
½ teaspoonful salt,
Dash pepper,
4 eggs,
1 tablespoonful warm water.

Remove the fat and tubes from a kidney and chop fine. Place in a frying pan with butter, salt, and pepper, and shake over a hot fire until the meat is golden brown. Beat the eggs without separating; add the warm water. Heat the butter in a spider, pour in the eggs, and shake over the fire till the mixture begins to set. Draw back—so the omelet may set without burning; turn the cooked kidney over the center, fold up, and serve on a hot platter.

Veal Kidneys Deviled.

Split in half 3 veal kidneys and take out the fibrous parts. Spread both sides with a mayonnaise, season highly, roll in bread crumbs, dip in melted butter, and broil over a hot fire. Serve at once.

Fried Sweetbreads.

1 pair sweetbreads,
1 tablespoonful butter,
1 tablespoonful flour,
1 cupful milk,
Salt and pepper.

Parboil the sweetbreads; when cold, dip them in beaten egg and cracker crumbs, sprinkle salt over them, and fry in hot fat. Stir together the butter and flour, then set the pan back a little and add gradually the milk; stir until smooth. Season with salt and pepper, finely chopped celery, and cook about two minutes. Strain the sauce over the sweetbreads.

Sweetbread Croquettes.

2 sweetbreads,
1 can mushrooms,
1 tablespoonful flour,
1 tablespoonful butter,
½ cupful cream,
2 yolks eggs.

Parboil the sweetbreads and cut them in small pieces; also cut the mushrooms. Put into a saucepan the flour and butter, and when made smooth, add the cream; heat, then add the sweetbreads and mushrooms.

Sweetbreads à la Newburg.

1 cupful cream,
1½ cupfuls sweetbreads,
Yolks 3 eggs,
½ teaspoonful salt,
Few grains cayenne.

Heat the cream; add the sweetbreads parboiled and cut in cubes. Beat the yolks of the eggs; add the salt and cayenne, and stir into the cream. Stir until thickened slightly; serve at once.

Sweetbread Fritters.

Parboil sweetbreads, cut in small pieces, season with salt, pepper, and chopped parsley; dip in fritter batter and fry in deep fat.

CHAPTER XLV

VEAL LEFT-OVERS

Veal is the flesh of an immature creature, and will not keep fresh as long as that of an older animal. A left-over of beef may be kept a day or two before serving again; it is better to see to the condition of veal twenty-four hours after cooking, especially in hot weather, and serve it as soon as convenient. Veal has little flavor, and requires considerable seasoning. Brown sauce is the general accompaniment to veal at the first cooking. Save every spoonful of sauce to use with it when warming over. If there is no brown gravy, white sauce may take its place. Veal makes an excellent ragout, seasoned with onion juice and cayenne, minced and poured on toast for breakfast; in a salad or croquettes, it tastes very much like chicken. Add to it a few mushrooms or 2 or 3 spoonfuls left-over sweetbreads, and you have delicious rissoles. It is excellent combined with oysters in a scallop. When preparing it for a salad, be careful to reject all morsels of gristle as well as brown or hard meat. One-half measure each of cold veal and finely chopped white cabbage is delicious with a horse-radish dressing. Marinate for two hours, else you will find the salad a tasteless one.

Nut Balls.

- 1 cupful cold chopped veal,
- 12 chopped blanched almonds,
- ½ teaspoonful salt,
- 1 egg,
- Pepper,
- Paprika,
- 1 cupful tomato sauce.

Mix the meat, almonds, and seasoning, and moisten with the well-beaten egg. Roll into balls the size of a walnut and set in a baking pan. Pour over them the hot tomato sauce. Cook in a hot oven for twenty minutes. Serve on a platter garnished with water cress.

Windermere Croquettes (English recipe).

- 1½ cupfuls milk,
- 1½ tablespoonfuls butter,
- 3 tablespoonfuls flour,
- 1 teaspoonful salt,
- Dash cayenne,
- 2 cupfuls cold chopped veal,
- 1 tablespoonful chopped parsley,
- ½ cupful cold rice,
- Yolks 3 hard-boiled eggs.

Make a white sauce from the milk, flour, butter, and seasonings. To 1 cupful sauce add the chopped meat and parsley. Spread on a plate to cool. Into the ½ cupful sauce beat the rice and the yolks of the eggs pushed through a potato ricer. Spread on a plate to cool. Take a tablespoonful meat mixture and flatten into a cake. Inside this put a teaspoonful rice mixture rolled in a tiny ball. Wrap the meat around it till covered. Roll in flour, egg, crumbs, and fry in deep fat. Pile cannon-ball fashion on a platter. Garnish with parsley.—Mary Kendall.

Calf's Liver Terrapin with Mushrooms.

- 2 cupfuls cold liver,
- 1 cupful stock,
- 2 tablespoonfuls butter,
- 3 eggs,
- ¼ teaspoonful salt,

¼ teaspoonful paprika,
¼ teaspoonful kitchen bouquet,
½ teaspoonful mustard,
2 drops McIlhenny's Tabasco Sauce,
1 cupful mushrooms,
2 truffles.

Boil the eggs hard. Rub the yolks smooth with the butter, salt, paprika, kitchen bouquet, mustard, and tabasco. Add the liver cut in small pieces and the stock. Cook five minutes, add the mushrooms and truffles, and serve garnished with whites of eggs cut in rings.

Veal Omelet.

If you have a cupful of cold roast veal left over, chop it fine, season with pepper, salt, and a dash of paprika; then tuck it between the folds of an omelet. Pour over it before sending to the table a cup of hot, well-seasoned tomato sauce.

CHAPTER XLVI

PORK

Roast Pork.

SELECT a piece of loin from a young pig, 3 pounds in weight; score the rind across one eighth of an inch apart, season with ½ tablespoonful salt and ¼ teaspoonful pepper; lay the pork in a roasting pan, place it in a medium hot oven, roast till light brown, basting with its own gravy; then add ½ cupful boiling water; continue to roast and baste till nearly done, turn the meat over, so the rind lies in the gravy, roast ten minutes, turn it again, so the rind is on the top; let it remain five minutes longer in the oven, transfer to a hot dish, free the gravy from fat, mix 1 teaspoonful cornstarch with ½ gill cold water, add it to the gravy, stir two minutes, add sufficient boiling water to make creamy sauce, strain, and serve with the meat.

Pork Tenderloins with Sweet Potatoes.

Wipe tenderloins, put in a dripping pan and brown quickly in a hot oven; then sprinkle with salt and pepper, and bake forty-five minutes, basting every fifteen minutes.

Pare six potatoes and parboil ten minutes, drain, put in pan with meat, and cook until soft, basting when basting meat.—FANNIE M. FARMER.

Pork Chops, Sauce Robert.

Take 8 rib chops, trim them neatly; have ready some finely chopped onion and parsley; sprinkle each chop on both sides with this, also salt and pepper, and beat lightly with a broad knife, to make all adhere. Dip each one into slightly beaten egg, then roll into fine bread crumbs; let stand five minutes; dip into melted butter, and roll again in the crumbs. Arrange in a wire broiler and broil seven minutes over a clear fire. Chop fine 2 large onions, place in a stewpan with 1 tablespoonful butter, and cook slowly until well colored; add 1 tablespoonful flour, stir, and brown again, add slowly 1½ cupfuls beef stock and 2 tablespoonfuls vinegar. When smooth and thick, simmer until reduced to 1 cupful, add 1 teaspoonful mixed mustard, salt, and pepper to taste. Pour this around the chops as they are dished.

Bobble Gash (German recipe).

1 pound lean pork,
1 pound veal,
1 tablespoonful lard,
3 onions,
5 potatoes,
1 cupful cream,
1 tablespoonful flour.

Cut the pork and veal in small pieces. Put the lard in a kettle; when hot, add the onions sliced. As they commence to brown, drop in the meat and stir constantly until brown; then cover with water and boil three fourths of an hour. Season with salt and pepper. Pare and cut in small dice the potatoes; when boiled, add them to the meat with the cream. Thicken with flour.

Boston Pork and Beans.

Pick over and wash a quart of dried beans the night before you bake them. Put them to soak in cold water. In the morning, pour off the water, put them in a kettle, then cover with plenty of cold water, and set to boil. Cook till perfectly tender; turn off the bean water; put them into a pot; score in lines the rind of a piece of pork and bury it, all but the surface of the rind, in the middle of the beans. Add enough boiling water to the beans to cover. Stir in 2 tablespoonfuls molasses and a teaspoonful fresh mustard. Cover the pot and put in the oven. Bake moderately, but steadily, five hours. If the water wastes away so as to be below the surface of the beans, supply enough just to cover them. Toward the end of the time, it may be allowed to dry down enough to permit the pork to brown. Uncover the pot for a little while for this purpose.

Roast Pig.

A pig for roasting should not weigh over 6 or 7 pounds after being cleaned. When it has been prepared by the butcher, lay it in cold water for fifteen minutes, then wipe dry, inside and out. Make a stuffing as for a turkey, adding two beaten eggs. Stuff the pig to his original size and shape. Sew him up, bend his fore legs backward, his back legs forward under him, and skewer into shape. Dredge with flour and set, with a little salt water, into a covered roaster. At the end of twenty minutes remove the cover again, rub the pig with butter, and brown for ten minutes. Serve very hot with apple sauce.

Homemade Sausage.

Take of lean young pork 1½ pounds tenderloin, the rest any lean cut, 4 pounds, and fat, 2 pounds; put it through a sausage grinder—twice, perhaps three times, until of the desired fineness. Use for each pound of meat, 1 teaspoonful powdered, dried leaf sage, 1 teaspoonful salt, ⅓ teaspoonful pepper, and ⅓ nutmeg; nutmeg may be omitted if preferred. A quantity of sausage may be made at a time and preserved for regular use if one has a cold storeroom in which to keep it. It should be packed in jars and covered an inch thick with melted lard, which will preserve it.

Sauerkraut with Spareribs.

Cover the kraut with cold water, add a little salt if necessary, and place to boil three hours before using it. About an hour before it is done, put spareribs in and let them boil until the meat falls from the bones. Remove the spareribs, and stir in the kraut a grated raw potato from which the water has been drained. Let it come to a boil after this, being careful it does not burn; remove from stove, and serve.

To Boil a Ham.

Twenty-four hours before a ham is to be used, scrub it thoroughly with a vegetable brush and cold, weak borax water. Put in cold water and soak twenty-four hours. If it is to be baked, it requires four hours' boiling. Use a big kettle, as the ham must be covered all over with water. Let it come to the boil very slowly. Remove the scum. When it begins to boil, add 12 whole cloves, 1 bay leaf, 12 peppercorns, the outside stalks of 1 bunch celery, 2 chopped onions, 2 cloves garlic, 1 chopped carrot and turnip, 2 blades mace, 12 allspice berries, and 1 quart cider or a cupful vinegar. Never allow the ham to boil, merely simmer slowly; that is one secret of making it perfectly tender. Allow twenty-five minutes or half an hour to the pound. If the ham is to be used cold, you can add to its tender juiciness by allowing it to stand in the pot liquor till nearly cold. Then lift it out, peel off the skin and roll in dried bread crumbs with which 3 tablespoonfuls brown sugar have been sifted. Set it in the oven till the crumbs form a crisp brown crust. If the ham is to be baked, take it from the water, drain thoroughly, then take off the skin except around the shank, where it may be cut in vandykes with a sharp-pointed knife. Cover with crumbs and stick it full of cloves, set in a moderate oven, and bake two hours. If you prefer the ham glazed, allow it to cool as for boiled ham, then skin, wipe dry, and brush all over with beaten egg. Mix 1 cupful sifted cracker crumbs, a dash salt and pepper, 2 tablespoonfuls melted butter, and cream enough to make crumbs into a paste. Spread it evenly over the ham, set in a moderate oven, and bake till brown; serve hot with brown sauce. When a baked or boiled ham goes to the table, wrap about the unsightly bone a ruffle of white tissue paper, and garnish with hard-boiled eggs cut in quarters.

Ham Steak.

Put slices of raw ham in a frying pan with ½ cupful water to make them tender. When the water has boiled out and the ham is light brown on both sides, dust with flour and pour on the following dressing, previously made: A cupful milk and cream mixed, a little butter, a teaspoonful mustard, and a dash McIlhenny's Tabasco Sauce. As soon as it boils, serve.

Broiled Ham and Eggs.

Slice the ham thin, take off the rind, and soak the slices in hot water. Broil carefully and place on a hot platter. Break as many eggs as you require into a pan of boiling water; when the white is done, dip out carefully and lay the egg on ham. Sprinkle pepper and salt over each egg and serve.

Sausage Rolls.

Make a dough as for baking-powder biscuit; roll out and cut in large rounds with a biscuit cutter; lay sausage meat on half of each piece; turn the other half over and pinch together; bake half an hour. Serve with brown sauce poured around it.

Toad in the Hole (English recipe).

- 1 cupful flour,
- 1 egg,
- 1 cupful milk,
- Salt and pepper,
- 1 teaspoonful Calumet baking powder,
- 2 tablespoonfuls butter,
- Sausages.

Put the flour in a basin with the salt and make a well in the center. Break the egg and put it in with a quarter of the milk. Beat well, then add the remainder of the milk by degrees, beating all the time. Melt the butter in a pudding tin. Parboil the sausages, cut them in halves, and put them in the tin. Add the baking powder to the batter, and pour it over the sausages. Bake in a hot oven half an hour.

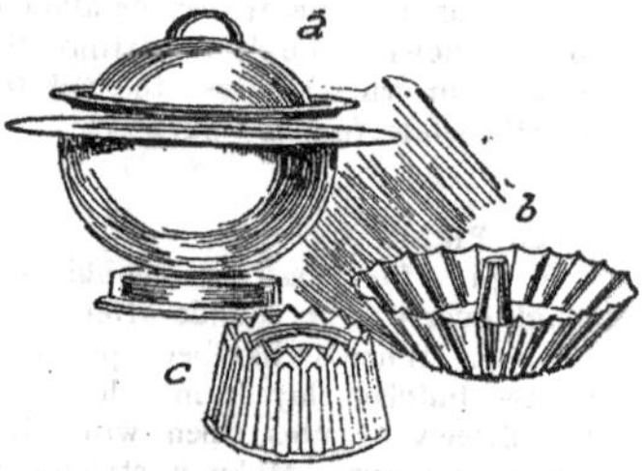

a, Bread Raiser; b, Fluted Cake Tin with Tube in Center; c, Crown Mold for Jellies.

Sausage and Apple.

Prick the skins of the sausages, simmer in a frying pan fifteen minutes, drain, and brown in the oven; make a sirup of 1 cupful each sugar and water, and in it cook pared apples, cut lattice fashion, a few at a time, to preserve the shape. Serve the sausage on the apple.

Broiled Pigs' Feet.

Scrape the feet and wash them thoroughly, soak in cold water two hours, then wash and scrape again. Split each in half lengthwise, and tie the pieces separately in pieces of cheese cloth. Place in a deep saucepan, cover with boiling water, add 1 tablespoonful salt, and simmer slowly until the feet are tender, usually about four hours. Take them from the liquor and set aside until cold; remove the cloths; they are ready then to be broiled in the following:

- 2 tablespoonfuls butter,
- 1 tablespoonful lemon juice,
- ½ teaspoonful salt,

Dash McIlhenny's Tabasco Sauce,
½ tablespoonful finely chopped parsley.

Cream the butter. Work gradually into it lemon juice, salt, tabasco, and parsley. After removing the cloth from each piece, brush with melted butter and dust with salt and pepper. Broil over a clear fire for six minutes. Transfer to a hot platter, and spread with prepared butter. The pigs' feet may be prepared the day before needed.

Fried Salt Pork, Cream Gravy.

½ pound salt pork,
1 cupful cream,
1 teaspoonful flour,
Pinch pepper.

Wash the pork, trim off the rind, and with a sharp knife cut in thin slices. Spread in a large spider and place at the side of the fire until the fat is well fried out, then draw gradually forward until the slices begin to color. Transfer them to a heated platter and keep hot. Pour off most of the fat, leaving about 2 tablespoonfuls in the pan; stir into this the cream, and when it comes to the boiling point, thicken slightly with flour blended with a little cold milk. Season with pepper; boil up once, and pour over the pork.

CHAPTER XLVII

PORK AND HAM LEFT-OVERS

COLD pork, in the estimation of some persons, is better than when it is hot. Serve it in neatly cut slices for tea or luncheon at the second meal, then take stock of the remains and look to the future. Roast-pork bones make an excellent brown stock, almost as rich as that of roast beef. Trim the scraps from the bones and consign them to the soup kettle. Cut with a keen knife all the fat from the meat that is not to be served cold. This fat rendered down makes an excellent dripping to sauté potatoes. Chop, and allow it to melt, strain, and set away in the refrigerator. The tender white meat of pork makes a salad which tastes very much like chicken. Sometimes if one has a few bits of chicken left over, they may be combined with the pork, cut in neat cubes, and the fraud can scarcely be detected. Pork makes excellent croquettes or is good sliced and reheated in a cup of its brown gravy. It may be minced, enriched by a few spoonfuls of gravy, and poured on toast for a breakfast dish. Cold ham has a multitude of uses. A few scraps may be converted into a delicious sandwich or gives an excellent flavor to a salad omelet or egg dish. Even cold sausage has its uses, while a slice or two of cold broiled bacon put through a meat chopper and added to croquette mixtures provides an agreeable seasoning.

Ham Soufflé.

Take 2 cupfuls cold minced ham, add the white of 1 egg and beat till smooth. Then put in a dash of paprika, 1 cupful whipped cream, and 2 whites of eggs beaten stiff. Pour into an oiled melon mold, bake, and serve with tomato sauce poured around it.

Ham Griddlecakes.

1 cupful minced ham,
2 cupfuls stale bread crumbs,
2 eggs,
Pepper,
1 cupful scalded milk.

Mix the ham and crumbs with the milk and well-beaten eggs. Drop by spoonfuls on a hot buttered griddle.

Ham Balls.

Mince remains of lean ham, and mix with an equal quantity of mashed potatoes. Mold into small, flat cakes, roll in flour, and brown in a spider with slices of salt pork fried out.

Ham Toast.

2 cupfuls cold ham,
2 eggs,
½ cupful cream,
⅛ teaspoonful mustard,
Pepper.

Chop very fine the cold ham, add the well-beaten eggs, cream, a little pepper and mustard. Heat this mixture till almost at the boiling point, and spread on slices of buttered toast.

Shredded Ham.

½ tablespoonful butter,
5 tablespoonfuls currant jelly,
Dash cayenne,
1 cupful cold ham.

Cut the ham into narrow strips. Put the butter and currant jelly in a saucepan. As soon as they are melted, add the cayenne and ham, and simmer five minutes.

Ham Sandwiches.

2 cupfuls finely chopped ham,
1 cucumber pickle,
2 teaspoonfuls made mustard,
2 tablespoonfuls butter,
¼ teaspoonful pepper.

Put the ham through a meat chopper, using the finest knife. Mix perfectly smooth with the butter and seasonings and spread between slices of bread from which the crusts have been cut.

Ham-and-Potato Pie.

1 cupful cream sauce,
2 cupfuls cold potatoes,
1½ cupfuls cold chopped ham,
½ cupful dried bread crumbs.

Chop the ham coarsely and cut the potatoes into dice. Butter a vegetable dish, put in a layer of cold potato, then a layer of ham, and pour over it ½ cupful cream sauce. Cover with another layer of potato and ham. Pour in the remainder of the sauce, and cover with buttered crumbs. Bake twenty minutes.

Block Island Croquettes.

1 cupful minced ham,
1 cupful stale bread crumbs,
2 cupfuls chopped cold potatoes,
1 tablespoonful butter,
1 egg.

Mix the ham, crumbs, and potatoes with the butter and egg, make into small balls, flour, egg, crumb, and fry in hot fat.

Pork Cutlets.

2 cupfuls chopped cold pork,
2 eggs,
½ cupful cracker crumbs,
1 teaspoonful minced parsley,
1 teaspoonful minced onion,
1 tablespoonful cream,
Pepper and salt.

Beat the eggs thoroughly, mix with the cream, stir in the chopped pork, cracker crumbs, onion, parsley, and seasoning. Form into cutlet-shaped croquettes, roll in flour, egg, and crumbs. At the small end of the croquette stick in a few inches of macaroni. Fry in deep fat, and serve with tomato sauce.

CHAPTER XLVIII

POULTRY

In selecting a chicken, feel of the breastbone; it ought to be smooth and soft as cartilage and bend easily. A young chicken has soft feet, a smooth skin, and abundance of pin-feathers. Long hairs, coarse scales on the feet, and an ossified breast-bone are pretty sure signs that it is an old fowl. By the same marks you may choose a tender, young turkey, also ducks. To dress and clean poultry, hold the bird over a flame, either alcohol, gas, or burning paper, and blaze off all the hair and down. Cut off the head and pick out the pin-feathers with a fine-pointed knife. With an old fowl or turkey it is worth while to pull the tendons. This operation makes the dark meat so much more tender. Find the portion just behind the leg joint where there are a bunch of tendons, with a fine-pointed scissors, cut very carefully the cartilage skin that covers them, and strip it down till you leave exposed the bunch of white sinews. If the bird is fairly tender, they can be pulled by inserting a stout steel skewer, lifting each tendon by itself and twisting it until it snaps. A turkey will frequently require something as strong as a screw-driver. To admit the hand, make an incision through the skin just below the breastbone and remove the gizzard, heart, etc.; be very careful not to break the gall bladder, as even a drop of its contents would give a bitter flavor to everything it touches. Pull out the lungs—they lie inside the ribs—also the kidneys, crop, and windpipe. Draw the neck skin down and cut the neck off close to the body, leaving skin enough to cover the opening. Cut out the oil bag in the tail, then wash the fowl by allowing cold water to run through it. If the chicken is to be cut up, sever the skin between the leg and body, bend the leg back, and cut through the flesh. Separate the second joint from the drumstick, take off the limbs and cut the breast away from the back, starting just below the breastbone and letting the knife pass between the small ribs on either side through to the collar bone. When trussing a fowl for roasting or boiling, draw the legs close to the body and insert a skewer under the middle joint, running it straight through until it comes out opposite. Cross the drumsticks, tie them with a long string together and fasten to the tail. Put the wings close to the body and keep them in place by a second skewer. Draw the skin of the neck under the back and pin down with a toothpick. Now turn the bird on its breast, take the string attached to the tail and tie to the lower skewer, cross it, draw through the upper skewer, and cut off the ends.

Braised Chicken.

Truss a plump chicken, fry in the fat of salt pork, place on a trivet in a deep pan; into the fat put a carrot cut in squares, ½ onion, ½ bay leaf, and a sprig parsley. Add 2 tablespoonfuls butter and allow the vegetables to fry delicately brown. Pour this over the chicken. Add 2 cupfuls hot chicken broth, cover, and set in a moderate oven. Baste frequently, adding water to the stock, if necessary. Lift the chicken to a hot platter, skim off the fat, thicken the gravy and season, then strain over the fowl.

Broiled Chicken.

Sprinkle a chicken, which has been cut up, with salt and pepper, dip into melted butter, then place in a broiler. Cook twenty minutes over a bright fire, turning the broiler so the pieces may be equally brown. Put on a platter spread with soft butter, sprinkle with pepper and salt, and set in the oven for a few minutes before serving.

Grilled Chicken.

Choose small chickens, split down the back, and soak each in olive oil, seasoned with salt and pepper, for an hour or two. Coat with flour, and broil over a clear fire till done. Into a saucepan put 1 cupful water and an onion; let cook fifteen minutes, take out the onion, and pour the sauce over thin slices of toast, on which arrange the chickens. Garnish with fried parsley.

Chicken with Dumplings (New England recipe).

3 or 4 pound chicken,
1 tablespoonful salt,
1 teaspoonful pepper,
2 onions,
1 tablespoonful flour,
2 tablespoonfuls butter,
½ cupful milk,
2 cupfuls prepared flour.

Cut chicken in 10 pieces and place in saucepan. Add salt, pepper, and onion, cover with boiling water, and cook till tender; then mix flour with butter, and thicken the gravy. Ten minutes before serving, mix prepared flour with butter and milk, and 2 eggs beaten to a stiff froth; cut with a tablespoon small portions from the dough, drop them into the gravy, cover, and boil six minutes; remove the saucepan to side of stove, where they may stop boiling. In serving, arrange the chicken on a platter, and lay the dumplings in a circle around it. Sprinkle 1 tablespoonful chopped parsley over the whole, and serve. This dough will make 12 dumplings.

Chicken Baked in Milk.

Prepare a chicken as though for roasting. Mix a dressing — using crumbed bread, butter, salt, and pepper. Stuff the chicken with this mixture; place it in a baker. In the bottom of the pan put 2 quarts rich milk; cover, and bake slowly, until the chicken is very tender, turning and basting as often as necessary. Thicken the gravy in the pan, seasoning with salt and pepper.

Chicken in Casserole.

2½-pound chicken,
1 can mushrooms,
1 carrot,
1 onion,
1 stalk celery,
1 tablespoonful chopped parsley,
1 teaspoonful salt,
½ teaspoonful pepper,
1 teaspoonful beef extract,
1 tablespoonful flour,
2 cupfuls boiling water.

Clean and truss the chicken, and steam until tender. Melt the butter in a frying pan, add the vegetables chopped fine, cook five minutes, then add the flour. Dissolve the beef extract in boiling water, add the seasonings, and pour it into the frying pan. Cook five minutes. Put the chicken in a *casserole*, dredge with flour, dust with salt and pepper, and pour the contents of the frying pan over it. Place it in the oven, and cook until the chicken is thoroughly browned. Remove from the oven, cover, and serve in the casserole.

Panned Chicken.

Prepare a chicken as for broiling, slightly flatten it, cover with bits of butter, and place in a moderate oven. When nearly done, sprinkle with salt and pepper and dredge with flour; return to the oven and brown, first on one side, then on the other. Keep hot while you make the sauce. Pour a cupful hot milk into the pan, and add 1 tablespoonful grated bread crumbs, also a few drops onion juice. Stir the sauce vigorously, let it boil one minute, turn over the chicken, garnish with parsley, and serve.

Fried Chicken (Southern recipe).

Cut a young chicken into neat pieces, drop in cold water, then roll in flour seasoned with salt and pepper. Put it in a saucepan with fat which has been fried out of salt pork, and cook, turning once or twice till it is well browned. Skim off as much of the fat as possible, add a cupful cream or rich milk, thicken with a little flour, seasoning if necessary, and strain over the chicken.

Chicken with Almond Sauce (Southern recipe).

1 young chicken,
1 tablespoonful lard,
1 tablespoonful flour,
2 cupfuls cream,
1 tablespoonful finely chopped parsley,
1 cupful chopped blanched almonds.

Cut up the chicken as for fricassee; fry golden brown in hot lard. Put it on a hot platter and make the sauce. Thicken the lard (in which the chicken was fried) with the flour; when the flour is cooked, add the cream, parsley, and almonds. Let it boil five minutes, and pour around the chicken.

Chicken with Peanuts (Spanish recipe).

Cut a young chicken into small pieces, roll in flour, and fry brown in lard or butter. When the chicken is done, pour over it a cupful sweet cream and sprinkle liberally with roasted peanuts coarsely powdered.

Creamed Chicken and Sweetbreads.

4-pound chicken,
4 sweetbreads,
1 can mushrooms,
1 quart cream,
4 tablespoonfuls butter,
5 tablespoonfuls flour,
½ grated onion,
Nutmeg, salt, and pepper.

Boil chicken and sweetbreads; when cold, cut them up. In a saucepan put cream; in another butter and flour. Stir until melted, then pour on the hot cream, stirring until it thickens; add onion and nutmeg, and season highly with pepper and salt. Put chicken and other ingredients, with sweetbreads and mushrooms, in a baking dish, cover with bread crumbs and butter, then bake twenty minutes.

Chicken Pie.

Stew a cut-up chicken in enough boiling water to cover, adding pepper and salt. When parboiled, remove to a deep earthen dish and cover with a crust. Use a recipe for rich baking-powder biscuit. Instead of putting a blanket of the dough on top of the pie, cut it into rounds, as for biscuit. Have the chicken laid lightly so the gravy will not touch the dough, and cover as closely as possible. Bake in a moderate oven until the crust is well risen and brown. This is an improvement on the old style of all-over crust, partly because it allows plenty of escape for steam. The biscuit can be easily served, and the paste is not made heavy by cutting with a knife.

Roast Turkey.

Remove the crusts from a stale loaf of bread. Break the loaf in the middle and grate or rub the bread into fine crumbs. Season highly with salt and pepper. Add a cup of diced celery, cooked tender. With a fork mix celery and seasoning through the crumbs, then sprinkle with them 3 or 4 tablespoonfuls melted butter. With a spoon put the prepared crumbs in the place from which the crop was removed until the breast becomes plump. Put the remaining crumbs in the body. Do not pack the crumbs closely either in crop or body, but allow room for them to swell when moistened by the steam from the turkey in cooking. Fold back the wings. Press the legs close to the body, crossing the drumsticks in front of the tail. With small skewers and strong cord fasten in proper shape. Place the turkey, back up, on a rack in the roasting pan. When the back is browned, turn the turkey over, and when the breast and sides are nicely browned, baste with a thin gravy every ten or fifteen minutes until the fowl is cooked. An 8-pound turkey will cook in two hours. Use the water in which the celery was cooked to make basting gravy for the turkey.—EMMA P. EWING.

Roast Chicken.

4-pound chicken.
1 teaspoonful salt,
1 tablespoonful butter,
1 tablespoonful cornstarch,
½ cupful boiling water.

Singe the chicken, wash it quickly in cold water, then dry with a towel; season inside and out with salt, fill the body and crop with bread dressing, sew it up, and spread butter over the breast. Cover the breast with thin slices of larding pork; bend the wings backward, put skewers through the thigh and body, and place it in a roasting pan. Set the pan in a medium-hot oven and roast until the chicken has become a fine brown all over, basting frequently with its own gravy; then add ½ cupful boiling water; continue the roasting and basting till the chicken is done, which will take from one to two hours, according to the age of the fowl. If the gravy gets too brown, add a little more water. The chicken feet, neck, and giblets may be used to make rice soup. Shortly before serving, lay the chicken on a dish, remove the skewers and thread, free the gravy from fat, mix the cornstarch with cold water, add it to the gravy, stir, and cook for a few minutes; then add sufficient boiling water to make a creamy sauce. Cook three minutes, strain, chop the boiled giblets fine and add to the sauce.

Bread Dressing.

½ pound stale bread,
2 tablespoonfuls butter,
2 tablespoonfuls chopped onion,
1 teaspoonful salt,
½ teaspoonful pepper,
1 teaspoonful thyme,
1 egg.

Soak bread in cold water, place a saucepan with butter and onions over the fire; cook five minutes without browning; inclose the bread in a towel and press out all the water, add it to the saucepan, stir over the fire five minutes, then remove; when cold, add salt, pepper, thyme, and egg; mix well and use as stuffing.

Roast Duck.

Pick, singe, and wipe outside of duck. Salt and pepper the inside after carefully drawing and wiping. Cut off the wings at the second point and truss the duck neatly. Roast in a very hot oven from one and a half to two hours in a baking pan containing a little water; baste frequently. Celery, onions, or apples, cored and quartered, are sometimes placed inside the duck to improve the flavor.

CHAPTER XLIX

LEFT-OVER CHICKEN AND TURKEY

CHICKEN, even at twenty cents a pound, is not more extravagant than roast beef, when one considers that every morsel of it can be used, even to the bleaching of the bones in a soup. The carcasses of two good chickens or one turkey will make a quart or two of excellent stock. This means, of course, that every bone, the giblets, and every morsel of skin shall be saved. A careful housewife gathers all these remains into a clean bowl and they stand in the refrigerator until ready to be used. Cover them with cold water, add the seasonings suitable for chicken soup, and set far back on the stove, where it will take at least an hour to begin to simmer. In four hours it will be ready to strain. Never add salt to a soup till after it has cooked. Cool the stock as quickly as possible, but never by putting it steaming hot into the refrigerator. I have seen that plan followed in more than one household; then I have heard the cook exclaim in wonder over spoiled stock and other foods ruined. Still, the sooner stock cools, the longer it will keep. Do not break the cake of fat on top until ready to use; it excludes the air and helps keep the soup sweet.

There is no meat so suitable for *réchauffés* as chicken. It makes excellent croquettes and timbales. Creamed, it loses none of its delicate flavor. It is excellent in *pâtés* or on toast. It is good scalloped, deviled, curried, in fritters, or as *soufflé*, while on hot summer days it appeals to the appetite as a salad, in aspic jelly, in a *mousse*, or potted. The meat of turkey, game, duck, and goose may be treated in many instances as chicken. The flavor of a turkey salad is not as delicate as a chicken salad, still it is a dish not to be despised. The same rule ought to apply to the warming over of poultry as to other meats. Do not *cook* it a second time; all it requires is *reheating*.

Scalloped Turkey.

Into small ramequin dishes sprinkle dried bread crumbs browned in butter. Over this put a layer, one and a half inches deep, of chopped, cold turkey moistened by a spoonful giblet gravy. Cover with browned crumbs, and bake till chestnut brown.

Chicken-and-Ham Mold.

2 cupfuls cold chopped chicken,
1 cupful chopped ham,
1 cupful cold boiled macaroni,
2 eggs,
1 tablespoonful butter,
1 cupful gravy,
Pepper and salt.

Mix the chicken, ham, and macaroni, moisten with the eggs, melted butter and gravy, season highly. Butter a mold, pour the mixture in, put on cover tightly, and boil two hours. Dip the mold into cold water for a minute and turn out on a hot dish. Serve with tomato sauce.

Chicken Omelet.

2 tablespoonfuls milk,
4 eggs,
Salt and pepper,
1 cupful chopped cold chicken.

Beat the eggs till light, add milk and seasoning. Just before pouring into the pan, add the chicken to the egg mixture. Melt the butter in an omelet pan, cook, and fold exactly like an omelet.

Chicken Gallosch (Hungarian recipe).

2 potatoes (raw),
1 tablespoonful butter,
½ teaspoonful paprika,
1 cupful brown stock,
½ teaspoonful salt,
½ clove garlic,
1 cupful cold chicken.

Pare 3 small potatoes, cut into dice, and fry in melted butter in the spider. Toss about in the butter till they begin to brown, add the seasoning, stock, and chicken. Simmer slowly. Serve as soon as the potatoes are soft.

a, Spoon for Beating Cake; b, Wire Toaster; c, Purée Sieve.

Chicken and Macaroni (Italian recipe).

1 cupful cold macaroni,
2 cupfuls cold chicken,
6 mushrooms,
½ cupful cream,
½ cupful chicken stock,
½ cupful dried bread crumbs,
Pepper and salt,
1 tablespoonful butter.

Into a buttered dish put a layer of macaroni, then a layer of chicken cut in small strips. Sprinkle with pepper and salt and the mushrooms cut in quarters. Cover with a layer of macaroni, another of chicken, then pour over it the cream and stock. Sprinkle buttered bread crumbs over the top, and bake brown. If it browns too quickly, cover with a plate, and pour a little more stock in.

Chicken Soufflé.

2 tablespoonfuls flour,
2 tablespoonfuls butter,
1 teaspoonful salt,
⅛ teaspoonful pepper,
2 cupfuls scalded milk,
2 cupfuls cold chicken,
½ cupful stale bread crumbs,
1 tablespoonful chopped parsley,
3 eggs.

Make a white sauce from the butter, flour, salt, pepper, and milk. Add the crumbs, and cook until thick. Take from the fire and stir in the chicken, parsley, and yolks of the eggs beaten till thick and lemon-colored. Whip the whites until stiff and dry and fold in. Pour in a buttered dish and set in a pan of hot water to bake in a hot oven thirty-five minutes.

Chicken Croquettes.

1½ cupfuls chopped chicken,
¼ cupful chopped ham,
6 chopped mushrooms,
4 tablespoonfuls flour,
2 tablespoonfuls butter,
1 cupful chicken stock,
1 tablespoonful cream,
Pepper and salt,
Nutmeg,
1 teaspoonful lemon juice.

Put in a saucepan the flour and butter. Mix till the butter absorbs the flour, then add stock made from boiling up the bones of the chicken, and stir till it becomes a thick paste. Add cream, pepper and salt enough to season, a little nutmeg and lemon juice. Stir in the chopped chicken and mushrooms. Mix well and turn on a plate to cool. When quite cold, roll a tablespoonful mixture in oblong shape, dip in egg and bread crumbs, and fry in hot fat.—MARGARET BAILEY.

CHAPTER L

MEAT OR FISH SAUCES

Celery Sauce.

1 tablespoonful flour,
2 tablespoonfuls butter,
2 cupfuls milk,
1 head celery.

Cut celery into pieces two inches long and boil in salted water for an hour. Mix smoothly flour, butter, and milk, stir until boiling; add the celery pulp, season with salt and pepper and a little mace; let it boil quickly for two minutes. Strain.

Anchovy Sauce.

Bone 4 anchovies and bruise in a mortar to a smooth paste; stir them in a drawn-butter sauce, simmer five minutes, or stir in 2 teaspoonfuls essence of anchovy. A little cayenne is an improvement.

Cardinal Sauce.

2 tablespoonfuls butter,
1 tablespoonful flour,
2 cupfuls stock,
$\frac{1}{2}$ teaspoonful onion juice,
1 bay leaf.

Cardinal sauce is, as a rule, made from lobsters and colored with coral; so, if possible, purchase lobsters containing coral. Boil the lobster, open and remove the coral, and press it through a sieve. Put the butter into pan and let melt. Add flour without browning, then add stock, onion juice, and bay leaf. Stir constantly until it boils. Take out bay leaf, add salt and pepper, the coral, and a little of the red part of the lobster chopped fine.

Sauce Soubise.

3 onions,
2 tablespoonfuls butter,
1 tablespoonful flour.

Peel and chop onions, simmer with butter for three quarters of an hour, but do not let them color very much. Add flour, salt, pepper, and a pinch of mace, and mix all together; moisten with a cup of fish liquor and the same quantity of hot cream or milk. Serve in tureen.

Sauce Allemande.

4 tablespoonfuls butter,
4 tablespoonfuls flour,
2 cupfuls white stock,
Yolks 3 eggs.

Melt butter and mix thoroughly with flour over a gentle fire; add stock and a little salt and pepper; stir, boil fifteen minutes, remove from fire, skim off grease carefully, add eggs mixed in a little water, and stir in with egg beater to make sauce light.

Spanish Sauce.

4 tablespoonfuls butter,
4 tablespoonfuls flour,
2 cupfuls white stock,
$2\frac{1}{2}$ tablespoonfuls lean raw ham,
1 carrot,
1 onion sliced,
1 stalk celery,
2 cloves.

Melt butter in saucepan, add flour, and stir over a gentle fire until nicely browned; mix with white stock, ham, carrot, sliced onion, celery, cloves, a pinch of salt and pepper; stir until beginning to boil, then simmer gently on back of stove for one hour; skim off grease before serving.

Sauce Piquante.

4 tablespoonfuls butter,
1 small carrot,
6 shallots,

1 bunch savory herbs,
Parsley,
½ bay leaf,
2 slices lean bacon,
2 cloves,
6 peppercorns,
1 blade mace,
3 allspice berries,
4 tablespoonfuls vinegar.
1 cupful stock,
½ teaspoonful sugar,
Cayenne and salt to taste.

Put the butter into saucepan with the carrot and shallots cut into small pieces, add the herbs, bay leaf, spices, and ham minced fine; let these ingredients simmer slowly until the bottom is covered with a brown glaze, keep stirring and put in remaining ingredients, simmer gently fifteen minutes, skim off every particle of fat. This is an excellent recipe when a sharp but not too acid sauce is required.

Cucumber Cream Sauce.

1 cucumber,
½ teaspoonful salt,
½ teaspoonful chopped parsley,
½ teaspoonful chopped onion,
1 tablespoonful tarragon vinegar,
¾ cupful cream.

Chop cucumber, season with salt, parsley, onion, and vinegar. Mix thoroughly and drain in colander half an hour. When ready to serve, add cream beaten stiff.

Sauce Tartare.

1 cupful mayonnaise,
2 sweet pickled cucumbers,
3 olives,
1 tablespoonful chopped water cress,
1 teaspoonful capers,
½ teaspoonful onion juice.

Stir into the mayonnaise the cucumbers, olives, water cress, capers, and onion juice.

Brown Sauce.

1 tablespoonful butter,
1 tablespoonful flour,
2 cloves,
1 bay leaf,
1 teaspoonful chopped onion,
1 teaspoonful chopped parsley.

Heat stock; blend together butter and flour, add to hot stock with cloves, bay leaf, parsley, and onion. Cook for a few minutes. Strain, and serve hot with cannelon of beef or rolled beef.

Hollandaise Sauce.

½ cupful butter,
Yolks 2 eggs,
⅓ cupful boiling water,
¼ teaspoonful salt,
Dash cayenne,
1 tablespoonful lemon juice.

Cream the butter, add yolks of eggs one at a time, beating it thoroughly, then add water. Cook in a double boiler till it thickens to the consistency of a custard. The seasoning, which consists of salt, cayenne, and lemon juice, is added just before the boiler is lifted from the fire.

Bechamel Sauce.

1½ cupfuls white stock,
1 slice onion,
1 slice carrot,
Bit bay leaf,
Sprig parsley,
6 peppercorns,
4 tablespoonfuls butter,
4 tablespoonfuls flour,
1 cupful scalded milk,
Salt and pepper.

Cook white stock twenty minutes with onion, carrot, bay leaf, parsley, and peppercorns, then strain. It should be cooked down to about 1 cupful liquor. Melt butter, add flour, add the hot sauce to scalded milk, and season.

White Mushroom Sauce.

4 tablespoonfuls butter,
1 slice carrot,
1 slice onion,
Bit bay leaf,
Sprig parsley,

6 peppercorns,
4 tablespoonfuls flour,
2 cupfuls white stock,
½ can mushrooms,
½ teaspoonful lemon juice,
Salt and pepper.

Melt butter, add carrot, onion, bay leaf, parsley, peppercorns, flour, and, slowly, white stock. Cook five minutes, remove seasonings, and add mushrooms cut in pieces. Add lemon juice, salt, and pepper.

Shrimp Sauce.

1 cupful shrimps,
1 tablespoonful butter,
1 tablespoonful flour,
Salt, pepper, paprika,
1 teaspoonful anchovy paste.

Pound shrimps, skins and all, in a mortar. Boil afterwards for ten minutes in a cupful water. Press the liquor through a *purée* strainer. Mix butter and flour to a paste; pour over it the shrimp liquor. Season with salt, pepper, and paprika; add anchovy paste. Just before serving, add six shrimps cut in inch pieces.

Drawn-Butter Egg Sauce.

1 tablespoonful butter,
1 tablespoonful flour,
1 cupful fish stock,
6 slices hard-boiled egg,
Salt and pepper.

Cook together until well mixed the butter and flour. Add fish stock. Simmer five minutes, season with salt and pepper, and serve in a tureen in which have been placed the slices of hard-boiled egg.

Thin White Sauce.

2 cupfuls milk,
2 tablespoonfuls butter,
2 tablespoonfuls flour,
Pepper and salt.

Put the butter in a small saucepan, and let it melt over a slow fire. Add the flour, and blend to a paste with a wire whisk. Add the seasonings, then the scalded milk, and beat till the sauce gets creamy.

Tomato Sauce.

½ can tomatoes,
1 slice onion,
¼ cupful butter,
3 tablespoonfuls flour,
Pepper and salt.

Cook the tomatoes with onion for ten minutes, squeeze through a potato ricer, and to the pulp add the butter and flour rubbed to a paste, also the seasoning, then beat till creamy.

Horse-Radish Sauce.

¼ cupful grated horse-radish,
4 tablespoonfuls powdered cracker,
½ cupful cream,
1 tablespoonful powdered sugar,
½ teaspoonful mustard,
2 tablespoonfuls vinegar,
1 teaspoonful salt,
¼ teaspoonful pepper.

Blend all the ingredients together, heat over boiling water, and serve with boiled beef.

Cold Horse-Radish Sauce.

3 tablespoonfuls grated horse-radish,
1 tablespoonful vinegar,
Dash McIlhenny's Tabasco Sauce,
¼ teaspoonful salt,
½ cupful thick cream.

Mix the horse-radish, vinegar, and seasonings, then beat in with a fork the cream, which has been whipped to a stiff froth.

Mint Sauce.

¼ cupful sugar,
½ cupful vinegar,
1 cupful fresh mint.

Strip the mint free from its tough leaves and stalks; chop it slightly, wash and put in the vinegar, melt the sugar in a tablespoonful boiling water, add it to the sauce, and serve cold with roast lamb.

CHAPTER LI

VEGETABLES

Potatoes, peas, corn, beans, and many of the vegetables which are universally used, receive fair treatment, but in American kitchens there is still much to learn on the subject of how to make the best of what a country cook calls "greens." In the spring, one craves this sort of food for the well-being of the body and because appetite demands it. The earth yields with the seasons exactly the sort of food we ought to eat, and eat liberally, for it is nature's own medicine. First, let us divide vegetables into classes. There are such cereals as rice, then corn, and legumes, which include the large family of beans, peas, and lentils. In the root class we have beets, carrots, parsnips, turnips, and radishes. Green vegetables include a variety of things herbaceous, from cabbage to dandelions. In bulbs there is the onion family and garlic; then what are called fruit vegetables, eggplant, peppers, okra, cucumbers, and squash. There is also the fungous class, such as mushrooms and truffles. Each class has a different food value; they require different treatment in cookery and are suited to accompany different foods, although our nation would be in no way the loser, either in health or economy, if it learned, like the French people, to make an excellently cooked vegetable serve for one course.

Before we consider the cooking of vegetables, let us study what their properties are and what they do for our bodies. Every vegetable contains more or less of what is called cellulose tissue. This helps to keep the stomach and intestines perfectly healthy. For instance, when we eat meat, we put into our stomachs a highly concentrated food that requires the addition of other foods, bulky and less easily digested, to make a perfectly balanced meal. Strange as it may seem, the value of vegetables lies in the fact that they are made up largely of a membranous substance so bulky and full of refuse that the stomach expels it to the intestines almost in an unchanged condition. Meanwhile, the blood has taken to itself such mineral matter and salts as are necessary to the human system. While digestion is in progress, the loose mass of cellulose is keeping up the peristaltic action that goes on for several hours after eating in the healthy stomach. It is not necessary that there be nourishment in everything we eat. We require the pure distilled water and salts of green vegetables just as much as we do the proteid of meat and the nitrogen of legumes.

To get the fullest value from vegetables, they must be fresh. The country woman, who can pick green things from her garden before the dew has dried from them, is lucky indeed. The best that can be done by a city housewife is to do her own marketing intelligently and carefully. In marketing, beware of root vegetables which are overclean about the roots. The greengrocer has his method of reviving stale goods; roots are soaked from a withered condition back to a fresh appearance. Cabbage and lettuce are skillfully stripped of their outer leaves, and although dirty, sandy spinach is less attractive in looks than cleaner leaves, it is apt to be fresher than that which has been revived by washing. Even cucumbers, eggplant, and tomatoes can be revived by an ice-water bath. Within thin, membranous walls vegetables inclose a semifluid mass that stores up minute cells of starch or other material. As soon as the tender growth of the young plant is over, these cells grow woody and tough.

You can readily see this process in old asparagus, something we hesitate to eat; yet in thousands of families stale vegetables, which have developed the same conditions as if they were old, are used for economy's sake. It would really, in such a case, be better to omit vegetables from a menu. One is eating woody fiber, which can be torn apart like threads, and is almost as easy as thread to digest. Suppose we see for ourselves just what this fibrous mass is like. Take two messes of peas, one of them green things fresh from the pod. Cook in boiling water. They will be ready for the table in ten minutes, but first make them into a *purée* by forcing the pulp through a potato ricer. They contain little but pulp. Nothing except skins is left in the strainer. The value of fresh green peas lies in the sugar and mineral salts they contain. Now, take old dried peas such as are used as a base for soup. They have been soaking for twenty-four hours in cold water. Afterwards long, slow cooking softens them so they can be squeezed through the ricer. Then it actually takes muscle to get a *purée* from them, and it is small in proportion to the residue retained by the strainer. They are not only the dry, husky skins of the peas, but a quantity of pure waste which no stomach can properly digest. Still, this pulp made into a soup is a nutritious dish. That is why so many people with slow digestion can take in soup such vegetables as corn, tomato, beans, lentils, and celery, when the vegetable in its entirety would cause no end of distress.

Every vegetable is almost lacking in fat; the legumes have the largest proportion, and they average only three per cent. Therefore, fat in some form is added to every vegetable dish. We beat cream or butter into mashed potatoes, bake beans with a bit of pork on top of them, and pour oil over salads.

Now to the various methods of preparation and cooking of vegetables. Probably root vegetables are used most largely in every household. Keep two utensils for their thorough cleaning, a small stiff brush, and a square of rough burlap. The brush scrubs earth from every crevice. Burlap is also a splendid cleaner. Put your vegetables into cold water and rub them thoroughly with it. It will bring the skin off clean from new potatoes. Carrots, parsnips, and salsify require scraping after they have had a rubbing with the burlap. Turnips, kohl-rabi, and celeriac should be pared. Beets must be well cleansed, but not broken anywhere, not even have the tops cut, or they will "bleed," thus losing their fine sweet flavor. With most of the root vegetables, except potatoes, white and sweet, the only method for cooking is to boil them by dropping them into water at a bubbling boil. Turnips, carrots, parsnips, kohl-rabi, and celeriac will cook in half an hour if they are young and fresh; winter vegetables require from forty to sixty minutes. Young beets take an hour; old beets require boiling all day. The best way to cook them is to consign them to the fireless cooker. You can make these root vegetables as palatable as skilled French cooks do by the simple process of blanching.

Blanching means bleaching; it removes from winter vegetables their strong, acrid flavor. Then it improves their quality. Let us blanch turnips, for instance; then you can apply the same process to a variety of vegetables. Have a large saucepan with 2 quarts water at a rapid boil; add 1 tablespoonful salt; drop into it the pared turnips and bring the water back to the boiling point as quickly as possible. Cook rapidly, uncovered, for thirty minutes. Drain off the water, put the turnips in a strainer, and cool them under the cold-water faucet; then set away in a covered dish until you are ready to prepare them for the table. Cut them into rather large pieces, put in a saucepan with a tablespoonful butter, a dash pepper, a teaspoonful salt, and 4 tablespoonfuls meat stock or milk. Cook over a hot fire until the vegetables have absorbed both seasonings and liquid. Serve at once.

Blanching of vegetables means a saving of time, because they may be cooked in the leisurely hours of the morning, then quickly reheated when dinner is being prepared. Cabbage, cauliflower, Brussels sprouts, string beans, peas, onions, celery, kohl-rabi, carrots, parsnips, spinach, Swiss chard, artichokes, and salsify are vegetables which may be blanched before the final cooking.

Before using vegetables which form heads, such as lettuce, cabbage, cauliflower, kale and Brussels sprouts, cleanse thoroughly by soaking half an hour, head down, in cold, salted water, with a few tablespoonfuls vinegar in it. This makes insects or worms concealed among the curly leaves crawl out. Spinach requires no end of washing. The best way to cleanse it is to keep filling two pans with cold water and washing the greens till not a grain of sand settles in the bottom. Celery also requires thorough washing, as considerable dirt clings to both stalks and roots during the blanching process.

Different vegetables require different methods of boiling. All of them should be dropped into water which is vigorously bubbling. For a few minutes the process will be interrupted, but set it over a hot part of the stove, where it will begin to boil again rapidly. This must be continued for herbaceous vegetables, young peas, and beans. Root vegetables and cauliflower require gentler treatment. To quote a French cook, "Do not let the water grin; keep it smiling."

As soon as vegetables are tender, lift them off the fire and drain, never allowing anything to stay in hot water a minute after it has been cooked. This soaking process is what so often makes vegetables indigestible, when, if properly treated, they would be perfectly wholesome. While cooking vegetables of any kind, leave the saucepan uncovered; volatile bodies liberated by heat pass off in steam. Cabbage and onions closely lidded are sure to fill the house with an unpleasant odor as soon as they are uncovered; if cooked without a lid, odors are scarcely noticeable. When peas and beans are so ripe as to be slightly tough, they may still be made appetizing and digestible if ½ teaspoonful soda is added to the water. This helps to make them tender as well as retain the color, but beware of adding too much soda; it will give the food an exceedingly nasty flavor. When possible, a skilled cook boils every vegetable in distilled water. The country cook who has clean, soft, cistern water at her command, should always use it in boiling vegetables. The housewife who is compelled to use very hard water to cook vegetables should soften it slightly by adding a dash of soda.

Vegetables are invaluable for making cream soups. Take green peas, for instance. Boil 1 quart peas and 1 small onion in 3 pints water. When soft, squeeze the *purée* through a potato ricer; add it to the liquor in which the vegetables were boiled. Rub together 1 tablespoonful flour with 2 tablespoonfuls butter. This makes sufficient thickening. Season with 2 level teaspoonfuls salt and ⅛ teaspoonful pepper; then add 1 quart scalding-hot milk. Cook ten minutes, stirring frequently. Serve with croutons or wafers. The outside stalks of celery, corn, beans, onions, potatoes, cauliflower, spinach, leeks, tomatoes, or lettuce may often be economically converted into cream soups. In this way a vegetable left-over is deliciously re-served.

Boiling potatoes is such an everyday task that it seems almost unnecessary to offer a recipe for it, yet how seldom do we find a cook make the best of potatoes. If potatoes are "new," they should merely have their skins rubbed off with the burlap scrubber; if old, wash them well, soak half an hour in cold water, then pare off a ring lengthwise around the potato. This allows the skin to be taken off easily after boiling. Put them in a saucepan with plenty of boiling water, add a tablespoonful salt, boil another fifteen minutes, then drain off every drop of water, and leave them to dry for ten minutes covered with a folded towel. A favorite method for serving many vegetables is in cream sauce. A dish of creamed cauliflower will illustrate how potatoes, carrots, cabbage, peas, parsnips, artichokes, salsify, celery, onions, Brussels sprouts, and asparagus may be cooked. Blend 1 tablespoonful butter with 1 tablespoonful flour; then add gradually 1 pint hot milk, and beat till creamy. Add 1 teaspoonful salt, a dash pepper, and a small head blanched cauliflower broken into branches. Set it at the back of the stove where it may cook slowly for ten minutes.

The best way to cook spinach for preserving its refreshing and laxative qualities is not to add water, for after thorough washing the leaves retain enough moisture to steam it. Put it dry in a saucepan over the fire; in ten minutes it will be ready to drain and chop. Afterwards return it to the pan and season with 2 tablespoonfuls butter and a teaspoonful salt. Let it simmer ten minutes before serving. Old, tough spinach is better if blanched before it is seasoned and served.

Boiled Lettuce.

Wash 4 or 5 heads lettuce, removing thick, bitter stalks and retaining all the sound leaves. Cook in boiling salted water for ten or fifteen minutes, then blanch in cold water. Drain, chop lightly, and heat in a stewpan with butter and pepper to taste, or the chopped lettuce may be heated with a pint of white sauce seasoned with salt, pepper, and grated nutmeg. After simmering for a few minutes in the sauce, draw to a cooler part of the range and stir in well-beaten yolks of 2 eggs.

Beet Greens.

Wash thoroughly, put into a stewpan, and cover with boiling water. Add a teaspoonful salt for every 2 quarts greens. Boil rapidly for thirty minutes. Drain off the water, chop rather coarsely, season with butter and salt.

Asparagus Tips in Cream.

Cut the tender part of asparagus into short pieces. Add boiling water enough to cover the vegetable, and cook fifteen minutes. Serve in a cream dressing.

Boiled Peas with Butter.

Put 1 quart shelled peas in a stewpan and add enough boiling water to cover them generously. When they begin to boil, draw back where the water will bubble gently. When tender, add 1 teaspoonful salt and 3 tablespoonfuls butter. Cook ten minutes longer. If the peas are not the sweet kind, add a teaspoonful sugar.

Peas with Pork.

1 quart peas,
4 ounces pork,
1 tablespoonful butter,
½ cupful water,
2 small white onions,
⅛ teaspoonful pepper.

Cut pork into small bits. Put butter into stewpan; when it melts add the pork and cook gently until light brown, then add the water, peas, onion, and pepper. This is a good way to cook peas when they are old.

Peas with Lettuce (French recipe).

1 quart peas,
2 tablespoonfuls butter,
1 head lettuce (the heart),
1 small onion,
1 teaspoonful sugar,
½ cupful water.

Put the vegetables into a stewpan, cover, and cook for five minutes. Draw the pan back where the contents will simmer slowly for half an hour, drain, season, and serve hot.

Sugar Peas in the Pod.

Gather the pods while the peas are very small. String them like beans and cut into two or three lengths. Cover with boiling water, and boil gently twenty-five or thirty minutes. Season with salt and butter, and serve at once.

Shelled Beans Stewed.

1 quart shelled beans,
¼ pound salt pork,
1 onion,
½ teaspoonful pepper,
1 tablespoonful flour,
1 quart boiling water,
Salt to taste.

Cut the pork in slices and fry ten minutes in a stewpan. Add the onion, cut fine, cook twenty minutes. Cover the beans with boiling water and boil ten minutes. Drain off the water. Put the beans and flour in the stewpan with the pork and onion, and stir over the fire five minutes. Add the boiling water and pepper. Place the saucepan where its contents will simmer for two hours.

Green Lima Beans.

Cover 1 quart shelled beans with boiling water. Place on the fire where they will boil up quickly, then draw back where they will simmer until done. When tender, pour off part of the water. Season with a teaspoonful salt and 2 tablespoonfuls butter.

Dried Beans Sautéd.

Soak beans over night, and cook until tender, but not broken. Drain when soft. For 1 quart beans put 3 tablespoonfuls butter in a stewpan. When hot, put in the beans, which have been seasoned with a tablespoonful salt and ½ teaspoonful pepper. Cook for fifteen minutes, frequently turning the beans with a fork. Cover, and let cook slowly for half an hour. If they are liked moist, add a cupful meat broth, then cook for half an hour.

Baked Lentils.

1 quart lentils,
1 quart water,
6 ounces mixed salt pork,
1 clove garlic or 1 small onion,
1 teaspoonful salt,
¼ teaspoonful pepper.

Pick over and wash the lentils. Soak in cold water over night. In the morning pour off the water and put them in a stewpan with 2 quarts cold water and place on the fire. As soon as the water begins to boil, the lentils will rise to the top. Take them off with a skimmer and put in a deep earthen dish, with the pork and onion in the center. Mix the pepper and salt with a quart boiling water and add. Put the dish in a moderate oven, and cook slowly four or five hours. The lentils must be kept moist, and it may be necessary to add a little water from time to time.—MARIA PARLOA.

Stewed Okra.

Use only the small green pods, not more than two and a half inches long. Wipe the pods, cut off the stems and tips, if the latter be discolored. Put them into boiling salted water and cook gently for twenty to thirty minutes. Drain off the water, add 1 tablespoonful butter, 1 tablespoonful vinegar, and a little pepper and salt. Let them simmer at the back of the range until the butter is absorbed, then turn out without breaking the pods, and serve hot.

Baked Hubbard Squash.

Select a thoroughly ripened squash, cut in halves and remove the seeds, scraping the inside thoroughly. Bake one and a half hours in a moderate oven, remove the thin brown skin and with a spoon scrape the squash out of the shell into a hot dish, mashing it with butter, salt, and pepper to taste.

Scalloped Onions.

Boil 6 or 8 onions till tender, changing the water once. Separate them with a fork and arrange in layers in a buttered earthen dish, alternating the layers with buttered bread crumbs. Season with salt and pepper, pour over milk to nearly cover, spread with melted butter, and brown in a moderate oven.

Yankee Fried Parsnips.

Scrape parsnips thoroughly and parboil in salted water; cut in slices lengthwise, dip each piece in molasses, and fry in fat.

Tomatoes Stuffed with Succotash.

Wash, wipe, and remove a thin slice from the stem end of 6 tomatoes, scoop out the inside, sprinkle with salt, invert, stand half an hour. Mix the pulp with 1 cupful succotash; stuff the tomatoes and arrange them in a buttered pan, sprinkle the top of each with buttered cracker crumbs. Bake in a hot oven twenty minutes. Baste with melted butter.

Peppers with Macaroni (Italian recipe).

Cut the tops from green peppers, remove seeds and core, and let stand ten minutes in boiling water. Chop cooked macaroni into small pieces and mix with a thin cream sauce. Drain the peppers, fill with macaroni, adding to each a generous spoonful of grated cheese. Bake in a granite dish with very little water until the peppers are tender. Serve with tomato sauce made from fresh or canned tomatoes pressed through a sieve and thickened with melted butter to which a tablespoonful flour has been added. Salt and a few drops of onion juice should be added, but no pepper.

Fried Turnips.

Peel the turnips, cut in inch cubes, boil until tender, drain, and fry in butter until golden brown on both sides.

Potatoes Hashed with Green Peppers.

To hashed brown potatoes add chopped bacon in the proportion of one slice to each person, and minced red or green peppers.

Stuffed Cucumbers and White Sauce.

Peel large cucumbers and cut lengthwise; scoop out the centers; fill with bread-crumb stuffing, plain or mixed with chopped meat; put side by side in a pan, and bake in a hot oven, basting frequently with melted butter and hot water. When the cucumbers are soft, remove, and put a spoonful white sauce over each as it is served.

Corn Custard.

6 ears corn,
3 eggs,
1 cupful milk,
½ teaspoonful salt,
Dash cayenne.

Scrape the corn from the ears, beat the eggs, add the milk to the corn, then add a seasoning of salt and cayenne, and mix the eggs in lightly; bake in a deep buttered dish in a pan of hot water in the oven till a knife blade put into the custard comes out dry. Serve at once.

Pepper Rings.

Cut a large pepper in 4 rings, removing the seeds; boil fifteen minutes; cut 4 rounds of stale bread and brown them in the oven. Butter the slices, lay a ring of pepper on each and fill the center with well-seasoned, cold minced meat. Moisten with water in which the pepper was boiled, adding salt and butter to season, and set in the oven.

Chile con Carne (a Mexican recipe).

Soak 1 pint dried Lima beans over night; in the morning arrange in the bean pot with 1 pound solid lean beef, 2 ounces sweet fat or suet, a red pepper cut in rings, and ½ onion, shaved. Cover with water, season with salt, ½ teaspoonful mustard wet up with vinegar, a dash McIlhenny's Tabasco Sauce, and bake slowly in a moderate oven for three or four hours.

To Boil Cabbage.

Cut a head of cabbage in 4 parts. Soak half an hour in a pan of cold water to which has been added a tablespoonful salt; this will draw out insects or worms that may be hidden in the leaves. After soaking, cut in slices. Have a large stewpan half full of boiling water; put in the cabbage, pushing it under the water with a spoon. Add 1 tablespoonful salt, and cook twenty-five to forty minutes. Turn into a colander and drain; put in a chopping bowl and mince. Season with butter, pepper, and more salt if required. Allow a tablespoonful butter to a pint cooked vegetable.

Cabbage Cooked with Pork.

For a small head of cabbage use ½ pound salt pork. Boil the pork gently for three or four hours. Prepare the cabbage, and boil rapidly till tender. Serve the pork with the cabbage.

Creamed Cabbage.

2 cupfuls boiled and minced cabbage,
1 cupful hot milk,
1 tablespoonful butter,
1 teaspoonful flour,
½ teaspoonful salt,
⅛ teaspoonful pepper.

Put the cabbage, hot milk, salt, and pepper in a stewpan. Beat the butter and flour together until creamy, then stir into the contents of the stewpan. Simmer ten minutes; serve very hot.

Cabbage and Potato Purée.

2 cupfuls boiled finely minced cabbage,
6 medium-sized potatoes,
2 tablespoonfuls butter,
2 teaspoonfuls salt,
½ teaspoonful pepper,
1 cupful hot milk.

Peel the potatoes and put them in a stewpan with enough boiling water to cover. Cook thirty minutes. Pour off the water and mash fine. Beat in the hot milk, seasoning, and cabbage. Cook five minutes longer.

Boiled Cauliflower.

Remove the green leaves and the greater part of the stalk. Put the head in a pan of cold water which contains to each quart a teaspoonful salt and a teaspoonful vinegar. Let it soak an hour or more. Put the cauliflower in a large stewpan, stem down, and cover with boiling water. Add a tablespoonful salt, and cook with the cover of the saucepan partially off, boiling gently all the time. A large, compact head requires half an hour, small heads from twenty to twenty-five minutes. Cauliflower begins to deteriorate the moment it is overcooked.

Creamed Cauliflower.

2 cupfuls cooked cauliflower,
2 cupfuls milk,
1 teaspoonful salt,
⅛ teaspoonful pepper,
1 tablespoonful butter,
½ tablespoonful flour,
3 slices toasted bread.

Break the cauliflower into branches and season with half the salt and pepper. Put the butter in a saucepan. When hot, add the flour, and stir until smooth, then add the milk, stirring all the time. When the sauce boils, add salt, pepper, and cauliflower. Cook ten minutes; serve on toast.

Brussels Sprouts Blanched.

Remove wilted or yellow leaves from the sprouts, cut the stocks close to the head, and soak in salted cold water for an hour or more. Drain and put into boiling water. Allow 1 teaspoonful salt to 2 quarts water. Boil rapidly for fifteen minutes. When done, turn into a colander and pour cold water over them. They are ready now to serve with any kind of sauce, or can be seasoned with butter, salt, and pepper.

Brussels Sprouts Sautéd.

1 quart Brussels sprouts,
3 tablespoonfuls butter,
½ teaspoonful salt,
¼ teaspoonful pepper.

Blanch the sprouts and drain well. Put them in a saucepan with butter and other seasonings. Place over a hot fire and shake frequently. Cook five minutes; serve hot.

Kale Boiled with Pork.

Cook kale the same as cabbage with pork.

Minced Kale (Scotch recipe).

Remove old or tough leaves. Wash the kale thoroughly and drain; then put to cook in a kettle of boiling water to which has been added 1 tablespoonful salt to 4 quarts water. Boil rapidly till tender. Pour off the water, and chop the kale fine; put back into the kettle, add 1 tablespoonful butter and 2 tablespoonfuls meat broth for each pint minced vegetable. Cook ten minutes, and serve at once. The time required for cooking kale varies from thirty to fifty minutes.

To Boil Spinach.

To clean spinach, cut off the roots, break the leaves apart and drop in a pan of water, rinsing them well. Continne washing in clean water until there is no sand left in the bottom of the pan. Drain and blanch. For ½ peck spinach have 3 quarts boiling water and 1 tablespoonful salt. Let it cook ten minutes, counting from the time it begins to boil. Put the spinach in a colander, and pour cold water over it. Drain well, and chop.

Spinach with Cream.

2 cupfuls boiled spinach,
2 tablespoonfuls butter,
1 tablespoonful flour,
1 teaspoonful salt,
½ teaspoonful pepper,
1 cupful scalded cream.

Mince the spinach. Put the butter in a saucepan on the fire. When hot, add the flour and stir until smooth, then add the minced spinach and salt and pepper. Cook five minutes; then add cream, and cook three minutes longer.

Spinach with Egg.

2 cupfuls boiled spinach,
3 tablespoonfuls butter,
½ teaspoonful pepper,
2 eggs,
3 teaspoonfuls salt.

Drain the blanched spinach and chop fine, return to the saucepan, and add salt, pepper, and butter. Place on the fire, and cook ten minutes. Heap in a mound on a hot dish, and garnish with hard-boiled eggs cut in slices.

Spinach Cooked without Water.

Young, tender spinach can be cooked without water. When well washed, put in a stewpan over the fire; cover, and cook for ten minutes. Turn it several times during the cooking. Put it in a chopping bowl and mince fine. Return to the stewpan and add seasonings, allowing for ½ peck spinach 2 generous tablespoonfuls butter and a teaspoonful salt. Simmer ten minutes; if very tender, five minutes will be sufficient.

Cucumber Sautéd.

Boil pared and quartered cucumbers for three minutes. Drain the pieces, and season with salt and pepper. Roll in flour, and cook in a saucepan with butter for twenty minutes. This dish may be varied by adding minced parsley and chives about five minutes before the cooking is finished.

Stewed Tomatoes.

Peel tomatoes and cut in small pieces. Put into a stewpan on the fire. Boil gently twenty minutes or half an hour. Season five minutes before the cooking is finished. Allow for each quart tomato 1 teaspoonful salt and sugar and 1 tablespoonful butter.

Scalloped Tomatoes.

2 cupfuls peeled and cut tomatoes,
2 cupfuls grated bread crumbs,
1 level teaspoonful salt,
1 tablespoonful butter,
Dash pepper.

Reserve 3 tablespoonfuls bread crumbs, and spread the remainder on a pan. Brown in the oven. Mix the tomato, browned crumbs, salt, pepper, and half the butter together, and put in a shallow baking dish. Spread the unbrowned crumbs on top, and

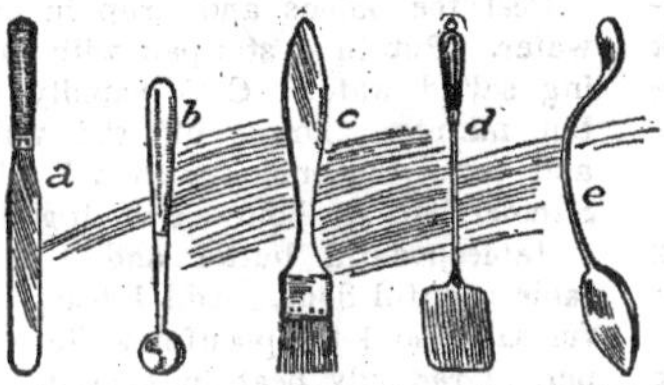

a, Teller Knife; b, Cutter for Potato Balls; c, Butter Brush for Greasing Cake Tins; d, Pancake Turner; e, Bent Spoon for Giving Medicine.

dot with the remainder of the butter, cut into bits. Bake in a moderately hot oven half an hour.

Stuffed Green Peppers (Italian recipe).

6 sweet peppers,
1 pint soaked stale bread,
2 teaspoonfuls salt,
1 tablespoonful fine herbs,
½ teaspoonful sweet basil and summer savory,
2 tablespoonfuls butter.

Cut off the stem end of the pepper and remove the interior, being careful to take out every seed. Fill the peppers with the dressing. Place them on end in a shallow dish, and pour around them a sauce prepared as follows:

1 tablespoonful butter,
1 tablespoonful flour,
1½ cupfuls meat stock,
1 teaspoonful salt.

Heat the butter; add the flour. Stir until smooth and brown, then add the meat stock. Season with salt. Cook five minutes, pour around the stuffed peppers. Put the dish in a moderately hot oven and bake the peppers one hour, basting with the sauce in the dish. Peppers may be filled with a well-seasoned dressing of chopped meat, with or without the addition of bread crumbs or rice.

Beans in a Casserole (Spanish recipe).

2 cupfuls white or pink beans,
1 onion,
Small piece pork or bacon,
1 cupful canned tomatoes,
2 shredded chili peppers,
Dash McIlhenny's Tabasco Sauce.

Soak the beans over night. In the morning boil fifteen minutes and drain. Fry the onion with the pork or bacon. Add these to the beans, also the tomato, peppers, salt, and sufficient hot water to cover well. Boil briskly for ten minutes, then put in a casserole, and bake in a slow oven four hours.

Cauliflower Browned.

Soak cauliflower in cold water for a few hours, boil one hour in salted water, drain, and sprinkle with a few drops of vinegar mixed with salt and pepper, and dust with soft bread crumbs fried in butter till brown.

Boiled Turnips.

Peel and slice the turnips; drop in a stewpan with boiling water enough to cover. Cook until tender, then drain. Mash with a wooden vegetable masher. Season with salt, butter, and pepper. Serve at once.

Hashed Turnips.

Chop drained turnips in large pieces. Return to the stewpan, and for 1½ pints turnips add a teaspoonful salt, ¼ teaspoonful pepper, a tablespoonful butter, and 4 tablespoonfuls water. Cook over a hot fire until the turnips have absorbed the seasonings. Serve at once. Or the salt, pepper, butter, and a tablespoonful flour may be added to the hashed turnips, then the stewpan be placed over the hot fire and shaken frequently to toss up the turnips. When the turnips have been cooking five minutes in this manner, add ½ pint meat stock or milk, and cook ten minutes.

Carrots with White Sauce.

Scrape carrots lightly, then cut into large dice. Put in a stewpan with salted water and boil until tender. Young carrots will cook in thirty minutes, old ones in forty-five. Drain, put back in the stewpan, and for every pint add 1 tablespoonful butter, 1 teaspoonful sugar, ½ teaspoonful salt, and 1 gill meat stock. Cook until they have absorbed the seasonings and liquid.

Salsify.

To prevent salsify from turning dark, drop it as soon as pared and cut into a mixture of flour and water made slightly acid with vinegar. Cook thirty minutes, drain, and serve in a white sauce. Or mix 1 tablespoonful butter, ½ teaspoonful salt, 1 teaspoonful lemon juice, and 1 teaspoonful minced parsley. Add this to the drained salsify, and serve at once.

Beets with Butter.

Wash beets, being careful not to break the skins. Put in a stewpan, cover with boiling water, and boil until tender. Young beets will cook in one hour. When tender, take from the boiling water and drop into cold water. Rub off the skins. Cut in thin slices and season with salt and butter. Serve at once.

Boiled Kohl-Rabi.

Wash and pare the vegetable, then cut in thin slices. Put in salted boiling water and boil until the vegetable is tender. This will take from thirty to fifty minutes. Pour off the water, and season with butter, salt, and pepper.

Stewed Celery.

Remove the leaves from the stalks. Scrape rusted or dark spots, cut into pieces three inches long, and put in boiling water. Add 1 teaspoonful salt for 2 quarts water. Boil rapidly fifteen minutes. Pour off the water, rinse with cold water, then drain. Finish in the following manner: Put the celery in the stewpan with 1 tablespoonful butter, and 1 teaspoonful salt for each quart celery. Cover, and cook slowly for fifteen minutes. Shake the pan frequently while the celery is cooking. Serve hot.—MARIA PARLOA.

Boiled Onions in White Sauce.

Peel the onions and drop in cold water. Put in a stewpan with boiling salted water. Cook rapidly for ten minutes. Drain off the water and cover the onions with hot milk. Simmer half an hour. Beat together 1 tablespoonful butter and 1 level tablespoonful flour. Add 1 teaspoonful salt and ¼ teaspoonful white pepper. Gradually beat in ½ cupful of the milk in which the onions are cooking. When smooth, stir the mixture into the onions and milk. Let it cook ten minutes longer.

Stewed Onions.

Cut the onions in slices and boil in salted water ten minutes. Drain, add 2 tablespoonfuls butter, 1 teaspoonful salt, ¼ teaspoonful pepper. Cover the stewpan, and cook over a hot fire five minutes, shaking the pan occasionally. Set it back where it will cook slowly for forty minutes.

Stewed Cucumbers.

Stew pared cucumbers, cut in quarters, for fifteen minutes, with a little water and a small minced onion. Pour off the water; stir in flour, butter, and salt; heat for two or three minutes, then serve.

Baked Eggplant.

For baked eggplant make a dressing as for stuffed peppers, except that a little more salt, pepper, and butter are used. Cut the eggplant in two lengthwise, scrape out the inside, and mash fine, then mix with the dressing and return to the shells. Place on a pan in the oven. Cook forty-five minutes.—MARIA PARLOA.

Fried Eggplant.

Cut the vegetable in slices half an inch thick and pare. Sprinkle with salt and pile them upon one another; put a plate with a weight on top. Let them rest an hour, then remove weight and plate. Add 1 tablespoonful water, ½ tablespoonful salt, and ¼ teaspoonful pepper to an egg. Beat well. Dip the slices of eggplant in the egg, then in dried bread crumbs. Fry in deep fat.

Broiled Eggplant.

The eggplant is sliced and drained; then spread the slices on a dish, season with pepper, baste with salad oil, sprinkle with dried bread crumbs, and broil.

Summer Squash.

Wash the squash, cut into small pieces, and cook in boiling water or steam. The cooked squash is mashed fine and seasoned with salt, pepper, and butter.

Boiled Corn on the Cob.

Free the corn from husks and "silk." Drop into boiling water, and cook ten minutes.

Corn Cut from Cob.

Corn may be cut from the cob and heated with butter, pepper, and a little milk. First cook the ears five minutes in boiling water to set the juice. Then with a sharp knife cut through the center of each row of grains, and with the back of a knife press the grains from the hulls. Put it in a saucepan and season with salt, pepper, and butter. Add enough hot milk to moisten well, and cook ten minutes.

Beans with Gravy (Mexican recipe).

Soak 2 cupfuls beans over night; in the morning add a small onion and boil gently until soft; take out the onion and drain the beans. Put a

Beans à la Bretonne (French recipe).
Boil ½ pint haricot beans till tender; slice 4 large onions, and fry them in butter till brown. Put the beans and onions together in a stewpan, and add a little strong stock, pepper and salt, and finely minced parsley. Serve hot.

Beans à la Poulette (French recipe).
Put young, tender beans in a stewpan with plenty of water, and a handful salt, and set them over a strong fire. When done, blanch, drain, and put in a stewpan with a bit of butter, an onion or two cut in dice, and previously fried in butter. Sprinkle in a tablespoonful flour; let them stew a few minutes, but do not allow them to brown; add a spoonful stock, some minced parsley and green onions, with salt and pepper. Let them come to a boil, stirring well, and thicken with the yolks 2 eggs, beaten in a little cream. Just before serving, add the juice of a lemon.

Turnips Glacé au Sucre (French recipe).
Clean young, tender turnips, put them in a stewpan with a small piece of butter, 2 tablespoonfuls sugar, a little salt, and ½ pint stock. Simmer forty minutes. When nearly done, place the stewpan over a brisk fire to reduce the sauce to a glaze, rolling the turnips about in it, but with great care to avoid breaking them; dish, and pour the glazed sauce over them.

Stewed Red Cabbage.
Split a red cabbage, cut in thin slices, soak in salt and water, then put in a saucepan with some stock and a little butter blended with flour; add pepper and salt, a glass of vinegar, and a bit of bacon. Stew till tender, take out the bacon, and serve.

Shredded Red Cabbage (Dutch recipe).
Cut a red cabbage in shreds and boil till tender; drain as dry as possible; put in a stewpan with a tablespoonful pure olive oil, a tablespoonful butter, 3 tablespoonfuls vinegar and water, an onion cut small, some pepper and salt. Let it simmer till all the liquor evaporates. This is eaten in Holland hot or cold.

Choufleurs au Gratin (French recipe).
1 cauliflower,
2 tablespoonfuls grated Parmesan cheese,
2 tablespoonfuls butter,
Dash pepper and salt,
2 tablespoonfuls lemon juice,
Yolks 2 eggs.

Boil the cauliflower, drain, put it on the dish in which it is to be served; prepare a sauce of the cheese, butter, pepper, and salt, lemon juice, and yolks of eggs beaten; beat and mix together, pour it over the cauliflower, grate Parmesan cheese over the top, put in the oven, and bake twenty minutes. Brown the top.

Artichokes à la Crême (French recipe).
Boil artichokes in salted water; when they are done, drain. About half an hour is sufficient to cook them if they are tender. Toss in butter in a stewpan, add some cream and a little chopped parsley. Thicken the sauce with the yolk of an egg; season with salt and cayenne.

Leland Tomatoes (English recipe).
Wipe 4 tomatoes, pare, and cut in 3 slices. Sprinkle with salt and pepper, dredge generously with flour, and sauté in butter, first on one side, then on the other. Remove to a hot serving dish and pour over them the following sauce: Melt 2½ tablespoonfuls butter, add 2½ teaspoonfuls flour, and stir until blended; then pour on, while stirring or beating constantly, 1 cupful milk. Bring to the boiling point, season with salt and pepper.

Tomato Surprise.
6 tomatoes,
2 hard-boiled eggs,
2 tablespoonfuls red pepper,
2 tablespoonfuls green pepper,
1 shallot,

1 clove garlic,
4 anchovies.

Wipe the tomatoes, cut a slice from the stem end of each, scoop out the inside, invert, and stand thirty minutes. Add the eggs, peppers, shallot, garlic and anchovies finely chopped. Moisten with mayonnaise dressing. Fill the tomato cases with the mixture, mask with mayonnaise, and garnish with anchovies. Serve as a first course at dinner.

Broiled Tomatoes.

Wipe and cut tomatoes in halves crosswise; then cut a thin slice from the rounding part of each. Sprinkle with salt and pepper, dip in crumbs, egg, and crumbs again, place in a well-buttered broiler, and broil six to eight minutes.

Baked Tomatoes.

Wipe 6 smooth, medium-sized tomatoes and remove a thin slice from the stem end of each. Take out the seeds and pulp and drain off most of the liquid. Add to the pulp an equal quantity of buttered cracker crumbs, and season with salt, pepper, and a few drops of onion juice. Refill the tomatoes with the mixture, place in a buttered pan, sprinkle with buttered cracker crumbs, and bake twenty minutes in a hot oven.

Deviled Tomatoes.

4 tablespoonfuls butter,
2 teaspoonfuls powdered sugar,
1 teaspoonful mustard,
½ teaspoonful salt,
Few grains cayenne,
Yolk hard-boiled egg,
1 egg slightly beaten,
2 tablespoonfuls vinegar.

Wipe, peel, and cut tomatoes in slices. Sprinkle with salt and pepper, dredge with flour, and sauté in butter. Remove to a hot serving dish, and pour over a dressing made from the above ingredients. Cook over hot water, stirring constantly, until the mixture thickens.

Fried Corn.

Scrape corn carefully from the cob. Cut through the center of the kernel, so that all the pulp and juices may be extracted without the removal of the hulls. Sift a little flour over the corn, with salt and pepper to taste. Place some slices of bacon over the fire in frying pan, until all the grease has been extracted. Remove the meat and put the corn in the pan to fry in the bacon fat until it becomes delicately brown and tender; it must be stirred constantly for fifteen or twenty minutes.

Corn Patties Garnished with Husks.

Green corn,
3 eggs,
1 cupful fine cracker crumbs,
½ teaspoonful sugar,
Pepper and salt.

This calls for enough green corn after it has been grated to make a pint. To the corn add 2 eggs and the cracker crumbs, season with salt and pepper—about ¼ teaspoonful pepper and a teaspoonful salt. Add the sugar and form the mixture into cakes about the size of a large oyster; then roll in egg and afterwards in cracker crumbs. Wash the corn husks and shred the ends with a fork for about two inches. Arrange them on a platter with the fringe hanging over the sides. Cook the patties in smoking-hot lard until brown and crisp; then heap in a mound in the center of the platter and serve at once.—MARIA PARLOA.

Vegetarian Sausages.

1½ cupfuls Lima beans,
2 tablespoonfuls butter,
1 teaspoonful salt,
Dash McIlhenny's Tabasco Sauce.

Soak the beans over night, cook in salted water until soft. Drain perfectly dry, then squeeze the pulp through a potato ricer. Beat in the butter and seasonings. If not moist enough, add a beaten egg or as much of it as required, make the paste so soft it can be rolled into croquettes. Shape like small sausages, dip in beaten egg and flour, then fry in butter, rolling the sausages over in the pan till brown on all sides. Serve with cold slaw.

Beans à la Bretonne (French recipe).

- ½ pint haricot beans,
- 4 large onions,
- 2 tablespoonfuls butter,
- 1 cupful brown stock,
- Dash McIlhenny's Tabasco Sauce,
- 1 teaspoonful salt,
- 1 teaspoonful finely minced parsley.

Boil the beans till tender; slice the onions thin, and fry in butter till brown. Put the beans and onions in a stewpan and add the stock, pepper, salt, and parsley. Serve very hot.

French Beans à la Poulette (French recipe).

Put young, tender beans in a stewpan with plenty of salted water. When cooked, blanch, drain, and return to stewpan with a bit of butter. Sprinkle in a tablespoonful flour; let them stew a few minutes, but do not allow them to brown; add a tablespoonful stock, minced parsley, and green onions with salt and pepper. Let them come to a boil, stir well, thicken with yolks 2 eggs, beaten in a little cream. Just before serving, add juice of a lemon.

Curried Onion.

Fry sliced onions in butter or fat; salt and pepper, then add 1 teaspoonful curry, 2 raw eggs, and a few drops lemon juice. Serve hot.

CHAPTER LII

LEFT-OVER VEGETABLES

The possibilities for utilizing cold vegetables are greater than for any dish that comes to the American table. Almost every vegetable in common use, from the ragged outside leaves of lettuce to a cupful cold string beans, may reappear as a tasty hot dish or a tempting salad. Left-over spinach, corn, lettuce, tomato, string beans, peas, squash, cauliflower, carrots, onions, or beans may be converted into savory soups, and nearly every vegetable in the market when cold can reappear as a salad. If the left-overs are many and small, the result may be a Macedoine salad. This is the name given to a salad in which cold boiled vegetables are combined. Each vegetable is kept separate, and generally the dish can be arranged in such a charming scheme of color that it is a pleasure to the eye. Vegetables may be cut in cubes, strips, triangles, tiny balls, or in fancy shapes, formed by a vegetable cutter. During the summer, when young beets, turnips, carrots, and green vegetables are at their best, these salads may be had in perfection. If left-overs of vegetables come from the table coated with cream sauce or mayonnaise, put each by itself in a colander. Wash off in cold water, drain thoroughly, chill before using, and it will be as good as if freshly cooked. Plenty of a crisp green vegetable, lettuce, water cress, or parsley, is necessary to make a Macedoine salad perfect.

Spinach in Molds.

2 cupfuls cold spinach,
Pepper and salt,
1 tablespoonful lemon juice,
1 tablespoonful melted butter.

Drain the spinach and chop fine. Season and stir in the melted butter. Butter Dario molds and pack in the mixture. Set on ice until chilled. Remove from the molds and arrange the spinach on thin slices of cold boiled tongue cut in rounds. Garnish the base of each with parsley, and serve on top a spoonful sauce tartare.

Baked-Bean Sandwiches.

½ cupful baked beans,
1 tablespoonful horse-radish,
1 teaspoonful celery and parsley minced fine,
½ teaspoonful onion juice,
¼ teaspoonful mustard,
Dash McIlhenny's Tabasco Sauce.

Press the beans through a potato ricer, mix with the seasoning, and spread between slices of entire-wheat bread.

Corn Soup.

1 quart veal stock,
1 cupful green corn cut from the cob and chopped.

Add the corn to the stock and simmer slowly for twenty minutes. Add pepper and salt to taste, thicken slightly, and strain.

Pea Soup.

2 cupfuls cold green peas,
4 cupfuls veal stock,
1 slice onion,
1 teaspoonful salt,
⅛ teaspoonful pepper,
2 tablespoonfuls butter,
2 tablespoonfuls flour.

Add the peas and onion to the stock and simmer till they begin to fall to pieces. Rub through a sieve, reheat, season, and bind with butter and flour rubbed together. Peas that are too old to serve as a vegetable may be used for soup.

Cream-of-Corn Soup.

2 cupfuls cold corn,
2 cupfuls boiling water,
2 cupfuls milk,
1 slice onion,
Sprig parsley,
2 tablespoonfuls butter,
2 tablespoonfuls flour,
Pepper and salt.

Put the corn through a meat chopper. Add the boiling water and simmer for twenty-five minutes. Rub through a sieve. Scald the milk with the onion and parsley. Remove the seasonings, and pour the milk over the corn pulp. Melt the flour and butter together and use for binding. Season with pepper and salt.

Baked-Bean Soup.

3 cupfuls cold baked beans,
2 cupfuls water,
4 cupfuls stock,
2 slices onion,
3 stalks celery,
1½ cupfuls canned tomatoes,
2 drops McIlhenny's Tabasco Sauce,
Salt and pepper,
2 tablespoonfuls butter,
2 tablespoonfuls flour.

Put the beans, celery, onion, tomatoes, with the stock and water, into a saucepan and simmer half an hour. Rub through a sieve, leaving nothing in the sieve except the skins of the beans and the seeds of the tomato. Add the seasonings, bind with the butter and flour melted together.

Wilted Lettuce.

1 slice ham,
½ cupful vinegar,
1 egg,
½ teaspoonful mustard,
Pepper and salt,
Outside leaves 2 heads lettuce.

Fry a slice of ham with some fat on. When done, remove the ham, leaving the fat gravy in the frying pan Have ready the vinegar, beaten egg, mustard and pepper and salt to taste. Add the egg to the vinegar slowly so it will not curdle. When well mixed, pour slowly into the ham gravy, stirring well. Let it come to a boil. Put the lettuce in with a fork, toss and thoroughly mix with the hot mixture in the frying pan for two minutes. Cover the pan for two minutes, then turn out in a deep dish.

Vegetable Hash.

From the remains of a boiled dinner there are generally enough left-overs to make a vegetable hash.

a, Meat Chopper; b, Wire Spoon for Beating Sauces; c, Potato Ricer; d, Glass Measuring Cup; e, Cream Whip.

Chop coarsely cabbage, turnips, parsnips, potatoes, and ½ a carrot. Combine in equal quantities and to each pint of the vegetable use a tablespoonful butter melted in a spider. Pepper and salt to taste and add 2½ tablespoonfuls brown stock. Cook slowly, and let it just come to a boil. Serve hot with pickled beets.

Sauce Robert.

2 drops McIlhenny's Tabasco Sauce,
8 tablespoonfuls oil mayonnaise,
4 tablespoonfuls French mustard,
2 tablespoonfuls vinegar,
2 cold boiled onions.

Chop the onions fine and mix with the other ingredients. This is a delicious accompaniment to pork tenderloin, veal cutlet, lamb chops, or a steak.

Cabbage Jelly (German recipe).

Drain cold boiled cabbage perfectly dry, chop fine, add butter, pepper, and salt to taste. Press the whole closely into a small pudding dish, and bake an hour.

Corn Omelet.

1 cupful cold corn,
3 eggs,
¼ cupful milk,
½ teaspoonful salt,
Dash pepper,
1 tablespoonful butter.

Chop the corn slightly. Beat the yolks of the eggs till thick, mix with the milk, salt and pepper. Add the corn and fold in the whites of the eggs beaten dry. Melt the butter in an omelet pan, pour in the mixture, and cook exactly as you would an omelet.

Corn Fritters.

1 cupful cold chopped corn,
1 cupful milk,
1 teaspoonful Calumet baking powder,
Yolks 2 eggs,
4 tablespoonfuls flour,
½ teaspoonful salt,
¼ teaspoonful pepper,
Whites 2 eggs.

Beat the yolks till thick and lemon-colored, add the milk and seasoning, then the corn, flour, and baking powder. Last of all, cut in the whites of eggs beaten to a stiff froth. Drop from a tablespoon into hot lard, and fry a delicate brown.

Curried Vegetables.

1 cupful cold potatoes,
1 cupful cold carrots,
½ cupful cold turnips,
½ cupful cold peas,
2 tablespoonfuls butter,
2 slices onion,
2 tablespoonfuls flour,
¾ tablespoonful salt,
½ teaspoonful curry powder,
¼ teaspoonful pepper,
Dash celery salt,
1 cupful milk,
1 teaspoonful chopped parsley.

Cut the potatoes, carrots, and turnips into tiny cubes; add the peas. Pour over them the onion cooked in the butter for five minutes. Add flour, and seasonings, and pour on slowly the scalded milk. Sprinkle with finely chopped parsley.

Spinach Réchauffé (French recipe).

2 cupfuls cold spinach,
4 tablespoonfuls butter,
3 tablespoonfuls flour,
⅔ cupful chicken stock,
1 teaspoonful powdered sugar,
Salt and pepper,
Grated nutmeg,
Grated lemon rind.

Chop the spinach fine, reheat in a double boiler with the butter, in which has been melted the flour and chicken stock. Add the seasonings.

Baked-Bean Rarebit.

2 tablespoonfuls butter,
½ teaspoonful salt,
¼ teaspoonful paprika,
1 cupful cold baked beans,
½ cupful milk,
2 drops McIlhenny's Tabasco Sauce,
⅔ cupfuls chopped cheese.

Press the beans through the potato ricer and sprinkle the pulp with the seasonings. Put in an omelet pan with the butter, and when hot add the milk and cheese. Stir till thoroughly blended. Serve on slices of toast laid on very hot plates.

Onion Soufflé.

½ cupful stale bread crumbs,
1 teaspoonful chopped parsley,
1 cupful cold boiled onions,
Yolk 1 egg,
1 tablespoonful butter,
1 tablespoonful flour,
¼ teaspoonful salt,
Paprika,
1 cupful milk,
Whites 2 eggs.

Chop the onions fine. Make a white sauce from the butter, flour, seasonings, and milk. When it boils, add to it the bread crumbs, parsley, chopped onion, and beaten yolk of the egg. Beat the whites of the eggs to a stiff froth and fold them into the onion mixture. Pour into a buttered dish and bake fifteen minutes in a moderate oven. Serve with cream sauce.

Scalloped Tomatoes and Onions.

1½ cupfuls cold boiled onions,
6 tomatoes,
Pepper and salt,
1 cupful buttered crumbs.

Cut the tomatoes into thin slices and chop the onions fine. Butter a baking pan. Put in a layer of sliced tomatoes, season with pepper and salt. Cover with a sprinkling of buttered crumbs, cover with sliced onions, then a layer of tomatoes. Make the last layer onion slices covered liberally with crumbs. Bake in a moderate oven three quarters of an hour.

Monday's Soup.

½ can tomatoes,
6 boiled or baked potatoes,
½ onion,
1 stalk celery,
Few celery tops,
Pepper and salt,
1 tablespoonful vinegar,
1 cupful hot milk,
Pinch soda.

Boil vegetables together until they are soft. Put through a potato ricer, add pepper, salt, and soda. Just before serving pour in the milk with a pinch of soda dissolved in it. Sift over the top dry bread crumbs.

Green-Pea Soup.

Take what remains of the peas cooked for dinner the day before and a little of any kind of soup left, and boil together until the peas are soft. If you have a heaping cupful peas you can make soup enough for four or five persons. Put in salt and pepper and onion. The quantity of each must depend upon the character of the soup which you have put in. Put a tablespoonful butter into a frying pan, and when it is hot, put a handful stale bread cut in dice. Stir until they are quite brown. Strain the soup, rubbing the peas through a colander. Sprinkle in a little chopped parsley and a few celery tops cut up fine. Put the fried bread in the tureen, and pour in the soup.

Savory Cauliflower (Dutch recipe).

Steam cold boiled cauliflower until it is hot, and pour over it a sauce made as follows: Boil 1 cupful thin cream, thicken by adding 1 teaspoonful flour, stirred smooth in a little cold cream; let the mixture boil up, stirring constantly, add a pinch salt, a little pepper, and a small quantity nutmeg.

Cauliflower au Fromage (French recipe).

Put cold boiled cauliflower in a bake dish, and turn over it enough drawn butter to moisten; grate cheese over the top, cover with sifted bread crumbs, put small bits of butter on top, and bake until light brown.

Asparagus Omelet.

Put a tablespoonful butter in a frying pan; when melted, pour in 3 eggs which have been beaten just enough to mix the yolks with the whites; stir constantly; when the mixture thickens, take from the fire, season with salt and pepper, and stir into it what you have left of cold boiled asparagus cut into small bits.

Boiled Potatoes.

In boiling potatoes, choose tubers, if possible, which are of the same size. When this cannot be done, put the larger potatoes at the bottom of the saucepan, the small ones on top. Wash, pare, and put in cold water to prevent them from becoming discolored. During the winter, when potatoes grow old and soft, soak for two hours before cooking. Put in boiling salted water and cook until soft. Drain and serve in a dish with folded napkin over them.

Baked Potatoes.

Select the smoothest and most wholesome potatoes for baking. Scrub with a vegetable brush and lay in a baking pan. They will require forty minutes in a hot oven. Serve immediately or they are apt to become soggy.

Mashed Potatoes.

Take boiled potatoes and put them through a potato ricer, add butter, milk, pepper, and salt, and beat with a fork until fluffy. Heap lightly in a dish and, if you wish, brown them over the top.

Scalloped Potatoes.

Cut potatoes in thin slices, put in layers in a baking dish sprinkled with pepper and salt, dredged with flour, and with a little butter here and there. Pour hot milk over it, until the milk can be seen through the potatoes, sprinkle with bread crumbs and bake in a hot oven for an hour.

Potatoes Baked on Half Shell.

Bake 6 or 8 good-sized potatoes; as soon as they are soft, cut in halves lengthwise, scoop out the inside, mix with butter, cream, pepper, and salt, and the whites of 2 eggs beaten to a stiff froth. Whip the potato until white and fluffy, then put back into the skins and rake them with a fork until they have a rough appearance on top. Return to the oven, and bake until brown on top.

Potato Omelet.

Prepare mashed potatoes; put them in a spider in which a tablespoonful butter has been melted, smooth with a palette knife, allow them to cook a few minutes over a moderate fire; when delicately crusted underneath, score in the center, fold omelet fashion, then put on a hot platter.

Potatoes a la Hollandaise (French recipe).

1½ cupfuls white stock,
3 cupfuls potato cubes,
4 tablespoonfuls butter,
½ teaspoonful salt,
Dash McIlhenny's Tabasco Sauce,
1 tablespoonful lemon juice,
1 tablespoonful shredded parsley.

Pare the potatoes, cut into small cubes, and soak for half an hour in cold water. Cook until almost soft in the white stock, drain, and add the lemon juice, butter, and seasonings. Cover the saucepan and set back on the stove where it will not cook for five minutes. Serve in a vegetable dish sprinkled with the parsley.

Roasted Brown Potatoes.

Wash and pare potatoes, soak in cold water, boil for seven minutes, then remove from the kettle and lay in the gravy of a roast about half an hour before the meat is to be taken from the oven. Baste with fat two or three times. Sweet potatoes may be cooked in the same way.

Chambrey Potatoes (French recipe).

Wash and pare potatoes, then cut into thin flakes on a vegetable slicer, soak for half an hour in ice water, drain, and dry in a towel. In an iron spider fry out a couple slices salt pork, cook 2 slices onion delicately brown, lift out the onion, then put in the potatoes, having the spider more than half full, season with pepper and salt and dot over the top with bits of butter. Set the spider back on the stove where there is moderate heat. Cover tightly until the potatoes are softened and brown. Occasionally, while cooking, turn them over to prevent burning.

Hongroise Potatoes (French recipe).

1 cupful scalded milk,
4 tablespoonfuls butter,
3 cupfuls potato cubes,
2 tablespoonfuls flour,
½ teaspoonful salt,
½ teaspoonful lemon juice,
Dash McIlhenny's Tabasco Sauce.

Soak the potato cubes in ice water half an hour. Parboil three minutes, and drain. Put the butter in a spider, and sauté the potatoes delicately brown. Add the seasonings, dust on the flour, and pour in the hot milk; allow it to cook for a few minutes, then turn into a hot dish and sprinkle with shredded parsley.

Potatoes Brabanconne (French recipe).

Into 2 cupfuls mashed potatoes, stir a tablespoonful finely chopped chives, 1 teaspoonful chopped parsley, a dash pepper, teaspoonful salt, 2 teaspoonfuls butter, and a tablespoonful cream. Turn out on a platter, shape into a mound, dust over it grated cheese and stale bread crumbs. Cover with bits of butter, and brown in the oven.

POTATOES WHICH ARE FRIED

Saratoga Chips.

Pare potatoes, slice into thin shavings on a vegetable cutter, and allow to soak in ice water for an hour. Lift from the water, dry in a towel, fry in deep fat or oil until they curl and are delicately brown. Shake as free from fat as possible before lifting frying basket from the kettle, and put to drain on absorbent paper. Dust with salt. Be careful that the fat is not too hot, as the potatoes must cook before they brown, also allow the fat to reheat each time before frying another portion of potatoes.

French Fried Potatoes.

Wash and pare potatoes, cut them into lengthwise strips, and soak an hour in ice water. Drain and dry, then fry in hot fat. When taken from the kettle, shake them on a sheet of brown paper to absorb the fat, and dust with salt. Be careful not to cook too many potatoes at a time, as the fat is apt to become chilled and the potatoes grease-soaked.

Fried Potato Balls.

2 cupfuls hot mashed potatoes,
½ teaspoonful salt,
¼ teaspoonful celery salt,
Dash cayenne,
1 tablespoonful butter,
1 egg,
1 teaspoonful shredded parsley.

Into the hot potatoes beat the butter and seasonings. Allow it to cool for a few minutes, then add the parsley and egg. Whip with a fork until thoroughly blended, roll between the hands into small balls, dip in flour, fry in hot fat, and drain on brown paper.

Potato Croquettes.

Prepare mashed potatoes as for fried balls, adding a little onion juice and a dash McIlhenny's Tabasco, make into cork-shaped croquettes, roll in flour, egg, and finely sifted bread crumbs. Fry delicately brown in hot fat, then drain and absorb on paper.

Kartoffelklösse (German recipe).

3 cupfuls mashed potatoes,
1 cupful toasted bread crumbs,
2 eggs,
Dash pepper,
1 teaspoonful salt,
1 tablespoonful chopped parsley,
¼ teaspoonful nutmeg.

Beat the bread crumbs into the mashed potatoes, add the seasoning and parsley, moisten with the yolks of eggs beaten thick and lemon-colored. Whip the whites of eggs to a stiff froth, then blend with the potato. Mold into small balls and fry until delicately brown in hot fat. Kartoffelklösse has sometimes a teaspoonful baking powder added to the mixture and they are boiled like dumplings in salted water, when they puff up till half as large again; then they are served with tomato sauce poured about them and a sprinkling of crisp, buttered bread crumbs.

SWEET POTATOES

Boiled Sweet Potatoes.

Select potatoes which are of about the same size; if wished, they may be boiled in skins and peeled before going to the table, or pare them, and cook twenty minutes in salt water.

Baked Sweet Potatoes.

Wash potatoes, wipe, dry, and bake quickly in a hot oven. If they cannot be served immediately, prick with a fork and allow the steam to escape to prevent becoming soggy.

Sweet Potato (Southern style).

Bake medium-sized potatoes; when they are soft, cut in two lengthwise and scoop out the inside with a spoon. Put it through a potato ricer, have butter, salt, pepper, and enough thick cream to moisten. Whip with a fork until light and fluffy, refill the skins, heaping the potato into rough little mounds, and bake delicately brown.

Sweet Potatoes in Cream (Southern recipe).

When baking sweet potatoes, remove a large one from the oven while still firm. When cool, pare it, and chop to the size of peas; season with salt and butter and heap lightly in a buttered baking dish. Pour over it 3 or 4 tablespoonfuls cream, spread the top with melted butter and dust with powdered sugar.

Sweet-Potato Croquettes.

Two cupfuls mashed, boiled, steamed, or baked potatoes; add the beaten yolks of 2 eggs, and season to taste. When cold, form into small croquettes, roll in egg and bread crumbs, and fry in hot lard to an amber color. Serve on a napkin.

Broiled Sweet Potatoes.

Steam, pare, and cut in slices three eighths of an inch thick, lay the slices in a double broiler; salt, cover with melted butter, and broil over a slow fire.

Glazed Sweet Potatoes.

Boil sweet potatoes until nearly cooked, then peel and cut into quarters lengthwise. Lay on a baking platter, sprinkle over them salt, brown sugar, and melted butter, add a few tablespoonfuls boiling water. Set in a hot part of the oven, and bake till the potatoes are covered with a thin brown glaze.

CHAPTER LIV

LEFT-OVER POTATOES

STUDY all sorts of methods for making warmed-up potatoes good and so different that they will not taste alike twice. One day there may be a suspicion of onion about the dish, another the rich flavor given by a spoonful beef extract, a dash chives, parsley, cayenne, or celery, or they may appear *au gratin* with a delicate cheese flavor. Mashed potato may be warmed again or reappear in a dozen different ways.

There are a few rules to remember in the keeping of left-over potatoes. Never put them hot into the refrigcrator. Do not allow them to stand in an uncovered dish. They will acquire a tough, disagreeable skin, and are reduced to nothing by paring. Use cold potatoes before they are two days old. In hot weather they will not keep more than twenty-four hours. The sense of smell will speedily reveal to you if they have soured.

In hot weather use potatoes as often as possible in a salad. In this, too, seek variety. There are endless recipes for potato salads. Do not make a salad of old potatoes, the newer they are the more satisfactory the salad. In Germany, potatoes for a salad are always boiled in their skins, and it is a fact that they taste better than when pared before cooking. The neatest method for preparing them is to cut the potatoes into cubes about half an inch square or in tiny balls with a potato scoop. Do not cut them too thin or small. They break, and nothing looks more uninviting than a mushy potato salad.

Potatoes absorb a great deal of dressing, and they ought to marinate at least an hour before being served. One of the most acceptable of potato salads is a combination of potato and pickled beet with Worcestershire Sauce and onion juice. Another is made with finely sliced onions as a flavor, and a sprinkling of chopped tarragon, parsley, and chervil. A third has celery and chopped cabbage with minced pickle and a hard-boiled egg. Mushrooms and minced pickle are a favorite addition to a potato salad, while lettuce or celery enters into the make-up of others. There are a few things among vegetables that will combine well with potatoes. Cold peas are good, so are tomatoes, green peppers, olives, asparagus, red cabbage, cauliflower, capers, turnips, carrots, cucumbers, or string beans. Sometimes a relish is added to the potato salad by a few slices of salt salmon, several anchovies, or sardines.

Sweet potatoes may be put through the potato ricer and converted into croquettes or a pudding or pie. They may be glazed with sugar and butter, warmed in cream, or make an excellent *soufflé*. Another way is to cut them in thick slices, dip in flour, egg, and crumbs, and fry in deep fat, or slice them into a fritter batter, and fry.

Delmonico Potatoes.

5 cold potatoes,
1 tablespoonful butter,
1 tablespoonful flour,
1 cupful milk,
½ teaspoonful salt,
Dust pepper,
½ cupful grated cheese.

Cut the potatoes into fine dice, make a white sauce from the butter, flour, milk, and seasonings, and toss the potatoes lightly into the sauce. Turn into a baking dish, sprinkle with grated cheese, and bake till light brown.

Potato Puffs.

2 cupfuls finely chopped cold potatoes,
2 tablespoonfuls cream,
1 egg,
Pepper and salt,
2 tablespoonfuls flour.

Mix the potatoes thoroughly with the seasonings, flour, egg, and cream. Drop by spoonfuls in hot fat in a spider.

Stewed Potatoes.

Cut cold potatoes in neat small slices. Scald 1 cupful milk, 1 tablespoonful butter, and seasoning of salt and pepper. Add the potato. Let it boil up, and serve very hot.

Lyonnaise Potatoes.

1 onion,
2 tablespoonfuls butter,
5 cold potatoes,
Pepper and salt.

Chop the onion, and fry five minutes in the butter. Into this put 5 potatoes cut into dice, season with pepper and salt. Serve when brown and crisp.

Browned Potato.

Boil a pint or 2 of the tiny potatoes left in a barrel and let them cool. Skin and sauté in 2 tablespoonfuls clarified butter. Pepper and salt while in the spider. When well browned, put in a heated vegetable dish and sprinkle with chopped parsley.

Creamed Potatoes.

2 cupfuls cold boiled potatoes,
1¼ cupfuls white sauce.

Cut the potatoes into fine slices, and heat in the white sauce.

Chartreuse Potatoes.

3 cupfuls cold boiled potatoes,
Pepper and salt,
½ teaspoonful onion juice,
½ cupful flour,
½ teaspoonful salt,
½ cupful milk,
1 egg.

Mix the flour, salt, and pepper. Add the milk gradually and well-beaten egg. Cut the potatoes into quarter-inch slices. Sprinkle with salt, pepper, and onion juice. Put together in pairs. Dip into the batter. Fry in deep fat and drain.

Potatoes with Hard-Boiled Eggs.

6 cold boiled potatoes,
6 hard-boiled eggs,
Pepper and salt,
2 cupfuls thin white sauce,
½ cupful buttered cracker crumbs.

Cut the potatoes and eggs into quarter-inch slices. Put a layer of potatoes in a buttered baking dish. Sprinkle with pepper and salt. Cover with a layer of eggs cut in slices, then a layer of potatoes. Pour over it the white sauce. Cover with crumbs, and bake until brown.

Whipped Potato.

If you have 2 cupfuls cold mashed or riced potato, put a tablespoonful butter and 4 tablespoonfuls milk or cream in the double boiler, then add the potato. Leave the lid off. In ten minutes it will be hot. Beat with a silver fork till light and fluffy. Serve as ordinary mashed potato or use it as a border for any dish. It tastes like newly cooked potato.

Duchesse Potatoes.

2 cupfuls cold mashed potatoes,
1 egg,
2 tablespoonfuls cream.

Beat the yolk of the egg till very thick, add the cream to it, and work into the potatoes. Shape in small pyramids. Rest each one on the broad end in a buttered tin. Beat the white of the egg slightly; add to it a teaspoonful milk and brush each cone with the mixture. Bake till golden brown. Serve on a hot platter garnished with parsley.

Potato Croquettes.

3 cupfuls cold mashed potatoes
1 tablespoonful butter,
½ cupful cream,
Whites 2 eggs,

Salt and pepper,
Grating nutmeg.

Warm the potatoes, add the butter, cream, well-beaten eggs, salt and pepper to taste, and a slight grating of nutmeg. Let the mixture cool, then shape, roll in egg and cracker crumbs, and fry.

Potato Scones (Scotch recipe).

Take cold mashed potatoes, moisten with cream, and work in sufficient flour, with which baking powder is mixed, to make a firm dough, adding a pinch salt. Roll out the potato paste, sprinkle with dry flour, roll in beaten egg, again in flour, cut into rounds, and bake on a hot griddle for ten minutes; butter while hot, and serve.

Potato-and-Tomato Salad.

1 cupful boiled new potatoes,
1 cupful fresh tomatoes,
1 green pepper.

Cut the potatoes in neat cubes, the tomatoes in quartered slices. Arrange in layers on a nest of lettuce leaves, sprinkle each layer with chopped green pepper, salt, and powdered sugar. Pour over it a French dressing.

Glazed Sweet Potatoes.

6 cold sweet potatoes,
2 tablespoonfuls butter,
2 tablespoonfuls brown sugar,
Pepper and salt.

Pare the potatoes and cut in two lengthwise, dusting with pepper and salt. Melt the butter and sugar together; dip the slices of potatoes in this. Arrange in a baking pan, and bake till they are rich brown.

Sweet Potatoes (Cuban recipe).

8 cold sweet potatoes,
½ cupful water,
1 cupful brown sugar,
1 teaspoonful butter.

Pare cold sweet potatoes that have been boiled or baked. Put them in a sirup made from the water, sugar, butter, and a dust of cinnamon. Bake until the potatoes are covered with a fine, brown glaze.

Sweet-Potato Salad.

2 cupfuls cold sweet potatoes,
1 cupful celery,
6 olives,
1 tablespoonful minced parsley.

Cut the potatoes into small cubes and the celery into inch pieces. Mix and finish with French dressing. Sprinkle with sliced olives and parsley.

Sweet Potatoes au Gratin.

1½ pints cold sweet potato,
2 tablespoonfuls brown sugar,
2 tablespoonfuls butter,
Pepper and salt,
½ cupful buttered crumbs.

Cut the potatoes into tiny cubes and arrange in a loose layer in the bottom of a buttered baking dish. Sprinkle with pepper, salt, sugar, and morsels of butter. Repeat with another layer of potato; on top put a layer of buttered crumbs. Bake till well browned.

Hashed Brown Potatoes.

⅓ cupful fat salt pork,
2 cupfuls cold boiled potatoes,
⅛ teaspoonful pepper,
⅛ teaspoonful salt.

Try out the fat salt pork, cut in small cubes, remove scraps. Add the potatoes, finely chopped, pepper, and salt. Mix potatoes thoroughly with fat; cook three minutes, stirring constantly; brown underneath. Fold as an omelet, and turn on hot platter.

Curried Potatoes.

¼ cupful butter,
1 small onion,
3 cupfuls cold boiled potato cubes,
¾ cupful white stock,
½ tablespoonful curry powder,
Juice 1 lemon,
Salt and pepper.

Cook the butter with the onion until yellow; add the potato and cook until it has absorbed butter, then add the stock, curry powder, lemon juice, salt and pepper to taste.—FANNIE M. FARMER.

CHAPTER LV

SALADS

It is not so many years ago that salads were considered a luxury only to be found on the tables of the wealthy; to-day a wider knowledge of cookery has taught the housewife who has to set a table with a small income that there is no more economical, wholesome dish than a well-made salad. She is beginning to realize, as the French do, that almost anything can be put into a salad, and that even cheap materials with a mayonnaise or a simple French dressing make a palatable as well as a cheap and most sightly dish. There are four essentials to a good salad; everything that goes into it must be ice cold, the green vegetable used must be perfectly clean and crisp, the ingredients of a mayonnaise must be properly proportioned and thoroughly blended and the salad materials should be well mixed just before the dish is served. If these rules are followed, a simple head of lettuce with a plain French dressing is a perfect dish. No nicer way can be found to serve a vegetable salad than to bring the materials to the table crisp, fresh, and green, and dress it at the time it is to be served. For this purpose a large salad bowl, accompanied by a wooden knife and fork, and a small tray containing a cruet of oil and vinegar with pepper and salt, are a necessity.

For nearly every salad, lettuce is used as a base. If a whole head is not required at once, it may be kept fresh for several days. As soon as it comes from the market, sprinkle it and put it away tightly covered in the refrigerator. A good receptacle to keep for lettuce is a 5-pound lard pail with a tight lid. When required, clip off with shears the ragged, withered ends of the outside leaves, for often the portion nearest the stem is good enough to put into the base of the salad, to eke out quantity even if it is not to be eaten. Separate the rest of the leaves, wash thoroughly, and leave them for fifteen minutes to crisp in ice-cold water. Look over each leaf carefully in search of dirt or any of the insects that are to be found clinging to green stuff. Dry by shaking lightly in a wire basket, seeing that none of the leaves are bruised or broken.

Cold cooked vegetables or any left-over that is to be utilized in a salad, such as string beans, potatoes, or peas, are best if marinated for an hour or two before being used in a French dressing, leaving them in a cold place. If the salad is to be Macedoine, make a blend of various vegetables, marinate each one by itself, and only put together before sending to the table. Meat that is to go in a salad is much improved by standing for a short time in French dressing before using. Fish should be flaked or cut in neat cubes.

There is a strong prejudice among many people against oil. This is owing largely to the fact that sometimes one may have tasted a mayonnaise made of strong rancid oil. If you appreciate a salad, it pays to become a judge of good oil. Our California oils are now of the finest quality and are sold at a more moderate price than Italian oils. Good oil has a fresh, pleasant odor and a pale-green tinge. For people who really find the taste of oil obnoxious, there are various recipes for a boiled dressing in which butter takes the place of oil and makes very good salad. A cook can make a blend of boiled dressing with a tablespoonful oil mayonnaise in which it is almost impossible to detect any taste of oil. An excellent way is to make a pint of each dressing (if a salad comes to the table once each day, as it should) and keep them in the refrigerator tightly corked. Sometimes a few tablespoonfuls cream, whipped stiff, add a certain deliciousness to a mayonnaise that nothing else can give. It is especially nice where sour apples or celery are blended. Do not use "any old vinegar" in a salad; the best is none too fine; a colorless white-wine vinegar is required for any sort of mayonnaise.

During the summer, when all sorts of fresh green vegetables are abundant, it is a good plan while cooking what is to be used for dinner to double the amount needed and have something left for the next day's salad. This applies to such vegetables as green peas, string beans, cauliflower, turnips, carrots, new potatoes, spinach, asparagus, artichokes, beets, okra, or Brussels sprouts. In winter there need be no dearth of salads, for we have constantly with us cabbage, celery, and many of the boiled vegetables, as well as apples.

Every salad must be gently handled. It cannot be stirred as one would do when cooking a dish nor should it be molded or pattied. To break lettuce leaves makes them not only unsightly, but renders them tough. Pour the dressing over what ingredients are to be served in salad fashion, and toss with two forks till each particle is coated with mayonnaise or a French dressing, still not made mussy or broken. A variety of flavorings is a boon to the housewife who has not a great number of materials within her reach. Day by day even a plain potato or lettuce salad may be made a different dish by the use of some small addition as a flavor, such as chives or tiny pickled onions strewn over it, or make a difference in the seasoning, a mere hint of garlic one day, tarragon vinegar the next, or mint which can be added to a salad or two. The cook can make very cheaply for herself a number of flavored vinegars which will serve for a long time. To obtain any flavor, put the herb desired in a bottle, cover with white-wine vinegar,

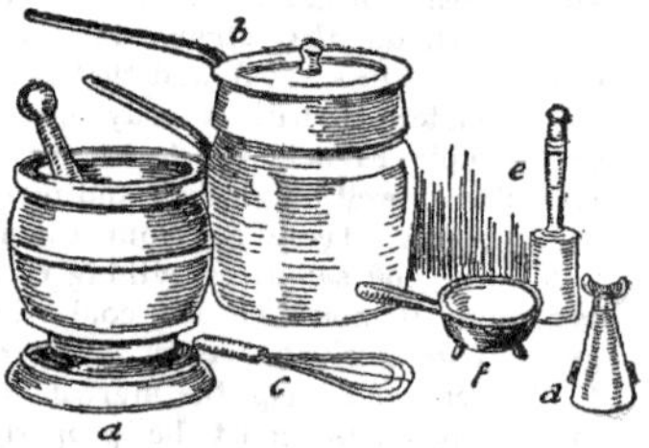

a, Mortar and Pestle; b, Double Boiler; c, Whisk for Beating Eggs; d, Ice-cream Mold; e, Potato Masher; f, Handled Casserole, Individual Size.

cork, and set the bottle in cold water, bringing it to a boil. Tarragon, chervil, nasturtium, cucumber, sweet basil, chives, onion, celery, summer savory, garlic, or peppers can be used in this way.

Oil Mayonnaise.

Yolk 1 egg,
1 teaspoonful salt,
1 teaspoonful powdered sugar,
1 tablespoonful lemon juice,
1 cupful olive oil,
1 teaspoonful mustard,
1 tablespoonful vinegar,
Dash McIlhenny's Tabasco Sauce.

Rub a bowl with the cut side of an onion, set in a pan of ice water, put in the dry ingredients and stir them together, then mix to a paste with a teaspoonful vinegar. Blend with the yolk of egg, stirring till perfectly smooth. Now, begin to put in the oil, a few drops at a time, beating constantly with a Dover egg beater. Alternate the oil with a little vinegar and lemon juice, until all ingredients have been used. When finished, the mayonnaise ought to be like a thick jelly.

DRESSING OR SAUCES FOR SALADS

French Dressing.

1 tablespoonful vinegar,
4 tablespoonfuls olive oil,
¼ teaspoonful salt,
⅛ teaspoonful pepper.

Put the salt and pepper in the salad bowl, or in a small bowl if the sauce is to be served separately. Add a little oil, stir well, then gradually add the remainder of the oil, beating constantly. Last of all stir in the vinegar, which should be diluted with water ii very strong. This dressing may be modified to suit different vegetables.

Cooked Salad Dressing.

2 eggs,
½ cupful vinegar,
1 cupful milk,
1 tablespoonful oil or butter,
1 teaspoonful salt,
⅛ teaspoonful pepper.

Put the oil and dry ingredients in a bowl and mix well. Add the eggs, and beat for five minutes. Now add the milk, place the bowl in a pan of boiling water, and cook till the sauce thickens like thin cream. Stir the sauce constantly while cooking, and bottle what you do not require for immediate use. If butter is substituted for oil, add it just before taking the dressing from the fire.

Sour-Cream Dressing.

1 cupful sour cream,
2 tablespoonfuls lemon juice,
2 tablespoonfuls vinegar,
1 scant tablespoonful sugar,
1 teaspoonful salt,
¼ teaspoonful pepper,
1 teaspoonful mixed mustard.

Beat the cream with an egg beater until thick. Mix the other ingredients and gradually add the cream, beating all the while.

Catsup Cream Dressing.

1 cupful cream,
½ cupful tomato catsup,
2 tablespoonfuls olive oil,
2 tablespoonfuls vinegar,
1 tablespoonful sugar,
1 teaspoonful salt.

Mix the dry ingredients, oil, salt, and vinegar together, then add the catsup and cream, beating it in gradually.

Cream Dressing.

½ tablespoonful salt,
½ tablespoonful mustard,
¾ tablespoonful sugar,
1 egg slightly beaten,
2½ tablespoonfuls melted butter,
¾ cupful sugar,
¼ cupful vinegar.

Mix dry ingredients, add vinegar very slowly. Cook over boiling water, stirring until the mixture thickens, strain, and cool. Add before using it an equal quantity of whipped cream.

Chicken-Salad Dressing.

½ cupful rich chicken broth,
½ cupful vinegar,
Yolks 5 eggs,
2 tablespoonfuls mixed mustard,
1 teaspoonful salt,
¼ teaspoonful pepper,
Few grains cayenne,
½ cupful thick cream,
¼ cupful melted butter.

Reduce stock in which a fowl has been cooked to ½ cupful. Add vinegar, yolks of eggs slightly beaten, mustard, salt, pepper, and cayenne. Cook over boiling water, stirring constantly until mixture thickens. Strain, add cream and melted butter, then cool.—Fannie M. Farmer.

Oil Dressing, Boiled.

1½ teaspoonfuls mustard,
1 teaspoonful salt,
2 teaspoonfuls powdered sugar,
Dash McIlhenny's Tabasco Sauce
2 tablespoonfuls oil,

¼ cupful vinegar diluted with cold water to make ½ cupful,
2 eggs slightly beaten.

Mix dry ingredients, add egg and oil gradually, stirring constantly until thoroughly blended; then add diluted vinegar. Cook over boiling water until mixture thickens.

Tomato Mayonnaise.

2 solid tomatoes,
Yolks 2 hard-boiled eggs,
Yolk 1 raw egg,
½ cupful oil.
2 drops McIlhenny's Tabasco Sauce,
3 drops onion juice.

Peel the tomatoes; cut them in halves and press out all the seeds, retaining the solid portion. Chop and press through a sieve. Mash the yolks of the hard-boiled eggs until very fine; add the yolk of the raw egg; when thoroughly mixed, add the oil a little at a time. When thick and smooth, add the dry pulp of the tomato (which has been draining while you are making the dressing). Add the tabasco and onion juice. This is a delicious dressing for cold beef or mutton.

Sidney Smith's Salad Dressing.

1 boiled or baked potato,
Yolk 2 raw eggs,
½ teaspoonful salt,
Dash McIlhenny's Tabasco Sauce,
6 tablespoonfuls oil,
2 teaspoonfuls tarragon vinegar,
1 teaspoonful lemon juice.

Press the freshly boiled or baked potato through a potato ricer; rub it down with a palette knife until perfectly smooth; drop in the yolk of 1 egg; rub thoroughly; then add the second yolk and rub again. Add the salt and pepper, oil, vinegar, and lemon juice. This dressing is improved by a suspicion of garlic or onion, and is excellent with celery or tomatoes.

SALADS

Water Cress and String-Bean Salad.

Arrange water cress on a flat dish; in the middle put a small heap of cream-cheese balls; around these lay in regular piles cooked and seasoned string beans; cover with French dressing.

Cucumber-and-Tomato Salad in Cucumbers.

Cut lengthwise large cucumbers; scoop out the centers in good-sized bits; mix with equal parts of peeled tomatoes cut into small bits, and refill the cucumber shells. Set on lettuce, and cover with French dressing.

Crab Salad.

1 dozen crabs,
1 cupful mayonnaise
2 heads lettuce,
1 green pepper.

Put the crabs in warm water, add a tablespoonful salt, stand the kettle over a brisk fire, and boil thirty minutes. When cold, pick out the meat and put it away until wanted. Wash and dry the lettuce carefully. Stand on the ice until wanted. When ready to serve, mix the crab meat, pepper cut into fine strips, and mayonnaise lightly together. Garnish the dish with lettuce leaves, place the mixture in the center, and serve.

Camp Salad.

Prepare a mixture of salad vegetables, or the following; lettuce torn into bits, dandelion nicely bleached, chives, and parsley minced fine, tiny cooked string beans or peas, a small onion or a bit of leek, and a tomato or a bit of celery. Cut 6 or 8 thin slices of bacon into bits and let them cook in a spider until crisp. Add 1 tablespoonful tarragon vinegar; pour the hot fat with the bacon over the salad mixture, and serve at once.

Celery, Apple, and Nut Salad.

Clean the celery and lettuce and set it to crisp in a wet napkin on the ice. When ready to serve, cut the celery in thin, crescent-shaped pieces; cut the apples in eighths, remove core, skin and slice crosswise in thin pieces, then crumble the pecans or walnuts. Take equal parts celery and apple and ½ part nuts. Mix with mayonnaise to hold together. Arrange the mixture on a platter in a mold with lettuce around the edge, cover with mayonnaise and garnish with thin rings or crescents of red-skinned apples and celery tips.

Ensalada (Mexican recipe).

Slice 2 Spanish onions in thin rings, cut 2 fresh chilis across in rings, removing the seeds, and slice 3 ripe, firm tomatoes. Put these in alternate layers in a shallow bowl, sprinkle parsley and bread crumbs over the top, and cover with a dressing made of 3 parts oil to 1 vinegar, seasoned with salt. Serve ice cold.—MAY E. SHERWOOD.

Summer Salad.

2 stalks celery,
2 seeded green peppers,
2 tomatoes,
2 tablespoonfuls cream,
2 tablespoonfuls mayonnaise,
Vinegar,
Salt and pepper.

Finely slice the celery and peppers, add the tomatoes skinned and cut in quarters. Beat the cream until stiff, add to the mayonnaise, with vinegar, salt, and pepper to taste. Mix with the vegetables, and arrange on a bed of escarole.

No-name Salad.

Make a mayonnaise, a small amount of aspic, and a French dressing. Flake any cold cooked fish, either of one kind or mixed, and lay for an hour in a deep plate sprinkled with oil and vinegar. Line a plain, flat-topped mold with liquid aspic by pouring in a small quantity and tipping the mold in a bed of cracked ice till every part is thickly coated; then set on ice. Ornament the bottom (which will be the top) with a round of truffles in the center and a dozen shrimps radiating from it, decorate the sides with a ring of shrimps alternating with slices of truffle; set these with a little more aspic. Add to the mayonnaise its own bulk of the jelly and put in the mold a layer of the mixture, then a layer of fish just as you lift it from the marinade; strew with capers, add another layer of sauce, then fish, till the mold is full; garnish with cauliflower and water cress seasoned with French dressing.—ANNE WARNER.

Salmon Salad.

Place on a bed of lettuce the contents of ½ can salmon, freed from oil and bones, and flaked. Pour over the fish boiled salad dressing or mayonnaise, then garnish with slices of hard-boiled eggs and lemon.

Garcia Salad (Spanish recipe).

Cut celery, apples, and fresh tomatoes in thin strips about two inches long; serve on lettuce leaves with French dressing. A slice of truffle on the top adds to the appearance and flavor.—GOOD HOUSEKEEPING.

Bavarian Salad.

Shred very fine 2 heads lettuce, chop 2 onions fine, and cut 1 cold beet into cubes. Make a layer of the lettuce, toss together the beets and onion and pile on lettuce. Marinate with a French dressing, pour over the top an oil mayonnaise, garnish with sliced olives.

Potato-and-Pepper Salad.

3 large cold potatoes,
1 green pepper,
4 tablespoonfuls vinegar,
2 tablespoonfuls ice water,
¼ teaspoonful powdered sugar,
Dash pepper,
½ teaspoonful salt,
2 tablespoonfuls oil.

Cut the potatoes into half-inch dice. Remove the seeds from the pepper and chop fine. Mix the vinegar, water, sugar, salt, and pepper. Put a layer of potatoes into the salad dish, then a layer of chopped pepper, and sprinkle over it a tablespoonful oil. Put in another layer of potatoes and peppers, add the other tablespoonful oil, and pour over all the vinegar. Set in the refrigerator for fifteen minutes to marinate.—MARIA WILLETT HOWARD.

Chicken Molded with Mayonnaise.

Stew a 4-pound chicken in 2 quarts cold water, add 4 slices carrot, 1 onion stuck with 8 cloves, 2 stalks celery, bit bay leaf, ½ teaspoonful peppercorn, 1 teaspoonful salt. Bring quickly to the boil till tender. Remove meat from bones and chop (there should be 2½ cupfuls. Reduce stock to 1 cupful, cool, soak 1½ teaspoonfuls granulated gelatin in 2 teaspoonfuls cold water and dissolve in stock which has been reheated; add to meat, season with salt, pepper, celery salt, and onion juice. Pack in buttered ½-pound baking-powder tins and chill. Remove from molds, cut in rounds, put on lettuce, and garnish with mayonnaise.—FANNIE M. FARMER.

Tomato-and-Pea Salad.

Scoop out skinned tomatoes, fill with cold boiled peas and English walnuts marinated with French dressing or mayonnaise. Serve on lettuce.

Cucumber Salad.

Pare cucumbers and cut crosswise in quarter-inch slices. Let them stand in ice water an hour, then take a sharp knife and pare round and round the slices very thinly, just as an apple would be pared, until there is a long, thin-curled strip. Put these strips on ice to harden, then put each one on a single lettuce leaf and serve on small plates. Put a spoonful mayonnaise on each plate and pass prepared horse-radish, vinegar, and oil with it. Brown bread cut in long narrow strips and spread with soft cheese is delicious with this salad. Most soft cheeses must be thinned with cream to make them spread easily.

Grand Union Cabbage.

Select a small, heavy cabbage and roll back the outside leaves. Cut out the center, leaving the shell entire. With a sharp knife slice the heart of the cabbage thin and soak in ice water till crisp. Drain and dry between towels. Add 2 green peppers cut in fine strips and mix with a French dressing. Pour over the cabbage and peppers, then refill the cabbage bowl. —STELLA A. DOWNING.

English-Walnut-and-Chicken Salad.

For this salad there will be required 24 English walnuts, onion, parsley, chicken liquor, celery, cold cooked chicken, French dressing, and mayonnaise. Take 1 pint chicken and 1 pint celery cut into dice, and parboil the English walnuts long enough to remove the skins. In boiling the nuts, add a slice onion, a sprig parsley, and a little chicken liquor, then drain, remove the brown skins, and mix them with the celery and chicken. Pour over this a cupful French dressing and put in the refrigerator for an hour or more. At serving time stir ½ pint mayonnaise into this. Make shells of crisp lettuce leaves, put a tablespoo..ful salad into each and a teaspoonful mayonnaise on top, and serve.—ELLA E. WOODBRIDGE.

Olla Podrida Salad (a Spanish salad).

2 small apples,
2 medium-sized onions,
6 tomatoes,
2 cold boiled potatoes,
1 tablespoonful vinegar,
2 tablespoonfuls oil,
Little powdered sugar,
Salt and pepper,
2 hard-boiled eggs,
Dash McIlhenny's Tabasco Sauce.

Peel the apples and onions, and chop fine. Peel and chop 3 tomatoes, mixing the pulp with the apples and onions. Rub a few bread crumbs on a clove garlic, and add them to the salad, also the potatoes, which have been sliced and chopped. Add to the salad the vinegar, oil, sugar, salt, pepper, and tabasco. Mix thoroughly together, and let stand about an hour. Cut the remainder of the tomatoes in slices, also the eggs, arrange on top of the salad, then mask with mayonnaise.

Egg Salad.

Boil the eggs hard, remove the shells, cut in halves lengthwise, and take out the yolks. Mash the yolks, using a silver fork; season with minced chowchow; add a little mustard sauce, a dash McIlhenny's Tabasco Sauce, melted butter, salt and pepper, and, if desired, minced olives. Return to the whites of eggs, arrange on a bed of lettuce or cress, dress with French dressing or mayonnaise. If no olives have been used in filling the eggs, a few pimolas scattered over the salad add to its decoration.

Jardinière Salad.

Cut into fine strips new turnips, carrots, and potatoes, and put them with a few green peas into a saucepan to fry lightly in a little butter. Cover with chicken stock and cook till quite tender. Drain and put in a salad dish. Pour over them French dressing. Set aside for an hour; in serving, coat with mayonnaise.

Beet Salad in Cups.

Boil the largest beets you can find with their skins on; peel them as soon as the beets are done. Cut a slice off the top and scoop out the center to form a cup. Chop celery fine, cut cucumbers in dice, and use a portion of the chopped beet. Mix and fill the beet cups. Put a spoonful mayonnaise on top. Place the cups on lettuce leaves, and serve ice cold.

Neufchâtel Salad.

2 rolls Neufchâtel cheese,
2 tablespoonfuls finely chopped olives,
1 tablespoonful cream,
Salt,
Cayenne,
1 teaspoonful capers,
1 pimento cut in strips.

Mash the cheese, add the olives, capers, and pimentoes; moisten with cream, season with salt and cayenne, form into small balls. Marinate with a French dressing. Serve on shredded lettuce, and garnish with pimentoes cut in strips.

Cauliflower Salad.

Stand a firm white cauliflower in salt water for half an hour, then cook it in boiling water until tender but not quite done. Drain, cool, cut into sprigs and arrange neatly in a salad bowl lined with lettuce leaves. Mash the yolks of 4 hard-boiled eggs and cut the whites into petals; arrange these like daisies over the cauliflower, and pour over a plain French dressing. Serve very cold.—Mary Foster Snider.

Salad in Boats.

Select 6 fresh cucumbers all the same size. Pare, cut in halves lengthwise, scoop out the centers, and lay in water till wanted. Dry and fill with a mixture of sweetbread and peas, dressed with mayonnaise. Set on a green lettuce leaf or individual plates.—Anne Warner.

Spinach Salad on Tongue.

Pick over, wash, and cook ½ peck spinach. Drain and chop fine. Season with salt, pepper, and lemon juice, and add 1 tablespoonful melted butter. Butter small tin molds slightly and pack solidly with the mixture. Chill, remove from mold, and arrange on thin slices of cold boiled tongue, cut in circular pieces. Garnish base of each with parsley, and serve on top of each sauce tartare.—Stella A. Downing.

Sweetbread Salad.

1 cupful mayonnaise,
1 pair sweetbreads,

1 cupful celery,
1 head lettuce.

Soak the sweetbreads in cold water for twenty minutes, then parboil in salted water. Cool and cut in slices, mix with 1 cupful celery cut in small pieces, cover with French dressing, and chill for half an hour. Serve in nests made of the inner leaves of lettuce, and garnish with mayonnaise.

Tomato Jelly with Celery Salad.

2 cups tomatoes,
1 slice onion,
1 teaspoonful salt,
⅛ teaspoonful pepper,
2 tablespoonfuls granulated gelatin,
½ cupful cold water.

Cook the tomatoes with the onion, salt, and pepper twenty minutes, then strain; add the gelatin, which has been soaked in cold water, and stir until dissolved; pour into a border mold which has been previously dipped in cold water. Serve with a garnish of white lettuce, and fill the center with celery salad.

Potato Salad (German recipe).

Cut cold boiled, rather waxy, potatoes into moderately thick slices, put in a bowl, and add to every pound a tablespoonful vinegar, 2 tablespoonfuls oil, ½ teaspoonful salt, ¼ teaspoonful pepper, and a little minced parsley. Slices of beet root and onions are a great improvement to the salad.

Ox-Cheek Salad (German recipe).

The bones having been removed, the ox cheek is rubbed thoroughly with salt, and put into a deep dish in salt for a week. It is then boiled in plenty of water with vegetables and a sprig parsley for five hours. The liquor poured from this makes an excellent soup. The meat is cut into dice and put into a salad bowl, with new potatoes also diced, and the same quantity of beet root and celeriac blanched for five or six minutes in salt water. Mix the vegetables, season with salad dressing and a spoonful whole capers.

Salad of Shad Roe and Cucumbers.

Cover a pair of shad roes, a sliced onion, and a bay leaf with boiling water to which has been added lemon juice or vinegar, and cook for twenty minutes. Drain and dry the roes, cover them with a tablespoonful lemon juice, 2 tablespoonfuls oil, and a dash pepper and salt. When cold, cut into small cubes (if they are not too tender). Rub a salad bowl with a clove garlic. Cut a thoroughly chilled cucumber in dice. Put a bed of lettuce into the bowl. Arrange the cucumber and lettuce, and over that the roe, well drained from the marinade. Garnish with a few delicate tips of lettuce and whole cucumber slices. Serve very cold.

Red-Apple Salad.

Select large red apples of uniform size, scoop into cups, and put in cold water in which there is a little lemon juice until time to fill them. Mix the chopped apple with celery, grapefruit carpels, and mayonnaise dressing, and fill the apples. Garnish with Maraschino cherries and broken walnuts, and lay on leaves of lettuce. Serve with wafers spread with cream cheese.

Potato-Salad Balls.

Add to left-over mashed potatoes 2 or 3 tablespoonfuls vinegar, the same of oil, and 2 teaspoonfuls grated onion. Make into little balls by using butter-ball paddles. These may be served with croquettes or patties. Or they may be placed on a leaf of lettuce as a salad course with a spoonful mayonnaise.

Pepper-and-Chicken Salad.

1 cupful tender green pepper,
1 cupful chopped celery,
2 cupfuls chicken,
2 hard-boiled eggs,
1 cucumber pickle,
Salt and pepper.

Chop the peppers fine, add the celery and chicken, mix well; add the eggs, cucumber pickle, salt, and pepper to taste. Set away to chill. When ready to serve, pour over it a rich mayonnaise. Garnish with parsley and olives.

Salad Provençal (French recipe).

1 cold carrot,
1 cold turnip,
1 cupful cold chicken meat,
12 mushrooms,
½ cupful asparagus tips,
½ cupful Brussels sprouts.

Cut the carrot, turnip, and chicken into inch strips. Mix lightly with a fork. Arrange in a nest of lettuce leaves on a flat dish. Moisten with mayonnaise and mask the top with a few spoonfuls. Garnish with cluster of mushrooms, asparagus tips, and Brussels sprouts.

Chiffonade Salad (French recipe).

1 head lettuce,
½ cupful cold beets,
½ cupful cold carrots,
½ cupful cold string beans,
1 tablespoonful chives.

Make a nest of lettuce and cut the vegetables into neat cubes. Chop the chives fine, scatter them on top, marinate with a French dressing.

Beet-and-Cabbage Salad

½ head raw cabbage,
6 cold beets,
Pepper and salt.

Shred the cabbage finely, soak for half an hour in iced water, drain thoroughly. Mix with the beets cut into fine cubes. Sprinkle with salt, pepper, and minced onion. Serve with French dressing.

Moscow Salad (Russian recipe).

1 cupful cold red beets,
1 cupful cold potatoes,
2 onions,
1 cupful celery,
1 head chicory,
1 teaspoonful capers,
1 teaspoonful pickled nasturtium seeds,
6 olives.

Cut the beets and potatoes into fine cubes, slice the onions fine, cut the celery into inch-length pieces, tear the chicory into fine strips, cut the olives into thin slices. Toss lightly together, add the capers and nasturtium seeds. Lay in lettuce leaves. Serve with French dressing or mayonnaise. Garnish with rings of hard-boiled eggs and sprinkle over the top a tablespoonful yolk of egg put through a potato ricer.—HELEN SASMORSKY.

Aspic Salad (Russian recipe).

1 cupful green peas,
½ cupful cold carrots,
1 tablespoonful capers,
1 cupful aspic jelly.

Cut the carrots into tiny cubes. Ornament the bottom of a mold with the peas, carrot, and capers, and fix them with aspic jelly. When hard, fill the mold with jelly. Let it grow solid, then scoop out a small hollow with a hot spoon and fill with mayonnaise.

Red-Vegetable Salad (Russian recipe).

2 cupfuls cold beets,
2 cupfuls cold boiled potatoes,
2 cupfuls raw red cabbage,
1 teaspoonful salt,
6 tablespoonfuls oil.

Chop the beets and potatoes fine. Pour over them the red vinegar in which the beets have been pickled. Add the cabbage shredded very fine. Sprinkle with salt and oil. Toss together, and stand in the refrigerator half an hour before serving. Just before serving, add ½ cupful French dressing flavored with onion juice.

Cauliflower-and-Potato Salad.

2 cupfuls cold potatoes,
½ cupful cold cauliflower.

Cut the potato into fine cubes and mince the cauliflower coarsely. Toss lightly, and serve with a French dressing. Garnish with slices of cucumber.

Summer Salad.

6 tomatoes,
3 cucumbers,
1 onion,
3 green peppers,
2 apples.

Slice the tomatoes, cucumbers, and apples; chop the onion and peppers fine. Blend with a French dressing. —May Irwin.

Baked-Bean Salad.

2 cupfuls cold baked beans,
3 ripe tomatoes,
3 tablespoonfuls vinegar,
6 tablespoonfuls oil,
¼ teaspoonful mustard,
Dash McIlhenny's Tabasco Sauce,
½ teaspoonful onion juice.

Make a dressing from the vinegar, oil, and seasonings. Heap the beans on lettuce, garnish with sliced tomatoes and over all pour the dressing.

Tomato Salad (German recipe).

Peel medium-sized tomatoes, remove a thin slice from the top of each, take out the seeds and some of the pulp, sprinkle inside with salt, invert, and let stand thirty minutes. Shred ½ head small cabbage. Let stand two hours in 1 quart cold water to which 2 tablespoonfuls salt have been added. Cook slowly for thirty minutes ½ cupful each cold water and vinegar, a bit bay leaf, ½ teaspoonful peppercorns, ¼ teaspoonful mustard seed, and 6 cloves. Strain, and pour over the cabbage drained from salt water. Let stand for two hours, again drain, and refill the tomatoes.

Tomato-Pineapple Salad.

Peel medium-sized tomatoes, remove a thin slice from the top of each, take out the seeds and some of the pulp. Sprinkle inside with salt, invert, and let stand thirty minutes. Fill the tomatoes with fresh pineapple cut in small cubes and English walnut meats, using ⅔ pineapple and ⅓ nut meats, mixed with mayonnaise. Garnish with mayonnaise halves of nut meats and slices cut from the tops of tomatoes. Serve on a bed of lettuce leaves.

Shaddock Salad.

2 green peppers,
1 head romaine,
Pulp 1 large grape fruit,
3 tomatoes.

Cook the peppers in boiling water; cool, and shred. Shred the romaine; remove the pulp from the grape fruit; peel the tomatoes and cut in quarters lengthwise. Arrange in a salad bowl, and pour over French dressing.

CHAPTER LVI

PUDDINGS MADE FROM STALE BREAD AND CAKE

THE variety of puddings into which stale bread enters is endless. It begins with the old-fashioned, económical pandowdy and ends with the queen of puddings, rich in jam and lovely in merinque. For puddings, use only stale bread or crumbs, rejecting crusts. Do not add the oven-dried crumbs, or you will have a pudding as tough as a door mat. Left-overs of fruit, fresh berries, peaches, plums, gooseberries, apples, prunes, apricots, almost anything can enrich a bread pudding. A cupful canned or stewed fruit or a few spoonfuls jam or marmalade give a morsel of delicious flavoring. The good cook uses common sense and the material she has at hand. If the recipe calls for red raspberries and she has nothing but dried apples, she can season them with spices, and the dessert will be a success. The base of any bread pudding light as a *soufflé* and large enough for a family of 4 consists of 1 cupful stale-bread crumbs, 2 cupfuls milk, and 1 egg. This may be enriched by almonds, chocolate, nut meats, raisins, currants, and peel or fruit of any description.

Stale cake, especially sponge cake or lady's fingers, may be converted into delicious puddings.

Where the pudding is to be steamed or baked, cut the cake in fingers or break it into crumbs. If the pudding is to be soaked with wine, have a custard, fruit juice, or cream poured over it, after cutting it in slices. Reject icing; it generally makes a pudding sweeter than is desirable. A good plain pudding is made by putting slices of stale cake in a steamer and, when moist, serving with a spoonful strawberry or marmalade sauce. It may be covered when cold with hot stewed berries and served with cream. Stale sponge cake serves as a foundation for charlotte russe and cabinet pudding, or, if steamed, may be covered with strawberries and whipped cream, when it makes an excellent imitation of strawberry shortcake.

Bread-Plum Pudding.

1 cupful suet,
1 cupful raisins,
1 cupful currants,
½ cupful citron and candied orange peel,
1 cupful sugar,
3 cupfuls stale-bread crumbs,
4 eggs,
½ cupful milk,
1 teaspoonful cinnamon,
½ teaspoonful each allspice, cloves, and nutmeg,
Grated rind 1 lemon.

Chop the suet fine. Seed the raisins. Slice the citron and orange peel, mix with the currants, sugar, and bread crumbs, moisten with eggs well beaten, and milk, then add the seasonings. Pour into a buttered mold. Steam four hours, and serve with hard sauce.

Orange Pudding.

1⅓ cupfuls stale-bread crumbs,
1 cupful cold water,
1 cupful sugar,
1 cupful orange juice,
Juice ½ lemon,
2 eggs,
1 tablespoonful melted butter,
¼ teaspoonful salt,
2 tablespoonfuls powdered sugar,
½ teaspoonful orange extract.

Soak the crumbs in water twenty minutes, then add the sugar, orange, and lemon juice, the yolks of eggs slightly beaten, the butter and salt. Beat till thoroughly mixed, pour in a buttered dish, and bake in a moderate oven till the pudding is firm. Allow it to cool slightly and cover with

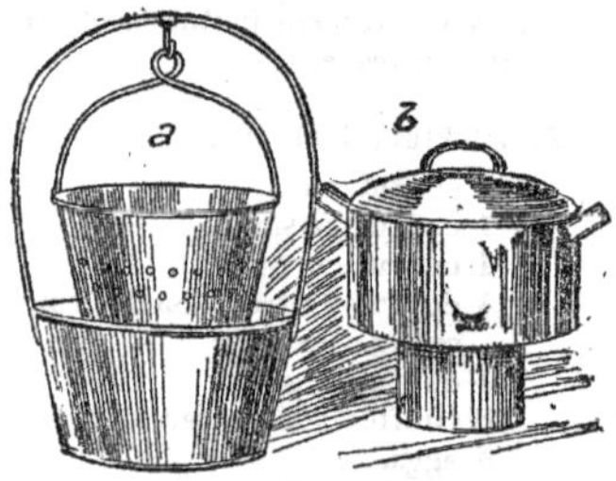

a, Saratoga Chip Kettle; b, Tea Kettle Steamer.

a meringue made from the whites of the eggs, sugar, and orange flavoring. Brown delicately, and serve hot or cold.

Walnut Pudding.

- Meats from 12 English walnuts,
- 1 cupful stale brown-bread crumbs,
- 2 cupfuls milk,
- 2 tablespoonfuls sugar,
- 3 eggs,
- 1 teaspoonful McIlhenny's Mexican Vanilla.

Scald the milk in a double boiler, and add to it the crumbs and chopped walnut meats. Allow the mixture to simmer gently five minutes, then take from the fire. When cool, stir in the yolks of eggs beaten with the sugar. Add vanilla and the whites of eggs beaten to a stiff froth. Pour in a buttered mold, and bake thirty minutes. Serve hot with vanilla sauce or hard sauce.—MARGARET BAILEY.

Lemon-Meringue Pudding.

- 2 cupfuls stale-bread crumbs,
- 2 cupfuls cold water,
- 1 lemon,
- ⅔ cupful sugar,
- 3 eggs,
- ½ cupful chopped suet,
- 3 tablespoonfuls powdered sugar.

Soak the crumbs in water thirty minutes, then add juice and grated rind of the lemon. Beat the yolks of eggs till thick and lemon-colored, add sugar and suet, and mix thoroughly. Add the other ingredients. Bake an hour. Beat the whites of eggs to a dry froth and make a meringue with 3 tablespoonfuls powdered sugar. Heap lightly on top of the pudding, dust with powdered sugar, and brown delicately. Serve with a liquid sauce.

Prune-and-Bread Pudding.

- 2 cupfuls prunes,
- 6 slices buttered bread,
- 2 eggs,
- 4 tablespoonfuls sugar,
- 2 cupfuls milk,
- Nutmeg.

Soak the prunes over night, and in the morning remove the stones. Cover the bottom of a buttered baking dish with a layer of buttered bread cut in wide fingers. Cover with prunes and a dust of nutmeg and sugar. Put in another layer of buttered bread, then prunes with sugar and nutmeg. Let the crust be bread with the buttered side up. Beat the eggs well, add the milk, and pour over the pudding. Bake an hour, covering the pudding with a plate for half an hour, then leaving it uncovered to crust. Serve with hard sauce or lemon sauce.

Apple-Custard Pudding.

- 2 cupfuls pared and quartered apples,
- 1 cupful stale-bread crumbs,
- 4 tablespoonfuls sugar,
- 1 tablespoonful flour,
- 1 tablespoonful butter,
- 1 egg,
- ½ lemon,
- ½ cupful water.

Put the apples with water in a granite saucepan and cook till the fruit mashes easily. Remove from the fire, add sugar, butter, and the grated rind and juice of a lemon. Mix the flour with bread crumbs and stir into the mixture. Beat the egg till light, and add it last. Turn into a buttered dish, and bake in a moderate oven three quarters of an hour. Serve hot with hard sauce.

Fig Pudding.

1 cupful chopped figs,
½ cupful finely chopped suet,
1 cupful chopped apple,
½ cupful brown sugar,
½ cupful stale-bread crumbs,
¼ cupful milk,
2 eggs,
¾ cupful flour.

To the suet add the sugar, apple, and figs. Pour the milk over the bread crumbs, and add the yolks of eggs well beaten. Combine the mixtures, add the flour and the whites of eggs beaten until stiff. Turn into a greased pudding mold and steam in a covered steamer four hours.

Orange-Marmalade Pudding.

1 cupful stale-bread crumbs,
1 cupful orange marmalade,
½ cupful chopped suet,
1 teaspoonful Calumet baking powder,
1 cupful flour,
½ cupful sugar,
1½ cupfuls milk.

Toss the dry ingredients together. Add the suet and marmalade, then stir in the milk and egg. Beat five minutes. Put into a buttered mold, cover tightly, and steam two hours.

Scalloped Apples.

6 large tart apples,
2 cupfuls stale-bread crumbs,
2 tablespoonfuls molasses,
½ cupful hot water.

Pare the apples and cut in generous slices. Into a buttered baking dish put a layer of bread crumbs, then a layer of sliced apples, and a top layer of crumbs. Add the hot water to the molasses and pour it over the pudding. Bake twenty minutes.

Bread Pudding with Raspberry Sauce.

2 cupfuls stale-bread crumbs,
2 cupfuls milk,
3 eggs,
Salt.

Soak the crumbs half an hour in milk. Beat the yolks of the eggs till thick and lemon-colored and add to the soaked crumbs with a pinch salt. Cut in the whites of eggs beaten to a stiff froth, and bake, setting in a pan of hot water in a moderate oven, forty minutes. Put no sugar in this pudding; the sauce supplies all the necessary sweetness.

Raspberry Sauce.

3 tablespoonfuls powdered sugar,
1½ tablespoonfuls butter,
1 cupful red raspberries,
Juice 1 lemon.

Cream the sugar and butter together. Mash the fruit, and beat in with the sugar and butter. Add the lemon juice, and beat till very light and frothy.

Apple Dowdy.

½ loaf stale brown bread,
8 large tart apples,
½ teaspoonful cinnamon,
¼ cupful dark-brown sugar,
½ cupful cold water,
2 tablespoonfuls butter.

Cut the bread in thin slices and pare off the crusts. Butter each slice. Lay them into a buttered baking dish till it is neatly lined. Inside put the apples, pared and sliced, sugar, cinnamon, dust of salt, and pour water over all. Cover the top with bread, buttered side up. Bake slowly an hour. Serve hot with liquid or hard sauce.

Chocolate Soufflé.

1 cupful stale-bread crumbs,
2 cupfuls scalded milk,
1 square Runkel's Chocolate,

⅔ cupful sugar,
1 egg,
Dash salt,
½ teaspoonful McIlhenny's Mexican Vanilla.

Pour the milk over the crumbs and allow them to swell half an hour. Melt the chocolate in a bowl in the mouth of a boiling kettle, add to the sugar, and scrape it into the soaked bread, beating well. Add the salt, vanilla, and egg slightly beaten. Turn into a buttered dish and bake three quarters of an hour. Serve hot.

Jam Pudding.

Stale bread,
2 cupfuls milk,
½ cupful sugar,
Salt,
1 egg.

Cut stale bread in slices, remove crusts, spread with butter or cream, and quince or plum jelly; put together like sandwiches. Place in a baking dish in layers. Pour over a custard of milk, egg, sugar, and a little salt. Bake, covered, half an hour; then uncover, and brown. Serve warm or cold, with cream.

Caramel Pudding.

2 cupfuls bread crumbs,
1½ cupfuls milk,
2 tablespoonfuls butter,
3 eggs,
1 cupful sugar,
1 tablespoonful caramel.

Mix together, and add whites of eggs beaten with tablespoonful sugar just before pouring into mold. Steam three hours in a buttered mold. Serve with apple jelly and caramel sauce.

Apricot Pudding.

1 cupful stale-bread crumbs,
1 cupful fresh or preserved apricots cut in dice,
½ cupful sugar,
¼ cupful butter,
½ cupful water,
½ cupful apricot sirup.

Butter a baking dish; cover the bottom with layer of crumbs, over it place the fruit; cover with crumbs, dot with bits of butter, then apricots, and so on, until the dish is full. The upper layer should be of crumbs, covered thickly with bits of butter. Pour over a portion of the liquid, or add it in mixing the pudding; place in a pan of water, and bake half an hour; take from the water, and finish baking fifteen or twenty minutes. Serve with cream or apricot sauce.

Brown-Bread Pudding.

1 cupful brown-bread crumbs,
2 cupfuls milk,
3 eggs,
2 tablespoonfuls maple sugar.

Soak the crumbs in ½ cupful milk fifteen minutes; make a custard of the remainder of the milk, eggs, and sugar; pour it hot over the crumbs; beat the whites of 2 eggs, with 1 tablespoonful sugar and 1 or 2 tablespoonfuls thick cream; stir lightly into the custard. Bake half an hour in a moderate oven; eat with cream.

Cocoanut Pudding.

2 cupfuls scalded milk,
3 eggs,
1 tablespoonful cornstarch,
1 tablespoonful sugar,
½ cupful grated cocoanut,
2 tablespoonfuls powdered sugar.

Cut stale bread in slices, spread with butter and honey, and cover with grated cocoanut. Line a baking dish with the sandwiches. Pour over a custard made with milk, eggs, cornstarch, sugar, grated cocoanut, and a little salt. Bake in a moderate oven half or three quarters of an hour. Cover with a meringue of the whites of 3 eggs and powdered sugar. Brown delicately. Serve with cream.

Chocolate Whips.

3 eggs,
2 tablespoonfuls sugar,
1 tablespoonful Runkel's Chocolate grated,

1 tablespoonful sugar,
1 tablespoonful hot water,
2 cupfuls milk.

Beat the yolks of the eggs and sugar till light. Dissolve sugar and chocolate in hot water; when dissolved, add slowly milk heated to boiling; pour this mixture over the beaten eggs and sugar, and cook in a double boiler, stirring constantly until it thickens. When cool, flavor with McIlhenny's Vanilla and place on ice. When ready to serve, half fill small punch glasses with the custard and whipped cream, sweetened and flavored, over it.

Sponge Cake à la Chantilly.

1 stale sponge cake,
2 cupfuls fresh or canned fruit,
1 cupful cream,
2 tablespoonfuls powdered sugar,
½ teaspoonful McIlhenny's Mexican Vanilla.

From the top of a stale sponge cake cut a thin slice. Remove the inside, leaving a wall one and a half inches thick. Into this put any fresh fruit sprinkled with sugar, or canned fruit from which the bulk of the juice has been drained. Beat the cream till thick. Add the sugar and vanilla, and pour over the cake just before serving. Save the inside of the loaf; it may be utilized in various ways.

Cocoanut Sponge Pudding.

2 cupfuls scalded milk,
1½ cupfuls sponge-cake crumbs,
1 cupful grated cocoanut,
1 cupful sugar,
Grating nutmeg,
1 tablespoonful rose water,
3 eggs.

Pour the hot milk over the sponge-cake crumbs, sugar, beaten yolks of eggs, cocoanut. Allow it to stand half an hour. Add the nutmeg, rose water, and whites of eggs beaten to a dry froth. Bake three quarters of an hour in a buttered mold. Serve with wine sauce.—MARGARET BAILEY.

Marmalade Sponge Cake.

1 stale sponge cake,
4 dry lady's fingers,
1 cupful powdered sugar,
½ cupful butter,
¾ cupful orange marmalade.

Cut a stale sponge cake in two, in layer style, and set it in a steamer ten minutes. Make a hard sauce by creaming the butter gradually, adding the sugar, and beating it till smooth and white. Add the marmalade at the last. Dry the lady's fingers in a moderate oven till light brown, then roll into crumbs with a rolling-pin. Spread the hard sauce on a layer of the cake, cover with the other half of the cake, spread with the remainder of the sauce, and scatter thickly with sifted lady's finger crumbs. Serve immediately. Almost any kind of jam can be used instead of orange marmalade. If it is a very rich, sweet preserve, use ¼ cupful less sugar. The sauce is also excellent if made with ¼ cupful orange juice beaten into the hard sauce, 1 tablespoonful lemon juice, and ½ teaspoonful orange extract.

Cream in a Crust.

Make a sponge cake, and bake in a solid loaf, either round or oblong. When cool, take out the center, leaving the crust an inch thick on the sides and bottom. Make an icing of 2 ounces chocolate, a cupful sugar, ½ cupful water, and McIlhenny's Vanilla to flavor. Melt the chocolate and add to it slowly the sugar and water boiled to a sirup which will spin a thread. Flavor, and brush with it at once the entire cake, inside and out, until it is well coated. Just before serving, fill with rich, sweet cream (about a cupful), whipped, sweetened, and flavored.

Pineapple Pudding.

Slices of stale cake,
1 pineapple,
½ cupful sugar,
1 cupful cold water.

Courtesy, The Kellogg Fruit Co.

Line a buttered pudding dish with slices of stale cake. Pare and slice the pineapple thinly. Cover each layer of cake with the fruit, sprinkling it with sugar; cover with cake, then pineapple. Make the top layer cake, and over all pour the water. Cover, and bake slowly two hours. Eat hot with hard sauce.

Cabinet Pudding.

3 cupfuls cake,
1 cupful milk,
2 eggs,
Salt,
2 tablespoonfuls sugar,
¾ cupful raisins, nut meats, and citron.

Butter a quart melon mold and scatter over it a few currants, raisins, nut meats, or tiny bits of citron. Fill the mold almost to the top with broken bits of cake, and sprinkle a little fruit through it if the pieces are of plain cake. Beat 2 eggs, stir in 2 tablespoonfuls sugar, a dash salt, and the milk. Pour this custard over the cake in the mold, turning in a little at a time to allow the cake to absorb the liquid, until all the custard is used. Put on cover and place the mold in a kettle of boiling water, not allowing the water to come quite to the top of the mold. Place a lid on the kettle and let it boil an hour. Serve the pudding hot, with wine or fruit sauce.

Crumb Pudding.

3 eggs,
½ cupful sugar,
⅓ cupful soft bread crumbs,
½ cupful farina,
½ cupful broken nut meats,
½ cupful butter,
½ cupful powdered sugar,
2 tablespoonfuls milk,
1 teaspoonful McIlhenny's Mexican Vanilla.

Beat the yolks of eggs until light and lemon-colored. Gradually add sugar, bread crumbs, and farina. Mix perfectly, fold in the whites of eggs beaten stiff, and nut meats. Pour into 2 layer-cake pans which have been buttered and floured. Bake half an hour in a slow oven. When slightly cooled, put the layers together with a creamy sauce made as follows: Cream ½ cupful butter, add gradually ½ cupful powdered sugar and 2 tablespoonfuls milk, add drop by drop. Flavor with 1 teaspoonful McIlhenny's Vanilla. Serve hot.—KATHERINE A. FRENCH.

Peach Crumb Pudding.

1 pint stale-bread crumbs,
1 tablespoonful melted butter,
2 eggs,
½ cupful sugar.

On a pint of stale-bread crumbs pour boiling water and stir in melted butter. After standing till thoroughly soaked, add eggs and sugar. On the bottom of a buttered dish put a thin layer of this batter, over it a layer of sliced peaches, and so on, dredging each layer of peaches with sugar, till the dish is full, having batter at the top. About an hour in a moderate oven will be required for the baking. Serve with sweetened cream.

Suet Cherry Roly-Poly.

5 ounces suet,
½ pound flour,
¼ teaspoonful salt.

Remove the fiber and skin from suet, chop fine, add flour and salt, mix well. Add sufficient cold water to make it stick, and roll out on a well-floured board. Cover with pitted cherries, dust with sugar, and roll quickly; tie in a well-floured cloth, leaving room for it to swell. Place in a kettle of boiling water and keep it boiling steadily two hours, or it may be steamed two hours and a half. Serve hot with any sweet sauce, or sweetened cream.

Marmalade Pudding.

½ pound bread crumbs,
¼ pound brown sugar,
½ pound suet,
4 eggs,
1 small jar orange marmalade.

Mix together, put in a mold with tight-fitting cover, and boil three hours.

Huckleberry Pudding.

Line pudding dish with buttered slices of bread. Fill with huckleberries, sprinkle over sugar and the grated rind and juice of a lemon. Place on top of buttered bread. Set in a pan of water in a hot oven; cover the pudding with a plate, and bake one and a half hours. When the pudding is done, cover with a meringue made of the whites of 2 eggs beaten to a stiff froth and 2 tablespoonfuls powdered sugar. Return to the oven to brown lightly, and serve hot.

Plain Plum Pudding.

4 cupfuls flour,
1 pound currants,
2 cupfuls sugar,
1 pound raisins,
½ pound candied lemon peel chopped fine,
1 pound suet chopped fine,
1 teaspoonful Calumet baking powder,
Nutmeg and cinnamon.

Sift the flour, baking powder, spices, and salt; add other ingredients. When well mixed, add sufficient cold water or milk to make a batter just thick enough to spoon into the mold. Leave room for it to rise. Cover closely, and boil six hours.

Fluff Pudding.

2 tablespoonfuls gelatin,
2 cupfuls cream,
1 teaspoonful McIlhenny's Mexican Vanilla,
2 cupfuls milk,
8 eggs,
¾ cupful sugar.

Soak the gelatin in cold water half an hour. Scald the milk, and dissolve the gelatin in it. Beat the yolks and sugar together, stir into the boiling milk, and cook two minutes. Take from the fire, add the vanilla, and turn into a bowl to cool. Stand the bowl in a pan of cracked ice, and stir constantly until it thickens; then add the whipped cream; turn into a mold and set away to harden. Serve with whipped cream.

Snow Pudding.

2 tablespoonfuls gelatin,
1 cupful sugar,
2 eggs,
Juice 2 lemons,
2 cupfuls milk,
1 teaspoonful McIlhenny's Mexican Vanilla,
1 cupful boiling water.

Let the gelatin soak half an hour in cold water, pour over it boiling water, add sugar, and stir till dissolved; add the lemon juice, and strain; set in ice water. When cold, whip with an egg beater until white as snow; beat the whites of eggs to a stiff froth, and stir them in. Dip a mold in cold water, pour the pudding into it, and set in a cold place till it hardens.

Sauce for Pudding.

Scald the milk; beat the yolks of eggs and a ½ cupful sugar together, stir into the boiling milk. Cook two minutes, add vanilla, and pour out to cool. Dish the pudding with the sauce poured about it.

Bananas and Tapioca.

¼ cupful minute tapioca,
1 pint boiling water,
¾ cupful sugar,
¼ teaspoonful salt,
Juice 2 lemons,
Whites 2 eggs,
5 bananas,
Whipped cream.

Mix the sugar and tapioca, stir into the boiling water and salt; cook, stirring occasionally, until the tapioca is transparent, then add the lemon juice and fold in the whites of eggs. When the eggs are evenly distributed throughout the mixture, fold in the pulp of the bananas cut in thin slices. Serve with cream, whipped or plain.

Orange Tapioca Fluff.

½ cupful minute tapioca,
1 cupful sugar,
1 pint water,
3 oranges,
2 eggs.

Boil tapioca, sugar, and water in a double boiler till clear, stirring often. Add the orange juice about three minutes before removing from the stove. When cool and beginning to "jell," stir into it the well-beaten whites of eggs. Serve with a soft custard.

Raspberry Jelly.

3 tablespoonfuls minute tapioca,
3 tablespoonfuls sugar,
2 cupfuls hot water,
Juice 1 lemon,
1 cupful raspberry juice.

Cook tapioca until clear with sugar in boiling water, add the lemon juice and raspberry juice. When beginning to "jell," beat smooth with a spoon.

Danish Pudding.

3 cupfuls hot water,
½ cupful minute tapioca,
1 teaspoonful salt,
½ cupful sugar,
1 tumbler currant jelly.

Cook the tapioca and water fifteen minutes. Add sugar, salt, and currant jelly. Stir until jelly is dissolved. Pour into glass dish and keep on ice. Serve very cold with sugar and cream. In summer 1 pint ripe strawberries used in place of jelly makes a pleasing change.

Grape Blancmange.

1 cupful grape juice,
3 tablespoonfuls cornstarch,
Whites 3 eggs,
½ cupful sugar,
Yolks 3 eggs,
1 teaspoonful McIlhenny's Mexican Vanilla,
1 pint milk.

Put the grape juice and 1 cupful water in a double boiler; when boiling, stir in the cornstarch previously dissolved in cold water; cook five minutes, stirring till smooth and thick; remove from fire, fold in the stiffly beaten whites and sugar. Make a custard of the yolks of eggs, sugar to sweeten, a teaspoonful vanilla and milk, and serve with the grape blancmange. Turn it from the mold into a glass dish, and pour the custard around it.

Winter Fruit Pudding.

2 tablespoonfuls gelatin,
6 oranges,
1 can pineapple,
3 bananas,
Sugar to taste.

Slice the bananas, cut the pineapple in small pieces, and spoon the pulp from the oranges. Drain off the juice; in part of this soak the gelatin five minutes, stand in hot water until dissolved, add to the rest of the juice, and pour over the fruit arranged in a salad bowl. Set on ice until jellied, then sprinkle with grated cocoanut.

Coffee Jelly.

2 tablespoonfuls gelatin,
½ cupful cold water,
3 cupfuls coffee,
¾ cupful sugar,

Soak the gelatin in cold water five minutes and dissolve in the hot coffee; add the sugar, stir until dissolved, and turn into a mold. Serve with whipped cream.

Cocoanut Cream Tapioca.

1 quart hot milk,
2 tablespoonfuls minute tapioca,
3 tablespoonfuls cocoanut,
1 cupful sugar,
2 tablespoonfuls powdered sugar,
Yolks 3 eggs.

Boil fifteen minutes in a double boiler, stirring frequently, the milk, tapioca, cocoanut, and sugar. Add the beaten yolks of eggs and remove at once from the stove. Cover with whites of eggs beaten to a stiff froth with powdered sugar, and brown in a quick oven.

Indian Tapioca Pudding.

2 tablespoonfuls minute tapioca,
1 quart milk,
3 tablespoonfuls cornmeal,
½ cupful molasses,
1 tablespoonful butter,
1 tablespoonful cinnamon,
Nutmeg to taste,
1 egg,
1 cupful cold milk.

Cook tapioca in milk ten minutes. While boiling, stir in cornmeal wet with a little milk, molasses, butter, salt, cinnamon, nutmeg, and egg. Pour in a dish, add cold milk, and bake two hours.

Coffee Tapioca.

3 cupfuls coffee infusion,
½ cupful minute tapioca,
½ cupful sugar,
Salt,
1 teaspoonful McIlhenny's Mexican Vanilla.

Cook tapioca in coffee fifteen minutes with sugar and salt. Flavor with vanilla, and serve cold with cream and sugar.

Apple Tapioca.

6 tart apples,
1 cupful sugar,
Salt,
½ cupful minute tapioca,
1 quart water.

Pare and quarter apples. Place in dish and pour over sugar and salt. Cook tapioca in double boiler in a quart water with pinch salt fifteen minutes. Pour this over the apples. Cover the dish, and bake half an hour. Serve with cream and sugar.

Rothe Grütze (German recipe).

½ cupful minute tapioca,
1 cupful sugar,
¼ teaspoonful salt,
1½ cupfuls hot water,
2 cupfuls rhubarb.

Put tapioca in double boiler with sugar, salt, and hot water. Add rhubarb that has been washed and cut in small pieces, without peeling. Cook till the rhubarb is tender. Mash with a fork, and pour, while hot, into a cold, wet earthen or granite mold. Keep in a cold place a few hours, turn out, and serve with cream. This may be molded in individual cups.

Hot Chocolate Pudding.

2 cupfuls stale-bread crumbs,
2 cupfuls milk scalded,
1½ ounces chocolate,
½ cupful sugar,
1 egg,
Dash salt,
1 teaspoonful McIlhenny's Mexican Vanilla.

Pour the hot milk, in which the chocolate has been melted, over the bread crumbs, add to it sugar and salt. Beat the yolk of egg till thick and lemon-colored, stir it in, add the vanilla, last of all the white of egg beaten to a stiff froth. Pour the mixture into buttered custard cups, set in a pan of boiling water, then in a moderate oven bake about half an hour. Serve hot with hard sauce.

Chocolate Tapioca.

½ cupful minute tapioca,
½ cupful sugar,
½ teaspoonful salt,
3 cupfuls milk,
1 ounce chocolate,
½ teaspoonful McIlhenny's Mexican Vanilla.

Soak the tapioca over night, scald the milk in a double boiler, add the tapioca, sugar, and melted chocolate. Cook half an hour, stirring frequently. When taken from the fire, add the vanilla, and pour into a mold. Serve the pudding ice cold, with whipped cream or chilled custard.

Baked Chocolate Custard.

2 cupfuls milk,
1 ounce chocolate,
2 eggs,
¼ cupful sugar,
Dash salt,
½ teaspoonful McIlhenny's Mexican Vanilla,

Melt the chocolate in a double boiler. Pour the milk in and let it come to the scalding point. Pour over the slightly beaten eggs and the sugar and salt, strain into a buttered mold or custard cups; set them in a pan of hot water and bake in a moderate oven until a knife can be put into the middle of the custard and come out clean. Serve ice cold.

Chocolate Spanish Cream.

1 tablespoonful granulated gelatin,
3 cupfuls milk,
Whites 3 eggs,
Yolks 3 eggs,
½ cupful sugar,
Dash salt,
1 teaspoonful McIlhenny's Mexican Vanilla,
1½ squares chocolate.

Melt the chocolate in a double boiler, add the sugar, and pour over it the scalded milk; beat till perfectly blended, then pour over the beaten egg yolks and back into the boiler, cooking till it thickens like a custard. Remove from the stove, add the salt, vanilla, and whites of eggs beaten to a stiff froth. Turn into individual molds which have been dipped in cold water, and chill. Serve with a garnish of whipped cream.

Chocolate Charlotte.

1 tablespoonful granulated gelatin,
¼ cupful cold water,
⅔ cupful scalded cream,
1½ squares chocolate,
3 tablespoonfuls hot water,
⅔ cupful sugar,
Whip 3 cupfuls cream.
1 teaspoonful McIlhenny's Mexican Vanilla,
6 lady's fingers.

Melt the chocolate in a double boiler, add half the sugar, dilute with boiling water, and put in the soaked gelatin. Stir till dissolved, add the scalded cream, and pour into a bowl; set in a pan of ice water and stir till it begins to thicken. Fold in the whip from the cream. Separate the lady's fingers and place them around the inside of a mold, crust side out. Turn in the chocolate mixture, and set it on ice. When very cold, turn out on a platter and garnish with whipped cream.

Chocolate Blancmange.

2 cupfuls scalded milk,
5 tablespoonfuls cornstarch,
½ cupful sugar,
Dash salt,
⅓ cupful cold milk,
1½ squares chocolate,
3 tablespoonfuls hot water,
Whites 3 eggs,
1 teaspoonful McIlhenny's Mexican Vanilla.

Mix the cornstarch, sugar, and salt in the cold milk, pour it into the scalded milk in a double boiler. Cook ten minutes, stirring constantly till it thickens, add the chocolate melted in the hot water, beat until smooth, add the whites of the eggs beaten stiff and vanilla, pour into a mold, and chill. Serve with whipped cream.

Chocolate Pudding.

6 eggs,
1 cupful sugar,
½ teaspoonful McIlhenny's Mexican Vanilla,
¼ pound Runkel's sweet chocolate grated,
1 cupful almonds chopped fine without blanching,
1 cupful sifted bread crumbs,
1 teaspoonful Calumet baking powder.

Beat until light and thick the yolks of eggs, sugar, vanilla, chocolate, almonds, bread crumbs, whites of eggs, and baking powder. Butter a pudding form, turn into it the mixture, and bake in a moderate oven thirty to forty minutes. Serve with meringue sauce. To make meringue sauce, boil together ½ cupful sugar and ½ cupful water until the mixture forms a soft ball when dropped in cold water, then turn it slowly over the whites of 2 eggs. Beat well, and

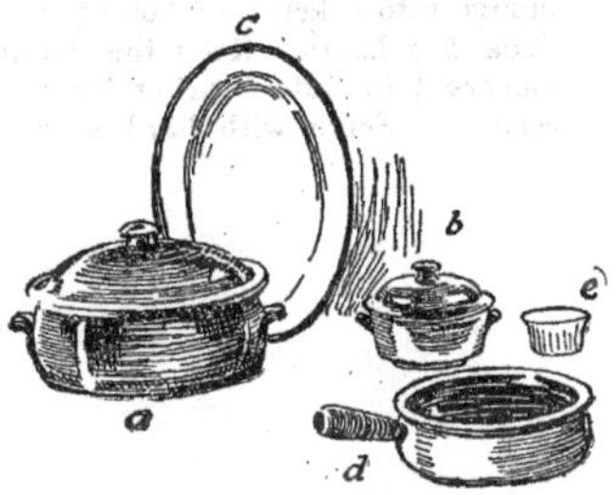

a, Covered Baking Dish; b, Small Covered Casserole; c, Shallow Baking Dish; d, Clay Casserole; e, Individual Ramequin.

flavor with vanilla. Turn out the pudding, and pile the sauce around its base, completely encircling it, and decorate, if desired, with chocolate candies.

Charlotte Russe.

- 1 quart thin cream,
- ¾ cupful powdered sugar,
- 1 teaspoonful McIlhenny's Mexican Vanilla,
- 12 lady's fingers,
- 2 tablespoonfuls gelatin.

Soak the gelatin in cold water half an hour. Beat the cream, and drain off the whip on a sieve. Line a mold with lady's fingers. Pour the cream in a basin and set it in a pan of ice water. Add to the soaked gelatin enough boiling water to dissolve it. Add the sugar carefully to the cream, then the vanilla, and last strain in the gelatin. Commence to stir immediately; stir from the sides and bottom of the basin until it begins to thicken, then pour into molds, and set on ice to harden.

Poor Man's Pudding.

- 2 cupfuls milk,
- 4 tablespoonfuls rice,
- ¼ cupful brown sugar,
- Dash salt,
- ½ teaspoonful cinnamon,
- 1 tablespoonful butter.

Wash the rice, add milk, sugar, butter, and seasoning. Bake several hours, stirring frequently till it is moist and brown.

Cottage Pudding.

- ⅓ cupful butter,
- 1 cupful sugar,
- 1 egg,
- 2½ cupfuls flour,
- 3 teaspoonfuls Calumet baking powder.

Cream the butter, add sugar gradually, and the egg well beaten; mix and sift flour, baking powder, and salt; add alternately with milk to first mixture; turn into gem pans, bake thirty minutes. Serve with vanilla sauce.

Steamed Apple Pudding.

- 2 cupfuls flour,
- 4 teaspoonfuls Calumet baking powder,
- ½ teaspoonful salt,
- 2 tablespoonfuls butter,
- ¾ cupful milk,
- 4 apples cut in eighths.

Mix and sift the ingredients; rub in the butter, add milk gradually, toss on a floured board, pat and roll out, place apples on middle of dough, and sprinkle with sugar mixed with a dash of nutmeg and salt. Wrap the dough around the apples and lift into buttered molds. Cover and steam an hour and a half, and serve with vanilla sauce.

Snowballs.

- ½ cupful butter,
- 1 cupful sugar,
- ½ cupful milk,
- 2¼ cupfuls flour,
- 3½ teaspoonfuls Calumet baking powder.
- Whites 3 eggs.

Cream the butter, add sugar gradually, then the milk and flour mixed and sifted with baking powder; last the whites of eggs beaten to a stiff froth. Steam thirty-five minutes in buttered cups; serve with strawberry hard sauce.

English Plum Pudding.

1½ cupfuls flour,
1½ cupfuls stale-bread crumbs,
¾ pound raisins,
¾ pound currants,
¾ pound suet,
1¼ cupfuls sugar,
1 cupful molasses,
3 ounces candied orange peel,
1 teaspoonful nutmeg,
1 teaspoonful mace,
6 eggs,
1 teaspoonful salt.

Mix all the dry ingredients, add the eggs well beaten, and stir ten minutes. Turn into a floured pudding cloth or mold. If the cloth is used, tie securely, leaving some space to allow the pudding to swell, and plunge into a kettle of boiling water. Cook five hours. Keep the pudding immersed in water during the entire cooking. Serve with hard sauce.

CHAPTER LVII

PUDDING SAUCES

(Hot Sauces)

Chocolate Sauce.

1 cupful water,
½ cupful sugar,
1 stick cinnamon,
1 square Runkel's Chocolate,
½ cupful milk,
1½ tablespoonfuls cornstarch,
Dash salt,
1 teaspoonful McIlhenny's Mexican Vanilla.

Cook together the water, sugar, and cinnamon, strain, add the chocolate which has been dissolved in hot milk, thicken with cornstarch, wet in a little water. Add the salt and beat till creamy. After taking off the fire, add the vanilla and serve hot. This is a very nice sauce to use with a hot plain pudding of any kind or with vanilla ice cream frozen hard.

Foamy Sauce.

½ cupful powdered sugar,
3 whites eggs,
1 teaspoonful McIlhenny's Mexican Vanilla,
1 cupful boiling water.

Beat the whites of eggs to a stiff froth, add the powdered sugar, flavoring, and water, stir carefully, and serve very hot.

Orange Sauce.

2 tablespoonfuls butter,
Yolks 4 eggs,
3 tablespoonfuls powdered sugar,
¾ cupful thick cream,
¾ cupful orange juice,
Grated rind 1 orange.

Cream the butter and whip the sugar into it, put in a double boiler, add the yolks of eggs well beaten with the cream, stir constantly till it is like a thick custard, then take from the fire, and blend in orange juice and rind.

Fruit Sauce.

½ cupful sugar,
1 cupful boiling water,
1 tablespoonful arrowroot,
½ can any preserved fruit.

Boil sugar and water together, add the fruit, which may be anything you happen to have—strawberries, peaches, apricots, raspberries (red), or quinces will make a nice sauce. Cook in the sirup a few minutes, then press the pulp through a potato ricer, put back on the fire in a saucepan; when boiling, thicken with the arrowroot dissolved in cold water, beat till thick and creamy. This sauce may be served hot with any hot pudding, or when thoroughly chilled it is nice with cold rice or vanilla ice cream.

Hard Sauce.

½ cupful butter,
1 cupful powdered sugar,
Little nutmeg.

Beat butter well, stir in slowly sugar, and beat to a cream. Pile on a plate, and grate over a little nutmeg. Keep cool.

Strawberry Sauce.

1 tablespoonful butter,
1½ cupfuls powdered sugar,
White 1 egg,
1 pint mashed strawberries.

Beat butter to a cream. Add gradually sugar and the whites of eggs. Beat till very light, and just before serving add strawberries.

Soft Custard.

2 cupfuls scalded milk,
Yolks 4 eggs,
2 tablespoonfuls sugar,
½ teaspoonful salt.

Cook over hot fire till it will mask the spoon, strain, cool, and flavor. Some puddings are improved by having the sugar browned as for caramel sauce.

Maple Sauce.

½ pound maple sugar,
½ cupful water,
Whites 2 eggs,
½ cupful thick cream,
1 teaspoonful lemon juice.

Boil water and sugar till it will spin. Whisk boiling hot into the beaten whites of eggs, add cream and lemon juice.

Crême d'Amande Sauce (French recipe).

2 cupfuls sweet cream,
2 ounces sweet almond,
2 drops extract bitter almond,
¼ cupful powdered sugar,
1 teaspoonful rose water.

Chop almonds which have been blanched and browned in the oven, pound them very fine. Add sugar, almonds, and rose water to the cream. Beat until the sauce is very light.

Aigre Diouz (French recipe).

2 cupfuls sour cream,
Juice and grated rind 1 lemon,
Sugar to taste.

Beat hard and long until the sauce is very light.

Currant-Jelly Sauce.

½ cupful currant jelly,
Whites 3 eggs,
½ cupful powdered sugar,
½ cupful thick cream.

Beat the whites of eggs to a stiff froth, add sugar by degrees, and beat well. Soften the jelly by heating in a bowl set in hot water. When soft enough to drop from a spoon, beat it into the eggs and sugar. Add the cream. Stir in 2 tablespoonfuls jelly cut in dice, and serve.

Lemon Sauce.

1 cupful sugar,
½ cupful water,
Rind and juice 2 lemons,
Yolks 3 eggs.

Boil the water, sugar, juice, and rind of lemons all together ten minutes. Beat the yolks of eggs. Strain the sirup, stir the eggs into it, set the saucepan in boiling water, and beat rapidly until thick and smooth; remove from the water, and beat five minutes.

Orange Sauce.

1 cupful sugar,
1 cupful water,
½ teaspoonful cornstarch,
¾ cupful orange juice,
Juice 1 lemon,
1 cupful orange pulp.

Make a sirup of sugar and water, and thicken with cornstarch. Take from the fire, cool, add orange juice, juice of lemon, and orange pulp. Serve ice cold.

Vanilla Sauce.

1 cupful sugar,
1 cupful water,
1 apple,
Pinch cinnamon,
½ teaspoonful McIlhenny's Mexican Vanilla,
½ teaspoonful arrowroot,
1 cupful whipped cream.

Mix the sugar and water, and put over the fire. Peel and core the apple, slice, cut into dice, and put at once in the hot sirup. Simmer gently until soft. Take out, thicken the sirup with arrowroot, cook five minutes, strain, add whipped cream.

(Cold Sauces)

Egg Sauce.

3 eggs,
1 cupful sugar,
1 teaspoonful McIlhenny's Mexican Vanilla.

Separate the eggs and beat the yolks till thick and lemon-colored, adding the sugar gradually. Whip the eggs to a stiff froth, blend with the yolks, flavor with the vanilla, and serve ice cold.

Whipped-Cream Sauce.

1 cupful double cream,
½ cupful powdered sugar,
White 1 egg,
1 teaspoonful McIlhenny's Mexican Vanilla.

Beat the cream till perfectly stiff, adding the sugar gradually. Blend in the white of egg beaten to a froth, flavor with the vanilla, and serve cold.

Jelly Sauce.

Yolks 3 eggs,
½ cupful powdered sugar,
2 cupfuls hot milk,
1 tablespoonful gelatin,
1 teaspoonful McIlhenny's Mexican Vanilla.

Beat the yolks of eggs till very thick, adding the sugar gradually, pour over it the milk, cook to a creamy custard, then add the gelatin dissolved in a little cold water, and flavor with vanilla.

Pistachio Sauce.

1 cupful sugar,
1 tablespoonful cornstarch,
2 cupfuls boiling water,
1 teaspoonful pistachio,
½ cupful chopped pistachio nuts.

Boil the sugar and water together five minutes, thicken with cornstarch dissolved in cold water, flavor with pistachio, and stir in the nuts, and chill. If desired, this sauce may be served hot with a hot pudding.

Creamy Sauce.

1 teaspoonful butter,
2 cupfuls powdered sugar,
1 egg,
½ cupful thick cream,
1 teaspoonful McIlhenny's Mexican Vanilla.

Rub to a cream butter, sugar, and egg, add cream and vanilla. If it should separate, set it over hot water and stir until smooth again. Keep on ice till wanted.

Plain Hot Sauce.

2 cupfuls water,
1 cupful sugar,
1 tablespoonful cornstarch,
1 teaspoonful butter,
1 lemon.

Boil sugar, and water, stir in cornstarch, wet with water, butter, 1 lump of sugar well rubbed on lemon rind, or any flavoring preferred. Care must be taken to cook cornstarch well or it will taste raw.

CHAPTER LVIII

FROZEN DESSERTS

To the country housewife who has access to plenty of ice, milk, cream, and fruit, raw or preserved, frozen desserts are not a luxury; besides, they require no more time to make than a pie. In hot weather at least they are very much to be preferred to pastry desserts, both hygienically and from a palatable standpoint. Cream is by no means a necessity in the making of frozen dishes—fruit can be frozen, delicious sherbets may be made from milk or fruit-flavored water, and are as inexpensive as they are good. In a home where there are children, the little ones will gladly come to aid during the freezing process when ice cream is in prospect, as every mother knows.

First, there is the necessity of a good freezer. Never economize by purchasing a cheap one; the best is the truest economy in the end. Also provide a strong burlap bag and a mallet for smashing ice, as well as a dipper to measure salt and ice, for half the rapidity of the freezing process depends on the proper proportions being used. In winter, snow can be utilized instead of ice; if the salt does not act rapidly upon it, add a cupful cold water. Before pouring the stuff to be frozen into the can, adjust every part and give the crank a few twirls to insure the freezer being in first-class order. Then fill the can, adjust it again, and put in the crushed ice and salt in proper quantities. If there is only a small quantity to be frozen, the salt and ice need come no higher than the mixture inside. Never fill the can to the top; it will make a cream coarse-grained or it will spill out. At first, turn the crank steadily but rather slowly. When frozen to a mush, turn more rapidly, adding more salt and ice if necessary. Never draw off the brine till the freezing process is accomplished, then remove the top and dasher, and pack solidly with a spoon, put a cork dipped in lard into the hole at the top so there will not be the slightest danger of brine working in, and repack the freezer with 4 measures ice to one salt. Cover with newspapers or a piece of carpet and leave it, if possible, for two hours to mellow and ripen. If nuts, fruit, or liquors are to be added to frozen stuff, do not put them in till the mixture is a mush. When serving time comes, remove the can, wipe it off carefully before opening to make sure not a drop of brine can get inside, take off the lid, run a palette knife around the edge of the cream, invert the can on a platter, and the contents will slip out. If it should prove refractory, wring a cloth from hot water, wrap it about the can, and there will be no further trouble.

Keep your freezer in perfect order. After using, wash it thoroughly and set the pieces in a moderate oven or over the stove to get perfectly dry. Occasionally a drop of oil is needed to make it work well. There is a small hole in the cap covering the gear; look into this end and turn the crank till you discover another hole in the top gear of the frame. Let a few drops of machine oil drop into it.

Frozen dishes may be classified thus:

Water Ice.—Sweetened fruit juice, diluted with water, requires 3 level measures ice to 1 salt.

Sherbet.—A water ice, to which has been added a small quantity of dissolved gelatin or beaten whites of eggs.

Frappé.—Water ice frozen to the consistency of mush. Frappé requires equal quantities of ice and salt to give it a granular consistency.

Punch.—A water ice, to which has been added spirits or spices for stronger flavoring.

Frozen Fruits.—Fruit pulp frozen where one or several kinds of fruits have been used.

Philadelphia Ice Cream.—A custard foundation thin cream, and flavoring.

Mousse (Parfait or Fruit Pudding).—Heavy cream, whipped stiff, sweetened, flavored, poured in a mold, packed in ice and salt (2 parts ice to 1 salt), and allowed to stand three or four hours. Mousse is also made from the whip off thin cream folded into a mixture containing a small quantity of gelatin.

WATER ICES

Cider Ice.

1 quart cider,
1 cupful orange juice,
¼ cupful lemon juice,
1½ cupfuls sugar.

Dissolve the sugar in the cider, add the fruit juice, mix the ingredients, and freeze.

Orange Ice.

4 cupfuls water,
2 cupfuls orange juicc,
2 cupfuls sugar,
¼ cupful lemon juice,
Grated rind 2 oranges.

Boil sugar and water twenty minutes. Add fruit juices and grated rind; cool, strain, and freeze.

Apple Water Ice.

6 large tart apples,
2 cupfuls sugar,
4 cupfuls water,
2 lemons.

Put the apples, sugar, and water on to boil, add the grated yellow rind of 1 lemon. Cook until the apples are reduced to a pulp, take from the fire, drain carefully, without squeezing, add the juice of the lemons; when cold, freeze.

Currant Water Ice.

2 cupfuls red-currant juice,
2 cupfuls sugar,
2 cupfuls boiling water.

Add the sugar to the boiling water, and stir until dissolved. When cold, add the currant juice, and freeze.

Pineapple Water Ice.

2 large yellow pineapples,
3 cupfuls sugar,
4 cupfuls water,
Juice 2 lemons.

Pare the pineapples, grate them, and add the juice of the lemons. Boil the sugar and water together five minutes. When cold, add the pineapple, strain through a fine sieve, and freeze.

Raspberry Water Ice.

1 quart red raspberries,
4 cupfuls water,
Juice 2 lemons,
2 cupfuls sugar.

Add the sugar and lemon juice to the berries, stir, and stand an hour; then mash, add the water, strain through a cloth, and freeze.

Strawberry Water Ice.

1 quart strawberries,
2 cupfuls sugar,
4 cupfuls water,
Juice 2 lemons.

Add the sugar and lemon juice to the strawberries, mash them, and stand an hour; add the water, strain through a cloth, and freeze.

Grape Water Ice.

3 pounds Concord grapes,
4 cupfuls water,
2 cupfuls sugar.

Boil the sugar and water together five minutes. Pulp the grapes, add the pulps and skins to the sirup; stand to cool. When cold, press through a fine sieve, being careful not to mash the seeds, and freeze.

Ginger Water Ice.

6 ounces preserved ginger,
1 quart lemon water ice.

Pound 4 ounces ginger to a paste. Cut the remaining 2 ounces into very thin slices and stir these into the water ice. Repack, and stand to ripen.

Lemon Water Ice.

4 large juicy lemons,
4 cupfuls water,
1 orange,
2½ cupfuls sugar.

Put the sugar and water on to boil. Chip the yellow rind from 3 lemons and the orange, add to the sirup, boil five minutes, and stand to cool. Squeeze the juice from the orange and lemons, add to the cold sirup, strain through a cloth, and freeze.

Barberry Water Ice.

4 large juicy lemons,
4 cupfuls water,
1 orange,
2½ cupfuls sugar,
1 cupful barberry juice.

Add ½ pint barberry juice, slightly sweetened, to the recipe for lemon water ice, before freezing.

Pomegranate Water Ice.

1 dozen ripe pomegranates,
2 cupfuls water,
2 cupfuls sugar.

Cut the pomegranates into halves, remove the seeds carefully from the inside bitter skin, press in a sieve without breaking the seeds. Add the sugar to the juice, and stir until dissolved, add the water, strain, and freeze.

Quince Water Ice.

3 large ripe quinces,
4 cupfuls water,
1 cupful sugar.

Pare the quinces and cut into thin slices, add with the sugar to the water, cover the saucepan, cook fifteen minutes, strain, and freeze.

Italian Tutti-Frutti.

1 pound mixed French candied fruits,
4 cupfuls water,
2½ cupfuls sugar,
3 lemons,
4 oranges.

Chop the fruit fine. Put the sugar and water with chipped rinds of 2 lemons and 1 orange to boil five min-

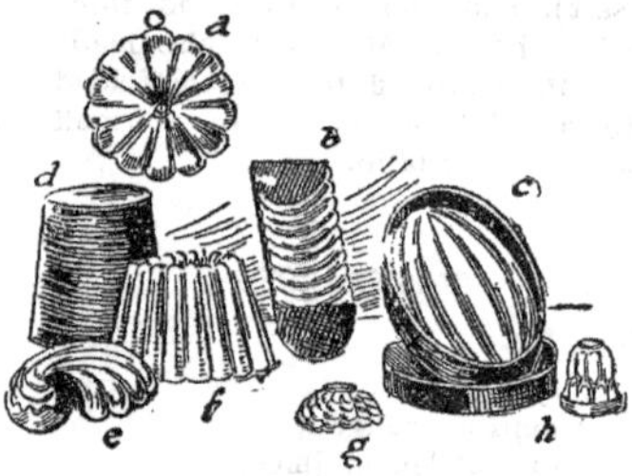

a Round Fluted Mold; b, French Bread Pan; c, Melon Mold; d, Pudding Mold; e, Shell Mold for Jelly; f, Deep Fluted Mold; g, Individual Shell Mold for Jelly or Cream; h, Individual Jelly Mold.

utes. When cold, add the juice of 2 lemons and oranges, strain, and freeze very hard; then stir in the fruit, stand thirty minutes, and it is ready to serve.

SHERBETS

Lemon Sherbet.

4 lemons,
2 cupfuls sugar,
1 quart boiling water.

Shave off the peel from 2 lemons. Put the parings into a bowl, add the boiling water, and let stand ten minutes closely covered. Cut the lemons in halves, remove the seeds, squeeze out the juice, and add with the sugar to the water. Strain and freeze.

Lemon Sherbet with Gelatin.

1 tablespoonful gelatin,
3½ cupfuls cold water,
6 lemons,
1 cupful sugar,
½ cupful boiling water.

Soak the gelatin in ½ cupful cold water twenty minutes. Put the sugar and remaining cold water into a pitcher. Pare the lemons, cut in halves, remove the seeds, and press out the juice with a lemon squeezer; add it to the sirup. Dissolve the soaked gelatin in the boiling water, and add to the other mixture. Strain and freeze.

Apple Sherbet.

2 cupfuls sugar,
Juice 2 lemons,
1 pound apples,
1 quart water,
White 1 egg,
1 tablespoonful powdered sugar.

Put the sugar, water, and rind of 1 lemon, chipped, on to boil. Pare, core, and quarter the apples, add them to the sirup, and cook until tender; press through a fine sieve, add the juice of lemons, and, when cold, freeze the same as ice cream. Beat the white of 1 egg until frothy, add a tablespoonful powdered sugar, and beat until white and stiff. Remove the dasher, stir in the meringue, and repack.

Apricot Sherbet.

1 quart apricots,
1 lemon,
1 cupful sugar,
1 cupful water.

Boil the sugar and water five minutes. Press the apricots through a sieve, add to the sirup, and lemon juice. When cold, freeze. Peach sherbet is made in the same manner.

Banana Sherbet.

1 dozen red-skinned bananas,
2 cupfuls sugar,
2 oranges,
1 quart water.

Boil the sugar and water five minutes, and add the juice of the oranges; when cold, stir in the bananas mashed fine, and freeze.

Cherry Sherbet.

1 quart sour cherries,
2 cupfuls sugar,
1 quart water.

Boil the sugar and water fifteen minutes. Stone the cherries, and add to the sirup when cold. Press through a sieve, and freeze.

Ginger Sherbet.

4 large juicy lemons,
1 quart water,
1½ pounds sugar.

Make a lemon sherbet; when frozen, add a tablespoonful sirup from preserved Canton ginger.

Orange Sherbet.

1 pint orange juice,
2 tablespoonfuls gelatin,
2 cupfuls sugar,
1 quart water.

Cover the gelatin with a little cold water and soak half an hour. Boil the sugar and water five minutes, add the gelatin, and allow to cool. Add the orange juice, and freeze.

Raspberry-and-Currant Sherbet.

1 quart raspberries,
½ pint currant juice,
2 cupfuls sugar,
1 quart water.

Boil the sugar and water five minutes. When cold, add the currant juice and the raspberries, mashed; strain through a cloth, and freeze.

Pineapple Sherbet.

2 large pineapples or 1 quart can,
2½ cupfuls sugar,

Juice 2 lemons,
1 quart water.

Grate the pineapple. Boil the sugar and water five minutes, add the pineapple and juice of lemons. Strain and freeze.

Pomona Sherbet.

1 pint orange juice,
1 quart new cider,
2 cupfuls sugar.

Mix the cider and orange juice, stir in the sugar until thoroughly dissolved; strain and freeze.

Strawberry Sherbet.

1 quart red strawberries,
2 cupfuls sugar,
1 quart water,
Juice 2 lemons.

Boil the sugar and water. Add the lemon juice to the strawberries and mash them. When the sirup is cold, pour it over the strawberries, strain and freeze.

Pomegranate Sherbet.

2 cupfuls sugar,
1 teaspooonful gelatin,
1 quart water,
½ dozen blood oranges,
1 lemon.

Prepare a sirup as for lemon sherbet; when cold, add lemon juice, freeze.

Peach Sherbet.

2 cupfuls sugar,
1 teaspoonful gelatin,
2 oranges,
1 quart water,
¼ peck peaches,
1 lemon.

To a sirup prepared as for lemon sherbet, add a pint peach pulp, also the orange and lemon juice.

Blackberry Sherbet.

2 quarts blackberries,
1 tablespoonful gelatin,
2 cupfuls granulated sugar,
2 lemons.

Crush 2 quarts juicy blackberries with a cupful granulated sugar. Let stand an hour. Put the fruit and sugar through a vegetable press and strain the juice. There should be at least 1½ pints. To this add another cupful sugar and a pint water, and stir until the sugar is dissolved. Have ready a tablespoonful gelatin which has been soaked half an hour in cold water, then dissolved in a little boiling water. Put this with the other ingredients, add the lemon juice, and freeze.

Milk Sherbet.

1 teaspoonful gelatin,
1½ cupfuls sugar,
1 quart milk,
Juice 4 lemons,
Juice 1 orange.

Soften the gelatin in ½ cupful milk, dissolve over hot water, and strain into the rest of the milk; turn the milk into the can of the freezer packed for freezing; when thoroughly chilled, add the fruit juice and sugar stirred together; freeze.

FRAPPÉS

Iced Chocolate.

4 ounces Runkel's Sweet Chocolate,
Scant ½ cupful sugar,
1 cupful water,
1 quart cream,
1 teaspoonful McIlhenny's Mexican Vanilla.

Put the chocolate, water, and sugar in a saucepan to melt; stir until perfectly smooth. Put the cream in a double boiler, and when hot, add gradually to the chocolate mixture, and beat until thoroughly mixed; when cold, strain, add the vanilla, and freeze.

Iced Coffee.

1⅜ cupfuls sugar,
2 cupfuls water,
2 cupfuls black coffee,
1 quart cream.

Boil the sugar and water together five minutes, add the coffee, then the cream, and when cold, freeze. Serve in glasses.

Iced Lemonade.

2 cupfuls sugar,
4 cupfuls water,
Juice 4 large lemons.

Melt the sugar and water together, add the lemon juice, and freeze to the consistency of soft snow. Serve in lemonade glasses.

Iced Raspberry Vinegar.

Sugar,
1 quart water,
Raspberry vinegar.

Mix the sugar, raspberry vinegar, and water according to taste, making it a little oversweet; freeze.

Coffee Frappé.

8 cupfuls water,
2 cupfuls sugar,
1 cupful coffee,
White 1 egg.

Put the coffee in a farina boiler, pour boiling water over it, stir occasionally five minutes, then strain through fine muslin, add the sugar, and stir until dissolved. When cold, add the white of egg unbeaten, and freeze to the consistency of wet snow. Serve in punch glasses. Tea frappé may be made after the same fashion.

Orange Granite.

6 oranges,
2 cupfuls orange juice,
2 cupfuls sugar,
2 cupfuls water.

Boil the sugar and water five minutes. Peel the oranges, remove every particle of white skin, separate the carpels and carefully remove the seeds. Drop these into the hot sirup, and stand an hour, then drain the sirup into another vessel, add the orange juice, mix, strain, and freeze. When frozen rather stiff, add the pieces of oranges, and serve in glasses.

Strawberry Granite.

2 cupfuls orange juice,
2 cupfuls strawberry juice,
1 quart whole strawberries,
3 cupfuls sugar,
3 cupfuls water.

Boil the sugar and water five minutes. Drop the strawberries into this sirup, lift them carefully with a skimmer, and place on a platter to cool; then add to the sirup the strawberry and orange juice. Strain and freeze. When frozen, stir in the strawberries, and serve in glasses.

FROZEN FRUITS

Frozen Apricots.

1 quart can apricots,
2 tablespoonfuls gelatin,
2 cupfuls sugar,
2 cupfuls cream.

Drain the apricots, cut them in pieces, measure the sirup, and add sufficient water to make 1½ pints; add the sugar. Cover the gelatin with a little cold water and soak half an hour. Boil the sugar, sirup, and water together five minutes, skim carefully, add the gelatin, stir until dissolved, add the apricots, and stand to cool; then freeze, stirring slowly. When frozen, remove the dasher and add the cream whipped. Repack, cover, and stand two hours. Dried apricots, carefully cooked, can be used.

Frozen Bananas.

1 dozen red-skinned bananas,
2 cupfuls sugar,
2 cupfuls water,
Juice 2 oranges,
2 cupfuls cream.

Peel the bananas, cut them in slices, then mash fine. Boil the water and sugar five minutes, strain, and when cool, add the orange juice and bananas. Freeze, turning slowly. When frozen, remove the dasher and stir in carefully the cream whipped. Repack, and put away to ripen.

Frozen Peaches.

2 pounds peaches,
4 cupfuls water,
6 peach kernels,
3 cupfuls sugar.

Pare the peaches and take out the stones. Pound the kernels to a paste, add them with the sugar to the water, boil five minutes, strain, and cool. When cold, add the peaches, mashed, and freeze. Repack, and stand to ripen.

Frozen Cherries.

2 quarts morello cherries,
4 cupfuls sugar,
4 cupfuls water.

Stone the cherries, mix them with the sugar, and stand an hour; add the water, stir until the sugar is thoroughly dissolved, put in the freezer, and turn rapidly until frozen.

Frozen Pineapples.

2 large pineapples,
4 cupfuls sugar,
4 cupfuls water.

Pare the pineapples, cut out the eyes, and grate the flesh, rejecting the core; add the sugar and water, stir until the sugar is dissolved, and freeze.

Frozen Raspberries.

1 quart raspberries,
2 cupfuls sugar,
Juice 2 lemons,
4 cupfuls water.

Add the sugar and lemon juice to the berries, mash, and stand an hour; add the water, stir until the sugar is dissolved, and freeze.

Frozen Strawberries.

1 quart strawberries,
Juice 2 lemons,
2 cupfuls sugar,
4 cupfuls water.

Add the sugar and lemon juice to the berries, and stand an hour. Mash the berries, add the water, stir until the sugar is thoroughly dissolved, and freeze slowly.

ICE CREAM

Coffee Cream.

½ cupful very strong coffee,
1 pint milk,
3 pints cream,
2 cupfuls sugar.

Heat the milk and half the cream in a double boiler. Put in the coffee and sugar, and stir until the latter is dissolved. Take from the fire, and when cool, put into the freezer with the uncooked cream. If you wish to have a light, more spongy cream, you may whip the uncooked cream, and stir this into the contents of the freezer when these have begun to congeal. Freeze, and when solid, pack for an hour before serving.

Lemon Cream.

1 pint cream,
⅛ teaspoonful salt,
1 cupful sugar,
1 lemon.

Pare the rind off a lemon, cut in halves, remove the seeds, and squeeze out the juice. Strain the juice and mix it with the same amount of sugar. Boil until clear, stir through the cream, and freeze.

Vanilla Ice Cream.

3 cupfuls milk,
1½ cupfuls whipped cream,
¾ cupful sugar,
2 eggs,
1 tablespooonful McIlhenny's Mexican Vanilla.

Beat the eggs with the sugar, scald the milk, blend, and pour the mixture in a double boiler. Cook a few minutes to set the eggs, but not so the mixture thickens like a custard. Remove from the fire, cool, add the cream and vanilla. When cold, freeze.

Pistachio Cream.

1 quart cream,
¼ pound pistachio nuts,
1 quart milk,
1½ cupfuls sugar,
1 dessertspoonful pistache extract.

Shell the nuts and remove the outside skins; chop fine and rub to a paste, adding gradually the extract. Add the sugar to the milk, and stir in a double boiler until the sugar is dissolved and the milk hot. Stand until cold. Add a little cream gradually to the nuts, continue rubbing constantly to a smooth paste, then add the entire quantity of cream. If the nuts are pale, add 2 drops green coloring. Add this to the milk, and freeze.

Bisque Ice Cream.

Yolks 8 eggs,
1½ pints cream,
Juice 1 orange,
½ cupful sugar,
¼ saltspoonful salt,
¼ pound macaroons.

Beat the first 3 ingredients with a wire whip until the mixture is very smooth. Pour it into a saucepan, place over a slow fire, and stir constantly until it is a custard. Do not let it boil. Strain into a bowl which has been chilled; stir two minutes and freeze. Remove dasher, flavor with ½ teaspoonful grated rind of orange or lemon, add the cream whipped stiff, and the macaroons crushed fine. Pack in ice and salt.

Strawberry Ice Cream.

1 quart strawberries,
1 quart cream,
2 cupfuls sugar.

Put half the sugar and half the cream in a double boiler over the fire; when the sugar dissolves, cool. Mash the strawberries, adding half the sugar, then stand an hour. Press through a colander. Add remaining half the cream to the sweetened cream and freeze moderately stiff, then add the berries, and repack. If canned strawberries are used, half the sugar may be omitted.

Pineapple Cream.

1 quart cream,
2 cupfuls sugar,
Juice 1 lemon,
1 large pineapple or 1 pint can.

Scald the cream with half the sugar, stir until sugar is dissolved, and cool. Grate the pineapple, mix with the rest of the sugar, and stir until dissolved. Add the remaining pint cream to sweetened cream, and freeze; add the lemon juice to the pineapple, and stir into the frozen cream; beat thoroughly and pack. If canned pineapple is used, add the lemon juice, and stir into the cream when cold.

Ginger Cream.

6 ounces preserved ginger,
2 tablespoonfuls lemon juice,
1 pint cream,
¾ cupful sugar.

Pound the sugar to a paste with the lemon juice. Mix sugar and cream, add to the ginger, press through a sieve, and freeze.

Cocoanut Cream.

1 quart cream,
1 cupful sugar,
1 tablespoonful McIlhenny's Mexican Vanilla,
1 cocoanut grated.

Scald half the cream with the sugar. When cool, add the rest of cream, vanilla, and cocoanut; freeze.

Vanilla Cream with Extract.

1 quart cream,
1 cupful sugar,
2 tablespoonfuls McIlhenny's Mexican Vanilla.

Scald half the cream with sugar. When cold, add the remainder of the cream, vanilla, and freeze.

Ice Cream from Condensed Milk.

1 can condensed milk,
3 tablespoonfuls cornstarch,
1 tablespoonful McIlhenny's Mexican Vanilla.

Add sufficient boiling water to 1 can condensed milk to make it the proper consistency. Moisten 3 tablespoonfuls cornstarch with a little cold milk, add to the mixture, stir and cook five minutes, and take from the fire; when cold, add vanilla extract to flavor; freeze.

Arrowroot Cream.

1 pint cream,
1 quart milk,
1½ cupfuls sugar,
2 tablespoonfuls arrowroot,
1 tablespoonful McIlhenny's Mexican Vanilla.

Moisten the arrowroot with a little milk; put the remainder in a double boiler; when hot, add the arrowroot, stir and cook ten minutes, add the sugar, take from the fire, add the cream and vanilla. When cold, freeze.

Gelatin Cream.

1 quart cream,
1 pint milk,
1½ cupfuls sugar,
½ box gelatin,
2 tablespoonfuls McIlhenny's Mexican Vanilla.

Cover the gelatin with the milk and stand in a cool place thirty minutes; put it in a double boiler; when hot, add the sugar, strain, add the cream and vanilla, and freeze.

Caramel Cream.

1 quart cream,
1 cupful sugar,
6 eggs,
3 tablespoonfuls caramel,
1 teaspoonful McIlhenny's Mexican Vanilla.

Beat the yolks of eggs and the sugar together until light. Whisk the whites to a stiff froth, stir them into the yolks and sugar. Scald the cream, then stir and cook until the mixture begins to thicken. Take from the fire, and strain; when cold, add the vanilla, and freeze.

Almond Cream.

Yolks 6 eggs,
1 quart cream,
2 ounces Jordan almonds,
1½ cupfuls sugar.

Blanch the almonds and chop them fine. Put 2 tablespoonfuls granulated sugar with the chopped almonds in a saucepan, stir over the fire until the almonds are red brown, take from the fire and when cool, pound them to a paste. Put the cream in a double boiler. Beat the eggs and sugar together until light, add to the hot cream, stir until thickened, take from the fire, add the pounded almonds, and freeze.

Brown-Bread Ice Cream.

2 slices brown bread,
¾ cupful sugar,
2 lady's fingers,
½ pint milk,
1 pint cream.

Put the bread in the oven and brown, roll, and sift. Dry and roll the lady's fingers. Put the cream, milk, and sugar in a double boiler, and stir until the sugar is dissolved; when cold, freeze. When frozen, add the sifted crumbs, and repack.

Raspberry-Jam Cream.

1 pound raspberry jam,
Juice 1 lemon,
1 pint cream,
1 gill milk.

Mix the lemon juice with the raspberry jam, add gradually the milk and cream, strain through a sieve, and freeze.

Burnt-Almond Cream.

1 quart cream,
1 cupful sugar,
4 ounces shelled almonds,

1 teaspoonful caramel,
1 tablespoonful McIlhenny's Mexican Vanilla.

Blanch and roast the almonds, then pound them in a mortar to a paste. Put half the cream and the sugar on to boil, stir until the sugar is dissolved, add the remaining pint of cream and the almonds; when cold, add the caramel and vanilla; freeze.

Chocolate Cream.

2 cupfuls scalded milk,
1 tablespoonful flour,
1 egg,
⅓ cupful boiling water,
1½ cupfuls sugar,
⅛ teaspoonful salt,
2 squares Runkel's Chocolate,
1 quart thin cream,
1 teaspoonful McIlhenny's Mexican Vanilla.

Mix 1 cupful sugar with the flour and salt. Add the egg slightly beaten, and gradually the milk. Cook over hot water twenty minutes, stirring constantly at first. Put chocolate in saucepan, place over hot water, and when melted, add remaining sugar and boiling water. Add chocolate mixture to hot custard. Cool, add cream and flavoring, strain and freeze. One third cupful Runkel's Prepared Cocoa may be used in place of chocolate.

Apricot Cream.

1 quart cream,
1½ cupfuls sugar,
1 quart apricots or 1 pint can.

Put half the cream to heat in a double boiler. When hot, add the sugar, and stir until dissolved. Take from the fire, add the remaining half of the cream, and when cold, freeze. Mash the apricots and stir them quickly into the frozen cream; turn the crank rapidly for five minutes; pack.

Banana Cream.

8 bananas,
1 quart cream,
1 cupful cream.

Peel and mash the bananas. Put 1 pint cream to scald in a double boiler. When hot, add the sugar, stir until dissolved, and cool. Beat and stir the bananas to a smooth paste, add to the cream and sugar; then add the remainder of cream, and freeze.

Mandarin Cream.

1 quart cream,
1 cupful sugar,
Juice 12 mandarins,
Rind 2 mandarins.

Put half the cream to scald in a double boiler, add the sugar, and stir until dissolved. When cool, add the juice and rind of mandarins and the remaining half of cream; freeze.

Raspberry Cream.

1 quart cream,
2 cupfuls sugar,
1 quart raspberries,
Juice 1 lemon.

Put half the sugar and cream to boil; when sugar is dissolved, cool; add the rest of sugar and lemon juice to the berries, stand an hour, then strain. Add the remaining half of the cream to the sweetened cream, and freeze; when frozen, stir in the fruit juice, beat thoroughly, and pack.

Peach Cream.

1 quart cream,
¼ peck peaches,
1½ cupfuls sugar,
1 lemon.

Scald 1 quart thin cream and 1 cupful sugar; when cold, freeze to a mush, then add 1½ cupfuls peach pulp, mixed with ½ cupful sugar, and the juice of ½ lemon; finish freezing.

Blackberry Ice Cream.

1 quart milk,
1 quart blackberries,
1 lemon,
1 pint double cream,
1 cupful sugar,
1 tablespoonful cornstarch.

Stir cornstarch, mixed with the sugar, into the milk, which has been previously scalded. Cook until the mixture thickens. The mixture will be as thick as thin cream. Add the cream, and when cold, freeze to a mush. A tablespoonful lemon extract may be added before freezing. Crush a basket of ripe, juicy blackberries, and press through a *purée* sieve to remove the seeds. Mix the pulpy juice, of which there should be a pint, with a cupful sugar, and set on the ice to chill. Add to the half-frozen mixture, and finish freezing.

PARFAIT, MOUSSE, AND FROZEN PUDDING

Apricot Pudding.

1 quart cream,
Yolks 4 eggs,
1½ cupfuls sugar,
12 apricots.

Scald 1 pint cream. Beat together the egg yolks, and sugar, stir into hot cream, cook one minute, take from the fire, and add the remaining pint cream. When frozen, stir in the apricots, which should be pared and cut in small pieces. Peach pudding may be made in the same manner.

Queen Pudding.

Line a melon mold two inches deep with vanilla ice cream or strawberry water ice. Have ready a pint frozen peaches; fill these into the center, cover with ice cream, put on the lid, bind the edges with a strip of buttered cloth, pack and stand two hours. When ready to serve, wipe the outside of the mold with a warm towel, and turn the pudding out on a large dish. Dust with grated macaroons, and serve immediately.

Chesterfield Cream.

1¾ cupfuls sugar,
Rind 1 lemon,
1 pint preserved damsons,
1½ pints cream,
Yolks 3 eggs,
2 inch stick cinnamon.

Scald the cream with the cinnamon and the rind of lemon chipped. Beat the sugar and yolks together, add to the hot cream, cook one minute, strain, and when cold, freeze. When

a, Extension Strainer; b, Small Wire Strainer.

frozen, stir in an extra pint cream whipped. Stand two hours. Serve with preserved damsons around it.

Macedoine of Fruit.

2 cupfuls sugar,
1 quart water,
3 bananas,
Juice 2 oranges,
1 lemon,
1 small pineapple,
12 large strawberries,
1 gill strawberry jelly,
2 tablespoonfuls gelatin.

Cover the gelatin with a little cold water, and soak half an hour. Boil the sugar and water together ten minutes, add the gelatin, orange, and lemon juice, bananas cut into small pieces, pineapple picked into small pieces, strawberries cut into halves, and jelly cut into blocks. Freeze, turning the crank very slowly.

Frozen Orange Soufflé.

1 quart cream,
1 pint orange juice,
Yolks 6 eggs,
2 cupfuls sugar,
½ box gelatin.

Cover the gelatin with ½ cupful cold water, and soak an hour, then dissolve in ½ cupful boiling water. Mix the orange juice and the sugar together. Whip the cream. Beat the yolks until light, add them to the orange juice and sugar; add the gelatin, strain, and freeze. When frozen, remove dasher, stir in the whipped cream, and stand two hours to ripen.

Frozen Strawberry Soufflé.

1 pint strawberry juice,
1½ cupfuls sugar,
½ box gelatin,
½ cupful cold water,
Yolks 6 eggs,
1 quart cream.

Mix the strawberry juice and sugar until they form a sirup. Cover the gelatin with cold water, and soak half an hour, then add a cupful boiling water, and stir until dissolved. Beat the yolks of eggs, add them to the sirup, also the gelatin, and freeze. When frozen, stir in lightly the cream whipped to a stiff froth; repack.

Frozen Pudding.

1 quart milk,
20 large raisins,
Yolks 4 eggs,
1 cupful sugar,
2 ounces citron,
2 ounces almonds,
1 tablespoonful McIlhenny's Mexican Vanilla.
1 ounce preserved ginger.

Put the milk and raisins in a double boiler and cook twenty minutes. Beat the yolks and sugar together, add to the hot milk, cook one minute, and strain. When cold, add the citron chopped fine, the almonds blanched and grated, the vanilla and ginger cut into small pieces; freeze.

Orange Mousse.

6 oranges,
1 pint cream,
1½ cupfuls sugar,
1 candied orange.

Squeeze orange juice into a saucepan with the sugar; add the rind of 1 orange, cut in pieces and 2 tablespoonfuls water. Place over the fire, stir with a wooden spoon until melted, strain, cool, and freeze. When frozen, remove dasher and add 1 pint cream whipped stiff, also the candied orange cut into small pieces. Pack in ice and salt for an hour and a half. Garnish with small pieces candied orange cut in thin strips, alternating with angelica cut in the same fashion. Finish with a row of sliced oranges cut in halves and lapping over each other.

Tutti-Frutti.

2 cupfuls milk,
Yolks 5 eggs,
2½ cupfuls thin cream,
¾ cupful sugar,
⅛ teaspoonful salt,
1½ tablespoonfuls McIlhenny's Mexican Vanilla,
1¾ cupfuls fruit cut in small pieces.

Make a custard of first 4 ingredicnts, strain, and cool. Add the cream and flavoring, then freeze to the consistency of mush, add the fruit, and continue freezing. Mold, pack in salt and ice, and let stand two hours. Candied cherries, pineapple, figs, sultana raisins, and citron may be used.

Pineapple Mousse.

1 teaspoonful gelatin,
1 pint double cream,
1 cupful scalded pineapple juice,
¾ cupful sugar,
Juice ½ lemon.

Soften the gelatin in 3 tablespoonfuls cold water five minutes and dissolve in the hot pineapple juice; add the sugar and let cool, then add the lemon juice and the cream; beat the mixture with an egg beater until thick. Turn into a chilled mold; press the cover down over wrapping paper, and let stand packed in equal measures of ice and salt three or four hours. Turn from the mold and surround with half slices pineapple sugared or dressed with a cold sugar sirup.

Frozen Custard.

1 quart milk,
4 eggs,
1 cupful sugar,

1 tablespoonful McIlhenny's Mexican Vanilla,
2 tablespoonfuls cornstarch.

Scald the milk. Moisten the cornstarch with a little cold milk, add it to the hot milk, and stir until it begins to thicken. Beat the eggs and sugar together, add to the hot milk, cook one minute, take from the fire, add vanilla, when cold, freeze.

Frozen Coffee Custard.

4 eggs,
½ pint cream,
1 cupful sugar,
1 pint milk,
½ pint strong coffee.

Scald the milk. Beat the eggs and sugar together until light; add them to the hot milk, cook, and instantly take from the fire, add the cream and coffee. When cold, freeze.

Frozen Chocolate Custard.

4 eggs,
1 pint cream,
1 pint milk,
1 cupful sugar,
2 ounces Runkel's Chocolate,
1 teaspoonful McIlhenny's Mexican Vanilla.

Put the milk over the fire in a double boiler; add the chocolate grated. Beat the eggs and sugar until light, add to the hot milk, cook one minute, take from the fire, add the cream and a teaspoonful vanilla. When cold, freeze.

Stuffed Mousse.

1 quart strawberry water ice,
1 pint cream,
1 teaspoonful McIlhenny's Mexican Vanilla,
½ cupful powdered sugar.

Whip the cream to a stiff froth, drain, sprinkle over it the sugar and vanilla, mix carefully. Pack a 2-quart melon mold in salt and ice, line with the strawberry water ice, reserving enough to cover bottom of the mold. Turn the whipped cream into the center, cover the water ice over the bottom, put on the lid, bind with a strip of buttered muslin, cover with salt and ice, and stand three or four hours.

Nesselrode Pudding.

1 pint large chestnuts,
1 pint cream,
1 pint water,
Yolks 6 eggs,
2 cupfuls sugar,
½ pint grated pineapple,
1 pound mixed French candied fruit,
1 teaspoonful McIlhenny's Mexican Vanilla.

Boil the chestnuts until tender, remove the shells and brown skins, press the pulp through a colander. Boil the sugar and water together five minutes. Beat the yolks of eggs until light, add to the boiling sirup, take from the fire, and beat until thick and cool. When cool, add the candied fruit chopped fine, the vanilla, pineapple, and chestnuts. When frozen, remove the dasher, and stir in the cream, whipped to a stiff froth.

Iced Rice Pudding.

½ cupful rice,
1 pint milk,
1 quart cream,
2 cupfuls sugar,
Yolks 6 eggs,
1 teaspoonful McIlhenny's Mexican Vanilla.

Boil rice in 1 pint cold water; drain, cover with the milk, and boil half an hour longer. While this is boiling, whip the cream. After you have whipped all you can, add the remainder and what has drained from the other to the rice and milk. Stand the whipped cream in a cold place. Press the rice through a sieve, and return to the double boiler. Beat the yolks and sugar together, pour over the rice, stir, return again to the fire, and cook two minutes, or until it begins to thicken. Add the vanilla, stir in the whipped cream, remove the dasher, smooth down the pudding, repack, and stand two hours.

Compote of Oranges.

1 dozen sweet oranges,
2 cupfuls sugar,
Juice ½ lemon,
1 gill water.

Put the sugar and water to boil; cook five minutes, skim, and add the lemon juice. Peel the oranges, cut in halves crosswise and cut out the cores with a sharp knife; put a few pieces at a time in the hot sirup, and lay them out singly on a flat dish; pour over them the remaining sirup and stand on ice to cool. To dish the pudding, lift out the can and carefully wipe off the brine. Wipe the bottom with a towel dipped in boiling water, put a dish over the top of it, turn it upside down, and remove the can. Heap the oranges on top and arrange them around the base of the pudding, pour the sirup over them, and serve.

Purée of Apricots.

1 quart can apricots,
1 cupful sugar,
Yolks 6 eggs,
1 pint cream.

Mash the apricots, beat the yolks of eggs and sugar together until light, then add them with the cream to the apricots; turn into a double boiler, and stir until the eggs begin to thicken. Strain, and whip to the consistency of sponge-cake batter. When cool, turn into a mold and set in ice and salt three hours.

Plombière.

½ pound Jordan almonds,
Yolks 7 eggs,
1 quart cream,
½ cupful sugar.

Blanch and pound the almonds to a paste. Scald the cream in a double boiler, add the almonds, egg yolks and sugar beaten to a cream, and stir over the fire until they begin to thick; beat for three minutes. Strain and freeze. When frozen, remove the dasher, make a small well in the center, fill with apricot jam, cover, and stand two hours.

Montrose Pudding.

1 quart cream,
Yolks 6 eggs,
1 cupful sugar,
1 tablespoonful McIlhenny's Mexican Vanilla,
1 pint strawberry water ice.

Scald the cream, beat the yolks and sugar, stir into the boiling cream, and cook until it thickens. Take from the fire, add the remaining pint cream and the vanilla, stand until cool, and freeze. When frozen, pack into a round mold, leaving a well in the center. Fill with strawberry water ice, cover with some of the pudding you have taken out. Pack in salt and ice, and let stand two hours. Serve with the following sauce poured around it:

Vanilla Sauce.

1 tablespoonful gelatin,
1 pint cream,
Yolks 3 eggs,
¼ cupful sugar,
1 teaspoonful McIlhenny's Mexican Vanilla.

Cover the gelatin with a little cold water and soak half an hour. Scald the cream. Beat the yolks and sugar together, add the boiling cream, stir until it thickens, add the gelatin, stir until it dissolves; take from the fire, add the vanilla, and stand in a cold place until wanted.

Frozen Chocolate with Whipped Cream.

2 squares Runkel's Chocolate,
1 cupful sugar,
Dash salt,
1 cupful milk,
3 cupfuls thin cream,
1 teaspoonful McIlhenny's Mexican Vanilla.

Melt the chocolate, scald the milk with the sugar and salt, and pour it over the chocolate. Add the cream, cool, freeze, and serve in glasses with a spoonful whipped cream in each.

Chocolate Sauce to Serve with Vanilla Ice Cream.

1½ cupfuls water,
½ cupful sugar,
6 tablespoonfuls Runkel's Chocolate,
1 tablespoonful cornstarch,
½ cupful cold water,
Dash salt,
½ tablespoonful McIlhenny's Mexican Vanilla.

Boil the water and sugar five minutes. Dissolve the cornstarch in cold water, add the grated chocolate, combine the mixtures, and cook in a double boiler till creamy. Flavor with vanilla, and serve hot with vanilla cream frozen very hard.

Frozen Plum Pudding.

1 quart chocolate ice cream,
¾ cupful candied fruit,
½ cupful blanched and chopped almonds,
½ cupful raisins,
½ cupful macaroon crumbs toasted,
¼ cupful shredded figs,
¼ cupful chopped walnuts.

Make the cream as directed in recipe for chocolate ice cream; when almost frozen, take off the lid, put in the fruit, turn the crank five minutes, then pack. This cream is so rich that it is at its best when served in small portions with a garnish of whipped cream.

Chocolate Mousse.

2 squares Runkel's Chocolate,
1¼ cupfuls sugar,
1 cupful cream,
¾ tablespoonful granulated gelatin,
3 tablespoonfuls boiling water,
1 teaspoonful McIlhenny's Mexican Vanilla,
1 quart cream.

Melt the chocolate with ½ cupful sugar and add 1 cupful cream. Scald, then put in the gelatin dissolved in cold water, the rest of the sugar, vanilla, and a dash of salt. Strain into a bowl and set in a pan of ice water. Stir occasionally till it thickens, then add the whip from the rest of the cream. Pour into a mold, rubbing inside the lid of the mold with lard to form a waterproof coating so no brine can enter, pack in ice and salt, and let stand four hours.

Continental Pudding.

1½ pints baked Indian-meal pudding,
1 pint thick cream,
1 cupful sugar,
1 tablespoonful caramel,
½ teaspoonful cinnamon.

Stir the ingredients to a smooth paste, whip the cream, beat in the sugar, add the spice, mix with the pudding, and freeze without beating, scraping the frozen mixture from the sides of the can, and stirring smooth. Serve, when frozen, with cream.

Angel-Cake Glacé.

1 quart cream,
Whites 6 eggs,
1¼ cupfuls sugar,
1 teaspoonful McIlhenny's Mexican Vanilla,
¾ cupful water,
½ cupful finely sifted angel-cake crumbs.

Cook the cream in a farina boiler, add sugar and flavoring, cool, strain, and freeze. Reserve ½ pound sugar and whites 4 eggs. Cook the sugar and water to the same degree required for boiling icing, and pour hot upon the whites beaten to the stiffest possible froth. Stir this icing, with the cake crumbs, gently into the frozen cream. Line the bottom of a mold with slices of angel cake; upon these place a layer of the cream, then cake, so on until the mold is full.

Cover tightly, and pack in ice three hours.

Fruit-Cake Glacé.

1 pint cream,
Yolks 4 eggs,
1 cupful sugar,
½ teaspoonful McIlhenny's Mexican Vanilla,
½ teaspoonful mixed spices,
2 ounces browned almond paste,
4 macaroons,
2 ounces dried and pounded fruit cake,
1 ounce chocolate,
1 tablespoonful caramel.

Make a custard of the cream, yolks, and sugar; add vanilla, sugar, spices, chocolate, and caramel; freeze, then stir in nuts and crumbs, mold in a cake pan—any ordinary oblong pan, two or two and a half inches deep, freeze in salt and ice. Turn out on platter, cover half an inch with almond paste mixed with little boiled icing. Serve in slices, with soft custard.

CHAPTER LIX

PUFF PASTE

If you have a marble slab to work on when making puff paste, your work will be easier. A rolling-pin with movable handles makes the touch lighter. There can be no heavy-handed methods, or you will have a solid, indigestible substance. Scald an earthen bowl, fill with ice water; wash your hands in hot water, then in cold. Work 1 pound butter in a bowl cold water until it is waxy and nearly all the salt is washed out of it. Take out the butter, pat and squeeze till the water flies. Measure from it 2 level tablespoonfuls, mold the rest into an oblong cake, then set it where it will grow hard and cold. Sift 1 pound flour with ½ teaspoonful salt into the bowl. Rub between the fingers and thumb the 2 tablespoonfuls butter. Mix with ice water, stirring constantly till you have a soft dough. Turn out on a marble slab, which has been dusted with flour. Knead with an even, light touch, till it feels elastic; then cover with a napkin, and set away to "ripen" five minutes. When the dough is ripened, you may begin work on it. Put the paste on the slab and, with the lightest possible pats from the rolling-pin, shape it about half as wide as it is long, keeping the corners square. At one end lay the hardened piece of butter. Over this fold the rest of the dough. Tuck lightly around the edges, inclosing all the air possible. With light taps from the rolling-pin break up the butter, spreading it and rolling the paste into a longer strip. Be careful to keep the sides and ends of the paste even, and to break as few air bubbles as possible. When the strip is almost as long as the slab, fold it like the letter Z, and begin again rolling, folding, and turning until the process has been repeated six times. If the paste shows the least symptom of being soft, or the butter of breaking through, set it away to chill before you finish the process. Roll always in one direction, from you, with a long, sweeping motion. By cutting the paste across after the work is completed, you may see the texture which gives you a crust eight times as high after baking as before it was set in an oven. You will notice layer after layer of a waferlike thickness of butter and paste with tiny bubbles between. Wrap it in parchment paper and set away in a covered dish overnight. It will be all the more tender and flaky for twenty-four hours of "ripening." During the winter a batch of puff paste, wrapped and covered, may be kept for several weeks in a very cold place. Use it as desired, baking *patés, vol au vents,* or tarts as required. These will keep five or six days after making, being reheated before they are filled.

The oven for baking puff paste should be as hot as for rolls, with the greatest heat underneath, so the *paté* can rise to its full height before browning. As heat touches the pastry the bubbles expand, lifting the thin layers higher and higher. When it has reached its height, and is baked delicately brown, you have what is properly called puff paste.

NOTES ABOUT PUFF PASTE

When using a cutter, always dip in flour between each cutting; it will insure neat edges.

If the work has to be done in a warm room, chill the paste between three pans, the upper one filled with broken ice, the second one set into another large pan, also filled with ice. Puff paste is always in good condition if it slips easily on the slab.

Should you wish to use is for a pie, bake it *vol-au-vent* fashion over the bottom of a pie-plate first, and fill after baking, or use ordinary pie paste for the bottom when the filling is to be baked.

Build up the sides with puff paste; rich pastry never makes a good undercrust—it soaks.

When baking small pieces such as *paté* tops or cheese straws, do not put them in a pan with the larger pieces; they bake in less than half the time required by the others.

If you wish pastry to have a glazed appearance, brush over with beaten egg before putting it in the oven.

Utilize trimmings for smaller things; never add them to the larger pieces of paste.

Use the sharpest knife for cutting pastry; if it is dragged ever so slightly in the cutting it will not rise well. Also, in making two layers of pastry adhere, never press it together or you will have a heavy spot.

Always have puff paste ice cold when it is put in the oven. Let the heat be greatest at the bottom when the paste is put in; it must rise before it begins to brown.

PUFF-PASTE DAINTIES

Vol au Vent.

Lay a mold upon a round of puff paste, rolled about half an inch thick, and cut out a circle as big as you think will be required to cover it. Set the mold upside down and tuck down the paste, handling carefully. Do not cover scantily anywhere or it will crack. Prick all over with a fork and set away in a cold place to chill thoroughly. Find a plate or saucer which fits the top of the mold and cover with puff paste. Cut from the trimmings stars, hearts, crescents, or any forms you can produce with a paste jagger. Brush the paste on the saucer lightly with cold water, and stick on the ornaments in any style desired. Chill the *vol au vent* and lid for half an hour, then bake in an oven which is very hot at first, but cooled slightly when the pastry has risen and is beginning to brown. Watch the baking with great care, as the paste will burn or become unshapely if not turned occasionally. A *vol au vent* may be filled with any cream mixture or with a cooked, chilled fruit and rich sirup.

Patês.

Roll out the paste half an inch thick; shape two rounds with a *paté* cutter. From one round cut a smaller piece. Use the ring left to lay on the other round, brushing with water to make it stick. Bake and fill with a creamed mixture, using the small round as a lid.

Cream Horns.

Cream horns are made on fine-pointed tubes which are called ladylock irons. Cut the paste into ribbons with a knife or jagger and begin to wind at the small end, the edges scarcely touching. Bake delicately brown. They may be filled with cream and chicken or oysters and served as an *entrée*, or with whipped cream as a dessert.

Cheese Straws.

Season some grated cheese with paprika and salt, then dust it over a piece of puff paste. Fold the paste and roll two or three times. Cut out in rings with a doughnut cutter or in straws with a jagger. The straws may be braided or baked singly.

Flaky Pie Crust.

- 3 cupfuls flour,
- ½ cupful butter,
- ¾ cupful ice water,
- ½ cupful lard.

Sift the flour into a chopping bowl, add the butter and lard, and chop with a knife until no piece of the shortening larger than a pecan can be seen. Sprinkle the water here and there through the flour, and mix with a fork into a soft dough. Drop on a floured board, dust lightly with flour, press down with the rolling-pin, and roll back and forth until the paste becomes an oblong sheet not more than half an inch in thickness. Slip a broad-bladed knife under each end of this sheet, and fold over toward the center, thus forming three layers of the paste. Lift, with the knife, from the board, dust with fresh flour; lay the paste down again, dust with flour, roll, and again fold over as before. Repeat the operation, and the paste is ready to use. When ice water is added to the flour and shortening, the shortening becomes distributed through the flour in small balls and is not packed together in a mass, and when the dough is drawn together and lightly pressed with the rolling-pin these balls flatten into flakes, which, by repeated foldings, are piled one upon another, and by gently rolling become thinner and more delicate. Three rollings and foldings are as much as these flakes will bear. Rolling and folding a great number of times causes them to become broken and packed, so that the paste will not rise and puff up, as it should, in baking. It is well to let the paste lie on ice, or in a cold place, for an hour before rolling it out for pies, as its quality is improved by so doing; and if the weather is warm it may advantageously be placed on ice ten minutes between each rolling out. If a teaspoonful baking powder be sifted with the flour, less shortening can be used, but the pastry will not be as crisp and delicate.—Emma P. Ewing.

Apple Pie.

Roll pie crust to the thickness desired. Place upon a pie pan, shaping it carefully, and cut round the edges with a sharp knife. Cover the bottom of the crust with a thin layer of sugar, dust with flour, then fill the crust with quarters of pared and cored apples. Dust with salt, add plenty of sugar—if the apples are very tart—roll an upper crust and lay over them, trim around the edges, press the upper and lower crusts together, bake until the apples are soft and the top and bottom crusts are nicely browned.

Raspberry Pie.

To 2 cupfuls raspberries add 1 cupful ripe currants and 1 cupful granulated sugar, with which a tablespoonful flour has been mixed; stir together. Line a plate with flaky pie crust, put in the fruit, cover with a tolerably thick sheet of paste, make several incisions for the escape of steam, and bake till the crusts are nicely browned. Serve cool.

Cherry Pie.

2 cupfuls sour cherries,
1 cupful granulated sugar,
1 tablespoonful flour.

Pick over and wash the cherries, add sugar and flour, mix together. Line a pan with paste, fill with the cherries, and cover with a sheet of paste, rolled twice as thick as ordinary pie crust. Make incisions near the center for the escape of steam, and bake till brown. If the cherries are sweet, use less sugar.

Pumpkin Pie.

2 cupfuls stewed pumpkin,
1 cupful rich milk,
½ cupful molasses,
½ cupful granulated sugar,
1 tablespoonful melted butter,
1 tablespoonful ginger,
1 teaspoonful salt,
2 eggs.

Stir well together, line a deep tin pie pan with paste rolled moderately thick, sift a little flour evenly over the bottom, and fill three quarters full with the prepared mixture. Bake until the pie is brown in the center. In preparing the pumpkin, use very little water. Cover the kettle in which it is cooking, and stew until the pumpkin is perfectly soft, then remove the cover and continue the stewing, stirring frequently until the moisture evaporates and the pumpkin becomes a smooth paste. Rub through a fine sieve.

Sweet-Potato Pie.

2 cupfuls boiled sweet potato,
2 tablespoonfuls butter,
2 tablespoonfuls lemon juice,
1 cupful sugar,
Grated rind ½ lemon,
1 tablespoonful ginger,
1 tablespoonful cinnamon,
1 teaspoonful salt,
½ grated nutmeg,
2 cupfuls milk,
Yolks 3 eggs,

Rub potatoes through a sieve, add butter, lemon juice, sugar in which have been mixed the grated rind of lemon, ginger, cinnamon, salt, and grated nutmeg. Stir well together, add milk and the beaten yolks of eggs, and last the whites of eggs beaten stiff. Fit the paste to the pan, dust with flour, fill, and bake.

Custard Pie.

½ cupful granulated sugar,
1 tablespoonful cornstarch,
2 cupfuls milk,
3 eggs,
Pinch salt.

Add cornstarch to sugar, mix well, stir it into milk, boiling hot, and simmer five minutes. When cool, add eggs, well beaten, and salt. Line a deep pie pan with paste, dust with flour, and fill three quarters full with the mixture. Bake in a moderate oven until firm in the center. Grate nutmeg over the top, and serve cool.

Crumb Lemon Pie.

½ cupful lemon juice,
½ cupful sugar,
2 tablespoonfuls butter,
3 eggs,
Grated peel 1 lemon,
1 cupful stale sponge-cake crumbs.

Strain the lemon juice over the crumbs and soak half an hour, cream the butter, add half the sugar, then, one at a time, the yolks of eggs, then the balance of the sugar, with the lemon peel, and a pinch salt. With a fork mix the crumbs well with the lemon juice, and stir them into the butter and sugar, beating well, then add the whites of eggs beaten stiff. Bake, and serve like custard pie.

Lemon Pie.

2 cupfuls boiling water,
1½ cupfuls sugar,
½ cupful lemon juice,
1 tablespoonful butter,
1 tablespoonful cornstarch,
Grated peel 1 lemon,
Yolks 3 eggs.

Mix the sugar and cornstarch well together, add them to the boiling water, and cook five minutes. Remove from the fire, add butter, lemon juice, peel, and lastly the eggs beaten very lightly. Line a deep pan with the paste, dust with flour, fill three fourths full with the mixture, and bake in a moderate oven till firm in the center. When cool, cover with a meringue made from whites of eggs.

Vanilla Cream Pie.

1 tablespoonful cornstarch,
½ cupful sugar,
2 cupfuls boiling milk,
1 tablespoonful butter,
1 teaspoonful McIlhenny's Mexican Vanilla.

Mix together cornstarch, sugar, and boiling milk. Cook five minutes, then add, stirring rapidly while adding, well-beaten eggs. Continue cooking until the egg is delicately cooked but not curdled, remove from the fire and stir butter into the mixture. When the butter is perfectly mixed with the custard, add the vanilla, and pour into a freshly baked tart shell. Orange cream pie and lemon pie may be made by using orange or lemon extract in place of vanilla.—EMMA P. EWING.

Lemon-and-Raisin Pie.

1 cupful chopped raisins,
Juice and rind 1 lemon,
1 cupful sugar,
1 cupful water,
1 teaspoonful cornstarch.

Boil the mixture ten minutes; bake between double crusts.

Green-Currant Pie.

1 cupful green currants,
½ cupful sugar,
1 tablespoonful butter,
Yolks 2 eggs,
1 tablespoonful flour,
1 tablespoonful water.

Mash currants and sugar, using a wooden potato masher. Beat to a cream butter and sugar, then add in successive order the yolks of eggs, flour, water, and the mashed currants. Line a deep pan with pastry, fill with the currant mixture, and bake. When done, cool slightly and cover with a meringue made of the whites of 2 eggs, 2 tablespoonfuls sugar, and vanilla to flavor. Bake in a slow oven until delicately brown.

Apple Pie with Pineapple Flavor.

3 tablespoonfuls grated pineapple,
1 tablespoonful water,
3 tablespoonfuls sugar.

Bake an apple pie in the usual way, but without sweetening. While it is baking, take the pineapple, water, and sugar, and simmer together till the fruit looks clear. When the pie is taken from the oven, remove the top crust, spread the pineapple over the apple, replace the cover, and set the pie away to cool.

German Cherry Pie.

Make a cherry pie as usual, but omit the upper crust. When nearly done, beat an egg light and add it to a scant ½ cupful cream and a tablespoonful sugar. Pour over the top of pie, return to the oven, and bake until the custard is set.

Date Pie.

1 pound dates,
3 eggs,
1 teaspoonful cinnamon,
2 cupfuls milk,
1 cupful sugar.

Soak dates in warm water overnight, then stew and sift the same as pumpkin. Into the pulp stir beaten eggs, cinnamon, milk, and sugar. Bake in one crust.

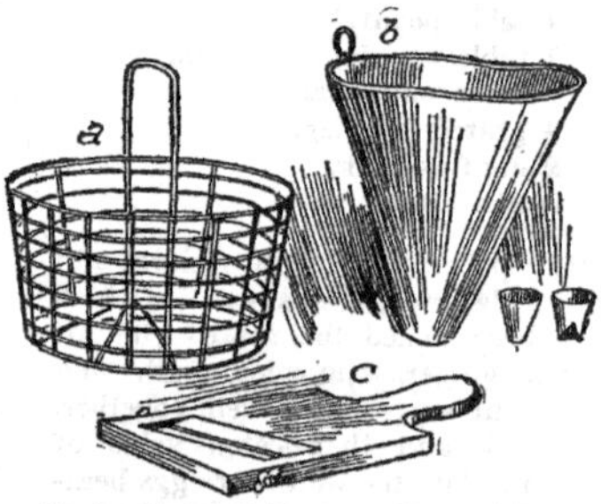

a, Frying Basket; b, Meringue Bag with Pastry Tubes; c, Vegetable Plane.

Fig Pie.

½ pound figs,
1 cupful water,
Whites of 2 eggs,
2 tablespoonfuls sugar,
1 tablespoonful lemon juice.

Make a rich bottom crust. Chop figs fine, cook with cupful water. Sweeten and flavor with lemon. When the figs are smooth, put into the crust and bake. Take a meringue of whites of 2 eggs, beaten stiff, with 2 tablespoonfuls powdered sugar, flavor with McIlhenny's Mexican Vanilla, and as soon as the crust is baked, spread this over the top; let brown a minute or two.

Gooseberry Pie.

Cut off the blossoms and stems of berries and fill a pie dish lined with plain paste, spreading over the top one third as much sugar as berries used. Slightly dredge with flour, and cover with a thin crust pricked with a fork. Bake half an hour.

Prune Pie.

½ pound prunes,
½ cupful sugar,
½ cupful currant jelly or 1 teaspoonful lemon juice.

Stew prunes, remove stones, stir in sugar, currant jelly, or lemon juice. Dust flour over the fruit, and bake with an upper crust.

Strawberry Pie.

Line a pie plate with thin paste and set in the oven till nearly baked. Take from the oven and fill with sugared berries, dredge with flour, cover the top crisscross with narrow strips of paste, return to the oven, and finish baking.

Torto Frutas (Mexican).

Line the sides of a baking dish with puff paste; cover the bottom with sliced pineapple; next a layer of sliced oranges, then sliced bananas, then a few slices lemon. Sift sugar between each layer. Repeat the layers until the dish is full, and cover the top layer with chopped nuts. Lay over the top narrow strips of the pastry, and bake slowly an hour.—MAY E. SOUTHWORTH.

Cocoanut Pie.

2 cupfuls hot milk,
2 well-beaten eggs,
½ cupful sugar,
1 cupful grated cocoanut,
1 teaspoonful McIlhenny's Mexican Vanilla.

Line a plate with paste, pour milk over eggs, set the bowl containing the mixture in boiling water, stir till thick, then take it out and stir in sugar, cocoanut, and vanilla. Fill the pie plate. Sprinkle top of pie with cocoanut, and bake till delicately brown.

Orange Pie.

1 cupful powdered sugar,
1 tablespoonful butter,
2 tablespoonfuls cornstarch,
½ cupful cold milk,
Grated rind and juice 1 orange,
1 egg,
2 oranges.

Beat sugar and butter together till light. Moisten cornstarch with milk, cook and stir one minute, pour quickly on butter and sugar; add the rind and juice of orange; mix well-beaten egg; peel oranges, cut into slices, and cut each slice into quarters. Line plate with paste, and bake in a quick oven until done. Stir the orange slices quickly into the custard mixture, fill the baked crust with this, and place in a quick oven a few minutes to brown. While it is browning, beat the whites of 2 eggs until light, add 2 tablespoonfuls powdered sugar, and beat until stiff. Spread this over the pie; dust thickly with powdered sugar, and stand again in the oven until delicately brown.

Dried-Apple Pie.

Soak the apples, put in a brown earthen pot, cover with water; cover the pot, and bake four or five hours; sweeten with sugar or molasses the last half hour and mash well with a spoon; when the apples are thoroughly cooked, flavor with lemon juice and add a little butter. The pie can be baked between two crusts, or bands of the paste can be placed over the top.

Banana Pie.

Yolks 2 eggs,
½ cupful sugar,
2 large bananas.

Beat the yolks of eggs and sugar to a cream. Peel and mash bananas, beat into the eggs together with milk. Bake with one crust; when done, cover with a meringue made of the 2 whites, and 2 tablespoonfuls sugar. Serve cold.

Rhubarb Pie.

Wash rhubarb, cut in half-inch pieces, put in deep pie plate having narrow strip of paste around the edge, sprinkle with sugar mixed with flour, allowing ½ cupful sugar and 2 tablespoonfuls flour to every cupful rhubarb. Cover with paste, and bake like apple pie. All juicy fruit pies should be made in the same way.

Chocolate Pie.

2 cupfuls scalding milk,
3 eggs,
4 tablespoonfuls sugar,
½ cupful Runkel's Chocolate,
1 teaspoonful McIlhenny's Mexican Vanilla.

Make a custard by pouring milk gradually upon eggs that have been well beaten and sugar. Return to fire, stir in chocolate, remove from fire, add vanilla, and pour the mixture into a pie plate lined with puff paste. Bake until set. Make a meringue of the whites of eggs and a tablespoonful powdered sugar, and spread on top of the pie. Brown delicately.

Chocolate-Cream Pie.

1 tablespoonful cornstarch,
½ cupful sugar,
2 cupfuls scalding milk,
3 eggs,
1½ squares Runkel's Chocolate,
1 tablespoonful butter,
1 teaspoonful McIlhenny's Mexican Vanilla.

Melt the chocolate in a double boiler with the sugar, pour over it the scalding milk, add the cornstarch, and cook five minutes; then beat in the whipped eggs. Cook till the mixture is custardy, add a dash salt, also butter and vanilla, pour into a freshly baked pie shell. Serve ice cold. If you wish to enrich this delicious pie, you may serve it with a meringue or a top of whipped cream.

Mince-Meat.

2¼ pounds round of beef,
2 quarts chopped apples,
½ pint chopped suet,
1½ pints raisins,
1 pint currants,
¼ pound citron,
1 quart sugar,
½ pint molasses,
3 pints cider,
2 tablespoonfuls salt,
4 tablespoonfuls cinnamon,
1 tablespoonful allspice,
1 tablespoonful mace,
1 teaspoonful cloves,
4 nutmegs grated,
4 lemons.

Put the beef in a small stewpan and cover with boiling water. Cook three hours, having the water only bubble at one side of the stewpan. Take from the fire and let the meat cool in the water, with the cover off the pan. When cold, remove fat and gristle, and chop the meat rather fine. Put it in a large bowl with all the other ingredients, except the cider, and mix thoroughly. Now, add the cider, and let the mixture stand in a cold place overnight. In the morning turn the mince-meat into a porcelain kettle and heat slowly to the boiling point; then simmer gently an hour. Put the mixture into stone jars and set away in a cold place; or it may be put in glass jars and sealed. It will keep for years in this way. When the pies are being made, 1 tumbler jelly or marmalade to 3 or 4 pies will be found a great improvement.—MARIA PARLOA.

CHAPTER LX

COOKIES, CAKES, AND DOUGHNUTS

Maple Hermits.

¾ cupful maple sugar,
½ cupful butter,
2½ cupfuls flour,
1 egg,
1 tablespoonful milk,
¼ teaspoonful cloves,
1 teaspoonful cinnamon,
½ teaspoonful soda,
½ cupful currants.

Beat the butter to a cream, and gradually beat in the sugar and spices. Dissolve the soda in the milk, and beat this into the sugar and butter. Add the egg well beaten, finally the flour and currants. Roll out an inch thick, and cut in squares. Bake in a quick oven twelve minutes.

Sugar Cookies.

2 cupfuls sugar,
1 cupful butter,
3 eggs,
3 cupfuls flour,
1 teaspoonful Calumet baking powder,
1 teaspoonful nutmeg,
½ teaspoonful cloves.

Cream butter and sugar, beat in the whipped eggs and spices, add the flour gradually, working it in until the dough is stiff enough to roll. Sprinkle flour over a pastry board. Make a ball of the dough, and lay it on the board. Rub the rolling-pin with flour and roll out the dough into a sheet quarter of an inch thick. Cut in round cakes, sift granulated sugar over each, and bake quickly.

Ginger Snaps.

2 cupfuls molasses,
1 cupful sugar,
1 cupful butter,
5 cupfuls flour,
1 teaspoonful ground ginger,
1 teaspoonful allspice,

Stir molasses, sugar, and butter together in a bowl set in hot water till very light. Mix in spices and flour, and roll in a thin sheet. Cut into small cakes, and bake quickly.

Chocolate Dominoes.

½ cupful pecan meat,
½ cupful English-walnut meat,
½ cupful figs,
½ cupful dates,
Grated rind 1 orange,
1 tablespoonful orange juice,
1 square Runkel's Chocolate.

Mix the nuts, dates, and figs, and put them through a food chopper. Wet with the orange juice, mix in the grated rind, and roll in a ball. Lay it on the baking board, which has been covered with sifted confectioner's sugar, and roll half an inch thick. Cut into shapes the size of a domino, and spread with melted chocolate. On top lay little rounds cut from blanched almonds to imitate dominoes.

Sour-Cream Cookies.

1 cupful sour cream,
1 teaspoonful soda,
1 cupful sugar,
Dash salt,
Flour,
½ teaspoonful nutmeg.

Mix the ingredients with enough flour to roll. Roll thin, and bake a nice brown.

Oklahoma Rocks.

2 cupfuls brown sugar,
½ cupful butter,
3 eggs,
Salt,
1 pound chopped nuts,
1 pound raisins,
1 teaspoonful soda in ⅓ cupful boiling water,
1 teaspoonful cinnamon,
½ teaspoonful cloves,
Flour to make stiff.

Mix the ingredients as given, and drop in spoonfuls on a greased baking pan.

Egg Cookies.

1 cupful sour cream,
1 cupful sugar,
1 teaspoonful soda,
Dash salt,
1 teaspoonful McIlhenny's Mexican Vanilla,
Flour enough to make soft dough.

Mix the cream, sugar, and soda with flour, a dash salt and a little vanilla, then flour enough to roll thin easily without sticking.

Boston Cookies.

1 cupful butter,
1½ cupfuls sugar,
3 eggs,
1 teaspoonful soda,
1½ teaspoonfuls hot water,
3¼ cupfuls flour,
½ teaspoonful salt,
1 teaspoonful cinnamon,
1 cupful chopped walnuts,
½ cupful currants,
½ cupful seeded chopped raisins.

Cream the butter, add the sugar gradually and eggs well beaten. Add soda dissolved in water, half the flour mixed and sifted with salt and cinnamon, then add nut meats, fruit, and remaining flour. Drop by spoonfuls an inch apart on a buttered sheet, and bake in a moderate oven.—Fannie M. Farmer.

Christmas Fruit Cookies.

½ cupful lard,
½ cupful butter,
1 cupful sugar,
2 beaten eggs,
½ cupful milk,
2 cupfuls flour,
½ teaspoonful soda,
¾ cupful currants,
¾ cupful raisins,
2 cupfuls uncooked rolled oats.

Cream the butter and lard, add the sugar, eggs, milk, flour, soda, currants, raisins, and rolled oats. Mix thoroughly, drop a teaspoonful at a time in unbuttered pans, and bake in a slow oven.

Chocolate Hearts.

3 ounces Runkel's Chocolate,
1 pound powdered sugar,
Whites 3 eggs,
1 teaspoonful McIlhenny's Mexican Vanilla.

Melt the chocolate by standing over hot water; add the sugar, and mix thoroughly; work to a stiff paste with the unbeaten whites of eggs, then add the vanilla. If the paste seems too soft, add more sugar. Break off in small pieces and roll a quarter of an inch thick, sprinkling the board and paste with granulated sugar instead of flour. Cut with a heart-shaped cake cutter, and place on pans oiled just enough to prevent sticking. Bake in a moderate oven. When done, they will feel firm to the touch, a solid crust having formed over the top. They should be very light, and will loosen easily from the pan after being allowed to stand a moment to cool.

Chocolate Cookies.

1 cupful butter,
1 cupful brown sugar,
2 eggs,
1 teaspoonful cinnamon,
½ teaspoonful cloves,

1 cupful almonds cut fine, without blanching,
1 cupful currants cleaned and dried),
2 ounces Runkel's Chocolate,
½ cupful milk,
2 teaspoonfuls Calumet baking powder,
Flour.

Mix butter, sugar, eggs, cinnamon, cloves, almonds, currants, the chocolate dissolved in ½ cupful milk, and flour enough to roll; before adding the flour, put in baking powder. Mix in the order given; roll out about an eighth of an inch thick; shape with cake cutter, and bake in a moderate oven. Make a thick sirup of ½ cupful each granulated sugar and water boiled together, and brush the cakes with this sirup as soon as they are taken from the oven.

Springerlein (German recipe).

1 cupful powdered sugar,
4 eggs,
Grated rind 1 lemon,
4 cupfuls flour,
½ teaspoonful Calumet baking powder.

Beat the eggs thoroughly with the sugar, add the rind of lemon, flour, and baking powder sifted with the flour, and mix quickly into loaf shape without much handling. Set in a cool place two hours. Flour a baking board, roll out dough to quarter of an inch thick, dust the mold with flour, press the springerlein on it tightly but firmly, then turn it over and carefully remove the cakes. Cut off surplus dough, put in the remainder, and mold more. Use as little flour as possible in rolling out. Put a cloth on the table, sprinkle it with aniseed, lay the cakes on it, and stand twelve hours in a cool room. Bake in buttered pans.

One, Two, Three, Four Cookies.

1 cupful butter,
2 cupfuls sugar,
3 cupfuls flour,
4 eggs,
1½ teaspoonfuls Calumet baking powder,
½ teaspoonful salt,
2 tablespoonfuls caraway seed.

Cream the butter and add half the sugar. Beat the yolks, add the remaining half of the sugar, and beat with the butter, then add the beaten whites. Mix the soda, cream of tartar, spice, and salt with the flour, and stir into the butter mixture. Take a teaspoonful dough, make into a ball with floured hands, place the balls in a pan, press or flatten into a round cake, and bake ten minutes.

Cream Cakes.

1 cupful hot water,
½ teaspoonful salt,
½ cupful butter,
1½ cupfuls flour,
5 eggs, yolks and whites beaten separately.

Boil the water, salt, and butter. When boiling, add the flour, and stir well five minutes; when cool, add the eggs. This is such a stiff mixture, many find it easier to mix with the hand, and some prefer to add the eggs whole, 1 at a time. When well mixed, drop from a tablespoonful on a buttered baking pan, some distance apart. Bake twenty to thirty minutes, or till brown and well puffed. Split when cool, and fill with cream.

Éclairs.—Bake the cream-cake mixture in pieces four inches long and one and a half wide. When cool, split and fill with cream. Ice with chocolate or vanilla frosting.

Cream for Cream Cakes and Éclairs.

1 pint boiled milk,
2 tablespoonfuls cornstarch,
3 eggs well beaten,
¾ cupful sugar,
1 saltspoonful salt or 1 teaspoonful butter.

Wet the cornstarch in cold milk, and cook in the boiling milk ten minutes. Beat the eggs; and add the sugar and the thickened milk. Cook in a double boiler five minutes. Add the salt or butter, and when cool, flavor with lemon, vanilla, or almond.

Chocolate Fingers.

3 eggs,
1 cupful sugar,
¼ cupful boiling water,
1 cupful flour.

(For Icing.)

3 cupfuls granulated sugar,
1 cupful water,
3 ounces Runkel's Chocolate,
½ teaspoonful McIlhenny's Mexican Vanilla.

Beat the yolks of eggs and sugar until light, add in succession the flour, water, and whites beaten until stiff. Bake in moderate oven, in an oblong sheet, about half an inch thick; cut, when done, into strips about three and a half inches wide.

To make the icing, boil the sugar and water until it spins a thread, then pour in a thin stream over the chocolate, which should be melted by standing over hot water; mix well and flavor with vanilla. Let the mixture cool slightly, beat with a wooden spoon until it grains, then stand in a pan of boiling water and stir constantly until it melts. Keep in hot water while coating the cakes. Dip each cake in the melted mixture, then in a saucer containing granulated sugar. Place, without touching each other, on a clean plate. If the chocolate mixture gets too thick, add from time to time a few drops hot water, keeping it melted during the process.

Nun's Gems.

1 cupful sugar,
1 cupful butter,
5 eggs,
½ teaspoonful cinnamon,
1 teaspoonful McIlhenny's Mexican Vanilla,
Grated rind 1 lemon,
2 cupfuls flour,
1 teaspoonful Calumet baking powder,
1 cupful grated cocoanut.

Cream the butter and sugar, mix the beaten yolks of eggs, and add the lemon, cinnamon, and vanilla. Sift the flour and baking powder, mix with the batter, then fold in the cocoanut, and the whites of eggs whipped to a stiff froth. Bake half an hour in gem pans; when cool, dip each cake in white or chocolate frosting.

Macaroons.

1½ cupfuls almond paste,
Whites 2 eggs,
1 cupful powdered sugar.

Mix the paste and sugar, then stir in the whites of eggs, which have been beaten stiff. Work with a spoon until the mixture is thoroughly blended, drop small teaspoonful paste into a pan which has been lined with buttered paper, put half a peanut in the center of each, and bake in a moderate oven until delicately brown. Lift the pan from the oven, take out the paper with the macaroons, lay for a minute on a damp towel, then with a palette knife you can slip each one off.

Cinnamon Strips.

2 cupfuls brown sugar,
4 eggs,
½ cupful shredded almonds,
Grated peel 1 lemon,
1 tablespoonful cinnamon,
1 teaspoonful cloves,
4 cupfuls flour.

Cream the sugar and eggs till they are a light froth, add the shredded almonds, lemon peel, and spices, sift in the flour, mix to a stiff batter, roll out on a floured baking board, cut into long strips, and bake until brown.

Chocolate Strips.

½ cupful butter,
1 cupful sugar,
2 eggs,

1½ squares Runkel's Chocolate,
1 teaspoonful McIlhenny's Mexican Vanilla,
1¼ cupfuls flour.

Cream the butter, sugar, and eggs, add the chocolate and vanilla, then the flour, beat thoroughly, pour into a shallow pan in a thin layer. Bake quickly, brush with white of egg, and dust with powdered sugar; while hot, cut into narrow strips.

CAKES MADE FROM SOUR MILK

Mrs. Moberly's Sour-Cream Cake.

1 cupful sugar,
2 eggs,
1 cupful sour cream,
½ teaspoonful soda,
2 cupfuls flour,
1½ teaspoonfuls baking powder,
1 teaspoonful lemon extract.

Beat sugar, egg yolks, and cream very light; sift in flour, soda, and baking powder. Flavor, add whites of eggs beaten to a stiff froth in a loaf cake.

Cocoa Cake.

½ cupful butter,
2 cupfuls coffee sugar,
2 eggs,
1 cupful sour milk,
1 scant teaspoonful Calumet baking soda,
2 cupfuls flour,
½ cupful Runkel's Cocoa.

Beat the butter and sugar to a cream, then add the other ingredients. Bake in a moderate oven. Cover with chocolate icing.

Dried-Apple Cake.

2 cupfuls molasses,
3 cupfuls dried apples,
1 cupful butter,
1 cupful sugar,
1 cupful sour milk,
1 teaspoonful soda,
4 eggs,
4 cupfuls flour,
1 cupful currants,
1 cupful raisins,
1 teaspoonful cloves,
1 teaspoonful cinnamon,
1 nutmeg.

Soak apples in as little water as possible over night; in the morning chop fine and boil half an hour in molasses. When cold, add butter, sugar and milk dissolved with soda, eggs, flour, fruit, and spices. Bake in a slow oven.

Spice Cake.

1 cupful sugar,
2 eggs,
4 tablespoonfuls butter,
½ cupful sour milk,
½ cupful strong coffee,
1 teaspoonful soda,
1 teaspoonful Calumet baking powder,
2½ cupfuls flour,
1 teaspoonful cinnamon,
1 teaspoonful nutmeg.

Cream sugar and butter, and add the milk, coffee, soda, baking powder, flour, spice, cinnamon, and nutmeg. Bake in a medium-sized pan, and frost with powdered sugar mixed with cream.

Devil's Cake.

2 cupfuls dark-brown sugar,
½ cupful butter,
½ cupful sour milk,
½ teaspoonful soda,
3 cupfuls flour,
1 teaspoonful Calumet baking powder,
2 eggs,
½ cupful Runkel's Chocolate, ground.

Beat the butter and sugar until smooth. Add the milk, soda dissolved in a little warm water, then the flour, which has been sifted twice with the baking powder. Add the eggs well beaten. Stir thoroughly and add the chocolate. This makes three good-sized layers. Filling — 2 cupfuls brown sugar, ⅓ cupful butter, ½ cupful sweet milk. Boil until it will thread, and spread between layers. If a very large cake is desired, two white layers may be added flavored with orange.

Training-Day Ginger Cake.

½ cupful butter,
1 cupful granulated sugar,
1 egg,
1 cupful New Orleans molasses,
1 cupful sour milk,
1 teaspoonful soda,
3 cupfuls pastry flour,
1 tablespoonful ginger.

Beat the butter to a cream, add the sugar and egg well beaten, the molasses, then the sour milk, to which the soda has been added and both stirred until the milk foams and there are no lumps remaining. Sift the flour and ginger, beat thoroughly, and turn into a shallow baking pan. Bake in a moderate oven; when it is well done, remove from the oven and spread with a thick layer of raw molasses. Return to the oven for a short time till the coating of the molasses has set, when the cake may be cut into squares.

Crumb Gingerbread.

1 teaspoonful soda,
4 cupfuls flour,
1 cupful butter,
2 cupfuls sugar,
1 cupful sour milk,
2 eggs,
½ grated nutmeg,
½ teaspoonful cinnamon,
1 teaspoonful ginger.

Rub the flour and butter together until they are reduced to crumbs, as flour and lard are worked together for pie crust; then add the sugar and stir this in till the mixture is once more crumbly. Measure out 2 cupfuls crumbs, and set away in a cold place until the batter is made. Into what remains of the crumbs stir in two well-beaten eggs, and add the sour milk and soda. When the soda is dissolved and the milk foams, turn it into the mixing bowl with the rest. Add to the batter the nutmeg, cinnamon, and ginger. Butter a dripping pan and measure out 1 cupful crumbs that was set aside; spread evenly on the bottom of the pan, pour the batter over them as evenly as possible; spread the rest of the crumbs on top, and bake in a moderately hot oven; when done, cut into squares, and keep in a closely covered jar.

Aunt Dinah's Cake.

¼ cupful butter,
½ cupful sugar,
½ cupful molasses,
2 cupfuls flour,
½ cupful sour milk,
½ teaspoonful ginger,
⅛ teaspoonful salt,
1 teaspoonful cinnamon,
½ teaspoonful soda,
¼ nutmeg grated,
Juice and rind ½ lemon,
1 egg.

Beat the butter and sugar to a cream, add the spices, lemon, and molasses. Dissolve the soda in 1 tablespoonful cold water, and stir into the sour milk. Add this and the egg well beaten, then the flour, and beat briskly. Pour into a well-buttered pan, and bake in a moderate oven fifty minutes. This cake will keep moist some time. One half cupful stoned raisins and ½ cupful currants may be stirred lightly into the batter just before it is put in the pan, if you wish a fruit cake.

Blackberry-Jam Cake.

½ cupful butter,
⅔ cupful sugar,
1 cupful flour,
⅔ cupful stoned raisins,
⅔ cupful blackberry jam,
2 tablespoonfuls sour cream or milk,
½ teaspoonful soda,
½ nutmeg grated,
2 eggs.

Beat the butter to a cream, then beat in the sugar. When very light, beat in the jam and nutmeg. Dissolve the soda in 1 tablespoonful cold water, and add it to the sour cream. Add this and the egg well beaten to the other ingredients. Now add the flour and beat for half a minute. Sprinkle a tablespoonful flour over the raisins, and stir them in lightly. Pour the batter into a well-buttered pan, and bake fifty minutes. This

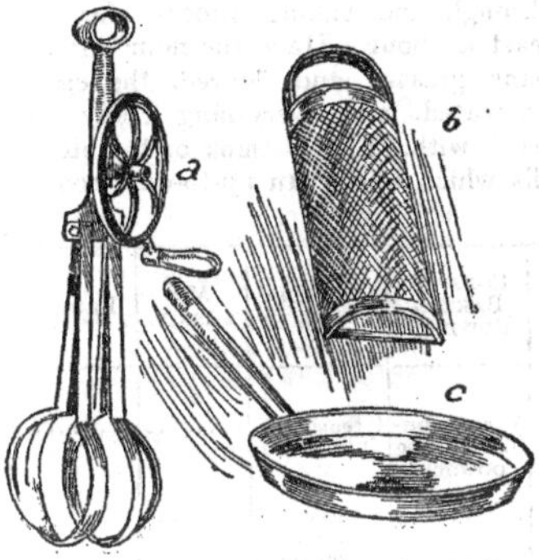

a, Dover Egg-beater; b, Grater; c, Omelet Pan.

makes one small loaf. This cake may be put away to be used as a pudding when convenient. Steam it an hour, and serve with a wine sauce. It is almost as good as a plum pudding.

Maple-Sugar Gingerbread.

1 egg,
1 cupful thick maple sirup,
2 cupfuls flour,
½ cupful sour milk,
¼ cupful butter,
½ teaspoonful ginger,
½ teaspoonful soda,
¼ teaspoonful salt,
Rind and juice ½ lemon.

Beat the butter to a cream, and add the sirup and flavoring. Dissolve the soda in 1 tablespoonful cold water and stir into the sour milk. Add this and the egg well beaten to the other ingredients, then the flour. Beat well; pour into a buttered pan. This quantity will make one small loaf or a thin sheet. If baked in a loaf, leave in oven fifty minutes; if in a sheet, twenty-five minutes.—Miss Parloa.

Holiday Cake.

1 cupful butter,
1 cupful sugar,
1 cupful molasses,
½ teaspoonful salt,
1 teaspoonful mixed spices,
1 egg,
1 cupful sour milk,
1 teaspoonful soda,
Flour,
1 cupful raisins and currants,
Small quantity citron.

Mix together the butter, sugar, molasses, salt, spices, and egg; beat well, then add the sour milk with the soda stirred in, and flour enough to make quite thick; add the raisins, currants, and citron. This makes two medium loaves, and will keep for weeks.

Marble Layer Cake.

⅓ cake Runkel's Chocolate,
1 teaspoonful baking soda,
½ cupful warm water,
2 cupfuls maple sugar,
2 eggs,
½ cupful butter,
1 cupful sour milk,
2½ cupfuls flour.

Melt the chocolate over hot water, dissolve the soda in the warm water; beat the butter to a cream. Add the eggs beaten without separating, and beat in gradually the sugar—beat for at least ten minutes. Pour the soda and water in the sour milk; add this with the melted chocolate to the egg mixture; now stir in the flour. Beat and bake in three layers. When cold, put together with maple or caramel filling.

CHAPTER LXI

CAKE

If one has mastered the art of measuring, mixing, and baking cake, there are only four cakes you have to know: sponge, butter, fruit, and raised cake.

Every other cake among a hundred recipes belongs to one of these classes; there is only a slight variation in its being richer or plainer, differently flavored, or differently named. When children are taught cake making in a cooking school, the teacher tabulates for them on a blackboard quantities and directions, something after the fashion illustrated here:

One of the most important things to learn about cake making is to have all the utensils and ingredients on hand before you begin work. The cake process will not wait, if you have to search for things. A half-beaten batter will fall flat before you are ready to attend to it again. Make up the fire so the oven will carry you through the baking process for at least an hour. Have the flour sifted, pans greased and floured, the eggs separated, and everything ready to work with. Let us think of the utensils which to-day an up-to-date cooking school demands for cake making. There is a bowl for beating the batter. I prefer the white enamel bowl to one made of earthenware, partly because it is light enough to handle easily, then it is unbreakable, and it can be kept beautifully clean. This bowl must be deep and narrow enough

Name of Cake.	Butter.	Sugar.	Eggs.	Milk.	Flour	Soda or Baking Powder	Flavoring.	Molasses.	Fruit.
Loaf or Layer Butter Cake.......	$\frac{2}{3}$ cupful.	2 cupfuls.	4	1 cupful.	$3\frac{1}{2}$ cupfuls.	5 teaspoonfuls baking powder.	1 teaspoonful vanilla	....	....
Sponge Cake	......	1 cupful.	4	......	1 cupful.	....	1 tablespoonful lemon juice	....	.....
Dark Fruit Cake........	$\frac{1}{2}$ cupful.	$\frac{3}{4}$ cupful. brown sugar.	2	$\frac{1}{2}$ cupful.	2 cupfuls.	$\frac{1}{2}$ teaspoonful soda.	1 teaspoonful cinnamon; $\frac{1}{2}$ teaspoonful all-spice; $\frac{1}{4}$ teaspoonful mace; $\frac{1}{4}$ teaspoonful cloves; $\frac{1}{2}$ teaspoonful lemon extract.	$\frac{1}{2}$ cupful.	$\frac{3}{4}$ cupful raisins; $\frac{3}{4}$ cupful currants; $\frac{1}{2}$ cupful citron.

It seems such an excellent method, that I printed for my own kitchen a large card holding our favorite recipes, and it has saved maids, as well as myself, much time in looking up recipes. I left some space at the bottom, and occasionally add to it new and good ones.

at the bottom to allow the spoon to turn over the ingredients and do its work thoroughly. The ideal cake-mixing spoon is a wooden one with a slitted bowl, just long enough for the top of the handle to reach your elbow. The old-fashioned spoon collects butter and sugar in a lump, while a slitted spoon constantly drives the creamed mass through it, and that, of course, makes it lighter. The slitted spoon beats without any noise, and leaves no black marks on the bowl. Then for the other utensils, you need a good flour sifter, cake pans which have been used long enough to become rather black—for new tin will never make a good crust—two glass measuring cups, a small bowl, a Dover egg beater with which to beat the yolks of eggs, a large pliable Teller knife, a flat wire egg whipper, which is called the Daisy beater, and a wire cake cooler, with feet which raise it high enough for the air to circulate around the cake and carry off the steam.

The only way always to have a good cake is to stick to the level measurements, as is taught to-day in all the leading cooking schools. Flour, sugar, butter, indeed every ingredient, is leveled off perfectly flat with the Teller knife. Grease your cake tin with lard or olive oil, using a butter brush (butter is not satisfactory for this, as it blackens the crust), then sprinkle flour inside the tin. Jar the pan lightly on the table, tipping it around so the flour will adhere to the greased surface. This gives a perfectly even surface to the bottom of the cake. If you wish to line the tin with paper, use parchment paper, which comes by the roll. Lay the tin upon it, top down, mark around with a pencil, then cut it an inch or two larger. Fringe the paper with a scissors down to the pencil line, and slip into a greased pan. Paper is frequently used with a fruit cake, because that cake burns more readily than any other. By using it

Before we begin the process of cake mixing, let us see what makes a cake light. Compared with the making of bread, cake raising is a swift process. It is brought about partly by blending an acid with an alkali. Air bubbles are created that make the mixture frothy before it is poured into the pans; heat begins to expand the bubbles and later to set them. Eggs thoroughly well beaten add further to the lightness of cake, for air is entangled liberally when the albumen is whipped.

According to what other ingredients are used in a cake, we add baking powder, soda, and cream of tartar, or soda alone for the raising power. Baking powder is simply a scientific mixture of cream of tartar and soda with the addition of a little flour to preserve it from getting lumpy. It must always be used with sweet milk. The same combination, of course, is made with cream of tartar and soda, the formula generally given in older cookbooks. Soda alone is used when there is some powerful acid in the liquid, such as sour milk or molasses. If one has nothing but sweet milk on hand and no cream of tartar, the soda will do its work almost as well by adding a small quantity of vinegar or lemon juice.

It is never economy to use poor ingredients in cake. Strong butter and eggs that are not absolutely fresh cannot have their flavor concealed by the most liberal addition of vanilla. Also, when you possibly can, use pastry flour. You can easily tell the difference between it and the flour with which we make bread, by gathering up a handful. It will stick together in a lump within your hand, while bread flour falls apart. Bread flour may be used in a contingency, but after measuring it, take out 2 level tablespoonfuls from each cupful as your batter is liable to be too thick, and the cake may crack as soon as it begins to crust.

eggs, drop the yolks into a mixing bowl, and the whites upon a large platter. If the eggs have been kept in a refrigerator or cold pantry, they will froth much more quickly. With the wooden spoon, beat the yolks steadily till they begin to grow thick and lemon-colored, adding gradually 1 cupful sugar. Put in 1 tablespoonful lemon juice and the grated rind of ½ lemon, then 1 cupful sifted flour with ¼ teaspoonful salt in it. This amount of salt ought to be added to every cake. It overcomes the flat taste which it would otherwise have. Beat the batter thoroughly, till it is bubbly and well mixed. If an assistant, meantime, has been whipping the whites of eggs for you, so much the better. A Dover egg beater does not begin to achieve the amount of frothy white you can get by whipping with a Daisy egg beater. Tip the platter slightly downward as it begins to froth. Swing the arm upward and downward; turn over the mass of froth, which will grow larger every second. When the latter is fairly heaped and every foam speck has a dry appearance, it is ready to add to the batter. Scrape it with a Teller knife and with this useful utensil, cut the froth in, across this way and that, lifting it lightly, until it is thoroughly blended and looks like delicate foam. If it should be beaten at this point, you will simply destroy all the bubbles of albumen you achieved by the whipping process. Scrape every particle of cake batter with the knife cleanly from the bowl into a cake pan, preferably a deep one. Let the mixture rise a little higher on the sides than in the middle, then set to bake in a slow oven.

The first process in baking is to get a cake thoroughly heated through, during which time it ought to rise steadily without crusting. When it has been half an hour in the oven, the rising process should have finished and a delicate crust have begun to form on top. The last half hour is given to its becoming solid, brown, and crusty.

Fudge Cake.

(An original recipe from the Copper Kettle Lunch Room at Smith College.)

- 1 cupful sugar,
- ½ cupful butter,
- 2 eggs,
- ½ cupful milk,
- 1½ cupfuls flour,
- 2½ teaspoonfuls Calumet baking powder,
- 2 ounces melted chocolate.

Cream together the butter and sugar, add the beaten yolks of eggs, then the milk and flour sifted with the baking powder. Beat well, add chocolate and the whites of eggs whipped to a stiff froth. Bake in a shallow pan in a moderate oven. When cool, pour over it a fudge frosting and mark in squares before the frosting has hardened.

Fudge Frosting.

- 2 cupfuls sugar,
- ½ cupful milk,
- 1 tablespoonful butter,
- ¾ cupful Runkel's Chocolate, grated,
- 1 teaspoonful McIlhenny's Mexican Vanilla,
- 1 cupful chopped walnuts.

Put the sugar, milk, butter, and chocolate into a granite saucepan and stir occasionally till the mixture reaches the boiling point. Boil without stirring eight minutes, then take from the fire and beat till creamy. At this point add the nuts and vanilla, then pour over the cake. This recipe makes a delicious fudge.

Feather Cake.

- 4 tablespoonfuls butter,
- 1 cupful sugar,
- 1½ cupfuls flour,
- 2½ teaspoonfuls baking powder,
- 2 eggs,
- ½ cupful milk,
- 1 teaspoonful McIlhenny's Mexican Vanilla.

Put butter in mixing bowl, work it with a spoon till creamy, add sugar gradually, and continue creaming. Sift flour and baking powder together; separate yolks of eggs from whites, beat yolks till light-colored and thick, then add milk and egg mixture to creamed butter and sugar, alternately with flour. Add flavoring, stir and beat well; lastly add whites of eggs beaten stiff. Put in a shallow greased and floured pan, or one lined with buttered paper. Bake about thirty minutes or till cake shrinks from the pan, and does not stick when tried with a straw. The feather cake may be varied and made into a number of different kinds, for instance:

Spice Cake.—Before adding the beaten whites, put in ¾ cupful seeded raisins that have been washed, dried, cut in halves, and rolled in a little of the flour reserved for the purpose. Flavor with ¼ teaspoonful ground cloves, ½ teaspoonful cinnamon, and a grating nutmeg instead of vanilla.

Marble Cake.—Color half the feather-cake mixture with ½ tablespoonful Runkel's Chocolate melted. Mix the white and dark part when putting it in the pan, so they will be well mingled though distinct.

Ribbon Cake.—To one third the feather-cake mixture add ½ teaspoonful mixed spices and ½ cupful seeded raisins cut in pieces. Bake in a shallow pan, and the remainder in two other shallow pans. When done, put the fruit cake between the others with a layer of jelly or frosting between.

Layer Cake.—Bake feather-cake mixture in round tins and put a cream, chocolate, or other filling between.

Nursery Cake.

- 3 tablespoonfuls butter,
- 1 cupful sugar,
- 1 egg,
- 1 cupful cold water,
- 2 cupfuls flour,
- 4 teaspoonfuls Calumet baking powder,
- 1 teaspoonful McIlhenny's Mexican Vanilla.

Cream the butter, add half the sugar, and continue creaming. Beat egg till light and add with the water and rest of the sugar to the creamed butter. Add flour mixed with baking powder. Flavor, beat well, and bake in a shallow pan about half an hour.

Surprise Cake.

- 4 tablespoonfuls butter,
- 1 cupful sugar,
- 1 egg,
- 1 cupful milk,
- 2 cupfuls flour,
- 4 teaspoonfuls baking powder,
- 1 teaspoonful McIlhenny's Mexican Vanilla.

Mix carefully, and bake like nursery cake.

Plain Wedding Cake.

- ½ cupful butter,
- 1½ cupfuls sugar,
- Yolks 3 eggs,
- ½ cupful milk,
- 2½ cupfuls flour,
- 3½ teaspoonfuls Calumet baking powder,
- 1 teaspoonful cinnamon,
- ½ teaspoonful ground cloves,
- ½ teaspoonful grated nutmeg,
- ½ teaspoonful powdered mace,
- ¾ cupful seeded raisins washed, dried, and cut in pieces,
- ¾ cupful currants washed, and dried,
- ¼ pound citron cut in small, thin pieces,
- Whites 3 eggs.

Roll fruit in ½ cupful flour, and sift the rest with baking powder and spices. Mix like feather cake, adding the floured fruit just before the stiffly beaten whites of eggs. Bake in a thick loaf, in a moderate oven. Cover with a plain, white icing.

Lemon Sponge Cake.

Yolks 2 eggs,
1 cupful sugar,
⅜ cupful hot water,
1 teaspoonful lemon juice,
Grated rind 1 lemon,
1 cupful flour,
1½ teaspoonfuls Calumet baking powder;
½ teaspoonful salt,
Whites 2 eggs.

Beat yolks till light-colored and thick, add half the sugar gradually, and continue beating; then the hot water, the rest of the sugar, the lemon juice and rind. Beat well, add flour, mixed with baking powder and salt; lastly cut and fold in the stiffly beaten whites of eggs. Put in shallow greased and floured pan, and bake in a moderately hot oven twenty-five minutes.

Chocolate Cake.

1 cupful sugar,
½ cupful butter,
2 eggs,
½ cupful milk,
1½ cupfuls flour,
2½ teaspoonfuls Calumet baking powder,
2 squares Runkel's Chocolate,
½ teaspoonful McIlhenny's Mexican Vanilla,
Dash salt.

Beat the butter and sugar together to a cream, add the yolks of eggs which have been well beaten, then the milk, the flour sifted with the baking powder and salt. Beat till light and frothy, add the vanilla and melted chocolate, last the whites of eggs whipped stiff. Bake in a long narrow pan, and when cool, cover with a white frosting.

Chocolate Layer Cake.

¾ cupfuls sugar,
2 tablespoonfuls butter,
1 egg,
½ cupful milk,
1⅓ cupfuls flour,
2 teaspoonfuls Calumet baking powder,
Dash salt,
½ teaspoonful McIlhenny's Mexican Vanilla.

Cream the butter and sugar together; add the egg beaten to a froth, then the milk, flour sifted with baking powder, and vanilla. Bake in one deep layer cake tin; when the cake is cool, split in two shortcake fashion, and cover the smooth top of each layer with a chocolate frosting.

Cocoa Sponge.

½ cupful butter,
1 cupful sugar,
3 eggs,
¼ cupful Runkel's Cocoa,
1 teaspoonful cinnamon,
¼ teaspoonful cloves,
½ cupful milk,
2 cupfuls flour,
3 teaspoonfuls Calumet baking powder.

Cream the butter and sugar, beat in the cocoa, the yolks of eggs well beaten, cinnamon, cloves, and milk, then the flour sifted with the baking powder; last add the whites of eggs whipped to a stiff froth. Bake in a moderate oven.

Devil's Food.

2 cupfuls sugar,
½ cupful butter,
4 eggs,
1 cupful milk,
2⅓ cupfuls flour,
4 teaspoonfuls Calumet baking powder,
2 squares Runkel's Chocolate,
½ teaspoonful McIlhenny's Mexican Vanilla.

Beat the butter and sugar to a cream, add the well-beaten yolks of eggs, then alternately mix with milk and flour sifted with the baking powder, stir in the melted chocolate and vanilla, then the whites of eggs, whip to a dry froth. Bake fifty minutes in a long narrow pan. Cover with a boiled white icing.

Chocolate Marshmallow Cake.

Use the recipe given either for chocolate cake, devil's food, or cocoa sponge, and bake in a shallow pan, letting the batter half fill. It ought to rise to the top of the pan. As soon as the hot cake is taken from the oven, turn it out and cover the top with marshmallows, which have been pulled apart; the soft inside of the sweetmeats will run together into a sort of frosting. When cool, pour over them a frosting made of Runkel's Sweet Chocolate melted over hot water.

Spanish Cake.

1 cupful sugar,
½ cupful butter,
2 eggs,
½ cupful milk,
1¾ cupfuls flour,
2 teaspoonfuls Calumet baking powder,
Dash salt,
1 teaspoonful cinnamon.

Cream the butter and sugar, beat in the yolks of eggs, then the flour, with which has been sifted cinnamon, salt, and baking powder, alternating with it the milk; the whites of eggs whipped to a stiff froth may be added the last thing. Bake in a large shallow pan and cover the top with caramel frosting.

Coffee Cake.

2 cupfuls sugar,
1 cupful butter,
2 tablespoonfuls molasses,
1¼ cupfuls cold coffee,
3¾ cupfuls flour,
1 teaspoonful cinnamon,
½ teaspoonful cloves,
½ teaspoonful nutmeg,
½ teaspoonful allspice,
5 teaspoonfuls Calumet baking powder,
¾ cupful raisins,
¾ cupful currants,
¼ cupful citron,
5 eggs.

Cream the butter and sugar, add the molasses and well-beaten yolks of eggs, then sift together the flour, spices, and baking powder. Beat in alternately with the coffee. Dredge the fruit with flour, stir it in, then the whites of eggs. Pour into deep cake tins and bake slowly in a moderate oven.

Pound Cake.

2 cupfuls butter,
2 cupfuls sugar,
10 eggs,
4 cupfuls flour,
½ teaspoonful mace,
2 tablespoonfuls milk.

Cream the butter and sugar, add the yolks of eggs beaten till thick, then the milk, flour, and whites of eggs. Pour into a square tin and bake an hour.

Angel Cake.

1 cupful whites of eggs,
Dash salt,
1 cupful sugar,
1 teaspoonful almond extract,
½ teaspoonful McIlhenny's Mexican Vanilla,
1 cupful flour,
1 teaspoonful cream of tartar.

Whip the whites of eggs on a large platter until they become a heap of dry froth. Then blend the sugar with them very carefully so the bubbles will not break. Sift the flour and cream of tartar three times and add to the egg mixture, stirring as little as possible, so as to keep it very frothy. Add the flavoring, pour into an unbuttered pan with a center tube, and bake forty minutes in a moderate oven. Do not move the cake until you are ready to take it from the oven, as it is very easy to make it fall. Invert the pan on a cake cooler and brush the cake with the white of egg beaten with a few tablespoonfuls powdered sugar. Allow this covering to harden before you frost it.

Sunshine Cake.

Yolks 5 eggs,
1 cupful sugar,
Dash salt,
¾ cupful flour,
½ teaspoonful cream of tartar,
Whites 7 eggs,
1 lump sugar,
1 teaspoonful lemon juice,
1 tablespoonful orange juice.

Beat the yolks of eggs till thick and lemon-colored, and add the sugar and flour, sifted with the cream of tartar and salt. Rub the lump of sugar over the rind of lemon, then dissolve it in the fruit juice; this constitutes the flavoring which may be stirred in and followed by the whites of eggs whipped to a dry froth. Bake the cake in a deep pan.

New England Raspberry Cake.

½ cupful butter,
1 cupful sugar,
Yolks 2 eggs,
⅔ cupful milk,
2 cupfuls flour,
1 teaspoonful Calumet baking powder.

This old-fashioned, delicious cake is baked in layers. Mix the butter and sugar to a cream, add the yolks of eggs well beaten and the milk; then stir in the flour, in which has been sifted the baking powder. Bake in jelly-cake pans. For the filling, crush slightly 1 quart raspberries, add whites 2 eggs, 1 cupful powdered sugar, and a few drops lemon juice. Whip until thick; spread between layers and over the top. To be eaten with cream.

Lady Baltimore Cake.

1 cupful butter,
2 cupfuls powdered sugar,
1 cupful milk,
Juice 1 lemon,
Whites 6 eggs,
4 cupfuls flour,
2 teaspoonfuls Calumet baking powder.

Rub the butter and sugar to a cream, and add the milk; when well mixed, stir in the juice of the lemon and whip very light; stir in alternately the stiffened whites of eggs and flour, sifted with the baking powder. Bake in jelly-tins. When cold, put together with this filling, and frost the top: Boil 3 cupfuls granulated sugar with a ½ cupful water until a drop hanging from the tip of a spoon threads in the air. Pour while hot over the whites 3 eggs whipped to a standing froth. Whip until you have a thick cream and stir in gradually a cupful each minced raisins and chopped pecans with 5 figs that have been soaked soft in lukewarm water, then dried and minced.

Cocoanut Cake.

1 cupful sugar,
½ cupful butter,
¾ cupful milk,
3 eggs,
2½ cupfuls flour,
2 teaspoonfuls Calumet baking powder,
1 grated cocoanut.

Cream the sugar and butter; take the milk of the cocoanut and, if not enough, add sweet milk to make ¾ cupful. Add the beaten yolks, then flour and baking powder sifted, then beaten whites, and lastly the grated cocoanut, reserving some for the frosting of the loaf. This is to be baked in a deep tin.

Orange Cake.

2 cupfuls sugar,
½ cupful butter,
½ cupful cold water,
Yolks 5 eggs,
2½ cupfuls flour,
2 teaspoonfuls baking powder,
Juice and rind 1 orange,
Whites 3 eggs.

Bake in layers; use boiled icing flavored with orange juice.

Gingerbread with Chocolate Glaze:

¾ cupful butter,
1 cupful sugar,
3 cupfuls flour,
1 cupful dark molasses,
1 cupful black coffee,
1 teaspoonful ginger,
½ teaspoonful cloves,
1 teaspoonful bicarbonate of soda,
3 eggs.

Mix the spices with the molasses. Dissolve the soda in a little boiling water and add to the coffee. Cream the butter and sugar, add the eggs, one at a time, and beat each one well. Add the molasses, then the coffee and flour, a little at a time, alternately. Bake in bread tins in a moderate oven forty to sixty minutes, or until the cake leaves the sides of the pans.

Gingerbread with Whipped Cream.

Use the gingerbread recipe given above, substituting a cupful boiling water for the coffee and using half butter and half lard; or 2 cupfuls molasses may be used, and the sugar omitted. In the latter case 2 teaspoonfuls soda instead of one should be dissolved in a cupful boiling water. Serve the cake very fresh, and cover the top just before serving with whipped cream. The cake may be broken into squares, and the pieces fitted together and covered entirely with whipped cream. It can then be served as a dessert.—MARY RONALD.

Quick Cake.

⅓ cupful soft butter,
1⅓ cupfuls brown sugar,
2 eggs,
½ cupful milk,
1¾ cupfuls flour,
3 teaspoonfuls baking powder,
½ teaspoonful cinnamon,
½ teaspoonful grated nutmeg,
½ pound dates stoned and cut in pieces.

Put ingredients in a bowl and beat all together for three minutes, using a wooden cake spoon. Bake in a buttered and floured cake pan thirty-five to forty minutes. If directions are followed, this makes a most satisfactory cake; but if the ingredients are added separately, it will not prove a success.—FANNIE M. FARMER.

Black Angel Cake.

1 cupful Runkel's Chocolate grated,
½ cupful milk,
2 cupfuls brown sugar,
Yolk 1 egg,
1 teaspoonful McIlhenny's Mexican Vanilla,
½ cupful butter,
2 cupfuls flour,
2 eggs,
2 teaspoonfuls Calumet baking powder.

Stir together in a saucepan the grated chocolate, milk, 1 cupful sugar, yolk 1 egg, and teaspoonful vanilla; cook slowly and cool. Take 1 cupful sugar, the butter, flour, milk, 2 eggs—cream butter and sugar with yolks of eggs; add milk, sifted flour, whites of eggs beaten stiff, beat together, then stir in the custard, lastly add the soda, dissolved in warm water. This cake will keep a long time. Another way is to bake in layers with the following filling: One cupful brown sugar, 1 cupful white sugar, 1 cupful water, 1 tablespoonful vinegar. Boil until like candy, then stir in beaten whites 2 eggs and ¼ pound marshmallows, boil again and place on cake, letting each layer cool before adding another.

Pork Cake.

1 pound salt pork,
2 cupfuls boiling water,
2 cupfuls dark-brown sugar,
1 cupful molasses,
1 teaspoonful soda,
1 pound raisins,
1 pound chopped dates,
¼ pound citron shaved fine,
4 cupfuls flour,
1 teaspoonful cinnamon,
1 teaspoonful cloves,
1 teaspoonful allspice,
1 teaspoonful nutmeg.

Chop the pork so fine as to look almost like lard, pour on it the boiling water, add the sugar, molasses, and soda, stir in the raisins, dates, and citron. Add the flour with the spices, pour the batter in loaf-cake pan, and bake in a moderate oven.

Apple Sauce Cake.

1 cupful butter,
2 cupfuls sugar,
4 eggs,
3 cupfuls flour,
1½ teaspoonfuls Calumet baking powder,
1 cupful milk,
6 apples,
6 ounces sugar,
1 teaspoonful butter.

Rub butter and sugar to a cream, add 2 eggs at a time, beating hard. Sift flour and baking powder together, add with milk, and mix into a batter. Bake in jelly-cake tins. Have apples peeled and sliced, and put on fire with sugar; when tender, rub through fine sieve, and add butter. When cold, use to spread between layers. Cover cake plentifully with sugar sifted over top.

Banana Cake.

½ cupful butter,
1 cupful sugar,
½ cupful milk,
2 scant cupfuls flour,
1½ teaspoonfuls Calumet baking powder,
Whites 4 eggs,
½ teaspoonful McIlhenny's Mexican Vanilla.

Mix flour and baking powder. Cream butter and sugar, add milk and flour alternately, then vanilla and beaten whites. Bake in 3 layer tins in hot oven. To boiled icing add ½ cupful finely sliced bananas and use as filling. Dust top with powdered sugar.

Geranium Cake.

½ cupful butter,
1 cupful sugar,
⅔ cupful water,
¼ teaspoonful salt,
2 cupfuls flour,
1 teaspoonful Calumet baking powder,
Whites 4 eggs.

Mix flour, salt, and baking powder. Cream butter and sugar, add alternately the water and flour, then whites of eggs, and whip hard five minutes. Line loaf pan with buttered paper, and rose-geranium leaves. Bake in a moderate oven. The leaves can be pulled off with the paper.

Lemon Queen Cake.

2 cupfuls sugar,
2 cupfuls flour,
1 cupful butter,
6 eggs,
2 lemons,
½ teaspoonful soda,
½ teaspoonful salt.

Mix salt and soda with flour. Beat butter to a light cream, and add lemon rind. Beat half the sugar into it. Beat yolks of eggs, then whites, then both together. Add sugar to the eggs and beat well. Put in lemon juice last. Bake in small cake tins.

White Fruit Cake.

¾ cupful butter,
1½ cupfuls sugar,
3 eggs,
2½ cupfuls flour,
2 teaspoonfuls Calumet baking powder,
½ cupful sweet cream,
1½ pounds raisins,
1 pound currants,
½ cupful citron,
½ cupful orange peel,
½ teaspoonful nutmeg,
Dash salt.

Cream the butter and sugar, add the beaten egg yolks, then alternately the cream and flour sifted with baking powder. Stir in the fruit, which has been dredged with flour, also the nutmeg, last of all the whites of eggs beaten to a stiff froth. Bake in deep pans lined with paraffin paper.

Walnut Mocha Cake.

½ cupful butter,
1 cupful sugar,
½ cupful cold coffee,
1¾ cupfuls flour,
2½ teaspoonfuls Calumet baking powder,
Whites 3 eggs,
1 cupful broken walnut meats.

Cream the butter and sugar, mix alternately the cold coffee and flour sifted with the baking powder, then stir in the walnut meats and whites of eggs beaten stiff. Bake in a deep pan and cover with White-Mountain Frosting, garnished with half walnuts.

Cider Cake.

2 cupfuls sugar,
1 cupful butter,
3 eggs,
¾ cupful cider,
4 cupfuls flour,
1 teaspoonful cloves,
1 teaspoonful soda.

Cream the butter and sugar, beat in the yolks of eggs, sift together the flour, soda, and spice, and mix alternately with the cider; last add the whites of eggs whipped to a stiff froth.

Neapolitan Cake.

2 cupfuls sugar,
1 cupful butter,
3 eggs,
1 cupful milk,
3 cupfuls flour,
1½ teaspoonfuls Calumet baking powder.

Make this cake exactly after the directions given for other cakes, then divide the batter into 3 equal parts. Color one third brown with a square of Runkel's Chocolate melted, another part pink with a morsel of pink coloring paste dissolved in ½ teaspoonful McIlhenny's Vanilla, leave the third part uncolored; pour each portion into a layer-cake tin and bake in a moderate oven. Lay on a platter first the white cake, then the chocolate, then the pink, putting each one together with White-Mountain Frosting; cover the top thickly with the same icing.

Citron Cake.

½ cupful butter,
1 cupful sugar,
3 eggs,
½ cupful milk,
3 cupfuls flour,
1 cupful citron,
1½ teaspoonfuls Calumet baking powder.

Cream the butter and sugar, add the beaten egg yolks, then the flour sifted with the baking powder, alternately with the milk. Whip the whites of eggs to a dry froth, blend into the cake batter, add the finely shaved citron, and bake an hour in a moderate oven.

Huckleberry Cake.

½ cupful butter,
1 cupful sugar,
3 eggs,
¾ cupful milk,
2 teaspoonfuls Calumet baking powder,
2 cupfuls flour,
1 cupful huckleberries.

Cream the butter and sugar, add the beaten eggs, milk and flour sifted with the baking powder. Stir in a cupful huckleberries dredged with flour, and bake in a moderate oven in a deep cake pan. This cake may be eaten cut in slices or served hot as a dessert with vanilla sauce.

Cocoanut-and-Citron Cake.

¼ cupful butter,
1 cupful sugar,
2 eggs,
1½ cupfuls flour,
2 teaspoonfuls Calumet baking powder,
½ cupful milk.

Cream the butter and sugar, add the beaten egg yolks, then the milk with the flour and baking powder; last of all stir in the whites of eggs whipped to a stiff froth. Bake the cake in two layers. Prepare the frosting after this fashion: Whip ½ pint double cream till stiff, blend with ½ cupful powdered sugar and stir in 2 cupfuls finely grated cocoanut. Spread between the cake, also on top, scattering it with shaved citron. This cake must be eaten soon after it is made, else it becomes sour and soggy.

Gold Cake.

¼ cupful butter,
½ cupful sugar,
Yolks 5 eggs,
1 teaspoonful orange extract,
⅞ cupful flour,
1½ teaspoonfuls Calumet baking powder,
¼ cupful milk.

Cream the butter, add sugar slowly, and continue beating. Add the yolks of eggs beaten until thick and lemon-colored, and the orange extract. Mix and sift the flour with the baking powder, and add alternately with milk to the first mixture. Bake in a buttered and floured tin.

Hickory Cake.

1 cupful butter,
2 cupfuls sugar,
1 cupful cold water,
Yolks 4 eggs,
1 teaspoonful ground mace and cinnamon mixed,
2 teaspoonfuls Calumet baking powder,
3 cupfuls flour,
2 cupfuls hickory-nut kernels.

Cream the butter with the sugar, add the cold water, well beaten yolks of eggs, mace, and cinnamon, baking powder and flour, stirred in alternately with the stiffened whites of eggs. Add the nuts, thoroughly dredged with flour. Stir in quickly, and turn into a loaf tin. Bake in a steady oven, covering the cake with brown paper for the first half hour it is in the oven. When cold, turn out, and cover with a plain icing. Arrange half kernels of hickory nuts at regular intervals on top of the icing.

Ground-Rice Cake.

Yolks 12 eggs,
Whites 6 eggs,
Grated peel 2 lemons,
2 cupfuls ground rice,
2 cupfuls flour,
2 cupfuls sugar.

Beat the yolks and whites of eggs with the lemon, mix in the rice, flour, sugar; beat up with the eggs, using a wooden spoon; butter a pan, and bake in a moderate oven half an hour.

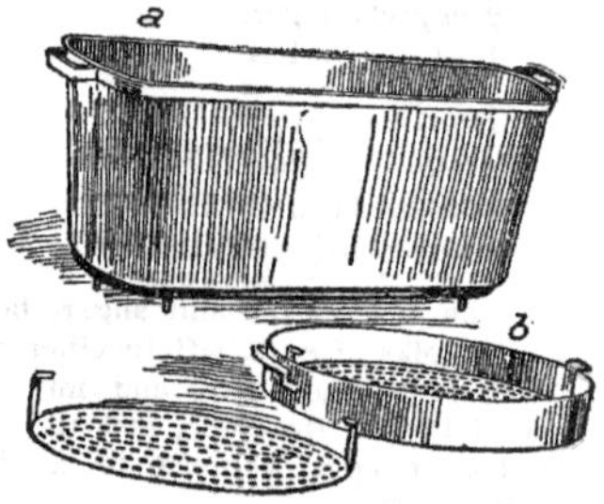

a, Ham Boiler; b, Fish Kettle with Removable Tray.

Jelly Roll.

3 eggs,
1 cupful sugar,
½ teaspoonful milk,
1 teaspoonful baking powder,
¼ teaspoonful salt,
1 cupful flour,
1 tablespoonful melted butter.

Beat eggs until light, add sugar gradually, milk, flour mixed and sifted with baking powder and salt, then butter. Line the bottom of a dripping pan with paper; butter paper and sides of pan. Cover bottom of pan with mixture, and spread evenly. Bake twelve minutes in a moderate oven. Take from oven and turn on a paper sprinkled with powdered sugar. Quickly remove paper, and cut off a thin strip from sides and ends of cake. Spread with jelly or jam which has been beaten to consistency to spread easily, and roll. After cake has been rolled, wrap paper around cake that it may better keep in shape. The work must be done quickly, or cake will crack in rolling.

Homemade Wedding Cake.

2 cupfuls butter,
2 cupfuls light-brown sugar,
12 eggs,
1 cupful molasses,
4 cupfuls flour,
1½ teaspoonfuls mace,
4 teaspoonfuls allspice,
4 teaspoonfuls cinnamon,
1 grated nutmeg,
½ teaspoonful soda,
3 pounds raisins,
1½ pounds citron,
2 pounds sultana raisins,
1 pound currants,
½ candied lemon peel,
½ candied orange peel,
4 squares Runkel's Chocolate,
1 tablespoonful hot water,
1 cupful milk.

Before beginning to make the cake, prepare the fruit required, seed the raisins, and cut them into halves with a scissors. Shave the citron, orange, and lemon peel into thin strips. Dredge them with flour, and set the chocolate to melt over boiling water. Sift together the flour, spices, and soda, and separate the eggs. Cream the butter and sugar very light, add the yolks of eggs beaten till stiff and lemon-colored, stir in the molasses, then the milk. Sift in the flour and spices, beat thoroughly, add the fruit, melted chocolate, whites of eggs whipped to a stiff froth, and the soda dissolved in hot water. Pour into a large round pan, which has been lined with paraffin paper and steam four hours. An excellent method to thoroughly cook such a large, rich cake as this to the heart is to steam it for an hour, then set into the fireless cooker, and leave it there over night. The saucepan which fits into the United States Cooker is almost the size to contain this recipe, and the cake could be baked right in it. When the steaming process is finished, the cake needs drying. Take off the lid, and leave it uncovered an hour or two in an oven which is merely warm. Turn out on a cake cooler, and when cold, ice with White Mountain Frosting.

Chocolate Snow Cake.

¼ cupful butter,
1 cupful sugar,
½ cupful milk,
1⅝ cupfuls flour,
2½ teaspoonfuls Calumet baking powder,
Whites 2 eggs,
½ teaspoonful McIlhenny's Mexican Vanilla.

Cream the butter and sugar, add the milk alternately with the flour and baking powder sifted together. Flavor with vanilla, and cut in the whites of eggs beaten to a stiff froth. Bake in layer tins. Fill with chocolate filling, and cover with chocolate frosting.

CAKES RAISED BY YEAST

Old-Fashioned Raised Cake.

½ pound currants,
6 cupfuls flour,
2 cupfuls warm milk,
½ yeast cake,
1 teaspoonful salt,
½ cupful butter,
2 cupfuls sifted brown sugar,
4 eggs,
1 tablespoonful mixed spice,
1 cupful raisins.

Mix salt with half the flour; add yeast, then gradually warm milk, beating to a batter, and set to rise over night. In the morning cream the butter and sugar, add also spice and beaten eggs to the risen batter, put in the remainder of the flour, gradually mixing thoroughly with the hand. Add fruit last. Let it rise until perfectly light. Scrape down and stir; fill pans two thirds full; let stand in a warm place. It will not rise perceptibly in the pans, but the process will have begun afresh in them and will complete in the baking. Bake an hour or more.

Loaf Cake without Eggs.

- 2 cupfuls warm milk,
- 3 cupfuls sugar,
- 1 cake yeast,
- 1 cupful butter,
- 1 cupful lard,
- Raisins,
- Spices,
- 1 teaspoonful Calumet baking powder,
- Flour.

Dissolve the yeast in a cupful water, add to the milk and 1 cupful sugar; make a stiff batter and let it rise over night; then add the rest of the sugar, butter, and lard; also raisins and spices and the baking powder. Let it rise again before baking.

Long Meadow Loaf Cake.

- 5 cupfuls sugar,
- 1½ cupfuls butter,
- 1 cupful lard,
- 4 cupfuls warm milk,
- 1 yeast cake,
- Whites 4 eggs,
- Flour,
- 1 teaspoonful nutmeg,
- 1 teaspoonful soda,
- 1½ pounds raisins,
- ½ pound citron.

Cream the sugar, butter, and lard. Mix thoroughly, divide, and to the smaller part of this mixture add the warm milk, yeast dissolved in the milk, and flour enough to make a batter which will be hard to stir with a spoon. Let it rise over night in a warm place. In the morning add the rest of the sugar and shortening, the whites of eggs, nutmeg, and soda. Let it rise again till light—it may take four hours—then add the raisins and citron. When risen the last time, bake slowly an hour.—Mrs. E. Brewer.

English Whigs.

- ½ cupful butter,
- 6 cupfuls flour,
- 3 eggs,
- ½ yeast cake,
- 2 cupfuls milk,
- 1 cupful sugar,
- ½ pound currants.

Rub the butter into the flour, beat the eggs with the yeast, the batter, and add the milk; beat all until smooth, cover the batter and let it stand three hours; then stir in the sugar and currants. Allow it to stand an hour, then pour in small tins, fill half full, and stand till risen. A quarter of an hour in a quick oven is sufficient to bake them.

Irish Barn Bake.

- 2 cupfuls bread dough,
- 2 ounces caraway seed,
- 1 cupful sugar,
- 4 eggs,
- ½ cupful butter.

Add as much flour to the dough as will make it a fit consistency to mold. Shape into loaves, let them rise, and bake.

Yorkshire Cake.

- 3 pounds flour,
- 1½ pints warm milk,
- 5 ounces butter,
- 1 yeast cake,
- 3 eggs.

Beat the flour, milk, yeast cake. and eggs well together, and let it rise; then form the cakes round; place them on the baking tins and let them rise again before putting them in the oven, which must be of a moderate heat. The butter may be warmed with the milk and added.

CHAPTER LXII

CAKE FILLINGS AND ICINGS

Whipped-Cream Filling.

Pour a cupful double cream into a bowl and whip with a Dover egg beater till stiff. Stop as soon as it begins to be quite thick or it will change to butter. Sweeten with 2 tablespoonfuls powdered sugar and flavor with ½ teaspoonful McIlhenny's Mexican Vanilla. This may be spread between layers of cake, then the top ornamented with a little of the cream squeezed through a pastry bag.

Maple-Cream Filling.

Boil ¼ cupful maple sirup until quite thick. Then add to it a teaspoonful granulated gelatin which has been dissolved in 2 tablespoonfuls cold water. Allow it to cool, and as soon as it begins to thicken, beat with a fork, then add it to a cupful thick cream which has been beaten stiff.

Chocolate-Cream Filling.

1 cupful sugar,
⅓ cupful flour,
Dash salt,
2 eggs,
1 teaspoonful McIlhenny's Mexican Vanilla,
¼ square Runkel's Chocolate,
2 cupfuls milk.

Put into a bowl the sugar, flour, and salt, blend thoroughly, then mix with the eggs well beaten. Scald the milk in a double boiler and add to it the egg mixture, beating steadily till it thickens. As soon as it is taken from the fire, stir in the melted chocolate and vanilla. Pour between layers of a cake when it has cooled.

Caramel Filling.

1 tablespoonful butter,
½ cupful sugar,
¾ cupful cream,
¼ cupful caramel,
1 teaspoonful McIlhenny's Mexican Vanilla.

Boil together the butter, sugar, and cream until it spins a thread. Then add the caramel and vanilla, beat until cool, and pour between the cake.

Cream Filling.

1½ cupfuls milk,
1 teaspoonful butter,
Dash salt,
2 eggs,
½ cupful sugar,
3 tablespoonfuls cornstarch,
1 teaspoonful McIlhenny's Mexican Vanilla.

Scald the milk with the butter, sugar, and salt; add the eggs beaten together with the cornstarch. As soon as the mixture becomes creamy, beat it thoroughly, cool, and add the vanilla. To make a coffee filling, use this recipe exactly as given, only adding ½ cupful very strong black coffee and leaving out ½ cupful hot milk.

Orange Filling.

Juice and grated rind 1 orange,
1 teaspoonful lemon juice,
1 teaspoonful orange extract,
Whites 2 eggs,
½ cupful powdered sugar,
1 teaspoonful gelatin,
2 tablespoonfuls cold water.

Put the gelatin to soak in the cold water, then set it into a bowl of boiling water until it dissolves, and add to the juice of the fruit. As soon as it begins to thicken, beat with a fork till fluffy, and mix with the powdered sugar and whites of eggs beaten to a stiff froth.

Peach Filling.

1 cupful whipped cream,
½ cupful powdered sugar,
1 cupful peach pulp.

Cut up 2 or 3 very ripe, juicy peaches and squeeze them through a potato ricer. Add to the pulp the sugar and cream beaten to a stiff froth. Blend thoroughly and put between layer cake. All recipes where whipped cream is added to a filling ought to be eaten as soon as possible after being made. The liquor soaks into a cake if it stands any time.

Red-Raspberry Filling.

½ cupful red raspberries,
White 1 egg,
⅓ cupful powdered sugar,
1 cupful thick cream.

Whip the cream to a stiff froth, also the white of egg. Put the two together and with a fork stir the sugar in, blending it perfectly. At the last, just before spreading the cake, stir in the raspberries thoroughly mashed. Strawberries may be used in the same way or the pulp of fresh apricots.

Tutti-Frutti Filling.

1 cupful whipped cream,
½ cupful powdered sugar,
1 cupful combination chopped walnuts, almonds, dates, raisins, and shaved citron.

Whip the cream very stiff, beat in the sugar, then add the nuts and fruit, blending it thoroughly with a fork.

Plain Icing.

Pour 2 tablespoonfuls whipped cream into a bowl and sift over it sufficient confectioner's sugar to make an icing thick enough to spread. Flavor with any extract or fruit juice you desire to use.

Egg Icing.

White 1 egg,
1 cupful confectioner's sugar,
1 teaspoonful lemon juice.

Whip the white of egg until frothy, beat in the lemon juice, then the sugar, until the icing is of a consistency that will spread.

White-Mountain Icing.

1 cupful granulated sugar,
1 teaspoonful McIlhenny's Mexican Vanilla,
⅓ cupful water,
White 1 egg.

Bring the water to the boil, add the sugar, and let the sirup cook without stirring until it will thread when lifted on the tip of a spoon. Pour it boiling hot over the white of egg which has been beaten to a stiff froth. Whip the mixture till it is soft and creamy, add the flavoring, and pour over the cake, spreading it smooth with a palette knife dipped in cold water.

Chocolate Frosting.

⅓ cupful cream,
1½ squares Runkel's Chocolate,
1 egg,
½ teaspoonful butter,
½ teaspoonful McIlhenny's Mexican Vanilla,
Confectioner's sugar.

Put the chocolate in a bowl to melt over hot water, scald the cream and pour over it, add the beaten yolk of egg and butter. Beat with a fork and sift in enough confectioner's sugar to make it of the proper consistency; last of all put in the vanilla, and spread over the cake. This frosting used on layers of white cake with chocolate filling between makes a delicious combination.

Orange Frosting.

Rind 1 orange,
3 tablespoonfuls orange juice,
1 teaspoonful lemon juice,
Confectioner's sugar.

Sift into the orange juice and rind enough confectioner's sugar to make this frosting spread.

Coffee Frosting.

Use the recipe given for White-Mountain frosting, only substitute ⅓ cupful strong coffee for boiling water, and leave out any flavoring.

Caramel Frosting.

½ cupful cream,
Dash salt,
2 tablespoonfuls caramel,
1 cupful light-brown sugar.

Boil together the brown sugar and cream for five minutes, then add the caramel and salt. Beat till cool and creamy, and pour while warm over the cake.

Maple-Sugar Frosting.

4 tablespoonfuls boiling water,
½ pound maple sugar,
White 1 egg.

Boil the sugar and water together till it spins a thread. Pour over the white of egg beaten till stiff, and whip till thick enough to spread.

Fondant Icing.

2 cupfuls sugar,
¼ teaspoonful cream of tartar,
1 cupful boiling water,
1 tablespoonful McIlhenny's Mexican Vanilla.

Mix the sugar and cream of tartar together, pour the water over it, and boil till it forms a little soft ball when dropped into cold water. Pour it out on an oiled platter, beat and knead till of the consistency of lard. Allow it to cool. When ready to use, soften it over boiling water, stirring with a fork till it is creamy. Add the flavoring, and pour over the cake. By first using this icing on a cake, then covering when hard and smooth with Runkel's Sweet Chocolate melted, you have what is called a chocolate-cream icing.

Decorating Icing.—Whip the whites of 2 eggs to a very stiff froth, then add slowly powdered sugar until the mixture is so stiff that every point and thread left by the beater will hold its place. It requires beating a long time. It is the same as meringue mixture, except that it is made hard with sugar instead of by drying, and takes about ½ cupful sugar to each egg.—Mary Ronald.

CHAPTER LXIII

FIRELESS COOKERY

FIRELESS COOKER

The United States Fireless Cooker attracted my attention and has my indorsements for three reasons: First, it is cheap, practical, and easily manipulated; second, it has no fabric or other lining to require extra care or to become foul; and last, because the inner vessel can be renewed at any time at little cost. The whole contrivance is so simple, so perfect, so easily understood, that it can be manipulated by a child.

The idea of cooking without fire should meet with approval from every housewife. It seems strange at first—paradoxical, almost a joke —but when the fact is demonstrated by an easily managed, simple contrivance, the truth is confirmed—*we can really cook without fire.* And not one, but many kinds of food.

Cooks have always known that food would keep hot for a long time if carefully covered. This fact induced some one to go just a step beyond and make a nonconducting cover that would retain the heat at a uniform temperature for many hours; and this is the principle of the fireless cooker.

Meats retain their flavor, and become tender more quickly if cooked below the boiling point. "Boiled" meats, to be perfect, should, after the first boiling, be cooked at a temperature of 180°; to maintain this temperature over a fire requires eternal vigilance, and even then is difficult to control. With a fireless cooker one need not give the meat a thought from the time it goes in the cooker until time for dinner.

It is to be especially recommended for vegetables that emit an odor while cooking, as cabbage, cauliflower, onions, and sauerkraut. Imagine surprising your family with a cabbage or sauerkraut dinner!

It is worth double its cost for cereals alone. One may have a well-cooked cereal without fire or rush in the morning. Your breakfasts can be put on the table in ten minutes.

It saves time. One can prepare dinner while the breakfast dishes are being washed. When ready to leave the kitchen, put the cooking vessel with its *boiling* contents in the cooker and go where you please until dinner time.

Foods do not become overcooked nor water-soaked if the dinner, from necessity, is pushed on an extra hour. *Do not open the cooker; let it alone until you are ready to serve its contents.* Nothing can be overdone when cooked in the United States Fireless Cooker.

It retains the nutrition and the natural flavors of all foods. There is no chance for escape.

It does away with that most unpleasant pot washing. It saves half the usual fuel.

It saves the housewife hours of time and worry.

It makes tough meat tender and palatable, and in this way saves many a dollar in a year in the cost of meat alone.

It is indispensable to the summer camp, house boat, or yacht. The fisherman or the camper may stay out an extra hour without keeping anyone waiting or spoiling the dinner.

To insure the best results with the United States Fireless Cooker, make sure that all foods are *boiling hot* in the cooking vessel when you place it in the cooker. The object of the cooker is simply to maintain the heat and continue the cooking. Large pieces of meat must be boiled sufficiently long to be thoroughly heated to the center or they will cool the water after the cooking vessel has been packed in the cooker. The best results are obtained when the cooking vessel is nearly or quite full.

If things are to be served boiling hot, stand the cooking vessel over the fire while you are arranging the table.

I am using the United States Fireless Cooker in both my kitchens, and would not, for many times its cost, give it up. Even with a gas stove, I prefer the cooker for long, slow cooking.

It steams fruit cakes to perfection —no watching, no boiling dry, no replenishing of water. Four hours in the cooker and one hour in the oven finishes them. Think of the time, worry, and fuel saved between this method and a "four hours' baking in a very slow oven."

I also found it most useful in the cooking of tripe, which requires hours of slow cooking to make it tender. Even then one has to watch it carefully or it will boil dry and scorch. A night in the cooker makes it very tender and ready to dress in many attractive ways.

What I have accomplished in saving, time, fuel, worry, and money by the use of the United States Fireless Cooker will, I trust, be sufficient to show every housewife an easier and better way.

(Signed) Sarah Tyson Rorer.

October, 1908.

FIRELESS COOKERY

Until one has become initiated into the secret of fireless cookery, it is hard to understand how food can be prepared by such a method. When one has mastered the science of cooking without fire, the whole process becomes very simple. It is requisite that, first of all, the dish which is being cooked should be brought to the boiling point and allowed to stand on the fire long enough for the heat to penetrate to the very heart of the food. It is then lifted, with the cover set on so tightly that no heat can escape, into the cooker, which is closed securely until several hours afterwards, when the food is brought to the table. During these hours the cooking is going on at a temperature of about 170°, the point required for slow cooking. For certain dishes, such as soups, stews, and the boiling of a tough piece of meat or fowl, there is no better way to render them palatable and nourishing.

Of all the cookers that have been put on the market, the wisest choice is the United States Fireless Cooker. The utensil is a heavy fiber pail containing two saucepans with tight lids, which can be set on top of each other. The cover is put on securely, then the cooker is left to do its work until it is time for the food to be ready. When a large piece of meat, such as a ham, corn beef, or a heavy fowl is to be cooked, it is brought to the boil in a large, deep pail which takes the place of the two smaller ones. In this cooker there are no cushions to retain odors or dampness; it can be kept perfectly clean by washing and airing each time it is used, and it is practically indestructible.

Some of the advantages of fireless cookery are these: During hot weather there is emancipation from an overheated kitchen. Food can be brought to the boil over a gas stove, the flame turned out, then the preparation of the meal can go on without any further attention. This means a saving of at least eighty per cent in fuel.

The perfect preparation of cheap cuts of meat, which could not be done over a hot stove.

There is no odor whatever while the food is being prepared. This allows the cooking of cabbage, onions, cauliflower, ham, corn beef, sauerkraut, and various other foods, which are apt to fill a house with most unpleasant smells.

It is almost impossible to overcook any food which has been properly prepared and then placed in the cooker; even if the time allotted for a certain dish has passed, it will be benefited instead of spoiled.

The washing of heavy, greasy, scorched pots and pans is no longer a necessity. There can be no burning of anything in the cooker.

The housewife who masters the secrets of fireless cookery can plan her meals exactly to the minute.

Breakfast can be prepared the night before, and found in the morning deliciously cooked and hot. This is especially true of such coarse-grained cereals as oatmeal, cornmeal, and cracked wheat, which demand hours of steaming over a hot stove to become fit for human food. Also there is a saving in the amount of cereal used, as it swells to its largest capacity.

The fireless cooker is a boon for the man or woman who requires a hot meal during the night; by close calculation a dish can be put in and be ready at any moment required.

The cooker is as useful for keeping frozen food chilled as for preserving heat in a hot dish. Instead of taking the labor to repack ice cream, put a can containing the frozen mixture into the cooker, pour around it some of the crushed ice and salt, fill up the space with cold brine, set on the cover, and the cream will remain in perfect condition for several hours.

Even when one has a small family which cannot use the quantity contained in one of the saucepans which fit into the cooker, equally good results may be obtained by preparing the dish in a granite pan, bringing it to the proper amount of heat, pouring water about it and allowing the water to boil. Set the cover on, put the utensil in the cooker, fit in the lid, and give the dish the time required.

A FEW RULES FOR SUCCESSFUL COOKING

In every case have the saucepan so full of food or water that it just allows the lid to fit in. When vacant space is left, heat escapes.

Never open the cooker until the required time has expired. If you do, it will be necessary to reheat the dish over the stove.

When any food seems to be extraordinarily tough, such as old beets, or a sinewy fowl, allow an hour or two more than the time directed.

An excellent method in preparing a number of dishes which require a long time to cook, is to set them in a cooker at night and leave them shut up tight until morning.

Various dishes, such as veal loaf, baked beans, and fruit cake, are at their best when brought to the baking point in the oven, then finished in the fireless cooker, being set inside the saucepan with boiling water, reaching nearly to the top of the inner utensil.

Boston bread can be made to perfection in this way by letting the loaf dry in the oven for fifteen minutes after taking from the cooker.

When you wish to brown the top of anything, as if it had been baked, set it under the flame in a gas oven for a few minutes, watching it closely.

When you have only one food to cook, fill the other saucepan with boiling water and set under or over the one containing food. It helps to keep the heat to point required.

Kind.	Quantity.	Water.	Time on Stove.	Time in Cooker.
Coarse hominy	1 cupful.	6 cupfuls.	30 minutes.	Over night.
Farina	1 cupful.	6 cupfuls.	10 minutes.	3 hours.
Wheatlet	1 cupful.	3½ cupfuls.	10 minutes.	3 hours.
Rice	1 cupful.	4 cupfuls.	5 minutes.	3 hours.
Macaroni	1 cupful.	3 cupfuls.	10 minutes.	2 hours.
Spaghetti	1 cupful.	3 cupfuls.	10 minutes.	2 hours.
Vermicelli	1 cupful.	2½ cupfuls.	5 minutes.	2 hours.

TIME-TABLE FOR COOKING SOUPS ABOVE

Soup.	Time on Stove.	Time in Cooker.
Consommé	15 minutes.	Over night.
Brown Stock	30 minutes.	Over night.
Tomato	10 minutes.	5 hours.
Soup à la Reine	30 minutes.	Over night.
Potato Cream	10 minutes.	2½ hours.
Soup Bègue	20 minutes.	6 hours.
Soup à la Menestra	10 minutes.	2 hours.
Ox Tail	20 minutes.	Over night.
White Soup Stock	30 minutes.	6 hours.
Beef Bouilli	25 minutes.	Over night.
Veal	20 minutes.	5 hours.
Sportsman's Broth	30 minutes.	7 hours.
Purée de Lentilles	20 minutes.	6 hours.
Chicken	20 minutes.	5 hours.
Sheep's Head Broth	30 minutes.	Over night.
Cock-a-Leekie	30 minutes.	Over night.
Friar's Chicken	30 minutes.	7 hours.
Rabbit	20 minutes.	6 hours.
Okra Gumbo	20 minutes.	6 hours.
Beef Gumbo	20 minutes.	5 hours.
Cream of Celery	10 minutes.	3 hours.
Cream of Corn	7 minutes.	3 hours.
Leek	10 minutes.	3 hours.
Hotchpotch	15 minutes.	5 hours.
Cream of Onion	5 minutes.	3 hours.
Soup Normandie	5 minutes.	2 hours.
Soup Maigre	10 minutes.	6 hours.
Purée of Celeriac	5 minutes.	2 hours.
Split Pea	10 minutes.	6 hours.
Green Pea	10 minutes.	3 hours.
Winter Okra	10 minutes.	6 hours.
Corn Chowder	10 minutes.	4 hours.
Dried Bean	15 minutes.	Over night.
Clam Chowder	10 minutes.	2 hours.
Black Bean	20 minutes.	Over night.
Onion Chowder	10 minutes.	2 hours.
Old-fashioned Bean	25 minutes.	Over night.
Herb	10 minutes.	2 hours.

VEGETABLES.

Vegetables.	Time on Stove.	Time in Cooker.
Beet Greens	10 minutes.	3 hours.
String Beans	10 minutes.	3 hours.
Green Peas	7 minutes.	3 hours.
Lima Beans	10 minutes.	4 hours.
Dried Beans	20 minutes.	Over night.
Okra	10 minutes.	2 hours.
Squash	15 minutes.	Over night.
Summer Squash	10 minutes.	4 hours.
Tomatoes	10 minutes.	3 hours.
Cabbage	15 minutes.	5 hours.
Cauliflower	15 minutes.	3 hours.
Green Corn	8 minutes.	3 hours.
Onions	10 minutes.	3 hours.
Spring Beets	10 minutes.	3 hours.
Winter Beets	30 minutes.	Over night.
Turnips	10 minutes.	5 hours.
Asparagus	5 minutes.	1½ hours.
Carrots	10 minutes.	4 hours.
Brussels Sprouts	10 minutes.	2 hours.
Spinach	10 minutes.	2 hours.
Kale	10 minutes.	3 hours.
Salsify	10 minutes.	2 hours.
Kohl Rabi	10 minutes.	2½ hours.
Boston Baked Beans	2 hours.	Over night.

MEAT.

Meat.	Time on Stove.	Time in Cooker.
Beef Stew	1 hour.	8 hours.
Boiled Ham	1 hour.	Over night.
Boiled Tongue	1 hour.	Over night.
Year Old Fowl	30 minutes.	6 hours.
Brown Fricasse of Veal	30 minutes.	5 hours.
Chop Suey	10 minutes.	8 hours.
Veal Birds	30 minutes.	5 hours.
Veal Loaf	45 minutes.	5 hours.
New England Boiled Dinner	1 hour.	12 hours.
Roast Loin of Lamb	30 minutes.	6 hours.
Pot Roast	1 hour.	10 hours.
Chicken Curry	30 minutes.	6 hours.
Beef à la Mode	15 minutes.	10 hours.
Beef Goulash	30 minutes.	6 hours.
Tripe	20 minutes.	4 hours.
Stuffed Steak	30 minutes.	6 hours.
Roast Veal	45 minutes.	6 hours.
Boiled Chicken	20 minutes.	6 hours.

PUDDINGS.

Puddings.	Time on Stove.	Time in Cooker.
Plum	1 hour.	Over night.
Baked Custard	20 minutes.	3 hours.
Cabinet	20 minutes.	4 hours.
Rice Pudding	10 minutes.	3 hours.
Apple Tapioca	10 minutes.	3 hours.
Fig	30 minutes.	6 hours.
Brown Betty	30 minutes.	4 hours.
Steamed Fruit	30 minutes.	4 hours.
Bread	30 minutes.	2 hours.
Cream Tapioca	20 minutes.	3 hours.

A FEW RECIPES FOR FIRELESS COOKERY

Beef Stew.

4 pounds beef,
2½ quarts cold water,
2 carrots,
2 onions,
1½ quarts sliced potatoes,
½ cupful rice,
1 tablespoonful salt,
4 chili peppers.

Choose a slice of beef from the top of a round, containing a bit of marrow bone. Put the marrow into the spider, and when fried out, add the meat, cut into pieces, large enough to make a portion; let them cook, turning constantly, until brown. Put part of the meat which has not been browned with the bone into the cold water in the pan of the cooker, and add the brown meat. Rinse out the spider to get all the brown gravy possible, cover the pail, and let it simmer an hour. Cut the carrots into slices, also the onions and potatoes, and parboil for five minutes. Drain, blanch in cold water, and add to the meat. Put the rice over the fire in cold water, let it boil five minutes, put it also in the pail, then add the salt and peppers, cover closely, and cook twenty minutes. Put the pail into the cooker, shut down the lid, and leave it eight hours.

Boiled Ham.

If the ham is very salty soak it over night in cold water, put it into the pail in the morning, cover with cold water, put the lid on tightly, and bring to the boiling point. Cook ten minutes hard, then simmer for fifteen more, set it into the cooker, and leave it there over night.

Chop Suey.

1 quart lean pork and chicken,
1 onion,
1 pint celery,
2 tablespoonfuls cornstarch,
2 tablespoonfuls molasses,
1½ teaspoonfuls salt,
1 tablespoonful China soy,
½ cupful fresh mushrooms.

Cut the pork and chicken into small pieces, put any bones that remain in a cheese-cloth bag, tie it up and drop in pail of cooker. Cover with cold water and let it come very slowly to the boil. Fry out a piece of fat, salt pork in a spider, and brown the meat. Add it to the water in the pail, also the onion, the celery cut in inch lengths, bring to the boiling point, then simmer slowly for one hour. Dissolve the cornstarch in a little water and stir it in. Add the molasses, salt, and soy. Cook ten minutes longer, set the pail, tightly covered, into the cooker; leave it there eight hours. When served, lift out the cheese-cloth bag with the bones. Serve chop suey with boiled rice, Saratoga chips, and toast.

New England Boiled Dinner.

Put the corned beef on to cook at six in the morning if you want it for a six-o'clock dinner. Cover with cold water, put on lid securely, and simmer for half an hour. Then set it in the cooker. Pare potatoes, cut up cabbage in quarters, pare some turnips and slice them, and let each vegetable cook separately for ten minutes. Drain and blanch. Lift the meat from the cooker, put the vegetables into the pail, cover, and boil ten minutes. Return to the cooker until six o'clock.

Pot Roast.

¼ pound salt pork,
5 pounds round steak,
3 cupfuls boiling water,
Salt pepper, and flour.

Rub the meat on all sides with salt, pepper, and flour, fry out salt pork in a spider and brown the meat in it. Set a trivet into the pail of the cooker, pour in 2 cupfuls boiling water, which has been used to rinse the spider, let it boil five minutes, then cook gently on top of the stove for one hour. Remove to the fireless cooker and allow it ten hours. If vegetables are desired, parboil them, lay them under the meat in the gravy, and strain out before it is thickened.

Steamed Pudding.

½ pound beef suet,
½ cupful flour,
1 teaspoonful cinnamon,
1 teaspoonful mace,
⅛ teaspoonful salt,
½ teaspoonful cloves,
½ pound Sultana raisins,
½ pound currants,
½ pound citron,
½ cupful sugar,
1½ cupfuls soft bread crumbs,
3 eggs,
½ cupful milk.

Chop the suet fine, mix with the flour and spices, then add the fruit, sugar, and bread crumbs. Wet with the milk and eggs, stir hard, and turn the mixture into a greased mold. Set it into the pail of the cooker. Surround with boiling water, give it one hour on the stove and all night in the cooker.

Stewed Prunes.

1 pound prunes,
¼ cupful sugar,
1 cupful water.

Wash the prunes thoroughly, soak for two hours, put them into a granite dish, adding the sugar and water. Cook on top of the stove fifteen minutes, then remove to the pail of the cooker, pour boiling water in until it nearly reaches the top of the pail of prunes, cover tightly. Let the water boil five minutes, then set into the cooker and leave over night.

Cup Custard.

3 cupfuls milk,
½ cupful sugar,
Pinch salt,
3 eggs.

Scald the milk, pour it over the sugar and salt, stir in the well-beaten eggs, pour into custard cups, and grate a little nutmeg on top of each. Set the cups into the pail of the cooker, pour boiling water around them, and boil for ten minutes. Place them in the fireless cooker three hours. If you wish to serve custard with the top browned, set it under the flame of the gas stove for a few minutes. Serve ice-cold.

CHAPTER LXIV

FAVORITE DISHES IN FAMOUS HOMES

In addition to the large variety of recipes in this book, we present contributions from the wives of famous men in all parts of America. The wife of President Taft and Vice-President Sherman each commend their favorite dish, while from wives of U. S. Senators and the Governors of various States come excellent recipes. The value of such recipes consists not only in an interesting study of what are favorite dishes in famous homes, but in a most valuable addition to the cookery encyclopedia of every housewife. Many of the recipes are for fine old-fashioned dishes, such as toothsome gingerbread, brown bread, and an excellent mince-meat. Here we find food peculiar to a certain part of the country, such as the Governor of Florida's fried okra, or a toothsome chicken pie, suggested by Mrs. Dawson, the wife of the Govcruor of West Virginia. There are various recipes which are unlike any found in ordinary cookbook literature; for instance, a delicious angel-food pudding, Mrs. Chester Long's favorite cake, Hamburg cookies, Frankfort pudding, potato cake, and raspberry buns. Each recipe is well worth trying, and, once tried, it will become a favorite in thousands of homes.

From Mrs. William H. Taft.

Sponge Pudding.

¼ cupful sugar,
½ cupful flour,
¼ cupful butter,
1 pint boiled milk,
5 eggs.

Mix sugar and flour, wet with a little cold water and stir into the boiling milk. Cook until it thickens and is smooth. Add the butter and when well mixed stir it into the well-beaten yolks of the eggs. Then add the whites beaten stiff and bake in a shallow dish or cups, placing them in a pan of hot water while in the oven. Serve with creamy sauce.

From Mrs. J. S. Sherman, wife of Vice-President.

Saratoga Pudding.

2 cupfuls coarse bread crumbs,
4 eggs,
1 quart sweet milk,
1 cupful sugar,
Pinch salt,
½ cupful raisins,
Butter, size of walnut,
Flavoring, milk or vanilla.

After baking, spread with layer currant jelly before putting on meringue.

From Mrs. Reed Smoot, wife of U. S. Senator from Utah.

Five-Egg Orange Cake.

5 eggs,
½ cupful butter,
1 cupful sugar,
¾ cupful milk,
3 cupfuls flour,
1½ teaspoonfuls vanilla,
1½ teaspoonfuls baking powder.

Beat sugar and butter to a cream, drop in yolks of eggs, thoroughly beaten, add 1 cupful flour, milk, then another cupful flour, beating thoroughly all the time. Add rest of flour, with whites of eggs beaten to a stiff froth. Bake in layer tins in moderate oven.

Filling for the Cake

Beat white of 1 egg to a stiff froth, and add 1 teacupful pulverized sugar; grate the outside of an orange down to the white, squeeze out juice, and add to frosting.

From Mrs. Joseph W. Bailey, wife of U. S. Senator from Texas.

Stuffed Tomatoes.

Take fresh, firm tomatoes, and cut pulp from them with a sharp knife. Mix together chopped cucumber, onion to taste, cabbage, pepper, celery and salt, with some pulp of tomato. Place this mixture in scooped tomatoes and serve on lettuce with a garnish of mayonnaise.

From Mrs. J. W. Burrows, wife of U. S. Senator from Michigan.

Delicious Fruit Punch.

Sweeten juice of 8 lemons and 4 oranges to taste. Just before serving, place a square of ice in a punch bowl and pour over it sweetened juice, then add 2 quarts Apollinaris water or White Rock, and garnish with a bunch of grapes laid on ice. A gill of raspberry or blackberry juice left over from canned fruit adds a beautiful color to the punch as well as a fine flavor.

From Mrs. B. R. Tillman, wife of U. S. Senator from South Carolina.

Tillie's Gingerbread.

1 cupful sugar,
1 cupful butter,
4 eggs,
2 cupfuls molasses,
4 cupfuls sour milk,
2 teaspoonfuls soda,
2 teaspoonfuls cinnamon,
2 teaspoonfuls salt,
2 teaspoonfuls ground ginger,
5 cupfuls flour.

Cream together butter and sugar, add eggs well beaten, molasses, then sour milk, and, last, flour with which has been sifted spices, salt, and soda. Bake in moderate oven.

From Mrs. Robert J. Gamble, wife of U. S. Senator from South Dakota.

Hamburg Cookies.

1 pound granulated sugar,
12 eggs,
3 pounds butter,
1 ounce carbonate ammonia,
10c. worth oil of lemon.

Powder ammonia, dissolve in 1 egg, add balance of eggs and sugar, and beat for an hour. Add flour, lemon, and butter (not melted); mix with enough flour to make dough as stiff as can be rolled. Keep it on ice till ready to roll. With a cooky cutter shape like lady's fingers. Sprinkle pans with flour before putting in cookies, and bake. The butter should have all the salt washed out of it twenty-four hours before using. This makes a delicious cooky when putting up boxes of cake at the Christmas season. They are very delicate and will keep for weeks. It looks like an expensive recipe, but is not when you consider the quantity of cookies it makes.

From Mrs. John Sharp Williams, wife of U. S. Senator from Mississippi.

Candy.

Have two saucepans; into one put 3 cupfuls granulated sugar, 1 cupful thick sirup, and ⅔ cupful water. Into the other pan put 1 cupful granulated sugar and a gill water. Allow contents of both pans to cook until sirup will spin a thread or make a soft ball between the fingers when dropped in cold water. When both are ready, turn slowly sirup in first pan over stiffly beaten whites 3 eggs, and beat constantly during process. Into second sirup stir 1 cupful chopped nuts, add to other, and pour frothy mass into buttered tins to cool. When cold, mark in blocks with very sharp knife.

From Mrs. Chester I. Long, wife of U. S. Senator from Kansas.

A Favorite Cake.

4 eggs,
2 tablespoonfuls baking powder,
1 cupful milk,
1 cupful butter.

Cream butter and sugar, add yolks of eggs and milk, then flour sifted with baking powder. After heating these thoroughly, add stiffly beaten whites of eggs. Bake in three layers and put together with following filling:

1 quart double cream,
1 pound pecans,
1 pound seeded raisins.

Whip cream to a froth, sweeten, and put between layers. Chop nuts and raisins and sprinkle over cream between each, also on top. This makes a cake which may be served alone as a dessert. It is a favorite with all our friends.

From Mrs. P. J. McCumber, wife of U. S. Senator from North Dakota.

Chocolate Cookies.

Beat to a cream ½ cupful butter and 1 tablespoonful lard; gradually beat into this 1 cupful sugar. Add 1 teaspoonful cinnamon, 2 ounces chocolate (melted over steam), 1 beaten egg, and ½ teaspoonful soda dissolved in 2 tablespoonfuls sour milk. Stir in 2½ cupfuls flour. Roll thin and cut with cooky cutter. Bake in hot oven. When cold, spread chocolate frosting on each cooky; on top of each put half a walnut meat.

From Mrs. Nathan Bay Scott, wife of U. S. Senator from West Virginia.

Old-Fashioned Pound Cake.

1 pound butter,
1 pound sugar,
10 eggs,
1 pound flour.

Butter and sugar are first creamed, then yolks of eggs added, then flour. The rule is to beat for an hour, but sometimes you get tired before hour is up. Last, fold in whites of eggs beaten to a stiff froth; bake slowly an hour.

From Governor Albert W. Gilchrist of Florida

Fried Okra.

Take several pods tender okra, wash thoroughly, and cut into thin pieces crosswise; beat 2 eggs, season with salt and pepper, dip okra first into sifted meal, then into egg, again into meal, and fry in butter.

From Mrs. B. B. Brooks, wife of Governor of Wyoming.

Drop Cakes.

1½ cupfuls brown sugar,
1 cupful butter,
1½ cupfuls sweet milk,
3 eggs,
1 teaspoonful each, cinnamon, cloves, allspice, and nutmeg,
1 cupful chopped raisins,
1 cupful broken English walnuts,
2 teaspoonfuls baking powder.

Cream sugar and butter, add well-beaten eggs, then milk. Sift spices and baking powder with enough flour to make a batter that will drop from a spoon, add mixture, stir in nuts and raisins, beat well, then drop by teaspoonfuls on a greased pan and bake in hot oven.

From Mrs. Henry B. Quinby, wife of Governor of New Hampshire.

Breakfast Gems.

3 eggs,
1 teaspoonful sugar,
1 coffeecupful sweet milk,
1 cupful warm water,
4 tablespoonfuls yeast,
Flour enough to make a stiff batter.

Beat yolks of eggs and sugar, stir in milk, water, and yeast. Beat well and set in a warm place to rise. When light, beat whites of eggs to a stiff froth and stir into batter, with a pinch of salt. Bake in greased gem pans. If wanted for breakfast, mix batter night before.

From Mrs. Edwin Lee Norris, wife of Govenor of Montana.

Molasses Pudding.

1 cupful molasses,
1 cupful butter,
1 cupful hot water,
1 teaspoonful soda,
3 cupfuls flour,
1 cupful raisins.

Cream butter, add molasses, then hot water; beat in flour with which soda has been sifted, stir in raisins, put in a greased mold, and steam three hours.

Sauce for Molasses Pudding.

1 cupful butter,
1 cupful sugar,
2 eggs.

Cream butter and sugar, then add thoroughly beaten eggs. Stir together, set over fire in cold water, let water come to boil, and serve sauce hot. A glass of sherry or brandy may be added, though we prefer it without.

From Mrs. W. M. O. Dawson, wife of Governor of West Virginia.

Chicken Pie.

Meat of 1 chicken cooked,
1 can mushrooms,
1½ pints potato balls parboiled,
6 hard-boiled eggs,
1 heaping tablespoonful minced parsley,
1½ pints cream dressing.

Cut chicken meat as for a salad, put in bottom of baking dish, cover with mushrooms, then with potato balls. Season to taste. Sprinkle over it minced whites of eggs, then minced yolks. Scatter with minced parsley, and cover with dressing. On top put a cover of small biscuits as large as a finger ring. Bake three quarters of an hour.

From Mrs. F. M. Warner, wife of Governor of Michigan.

Pinafore Cake.

1 cupful sugar,
½ cupful butter (scant),
½ cupful milk (scant),
2 cupfuls flour,
2 teaspoonfuls baking powder,
Whites 3 eggs.

Cream butter and sugar, add milk, flour sifted with baking powder, then whites of eggs whipped to a stiff froth, also 2 tablespoonfuls cold water and ½ teaspoonful lemon flavoring. Put half of this mixture into a layer-cake pan; to what is left add 1 teaspoonful strawberry coloring. When both cakes are baked, put together with following filling:

Filling

Yolks 3 eggs,
½ cupful sugar,
1 cupful milk,
1 tablespoonful cornstarch (scant).

Heat milk in a double boiler, add eggs and cornstarch, cook till it thickens, add pinch of salt and any flavoring desired, and put between layers of cake.

From Mrs. A. C. Shallenberger, wife of Governor of Nebraska.

Amber Cream.

1 quart milk,
½ package gelatin,
1 cupful sugar,
Yolks 6 eggs,
Whites 6 eggs,
1 teaspoonful vanilla.

Dissolve gelatin in a little cold water, let milk come to boiling point and melt gelatin in it. Add sugar and well-beaten yolks of eggs, stirring constantly till well blended, cook in a double boiler till it thickens, then turn in whites of eggs whipped to a stiff froth. Flavor with vanilla. Pour into cups or a fancy mold and set in a cold place over night. When ready to serve, turn out on a plate or sauce dish.

From Mrs. John F. Shafroth, wife of Governor of Colorado.

Cucumber Mangoes (Prize recipe).

Soak in strong brine nine days as many large green cucumbers as you wish to use. Then lay them forty-eight hours in clear water. Cut a slit lengthwise in each, scoop out seeds, wipe dry and fill with stoned raisins, lemon cut in long, thin strips, and 6 or 8 whole cloves. Sew up slit, pack cucumbers in a stone jar and cover with a boiling sirup made after following recipe: Add to 1 quart vinegar 5 pounds sugar, also mace, cinnamon, and cloves to taste. Reheat sirup and pour boiling hot over cucumbers for nine successive mornings.

From Mrs. J. S. Sanders, wife of Governor of Louisiana.

Strawberry Ambrosia.

Select large, ripe strawberries. Arrange in a glass bowl with alternate layers coarsely chopped pineapple. Sprinkle between layers plenty of powdered sugar and freshly grated cocoanut, then pour over top 1 cupful orange juice. Set on ice, and serve very cold.

From Mrs. M. R. Patterson, wife of Governor of Tennessee.

English Pudding.

Yolks 4 eggs,
2 tablespoonfuls sugar,
1 tablespoonful cornstarch,
1 pint milk,
1 teaspoonful vanilla.

Stir on fire in a double boiler milk, eggs, sugar, and cornstarch till it thickens, then add whites of eggs beaten to a stiff froth. Put in a deep dish a layer of fruit, then one of macaroons, and pour custard on top. When cold, cover with a thin layer of jelly and 1 pint whipped cream.

Almond Cream.

Mash 12 vanilla wafers with a rolling-pin, and pour over them a wineglass of whisky. When soft, add 1 quart sweet milk and sweeten to taste. Whip 1 quart cream, sweeten to taste, flavor with a teaspoonful extract of almond, mix with first concoction, and freeze.

From Mrs. Augustus E. Willson, wife of Governor of Kentucky.

Frankfort Pudding.

Make a plain ice cream as follows: Put 1 pint new milk in a double boiler; when gradually hot, add to 2 tablespoonfuls flour a little milk; stir until free from lumps, add to scalded milk and boil until a little thicker than custard. Strain into 1 quart rich cream; add 2 cupfuls powdered sugar, whites 2 eggs (unbeaten), and 2 teaspoonfuls vanilla. Freeze, line a mold with ice cream, and fill center with following mixture:

The night before you wish to use them, take ½ pound candied cherries and cut into small pieces, and ½ pound French chestnuts shelled, blanched, boiled until soft, and cut into small pieces. Let these stand over night in sherry to cover them. Mix lightly with 1 quart whipped cream and fill the center of mold; close it and set in salt and ice four hours. Serve with a sauce of whipped cream flavored with sherry.

From Mrs. Bert M. Fernald, wife of Governor of Maine.

Chocolate Cake.

Melt ½ cupful butter, and gradually add 1½ cupfuls sugar. Scrape ¼ pound chocolate fine, add 3 teaspoonfuls sugar and 3 tablespoonfuls hot water; stir over steam until smooth. Add to sugar and butter, then drop in yolks 3 eggs, stir, and add whites 3 eggs beaten to a stiff froth. Add ½ cupful milk in which ½ teaspoonful soda is dissolved, and lastly 1½ cupfuls flour in which is mixed 1 teaspoonful cream tartar and a little salt. Flavor with vanilla.

Frosting

1½ cupfuls sugar,
½ cupful water.

Boil until it threads, add to the beaten white 1 egg, a few drops at a time, and stir constantly; flavor.

From Mrs. G. H. Prouty, wife of Governor of Vermont.

Maple Parfait.

1 cupful maple sirup,
Yolks 6 eggs,
1 pint cream.

Heat sirup to boiling point, pour slowly onto beaten egg yolks and the whip from cream, turn into a mold and pack in equal measures of finely crushed ice and rock salt. Let stand four hours and serve with chopped browned almonds.

From Mrs. Albert B. Cummins, wife of U. S. Senator from Iowa.

Almond Tart.

Yolks 9 eggs,
1 pound sugar,
¾ pound grated almonds,
2 cupfuls grated lady's fingers,
1 teaspoonful vanilla,
1 teaspoonful baking powder,
Juice and rind 1 lemon,
Whites 9 eggs,

Mix ingredients in order given, and bake in two layers in moderate oven.

Filling for Tart

1 pound chopped walnuts,
Whites 2 eggs,
Lemon juice and sugar to taste.

From Mrs. Robert L. Taylor, wife of U. S. Senator from Tennessee.

Steamed Corn Bread.

2 cupfuls sweet milk,
1 cupful butter,
3 cupfuls cornmeal,
1 cupful flour,
1 egg,
1 teaspoonful soda,
1 teaspoonful salt,
½ cupful molasses.

Mix ingredients, beat thoroughly, and pour into pail, with tight-fitting lid. Cook in vessel of boiling water two and a half hours. Turn out on a pan, and brown in oven.

From Mrs. Robert S. Vessey, wife of Governor of South Dakota.

Brown Bread.

1 cupful sweet milk,
2 cupfuls sour milk,
2 cupfuls cornmeal,
1 cupful flour,
½ cupful molasses,
1½ teaspoonfuls soda,
1 teaspoonful salt.

Sift dry materials, pour in molasses and milk, then beat hard and pour in a greased mold. Steam three hours and dry in a hot oven a few minutes. This mixture is very thin, but makes a delicious bread.

From Mrs. G. W. Donaghey, wife of Governor of Arkansas.

White Loaf Cake.

1 cupful butter,
2 cupfuls sugar,
1 cupful sweet milk,
2 teaspoonfuls baking powder,
5 cupfuls flour,
Whites 13 eggs.

Cream butter and sugar, sift baking powder with flour, and alternately add it with milk to sugar and butter. Last of all, cut in whites of eggs whipped to a stiff froth. Bake in layer-cake pans.

Filling for Cake

2 cupfuls sugar,
Whites 2 eggs,
½ pound marshmallows,
1 pound English walnuts.

Cook sugar with ¾ cupful water. When it threads, pour over whites of eggs not beaten very much and marshmallows. Shell walnuts, break slightly, add to filling, and put between layers of cake.

From Mrs. John Burke, wife of Governor of North Dakota.

Angel-Food Pudding.

2 eggs,
1 cupful powdered sugar,
1 tablespoonful flour,
1 teaspoonful baking powder,
1 cupful broken walnut meats,
1 cupful dates.

Beat together thoroughly eggs, sugar, flour, and baking powder, add nuts and dates. Pour into a baking dish, set it in a pan of boiling water and bake about half an hour. Let it cool, still standing in the water, chill, and serve with whipped cream.

This pudding is a great favorite with children.

From Mrs. Samuel G. Cosgrove, wife of Governor of Washington.

Potato Cake.

¾ cupful butter,
2 cupfuls sugar,
Yolks 4 eggs,
1 cupful hot mashed potato,
2 squares chocolate,
½ cupful milk,
2 cupfuls flour,
3½ teaspoonfuls baking powder,
1 teaspoonful each cinnamon and nutmeg,
½ teaspoonful ground cloves,
1 cupful chopped walnut meats,
Whites 4 eggs.

Cream together butter and 1 cupful sugar, beat to a froth yolks of eggs with remainder of sugar, then blend both mixtures thoroughly together. Add potatoes, chocolate melted over hot water, and alternately milk with flour, which has been sifted with baking powder and spices. Last, add whites of eggs whipped to a stiff froth and walnut meats. Bake in layers or a loaf cake as desired, and cover with a chocolate or a white frosting.

From Mrs. W. R. Stubbs, wife of Governor of Kansas.

Pickled Peaches.

1 gallon peeled peaches,
3 pounds sugar,
1 pint pure cider vinegar,
2 dozen cloves,
6 sticks cinnamon.

Boil vinegar, sugar, cinnamon, and cloves fifteen minutes, then pour liquor over peaches and let stand over night in stone jar covered with a plate. Next morning pour off liquor and heat to boiling point, then add peaches to boiling liquor and let cook slowly until tender. Seal in glass jars.

From Mrs. Parker Morgan, one of the 400.

Raspberry Buns.

1 pound flour,
½ pound lard,
6 ounces sugar,
½ teaspoonful salt,
1½ teaspoonfuls baking powder,
1 egg,
A little milk.

Place flour in a bowl and rub lard in thoroughly; add salt, sugar, and baking powder. Beat egg well and add sufficient milk to make the whole into a rather stiff paste. Knead lightly, and roll out about a quarter of an inch thick, cut into rounds and wet the edges. Place a little jam in the center of each and fold over. Pinch the edges together and flatten slightly, put on a greased baking sheet, and bake in a quick oven twenty minutes.

From Mrs. Jesse Knight of Utah.

Mince-Meat.

½ pound butter,
2½ pounds brown sugar,
3 pounds boiled beef neck,
1½ pounds suet,
2½ pounds white sugar,
2 tablespoonfuls cinnamon,
2 tablespoonfuls nutmeg,

2 tablespoonfuls mace,
2 tablespoonfuls allspice,
2 tablespoonfuls salt,
Juice and rind 3 lemons,
6 pounds raisins, seeded,
3 pounds currants,
1 pound citron,
1 tablespoonful almond extract,
8 pounds apples,
1 pint brown sherry,
1 pint brandy.

Rub butter and brown sugar together; chop beef neck after boiling till tender enough to fall from bone; grind or chop finely suet. Add spices to white sugar, grate rind of lemons, being careful not to get any white, and mix grated rind into sugar and spices. Seed raisins, wash and dry currants, chop citron finely, peel and chop apples. Mix all thoroughly together, adding sherry, brandy, and almond extract last. Put in glass jars; it will keep indefinitely.

From Mrs. Thomas P. Gore, wife of Senator from Oklahoma.

Braised Veal.

Slice veal steak into strips from one to one and one half inches thick. Season well to taste, and roll up and skewer with toothpicks. Fry them in hot butter till browned on both sides—be sure not to scratch. Place them in a roaster and sprinkle with butter, add enough water—cream and water is better, but in that case do not use butter. Bake from two to four hours in a moderate oven. Be careful not to burn.

This recipe was originated by a friend of mine, Mrs. Thomas H. Dunn of Oklahoma, and from experience I know just how delicious it is.

The following recipe was given by one of the best cooks in America.

Chicken Fricassee.

Cut a fowl up into pieces, put it in a saucepan covered with boiling water and cook very slowly till tender. When half done, season with salt and pepper. Lift out the pieces, allow them to drain, sift with flour to which a little salt and pepper has been added, then sauté slowly in pork fat. Arrange the chicken in pieces upon toast, or if liked better, fix New England style, with a circle of baking powder biscuits about them heaped on a platter. In arranging the chicken, lay it on the platter as much as possible in the shape of a whole bird, having the breast in the centre, legs and wings in the natural position and back underneath; this makes it easy to serve. To the liquor from the chicken add a cup of cream or three tablespoonfuls of butter and thicken with a quarter of a cup of flour dissolved in cold water. Strain over the chicken and biscuits. If there is more gravy than the platter will hold serve it in a gravy boat.

CHAPTER LXV

SOME KITCHEN KINKS

INSTEAD of shelling peas, throw them, pods and all, into a kettle of boiling water, after washing and discarding all spoiled ones. When they are done the pods will rise to the surface, while the peas will stay at the bottom of the kettle. Peas cooked in this manner have a fine flavor.

To hasten the baking of potatoes, I let them stand a few minutes in hot water, after washing them clean.

If you relish celery in soup and live where it cannot be secured the year round, dry the celery leaves as you get them and put them away in a fruit jar. When preparing soup, tie a few of the leaves in a cloth, and drop it into the kettle. You will find that the soup will have even more of the taste of celery than when using the stalk.

In making peanut butter, I mix the ground peanuts with cream or milk instead of olive oil, if I only desire a small quantity. It is delicious, although it does not keep longer than a few days.

Ham may be kept from getting hard and dry on the outside thus: take some of the fat part of the ham and fry it out. Let it get hard then spread on the cut end of the ham; half an inch thick is not too much. This excludes air. Hang in a cool place. When I want to slice ham I scrape off this fat, and afterwards put it on again as before.

If your omelets burn because you have no "omelet pan," put a tablespoonful of common salt in the frying skillet. Put it on the stove and heat very hot. Empty salt from the pan, wipe it with a dry cloth. Cook the omelet with a small quantity of butter, and it will not burn easily.

Changing the water two or three times will keep potatoes from turning dark, and if they have been frostbitten this will improve them.

Before trying to break a cocoanut put it in the oven to warm. When heated a slight blow will crack it, and the shell will come off easily.

A layer of absorbent cotton in the mouth of fruit cans is an excellent preventive against mold. If mold should form, it will cling to the cotton and leave the fruit clean.

A delicious kind of sandwich was served with coffee at a recent club meeting. It took the fancy of each and every one. After tasting, some one asked the hostess of what it was made. She politely replied, "The recipe was sent to me from a friend in an Eastern city, with the strict injunction I should not publish it." Immediately all began guessing. A nod from the hostess informed one girl she had guessed right. Here is the recipe: One cake of Philadelphia cream cheese, mixed with canned Spanish peppers, chopped fine. One large pepper is sufficient for one cake of cheese.

To keep cream sweet heat it to almost boiling point, put it in a glass bottle or earthen vessel, cover, and set aside to cool. Cream thus treated will keep sweet and fresh several days, in moderate weather, and over the second day in warm weather.

When making fudge, stir in half a pound of marshmallows before you turn it into the tin to cool. They melt immediately and make the candy as smooth and creamy as can be.

If you want nicely flavored butter, with the buttermilk well worked out, try putting in a teaspoonful of clear honey to about three pounds of butter. You can not taste the honey but it improves the butter.

When using grated or sliced pineapple for sauce the juice of half a lemon with sugar and water added gives a delicious flavor.

To give frosting a nice flavor add a bit of butter, the size of a hickory nut. It will also prevent the frosting from becoming hard too soon.

To prevent staining your fingers, while paring potatoes keep the potatoes in cold water.

Gruels are more tempting to the sick if whipped to a froth with an egg-beater before serving in a pretty cup.

When baking cookies, use a large round pancake griddle to bake them on. First heat it on top of the range, and have it well greased.

If a kitchen window is kept open two inches at the top while frying foods, boiling cabbage or other odorous vegetables, the unpleasant odor will go out of the window instead of spreading through the house.

After boiling salt ham or tongue remove it from the fire and plunge at once in cold water. This instantly loosens the skin, which then pulls off without any trouble. Treat beets the same way.

Try baking bread in a meat roaster with a top. This keeps the bread from browning on the upper side before it is done through—thus browning it evenly all over.

Prune pies are improved by adding one teaspoonful of vinegar to each pie. Prunes are rather flat tasting so the vinegar cuts the sweetness.

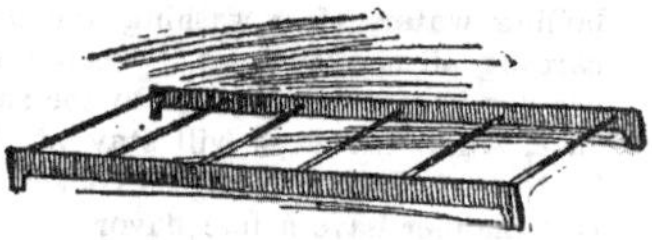

Rack to Set Under Hot Kettles.

On making cake when fresh milk, buttermilk, molasses, and sour milk, are lacking, use a cup of apple sauce into which has been stirred a teaspoonful of baking soda. Besides being an excellent substitute, the sauce makes a delicious spice cake, and without eggs, too.

When spreading butter on sandwiches or toast, do not try to soften the butter, but heat a silver knife by placing it in boiling water. The difficulty is overcome at once.

When a recipe calls for sugar and flour, instead of moistening the flour with water or milk, stir flour and sugar together in the dry state. Then no lumps will be seen.

If one cannot afford much cream when making ice cream, a small quantity will go farther and be richer if whipped or scalded. In summer, milk sherbet, made with lemons and gelatin, is inexpensive, very delicious, and a refreshing substitute for cream.

Much can be done at night in preparation for breakfast. For instance, if baked potatoes are to be included in the *menu,* wash them; and sift flour or meal for muffins.

When we bake apples in the usual way, after coring and putting in sugar and water, the juice runs into the dish and is burned or wasted, as it naturally will not stay in the hole. After coring, cut the apple in two, and make the center of the trench in the apple deeper; fill it with sugar, laying the cut half of each one upwards.

To economize stove space when making rice soup I place a cup containing the rice in the soup kettle. It serves the purpose of a double boiler. It also prevents scorching or the soup boiling over, the latter generally being caused by the addition of rice.

To keep cheese moist, wrap it in a soft cloth wrung out of vinegar, and keep in an earthen jar, with the cover slightly raised.

To clean lettuce is often a nuisance, because of tiny green insects or their eggs in it. Turn on the cold water faucet slightly, put your thumb against it so the stream squirts *with force,* and hold each leaf, with the broad end in the hand, under the water for a few seconds. Rinse, and it is ready for the table.

In the cooking departments of women's magazines, I find one class of housekeepers completely ignored, perhaps unwittingly. It comprises the millions who inhabit lofty plateaus and mountains. Perhaps lowland women do not know that we who come to these high altitudes (Telluride, Colorado), have to learn all over again how to cook. I have seen hundreds of recipes in cookbooks and magazines that would fail altogether here. For instance—I have boiled potatoes in Ohio (near the sea level) in twenty-five minutes. In Denver, at an altitude of five thousand feet, it takes thirty-five minutes. In Leadville, Colorado, at ten thousand feet, forty-five minutes. This is because of water boiling at a lower temperature in high altitudes. Where I now live, at an altitude of nine thousand feet, I boil potatoes nearly an hour in water merely at the boiling point, and find they are not tender, so the water must be much hotter than at the boiling point to cook them. Other vegetables must be cooked longer. It is impossible to cook until tender some of the garden peas that are on sale here in the summer, and we have to depend almost wholly on factory canned peas.

A woman must learn over again to bake cake if she has just come from a low altitude. No Eastern cookbook can be depended upon. The ladies of this town have published a cookbook of their own reliable recipes. It is eagerly bought by newcomers from low altitudes. In baking cake, you must use more flour and less shortening.

Nothing else sweetens vessels in which milk has been kept so well as a solution of baking soda and hot water, in the proportion of a level teaspoonful to a quart of warm water. Let the solution stand in the vessels long enough to get cold. Pudding dishes or pots and pans which have been burned are easily cleaned this way.

If the refrigerator is stored away and the cellar is warm from the heating plant there, an excellent way to keep lettuce crisp and tender, is to wrap each head separately in a piece of old linen, wet in cold water. Moisten the linen every day, and you can keep lettuce for two weeks. The inner leaves will be yellow and crisp, and there will be no wasting of outer leaves.

Sometimes it is impossible to obtain sour milk for a favorite dish. A mountain mine cook told me his method of obtaining sour milk was to dilute condensed milk, which is invariably used at the mines, until it was like ordinary skimmed milk. Then he added a little sugar, and kept it in a warm place until it soured, even elabbered.

When using lemons in a way that does not call for the rind, I pare off the yellow portion carefully, put it through the meat chopper with the finest plate, and spread it out to dry. Then I put into a corked bottle, and it frequently saves grating peel when one is in a hurry, or makes a pleasant flavoring when a fresh lemon is not at hand.

Wash and slice ten stalks of rhubarb, cut and core three medium-sized apples, then stew apples and rhubarb together. Hang up in a jelly bag. For every pint of juice take a pint of sugar; boil till it jellies and pour into tumblers.

If you cut cheese in long strips and put in a glass jar, screwing the lid on tight, it will keep fresh till the last bit is used. It can be kept in the ice box in this way without harming other food.

When I use oranges or lemons, if the rind is fresh and wholesome, I pare it thin, so as to get none of the bitter white inner skin, and put it in a glass jar of granulated sugar. When the sugar has absorbed enough oil of the fruit skin to make it moist, it is ready to use for flavoring cakes, puddings, etc. The bits of rind give a delicious flavor to pudding sauces.

If you wish to prevent citron, raisins, or currants from sinking to the bottom of your cake, have them well warmed in the oven before adding them to the batter.

When spinach and dandelion are expensive, try cooking celery leaves exactly as you would other greens, boiling them in salted water, then chopping slightly and seasoning with butter, pepper, and salt. By saving the leaves from three or four bunches and keeping them bouquet fashion, with their stalks in water, you may soon accumulate enough leaves for a small, savory dish of celery greens.

Here are some uses for salt: To beat eggs quickly add a pinch of salt. This also applies when whipping cream. Place salt in the oven under the baking tins, in order to prevent the scorching of their contents. Put salt in the water when you wish to cool a dish quickly. Use salt to remove ink stains from carpet, when the ink is fresh. Salt sprinkled on the pantry shelves will drive away ants.

Before cooking mushrooms I always distinguish them from poisonous fungi by sprinkling salt on the spongy part, or gills. If they turn yellow, they are poisonous; if black, they are wholesome.

Boil oyster plant, parsnips, and such vegetables, with thin skins on; then peel when cold. The flavor is preserved and your hands are not stained.

For boiling meats I always use a lard can in preference to a kettle. For a smaller piece of meat, or a chicken, there is nothing better than a tin bucket with a tight-fitting cover. It confines the steam and not only cooks more quickly, but the meat is juicier and more tender.

When poaching eggs add a little vinegar to the water, besides salt. This sets the eggs and keeps them in good shape.

A pinch of soda, put in green vegetables while they are boiling, acts like magic. It makes string-beans deliciously tender; it keeps the fine color of spring peas, while a more generous pinch performs a miracle for cabbage, causing it to cook in about half the usual time, and keeping it as fresh and green as when it came from the garden.

In making mayonnaise, I find that using vinegar which has been poured over pickles, beets, or cucumbers, instead of fresh vinegar, adds a pleasant flavor to salads.

If pastry is considered unwholesome, those who are fond of pumpkin or squash pies will find a good substitute by baking them as custards. I use the same recipe as for a filling for a pie, only add a little more milk, then bake it in custard cups set in a pan of water. The result is a creamy, delicious dessert.

When steaming a pudding, place the steamer over the saucepan in which you are boiling potatoes. One gas burner will cook both pudding and potatoes.

When beating eggs separately beat the white first, then "steal" a little bit of it to start the yolks. The result is the yolks will not stick to the beater, as is generally the case, and they will get light twice as quickly.

To insure success with salt-rising bread in cold weather, keep the night yeast in a box of hay. A small wooden box with a close-fitting lid is best for this purpose. Put hay into the bottom of the box and around the sides. In the middle of this set your yeast, then cover with hay. This will keep the yeast from a chill. Good bread will be the result.

When serving afternoon tea, try using slices of orange instead of the inevitable lemon. The flavor is very delicious, especially when combined with green tea. Fresh sliced cucumbers also give an agreeable flavor to hot tea if a dash of rum be added to the beverage.

Set a glass of jelly in a pan of boiling water for two minutes or more. Let the water reach to the top of the glass. Then plunge into cold water. Take it out of that immediately and turn bottom up on a cut-glass nappy or saucer. It will be prettily molded.

To grind coffee and soak it some hours before boiling is a decided economy, but it ***must not be soaked in the pot.*** The acid in the coffee acting on the metal pot turns the coffee dark and gives it an unpleasant flavor. You can easily test this at breakfast time by putting a drop of coffee on the steel carver. Soak the coffee in a closed earthen vessel.

I save all paraffin paper from cracker boxes and cut it up to fit cake tins. After a pan is greased I put a sheet of paper in the bottom, and it keeps the cake from sticking to the pan. It is better to let the paper stay on cake after it is baked, until it is cold, unless frosting is to be used.

Corn-meal mush will brown very quickly when fried, if a little sugar is put in the water while boiling.

When mixing mustard, add a few drops of oil or sweet oil. This will prevent the unsightly black surface of the interior of your mustard jar. The paste will retain its original bright yellow color as long as a partiele remains.

New popcorn, or popcorn that is damp, should not be dried out before popping, as is usually done. If you have recently gathered your corn, or if it has been left in a damp room, and you wish to use it right away, shell a few ears and put it in a bowl of water for ten minutes. It will pop readily, and the flakes will be crisp and nice.

When picking a fowl, particularly if there are many pin feathers, the work can be simplified by plunging it into hot water for a few seconds, then wrapping in a piece of burlap and allowing it to stand for three or four minutes. When picking, uncover only a portion at a time, so that the rest will remain warm and damp, and the feathers, great and small, can be stripped off in an amazingly short time.

Use lemon peel, after the juice has been partly squeezed out, to rub stains from silverware; also to remove fruit stains from your fingers.

If you do not want liquor in your mince meat, use one pint of clear, strong coffee to each gallon of mince meat.

Warm jelly glasses before putting in the jelly, as it helps it to thicken, or set them in the sun.

As a relish and a garnish to serve with a light meat course, such as chicken croquettes or timbales, nothing is more refreshing than small individual molds of very tart lemon jelly, in which are molded a few nut meats. The jelly can be tinted to carry out any color scheme.

APPENDIX CHAPTER I

ECONOMICAL USE OF MEAT IN THE HOME*

By

C. F. LANGWORTHY, Ph.D.

Expert in Charge of Nutrition Investigations, Office of Experiment Stations

AND

CAROLINE L. HUNT, A.B.

Expert in Nutrition, Office of Experiment Stations

GENERAL METHODS OF PREPARING MEAT FOR THE TABLE

The advantages of variety in the methods of preparing and serving are to be considered even more seriously in the cooking of the cheaper cuts than in the cooking of the more expensive ones, and yet even in this connection it is a mistake to lose sight of the fact that, though there is a great variety of dishes, the processes involved are few in number.

An experienced teacher of cooking, a woman who has made very valuable contributions to the art of cookery by showing that most of the numerous processes outlined and elaborately described in the cook books can be classified under a very few heads, says that she tries "to reduce the cooking of meat to its lowest terms and teach only three ways of cooking. The first is the application of intense heat to keep in the juices. This is suitable only for portions of clear meat where the fibers are tender. By the second method the meats are put in cold water and cooked at a low temperature. This is suitable for bone, gristle, and the toughest portions of the meat, which for this purpose should be divided into small bits. The third is a combination of these two processes and consists of searing and then stewing the meat. This is suitable for halfway cuts, i. e., those that are neither tender nor very tough." The many varieties of meat dishes are usually only a matter of flavor and garnish.

In other words, of the three processes the first is the short method; it aims to keep all the juices within the meat. The second is a very long method employed for the purpose of getting all or most of the juices out. The third is a combination of the two not so long as the second and yet requiring so much time that there is danger of the meat being rendered tasteless unless certain precautions are taken such as searing in hot fat or plunging into boiling water.

It is commonly said that the cooked meat fibers are harder or less tender than the raw, which seems a natural assumption since the meat protein, like egg albumen, is coagulated by heat, and furthermore, the water is forced out from the individual muscle fibers and they are shortened and thickened by the application of heat. * * *

A good idea of the changes which take place while meat is being cooked can be obtained by examining a piece of flesh which has been "cooked to pieces," as the saying goes. In

* U. S. Department of Agriculture. Farmers' Bulletin No. 391.

this the muscular fibers may be seen completely separated one from another, showing that the connective tissue has been destroyed. It is also evident that the fibers themselves are of different texture from those in the raw meat. In preparing meat for the table it is usual to stop short of the point of disintegration, but while the long process of cooking is going on the connective tissue is gradually softening and the fibers are gradually changing in texture. The former is the thing to be especially desired, but the latter is not. For this reason it is necessary to keep the temperature below the boiling point and as low as is consistent with thorough cooking, for cooks seem agreed, as the result of experience shows, that slow gentle cooking results in better texture than is the case when meat is boiled rapidly. This is the philosophy that lies back of the simmering process.

When meat is cooked by roasting, broiling, or any other similar process the meat juices brown with the fat, producing substances which to most of us are agreeable to the senses of smell and taste alike. When meats are cooked in hot water such highly flavored substances are not so evident to the sense of smell, but nevertheless bodies of agreeable flavor which are perceptible to the palate are developed in the meat during the cooking process and are of similar value in promoting digestion.

The chief loss in weight when meat is cooked is due to the driving off of water. When beef is cooked by pan broiling—that is, searing in a hot, greased pan, a common cooking process—no great loss of nutrition results, particularly if the fat and other substances adhering to the pan are utilized in the preparation of gravy. When beef is cooked by boiling, there is a loss of 3 to 20 per cent of material present, though this is not an actual loss if the broth is utilized for soup or in some similar way. Even in the case of meat which is used for the preparation of beef tea or broth, the losses of nutritive material are apparently small though much of the flavoring matter has been removed. The amount of fat found in broth varies directly with the amount originally present in the meat; the fatter the meat the greater the quantity of fat in the broth. The loss of water in cooking varies inversely with the fatness of the meat; that is, the fatter the meat the smaller the shrinkage due to loss of water. In cooked meat the loss of various constituents is inversely proportional to the size of the cut. In other words, the smaller the piece of meat the greater the percentage of loss. Loss also appears to be dependent somewhat upon the length of time the cooking is continued. When pieces of meat weighing 1½ to 5 pounds are cooked in water somewhat under the boiling point there appears to be little difference in the amount of material found in broth whether the meat is placed in cold water or hot water at the beginning of the cooking period. When meat is roasted in the oven the amount of material removed is somewhat affected by the character of the roasting pan and similar factors, thus the total loss in weight is naturally greater in an open than in a closed pan as the open pan offers more opportunity for the evaporation of water. Judging from the average results of a considerable number of tests it appears that a roast weighing 6 pounds raw should weigh 5 pounds after cooking, or in other words the loss is about one-sixth of the original weight. This means that if the raw meat costs 20 cents per pound the cooked would represent an increase of 4 cents a pound on the original cost; but this increase would of course be lessened if all the drippings and gravy are utilized. With the quantities used in the ordinary home the relative losses sustained in different methods of cooking meat are not great enough to be of particular importance with reference to economical management.

However, in public institutions where a small saving per day for each inmate represents a large item in the course of a year, it may be desirable to select methods involving the least loss, which would mean that the advantage would lie with stewing and boiling rather than with broiling and roasting, so far as the relative losses of material are concerned. The relative economy of different methods of cookery depends very greatly upon the kind of fuel, the form of stove and oven, and other similar factors. These vary so much under different home conditions that it is difficult to draw general deductions though the subject has often been investigated. However, it may be said that it is often possible to effect a saving if the housewife can so plan the cooking of meat and other foods as to take full advantage of the heat supplied by the fuel used.

REDUCING THE EXPENSE FOR MEAT IN THE DIET

The expense for meat in the home may be reduced * * * by careful attention to the use of meat, bone, fat, and small portions commonly trimmed off and thrown away and the utilization of left-over portions of cooked meat; and the use of the less expensive kinds.

UTILIZING THE FAT, BONE, AND TRIMMINGS IN MEATS, AND THE LEFT-OVER COLD MEATS

In the percentage of fat present in different kinds and cuts of meat, a greater difference exists than in the percentage of proteids. The lowest percentage of fat ordinarily found in meat is 8.1 per cent, as in the shank of beef; the highest is 32 per cent in pork chops. The highest priced cuts, loin and ribs of beef, contain 20 to 25 per cent. If the fat of the meat is not eaten at the table, and is not utilized otherwise, a pecuniary loss results. If butter is the fat used in making crusts for meat pies, and in preparing the cheaper cuts, there is little economy involved; the fats from other meat should therefore be saved, as they may be used in place of butter in such cases, as well as in preparing many other foods. The fat from sausage or from the soup kettle, or from a pot roast, which is savory because it has been cooked with vegetables, is particularly acceptable. Sometimes savory vegetables, onion, or sweet herbs are added to fat when it is tried out to give it flavor.

Some illustrations of methods of preparing such cooking fats follow:

Trying Out Fat.—A double boiler is the best utensil to use in trying out small portions of fat. There is no danger of burning the fat and the odor is much less noticeable than if it is heated in a dish set directly over the fire.

Clarifying Fat.—Excepting where the purpose of clarifying fat is to remove flavors, a good method to follow is to pour boiling water over the fat, to boil thoroughly, and then to set it away to cool. The cold fat may be removed in a solid cake and any impurities clinging to it may be scraped off, as they will be found at the bottom of the layer. By repeating this process two or three times a cake of clean, white fat may be obtained.

A slight burned taste or similar objectionable flavors often can be removed from fat by means of potatoes. After melting the fat, put into it thick slices of raw potato; heat gradually. When the fat ceases to bubble and the potatoes are brown, strain through a cloth placed in a wire strainer.

Savory Drippings.—When rendering the drippings of fat meat, add a small onion (do not cut it), a few leaves of summer savory and thyme, a teaspoonful of salt, and a little pepper. This is enough for a pint of fat. Keep the drippings covered and in a cool place.

Uses for Bones.—Almost any meat bones can be used in soup making, and if the meat is not all removed from them the soup is better. But some bones, especially the rib bones, if they have a little meat left on them, can be grilled or roasted into very palatable dishes. The "sparerib" of southern cooks is made of the rib bones from a roast of pork, and makes a favorite dish when well browned. The braised ribs of beef often served in high-class restanrants are made from the bones cut from rib roasts. In this connection it may be noted that many of the dishes popular in good hotels are made of portions of meat such as are frequently thrown away in private houses, but which with proper cooking and seasoning make attractive dishes and give most acceptable variety to the menu. An old recipe for "broiled bones" directs that the bones (beef ribs or sirloin bones on which the meat is not left too thick in any part) be sprinkled with salt and pepper (Cayenne), and broiled over a clear fire until browned. Another example of the use of bones is boiled marrow bone. The bones are cut in convenient lengths, the ends covered with a little piece of dough over which a floured cloth is tied, and cooked in boiling water for two hours. After removing the cloth and dough, the bones are placed upright on toast and served. Prepared as above, the bones may also be baked in a deep dish. Marrow is sometimes removed from bones after cooking, seasoned, and served on toast.

Trimmings from meat may be utilized in various "made dishes," of which examples will be given further on, or they can always be put to good use in the soup kettle. It is surprising how many economies may be practiced in such ways and also in the table use of left-over portions of cooked meat if attention is given to the matter. Many of the recipes given in this bulletin involve the use of left-overs. Others will suggest themselves or may be found in all the usual cookery books.

Extending the Flavor of Meat.—Common household methods of extending the meat flavor through a considerable quantity of material which would otherwise be lacking in distinctive taste are to serve the meat with dumplings, generally in the dish with it, to combine the meat with crusts, as in meat pies or meat rolls, or to serve the meat on toast and biscuits. Borders of rice, hominy, or mashed potatoes are examples of the same principles applied in different ways. By serving some preparation of flour, rice, hominy, or other food rich in starch with the meat we get a dish which in itself approaches nearer to the balanced ration than meat alone and one in which the meat flavor is extended through a large amount of the material.

Throughout the measurements given in the recipe call for a level spoonful or a level cupful, as the case may be.

A number of recipes for meat dishes made with dumplings and similar preparations follow:

Meat Stew with Dumplings.

Stew.

5 pounds of a cheaper cut of beef.
4 cups of potatoes cut into small pieces.
⅔ cup each of turnips and carrots cut into ½-inch cubes.
½ onion, chopped.
¼ cup of flour.
Salt and pepper.

Cut the meat into small pieces, removing the fat; try out the fat and brown the meat in it. When well browned, cover with boiling water, boil for five minutes and then cook in a lower temperature until the meat is done. If tender, this will require about three hours on the stove or five hours in the fireless cooker. Add carrots, turnips, onions, pepper and salt during the last hour of cooking, and the potatoes fifteen minutes before serving. Thicken with the flour diluted with cold water. Serve with dumplings (see below). If this dish is made in the fireless cooker, the mixture must be reheated when the vegetables are put in. Such a stew may also be made of mutton. If veal or pork is used the vegetables may be omitted or simply a little onion used. Sometimes for variety the browning of the meat is dispensed with. When white meat, such as chicken, veal, or fresh pork, is used, the gravy is often made rich with cream or milk thickened with flour. The numerous minor additions which may be introduced give the great variety of such stews found in cookbooks.

Dumplings.

2 cups flour.
4 teaspoonfuls baking powder.
⅔ cup milk or a little more if needed.
½ teaspoonful salt.
2 teaspoonfuls butter.

Mix and sift the dry ingredients. Work in the butter with the tips of fingers, add milk gradually, roll out to a thickness of one-half inch and cut with biscuit cutter. In some countries it is customary to season the dumplings themselves with herbs, etc., or to stuff them with bread crumbs fried in butter instead of depending upon the gravy to season them.

A good way to cook dumplings is to put them in a buttered steamer over a kettle of hot water. They should cook from twelve to fifteen minutes. If it is necessary to cook them with the stew, enough liquid should be removed so that they may be placed upon the meat and vegetables.

Sometimes the dough is baked and served as biscuits over which the stew is poured. If the stew is made with chicken or veal it is generally termed a fricassee.

Ragout of Mutton with Farina Balls.

1½ pounds neck of mutton cut into small pieces.
1 tablespoonful butter.
1 tablespoonful flour.
1 onion.
1 carrot.
½ can peas.
2 cups hot water.
1 teaspoonful salt.
¼ teaspoonful pepper.
1 bay leaf.
Sprig parsley.
1 clove.

Farina Balls.

¼ cup farina.
1 cup milk.
¼ teaspoonful salt.
⅛ teaspoonful pepper
Onion juice.
Yolk 1 egg.

Put butter in frying pan. When melted add flour and brown. Add carrot and onion, cut in dice. Remove vegetables and add meat, searing well. To meat and vegetables add hot water and seasonings. Put in a suitable kettle, cover and simmer two hours. Add peas ten minutes before serving in a dish with farina balls made as follows:

Cook farina and milk in double boiler one hour. Add seasoning and well-beaten yolk. Stir well and cool. When cold roll into balls. Dip in egg and crumbs and fry in deep fat. Rice may be used in a similar way.

MEAT PIES AND SIMILAR DISHES

Meat pies represent another method of combining flour with meat. They are ordinarily baked in a fairly deep dish the sides of which may or may not be lined with dough. The cooked meat, cut into small pieces, is put into the dish, sometimes with small pieces of vegetables, a gravy is poured over the meat, the dish is covered with a layer of dough, and then baked. Most commonly the dough is like that used for soda or cream-of-tartar biscuit, but sometimes shortened pastry dough, such as is made for pies, is used. This is especially the case in the fancy individual dishes usually called patties. Occasionally the pie is covered with a potato crust in which case the meat is put directly into the dish without lining the latter. Stewed beef, veal, and chicken are probably most frequently used in pies, but any kind of meat may be used, or several kinds in combination. Pork pies are favorite dishes in many rural regions, especially at hog-killing time, and when well made are excellent.

If pies are made from raw meat and vegetables longer cooking is needed than otherwise, and in such cases it is well to cover the dish with a plate, cook until the pie is nearly done, then remove the plate, add the crust, and return to the oven until the crust is lightly browned. Many cooks insist on piercing holes in the top crust of a meat pie directly it is taken from the oven.

Twelve O'Clock Pie.

This is made with shoulder of mutton, boiled with carrot and onion, then cut up, mixed with potatoes separately boiled and cut up, and put into a baking dish. The crust is made by mixing smoothly mashed potatoes to which a tablespoonful of shortening has been added, with enough flour and water to make them roll out easily. A pie made of a pound of meat will require 5 or 6 small boiled potatoes, a cupful of mashed potatoes, and 8 or 10 tablespoonsful of flour, and should be baked about twenty minutes in a hot oven. Salt, pepper, and other seasoning, as onion and carrot, may be added to taste. A teaspoonful of baking powder makes the crust lighter.

Meat and Tomato Pie.

This dish presents an excellent way of using up small quantities of either cold beef or cold mutton. If fresh tomatoes are used, peel and slice them; if canned, drain off the liquid. Place a layer of tomato in a baking dish, then a layer of sliced meat, and over the two dredge flour, pepper and salt; repeat until the dish is nearly full, then put in an extra layer of tomato and cover the whole with a layer of pastry or of bread or cracker crumbs. When the quantity of meat is small, it may be "helped out" by boiled potatoes or other suitable vegetables. A few oysters or mushrooms improve the flavor especially when beef is used. The pie will need to be baked from half an hour to an hour according to its size and the heat of the oven.

Meat and Pastry Rolls.

Small quantities of cold ham, chicken, or other meat may be utilized for these. The meat should be chopped fine, well seasoned, mixed with enough savory fat or butter to make it "shape," and formed into rolls about the size of a finger. A short dough (made, say, of a pint of flour, 2 tablespoonfuls of lard, 1 teaspoonful of baking powder, salt, and milk enough to mix) should be rolled thin, cut into strips, and folded about the meat rolls, care being taken to keep the shape regular. The rolls should be baked in a quick oven until they are a delicate brown color and served hot.

Meat Turnovers.

Almost any kind of chopped meat may be used in these, and if the quantity on hand is small may be mixed with potato or cooked rice. This filling should be seasoned to taste with salt and pepper, onion, or whatever is relished, and laid on pieces of short biscuit dough rolled thin and cut into circles about the size of an ordinary saucer. The edges of the dough should be moistened with white of egg, the dough then folded over the meat, and its edges pinched closely together. If desired, the tops of the turnovers may be brushed over with yolk of egg before they are placed in the oven. About half an hour's baking in a hot oven is required. Serving with a brown sauce increases the flavor and moistens the crust.

MEAT WITH MACARONI AND OTHER STARCHY MATERIALS

Macaroni cooked with chopped ham, hash made of meat and potatoes, or meat and rice, meat croquettes—made of meat and some starchy materials like bread crumbs, cracker dust, or rice—are other familiar examples of meat combined with starchy materials. Pilaf, a dish very common in the Orient and well known in the United States, is of this character and easily made. When there is soup or soup stock on hand it can be well used in the pilaf.

Turkish Pilaf.

½ cup of rice.
¾ cup of tomatoes stewed and strained.
1 cup stock or broth.
3 tablespoonsful of butter.

Cook the rice and tomatoes with the stock in a double boiler until the rice is tender, removing the cover after the rice is cooked if there is too much liquid. Add the butter and stir it in with a fork to prevent the rice from being broken. A little catsup or Chili sauce with water enough to make three-quarters of a cup may be substituted for the tomatoes. This may be served as a border with meat, or served separately in the place of a vegetable, or may make the main dish at a meal, as it is savory and reasonably nutritious.

Meat Cakes.

1 pound chopped veal.
¼ pound soaked bread crumbs.
2 tablespoonfuls savory fat or butter.
1 teaspoonful chopped onion.
1½ teaspoonsful salt.
Dash of pepper.

Mix all the ingredients except the butter or fat and shape into small round cakes. Melt the fat in a baking pan and brown the cakes in it, first one side and then the other. Either cooked or raw veal may be used. In the case of raw meat the pan should be covered so that the heat may be retained to soften the meat.

Stew from Cold Roast.

This dish provides a good way of using up the remnants of a roast, either of beef or mutton. The meat should be freed from fat, gristle, and bones, cut into small pieces, slightly salted, and put into a kettle with water enough to nearly cover it. It should simmer until almost ready to break in pieces, when onions and raw potatoes, peeled and quartered, should be added. A little soup stock may also be added if available. Cook until the potatoes are done, then thicken the liquor or gravy with flour. The stew may be attractively served on slices of crisp toast.

Meat with Beans.

Dry beans are very rich in protein, the percentage being fully as large as that in meat. Dry beans and other similar legumes are usually cooked in water, which they absorb, and so are diluted before serving; on the other hand, meats by the ordinary methods of cooking are usually deprived of some of the water originally present—facts which are often overlooked in discussing the matter. Nevertheless, when beans are served with meat the dish is almost as rich in protein as if it consisted entirely of meat.

Pork and beans is such a well-known dish that recipes are not needed. Some cooks use a piece of corned mutton or a piece of corned beef in place of salt or corned pork or bacon or use butter or olive oil in preparing this dish.

In the Southern States, where cowpeas are a common crop, they are cooked in the same way as dried beans. Cowpeas baked with salt pork or bacon make an excellent dish resembling pork and beans, but of distinctive flavor. Cowpeas boiled with ham or with bacon are also well-known and palatable dishes.

Recipes are here given for some less common meat and bean dishes:

Mexican Beef.

The Mexicans have a dish known as "Chili con carne" (meat with Chili pepper), the ingredients for which one would doubtless have difficulty in obtaining except in the southwestern United States. However, a good substitute for it may be made with the foods available in all parts of the country. The Mexican recipe is as follows:

Remove the seeds from two Chili peppers, soak the pods in a pint of warm water until they are soft, scrape the pulp from the skin and add to the water. Cut two pounds of beef into small pieces and brown in butter or drippings. Add a clove of garlic and the Chili water. Cook until the meat is tender, renewing the water if necessary. Thicken the sauce with flour. Serve with Mexican beans either mixed with the meat or used as a border.

In the absence of the Chili peppers, water and Cayenne pepper may be used, and onions may be substituted for garlic. For the Mexican beans, red kidney beans either fresh or canned make a good substitute. If the canned beans are used they should be drained and heated in a little savory fat or butter. The liquid may be added to the meat while it is cooking. If the dried beans are used they should be soaked until soft, then cooked in water until tender and rather dry, a little butter or dripping and salt being used for seasoning or gravy. White or dried Lima beans may be used in a similar way.

Haricot of Mutton.

- 2 tablespoonsful of chopped onions.
- 2 tablespoonsful of butter or drippings.
- 2 cups of water, and salt and pepper.
- 1½ pounds of lean mutton or lamb cut into 2-inch pieces.

Fry the onions in the butter, add the meat, and brown; cover with water and cook until the meat is tender. Serve with a border of Lima beans, seasoned with salt, pepper, butter, and a little chopped parsley. Fresh, canned, dried, or evaporated Lima beans may be used in making this dish.

Roast Pork with Cowpeas.

For this dish a leg of young pork should be selected. With a sharp knife make a deep cut in the knuckle and fill the opening with sage, pepper, salt, and chopped onion. When the roast is half done scar the skin but do not cut deeper than the outer rind. When the meat is nearly cooked pour off the excess of fat and add a quart of *white* cowpeas which have been previously parboiled or "hulled" and cook slowly until quite done and the meat is brown. Apple sauce may be served with this dish.

Meat Salads.

Whether meat salads are economical or not depends upon the way in which the materials are utilized. If in chicken salad, for example, only the white meat of chickens especially bought for the purpose and only the inside stems of expensive celery are used, it can hardly be cheaper than plain chicken. But, if portions of meat left over from a previous serving are mixed with celery grown at home, they certainly make an economical dish, and one very acceptable to most persons. Cold roast pork or tender veal—in fact, any white meat can be utilized in the same way. Apples cut into cubes may be substituted for part of the celery; many cooks consider that with the apple the salad takes the dressing better than with the celery alone. Many also prefer to marinate (i. e., mix with a little oil and vinegar) the meat and celery or celery and apples before putting in the final dressing, which may be either mayonnaise or a good boiled dressing.

Meat with Eggs.

Occasionally eggs are combined with meat, making very nutritious dishes. Whether this is an economy or not of course depends on the comparative cost of eggs and meat.

In general, it may be said that eggs are cheaper food than meat when a dozen cost less than 1½ pounds of meat, for a dozen eggs weigh about 1½ pounds and the proportions of protein and fat which they contain are not far different from the proportions of these nutrients in the average cut of meat. When eggs are 30 cents a dozen they compare favorably with round of beef at 20 cents a pound.

Such common dishes as ham and eggs, bacon or salt pork and eggs, and omelette with minced ham or other meat are familiar to all cooks.

Roast Beef with Yorkshire Pudding.

The beef is roasted as usual and the pudding made as follows:

Yorkshire Pudding.

3 eggs.
1 pint milk.
1 cupful flour.
1 teaspoonful salt.

Beat the eggs until very light, then add the milk. Pour the mixture over the flour, add the salt, and beat well. Bake in hissing hot gem pans or in an ordinary baking pan for forty-five minutes, and baste with drippings from the beef. If gem pans are used, they should be placed on a dripping pan to protect the floor of the oven from the fat. Many cooks prefer to bake Yorkshire pudding in the pan with the meat; in this case the roast should be placed on a rack and the pudding batter poured on the pan under it.

Corned Beef Hash with Poached Eggs.

A dish popular with many persons is corned beef hash with poached eggs on top of the hash. A slice of toast is sometimes used under the hash. This suggests a way of utilizing the small amount of corned-beef hash which would otherwise be iusufficient for a meal.

Housekeepers occasionally use up odd bits of other meat in a similar way, chopping and seasoning them and then warming and serving in individual baking cups with a poached or shirred egg on each.

Ham and Poached Eggs with Cream Sauce.

A more elaborate dish of meat and eggs is made by placing a piece of thinly sliced boiled ham on a round of buttered toast, a poached egg on the ham, and covering with a highly seasoned cream or a Hollandaise sauce. A slice of tongue may be used instead of the ham. If preferred, a well-seasoned and rather thick tomato sauce or curry sauce may be used.

Stuffing or Forcemeat.

Another popular way to extend the flavor of meat over a large amount of food is by the use of stuffing or forcemeat (a synonym more common in England than in the United States). As it is impossible to introduce much stuffing into some pieces of meat even if the meat is cut to make a pocket for it, it is often well to prepare more than can be put into the meat and to cook the remainder in the pan beside the meat. Some cooks cover the extra stuffing with buttered paper while it is cooking and baste it at intervals.

Some recipes for meat dishes of this character follow, and others will be found in cookbooks.

Mock Duck.

Mock duck is made by placing on a round steak a stuffing of bread crumbs well seasoned with chopped onions, butter, chopped suet or dripping, salt, pepper, and a little sage, if the flavor is relished. The steak is then rolled around the stuffing and tied with a string in several places. If the steak seems tough, the roll is steamed or stewed until tender before roasting in the oven until brown. Or it may be cooked in a casserole or other covered dish, in which case a cupful or more of water or soupstock should be poured around the meat. Mock duck is excellent served with currant or other acid jelly.

Mock Wild Duck.

- 1 flank steak, or
- 1½ pounds round steak cut ½-inch thick.
- 2 lamb kidneys.
- ¼ cup butter or drippings.
- ½ cup cracker crumbs.
- 1 tablespoonful minced onion.
- Salt, pepper, and powdered thyme, sage, and savory.
- 2 tablespoonsful flour.
- 1 tablespoonful sugar.
- 3 cupfuls water or stock.

Trim the kidneys of all fat, cords, and veins. Cut into small pieces and spread evenly over one side of the steak together with the crumbs, onion, and seasonings. Roll and tie with a cord. Brown the roll in fat, then remove and make a gravy by heating the flour in the fat and adding three cupfuls of stock or water and the sugar. Put the meat into the gravy and cook slowly until tender in a covered baking dish, a steamer, or a fireless cooker. If steamed or cooked in a fireless cooker, the roll should be browned in the oven before serving.

Veal or Beef Birds.

A popular dish known as veal or beef birds or by a variety of special names is made by taking small pieces of meat, each just large enough for an individual serving, and preparing them in the same way as the mock duck is prepared.

Sometimes variety is introduced by seasoning the stuffing with chopped olives or tomato. Many cooks prepare their "birds" by browning in a little fat, then adding a little water, covering closely and simmering until tender.

UTILIZING THE CHEAPER CUTS OF MEAT IN PALATABLE DISHES

When the housekeeper attempts to reduce her meat bill by using the less expensive cuts, she commonly has two difficulties to contend with—toughness and lack of flavor. It has been shown how prolonged cooking softens the connective tissues of the meat. Pounding the meat and chopping it are also employed with tough cuts, as they help to break the muscle fibers. As for flavor, the natural flavor of meat even in the least desirable cuts may be developed by careful cooking, notably by browning the surface, and other flavors may be given by the addition of vegetables and seasoning with condiments of various kinds.

Methods of preparing inexpensive meat dishes will be discussed and practical directions for them will be given in the following sections. As often happens, two or three methods may be illustrated by the same dish, but the attempt has been made to group the recipes according to their most salient feature.

Prolonged Cooking at Low Heat.

Meat may be cooked in water in a number of ways without being allowed to reach the boiling point. With the ordinary kitchen range this is accomplished by cooking on the cooler part of the stove rather than on the hottest part, directly over the fire. Experience with a gas stove, particularly if it has a small burner known as a "simmerer," usually enables the cook to maintain temperatures which are high enough to sterilize the meat if it has become accidentally contaminated in any way and to make it tender without hardcuing the fibers. The double boiler would seem to be a neglected utensil for this purpose. Its contents can easily be kept up to a temperature of 200° F., and nothing will burn. Another method is by means of the fireless cooker. In this a high temperature can be maintained for a long time without the application of fresh heat. Still another method is by means of a closely covered baking dish. Earthenware dishes of this kind suitable for serving foods as well as for cooking are known as casseroles. For cooking purposes a baking dish covered with a plate or a bean jar covered with a saucer may be substituted. The Aladdin oven has long been popular for the purpose of preserving temperatures which are near the boiling point and yet do not reach it. It is a thoroughly insulated oven which may be heated by a kerosene lamp or a gas jet.

In this connection directions are given for using some of the toughest and least promising pieces of meat.

Stewed Shin of Beef.

4 pounds of shin of beef.
1 medium sized onion.
1 whole clove and a small bay leaf.
1 sprig of parsley.
1½ tablespoonfuls of flour.
1 small slice of carrot.
½ tablespoonful of salt.
½ teaspoonful of pepper.
2 quarts of boiling water.
1½ tablespoonfuls of butter or savory drippings.

Have the butcher cut the bone in several pieces. Put all the ingredients but the flour and butter into a stewpan and bring to a boil. Set the pan where the liquid will just simmer for six hours, or after boiling for five or ten minutes, put all into the fireless cooker for eight or nine hours. With the butter, flour, and one-half cupful of the clear soup from which the fat has been removed, make a brown sauce; to this add the meat, the marrow removed from the bone. Heat and serve. The remainder of the liquid in which the meat has been cooked may be used for soup.

Boiled Beef with Horse-radish Sauce.

Plain boiled beef may also be served with horse-radish sauce, and makes a palatable dish. A little chopped parsley sprinkled over the meat when served is considered an improvement by many persons. For the sake of variety the meat may be browned like pot roast before serving.

Scotch Broth.

3 pounds mutton.
2 tablespoonsful of pearl barley.
2 tablespoonsful of minced onion.
2 tablespoonsful of minced turnip.
2 tablespoonsful of minced carrot.
2 tablespoonsful of minced celery.
2 tablespoonsful of salt.
1 teaspoonful of pepper.
1 tablespoonful of minced parsley.
3 quarts cold water.

Remove the bones and all the fat from the mutton, cut the meat into small pieces and put it into a stewpan with the water, chopped vegetables, barley, and all the seasoning excepting the parsley. It will be found convenient to tie the bones in a piece of thin white cloth before adding them to the other ingredients. Bring the stew to a boil, quickly skim it and allow it to simmer for three hours, thicken with the flour, and add the chopped parsley.

Stuffed Heart.

Wash the heart thoroughly inside and out, stuff with the following mixture, and sew up the opening: One cup broken bread dipped in fat and browned in the oven, 1 chopped onion, and salt and pepper to taste.

Cover the heart with water and simmer until tender or boil ten minutes and set in the fireless cooker for six or eight hours. Remove from the water about one-half hour before serving. Dredge with flour, pepper, and salt, or sprinkle with crumbs and bake until brown.

Braised Beef, Pot Roast, and Beef à la Mode.

The above names are given to dishes made from the less tender cuts of meat. They vary little either in composition or method of preparation. In all cases the meat is browned on the outside to increase the flavor and then cooked in a small amount of water in a closely covered kettle or other receptacle until tender. The flavor of the dish is secured by browning the meat and by the addition of the seasoning vegetables. Many recipes suggest that the vegetables be removed before serving and the liquid be thickened. As the vegetables are usually extremely well seasoned by means of the browned fat and the extracts of the meat, it seems unfortunate not to serve them.

Of course, the kind, quality, and shape of the meat all play their part in the matter. Extra time is needed for meats with a good deal of sinew and tough fibers such as the tough steaks, shank cuts, etc.; and naturally a fillet of beef, or a steak from a prime cut, will take less time than a thick piece from the shin. Such dishes require more time and perhaps more skill in their preparation and may involve more expense for fuel than the more costly cuts, which like chops or tender steaks may be quickly cooked, but to the epicure, as well as to the average man, they are palatable when rightly prepared.

Bean-pot Roast.

3 pounds mutton (shoulder), or
3 pounds round, or chuck steak.
1 cup carrots cut into small pieces.
1 cup potatoes cut into small pieces.
¼ cup sliced onion.

Cover the meat with boiling water. Place the cover on the bean pot and let the meat cook in a moderate oven for two hours; then add the vegetables cut in half-inch cubes, with 2 teaspoonfuls salt; cook until the vegetables are tender, which will require about one hour; then serve, pouring a sauce over the meat, made from 1 cup of the liquid in which the meat was cooked, thickened with 2 tablespoonsful of flour.

Hungarian Goulash.

2 pounds top round of beef.
A little flour.
2 ounces salt pork.
2 cups tomatoes.
1 stalk celery.
1 onion.
2 bay leaves.
6 whole cloves.
6 peppercorns.
1 blade mace.

Cut the beef into 2-inch pieces and sprinkle with flour; fry the salt pork until light brown; add the beef and cook slowly for about thirty-five minutes, stirring occasionally. Cover with water and simmer about two hours; season with salt and pepper or paprika.

From the vegetables and spices a sauce is made as follows: Cook in sufficient water to cover for twenty minutes; then rub through a sieve, and add to some of the stock in which the meat was cooked. Thicken with flour, using 2 tablespoonsful (moistened with cold water) to each cup of liquid, and season with salt and paprika.

Serve the meat on a platter with the sauce poured over it. Potatoes, carrots, and green peppers cooked until tender, and cut into small pieces or narrow strips, are usually sprinkled over the dish when served, and noodles may be arranged in a border upon the platter.

Goulash is a Hungarian dish which has come to be a favorite in the United States.

Casserole Cookery.

A casserole is a heavy earthenware dish with a cover. A substitute for it can easily be improvised by using any heavy earthenware dish with a heavy plate for the cover. A casserole presentable enough in appearance to be put on the table serves the double purpose of baking and serving dish.

A suitable cut of beef or veal, and it may well be one of the cheaper cuts, as the long, slow cooking insures tenderness, may be cooked in a casserole.

Poultry and other meats besides beef or veal can be cooked in this manner. Chicken cooked in a casserole, which is a favorite and expensive dish in good hotels and restaurants, may be easily prepared in the home, and casserole cookery is to be recommended for tough chicken.

The heat must be moderate and the cooking must occupy a long time. Hurried cooking in a casserole is out of the question. If care is taken in this particular, and suitable seasonings are used, few who know anything of cooking should go astray.

Chopped meat also may be cooked in a casserole and this utensil is particularly useful for the purpose, because the food is served in the same dish in which it is cooked and may easily be kept hot, a point which is important with chopped meats, which usually cool rapidly.

Casserole Roast.

3 or 4 pounds of round or rump of beef.
A slice of salt pork.
A few peppercorns.
One-fourth each of a carrot, a turnip, an onion, and a head of celery cut into small pieces.

Try out the pork. Brown the meat on both sides in the fat. Put in a casserole with the vegetables around it, add 2 cupsful of water or stock. Cover and cook in a hot oven three hours, basting occasionally. A sauce or gravy can be made with water, flour, and some of the juice left in the casserole.

Casserole or Italian Hash.

Boil one-fourth pound of macaroni, drain and put into a buttered casserole, add a little butter and grated cheese. Push the macaroni to the sides of the dish and fill the center with chopped cooked meat seasoned to suit the taste of the family. A little sausage gives a good flavor to this dish. Place in the oven until hot throughout and serve.

A very good modification of this is made by using raw instead of cooked meat. For this one-half pound of round steak is sufficient for a family of six. This should be cut into small pieces, browned, and cooked until tender in water with the onions and other seasonings. An hour before the cooking is complete, add one-half can of tomatoes. Before serving, the meat may be mixed with the sauce, and the whole is poured over the macaroni.

MEAT COOKED WITH VINEGAR

Dishes of similar sort as regards cooking, but in which vinegar is used to give flavor as well as to soften the meat and make it tender, are the following:

Sour Beef.

Take a piece of beef from the rump or the lower round, cover with vinegar or with a half-and-half mixture of vinegar and water, add sliced onion, bay leaves, and a few mixed whole spices and salt. Allow to stand a week in winter or three or four days in summer; turn once a day and keep covered. When ready to cook, brown the meat in fat, using an enameled iron pan, strain the liquid over it and cook until tender; thicken the gravy with flour or ginger snaps (which may be broken up first), strain it, and pour over the sliced meat. Some cooks add cream.

Sour Beefsteak.

Round steak may be cooked in water in which there is a little vinegar, or if the time is sufficient, it may be soaked for a few hours in vinegar and water and then cooked in a casserole or in some similar way.

POUNDED MEAT

Pounding meat before cooking is an old-fashioned method of making it tender, but while it has the advantage of breaking down the tough tissues it has the disadvantage of being likely to drive out the juices and with them the flavor. A very good way of escaping this difficulty is pounding flour into the meat; this catches and retains the juices. Below are given the recipes for two palatable dishes in which this is done:

Farmer Stew.

Pound flour into both sides of a round steak, using as much as the meat will take up. This may be done with a meat pounder or with the edge of a heavy plate. Fry in drippings, butter, or other fat in a Scotch bowl, or if more convenient in an ordinary iron kettle or a frying pan; then add water enough to cover it. Cover the dish very tightly so that the steam can not escape and allow the meat to simmer for two hours or until it is tender. One advantage of this dish is that ordinarily it is ready to serve when the meat is done as the gravy is already thickened. However, if a large amount of fat is used in the frying, the gravy may not be thick enough and must be blended with flour.

Spanish Beefsteak.

Take a piece of round steak weighing 2 pounds and about an inch thick; pound until thin, season with salt and Cayenne pepper, cover with a layer of bacon or salt pork, cut into thin slices, roll and tie with a cord. Pour around it half a cupful of milk and half a cupful of water. Place in a covered baking dish and cook two hours, basting occasionally.

CHOPPED MEAT

Chopping meat is one of the principal methods of making tough and inexpensive meat tender, i. e., dividing it finely and thus cutting the connective tissue into small bits. Such meats have another advantage in that they may be cooked quickly and economically.

In broiling chopped meat the fact should be kept in mind that there is no reason why it should not be cooked like the best and most expensive tenderloin. The only reason that ever existed for difference in treatment was the toughness of the connective tissue, and this feature has been overcome by the chopping. The ideal to be reached in broiling steak is to sear the surface very quickly, so that the juices which contain the greater part of the flavoring of the meat shall be kept in, and then to allow the heat to penetrate to the inside until the whole mass is cooked to the taste of the family. To pass the point where the meat ceases to be puffy and juicy and becomes flat and hard is very undesirable, as the palatability is then lost. Exactly the same ideal should be kept in mind in broiling chopped meat. If this were always done, hard, compact, tasteless balls or cakes of meat would be served less often. To begin with, the broiler should be even more carefully greased than for a whole steak. This makes it possible to form the balls or cakes of chopped meat with very little pressure without running the risk of having them pulled to pieces by adhering to the wires of the broiler. They should be heated on both sides even more quickly than the steak, because the chopping has provided more ways of escape for the juice, and these openings should be sealed as soon as possible. The interior should be cooked to the taste of the family just as the steak is.

In regard to broiling it may incidentally be noted that housekeepers often make themselves unnecessary work when broiling under gas by allowing the juice from steaks or meat balls to drop into the large pan under the rack. A smaller pan set in the larger one may be made to catch all the juice and fat and is much easier to wash. It serves also to economize the gravy.

Chopped raw meat of almost any kind can be very quickly made into a savory dish by cooking it with water or with water and milk for a short time, then thickening with butter and flour, and adding different seasonings as relished, either pepper and salt alone, or onion juice, celery, or tomato. Such a dish may be made to "go further" by serving it on toast or with a border of rice or in some similar combination.

Tough Portions of Porterhouse Steak.

Before speaking of the cooking of the cuts that lack tenderness throughout, it may be well to refer to the fact that the flank end of the porterhouse is to be classed with the toughest of cuts and with those which, when cooked alone, are with difficulty made tender even by long heating. Mock duck, which is commonly made out of flank steak, can be rendered tender enough to be palatable only by long steaming or cooking in water and yet people quite generally broil this part of the steak with the tenderloin and expect it to be eaten. The fact is that to broil this part of the porterhouse steak is not good management. It is much more profitable to put it into the soup kettle or to make it into a stew. In families where most of the members are away during the day the latter is a good plan, for the end of a steak makes a good stew for two or three people. This may be seasoned with vegetables left from dinner, or two or three olives cut up in gravy will give a very good flavor; or a few drops of some one of the bottled meat sauces, if the flavor is relished, or a little Chili sauce may be added to the stew. But if the tough end of a porterhouse is needed with the rest, a good plan is to put it through a meat grinder, make it into balls, and broil it with the tender portions. Each member of the family can then be served with a piece of the tenderloin and a meat ball. If the chopped meat is seasoned with a little onion juice, grated lemon rind, or chopped parsley, a good flavor is imparted to the gravy.

Hamburg Steak.

This name is commonly given to inexpensive cuts of beef chopped, seasoned a little, shaped into small balls or into one large thin cake, and quickly broiled in the way that a tender steak would be. Owing to the quick cooking much of the natural flavor of the meat is developed and retained. The fact should be kept in mind that Hamburg steak must be made from fresh, well-ground meat. It is much safer to chop the meat at home, as chopped meat spoils very quickly. Much depends, too, upon browning it sufficiently to bring out the flavors. Many cooks think that Hamburg steak is improved if the meat is mixed with milk before it is cooked.

In some parts of the country, and particularly in some of the Southern States, two kinds of beef are on sale. One is imported from other parts of the country and is of higher price. The other, known locally as "native beef," is sometimes lacking in flavor and in fat and is usually tougher. Southern native beef such as is raised in Florida is almost invariably, however, of extremely good flavor, due presumably to the feed or other conditions under which it is raised. By chopping such meat and cooking it as Hamburg steak, a dish almost as palatable as the best cuts of the more expensive beef may be obtained. In such cases, however, it is desirable because of the low percentage of fat to add suet or butter to the meat. The reason for this is that in the cooking the water of the juice when unprotected by fat evaporates too quickly and leaves the meat dry. This may be prevented by adding egg as well as fat, for the albumen of the egg hardens quickly and tends to keep in the juices. The proportion should be 1 egg to 1½ pounds of meat.

Savory Rolls.

Savory rolls in great variety are made out of chopped meat either with or without egg. The variety is secured by the flavoring materials used and by the sauces with which the baked rolls are served. A few recipes will be given below. While these definite directions are given it should be remembered that a few general principles borne in mind make recipes unnecessary and make it possible to utilize whatever may happen to be on hand. Appetizing rolls are made with beef and pork mixed. The proportion varies from two parts of beef and one of pork to two of pork and one of beef. The rolls are always improved by laying thin slices of salt pork or bacon over them, which keep the surface moistened with fat during the roasting. These slices should be scored on the edge, so that they will not curl up in cooking. The necessity for the salt pork is greater when the chopped meat is chiefly beef than when it is largely pork or veal. Bread crumbs or bread moistened in water can always be added, as it helps to make the dish go farther. When onions, green peppers, or other vegetables are used, they should always be thoroughly cooked in fat before being put in the roll, for usually they do not cook sufficiently in the length of time it takes to cook the meat. Sausage makes a good addition to the roll, but it is usually cheaper to use unseasoned pork meat with the addition of a little sage.

Cannelon of Beef.

This dish is prepared by making chopped beef into a roll and baking it wrapped in a buttered paper, a method designed to keep in the steam and so insure a moist, tender dish. The paper must be removed before serving. The roll should be basted occasionally with butter and water or drippings and water. In preparing the roll an egg may be added for each pound and a half of meat, and chopped parsley, onion juice, lemon peel, or finely chopped green peppers make good seasoning. A thickened gravy may be made from the drippings, the liquid used being either water or tomato juice.

Strips of pork laid on the roll may be substituted for the buttered paper and basting.

Filipino Beef.

1 pound round beef.
½ pound lean fresh pork.
1 small onion.

1 green pepper.
1 teaspoonful of salt.
1 cup of soft stale bread crumbs.
1 egg.
2 cups of stewed tomatoes.
2 slices of bacon.
2 tablespoonfuls of butter.
4 tablespoonfuls of flour.

Remove the seeds from the pepper and put it through the meat grinder with the meats and the onion. Add crumbs, egg, and salt. Make into a roll, place in a shallow baking dish, pour the strained tomatoes around it, put the bacon on top, and bake forty minutes, basting with the tomatoes. Thicken the gravy with the flour cooked in the butter. A little seasoning such as a bit of bay leaf, a clove, and a small piece of onion improves the tomato sauce. As the pepper and onion are not likely to be cooked as soon as the meat, it is well to fry them in a little fat before adding to the other ingredients.

This dish will serve 6 to 8 people. When the meat is 20 cents a pound and every other item is valued at usual town market prices, the dish costs about 50 cents. If the meat costs only 10 cents per pound and vegetables from the garden are used the initial cost of the dish will be small. Since no vegetable except potatoes or rice need be served with this dish, it may be said to answer the purpose of both meat and vegetable.

Mock Rabbit.

½ pound round steak, and
1 pound sausage;
or
1 pound round steak, and
½ pound sausage meat.
3 slices of bread moistened with water.
1 egg.
1 onion.
¼ pound salt pork.
Pepper and salt.

Chop the meat. Chop the onion and cook (but do not brown) it in the fat tried out of a small portion of the pork. Add the bread and cook a few minutes. When this is cool, mix all the ingredients and form into a long round roll. The surface can easily be made smooth if the hand is wet with cold water. Lay the remaining pork cut in thin slices on top and bake forty minutes in a hot oven. The sausage may be omitted if desired and other seasoning used.

Veal Loaf.

3 pounds veal.
1 pound salt pork.
6 soda crackers rolled fine.
3 eggs well beaten.
¼ teaspoonful pepper.
½ teaspoonful salt.

Chop the meat mixed with the other ingredients, shape, and bake three hours, basting occasionally with pork fat. Use one-fourth cut of fat for this purpose. If the roll is pierced occasionally the fat will penetrate more effectually. Veal loaf may also be cooked in bread pans. Some persons cook the veal before chopping.

DEVELOPING AND IMPROVING FLAVOR OF MEAT

The typical meat flavors are very palatable to most persons, even when they are constantly tasted, and consequently the better cuts of meat in which they are well developed can be cooked and served without attention being paid especially to flavor. Careful cooking aids in developing the natural flavor of some of the cheaper cuts, and such a result is to be sought wherever it is possible. Browning also brings out flavors agreeable to most palates. Aside from these two ways of increasing the flavor of the meat itself there are countless ways of adding flavor to otherwise rather tasteless meats.

The flavors may be added in preparing the meat for cooking, as in various seasoned dishes already described, or they may be supplied to cooked meat in the form of sauces.

Retaining Natural Flavor.

As has already been pointed out, it is extremely difficult to retain the flavor-giving extractives in a piece of meat so tough as to require prolonged cooking. It is sometimes partially accomplished by first searing the exterior of the meat and thus preventing the escape of the juices. Another device, illustrated by the following recipe, is to let them escape into the gravy which is served with the meat itself. A similar principle is applied when roasts are basted with their own juice.

Round Steak on Biscuits.

Cut round steak into pieces about one-half inch square, cover with water and cook it at a temperature just below the boiling point until it is tender, or boil for five minutes, and while still hot put into the fireless cooker and leave it for five hours. Thicken the gravy with flour mixed with water allowing 2 level tablespoonsful to a cup of water. Pour the meat and gravy over split baking powder biscuits so baked that they have a large amount of crust.

Flavor of Browned Meat or Fat.

Next to the unchanged flavor of the meat itself comes the flavor which is secured by browning the meat with fat. The outside slices of roast meat have this browned flavor in marked degree. Except in the case of roasts, browning for flavor is usually accomplished by heating the meat in a frying pan in fat which has been tried out of pork or in suet or butter. Care should be taken that the fat is not scorched. The chief reason for the bad opinion in which fried food is held by many is that it almost always means eating burned fat. When fat is heated too high it splits up into fatty acids and glycerin, and from the glycerin is formed a substance (acrolein) which has a very irritating effect upon the mucous membrane. All will recall that the fumes of scorched fat make the eyes water. It is not surprising that such a substance, if taken into the stomach, should cause digestive disturbance. Fat in itself is a very valuable food, and the objection to fried foods because they may be fat seems illogical. If they supply burned fat there is a good reason for suspicion. Many housekeepers cook bacon in the oven on a wire broiler over a pan and believe it more wholesome than fried bacon. The reason, of course, is that thus cooked in the oven there is less chance for the bacon becoming impregnated with burned fat. Where fried salt pork is much used good cooks know that it must not be cooked over a very hot fire, even if they have never heard of the chemistry of burned fat. The recipe for bean-pot roast and other similar recipes may be varied by browning the meat or part of it before covering with water. This results in keeping some of the natural flavoring within the meat itself and allowing less to go into the gravy. The flavor of veal can be very greatly improved in this way.

The following old-fashioned dishes made with pork owe their savoriness chiefly to the flavor of browned fat or meat:

Salt Pork with Milk Gravy.

Cut salt or cured pork into thin slices. If very salt, cover with hot water and allow it to stand for ten minutes. Score the rind of the slices and fry slowly until they are a golden brown. Make a milk gravy by heating flour in the fat that has been tried out, allowing 2 tablespoonsful of fat and 2 tablespoonsful of flour to each cup of milk.

This is a good way to use skim milk, which is as rich in protein as whole milk. The pork and milk gravy served with boiled or baked potatoes makes a cheap and simple meal, but one that most people like very much. Bacon is often used in place of salt pork in making this dish.

Fried Salt Pork with Salt Codfish or "Salt-Fish Dinner."

½ pound salt pork.
1 pound codfish.
2 cups of milk (skim milk will do).
4 tablespoonsful flour.
A speck of salt.

Cut the codfish into strips, soak in lukewarm water and then cook in water until tender but do not allow the water to come to the boiling point except for a very short time as prolonged boiling may make it tough. Cut the pork into one-fourth inch slices and cut several gashes in each piece. Fry very slowly until golden brown, and remove, pouring off the fat. Out of 4 tablespoonsful of the fat, the flour, and the milk make a white sauce. Dish up the codfish with pieces of pork around it and serve with boiled potatoes and beets. Some persons serve the pork, and the fat from it, in a gravy boat so it can be added as relished.

Flavoring Vegetables, Herbs, Spices, Etc.

Many flavorings are used in meat dishes, some of which are familiar to all cooks—onions, carrots, turnips, and garlic being perhaps the most widely known. Butter, too, may be regarded as one of the most common seasonings, and of course makes the dish richer. Meat extract is also used for flavoring many meat dishes and other foods, as are also, though less commonly, similar extracts made from clams or other "sea food." The following list includes these with various others, a number of which it is convenient to keep always on hand: Onions, carrots, green peppers, parsnips, turnips, tomatoes, fresh, canned or dried; celery tops and parsley, either fresh or dried; sage, savory, thyme, sweet marjoram, bay leaf, garlic, lemon rind, vinegar, capers, pickles, olives, currant jelly, curry powder, cloves, pepper corns, celery seed, meat extract, Chili sauce, pepper sauce or some similar hot or sharp sauce, and some kind of good commercial meat sauce. Some hints regarding the use of such flavorings follow:

Flavor of Fried Vegetables.—Most of the stews, soups, braised meats, and pot roasts are very much improved if the flavoring vegetables which they contain, such as carrots, turnips, onions, celery, or green peppers, are fried in a little fat before being cooked with the meat. This need not complicate the preparation of the meat or increase the number of utensils used, for the meat itself is usually seared over in fat, and the vegetables can be cooked in the same fat before the browning of the meat.

Onion Juice. — Cookbooks usually say that onion juice should be extracted by cutting an onion in two and rubbing the cut surface against a grater. Considering how hard it is to wash a grater, this method has its drawbacks. Small amounts of juice may be obtained in the following simpler way: Peel the onion and extract a few drops of juice by pressing one side with the dull edge of a knife.

Green Peppers. — The flavor of green peppers gives an acceptable variety. The seed should always be removed. The peppers should be chopped and added to chopped meat or other meat dishes. Meat mixed with bread crumbs may be baked in the pepper shells and the stuffed peppers served as a separate dish.

Parsley.—It is easy to raise parsley by growing it in a pot in the kitchen window and thus to have it always on hand fresh, or the leaves may be kept for a long time if sealed up in a fruit jar and stored in a cool place.

Parsley, mint, and celery tops may all be dried, rubbed into fine bits, and kept in air-tight jars. Recipes usually say to chop fresh parsley with a sharp knife on a board. But a board is a hard thing to wash and a plate serves the purpose quite as well.

Bay Leaf.—Bay leaf is one of the best and at the same time one of the most abused flavors. In small quantities it gives a very pleasant flavor to soups and gravies but in large quantities it gives a rank resin-like taste. Remember that half of a bay leaf is the allowance for 3 quarts of soup stock. This will indicate how small a quantity should be used for the portion of gravy usually served at a meal. With this precaution in mind, bay leaf may be recommended as a flavoring for many sauces, particularly tomato sauce.

A Kitchen Bouquet.—A "bouquet" such as is often referred to in recipes may be made as follows: A sprig each of parsley, savory, and thyme, one small leaf of sage, and a bay leaf. This will flavor 1 gallon of soup when cooked in it for an hour and should not remain in it longer.

Horse Radish.—Horse radish, like mustard, is more often served with meat than used to flavor it during cooking. A very palatable sauce, especially good with boiled beef, is made by adding grated horse radish and a little vinegar to a little whipped cream, or as follows: Thicken milk with cracker crumbs by heating them together in a double boiler, using 3 tablespoonsful of cracker crumbs to 1½ cups of milk. Add one-third of a cup of grated horse radish, 3 tablespoonsful of butter, and one-half teaspoonful of salt; or thicken with butter and flour some of the water in which the meat was boiled, add a generous quantity (1 or 2 tablespoonsful) of grated horse radish, boil a short time, and serve. This recipe is the most usual in German homes where the sauce is a favorite.

Acid Flavoring.—Vinegar, lemon juice, and sour jelly, like currant, are often used to flavor the thick gravies which are a part of meat stew or which are served with it. Vinegar is an old-fashioned relish which was often added to bacon or salt pork and greens, pork and beans, corned beef and cabbage, and similar dishes. These flavors combine well with that of brown flour, but not with onions or other vegetables of strong flavor. The idea that vinegar used in small quantities is unwholesome seems to be without foundation.

Pickles.—Chopped pickles are sometimes added to the gravy served with boiled mutton. They are cheaper than capers and serve somewhat the same purpose. Chopped pickles are also very commonly used in sauces for fish and in many others to give a distinctive flavor.

Olives.—Chopped olives also make a welcome variety in meat sauce, and are not expensive if they are bought in bulk. They will not spoil if a little olive oil is poured on the top of the liquor in which they are kept. This liquor should always completely cover them.

Chili Sauce, Commercial Meat Sauces, Etc.—Recipes often may be varied by the addition of a little Chili sauce, tomato catsup, or a commercial meat sauce. These may be called emergency flavors and used when it is not convenient to prepare other kinds of gravies.

Sausage. — A little sausage or chopped ham may be used in chopped beef.

Curry Powder.—This mixture of spices which apparently originated in India, but which is now a common commercial product everywhere, is a favorite flavoring for veal, lamb, or poultry. The precaution mentioned in connection with bay leaves, however, should be observed. A small amount gives a good flavor. It is usually used to season the thick sauces with which meats are served or in which they are allowed to simmer. While the term "curry" is usually employed to describe a particular mixture of spices made up for the trade it has another meaning. The words "curry" or "curried" are sometimes used to describe highly seasoned dishes of meat, eggs, or vegetables prepared by methods that have come from India or other parts of the East.

India Curry.

1½ pounds veal.
½ cup of butter or drippings.
2 onions or less.
½ tablespoonful curry or less.

Brown meat either without fat or with very little and cut into small pieces.

Fry the onions in the butter, remove them, add the meat and curry powder. Cover the meat with boiling water and cook until tender. Serve with a border of rice. This dish is so savory that it can be made to go a long way by serving with a large amount of rice. The two onions and one-half tablespoonful of curry powder are the largest amount to be used. Many persons prefer less of each.

In preparing the rice for this dish perhaps no better method can be given than the following:

"Wash 1 cupful of rice in several waters, rubbing the grains between the hands to remove all the dirt. Put the washed rice in a stewpan with 2½ cupsful of water and 1 teaspoonful of salt. Cover and place where the water will boil. Cook for twenty minutes, being careful not to let it burn. At the end of this time put the stewpan on a tripod or ring and cover the rice with a fold of cheese cloth. Let it continue to cook in this manner an hour, then turn into a hot vegetable dish. The rice will be tender, dry and sweet, and each grain will separate. During the whole process of cooking, the rice must not be stirred. If a tablespoonful of butter is cut up and scattered over the rice when it has cooked twenty minutes the dish will be very much improved."

The butter is not necessary when the rice is served with India curry but may be included in dishes where less fat is used.

Curry of Veal.

2 tablespoonfuls butter or drippings.
1½ pounds veal.
½ onion, chopped.
1 pint milk.
1 tablespoonful flour.
1 teaspoonful curry powder.
Salt and pepper.

Fry the onions in the butter or drippings, remove, and fry the veal until it is brown. Transfer the meat to the double boiler, cover with milk and cook until the meat is tender. Add the curry powder a short time before the meat is done and thicken the milk with flour before serving.

SAUCES

The art of preparing savory gravies and sauces is more important in connection with the serving of the cheaper meats than in connection with the cooking of the more expensive.

There are a few general principles underlying the making of all sauces or gravies, whether the liquid used is water, milk, stock, tomato juice, or some combination of these. For ordinary gravy 2 level tablespoonsful of flour or 1½ tablespoonsful of cornstarch or arrowroot is sufficient to thicken a cupful of liquid. This is true excepting when, as in certain recipes given elsewhere, the flour is browned. In this case about one-half tablespoonful more should be allowed, for browned flour does not thicken so well as unbrowned. The fat used may be butter or the drippings from the meat, the allowance being 2 tablespoonsful to a cup of liquid.

The easiest way to mix the ingredients is to heat the fat, add the flour, and cook until the mixture ceases to bubble, and then to add the liquid. This is a quick method and by using it there is little danger of getting a lumpy gravy. Many persons, however, think it is not a wholesome method and prefer the old-fashioned one of thickening the gravy by means of flour mixed with a little cold water. The latter method is of course not practicable for brown gravies.

Considering the large amount of discussion about the digestibility of fried food and of gravies made by heating flour in fat, a few words on the subject at this point may not be out of order. It is difficult to see how heating the fat before adding the flour can be unwholesome, unless the cook is unskillful enough to heat the fat so high that it begins to scorch. Overheated fat, as has already been pointed out, contains an acrid irritating substance called "acrolein," which may be readily considered to be unwholesome. It is without doubt the production of this body by overheating which has given fried food its bad name. Several ways of varying the flavor of gravies and sauces were suggested in the preceding section. One other should be especially mentioned here.

The Flavor of Browned Flour.

The good flavor of browned flour is often overlooked. If flour is cooked in fat until it is a dark brown color a distinctive and very agreeable flavor is obtained. This flavor combines very well with that of currant jelly and a little jelly added to a brown gravy is a great improvement. The flavor of this should not be combined with that of onions or other highly flavored vegetables. A recipe for a dish which is made with brown sauce follows:

Mock Venison.

Cut cold mutton into thin slices and heat in a brown sauce made according to the following proportions:

2 tablespoonsful butter.
2 tablespoonsful flour.
1 tablespoonful of bottled meat sauce (whichever is preferred).
1 tablespoonful red currant jelly.
1 cupful water or stock.

Brown the flour in the butter, add the water or stock slowly, and keep stirring. Then add the jelly and meat sauce and let the mixture boil up well.

APPENDIX CHAPTER II

CHEESE AND ITS ECONOMICAL USES IN THE DIET *

By

C. F. LANGWORTHY, Ph.D.

Expert in Charge of Nutrition Investigations, Office of Experiment Stations

AND

CAROLINE L. HUNT, A.B.

Expert in Nutrition, Office of Experiment Stations

KINDS OF CHEESE USED IN AMERICAN HOMES

The American factory cheese—the so-called American cream cheese—is of the English Cheddar type, and as it is the most commonly used of all the commercial varieties in the United States, may be taken as a standard. Other types are, however, well known, particularly in cities and large towns where there are well stocked markets and stores, and it is interesting to note also, at least briefly, the characteristics of some of them.

Cheddar and American Full Cream Cheese.

Cheddar cheese—named from the English village where it originated—is a comparatively old type of cheese, very popular in England and also in the United States. The name is now more fitly applied to a process than to any particular shape.

Cheddar cheese is made from sweet cows' milk, which may be skimmed, partly skimmed, or unskimmed. If made from unskimmed milk the cheese is called "full cream." If cream is removed the cheese is designated "part-skim" or "skim," as the case may be.

Cheese of Cheddar type as made in the United States is perhaps most often marketed in large, flat, round forms, 13 to 16 inches in diameter, about 5 or 6 inches in height, and weighing 26 to 32 pounds each, though other shapes and sizes are also fairly common. It is usually pale to darker yellow in color, though it may be white when uncolored. When fresh it is mild in flavor, but when well ripened has a characteristic and sharp taste. The new cheese is soft, though not waxy, in texture, and may be easily shaved or broken into small pieces. When well ripened it may be finely grated.

These characteristics, together with its distinctive and peculiar flavor and its wide distribution in the markets, are qualities which help to make it the variety most commonly used in the United States.

Sage cheese is a variety of Cheddar cheese, which is flavored with sage and is further characterized by the green mottled appearance formerly due to bits of sage leaf but now generally obtained in another way.

English Dairy Cheese.

From the standpoint of the cook who frequently wishes to use grated cheese this variety is important.

* U. S. Department of Agriculture. Farmers' Bulletin No. 487.

Though made in much the same way as Cheddar, it differs from it, in that the curd is heated to a somewhat higher temperature, and the cheese is therefore harder. It commonly sells for somewhat more per pound than the standard or American factory variety and is likely to be found only in the larger markets.

Soft Cream Cheeses.

Cream cheese true to name is made from rich cream thickened by souring or from sweet cream thickened with rennet. The whey is removed by draining. It is then covered, salted, and turned occasionally, being ready for market in 5 to 10 days. A variety is also made with rennet from cream of low fat content, as well as a number of other special sorts much more common in France than in the United States.

The term "cream cheese," however, is an elastic one and includes many varieties which are sold under special trade names. Such cheese is common in most markets.

Soft cream cheese differs from standard cheese, so far as composition is concerned, in having more water and fat and less protein, water usually making up about one-half of the total weight. It differs also in being much more perishable. These cheeses commonly sell for 10 or 15 cents each, which is about 40 to 50 cents a pound.

Of late there have been on the market varieties of such cheese or of Neufchâtel, made by combining the cheese with chopped pimiento. These bring a relatively high price in market and may be easily prepared at home if this seems more convenient.

Neufchâtel Cheese.

This very popular variety—named from a town in northeastern France —is similar in appearance and in the way it is marketed to soft cream cheese. It is made either from whole or skim milk curdled with rennet. After draining and pressing, it is kneaded thoroughly, formed into small rolls or blocks, and then ripened until special molds develop, which requires about four weeks. It is then wrapped in tinfoil and marketed.

Parmesan Cheese.

This is a name given outside of Italy to a very hard cheese which in that country is said to be known as Grana, a name given because of the granular appearance which it has after it has been broken. It is sometimes sold in grated form and brings a relatively high price, but is more commonly sold ungrated. When well made it will keep for years and may be easily broken and grated. It is very generally used in Europe for serving with soups, for seasoning macaroni, and for other similar purposes, and is quite common in American markets.

Sap Sago.

This is a skim milk cheese made in Switzerland, which is suitable for grating. It contains, for every 4 pounds of cheese, 1 pound of a clover (*Melilotus cœruleus*) grown in Switzerland. It is greenish in color and has an unusual flavor. It is not high priced.

Gorgonzola and Roquefort.

These are highly flavored cheeses characterized by the presence of molds through their entire mass. Roquefort is made from the milk of sheep; Gorgonzola, from cows' milk.

Potted or Sandwich Cheeses.

Ordinary cheese is often mixed with butter or oil in the proportion of 5 parts of cheese to 1 of butter or oil, by weight. The mixture is sometimes seasoned with mustard or with curry powder. Such cheeses, unseasoned or seasoned, are on the market in great variety. Potted cheese may be easily prepared at home if the housekeeper wishes to take the trouble.

Swiss Cheese (Emmentaler, Gruyère, Etc.).

This term as used in America is somewhat vague. Different names are given to the varieties according to the districts of Switzerland in which they are made, but they are all similar and characterized by a mild, sweetish flavor and the presence of large holes or "eyes." Foreign and domestic brands are to be found in most markets. They are suitable for cooking purposes, as well as for use without being cooked, and are much used in this way in Europe and well known and liked in the United States.

Edam Cheese.

This is a cheese made in Holland. It is molded in spherical form, and the outside is usually dyed red. It is usual in this country to cut off a section of the top, which serves as a lid, and to scoop out the inside as needed. In Holland it is frequently served in slices, particularly when it is fresh. Edam cheese is seldom used in cookery in American homes, though thrifty housewives, after the greater part of the cheese has been removed, often stuff the hollow shell with cooked and seasoned macaroni, rice, or something similar and bake.

Brie and Camembert Cheese.

These are very soft rennet cheeses of foreign origin and of somewhat smaller nutritive value than standard cheese, and of strong flavor and odor. They are not often used in cookery, but are used as an accompaniment to other foods.

Cottage Cheese.

Cottage cheese and other sour milk and cream cheeses, junket, Devonshire cream, and a number of other cheese-like products are described in the section which deals with homemade cheese.

The Care of Cheese in the Home.

One of the best ways of keeping cheese which has been cut is to wrap it in a slightly damp cloth and then in paper, and to keep it in a cool place. To dampen the cloth, sprinkle it and then wring it. It should seem hardly damp to the touch. Paraffin paper may be used in place of the cloth. When cheese is put in a covered dish, the air should never be wholly excluded, for if this is done, it molds more readily.

In some markets it is possible to buy small whole cheeses. These may be satisfactorily kept by cutting a slice from the top, to serve as a cover, and removing the cheese as needed with a knife, a strong spoon, or a cheese scoop. It is possible to buy at the hardware stores knobs which inserted in the layer cut from the top make it easy to handle. The cheese below the cover should be kept wrapped in a cloth.

Cheese as a Food.

Cheese is used in general in two ways—in small quantities chiefly for its flavor and in large quantities for its nutritive value as well as for its flavor. Some varieties of cheese are used chiefly for the first purpose, others chiefly for the second. Those which are used chiefly for their flavor, many of which are high priced, contribute little to the food value of the diet, because of the small quantity used at a time. They have an important part to play, however, in making the diet attractive and palatable. The intelligent housekeeper thinks of them not as necessities, but as lying within what has been called "the region of choice." Having first satisfied herself that her family is receiving sufficient nourishment, she then, according to her means and ideas of an attractive diet, chooses among these foods and others which are to be considered luxuries.

Those cheeses, on the other hand, which are suitable to be eaten in large quantities and which are comparatively low priced are important not only from the point of view of flavor, but also from the point of view of their nutritive value. Among such cheeses the one which, as noted above, is known to the trade as standard factory cheese and to the housewife as American cheese stands out preeminently. Therefore when the word "cheese" is used without specification in the following pages it may be taken to refer to this particular variety.

The Use of Cheese in the Diet.—It has been the purpose, in preparing this discussion of cheese, to consider ways in which mild flavored sorts may serve as staple articles of diet, rather than the use of highly flavored varieties as appetizers and as accompaniments of other foods. The use of highly flavored cheese as a condiment is customary and may profitably be extended, since it offers a simple way of adding to the attractiveness of the diet. The variety of the cheese selected is a matter of choice, some persons preferring such kinds as well-ripened American full cream cheese or the potted cheeses, and others such sorts as Roquefort, Camembert, and other varieties. From the physiologist's standpoint, cheese used in this way for its flavor should really form a part of a well-balanced meal rather than be added to a meal which already supplies an abundance of nutritive material. In other words, condimental cheeses may better accompany a moderate than a very generous menu.

In considering the use of cheese in quantity as an integral part of the diet there are many possibilities from simple combinations like bread and cheese to elaborate dishes in which cheese is used as a flavor and as a principal constituent.

As has been pointed out, cheese, being rich in both protein and fat, would logically replace such foods as meat, fish, and eggs, when taken in quantity, rather than cereal foods characterized by a large amount of starch, or succulent foods, such as vegetables and fruits. In planning menus of which cheese forms a large part the housekeeper should bear these facts in mind.

Bill-of-Fare Making with Cheese as the Central Food.—Since meat has so generally been the chief protein food of a meal, and the kind selected usually has determined the choice of vegetables and condiments, it is not strange that very many housekeepers should be inexperienced and consequently unskillful in planning meals in which cheese is substituted for meat when for any reason they may desire to make such a change. In seeking skill they might take a suggestion from the experiments to which reference has been made, and also from a case investigated and reported by the Office of Experiment Stations, of a man who lived for months upon a diet of bread, fruit, and cheese, and who remained in good health and active, and did not weary of the monotony of the diet.

The first two articles of the diet mentioned, namely, the bread and the cheese, could have been taken in such amounts as to constitute what is usually considered a balanced ration, i. e., in such amounts as to supply the right quantity of muscle forming foods in comparison with the energy value. The bread and cheese taken with the fruit, however, make a ration which is well balanced not only in the older and more widely accepted sense, but also in the more modern sense that it makes an attractive and palatable combination of foods, as well as a balanced ration, and thus favors digestion. The watery and refreshing fruits or succulent vegetables with their large supply of cellulose are a pleasant contrast to the concentrated and fatty cheese.

Housekeepers would probably find that if in planning menus of which a cheese dish is the chief feature they were to take pains to supply also crisp, watery vegetables, water cress, celery, lettuce, served with a dressing or with salt alone, or simple fruit salads, and would give preference to refreshing fruits, either fresh or cooked, rather than to what are known as heavy desserts, they would in general be more successful in pleasing those who are served.

There is another point also to be considered in combining cheese with other foods. Whether it is raw or cooked it is likely to be somewhat soft, and so seems to call for the harder kinds of bread—crusty rolls or biscuit, zwieback, toast, pulled bread, rye bread, the harder brown breads, or crackers, and some of the numerous crisp ready-to-eat cereal breakfast foods. Brittle cookies, too, seem more suitable than rich soft cakes or puddings for the dessert in such meals.

A few bills of fare are given below which experience has shown to represent combinations of dishes which are palatable and which, if eaten in usual amounts, will supply protein and energy in proportions which accord with usual dietary standards. Menus such as these are more commonly served at lunch or at supper, but they might equally well be served for dinner, the selection of dishes for any meal being of course chiefly a matter of custom and convenience for those who have any range of choice.

Suggested bills of fare in which cheese dishes are the chief source of protein and fat.

MENU No. 1.

Macaroni and cheese.
Raisin bread or date bread.
Orange and water cress salad.
Baked apples.
Sugar cookies.
Cocoa.

MENU No. 2.

Cheese fondue.
Toast, zwieback, or thin and crisp baking-powder biscuit.
Celery.
Potatoes, baked. boiled, or fried in deep fat.
Peas, or some other fresh vegetable.
Coffee.
Fruit salad with crisp cookies or meringues.

MENU No. 3.

Clear soup.
Baked eggs with cheese or Boston roast.
Baked potatoes.
Lettuce salad.
A sweet jelly, crab apple or quince for example, or a preserve.
Rye bread.
Orange or banana shortcake.
Tea.

These bills of fare should be taken as suggestive merely and not as a solution of the problem. In fact, the whole art of making bills of fare needs developing. There is abundant evidence that overeating, where it exists, is frequently due to the fact that meals are not skillfully planned. People often continue eating after they have taken enough in total bulk because they have not had all they want of some particular kind of food. The meal has contained too large a percentage of proteid or too much starch; has been too moist or too dry; too highly flavored or not sufficiently flavored. Bill-of-fare making calls not only for knowledge of food values but also for skill in combining flavors and textures.

In this discussion of menu making, and of the use of cheese as an integral part of the diet, the aim has been to suggest ways of using cheese to add to the palatability of meals made up of usual dishes, and to suggest dishes containing cheese which could serve as substitutes for meat dishes when so desired, and also for dishes of many sorts to be used as taste suggests and in which the nutritive value as well as the flavor is increased by the addition of cheese. If cheese is used and in quantity, it is obvious that some other proteid and fat foods should be diminished, in order that the meal or day's menu may not be unduly hearty.

For the convenience of the housekeeper, a number of recipes for cheese dishes are given in later pages, these being preceded by directions for making cottage cheese and other similar cheeses which are usually made in the home.

Homemade Cheese.

Even as late as a generation or two ago cheese of different kinds was made at home for family use, as sour-milk or cottage cheese still is, and cheese making was very generally a farm industry, cheese like butter, being sold by the farmer who made it. Cottage cheese is very commouly homemade. Most types of cheese, however, are now as a rule made on a large scale in factories where advantage may be taken of labor-saving devices.

Curds and Whey.

Cheese curds and whey, an old-fashioned dish, which is often spoken of in accounts of life in earlier times, sometimes refers to sour-milk curds and sometimes to curd separated with rennet. This dish when made with rennet is much like junket and though far less common to-day than was once the case is wholesome and palatable.

Cottage Cheese.

This cheese is very commonly prepared in the home, and the process of making it is very simple. It consists merely of curdling the milk, separating the curd from the whey, seasoning, and pressing it.

The curd is formed by the souring of the milk, and the process is hastened if the milk is kept warm, the best temperature being about blood heat, 96° F. A temperature much above this should be avoided, as the curd is likely to become hard and tough if much heated. The danger is usually not that the whole will be overheated but that the portion nearest the fire will be. In the old-fashioned kitchen there was usually a place where the milk could stand till it was uniformly warm throughout. With our present cooking arrangements it is often desirable to hasten the process. This may be done by setting the milk into a pan of warm water or by pouring hot water directly into the milk itself. The effect of the latter method is to remove much more of the acid than when the whey is left undiluted. Some consider this a great advantage.

If, for any reason, the curd is overheated, it should be put through a meat chopper. This will insure cottage cheese of excellent texture.

If the milk is thoroughly chilled before the whey is drained off it retains more of the fat than if this is done when warm. Under no circumstances, however, is much of the fat retained in cottage cheese. It is therefore more economical to make it out of skim milk and to add the fat to the curd in the form of butter or cream.

Chopped parsley, caraway seeds, chopped olives, and pimiento may all be used for flavoring if such flavored cheese is preferred to plain cottage cheese.

Cottage cheese is most commonly consumed immediately, but if made in quantity for commercial purposes, it may be packed in tubs and placed in cold storage. Sometimes it is formed into rolls or blocks and wrapped in tinfoil when marketed. Such cheese is used without ripening.

Though cottage cheese is usually made by allowing the milk to sour naturally, it is sometimes more convenient to curdle the milk by adding rennet, and some housekeepers have a preference for cottage cheese thus made, since the flavor is milder and the acid taste which it possesses when made from sour milk is lacking.

Sour-Cream Cheese.

When cream is to be made into cheese similar to cottage cheese, it should be drained without having previously been heated. The drainage is facilitated by moistening the cloth in salt water before the cream is poured in. The curd is formed either by souring or by the addition of rennet.

Uncooked Curd, or French Cottage Cheese.

The French make cheese from sour milk without heating it. They pour the milk into earthen molds which have holes in the bottom. A very fine sieve may be used instead of the molds. The whey drips out and the curd assumes a custardlike consistency and takes the shape of the mold. When sufficiently stiff, the cheese is chilled, and is eaten with sweet cream and sugar. It is a staple dessert in many French families, especially in hot weather, and is delicious served with acid fruit, such as currants, or with strawberries.

Junket.

If cottage cheese is made from sweet milk and rennet and served without breaking and separating the curd and whey, the dish is called junket. It is customary to season it a little, as with grated nutmeg or with cinnamon and sugar.

Buttermilk Cheese.

To make buttermilk cheese, heat buttermilk to about 130° or 140° F. Allow it to cool and strain it. As the curd will settle to the bottom, most of the whey may be poured off before the draining is begun.

This cheese is, of course, almost wholly without fat and yet, probably because the particles of curd are very finely divided, it has a smooth consistency, which suggests the presence of fat. It may be served seasoned with salt only, or it may be mixed with butter or cream and seasonings. It is suitable for combining with olives and pimientos, as elsewhere recommended, or for any use to which the ordinary cream cheeses are put.

Buttermilk Cream.

By controlling the temperature in heating the buttermilk and not allowing it to go above 100° F., a compound is made which after draining has the consistency of a very thick cream. It is claimed that this "cream" is suitable for eating on bread in place of butter.

The recipes given on other pages suggest ways of making a salad dressing out of buttermilk cream.

Devonshire Cream.

Devonshire cream somewhat resembles sweet cream in flavor and consistency. It is very much liked in England, where it is commonly eaten with fresh or preserved fruit, but it is not so well known in America.

To make Devonshire cream, allow a pan of whole milk to stand for 24 hours in a cool place or for 12 hours in a warmer place. Place the pan on the cooler part of the stove and heat until the milk is very hot, but not to the boiling point. If heated too much a thick skin will form on the surface. The more slowly the milk is heated the better. Having been heated, the milk should be kept in a cool place for 24 hours and then skimmed. The thick cream obtained has a characteristic flavor and texture.

CHEESE DISHES AND THEIR PREPARATION.

The list of cheese dishes in the culinary literature of this and other countries is a long one, but most of them are variations of a comparatively small number of general types. Those which have been selected and studied experimentally represent the principal types and in many cases have been adapted to American methods of preparations and tastes. In some instances, this has resulted in new and perhaps more rational combinations than those which served as models.

For convenience, the cheese dishes included in this bulletin have been grouped under the following heads:

(1) Cheese dishes which may serve as meat substitutes.

(2) Cheese soups and vegetables cooked with cheese.

(3) Cheese salads, sandwiches, and similar dishes.

(4) Cheese pastry, cheese sweets, and similar dishes.

Variety may be obtained in the recipes by varying the flavorings. Among the best flavorings for cheese dishes are onion, chives, and the ordinary green sweet pepper. Since the cheese needs very little cooking, however, and onion or the pepper needs a great deal, they should always be previously cooked, either by stewing in a very little water, or by cooking in butter. The seeds of the pepper, of course, should be removed before cooking. Where chopped celery is used, as it may be in most of these dishes, it, too, should be cooked beforehand until tender. Other good flavors are mustard, curry powder, onion juice, chopped olives, pimiento, and, according to European recipes, nutmeg or mace.

In preparing the cheese it often has been found convenient to use a very coarse grater, having slits instead of the usual rounded holes. Such a grater, in spite of its name, shaves the cheese instead of grating it. When the cheese is soft this is an advantage, since the grater does not become clogged.

CHEESE DISHES WHICH MAY BE USED IN THE SAME WAY AS MEAT

Meat is wholesome and relished by most persons, yet it is not essential to a well-balanced meal and there are many housekeepers who for one reason or another are interested in lessening the amount of meat which they provide or to substitute some other foods for it. The problem with the average family is undoubtedly more often the occasional substitution of other palatable dishes for the sake of variety, for reasons of economy, or for some other reason than the general replacement of meat dishes by other things.

Foods which are to be served in place of meat should be rich in protein and fat and should also be savory. Cheese naturally suggests itself as a substitute for meat, since it is rich in the same kinds of nutrients which meat supplies, is a staple food with which everyone is familiar, and is one which can be used in a great variety of ways. In substituting cheese for meat, especial pains should be taken to serve dishes which are relished by the members of the family. A number of recipes for dishes which contain cheese are given below. They are preceded by several recipes for cheese sauces which, as will appear, are called for in the preparation of some of the more substantial dishes.

Cheese Sauce No. I.

1 cupful of milk.
2 tablespoonsful of flour.
1 ounce of cheese (1/4 cupful of grated cheese).
Salt and pepper.

Thicken the milk with the flour and just before serving add the cheese, stirring until it is melted.

This sauce is suitable for use in preparing creamed eggs, or to pour over toast, making a dish corresponding to ordinary milk toast, except for the presence of cheese. It may be seasoned with a little curry powder and poured over hard boiled eggs.

Cheese Sauce No. II.

Same as cheese sauce No. I, except that the cheese is increased from 1 to 2 ounces.

This sauce is suitable for using with macaroni or rice, or for baking with crackers soaked in milk.

Cheese Sauce No. III.

Same as cheese sauce No. I, except that two cupsful of grated cheese or

8 ounces are used. This may be used upon toast as a substitute for Welsh rarebit.

Cheese Sauce No. IV.

Same as cheese sauce No. II, save that 2 tablespoonsful of melted butter are mixed with the flour before the latter is put into the milk. This sauce is therefore very rich in fat and has only a mild flavor of cheese.

Among the recipes for dishes which may be used like meat, the first 30 are such that, eaten in usual quantities, they will provide much the same kind and amount of nutritive material as the ordinary servings of meat dishes used at dinner. In several cases there is a resemblance in appearance and flavor to common meat dishes, which would doubtless be a point in their favor with many families.

While, chiefly owing to custom, it may not accord with the taste of the family to serve cheese dishes at dinner in place of meat, it is much more in accord with usual dietary habits in American homes to serve such dishes at least occasionally for lunch, for supper, or for breakfast; that is, for a less formal meal than dinner. The last group of recipes in this section, beginning with "breakfast cereals with cheese," supply rather smaller proportions of nutritive materials than those in the first group and so may be more suitable for use at the less hearty meals. There is no hard and fast line to be drawn between the two groups, however, and many of the recipes may be used interchangeably.

In the recipes calling for large amounts of cheese the food value is given, not in figures, but in comparison with beef of average composition and average percentage of waste. This comparison is necessarily rough owing to the varying composition of the foods and the varying weights of such ingredients as a cupful of grated cheese or bread crumbs. In making the comparisons, beef of average composition has been considered to have 15.2 per cent of protein, and a fuel value of 935 calories per pound; ordinary American cheese has been considered to have 26 per cent of protein and a fuel value of 1,965 calories per pound. After many weighings, 4 ounces was decided to be the average weight of a cupful of cheese and 2½ ounces the average weight of a cupful of bread crumbs. These weights have been taken, therefore, in calculating the food value of dishes. When cheese is very soft, however, it may be pressed into a cup and measured like butter. Under these circumstances, the weight of a cupful of cheese may be considered one-half a pound. The price of cheese is taken as 22 cents a pound, of butter 25 cents a pound, of eggs 25 cents a dozen, in this and all similar calculations in this bulletin. Prices vary with time, place, and season. Those mentioned above are such as were paid for materials at the time the experiments here summarized were made and are not extreme values in either direction. Like all such estimates, the calculations are only relative, and the housekeeper who wishes to estimate the comparative cost of the cheese dishes and other foods can readily do so by taking into account the amount of materials used and the prices paid for ingredients at any particular time.

Cheese Fondue No. I.

1⅓ cupsful of soft, stale bread crumbs.
6 ounces of cheese (1½ cupsful of grated cheese or 1⅓ cupsful of cheese grated fine or cut into small pieces).
4 eggs.
1 cupful of hot water.
½ teaspoonful of salt.

Mix the water, bread crumbs, salt and cheese; add the yolks thoroughly beaten; in this mixture cut and fold the whites of eggs beaten until stiff. Pour into a buttered baking dish and cook 30 minutes in a moderate oven. Serve at once.

The food value of this dish, made with the above quantities, is almost exactly the same as that of a pound of beef of average composition and a pound of potatoes combined. It contains about 80 grams of proteids and has a fuel value of about 1,300 calories. Estimated cost, 18 cents, calculated as explained elsewhere.

Cheese Fondue No. II.

- 1⅓ cupsful of hot milk.
- 1⅓ cupsful of soft, stale bread crumbs.
- 1 tablespoonful of butter.
- 4 eggs.
- ⅓ of a pound of cheese (1⅓ cupsful of grated cheese or 1 cupful of cheese cut into small pieces).
- ½ teaspoonful of salt.

Prepare as in previous recipe.

The protein value of this dish is equal to that of 1⅛ pounds of potato and beef, the fuel value, however, being much in excess of these. Calculated cost, 22 cents.

In making either of these fondues, rice or other cereals may be substituted for bread crumbs. One-fourth cupful of rice measured before cooking, or one cupful of cooked rice or other cereals, should be used.

A comparison of the recipes for the two fondues may indicate the general principle on which the recipes in this bulletin have been worked out. The second recipe is one commonly found in cookbooks. In the first one, the butter has been omitted and water substituted for milk and the amount of cheese is slightly increased. This makes a somewhat cheaper dish and one which is less rich because its percentage of fat is not so great. For this reason it is easier to adjust to the ordinary bill of fare. A dish in which there is combined cheese with its large percentage of fat, butter with its 85 per cent of fat, and eggs with their 10 per cent of fat, is too rich to admit of being combined rationally with other fatty dishes. It therefore limits the number of dishes that may be served with it, making milk soup, for example, or dishes containing white sauce or those containing much butter or oil seem out of place. The omission of butter from the ordinary recipes and the substitution of water or skimmed milk for whole milk may perhaps be the means of making cheese dishes more wholesome and more generally acceptable.

Another advantage of omitting butter from cheese dishes and of substituting water or skimmed milk for whole milk is that it makes it possible to increase the amount of cheese without making the dish too rich. This is of advantage to those who like the flavor of cheese, and also, because it tends to increase the tissue forming value of the dish, particnlarly if skimmed milk is used rather than water.

Boiled Fondue.

- 1½ cupsful of bread crumbs.
- 1½ cupsful of milk.
- 1½ cupsful of cheese cut into small pieces.
- 1 egg.
- 2 tablespoonsful of butter.
- 6 ounces of crackers.

Soak the bread in the milk. Melt the butter and add the cheese. When the cheese has melted add the soaked crumbs, the eggs slightly beaten, and the seasoning. Cook a short time and serve on toasted crackers.

Since it consists of essentially the same ingredients, the food value of this dish is obviously much the same as that of fondue made in other ways.

Rice Fondue.

- 1 cupful of boiled rice.
- 2 tablespoonsful of milk.
- 4 eggs.
- 1 cupful of grated cheese.
- ½ teaspoonful of salt.
- 1 teaspoonful of some commercial meat sauce, or similar flavoring.

Heat the rice in the milk, add the other ingredients, and cook slowly until the cheese is melted. Serve on crackers or toast.

The food value is not far from that of a pound of beef of average composition, and the calculated cost is 15 cents.

Corn and Cheese Soufflé.

- 1 tablespoonful of butter.
- 1 tablespoonful of chopped green pepper.
- ¼ cupful of flour.
- 2 cupsful of milk.
- 1 cupful of chopped corn.
- 1 cupful of grated cheese.
- 3 eggs.
- ½ teaspoonful of salt.

Melt the butter and cook the pepper thoroughly in it. Make a sauce out of the flour, milk, and cheese as explained elsewhere; add the corn, cheese, yolks, and seasoning; cut and fold in the whites beaten stiffly; turn into a buttered baking dish and bake in a moderate oven 30 minutes.

Made with skimmed milk and without butter, this dish has a food value slightly in excess of a pound of beef and a pound of potatoes. Calculated cost about 20 cents.

Welsh Rabbit.

- 1 tablespoonful of butter.
- 1 teaspoonful of cornstarch.
- ½ cupful of milk.
- ½ pound of cheese, cut into small pieces.
- ¼ teaspoonful each of salt and mustard.
- A speck of cayenne pepper.

Cook the cornstarch in the butter; then add the milk gradually and cook two minutes; add the cheese and stir until it is melted. Season and serve on crackers or bread toasted on one side, the rabbit being poured over the untoasted side. Food value is that of about three-fourths of a pound of beef. Calculated cost, 13 cents.

Tomato Rabbit.

- 2 tablespoonsful of butter.
- 2 tablespoonsful of flour.
- ¾ cupful of milk.
- ¾ cupful of stewed and strained tomatoes.
- ⅛ teaspoonful of soda.
- 1 pound of cheese
- 2 eggs, slightly beaten.
- Salt, mustard, cayenne pepper.

Cook the butter and the flour together, add the milk, and as soon as the mixture thickens add tomatoes and soda. Then add cheese, eggs, and seasoning. Serve on toasted whole wheat or Graham bread.

Green Corn, Tomato, and Cheese.

- 1 tablespoonful of butter.
- 2 cups of grated cheese.
- ¾ cup of canned or grated fresh corn.
- 1 ripe pimiento.
- ½ cup of tomato purée.
- 2 egg yolks.
- 1 teaspoonful of salt.
- ½ teaspoonful of paprika.
- 1 clove of garlic.
- 4 slices of bread.

Into the melted butter stir the cheese until it, too, is melted. Then add the corn and pimiento, stir for a moment and add the egg yolks beaten and mixed with the tomato juice and the salt and paprika. Have ready the bread toasted on one side and very lightly rubbed on its untoasted side with the garlic cut in two. Pour the mixture over the untoasted side of the bread and serve at once. A poached egg is sometimes placed on top of each portion, making a very nutritious combination.

Macaroni and Cheese No. I.

- 1 cupful of macaroni, broken into small pieces.
- 2 quarts of boiling water.
- 1 cupful of milk.
- 2 tablespoonsful of flour.
- ¼ to ½ pound of cheese.
- ½ teaspoonful of salt.
- Speck of cayenne pepper.

Cook the macaroni in the boiling salted water, drain in a strainer, and pour cold water over it to prevent the pieces from adhering to each other. Make a sauce out of the flour, milk, and cheese. Put the sauce and macaroni in alternate layers in a buttered baking dish, cover with buttered crumbs, and heat in oven until crumbs are brown.

Macaroni and Cheese No. II.

A good way to prepare macaroni and cheese is to make a rich cheese sauce and heat the macaroni in it. The mixture is usually covered with buttered crumbs and browned in the oven. The advantage of this way of preparing the dish, however, is that it is unnecessary to have a hot oven, as the sauce and macaroni may be reheated on the top of the stove.

Macaroni with Cheese and Tomato Sauce.

Boiled macaroni may be heated in tomato sauce and sprinkled with grated cheese just before serving.

Italian Macaroni and Cheese.

1 cupful of macaroni broken into small pieces.
2 quarts of boiling salted water.
½ onion.
2 cloves.
1½ cupsful of tomato sauce.
½ cupful or more of grated cheese.

Cook the macaroni in the boiling salted water with the onion and cloves. Drain, remove the onion and cloves, reheat in tomato sauce, and serve with grated cheese.

Cheese and Macaroni Loaf.

½ cupful of macaroni broken into small pieces.
1 cupful of milk.
1 cupful of soft bread crumbs.
1 tablespoonful of butter.
1 tablespoonful of chopped green pepper.
1 teaspoonful each of chopped onion and parsley.
3 eggs.
1 teaspoonful of salt.
½ cupful of grated cheese.

Cook the macaroni in boiling salted water until tender, and rinse in cold water. Cook the parsley, onion, and pepper in a little water with the butter. Pour off the water or allow it to boil away. Beat the egg, white and yolk separately. Mix all the ingredients, cutting and folding in the stiffly beaten whites at the last. Line a quart baking dish with buttered paper; turn the mixture into it; set the baking dish in a pan of hot water, and bake in a moderate oven from one-half to three-fourths of an hour. Serve with tomato sauce.

Baked Rice and Cheese No. I.

1 cupful of uncooked rice and
4 cupsful of milk;
or,
3 cupsful of cooked rice and
1 cupful of milk.
2 tablespoonsful of flour.
½ pound of cheese.
½ teaspoonful of salt.

If uncooked rice is used, it should be cooked in 3 cupsful of milk. Make a sauce with one cupful of milk, add the flour, cheese, and salt. Into a buttered baking dish put alternate layers of the cooked rice and the sauce. Cover with buttered crumbs and bake until the crumbs are brown. The proteids in this dish, made with rice cooked in milk, are equal to those of nearly 1¾ pounds of average beef. If skimmed milk is used, the fuel value is equal to nearly 3½ pounds of beef. Whole milk raises the fuel value still higher. Estimated cost 28 cents.

Baked Rice and Cheese No. II.

¼ pound of cheese grated or cut into small pieces.
1 cupful of rice.
Milk as needed.

Cook the rice; put into a buttered baking dish alternate layers of rice and cheese; pour over them enough milk is used to pour over it, this the rice; cover with buttered crumbs and brown.

If the rice is cooked in milk either whole or skimmed, and one cup of milk is used to pour over it, this dish has as much protein as 1¼ pounds of beef of average composition. and a much higher fuel value.

Baked Crackers and Cheese No. I.

- 9 or 10 butter crackers or Boston crackers.
- ¼ pound of cheese or 1 cupful of grated cheese.
- 1½ cupsful of milk.
- ¼ teaspoonful of salt.
- Flour.

Split the crackers, if the thick sort are selected, or with a sharp knife cut them into pieces of uniform size. Pour the milk over them and drain it off at once. With the milk, flour, cheese, and salt, make a sauce. Into a buttered baking dish put alternate layers of the soaked crackers and sauce. Cover with bread crumbs and brown in the oven, or simply reheat without covering with crumbs.

The above is a very satisfactory substitute for macaroni and cheese, and can be prepared in less time.

Baked Crackers and Cheese No. II.

- 9 or 10 butter crackers or soda crackers.
- 2 cupsful of hot milk, whole or skimmed.
- 1 cupful of grated cheese.
- ¼ teaspoonful of salt.

This is more quickly prepared than the preceding recipe, but as the milk is likely to curdle, it has not so good a consistency.

Soak the crackers in the milk; place them in a buttered baking dish in alternate layers with the cheese; pour the remaining milk over them and bake. This dish may be covered with buttered crumbs. Variety may be secured, in either this recipe or the preceding one, by putting a very small amount of mixed mustard on each cracker.

Cheese Rolls.

A large variety of rolls may be made by combining legumes, either beans of various kinds, cowpeas, lentils, or peas, with cheese of various kinds, and adding bread crumbs to make the mixture thick enough to form into a roll. Beans are usually mashed, but peas or small Lima beans may be combined whole with bread crumbs and grated cheese, and enough of the liquor in which the vegetables have been cooked may be added to get the right consistency. Or, instead of beans or peas, chopped spinach, beet tops, or head lettuce may be used. Home-made cottage cheese, and the soft cream cheese of commerce, standard cheese, or English dairy may be used.

Boston Roast.

- 1 pound can of kidney beans or equivalent quantity of cooked beans.
- ½ pound of grated cheese.
- Bread crumbs.
- Salt.

Mash the beans or put them through a meat grinder. Add the cheese and sufficient bread crumbs to make the mixture stiff enough to be formed into a roll. Bake in a moderate oven, basting occasionally with butter and water. Serve with tomato sauce. This dish may be flavored with onions, chopped and cooked in butter and water.

Pimiento and Cheese Roast.

- 2 cupsful of cooked Lima beans.
- ¼ pound of cream cheese, commercial or home made.
- 3 canned pimientos chopped.
- Bread crumbs.

Put the first three ingredients through a meat chopper. Mix thoroughly and add bread crumbs until it is stiff enough to form into a roll. Brown in the oven, basting occasionally with butter and water.

Nut and Cheese Roast.

1 cupful of grated cheese.
1 cupful of chopped English walnuts.
1 cupful of bread crumbs.
2 tablespoonsful of chopped onion.
1 tablespoonful of butter.
Juice of half a lemon.
Salt and pepper.

Cook the onion in the butter and a little water until it is tender. Mix the other ingredients and moisten with water, using the water in which the onion has been cooked. Pour into a shallow baking dish and brown in the oven.

Cheese and Spinach Roll.

2 quarts of spinach.
1 cupful of grated cheese.
1 tablespoonful of butter.
Salt.
Bread crumbs.

Cook the spinach in water for 10 minutes. Drain off the water, add the butter, cook until tender, and chop. Add the cheese and the eggs, and bread crumbs enough to make a mixture sufficiently stiff to form into a roll, or leave more moist and cook in a baking dish.

Vegetable and Cheese Rolls.

For the spinach of the above recipe there may be substituted beet tops, Swiss chard, or the outer leaves of lettuce.

Cheese Used in the Stuffing of Meats.

The mixtures in the preceding two recipes may be used for stuffing veal or beef. Eggs may be added if desired, and chopped onions or parsley may be cooked with the greens. In Italy roasts thus prepared are sprinkled with a little finely chopped garlic, and covered with celery tops and thin slices of bacon or fat pork before roasting.

Creamed Cheese and Eggs.

3 hard boiled eggs.
1 tablespoonful of flour.
1 cupful of milk.
½ teaspoonful of salt.
Speck of cayenne.
¼ cupful or 1 ounce grated cheese.
4 slices of toast.

Make a thin white sauce with the flour and milk and seasonings. Add the cheese and stir until melted. Chop the whites and add them to the sauce. Pour the sauce over the toast, force the yolks through a potato ricer or strainer, sprinkle over the toast.

Baked Eggs with Cheese.

4 eggs.
1 cupful, or 4 ounces, of grated cheese.
1 cupful of fine, soft, stale bread crumbs.
¼ teaspoonful salt.
A few grains of cayenne pepper.

Break the eggs into a buttered baking dish or into ramekins and cook them in a hot oven until they begin to turn white around the edge. Cover with the mixture of crumbs, cheese, and seasonings. Brown in a very hot oven. In preparing this dish it is essential that the oven be very hot or the egg will be too much cooked by the time the cheese is brown. To avoid this, some cooks cover the eggs with white sauce before adding crumbs.

The food value of the dish is very close to that of a pound of beef of average composition. The estimated cost is about 14 cents.

For those who are particularly fond of cheese the amount of cheese in this recipe may be very much increased, thus making a much more nourishing dish. Or, the amount may be reduced so as to give hardly more than a suggestion of the flavor of cheese.

Scrambled Eggs with Cheese.

½ pound of cheese grated or cut into small pieces.
8 eggs.
1 tablespoonful of chopped parsley.
A pinch of nutmeg.
½ teaspoonful of salt.

Beat the eggs slightly, mix them with the other ingredients, and cook over a very slow fire, stirring constantly, so that the cheese may be melted by the time the eggs are cooked. In food value the dish is equal to nearly 2 pounds of average beef. The calculated cost is about 30 cents.

Swiss Eggs.

4 eggs.
½ cupful of cream.
1 tablespoonful of butter.
Salt and pepper.
¼ cupful of grated cheese.

Heat the butter and cream together, break in the eggs whole, sprinkle with salt and pepper. When nearly done, add the cheese. Serve on buttered toast. Strain the cream over the toast.

Cheese Omelet No. I.

Cheese may be introduced into omelets in several ways. An ordinary omelet may be served with thin cheese sauce made in the following proportions:

1½ tablespoonsful of flour.
1½ tablespoonsful of cheese.
1 cupful of milk.

This sauce may also be added to omelets in which boiled rice, minced meat, or some other nutritious material has been included.

Cheese Omelet No. II.

Grated cheese may be sprinkled over an ordinary omelet before it is served.

Cheese Omelet.

Yolks of 2 eggs.
2 tablespoonsful of hot water.
1 cupful of grated cheese.
Salt and pepper.
Whites of 4 eggs.
1 tablespoonful of butter.

Beat the yolks until lemon colored and add the hot water and the seasoning. Beat the whites until they are stiff, and add the cheese. Cut and fold the two mixtures together. Heat the butter in omelet pan and cook the mixture very slowly until it is brown on the underside. If possible, cook the top of the omelet in the oven or by means of a hot plate held over it.

Breakfast Cereals with Cheese.

That cheese combined with cereal foods makes a rational dish as regards the proportion of nutrients it supplies has been pointed out on another page. Cheese and some of the crisp "ready to serve" cereal breakfast foods is a combination which is common, the cheese being melted with the cereal food, or simply served with it.

There are many who relish a piece of cheese with the cooked cereal so commonly eaten for breakfast and find such a combination satisfying to appetite and taste. Oatmeal or some other home cooked breakfast cereal prepared with cheese is palatable, and such dishes have an advantage in that they may be served without cream and sugar. Since such a dish contains considerably more protein than the breakfast cereals as ordinarily served, it has a further advantage in that it may well serve as the principal item of a breakfast menu, instead of a preliminary to other courses. Such a combination as cereals cooked with cheese, toast, fruit, and tea, coffee, or chocolate, makes a palatable as well as nutritious breakfast and one which does not require much work to prepare and to clear away. A recipe for preparing oatmeal with cheese follows. Wheat breakfast foods, either parched or unparched, corn meal, and hominy may be prepared in the same way.

Oatmeal with Cheese.

2 cupsful of oatmeal.
1 cupful of grated cheese.
1 tablespoonful of butter.
1 level teaspoonful of salt.

Cook the oatmeal as usual. Shortly before serving, stir in the butter and add the cheese, and stir until the cheese is melted and thoroughly blended with the cereal.

The cheese should be mild in flavor and soft in texture. The proportion of cheese used may be increased if a more pronounced cheese flavor is desired.

Cheese with Mush.

Cheese may be added to cornmeal mush or to mush made from any of the corn or wheat preparations now on the market. The addition of cheese to cornmeal mush is partienlarly desirable when the mush is to be fried.

Fried Bread with Cheese No. I.

6 slices of bread.
1 cupful of milk.
2 ounces of cheese, or ½ cupful of grated cheese.
½ teaspoonful of salt.
½ teaspoonful of potassium bicarbonate.
Butter or other fat for frying.

Scald the milk with the potassium bicarbonate; add the grated cheese, and stir until it dissolves. Dip the bread in this mixture and fry it in the butter. The potassium bicarbonate helps to keep the cheese in solution. It is desirable, however, to keep the milk hot while the bread is being dipped.

Fried Bread with Cheese No. II.

Cut stale bread into thin pieces. Put two pieces together with grated cheese between them; dip into a mixture of egg and milk and fry in butter or other fat.

Roman Gnocchi.

2 cupsful of milk.
¼ cupful of flour.
¼ cupful of cornstarch.
2 cupsful of milk.
2 egg yolks.
¾ cupful of grated cheese.
Salt.

Melt the butter; cook the cornstarch thoroughly, and then the flour in the butter; add the milk gradually; cook three minutes, stirring constantly; add the yolks and one-half cupful of the cheese. Pour into a buttered shallow pan and cool. Cut into squares; place them on a platter a little distance apart; sprinkle with remaining cheese, and brown in the oven.

The proteid value is that of three-fourths of a pound of average beef, the fuel value that of 1¾ pounds. Calculated cost 17 cents.

Cheese Soufflé.

2 tablespoonsful of butter.
3 tablespoonsful of flour.
½ cupful of milk (scalded).
½ teaspoonful of salt.
A speck of cayenne.
¼ cupful of grated cheese.
3 eggs.

Melt the butter; add the flour and, when well mixed, add gradually the scalded milk. Then add salt, cayenne, and cheese. Remove from the fire and add the yolks of the eggs, beaten until lemon colored. Cool the mixture and fold into it the whites of the eggs, beaten until stiff. Pour into a buttered baking dish and cook 20 minutes in a slow oven. Serve at once.

The proteid value of this recipe is equal to that of a half pound of beef; the fuel value is equal to that of three-fourths of a pound.

Cheese Soufflé with Pastry.

2 eggs.
⅔ cupful of thin cream.
1 cupful of grated cheese.
½ cupful of Swiss chèese cut into small pieces.
Salt, cayenne pepper, and nutmeg.

Add the eggs to the cream and beat slightly, then add the cheese and seasoning. Bake 15 minutes in a hot oven, in patty tins lined with puff paste.

Cheese Croquettes.

3 tablespoonsful of butter.
¼ cupful of flour.
⅔ cupful of milk.
Yolks of 2 eggs.
1 cupful of cheese cut in very small pieces.
½ cupful grated cheese.
Salt and pepper.

Make with a white sauce, using the butter, flour, and the milk. Add the unbeaten yolks and stir until well mixed, then add the grated cheese. As soon as the cheese melts, remove from the fire, fold in the pieces of cheese, and add the seasoning. Spread in a shallow pan and cool. Cut into squares or strips, cover with an egg and crumb mixture, and fry in deep fat.

Fried Cheese Balls.

1½ cupsful of grated cheese.
1 tablespoonful of flour.
The whites of 3 eggs.
Salt, pepper, cracker dust.

Beat the whites of the eggs; add the other ingredients; make into balls and roll in cracker dust. If the amount of flour is doubled, the mixture may be dropped from a spoon and fried without being rolled in crumbs.

CHEESE SOUPS AND VEGETABLES COOKED WITH CHEESE

In these dishes the cheese is used not only to add nutritive value, but also to give its characteristic flavor either to materials otherwise rather mild in taste (as in potatoes with cheese) or to combine its flavor with that of some more highly flavored vegetables (as in cheese and vegetable soup). The ingenious housekeeper whose family is fond of cheese can doubtless think of many desirable ways of making such combinations besides those given in the following recipes:

Milk and Cheese Soup.

3 cupsful of milk, or part milk and part stock.
1½ tablespoonsful of flour.
1 cupful of grated cheese.
Salt and paprika.

Thicken the milk with the flour, cooking thoroughly. This is best done in a double boiler, with frequent stirrings. When ready to serve, add the cheese and the seasoning.

The proteids in this soup are equal in amount to those in five-sixths of a pound of beef of average composition; its fuel value is higher than that of a pound of beef.

Cheese and Vegetable Soup.

2 cupsful of stock.
2 tablespoonsful of finely chopped carrots.
1 tablespoonful of chopped onion.
A very little mace.
2 tablespoonsful of butter.
2 tablespoonsful of flour.
1½ teaspoonsful of salt.
1 cupful of scalded milk.
¼ cupful of grated cheese.

Cook the vegetables a short time in one-half of the butter, add the stock and the mace, boiling 15 or 20 minutes. Strain and add the milk. Thicken with flour cooked in the remaining butter. Just before serving, stir in the cheese and cook until it is melted.

Scalloped Potatoes with Cheese No. I.

Put into a buttered baking dish alternate layers of cheese sauce No. I and cold boiled potatoes, sliced or cut into dice. Cover with buttered crumbs and bake.

Scalloped Potatoes with Cheese No. II.

Put into a buttered baking dish alternate layers of white sauce and cold boiled potatoes, either sliced or cut into dice. Put over the top a layer of grated cheese and then a layer of buttered bread crumbs. Brown in the oven.

Scalloped Cabbage or Cauliflower with Cheese.

Cauliflower or cabbage may be scalloped according to either of the recipes given for scalloped potatoes and cheese. Sometimes a cauliflower is boiled whole, spread with grated cheese, then with buttered bread crumbs. It is browned in the oven and served with white sauce poured around it.

Cheese with Potato Puffs.

1 cupful of mashed potatoes.
¼ cupful of milk.
1 egg.
½ teaspoonful of salt.
½ cupful of grated cheese.

Beat the potatoes and milk together until thoroughly mixed. Add the egg and the salt and beat thoroughly. Finally add the cheese. Bake in muffin tins in a slow oven 10 or 15 minutes.

A similar dish may be made by scooping out the inside of a baked potato and mixing it with cheese as above. Fill the potato-skin shell with the mixture, return to the oven, and bake until light brown.

Potatoes with Cheese Sauce.

Cut boiled potatoes into cubes and serve with cheese sauce No. I. This is one of the cheese and vegetable dishes most frequently found on restaurant menus.

CHEESE SALADS, SANDWICHES, AND SIMILAR CHEESE DISHES

Cheese of one sort or another is a very common accompaniment of salads, and the combination is rational as well as palatable, for the constituents of the succulent foods—chiefly water and cellulose—supplement the protein and fat of the cheese. Cheese is often used also as a part of the salad.

A number of recipes are given below for cheese salads and other cheese dishes which may be served with dinner or other regular meals, or served as part of a special lunch or special supper. Many of the cheese dishes discussed in other sections are also commonly used for such occasions when something savory is desired which can be easily and quickly prepared.

Cheese with Salads.

Cheese or cheese dishes are an acceptable addition to salads. Neufchâtel or other cream cheese, either plain or mixed with pimientos and olives may be passed with lettuce or may be cut into slices and served on lettuce.

Cheese balls are often served with salad. They are made of some soft cream cheese, and are frequently combined with chopped chives, olives, sweet peppers, chopped nuts, etc., for the sake of adding flavor. Cooked egg yolk, spinach extract, etc., are sometimes mixed in for the sake of color. If the balls are rolled in chopped chives or parsley, both flavor and color are supplied.

Plain Cheese Salad.

Cut Edam or ordinary American cheese into thin pieces, scatter them over lettuce leaves, and serve with French dressing.

Olive and Pimiento Sandwich or Salad Cheese.

Mash any of the soft cream cheeses and add chopped olives and pimientos in equal parts. This mixture requires much salt to make it palatable to most palates, the amount depending chiefly on the quantity of pimiento used. The mixture may be spread between thin slices of bread or it may be made into a roll or molded, cut into slices, and served on lettuce leaves with French dressing.

Cheese and Tomato Salad.

Stuff cold tomatoes with cream cheese and serve on lettuce leaves with French dressing.

Cheese and Pimiento Salad.

Stuff canned pimientos with cream cheese, cut into slices, and serve one or two slices to each person on lettuce leaves with French dressing.

Cheese Jelly Salad.

½ cupful of grated cheese.
1 tablespoonful of gelatin.
1 cupful of whipped cream.
Salt and pepper to taste

Mix the cheese with the whipped cream, season to taste with salt and pepper, and add to the gelatin dissolved in a scant cupful of water. This may be molded in a large mold or in small molds.

When the jelly begins to harden, cover with grated cheese. The jelly should be served on a lettuce leaf, preferably with a cream dressing or a French dressing, to which a little grated cheese has been added.

Cheese Salad and Preserves.

Epicures have devised a dish which consists of lettuce with French dressing served with cream cheese and thick preparations of currants or other fruits preserved in honey or sugar, which, owing to the fact that the seeds have been extracted by a laborious process, are fairly expensive. The soft cheese often found in market is also relatively expensive. There is a suggestion in this dish, however, for others which are much less costly. Buttermilk cream, or ordinary cottage cheese served with lettuce or other green salad and a small amount of rich homemade preserves, is a combination with much the same character, and also very appetizing.

Deviled Eggs with Cheese.

In making deviled eggs, either to be eaten alone or upon lettuce leaves in the form of salad, a little grated cheese may be mixed with the yolks in addition to the usual salad dressing and flavorings with which the yolks are mixed.

Cheese and Celery.

Cut stalks of celery having deep grooves in them into pieces about 2 inches long. Fill the grooves with cream cheese salted or flavored with chopped pimientos, and serve with bread and butter as a salad course or serve as a relish at the beginning of a meal.

Although not cheese dishes, strictly speaking, the following salad dressings made with buttermilk cream may be included in this section.

Buttermilk Salad Dressing.

½ cupful of buttermilk cream.
1 tablespoonful of vinegar.
¼ teaspoonful of salt.
Cayenne pepper.

This dressing is particularly suitable for serving with cucumbers.

Buttermilk Cream Horseradish Salad Dressing.

To buttermilk cream add a little grated horseradish and vinegar and salt. Serve on whole or sliced tomatoes.

Cheese Sandwiches.

Mash or grate American cheese, add salt, a few drops of vinegar and paprika, and a speck of mustard. Mix thoroughly and spread between thin slices of bread.

Cheese and Anchovy Sandwiches.

To the mixture mentioned in the preceding recipe, add a little anchovy essence. Sardines mashed or rubbed into a paste or any other fish paste may be used in a similar way.

Cuban Sandwiches.

This sandwich may be described as a kind of club sandwich with cheese. It is usually made large so that it is necessary to eat it with a knife and fork. It may be made in such proportions as to supply a large amount of nourishment.

Cut the crusts from slices of bread. Between two slices lay first lettuce with a little salad dressing or salt on it, then a slice of soft mild cheese and finally thin slices of dill pickles or a little chopped pickle.

Toasted Cheese Sandwiches.

Plain bread and butter sandwiches with fairly thick slices of cheese put between the slices are frequently toasted, and on picnics, or at chafing dish suppers, are often browned in a pan in which bacon has just been fried.

CHEESE PASTRY, CHEESE SWEETS, AND SIMILAR DISHES

In the foregoing pages a large number of recipes have been included in which cheese is combined with materials without cooking, as in salads, or used in cooked dishes of creamy or custard-like consistency, as in soufflés and Welsh rabbit or in combination with vegetables or cereals, such as rice.

There are a number of cheese dishes of quite different character in which the cheese is combined with dough, batter, or pastry in various ways, and a number of dishes in which cheese or cheese curd is used in combinations suitable for dessert. Such sweet dishes were once much more common than they are to-day, as reference to old cookery books will show, but some of them are well worth retaining.

In cheese sweets, flavor and richness are both contributed by the cheese.

When cheese is used in pastry or dough it may serve simply as a flavor, as in cheese sticks or cheese straws, or it may wholly or in part replace with its fat the usual shortening, as butter or other fat, and with its protein (casein) the protein (albumin) of eggs. As an illustration of such a use of cheese, cheese gingerbread may be cited.

Using cheese in this way is often an economy when eggs are scarce. Better results will be obtained if soft cheese is used which can be worked into the dough in much the same way as butter or other shortening. To those who like cheese the flavor which it imparts would be an advantage. However, if a very mild cheese is used in combination with molasses or spice the dish differs a little in flavor from one prepared in the usual way.

Cheese Biscuit No. I.

2 cupsful of flour.
4 teaspoonsful of baking powder.
2 tablespoonsful of lard or butter.
⅞ of a cup of milk.
¼ teaspoonful of salt.
Grated cheese sufficient to give desired flavor.

Mix all the ingredients excepting the cheese as for baking powder biscuits. Roll thin, divide into two parts, sprinkle one half with grated cheese, lay the other half of the dough over the cheese, cut out with a small cutter, and bake.

Cheese Biscuit No. II.

- 1/4 pound of soft cheese.
- 2 cupsful of flour.
- 1 cupful of water.
- 4 teaspoonsful of baking powder.
- 1 1/2 teaspoonsful of salt.

Mix and sift the dry ingredients, then work in the cheese with a fork or with the fingers, and add the water gradually. The approximate amount of water has been given; it it impossible to give the exact amount, as flour differs in its capacity for taking up moisture. Toss the dough on a floured board and roll out and cut with a biscuit cutter. Place in a buttered pan and bake in a quick oven from 12 to 15 minutes. The biscuit may be sprinkled with cheese before being put into the oven.

If the cheese is sufficiently soft it can be measured just as butter is. This recipe, then, would call for 1/2 cupful.

Cheese Drops.

- 2 1/2 tablespoonsful of milk.
- 1 teaspoonful of butter.
- 1 1/4 cupsful of flour.
- 1/8 teaspoonful of salt.
- 1 egg.
- 2 tablespoonsful of grated Parmesan cheese or dry American cheese.

Heat the butter and milk to boiling point, add the flour and the salt and stir thoroughly. Remove from the fire, add the egg and cheese and stir until well mixed. When cold, drop in small pieces in deep fat and brown. This makes a good addition to any clear soup or to consommé.

Cheese Wafers.

Spread grated cheese on thin crackers, heat in the oven until the cheese is melted. Serve with soup or salad.

Cheese Relish.

Spread bread which has been toasted or fried in deep fat with grated cheese, or with grated cheese mixed with a little mustard, then heat in the oven until the cheese is melted. This may be served with salad, or as a relish to give flavor to some dish such as boiled rice or hominy, which has no very marked flavor.

Cheese Straws.

Roll out plain or puff paste until one-fourth of an inch thick. Spread one-half of it with grated cheese. Fold over the other half and roll out again. Repeat the process three or four times. Cut into strips and bake. Serve with soup or salad.

Salad Biscuit.

- 1/2 pound of cheese.
- 2 cupsful of flour.
- 4 teaspoonsful of baking powder.
- 1 1/2 teaspoonsful of salt.
- 1 cupful of water.

Mix as for cheese biscuits No. I or No. II, depending on whether the cheese is hard or soft.

Cheese Gingerbread No. I.

- 1 cupful of molasses.
- 4 ounces of cheese.
- 1 teaspoonful of soda.
- 1/2 cupful of water.
- 2 cupsful of flour.
- 2 teaspoonsful of ginger.
- 1/2 teaspoonful salt.

Heat the molasses and the cheese in a double boiler until the cheese is melted. Add the soda and stir vigorously. Mix and sift dry ingredients and add them to the molasses and cheese alternately with the water. Bake 15 minutes in small buttered tins.

Cheese Gingerbread No. II.

½ cupful of molasses.
½ cupful of sugar.
4 ounces of cheese.
2 cupsful of flour.
1 teaspoonful of soda.
2 teaspoonsful of ginger.
½ teaspoonful of salt.
¾ cupful of water.

Rub the cheese and the sugar together. Add the molasses. Mix and sift the dry ingredients and add them to the cheese mixture alternately with the water.

Cheese Custard.

1 cupful of grated cheese.
½ cupful of cream or rich milk.
Yolks of 2 eggs.
A speck of salt and of paprika.

Mix the cream and the cheese and heat until the cheese is melted. Remove from the fire and add the yolks of the eggs. Bake in paper cases or buttered ramekins. Serve with jelly or preserves.

Cheese Cakes.

1 quart of milk.
Rennet.
1 ounce of sugar.
Yolks of 2 eggs.
A speck of nutmeg.
1½ ounces of butter.
1 ounce of dried currants or small raisins.

Warm the milk and add the rennet, using the amount prescribed on the package. Let the milk stand until the curd forms, then break up the curd and strain off the whey. Add the other ingredients to the curd; line patty tins with pastry, fill them with the mixture, and bake.

Brown Betty with Cheese.

Arrange in a deep earthenware baking dish, alternate layers of bread crumbs and thinly sliced apples. Season with cinnamon, also a little clove if desired and brown sugar. Scatter some finely shaved mild full cream cheese over each layer of apple. When the dish is full, scatter bread crumbs over the top and bake 30 to 45 minutes, placing the dish in a pan of water so that the pudding will not burn.

If preferred, this may be sweetened with molasses mixed with an equal amount of hot water and poured over the top, a half cupful of molasses being sufficient for a quart pudding dish full.

Cheese may be used in place of butter in a similar way in other apple puddings. Apple pie made with a layer of finely shaved cheese over the seasoned apple and baked in the usual way is liked by many who are fond of cheese served with apple pie.

APPENDIX CHAPTER III

PREPARATION OF VEGETABLES FOR THE TABLE *

By

MARIA PARLOA.

GENERAL PRINCIPLES

Vegetables are baked, roasted, fried, or boiled, are used for making a great variety of dishes, and are prepared for the table in other ways; but the most common method of cooking them is in boiling water. Steaming is not infrequently resorted to as a method of cooking vegetables and is, of course, similar in principle to boiling in water.

The simpler the methods of cooking and serving vegetables the better. A properly grown and well-cooked vegetable will be palatable and readily digestible. Badly cooked, water-soaked vegetables very generally cause digestive disturbances, which are often serious. Nearly every vegetable may be cooked so that with plain bread it may form a palatable course by itself, if it is desired to serve it in this manner.

All green vegetables, roots, and tubers should be crisp and firm when put on to cook. If for any reason a vegetable has lost its firmness and crispness, it should be soaked in very cold water until it becomes plump and crisp. With new vegetables this will be only a matter of minutes, while old roots and tubers often require many hours. All vegetables should be thoroughly cleaned just before being put on to cook. Vegetables that form in heads, such as cabbage, cauliflower, and Brussels sprouts, should be soaked, heads turned down, in salted cold water, to which a few spoonsful of vinegar may be added. If there are any worms or other forms of animal life in these vegetables, they will crawl out. To secure the best results all vegetables except the dried legumes must be put in boiling water, and the water must be made to boil again as soon as possible after the vegetables have been added, and must be kept boiling until the cooking is finished. Herbaceous vegetables should boil rapidly all the time. With tubers, roots, cauliflower, etc., the ebullition should not be so violent as to break the vegetables. Green beans and peas when removed from the pod must also be cooked gently, i. e., just simmer. When the pods and all are used they are to be cooked rapidly, like the herbaceous vegetables.

To secure the most appetizing and palatable dishes, only fresh tender vegetables should be cooked. If, however, green beans, peas, etc., have grown until a little too old and it still seems best to gather them, a very small piece of baking soda added to the water in which they are boiled makes them more tender, it is commonly believed, and helps to retain the color. Too much soda injures the flavor, and an excess must be carefully avoided. A little soda may also be used to advantage if the water is quite hard. Peas may be boiled for fifteen or twenty minutes in the water to which the soda has been added, then to be cooked the same as peas with pork.

During the cooking of all vegetables the cover must be drawn to one side of the stewpan to allow the volatile bodies liberated by the heat to pass off in the steam. All vegetables should be thoroughly cooked, but the cooking should stop while the vegetable is still firm. This, of course, does

*U. S. Department of Agriculture. Farmers' Bulletin No. 256.

not apply to vegetables that are cooked in soups, purées (thick strained soups), etc. The best seasoning for most vegetables is salt and good butter. Vegetables that are blanched and then cooked with butter and other seasonings and very little moisture are more savory and nutritious than when all the cooking is done in a good deal of clear water.

Blanching Vegetables.—Blanching, which in cookery is entirely different from the bleaching or blanching of green vegetables in the garden, is a cooking process often used with vegetables, since it removes the strong or acrid taste and improves the quality. It is also convenient, since blanching may be done at any time, and the cooking completed in a very short time when the dish is to be served.

Have a large stewpan half full of rapidly boiling water. Add a tablespoonful of salt for every 2 quarts of water. Have the vegetables cleaned and well drained. Drop them into the boiling water, and bring the water back to the boiling point as quickly as possible. Boil rapidly, with the cover partially or wholly off the stewpan, five to twenty minutes, depending upon the vegetable, then drain off the water. If the cooking of the vegetable is not to be finished at once, pour cold water over the vegetable to cool it quickly, then drain and set aside until needed. If the cooking is to be continued at once, it will not be necessary to rinse the vegetable with cold water. To complete the cooking the vegetable should be put in a small stewpan with butter or drippings and the other seasonings and cooked gently until done. A few spoonsful of liquid will be required for every quart of very juicy vegetables, and half a pint of liquid for drier vegetables. The stewpan is to be covered, only a slight opening being left for ventilation. All vegetables cooked in this manner should be cut up rather small either before or after the blanching.

Waste in Preparing Vegetables.—In preparing vegetables for the table there is almost always a larger or smaller loss due to inedible matter, skins, roots, seeds, etc., and also a waste of good material, which is caused by careless paring, etc., all these losses being grouped together in reporting analyses under the name "refuse." The amount of refuse varies greatly in different vegetables. The amount may be very small (7 per cent) in such vegetables as string beans; medium (10 per cent to 15 per cent) in such vegetables as onions, cabbage, leeks, lettuce, cucumbers; or high (50 per cent) in such vegetables as beans in pod, pumpkins, and squash. With tubers, such as potatoes, the average amount of refuse is 20 per cent, and with such roots as turnips 30 per cent.

In preparing vegetables for the table the careful cook will remove all inedible portions and will see to it that the total amount of refuse is as small as is consistent with good quality. Thin paring of potatoes and other vegetables is an economy which it is worth while to practice, and is an easy way of decreasing useless loss. * * *

Changes that Take Place in Cooking Vegetables.—Briefly, these are the principal changes that take place in vegetables during cooking: The cellular tissue is softened and loosened; the nitrogenous substances are coagulated; the starch granules absorb moisture, swell, and burst; a flavors and odors are developed.

As long as the vegetable is kept at a temperature above 125° F. changes continue to go on in the vegetable substance. The most marked of these are in the starch and in the odor, color, and flavor of the vegetable. Starch will not dissolve in cold water, but pure starch gelatinizes readily in hot water, and if the temperature is high enough will become gummy and opaque. If starch is cooked in just moisture enough to swell and burst its granules and is then kept hot, but without additional moisture, a change will continue to take place, though the starch will remain dry and glistening. The flavor grows sweeter and more nutty the longer the starchy food cooks in dry heat. (See Boiled Potatoes, Boiled Rice.) It is only vegetables that are composed largely of starch that can be kept hot in this manner without acquiring a strong taste and poor color. Potatoes, if kept in a closely covered vessel or with the unbroken skins on, will become soggy and dark and have a rank flavor. This is owing to the retention of moisture, which changes some of the starch to a sticky gummy mass, and very probably to the noxious volatile bodies which are generated by heat and should be allowed to pass away. If the skins are broken and the vessel ventilated, potatoes may be kept warm a long time without spoiling. * * *

Overcooking changes and toughens the texture of vegetable foods and destroys the chlorophyll and other coloring matters and volatilizes or injures the bodies which contribute to the flavor. Overcooked vegetables are inferior in appearance and flavor and often indigestible (that is, promotive of digestive disturbance) as well as unpalatable.

SUCCULENT VEGETABLES

Cabbage.—Because of the relatively large amount of sulphur which cabbage contains it is apt to be indigestible and cause flatulence when it is improperly cooked. On the other hand, it can be cooked so that it will be delicate and digestible. It is one of our most useful vegetables, being available during the late fall, winter, and spring months, when other green vegetables are difficult to procure. The quickest and simplest methods of cooking cabbage are the best. The essentials for the proper cooking of this vegetable are plenty of boiling water, a hot fire to keep the water boiling all the time, and thorough ventilation, that the strong-smelling gases, liberated by the high temperature, may be carried off in the steam.

Young cabbage will cook in twenty-five or thirty minutes; late in the winter it may require forty-five minutes. The vegetable when done should be crisp and tender, any green portion should retain the color, and the white portion should be white and not yellow or brown. Overcooked cabbage or cauliflower is more or less yellow, has a strong flavor, and is very inferior to the same dish properly cooked. In addition, overcooking is a cause of digestive disturbance.

To Boil Cabbage.—Cut a small head of cabbage into four parts, cutting down through the stock. Soak for half an hour in a pan of cold water to which has been added a tablespoonful of salt; this is to draw out any insects that may be hidden in the leaves. Take from the water and cut into slices. Have a large stewpan half full of boiling water; put in the cabbage, pushing it under the water with a spoon. Add one tablespoonful of salt and cook from twenty-five to forty-five minutes, depending upon the age of the cabbage. Turn into a colander and drain for about two minutes. Put in a chopping bowl and mince. Season with butter, pepper, and more salt if it requires it. Allow a tablespoonful of butter to a generous pint of the cooked vegetable. Cabbage cooked in this manner will be of delicate flavor and may be generally eaten without distress. Have the kitchen windows open at the top while the cabbage is boiling, and there will be little if any odor of cabbage in the house.

Cabbage Cooked with Pork.—For a small head of cabbage use about half a pound of mixed salt pork. Boil the pork gently for three or four hours. Prepare the cabbage as for plain boiled cabbage. Drain well and put on to boil with the pork. Boil rapidly for twenty-five to forty-five minutes. Serve the pork with the cabbage. The vegetable may require a little more salt.

Smoked bacon or ham may be substituted for the pork. Cabbage may be cooked in water in which corned beef was boiled.

Creamed Cabbage.

1 pint boiled and minced cabbage.
½ pint hot milk.
1 tablespoonful butter.
1 teaspoonful flour.
½ teaspoonful salt.
½ teaspoonful pepper.

Put the cabbage, hot milk, salt, and pepper in a stewpan and on the fire. Beat the butter and flour together until creamy, then stir into the contents of the stewpan. Simmer ten minutes, being careful not to scorch the sauce; serve very hot.

Cabbage with Sausage.

6 sausages.
1 quart minced cabbage.
½ teaspoonful pepper.
Salt. if necessary.

Fry the sausages crisp and brown. Take from the frying pan and pour off all but three tablespoonsful of the fat. Put the minced cabbage in the frying pan and cook six minutes. Arrange in a hot dish and garnish with the sausages. Serve mashed potatoes with this dish.

Purée of Cabbage and Potatoes.

1 pint boiled finely-minced cabbage.
6 medium-sized potatoes.
2 tablespoonsful butter or savory drippings.
2 teaspoonsful salt.
½ teaspoonful pepper.
½ pint hot milk.

Peel the potatoes and put them in a stewpan with boiling water enough to cover them. Cook just thirty minutes. Pour off the water and mash fine and light. Beat in the hot milk, seasoning, and cabbage. Cook about five minutes longer.

Cauliflower.—This vegetable, which a few years ago was a luxury, is now cultivated by nearly all market gardeners, and is within the means of all housekeepers. It is a most delicious vegetable, when properly cooked, and vile when improperly cooked, which generally means when overcooked.

Remove all the large green leaves and the greater part of the stalk. Put the head down in a pan of cold water which contains to each quart a teaspoonful of salt and a teaspoonful of vinegar. Let it soak in this water an hour or more. This is to draw out worms, if any should be hidden in the vegetable. When ready to cook the cauliflower put it into a large stewpan, stem end down, and cover generously with boiling water. Add a tablespoonful of salt and cook with the cover of the saucepan partially off, boiling gently all the time. A large, compact head will require a full half hour, small heads from twenty to twenty-five minutes. If the flowers are loose the heat penetrates to all parts quickly. When compact a little extra time should be allowed for the cooking, but the time must never exceed the half hour. The cauliflower begins to deteriorate the moment it begins to be overcooked. Overcooking, which is very common, can be told by the strong flavor and dark color. It makes the vegetable not only unpleasant to the eye and palate, but indigestible also. If this vegetable must be kept warm for any length of time, cover the dish with a piece of cheese cloth. In hotels and restaurants it is better to blanch it, chill with cold water, and then heat in salted boiling water when needed.

Creamed Cauliflower.

1 pint cooked cauliflower.
1 pint milk.
1 teaspoonful salt.

⅓ teaspoonful pepper.
1 tablespoonful butter.
½ tablespoonful flour.
3 slices toasted bread.

Have the cooked cauliflower broken into branches and seasoned with half the salt and pepper. Put the butter in a saucepan and on the fire. When hot add the flour and stir until smooth and frothy, then gradually add the milk, stirring all the time. When the sauce boils add the salt, pepper, and the cauliflower. Cook 10 minutes and dish on the slices of toast. Serve very hot.

Broccoli.—This vegetable is a species of cauliflower and can be cooked and served in the same manner.

Brussels Sprouts.—This is a species of cabbage, which forms in many small heads about the size of an English walnut on the stock of the plant. It is fairly common in most large markets and is worthy of more extended use than it has commonly met with in the United States.

Brussels Sprouts Blanched.—Remove the wilted or yellow leaves from the little heads or "sprouts," cut the stock close to the head, and soak in salted cold water for an hour or more. Drain well and put into plenty of boiling salted water. Allow one teaspoonful of salt to two quarts of water. Boil rapidly for fifteen or twenty minutes, the time depending on the size of the heads. When done turn into a colander and pour cold water over the heads. They are now ready to cook in butter, or to serve with any kind of sauce. Or the boiling water may be drained from the sprouts, which can then be seasoned with butter, salt, and pepper.

Brussels Sprouts Sauté.

1 quart Brussels sprouts.
3 tablespoonfuls butter.
½ teaspoonful salt.
¼ teaspoonful pepper.

To sauter a food is to cook it quickly in a frying pan in a little fat. Blanch the sprouts and drain well. Put them into a broad-bottomed saucepan with the butter and other seasonings. Place over a hot fire and shake frequently. Cook five minutes. Serve hot.

Kale, or Borecole.—There are several varieties of this vegetable. The dwarf, green-curled kale is the best for the table and is a fall and spring vegetable. The leaves are sweeter and more tender after having been touched by the frost. In the North the roots may be banked with earth at the beginning of winter and when extreme cold weather sets in the plants may be covered lightly with hay or straw. In the spring the old stalks will produce young shoots that make delicious greens.

Kale Boiled with Pork.—Cook the kale the same as cabbage with pork.

Minced Kale.—Remove all the old or tough leaves. Wash the kale thoroughly and drain, then put on to cook in a kettle of boiling water, to which has been added salt in the proportion of 1 tablespoonful to 4 quarts of water. Boil rapidly, with the cover off the kettle, until the vegetable is tender. Pour off the water, and chop the kale rather fine; then put back into the kettle and add 1 tablespoonful of butter and 2 of meat broth or water for each pint of the minced vegetable. Add more salt if required. Cook for ten minutes and serve at once. The time required for cooking kale varies from thirty to fifty minutes. If young and fresh from the garden it will cook in thirty minutes.

Sea Kale. — This is a delicious spring vegetable. It requires practically the same culture as asparagus, and the young shoots are cooked in the same way as this vegetable. Sea kale may be cut the third year from the planting of the seed. Cutting should not be continued after the flower heads begin to form. The flower heads may be cooked the same as broccoli.

Spinach.—This vegetable is a great

resource in cold weather when green vegetables are scarce.

The common spinach, which is the sort usually met with in gardens or markets, goes to seed quickly in hot weather, but New Zealand spinach, which is a very different plant from ordinary spinach and far less well known in the United States, yields tender greens all summer. The shoots should be cut regularly; if not, the old shoots become tough and rank flavored.

Spinach has little food value, but its refreshing and slightly laxative qualities make it a valuable adjunct to the more substantial foods. It contains little starch and only a suggestion of sugar, and is therefore one of the vegetables that physicians include in the bill of fare of many invalids who require a diet without these carbohydrates.

Like most other vegetables, it is rarely cooked to perfection, yet it is not difficult to prepare. Except for special reasons the simplest methods are the best for this vegetable. No matter how cheap the raw spinach may be, it is always expensive in two things—labor and butter. It takes a good deal of time, water, and patience to wash it clean, and no other vegetable requires so much butter if it is to be at its best. Where strict economy must be practiced, sweet drippings from roast beef or chicken can be substituted for the butter.

To clean the spinach cut off the roots, break the leaves apart and drop them into a large pan of water, rinse them well in this water and put them in a second pan of water. Continue washing in clean waters until there is not a trace of sand on the bottom of the pan in which the vegetable was washed. If the spinach is at all wilted let it stand in cold water until it becomes fresh and crisp. Drain from this water and blanch. For half a peck of spinach have in a large saucepan 3 quarts of boiling water and 1 tablespoonful of salt. Put the drained spinach in the boiling water and let it boil ten minutes, counting from the time it begins to boil. When it begins to boil draw the cover of the saucepan a little to one side to allow the steam to escape. At the end of ten minutes pour the spinach into a colander, and when the hot water has passed off pour cold water over it. Let it drain well and mince coarse or fine, as is suitable for the manner in which it is to be served.

One peck of spinach will make about 1½ pints when blanched and minced.

Spinach with Cream.

½ peck spinach.
2 tablespoonfuls butter.
1 tablespoonful flour.
1 teaspoonful salt.
½ teaspoonful pepper.
½ pint cream or milk.

Blanch and mince the spinach. Put the butter in a saucepan and on the fire. When hot add the flour and stir until smooth and frothy, then add the minced spinach and the salt and pepper. Cook for five minutes, then add the milk or cream, hot, and cook three minutes longer. Serve.

Spinach with Egg.

½ peck spinach.
3 tablespoonfuls butter.
½ teaspoonful pepper.
2 eggs.
3 teaspoonfuls salt.

Wash and blanch the spinach, using two teaspoonfuls of the salt in the water in which the vegetable is boiled. Drain the blanched spinach and chop rather fine, return it to the saucepan, and add the salt, pepper, and butter. Place on the fire and cook ten minutes. Heap in a mound on a hot dish and garnish with the hard-boiled eggs, cut in slices.

Spinach Cooked without Water.—Fresh spinach when washed holds enough water for cooking. Put the spinach in a stewpan and on the fire; cover and cook ten minutes. Press down and turn the spinach over several times during the cooking. At the end of ten minutes turn the spinach into a chopping bowl, and mince rather fine. Return to the stewpan and add the seasonings, allowing for half a peck of spinach two generous tablespoonfuls of butter and a teaspoonful of salt. Simmer ten minutes; or if very tender five minutes will be sufficient.

Spinach cooked in this manner will retain all its salts. It will be more laxative and the flavor stronger than when blanched (boiled in water). In young, tender spinach this is not objectionable, but when the overgrown vegetable is cooked in its own moisture the flavor is strong and somewhat acrid.

Lettuce.—If lettuce has grown until rather too old for salad, it may be cooked, and makes a fairly palatable dish.

Boiled Lettuce.—Wash four or five heads of lettuce, carefully removing thick, bitter stalks and retaining all sound leaves. Cook in plenty of boiling salted water for ten or fifteen minutes, then blanch in cold water for a minute or two. Drain, chop lightly, and heat in a stewpan with some butter, salt and pepper to taste. If preferred, the chopped lettuce may be heated with a pint of white sauce seasoned with salt, pepper, and grated nutmeg. After simmering for a few minutes in the sauce, draw to a cooler part of the range and stir in the well-beaten yolks of two eggs. See, also, "Peas with lettuce."

Swiss Chards.—This vegetable is a variety of beet in which the leaf stalk and midrib have been developed instead of the root. It is cultivated like spinach, and the green, tender leaves are prepared exactly like this vegetable. The midribs of the full-grown leaves may be cooked like celery.

Beet Greens.—Beets are usually thickly sowed, and as the young beet plants begin to grow they must be thinned out. The young plants pulled from the bed make delicious greens, particularly if the root has attained some little size. Unfortunately, of late years the leaves are attacked by insects; therefore, they must be examined leaf by leaf, and all which are infested rejected. Do not separate the roots from the leaves. Wash thoroughly in many waters. Put into a stewpan and cover generously with boiling water. Add a teaspoonful of salt for every two quarts of greens. Boil rapidly until tender. This will be about thirty minutes. Drain off the water, chop rather coarse, season with butter and salt.

The vegetable may be boiled with pork as directed for "Cabbage and pork."

Asparagus.—This delicious spring vegetable should be treated very simply, yet carefully.

Cut off the woody part, scrape the lower part of the stalks. Wash well and tie in bunches. Put into a deep stewpan, with the cut end resting on the bottom of the stewpan. Pour in boiling water to come up to the tender heads, but not to cover them. Add a teaspoonful of salt for each quart of water. Place where the water will boil. Cook until tender, having the cover partially off the stewpan. This will be from fifteen to thirty minutes, depending upon the freshness and tenderness of the vegetable. Have some slices of well toasted bread on a platter. Butter them slightly. Arrange the cooked asparagus on the toast, season with butter and a little salt and serve at once. Save the water in which the asparagus was boiled to use in making vegetable soup.

Another method of cooking asparagus is to cut all the tender part into short pieces. Add boiling water enough to just cover the vegetable and place where the water will boil. Cook until tender (about fifteen minutes), season with salt and butter, and serve in the greater part of the juice.

If preferred, a cream dressing may be served with asparagus.

Globe Artichoke.—The large flower bud of the *Cynara scolymus* is known as the globe or French artichoke. The flower buds must be used before they open. The edible portion consists of the thickened portion at the base of the scales and the receptacle to which the leaf-like scales are attached. In cookery books the receptacles are always spoken of as the bottoms. The parts of the flower in the center of the bud are called the "choke" and must always be removed.

When the artichoke is very young and tender the edible parts may be eaten raw as a salad. When it becomes hard, as it does very quickly, it must be cooked. When boiled it may be eaten as a salad or with a sauce. The scales are pulled with the fingers from the cooked head, the base of each leaf dipped in the sauce and then eaten. The bottoms (receptaeles), which many consider the most delicate part of the artichoke, may be cut up and served as a salad, or they may be stewed and served with a sauce. To prepare the artichoke remove all the hard outer leaves. Cut off the stem close to the leaves. Cut off the top of the bud. Drop the artichokes into boiling water and cook until tender, which will take from thirty to fifty minutes, then take up and remove the choke. Serve a dish of French salad dressing with the artichokes, which may be eaten either hot or cold. Melted butter also makes a delicious sauce for the artichokes if they are eaten hot.

Spring Greens.—After months of a very limited supply of herbaceous vegetables, which is the usual condition in the northern regions of the United States, there is a craving for "greens." In almost all localities many of the common weeds are tender and well-flavored when very young. If one has a garden, it can be so managed that there shall be an abundance of fresh roots and greens until the time when the regular garden products are ready. There are a number of plants that may be left in the garden over winter for early spring use. Jerusalem artichokes, parsnips, salsify, leeks, and potato onions will give roots or buds as soon as the frost will permit digging. For greens there are such plants as curled green kale, and cabbage. The roots of these plants should be well earthed up, and when the real hard freezing weather comes the plants must be covered with hay or straw.

Spinach and kale, or German winter greens, may be sown in September. When the hard freezing weather comes protect them with leaves, straw, etc. Sorrel, if properly protected, will make a rapid growth as soon as anything begins to grow. It makes delicious greens by itself, or it may be cooked with other greens. It also makes a refreshing salad. The young shoots of the milkweed are almost as delicious as asparagus, when cooked according to the second method for cooking asparagus. In fact, the milkweed and asparagus may be cut up and cooked together.

The white goosefoot (*Chenopodium album*), better known by the common names "pigweed" and "lamb's quarters," grows in almost all cultivated land. When very young it makes good greens, and should be cooked like spinach. The dandelion, when gathered before the flower bud has attained any size, makes tender greens, and is greatly liked by many people because of its pleasant, bitter flavor. The cultivated dandelion is larger leaved, more tender, and of a milder flavor, and is also a fine salad if blanched like celery. A small bed of this vegetable will give a generous return in the spring, for the small amount of care it requires.

The marsh marigold, commonly called "cowslip," is found in many regions in marshy places. In the early spring this plant makes good greens. Cook the same as spinach. Purslane is a weed common in most gardens and is very palatable as a pot herb. It is also cooked like spinach.

In the Southern States the young shoots of the pokeberry or poke tops are favorite greens, and are cooked like asparagus, while turnip sprouts, cabbage sprouts, and collards are favorite greens of garden origin.

In some regions of Europe young hop sprouts are much prized, being cooked like asparagus. Though eaten to some extent, they do not seem to be known to many housewives in this country.

Every locality produces some wild plants that are safe and pleasant to use as greens. It is important, however, that the wild greens shall be gathered by persons who are familiar with the plants.*

PEAS

Green Peas.—This vegetable should be gathered when the seeds are about half grown, and it should be cooked as soon as possible after gathering. When the peas are thus young and tender they are best simply boiled and seasoned with salt and good butter. Some varieties of peas lack sweetness, and in this case a little sugar in the water in which they are cooked improves the flavor. Overcooking spoils the color and flavor of the vegetable. Peas should always be boiled slowly, and with the cover partially off the stewpan. It is impossible to give the exact time of cooking this vegetable, since so much depends upon the maturity of the peas, the length of time they have been picked, etc. Young, tender peas will generally cook in twenty or thirty minutes, and the seasoning should be added while they are still firm and crisp. If the peas are cooked until the green color of the chlorophyll is destroyed they are overdone and their delicate flavor is spoiled. When peas are overgrown and a little hard they should be cooked by the rule "Peas with pork." When this rule is followed a pinch of delicate, small, white onions may be added to the peas and other ingredients and will give a very savory dish.

Boiled Peas with Butter.—Put one quart of shelled peas in a stewpan and add enough boiling water to cover them generously. Place over a hot fire and when they begin to boil draw back where the water will bubble gently. Until the peas are done cook with the cover partially off the stewpan. When the peas are tender add one teaspoonful of salt and three tablespoonfuls of good butter. Cook ten minutes longer. If the peas are not the sweet kind add a teaspoonful of sugar with the salt and butter.

Peas with Pork.

1 quart peas.
4 ounces pork.
1 tablespoonful butter.
1 gill water (½ cupful).
2 small white onions.
⅛ teaspoonful pepper.

Cut pork into small bits. Put butter into stewpan and on the fire. When the butter is melted add the pork and cook gently until a light brown, then add the water, peas, onion, and pepper. This is a good way to cook peas when they are a little old and hard.

Peas with Lettuce.

1 quart peas.
2 tablespoonfuls butter.
1 head lettuce—the heart.
1 small onion.
1 teaspoonful sugar.
½ gill water.

Put all the ingredients into a stewpan, cover and place over the fire and cook for five minutes, tossing the vegetables several times. Now draw the pan back where the contents will simmer slowly for half an hour.

Purée of Dried or Split Peas.—Soak one quart of dried peas over night and follow the directions for purée of dried beans.

Sugar Peas.—The green pods of the sugar pea may be prepared like string beans.

---

* For a discussion of wild plants used as pot herbs, see "Some Additions to our Vegetable Dietary," by F. V. Coville, U. S. Dept. Agr. Yearbook 1895, p. 205.

Gather the pods while the seeds are still very small. String them like beans and cut into two or three lengths. Cover with boiling water and boil gently until tender. If they are young and fresh they will cook in twenty-five or thirty minutes. Pour off some of the water, which will serve for soup. Season with salt and butter and serve at once. When the pods are fresh and tender they have an exquisite flavor. When the seeds have grown large and the pods become tough they may be shelled and cooked like any other variety of peas. The seeds of the sugar pea are tender and fine flavored.

BEANS

Beans are served as a vegetable in three stages of growth, namely, the tender young pods, the fresh seeds, and the dried seeds. The pods are known as green or string beans and as butter beans, depending upon the variety. String beans make one of our most delicious vegetables, if young and properly cooked. They should be gathered before the seeds begin to form. In this state the bean is sweet, delicate, and tender, but not a highly nutritious food. Shelled beans, both dried and fresh, particularly the former, contain a large percentage of nitrogenous matter. The dried, ripe, shelled beans are apt to produce flatulence and sometimes colic. This trouble is largely due to the hull or skin and the germ, and may be remedied in a great measure by proper cooking, and, when possible, the removal of the hulls. The best forms in which to eat dried beans are in soups and purées. Beans that have been thoroughly stewed or baked under the right conditions may be eaten by people who live a good deal out of doors. Fat of some kind is necessary in the cooking of beans. The fat has a softening influence on the composition of the beans, and, since this vegetable has a very small percentage of fat, it is very desirable to supply this element either when cooking or when serving the vegetable. When possible, beans should be cooked in soft water. Dried beans are always hard when raw and have a strong acrid flavor. To soften them and remove the strong flavor, the vegetable should be soaked in cold water, and then brought to the boiling point in fresh cold water. This water should be thrown away and the cooking be finished in fresh water. A little soda in the water in which the beans are soaked and in the water in which they are first scalded will help to soften and sweeten the vegetable.

Green or String Beans.—Formerly it was difficult to find the slender, stringless green beans, but to-day the progressive market gardeners make a point of raising beans of this kind. Unfortunately, not all market gardeners and farmers are progressive, and many still raise a coarse, fibrous bean that is a disappointment to the consumer. In the very early stage of the pod almost any kind of bean will be good, if properly cooked, but all except the stringless kind must have their strings carefully removed. The pods should be gathered while small and tender. If for any reason they become wilted, they must be made crisp and fresh by being soaked in cold water. The beans that are brought from the South in cold weather are usually more or less wilted. They should be freed from strings, cut up, and soaked at least twelve hours in cold water. They will then cook like fresh beans.

To Blanch Green Beans.—Green beans should always be blanched. To do this drain them from the cold water and put them into water that is boiling rapidly, allowing a teaspoonful of salt to two quarts of water. Boil rapidly, with the cover partially off the saucepan, for twenty minutes. Turn into a colander and let cold water run upon them. They are now ready to be finished in any manner you like. The blanching can be done in the morning while the fire is good and the beans be finished for dinner at the proper time.

Green Beans, Plain.

1 quart beans.
½ pint water.
1 generous tablespoonful butter.
1 level teaspoonful salt.

String the beans if necessary and cut them into two-inch lengths. Blanch them as directed. Drain and put in the saucepan with the water, salt, and butter. Cook for ten minutes over a hot fire, turning the contents of the saucepan from time to time. Serve very hot. If the beans are not tender it may take fifteen minutes to cook them, but under all circumstances be careful not to overcook, as this ruins the flavor. If overcooked, green beans become yellow or brown.

Green Beans Boiled with Pork.—Boil about a quarter of a pound of pork for five hours. Have the beans free from strings and cut about 2 inches long. Cook them with the pork until tender (about half an hour).

Green Beans with Pork (French Method).

1 quart boiled beans.
2 ounces pork.
1 pint hot water.
1 teaspoonful flour.

Cut the pork into small dice and put in the stewpan. Cook slowly for twenty minutes, then add the water. Mix the flour with a few spoonfuls of cold water; stir into the pork and water. Place the stewpan where the contents will cook slowly for an hour. At the end of this time add the beans and cook half an hour. Taste to see if more salt is required. A tablespoonful of butter added just before serving is a great acquisition to this dish.

Butter beans, the varieties of string beans which are pale yellow in color, may be cooked like the green string beans.

Scarlet Runner Beans.—In Great Britain the scarlet runner beans, which are raised in the United States almost exclusively as an ornamental plant, are highly prized for the table. The tender green pods are "whittled" into small sections (after stringing) and cooked in water until just tender. Like other green vegetables, they lose their color and delicate flavor if overcooked. These beans are at their best seasoned only with butter and salt.

Shelled Kidney Beans.—All the varieties of this bean, when gathered while the seeds are still tender, may be cooked like the Lima beans. They may also be boiled with pork like green beans. It takes from one to two hours to cook kidney beans.

Stewed Shelled Beans.

1 quart shelled beans.
¼ pound salt pork.
1 onion.
½ teaspoonful pepper.
1 tablespoonful flour.
1 quart boiling water.
Salt to taste.

Cut the pork in slices and fry it slowly ten minutes in a stewpan. Add the onion, cut fine, and cook twenty minutes very slowly. Cover the beans with boiling water and boil ten minutes. Drain off the water. Put the beans and flour in the stewpan with the pork and onion, and stir over the fire for five minutes. Add the quart of boiling water and the pepper. Place the saucepan where its contents will simmer for two hours. Taste to see if salt enough; if not, add salt.

This method of cooking new shelled beans gives a savory and substantial dish.

Green Lima Beans.—Cover 1 quart of the shelled beans with boiling water. Place on the fire where they will boil up quickly, then draw back where they will just simmer until done. When tender pour off a part of the water. Season the beans with a teaspoonful of salt and 2 heaping tablespoonfuls of butter.

Or drain the water from the beans. Put the butter in a saucepan with 1 tablespoonful of flour. Stir over the fire until smooth and frothy, then add the beans and stir over the fire for five minutes. Draw back and add half a pint of water, meat stock, or milk. Simmer ten minutes. If liked, a teaspoonful of fine herbs may be added a few minutes before serving. It will take from forty-five to sixty minutes to boil the beans sufficiently.

Dried Beans.—All dried beans require the same preliminary treatment, no matter how they are to be finally cooked and served. Look them over carefully to remove all dirt and pebbles, then wash clean. Soak them overnight in plenty of cold water. In the morning pour off the water and put them in a stewpan with cold water enough to cover them generously. Let them come to the boiling point in this water, then drain. If the beans are old and hard, for each quart put a piece of soda about the size of a large bean in the water in which they are soaked overnight, also in the first water in which they are boiled.

The scalded and drained beans should be put back in the stewpan and covered generously with boiling water. Add 1 tablespoonful of salt for 1 quart of beans. They should now cook slowly, with the cover partially off the stewpan until they have reached the required degree of tenderness. For stewed and baked beans the cooking must stop when the skins begin to crack. For beans served with a sauce they should cook until perfectly tender, but they must not be broken or mushy. For purées and soups they should be cooked until very soft.

Purée of Dried Beans.

Cook 1 quart of beans in water until very soft, then drain well (saving the water) and rub through a purée sieve. Put 1 pint of the strained beans in a stewpan with 2 tablespoonfuls of butter or savory drippings, 1 teaspoonful of sugar, 1 teaspoonful of salt, one-fourth of a teaspoonful of pepper, and hot milk enough to make the purée like thick mush. About half a pint of milk will be right. Cook in the double boiler for one hour, stirring often and adding more milk if too dry. Heap the purée in the center of a hot platter. Garnish with a circle of fried sausages, pork chops, mutton chops, or any fat meat. The purée may be served as a vegetable, with any kind of meat. A soup may be made with the water in which the beans were cooked and the remainder of the strained beans.

Dried Beans Sauté.

Cook the beans until tender, but not broken. Drain off the water and save it for soup. For 1 quart of beans put 3 tablespoonfuls of savory drippings or butter in a large-bottomed stewpan. When the fat is hot put in the drained beans, which have been seasoned with a tablespoonful of salt and half a teaspoonful of pepper. Cook over a hot fire for fifteen minutes, frequently turning the beans over with a fork. Cover and let them cook for half an hour where they will not burn. If the beans are liked moist add a cupful of meat broth, milk, or water before putting them to cook for the last half hour.

This dish may be made more savory by frying a tablespoonful of minced chives, shallot, or onion in the butter or fat before adding the beans. A tablespoonful of fine herbs may also be added to the beans to make them more savory.

Dried Beans with Sauce.

The well-cooked and drained beans may be moistened with any good sauce and cooked for half an hour.

Dried Beans in Salad.

Season the cooked and drained beans with any of the salad dressings described elsewhere and serve as a salad.

Baked Beans.

Cook the dried beans gently until the skins begin to break, then drain off the water. Put a layer of beans in a bean pot or deep earthen dish, and on this layer, in the center of the dish, place a piece of salt pork ("streak of fat and streak of lean") having the rind side up, using for 1 quart of beans a half pound of pork; the rind should be scored. Fill up the dish with the beans and add seasonings and water to cover the beans. The simplest seasoning is 1 tablespoonful of salt and half a teaspoonful of pepper to a quart of beans. Mix the salt and pepper with the water. If liked, a tablespoonful of mustard may be added as well as a tablespoonful or more of molasses and an onion. Instead of the pork a piece of salt or fat beef or mutton may be employed. In this case there should be from 1½ to 2 pounds of the meat per quart of beans. If fresh meat be used, add more salt to the beans. If, on the other hand, salt meat is used, probably 1 teaspoonful of salt will be enough.

When mutton is employed trim off every particle of the skin.

Bake the beans in a very moderate oven for eight or ten hours. Add a little boiling water from time to time, but never enough to bring the water beyond the top of the beans. Any kind of bean may be baked in this manner. However, the small pea bean is the best for "Boston baked beans." The Lima and large white beans are best for the deep earthen dish. Do not cover the beans while baking.

Lentils.—Lentils may be cooked in purées, soups, etc., like dried beans.

Baked Lentils.

1 quart lentils.
1 quart water.
6 ounces mixed salt pork.
1 clove of garlic or 1 small onion.
1 generous teaspoonful salt.
½ teaspoonful pepper.

Pick over and wash the lentils. Soak in cold water overnight. In the morning pour off the water and put the lentils in a stewpan with two quarts of cold water and place on the fire. As soon as the water begins to boil the lentils will rise to the top. Take them off with a skimmer and put them in a deep earthen dish, with the pork and onion in the center. Mix the pepper and salt with a quart of boiling water and add. Put the dish in a moderate oven, and cook slowly for four or five hours. The lentils must be kept moist, and it may be necessary to add a little water from time to time. If the pork is not very salt the dish may require a little more salt.

Stewed lentils are prepared in about the same manner, but using more water. Instead of pork, fat corned beef or the shank of a ham may be employed.

Cowpeas. — Cowpeas (a common leguminous vegetable in the southern United States), also called black-eye peas, Whip-poor-will peas, Lady peas, cornfield peas, etc., are most excellent cooked like shelled beans when green. The young pods are also served like string beans. The ripe, dry beans, which are also very palatable and nutritious, may be cooked like dried beans or lentils.

POTATOES

There are many varieties of this vegetable. Tastes differ as to the most desirable kinds. In America and in England the white, mealy varieties are the most prized. On the Continent of Europe the "Yellow Holland" is a favorite variety. The white potato, when light and dry, is of delicate flavor and thought to be easy of digestion. It is especially suited for boiling, steaming, and baking, and for soups and purées. The yellow potatoes are more suitable for preparations in which it is desirable that the whole or pieces of potatoes shall retain their shape when cooked. Such potatoes are the best kind to use for salads, ragouts, hash, and for the fried potato known as "Pommes de terre soufflée," which is like a Saratoga chip, except that it puffs up like a little sack filled with air. In general the yellow potato has a richer flavor than the white.

The potato is in such common use that it would seem as if all its characteristics would be well understood and it would be cooked in perfection. Unfortunately, the contrary is true, and perhaps no other vegetable is so carelessly cooked as a rule.

The potato is a starchy food that contains enough moisture in its composition to cook the starch. This moisture is in the form of a watery juice, in which is dissolved the nitrogenous matter, the various salts, sugar, gum, etc. The starch cells are surrounded and penetrated by this watery bath. In cooking, the nitrogenous juice is coagulated in part at least by the heat, the starch granules swell and burst, and the starch absorbs the watery part of the juice. When this stage is reached, if the moisture has been in the right proportion, all parts of the potato will present a light, dry, glistening appearance. Every one concedes that such a potato will not cause digestive disturbance. However, the moisture is not always in the right proportion. Ripe potatoes and potatoes grown on a well-drained or sandy soil will, as a rule, be dry and mealy if properly cooked. Potatoes grown in a wet season or in a heavy, damp soil as a rule contain too large a proportion of moisture for the starch. Old potatoes that are allowed to sprout will be watery, probably owing to the withdrawal of some of the starch for food for the growing sprouts.

A poisonous substance called solanin is found in or near the skin of potatoes which have grown exposed to the sun or a strong light. Solanin also develops when potatoes are allowed to sprout, and serious illness has been known to follow the eating of exposed and sprouted potatoes. The green color which a potato exposed to a strong light takes on is largely due to the grains of chlorophyll developed in the parts of the tuber exposed to the light. The strong flavor is probably due to some substance which develops along with the chlorophyll. It will be seen that potatoes intended for the table should not be exposed to strong light or be allowed to sprout.

Potatoes cooked in dry heat, as by baking in the oven, roasting in ashes, frying in deep fat, or steaming in their jackets retain all their salts and other constituents, and the flavor is more pronounced and savory than when cooked in water. But potatoes so cooked must be served just as soon as they are done, or else they will become soggy and bad flavored.

Potatoes cooked in the skin should be free from any blemish and washed absolutely clean. Old potatoes, that is, potatoes that are kept into the spring and early summer, are better for being soaked in cold water and peeled before cooking.

Boiled Potatoes.

The method and the time given for boiling potatoes are the same whether the potato be peeled, partially peeled, or left with the skin intact. If a dozen or two ordinary sized potatoes are put on the fire in a large stewpan and are covered generously with boiling water and a cover is immediately put on the stewpan, they will be cooked to the proper point in thirty minutes from the time the cover was put on the stewpan. Small potatoes will cook in two minutes less time, and very large potatoes will require about thirty-five minutes' cooking. If the potatoes are to be boiled in their skins, wash them until clean and then with a sharp knife cut a narrow band of the skin from the center of the potato. Cut a little bit of the skin from each end of the potato. If the potatoes are to be peeled use a very sharp knife and remove the thinnest possible layer. The skins may be scraped off, if preferred, and there are special knives for this purpose. Let the potatoes boil fifteen minutes, then add 1 tablespoonful of salt for every dozen potatoes. When the potatoes have been cooking thirty minutes, drain off every drop of water and let all the steam pass off. They are now ready to serve, though they will not be injured but in fact will be improved by being kept hot for an hour or more, if they are well ventilated in such a way that they dry rather than retain moisture.

When boiled or steamed potatoes must be kept warm for any length of time, place the stewpan on the range on a tripod or iron ring and cover the potatoes with one thickness of cheese cloth. This will protect them from the cold air and allow the moisture to pass off.

Steamed Potatoes.

Steamed potatoes are prepared as for boiling, put in a closed vessel having a perforated bottom, which is then put over a kettle of boiling water. The water must be kept boiling hard every moment. They will require from thirty to forty minutes to cook.

Baked Potatoes.

Select potatoes having a smooth, unmarred surface. Wash perfectly clean and let them drain. Put them in an old baking pan kept for this purpose—do not crowd them—and put in a hot oven. If the oven is large and hot and the potatoes of medium size, forty minutes will answer for the cooking. On the other hand, if the oven is filled with cold potatoes the temperature of the oven will be reduced quickly and it will require an hour to cook the potatoes. Baked potatoes should be served as soon as they are done. If they must be kept any time after the cooking is completed, break them in order that the moisture may escape. Keep them in a warm oven or covered with cheese cloth in a stewpan.

Reheating Potatoes.

Cold boiled, steamed, or baked potatoes may all be utilized in savory dishes. In reheating potatoes the following things must be kept in mind: The potatoes must be well seasoned to make them savory, they must be heated to as high a temperature as possible without burning them, and they must be served very hot. The cold potatoes may be sliced or be cut into small pieces, seasoned with salt and pepper and browned in a little savory drippings, or seasoned as before and heated in the frying pan with butter or the drippings. A little minced onion, or chives, or green pepper, or a tablespoonful of fine herbs may be added.

A tablespoonful of butter and a teaspoonful of flour may be stirred over the fire until the mixture is smooth and frothy. Add to this a pint of well-seasoned potatoes and stir the mixture with a fork for three minutes, then add half a pint of milk and cook until thoroughly heated, being careful not to burn. A pint and a half of cold potatoes cut in cubes and seasoned with salt and pepper may be heated in a pint of the white sauce described elsewhere.

Escalloped Potatoes.

This dish may be prepared by mixing a pint and a half of cold potatoes cut in cubes and seasoned with a teaspoonful of salt, one-fourth of a teaspoonful of pepper, and a pint of cream sauce. Put the mixture in a shallow baking dish, cover with grated bread crumbs, and dot with butter. Bake half an hour in a moderate oven.

Sweet Potatoes. — Southern and northern tastes differ as to what is a desirable quality in a sweet potato. In the South the moist potato is considered best. At the North the dry potato is more generally liked. The variety of potatoes grown for the northern market is commonly less sweet and moist than those grown for the South. However, long cooking will make any sweet potato moist.

Baked Sweet Potatoes.

Wash the potatoes and bake the same as white potatoes. Small ones will bake in half an hour, while very large ones will require an hour or more. If the potatoes are liked very moist and sweet, bake from an hour to two hours, depending on size.

Browned Sweet Potatoes.

Boil medium-sized sweet potatoes forty-five minutes. Peel them and cut in halves lengthwise. Put them in a baking pan and baste with savory drippings, and season with salt. Cook them in a hot oven for twenty minutes.

Fried Sweet Potatoes.

Cut the boiled potatoes in slices and fry brown in savory drippings. Or the potatoes may be cut in four parts lengthwise, put in a frying basket and be cooked for ten minutes in smoking hot fat. The fat must be deep enough to cover the potatoes.

Candied Sweet Potatoes.

Candied sweet potatoes are very popular on southern tables, and are extremely palatable when well prepared. Cut boiled sweet potatoes into long slices, place in an earthen dish, put lumps of butter on each slice, and sprinkle with sugar. Some cooks add a little water also. Bake until the sugar and butter have candied and the potatoes are brown.

OTHER ROOTS AND BULBS

Jerusalem Artichoke.—This vegetable is in season in the fall and spring, and may be cooked like kohlrabi and served in a white cream or sauce. The artichoke may also be cooked in milk.

When this is done, cut the washed and peeled artichoke into cubes, put in a stewpan, and cover with milk (a generous pint to a quart of cubes). Add one small onion and cook twenty minutes. Beat together one tablespoonful of butter and one level tablespoonful of flour, and stir this into the boiling milk. Then season with a teaspoonful of salt and one-fourth of a teaspoonful of pepper, and continue the cooking half an hour longer. The cooking should be done in a double boiler. The artichoke also makes a very good soup.

Turnips.—This vegetable is generally spoiled by overcooking. The flat, white summer turnip, when sliced, will cook in thirty minutes. If the cooking is prolonged beyond this time, the vegetable begins to deteriorate, growing dark in color and strong in flavor. The winter turnips require from forty-five to sixty minutes.

Boiled Turnips.

Have the turnips peeled and sliced. Drop the slices into a stewpan with boiling water enough to cover generously. Cook until tender, then drain well. They are now ready to mash or chop. If they are to be served mashed, put them back in the stewpan; mash with a wooden vegetable masher, as metal is apt to impart an unpleasant taste. Season with salt, butter, and a little pepper. Serve at once.

Hashed Turnips.

Chop the drained turnips into rather large pieces. Return to the stewpan, and for a pint and a half of turnips add a teaspoonful of salt, one-fourth of a teaspoonful of pepper, a tablespoonful of butter, and four tablespoonfuls of water. Cook over a very hot fire until the turnips have absorbed all the seasonings. Serve at once. Or the salt, pepper, butter, and a tablespoonful of flour may be added to the hashed turnips; then the stewpan may be placed over the hot fire and shaken frequently to toss up the turnips. When the turnips have been cooking five minutes in this manner add half a pint of meat stock or of milk and cook ten minutes.

Carrots.—The carrot is valuable as a vegetable and as a flavorer. When partially grown and fresh from the ground they have a delicious flavor, and are so tender that they may be cooked without water. As the carrot grows old the flavor grows stronger, and in the majority of varieties the heart grows hard and woody. When the carrot reaches this stage only the outer layers are desirable for food.

Carrots with White Sauce.

Scrape the carrots lightly; then cut into large dice or slices. Put into a stewpan with salted boiling water, allowing a teaspoonful of salt for a quart of water, and boil until tender. The young carrots will cook in thirty minutes and the old ones in forty-five. Drain, season with a little salt, put them in a vegetable dish, and pour the white sauce over them. Or the carrots may be cut into dice before cooking and boiled and drained as directed; then put them back in the stewpan, and for every pint add one tablespoonful of butter, one teaspoonful of sugar, half a teaspoonful of salt, and one gill of water or meat stock. Cook over a hot fire until the carrots have absorbed the seasonings and liquid.

Parsnips.—This vegetable, because of its pronounced taste, is probably not so generally liked as are most of the other roots. It is at its best in the early spring, when it has been in the ground all winter.

The simplest method of cooking the parsnip is to wash it clean, boil it, and then scrape off the skin. Now cut in slices and put in the vegetable dish. Season with salt and butter. When the parsnips are tender and just out of the ground they will cook in thirty-five minutes; when old it takes from forty to fifty minutes to cook them. The cooked and peeled parsnips may be chopped rather coarse, seasoned with salt, and put into a stewpan with hot milk enough to cover them. Place the stewpan on the range where the heat is moderate.

For a pint and a half of parsnips beat together one tablespoonful of butter and one teaspoonful of flour. Stir into the parsnips and milk. Simmer for ten minutes. Parsnips are often cut in slices after boiling and fried in butter.

Salsify.—This vegetable is sometimes called oyster plant, because the flavor suggests that of the oyster, particularly when the boiled vegetable is sliced and fried in butter. Salsify is one of the roots that may be left in the ground over winter, thus making this vegetable available for the late summer, fall, and spring.

To prevent this root from turning dark it must be dropped as soon as it is pared and cut into a mixture of flour and water made slightly acid with vinegar. For 6 good-sized roots mix together 1 tablespoonful of vinegar, 2 tablespoonfuls of flour, 1 teaspoonful of salt, and 3 pints of water. Wash and scrape the roots, then cut into slices about 3 inches long. Drop into the prepared water. Place the stewpan on the fire and cook the salsify thirty minutes, counting from the time it begins to boil. Drain and serve in a white sauce. Or mix together 1 tablespoonful of butter, half a teaspoonful of salt, 1 teaspoonful of lemon juice, and 1 teaspoonful of minced parsley or chervil. Add this to the drained salsify and serve at once.

Beets.—Beets are among our most useful vegetables, since they may be had all through the summer and may also be stored in good condition for winter use. Sometimes beets are cut in small pieces, after boiling, and served with white sauce, but the most common as well as the most palatable way of serving them is with butter.

Beets with Butter.

Wash the beets, being careful not to break the skin. Put into a stewpan and cover generously with boiling water and boil until tender. Young beets will cook in one hour. As the beets grow old the time of cooking must be increased. In winter this vegetable becomes so hard it may require four or more hours of steady boiling to soften it. It is then only suitable for pickling in vinegar after being thoroughly boiled.

When the young beets are cooked, take them from the boiling water and drop them into cold water. Rub off the skin. Cut the beets in thin slices and season with salt and butter. Serve at once.

Kohl-Rabi, or Turnip Cabbage.—This vegetable is a variety of the cabbage, but instead of the reserve nutritive matter of the plant being stored largely in the leaves or flowers, it is collected in the stem, which forms a turniplike enlargement just above the ground. Kohl-rabi is fine flavored and delicate, if cooked when very young and tender. It should be used when it has a diameter of not more than 2 or 3 inches. As it grows large it becomes tough and fibrous.

Boiled Kohl-Rabi.

Wash and pare the vegetables, then cut in thin slices. Put into slightly salted boiling water and boil, with the cover partially off the stewpan, until the vegetable is tender. This will take from thirty to fifty minutes. Pour off the water and season with butter, salt, and pepper.

Kohl-rabi may be boiled with pork in the same way as cabbage. The cold boiled vegetable may be served as a salad.

Celeriac.—This vegetable is also known as "knot celery" and "turnip-rooted celery." The roots, which are about the size of a white turnip, and not the stalks are eaten. They are more often used as a vegetable than as a salad.

Pare the celeriac, cut in thin, narrow slices, and put into cold water. Drain from this water and drop into boiling water and boil thirty minutes. Drain and rinse with cold water. The celeriac is now ready to be prepared and served the same as celery.

Purée of Celeriac.

1 quart celeriac cut in dice.
2 tablespoonfuls butter.
1 tablespoonful flour.
1 teaspoonful salt.
1 gill stock or cream.

Cook the celeriac thirty minutes in boiling water, rinse in cold water, then press through a purée sieve. Put the butter in a saucepan and on the fire. When hot add the flour and stir until smooth and frothy, and then add the strained celeriac and cook five minutes, stirring frequently. Add the salt and stock or cream and cook five minutes longer. If the purée seems dry, add more stock or cream. The vegetable varies as to the amount of moisture it requires. It should be eaten very hot. If used as a garnish, it is generally put in the center of the dish and the poultry or meat placed on it or around it. Otherwise it may be served on toast or fried bread as a dish by itself.

Celery.—The culture of this vegetable is so general that one can find it in large markets nearly every month of the year. Celery is at its best in the late fall and early winter, when the weather has been cold enough to crisp the blanched stalks. This plant is most useful as a salad and flavorer, but is perhaps most commonly eaten raw, without any dressing except salt, as an accompaniment of fish, meat, etc.

Only the tender, inner stalks should be eaten raw. The hard, outside stalks make a delicious and wholesome dish when properly cooked.

When thus used, celery should be blanched and served with a sauce.

Stewed Celery.

To blanch celery in cooking, remove all the leaves from the stalks. Scrape off all rusted or dark spots, cut into pieces about 3 inches long, and put in cold water. Have a stewpan of boiling water on the fire, wash and drain the celery and put in the boiling water. Add one teaspoonful of salt for every 2 quarts of water. Boil rapidly for fifteen minutes, having the cover partially off the stewpan. Pour off the water and rinse with cold water, then drain. The celery is now ready to finish in the following manner: Put the celery in the stewpan with one tablespoonful of butter, and one teaspoonful of salt for each quart of celery. Cover and cook slowly for fifteen minutes. Shake the pan frequently while the celery is cooking. Serve hot.

Onion.—This vegetable is the most useful of all our flavorers, and there is hardly a soup, stew, sauce, etc., that is not improved by the addition of the onion flavor. As a vegetable the onion may be prepared in a variety of ways. The white onions are the most delicate and are therefore more suitable as a vegetable than the yellow or red variety. The large Spanish onions and the Bermuda onion are also delicate and suitable for a table vegetable. If the stronger onions are used for this purpose they must be thoroughly blanched.

Boiled Onions in White Sauce.

Peel the onions and cut off the roots, dropping into cold water as fast as they are peeled. Drain from the cold water and put in a stewpan with boiling water to cover generously. Add a teaspoonful of salt for each quart of water. Boil rapidly for ten minutes, with the cover partially off the saucepan. Drain off the water and cover the onion with hot sweet milk (a quart of onions will require a pint of milk). Simmer for half an hour. Beat together one tablespoonful of butter and one level tablespoonful of flour. Add one teaspoonful of salt and one-fourth of a teaspoonful of white pepper. Gradually beat in about half a cupful of the milk in which the onions are cooking. When smooth, stir the mixture into the onions and milk. Let the dish cook ten minutes longer and serve.

Stewed Onions.

Cut the onions in slices and boil in salted water for ten minutes. Drain well and return to the stewpan.

For a quart and a half of onion, measured before it was boiled, add two tablespoonfuls of butter, one teaspoonful of salt, and one-fourth of a teaspoonful of pepper. Cover the stewpan and cook over a hot fire for five minutes, shaking the pan to prevent the onion from browning. Set the stewpan back where the contents will cook slowly for forty minutes. Drippings may be substituted for the butter, but, of course, the dish will not be so delicate in flavor.

MISCELLANEOUS VEGETABLES

Cucumbers. — The cucumber is much oftener eaten in the United States as a salad than cooked, yet it is a very palatable vegetable when stewed and served with a white sauce, or seasoned with butter, salt, and pepper, and served on toast. The pared and quartered cucumber should be cooked until tender in boiling salted water, which will require about fifteen minutes, and then served as directed. Cucumbers may also be cut in slices lengthwise and fried like summer squash or eggplant.

Stewed Cucumbers.

Stew pared cucumbers, cut in quarters or in thick slices, for fifteen minutes in a saucepan with a little water and a minced shallot or a small minced onion. Pour off the water; stir in a little flour, butter, and salt; heat for two or three minutes, and then serve.

Cucumber Sauté.

Boil pared and quartered cucumbers for three minutes only. Then drain the pieces and season with salt and pepper. Roll in flour and cook in a saucepan with butter for twenty minutes. This dish may be varied by adding minced parsley, chives, and chervil about five minutes before the cooking is finished.

Tomatoes.—The tomato, although not very nutritious, may be classed as one of our must useful vegetables. Raw, it makes an attractive and refreshing salad and may be served by itself or in combination with other vegetables, with meat or with fish. As a vegetable the tomato may be prepared in many ways. It makes a good foundation for soups and sauces. Made into catsup or pickles it serves as a relish. The addition of a little tomato gives a pleasant, acid flavor to many soups and sauces, and also to meat, fish, and vegetable dishes. If possible the tomatoes should ripen fully on the vines, as the flavor is much better than when picked green and then allowed to ripen.

When properly canned this vegetable keeps well and retains its natural flavor. The housekeeper who has a generous supply of canned tomatoes on hand will find them very valuable at all times of the year, but especially in the winter months when the variety of vegetables is not great.

Overcooking spoils the flavor and color of the tomato.

To Peel Tomatoes.

Put the ripe tomatoes into a dish and pour boiling water over them. Let them rest in the water about one minute; then pour the water off. The thin skin will now peel off readily.

When a quantity of tomatoes are to be peeled have a deep stewpan a little more than half filled with boiling water and on the fire where the water will continue to boil. Put the tomatoes in a frying basket and lower into the boiling water. Let the basket remain one minute in the water. There must, of course, be water enough to cover the tomatoes.

Stewed Tomatoes.

Peel the tomatoes and cut into small pieces. Put into a stewpan and on the fire. Boil gently for twenty minutes or half an hour, counting from the time it begins to boil. Season five minutes before the cooking is finished. Allow for each quart of tomato one generous teaspoonful each of salt and sugar and one tablespoonful or more of butter.

Escalloped Tomatoes.

1 pint peeled and cut tomatoes.
1 pint grated bread crumbs.
1 level teaspoonful salt.
1 tablespoonful butter.
A suggestion of pepper.

Reserve three tablespoonfuls of the bread crumbs, and spread the remainder on a pan. Brown in the oven, being careful not to burn them. Mix the tomato, browned crumbs, salt, pepper, and half the butter together, and put in a shallow baking dish. Spread the unbrowned crumbs on top, and dot with the remainder of the butter, cut into bits. Bake in a moderately hot oven for half an hour. The top of this dish should be brown and crisp.

Tomato Toast.

Boil one quart of peeled and cut tomatoes for ten minutes, then rub through a strainer. Return to the stewpan and add two level teaspoonfuls of salt, half a teaspoonful of pepper, and two tablespoonfuls of butter. Place on the fire and cook five minutes. Have the bottom of a hot platter covered with well-toasted slices of bread and pour the hot tomato over it. Serve at once. A dropped or poached egg may be put on each slice of toast.

Okra.—Though okra, a variety of Hibiscus with mucilaginous edible pods, will grow in most parts of the United States, it is much more commonly eaten in the Southern States than elsewhere. The young pods should be boiled in salted water until tender (about twenty minutes), drained, and heated for 5 minutes with cream (a scant cup to a quart of okra), a tablespoonful of butter, and salt and pepper. Okra is also a common ingredient of soups.

The cultivation of okra, methods of serving it, and related topics are discussed in a recent publication of the U. S. Department of Agriculture.

Green Peppers.—The sweet green pepper, though fairly common in our city markets, is not as widely known as a vegetable as it deserves. Sliced, it makes a very fine salad alone, or, more commonly, mixed with other salad plants like lettuce. Stuffed and baked peppers are very palatable.

Green Peppers Stuffed and Baked.

Use only tender sweet peppers. For six medium-sized peppers make a dressing in the following manner: Soak, in cold water, enough stale bread to make one pint when the water is pressed out. Season this with two teaspoonfuls of salt, one tablespoonful of fine herbs, about one-fifth of a teaspoonful each of sweet basil and summer savory, and two tablespoonfuls of butter or savory drippings.

Cut off the stem end of the pepper and remove all the interior, being careful to take out every seed. Fill the peppers with the dressing. Place them on end in a shallow baking dish and pour around them a sauce prepared as follows: Put into a saucepan and on the fire, one tablespoonful of drippings. When hot, add one level tablespoonful of flour. Stir until smooth and brown, then add, gradually, three gills of meat stock or water. Season with one level teaspoonful of salt. Cook five minutes, then pour around the stuffed peppers. Put the dish in a moderately hot oven and bake the peppers one hour, basting often with the sauce in the dish. Peppers may also be filled with a well-seasoned dressing of chopped meat, made with or without the addition of bread crumbs or rice.

Eggplant.—This vegetable, as well as potato and tomato, belongs to the nightshade family. Like all succulent green vegetables, it has little nutritive value. The common methods of cooking are by frying, broiling, and baking.

Baked Eggplant.

For baked eggplant make a dressing as for stuffed peppers, except that a little more salt, pepper, and butter are used. Cut the eggplant in two lengthwise, scrape out the inside, and mash it fine, then mix with the dressing and return to the shells. Place on a pan and in the oven. Cook forty-five minutes.

Fried Eggplant.

For fried eggplant cut the vegetable in slices about half an inch thick and pare. Sprinkle the slices with salt and pile them upon one another, put a plate with a weight on top of the slices. Let them rest for an hour, then remove weight and plate. Add one tablespoonful of water, half a tablespoonful of salt, and half a teaspoonful of pepper to an egg. Beat well. Dip the slices of eggplant in the egg, then in dried bread crumbs. Spread on a dish for twenty or more minutes. Fry till brown (in deep fat).

Broiled Eggplant.

The eggplant is sliced and drained as directed above. Then spread the slices on a dish, season with pepper, and baste with salad oil, sprinkle with dried bread crumbs and broil.

Squash.—The various varieties of the summer squash are generally cooked when so small and tender that the thumb nail can pierce the rind easily.

To prepare for the table wash the squash, cut into small pieces, and either cook in boiling water or steam it. It will cook in boiling water in half an hour. It takes about an hour to cook it in the steamer. The cooked squash is mashed fine and seasoned with salt, pepper, and butter. This method gives a delicate flavored but rather watery dish.

Summer squash is very palatable cut in slices and fried like eggplant.

It is claimed by many that the very young summer squashes, particularly the turban variety, or "cymlin" of the Southern States, are very delicate and palatable cooked whole. For this dish they should not be much larger than a silver dollar. In the opinion of the writer the crook-necked and other summer squashes are richer in flavor when grown to a large size. From the more mature squash remove the thin skin and seeds. Cut the squash in small pieces and put in a stewpan with boiling water enough to cover. Boil for half an hour. Drain, mash, and season with salt, pepper, and butter.

Cook winter squash in the same manner. Squash is one of the vegetables that require a good deal of butter.

Green Corn.—Green corn, a typical American food product, is a vegetable which, for most palates, is easily spoiled by overcooking, since the longer the cooking period the less pronounced the delicate corn flavor.

Boiled Corn on the Cob.

The most satisfactory way to serve green corn is on the cob. Free the corn from husks and "silk." Have a kettle of water boiling hard, drop the corn into the water and cook ten minutes. If only a few ears of corn are put in a kettle of boiling water, the temperature of the water is not lowered greatly and the corn will cook in eight minutes. On the other hand, if a large quantity of corn is crowded into a kettle of boiling water, the temperature is very much lowered and the time of cooking must be increased. When possible, surround the corn with a generous quantity of boiling water.

Corn Cut From Cob.

Corn may be cut from the cob and heated with butter, pepper, and a little milk. For this dish cook the ears five minutes in boiling water to set the juice. Then with a sharp knife cut through the center of each row of grains and with the back of a case knife press the grains of corn from the hulls. Put the corn in a saucepan and season with salt, pepper, and butter. Add enough hot milk to moisten well, and cook ten minutes. Serve at once.

The raw corn may be cut from the cob and treated in the same manner.

Succotash.

To a pint of corn cooked as above add a pint of cooked and seasoned shelled beans.

Vegetable Hash.—Hash may be made with one or many cooked vegetables, the vegetable or vegetables being used alone or combined with meat or fish. Potato is the most useful vegetable for a hash, as it combines well with the animal food or with other vegetables.

The conditions essential to a good hash are that the vegetables shall be cut fairly fine, but not so fine that the pieces shall lose their shape or stick together—that is, the particles should drop apart readily when shaken on a fork. Each vegetable must be cut up separately, then all be mixed. The vegetables, or vegetable, and meat or fish must be well seasoned with salt and pepper, and if liked there may be added a little minced onion, chives, parsley, chervil, or green pepper finely minced. The hash must be moistened a little with meat broth, milk, or water (not more than half a cupful for a quart of hash). When the hash is mixed, seasoned, and moistened put a tablespoonful of butter or savory drippings in a frying pan. When this is melted put in the hash, and spread evenly and lightly in the pan. Over this put little dots of butter or savory drippings, using about one tablespoonful in all. Cover the pan and place where the hash will not burn, but where the heat is fairly good, and cook half an hour, then fold and turn on a hot platter. A rich brown crust will have formed on the bottom of the hash if the heat was sufficient. Serve very hot. The plates on which hash is served should be hot.

Rice.—Wash 1 cupful of rice in several waters, rubbing the grains between the hands to remove all the dirt. Put the washed rice in a stewpan with 2½ cupfuls of water and 1 teaspoonful of salt. Cover and place where the water will boil. Cook for twenty minutes, being careful not to let it burn. At the end of this time put the stewpan on a tripod or ring and cover the rice with a fold of cheese cloth. Let it continue to cook in this manner an hour, then turn into a hot vegetable dish. The rice will be tender, dry, and sweet, and each grain will be separate. During the whole process of cooking the rice must not be stirred. If a tablespoonful of butter is cut up and sprinkled over the rice when it has cooked twenty minutes the dish will be very much improved.

Hominy and Corn Meal. — The large hominy, which is so common in the southern part of the United States, is frequently served as a vegetable, either boiled or fried in drippings. Fine hominy, which is more common in the northern part of the country, and which is often served as a vegetable, should be thoroughly washed, and cooked in boiling water in the proportion of 1 gill of hominy to a pint of water, to which a half teaspoonful of salt has been added. When cold, the boiled hominy may be cut in slices and fried. The slices will brown more readily if they are first rolled in flour.

Fried corn-meal mush is often served as a vegetable, with chicken and other meats, and is very palatable and useful when fresh vegetables are not common. It is interesting to note that in the Southern States rice and hominy are much oftener used as starchy vegetables in place of potatoes than in other parts of the country.

Vegetable Soups. — Nearly every vegetable grown may be employed in the preparation of soups, either as the foundation for the soup or as a garnish to any kind of meat stock. A few types of vegetable soups are here given. Meat, meat broth, or beef extract may be added to any of them if additional flavor is desired, but as they stand they are very satisfactory soups.

Mixed Vegetable Soup.

- 3 quarts water.
- 1 quart shredded cabbage.
- 1 pint sliced potato.
- ½ pint minced carrot.
- ½ pint minced turnip.
- ½ pint minced onion.
- 1 leek.
- 2 tomatoes.
- 2 tablespoonfuls minced celery.
- 2 tablespoonfuls green pepper.
- 2 tablespoonfuls butter or drippings.
- 3 teaspoonfuls salt.
- ½ teaspoonful pepper.

Have the water boiling hard in a stewpan and add all the vegetables except the potatoes and tomatoes. Boil rapidly for ten minutes, then draw back where it will boil gently for one hour. At the end of this time add the other ingredients and cook one hour longer. Have the cover partially off the stewpan during the entire cooking. This soup may be varied by using different kinds of vegetables.

Herb Soup.

½ pint finely shredded spinach.
¼ pint shredded sorrel.
¼ blanched and sliced leek.
The white heart leaves of a head of lettuce.
4 potatoes, medium size.
3 level teaspoonfuls salt.
4 tablespoonfuls butter.
1 tablespoonful chervil.
2 quarts boiling water.
½ pint bread cut in dice and fried in butter or browned in the oven.

Have the sorrel, spinach, and lettuce fresh, tender, and free from tough midribs. Wash and shred. Cut the washed leek into thin slices. Put in the stewpan with the butter and cook fifteen minutes, being careful not to brown. Now add the potatoes, salt, and boiling water. Place the stewpan where the contents will boil quickly, and when the soup begins to boil draw the stewpan back where the contents will boil gently for one hour. At the end of this time crush the potatoes with a fork, add the chervil, and simmer five minutes longer. Turn into the soup tureen, add the crisped bread, and serve.

If preferred, the soup may be rubbed through a purée sieve, returned to the fire, and when boiling hot be poured on the yolks of 2 eggs which have been beaten with 2 tablespoonfuls of milk.

This soup may be varied indefinitely. Any number of green vegetables can be employed in making it, care being taken to use only a small quantity of those of pronounced flavor.

Sorrel Soup.

3 pints boiling water.
3 tablespoonfuls butter.
⅓ cup shredded sorrel.
3 tablespoonfuls milk.
1 teaspoonful salt.
Yolk 2 eggs.
½ cupful bread cut in dice and dried in the oven or fried in butter.

Tear the tender green parts from the midribs of the cultivated sorrel; wash in cold water and shred very fine. Put half the butter in a stewpan and add the shredded sorrel. Place on the fire and cook five minutes, stirring frequently. Now add the boiling water and salt and boil ten minutes. Beat the yolks of the eggs well, then add the milk and pour into the soup tureen, and add the remaining half of the butter cut into bits. Gradually pour the boiling-hot soup in the soup tureen, stirring all the while to combine the hot mixture with the egg yolk. Add the bread dice and serve.

Leek Soup.

3 quarts boiling water.
2 cupfuls leeks, cut fine.
4 cupfuls potatoes, cut in dice.
2 tablespoonful butter or drippings.
3 teaspoonfuls salt.
½ teaspoonful pepper.
4 slices stale bread cut in small pieces.
4 tablespoonfuls minced onion.

Wash the leeks and cut off the roots. Cut the white part in thin slices. Pare the potatoes and cut in dice. Put them in a bowl of cold water. Put the butter, leeks, and onion in the soup pot and on the fire. Cook twenty minutes slowly, stirring frequently, then add the hot water, potatoes, and seasoning, and cook at least half an hour longer. Serve very hot. If it is convenient and liked, cook with the leeks and butter the white stalks of 4 or 5 cibols, or 1 shallot may be cut fine and cooked with the leeks.

This is a delicious and wholesome soup, and is even better reheated the second day than the first.

Cream of Leek Soup.

Make this soup as directed for leek soup, using only 3 pints of water. When it is cooked, rub through a sieve, return to the soup pot, and add 1 quart of hot milk. Beat with whisk until smooth. Half a cupful of the milk can be reserved cold and added to 2 well-beaten yolks of eggs. Stir this into the soup just as it is taken from the fire.

The yolks of the eggs make the soup very much richer.

Potato Soup.

- 8 medium-sized potatoes.
- ½ pint chopped celery.
- 4 tablespoonfuls minced onion.
- 1 tablespoonful butter.
- 1 tablespoonful flour.
- 1½ teaspoonfuls salt.
- ½ teaspoonful pepper.
- 1 teaspoonful minced chervil or parsley.
- 1 quart milk.

Pare the potatoes and put in a stewpan with the celery and onion. Cover with boiling water and put over a hot fire. Cook thirty minutes, counting from the time the pan is put over the fire. Reserve half a cupful of the milk cold, and put the balance to heat in the double boiler. Mix the flour with the cold milk and stir into the boiling milk. When the potatoes, etc., have been cooking thirty minutes pour off the water, saving it to use later. Mash and beat the vegetables until light and fine, then gradually beat in the water in which they were boiled, rub through the purée sieve and then put back on the fire. Add the salt and pepper. Beat with an egg whisk for three minutes, then gradually beat in the boiling milk. Add the butter and minced herbs and serve at once.

Cream of Celeriac Soup.

- 1 quart celeriac cut in cubes.
- 1 quart white stock.
- 1 pint cream.
- ½ pint canned peas.
- 2 tablespoonfuls butter.
- 2 tablespoonfuls salt.
- ½ tablespoonful pepper.
- Yolks of 2 eggs.

Follow the rule given for purée of celeriac, gradually adding the hot white stock, rub through a fine sieve, return to the fire, and add a cupful of canned peas. Reserve one cupful of the cream cold and add the remainder to the soup. Beat the yolks of the eggs well and add the cold cream to them, then stir the mixture into the soup. Draw back from the fire and beat with the whisk for one minute, then serve at once.

Tomato Soup.

- 1 quart peeled and finely cut tomatoes.
- 1 quart cold water.
- 1 onion.
- 1 tablespoonful sugar.
- 2 teaspoonfuls salt.
- ½ teaspoonful pepper.
- 2 tablespoonfuls butter.
- 4 tablespoonfuls cornstarch.
- 1 tablespoonful flour.

Mix the cornstarch with the water and put into a stewpan with all the other ingredients, except the butter and flour, the onion being left whole. Stir frequently until the soup boils, then cook half an hour, counting from the time it begins to boil. At the end of this time beat the butter and flour together until light and smooth and stir into the soup. Cook ten minutes longer, then take out the onion and serve the soup with toasted or fried bread. If a smooth soup is desired strain through a fine sieve. This is the simplest kind of tomato soup. It may be varied by the addition of rice, macaroni, beans, peas, and other vegetables. Instead of the fried bread stale bread may be cut in small pieces and put in the bottom of the soup tureen.

Okra and Tomato Soup.

1 pint sliced okra.
1½ pints tomatoes pared and cut fine.
2 quarts water.
3 tablespoonfuls rice.
3 tablespoonfuls minced onion.
1 green pepper, seeds removed and pepper cut fine.
3 teaspoonfuls salt.
¼ teaspoonful pepper.

Put all the ingredients into the soup pot and cook gently for two hours, then add two tablespoonfuls of butter or sweet drippings and serve. The bones from roast meat or broiled meat cooked with this soup add to the flavor.

Onion Chowder.

3 quarts boiling water.
1 pint minced onion.
1 quart potatoes cut in dice.
3 teaspoonfuls salt.
½ teaspoonful pepper.
3 tablespoonfuls butter or savory drippings.
1 tablespoonful fine herbs.

Cook the onion and butter together for half an hour, but slowly, so that the onion will not brown. At the end of this time add the boiling water, potatoes, salt, and pepper and cook one hour longer, then add the fine herbs and serve.

Green Pea Soup.

1 quart shelled peas.
3 pints water.
1 quart milk.
1 onion.
2 tablespoonfuls butter.
1 tablespoonful flour.
3 level teaspoonfuls salt.
½ teaspoonful pepper.

Put the peas in a stewpan with the boiling water and onion and cook until tender, which will be about half an hour. Pour off the water, saving for use later. Mash the peas fine, then add the water in which they were boiled, and rub through a purée sieve. Return to the saucepan, add flour and butter, beaten together, and the salt and pepper. Now gradually add the milk, which must be boiling hot. Beat well and cook ten minutes, stirring frequently.

Split Pea Soup.

1 pint split peas.
4 quarts water.
½ pound salt pork.
1 large onion.
2 tablespoonfuls celery.
1 tablespoonful flour.
1 tablespoonful butter.
1 teaspoonful pepper.
1 sprig parsley.

Pick the peas over, that there may be no blemished ones among them, then wash and soak in cold water over night. In the morning turn off the water and put them in the soup pot, with the cold water and salt pork. Simmer gently seven hours, being careful that the soup does not burn. When it has cooked six hours add the seasoning. Have a large wooden spoon to stir the soup. When done it should be thin enough to pour. By boiling it may become too thick; if so, add boiling water. When thoroughly cooked, the soup is smooth and rather mealy. If not cooked enough, after standing a few minutes the thick part will settle, and the top look watery. At the end of seven hours strain the soup through a sieve and return to a soup pot. Beat the flour and butter together until creamy, then stir into the soup and simmer half an hour longer. If the salt pork has not seasoned the soup sufficiently add a little salt. For some tastes the soup would be improved by the addition of a quart of hot milk.

Serve little squares of fried bread in a separate dish.

Dried Bean Soup.

1 pint dried beans.
4 quarts water.
1 large onion, minced fine.

4 tablespoonsful sweet drippings or butter which gives a better flavor.
3 tablespoonsful flour.
1 tablespoonful minced celery or a few dried celery leaves.
½ teaspoonful pepper.
2 teaspoonsful salt.

Wash the beans and soak them over night in cold water. In the morning pour off the water and put them in the soup pot with 3 quarts of cold water. Place on the fire and when the water comes to the boiling point pour it off (throw this water away). Add 4 quarts of boiling water to the beans and place the soup pot where the contents will simmer for four hours. Add the celery the last hour of cooking. Cook the onion and drippings slowly in a stewpan for half an hour. Drain the water from the beans (save this water) and put them in the stewpan with the onions and drippings. Then add the flour and cook half an hour, stirring often. At the end of this time mash fine and gradually add the water in which the beans were boiled until the soup is like thick cream. Then rub through a purée sieve and return to the fire; add the salt and pepper and cook twenty minutes or more. Any kind of beans may be used for this soup; the Lima beans give the most delicate soup, but the large or small white beans are very satisfactory and are less expensive than the Limas.

In cold weather the quantities of beans and flavorings may be doubled, but only 6 quarts of water are used. The resulting thick soup can be kept in a cold place and a portion boiled up as required and thinned with meat stock or milk.

Cream of Bean Soup.

Make as above, but add only enough of the water in which the beans were cooked to make the mixture like thin mush. Have this very hot and add boiling hot milk to make it like thick cream, about a quart of milk to 3 pints of the bean purée. Boil up at once and serve. It spoils a cream soup to let it cook many minutes after the milk is added.

Seasonings and Sauces for Vegetables.—Much of the excellence of well-cooked vegetables depends upon the proper use of seasonings and sauces. The seasoning selected should undoubtedly be suitable for the dish, but so much depends upon custom that only general suggestions can be made. The Italians and some other races are much fonder of garlic than Americans, the Germans of summer savory or "bohnenkraut" in string beans, and the English of mint with peas. Each housewife must select the seasonings which her family prefers and endeavor to use them in such a way that the special flavors may be most satisfactorily brought out.

Time of Cooking Flavorers.

When a soup, sauce, or vegetable is to be flavored with a herb or another vegetable the flavorer should be added toward the end of the cooking period. Since the oils and other bodies which give seasoning vegetables and herbs their flavor are volatile they are either driven off by long-continued cooking or rendered much less delicate in flavor. Herbs that are to be left in the dish or served with the dish must be added just before the food is served. The herbs generally served with the dish are chervil, parsley, tarragon, and chives.

Burnet, thyme, summer savory, sage, and sweet basil are cooked with the dish a short time, not over twenty minutes, and are then removed.

The little bunch of mixed herbs, the "bouquet garni," so often referred to in cook books, is made with two branches of parsley, a sprig each of thyme and summer savory, a small leaf of sage, and a small bay leaf, all tied together. This is cooked with the dish from ten to twenty minutes, then removed. The bay leaves must be purchased at the grocer's. Turnips, carrots, parsnips, celery, leeks, cibol, onions, etc., when used just as flavorers, should be tied in a bunch and cooked twenty or thirty minutes in the dish and then be removed.

When shallot and garlic are used they should never be cut, but separated into "cloves." One clove will be enough for a small quantity of soup, sauce, or ragout. Never fry shallot or garlic. Cook in the dish to be flavored about ten minutes, then remove.

Fried Vegetables for Seasoning.

Vegetables when used raw as a seasoning give a strong flavor, and only a little of each should be used. For flavoring soups, sauces, stews, etc., fried vegetables are far superior to the raw. To prepare them for use, clean and peel or scrape the vegetables, then cut them into small pieces, and put in a saucepan with butter or sweet fat, allowing two generous tablespoonsful of butter to a pint of vegetables. Place on a hot part of the range and stir until the butter and vegetables become hot. Partially cover the saucepan and set back, where the vegetables, which should be stirred often, will cook slowly for half an hour. At the end of this time place the pan on a hot part of the range and stir the contents until the butter begins to separate from the vegetables. Drain the butter, saving it with savory drippings, which every housewife should always have on hand and add the vegetables to the dish they are to flavor.

Fine Herbs.

In its broadest sense, the term "fine herbs" includes all the delicate, savory herbs, such as burnet, sweet basil, tarragon, and chervil. As commonly understood, three herbs enter into the seasoning known to cooks as "fine herbs"; these are parsley, chervil, and chives. They are minced fine and added to the sauce, soup, omelet, etc. For an omelet, they are stirred into the beaten eggs in the proportion of a teaspoonful to three eggs. When added to sauces, the herbs must be added just as they are about to be served. These three herbs combine well with almost any vegetable, fish, or meat. In general, herbs should be washed, placed on a clean board, and cut with a sharp knife.

Chervil and tarragon when employed in soup or salad should be torn leaf by leaf into small pieces.

Tarragon Vinegar.

Strip about three ounces of leaves from the branches of tarragon; put into a quart fruit jar and fill with good vinegar. Close and let stand for about twenty days, then strain. The best vinegar to use for this purpose is white wine vinegar, but good cider vinegar will also answer. The best time to make tarragon vinegar is about the last of August, when the plants are large and vigorous. Tarragon vinegar may be used for salads and sharp sauces, when the fresh herb is not available.

Butter with Vegetables.

It is almost universally conceded that vegetables require the addition of fat in order that they may be at their best, and there is no fat which is so suitable as butter for the majority of vegetables, judged by the texture of the dish and also by the flavor.

The American housekeeper has a way of looking upon the use of butter, milk, cream, and eggs in the preparation of vegetables, soups, and sauces as if these ingredients were simply "trimmings" and not food. But it should be remembered that these articles are valuable foods and naturally increase the food value of the dish of which they form a part. They are all, wholesome, and, although almost always more expensive than the vegetable foods with which they are combined, their use in reasonable quantities is certainly to be recommended.

Increasing the cost of the dish by the free use of butter, cream, etc., may after all be economy if the increase is intelligently made, and the vegetable soups, purées, etc., made "hearty" as well as appetizing by the addition of butter, eggs, etc., are combined with smaller quantities of meat and with light and simple desserts.

Savory Drippings.

As a substitute for butter in seasoning vegetables there is nothing better than sweet, savory drippings. Not all meats supply fats that are savory in the sense in which the word is employed here. The following fats may be employed alone or in combination for seasoning vegetables: The fat from fried sausages, ham, bacon, and pork, and from roast pork, veal, and chicken. Fats trimmed from poultry, veal, pork, and ham may be fried out carefully and saved for use in cooking vegetables. Such fats have a flavor which comes from seasoning, as in sausage, from smoke, as in ham and bacon, or from brown material, as in roast meat. The fat skimmed from the water in which poultry has been boiled and the fats skimmed from the gravies of most roast meats may be clarified and also employed in the preparation of vegetables for the table. Great care must be taken that all these fats are clean and sweet, and that the temperature at which they are fried out shall not be so high as to impair the flavor. Burned or scorched fat is not only unpleasant in flavor, but is a frequent cause of indigestion.

When rendering the trimmings of fat meat, add a small onion or a shallot (do not cut them), a few leaves of summer savory and thyme, a teaspoonful of salt, and a little pepper. This seasoning is enough for half a pint of fat. Keep the drippings covered, and in a cool, dry place.

Cream Sauce.

½ pint milk.
1 tablespoonful butter.
1 teaspoonful flour.
½ teaspoonful salt.
¼ teaspoonful pepper.

Heat the milk over boiling water; beat the butter and flour to a cream and stir into the hot milk. Cook five minutes, then add salt and pepper, and use. This sauce is suitable for boiled cauliflower, potatoes, carrots, etc. It is also a good sauce for escalloped dishes. This sauce may be modified by the addition of flavoring herbs.

Cream Mustard Sauce.

Make the cream sauce as directed above. Mix one tablespoonful of mustard with a teaspoonful of cold water and stir into the sauce about two minutes before serving. The quantity of mustard may be increased or diminished, as one may desire the flavor strong or mild.

White Sauce.

This sauce is made like the cream sauce, except that half a pint of white-meat broth is substituted for the milk, and two tablespoonsful of flour instead of one are used. The saucepan is put directly on the stove and the sauce is simmered ten minutes. White sauce, like cream sauce, may be modified by the addition of other flavors.

Tomato Sauce.

Cook one pint of peeled and cut tomatoes ten minutes, then rub through a strainer. Beat in a saucepan until smooth and light one tablespoonful of flour and one generous tablespoonful of butter. Gradually beat the hot tomato into this. Add the salt and pepper and cook ten minutes. This sauce may be served with macaroni, rice, etc., as well as with fish and meat. The flavor of the tomato sauce may be modified by the addition of onion, spice, or herbs.

Salads and Salad Dressings.—Nearly all vegetables may be served in the form of salad. The salads made with the raw vegetables are more refreshing and perhaps more generally relished than those made with cooked vegetables. The most common green salad plant in the United States is undoubtedly lettuce, and perhaps celery, alone or mixed with other materials, next. Endive, chicory, blanched dandelion, and other plants should also be used, as they give a pleasant variety to the menu. Such salads are garnished like lettuce. In most of our gardens the only sort of lettuce grown is some variety of the head lettuce. Roman lettuce, the "Salade Romaine" of Europe, which is fairly common in our city markets, is a delicious variety, which should be more generally used by American housekeepers.

Raw vegetables should be used only when they are young, tender, and fresh. When boiled green vegetables are used for a salad they should not be cooked so long that they lose crispness and flavor. Salad dressings are usually sharp or pungent sauce, with which the salad is moistened and seasoned, or "dressed." The most serviceable all-round salad dressing is what is known as French salad dressing. This is suitable for any vegetable salad, raw or cooked. Besides the dressing proper there are several herbs which are used as flavorers. In continental Europe some or all of these herbs are almost an invariable accompaniment of all lettuce salads and nearly all other green salads. These herbs are, in France, termed the fourniture of the salad, and it is a saying among the French that the fourniture is essential to all salads, while the use of garlic, hard boiled eggs, etc., is optional. The herbs generally employed in the fourniture are chervil, tarragon, chives, or cibol. These flavor deliciously lettuce and other tender green salads. They are also a great acquisition to soups, sauces, omelets, etc., one or more being employed to give special flavor to a dish. They may be readily cultivated in the kitchen garden.

Lettuce Salad with French Dressing.

2 heads lettuce.
2 or 3 sprays tarragon.
6 or 8 branches chervil.
1 tablespoonful minced chives or cibol, if the flavor be liked.
French dressing.

Remove all the green, tough leaves from the heads of lettuce. Break off the tender leaves one by one and rinse in cold water. Shake off the water and lay the leaves on a piece of cheese cloth and put the lettuce, wrapped lightly in the cheese cloth, on ice. At serving time, put the leaves in the salad bowl. Have the herbs torn into small bits and sprinkle over the lettuce. Sprinkle the dressing (a spoonful at a time) over the salad. Lift and turn the salad with the spoon and fork. Continue mixing in this manner until all the dressing has been used. The work must be done lightly and carefully that the lettuce shall not be crushed. Serve immediately. This is the French salad that so many travelers remember with great pleasure. The secret of its exquisite quality is that the lettuce is crisp and tender, delicate flavoring herbs are added to it, the vinegar is never strong, the oil is good, and, finally, the dressing is added just before the salad is served. In the heat of the summer, when head lettuce is not plenty, the tender young plants may be used. The flavor of the salad may be varied by the addition of other green salads and herbs, such as chicory, sorrel, borage, burnet, etc. When fresh tarragon is not available, tarragon vinegar may be employed.

Lettuce Salad with Cream Dressing.

1 large solid head lettuce.
1 tablespoonful vinegar.
½ teaspoonful salt.
¼ teaspoonful pepper.
4 tablespoonsful thick, sweet cream.

Remove the outer leaves from the head of lettuce, leaving only the crisp, clean, bleached leaves. Break the leaves one by one from the head, and if perfectly clean do not wash them. If not clean, wash quickly in cold water and drain. Tear each leaf into three or four pieces; put the shredded lettuce into a large towel or napkin and place on the ice or in a cold cellar. At serving time put the lettuce in a salad bowl. Mix the salt, pepper, and vinegar in the salad spoon and sprinkle over the lettuce; stir well, then add the cream, a spoonful at a time, and mix by tossing the lettuce lightly with the spoon and fork. Serve immediately.

Cabbage Salad.

Either red or white cabbage may be used for salad, and must be firm, crisp, and tender. Remove the outer leaves and cut the tender cabbage into fine shreds. Wash well and let soak in cold water for half an hour. Drain and season with French dressing or cooked salad dressing. Serve at once.

Cucumber Salad.

This vegetable should always be crisp and fresh when used. There is an old and widespread belief that cucumbers are more wholesome if the slices are soaked in cold water or in salted water before serving. Doubtless the distress which some persons experience after eating cucumbers is due to the fact that they are swallowed without proper mastication. It does not seem probable that there is any unwholesome property in this vegetable when we recall the extent to which it is eaten in some other countries and the good reputation which it bears there. In Persia the cucumber is most highly prized and is consumed in very large quantities. On account of its succulent character it is often used by travelers in place of water, as the water supply in many villages and towns is not above suspicion.

Cucumbers should be pared and sliced thin, and then may be dressed with oil and vinegar, like lettuce, or with a little vinegar, salt, and pepper. Cucumbers are at their best for salads when fairly young, and should not be used after the seeds have become hard and tough, as most persons consider them objectionable. A pleasant variation in the appearance of the dish may be easily obtained by slicing rather small cucumbers lengthwise instead of across, as is the more common method.

DRESSINGS OR SAUCES FOR SALADS

French Dressing.

1 tablespoonful vinegar.
4 tablespoonsful olive oil.
¼ teaspoonful salt.
⅛ teaspoonful pepper.

Put the salt and pepper in the salad bowl, or in a small bowl if the sauce is to be served separately. Add a little oil and stir well, then gradually add the remainder of the oil, stirring all the while. Last of all stir in the vinegar, which should be diluted with water if very strong.

This sauce may be modified to suit different vegetables. As it is given it is right for lettuce, chicory, cooked asparagus, cauliflower, artichoke, etc.

Cream may be substituted for the oil, but the salad is not so rich.

Cooked Salad Dressing.

2 eggs.
1 gill vinegar.
2 gills milk.
1 tablespoonful oil or butter.
1 teaspoonful salt.
1 teaspoonful mustard.
¼ teaspoonful pepper.

Put the oil and dry ingredients into a bowl and mix well. Add the eggs and beat for five minutes, then add the vinegar and beat one minute. Now add the milk, place the bowl in a pan of boiling water, and cook until the sauce thickens like thin cream. It will take about ten minutes. Stir the sauce constantly while cooking. Cool and bottle what you do not require for immediate use. This sauce is good for nearly all kinds of cooked vegetables.

If butter is substituted for the oil, add it just before taking the sauce from the fire.

Sour Cream Dressing.

½ pint sour cream.
2 tablespoonsful lemon juice.
2 tablespoonsful vinegar.
1 scant tablespoonful sugar.
1 teaspoonful salt.
¼ teaspoonful pepper.
1 teaspoonful or more mixed mustard.

Beat the cream with an egg beater until smooth, thick, and light. Mix the other ingredients together and gradually add to the cream, beating all the while.

This dressing may be modified to suit different vegetables. Having beaten sour cream for a foundation the seasoning may be anything desired, as, for example, the mustard and lemon may be omitted and the dressing be seasoned highly with any kind of catsup.

A sweet cream may be substituted for the sour; it should be quite thick.

Cream Salad Dressing.

1 cupful cream (sweet or sour).
½ cupful tomato catsup.
2 tablespoonsful olive oil.
2 tablespoonsful vinegar.
2 tablespoonsful sugar.
1 teaspoonful salt.

Mix the oil, salt, sugar, and vinegar together, then beat in the catsup and finally add the cream, beating it in gradually.

This dressing is very good for vegetables, or for fish salads.

INDEX

[N. B.—Single indentions of index references in the following pages indicate the omission of the word standing at the head of such indented matter; double indentions indicate the omission of two or more words. For example, in the line next following "Acid, acetic," the indention indicates the omission of the word "acid"; hence the next reference should be read, "Acid, citric," and similarly throughout. The single indention in the line next following, *"Baked and stuffed green peppers,"* indicates the omission of the word *"Baked"*; the double indention in the next line indicates the omission of the two words *"Baked bean;"* hence the third line should be read *"Baked bean salad,"* and so throughout the index. To facilitate quick reference, as a convenience to busy housekeepers, all *cooking recipes are printed in italics.*]